Modern Advanced Accounting

E. John Larsen
University of Southern California

6th edition

Modern Advanced Accounting

McGraw-Hill, Inc.

New York
St. Louis
San Francisco
Auckland
Bogotá
Caracas
Lisbon
London
Madrid
Mexico City
Milan
Montreal
New Delhi
San Juan
Singapore
Sydney
Tokyo
Toronto

This book is printed on acid-free paper.

4 5 6 7 8 9 0   DOC/DOC   9 9 8 7 6 5

ISBN 0-07-036595-4

This book was set in Times Roman by Progressive Typographers, Inc.
The editors were Alan Sachs and Linda Richmond;
the designer was Joan Greenfield;
the production supervisor was Friederich W. Schulte.
R. R. Donnelley & Sons Company was printer and binder.

Library of Congress Cataloging-in-Publication Data

Larsen, E. John.
  Modern advanced accounting/E. John Larsen.—6th ed.
     p.   cm.
  Includes index.
  ISBN 0-07-036595-4
  1. Accounting.   I. Title.
HF5635.M8756   1994   93-27419
657'046—dc20

Contents

liquidation. Equities of two partners are not sufficient to absorb their shares of loss from liquidation. Partnership is insolvent but partners are solvent. Partnership is insolvent and partners are insolvent.

Chapter 4
Accounting for Branches; Combined Financial Statements **133**

Preface

The sixth edition of *Modern Advanced Accounting* may be used in a one-semester or two-quarter course, at either the undergraduate level or the graduate level. The emphasis throughout the book is on accounting concepts and on analysis of the problems that arise in the application of these underlying concepts to specialized accounting entities—partnerships, branches, affiliated companies, governmental entities, nonprofit organizations, and estates and trusts—and on topics such as segments of business enterprises, interim reporting, reporting for the Securities and Exchange Commission, international accounting standards, accounting for multinational enterprises, and bankruptcy.

Significant revisions are occurring in accounting education, triggered in large part by the Accounting Education Change Commission (AECC), which has made the following recommendations:[1]

> The focus [of accounting education] should be on developing analytical and conceptual thinking, not on memorizing professional standards.
>
> [Accounting graduates] should know and understand the ethics of the profession and be able to make value-based judgments.
>
> [Accounting] [c]ourses should focus on both basic concepts and the application of these concepts in real-world environments, including international and ethical issues.
> . . . accounting programs should not focus primarily on preparation for professional examinations.
>
> [Students] should identify and solve unstructured problems that require use of multiple information sources.

In response to the foregoing, I have incorporated the following in the sixth edition of *Modern Advanced Accounting:*

---

[1] *Position Statement No. One,* "Objectives of Education for Accountants," AECC (Torrance, California: 1990), pp. 2–5.

1   A number of new cases requiring analytical and conceptual thinking on financial accounting and ethical issues, some of which require students to research suggested references.

2   Presentation of ethical issues in advanced accounting in Chapter 1, with an expanded discussion of the ethical codes of the Institute of Management Accountants, the Financial Executives Institute, and the American Institute of Certified Public Accountants.

3   A new chapter (No. 18) on *International Accounting Standards,* which also incorporates accounting for foreign currency transactions; and an expanded chapter (No. 19) on translation of foreign currency financial statements.

4   A substantial increase in the number of multiple-choice questions and other exercises and a reduction in the number of long, complex problems.

In addition, there is no reference to professional examinations in the sixth edition of *Modern Advanced Accounting.*

Other New Features of the Sixth Edition

Many chapters have been updated to include recent pronouncements by accounting rule-making bodies. For example, the following have been incorporated in this edition: (1) *FASB Statement No. 109,* ''Accounting for Income Taxes,'' in Chapter 10; (2) *GASB Statement No. 11,* dealing with the measurement focus and bias of governmental fund accounting, in Chapter 12;[2] *FASB Statements No. 117,* ''Financial Statements of Nonprofit Organizations'' and *No. 116,* ''Accounting for Contributions Received and Contributions Made,'' in Chapter 15; and (4) the following in Chapter 18:

> *FASB Statement No. 105,* ''Disclosure of Information about Financial Instruments with Off-Balance Sheet Risk . . .''

> *FASB Statement No. 107,* ''Disclosures about Fair Value of Financial Instruments''

> *International Accounting Standard (IAS) No. 21,* ''Accounting for the Effects of Changes in Foreign Exchange Rates''

> *IAS No. 22,* ''Accounting for Business Combinations''

> *IAS No. 27,* ''Consolidated Financial Statements and Accounting for Investments in Subsidiaries''

> *IAS No. 28,* ''Accounting for Investments in Associates''

> *IAS No. 31,* ''Financial Reporting of Interests in Joint Ventures''

---

[2] The author is aware that the Governmental Accounting Standards Board has deferred the effective date of *GASB Statement No. 11;* nonetheless, he has elected to include the standards in that statement in the book.

In addition to the foregoing, the sixth edition of *Modern Advanced Accounting* has the following new features:

A glossary of key terms (at the end of the book)

A single chapter (No. 15) on accounting for nonprofit organizations

Recognition of partners' salaries as an operating expense of the partnership in Chapter 2

Recognition by home office of realized gross profits resulting from branch sales in Chapter 4

A chart comparing purchase accounting with pooling-of-interests accounting for business combinations in Chapter 5

Illustrations of the preparation of consolidated financial statements without a working paper in Chapters 6 and 8

Reference to *FASB Discussion Memorandums* ". . . Consolidation Policy and Procedures" and "New Basis Accounting" in Chapter 6

Illustration of push-down accounting in Chapter 6

Illustration of sales and loans denominated in a foreign currency in Chapter 18

Translation from foreign functional currency to U.S. dollar of subsidiary's financial statements, and consolidation of subsidiary's translated statements with those of the parent company, in Chapter 19

A chart comparing remeasurement with translation of foreign currency financial statements in Chapter 19

Inclusion of relevant Securities and Exchange Commission *Accounting and Auditing Enforcement Releases* in the chapters to which they relate

Organization of Subject Matter

I anticipate that the organization of 18 of the 20 chapters into five parts will be useful to instructors and students. This arrangement should facilitate the planning and presentation of the subject matter and, I hope, make it easier for students to learn and retain the concepts and procedures presented. A brief description of the contents of each of the five parts follows.

Part One: Accounting for Partnerships and Branches
(Chapters 2 through 4)

Following ethical issues in Chapter 1, the first part deals with the accounting principles and procedures for partnerships, joint ventures, and branch operations. Partnerships (both general and limited) and joint ventures are covered in Chapters 2 and 3, which carry the student from the basic concepts of partnership accounting often presented in an introductory accounting course to the more complex problems of profit sharing, realignment of partners' equities, and liquidation. Chapter 4, which deals with home office–branch relationships and combined financial statements, provides a logical stepping-stone to the seven chapters dealing with business combinations and consolidated financial statements.

Part Two: Business Combinations and Consolidated Financial Statements (Chapters 5 through 11)

Since the issuance in 1987 of *FASB Statement 94,* ''Consolidation of All Majority-Owned Subsidiaries,'' no new pronouncements have been produced in the FASB's Consolidations and Related Matters project. Consequently, the changes in Part Two are minor, as described on page xix.

Part Three: Accounting for Nonbusiness Organizations (Chapters 12 through 15)

Apart from the new features in Part Three described on page xviii, Chapters 12 through 15 have been revised where appropriate to clarify the many complexities of accounting for governmental entities and nonprofit organizations.

Part Four: Accounting for Fiduciaries (Chapters 16 and 17)

The fourth section of the book includes chapters entitled ''Bankruptcy: Liquidation and Reorganization'' and ''Estates and Trusts.'' Although some instructors may not cover these two traditional topics in their courses, I believe that it is imperative to include them for those who wish to do so. Many accountants in today's practice environment must assist clients with problems of bankruptcy, liquidation, reorganization, and the accounting for estates and trusts.

Part Five: International Accounting (Chapters 18 and 19)

As indicated on page xviii, Chapters 18 and 19 are in part an outgrowth of recommendations by the Accounting Education Change Commission.

The three topics covered in Chapter 20 are unrelated to the subject matter of the five parts described above.

Review Questions, Exercises, Cases, and Problems

The learning and assignment material provided at the end of each chapter is divided into four groups: review questions, exercises, cases, and problems. Most end-of-chapter material has been tested in class by the author.

The review questions may be used by students as a self-testing and review device to measure their comprehension of key points in each chapter.

An exercise typically covers a specific point or topic and does not require extensive computations. Instructors may use the exercises to supplement problem assignments, for class discussion, and for examinations.

The cases require analytical reasoning but involve little or no quantitative data. Students are required to analyze business situations, to apply accounting principles, and to propose or evaluate a course of action. However, they are not required to prepare lengthy working papers or otherwise to manipulate accounting data on an extensive scale. The cases have proved to be an effective means of encouraging students to take positions in the argument of controversial accounting issues.

Several problems demonstrate the concepts presented in the theoretical discussion included in the chapter. Probably no more than a third of the problems would be used in a single course; consequently, ample opportunity exists to vary homework assignments from term to term.

Supplements with the Sixth Edition

As was the case with previous editions, the sixth edition of *Modern Advanced Accounting* is accompanied by a comprehensive package of supplementary items for both students and instructors.

For students

1   A student *Study Guide,* prepared by the author, is designed to help students measure their progress by providing immediate feedback. It contains an outline of the important points for each chapter, plus a variety of objective questions and short exercises and a case. Answers to the questions, exercises, and cases are at the end of each Study Guide chapter to help students evaluate their understanding of the subject matter.

2   *Accounting Work Sheets* for the problems are available for purchase by students. On these work sheets the organization names, problem numbers, numerous headings, and some preliminary data (such as trial balances) have been entered to save students' time and to facilitate review by the instructor.

3   A *Checklist of Key Figures* is provided for most problems. In this edition of *Modern Advanced Accounting* the checklist is on the inside front cover of the textbook. The purpose of the checklist is to aid students in verifying intermediate amounts in problem solutions and in discovering errors.

For instructors

1   A *Solutions Manual* is available from the publisher to adopters of the text. The Solutions Manual contains answers to all review questions, exercises, cases, and problems in the text. In addition, at the beginning of each chapter, there are short descriptions, time estimates, and difficulty ratings for each of the problems, to help instructors choose problems that best fit the needs of their individual courses in terms of scope, level, and emphasis.

2   A booklet of *Examination Questions,* with text material arranged chapter by chapter, is available at no charge. It contains true-or-false and multiple-choice questions, short problems, and a case for each chapter. Instructors should find the booklet a useful source of material for assembling examinations, because they may emphasize those topics or chapters that meet their course outline. Complete answers are provided for all questions, problems, and cases.

3   An *Instructor's Teaching Guide* is a teaching aid designed to assist instructors in preparing assignments and in covering the materials in class. The author's goals in providing this supplement were to make the task of instructors easier and to enable them to use their time more efficiently, so that the students' learning process would be enhanced.

4 *Overhead Transparencies* of problem solutions are available for many of the problems in the text. The transparencies are considered by many instructors to be an effective means of showing desired organization and format of solutions.

Acknowledgments

I express my deepest gratitude to the following:

My wife Kathleen, for her assistance in the planning and the completion of the sixth edition of *Modern Advanced Accounting*.

The McGraw-Hill, Inc., editorial staff—Executive Editor Alan Sachs, Senior Editing Supervisor Linda Richmond, Associate Editor Judy Howarth, and Editorial Assistant Linda Phillips—for their encouragement, patience, and overall professionalism.

The Financial Accounting Standards Board and the Governmental Accounting Standards Board, for permission to quote from *Statements, Discussion Memoranda, Interpretations,* and *Exposure Drafts.* All quotations used are copyrighted by the Financial Accounting Standards Board or the Governmental Accounting Standards Board, Norwalk, Connecticut, U.S.A., and are reprinted with permission. Copies of the complete documents are available from the Financial Accounting Standards Board or the Governmental Accounting Standards Board.

John Dreyer, Vice president, Corporate Communications, The Walt Disney Company, for permission to reproduce in Chapter 20 excerpts from the 1992 annual report of The Walt Disney Company.

Michael Davis of Lehigh University for careful checking of end-of-chapter review questions, exercises, cases, and problems and solutions thereto.

Reviewers of the sixth edition for their helpful comments and suggestions: J. Kevin Green, Washington and Lee University; Phillip J. Korb, University of Baltimore; Russ Langer, San Francisco State University; Victoria Rymer, University of Maryland; Maurice Stark, Kansas State University; Lawrence N. Waterbury, Quinnipiac College; and Jerome E. Zetts, Youngstown State University.

All the foregoing have contributed immeasurably to the creation of the sixth edition of *Modern Advanced Accounting*.

E. John Larsen

Ethical Issues in Advanced Accounting

Why begin the study of advanced accounting with a discussion of ethical issues? Because in recent years much attention has been devoted to the ethical conduct of accountants, both in industry and in public practice. Critics have alleged that ethical standards of accountants have deteriorated and that the interests of users of financial statements and financial reports have been subordinated to the desires of preparers of such reports to present the most favorable picture of the financial status of a reporting entity. Terms such as the following have been incorporated in the vocabulary of accountants:

"Cute accounting" to describe stretching the *form* of accounting standards to the limit, regardless of the *substance* of the underlying business transactions or events

"Cooking the books" to indicate fraudulent financial reporting

Many topics of advanced accounting have been the subject of both "cute accounting" and "cooking the books" by accounting executives of business enterprises. Because the controller, the chief accounting officer, and the accounting staffs of business enterprises have the primary responsibility for preparing and disseminating financial statements and financial reports to users thereof, this chapter deals with the establishment of ethical standards for those preparers. In subsequent chapters, Securities and Exchange Commission (SEC) enforcement actions dealing with wrongful application of accounting standards are described for topics covered in those chapters.

ETHICAL STANDARDS FOR PREPARERS OF FINANCIAL STATEMENTS AND FINANCIAL REPORTS

Until recently, most efforts to develop ethical standards for accountants have focused on CPAs in the practice of public accounting—primarily auditing. For example, although the first code of ethics of the American Institute of Certified Public Accountants (AICPA) was adopted in 1917, prior to 1988 few of its provisions applied to AICPA members in industry. The Institute of Management Accountants (IMA), an organization devoted primarily to the interests of accountants in industry, first issued its *Standards of Ethical Conduct for Management Accountants* in 1983. The Financial Executives Institute (FEI), an organization of financial vice presidents, controllers, and treasurers of business enterprises, first issued its *Code of Ethics* in 1985.

Presumably, the lack of formal ethical standards for management accountants and financial executives prior to 1983 stemmed from the view that the first line of defense against improper financial reporting was provided by independent CPAs who audited financial statements of business enterprises, and that preparers of those statements had only a secondary role in assuring quality financial reporting. This view was prevalent although the AICPA had long included the following statement in its pronouncements on auditing:[1]

> Management has the responsibility for adopting sound accounting policies, for maintaining an adequate and effective system of accounts, for the safeguarding of assets, and for devising a system of internal control that will, among other things, help assure the production of proper financial statements. The transactions which should be reflected in the accounts and in the financial statements are matters within the direct knowledge and control of management. The auditor's knowledge of such transactions is limited to that acquired through his examination. Accordingly, the fairness of the representations made through financial statements is an implicit and integral part of management's responsibility. The independent auditor may make suggestions as to the form or content of financial statements or he may draft them in whole or in part, based on management's accounts and records. However, his responsibility for the statements he has [audited] is confined to the expression of his opinion on them. The financial statements remain the representations of management.

Significant Events in the Establishment of Ethical Standards for Management Accountants and Financial Executives

The Seaview Symposium of 1970   An early effort to establish ethical standards for preparers of financial statements occurred at a 1970 symposium of members of the AICPA, the FEI, the Financial Analysts Federation, and the Robert Morris Associates (an organization of credit grantors), which took place at Seaview Country Club, Absecon, New Jersey. Papers and discussions at this symposium criticized the lack of a code of ethics for members of the FEI, given that the other three participating organizations had such codes.[2]

The Equity Funding Fraud of 1973   In 1973, a major fraud, of about nine years' duration, was discovered at Equity Funding Corporation of America (Equity), a seller of mutual fund shares that were pledged by the investors to secure loans to

---

[1] *Statement on Auditing Standards No. 1,* "Codification of Auditing Standards and Procedures," AICPA (New York: 1972), pp. 1–2.

[2] John C. Burton, ed., *Corporate Financial Reporting: Ethical and Other Problems,* AICPA (New York: 1972), pp. 7, 51–52, 109, 420–421.

finance life insurance premiums. During the nine-year period, at least $143 million of fictitious pre-tax income was generated, during a period in which Equity reported a total net income of $76 million, instead of the real pre-tax losses totaling more than $67 million.[3] The fraud was carried out by at least 10 executives of Equity, including the chief executive officer (CEO), chief financial officer (CFO), controller, and treasurer; several of the executives were CPAs with public accounting experience. The fraudulent conduct of these CPAs, all of whom presumably had at one time been subject to the AICPA's *Code of Professional Ethics* during their public accounting careers, furnished clear evidence of the need for ethics codes for management accountants and other financial executives.

Action by the IMA In 1983, the IMA issued *Standards of Ethical Conduct for Management Accountants,* the third in a series of *Statements on Management Accounting.* The IMA standards, which are presented in Appendix 1 (pages 8 through 10), cover the management accountant's obligations as to competence, confidentiality, integrity, and objectivity, and they provide guidance for resolutions of ethical conflict. Noteworthy in the preamble to the standards (page 8) is the management accountant's obligation not to condone violations of the standards by others in the organization.

Action by the FEI The *Code of Ethics* promulgated by the FEI in 1985 is in Appendix 2 (page 10). Although briefer than the IMA standards, the FEI's code covers essentially the same areas of professional conduct as do the IMA standards.

Treadway Commission Recommendations The National Commission on Fraudulent Financial Reporting (Treadway Commission), which had been sponsored by the AICPA, the IMA, the FEI, the American Accounting Association (composed primarily of accounting educators), and the Institute of Internal Auditors, issued its report in 1987. Defining *fraudulent financial reporting* as "intentional or reckless conduct, whether act or omission, that results in materially misleading financial statements,"[4] the Treadway Commission made 49 recommendations for curbing such reporting. The recommendations dealt with the public company; the independent public accountant; the SEC, financial institution regulators, and state boards of accountancy; and education. Stating that "the responsibility for reliable financial reporting resides first and foremost at the corporate level,"[5] the Treadway Commission included the following among its recommendations for the public company:[6]

> *Recommendation: Public companies should maintain accounting functions that are designed to meet their financial reporting obligations.*
>
> A public company's accounting function is an important control in preventing and detecting fraudulent financial reporting. The accounting function must be designed to allow the company and its officers to fulfill their statutory financial disclosure obligations.

---

[3] *Report of the Trustee of Equity Funding Corporation of America,* October 31, 1974, p. 12.
[4] *Report of the National Commission on Fraudulent Financial Reporting,* (New York: 1987), p. 2.
[5] Ibid., p. 6.
[6] Ibid., pp. 36–37.

As a member of top management, the chief accounting officer helps set the tone of the organization's ethical conduct and thus is part of the control environment. Moreover, the chief accounting officer is directly responsible for the financial statements, and can and should take authoritative action to correct them if necessary. He generally has the primary responsibility for designing, implementing, and monitoring the company's financial reporting system and internal accounting controls. The controller may serve as the chief accounting officer, or the chief financial officer also may perform the functions of a chief accounting officer.

The chief accounting officer's actions especially influence employees who perform the accounting function. By establishing high standards for the company's financial disclosures, the chief accounting officer guides others in the company toward legitimate financial reporting.

Moreover, the chief accounting officer is in a unique position. In numerous cases, other members of top management, such as the chief executive officer, pressure the chief accounting officer into fraudulently manipulating the financial statements. An effective chief accounting officer is familiar with the company's financial position and operations and thus frequently is able to identify unusual situations caused by fraudulent financial reporting perpetrated at the divisional level.

The chief accounting officer has an obligation to the organization he serves, to the public, and to himself to maintain the highest standards of ethical conduct. He therefore must be prepared to take action necessary to prevent fraudulent financial reporting. His efforts may entail bringing matters to the attention of the CEO, the CFO, the chief internal auditor, the audit committee, or the entire board of directors.

The Financial Executives Institute (FEI) and the [Institute of Management Accountants (IMA)] play active roles in enhancing the financial reporting process by sponsoring research, technical professional guidance, and continuing professional education and by participating in the shaping of standards. Both organizations also have promulgated codes of conduct that strongly encourage reliable financial reporting. Public companies should encourage their accounting employees to support these organizations and adhere to their codes of conduct.

Revision of AICPA Ethics Rules   In 1988, the members of the AICPA approved a revised *Code of Professional Conduct* to replace the *Code of Professional Ethics* that previously had been in effect. This action was triggered by the 1986 *Report of the Special Committee on Standards of Professional Conduct for Certified Public Accountants* (Anderson Committee), which recommended restructuring the AICPA's ethics code to improve its relevance and effectiveness.[7] A key element of the Anderson Committee recommendations was extension of applicability of the Rules of Professional Conduct of the revised *Code of Professional Conduct* to

---

[7] *Report of the Special Committee on Standards of Professional Conduct for Certified Public Accountants,* AICPA (New York: 1986), p. 1.

AICPA members who are not practicing in a CPA firm.[8] Thus, Rules 102, 201, 202, 203, 302, and 501 of the *Code of Professional Conduct* in Appendix 3 (pages 11 through 22) apply to *all* AICPA members, including those in private industry, governmental entities, and nonprofit organizations.

Analysis of Ethical Standards for Management Accountants and Financial Executives

A review of the contents of the IMA, FEI, and AICPA ethics pronouncements in Appendixes 1, 2, and 3 reveals several similarities. All three require members of the respective organizations to be competent, act with integrity and objectivity, maintain confidentiality of sensitive information, and avoid discreditable acts. The IMA and AICPA codes specifically prohibit conflicts of interest, but the FEI code only indirectly addresses such conflicts in its confidentiality provision. Only the IMA and FEI codes specifically require communication of complete information to users of their members' reports; AICPA members indirectly are comparably obligated by Rule 202.

Rule 203 of the AICPA code requires compliance with generally accepted accounting principles. One might prefer that both the IMA and the FEI codes had comparable explicit provisions, given management accountants' and financial executives' primary responsibility for financial statements and financial reports.

Other differences among the three ethics codes include the following:

1   The IMA standards in essence require members to *report* violations of the standards by members of their organizations to responsible officials of the organizations. The FEI and AICPA codes have no such requirements.

2   The FEI code requires members to conduct their *personal,* as well as their *business,* affairs with honesty and integrity. The IMA and AICPA standards do not address personal affairs.

The issues of *conflicts of interest* and *discreditable acts* are discussed further in the following sections.

Conflicts of Interest   A *conflict of interest* results when an individual reaps an inappropriate *personal* benefit from his or her acts in an *official* capacity. For example, a chief accounting officer might ''cook the books'' to overstate pre-tax income of the employer corporation in order to obtain a larger performance bonus. Alternatively, the controller of a publicly owned corporation might engage in *insider trading*[9] to maximize gains or minimize losses on purchases or sales of the employer corporation securities. For example, in *Accounting and Auditing Enforcement Release (AAER) 344* (December 10, 1991), the Securities and Exchange Commission (SEC) reported the permanent disbarment from practice before it of the controller, a CPA, of a publicly owned company, who had allegedly engaged in insider trading

---

[8] Ibid., p. 23.

[9] Section 21A of the Securities Exchange Act of 1934 defines *insider trading* as ''purchasing or selling a security while in possession of material, nonpublic information . . . or . . . communicating such information in connection with a securities transaction. . . .''

and thus avoided losses of more than $73,000 on sales of the employer company's common stock. According to the SEC, the controller had acted with senior management of the company to overstate the company's earnings by more than $38,000,000 over a two-and-one-half-year period. The controller was ordered to disgorge the $73,000 and pay a penalty of the same amount.

Discreditable Acts   None of the three ethics codes presented in appendixes to this chapter defines *discreditable acts.* Probably the term cannot be adequately defined or circumscribed; what might be a discreditable act to one observer would not be construed the same by another observer. For example, and returning to the FEI's requirement of integrity in its members' *personal* affairs, might an FEI member observing another member's substance abuse construe the act as discreditable to the abusive member, the member's employer, the FEI, or other members of the FEI? Such questions are difficult to answer in a society in which some condone personal actions that are condemned by others.

Concluding Observations

In considering episodes of "cooking the books," described in subsequent chapters, it should be kept in mind that, although the Treadway Commission opined that "The incidence of fraudulent financial reporting cannot be quantified with any degree of precision," [10] it also gave the following data:[11]

1   The number of SEC proceedings against reporting companies from 1981 to 1986 was less than one percent of the number of financial reports filed with the SEC during that period.

2   The Chairman of the Federal Deposit Insurance Corporation contended that management fraud (presumably including "cooking the books") contributed to one-third of bank failures.

3   Ten percent of total bankruptcies in a study authorized by the Treadway Commission involved fraudulent financial reporting.

4   Former SEC Chairman John Shad estimated that all fraudulent securities activities amount to a fraction of one percent of the $50 billion of corporate and government securities traded daily.

Thus, "cooking the books" episodes, though serious and despicable, apparently do not indicate a wholesale breakdown of ethical conduct by management accountants and financial executives of business enterprises.

An important question to consider is: Can the codes of conduct for management accountants and financial executives recently established or revised by the IMA, the FEI, and the AICPA help those key players in corporate financial reporting to resist pressures, often from top management but sometimes from within themselves, to falsify financial statements and financial reports? Or is it too much to expect such

---

[10] *Report of the National Committee on Fraudulent Financial Reporting,* p. 25.
[11] Ibid., pp. 25–26.

individuals, whose livelihoods and careers depend a great deal on what is in those statements and reports, to be completely impartial in their preparation? Ralph E. Walters, CPA, former Director of Professional Conduct for The California Society of Certified Public Accountants, has considered this thorny question as follows:[12]

> An obligation to be *impartial* seems to me to place a new and possibly unrealistic burden on the management accountant. Traditionally, most employees have felt an obligation, within the bounds of honesty and integrity, to put the best face upon their employer's affairs. For example, there is still some latitude in selection and judgment in the application of GAAP [generally accepted accounting principles]. Some managers consistently opt for the most aggressive principle or application. The aggregate effect is to bias the financial statements. They may be in accordance with GAAP, but the quality of earnings is suspect. They are not impartial. This condition is not uncommon in practice (it is a principal reason we need independent auditors). An accountant associated with this condition is literally violating the AICPA Code. The [IMA] Code is less clear.
>
> Is this interpretation realistic? Do management accountants generally understand this? I doubt it. In fairness to their members and to the public, the AICPA and the [IMA] need to put their heads together and agree how much objectivity management accountants can be expected to live with, including some examples in real-life situations. The positions should be consistent and must be made clear to all management accountants.

The questions raised in the foregoing paragraph are difficult to answer. However, the SEC has emphasized the importance of objectivity as follows, in rejecting the "good soldier" rationalization of unethical conduct by a corporate controller (a CPA):[13]

> . . . the Commission cannot condone [the controller's] conduct. [The controller] had or had available to him more than sufficient information to be aware that the financial statements he prepared and the periodic reports he signed were materially inaccurate. Under the circumstances, and as a senior level financial officer and the highest level CPA within [the corporation] involved in the financial reporting process, [the controller] owed a duty to [the corporation] and its shareholders not to assist in, or even acquiesce in, [the corporation's] issuance of such financial statements. Although [the controller] may have made the appropriate recommendations to his corporate supervisors, when those recommendations were rejected, [the controller] acted as the "good soldier," implementing their directions which he knew or should have known were improper.

At the beginning of their professional careers, students of advanced accounting might well reflect on their sense of ethical values and decide on a course of action if they find themselves in a position such as the foregoing one.

---

[12] Ralph E. Walters, "Ethics and Excellence," *Management Accounting,* January 1990, p. 12.
[13] *AAER 93,* ". . . In the Matter of Michael R. Maury" (March 26, 1986).

APPENDIX 1: STANDARDS OF ETHICAL CONDUCT FOR MANAGEMENT ACCOUNTANTS*

Management accountants have an obligation to the organizations they serve, their profession, the public, and themselves to maintain the highest standards of ethical conduct. In recognition of this obligation, the [Institute of Management] Accountants has promulgated the following standards of ethical conduct for management accountants. Adherence to these standards is integral to achieving the *Objectives of Management Accounting.*[1] Management accountants shall not commit acts contrary to these standards nor shall they condone the commission of such acts by others within their organizations.

Competence

Management accountants have a responsibility to:

●   Maintain an appropriate level of professional competence by ongoing development of their knowledge and skills.

●   Perform their professional duties in accordance with relevant laws, regulations, and technical standards.

●   Prepare complete and clear reports and recommendations after appropriate analyses of relevant and reliable information.

Confidentiality

Management accountants have a responsibility to:

●   Refrain from disclosing confidential information acquired in the course of their work except when authorized, unless legally obligated to do so.

●   Inform subordinates as appropriate regarding the confidentiality of information acquired in the course of their work and monitor their activities to assure the maintenance of that confidentiality.

●   Refrain from using or appearing to use confidential information acquired in the course of their work for unethical or illegal advantage either personally or through third parties.

Integrity

Management accountants have a responsibility to:

●   Avoid actual or apparent conflicts of interest and advise all appropriate parties of any potential conflict.

---

* From Institute of Management Accountants (formerly National Association of Accountants), *Statements on Management Accounting: Standards of Ethical Conduct for Management Accountants,* Statement No. 1C (10 Paragon Drive, Montvale, NJ 07645, June 1, 1983). Reprinted with permission.
[1] [Institute of Management Accountants], *Statements on Management Accounting: Objectives of Management Accounting,* Statement No. 1B (New York, June 17, 1982).

- Refrain from engaging in any activity that would prejudice their ability to carry out their duties ethically.

- Refuse any gift, favor, or hospitality that would influence or would appear to influence their actions.

- Refrain from either actively or passively subverting the attainment of the organization's legitimate and ethical objectives.

- Recognize and communicate professional limitations or other constraints that would preclude responsible judgment or successful performance of an activity.

- Communicate unfavorable as well as favorable information and professional judgments or opinions.

- Refrain from engaging in or supporting any activity that would discredit the profession.

Objectivity

Management accountants have a responsibility to:

- Communicate information fairly and objectively.

- Disclose fully all relevant information that could reasonably be expected to influence an intended user's understanding of the reports, comments, and recommendations presented.

Resolution of Ethical Conflict

In applying the standards of ethical conduct, management accountants may encounter problems in identifying unethical behavior or in resolving an ethical conflict. When faced with significant ethical issues, management accountants should follow the established policies of the organization bearing on the resolution of such conflict. If these policies do not resolve the ethical conflict, management accountants should consider the following courses of action:

- Discuss such problems with the immediate superior except when it appears that the superior is involved, in which case the problem should be presented initially to the next higher managerial level. If satisfactory resolution cannot be achieved when the problem is initially presented, submit the issues to the next higher managerial level.

    If the immediate superior is the chief executive officer, or equivalent, the acceptable reviewing authority may be a group such as the audit committee, executive committee, board of directors, board of trustees, or owners. Contact with levels above the immediate superior should be initiated only with the superior's knowledge, assuming the superior is not involved.

- Clarify relevant concepts by confidential discussion with an objective advisor to obtain an understanding of possible courses of action.

- If the ethical conflict still exists after exhausting all levels of internal review, the management accountant may have no other recourse on significant matters than to resign from the organization and to submit an informative memorandum to an appropriate representative of the organization.

Except where legally prescribed, communication of such problems to authorities or individuals not employed or engaged by the organization is not considered appropriate.

APPENDIX 2: FEI CODE OF ETHICS*

To be eligible for active membership in Financial Executives Institute, applicants must possess those personal attributes such as character, personal integrity and business ability that will be an asset to the Institute. They must also meet preestablished criteria indicating a high degree of participation in the formulation of policies for the operation of the enterprises they represent and in the administration of the financial functions. Members of the Institute are expected to follow this Code of Ethics.

As a member of Financial Executives Institute, I will:

● Conduct my business and personal affairs at all times with honesty and integrity.

● Provide complete, appropriate and relevant information in an objective manner when reporting to management, stockholders, employees, government agencies, other institutions and the public.

● Comply with rules and regulations of federal, state, provincial, and local governments, and other appropriate private and public regulatory agencies.

● Discharge duties and responsibilities to my employer to the best of my ability, including complete communication on all matters within my jurisdiction.

● Maintain the confidentiality of information acquired in the course of my work except when authorized or otherwise legally obligated to disclose. Confidential information acquired in the course of my work will not be used for my personal advantage.

● Maintain an appropriate level of professional competence through continuing development of my knowledge and skills.

● Refrain from committing acts discreditable to myself, my employer, FEI or fellow members of the Institute.

* From Financial Executives Institute, *Code of Ethics* (10 Madison Avenue, Morristown, NJ 07962–1938). Reprinted with permission.

APPENDIX 3: AICPA CODE OF PROFESSIONAL CONDUCT*

Composition, Applicability, and Compliance

The Code of Professional Conduct of the American Institute of Certified Public Accountants consists of two sections — (1) the Principles and (2) the Rules. The Principles provide the framework for the Rules, which govern the performance of professional services by members. The Council of the American Institute of Certified Public Accountants is authorized to designate bodies to promulgate technical standards under the Rules, and the bylaws require adherence to those Rules and standards.

The Code of Professional Conduct was adopted by the membership to provide guidance and rules to all members — those in public practice, in industry, in government, and in education — in the performance of their professional responsibilities.

Compliance with the Code of Professional Conduct, as with all standards in an open society, depends primarily on members' understanding and voluntary actions, secondarily on reinforcement by peers and public opinion, and ultimately on disciplinary proceedings, when necessary, against members who fail to comply with the Rules.

Section I: Principles
Preamble

Membership in the American Institute of Certified Public Accountants is voluntary. By accepting membership, a certified public accountant assumes an obligation of self-discipline above and beyond the requirements of laws and regulations.

These Principles of the Code of Professional Conduct of the American Institute of Certified Public Accountants express the profession's recognition of its responsibilities to the public, to clients, and to colleagues. They guide members in the performance of their professional responsibilities and express the basic tenets of ethical and professional conduct. The Principles call for an unswerving commitment to honorable behavior, even at the sacrifice of personal advantage.

Article I
Responsibilities

In carrying out their responsibilities as professionals, members should exercise sensitive professional and moral judgments in all their activities.

As professionals, certified public accountants perform an essential role in society. Consistent with that role, members of the American Institute of Certified Public Accountants have responsibilities to all those who use their professional services. Members also have a continuing responsibility to cooperate with each other to improve the art of accounting, maintain the public's confidence, and carry out the

---

* From American Institute of Certified Public Accountants, *Code of Professional Conduct.* Copyright © 1992 by American Institute of Certified Public Accountants, Inc. (New York). Reprinted with permission.

profession's special responsibilities for self-governance. The collective efforts of all members are required to maintain and enhance the traditions of the profession.

Article II
The Public Interest

Members should accept the obligation to act in a way that will serve the public interest, honor the public trust, and demonstrate commitment to professionalism.

A distinguishing mark of a profession is acceptance of its responsibility to the public. The accounting profession's public consists of clients, credit grantors, governments, employers, investors, the business and financial community, and others who rely on the objectivity and integrity of certified public accountants to maintain the orderly functioning of commerce. This reliance imposes a public interest responsibility on certified public accountants. The public interest is defined as the collective well-being of the community of people and institutions the profession serves.

In discharging their professional responsibilities, members may encounter conflicting pressures from among each of those groups. In resolving those conflicts, members should act with integrity, guided by the precept that when members fulfill their responsibility to the public, clients' and employers' interests are best served.

Those who rely on certified public accountants expect them to discharge their responsibilities with integrity, objectivity, due professional care, and a genuine interest in serving the public. They are expected to provide quality services, enter into fee arrangements, and offer a range of services — all in a manner that demonstrates a level of professionalism consistent with these Principles of the Code of Professional Conduct.

All who accept membership in the American Institute of Certified Public Accountants commit themselves to honor the public trust. In return for the faith that the public reposes in them, members should seek continually to demonstrate their dedication to professional excellence.

Article III
Integrity

To maintain and broaden public confidence, members should perform all professional responsibilities with the highest sense of integrity.

Integrity is an element of character fundamental to professional recognition. It is the quality from which the public trust derives and the benchmark against which a member must ultimately test all decisions.

Integrity requires a member to be, among other things, honest and candid within the constraints of client confidentiality. Service and the public trust should not be subordinated to personal gain and advantage. Integrity can accommodate the inadvertent error and the honest difference of opinion; it cannot accommodate deceit or subordination of principle.

Integrity is measured in terms of what is right and just. In the absence of specific rules, standards, or guidance, or in the face of conflicting opinions, a member should test decisions and deeds by asking: ''Am I doing what a person of integrity would do? Have I retained my integrity?'' Integrity requires a member to observe both the form and the spirit of technical and ethical standards; circumvention of those standards constitutes subordination of judgment.

Integrity also requires a member to observe the principles of objectivity and independence and of due care.

Article IV
Objectivity and Independence

A member should maintain objectivity and be free of conflicts of interest in discharging professional responsibilities. A member in public practice should be independent in fact and appearance when providing auditing and other attestation services.

Objectivity is a state of mind, a quality that lends value to a member's services. It is a distinguishing feature of the profession. The principle of objectivity imposes the obligation to be impartial, intellectually honest, and free of conflicts of interest. Independence precludes relationships that may appear to impair a member's objectivity in rendering attestation services.

Members often serve multiple interests in many different capacities and must demonstrate their objectivity in varying circumstances. Members in public practice render attest, tax, and management advisory services. Other members prepare financial statements in the employment of others, perform internal auditing services, and serve in financial and management capacities in industry, education, and government. They also educate and train those who aspire to admission into the profession. Regardless of service or capacity, members should protect the integrity of their work, maintain objectivity, and avoid any subordination of their judgment.

For a member in public practice, the maintenance of objectivity and independence requires a continuing assessment of client relationships and public responsibility. Such a member who provides auditing and other attestation services should be independent in fact and appearance. In providing all other services, a member should maintain objectivity and avoid conflicts of interest.

Although members not in public practice cannot maintain the appearance of independence, they nevertheless have the responsibility to maintain objectivity in rendering professional services. Members employed by others to prepare financial statements or to perform auditing, tax, or consulting services are charged with the same responsibility for objectivity as members in public practice and must be scrupulous in their application of generally accepted accounting principles and candid in all their dealings with members in public practice.

Article V
Due Care

A member should observe the profession's technical and ethical standards, strive continually to improve competence and the quality of services, and discharge professional responsibility to the best of the member's ability.

The quest for excellence is the essence of due care. Due care requires a member to discharge professional responsibilities with competence and diligence. It imposes the obligation to perform professional services to the best of a member's ability with concern for the best interest of those for whom the services are performed and consistent with the profession's responsibility to the public.

Competence is derived from a synthesis of education and experience. It begins with a mastery of the common body of knowledge required for designation as a certified public accountant. The maintenance of competence requires a commitment to learning and professional improvement that must continue throughout a member's professional life. It is a member's individual responsibility. In all engagements and in all responsibilities, each member should undertake to achieve a level of competence that will assure that the quality of the member's services meets the high level of professionalism required by these Principles.

Competence represents the attainment and maintenance of a level of understanding and knowledge that enables a member to render services with facility and acumen. It also establishes the limitations of a member's capabilities by dictating that consultation or referral may be required when a professional engagement exceeds the personal competence of a member or a member's firm. Each member is responsible for assessing his or her own competence — of evaluating whether education, experience, and judgment are adequate for the responsibility to be assumed.

Members should be diligent in discharging responsibilities to clients, employers, and the public. Diligence imposes the responsibility to render services promptly and carefully, to be thorough, and to observe applicable technical and ethical standards.

Due care requires a member to plan and supervise adequately any professional activity for which he or she is responsible.

Article VI
Scope and Nature of Services

A member in public practice should observe the Principles of the Code of Professional Conduct in determining the scope and nature of services to be provided.

The public interest aspect of certified public accountants' services requires that such services be consistent with acceptable professional behavior for certified public accountants. Integrity requires that service and the public trust not be subordinated to personal gain and advantage. Objectivity and independence require that members be free from conflicts of interest in discharging professional responsibilities. Due care requires that services be provided with competence and diligence.

Each of these Principles should be considered by members in determining whether or not to provide specific services in individual circumstances. In some instances, they may represent an overall constraint on the nonaudit services that might be offered to a specific client. No hard-and-fast rules can be developed to help members reach these judgments, but they must be satisfied that they are meeting the spirit of the Principles in this regard.

In order to accomplish this, members should

• Practice in firms that have in place internal quality-control procedures to ensure that services are competently delivered and adequately supervised.

• Determine, in their individual judgments, whether the scope and nature of other services provided to an audit client would create a conflict of interest in the performance of the audit function for that client.

● Assess, in their individual judgments, whether an activity is consistent with their role as professionals (for example, Is such activity a reasonable extension or variation of existing services offered by the member or others in the profession?).

Section II: Rules

Applicability

The bylaws of the American Institute of Certified Public Accountants require that members adhere to the Rules of the Code of Professional Conduct. Members must be prepared to justify departures from these Rules.

Interpretation of Applicability Section

[*The professional ethics executive committee has issued the following interpretation of the applicability section of the Code, effective November 30, 1989.*]

For purposes of the applicability section of the Code, a "member" is a member or international associate of the American Institute of CPAs.

1 The Rules of Conduct that follow apply to all professional services performed except (a) where the wording of the rule indicates otherwise and (b) that a member who is practicing outside the United States will not be subject to discipline for departing from any of the rules stated herein as long as the member's conduct is in accord with the rules of the organized accounting profession in the country in which he or she is practicing. However, where a member's name is associated with financial statements under circumstances that would entitle the reader to assume that U.S. practices were followed, the member must comply with the requirements of Rules 202 and 203.

2 A member may be held responsible for compliance with the rules by all persons associated with him or her in the practice of public accounting who are either under the member's supervision or are the member's partners or shareholders in the practice.

3 A member shall not permit others to carry out on his or her behalf, either with or without compensation, acts which, if carried out by the member, would place the member in violation of the rules.

Definitions

Client A client is any person or entity, other than the member's employer, that engages a member or a member's firm to perform professional services or a person or entity with respect to which professional services are performed. The term "employer" for these purposes does not include those entities engaged in the practice of public accounting.

Council The Council of the American Institute of Certified Public Accountants.

Enterprise For purposes of the Code, the term "enterprise" is synonymous with the term "client."

Financial Statements   Statements and footnotes related thereto that purport to show financial position which relates to a point in time or changes in financial position which relate to a period of time, and statements which use a cash or other incomplete basis of accounting. Balance sheets, statements of income, statements of retained earnings, statements of [cash flows] and statements of changes in owners' equity are financial statements.

Incidental financial data included in [consulting] services reports to support recommendations to a client and tax returns and supporting schedules do not, for this purpose, constitute financial statements; and the statement, affidavit, or signature of preparers required on tax returns neither constitutes an opinion on financial statements nor requires a disclaimer of such opinion.

Firm   A proprietorship, partnership, or professional corporation or association engaged in the practice of public accounting, including individual partners or shareholders thereof.

Holding Out   In general, any action initiated by a member that informs others of his or her status as a CPA or AICPA-accredited specialist constitutes holding out as a CPA. This would include, for example, any oral or written representation to another regarding CPA status, use of the CPA designation on business cards or letterhead, the display of a certificate evidencing a member's CPA designation, or listing as a CPA in local telephone directories.

Institute   The American Institute of Certified Public Accountants.

Interpretations of Rules of Conduct   Pronouncements issued by the division of professional ethics to provide guidelines concerning the scope and application of the Rules of Conduct.

Member   A member, associate member, or international associate of the American Institute of Certified Public Accountants.

Practice of Public Accounting   The practice of public accounting consists of the performance for a client, by a member or a member's firm, while holding out as CPA(s), of the professional services of accounting, tax, personal financial planning, litigation support services, and those professional services for which standards are promulgated by bodies designated by Council, such as Statements of Financial Accounting Standards, Statements on Auditing Standards, Statements on Standards for Accounting and Review Services, Statements on Standards for [Consulting] Services, Statements of Governmental Accounting Standards, Statements on Standards for Attestation Engagements, and Statement on Standards for Accountants' Services on Prospective Financial Information.

However, a member or a member's firm, while holding out as CPA(s), is not considered to be in the practice of public accounting if the member or the member's firm does not perform, for any client, any of the professional services described in the preceding paragraph.

Professional Services Professional services include all services performed by a member while holding out as a CPA.

Rules
Rule 101   Independence
A member in public practice shall be independent in the performance of professional services as required by standards promulgated by bodies designated by Council.

Rule 102   Integrity and Objectivity
In the performance of any professional service, a member shall maintain objectivity and integrity, shall be free of conflicts of interest, and shall not knowingly misrepresent facts or subordinate his or her judgment to others.

Rule 201   General Standards
A member shall comply with the following standards and with any interpretations thereof by bodies designated by Council.

A. *Professional Competence.* Undertake only those professional services that the member or the member's firm can reasonably expect to be completed with professional competence.

B. *Due Professional Care.* Exercise due professional care in the performance of professional services.

C. *Planning and Supervision.* Adequately plan and supervise the performance of professional services.

D. *Sufficient Relevant Data.* Obtain sufficient relevant data to afford a reasonable basis for conclusions or recommendations in relation to any professional services performed.

Rule 202   Compliance With Standards
A member who performs auditing, review, compilation, [consulting], tax, or other professional services shall comply with standards promulgated by bodies designated by Council.

Rule 203   Accounting Principles
A member shall not (1) express an opinion or state affirmatively that the financial statements or other financial data of any entity are presented in conformity with generally accepted accounting principles or (2) state that he or she is not aware of any material modifications that should be made to such statements or data in order for them to be in conformity with generally accepted accounting principles, if such statements or data contain any departure from an accounting principle promulgated by bodies designated by Council to establish such principles that has a material effect on the statements or data taken as a whole. If, however, the statements or data contain such a departure and the member can demonstrate that due to unusual circumstances the financial statements or data would otherwise have been misleading, the member

can comply with the rule by describing the departure, its approximate effects, if practicable, and the reasons why compliance with the principle would result in a misleading statement.

Rule 301   Confidential Client Information

A member in public practice shall not disclose any confidential client information without the specific consent of the client.

This rule shall not be construed (1) to relieve a member of his or her professional obligations under rules 202 and 203, (2) to affect in any way the member's obligation to comply with a validly issued and enforceable subpoena or summons, or to prohibit a member's compliance with applicable laws and government regulations, (3) to prohibit review of a member's professional practice under AICPA or state CPA society or Board of Accountancy authorization, or (4) to preclude a member from initiating a complaint with, or responding to any inquiry made by, the ethics division or trial board of the Institute or a duly constituted investigative or disciplinary body of a state CPA society or Board of Accountancy.

Members of any of the bodies identified in (4) above and members involved with professional practice reviews identified in (3) above shall not use to their own advantage or disclose any member's confidential client information that comes to their attention in carrying out those activities. This prohibition shall not restrict members' exchange of information in connection with the investigative or disciplinary proceedings described in (4) above or the professional practice reviews described in (3) above.

Rule 302   Contingent Fees

A member in public practice shall not

(1) Perform for a contingent fee any professional services for, or receive such a fee from, a client for whom the member or the member's firm performs
    (*a*) an audit or review of a financial statement; or
    (*b*) a compilation of a financial statement when the member expects, or reasonably might expect, that a third party will use the financial statement and the member's compilation report does not disclose a lack of independence; or
    (*c*) an examination of prospective financial information;
    or

(2) Prepare an original or amended tax return or claim for a tax refund for a contingent fee for any client.

The prohibition in (1) above applies during the period in which the member or the member's firm is engaged to perform any of the services listed above and the period covered by any historical financial statements involved in any such listed services.

Except as stated in the next sentence, a contingent fee is a fee established for the performance of any service pursuant to an arrangement in which no fee will be charged unless a specified finding or result is attained, or in which the amount of the fee is otherwise dependent upon the finding or result or such service. Solely for purposes of this rule, fees are not regarded as being contingent if fixed by courts or other public authorities, or, in tax matters, if determined based on the results of judicial proceedings or the findings of governmental agencies.

A member's fees may vary depending, for example, on the complexity of services rendered.

Rule 401   *[There are currently no rules in the 400 series.]*

Rule 501   Acts Discreditable

A member shall not commit an act discreditable to the profession.

Rule 502   Advertising and Other Forms of Solicitation

A member in public practice shall not seek to obtain clients by advertising or other forms of solicitation in a manner that is false, misleading, or deceptive. Solicitation by the use of coercion, over-reaching, or harassing conduct is prohibited.

Rule 503   Commissions and Referral Fees

A. *Prohibited Commissions*

A member in public practice shall not for a commission recommend or refer to a client any product or service, or for a commission recommend or refer any product or service to be supplied by a client, or receive a commission, when the member or the member's firm also performs for that client

(*a*)   an audit or review of a financial statement; or

(*b*)   a compilation of a financial statement when the member expects, or reasonably might expect, that a third party will use the financial statement and the member's compilation report does not disclose a lack of independence; or

(*c*)   an examination of prospective financial information.

This prohibition applies during the period in which the member is engaged to perform any of the services listed above and the period covered by any historical financial statements involved in such listed services.

B. *Disclosure of Permitted Commissions*

A member in public practice who is not prohibited by this rule from performing services for or receiving a commission and who is paid or expects to be paid a commission shall disclose that fact to any person or entity to whom the member recommends or refers a product or service to which the commission relates.

C. *Referral Fees*

Any member who accepts a referral fee for recommending or referring any service of a CPA to any person or entity or who pays a referral fee to obtain a client shall disclose such acceptance or payment to the client.

Rule 504   *[There is currently no rule 504.]*

Rule 505   Form of Organization and Name

A member may practice public accounting only in the form of organization permitted by state law or regulation whose characteristics conform to resolutions of Council.

A member shall not practice public accounting under a firm name that is misleading. Names of one or more past owners may be included in the firm name of a successor organization. Also, an owner surviving the death or withdrawal of all other owners may continue to practice under a name which includes the name of past owners for up to two years after becoming a sole practitioner.

A firm may not designate itself as "Members of the American Institute of Certified Public Accountants" unless all of its owners are members of the Institute.

Appendix A: Council Resolution Designating Bodies to Promulgate Technical Standards

Financial Accounting Standards Board

WHEREAS: In 1959 the Council designated the Accounting Principles Board to establish accounting principles, and

WHEREAS: The Council is advised that the Financial Accounting Standards Board (FASB) has become operational, it is

RESOLVED: That as of the date hereof the FASB, in respect of statements of financial accounting standards finally adopted by such board in accordance with its rules of procedure and the bylaws of the Financial Accounting Foundation, be, and hereby is, designated by this Council as the body to establish accounting principles pursuant to rule 203 and standards on disclosure of financial information for such entities outside financial statements in published financial reports containing financial statements under rule 202 of the Rules of the Code of Professional Conduct of the American Institute of Certified Public Accountants provided, however, any accounting research bulletins, or opinions of the accounting principles board issued or approved for exposure by the accounting principles board prior to April 1, 1973, and finally adopted by such board on or before June 30, 1973, shall constitute statements of accounting principles promulgated by a body designated by Council as contemplated in rule 203 of the Rules of the Code of Professional Conduct unless and until such time as they are expressly superseded by action of the FASB.

Governmental Accounting Standards Board

WHEREAS: The Governmental Accounting Standards Board (GASB) has been established by the board of trustees of the Financial Accounting Foundation (FAF) to issue standards of financial accounting and reporting with respect to activities and transactions of state and local governmental entities, and

WHEREAS: The American Institute of Certified Public Accountants is a signatory to the agreement creating the GASB as an arm of the FAF and has supported the GASB professionally and financially, it is

RESOLVED: That as of the date hereof, the GASB, with respect to statements of governmental accounting standards adopted and issued in July 1984 and subsequently in accordance with its rules of procedure and the bylaws of the FASB, be, and hereby is, designated by the Council of the American Institute of Certified Public Accountants as the body to establish financial accounting principles for state and local governmental entities pursuant to rule 203, and standards on disclosure of financial information for such entities outside financial statements in published financial reports containing financial statements under rule 202.

AICPA Committees and Boards

WHEREAS: The membership of the Institute has adopted rules 201 and 202 of the Rules of the Code of Professional Conduct, which authorizes the Council to designate bodies to promulgate technical standards with which members must comply, and therefore it is

Accounting and Review Services Committee

RESOLVED: That the AICPA accounting and review services committee is hereby designated to promulgate standards under rules 201 and 202 with respect to unaudited financial statements or other unaudited financial information of an entity that is not required to file financial statements with a regulatory agency in connection with the sale or trading of its securities in a public market.

Auditing Standards Board

RESOLVED: That the AICPA auditing standards board is hereby designated as the body authorized under rules 201 and 202 to promulgate auditing and attest standards and procedures.

RESOLVED: That the auditing standards board shall establish under statements on auditing standards the responsibilities of members with respect to standards for disclosure of financial information outside financial statements in published financial reports containing financial statements.

Management Consulting Services Executive Committee

RESOLVED: That the AICPA management consulting services executive committee is hereby designated to promulgate standards under rules 201 and 202 with respect to the offering of management consulting services, provided, however, that such standards do not deal with the broad question of what, if any, services should be proscribed.

AND FURTHER RESOLVED: That any Institute committee or board now or in the future authorized by the Council to issue enforceable standards under rules 201 and 202 must observe an exposure process seeking comment from other affected committees and boards, as well as the general membership.

Attestation Standards

RESOLVED: That the AICPA accounting and review services committee, auditing standards board, and management consulting services executive committee are hereby designated as bodies authorized under rules 201 and 202 to promulgate attestation standards in their respective areas of responsibility.

Appendix B: Council Resolution Concerning Form of Organization and Name

RESOLVED: That under rule 505, a member may practice public accounting in a business form other than a proprietorship or partnership only if such entity has the following characteristics:

1   *Ownership.* All owners shall be persons who hold themselves out to be certified public accountants or public accountants and who perform for clients one or more types of services performed by certified public accountants or public accountants. Owners shall at all times own their equity in their own right and shall be the beneficial owners of the equity capital ascribed to them.

2   *Transfer of Ownership.* Provision shall be made requiring any owner who ceases to be eligible to be an equity owner to dispose of all his or her interest within a reasonable period to a person qualified to be an owner or to the entity.

3   *Directors and Officers.* The principal executive officer shall be an owner and a member of the entity's governing body. Lay governing body members shall not exercise any authority whatsoever over professional matters.

4   *Conduct.* The form of organization shall not change the obligation of its owners, directors, officers, and other employees to comply with the Code of Professional Conduct established by the American Institute of Certified Public Accountants.

REVIEW QUESTIONS

1   What are "cute accounting" and "cooking the books"?

2   Why is the Equity Funding Corporation of America fraud significant for management accountants and financial executives?

3   Identify the four components of ethical conduct for management accountants, set forth in *Standards of Ethical Conduct for Management Accountants* of the Institute of Management Accountants.

4   How did the National Commission on Fraudulent Financial Reporting (Treadway Commission) define *fraudulent financial reporting?*

5   What Rules of Professional Conduct of the American Institute of Certified Public Accountants apply to all members of the AICPA, including management accountants?

6   Do the ethics codes of the Institute of Management Accountants and the Financial Executives Institute require their members to comply with generally accepted accounting principles? Explain.

7   What is *insider trading* of corporate securities?

8   Does the Securities and Exchange Commission accept a "good soldier" rationalization for fraudulent financial reporting? Explain.

9 What are the obligations of management accountants regarding *conflicts of interest?*

10 Does the *Code of Ethics* of the Financial Executives Institute require FEI members to maintain the confidentiality of information acquired in the course of their work in all circumstances? Explain.

11 Does the *Code of Professional Conduct* of the American Institute of Certified Public Accountants require AICPA members in industry to maintain the appearance of independence? Explain.

EXERCISE

Ex. 1-1 Select the best answer for each of the following multiple-choice questions:

1 The bylaws of the AICPA require members to adhere to the Code of Professional Conduct section entitled:
a Principles
b Rules
c Interpretations
d Ethics Rulings

2 A rule of the AICPA Code of Professional Conduct that does not apply to AICPA members in private industry is:
a Rule 101–Independence
b Rule 102–Integrity and objectivity
c Rule 201–General standards
d Rule 203–Accounting principles

3 Conduct of a member's personal affairs is addressed in the ethics code or codes of the:
a American Institute of Certified Public Accountants only
b Financial Executives Institute only
c Institute of Management Accountants only
d Three organizations cited above

4 According to the National Commission on Fraudulent Financial Reporting (Treadway Commission), the responsibility for reliable financial reporting lies first and foremost:
a At the corporate level
b With the SEC
c With independent auditors
d With state boards of accountancy

5 Does *fraudulent financial reporting* include:

	Cooking the books?	Cute accounting?
a	No	Yes
b	No	No
c	Yes	Yes
d	Yes	No

6   According to the AICPA, are financial statements of a business enterprise that have been drafted by the enterprise's independent auditors the representations of the enterprise's:

	Management?	*Independent auditors?*
a	Yes	Yes
b	Yes	No
c	No	Yes
d	No	No

7   *Standards of Ethical Conduct for Management Accountants* of the Institute of Management Accountants deal with all of the following except:
a Competence
b Confidentiality
c Independence
d Integrity
e Objectivity

8   The *Report of the National Commission on Fraudulent Financial Reporting* did not include recommendations for:
a Financial institution regulators
b Legal counsel of business enterprises
c Educators
d State boards of accountancy

9   Are conflicts of interest addressed *directly* in the ethics codes of the:

	IMA?	*FEI?*	*AICPA?*
a	Yes	Yes	Yes
b	Yes	No	Yes
c	No	Yes	Yes
d	No	No	Yes

10   Compliance with generally accepted accounting principles is required by the ethics code of the:
a AICPA only
b AICPA and FEI
c AICPA and IMA
d AICPA, FEI, and IMA

11   According to *Standards of Ethical Conduct for Management Accountants* of the Institute of Management Accountants, management accountants faced with significant ethical issues should first:
a Discuss the issue with the immediate superior, except when it appears the superior is involved.
b Clarify relevant concepts by confidential discussion with an objective adviser.
c Discuss the issue with the audit committee of the board of directors.
d Follow the established policies of the business enterprise bearing on the resolution of such issues.

12 The section of the American Institute of Certified Public Accountants Code of Professional Conduct that governs the performance of professional services by AICPA members is the:

a Principles

b Rules

c Bylaws

d Technical standards

CASES

Case 1-1 According to Ralph E. Walters (page 7 of the text): "An obligation to be *impartial* seems to me to place a new and possibly unrealistic burden on the management accountant."

Instructions

Do you agree with Walters? Explain.

Case 1-2 In a discussion of ethics for financial executives, student A opined that the Financial Executives Institute erred in requiring its members to conduct their *personal affairs* as well as their *business affairs* at all times with honesty and integrity. According to A, such a requirement is an unwarranted invasion of FEI members' privacy. Student B disagreed, stating that FEI members' conduct in business affairs is significantly affected by their conduct in personal affairs, and therefore conduct in both areas appropriately is subjected to the same high standards by the FEI.

Instructions

Do you agree with student A or student B? Explain.

Case 1-3 Vernon Cass, chief financial officer of Tingley Corporation, a publicly owned enterprise, asked his subordinate, John Conroy, CPA and controller of Tingley, if any accounting changes might be made before the forthcoming close of the fiscal year to enhance Tingley's earnings for the year. Conroy suggested that he might extend economic lives of plant assets, reduce the percentage used to estimate doubtful accounts expense based on net credit sales, and defer, rather than expense, certain advertising costs that consistently had been recognized as expenses in prior years. Cass instructed Conroy to formalize a proposal incorporating those suggestions, for consideration by the audit committee of Tingley's board of directors.

Instructions

Evaluate the actions of Vernon Cass and John Conroy. (Suggestion: Consider the provisions of *APB Opinion No. 20,* "Accounting Changes," and *Statement on Auditing Standards No. 57,* "Auditing Accounting Estimates," in your discussion.)

Case 1-4 The following excerpt is from *Standards of Ethical Conduct for Management Accountants* of the Institute of Management Accountants:

If [an] ethical conflict still exists after exhausting all levels of internal review, the management accountant may have no other recourse on significant matters

than to resign from the organization and to submit an informative memorandum
to an appropriate representative of the organization.

Instructions

What is your opinion of the foregoing excerpt? Explain.

Case 1-5   Certified public accountants (CPAs) typically are subject to codes of ethics or conduct enacted by state boards of accountancy that license the accountants.

Instructions

Given that CPAs are subject to oversight by state boards of accountancy, what is the
incentive—if any—for CPAs in management accounting to be members of the
AICPA, the FEI, and the IMA? Explain.

Part 1

Accounting for Partnerships and Branches

Partnerships, both general and limited, involve accounting problems not present in corporations. Limited legal life, owners who often are active in the operation of the business, varied net income and loss sharing arrangements, and unlimited liability of partners for unpaid debts of a partnership are a few of the features of partnerships that necessitate specialized accounting and reporting principles. Joint ventures, both incorporated and unincorporated, also have features that differentiate them from both corporations and general or limited partnerships and give rise to unique accounting practices.

Accounting for home office and branches or divisions of a single corporation requires separate accounting entities where no separate legal entities exist. A result is the need for working papers for combined financial statements of the single corporation.

2

Partnership Organization and Operation

Nature of Partnerships

Much of the following discussion of partnerships is based on the Uniform Partnership Act, which has been adopted by most of the states. This Act defines a ***partnership*** (often referred to as a *firm*) as *"an association of two or more persons to carry on, as co-owners, a business for profit."* In this definition, the term ***persons*** includes individuals and other partnerships, and in some states corporations may be partners. The creation of a ***general partnership*** requires no approval by the state; in fact, a partnership may be formed orally, although a carefully formulated written contract is highly desirable. (The special requirements for formation of a ***limited partnership*** are discussed in a subsequent section of this chapter.)

Partnerships traditionally are associated with the practice of law, medicine, public accounting, and other professions, and also with small business enterprises. In some states licensed professional persons such as CPAs are forbidden to incorporate because the creation of a corporate entity might weaken the confidential relationship between the professional person and the client. However, a number of states have approved legislation designed to permit ***professional corporations,*** which have various requirements as to professional licensing of stockholders, transfers of stock ownership, and malpractice insurance coverage.

ORGANIZATION OF A GENERAL PARTNERSHIP

Characteristics of a General Partnership

The basic characteristics of a partnership are summarized below and on page 32.

Ease of Formation   In contrast with a corporation, a general partnership may be created by an oral or a written contract between two or more persons, or may be ***implied by their conduct.*** This advantage of convenience and minimum expense in the formation of a partnership in some cases may be offset by certain difficulties inherent in such an informal organizational structure.

31

Limited Life   A general partnership may be ended by the death, retirement, bankruptcy, or incapacity of a partner. The admission of a new partner to the partnership legally ends the former partnership and establishes a new one.

Mutual Agency   Each partner has the authority to act for the partnership and to enter into contracts on its behalf. However, acts beyond the normal scope of business operations, such as the obtaining of a bank loan by a partner, generally do not bind the partnership unless specific authority has been given to the partner to enter into such transactions.

Unlimited Liability   The term *general partnership* refers to a firm in which all the partners are responsible for liabilities of the firm and all have authority to act for the firm. Partnership creditors having difficulty in collecting from the partnership may request payment from any partner who has personal financial resources in excess of personal liabilities. In a *limited partnership,* one or more of the partners have no responsibility for liabilities of the partnership. The activities of limited partners are somewhat restricted, and they must maintain an agreed investment in the partnership or withdraw completely. The Uniform Limited Partnership Act requires that the firm identify itself publicly as a limited partnership and that at least one member of the firm be a *general partner* who is responsible for unpaid liabilities of the firm.

Co-ownership of Partnership Assets and Earnings   When individuals invest assets in a partnership, they retain no claim to those specific assets but acquire an *ownership equity in net assets* of the partnership. Every member of a partnership also has an ownership equity in partnership earnings; in fact, participation in earnings and losses is one of the tests of the existence of a partnership.

Deciding between a Partnership and a Corporation

One of the most important considerations in choosing between a partnership and the corporate form of business organization is the income tax status of the enterprise and of its owners. A partnership pays no income tax but is required to file an annual *information return* showing its revenue and expenses, the amount of its net income, and the division of the net income among the partners. The partners report their respective shares of the *ordinary net income* from the partnership and such items as dividends and charitable contributions in their individual income tax returns, regardless of whether they received more or less than this amount of cash from the partnership during the year.

  A corporation is a separate legal entity subject to a corporate income tax. The net income, when and if distributed to stockholders as dividends, also is taxable income to stockholders. Certain corporations with few stockholders may elect to be taxed as partnerships, provided their net income or loss is assumed by their stockholders. These corporations file information returns as do partnerships, and their stockholders report in individual tax returns their respective shares of the year's net income or loss. Thus, a partnership may incorporate as a *Subchapter S Corporation* to gain the advantages of limited liability but at the same time elect to be taxed as a partnership. Income tax rates and regulations are subject to frequent change, and new interpretations of tax laws often arise. The tax status of the owners also is likely to change from year to year. For these reasons, management of a business enterprise should review the tax implications of the partnership and corporate forms of organization so that the enterprise may adapt most successfully to the income tax environment.

The burden of taxation is not the only factor influencing a choice between the partnership and the corporate form of organization. Perhaps the factor that most often tips the scales in favor of incorporation is the opportunity for obtaining larger amounts of capital when ownership may be divided into shares of capital stock, readily transferable, and offering the advantages inherent in the separation of ownership and management. Another reason for choosing the corporate form of organization is the limited liability of stockholders for unpaid debts of the corporation.

Is the Partnership a Separate Entity?

In accounting literature, the legal status of partnerships often has received more emphasis than the fact that they are business enterprises. It has been common practice to distinguish a partnership from a corporation by saying that a partnership was an "association of persons" and a corporation was a separate entity. Such a distinction stresses the *legal form* rather than the *economic substance* of the business organization. In terms of managerial policy and business objectives, partnerships are as much business and accounting entities as are corporations. Partnerships typically are guided by long-range plans not likely to be affected by the admission or withdrawal of a single partner. In these firms the accounting policies should reflect the fact that the partnership is an accounting entity apart from its owners.

Treating the partnership as an economic and accounting entity often will aid in developing financial statements that provide the most meaningful presentation of financial position and results of operations. Among the accounting policies to be stressed is continuity in asset valuation, despite changes in the income-sharing ratio and changes in ownership. Another appropriate policy may be recognizing as expenses the salaries for personal services rendered by partners who also hold managerial positions. In theoretical discussions, considerable support is found for treating every business enterprise as an accounting entity, apart from its owners, regardless of the form of organization. A managing partner under this view is both an employee and an owner, and the salary for the personal services rendered by a partner is an operating expense of the partnership.

The inclusion of partners' salaries among expenses has been opposed by some accountants on grounds that partners' salaries may be set at unrealistic levels and that a partnership is an association of individuals who are owners and not employees of the partnership, despite their managerial or other functions.

A partnership has the characteristics of a separate entity in that it may hold title to property, may enter into contracts, and in some states may sue or be sued as an entity. In practice, most accountants treat partnerships as separate entities with continuity of accounting policies and asset valuations not interrupted by changes in ownership.

The Partnership Contract

Although a general partnership may exist on the basis of an oral agreement or may be implied by the actions of its members, good business practice requires that the partnership contract be in writing. The most important points covered in a partner-ship contract are the following:

1   The date of formation and the planned duration of the partnership, the names of the partners, and the name and business activities of the partnership.

2   The assets to be invested by each partner, the procedure for valuing noncash investments, and the penalties for a partner's failure to invest and maintain the agreed amount of capital.

3   The authority of each partner and the rights and duties of each.

4   The accounting period to be used, the nature of accounting records, financial statements, and audits by independent public accountants.

5   The plan for sharing net income or loss, including the frequency of income measurement and the distribution of the income or loss among the partners.

6   The drawings allowed to partners and the penalties, if any, for excessive with-drawals.

7   Insurance on the lives of partners, with the partnership or surviving partners named as beneficiaries.

8   Provision for arbitration of disputes and liquidation of the partnership at the end of the term specified in the contract or at the death or retirement of a partner. Especially important in avoiding disputes is agreement on procedures such as bind-ing arbitration for the valuation of the partnership assets and the method of settle-ment with the estate of a deceased partner.

One advantage of preparing a partnership contract with the aid of attorneys and accountants is that the process of reaching agreement on specific issues will develop a better understanding among the partners on many issues that might be highly controversial if not settled at the outset. However, it is seldom possible to cover in a partnership contract every issue that may later arise. Revision of the partnership contract generally requires the approval of all partners.

Disputes arising among partners that cannot be resolved by reference to the partnership contract may be settled by binding arbitration or in the courts. A partner who is not satisfied with the handling of disputes always has the right to withdraw from the partnership.

Owners' Equity Ledger Accounts for Partners

Accounting for a partnership differs from accounting for a single proprietorship or a corporation with respect to the sharing of net income and losses and the maintenance of the owners' equity ledger accounts. Although it would be possible to maintain partnership accounting records with only one ownership equity account for each partner, the usual practice is to maintain three types of accounts. These ownership equity accounts consist of (1) *capital* accounts, (2) *drawing* or *personal* accounts, and (3) accounts for *loans* to and from partners.

The original investment by each partner is recorded by debiting the assets invested, crediting any liabilities assumed by the partnership, and crediting the partner's capital account with the current fair value of the ***net assets*** (assets minus liabilities) invested. Subsequent to the original investment, the partner's equity is ***increased*** by additional investments and by a share of net income; the partner's equity is ***decreased*** by withdrawal of cash or other assets and by a share of net losses.

Another possible source of increase or decrease in partners' ownership equity results from changes in ownership, as described in subsequent sections of this chapter.

The original investment of assets by partners is recorded by credits to the capital accounts; drawings by partners in anticipation of net income or drawings that are considered salary allowances are recorded by debits to the drawing accounts. However, a large withdrawal that is considered a permanent reduction in the ownership equity of a partner is debited directly to the partner's capital account.

At the end of each accounting period, the net income or net loss in the Income Summary ledger account is transferred to the partners' capital accounts in accordance with the partnership contract. The debit balances in the drawing accounts at the end of the period also are closed to the partners' capital accounts. Because the accounting procedures for partners' ownership equity accounts are not subject to state regulations as in the case of capital stock and other stockholders' equity accounts of a corporation, many acceptable deviations from the procedures described here are possible.

Loans to and from Partners

Occasionally, a partner may receive cash from the partnership with the intention of repaying this amount. Such a transaction may be debited to the Loans Receivable from Partners ledger account rather than to the partner's drawing account.

Conversely, a partner may make a cash payment to the partnership that is considered a loan rather than an increase in the partner's capital account balance. This transaction is recorded by a credit to Loans Payable to Partners and generally is accompanied by the issuance of a promissory note. Loans receivable from partners are displayed as assets in the partnership balance sheet and loans payable to partners are displayed as liabilities. The classification of these items as current or long-term generally depends on the maturity date, although these ***related party transactions*** may result in noncurrent classification of the partners' loans, regardless of maturity dates.

If a substantial unsecured loan has been made by a partnership to one of the partners and repayment appears doubtful, it is appropriate to offset the receivable against the partner's capital account balance. If this is not done, partnership assets and total partners' equity may be misleading. In any event, the disclosure principle requires separate listing of any receivables from partners.

Valuation of Investments by Partners

The investment by a partner in the firm often includes assets other than cash. It is imperative that the partners agree on the current fair value of nonmonetary assets at the time of their investment and that the assets be recognized in the accounting records at such values. Any gains or losses resulting from the disposal of such assets during the operation of the partnership, or at the time of liquidation, generally are divided according to the plan for sharing net income or losses. Therefore, equitable treatment of the individual partners requires a starting point of current fair values recorded for all noncash assets invested in the firm. Thus, partnership gains or losses from disposal of noncash assets invested by the partners will be measured by the difference between the disposal price and the current fair value of the assets when invested by partners, adjusted for any depreciation or amortization to the date of disposal.

INCOME-SHARING PLANS FOR GENERAL PARTNERSHIPS

Partners' Equity in Assets versus Share in Earnings

The equity of a partner in the net assets of the partnership should be distinguished from a partner's share in earnings. Thus, to say that David Jones is a one-third partner is not a clear statement. Jones may have a one-third equity in the net assets of the partnership but have a larger or smaller share in the net income or losses of the firm. Such a statement might also be interpreted to mean that Jones was entitled to one-third of the net income or losses, although his capital account represented much more or much less than one-third of the total partners' capital. To state the matter concisely, partners may agree on any type of *income-sharing plan (profit and loss ratio),* regardless of the amount of their respective capital account balances. The Uniform Partnership Act provides that if partners fail to specify a plan for sharing net income or losses, *it is assumed that they intended to share equally.* Because income sharing is of such great importance, it is rare to find a situation in which the partnership contract is silent on this point.

Division of Net Income or Loss

The many possible plans for sharing of net income or loss among partners of a general partnership may be summarized in the following categories:

1   Equally, or in some other ratio

2   In the ratio of partners' capital account balances on a particular date, or in the ratio of average capital account balances during the year

3   Allowing interest on partners' capital account balances and dividing the remaining net income or loss in a specified ratio

4   Allowing salaries to partners and dividing the resultant net income or loss in a specified ratio

5   Bonus to managing partner based on income

6   Allowing salaries to partners, allowing interest on capital account balances, and dividing the remaining net income or loss in a specified ratio

These alternative income-sharing plans emphasize that the value of personal services rendered by individual partners may vary widely, as may the amounts of capital invested by each partner. The amount and quality of managerial services rendered and the amount of capital invested often are important factors in the success or failure of a partnership. Therefore, provisions may be made for salaries to partners and interest on their respective capital account balances as a preliminary step in the division of net income or loss. Any remaining net income or loss then may be divided in a specified ratio.

Another factor affecting the success of a partnership may be that one of the partners has large personal financial resources, thus giving the partnership a strong credit rating. Similarly, partners who are well known in a profession or an industry may contribute importantly to the success of the partnership even though they may not participate actively in the operations of the partnership. These two factors may be incorporated in the income-sharing plan by careful selection of the ratio in which any remaining net income or loss is divided.

I now illustrate how each of the methods of dividing net income or loss may be applied. This series of illustrations is based on data for the A & B Partnership, which had a net income of $300,000 for the year ended December 31, Year 1, the first year of operations. The partnership contract provides that each partner may withdraw $5,000 on the last day of each month; both partners did so during Year 1. The drawings are recorded by debits to the partners' drawing accounts and are not a factor in the division of net income or loss; all other withdrawals, investments, and net income or loss are entered directly in the partners' capital accounts.

Partner A invested $400,000 on January 1, Year 1, and an additional $100,000 on April 1. Partner B invested $800,000 on January 1 and withdrew $50,000 on July 1. These transactions and events are summarized in the following capital, drawing, and Income Summary ledger accounts:

Ledger accounts for Year 1

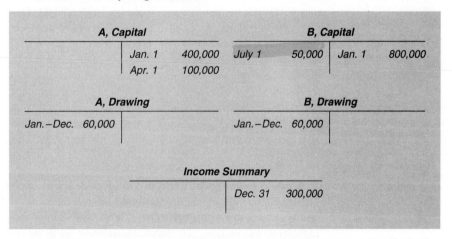

Division of Earnings Equally or in Some Other Ratio   Many partnership contracts provide that net income or loss is to be divided equally. Also, if the partners have made no specific agreement for income sharing, the Uniform Partnership Act provides that an intent of equal division is assumed. The net income of $300,000 for the A & B Partnership is transferred by a closing entry on December 31, Year 1, from the Income Summary ledger account to the partners' capital accounts by the following journal entry:

Journal entry to close
Income Summary
ledger account

Income Summary 300,000
    A, Capital   150,000
    B, Capital   150,000
To record division of net income for Year 1.

The drawing accounts are closed to the partners' capital accounts on December 31, Year 1 as follows:

Journal entry to close
drawing accounts

A, Capital 60,000
B, Capital 60,000
    A, Drawing   60,000
    B, Drawing   60,000
To close drawing accounts.

After the drawing accounts are closed, the balances of the partners' capital accounts show the ownership equity of each partner.

If the A & B Partnership had a net loss of, say, $200,000 during the year ended December 31, Year 1, the Income Summary ledger account would have a debit balance of $200,000. This loss would be transferred to the partners' capital accounts by a debit to each capital account for $100,000 and a credit to the Income Summary account for $200,000.

If A and B share earnings in the ratio of 60% to A and 40% to B and net income was $300,000, the net income would be divided $180,000 to A and $120,000 to B. The agreement that A should receive 60% of the net income (perhaps because of greater experience and personal contacts) would cause Partner A to absorb a larger share of the net loss if the partnership operated unprofitably. Some partnership contracts provide that a net income is to be divided in a specified ratio, such as 60% to A and 40% to B, but that a net loss is divided equally or in some other ratio. Another variation intended to compensate for unequal contributions by the partners provides that an agreed ratio (60% and 40% in this example) shall be applicable to a specified amount of income but that any additional income shall be shared in some other ratio.

Division of Earnings in Ratio of Partners' Capital Account Balances Division of partnership earnings in proportion to the capital invested by each partner is most likely to be found in partnerships in which substantial investment is the principal ingredient for success. To avoid controversy, it is essential that the partnership contract specify whether the income-sharing ratio is based on (1) the original capital investments, (2) the capital account balances at the beginning of each year, (3) the balances at the end of each year (before the distribution of net income or loss), or (4) the average balances during each year.

Continuing the illustration for the A & B Partnership, assume that the partnership contract provides for division of net income in the ratio of *original capital investments.* The net income of $300,000 for Year 1 is divided as follows:

Division of net income
in ratio of original
capital investments

> A: $300,000 \times \$400,000/\$1,200,000 = \$100,000$
>
> B: $300,000 \times \$800,000/\$1,200,000 = \$200,000$

The journal entry to close the Income Summary ledger account would be similar to the journal entry illustrated on page 38.

Assuming that the net income is divided in the ratio of capital account balances at the **end of the year** (before drawings and the distribution of net income), the net income of $300,000 for Year 1 is divided as follows:

Division of net income
in ratio of end-of-year
capital account
balances

> A: $300,000 \times \$500,000/\$1,250,000 = \$120,000$
>
> B: $300,000 \times \$750,000/\$1,250,000 = \$180,000$

Division of net income on the basis of (1) original capital investments, (2) yearly beginning capital account balances, or (3) yearly ending capital account balances may prove inequitable if there are material changes in capital accounts during the year. Use of average balances as a basis for sharing net income is preferable because it reflects the capital actually available for use by the partnership during the year.

If the partnership contract provides for sharing net income in the ratio of average capital account balances during the year, it also should state the amount of drawings each partner may make without affecting the capital account. In the continuing example for the A & B Partnership, the partners are entitled to withdraw $5,000 monthly. Any additional withdrawals or investments are entered directly in the partners' capital accounts and therefore influence the computation of the average capital ratio. The partnership contract also should state whether capital account balances are to be computed to the nearest month or to the nearest day.

The computations of average capital account balances to the nearest month and the division of net income for the A & B Partnership for Year 1 are on page 40.

Interest on Partners' Capital Account Balances with Remaining Net Income or Loss Divided in Specified Ratio   In the preceding section, the plan for dividing the entire net income in the ratio of partners' capital account balances was based on the assumption that invested capital was the dominant factor in the success of the partnership. However, in most cases the amount of invested capital is only one factor that contributes to the success of the partnership. Consequently, many partnerships choose to divide only a portion of net income in the capital ratio and to divide the remainder equally or in some other specified ratio.

To allow interest on partners' capital account balances at 15%, for example, is the same as dividing a part of net income in the ratio of partners' capital balances. If the partners agree to allow interest on capital as a first step in the division of net income, they should specify the interest rate to be used and also state whether interest is to be computed on capital account balances on specific dates or on average capital balances during the year.

A & B PARTNERSHIP
Computation of Average Capital Account Balances
For Year Ended December 31, Year 1

Partner	Date	Increase (decrease) in capital	Capital account balance	Fraction of year unchanged	Average capital account balances
A	Jan. 1	400,000	400,000	¼	100,000
	Apr. 1	100,000	500,000	¾	375,000
					475,000
B	Jan. 1	800,000	800,000	½	400,000
	July 1	(50,000)	750,000	½	375,000
					775,000

Total average capital account balances for A and B.   1,250,000

Division of net income:

To A: $300,000 × $475,000/$1,250,000.   114,000

To B: $300,000 × $775,000/$1,250,000.   186,000

Total net income   300,000

Again refer to the A & B Partnership with a net income of $300,000 for Year 1 and capital account balances as shown on page 37. Assume that the partnership contract allows interest on partners' average capital account balances at 15%, with any remaining net income or loss to be divided equally. The net income of $300,000 for Year 1 is divided as follows:

Division of net income with interest allowed on average capital account balances

	A	B	Combined
Interest on average capital account balances:			
A: $475,000 × 0.15	$ 71,250		$ 71,250
B: $775,000 × 0.15		$116,250	116,250
Subtotal.			$187,500
Remainder ($300,000 − $187,500) divided equally .	56,250	56,250	112,500
Totals.	$127,500	$172,500	$300,000

The journal entry to close the Income Summary ledger account on December 31, Year 1, is similar to the journal entry illustrated on page 38.

As a separate case, assume that the A & B Partnership had a net loss of $10,000 for the year ended December 31, Year 1. If the partnership contract provides for allowing interest on capital accounts, this provision *must be honored regardless of whether operations are profitable or unprofitable.* The only justification for omitting the allowance of interest on partners' capital accounts during a loss year would be in the case of a partnership contract containing a specific provision requiring such omission. Note in the following analysis that the $10,000 debit balance of the Income

Summary ledger account resulting from the net loss is increased by the allowance of interest to $197,500, which is divided equally between A and B:

Division of net loss		A	B	Combined
Interest on average capital account balances:				
A: $475,000 × 0.15......................		$ 71,250		$ 71,250
B: $775,000 × 0.15......................			$116,250	116,250
Subtotal.............................				$187,500
Resulting deficiency ($10,000 + $187,500)				
divided equally........................		(98,750)	(98,750)	197,500
Totals..............................		$(27,500)	$ 17,500	$ (10,000)

The journal entry to close the Income Summary ledger account on December 31, Year 1, is shown below:

Closing the Income Summary ledger account with a debit balance

```
A, Capital ................................................... 27,500
     Income Summary .........................................        10,000
     B, Capital .............................................        17,500
To record division of net loss for Year 1.
```

At first thought, the idea that a net loss of $10,000 should cause one partner's capital to increase and the other partner's capital to decrease may appear unreasonable, but there is sound logic to support this result. Partner B invested substantially more capital than did Partner A; this capital was used to carry on operations, and the partnership's incurring of a net loss in the first year is no reason to disregard B's larger capital investment.

A significant contrast between two of the income-sharing plans I have discussed (the capital-ratio plan and the interest-on-capital-accounts plan) is apparent if one considers the case of a partnership operating at a loss. Under the capital-ratio plan, the partner who invested more capital is required to bear a larger share of the net loss. This result may be considered unreasonable because the investment of capital presumably is not the cause of a net loss. Under the interest plan of sharing earnings, the partner who invested more capital receives credit for this factor and is charged with a lesser share of the net loss, or may even end up with a net credit.

I have considered interest allowances on partners' capital accounts as a technique for sharing partnership earnings equitably but as having no effect on the measurement of the net income or loss of the partnership. Interest on partners' capital accounts *is not an expense of the partnership,* but interest on loans from partners is recognized as expense and a factor in the measurement of net income or loss of the partnership. Similarly, interest earned on loans to partners is recognized as partnership revenue. This treatment is consistent with the point made on page 35 that loans to and from partners are assets and liabilities, respectively, of the partnership.

Another item of expense arising from dealings between a partnership and one of its partners is commonly encountered when the partnership leases property from a lessor who is also a partner. Rent expense is recognized by the partnership in such situations. The lessor, although a partner, also is a lessor to the partnership.

Salary Allowance with Resultant Net Income or Loss Divided in Specified Ratio

In discussing salaries to partners, I must distinguish between salaries and drawings. Because the term *salaries* suggests weekly or monthly cash payments for personal services that are recognized as operating expenses by the partnership, accountants should be specific in suggesting and defining the terminology used in accounting for a partnership. I use the term *drawings* in only one sense: a withdrawal of cash or other assets that reduces the partner's equity but has no part in the division of net income. I limit the word *salaries* in partnership accounting to mean an operating expense included in measuring net income or loss. When the term *salaries* is used with this meaning, the division of net income is the same, regardless of whether the salaries have been paid.

A partnership contract that authorizes partners to make regular withdrawals of specific amounts should state whether such withdrawals are intended to be a factor in the division of net income or loss. For example, assume that the contract states that Partner A may make drawings of $3,000 monthly and Partner B $8,000. If the intent is not clearly stated to include or exclude these drawings as an element in the division of net income or loss, controversy is probable, because one interpretation will favor Partner A and the opposing interpretation will favor Partner B.

Assuming that Partner A has more experience and ability than Partner B and also devotes more time to the partnership, it seems reasonable that the partners will want to recognize the more valuable contribution of personal services by A in choosing a plan for division of net income or loss. One approach to this objective would be to adopt an unequal ratio: for example, 70% of net income or loss to A and 30% to B. However, the use of such a ratio usually is not a satisfactory solution, for the same reasons mentioned in criticizing the capital ratio as a profit sharing plan. A ratio based only on personal services may not reflect the fact that other factors are important in determining the success of the partnership. A second point is that if the partnership incurs a loss, the partner rendering more personal services will absorb a larger portion of the loss.

A solution to the problem of recognizing unequal personal services by partners is to provide in the partnership contract for different salaries to partners, with the resultant net income or loss divided equally or in some other ratio. Applying this reasoning to the continuing illustration for the A & B Partnership, assume that the partnership contract provides for an annual salary of $100,000 to A and $60,000 to B, with resultant net income or loss to be divided equally. The salaries are paid monthly during the year. The net income of $140,000 for Year 1 is divided as follows:

Division of $140,000 net income after salaries expense

	A	B	Combined
Salaries	$100,000	$ 60,000	$160,000
Net income ($300,000 − $160,000) divided equally	70,000	70,000	140,000
Totals	$170,000	$130,000	$300,000

The journal entries required for the foregoing are as follows:

1   Monthly journal entries debiting Partners' Salaries Expense, $13,333 ($160,000 ÷ 12 = $13,333) and crediting A, Capital, $8,333 ($100,000 ÷ 12 = $8,333) and B, Capital, $5,000 ($60,000 ÷ 12 = $5,000)

2   Monthly journal entries debiting A, Drawing, $8,333 and B, Drawing, $5,000 and crediting Cash, $13,333

3   End-of-year journal entry debiting Income Summary, $140,000, and crediting A, Capital, $70,000 and B, Capital, $70,000

Bonus to Managing Partner Based on Income   A partnership contract may provide for a bonus to the managing partner equal to a specified percentage of income. The contract should state whether the basis of the bonus is net income without deduction of the bonus as an operating expense or income after the bonus. For example, assume that the A & B Partnership provides for a bonus to Partner A of 25% of net income and that the remaining income is divided equally. The net income is $300,000. After the bonus of $75,000 ($300,000 × 0.25 = $75,000) to A, the remaining $225,000 of income is divided $112,500 to A and $112,500 to B. Thus, A's share of income is $187,500 ($75,000 + $112,500 = $187,500), and B's share is $112,500; the bonus *is not* recognized as an expense.

If the partnership contract provided for a bonus of 25% of income *after the bonus* to Partner A, the bonus is computed as follows:

<table>
<tr><td>Bonus based on
income after bonus</td><td>

$Bonus + income\ after\ bonus = \$300,000$

$\qquad Let\ X = income\ after\ bonus$

$\qquad 0.25X = bonus$

$Then\ 1.25X = \$300,000\ income\ before\ bonus$

$\qquad\qquad X = \$300,000 \div 1.25$

$\qquad\qquad X = \$240,000$

$\qquad 0.25X = \underline{\$60,000}\ bonus\ to\ Partner\ A[1]$

</td></tr>
</table>

Thus, the pre-bonus income of $300,000 in this case is divided $180,000 to A and $120,000 to B, and the $60,000 bonus *is* recognized as an operating expense.

The concept of a bonus is not applicable to a net loss. When a partnership operates at a loss, the bonus provision is disregarded. The partnership contract also may specify that extraordinary items or other unusual gains and losses are to be excluded from the basis for the computation of the bonus.

---

[1] An alternative computation consists of converting the bonus percentage to a fraction. The bonus then may be computed by adding the numerator to the denominator and applying the resulting fraction to the income before the bonus. In the preceding example, 25% is converted to ¼; and adding the numerator to the denominator, the ¼ becomes ⅕ (4 + 1 = 5). One-fifth of $300,000 equals $60,000, the bonus to Partner A.

Salaries to Partners with Interest on Capital Accounts Many general partnerships divide net income or loss by allowing salaries to partners and also interest on their capital account balances. Any resultant net income or loss is divided equally or in some other ratio. Such plans have the merit of recognizing that the value of personal services rendered by different partners may vary, and that differences in amounts invested also warrant recognition in an equitable plan for sharing net income or loss.

To illustrate, assume that the partnership contract for the A & B Partnership provides for the following:

1 Annual salaries of $100,000 to A and $60,000 to B, recognized as operating expense of the partnership, with salaries to be paid monthly

2 Interest on average capital account balances, as computed on page 41

3 Remaining net income or loss divided equally

Assuming income of $300,000 for Year 1 before annual salaries expense, the $140,000 net income [$300,000 − ($100,000 + $60,000) = $140,000] is divided as follows:

Division of net income after salaries expense

	A	B	Combined
Interest on average capital account balances:			
A: $475,000 × 0.15	$71,250		$ 71,250
B: $775,000 × 0.15		$116,250	116,250
Subtotal.............................			$187,500
Resulting deficiency ($187,500 − $140,000)			
divided equally...........................	(23,750)	(23,750)	(47,500)
Totals...............................	$47,500	$ 92,500	$140,000

The journal entries to recognize partners' salaries expense, partners' withdrawals of the salaries, and closing of the Income Summary ledger account are similar to those described on page 43.

Financial Statements for a General Partnership

Income Statement Explanations of the division of net income among partners may be included in the income statement or in a note to the financial statements. This information is referred to as the *division of net income section* of the income statement. The following illustration for the A & B Partnership shows, in a condensed income statement for the year ended December 31, Year 1, the division of net income as shown above and the disclosure of partners' salaries expense, a *related party* item:

A & B PARTNERSHIP
Income Statement
For Year Ended December 31, Year 1

Net sales		$3,000,000
Cost of goods sold.		1,800,000
Gross margin on sales		$1,200,000
Partners' salaries expense	$160,000	
Other operating expenses	900,000	1,060,000
Net income		$ 140,000
Division of net income:		
Partner A		$ 47,500
Partner B		92,500
Total		$140,000

Note that because a partnership is not subject to income taxes, there is no income taxes expense in the income statement above. A note to the partnership's financial statements may disclose this fact and explain that the partners are taxed for their shares of partnership income, including their salaries.

Statement of Partners' Capital   Partners and other users of partnership financial statements generally want a complete explanation of the changes in the capital accounts each year. To meet this need, a *statement of partners' capital* is prepared. The following illustrative statement of partners' capital for the A & B Partnership is based on the capital accounts presented on page 37 and includes the division of net income for Year 1 illustrated in the income statement above.

A & B PARTNERSHIP
Statement of Partners' Capital
For Year Ended December 31, Year 1

	Partner A	Partner B	Combined
Partners' original investments, beginning of			
year.	$400,000	$800,000	$1,200,000
Additional investment (withdrawal) of capital .	100,000	(50,000)	50,000
Balances before salaries, net income, and			
drawings.	$500,000	$750,000	$1,250,000
Add: Salaries	100,000	60,000	160,000
Net income	47,500	92,500	140,000
Subtotals	$647,500	$902,500	$1,550,000
Less: Drawings	100,000	60,000	160,000
Partners' capital, end of year.	$547,500	$842,500	$1,390,000

Partners' capital at end of year is reported as owners' equity in the December 31, Year 1, balance sheet of the partnership, as illustrated below.

Balance Sheet A condensed balance sheet for the A & B Partnership on December 31, Year 1, is presented below:

A & B PARTNERSHIP
Balance Sheet
December 31, Year 1

Assets		Liabilities & Partners' Capital		
Cash.....................	$ 50,000	Trade accounts payable	$ 240,000	
Trade accounts receivable .	40,000	Long-term debt	370,000	
Inventories	360,000	Total liabilities	$ 610,000	
Plant assets (net).........	1,550,000	Partners' capital:		
		Partner A..... $547,500		
		Partner B..... 842,500	1,390,000	
		Total liabilities &		
Total assets	$2,000,000	partners' capital	$2,000,000	

Statement of Cash Flows A statement of cash flows is prepared for a partnership as it is for a corporation. This financial statement, the preparation of which is explained and illustrated in intermediate accounting textbooks, displays the net cash provided by operating activities, net cash used in investing activities, and net cash provided or used in financing activities of the partnership. A statement of cash flows for the A & B Partnership under the indirect method, which includes the net income from the income statement on page 45 and the investments and combined drawings from the statement of partners' capital on page 45, is presented on page 47.

Correction of Partnership Net Income of Prior Years

Any business enterprise, whether it be a single proprietorship, a partnership, or a corporation, will from time to time discover errors made in the measurement of net income in prior accounting periods. Examples include errors in the estimation of depreciation, errors in inventory valuation, and omission of accruals of revenue and expenses. When such errors are discovered, the question arises as to whether the corrections should be treated as part of the measurement of net income for the current accounting period or as *prior period adjustments* and entered directly to partners' capital accounts.

The correction of prior years' net income is particularly important when the partnership's income-sharing plan has been changed. For example, assume that in Year 1 the net income for the A & B Partnership was $300,000 and that the partners shared the net income equally, but in Year 2 they changed the income-sharing ratio to 60% for A and 40% for B. During Year 2, it was determined that the inventories at the end of Year 1 were overstated by $100,000 because of computational errors. The $100,000 reduction in the net income for Year 1 should be divided $50,000 to each partner, in accordance with the income-sharing ratio in effect for Year 1, the *year in which the error occurred.*

A & B PARTNERSHIP
Statement of Cash Flows (indirect method)
For Year Ended December 31, Year 1

Cash flows from operating activities:

Net income..		$ 140,000
Adjustments to reconcile net income to net cash provided by operating activities:		
Partners' salaries expense........................	$ 160,000	
Depreciation expense	20,000	
Increase in trade accounts receivable	(40,000)	
Increase in inventories...........................	(360,000)	
Increase in trade accounts payable	240,000	20,000
Net cash provided by operating activities		$ 160,000
Cash flows from investing activities:		
Acquisition of plant assets		($1,200,000)
Cash flows from financing activities:		
Partners' investments	$1,300,000	
Partner's withdrawal..............................	(50,000)	
Partners' drawings	(160,000)	
Net cash provided by financing activities.......................		1,090,000
Net increase in cash (cash at end of year)		$ 50,000

Exhibit 1 Noncash investing and financing activity:

Capital lease obligation incurred for plant assets		$ 370,000

Somewhat related to the correction of errors of prior periods is the treatment of nonoperating gains and losses. When the income-sharing ratio of a partnership is changed, the partners should consider the differences that exist between the carrying amounts of assets and their current fair values. For example, assume that the A & B Partnership owns marketable securities acquired for $20,000 that have appreciated in current fair value to $50,000 on the date when the income-sharing ratio is changed from 50% for each partner to 60% for A and 40% for B. If the securities were sold for $50,000 just prior to the change in the income-sharing ratio, the $30,000 gain would be divided $15,000 to A and $15,000 to B; if the securities were sold immediately after establishment of the 60:40 income-sharing ratio, the gain would be divided $18,000 to A and only $12,000 to B.

A solution sometimes suggested for such partnership problems is to revalue the assets to current fair value when the income-sharing ratio is changed or when a new partner is admitted or an old one retires. In some cases the revaluation of assets may be justified, but in general the continuity of historical cost valuations in a partnership is desirable for the same reasons that support the use of that valuation principle in accounting for corporations. A secondary objection to revaluation of assets is that, with a few exceptions such as marketable securities, satisfactory evidence of current fair value is seldom available. The best solution to the problem of a change in the ratio of income sharing usually is achieved by making appropriate adjustments to the partners' capital accounts rather than by a restatement of carrying amounts of assets.

CHANGES IN OWNERSHIP OF GENERAL PARTNERSHIPS

Accounting for Changes in Partners

Most changes in the ownership of a general partnership are accomplished without interruption of its operations. For example, when a large partnership promotes one of its employees to partner, there is usually no significant change in the finances or operating routines of the partnership. However, from a legal viewpoint a partnership is dissolved by the retirement or-death of a partner or by the admission of a new partner.

Dissolution of a partnership also may result from the bankruptcy of the firm or of any partner, the expiration of a time period stated in the partnership contract, or the mutual agreement of the partners to end their association.[2] Thus, the term *dissolution* may be used to describe events ranging from a minor change of ownership interest not affecting operations of the partnership to a decision by the partners to terminate the partnership.

Accountants are concerned with the *economic substance* of an event rather than with its *legal form.* Therefore, they must evaluate all the circumstances of the individual case to determine how a change in partners should be recorded. In the following sections of this chapter, I describe and illustrate the principal kinds of changes in the ownership of a partnership.

Accounting and Managerial Issues

Although a general partnership is ended in a legal sense when a partner withdraws or a new partner is admitted, the partnership often continues operations with little outward evidence of change. In current accounting practice, a partner's interest often is considered a share in the partnership that may be transferred, much as shares of a corporation's capital stock are transferred among stockholders, without disturbing the continuity of the partnership. For example, if a partner of a CPA firm retires or a new partner is admitted to the firm, the contract for the change in ownership should be planned carefully to avoid disturbing client relationships. In a large CPA firm with hundreds of partners, the decision to promote an employee to the rank of partner generally is made by a committee of partners rather than by action of all partners.

Changes in the ownership of a general partnership raise a number of accounting and managerial issues on which an accountant may serve as consultant. Among these issues are the setting of terms for admission of a new partner, the possible revaluation of existing partnership assets, the development of a new plan for the division of net income or loss, and the determination of the amount to be paid to a retiring partner.

---

[2] The *dissolution* of a partnership is defined by the Uniform Partnership Act as "the change in the relation of the partners caused by any partner ceasing to be associated in the carrying on as distinguished from the winding up of the business."

Admission of a New Partner

When a new partner is admitted to a firm of two or three partners, it is particularly appropriate to consider the fairness and adequacy of past accounting policies and the need for correction of errors in prior years' accounting data. The terms of admission of a new partner often are influenced by the level and trend of past earnings, because they may be indicative of future earnings. Sometimes accounting policies such as the use of the completed-contract method of accounting for construction-type contracts or the installment method of accounting for installment sales may cause the accounting records to convey a misleading impression of earnings in the years preceding the admission of a new partner.

Adjustments of the partnership accounting records may be necessary to restate the carrying amounts of assets and liabilities to current fair values before a new partner is admitted.

As an alternative to revaluation of the existing partnership assets, it may be preferable to evaluate any discrepancies between the carrying amounts and current fair values of assets and adjust the terms for admission of the new partner. In this way, the amount invested by the incoming partner may be set at a level that reflects the current fair value of the partnership, even though the carrying amounts of existing partnership assets remain unchanged in the accounting records.

The admission of a new partner to a partnership may be effected either by an *acquisition* of all or part of the interest of one or more of the existing partners or by an *investment* of assets by the new partner with a resultant increase in the net assets of the partnership.

Acquisition of an Interest by Payment to One or More Partners

If a new partner acquires an interest from one or more of the existing partners, the event is recorded by establishing a capital account for the new partner and decreasing the capital account balances of the selling partners by the same amount. No assets are received by the partnership; the transfer of ownership is a private transaction between two or more partners.

As an illustration of this situation, assume that L and M, partners of the L & M Partnership, share net income or losses equally and that each has a capital account balance of $60,000. Partner N (with the consent of M) acquires one-half of L's interest in the partnership by a cash payment to L. The journal entry to record this change in ownership follows:

N acquires one-half of L's interest in partnership	*L, Capital ($60,000 × ½)* *30,000*	
	N, Capital	*30,000*
	To record transfer of one-half of L's capital to N.	

The cash paid by N for half of L's interest may have been the carrying amount of $30,000, or it may have been more or less than the carrying amount. Possibly no cash price was established; L may have made a gift to N of the equity in the partnership. Regardless of the terms of the transaction between L and N, the journal entry illustrated on page 49 is all that is required in the partnership's accounting records; no change has occurred in the partnership assets, liabilities, or *total* partners' capital.

To explore further some of the implications involved in the acquisition of an interest by a new partner, assume that N paid $40,000 to L for one-half of L's $60,000 equity in the partnership. Some accountants have suggested that the willingness of the new partner to pay $10,000 [$40,000 − ($60,000 × ½) = $10,000] in excess of the carrying amount for a one-fourth interest in the total capital of the partnership indicates that the total capital is worth $40,000 ($10,000 ÷ 0.25 = $40,000) more than is shown in the accounting records. They reason that the carrying amounts of partnership assets should be written up by $40,000, or goodwill of $40,000 should be recognized with offsetting credits of $20,000 each to the capital accounts of the existing partners, L and M. However, most accountants take the position that the payment by N to L is a personal transaction between them and that the partnership, which has neither received nor distributed any assets, should prepare no journal entry other than an entry recording the transfer of one-half of L's capital to N.

What are the arguments for these two opposing views? Those who advocate a write-up of assets stress the *legal concept* of dissolution of the former partnership and formation of a new partnership. This change in identity of owners, it is argued, justifies a departure from the going-concern principle and the revaluation of partnership assets to current fair values to achieve an accurate measurement of the capital invested by each member of the new partnership.

The opposing argument, that the acquisition of an interest by a new partner requires only a transfer from the capital account of the selling partner to the capital account of the new partner, is based on several points. First, the partnership did not participate in negotiating the price paid by N to L. Many factors other than the valuation of partnership assets may have been involved in the negotiations between the two individuals. Perhaps N paid more than the carrying amount because N was allowed generous credit terms or received more than a one-fourth share in partnership net income. Perhaps the new partner was anxious to join the firm because of the personal abilities of L and M or because of the anticipated growth of the partnership. Based on these and other reasons, one may conclude that the cash paid for a partnership interest by a new partner to an existing partner does not provide sufficient evidence to support changes in the carrying amounts of the partnership's assets.

Investment in Partnership by New Partner

A new partner may gain admission by investing assets in the partnership, thus increasing the total assets and partners' capital of the partnership. For example, assume that X and Y, partners of the X & Y Partnership, share net income or loss equally and that each has a capital account balance of $60,000. Assume also that the carrying amounts of the partnership assets are approximately equal to current fair values and that Z owns land that might be used for expansion of partnership operations. X and Y agree to admit Z to the partnership by investment of the land; net income and losses of the new firm are to be shared equally. The land had cost Z $50,000, but has a current fair value of $80,000. The admission of Z is recorded by the partnership as follows:

New partner invests land

> Land.. 80,000
>   Z, Capital 80,000
>   To record admission of Z to partnership.

Z has a capital account balance of $80,000 and thus owns a 40% [$80,000 ÷ ($60,000 + $60,000 + $80,000) = 0.40] interest in the firm. The fact that the three partners share net income and losses equally does not require that their capital account balances be equal.

Bonus or Goodwill Allowed to Existing Partners

In a profitable, well-established firm, the existing partners may insist that a portion of the investment by a new partner be allocated to them as a bonus or that goodwill be recognized and credited to the existing partners. The new partner may agree to such terms because of the benefits to be gained by becoming a member of a firm with high earning power.

Bonus to Existing Partners   Assume that, in the C & D Partnership, C and D share net income and losses equally and have capital account balances of $45,000 each. The carrying amounts of the partnership net assets approximate current fair values. The partners agree to admit E to a one-third interest in capital and a one-third share in net income or losses for a cash investment of $60,000. The net assets of the new firm amount to $150,000 ($45,000 + $45,000 + $60,000 = $150,000). The following journal entry gives E a one-third interest in capital and credits the $10,000 **bonus** ($60,000 − $50,000 = $10,000) equally to C and D in accordance with their prior contract to share net income and losses equally:

Recording bonus to existing partners

> Cash.. 60,000
>   C, Capital ($10,000 × ½) 5,000
>   D, Capital ($10,000 × ½) 5,000
>   E, Capital ($150,000 × ⅓) 50,000
>   To record investment by E for a one-third interest in capital, with
>   bonus of $10,000 divided equally between C and D.

Goodwill to Existing Partners   In the foregoing illustration, E invested $60,000 but received a capital account balance of only $50,000, representing a one-third interest in the net assets of the firm. E might prefer that the full amount invested, $60,000, be credited to E's capital account. This might be done while still allotting E a one-third interest if **goodwill** is recognized by the partnership, with the offsetting credit divided equally between the two existing partners. If E is to be given a one-third interest represented by a capital account balance of $60,000, the indicated total capital of the partnership is $180,000 ($60,000 × 3 = $180,000), and the total capital of C and D must equal $120,000 ($180,000 × ⅔ = $120,000). Because their present combined capital account balances amount to $90,000, a write-up of $30,000 in the net assets of the partnership is recorded as follows:

Recording implied goodwill

Cash..	60,000	
Goodwill ($120,000 – $90,000)..............................	30,000	
C, Capital ($30,000 × ½).................................		15,000
D, Capital ($30,000 × ½).................................		15,000
E, Capital..		60,000

To record investment by E for a one-third interest in capital, with credit offsetting goodwill of $30,000 divided equally between C and D.

Evaluation of Bonus and Goodwill Methods   When a new partner invests an amount larger than the carrying amount of the interest acquired, the transaction should be recorded by allowing a bonus to the existing partners. The bonus method adheres to the valuation principle and treats the partnership as a going concern.

The alternative method of recording the goodwill implied by the amount invested by the new partner *is not considered acceptable by the author.* Use of the goodwill method signifies the substitution of estimated current fair value of an asset rather than valuation on a cost basis. The goodwill of $30,000 recognized in the foregoing example was not paid for by the partnership. *Its existence is implied* by the amount invested by the new partner for a one-third interest in the firm. The amount invested by the new partner may have been influenced by many factors, some of which may be personal rather than economic in nature.

Apart from the questionable theoretical basis for such recognition of goodwill, there are other practical difficulties. The presence of goodwill created in this manner is likely to evoke criticism of the partnership's financial statements, and such criticism may cause the partnership to write off the goodwill.[3] Also, if the partnership were liquidated, the goodwill would have to be written off as a loss.

Fairness of Asset Valuation   In the foregoing examples of bonus or goodwill allowed to the existing partners, it was assumed that the carrying amounts of assets of the original partnership approximated current fair values. However, if land and buildings, for example, have been owned by the partnership for many years, their carrying amounts and current fair values may be significantly different.

To illustrate this problem, assume that the net assets of the C & D Partnership, carried at $90,000, were estimated to have a current fair value of $120,000 at the time of admission of E as a partner. The previous example required E to receive a one-third interest in partnership net assets for an investment of $60,000. Why not write up the partnership's assets from $90,000 to $120,000, with a corresponding increase in the capital account balances of the existing partners? Neither a bonus nor the recognition of goodwill then would be necessary to record the admission of E to a one-

---

[3] According to *APB Opinion No. 17,* "Intangible Assets," only *acquired* goodwill should be recognized, and it must be amortized over a period of 40 years or less.

third interest for an investment of $60,000 because this investment is equal to one-third of the total partnership capital of $180,000 ($120,000 + $60,000 = $180,000).

Such restatement of asset values would not be acceptable practice in a corporation when the market price of its capital stock had risen. If one assumes the existence of certain conditions in a partnership, adherence to cost as a basis for asset valuation is as appropriate a policy as for a corporation. These specific conditions are that the income-sharing ratio should be the same as the share of equity of each partner and that the income-sharing ratio should continue unchanged. When these conditions do not exist, a restatement of net assets from carrying amount to current fair value may be the best way of achieving equity among the partners.

Bonus or Goodwill Allowed to New Partner

A new partner may be admitted to a partnership because it needs cash or because the new partner has valuable skills and business contacts. To ensure the admission of the new partner, the present firm may offer the new partner a larger equity in net assets than the amount invested by the new partner.

Bonus to New Partner   Assume that F and G, partners of the F & G Partnership who share net income and losses equally and have capital account balances of $35,000 each, offer H a one-third interest in net assets and a one-third share of net income or losses for an investment of $20,000 cash. Their offer is based on a need for more cash and on the conviction that H's personal skills and business contacts will be valuable to the partnership. The investment of $20,000 by H, when added to the existing capital of $70,000, gives a total capital of $90,000 ($20,000 + $70,000 = $90,000), of which H is entitled to one-third, or $30,000 ($90,000 × ⅓ = $30,000). The excess of H's capital account balance over the amount invested represents a $10,000 *bonus* ($30,000 − $20,000 = $10,000) allowed to H by F and G. Because F and G share net income or losses equally, the $10,000 bonus is debited to their capital accounts in equal amounts, as shown by the following journal entry to record the admission of H to the partnership:

Recording bonus to new partner

Cash	*20,000*	
F, Capital ($10,000 × ½)	*5,000*	
G, Capital ($10,000 × ½)	*5,000*	
H, Capital		*30,000*
To record admission of H, with bonus of $10,000 from F and G.		

In outlining this method of accounting for the admission of H, it is assumed that the net assets of the partnership were valued properly. If the admission of the new partner to a one-third interest for an investment of $20,000 was based on recognition that the net assets of the existing partnership were worth only $40,000, consideration should be given to writing down net assets by $30,000 ($70,000 − $40,000 = $30,000). Such write-downs would be appropriate if, for example, trade accounts receivable included doubtful accounts or if inventories were obsolete.

Goodwill to New Partner   Assume that the new partner H is the owner of a successful single proprietorship that H invests in the partnership rather than making an investment in cash. Using the same data as in the preceding example, assume that F and G with capital account balances of $35,000 each give H a one-third interest in net assets and net income or losses. The *identifiable* tangible and intangible net assets of the proprietorship owned by H are worth $20,000, but, because of its superior earnings record, a current fair value for the *total* net assets is agreed to be $35,000. The admission of H to the partnership is recorded as shown below:

New partner invests
single proprietorship
with goodwill

Identifiable Tangible and Intangible Net Assets...................	*20,000*	
Goodwill ($35,000 − $20,000).................................	*15,000*	
H, Capital		*35,000*
To record admission of H; goodwill is related to superior earnings of		
single proprietorship invested by H.		

The point to be stressed is that generally *goodwill* is recognized as part of the investment of a new partner *only when the new partner invests in the partnership a business enterprise of superior earning power.* If H is admitted for a cash investment and is credited with a capital account balance larger than the cash invested, the difference should be recorded as a bonus to H from the existing partners, or undervalued tangible or identifiable intangible assets should be written up to current fair value. Goodwill should be recognized only when substantiated by objective evidence, such as the acquisition of a profitable business enterprise.

Retirement of a Partner

A partner retiring from a general partnership usually receives cash or other assets from the partnership. It is also possible that a retiring partner might arrange for the sale of a partnership interest to one or more of the continuing partners or to an outsider. Because the accounting principles applicable to the latter situation already have been considered, the discussion of the retirement of a partner is limited to the situation in which the retiring partner receives assets of the partnership.

An assumption underlying this discussion is that the retiring partner has a right to withdraw under the terms of the partnership contract. A partner always has the *power* to withdraw, as distinguished from the *right* to withdraw. A partner who withdraws in violation of the terms of the partnership contract, and without the consent of the other partners, may be liable for damages to the other partners.

Computation of the Settlement Price   What is a fair measurement of the equity of a retiring partner? A first indication is the retiring partner's capital account balance, but this amount may need to be adjusted before it represents an equitable settlement price. Adjustments may include the correction of errors in accounting data or the recognition of differences between carrying amounts of partnership net assets and their current fair values. Before making any adjustments, the accountant should refer to the partnership contract, which may contain provisions for computing the amount to be paid a retiring partner. For example, these provisions might require an appraisal of assets, an audit by independent public accountants, or a valuation of the partnership as a going concern according to a prescribed formula. If the partnership has not maintained accurate accounting records or has not been audited, it is possible that the capital account balances are misstated because of incorrect depreciation expense, failure to provide for doubtful accounts expense, and other accounting deficiencies.

If the partnership contract does not contain provisions for the computation of the retiring partner's equity, the accountant may obtain authorization from the partners to use a specific method to determine an equitable settlement price.

In most cases, the equity of the retiring partner is computed on the basis of current fair values of partnership net assets. The gain or loss indicated by the difference between the carrying amounts of assets and their current fair values is divided in the income-sharing ratio. After the equity of the retiring partner has been computed in terms of current fair values for assets, the partners may agree to settle by payment of this amount, or they may agree on a different amount. The computation of an estimated current fair value for the retiring partner's equity is a necessary step in reaching a settlement. An independent decision is made whether to recognize the current fair values and the related changes in partners' capital in the partnership's accounting records.

Bonus to Retiring Partner   The partnership contract may provide for the computation of goodwill at the time of a partner's retirement and may specify the methods for computing the goodwill. Generally, the amount of the computed goodwill is allocated to the partners in the income-sharing ratio. For example, assume that L is to retire from the J, K & L Partnership. Each partner has a capital account balance of $60,000, and net income and losses are shared equally. The partnership contract provides that a retiring partner is to receive the balance of the retiring partner's capital account plus a share of any goodwill. At the time of L's retirement, goodwill in the amount of $30,000 is computed to the mutual satisfaction of the partners. *In the opinion of the author, this goodwill should not be recognized in the accounting records of the partnership* by a $30,000 debit to Goodwill and a $10,000 credit to each partners' capital account.

Serious objections exist to recording goodwill as determined in this fashion. Because only $10,000 of the goodwill is included in the payment for L's equity, the remaining $20,000 of goodwill *has not been paid for* by the partnership. Its display in the balance sheet of the partnership is not supported by either the valuation principle or reliable evidence. The fact that the partners ''voted'' for $30,000 of goodwill does not meet the need for reliable evidence of asset values. As an alternative, it would be possible to recognize only $10,000 of goodwill and credit L's capital account for the same amount, because this amount was paid for by the partnership as a condition of L's retirement. This method is perhaps more justifiable, but reliable evidence that goodwill exists still is lacking. The most satisfactory method of accounting for the retirement of partner L is to record the amount paid to L for goodwill as a $10,000 *bonus.* Because the settlement with L is for the balance of L's capital account of $60,000, plus estimated goodwill of $10,000, the following journal entry to record L's retirement is recommended:

<table>
<tr><td>Bonus paid to retiring
partner</td><td>L, Capital. . . . .
J, Capital ($10,000 × ½). . . . .
K, Capital ($10,000 × ½) . . . .
    Cash . . . .
To record payment to retiring partner L, including a bonus of $10,000.</td><td>60,000
5,000
5,000

70,000</td></tr>
</table>

The bonus method illustrated here is appropriate whenever the settlement with the retiring partner exceeds the carrying amount of that partner's capital. The agreement for settlement may or may not use the term *goodwill;* the essence of the matter is the determination of the amount to be paid to the retiring partner.

Bonus to Continuing Partners A partner anxious to escape from an unsatisfactory business situation may accept less than his or her partnership equity on retirement. In other cases, willingness by a retiring partner to accept a settlement below carrying amount may reflect personal problems. Another possible explanation is that the retiring partner considers the net assets of the partnership to be overvalued or anticipates less partnership net income in future years.

In brief, there are many factors that may induce a partner to accept less than the carrying amount of his or her capital account balance on withdrawal from the partnership. Because a settlement below carrying amount seldom is supported by objective evidence of overvaluation of assets, the preferred accounting treatment is to leave net asset valuations undisturbed unless a large amount of goodwill is carried in the accounting records. The difference between the retiring partner's capital account balance and the amount paid in settlement should be allocated as a *bonus* to the continuing partners.

For example, assume that M, N, and P, partners of the M, N & P Partnership, share net income or losses equally, and that each has a capital account balance of $60,000. N retires from the partnership and receives $50,000. The journal entry to record N's retirement follows:

<table>
<tr><td>Bonus to continuing
partners</td><td>N, Capital . . . .
    Cash . . . .
    M, Capital ($10,000 × ½). . . . .
    P, Capital ($10,000 × ½) . . . .
To record retirement of partner N for an amount less than carrying
amount of N's equity, with a bonus to partners M and P.</td><td>60,000
50,000
5,000
5,000</td></tr>
</table>

The final settlement with a retiring partner often is deferred for some time after the partner's withdrawal to permit the accumulation of cash, the measurement of net income to date of withdrawal, the obtaining of bank loans, or other acts needed to complete the transaction. The retirement of a partner does not terminate the retiring partner's responsibility for general partnership liabilities existing on the retirement date.

Death of a Partner   Partnership contracts often provide that partners shall acquire life insurance policies on each others' lives so that cash will be available for settlement with the estate of a deceased partner. A ***buy-sell agreement*** may be formed by the partners, whereby the partners commit their estates to sell their equities in the partnership and the surviving partners to acquire such equities. Another form of such an agreement gives the surviving partners an ***option to buy,*** or ***right of first refusal,*** rather than imposing on the partnership an obligation to acquire the deceased partner's equity.

LIMITED PARTNERSHIPS

The legal provisions governing limited partnerships are provided by the Uniform Limited Partnership Act. Among the ways in which a limited partnership differs from a general partnership are the following:

1   Limited partners have no obligation for unpaid liabilities of the limited partnership; only general partners have such liability.

2   Limited partners have no participation in the management of the limited partnership.

3   Limited partners may invest only cash or other assets in a limited partnership; they may not provide services as their investment.

4   The surname of a limited partner may not appear in the name of the partnership.

5   The formation of a limited partnership is evidenced by a ***certificate*** filed with the county recorder of the principal place of business of the limited partnership. The certificate includes many of the items present in the typical partnership contract of a general partnership (see page 34); in addition, it must include the name and residence of each general partner and limited partner; the amount of cash and other assets invested by each limited partner; provision for return of a limited partner's investment; any priority of one or more limited partners over other limited partners; and any right of limited partners to vote for election or removal of general partners, termination of the partnership, amendment of the certificate, or disposal of all partnership assets.

Membership in a limited partnership is offered to prospective limited partners in ***units*** subject to the Securities Act of 1933. Thus, unless provisions of that Act exempt a limited partnership, it must file a registration statement for the offered units with the Securities and Exchange Commission (SEC) and undertake to file periodic reports with the SEC. The SEC has provided guidance for such registration and reporting in ***Industry Guide 5: Preparation of Registration Statements Relating to Interests in Real Estate Limited Partnerships.***

Large limited partnerships that engage in ventures such as oil and gas exploration and real estate development and issue units registered with the SEC are termed ***master limited partnerships.***

Accounting for Limited Partnerships

The accounting for business transactions and events of limited partnerships parallels the accounting for general partnerships, except that limited partners do not have periodic drawings debited to a Drawings ledger account. With respect to additions and retirements of limited partners, who may be numerous, the limited partnership should maintain a subsidiary limited partners' ledger, similar to the stockholders' ledger of a corporation, with capital accounts for each limited partner showing investment units, increases for net income and decreases for net losses, and decreases for retirements.

Financial Statements for Limited Partnerships

In *Staff Accounting Bulletin 40,* the SEC provided standards for financial statements of limited partnerships filed with the SEC, as follows.[4]

> The equity section of a [limited] partnership balance sheet should distinguish between amounts ascribed to each ownership class. The equity attributed to the general partners should be stated separately from the equity of the limited partners, and changes in the number of equity units . . . outstanding should be shown for each ownership class. A statement of changes in partnership equity for each ownership class should be furnished for each period for which an income statement is included.
>
> The income statements of [limited] partnerships should be presented in a manner which clearly shows the aggregate amount of net income (loss) allocated to the general partners and the aggregate amount allocated to the limited partners. The statement of income should also state the results of operations on a per unit basis.

Although the foregoing standards are mandatory only for limited partnerships subject to the SEC's jurisdiction, they are appropriate for other limited partnerships.

To illustrate financial statements for a limited partnership, assume that Wesley Randall formed Randall Company, a limited partnership that was exempt from the registration requirements of the Securities Act of 1933, on January 2, Year 1. Wesley Randall, the general partner, acquired 30 units at $1,000 a unit, and 30 limited partners acquired a total of 570 units at $1,000 a unit. The limited partnership certificate for Randall Company provided that limited partners might withdraw their net equity (investment plus net income less net loss) only on December 31 of each year. Wesley Randall was authorized to withdraw $500 a month at his discretion, but he had no drawings during Year 1. Randall Company had a net income of $90,000 for Year 1, and on December 31, Year 1, two limited partners withdrew their entire equity interest of 40 units.

The following condensed financial statements (excluding a statement of cash flows) incorporate the foregoing assumptions and comply with the provisions of *Staff Accounting Bulletin 40:*

---

[4] *Staff Accounting Bulletin 40,* Topic F, Securities and Exchange Commission (Washington: 1981).

RANDALL COMPANY
(A Limited Partnership)
Income Statement
For Year Ended December 31, Year 1

Revenue..	$400,000
Costs and expenses	310,000
Net income..	$ 90,000

Division of net income ($150* per unit based on 600 weighted-average units outstanding):

To general partner (30 units)	$ 4,500
To limited partners (570 units)	85,500
Total..	$90,000

* $90,000 ÷ 600 units outstanding throughout Year 1 = $150

RANDALL COMPANY
(A Limited Partnership)
Statement of Partners' Capital
For Year Ended December 31, Year 1

	General partner		Limited partners		Combined	
	Units	Amount	Units	Amount	Units	Amount
Initial investment, beginning of year..........	30	$30,000	570	$570,000	600	$600,000
Add: Net income..........................		4,500		85,500		90,000
Subtotals	30	$34,500	570	$655,500	600	$690,000
Less: Redemption of units			40	46,000	40	46,000
Partners' capital, end of year...............	30	$34,500	530	$609,500	560	$644,000

RANDALL COMPANY
(A Limited Partnership)
Balance Sheet
December 31, Year 1

Assets		Liabilities & Partners' Capital		
Current assets	$ 240,000	Current liabilities		$ 100,000
Other assets	760,000	Long-term debt........................		256,000
		Total liabilities.......................		$ 356,000
		Partners' capital ($1,150* per unit based on 560 units outstanding):		
		General partner	$ 34,500	
		Limited partners..........	609,500	644,000
Total assets	$1,000,000	Total liabilities & partners' capital ...		$1,000,000

* $644,000 ÷ 560 = $1,150

SEC ENFORCEMENT ACTIONS DEALING WITH WRONGFUL APPLICATION OF ACCOUNTING STANDARDS FOR PARTNERSHIPS

In 1982, the Securities and Exchange Commission (SEC) initiated a series of *Accounting and Auditing Enforcement Releases* (AAERs) to report its enforcement actions involving accountants. Following are summaries of two AAERs dealing with violations of accounting standards for partnerships.

AAER 202   *AAER 202,* ''Securities and Exchange Commission v. William A. MacKay and Muncie A. Russell'' (September 29, 1988), deals with a general partnership formed by the former chief executive officer (CEO) and chief financial officer (CFO) (a CPA) of American Biomaterials Corporation, a manufacturer of medical and dental products. The SEC alleged that the partnership, Kirkwood Associates, ostensibly an executive search firm, had received more than $410,000 from American Biomaterials for nonexistent services. The partnership had no offices or employees, and its telephone number and address were those of a telephone answering and mail collection service. Although its CEO and CFO directly benefited from the $410,000 payments, American Biomaterials did not disclose this *related-party transaction* in its report to the SEC. The CEO and the CFO, without admitting or denying the SEC's allegations, consented to the federal court's permanently enjoining them from violating the federal securities laws.

AAER 214   In *AAER 214,* ''Securities and Exchange Commission v. Avanti Associates First Mortgage Fund 84 Limited Partnership et al.'' (January 11, 1989), the SEC reported on a federal court's entry of a permanent injunction against the general partner (a CPA) of a limited partnership that in turn was the general partner of a second limited partnership that made and acquired short-term first mortgage loans on real property. According to the SEC, the financial statements of the second limited partnership, filed with the SEC in *Form 10-K,* included a note that falsely reported the amount and nature of a related-party transaction. Correct reporting of the related-party transaction would have disclosed that the CPA had improperly profited from a kickback scheme involving payments made by borrowers from the limited partnership to a distant relative of the CPA. In a related enforcement action, reported in *AAER 220,* ''. . . In the Matter of Richard P. Franke . . .'' (March 24, 1989), the SEC permanently prohibited appearing or practicing before it by the CPA who had ostensibly audited the limited partnership's financial statements that were included in *Form 10-K.*

REVIEW QUESTIONS

1   In the formation of a general partnership, partners often invest nonmonetary assets such as land, buildings, and machinery, as well as cash. Should nonmonetary assets be recognized by the partnership at current fair value, at cost to the partners, or at some other amount? Explain.

2   Some CPA firms have thousands of staff members, and hundreds of partners, and operate on a national or an international basis. Would the corporate form of organization be more appropriate than the partnership form for such large organizations? Explain.

3 Explain the partnership balance sheet display of loans to and from partners and the accounting for interest on such loans.

4 Explain how partners' salaries should be displayed in the income statement of a general partnership, if at all.

5 List at least five items that should be included in a partnership contract.

6 List at least five methods by which net income or losses of a general partnership may be divided among partners.

7 The Ainsley & Burton Partnership admitted Paul Craig to a one-third interest in the firm for his investment of $50,000. Does this mean that Craig would be entitled to one-third of the partnership's net income or losses?

8 Duncan and Eastwick are negotiating a partnership contract, with Duncan to invest $60,000 and Eastwick $20,000 in the partnership. Duncan suggests that interest at 8% be allowed on average capital account balances and that any remaining net income or losses be divided in the ratio of average capital account balances. Eastwick prefers that the entire net income or losses be divided in the ratio of average capital account balances. Comment on these proposals.

9 The partnership contract of the Peel & Quay Partnership is brief on the sharing of net income and losses. It states: "Net income is to be divided 80% to Peel and 20% to Quay, and each partner is entitled to draw $2,000 a month." What difficulties do you foresee in implementing this contract? Illustrate possible difficulties under the assumption that the partnership had a net income of $100,000 in the first year of operations.

10 Muir and Miller operated the Muir & Miller Partnership for several years, sharing net income and losses equally. On January 1, Year 6, they agreed to revise the income-sharing ratio to 70% for Muir and 30% for Miller, because of Miller's desire for semiretirement. On March 1 the partnership received $10,000 in settlement of a disputed amount receivable on a contract completed in Year 5. Because the outcome of the dispute had been uncertain, no trade account receivable had been recognized. Explain the accounting treatment you would recommend for the $10,000 cash receipt.

11 Should the carrying amounts of a general partnership's assets be restated to current fair values when a partner retires or a new partner is admitted to the firm? Explain.

12 A new partner admitted to an established firm often is required to invest an amount of cash larger than the carrying amount of the interest in net assets the new partner acquires. In what ways might such a transaction be recorded? What is the principal argument for each method?

13 Two partners invested $2,000 each to form a general partnership for the construction of a shopping center. The partnership obtained a bank loan of $800,000 to finance construction, but no payment on this loan was due for two years. Each partner withdrew cash of $50,000 from the partnership from the proceeds of the loan. How should the investment of $4,000 and the withdrawal of $100,000 be displayed in the financial statements of the partnership?

14 A CPA firm was asked to express an auditors' opinion on the financial statements of a limited partnership in which a corporation was the general partner. Should the financial statements of the limited partnership and the auditors' report thereon include the financial statements of the general partner?

15 How do the financial statements of a limited partnership differ from those of a general partnership?

EXERCISES

Ex. 2-1 Select the best answer for each of the following multiple-choice questions:

1 Jill Evans paid $80,000 to general partner Sam Reed for one-half his interest (carrying amount $60,000) in the Palmer, Reed & Stowe Partnership. The appropriate journal entry (explanation omitted) for the Palmer, Reed, Stowe & Evans Partnership is:

a *Sam Reed, Capital*	80,000	
Jill Evans, Capital		80,000

b *Cash*.	80,000	
Sam Reed, Capital		20,000
Jill Evans, Capital		60,000

c *Cash*.	80,000	
Jill Evans, Capital		80,000

d *Sam Reed, Capital*	60,000	
Jill Evans, Capital		60,000

2 *Drawing* ledger accounts of a general partnership are:
a Expense accounts
b Contra-equity accounts
c Closed to the Income Summary account
d Displayed in the partnership's balance sheet

3 Is a general partnership's Interest Expense ledger account debited for:

	Interest on partners' capital included in income-sharing agreement?	Interest on partners' loans to the partnership?
a	Yes	Yes
b	Yes	No
c	No	Yes
d	No	No

4 Prior to the withdrawal of partner Ajax from the Ajax, Achilles & Odysseus Partnership, the partners agreed to increase, by a debit, the carrying amount of the general partnership's inventories to current fair values. The offsetting credit(s) is(are) to:

a Appraisal Capital

b Income Summary

c Unrealized Gain on Inventories

d The partners' capital accounts

5 On January 31, Year 2, partner Alex of the Alex, Bett, Carl & Dana Partnership withdrew $40,000 cash, in addition to the $10,000 monthly drawing authorized by the general partnership contract. Alex did not execute a promissory note for $40,000 payable to the partnership. The most appropriate journal entry (explanation omitted) for the partnership is:

a *Alex, Drawing*... 50,000
      Cash...   50,000

b *Salaries Expense*... 10,000
      Alex, Drawing.. 40,000
      Cash...   50,000

c *Loan Receivable from Alex*....................................... 40,000
      Alex, Drawing.. 10,000
      Cash...   50,000

d *Alex, Drawing*... 10,000
      Alex, Capital.. 40,000
      Cash...   50,000

6 May *goodwill* be recognized by a general partnership, under appropriate conditions, for the:

	Admission of a new partner to an existing partnership?	Retirement of a partner from an existing partnership?
a	Yes	Yes
b	Yes	No
c	No	Yes
d	No	No

7 Are partners' *drawings* (authorized by the partnership contract) displayed in a general partnership's

	Balance sheet?	Income statement?	Statement of partners' capital?	Statement of cash flows?
a	Yes	Yes	No	No
b	No	Yes	Yes	No
c	No	No	Yes	Yes
d	No	No	Yes	No

8 The income-sharing provision of the partnership contract of the Rand & Sand Partnership (a general partnership) provides for 6% interest on beginning-of-year capital account balances, with remaining income or loss divided 65% to Rand and 35% to Sand. If net income of the Rand & Sand Partnership for the year ended December 31, Year 4, was $80,000 and the partners' January 1, Year 4, capital account balances were $800,000 for Rand and $1,000,000 for Sand, Rand's share of the $80,000 net income is:

a $29,800

b $48,000

c $52,000

d Some other amount

9 The statement ''A partnership is an association of persons'' stresses:

a The legal form of a partnership

b The economic substance of a partnership

c Both the legal form and the economic substance of a partnership

d Neither the legal form nor the economic substance of a partnership

10 If a general partnership, whose partnership contract provides for interest on partners' capital account balances, incurs a net loss, the interest provision of the contract:

a Must be enforced

b Must be disregarded

c May be either enforced or disregarded

d Must be rescinded by the partners

11 Are the results of operations on a *per unit* basis displayed in the income statement of a:

	General partnership?	*Limited partnership?*
a	*Yes*	*Yes*
b	*Yes*	*No*
c	*No*	*Yes*
d	*No*	*No*

Ex. 2-2 Activity in the capital accounts of partners Webb and Yu for the year ended December 31, Year 10, follows:

	Webb, capital	*Yu, capital*
Balances, Jan. 1	*$40,000*	*$80,000*
Investment, July 1.................................	*20,000*	
Withdrawal, Oct. 1.................................		*40,000*

Net income of the Webb & Yu Partnership for the year ended December 31, Year 10, amounted to $48,000.

Prepare a working paper to compute the division of the $48,000 net income of the Webb & Yu Partnership under each of the following assumptions:

a The partnership contract is silent as to sharing of net income and losses.

b Net income and losses are divided on the basis of average capital account balances (not including the net income or loss for the current year).

c Net income and losses are divided on the basis of beginning capital account balances.

d Net income and losses are divided on the basis of ending capital account balances (not including the net income or loss for the current year).

Ex. 2-3 The partnership contract of the Ray, Stan & Todd Partnership provided that Ray was to receive a bonus equal to 20% of income and that the remaining income or loss was to be divided 40% each to Ray and Stan and 20% to Todd. Income of the Ray, Stan & Todd Partnership for Year 1 (before the bonus) amounted to $127,200.

Explain two alternative ways in which the bonus provision might be interpreted, and prepare a working paper to compute the division of the $127,200 income of the Ray, Stan & Todd Partnership for Year 1 under each interpretation.

Ex. 2-4 The partnership contract of the Jones, King & Lane Partnership provided for the division of net income or losses in the following manner:

(1) Bonus of 20% of income before the bonus to Jones
(2) Interest at 15% on average capital account balances to each partner
(3) Residual income or loss equally to each partner

Net income of the Jones, King & Lane Partnership for Year 3 was $90,000, and the average capital account balances for that year were Jones, $100,000; King, $200,000; and Lane, $300,000.

Prepare a working paper to compute each partner's share of the Year 3 net income of the Jones, King & Lane Partnership.

Ex. 2-5 The partnership contract of the Ann, Bud & Cal Partnership provides for the remuneration of partners as follows:

(1) Salaries of $40,000 to Ann, $35,000 to Bud, and $30,000 to Cal, to be recognized annually as operating expense of the partnership in the measurement of net income
(2) Bonus of 10% of income after salaries and the bonus to Ann
(3) Remaining net income or loss 30% to Ann, 20% to Bud, and 50% to Cal

Income of the Ann, Bud & Cal Partnership before partner's salaries and Ann's bonus was $215,000 for the year ended December 31, Year 8.

Prepare journal entries on December 31, Year 8, to (1) accrue partners' salaries and Ann's bonus and (2) close the Income Summary ledger account (credit balance of $100,000) of the Ann, Bud & Cal Partnership and divide the net income among the partners. Show supporting computations in the explanation for the second journal entry.

Ex. 2-6 The partnership contract for the Bates & Carter Partnership provided for salaries to partners and the division of net income or losses as follows:

(1) Salaries of $40,000 a year to Bates and $60,000 a year to Carter
(2) Interest at 12% a year on beginning capital account balances
(3) Remaining net income or loss 70% to Bates and 30% to Carter

For the year ended December 31, Year 4, the Bates & Carter Partnership had pre-salaries income of $200,000. Capital account balances on January 1, Year 4, were $400,000 for Bates and $500,000 for Carter; Bates invested an additional $100,000 in the partnership on September 30, Year 4. In accordance with the partnership contract, both partners drew their salary allowances in cash from the partnership during the year.

Prepare journal entries for the Bates & Carter Partnership on December 31, Year 4, to (1) accrue partners' salaries and (2) close the Income Summary (credit balance of $100,000) and drawing accounts. Show supporting computations in the journal entry closing the Income Summary account.

Ex. 2-7   Emma Neal and Sally Drew are partners of the Neal & Drew Partnership sharing net income or losses equally; each has a capital account balance of $200,000. Sally Drew (with the consent of Neal) sold one-fifth of her interest to her daughter Paula for $50,000, with payment to be made to Sally Drew in five annual installments of $10,000, plus interest at 15% on the unpaid balance.

Prepare a journal entry for the Neal, Drew & Drew Partnership to record the change in ownership, and explain why you would or would not recommend a change in the valuation of net assets in the accounting records of the Neal, Drew & Drew Partnership.

Ex. 2-8   On January 31, Year 6, Nancy Ross and John Clemon were admitted to the Logan, Marsh & Noble (CPA firm) partnership, which had net assets of $120,000 prior to the admission and an income-sharing ratio of Logan, 25%; Marsh, 35%; and Noble, 40%. Ross paid $20,000 to Carl Logan for one-half of his 20% share of partnership net assets on January 31, Year 6, and Clemon invested $20,000 in the partnership for a 10% interest in the net assets of the Logan, Marsh, Noble, Ross & Clemon Partnership. No goodwill was to be recognized as a result of the admission of Ross and Clemon to the partnership.

Prepare separate journal entries on January 31, Year 6, to record the admission of Ross and Clemon to the Logan, Marsh, Noble, Ross & Clemon Partnership.

Ex. 2-9   Partners A and B have capital account balances of $30,000 and $20,000, respectively, and they share net income and losses in a 3 : 1 ratio.

Prepare journal entries to record the admission of C to the A, B & C Partnership under each of the following conditions:

a C invests $30,000 for a one-fourth interest in net assets; the total partnership capital after C's admission is to be $80,000.

b C invests $30,000, of which $10,000 is a bonus to A and B. In conjunction with the admission of C, the carrying amount of the inventories is increased by $16,000. C's capital account is credited for $20,000.

Ex. 2-10   Lamb and Meek, partners of the Lamb & Meek Partnership who share net income and losses 60% and 40%, respectively, had capital account balances of $70,000 and $60,000, respectively, on June 30, Year 6. On that date Lamb and Meek agreed to admit Niles to the Lamb, Meek & Niles Partnership with a one-third interest in total partnership capital of $180,000 and a one-third share of net income or losses, for a cash investment of $50,000.

Prepare a working paper to compute the balances of the Lamb, Capital, Meek, Capital, and Niles, Capital ledger accounts on June 30, Year 6, following the admission of Niles to the Lamb, Meek & Niles Partnership.

Ex. 2-11   Floyd Austin and Samuel Bradford are partners who share net income and losses equally and have equal capital account balances. The net assets of the partnership have a carrying amount of $80,000. Jason Crade is admitted to the Austin, Bradford

& Crade Partnership with a one-third interest in net income or losses and net assets. To acquire this interest, Crade invests $34,000 cash in the partnership.

Prepare journal entries to record the admission of Crade in the accounting records of the Austin, Bradford & Crade Partnership under the:

a Bonus method

b Revaluation of net assets method, assuming partnership inventories are overstated

Ex. 2-12   On August 31, Year 9, Logan and Major, partners of the Logan & Major Partnership who had capital account balances of $80,000 and $120,000, respectively, on that date and who shared net income and losses in a 2 : 3 ratio, agreed to admit Nelson to the Logan, Major & Nelson Partnership with a 20% interest in net assets and net income in exchange for a $60,000 cash investment. Logan and Major were to retain their prior income-sharing arrangement with respect to the 80% remainder of net income (100% − 20% = 80%). On September 30, Year 9, after the closing of the partnership's revenue and expense ledger accounts, the Income Summary ledger account had a credit balance of $50,000.

Prepare journal entries for the Logan, Major & Nelson Partnership to record the admission of Nelson on August 31, Year 9, and to close the Income Summary ledger account on September 30, Year 9.

Ex. 2-13   On January 31, Year 2, partners of the Lon, Mac & Nan Partnership (a general partnership) had the following loan and capital account balances (after closing entries for January):

Loan receivable from Lon	$ 20,000 dr
Loan payable to Nan	60,000 cr
Lon, capital	30,000 dr
Mac, capital	120,000 cr
Nan, capital	70,000 cr

The partnership's income-sharing ratio was Lon, 50%; Mac, 20%; and Nan, 30%.

On January 31, Year 2, Ole was admitted to the partnership for a 20% interest in **total capital** of the partnership in exchange for an investment of $40,000 cash. Prior to Ole's admission, the existing partners agreed to increase the carrying amount of the partnership's inventories to current fair value, a $60,000 increase.

Prepare journal entries on January 31, Year 2, for the Lon, Mac, Nan & Ole Partnership to record the $60,000 increase in the partnership's inventories and the admission of Ole for a $40,000 cash investment.

Ex. 2-14   On May 31, Year 6, Ike Loy was admitted to the Jay & Kaye partnership (a general partnership) by investing Loy Company, a highly profitable proprietorship having identifiable tangible and intangible net assets of $600,000, at carrying amount and current fair value. Prior to Loy's admission, capital account balances and income-sharing percentages of Jay and Kaye were as follows:

	Capital account balances	Income-sharing percentages
Jay	$400,000	60%
Kaye	500,000	40%

The partnership contract for the new Jay, Kaye & Loy Partnership included the following provisions:

(1) Loy was to receive a capital account balance of $660,000 on his admission to the partnership on May 31, Year 6.
(2) Income for the year ended May 31, Year 7, and subsequent years was to be allocated as follows:
    (a) Bonus of 10% of income *after the bonus* to Loy
    (b) Resultant net income or loss 30% to Jay, 20% to Kaye, and 50% to Loy

Income *before the bonus* for the year ended May 31, Year 7, was $132,000.

Prepare journal entries for the Jay, Kaye & Loy partnership on May 31, Year 6, and May 31, Year 7 (the latter to accrue Loy's bonus and to close the Income Summary ledger account having a credit balance of $120,000).

Ex. 2-15 The inexperienced accountant for the Fox, Gee & Hay Partnership prepared the following journal entries during the year ended August 31, Year 10:

Year 9

Sept. 1	Cash	50,000	
	Goodwill	150,000	
	Fox, Capital ($150,000 × 0.25)		37,500
	Gee, Capital ($150,000 × 0.75)		112,500
	Hay, Capital		50,000

To record admission of Hay for a 20% interest in net assets, with goodwill credited to Fox and Gee in their former income-sharing ratio. Goodwill is computed as follows:

Implied total capital, based on Hay's investment ($50,000 × 5)	$250,000	
Less: Net assets prior to Hay's admission	100,000	
Goodwill	$150,000	

Year 10

Aug. 31	Income Summary	30,000	
	Fox, Capital ($30,000 × 0.20)		6,000
	Gee, Capital ($30,000 × 0.60)		18,000
	Hay, Capital ($30,000 × 0.20)		6,000

To divide net income for the year in the residual income-sharing ratio of Fox, 20%; Gee, 60%; Hay, 20%. Provision in partnership contract requiring $40,000 annual salary allowance to Hay is disregarded because income before salary is only $30,000.

Prepare journal entries for the Fox, Gee & Hay Partnership on August 31, Year 10, to correct the accounting records, which have not been closed for the year ended August 31, Year 10. Assume that Hay's admission to the partnership should have been recorded by the bonus method.

Ex. 2-16 On June 30, Year 2, the balance sheet of the King, Lowe & More Partnership and the partners' respective income-sharing percentages were as shown below.

KING, LOWE & MORE PARTNERSHIP
Balance Sheet
June 30, Year 2

Assets

Current assets	$185,000
Plant assets (net)	200,000
Total assets	$385,000

Liabilities & Partners' Capital

Trade accounts payable	$ 85,000
Loan payable to King	15,000
King, capital (20%)	70,000
Lowe, capital (20%)	65,000
More, capital (60%)	150,000
Total liabilities & partners' capital	$385,000

King decided to retire from the partnership on June 30, Year 2, and by mutual agreement of the partners the plant assets were adjusted to their total current fair value of $260,000. The partnership paid $92,000 cash for King's equity in the partnership, exclusive of the loan, which was repaid in full. No goodwill was to be recognized in this transaction.

Prepare journal entries for the King, Lowe & More Partnership on June 30, Year 2, to record the adjustment of plant assets to current fair value and King's retirement.

Ex. 2-17 The partners' capital (income-sharing ratio in parentheses) of the Nunn, Owen, Park & Quan Partnership (a general partnership) on May 31, Year 3, was as follows:

Nunn (20%)	$ 60,000
Owen (20%)	80,000
Park (20%)	70,000
Quan (40%)	40,000
Total partners' capital	$250,000

On May 31, Year 3, with the consent of Nunn, Owen, and Quan:

(1) Sam Park retired from the partnership and was paid $50,000 cash in full settlement of his interest in the partnership.
(2) Lois Reed was admitted to the partnership with a $20,000 cash investment for a 10% interest in the net assets of the Nunn, Owen, Quan & Reed Partnership.

No goodwill was to be recognized for the foregoing events.

Prepare journal entries on May 31, Year 3, to record the foregoing events.

Ex. 2-18 Macco Company, a limited partnership, was established on January 2, Year 1, with the issuance of 10 units at $10,000 a unit to Malcolm Cole, the general partner, and

40 units in the aggregate to five limited partners at $10,000 a unit. The certificate for Macco provided that Cole was authorized to withdraw a maximum of $24,000 a year on December 31 of each year for which net income was at least $100,000 and that limited partners might withdraw their equity for cash or promissory notes on December 31 of each year only. For Year 1 Macco had a net income of $300,000, and on December 31, Year 1, Cole withdrew $24,000 cash and a limited partner redeemed 10 units, receiving a two-year promissory note bearing interest at 10%.

Prepare a statement of partners' capital for Macco Company for the year ended December 31, Year 1.

CASES

Case 2-1   The X, Y & Z Partnership, whose partners share net income and losses equally, had an operating income of $30,000 for the first year of operations. However, near the end of that year, the partners learned of two unfavorable developments: (a) the bankruptcy of Sasha Company, maker of a two-year promissory note for $20,000 payable to Partner X that had been indorsed in blank to the partnership by Partner X at face amount as X's original investment, and (b) the appearance on the market of new competing patented devices that rendered worthless a patent that had been invested in the partnership by Partner Y at a value of $10,000 as part of Y's original investment.

The X, Y & Z Partnership had retained the promissory note made by Sasha Company with the expectation of discounting it when cash was needed. Quarterly interest payments had been received regularly prior to the bankruptcy of Sasha, but present prospects were for no further collections of interest or principal.

Partner Z argues that the $30,000 operating income should be divided $10,000 to each partner, with the $20,000 loss on the note debited to the capital account of Partner X and the $10,000 loss on the patent debited to the capital account of Partner Y.

Instructions

Do you agree with Partner Z? Explain.

Case 2-2   Carl Dobbs and David Ellis formed the Dobbs & Ellis Partnership on January 2, Year 5. Dobbs invested cash of $50,000, and Ellis invested cash of $20,000 and marketable securities (short-term investments) with a current fair value of $80,000. A portion of the securities was sold at carrying amount in January, Year 5, to provide cash for operations of the partnership.

The partnership contract stated that net income and losses were to be divided in the capital ratio and authorized each partner to withdraw $1,000 monthly. Dobbs withdrew $1,000 on the last day of each month during Year 5, but Ellis made no withdrawals during Year 5 until July 1, when he withdrew all the securities that had not been sold by the partnership. The securities that Ellis withdrew had a current fair value of $41,000 when invested in the partnership on January 2, Year 5, and a current fair value of $62,000 on July 1, Year 5, when withdrawn. Ellis instructed the accountant for the Dobbs & Ellis Partnership to record the transaction by reducing Ellis's capital account balance by $41,000, which was done. Income from operations of the Dobbs & Ellis Partnership for Year 5 amounted to $24,000.

Instructions

Determine the appropriate division of net income of the Dobbs & Ellis Partnership for Year 5. If the income-sharing provision of the partnership contract is unsatisfactory, state the assumptions you would make for an appropriate interpretation of the partners' intentions. Describe the journal entry, if any, that you believe should be made for the Dobbs & Ellis Partnership. (Disregard income taxes.)

Case 2-3   George Lewis and Anna Marlin are partners of the Lewis & Marlin Partnership who share net income and losses equally. They offer to admit Betty Naylor to the Lewis, Marlin & Naylor Partnership for a one-third interest in net assets and in net income or losses for an investment of $50,000 cash. The total capital of the Lewis & Marlin Partnership prior to Naylor's admission was $110,000. Naylor makes a counteroffer of $40,000, explaining that her investigation of the Lewis & Marlin Partnership indicates that many trade accounts receivable are past due and that a significant amount of the inventories is obsolete. Lewis and Marlin deny both these points. They contend that inventories are valued in accordance with generally accepted accounting principles and that the accounts receivable are fully collectible. However, after prolonged negotiations, the admission price of $40,000 proposed by Naylor is agreed upon.

Instructions

Explain two ways in which the admission of Naylor might be recorded by the Lewis, Marlin & Naylor Partnership, and indicate which method is preferable. Comment on the possibility of recognizing goodwill.

Case 2-4   Lowyma Company, a partnership of Ed Loeser, Peter Wylie, and Herman Martin, has operated successfully for many years, but Martin now plans to retire. In discussions of the settlement to be made with Martin, the point was made that inventories had been valued at last-in, first-out cost for many years. Martin suggested that the current replacement cost of the inventories be determined and the excess of this amount over the carrying amount be recognized as a gain to the partnership to be shared equally by the three partners. Loeser objected to this suggestion on grounds that any method of inventory valuation would give reasonably accurate results provided it were followed consistently and that a departure from the long-established method of inventory valuation used by the partnership would produce an erroneous earnings record for the life of the partnership to date.

Instructions

Evaluate the objections of Ed Loeser.

Case 2-5   A series of heavy net losses has resulted in the following balance sheet drafted by the controller of the Nobis, Ortho & Parr Partnership (a general partnership):

NOBIS, ORTHO & PARR PARTNERSHIP
Balance Sheet
July 31, Year 8

Assets

Current assets	$420,000
Plant assets (net)	550,000
Total assets	$970,000

Liabilities & Partners' Capital

Current liabilities		$380,000
Long-term debt		420,000
Total liabilities		$800,000
Art Nobis, capital	$ 130,000	
June Ortho, capital	(120,000)	
Carl Parr, capital	160,000	
Total partners' capital		170,000
Total liabilities and partners' capital		$970,000

Concerned about the partnership's high debt-to-equity ratio of 470.6% ($800,000 ÷ $170,000 = 470.6%), the partners consult with Jack Julian, CPA, controller of the partnership, who is a member of the AICPA, FEI, and IMA (see Chapter 1), regarding the propriety of converting partner Ortho's capital deficit to an account receivable. Ortho shows Julian a personal financial statement showing a net worth of more than $8 million; Ortho points out that the bulk of her assets are in long-term investments that are difficult to liquidate to obtain cash for investment in the partnership. Partner Ortho is willing to pledge high-grade securities in her personal portfolio of investments to secure the $120,000 amount.

Instructions

May Jack Julian ethically comply with the request of the partners of the Nobis, Ortho & Parr Partnership? Explain.

Case 2-6 Jean Rogers, CPA, is a member of the AICPA, the IMA, and the FEI (see Chapter 1); she is employed as controller of the Barnes, Egan & Harder Partnership (a general partnership). On June 30, Year 7, the end of the partnership's fiscal year, partner Charles Harder informed Rogers that the proceeds of a $100,000 personal loan to him by Local Bank on a one-year, 8% promissory note had been deposited in the partnership's checking account at Local Bank. Showing Rogers a memo signed by all three partners that approved the partnership's repayment of Harder's personal loan, including interest, Harder instructed Rogers to account for the loan proceeds as a credit to his partnership capital account and to recognize the partnership's subsequent payments of principal and interest on the loan with debits to Charles Harder, Drawing and Interest Expense, respectively.

Instructions

May Jean Rogers ethically comply with Charles Harder's request? Explain.

PROBLEMS

Pr. 2-1 Among the business transactions and events of the Oscar, Paul & Quinn Partnership, whose partners shared net income and losses equally, for the month of January, Year 4, were the following:

Jan. 2 With the consent of Paul and Quinn, Oscar made a $10,000 cash advance to the partnership on a 12% demand promissory note.

6 With the consent of Oscar and Paul, Quinn withdrew from the partnership merchandise with a cost of $4,000 and a selling price of $5,200, in lieu of a regular cash drawing. The partnership uses the perpetual inventory system.

13 The partners agreed that a patent with a carrying amount of $6,000, which had been invested by Paul when the partnership was organized, was worthless and should be written off.

27 Paul paid a $2,000 trade account payable of the partnership.

Instructions

Prepare journal entries for the foregoing transactions and events of the Oscar, Paul & Quinn Partnership and the January 31, Year 4, adjusting entry for the note payable to Oscar.

Pr. 2-2 The condensed balance sheet of the Gee & Hawe Partnership on December 31, Year 5, follows:

GEE & HAWE PARTNERSHIP
Balance Sheet
December 31, Year 5

Assets		Liabilities & Partners' Capital	
Current assets	$100,000	Liabilities	$300,000
Plant assets (net).	500,000	Louis Gee, capital	200,000
		Ray Hawe, capital	100,000
Total	$600,000	Total	$600,000

Gee and Hawe shared net income or losses 40% and 60%, respectively. On January 2, Year 6, Lisa Ivan was admitted to the Gee, Hawe & Ivan Partnership by the investment of the net assets of her highly profitable proprietorship. The partners agreed to the following current fair values of the identifiable net assets of Ivan's proprietorship:

Current assets	$ 70,000
Plant assets	230,000
Total assets	$300,000
Less: Liabilities	200,000
Net assets.	$100,000

Ivan's capital account was credited for $120,000. The partners agreed further that the carrying amounts of the net assets of the Gee & Hawe Partnership were equal to their current fair values and that the accounting records of the old partnership should be used for the new partnership. The following partner-remuneration plan was adopted for the new partnership:

(1) Salaries of $10,000 to Gee, $15,000 to Hawe, and $20,000 to Ivan, to be recognized as expenses of the partnership
(2) A bonus of 10% of income after deduction of partners' salaries and the bonus to Ivan
(3) Remaining income or loss as follows: 30% to Gee, 40% to Hawe, and 30% to Ivan

For the year ended December 31, Year 6, the Gee, Hawe & Ivan Partnership had income of $78,000 before partners' salaries and the bonus to Ivan.

Instructions

Prepare journal entries for the Gee, Hawe & Ivan Partnership to record the following (include supporting computations in the explanations for the entries):

a The admission of Ivan to the partnership on January 2, Year 6
b The partners' salaries, bonus, and division of net income for the year ended December 31, Year 6

Pr. 2-3   The Ross & Saye Partnership was organized and began operations on March 1, Year 1. On that date, Roberta Ross invested $150,000, and Samuel Saye invested land and building with current fair values of $80,000 and $100,000, respectively. Saye also invested $60,000 in the partnership on November 1, Year 1, because of its shortage of cash. The partnership contract includes the following remuneration plan:

	Ross	Saye
Annual salary (recognized as operating expense)	$18,000	$24,000
Annual interest on average capital account balances	10%	10%
Remainder	60%	40%

The annual salary was to be withdrawn by each partner in 12 monthly installments.

During the year ended February 28, Year 2, the Ross & Saye Partnership had net sales of $500,000, cost of goods sold of $280,000, and total operating expenses of $100,000 (including partners' salaries expense but excluding interest on partners' average capital account balances). Each partner made monthly cash drawings in accordance with the partnership contract.

Instructions

a Prepare a condensed income statement for the Ross & Saye Partnership for the year ended February 28, Year 2. Show the details of the division of net income in a supporting exhibit.
b Prepare a statement of partners' capital for the Ross & Saye Partnership for the year ended February 28, Year 2.

Pr. 2-4   Lucas and May formed the Lucas & May Partnership on January 2, Year 1. Their capital accounts showed the following changes during Year 1:

	Lucas, capital	May, capital
Original investments, Jan. 2, Year 1......................	$120,000	$180,000
Investments: May 1......................................	15,000	
July 1.......................................		15,000
Withdrawals: Nov. 1	(30,000)	(75,000)
Capital account balances, Dec. 31, Year 1	$105,000	$120,000

The income of the Lucas & May Partnership for Year 1, before partners' salaries expense, was $69,600. The income included an extraordinary gain of $12,000.

Instructions

Prepare a working paper to compute each partner's share of net income of the Lucas & May Partnership for Year 1 to the nearest dollar, assuming the following alternative income-sharing plans:

a The partnership contract is silent as to division of net income or loss.

b Income before extraordinary items is shared equally after allowance of 10% interest on average capital account balances (computed to the nearest month) and after salaries of $20,000 to Lucas and $30,000 to May recognized as operating expenses by the partnership. Extraordinary items are shared in the ratio of original investments.

c Income before extraordinary items is shared on the basis of average capital account balances, and extraordinary items are shared on the basis of original investments.

d Income before extraordinary items is shared equally between Lucas and May after a 20% bonus to May based on income before extraordinary items after the bonus. Extraordinary items are shared on the basis of original investments.

 Pr. 2-5 The Alex, Baron & Crane Partnership was formed on January 2, Year 1. The original cash investments were as follows:

Alex	$ 96,000
Baron...	144,000
Crane...	216,000

According to the partnership contract, the partners were to be remunerated as follows:

(1) Salaries of $14,400 for Alex, $12,000 for Baron, and $13,600 for Crane, to be recognized as operating expenses by the partnership

(2) Interest at 12% on the average capital account balances during the year

(3) Remainder divided 40% to Alex, 30% to Baron, and 30% to Crane

Income before partners' salaries for the year ended December 31, Year 1, was $92,080. Alex invested an additional $24,000 in the partnership on July 1; Crane withdrew $36,000 from the partnership on October 1; and, as authorized by the partnership contract, Alex, Baron, and Crane each withdrew $1,250 monthly against their shares of net income for the year.

Instructions

a Prepare a working paper to divide the $92,080 income before partners' salaries of the Alex, Baron & Crane Partnership for the year ended December 31, Year 1, among the partners. Show supporting computations.

b Prepare a statement of partners' capital for the Alex, Baron & Crane Partnership for the year ended December 31, Year 1.

Pr. 2-6   Partner Eng plans to withdraw from the Chu, Dow & Eng Partnership on July 10, Year 3. Partnership assets are to be used to acquire Eng's partnership interest. The balance sheet for the partnership on that date follows:

CHU, DOW & ENG PARTNERSHIP
Balance Sheet
July 10, Year 3

Assets		Liabilities & Partners' Capital	
Cash........................	$ 74,000	Liabilities	$ 45,000
Trade accounts receivable		Chu, capital.................	120,000
(net).......................	36,000	Dow, capital	60,000
Plant assets (net)...........	135,000	Eng, capital.................	50,000
Goodwill (net)...............	30,000		
Total.....................	$275,000	Total....................	$275,000

Chu, Dow and Eng share net income and losses in the ratio of 3 : 2 : 1, respectively.

Instructions

Prepare journal entries to record Eng's withdrawal from the Chu, Dow & Eng Partnership on July 10, Year 3, under each of the following assumptions:

a Eng is paid $54,000, and the excess paid over Eng's capital account balance is recorded as a bonus to Eng from Chu and Dow.

b Eng is paid $45,000, and the difference is recorded as a bonus to Chu and Dow from Eng.

c Eng is paid $45,000, and goodwill currently in the accounting records of the partnership, which arose from Chu's original investment of a highly profitable proprietorship, is reduced by the total amount implicit in the transaction.

d Eng accepts cash of $40,500 and plant assets (equipment) with a current fair value of $9,000. The equipment had cost $30,000 and was 60% depreciated, with no residual value. (Record any gain or loss on the disposal of the equipment in the partners' capital accounts.)

Pr. 2-7   The Yee & Zane Partnership has maintained its accounting records on the accrual basis of accounting, except for the method of handling uncollectible account losses. Doubtful accounts expense has been recognized only when specific trade accounts receivable were determined to be uncollectible.

The partners of the Yee & Zane Partnership are anticipating the admission of Arne to the firm on December 31, Year 4, and they retain you to review the partnership accounting records before this action is taken. You suggest that the firm change retroactively to the allowance method of accounting for doubtful accounts receivable so that the planning for admission of Arne may be based on the accrual basis of accounting. The following information is available:

Year trade accounts receivable originated	Trade accounts receivable written off			Additional estimated uncollectible accounts
	Year 2	Year 3	Year 4	
Year 1	$1,200	$ 200		
Year 2	1,500	1,300	$ 600	$ 450
Year 3		1,800	1,400	1,250
Year 4			2,200	4,800
Totals	$2,700	$3,300	$4,200	$6,500

The partners shared net income and losses equally until Year 4. In Year 4 the income-sharing plan was changed as follows: salaries of $8,000 and $6,000 to Yee and Zane, respectively, to be expensed by the partnership; the resultant net income or loss to be divided 60% to Yee and 40% to Zane. Income of the Yee & Zane Partnership for Year 4 was $52,000 before partners' salaries expense.

Instructions

a Prepare a journal entry for the Yee & Zane Partnership on December 31, Year 4, giving effect to the change in accounting method for doubtful accounts expense. Support the entry with an exhibit showing changes in doubtful accounts expense for the year ended December 31, Year 4.

b Assume that after you prepared the journal entry in **a** above, Yee's capital account balance was $48,000, Zane's capital account balance was $22,000, and Arne invested $30,000 for a 20% interest in net assets of the Yee, Zane & Arne Partnership and a 25% share in net income or losses. Prepare a journal entry for the Yee, Zane & Arne Partnership to record the admission of Arne by the bonus method.

Pr. 2-8 Following are financial statements and additional information for the Alef, Beal & Clarke Partnership:

ALEF, BEAL & CLARKE PARTNERSHIP
Income Statement
For Year Ended December 31, Year 2

Revenue:		
Fees..		$480,000
Gain on disposal of equipment		600
Total revenue...		$480,600
Expenses:		
Depreciation	$ 3,220	
Other..	427,670	
Total expenses		430,890
Net income..		$ 49,710

(continued)

ALEF, BEAL & CLARKE PARTNERSHIP
Income Statement (concluded)
For Year Ended December 31, Year 2

Division of net income:

Partner Alef...	$ 22,280
Partner Beal	5,150
Partner Clarke	22,280
Total	$ 49,710

ALEF, BEAL & CLARKE PARTNERSHIP
Statement of Partners' Capital
For Year Ended December 31, Year 2

	Alef	Beal	Clarke	Combined
Partners' capital, beginning of year	$ 9,805	$10,680	$12,089	$32,574
Add: Net income	22,280	5,150	22,280	49,710
Goodwill recognized on				
partner Beal's retirement ...	1,000	1,000	1,000	3,000
Subtotals....................	$33,085	$16,830	$35,369	$85,284
Less: Drawings	(16,735)	(4,830)	(15,700)	(37,265)
Retirement of partner Beal..		(12,000)		(12,000)
Partners' capital, end of year	$16,350	$ -0-	$19,669	$36,019

ALEF, BEAL & CLARKE PARTNERSHIP
Comparative Balance Sheets
December 31, Year 2 and Year 1

	Dec. 31, Year 2	Dec. 31, Year 1	Increase (decrease)
Assets			
Current assets:			
Cash	$ 8,589	$ 3,295	$ 5,294
Trade accounts receivable	12,841	8,960	3,881
Allowance for doubtful accounts	(930)	(1,136)	(206)*
Supplies	983	412	571
Total current assets	$21,483	$11,531	$ 9,952
Investments:			
Cash surrender value of life insurance			
policies	$ 4,060	$ 5,695	$(1,635)
Plant assets:			
Land.....................................	$ 4,200	$ 4,200	$ 0
Buildings and equipment...................	40,800	30,090	10,710
Accumulated depreciation of buildings and			
equipment................................	(12,800)	(13,480)	(680)†
Total plant assets	$32,200	$20,810	$11,390
Goodwill	$ 3,000		$ 3,000
Total assets	$60,743	$38,036	$22,707

** A **decrease** in the allowance and an **increase** in total current assets*
*† A **decrease** in accumulated depreciation and an **increase** in total plant assets*

(continued)

ALEF, BEAL & CLARKE PARTNERSHIP
Comparative Balance Sheets (concluded)
December 31, Year 2 and Year 1

	Dec. 31, Year 2	Dec. 31, Year 1	Increase (decrease)
Liabilities & Partners' Capital			
Current liabilities:			
Note payable to bank......................	$ 3,330		$ 3,330
Trade accounts payable	1,681	$ 2,984	(1,303)
Accrued liabilities	1,913	2,478	(565)
Current portion of long-term debt	5,600		5,600
Total current liabilities	$12,524	$ 5,462	$ 7,062
Long-term debt:			
Equipment contract payable, due $300 monthly plus interest at 6%................	$ 4,200		$ 4,200
Note payable to retired partner, due $2,000 each July 1 plus interest at 5%	8,000		8,000
Total long-term debt.....................	$12,200		$12,200
Total liabilities	$24,724	$ 5,462	$19,262
Partners' capital:			
Partner Alef	$16,350	$ 9,805	$ 6,545
Partner Beal.............................		10,680	(10,680)
Partner Clarke	19,669	12,089	7,580
Total partners' capital...................	$36,019	$32,574	$ 3,445
Total liabilities & partners' capital	$60,743	$38,036	$22,707

Additional Information for Year 2

(1) Alef, Beal, and Clarke shared net income and losses equally. On July 1, Year 2, after the $15,450 net income of the partnership for the six months ended June 30 had been divided among the partners, Beal retired from the partnership, receiving $2,000 cash and a 5%, five-year promissory note for $10,000 in full settlement of his interest. The partners agreed to recognize goodwill of $3,000 prior to Beal's retirement and to retain Beal's name in the partnership name. Alef and Clarke agreed to share net income and losses equally following Beal's retirement.

(2) Following Beal's withdrawal, the insurance policy on his life was canceled, and the partnership received the cash surrender value of $3,420.

(3) The partnership acquired equipment costing $15,210 on August 31 for $6,210 cash and an equipment contract payable $300 a month at the end of each month beginning September 30, Year 2, plus interest at 6%. The partnership made required payments when due.

(4) On September 30, the partnership disposed of equipment that had cost $4,500 for $1,200, recognizing a gain of $600.

(5) The partnership borrowed $3,330 from the bank on a six-month, 8% promissory note due April 15, Year 3.

Instructions

Prepare a statement of cash flows under the indirect method for the Alef, Beal & Clarke Partnership for the year ended December 31, Year 2. A working paper is not required.

Pr. 2-9   Southwestern Enterprises, a limited partnership, was formed on January 2, Year 1, with the issuance of 1,200 units, $1,000 each, as follows:

Laurence Douglas, general partner, 400 units	$ 400,000
10 limited partners, 800 units total	800,000
Total (1,200 units)	$1,200,000

The trial balance of Southwestern Enterprises on December 31, Year 1, the end of its first year of operations, is as follows:

SOUTHWESTERN ENTERPRISES
(A Limited Partnership)
Trial Balance
December 31, Year 1

	Debit	Credit
Cash	$ 20,000	
Trade accounts receivable	90,000	
Allowance for doubtful accounts		$ 10,000
Inventories	100,000	
Plant assets	1,500,000	
Accumulated depreciation of plant assets		100,000
Note payable to bank		20,000
Trade accounts payable		50,000
Accrued liabilities		30,000
Laurence Douglas, capital		400,000
Laurence Douglas, drawings	0	
Limited partners, capital		800,000
Limited partners, redemptions	260,000	
Net sales		1,400,000
Cost of goods sold	700,000	
Operating expenses	140,000	
Totals	$2,810,000	$2,810,000

Additional Information

(1) The Limited Partners, Capital and Limited Partners, Redemptions ledger accounts are controlling accounts supported by subsidiary ledgers.

(2) The certificate for Southwestern Enterprises provides that general partner Laurence Douglas may withdraw cash each December 31 to the extent of his unit participation in the net income of the limited partnership. Douglas had no drawings for Year 1. The certificate also provides that limited partners may withdraw their net equity only on June 30 or December 31 of each year. Two limited partners, each owning 100 units in Southwestern Enterprises, withdrew cash for their equity during Year 1, as shown by the Limited Partners, Redemptions ledger account on page 81.

Limited Partners, Redemptions

Date	Explanation	Debit	Credit	Balance
Year 1				
June 30	100 units @ $1,100	110,000		110,000 dr
Dec. 31	100 units @ $1,500	150,000		260,000 dr

(3) Net income of Southwestern Enterprises for the year ended December 31, Year 1, was subdivided as follows:

Six months ended June 30, Year 1......................................	$120,000
Six months ended Dec. 31, Year 1......................................	440,000
Net income, year ended Dec. 31, Year 1	$560,000

(4) The 10%, six-month bank loan had been received on December 31, Year 1.

(5) There were no disposals of plant assets during Year 1.

Instructions

Prepare an income statement, a statement of partners' capital, a balance sheet, and a statement of cash flows (indirect method) for Southwestern Enterprises (a limited partnership) for the year ended December 31, Year 1. Show net income per weighted-average unit separately for the general partner and the limited partners in the income statement, and show partners' capital per unit in the balance sheet. A working paper is not required for the statement of cash flows.

3

Partnership Liquidation; Joint Ventures

LIQUIDATION OF A PARTNERSHIP

The Meaning of Liquidation

The *liquidation* of a partnership means winding up its activities, usually by selling assets, paying liabilities, and distributing any remaining cash to the partners. In some cases, the partnership net assets may be sold as a unit; in other cases, the assets may be sold in installments, and most or all of the cash received must be used to pay partnership creditors. A business enterprise that has ended normal operations and is in the process of converting its assets to cash and making settlement with its creditors is said to be *in liquidation,* or in the process of being liquidated. This process of liquidation may be completed quickly, or it may require several months.

The term *liquidation* also is used in a narrower sense to mean the payment of liabilities; however, in this chapter it is used only in the broader sense of bringing to a close the activities of a partnership. Another term commonly used in liquidation is *realization,* which means the conversion of noncash assets to cash.

When the decision is made to liquidate a partnership, the accounting records of the partnership should be adjusted and closed, and the net income or loss for the final period of operations entered in the capital accounts of the partners.

The liquidation process usually begins with the realization of noncash assets. Absent provisions of the partnership contract to the contrary, the losses or gains from realization of assets are divided among the partners in the income-sharing ratio and entered in their capital accounts. The amounts shown as their respective equities at this point are the basis for settlement. However, before any payment to partners, all outside creditors of the partnership must be paid in full. If the cash obtained from the realization of assets is insufficient to pay liabilities in full, an unpaid creditor may act to enforce collection from the personal assets of any solvent general partner, regardless of whether that partner has a credit or a debit capital account balance. As pointed out in Chapter 2, a partnership is treated as an entity for many purposes such as changes in partners, but it may not use the shield of a separate entity to protect partners personally against the claims of unpaid partnership creditors.

Division of Losses and Gains during Liquidation

The underlying theme in accounting for the liquidation of a partnership may be stated as follows: ***Divide the loss or gain from the realization of noncash assets before distributing the cash.*** As assets are realized, any loss or gain is allocated to the partners' capital accounts in the income-sharing ratio. The income-sharing ratio used during the operation of the partnership also is applicable to the losses and gains during liquidation, unless the partners have a different agreement.

When the net loss or gain from liquidation is divided among the partners and outside creditors have been paid, the final balances of the partners' capital and loan ledger accounts will be equal to the cash available for distribution to them. ***Payments are then made in the amounts of the partners' respective equities in the partnership.***

Distribution of Cash or Other Assets to Partners

The amount of cash, if any, that a partner is entitled to receive in a liquidation cannot be determined until partners' capital accounts have been adjusted for any loss or gain on the realization of the assets. Strictly interpreted, this reasoning might indicate that no cash may be distributed to a partner until after all the assets have been realized, because the net loss or gain will not be known until the realization of all noncash assets has been completed. In the first section of this chapter is illustrated a series of liquidations in which the realization of assets is completed before any payments are made to partners. Also illustrated in another section is liquidation in installments; that is, payments to partners after a portion of the noncash assets has been realized and all liabilities to outsiders have been paid, but with the final loss or gain from realization of the remaining assets not known. The installment payments to partners are computed by a method that provides a safeguard against overpayment.

An important service by accountants to a partnership in liquidation is to determine the appropriate distribution of cash or other assets to individual partners after the partnership liabilities have been paid. The partners may choose to receive certain assets, such as automobiles or furniture, ***in kind*** rather than to convert such property to cash. Regardless of whether cash or other assets are distributed to partners, it is imperative to follow the rule that no distribution of assets may be made to partners until after all possible losses and liquidation costs have been considered. Failure to follow this rule may result in overpayments to one or more partners and underpayments to others. If the partners who receive the overpayments are unable to return the excess payments, the person who authorized such payments may be liable for any losses sustained by the other partners.

The Uniform Partnership Act lists the order for distribution of cash by a liquidating general partnership as (1) payment of creditors in full, (2) payment of loans from partners, and (3) payment of partners' capital account balances. The indicated priority of partners' loans over partners' capital appears to be a legal fiction. This rule is nullified for practical purposes by an established legal doctrine called the ***right*** *of offset.* If a partner's capital account has a debit balance (or even a potential debit balance depending on possible future realization losses), any credit balance in that partner's loan account must be offset against the deficit (or potential deficit) in the capital account. *However, if a partner with a loan account receives any cash, the payment is recorded by a debit to the loan account to the extent of the balance of that account.*

Because of the right of offset, the total amount of cash received by a partner during liquidation always will be the same as if loans to the partnership had been recorded in the partner's capital account. Furthermore, the existence of a partner's loan account will not advance the time of payment to any partner during the liquidation. Consequently, in the preparation of a *statement of realization and liquidation* (see page 85), the number of columns may be reduced by combining the amount of a partner's loan with the amount shown in the partner's capital account. Thus, the statement of realization and liquidation will include only one column for each partner; the first amount in the column will be the total equity (including any loans) of the partner at the beginning of liquidation.

Combining the capital and loan ledger account balances of a partner in the statement of realization and liquidation does not imply combining these accounts in the partnership ledger. Separate ledger accounts for capital and for loans should be maintained to provide a clear record of the terms under which assets were invested by the partners.

Final Settlement with Partners

The amount that each partner receives from the liquidation of a general partnership will be equal to (1) the capital invested, whether recorded in a capital account or in a loan account; (2) a share of operating net income or loss minus drawings; and (3) a share of loss or gain from the realization of noncash assets in the course of liquidation. Thus, each partner will receive in the liquidation the amount of *his or her equity in the partnership.* The amount of a partner's equity is increased by the positive factors of investing capital and sharing in net income; it is decreased by the negative factors of drawings and sharing in net losses. If the negative factors are larger, the partner will have a capital deficit (a debit balance in the capital account), and the partner must pay to the partnership the amount of such a deficit. Failure to make good a capital deficit by a payment to the partnership would mean that the partner had not complied with provisions of the partnership contract for sharing net income or losses. This would cause the other partners to bear more than their contractual share of losses and thus to receive less in liquidation than their equities in the partnership.

PAYMENTS TO PARTNERS AFTER ALL NONCASH ASSETS REALIZED

Equity of Each Partner Is Sufficient to Absorb Loss from Liquidation

Assume that A and B, who share net income and losses equally, decide to liquidate the A & B Partnership (a general partnership). A balance sheet on June 30, Year 5, just prior to liquidation, follows:

Balance sheet of
general partnership
prior to liquidation

A & B PARTNERSHIP
Balance Sheet
June 30, Year 5

Assets		Liabilities & Partners' Capital	
Cash.........................	$10,000	Liabilities.....................	$20,000
Other assets................	75,000	B, loan	20,000
		A, capital....................	40,000
		B, capital....................	5,000
Total.....................	$85,000	Total.....................	$85,000

As a first step in the liquidation, the noncash assets with a carrying amount of $75,000 realized cash of $35,000, with a resultant loss of $40,000 absorbed equally by A and B. Because B's capital account balance is only $5,000, the partnership's accountant exercises the right of offset by transferring $15,000 from B's loan ledger account to B's capital account. The statement of realization and liquidation below, covering the period July 1 through 15, Year 5, shows the division of the loss between the partners, the payment of outside creditors, and the distribution of the remaining cash to the partners. (The income-sharing ratio appears next to each partner's name.)

A & B PARTNERSHIP
Statement of Realization and Liquidation
July 1 through 15, Year 5

	Assets				Partners' capital	
	Cash	Other	Liabilities	B, loan	A(50%)	B(50%)
Balances before liquidation ...	$ 10,000	$ 75,000	$ 20,000	$ 20,000	$ 40,000	$ 5,000
Realization of other assets at a						
loss of $40,000	35,000	(75,000)			(20,000)	(20,000)
Balances....................	$ 45,000		$ 20,000	$ 20,000	$ 20,000	$(15,000)
Payment to creditors	(20,000)		(20,000)			
Balances....................	$ 25,000			$ 20,000	$ 20,000	$(15,000)
Offset B's capital deficit against						
B's loan....................				(15,000)		15,000
Balances....................	$ 25,000			$ 5,000	$ 20,000	$ -0-
Payments to partners	(25,000)			(5,000)	(20,000)	-0-

In the above statement of realization and liquidation, B's loan account balance of $20,000 and capital account balance of $5,000 might have been combined to obtain an equity of $25,000 for B. As stated earlier, such a procedure would be appropriate because the legal priority of a partner's loan account has no significance in determining either the total amount of cash paid to a partner or the timing of cash payments to partners during liquidation.

In the foregoing illustration, partner A received cash of $20,000 and partner B received $5,000. Neither partner received payment until after partnership creditors had been paid in full. Because the only partnership asset is $25,000 cash at this point, it is reasonable to assume that checks to A and B for $20,000 and $5,000, respectively, were prepared and delivered to the partners at the same time. It is apparent that a partner's loan account has no special significance in the liquidation process. Therefore, succeeding illustrations do not show a partner's loan ledger account in a separate column of the statement of realization and liquidation. Whenever a partner's loan account is involved, its balance may be combined with the partner's capital account balance in the statement of realization and liquidation.

Equity of One Partner Is Not Sufficient to Absorb That Partner's Share of Loss from Liquidation

In this case, the loss on realization of assets, when distributed in the income-sharing ratio, results in a debit balance in the capital account of one of the partners. It may be assumed that the partner with a debit balance has no loan account or that the total of the partner's capital account and loan account combined is less than the partner's share of the loss on realization. To fulfill an agreement to share a specified percentage of partnership losses, the partner must pay to the partnership sufficient cash to eliminate any capital deficit. If the partner is unable to do so, the deficit must be absorbed by the other partners as an additional loss to be shared in the same proportion as they have previously shared net income or losses among themselves. To illustrate, assume the balance sheet below for the D, E & F Partnership (a general partnership) just prior to liquidation:

Balance sheet for general partnership to be liquidated

D, E & F PARTNERSHIP
Balance Sheet
May 20, Year 10

Assets		Liabilities & Partners' Capital	
Cash.......................	$ 20,000	Liabilities....................	$ 30,000
Other assets................	80,000	D, capital...................	40,000
		E, capital...................	21,000
		F, capital...................	9,000
Total.....................	$100,000	Total....................	$100,000

The income-sharing ratio is D, 20%; E, 40%; and F, 40%. The other assets with a carrying amount of $80,000 realized $50,000 cash, resulting in a loss of $30,000. Partner F is charged with 40% of this loss, or $12,000 ($30,000 × 0.40 = $12,000), which creates a debit balance of $3,000 in F's capital account. In the following statement of realization and liquidation it is assumed that F pays the $3,000 to the partnership:

Illustration of completed liquidation of general partnership

D, E & F PARTNERSHIP
Statement of Realization and Liquidation
May 21 through 31, Year 10

	Assets			Partners' capital		
	Cash	*Other*	*Liabilities*	*D(20%)*	*E(40%)*	*F(40%)*
Balances before liquidation.........	$ 20,000	$ 80,000	$ 30,000	$ 40,000	$ 21,000	$ 9,000
Realization of other assets at a loss of $30,000..........	50,000	(80,000)		(6,000)	(12,000)	(12,000)
Balances...........	$ 70,000		$ 30,000	$ 34,000	$ 9,000	$ (3,000)
Payment to creditors	(30,000)		(30,000)			
Balances...........	$ 40,000			$ 34,000	$ 9,000	$ (3,000)
Cash received from F	3,000					3,000
Balances...........	$ 43,000			$ 34,000	$ 9,000	$ -0-
Payments to partners	(43,000)			(34,000)	(9,000)	-0-

Next, change one condition of the foregoing illustration by assuming that partner F was not able to pay the $3,000 capital deficit to the partnership. If the cash available after payment of creditors is to be distributed to D and E without a delay to determine the collectibility of the $3,000 claim against F, the statement of realization and liquidation would appear as illustrated below:

Illustration of incomplete liquidation of general partnership

D, E & F PARTNERSHIP
Statement of Realization and Liquidation
May 21 through 31, Year 10

	Assets			Partners' capital		
	Cash	*Other*	*Liabilities*	*D(20%)*	*E(40%)*	*F(40%)*
Balances before liquidation.........	$ 20,000	$ 80,000	$ 30,000	$ 40,000	$ 21,000	$ 9,000
Realization of other assets at a loss of $30,000..........	50,000	(80,000)		(6,000)	(12,000)	(12,000)
Balances...........	$ 70,000		$ 30,000	$ 34,000	$ 9,000	$ (3,000)
Payment to creditors	(30,000)		(30,000)			
Balances...........	$ 40,000			$ 34,000	$ 9,000	$ (3,000)
Payments to partners	(40,000)			(33,000)	(7,000)	
Balances...........				$ 1,000	$ 2,000	$ (3,000)

The cash payments of $33,000 to D and $7,000 to E leave both of them with a sufficient capital account credit balance to absorb their share of the additional loss if F is unable to pay $3,000 to the partnership. The income-sharing ratio is 20% for D and 40% for E; consequently, the possible additional loss of $3,000 would be charged to them in the proportion of ⅔, or $1,000, to D and ⅓, or $2,000, to E. The payment of the $40,000 cash available to partners is divided between them in a manner that reduces D's capital account balance to $1,000 and E's balance to $2,000.

If the $3,000 is later collected from F, this amount will be divided $1,000 to D and $2,000 to E. The foregoing statement of realization and liquidation then may be completed as follows:

Completion of liquidation; capital deficit paid by partner F

	Assets		Liabilities	Partners' capital		
	Cash	Other		D(20%)	E(40%)	F(40%)
Balances (from page 87)				$ 1,000	$ 2,000	$(3,000)
Cash received from F..............	$ 3,000					3,000
Payments to partners	(3,000)			(1,000)	(2,000)	

However, if the $3,000 receivable from F is uncollectible, the statement of realization and liquidation would be completed with the write-off of F's capital deficit shown as an additional loss absorbed by D and E as follows:

Completion of liquidation; partner F unable to pay capital deficit

	Assets		Liabilities	Partners' capital		
	Cash	Other		D(20%)	E(40%)	F(40%)
Balances (from page 87)				$ 1,000	$ 2,000	$(3,000)
Additional loss from F's uncollectible capital deficit......				(1,000)	(2,000)	3,000

Equities of Two Partners Are Not Sufficient to Absorb Their Shares of Loss from Liquidation

It already has been noted that inability of a partner to pay the partnership for a capital deficit causes an additional loss to the other partners. A partner may have sufficient capital, or combination of capital and loan accounts, to absorb any direct share of loss on the realization of noncash assets, but not sufficient equity to absorb additional actual or potential losses caused by inability of the partnership to collect the deficit in another partner's capital account. In brief, one capital deficit, if not collectible, may cause a second capital deficit that may or may not be collectible.

Assume that J, K, L, and M, partners of the J, K, L & M Partnership (a general partnership) share net income and losses 10%, 20%, 30%, and 40%, respectively. Their capital account balances for the period August 1 through 15, Year 4, are as shown in the statement of realization and liquidation below, supported by the exhibit that follows.

J, K, L & M PARTNERSHIP
Statement of Realization and Liquidation
August 1 through 15, Year 4

	Assets			Partners' capital			
	Cash	Other	Liabilities	J(10%)	K(20%)	L(30%)	M(40%)
Balances before liquidation.........	$ 20,000	$ 200,000	$ 120,000	$ 30,000	$ 32,000	$ 30,000	$ 8,000
Realization of other assets at a loss of $80,000	120,000	(200,000)		(8,000)	(16,000)	(24,000)	(32,000)
Balances	$ 140,000		$ 120,000	$ 22,000	$ 16,000	$ 6,000	$(24,000)
Payment to creditors	(120,000)		(120,000)				
Balances	$ 20,000			$ 22,000	$ 16,000	$ 6,000	$(24,000)
Payments to partners (**Exhibit 1** below).............	(20,000)			(16,000)	(4,000)		
Balances				$ 6,000	$ 12,000	$ 6,000	$(24,000)

Exhibit 1

J, K, L & M PARTNERSHIP
Computation of Cash Payments to Partners
August 15, Year 4

	Partners' capital			
	J(10%)	K(20%)	L(30%)	M(40%)
Capital account balances before distribution of cash to partners ..	$22,000	$16,000	$ 6,000	$(24,000)
Additional loss to J, K, and L if M's deficit is uncollectible (ratio of 10:20:30)	(4,000)	(8,000)	(12,000)	24,000
Balances......................	$18,000	$ 8,000	$ (6,000)	
Additional loss to J and K if L's deficit is uncollectible (ratio of 10:20) ..	(2,000)	(4,000)	6,000	
Amounts that may be paid to partners	$16,000	$ 4,000		

Exhibit 1 on page 89, which supports the statement of realization and liquidation on that page, shows that the $20,000 of available cash may be distributed $16,000 to J and $4,000 to K. If the $24,000 deficit in M's capital account proves uncollectible, the additional loss to be divided among the other three partners will cause L's capital account to change from a $6,000 credit balance to a $6,000 debit balance (deficit). Therefore, L is not eligible to receive a cash payment. If this deficit in L's capital account proves uncollectible, the balances remaining in the capital accounts of J and K, after the cash payments to them totaling $20,000, will be equal to the amounts ($2,000 and $4,000, respectively) needed to absorb the additional loss shifted from L's capital account.

Partnership Is Insolvent but Partners Are Solvent

If a partnership is *insolvent,* it is unable to pay all outside creditors, and at least one and perhaps all of the partners will have debit balances in their capital accounts. In any event, the total of the capital account debit balances will exceed the total of the credit balances. If the partner or partners with a capital deficit pay the required amount to the partnership, it will have cash to pay its liabilities in full. However, the partnership creditors may demand payment from *any solvent* partner individually, regardless of whether the partner's capital account has a debit balance or a credit balance. In terms of relationships with creditors, the partnership is not a separate entity. A partner who makes payments to partnership creditors receives a credit to his or her capital account. As an illustration of an insolvent partnership whose partners are solvent (have personal assets in excess of liabilities), assume that N, O, and P, who are partners of the N, O & P Partnership (a general partnership) and who share net income and losses equally, prepare the following balance sheet just prior to liquidation on May 10, Year 8:

Balance sheet for
general partnership to
be liquidated

N, O & P PARTNERSHIP
Balance Sheet
May 10, Year 8

Assets		*Liabilities & Partners' Capital*	
Cash......................	$ 15,000	Liabilities	$ 65,000
Other assets...............	85,000	N, capital...................	18,000
		O, capital...................	10,000
		P, capital...................	7,000
Total.....................	$100,000	Total.....................	$100,000

On May 12, Year 8, the other assets with a carrying amount of $85,000 realize $40,000 cash, which causes a loss of $45,000 to be divided equally among the partners. The total cash of $55,000 is paid to the partnership creditors, which leaves unpaid liabilities of $10,000. Partner N's capital account has a credit balance of $3,000 after absorbing one-third of the loss. Partners O and P owe the partnership $5,000 and $8,000, respectively. Assuming that on May 30, Year 8, O and P pay in the amounts of their deficiencies, the partnership will use $10,000 of the $13,000 available cash to pay the remaining liabilities and will distribute $3,000 to N. These events are summarized in the statement of realization and liquidation below.

N, O & P PARTNERSHIP
Statement of Realization and Liquidation
May 11 through 30, Year 8

	Assets			Partners' capital		
	Cash	Other	Liabilities	N(⅓)	O(⅓)	P(⅓)
Balances before liquidation . . .	$ 15,000	$ 85,000	$ 65,000	$ 18,000	$ 10,000	$ 7,000
Realization of other assets at a						
loss of $45,000	40,000	(85,000)		(15,000)	(15,000)	(15,000)
Balances.	$ 55,000		$ 65,000	$ 3,000	$ (5,000)	$ (8,000)
Partial payment to creditors . . .	(55,000)		(55,000)			
Balances.	$ -0-		$ 10,000	$ 3,000	$ (5,000)	$ (8,000)
Cash invested by O and P	13,000				5,000	8,000
Balances.	$ 13,000		$ 10,000	$ 3,000		
Final payment to creditors	(10,000)		(10,000)			
Balances.	$ 3,000			$ 3,000		
Payment to N	(3,000)			(3,000)		

Assume that there was some delay in collecting the $13,000 capital deficits from O and P, and during this period the creditors demanded and received payment of their $10,000 in claims from partner N. The payment by N would cause N's equity to increase to $13,000 from $3,000. When the $13,000 is received from O and P by the partnership, it would be paid to N.

Another alternative is that creditors might collect the final $10,000 due them directly from O or P. Payments by these partners to creditors would be credited to their capital accounts and thus would eliminate or reduce their debts to the partnership. As long as it is assumed that the partners with capital deficits make payment to the partnership or directly to partnership creditors, the results are the same. Creditors will be paid in full and partners will share losses on liquidation as provided in the partnership contract.

Partnership Is Insolvent and Partners Are Insolvent

In the foregoing illustration of an insolvent partnership, it was assumed that the partners were solvent and therefore able to pay their capital deficits to the partnership. Now consider an insolvent partnership in which one or more of the partners are insolvent. This situation raises a question as to the relative rights of two groups of creditors: (1) creditors of the partnership and (2) creditors of the partners as individuals. The relative rights of these two groups of creditors are governed by the provisions of the Uniform Partnership Act relating to the *marshaling of assets.* These rules provide that assets of the partnership (including partners' capital deficits) are first available to creditors of the partnership and that assets owned individually by the partners are first available to their personal creditors. After the liabilities of the partnership have been paid in full, the creditors of an individual partner have a claim against the assets (if any) of the partnership to the extent of that partner's equity in the partnership.

After the personal creditors of a partner have been paid in full from the personal assets of the partner, any remaining personal assets are available to partnership creditors, regardless of whether the partner's capital account has a credit balance or a debit balance. *Such claims by creditors of the partnership are permitted only when these creditors are unable to obtain payment from the partnership.*

To illustrate the relative rights of creditors of an insolvent partnership and personal creditors of an insolvent partner, assume that R, S, and T, partners of the R, S & T Partnership (a general partnership) who share net income and losses equally, have the partnership balance sheet below just prior to liquidation on November 30, Year 10.

Balance sheet of general partnership prior to liquidation

R, S & T PARTNERSHIP
Balance Sheet
November 30, Year 10

Assets		*Liabilities & Partners' Capital*	
Cash......................	$ 10,000	Liabilities	$ 60,000
Other assets...............	100,000	R, capital...................	5,000
		S, capital...................	15,000
		T, capital...................	30,000
Total.....................	$110,000	Total.....................	$110,000

Assume also that on November 30, Year 10, the partners have the following personal assets and liabilities apart from their equities in the partnership:

Partners' personal assets and liabilities

Partner	Personal assets	Personal liabilities
R..	$100,000	$25,000
S..	50,000	50,000
T..	5,000	60,000

The realization of other assets of the partnership results in a loss of $60,000, as shown in the statement of realization and liquidation on page 93 for the period December 1 through 12, Year 10.

The creditors of the partnership have received all the cash of the partnership and still have unpaid claims of $10,000. They cannot collect from S or T personally because the personal assets of these two partners are just sufficient or are insufficient to pay their personal liabilities. However, the partnership creditors may collect the $10,000 in full from R, who is solvent. By chance, R has a capital deficit of $15,000, but this is of no concern to creditors of the partnership, who may collect in full from any partner who has sufficient personal assets, regardless of whether that partner's

Liquidation of general partnership not completed

R, S & T PARTNERSHIP
Statement of Realization and Liquidation
December 1 through 12, Year 10

	Assets			Partners' capital		
	Cash	Other	Liabilities	R(⅓)	S(⅓)	T(⅓)
Balances before liquidation.......	$ 10,000	$ 100,000	$ 60,000	$ 5,000	$ 15,000	$ 30,000
Realization of other assets at a loss of $60,000 ..	40,000	(100,000)		(20,000)	(20,000)	(20,000)
Balances.........	$ 50,000		$ 60,000	$(15,000)	$ (5,000)	$ 10,000
Partial payment to creditors	(50,000)		(50,000)			
Balances.........			$ 10,000	$(15,000)	$ (5,000)	$ 10,000

capital account has a debit balance or a credit balance. The statement of realization and liquidation is now continued below to show R's payment of the final $10,000 owed to partnership creditors. Because the assumptions about R's finances showed that R had $100,000 of assets and only $25,000 of liabilities, R is able to invest in the partnership the additional $5,000 needed to offset R's capital deficit. This $5,000 cash is paid to partner T, the only partner with a capital account credit balance.

Continuation of statement of realization and liquidation for general partnership

			Partners' capital		
	Cash	Liabilities	R(⅓)	S(⅓)	T(⅓)
Balances (from above)		$ 10,000	$(15,000)	$(5,000)	$10,000
Payment by R to partnership creditors........		(10,000)	10,000		
Balances.........			$ (5,000)	$(5,000)	$10,000
Cash invested by R	$ 5,000		5,000		
Balances.........	$ 5,000			$(5,000)	$10,000
Payment to T (or T's creditors)	(5,000)				(5,000)
Balances.........				$(5,000)	$ 5,000

The continued statement of realization and liquidation now shows that S owes $5,000 to the partnership; however, S's personal assets of $50,000 are exactly equal to S's personal liabilities of $50,000. Under the Uniform Partnership Act, all the personal assets of S will go to personal creditors; therefore, the $5,000 deficit in S's capital account represents an additional loss to be shared equally by R and T. To conclude the liquidation, R, who is solvent, pays $2,500 to the partnership, and the $2,500 will be paid to T or to T's personal creditors, because T is insolvent. These payments are shown below to complete the statement of realization and liquidation for the R, S & T Partnership:

Completion of liquidation of general partnership

			Partners' capital	
	Cash	R(⅓)	S(⅓)	T(⅓)
Balances (from above).........			$(5,000)	$ 5,000
Write-off of S's capital deficit as uncollectible		$(2,500)	5,000	(2,500)
Balances		$(2,500)		$ 2,500
Cash invested by R............	$ 2,500	2,500		
Balances	$ 2,500			$ 2,500
Payment to T (or T's creditors)..	(2,500)			(2,500)

The final results of the liquidation show that the partnership creditors received payment in full because of the financial status of partner R. Because R was solvent, the personal creditors of R also were paid in full. The personal creditors of S were paid in full, thereby exhausting S's personal assets; however, because S failed to pay the $5,000 capital deficit to the partnership, an additional loss of $5,000 was absorbed by R and T. The personal creditors of T received all of T's personal assets of $5,000 and also $7,500 from the partnership, representing T's equity in the firm. However, T's personal creditors were able to collect only $12,500 ($5,000 + $7,500 = $12,500) on their total claims of $60,000.

INSTALLMENT PAYMENTS TO PARTNERS

In the foregoing illustrations of partnership liquidation, all the partnership noncash assets were realized and the total loss from liquidation was divided among the partners before any cash payments were made to them. However, the liquidation of some partnerships may extend over several months. In such extended liquidations the partners usually will want to receive cash as it becomes available rather than waiting until all noncash assets have been realized. Installment payments to partners are appropriate if necessary safeguards are used to ensure that all partnership creditors are paid in full and that no partners are paid more than the amount to which they would be entitled after all losses on realization of assets are known.

Liquidation in installments is a process of realizing some assets, paying creditors, paying the remaining available cash to partners, realizing additional assets, and making additional cash payments to partners. The liquidation continues until all noncash assets have been realized and all cash has been distributed to partnership creditors and partners.

The circumstances of installment liquidation vary; consequently, my approach is to emphasize the general principles guiding liquidation in installments rather than to provide illustrations of all possible liquidation situations. Among the variables that cause partnership liquidations to differ are the sufficiency of each partner's capital to absorb that partner's share of the possible losses remaining after each installment payment of cash, the shifting of losses from one partner to another because of inability to collect a capital deficit, the offsetting of loan account balances against capital deficits, and the possible need for setting aside cash to pay future liquidation costs or unrecorded partnership liabilities.

General Principles Guiding Installment Payments

The critical element in installment liquidations is that the liquidator authorizes cash payments to partners before all losses that may be incurred in the liquidation are known. If payments are made to partners and later losses cause deficits in the partners' capital accounts, the liquidator will have to request the return of the payments. If the payments cannot be recovered, the liquidator may be personally liable to the other partners for the loss caused them by the inappropriate distribution of cash. Because of this danger, the only safe policy for determining installment cash payments to partners is the following *worst-case scenario:*

1 Assume a total loss on all remaining noncash assets, and provide for all possible losses, including potential liquidation costs and unrecorded liabilities.

2 Assume that any partner with a potential capital deficit will be unable to pay anything to the partnership; thus, distribute each installment of cash as if no more cash will be forthcoming, either from realization of assets or from collection of capital deficits from partners.

Under these assumptions, the liquidator will authorize a cash payment to a partner only if that partner has a capital account credit balance (or in capital and loan accounts combined) in excess of the amount required to absorb a portion of the maximum possible loss that may be incurred on liquidation. A partner's ''share of the maximum possible loss'' would include any loss that may result from the inability of partners to pay any potential capital deficits to the partnership.

When installment payments are made according to these rules, the effect will be to bring the equities of the partners to the income-sharing ratio as quickly as possible. *When installment payments have proceeded to the point that the partners' capital account balances (equities) correspond with the income-sharing ratio, all subsequent payments may be made in that ratio,* because each partner's equity will be sufficient to absorb an appropriate share of the maximum possible remaining loss.

Determining Appropriate Installment Payments to Partners

The amounts of cash that may be distributed safely to the partners each month (or at any other point in time) may be determined by computing the impact on partners' equities (capital and loan account balances) of the maximum possible loss on noncash assets remaining to be realized and the resultant potential impact on partners' capital. To illustrate, assume that X, Y, and Z, partners of the X, Y & Z Partnership (a general partnership) who share net income and losses in a 4:3:2 ratio, decide to liquidate the partnership and to distribute cash in installments. The balance sheet for the X, Y & Z Partnership just prior to liquidation on July 5, Year 1, is as follows:

Balance sheet of general partnership prior to liquidation in installments

X, Y & Z PARTNERSHIP
Balance Sheet
July 5, Year 1

Assets		Liabilities & Partners' Capital	
Cash	$ 8,000	Liabilities	$ 61,000
Other assets	192,000	X, capital	40,000
		Y, capital	45,000
		Z, capital	54,000
Total	$200,000	Total	$200,000

To simplify the illustration, assume that noncash assets were realized as follows:

Realization of other assets by liquidating partnership

X, Y & Z PARTNERSHIP
Realization of Other Assets
July 6 through September 30, Year 1

Date	Carrying amount of assets realized	Loss on realization	Cash received by partnership
July 31	$ 62,000	$13,500	$ 48,500
August 31	66,000	36,000	30,000
September 30	64,000	31,500	32,500
Totals	$192,000	$81,000	$111,000

Thus, on July 31, Year 1, $56,500 ($8,000 + $48,500 = $56,500) of cash is available for distribution. The first claim to the cash is that of partnership outside creditors; because their claims total $61,000, the entire $56,500 available on July 31 is paid to creditors, leaving an unpaid balance of $4,500 ($61,000 − $56,500 = $4,500), and the partners receive nothing on that date.

On August 31, Year 1, $30,000 cash is available for distribution; the first $4,500 is paid to creditors, leaving $25,500 ($30,000 − $4,500 = $25,500) available for distribution to partners. Under the worst-case scenario described on page 95, the appropriate distribution of the $25,500 to partners is determined as follows:

Determination of cash distributions to partners, Aug. 31, Year 1		X	Y	Z
Capital account balances, July 5, Year 1		$40,000	$ 45,000	$ 54,000
Allocation of loss on July 31, Year 1, realization				
of noncash assets ($13,500)		(6,000)	(4,500)	(3,000)
Allocation of loss on Aug. 31, Year 1, realization				
of noncash assets ($36,000)		(16,000)	(12,000)	(8,000)
Capital account balances, Aug. 31, Year 1		$18,000	$ 28,500	$ 43,000
Allocation of maximum potential loss on remain-				
ing noncash assets ($64,000)		(28,445)	(21,333)	(14,222)
Potential capital account balances		($10,445)	$ 7,167	$ 28,778
Allocation of potential loss from uncollectibility of				
X's potential capital deficit in ratio of 3:2		10,445	(6,267)	(4,178)
Appropriate cash payments to partners, Aug. 31,				
Year 1		$ 0	$ 900	$ 24,600

A technique similar to that above would be used to determine the appropriate payment to partners of the $32,500 cash available on September 30, Year 1.

Preparation of a Cash Distribution Program

Although the method for determining cash payments to partners illustrated in the foregoing section is sound, it is somewhat cumbersome. Furthermore, it does not show at the beginning of the liquidation how cash might be divided among the partners as it becomes available. For these reasons, it is more efficient to prepare in advance a complete *cash distribution program* to show how cash may be divided during liquidation. If such a program is prepared, any amounts of cash received from the realization of partnership assets may be paid immediately to partnership creditors and the partners as specified in the program.

Using the data for the X, Y & Z Partnership illustrated on page 96, the following cash distribution program may be prepared; the working paper supporting the cash distribution program and an explanation of the preparation of the working paper are on pages 98 and 99.

X, Y & Z PARTNERSHIP
Cash Distribution Program
July 5, Year 1

		Creditors	X	Y	Z
First.	$ 61,000	100%			
Next.	24,000				100%
Next.	25,000			60%	40%
All over.	$110,000		4/9	3/9	2/9

X, Y & Z PARTNERSHIP
Working Paper for Cash Distributions to Partners during Liquidation
July 5, Year 1

	X	Y	Z
Capital account balances before liquidation	$40,000	$45,000	$ 54,000
Income-sharing ratio..........................	4	3	2
Divide capital account balances before liquidation by income-sharing ratio to obtain **capital per unit of income sharing** for each partner...........	$10,000	$15,000	$ 27,000
Required reduction in capital per unit of income sharing for partner Z to reduce Z's balance to equal the next largest balance (for partner Y). This is the amount of the first cash distribution to a partner **per unit of the partner's income sharing.** Because Z has 2 units of income sharing, Z receives the first $24,000 ($12,000 × 2 = $24,000)			(12,000)
Capital per unit of income sharing after payment of $24,000 to Z.................................	$10,000	$15,000	$ 15,000
Required reduction in capital per unit of income sharing for partners Y and Z to reduce their balances to equal partner X's balance, which is the smallest capital per unit of income sharing. The required reduction is multiplied by each partner's income-sharing ratio to compute the amount of cash to be paid. Thus, Y receives $15,000 ($5,000 × 3 = $15,000), and Z receives $10,000 ($5,000 × 2 = $10,000)		(5,000)	(5,000)
Capital per unit of income sharing after payment of $15,000 to Y and $34,000 to Z. **Remaining cash may be distributed in the income-sharing ratio**..	$10,000	$10,000	$ 10,000

Procedures for developing foregoing working paper:[1]

1   The "capital account balances before liquidation" represent the *equities* of the partners in the partnership, that is, the balance of a partner's capital account, plus or minus the balance (if any) of a loan made by a partner to the partnership or a loan made by the partnership to a partner.

---

[1] The procedure for preparing a cash distribution program illustrated herein may be used regardless of the number of partners involved or the complexity of the income-sharing ratio. For example, assume that partners share net income and loss as follows: A 41.2%, B 32.3%, C 26.5%. The income-sharing ratio may be stated as 412 for A, 323 for B, and 265 for C to apply the techniques illustrated in this section.

2 The capital account balance before liquidation for each partner is divided by each partner's income-sharing ratio to determine the amount of capital per unit of income sharing for each partner. This procedure is critical because it (**a**) identifies the partner with the largest capital per unit of income sharing who, therefore, will be the first to receive cash, (**b**) facilitates the ranking of partners in the order in which they are entitled to receive cash, and (**c**) provides the basis for computing the amount of cash each partner receives at various stages of liquidation. Because Z's capital per unit of income sharing is largest ($27,000), Z is the first partner to receive cash (after all partnership creditors have been paid), followed by Y, and finally by X.

3 Z receives enough cash to reduce Z's capital of $27,000 per unit of income sharing to $15,000, equal to the balance for Y, the second-ranking partner. To accomplish this, Z's capital per unit of income sharing must be reduced by $12,000, and because Z has two units of income sharing, Z receives $24,000 ($12,000 × 2 = $24,000) before Y receives any cash.

4 At this point, the capital per unit of income sharing for both Y and Z is $15,000, indicating that they are entitled to receive cash until their capital per unit of income sharing is reduced by $5,000 to the $10,000 balance for X, the lowest-ranking partner. Because Y has three units and Z has two units of income sharing, Y receives $15,000 ($5,000 × 3 = $15,000) and Z receives an additional $10,000 ($5,000 × 2 = $10,000) before X receives any cash. After Z receives $24,000, Y and Z would share any amount of cash available to a maximum amount of $25,000 in a 3 : 2 ratio.

5 After Y has received $15,000 and Z has received $34,000 ($24,000 + $10,000 = $34,000), the capital per unit of income sharing is $10,000 for each partner, and any additional cash is paid to the partners in the income-sharing ratio (4 : 3 : 2), because their capital account balances have been reduced to the income-sharing ratio. This is illustrated below:

	X(⁴⁄₉)	Y(³⁄₉)	Z(²⁄₉)
Capital account balances before liquidation......	$40,000	$ 45,000	$ 54,000
First payment of cash to Z.....................			(24,000)
Second payment of cash to Y and Z in 3 : 2 ratio .		(15,000)	(10,000)
Capital account balances (in income-sharing ratio of 4 : 3 : 2) after payment of total of $49,000 to Y and Z.....................................	$40,000	$ 30,000	$ 20,000

Only when installment payments reach the point at which partners' capital account balances correspond with the income-sharing ratio may subsequent cash payments be made in that ratio.

A cash distribution program such as the one on page 97 also may be used to ascertain an equitable distribution of noncash assets to partners. The current fair value of noncash assets such as marketable securities, inventories, or equipment distributed to partners is treated as equivalent to cash payments. If a distribution of noncash assets departs from the cash distribution program by giving one of the partners a larger distribution than that partner is entitled to receive, subsequent distributions should be adjusted to allow the remaining partners to ''make up'' the distribution prematurely made to one of the partners. In such cases, a ***revised cash distribution program must be prepared,*** because the original relationship among the partners' capital account balances has been disrupted.

Any losses or gains on the realization of assets during liquidation are allocated to the partners in the income-sharing ratio, unless the partnership contract specifies another allocation procedure. Thus, the degree to which the capital account balances do not correspond with the income-sharing ratio is not altered by such losses or gains. Consequently, losses or gains from the realization of assets in the course of partnership liquidation do not affect the cash distribution program prepared prior to the start of liquidation.

To illustrate how the cash distribution program on page 97 may be used, assume that the realization of other assets by the X, Y & Z Partnership (a general partnership) from July 6 through September 30, Year 1, is as shown on page 96. The cash available each month is paid to creditors and partners according to the cash distribution program on page 97. The distributions of cash are summarized below.

X, Y & Z PARTNERSHIP
Distributions of Cash to Creditors and Partners
July 6 through September 30, Year 1

			Partners' capital		
Date	*Cash*	*Liabilities*	*X(4/9)*	*Y(3/9)*	*Z(2/9)*
July 31 (includes $8,000 on hand on July 5)	*$ 56,500*	*$56,500*			
August 31	*30,000*	*4,500*			*$24,000* ⎫
				$ 900	*600* ⎬
September 30	*32,500*			*14,100*	*9,400* ⎫
			$4,000	*3,000*	*2,000* ⎬
Totals	*$119,000*	*$61,000*	*$4,000*	*$18,000*	*$36,000*

The entire cash balance of $56,500 available on July 31 is paid to creditors, leaving $4,500 in unpaid liabilities. When $30,000 becomes available on August 31, $4,500 is paid to creditors, leaving $25,500 to be paid to the partners according to the cash distribution program on page 97. The program requires Z to receive 100% of the first $24,000 available for distribution to partners, and for Y and Z to share the next $25,000 in a 3:2 ratio. On August 31 only $1,500 ($30,000 − $4,500 − $24,000 = $1,500) is available for payment to Y and Z; thus Y and Z receive $900 and $600, respectively. Of the $32,500 available on September 30, the first $23,500 is paid to Y and Z in a 3:2 ratio, or $14,100 and $9,400, respectively, in order to complete the distribution of $25,000 to Y and Z before X participates; this leaves $9,000 ($32,500 − $23,500 = $9,000) to be distributed to X, Y, and Z in the 4:3:2 income-sharing ratio.

A complete statement of realization and liquidation for the X, Y & Z Partnership follows. The journal entries to record the realization of assets and to complete the liquidation of the X, Y & Z Partnership are on this page and page 102.

X, Y & Z PARTNERSHIP
Statement of Realization and Liquidation
July 6 through September 30, Year 1

	Cash	Other	Liabilities	X(4/9)	Y(3/9)	Z(2/9)
	Assets			**Partners' capital**		
Balances before liquidation...	$ 8,000	$ 192,000	$ 61,000	$ 40,000	$ 45,000	$ 54,000
July 31 installment: Realization of other assets at a loss of $13,500 ...	48,500	(62,000)		(6,000)	(4,500)	(3,000)
Balances ...	$ 56,500	$ 130,000	$ 61,000	$ 34,000	$ 40,500	$ 51,000
Payment to creditors ...	(56,500)		(56,500)			
Balances ...	$ -0-	$ 130,000	$ 4,500	$ 34,000	$ 40,500	$ 51,000
Aug. 31 installment: Realization of other assets at a loss of $36,000 ...	30,000	(66,000)		(16,000)	(12,000)	(8,000)
Balances ...	$ 30,000	$ 64,000	$ 4,500	$ 18,000	$ 28,500	$ 43,000
Payment to creditors ...	(4,500)		(4,500)			
Balances ...	$ 25,500	$ 64,000		$ 18,000	$ 28,500	$ 43,000
Payments to partners ..	(25,500)				(900)	(24,600)
Balances ...	$ -0-	$ 64,000		$ 18,000	$ 27,600	$ 18,400
Sept. 30 installment: Realization of other assets at a loss of $31,500 ...	32,500	(64,000)		(14,000)	(10,500)	(7,000)
Balances ...	$ 32,500			$ 4,000	$ 17,100	$ 11,400
Payments to partners ..	(32,500)			(4,000)	(17,100)	(11,400)

Journal entries to record liquidation of general partnership in installments

Year 1
July 31 Cash.. 48,500
         X, Capital...................................... 6,000
         Y, Capital...................................... 4,500
         Z, Capital...................................... 3,000
              Other Assets................................ 62,000
         To record realization of assets and division of $13,500
         loss among partners in 4:3:2 ratio

(continued)

Journal entries to
record liquidation of
general partnership in
installments
(concluded)

July	31	Liabilities	56,500	
		Cash..		56,500
		To record payment to creditors.		
Aug.	31	Cash..	30,000	
		X, Capital.....................................	16,000	
		Y, Capital.....................................	12,000	
		Z, Capital.....................................	8,000	
		Other Assets............................		66,000
		To record realization of assets and division of $36,000		
		loss among partners in 4 : 3 : 2 ratio.		
	31	Liabilities	4,500	
		Y, Capital.....................................	900	
		Z, Capital.....................................	24,600	
		Cash................................		30,000
		To record payment to creditors and first installment to		
		partners.		
Sept.	30	Cash..	32,500	
		X, Capital.....................................	14,000	
		Y, Capital.....................................	10,500	
		Z, Capital.....................................	7,000	
		Other Assets............................		64,000
		To record realization of remaining assets and division of		
		$31,500 loss among partners in 4 : 3 : 2 ratio.		
	30	X, Capital...	4,000	
		Y, Capital.....................................	17,100	
		Z, Capital.....................................	11,400	
		Cash................................		32,500
		To record final installment to partners to complete the liq-		
		uidation of the partnership.		

Withholding of Cash for Liabilities and Liquidation Costs

As previously emphasized, partnership creditors are entitled to payment in full before anything is paid to partners. However, in some cases the liquidator may find it
more convenient to set aside sufficient cash required to pay certain recorded liabilities, and to distribute the remaining cash to the partners. The withholding of cash for
payment of recorded liabilities is appropriate when for any reason it is not practicable
or advisable (as when the amount of the claim is in dispute) to pay the liabilities
before cash is distributed to partners. An amount of cash set aside, and equal to
recorded unpaid liabilities, is not a factor in computing possible future liquidation

losses; the possible future loss is measured by the amount of noncash assets, any *unrecorded* liabilities, and any liquidation costs that may be incurred.

Any costs incurred during the liquidation of a partnership are deducted from partners' capital account balances to compute the cash available for distribution to partners. Costs of liquidation thereby are treated as part of the total loss from liquidation. However, in some cases, the liquidator may wish to withhold cash in anticipation of future liquidation costs. The amount of cash set aside for future liquidation costs or for payment of unrecorded liabilities should be combined with the amount of noncash assets in the computation of the maximum possible loss that may be incurred to complete the liquidation of the partnership.

Liquidation of Limited Partnerships

Most of the discussion of the liquidation of general partnerships, in the preceding sections of this chapter, applies to the liquidation of limited partnerships. However, the Uniform Limited Partnership Act provides that after outside creditors of a limited partnership have been paid, the equities of the limited partners must be paid before the general partner or partners may receive any cash. Further, the limited partners may agree that one or more of them may have priority over the others regarding payments in liquidation of the limited partnership.

INCORPORATION OF A PARTNERSHIP

Many partnerships evaluate the possible advantages to be gained by incorporating. Among such advantages are limited liability of stockholders, ease of attracting additional capital, and possible income tax advantages.

BLAIR & BENSON PARTNERSHIP
Balance Sheet
June 30, Year 10

Assets

Cash		$12,000
Trade accounts receivable	$28,100	
Less: Allowance for doubtful accounts	600	27,500
Inventories		25,500
Equipment	$60,000	
Less: Accumulated depreciation of equipment	26,000	34,000
Total assets		$99,000

Liabilities & Partners' Capital

Liabilities:		
Trade accounts payable		$35,000
Partners' capital:		
Blair, capital	$47,990	
Benson, capital	16,010	64,000
Total liabilities & partners' capital		$99,000

To assure that each partner receives an equitable portion of the capital stock issued by the new corporation, the assets of the partnership must be adjusted to current fair value before being transferred to the corporation. Any identifiable intangible asset or goodwill developed by the partnership is included among the assets transferred to the corporation.

To illustrate the incorporation of a partnership, assume that Blair and Benson, partners of the Blair & Benson Partnership who share net income and loss in a 4:1 ratio, organize B & B Corporation to take over the net assets of the partnership. The balance sheet of the partnership on June 30, Year 10, the date of incorporation, is on page 103.

After an appraisal of the equipment and an audit of the financial statements, it is agreed that the following adjustments are required to restate the net assets of the partnership to current fair value:

1 Increase the allowance for doubtful accounts to $1,000.

2 Increase the inventories to current replacement cost of $30,000.

3 Increase the equipment to its reproduction cost new, $70,000, less accumulated depreciation on this basis, $30,500; that is, to current fair value, $39,500.

4 Recognize accrued liabilities of $1,100.

5 Recognize goodwill of $10,000.

B & B Corporation is authorized to issue 10,000 shares of $10 par common stock. It issues 5,500 shares of common stock valued at $15 a share to the partnership in exchange for the net assets of the partnership. The 5,500 shares received by the partnership are divided between the partners on the basis of the adjusted balances of their capital accounts. (Partners may withdraw small amounts of cash to round their capital account balances to even amounts, thus avoiding the issuance of fractional shares of common stock.) This procedure completes the dissolution and liquidation of the partnership.

Although the accounting records of the partnership may be modified to serve as the records of the new corporation, it is customary to use a new set of accounting records for the corporation. If this alternative is followed, the procedures required are:

In Accounting Records of Partnership:

1 Prepare journal entries for revaluation of assets, including recognition of goodwill, if any.

2 Record any cash withdrawals necessary to adjust partners' capital account balances to round amounts. (In some instances the contract may require transfer to the corporation of all assets except cash.)

3 Record the transfer of assets and liabilities to the corporation, the receipt of the corporation's common stock by the partnership, and the distribution of the common stock to the partners in settlement of the balances of their capital accounts.

The journal entries to adjust and eliminate the accounting records of the Blair & Benson Partnership are illustrated below.

Journal entries for Blair & Benson Partnership

Inventories ($30,000 − $25,500).........................	4,500	
Equipment ($70,000 − $60,000).........................	10,000	
Goodwill	10,000	
Allowance for Doubtful Accounts ($1,000 − $600).........		400
Accumulated Depreciation of Equipment		
($30,500 − $26,000)................................		4,500
Accrued Liabilities Payable........................		1,100
Blair, Capital ($18,500 × 0.80)		14,800
Benson, Capital ($18,500 × 0.20)		3,700

To adjust assets and liabilities to agreed amounts and to divide net gain of $18,500 between partners in 4:1 ratio.

Receivable from B & B Corporation ($64,000 + $18,500).........	82,500	
Trade Accounts Payable.................................	35,000	
Accrued Liabilities Payable.............................	1,100	
Allowance for Doubtful Accounts.........................	1,000	
Accumulated Depreciation of Equipment.....................	30,500	
Cash		12,000
Trade Accounts Receivable		28,100
Inventories		30,000
Equipment		70,000
Goodwill		10,000

To record transfer of assets and liabilities to B & B Corporation.

Common Stock of B & B Corporation (5,500 × $15)	82,500	
Receivable from B & B Corporation		82,500

To record receipt of 5,500 shares of $10 par common stock valued at $15 a share in payment for net assets transferred to B & B Corporation.

Blair, Capital ($47,990 + $14,800; 4,186 × $15)	62,790	
Benson, Capital ($16,010 + $3,700; 1,314 × $15)..............	19,710	
Common Stock of B & B Corporation.....................		82,500

To record distribution of common stock of B & B Corporation to partners: 4,186 shares to Blair and 1,314 shares to Benson.

In Accounting Records of New Corporation:

1   Record the acquisition of assets and liabilities (including obligation to pay for the net assets) from the partnership at current fair values.

2   Record the issuance of common stock at current fair value in payment of the obligation to the partnership.

The journal entries in the accounting records of B & B Corporation on June 30, Year 10, are illustrated below:

Journal entries for
B & B Corporation

Cash.	12,000	
Trade Accounts Receivable	28,100	
Inventories	30,000	
Equipment	39,500	
Goodwill	10,000	
Allowance for Doubtful Accounts.		1,000
Trade Accounts Payable.		35,000
Accrued Liabilities Payable.		1,100
Payable to Blair & Benson Partnership		82,500

To record acquisition of assets and liabilities from Blair & Benson Partnership.

Payable to Blair & Benson Partnership	82,500	
Common Stock, $10 par (5,500 × $10).		55,000
Paid-in Capital in Excess of Par		27,500

To record issuance of 5,500 shares of common stock valued at $15 a share in payment for net assets of Blair & Benson Partnership.

B & B CORPORATION
Balance Sheet
June 30, Year 10

Assets

Cash.		$ 12,000
Trade accounts receivable	$28,100	
Less: Allowance for doubtful accounts	1,000	27,100
Inventories		30,000
Equipment.		39,500
Goodwill		10,000
Total assets		$118,600

Liabilities & Stockholders' Equity

Liabilities:		
Trade accounts payable		$ 35,000
Accrued liabilities payable.		1,100
Total liabilities		$ 36,100
Stockholders' equity:		
Common stock, $10 par, authorized 10,000 shares, issued and outstanding 5,500 shares	$55,000	
Additional paid-in capital.	27,500	82,500
Total liabilities & stockholders' equity		$118,600

Note that the allowance for doubtful accounts is recognized in the accounting records of B & B Corporation because the specific accounts receivable that may not be collected are not known. In contrast, the depreciation recognized by the Blair & Benson Partnership is disregarded by B & B Corporation because the ''cost'' of the equipment to the new corporation is $39,500. The balance sheet for B & B Corporation on June 30, Year 10, is shown on page 106.

JOIN VENTURES

A *joint venture* differs from a partnership in that it is limited to carrying out a single project, such as production of a motion picture or construction of a building. Historically, joint ventures were used to finance the sale or exchange of a cargo of merchandise in a foreign country. In an era when marine transportation and foreign trade involved many hazards, individuals *(venturers)* would band together to undertake a venture of this type. The capital required usually was larger than one person could provide, and the risks were too high to be borne alone. Because of the risks involved and the relatively short duration of the project, no net income was recognized until the venture was completed. At the end of the voyage, the net income or net loss was divided among the venturers, and their association was ended.

In its traditional form, the accounting for a joint venture did not follow the accrual basis of accounting. The assumption of continuity was not appropriate; instead of the determination of net income at regular intervals, the measurement and reporting of net income or loss awaited the completion of the venture.

Present-Day Joint Ventures

In today's business community, joint ventures are less common but still are employed for many projects such as (1) the acquisition, development, and sale of real property; (2) exploration for oil and gas; and (3) construction of bridges, buildings, and dams.

The term *corporate joint venture* also is used by many large American corporations to describe overseas operations by a corporation whose ownership is divided between an American company and a foreign company. Many examples of jointly owned companies also are found in some domestic industries. A corporate joint venture and the accounting for such a venture are described in *APB Opinion No. 18,* ''The Equity Method of Accounting for Investments in Common Stock,'' as follows:

> ''Corporate joint venture'' refers to a corporation owned and operated by a small group of businesses (the ''joint venturers'') as a separate and specific business or project for the mutual benefit of the members of the group. A government may also be a member of the group. The purpose of a corporate joint venture frequently is to share risks and rewards in developing a new market, product or technology; to combine complementary technological knowledge; or to pool resources in developing production or other facilities. A corporate joint venture also usually provides an arrangement under which each joint venturer may participate, directly or indirectly, in the overall management of the

joint venture. Joint venturers thus have an interest or relationship other than as passive investors. An entity which is a subsidiary of one of the "joint venturers" is not a corporate joint venture. The ownership of a corporate joint venture seldom changes, and its stock is usually not traded publicly. A minority public ownership, however, does not preclude a corporation from being a corporate joint venture.[2]

. . . .

The [Accounting Principles] Board concludes that the equity method best enables investors in corporate joint ventures to reflect the underlying nature of their investment in those ventures. ***Therefore, investors should account for investments in common stock of corporate joint ventures by the equity method,*** both in consolidated financial statements and in parent-company financial statements prepared for issuance to stockholders as the financial statements of the primary reporting entity. [Emphasis added.][3]

. . . .

When investments in common stock of corporate joint ventures or other investments of 50% or less accounted for under the equity method are, in the aggregate, material in relation to the financial position or results of operations of an investor, it may be necessary for summarized information as to assets, liabilities, and results of operations of the investees to be presented in the notes or in separate statements, either individually or in groups, as appropriate.[4]

Use of the term *joint venture* in this chapter is in the traditional meaning of a general partnership organized to carry out a single project of limited duration.

Accounting for a Corporate Joint Venture

The complexity of modern business, the emphasis on good organization and strong internal control, the importance of income taxes, the extent of government regulation, and the need for preparation and retention of adequate accounting records are strong arguments for establishing a separate set of accounting records for every corporate joint venture of large size and long duration. In the accounting records of the joint venture, each venturer's capital account is credited for the amount of cash or noncash assets invested by each. The fiscal year of the joint venture may or may not coincide with the fiscal years of the venturers, but the use of the accrual basis of accounting and periodic financial statements for the venture permit regular reporting of the share of net income or loss allocable to each venturer.

The accounting records of such a corporate joint venture include the usual ledger accounts for assets, liabilities, owners' equity, revenue, and expenses. The entire accounting process should conform to generally accepted accounting practices, from the recording of transactions to the preparation of financial statements.

Accounting for an Unincorporated Joint Venture

As indicated above, ***APB Opinion No. 18*** required venturers to use the equity method of accounting for investments in corporate joint ventures. That Opinion did

---

[2] *APB Opinion No. 18,* "The Equity Method of Accounting for Investments in Common Stock," AICPA (New York: 1971), pp. 348–349.
[3] Ibid., p. 355.
[4] Ibid., p. 361.

not address accounting for investments in ***unincorporated*** joint ventures. However, the AICPA subsequently interpreted ***APB Opinion No. 18*** as follows:[5]

> . . . because the investor-venturer [in an unincorporated joint venture] owns an undivided interest in each asset and is proportionately liable for its share of each liability, the provisions of [***APB Opinion No. 18*** related to the equity method of accounting] may not apply in some industries. For example, where it is the established industry practice (such as in some oil and gas venture accounting), the investor-venturer may account in its financial statements for its *pro rata* share of the assets, liabilities, revenues, and expenses of the venture.

In view of the foregoing, it appears that either of two alternative methods of accounting may be adopted by investors in unincorporated joint ventures; thus, some investors have the option of using either the ***equity method of accounting*** or a ***proportionate share method of accounting*** for the investments. The two methods may be illustrated by assuming that Arthur Company and Beatrice Company each invested $400,000 for a 50% interest in an unincorporated joint venture on January 2, Year 1. Condensed financial statements (other than a statement of cash flows) for the joint venture, Arbe Company, for Year 1 were as follows:

ARBE COMPANY
(A Joint Venture)
Income Statement
For Year Ended December 31, Year 1

Revenue	$2,000,000
Less: Cost and expenses	1,500,000
Net income	$ 500,000

Division of net income:

Arthur Company	$250,000
Beatrice Company	250,000
Total	$500,000

ARBE COMPANY
(A Joint Venture)
Statement of Venturers' Capital
For Year Ended December 31, Year 1

	Arthur Company	Beatrice Company	Combined
Investments, Jan. 2, Year 1	$400,000	$400,000	$ 800,000
Add: Net income	250,000	250,000	500,000
Venturers' capital, end of year	$650,000	$650,000	$1,300,000

[5] *The Equity Method of Accounting for Investments in Common Stock: Accounting Interpretation of APB Opinion No. 18,* No. 2, "Investments in Partnerships and Ventures," AICPA (New York: 1971).

ARBE COMPANY
(A Joint Venture)
Balance Sheet
December 31, Year 1

Assets

Current assets	$1,600,000
Other assets	2,400,000
Total assets	$4,000,000

Liabilities & Venturers' Capital

Current liabilities		$ 800,000
Long-term debt		1,900,000
Venturers' capital:		
Arthur Company	$650,000	
Beatrice Company	650,000	1,300,000
Total liabilities & venturers' capital		$4,000,000

Under the *equity method of accounting,* both Arthur Company and Beatrice Company prepare the following journal entries for the investment in Arbe Company:

Venturer's journal entries for unincorporated joint venture under *equity method of accounting*

Year 1			
Jan. 2	Investment in Arbe Company (Joint Venture)	400,000	
	Cash		400,000
	To record investment in joint venture.		
Dec. 31	Investment in Arbe Company (Joint Venture)	250,000	
	Investment Income		250,000
	To record share of Arbe Company net income ($500,000 × 0.50 = $250,000).		

Under the *proportionate share method of accounting,* in addition to the two foregoing journal entries, both Arthur Company and Beatrice Company prepare the journal entry on page 111 for their respective shares of the assets, liabilities, revenue, and expenses of Arbe Company.

Use of the equity method of accounting for unincorporated joint ventures is consistent with the accounting for corporate joint ventures specified by *APB Opinion No. 18.* However, information on material assets and liabilities of a joint venture may be relegated to a note to financial statements (see footnote 4 on page 108), thus resulting in *off–balance sheet financing.* The proportionate share method of accounting for unincorporated joint ventures avoids the problem of off–balance sheet financing but has the questionable practice of including *portions* of assets such as plant assets in each venturer's balance sheet.

Given the Financial Accounting Standards Board's statement that "Information about an enterprise gains greatly in usefulness if it can be compared with similar

Additional venturer's journal entry for unincorporated joint venture under ***proportionate share method of accounting***			
Year 1			
Dec. 31	*Current Assets ($1,600,000 × 0.50)............*	*800,000*	
	Other Assets ($2,400,000 × 0.50)..............	*1,200,000*	
	Costs and Expenses ($1,500,000 × 0.50)........	*750,000*	
	Investment Income	*250,000*	
	Current Liabilities ($800,000 × 0.50).......		*400,000*
	Long-Term Debt ($1,900,000 × 0.50)		*950,000*
	Revenue ($2,000,000 × 0.50)............		*1,000,000*
	Investment in Arbe Company (Joint Venture)		*650,000*
	To record proportionate share of joint venture's assets, liabilities, revenue, and expenses.		

information about other enterprises . . . ,'' [6] it is undesirable to have two significantly different generally accepted accounting methods for investments in unincorporated joint ventures. Accordingly, the FASB has undertaken a study of the accounting for investments in joint ventures, as well as the accounting for all investments for which the equity method of accounting presently is used.

SEC ENFORCEMENT ACTIONS DEALING WITH WRONGFUL APPLICATION OF ACCOUNTING STANDARDS FOR JOINT VENTURES

AAER 40 This AAER, ''Securities and Exchange Commission v. Chronar Corp.'' (October 3, 1984), reported a permanent injunction against a corporation engaged in research and development of solar photovoltaic technology and the design, development, and marketing of manufacturing processes and equipment for photovoltaic panels. The SEC alleged that the corporation had prematurely recognized revenue (under the proportionate share method of accounting) from a joint venture of which it was a 51% owner. The ''revenue'' was from the corporation itself, in transactions fraught with uncertainties. The result of the inappropriate recognition of revenue and related expenses of the joint venture by the corporation was a 48% understatement of the corporation's nine-month net loss reported to the SEC in its quarterly report on ***Form 10-Q.*** In a related enforcement action, reported in ***AAER 78,*** ''. . . In the Matter of Seidman & Seidman . . .'' (October 10, 1985), the CPA firm that had reviewed the corporation's nine-month financial statements was censured by the SEC and undertook to improve its professional standards.

AAER 102 The SEC reported in ***AAER 102,*** ''. . . In the Matter of Ray M. VanLandingham and Wallace A. Patzke, Jr.'' (June 20, 1986), the issuance of an

---

[6] *Statement of Financial Accounting Concepts No. 2,* ''Qualitative Characteristics of Accounting Information,'' FASB (Stamford: 1980), p. 45.

order requiring the chief accounting officer and the controller (both CPAs) of a corporate marketer of petroleum products to comply with provisions of the *Securities Exchange Act of 1934* and related rules. The SEC found that the two executives were responsible for the corporation's failure to write down by at least $100 million its investment (carried at $311 million) in a joint venture that operated an oil refinery. The write-down was necessitated by the corporation's unsuccessful efforts to sell its investment in the joint venture at a price significantly below the carrying amount of the investment.

REVIEW QUESTIONS

1 Alo and Bel, partners of the Alo & Bel Partnership, have capital accounts of $60,000 and $80,000, respectively. In addition, Alo has made an interest-bearing loan of $20,000 to the partnership. If Alo and Bel now decide to liquidate the partnership, what priority or advantage, if any, does Alo have in the liquidation with respect to the loan ledger account?

2 Explain the procedure to be followed in a partnership liquidation when a debit balance arises in the capital account of one of the partners.

3 In the liquidation of the Cor, Don & Ell Partnership, the realization of noncash assets resulted in a loss that produced the following balances in the partners' capital accounts: Cor, $25,000 credit; Don, $12,500 credit; and Ell, $5,000 debit. The partners shared net income and losses in a 5:3:2 ratio. All liabilities have been paid, and $32,500 of cash is available for distribution to partners. However, it is not possible to determine at present whether Ell will be able to pay in the $5,000 capital deficit. May the cash on hand be distributed without a delay to determine the collectibility of the amount due from Ell? Explain.

4 After realization of all noncash assets and distributing all available cash to creditors, the insolvent Fin, Guy & Han Partnership still had trade accounts payable of $12,000. The capital account of Fin had a credit balance of $16,000 and that of Guy had a credit balance of $2,000. Creditors of the partnership demanded payment from Fin, who replied that the three partners shared net income equally and had begun operations with equal capital investments. Fin therefore offered to pay the creditors one-third of their claims and no more. What is your opinion of the position taken by Fin? What is the balance of Han's capital account? What journal entry, if any, should be made in the partnership accounting records for a payment by Fin to the partnership creditors?

5 In the Ile, Job & Key Partnership, Ile is the managing partner. The partnership contract provides that Ile is to receive an annual salary of $12,000, payable in 12 equal monthly installments, and the resultant net income or loss is to be divided equally. On June 30, the partnership suspended operations and began liquidation. Because of a shortage of cash, Ile had not drawn any salary for the last two months of operations. How should Ile's claim for $2,000 of ''unpaid wages'' be accounted for in the liquidation of the partnership?

6 Lud and Moy, partners of the liquidating Lud & Moy Partnership, share net income and losses equally. State reasons for allocation of losses incurred in the realization of assets equally or in the ratio of capital account balances.

7 Explain the basic principle to be observed in the distribution of cash in installments to partners when the liquidation of a partnership extends over several months.

8 During the installment liquidation of a partnership, it is appropriate to estimate the loss from realization of noncash assets. What journal entries, if any, should be made to recognize in the partners' capital accounts their respective shares of the loss that may be incurred during the liquidation?

9 The Nom, Orr & Pan Partnership is to be liquidated over several months, with installment distributions of cash to the partners. Will the total amount of cash received by each partner under these circumstances be more, less, or the same amount as if the liquidator had retained all cash until all noncash assets had been realized and then had made a single cash payment to each of the partners?

10 Under what circumstances, if any, is it appropriate for a partnership undergoing installment liquidation to distribute cash to partners in the income-sharing ratio?

11 Rab, San, and Tay, partners of the Rab, San & Tay Partnership who share net income or losses equally, had capital account balances of $30,000, $25,000, and $21,000, respectively, when the partnership began liquidation. Among the assets was a note receivable from San in the amount of $7,000. All partnership liabilities had been paid. The first assets realized during the liquidation were marketable securities with a carrying amount of $15,000, for which cash of $18,000 was received. How should this $18,000 be divided among the partners?

12 When the Urb, Van & Woo Partnership began liquidation, the capital account credit balances were Urb, $38,000; Van, $35,000; and Woo, $32,000. When the liquidation was complete, Urb had received less cash than either of the other two partners. What factors might explain why the partner with the largest capital account balance might receive the smallest amount of cash in liquidation?

13 Yang and Zee, partners of the Yang & Zee Partnership, decided to incorporate the partnership as Yang-Zee Corporation. The entire capital stock of Yang-Zee Corporation was divided equally between Yang and Zee because they had equal capital account balances in the partnership. An appraisal report obtained on the date of incorporation indicated that the land and buildings had increased in value by 50% while owned by the partnership. Should the carrying amounts of those assets be increased to appraisal value or carried at original cost to the partnership when transferred to Yang-Zee Corporation's accounting records? Explain.

14 Explain how a *joint venture* differs from a general partnership.

15 What are *corporate joint ventures?* What accounting standards for such ventures were established in *APB Opinion No. 18,* ''The Equity Method of Accounting for Investments in Common Stock''?

16 Compare the *equity method of accounting* with the *proportionate share method of accounting* for an investment in an unincorporated joint venture.

EXERCISES

Ex. 3-1   Select the best answer for each of the following multiple-choice questions:

1   Which of the following statements is correct?
a The *liquidation* of a general partnership always is accompanied by the partnership's *dissolution.*
b The *dissolution* of a general partnership always is accompanied by the partnership's *dissolution.*
c The *liquidation* of a general partnership may or may not be accompanied by its *dissolution.*
d *Liquidation* and *dissolution* are synonyms with respect to general partnerships.

2   A deficit (debit balance) in a general partner's capital account represents, in that partner's personal financial statement, a:
a Contra-asset
b Liability
c Contra-equity
d Deficit

3   Does the computation of possible future liquidation losses of a general partnership include:

	Recorded unpaid liabilities?	*Unrecorded unpaid liabilities?*
a	Yes	Yes
b	Yes	No
c	No	Yes
d	No	No

4   According to the Uniform Partnership Act, a liquidating general partnership's mandatory sequence for making cash payments for (1) liabilities (other than partner's loans), (2) partners' capital account balances, and (3) partners' loans to the partnership is:
a (1),(2),(3)
b (2),(1),(3)
c (1),(3),(2)
d (3),(1),(2)

5   In the installment liquidation of a general partnership, the income-sharing ratio is used for cash payments to partners:
a At all times
b At no time
c After all noncash assets have been realized
d When the balances of the partners' capital accounts are in the income-sharing ratio

6   Is the balance of the Loan Payable to Partner Jones ledger account combined with the balance of the Partner Jones, Capital account of a liquidating general partnership in:

	The partnership's general ledger?	The partnership's statement of realization and liquidation?
a	Yes	Yes
b	Yes	No
c	No	Yes
d	No	No

7   In the liquidation of a general partnership, cash received by a partner having a loan receivable from the partnership is debited to the partner's:

a Loan account

b Capital account

c Drawing account

d Retained earnings account

8   The *marshaling of assets* provisions of the Uniform Partnership Act provide that unpaid creditors of an insolvent general partnership have first claim to assets of:

a The partnership

b A solvent partner

c An insolvent partner

d Either the partnership or a solvent partner, as elected by the creditor

9   May unpaid creditors of an insolvent liquidating general partnership obtain payment from a personally solvent partner whose partnership capital account has a:

	Debit balance?	Credit balance?
a	Yes	Yes
b	Yes	No
c	No	Yes
d	No	No

10   The ledger accounts of the liquidating Gill, Hall & James Partnership included Loan Receivable from Gill, $10,000 dr; Loan Payable to Hall, $20,000 cr; Gill, Capital, $30,000 dr; Hall, Capital, $60,000 cr; James, Capital, $50,000 cr. The partners share net income and losses 20%, 40%, and 40%, respectively. In the preparation of a cash distribution to partners during liquidation working paper, beginning capital per unit of income sharing amounts are:

	Gill	Hall	James
a	($40,000)	$80,000	$50,000
b	($20,000)	$20,000	$12,500
c	($15,000)	$15,000	$12,500
d	–0–	$80,000	$50,000

11   May a balance sheet prepared for a corporation on the date it was created from the incorporation of a general partnership display in stockholders' equity:

	Common stock?	Additional paid-in capital?	Retained earnings?
a	Yes	Yes	Yes
b	Yes	Yes	No
c	Yes	No	No
d	Yes	No	Yes

12 In the installment liquidation of a limited partnership, after outside creditors have been paid:

a The limited partners' equities must be paid before the general partner receives any cash.

b Both the limited partners' and the general partner's equities may be paid in installments.

c The limited partners may agree that the general partner has priority regarding installment payments of cash.

d The marshaling of assets legal provisions apply.

13 Prior to the beginning of liquidation, the liabilities and partners' capital of the Mann, Nunn & Ogg Partnership, whose partners shared net income and losses equally, consisted of Liabilities, $60,000; Loan Payable to Ogg, $21,000; Mann, Capital, $30,000; Nunn, Capital, $60,000; and Ogg, Capital, $39,000. If, after realization of all noncash assets and payment of all outsider liabilities, $60,000 cash was available for distribution to partners on January 31, Year 3, partner Ogg should receive:

a $60,000   **b** $39,000   **c** $30,000   **d** $21,000   **e** Some other amount

Ex. 3-2   After the realization of all noncash assets and the payment of all liabilities, the balance sheet of the liquidating Pon, Quan & Ron Partnership on January 31, Year 6, showed Cash, $15,000; Pon, Capital, ($9,000); Quan, Capital, $8,000; and Ron, Capital, $16,000, with ( ) indicating a capital deficit. The partners share net income and losses equally.

Prepare a journal entry for the Pon, Quan & Ron Partnership on January 31, Year 6, to show the payment of $15,000 cash in a safe manner to the partners. Show computations in the explanation for the journal entry.

Ex. 3-3   Archer and Bender, partners of the Archer & Bender Partnership who share net income and losses in a 60 : 40 ratio, respectively, decided to liquidate the partnership. A portion of the noncash assets had been realized, but assets with a carrying amount of $42,000 were yet to be realized. All liabilities had been paid, and cash of $20,000 was available for distribution to partners. The partners' capital account balances were $40,000 for Archer and $22,000 for Bender.

Prepare a working paper to compute the amount of cash (totaling $20,000) to be distributed to each partner.

Ex. 3-4   Carlo and Dodge started the Carlo & Dodge Partnership some years ago and managed to operate profitably for several years. Recently, however, they lost a lawsuit requiring payment of large damages and incurred unexpected losses on trade accounts receivable and inventories. As a result, they decided to liquidate the partnership. After all noncash assets were realized, only $18,000 was available to pay liabilities, which amounted to $33,000. The partners' capital account balances before the start of liquidation and their income-sharing percentages are shown below:

	Capital account balances	Income-sharing percentages
Carlo................	$23,000	55%
Dodge..............	13,500	45%

a Prepare a working paper to compute the total loss incurred on the liquidation of the Carlo & Dodge Partnership.

b Prepare a working paper to show how the final settlement should be made between the partners, after Carlo pays $15,000 to partnership creditors. Carlo is insolvent after paying the creditors, but Dodge has net assets, exclusive of partnership interest, in excess of $100,000.

Ex. 3-5 The balance sheet of the Rich, Stowe & Thorpe Partnership on the date it commenced liquidation was as follows, with the partners' income-sharing ratio in parentheses:

RICH, STOWE & THORPE PARTNERSHIP
Balance Sheet
September 24, Year 4

Assets		Liabilities & Partners' Capital	
Cash	$ 20,000	Liabilities	$240,000
Other assets	480,000	Rich, capital (40%).	80,000
		Stowe, capital (40%)	120,000
		Thorpe, capital (20%)	60,000
		Total liabilities & partners'	
Total assets.	$500,000	capital.	$500,000

On September 24, Year 4, other assets with a carrying amount of $360,000 realized $300,000 cash, and $320,000 ($20,000 + $300,000 = $320,000) cash was paid in a safe manner.

Prepare journal entries for the Rich, Stowe & Thorpe Partnership on September 24, Year 4.

Ex. 3-6 On June 3, Year 8, the partners of the Ace, Bay & Cap Partnership agreed (1) to liquidate the partnership, (2) to share gains and losses on the realization of noncash assets in the ratio 1:3:4, and (3) to disburse the $80,000 available cash on June 3 in a safe manner. In addition to cash, the June 3 balance sheet of the partnership had other assets, $100,000; liabilities, $50,000; Ace, capital, $60,000; Bay, capital, $40,000; and Cap, capital, $30,000. The partnership had no loans receivable from or payable to the partners.

Prepare a journal entry for the Ace, Bay & Cap Partnership on June 3, Year 8, to show the disbursement of $80,000 cash. Show computations in the explanation for the entry.

Ex. 3-7 After realization of a portion of the noncash assets of the Ed, Flo & Gus Partnership, which was being liquidated, the capital account balances were Ed, $33,000; Flo, $40,000; and Gus, $42,000. Cash of $42,000 and other assets with a carrying amount of $78,000 were on hand. Creditors' claims total $5,000. The partners share net income and losses in a 5:3:2 ratio.

Prepare a working paper to compute the cash payments (totaling $37,000) that may be made to the partners.

Ex. 3-8 When Hale and Ian, partners of the Hale & Ian Partnership who shared net income and losses in a 4:6 ratio, were incapacitated in an accident, a liquidator was appointed to wind up the partnership. The partnership's balance sheet showed cash, $35,000; other assets, $110,000; liabilities, $20,000; Hale, capital, $71,000; and Ian, capital, $54,000. Because of the specialized nature of the noncash assets, the liquidator anticipated that considerable time would be required to dispose of them. The costs of liquidating the partnership (advertising, rent, travel, etc.) were estimated at $10,000.

Prepare a working paper to compute the amount of cash (totaling $5,000) that may be distributed to each partner.

Ex. 3-9   The following balance sheet was available for the Jones, Kell & Lamb Partnership on March 31, Year 8 (each partners' income-sharing percentage is shown in parentheses):

JONES, KELL & LAMB PARTNERSHIP
Balance Sheet
March 31, Year 8

Assets		*Liabilities & Partners' Capital*	
Cash........................	$ 25,000	Liabilities...................	$ 52,000
Other assets................	180,000	Jones, capital (40%).........	40,000
		Kell, capital (40%)..........	65,000
		Lamb, capital (20%).........	48,000
Total.....................	$205,000	Total.....................	$205,000

a The partnership was being liquidated by the realization of other assets in installments. The first realization of noncash assets having a carrying amount of $90,000 realized $50,000, and all cash available after settlement with creditors was distributed to partners. Prepare a working paper to compute the amount of cash each partner should receive in the first installment.

b If the facts are as in **a** above, except that $3,000 cash is withheld for possible liquidation costs, how much cash should each partner receive?

c As a separate case, assume that each partner appropriately received some cash in the distribution after the second realization of noncash assets. The cash to be distributed amounted to $14,000 from the third realization of noncash assets, and other assets with a $6,000 carrying amount remained. Prepare a working paper to show how the $14,000 is distributed to the partners.

Ex. 3-10   On November 10, Year 3, May, Nona, and Olive, partners of the May, Nona & Olive Partnership, had capital account balances of $20,000, $25,000, and $9,000, respectively, and shared net income and losses in a 4 : 2 : 1 ratio.

a Prepare a cash distribution program for liquidation of the May, Nona & Olive Partnership in installments, assuming liabilities totaled $20,000 on November 10, Year 3.

b How much cash was paid to all partners if May received $4,000 on liquidation?

c If May received $13,000 cash pursuant to liquidation, how much did Olive receive?

d If Nona received only $11,000 as a result of the liquidation, what was the loss to the partnership on the realization of assets? (No partner invested any additional assets in the partnership.)

Ex. 3-11   Following is the balance sheet of the Paul & Quinn Partnership on June 1, Year 10:

PAUL & QUINN PARTNERSHIP
Balance Sheet
June 1, Year 10

Assets		*Liabilities & Partners' Capital*	
Cash......................	$ 5,000	Liabilities....................	$20,000
Other assets................	55,000	Paul, capital................	22,500
		Quinn, capital...............	17,500
Total....................	$60,000	Total....................	$60,000

Partners share net income and net losses as follows: Paul, 60%; Quinn, 40%. In June, other assets with a carrying amount of $22,000 realized $18,000, creditors were paid in full, and $2,000 was paid to partners in a manner to reduce their capital account balances closer to the income-sharing ratio. In July, other assets with a carrying amount of $10,000 realized $12,000, liquidation costs of $500 were paid, and cash of $12,500 was distributed to partners. In August, the remaining other assets realized $22,500, and final settlement was made between the partners.

Prepare a working paper to compute the amount of cash each partner should receive in June, July, and August, Year 10.

Ex. 3-12   On September 26, Year 2, prior to commencement of liquidation of the Orville, Paula & Quincy Partnership, the partnership had total liabilities of $80,000 and partners' capital account credit balances of $120,000 for Orville, $160,000 for Paula, and $80,000 for Quincy. There were no loans to or from partners in the partnership's accounting records. The partners shared net income and losses as follows: Orville, 30%; Paula, 50%; Quincy, 20%.

Prepare a cash distribution program for the Orville, Paula & Quincy Partnership on September 26, Year 2.

Ex. 3-13   On January 21, Year 7, the date the partners of the A, B & C Partnership decided to liquidate the partnership, its balance sheet showed cash, $33,000; other assets, $67,000; trade accounts payable, $20,000; loan payable to A, $12,000; A capital, $28,000; B capital, $18,000; and C capital, $22,000. The partnership's income-sharing ratio was A, 50%; B, 30%; C, 20%. The accountant for the partnership prepared the following cash distribution program (to facilitate installment payments to partners) on January 21, Year 7: First $20,000, 100% to creditors; Next $6,000, 100% to C; Next $14,000, 5/7 to A and 2/7 to C; all over $40,000, in income-sharing ratio. Based on the foregoing, the partners decided to pay the entire cash of $33,000 on January 21, Year 7, in a safe manner consistent with the Uniform Partnership Act.

Prepare a journal entry to record the A, B & C Partnership's payment of $33,000 cash on January 21, Year 7.

Ex. 3-14   The net equities and income-sharing ratios for the partners of the Ruiz, Salvo, Thomas & Urwig Partnership before liquidation on May 5, Year 5, were as follows:

	Ruiz	*Salvo*	*Thomas*	*Urwig*
Net equity in partnership..............	$36,000	$32,400	$8,000	$(100)
Income-sharing ratio	3	4	2	1

Assets were expected to realize cash significantly in excess of carrying amounts.

Prepare a program showing how cash should be distributed to the partners as it becomes available in the course of liquidation if liabilities of the partnership totaled $15,000 on May 5, Year 5.

Ex. 3-15   On September 30, Year 2, the partners of the Allen, Brown & Cox Partnership, who shared net income and losses in the ratio of 5 : 3 : 2, respectively, decided to liquidate the partnership. The partnership trial balance on that date was as follows:

ALLEN, BROWN & COX PARTNERSHIP
Trial Balance
September 30, Year 2

	Debit	Credit
Cash	$ 18,000	
Loan receivable from Allen	30,000	
Trade accounts receivable	66,000	
Inventories	52,000	
Machinery and equipment (net)	189,000	
Trade accounts payable		$ 53,000
Loan payable to Brown		20,000
Allen, capital		118,000
Brown, capital		90,000
Cox, capital		74,000
Totals	$355,000	$355,000

The partners planned a lengthy time period for realization of noncash assets in order to minimize liquidation losses. All available cash, less an amount retained to provide for future liquidation costs, was to be distributed to the partners at the end of each month.

Prepare a cash distribution program for the Allen, Brown & Cox Partnership on September 30, Year 2, showing how cash should be distributed to creditors and to partners as it becomes available during liquidation. Round amounts to the nearest dollar.

Ex. 3-16   The balance sheet of the Davis, Evans & Fagin Partnership on September 29, Year 7, included cash, $20,000; other assets, $262,000; liabilities, $50,000; and total partners' capital, $232,000. On that date, the three partners decided to dissolve and liquidate the partnership. The cash distribution program prepared by the partnership's accountant follows:

DAVIS, EVANS & FAGIN PARTNERSHIP
Cash Distribution Program
September 29, Year 7

	Total	Creditors	Davis	Evans	Fagin
First	$ 50,000	100%			
Next	34,000			100%	
Next	48,000			33⅓%	66⅔%
All over	$132,000		40%	20%	40%

On September 30, Year 7, noncash assets with a carrying amount of $140,000 were sold for $100,000 cash.

Prepare journal entries for the Davis, Evans & Fagin Partnership on September 30, Year 7, to record the realization of $140,000 of noncash assets and the payment of all available cash on that date in accordance with the cash distribution program.

Ex. 3-17 The balance sheet of the Venner & Wigstaff Partnership, immediately before the partnership was incorporated as Venwig Corporation, follows:

VENNER & WIGSTAFF PARTNERSHIP
Balance Sheet
September 30, Year 5

Assets		Liabilities & Partners' Capital	
Cash......................	$ 10,500	Trade accounts payable	$ 16,400
Trade accounts receivable ...	15,900	Venner, capital..............	60,000
Inventories	42,000	Wigstaff, capital.............	52,000
Equipment (net of $18,000 ac-			
cumulated depreciation)	60,000		
Total....................	$128,400	Total....................	$128,400

The following adjustments to the balance sheet of the partnership were recommended by a CPA before accounting records for Venwig Corporation were to be established:

(1) An allowance for doubtful accounts was to be established in the amount of $1,200.
(2) Short-term prepayments of $800 were to be recognized.
(3) The current fair value of inventories, $48,000, and the current fair value of equipment, $72,000, were to be recognized.
(4) Accrued liabilities of $750 were to be recognized.

Prepare a balance sheet for Venwig Corporation on October 1, Year 5, assuming that 10,000 shares of $5 par common stock were issued to the partners in exchange for their equities in the partnership. Fifty thousand shares of common stock were authorized to be issued.

Ex. 3-18 On January 2, Year 1, Yale Corporation and Zola Corporation each invested $500,000 in an unincorporated joint venture, Y-Z Company, the income or losses of which were to be shared equally. On December 31, Year 1, financial statements of Y-Z Company showed total revenue, $800,000; total costs and expenses, $600,000; total current assets, $600,000; net plant assets, $1,500,000; total current liabilities, $300,000; total long-term debt, $600,000; and total venturers' capital, $1,200,000. Neither venturer had drawings during Year 1.

a Prepare journal entries for Yale Corporation for the year ended December 31, Year 1, to record its investment in Y-Z Company under the equity method of accounting.

b Prepare an additional journal entry for Yale Corporation on December 31, Year 1, to complete the journal entries (together with those in **a**) required for the investment in Y-Z Company under the proportionate share method of accounting.

CASES

Case 3-1   The Berg, Hancock & Loomis Partnership was insolvent and in the process of liquidation under the Uniform Partnership Act. After the noncash assets were realized and
the resultant loss was distributed equally among the partners in accordance with the
partnership contract, their financial positions were as follows:

	Equity in partnership	Financial position other than equity in partnership	
		Assets	Liabilities
Jack Berg	$ 30,000	$110,000	$45,000
Diane Hancock	(21,000)	20,000	40,000
David Loomis.....................	(55,000)	55,000	45,000

Several partnership creditors remained unpaid, but the partnership had no cash.

Instructions

Explain the prospects for collection by:
a The creditors of the partnership.
b The creditors of each partner.
c Jack Berg from the other partners. Compute the total loss that Berg will incur on
the liquidation of the partnership.

Case 3-2   On November 15, Year 1, in beginning the liquidation of the Burt, Fong & Nunn
Partnership, the liquidator found that an 8% promissory note payable for $100,000
issued by the partnership had six months remaining until maturity on May 15, Year
2. Interest on the note had been paid to November 15. Terms of the note provided that
interest at 8% to the maturity date must be paid in full in the event the note was paid
in full prior to maturity. The partnership had paid all other liabilities and had on hand
cash of $150,000. The remaining noncash assets had a carrying amount of $200,000.
The liquidator believed that six months would be required to dispose of them and that
the realization of the noncash assets over this period would produce cash at least 25%
in excess of the carrying amount of the assets.

      Partner Burt made the following statement to the liquidator: ''I realize you may
not pay the partners until creditors have been paid in full, but I need cash for another
investment. So I'd like for you to pay the note and interest to May 15, Year 2,
immediately and to distribute the remaining cash to the partners.'' Partner Fong
objected to this proposal for immediate cash payments because it would entail a loss
of $4,000 ($100,000 × 0.08 × $\frac{6}{12}$ = $4,000). Fong argued that if such action were
taken, the total interest cost of $4,000 on the note should be debited to Burt's capital
account. Partner Nunn had no concern in the matter, but as a convenience agreed to
assume the note liability in return for a $102,000 cash payment from the liquidator.
To protect the note payee against loss, Nunn offered to pledge collateral of $104,000
in U.S. government bonds. The note payee expressed willingness to accept this
arrangement. Partner Nunn specified that the proposed payment of $102,000 would
be in Nunn's new role as a creditor and that it would not affect Nunn's right to
receive any cash distributions during liquidation.

Instructions

Evaluate the proposal by each partner. What action should be taken by the liquidator? Would your answer differ if the assumptions were changed to indicate a probable loss on the realization of the remaining noncash assets?

Case 3-3   Lois Allen and Barbara Brett began a partnership and shared net income and losses equally. Although the partners began business with equal capital account balances, Allen made more frequent cash withdrawals than Brett, with the result that her capital account balance became the smaller of the two. The partners decided to liquidate the partnership on June 30; on that date the accounting records were closed and financial statements were prepared. The balance sheet showed capital of $40,000 for Allen and capital of $60,000 for Brett. In addition, the balance sheet showed that Brett had made a $10,000 loan to the partnership.

    The liquidation of the partnership was managed by Allen, because Brett was hospitalized by illness on July 1, the day after partnership operations were suspended. The procedures followed by Allen were as follows: (1) realize all the noncash assets at the best prices obtainable; (2) pay the creditors in full; (3) pay Brett's loan; and (4) divide all remaining cash between Brett and herself in the 40 : 60 ratio represented by their capital account balances.

    When Brett was released from the hospital on July 5, Allen informed her that through good luck and hard work, she had been able to realize the noncash assets and complete the liquidation during the five days of Brett's hospitalization. Thereupon, Allen delivered two partnership checks to Brett. One check was for $10,000 in payment of the loan account; the other was in settlement of Brett's capital account balance.

Instructions

a Do you approve the procedures followed by Allen in the liquidation? Explain.

b Assume that the liquidation procedures followed resulted in the payment of $24,000 to Brett in addition to the payment of her loan in full. What was the partnership's gain or loss on the realization of assets? If you believe that other methods should have been followed in the liquidation, explain how much more or less Brett would have received under the procedure you recommend.

Case 3-4   The Wells, Conner & Zola Partnership, a CPA firm, has been forced to liquidate because of the personal bankruptcy of partner Lewis Zola, which caused the dissolution of the firm. On the date of Zola's bankruptcy filing, the partnership's balance sheet was as shown on page 124, with the partners' income-sharing percentages in parentheses.

    In a meeting with the three partners, you, as the partners' accountant, are asked to supervise the liquidation of the partnership. In response to partner John Wells's assertion that, according to his attorney, the partnership had to pay the note and interest payable to Wells after all trade accounts payable had been paid, you explain your understanding of the right of offset, which gives the Wells loan no priority over partners' capital. You point out that the amounts to be realized for the partnership's office equipment and library are uncertain and that in an enforced liquidation losses may be incurred on the realization of those assets. You also indicate that the partner-

WELLS, CONNER & ZOLA PARTNERSHIP
Balance Sheet
October 31, Year 7

Assets		*Liabilities & Partners' Capital*	
Cash......................	$ 60,000	Trade accounts payable.....	$140,000
Trade accounts receivable ...	120,000	Interest payable to Wells....	10,000
Office equipment (net)	240,000	10% note payable to Wells ..	100,000
Library (net)	90,000	Wells, capital (50%)	280,000
Goodwill (net)..............	40,000	Conner, capital (30%).......	80,000
		Zola, capital (20%)	(60,000)
		Total liabilities &	
Total assets	$550,000	partners' capital.........	$550,000

ship goodwill has no realizable value and should be written off to the partners' capital accounts at once.

Your statements cause consternation to partners John Wells and Kathleen Conner. Wells points out that he has been absorbing the majority of the partnership's recent operating losses, and that his loan to the partnership was necessitated by a cash shortage. Conner objects to sharing any part of the writeoff of goodwill, reminding Wells, Zola, and you that the goodwill was recognized in the admission of Zola to the former Wells & Conner partnership for his investment of his highly profitable CPA firm proprietorship. Noting that Zola's personal bankruptcy was most likely an outgrowth of his deteriorating relationship with Wells, partnership clients, and her, Conner strongly urges that Zola's capital account be charged for the entire $40,000 carrying amount of the goodwill.

After further acrimonious discussion, the three partners request you to "go back to the drawing board" and return with a recommendation on how best to resolve the issues raised by Wells and Conner. In response to your inquiry, both Wells and Conner emphasize that they intend to continue the practice of public accounting in some form; Zola states that he has no future career plans until the resolution of his bankruptcy filing.

Instructions

Prepare recommendations for the three partners in response to the issues they have raised. Include in your recommendations your views on the desirability of the partners' retaining an independent attorney to resolve the issues raised.

Case 3-5 Anne Sanchez, chief accounting officer of the Kane & Grant Partnership, is a member of the IMA, the FEI, and the AICPA (see Chapter 1). Partners Jane Kane and Lloyd Grant inform Sanchez of their plans to incorporate the highly profitable partnership, with a view of a public offering to outside investors in the future. Indicating their desire for the best possible balance sheet for the new partnership, they ask Sanchez to reconsider her insistence that the partnership account for its 50% investment in KG/WM Company, an unincorporated joint venture, by the proportionate share method. Partner Kane shows Sanchez the following comparative balance sheet data for the partnership under two methods of accounting for the investment in KG/WM Company:

KANE & GRANT PARTNERSHIP
Condensed Balance Sheets
April 30, Year 5

	Proportionate share method	Equity method
Assets		
Investment in KG/WM Company..................	$ 0	$ 600,000
Other assets.....................................	3,800,000	2,400,000
Total assets.................................	$3,800,000	$3,000,000
Liabilities & Partners' Capital		
Total liabilities	$2,000,000	$1,200,000
Partners' capital	1,800,000	1,800,000
Total liabilities & partners' capital......................................	$3,800,000	$3,000,000

Kane points out that under the proportionate share method of accounting for the investment in KG/WM Company, the Kane & Grant Partnership's debt-to-equity ratio is 111% ($2,000,000 ÷ $1,800,000 = 111%), while under the equity method of accounting for the investment the partnership's debt-to-equity ratio is only 67% ($1,200,000 ÷ $1,800,000 = 67%).

Instructions

May Anne Sanchez ethically comply with the request of Jane Kane and Lloyd Grant? Explain.

Case 3-6   The Financial Accounting Standards Board is studying the accounting for investments in both corporate joint ventures and unincorporated joint ventures.

Instructions

Do you favor requiring a *single* accounting method for investments in both corporate and unincorporated joint ventures? If so, what should the accounting method be? If not, should one accounting method be mandatory for investments in corporate joint ventures, and another method mandatory for investments in unincorporated joint ventures? Or should alternative accounting methods be available for investments in both types of joint ventures? Explain.

PROBLEMS

Pr. 3-1   During liquidation, the Doris, Elsie & Frances Partnership became insolvent. On January 17, Year 4, after all noncash assets had been realized and all available cash had been distributed to creditors, the balance sheet of the partnership was as follows:

DORIS, ELSIE & FRANCES PARTNERSHIP
Balance Sheet
January 17, Year 4

Liabilities & Partners' Capital

Trade accounts payable	$ 60,000
Doris, capital	120,000
Elsie, capital	(160,000)
Frances, capital.	(20,000)
Total liabilities & partners' capital	$ -0-

The partners shared net income and losses (including gains and losses in liquidation) in the ratio 20%, 50%, and 30%, respectively. On January 17, Year 4, when the financial positions of the partners were as shown below, Elsie and Frances invested in the partnership all cash available under the marshaling of assets provisions of the Uniform Partnership Act:

Partner	Assets*	Liabilities*
Doris	$ 60,000	$ 80,000
Elsie.	280,000	200,000
Frances.	250,000	240,000

* Excludes equity in partnership.

Instructions

Prepare journal entries for the Doris, Elsie & Frances Partnership on January 17, Year 4, to record the receipt of cash from Elsie and Frances, the appropriate distribution of the cash, and the completion of the partnership liquidation.

Pr. 3-2   Following is the balance sheet of the Olmo, Perez & Quinto Partnership on January 31, Year 5, the date the partners authorized liquidation of the partnership. There were no unrecorded liabilities.

OLMO, PEREZ & QUINTO PARTNERSHIP
Balance Sheet
January 31, Year 5

Assets		Liabilities & Partners' Capital	
Cash.	$ 10,000	Trade accounts payable.	$ 90,000
Loan receivable from Perez . .	50,000	Loan payable to Olmo	60,000
Other assets (net)	240,000	Olmo, capital.	140,000
		Perez, capital	(70,000)
		Quinto, capital	80,000
		Total liabilities & partners'	
Total assets	$300,000	capital.	$300,000

Additional Information for Year 5

(1) The partners' income (loss)-sharing ratio was Olmo, 40%; Perez, 40%; and Quinto, 20%.

(2) On February 1, noncash assets with a carrying amount of $180,000 realized $140,000, and all available cash was paid to creditors and to partners.

(3) On February 4, noncash assets with a carrying amount of $60,000 realized $50,000, and that amount was paid to partners.

(4) On February 5, Perez, who was insolvent, paid $30,000 on the loan from the partnership. Olmo and Quinto agreed that the partnership would receive no further cash from Perez, and they instructed the accountant to close the partnership's accounting records.

Instructions

Prepare journal entries for the Olmo, Perez & Quinto Partnership on February 1, 4, and 5, Year 5. Disregard costs of the liquidation. Round all amounts to the nearest dollar. (Preparation of a cash distribution program as a supporting exhibit is recommended.)

Pr. 3-3 The loan and capital account balances of the Hal, Ian, Jay & Kay Partnership were as follows on September 25, Year 7, the date that the partnership began liquidation:

	Debit	Credit
Loan receivable from Jay	$10,000	
Loan payable to Hal		$20,000
Hal, capital		50,000
Ian, capital		25,000
Jay, capital		70,000
Kay, capital		50,000

Partnership liabilities totaled $80,000 on September 25, Year 7. The partners shared net income and losses and realization gains and losses as follows: Hal, 20%; Ian, 25%; Jay, 30%; and Kay, 25%.

Instructions

Prepare a cash distribution program for the Hal, Ian, Jay & Kay Partnership on September 25, Year 7.

Pr. 3-4 Carson and Worden decided to dissolve and liquidate the Carson & Worden Partnership on September 23, Year 10. On that date, the balance sheet of the partnership was as shown below:

CARSON & WORDEN PARTNERSHIP
Balance Sheet
September 23, Year 10

Assets		Liabilities & Partners' Capital	
Cash	$ 5,000	Trade accounts payable	15,000
Other assets	100,000	Loan payable to Worden	10,000
		Carson, capital	60,000
		Worden, capital	20,000
Total	$105,000	Total	$105,000

On September 23, Year 10, noncash assets with a carrying amount of $70,000 realized $60,000, and $64,000 was distributed to creditors and partners, $1,000 being retained to cover possible liquidation costs. On October 1, Year 10, the remaining noncash assets realized $18,000 (net of liquidation costs), and all available cash was distributed to partners. Carson and Worden share net income and losses 40% and 60%, respectively.

Instructions

a Prepare a cash distribution program for the Carson & Worden Partnership on September 23, Year 10, to determine the appropriate distribution of cash to partners as it becomes available.

b Prepare journal entries for the Carson & Worden Partnership on September 23, Year 10, and October 1, Year 10, to record the realization of assets and distributions of cash to creditors and partners.

Pr. 3-5   The statement of realization and liquidation for the Luke, Mayo & Nomura Partnership was as follows:

LUKE, MAYO & NOMURA PARTNERSHIP
Statement of Realization and Liquidation
April 30 through June 1, Year 5

	Assets		Trade Accounts Payable	Partners' Capital		
	Cash	Other		Luke	Mayo	Nomura
Balances before liquidation (April 30, Year 5).........	$ 20,000	$ 200,000	$ 120,000	$ 10,000	$ 30,000	$ 60,000
Realization of other assets at a loss of $120,000 (May 9, Year 5).........	80,000	(200,000)		(40,000)	(40,000)	(40,000)
Balances................	$100,000		$ 120,000	(30,000)	(10,000)	$ 20,000
Payment to creditors (May 12, Year 5).............	(100,000)		(100,000)			
Balances................			$ 20,000	(30,000)	(10,000)	$ 20,000
Payment by Luke to Partnership creditors (May 18, Year 5).............			(20,000)	$ 20,000		
Balances................				(10,000)	(10,000)	$ 20,000
Cash invested by Luke and Mayo (May 25, Year 5) ...	$ 20,000			$ 10,000	$ 10,000	
Balances................	$ 20,000					$ 20,000
Payment to Nomura (June 1, Year 5).............	(20,000)					(20,000)

Instructions

Prepare journal entries (omit explanations) for the liquidation of the Luke, Mayo & Nomura Partnership on May 9, 12, 18, and 25 and June 1, Year 5. Use a single Other Assets ledger account.

Pr. 3-6   On December 31, Year 5, the accounting records of the Luna, Nava & Ruby Partnership included the following ledger account balances:

	(dr) cr
Luna, drawing...	$ (24,000)
Ruby, drawing..	(9,000)
Nava, loan...	30,000
Luna, capital..	123,000
Nava, capital..	100,500
Ruby, capital..	108,000

Total assets of the partnership amounted to $478,500, including $52,500 cash, and partnership liabilities totaled $150,000. The partnership was liquidated on December 31, Year 5, and Ruby received $83,250 cash pursuant to the liquidation. Luna, Nava, and Ruby shared net income and losses in a 5 : 3 : 2 ratio, respectively.

Instructions

a Prepare a working paper to compute the total loss from the liquidation of the Luna, Nava & Ruby Partnership on December 31, Year 5.

b Prepare a statement of realization and liquidation for the Luna, Nava & Ruby Partnership on December 31, Year 5.

c Prepare journal entries for the Luna, Nava & Ruby Partnership on December 31, Year 5, to record the liquidation.

Pr. 3-7 The following balance sheet was prepared for the Haye & Lee Partnership, immediately prior to liquidation:

HAYE & LEE PARTNERSHIP
Balance Sheet
March 31, Year 5

Assets		Liabilities & Partners' Capital	
Cash......................	$ 10,000	Liabilities...................	$ 27,000
Investments in common		Haye, capital...............	72,000
stocks....................	20,000	Lee, capital.................	31,000
Other assets...............	100,000		
Total....................	$130,000	Total....................	$130,000

Haye and Lee shared operating income or losses in a 2 : 1 ratio and gains and losses on investments in a 3 : 1 ratio. The transactions and events to complete the liquidation were as follows:

Apr. 1   Haye withdrew the investments in common stocks at an agreed current fair value of $44,000.

Apr. 3   Other assets and the trade name, Haley's, were sold to Wong Products for $200,000 face amount of 12% bonds with a current fair value of $180,000. The gain on this transaction was an investment gain.

Apr. 7   Wong Products 12% bonds with a face amount of $40,000 were sold for $35,600 cash. The loss on this transaction was an investment loss.

Apr. 8   Liabilities were paid.

Apr. 10 Haye withdrew $100,000 face amount and Lee withdrew $60,000 face amount of Wong Products 12% bonds at carrying amounts.

Apr. 15 Available cash was paid to Haye and to Lee.

Instructions

Prepare journal entries for the Haye & Lee Partnership to record the foregoing transactions and events. Disregard interest on the bonds of Wong Products.

Pr. 3-8   Following is the balance sheet for the Adams, Barna & Coleman Partnership on June 4, Year 5:

ADAMS, BARNA & COLEMAN PARTNERSHIP
Balance Sheet
June 4, Year 5

Assets		Liabilities & Partners' Capital	
Cash......................	$ 6,000	Liabilities	$ 20,000
Other assets..............	94,000	Barna, loan.................	4,000
		Adams, capital..............	27,000
		Barna, capital..............	39,000
		Coleman, capital	10,000
Total....................	$100,000	Total....................	$100,000

The partners shared net income and losses as follows: Adams, 40%; Barna, 40%; and Coleman, 20%. On June 4, Year 5, the other assets realized $30,700, and $20,500 had to be paid to liquidate the liabilities because of an unrecorded trade account payable of $500. Adams and Barna were solvent, but Coleman's personal liabilities exceeded personal assets by $5,000.

Instructions

a Prepare a statement of realization and liquidation for the Adams, Barna & Coleman Partnership on June 4, Year 5. Combine Barna's loan and capital account balances.

b Prepare journal entries for the Adams, Barna & Coleman Partnership to record the liquidation on June 4, Year 5.

c How much cash would other assets have to realize on liquidation in order for Coleman to receive enough cash from the partnership to pay personal creditors in full? Assume that $20,500 is required to liquidate the partnership liabilities.

Pr. 3-9   The accountant for the Smith, Jones & Webb Partnership prepared the following balance sheet immediately prior to liquidation of the partnership:

SMITH, JONES & WEBB PARTNERSHIP
Balance Sheet
April 30, Year 3

Assets		Liabilities & Partners' Capital	
Cash......................	$ 20,000	Liabilities	$ 80,000
Other assets..............	280,000	Smith, capital	60,000
		Jones, capital..............	70,000
		Webb, capital..............	90,000
Total....................	$300,000	Total....................	$300,000

During May, Year 3, noncash assets with a carrying amount of $105,000 realized $75,000, and all liabilities were paid. During June, noncash assets with a carrying amount of $61,000 realized $25,000, and in July the remaining noncash assets with a carrying amount of $114,000 realized $84,000. The cash available at the end of each month was distributed promptly. The partners shared net income and losses equally.

Instructions

Prepare a statement of realization and liquidation for the Smith, Jones & Webb Partnership covering the entire period of liquidation (May through July, Year 3) and a supporting working paper showing the computation of installment payments to partners as cash becomes available.

Pr. 3-10 Denson, Eastin, and Feller, partners of the Denson, Eastin & Feller Partnership, shared net income and losses in a 5:3:2 ratio, respectively. On December 31, Year 6, at the end of an unprofitable year, they decided to liquidate the partnership. The partners' capital account balances on that date were as follows: Denson, $22,000; Eastin, $24,900; Feller, $15,000. The liabilities in the balance sheet amounted to $30,000, including a loan of $10,000 payable to Denson. The cash balance was $6,000.

The partners planned to realize the noncash assets over a long period and to distribute cash when it became available. All three partners were solvent.

Instructions

Prepare a cash distribution program for the Denson, Eastin & Feller Partnership on December 31, Year 6, and answer each of the following questions; prepare a working paper to show how you reached your conclusions. (Each question is independent of the others.)

a If Eastin received $2,000 from the first distribution of cash to partners, how much did Denson and Feller each receive at that time?

b If Denson received a total of $20,000 as a result of the liquidation, what was the total amount realized by the partnership on the noncash assets?

c If Feller received $6,200 on the first distribution of cash to partners, how much did Denson receive at that time?

Pr. 3-11 After several years of successful operation of the Lord & Lee Partnership, partners Lord and Lee decided to incorporate the partnership and issue common stock to public investors.

On January 2, Year 5, Lord-Lee Corporation was organized with authorization to issue 150,000 shares of $10 par common stock, and it issued 20,000 shares for cash to public investors at $16 a share. Lord and Lee agreed to accept shares of common stock at $16 a share in amounts equal to their respective partnership capital account balances, after the adjustments indicated on page 132 and after making cash withdrawals sufficient to avoid the need for issuing less than a multiple of 100 shares to either of the two partners. In payment for such shares, the partnership's net assets were transferred to the corporation and common stock certificates were issued. Accounting records were established for the corporation.

The post-closing trial balance of the Lord & Lee Partnership on December 31, Year 4, follows:

LORD & LEE PARTNERSHIP
Post-Closing Trial Balance
December 31, Year 4

	Debit	Credit
Cash..	$ 37,000	
Trade accounts receivable..............................	30,000	
Inventories...	56,000	
Land..	28,000	
Buildings	50,000	
Accumulated depreciation of buildings		$ 17,000
Trade accounts payable.................................		10,000
Lord, capital...		63,000
Lee, capital		111,000
Totals	$201,000	$201,000

The partnership contract provided that Lord was to receive 40% of net income or losses and Lee was to receive 60%. The partners approved the following adjustments to the accounting records of the partnership on December 31, Year 4:

(1) Recognize short-term prepayments of $1,500 and accrued liabilities of $750.
(2) Provide an allowance for doubtful accounts of $12,000.
(3) Increase the carrying amount of land to current fair value of $45,000.
(4) Increase the carrying amount of inventories to replacement cost of $75,000.

Instructions

a Prepare a journal entry for the Lord & Lee Partnership on December 31, Year 4, to record the foregoing adjustments and on January 2, Year 5, to record the liquidation of the partnership.

b Prepare journal entries on January 2, Year 5, to record Lord-Lee Corporation's issuances of common stock to public investors, Lord, and Lee.

c Prepare a balance sheet for Lord-Lee Corporation on January 2, Year 5, after the foregoing transactions and events had been recorded.

4

Accounting for Branches; Combined Financial Statements

Branches and Divisions

As a business enterprise grows, it may establish one or more branches to market its products over a large territory. The term *branch* is used to describe a business unit located at some distance from the *home office.* This unit carries merchandise obtained from the home office, makes sales, approves customers' credit, and makes collections from its customers.

A branch may obtain merchandise solely from the home office, or a portion may be purchased from outside suppliers. The cash receipts of the branch often are deposited in a bank account belonging to the home office; the branch expenses then are paid from an *imprest cash fund* or a bank account provided by the home office. As the imprest cash fund is depleted, the branch submits a list of cash payments supported by *vouchers* and receives a check from the home office to replenish the fund.

The use of an imprest cash fund gives the home office considerable control over the cash transactions of the branch. However, it is common practice for a large branch to maintain its own bank accounts. The extent of autonomy and responsibility of a branch varies, even among different branches of the same business enterprise.

A segment of a business enterprise also may be operated as a *division,* which generally has more autonomy than a branch. The accounting procedures for a division not organized as a separate corporation *(subsidiary company)* are similar to those used for branches. When a business segment is operated as a separate corporation, consolidated financial statements generally would be required. Consolidated financial statements are described in Chapters 6 through 11; accounting and reporting problems for business segments are included in Chapter 20.

Start-Up Costs of Opening New Branches

The establishment of a branch often requires the incurring of considerable costs before significant revenue may be generated. Operating losses in the first few months are likely. Some business enterprises would prefer to capitalize such *start-up costs* on the grounds that such costs are necessary to successful operation at a new location. However, most enterprises recognize start-up costs in connection with the opening of a branch as expenses of the accounting period in which the costs are incurred. The decision should be based on the principle that net income is measured by matching expired costs with realized revenue. Costs that benefit future accounting periods are deferred and allocated to those periods. Seldom is there complete certainty that a new branch will achieve a profitable level of operations in later years.

Accounting System for a Branch

The accounting system of one business enterprise having branches may provide for a complete set of accounting records at each branch; policies of another such enterprise may keep all accounting records in the home office. For example, branches of drug and grocery chain stores submit daily reports and business documents to the home office, which enters all transactions by branches in computerized accounting records kept in a central location. The home office may not even conduct operations of its own; it may serve only as an accounting and control center for the branches.

A branch may maintain a complete set of accounting records consisting of journals, ledgers, and a chart of accounts similar to those of an independent business enterprise. Financial statements are prepared by the branch accountant and forwarded to the home office. The number and types of ledger accounts, the internal control structure, the form and content of the financial statements, and the accounting policies generally are prescribed by the home office.

The remainder of this chapter focuses on a branch operation that maintains a complete set of accounting records. Transactions recorded by a branch should include all controllable expenses and revenue for which the branch manager is responsible. If the branch manager has responsibility over all branch assets, liabilities, revenue, and expenses, the branch accounting records should reflect this responsibility. Expenses such as depreciation often are not subject to control by a branch manager; therefore, both the branch plant assets and the related depreciation ledger accounts generally are maintained by the home office.

Reciprocal Ledger Accounts

The accounting records maintained by a branch include a Home Office ledger account that is credited for all merchandise, cash, or other assets provided by the home office; it is debited for all cash, merchandise, or other assets sent by the branch to the home office or to other branches. The Home Office account is a quasi-ownership equity account that shows the net investment by the home office in the branch. At the end of an accounting period when the branch closes its accounting records, the Income Summary account is closed to the Home Office account. A net income increases the credit balance of the Home Office account; a net loss decreases this balance.

In the home office accounting records, a *reciprocal ledger account* with a title such as Investment in Branch is maintained. This noncurrent asset account is debited for cash, merchandise, and services provided to the branch by the home office, and for net income reported by the branch. It is credited for cash or other assets received from the branch, and for net losses reported by the branch. Thus, the Investment in Branch account reflects the *equity method of accounting.* A separate investment account generally is maintained by the home office for each branch. If there is only one branch, the account title is likely to be Investment in Branch; if there are numerous branches, each account title includes a name or number to identify each branch.

Expenses Incurred by Home Office and Allocated to Branches

Some business enterprises follow a policy of notifying each branch of expenses incurred by the home office on the branch's behalf. As stated on page 134, plant assets located at a branch generally are carried in the home office accounting records. If a plant asset is acquired by the home office for the branch, the journal entry for the acquisition is a debit to an appropriate asset account such as Equipment: Branch and a credit to Cash or an appropriate liability account. If the branch acquires a plant asset, it debits the Home Office ledger account and credits Cash or an appropriate liability account. The home office debits an asset account such as Equipment: Branch and credits Investment in Branch.

The home office also usually acquires insurance, pays property and other taxes, and arranges for advertising that benefits all branches. Clearly, such expenses as depreciation, property taxes, insurance, and advertising must be considered in determining the profitability of a branch. A policy decision must be made as to whether these expense data are to be retained at the home office or are to be reported to the branches so that the income statement prepared for each branch will give a complete picture of its operations. An expense incurred by the home office and allocated to a branch is recorded by the home office by a debit to Investment in Branch and a credit to an appropriate expense ledger account; the branch debits an expense account and credits Home Office.

If the home office does not make sales itself but functions only as an accounting and control center, most or all of its expenses may be allocated to the branches. To facilitate comparison of the operating results of the various branches, the home office may charge each branch interest on the capital invested in that branch. Such interest expense recognized by the branches would be offset by interest revenue recognized by the home office and would not appear in the *combined* income statement of the business enterprise as a whole.

Alternative Methods of Billing Merchandise Shipments to Branches

Three alternative methods are available to the home office for billing merchandise shipped to its branches. The shipments may be billed (1) at home office cost, (2) at a percentage above home office cost, or (3) at the retail selling price. The shipment of merchandise to a branch does not constitute a *sale,* because ownership of the merchandise does not change.

Billing *at home office cost* is the simplest procedure and is widely used. It avoids the complication of unrealized gross profit in inventories and permits the financial statements of branches to give a meaningful picture of operations. However, billing merchandise to branches at home office cost attributes all gross profits of the enterprise to the branches, even though some of the merchandise may be manufactured by the home office. Under these circumstances, home office cost may not be the most realistic basis for billing shipments to branches.

Billing shipments to a branch *at a percentage above home office cost* (such as 110% of cost) may be intended to allocate a reasonable gross profit to the home office. When merchandise is billed to a branch at a price above home office cost, *the net income reported by the branch is understated and the ending inventories are overstated for the enterprise as a whole.* Adjustments must be made by the home office to eliminate the excess of billed prices over cost *(intracompany profits)* in the preparation of combined financial statements for the home office and the branch.

Billing shipments to a branch *at retail selling prices* may be based on a desire to strengthen internal control over inventories. The Inventories ledger account of the branch shows the merchandise received and sold at retail selling prices. Consequently, the account will show the ending inventories that should be on hand at retail prices. The home office record of shipments to a branch, when considered along with sales reported by the branch, provides a perpetual inventory stated at selling prices. If the physical inventories taken periodically at the branch do not agree with the amounts thus computed, an error or theft may be indicated and should be investigated promptly.

Separate Financial Statements for Branch and for Home Office

A separate income statement and balance sheet should be prepared for a branch so that management of the enterprise may review the operating results and financial position of the branch. The branch's income statement has no unusual features if merchandise is billed to the branch at home office cost. However, if merchandise is billed to the branch at retail selling prices, the branch's income statement will show a net loss approximating the amount of operating expenses. The only unusual aspect of the balance sheet for a branch is the use of the Home Office ledger account in lieu of the ownership equity accounts for a separate business enterprise. The separate financial statements prepared for a branch may be revised at the home office to include expenses incurred by the home office allocable to the branch and to show the results of branch operations after elimination of any intracompany profits on merchandise shipments.

Separate financial statements also may be prepared for the home office so that management will be able to appraise the results of its operations and its financial position. However, it is important to emphasize that separate financial statements of the home office and of the branch are prepared *for internal use only;* they do not meet the needs of investors or other external users of financial statements.

Combined Financial Statements for Home Office and Branch

A balance sheet for distribution to creditors, stockholders, and government agencies must show the financial position of a business enterprise having branches as a *single entity.* A convenient starting point in the preparation of a combined balance sheet consists of the adjusted trial balances of the home office and of the branch. A working paper for the combination of these trial balances is illustrated on page 140.

The assets and liabilities of the branch are substituted for the Investment in Branch ledger account included in the home office trial balance. Similar accounts are combined to produce a single total amount for cash, trade accounts receivable, and other assets and liabilities of the enterprise as a whole.

In the preparation of a combined balance sheet, reciprocal ledger accounts are eliminated because they have no significance when the branch and home office report as a single entity. The balance of the Home Office account is offset against the balance of the Investment in Branch account; also, any receivables and payables between the home office and the branch (or between two branches) are eliminated.

The operating results of the enterprise (the home office and all branches) are shown by an income statement in which the revenue and expenses of the branches are combined with corresponding revenue and expenses for the home office. Any intracompany profits or losses are eliminated.

Illustrative Journal Entries of Operation of a Branch Assume that Smaldino Company bills merchandise to Branch X *at home office cost* and that Branch X maintains complete accounting records and prepares financial statements. *Both the home office and the branch use the perpetual inventory system.* Equipment used at the branch is carried in the home office accounting records. Certain expenses, such as advertising and insurance, are incurred by the home office on behalf of the branch and are billed to the branch. Transactions and events during the first year (Year 1) of operations of Branch X are summarized below:

(1) Cash of $1,000 was forwarded by the home office to Branch X.
(2) Merchandise with a home office cost of $60,000 was shipped by the home office to Branch X.
(3) Equipment was acquired by Branch X for $500, to be carried in the home office accounting records. (Other plant assets for Branch X generally are acquired by the home office.)
(4) Credit sales by Branch X amounted to $80,000; the branch's cost of the merchandise sold was $45,000.
(5) Collections of trade accounts receivable by Branch X amounted to $62,000.
(6) Payments for operating expenses by Branch X totaled $20,000.
(7) Cash of $37,500 was remitted by Branch X to the home office.
(8) Operating expenses incurred by the home office and charged to Branch X totaled $3,000.

These transactions and events are recorded by the home office and by Branch X as follows (explanations for the journal entries are omitted):

Typical home office and branch transactions and events (perpetual inventory system)	Home Office Accounting Records Journal Entries		Branch Accounting Records Journal Entries	
	(1) Investment in		Cash 1,000	
	Branch X 1,000		Home Office	1,000
	Cash	1,000		
	(2) Investment in		Inventories 60,000	
	Branch X 60,000		Home Office	60,000
	Inventories . .	60,000		
	(3) Equipment:		Home Office 500	
	Branch X 500		Cash	500
	Investment in			
	Branch X . .	500		

(continued)

Home Office Accounting Records Journal Entries	Branch Accounting Records Journal Entries

(4) None	*Trade Accounts*
	  Receivable....... *80,000*
	Cost of Goods Sold *45,000*
	      Sales....... *80,000*
	      Inventories.. *45,000*

(5) None	*Cash ....* *62,000*
	  Trade
	  Accounts
	    Receivable. *62,000*

(6) None	*Operating*
	  Expenses........ *20,000*
	    Cash *20,000*

(7) Cash *37,500*
    Investment in
      Branch X...   *37,500*
	Home Office....... *37,500*
	    Cash *37,500*

(8) Investment in
    Branch X.........   *3,000*
    Operating
      Expenses....   *3,000*
	Operating
	  Expenses........ *3,000*
	    Home Office *3,000*

If a branch obtains merchandise from outsiders as well as from the home office, the merchandise acquired from the home office may be recorded in a separate Inventories from Home Office ledger account.

In the home office accounting records, the Investment in Branch X ledger account has a debit balance of $26,000 [before the accounting records are closed and the branch net income of $12,000 ($80,000 − $45,000 − $20,000 − $3,000 = $12,000) is transferred to the Investment in Branch X ledger account], as illustrated below:

Reciprocal ledger account in accounting records of home office, prior to equity-method adjusting entry

	Investment in Branch X			
Date	**Explanation**	**Debit**	**Credit**	**Balance**
Year 1	Cash sent to branch	1,000		1,000 dr
	Merchandise billed to branch at home office cost	60,000		61,000 dr
	Equipment acquired by branch, carried in home office accounting records		500	60,500 dr
	Cash received from branch		37,500	23,000 dr
	Operating expenses billed to branch	3,000		26,000 dr

In the accounting records of Branch X, the Home Office ledger account has a credit balance of $26,000 (before the accounting records are closed and the net income of $12,000 is transferred to the Home Office account), as shown below:

Reciprocal ledger
account in accounting
records of Branch X,
prior to closing entry

Home Office					
Date	Explanation	Debit	Credit	Balance
Year 1	Cash received from home office		1,000	1,000 cr
	Merchandise received from home of-fice		60,000	61,000 cr
	Equipment acquired	500		60,500 cr
	Cash sent to home office	37,500		23,000 cr
	Operating expenses billed by home of-fice		3,000	26,000 cr

Working Paper for Combined Financial Statements

A working paper for combined financial statements has three purposes: (1) to combine ledger account balances for like assets and liabilities, (2) to eliminate any intracompany profits or losses, and (3) to eliminate the reciprocal accounts.

Assume that the perpetual inventories of $15,000 ($60,000 − $45,000 = $15,000) at the end of Year 1 for Branch X had been verified by a physical count. The working paper illustrated on page 140 for Smaldino Company is based on the transactions and events illustrated on pages 137 and 138 and additional assumed data for the home office trial balance. All the routine year-end adjusting entries (except the home office entries on page 142) are assumed to have been made, and the working paper is begun with the adjusted trial balances of the home office and Branch X. Income taxes are disregarded in this illustration.

Note that the $26,000 debit balance of the Investment in Branch X ledger account and the $26,000 credit balance of the Home Office account are the balances *before the respective accounting records are closed,* that is, before the $12,000 net income of Branch X is entered in these two reciprocal accounts. In the Elimination column, elimination (*a*) offsets the balance of the Investment in Branch X account against the balance of the Home Office account. *This elimination appears in the working paper only;* it is not entered in the accounting records of either the home office or Branch X because its only purpose is to facilitate the preparation of combined financial statements.

Combined Financial Statements Illustrated The working paper on page 140 provides the information for the combined financial statements (excluding a statement of cash flows) of Smaldino Company on page 141.

SMALDINO COMPANY
Working Paper for Combined Financial Statements of Home Office and Branch X
For Year Ended December 31, Year 1
(Perpetual Inventory System: Billings at Cost)

| | Adjusted trial balances | | | |
	Home office	Branch	Elimination	Combined
	Dr (Cr)	Dr (Cr)	Dr (Cr)	Dr (Cr)
Income statement				
Sales..	(400,000)	(80,000)		(480,000)
Cost of goods sold...........................	235,000	45,000		280,000
Operating expenses	90,000	23,000		113,000
Net income (to statement of retained earnings below).....................................	75,000	12,000		87,000
Totals	-0-	-0-		-0-
Statement of retained earnings				
Retained earnings, Jan. 1, Year 1	(70,000)			(70,000)
Net (income) (from income statement above) ...	(75,000)	(12,000)		(87,000)
Dividends declared	40,000			40,000
Retained earnings, Dec. 31, Year 1 (to balance sheet below)				117,000
Totals				-0-
Balance sheet				
Cash..	25,000	5,000		30,000
Trade accounts receivable (net)..............	39,000	18,000		57,000
Inventories..................................	45,000	15,000		60,000
Investment in Branch X	26,000		(a) (26,000)	
Equipment..................................	150,000			150,000
Accumulated depreciation of equipment........	(10,000)			(10,000)
Trade accounts payable......................	(20,000)			(20,000)
Home office.................................		(26,000)	(a) 26,000	
Common stock, $10 par......................	(150,000)			(150,000)
Retained earnings (from statement of retained earnings above)				(117,000)
Totals	-0-	-0-	-0-	-0-

(a) To eliminate reciprocal ledger account balances.

SMALDINO COMPANY
Income Statement
For Year Ended December 31, Year 1

Sales	$480,000
Cost of goods sold	280,000
Gross margin on sales	$200,000
Operating expenses	113,000
Net income	$ 87,000
Earnings per share of common stock	$ 5.80

SMALDINO COMPANY
Statement of Retained Earnings
For Year Ended December 31, Year 1

Retained earnings, beginning of year	$ 70,000
Add: Net income	87,000
Subtotal	$157,000
Less: Dividends ($2.67 per share)	40,000
Retained earnings, end of year	$117,000

SMALDINO COMPANY
Balance Sheet
December 31, Year 1

Assets

Cash		$ 30,000
Trade accounts receivable (net)		57,000
Inventories		60,000
Equipment	$150,000	
Less: Accumulated depreciation	10,000	140,000
Total assets		$287,000

Liabilities & Stockholders' Equity

Liabilities:		
Trade accounts payable		$ 20,000
Stockholders' equity:		
Common stock, $10 par, 15,000 share authorized, issued, and outstanding	$150,000	
Retained earnings	117,000	267,000
Total liabilities & stockholders' equity		$287,000

Home Office Adjusting and Closing Entries and Branch Closing Entries The home office's equity-method adjusting and closing entries for branch operating results and the branch's closing entries on December 31, Year 1, are shown below (explanations for the entries are omitted):

Adjusting and closing entries (perpetual inventory system)

Home Office Accounting Records Adjusting and Closing Entries		Branch Accounting Records Closing Entries	
None		Sales 80,000	
		Cost of Goods	
		Sold	45,000
		Operating	
		Expenses ...	23,000
		Income	
		Summary....	12,000
Investment in		Income Summary ... 12,000	
Branch X.......... 12,000		Home Office..	12,000
Income:			
Branch X....	12,000		
Income: Branch X ... 12,000		None	
Income			
Summary....	12,000		

Billing of Merchandise to Branches at Prices above Home Office Cost

As stated on page 135, the home offices of some business enterprises bill merchandise shipped to branches at home office cost plus a markup percentage (or alternatively at retail selling prices). Because both these methods involve similar modifications of accounting procedures, a single example illustrates the key points involved, using the illustration for Smaldino Company on page 137 with one changed assumption: the home office bills merchandise shipped to Branch X at a markup of 50% above home office cost, or 33⅓% of billed price.[1]

Under this assumption, the journal entries for the first year's events and transactions by the home office and Branch X are the same as those presented on pages 137 and 138 except for the journal entries for shipments of merchandise from the home office to Branch X. These shipments ($60,000 cost + 50% markup on cost = $90,000) are recorded under the perpetual inventory system on page 143.

In the accounting records of the home office, the Investment in Branch X ledger account on page 143 now has a debit balance of $56,000 before the accounting records are closed and the branch net income or loss is entered in the Investment in Branch X account. This amount is $30,000 larger than the $26,000 balance in the prior illustration (page 138). The increase represents the 50% markup over cost ($60,000) of the merchandise shipped to Branch X.

---

[1] Billed price = cost + 0.50 cost; therefore, markup on billed price is 0.50/(1 + 0.50), or 33⅓%.

Journal entries for shipments to branch at prices above home office cost (perpetual inventory system)

Home Office Accounting Records Journal Entries		Branch Accounting Records Journal Entries	
(2) Investment in		Inventories......... 90,000	
Branch X 90,000		Home Office ..	90,000
Inventories....	60,000		
Allowance for			
Overvaluation			
of Inventories:			
Branch X	30,000		

Reciprocal ledger account in accounting records of home office, prior to equity-method adjusting entry

Investment in Branch X

Date	Explanation	Debit	Credit	Balance
Year 1	Cash sent to branch	1,000		1,000 dr
	Merchandise billed to branch at markup of 50% over home office cost, or 33⅓% of billed price	90,000		91,000 dr
	Equipment acquired by branch, carried in home office accounting records		500	90,500 dr
	Cash received from branch		37,500	53,000 dr
	Operating expenses billed to branch	3,000		56,000 dr

In the accounting records of Branch X, the Home Office ledger account now has a credit balance of $56,000, before the accounting records are closed and the branch net income or loss is entered in the Home Office account, as illustrated below:

Reciprocal ledger account in accounting records of Branch X, prior to closing entry

Home Office

Date	Explanation	Debit	Credit	Balance
Year 1	Cash received from home office		1,000	1,000 cr
	Merchandise received from home office		90,000	91,000 cr
	Equipment acquired	500		90,500 cr
	Cash sent to home office	37,500		53,000 cr
	Operating expenses billed by home office		3,000	56,000 cr

Branch X recorded the merchandise received from the home office at billed prices of $90,000; the home office recorded the shipment by credits of $60,000 to Inventories and $30,000 to Allowance for Overvaluation of Inventories: Branch X. Use of the allowance account enables the home office to maintain a record of the cost of merchandise shipped to Branch X, as well as the amount of the unrealized gross profit on the shipments.

At the end of the accounting period, Branch X reports its inventories (at billed prices) at $22,500. The cost of these inventories is $15,000 ($22,500 ÷ 1.50 = $15,000). In the home office accounting records, the required balance of the Allowance for Overvaluation of Inventories: Branch X ledger account is $7,500 ($22,500 − $15,000 = $7,500); thus, this account balance must be reduced from its present amount of $30,000 to $7,500. The reason for this reduction is that *the 50% markup of billed prices over cost has become realized gross profit to the home office with respect to the merchandise sold by the branch.* Consequently, at the end of the year the home office reduces its allowance for overvaluation of the branch inventories to the $7,500 excess valuation contained in the ending inventories. The debit adjustment of $22,500 in the allowance account is offset by a credit to the Realized Gross Profit: Branch X Sales account, because it represents additional gross profit of the home office resulting from sales by the branch.

These matters are illustrated in the home office end-of-period adjusting and closing entries on page 146.

Working Paper When Billings to Branches Are at Prices above Cost

When a home office bills merchandise shipments to branches at prices above home office cost, preparation of the working paper for combined financial statements is facilitated by an analysis of the flow of merchandise to a branch, such as the following for Branch X of Smaldino Company:

	Billed price	Home office cost	Markup (50% of cost; 33⅓% of billed price)
SMALDINO COMPANY Flow of Merchandise for Branch X During Year 1			
Beginning inventories			
Add: Shipments from home office	$90,000	$60,000	$30,000
Available for sale	$90,000	$60,000	$30,000
Less: Ending inventories	22,500	15,000	7,500
Cost of goods sold.	$67,500	$45,000	$22,500

The foregoing analysis provides in the Markup column the information needed for the Eliminations column in the working paper for combined financial statements on page 145.

The following working paper differs from the working paper on page 140 by the inclusion of an elimination to restate the ending inventories of the branch to cost. Also, the income reported by the home office is adjusted by the $22,500 of merchandise markup that was realized as a result of sales by the branch. As stated on page 139, the amounts in the Eliminations column appear only in the working paper. The amounts represent a mechanical step to aid in the preparation of combined financial statements and are not entered in the accounting records of either the home office or the branch.

SMALDINO COMPANY
Working Paper for Combined Financial Statements of Home Office and Branch X
For Year Ended December 31, Year 1
(Perpetual Inventory System: Billings above Cost)

	Adjusted trial balances		Eliminations	Combined
	Home office	Branch		
	Dr (Cr)	Dr (Cr)	Dr (Cr)	Dr (Cr)
Income statement				
Sales.......................................	(400,000)	(80,000)		(480,000)
Cost of goods sold........................	235,000	67,500	(a) (22,500)	280,000
Operating expenses.......................	90,000	23,000		113,000
Net income (loss) (to statement of retained				
earnings below)	75,000	(10,500)	(b) 22,500	87,000
Totals	-0-	-0-		-0-
Statement of retained earnings				
Retained earnings, Jan. 1, Year 1	(70,000)			(70,000)
Net (income) loss (from income statement				
above).....................................	(75,000)	10,500	(b) (22,500)	(87,000)
Dividends declared	40,000			40,000
Retained earnings, Dec. 31, Year 1 (to bal-				
ance sheet below)				117,000
Totals				-0-
Balance sheet				
Cash	25,000	5,000		30,000
Trade accounts receivable (net)	39,000	18,000		57,000
Inventories................................	45,000	22,500	(a) (7,500)	60,000
Investment in Branch X....................	56,000		(c) (56,000)	
Allowance for overvaluation of inventories:				
Branch X	(30,000)		(a) 30,000	
Equipment	150,000			150,000
Accumulated depreciation of equipment.....	(10,000)			(10,000)
Trade accounts payable	(20,000)			(20,000)
Home office		(56,000)	(c) 56,000	
Common stock, $10 par	(150,000)			(150,000)
Retained earnings (from statement of re-				
tained earnings above)				(117,000)
Totals	-0-	-0-	-0-	-0-

(a) To reduce ending inventories and cost of goods sold of branch to cost, and to eliminate unadjusted balance of Allowance for Overvaluation of Inventories: Branch X ledger account.

(b) To increase income of home office by portion of merchandise markup that was realized by branch sales.

(c) To eliminate reciprocal ledger account balances.

Combined Financial Statements   Because the amounts in the Combined column of the working paper on page 145 are the same as in the working paper prepared when the merchandise shipments to the branch were billed at home office cost, the combined financial statements are identical with those illustrated on page 141.

Home Office Adjusting and Closing Entries and Branch Closing Entries   The December 31, Year 1, adjusting and closing entries of the home office are illustrated below:

<table>
<tr><td align="left">End-of-period home
office adjusting and
closing entries</td><td colspan="3" align="center">**Home Office Accounting Records**
Adjusting and Closing Entries</td></tr>
<tr><td></td><td>Income: Branch X..</td><td>10,500</td><td></td></tr>
<tr><td></td><td>   Investment in Branch X...............................</td><td></td><td>10,500</td></tr>
<tr><td></td><td>To record net loss reported by branch.</td><td></td><td></td></tr>
<tr><td></td><td>Allowance for Overvaluation of Inventories: Branch X ....</td><td>22,500</td><td></td></tr>
<tr><td></td><td>   Realized Gross Profit: Branch X Sales ....</td><td></td><td>22,500</td></tr>
<tr><td></td><td>To reduce allowance to amount by which ending inventories of branch exceed cost.</td><td></td><td></td></tr>
<tr><td></td><td>Realized Gross Profit: Branch X Sales.........................</td><td>22,500</td><td></td></tr>
<tr><td></td><td>   Income: Branch X.....................................</td><td></td><td>10,500</td></tr>
<tr><td></td><td>   Income Summary ....</td><td></td><td>12,000</td></tr>
<tr><td></td><td>To close branch net loss and realized gross profit to Income Summary ledger account. (Income tax effects are disregarded.)</td><td></td><td></td></tr>
</table>

After the foregoing journal entries have been posted, the ledger accounts in the home office general ledger used to record branch operations are as follows:

End-of-period balances in accounting records of home office

	Investment in Branch X			
Date	**Explanation**	**Debit**	**Credit**	**Balance**
Year 1	Cash sent to branch	1,000		1,000 dr
	Merchandise billed to branch at markup of 50% above home office cost, or 33⅓% of billed price	90,000		91,000 dr
	Equipment acquired by branch, carried in home office accounting records		500	90,500 dr
	Cash received from branch		37,500	53,000 dr
	Operating expenses billed to branch	3,000		56,000 dr
	Net loss for Year 1 reported by branch		10,500	45,500 dr

Allowance for Overvaluation of Inventories: Branch X

Date	Explanation	Debit	Credit	Balance
Year 1	Markup of merchandise shipped to branch during Year 1 (50% of cost)		30,000	30,000 cr
	Realization of 50% markup on merchandise sold by branch during Year 1	22,500		7,500 cr

Realized Gross Profit: Branch X Sales

Date	Explanation	Debit	Credit	Balance
Year 1	Realization of 50% markup on merchandise sold by branch during Year 1		22,500	22,500 cr
	Closing entry	22,500		-0-

Income: Branch X

Date	Explanation	Debit	Credit	Balance
Year 1	Net loss for Year 1 reported by branch	10,500		10,500 dr
	Closing entry		10,500	-0-

In the *separate* balance sheet for the home office, the $7,500 credit balance of the Allowance for Overvaluation of Inventories: Branch X ledger account is deducted from the $45,500 debit balance of the Investment in Branch X account, thus reducing the carrying amount of the investment account to a cost basis with respect to shipments of merchandise to the branch. In the *separate* income statement for the home office, the $22,500 realized gross profit on Branch X sales may be displayed following gross margin on sales, $165,000 ($400,000 sales − $235,000 cost of goods sold = $165,000).

The closing entries for the branch at the end of Year 1 are as follows:

Closing entries for Branch X (perpetual inventory system)

Branch Accounting Records
Closing Entries

Sales	80,000	
Income Summary	10,500	
Cost of Goods Sold		67,500
Operating Expenses		23,000
To close revenue and expense ledger accounts.		
Home Office	10,500	
Income Summary		10,500
To close the net loss in the Income Summary account to the Home Office account.		

After these closing entries have been posted by the branch, the Home Office ledger account in the accounting records of Branch X below has a credit balance of $45,500, the same as the debit balance of the Investment in Branch X account in the accounting records of the home office.

Compare this ledger account with Investment in Branch X account on page 146

	Home Office				
Date	**Explanation**	**Debit**	**Credit**	**Balance**
Year 1	Cash received from home office		1,000	1,000 cr
	Merchandise received from home office		90,000	91,000 cr
	Equipment acquired	500		90,500 cr
	Cash sent to home office	37,500		53,000 cr
	Operating expenses billed by home office		3,000	56,000 cr
	Net loss for Year 1	10,500		45,500 cr

Treatment of Beginning Inventories Priced above Cost

The working paper on page 145 shows how the ending inventories and the related allowance for overvaluation of inventories were handled. However, because Year 1 was the first year of operations for Branch X, no beginning inventories were involved.

Perpetual Inventory System   Under the perpetual inventory system, no special problems arise when the beginning inventories of the branch include an element of unrealized gross profit. The working paper eliminations would be similar to those illustrated on page 145.

Periodic Inventory System   I continue the illustration for Smaldino Company for a second year of operations (Year 2) to demonstrate the handling of beginning inventories carried by Branch X at an amount above home office cost. However, I now assume that both the home office and Branch X adopted the periodic inventory system in Year 2. When the periodic inventory system is used, the home office credits Shipments to Branch (a contra account to Purchases) for the home office cost of merchandise shipped and Allowance for Overvaluation of Inventories for the markup over home office cost. The branch debits Shipments from Home Office (analogous to a Purchases account) for the billed price of merchandise received.

The beginning inventories for Year 2 were carried by Branch X at $22,500, or 150% of the cost of $15,000 ($15,000 × 1.50 = $22,500). Assume that during Year 2 the home office shipped merchandise to Branch X that cost $80,000 and was billed at $120,000, and that Branch X sold merchandise for $150,000 that was billed at

$112,500. The journal entries (explanations omitted) to record the shipments and sales under the periodic inventory system are illustrated below:

Journal entries for shipments to branch at a price above home office cost (periodic inventory system)

Home Office Accounting Records Journal Entries		Branch Accounting Records Journal Entries	
Investment in		Shipments from	
Branch X..........	120,000	Home Office........	120,000
Shipments to		Home Office ..	120,000
Branch X	80,000		
Allowance for			
Overvaluation			
of Inventories:			
Branch X	40,000		
None		Cash (or Trade	
		Accounts	
		Receivable)	150,000
		Sales.........	150,000

The branch inventories at the end of Year 2 amounted to $30,000 at billed prices, representing cost of $20,000 plus a 50% markup on cost ($20,000 × 1.50 = $30,000). The flow of merchandise for Branch X during Year 2 is summarized below:

SMALDINO COMPANY
Flow of Merchandise for Branch X
During Year 2

	Billed price	Cost	Markup (50% of cost; 33⅓% of billed price)
Beginning inventories (see page 144)..................	$ 22,500	$ 15,000	$ 7,500
Add: Shipments from home office	120,000	80,000	40,000
Available for sale...........	$142,500	$ 95,000	$ 47,500
Less: Ending inventories	(30,000)	(20,000)	(10,000)
Cost of goods sold	$112,500	$ 75,000	$ 37,500

The activities of the branch for Year 2 and end-of-period adjusting and closing entries are reflected in the four home office ledger accounts on page 150.

In the accounting records of the home office at the end of Year 2, the balance required in the Allowance for Overvaluation of Inventories: Branch X ledger account is $10,000, that is, the billed price of $30,000 less cost of $20,000 for merchandise in the branch's ending inventories. Therefore, the allowance account balance is reduced from $47,500 to $10,000. This reduction of $37,500 represents the 50% markup of

End-of-period balances
in accounting records
of home office

Investment in Branch X

Date	Explanation	Debit	Credit	Balance
	Balance, Dec. 31, Year 1 (see page 146)			45,500 dr
Year 2	Merchandise billed to branch at markup of 50% above home office cost, or 33⅓% of billed price	120,000		165,500 dr
	Cash received from branch		113,000	52,500 dr
	Operating expenses billed to branch	4,500		57,000 dr
	Net income for Year 2 reported by branch	10,000		67,000 dr

Allowance for Overvaluation of Inventories: Branch X

Date	Explanation	Debit	Credit	Balance
	Balance, Dec. 31, Year 1 (see page 147)			7,500 cr
Year 2	Markup of merchandise shipped to branch during Year 2 (50% of cost)		40,000	47,500 cr
	Realization of 50% markup on merchandise sold by branch during Year 2	37,500		10,000 cr

Realized Gross Profit: Branch X Sales

Date	Explanation	Debit	Credit	Balance
Year 2	Realization of 50% markup on merchandise sold by branch during Year 2		37,500	37,500 cr
	Closing entry	37,500		-0-

Income: Branch X

Date	Explanation	Debit	Credit	Balance
Year 2	Net income for Year 2 reported by branch		10,000	10,000 cr
	Closing entry	10,000		-0-

merchandise above cost that was realized by Branch X during Year 2 and is credited to the Realized Gross Profit: Branch X Sales account.

The Home Office account in the branch general ledger shows the following activity and closing entry for Year 2:

Reciprocal ledger account in accounting records of Branch X

Home Office

Date	Explanation	Debit	Credit	Balance
	Balance, Dec. 31, Year 1 (see page 148)			45,500 cr
Year 2	Merchandise received from home office		120,000	165,500 cr
	Cash sent to home office	113,000		52,500 cr
	Operating expenses billed by home office		4,500	57,000 cr
	Net income for Year 2		10,000	67,000 cr

The working paper for combined financial statements under the periodic inventory system, which reflects pre-adjusting and pre-closing balances for the reciprocal ledger accounts and the Allowance for Overvaluation of Inventories: Branch X account, is shown below and on page 152.

SMALDINO COMPANY
Working Paper for Combined Financial Statements of Home Office and Branch X
For Year Ended December 31, Year 2
(Periodic Inventory System: Billings above Cost)

	Adjusted trial balances		Eliminations	Combined
	Home office	Branch		
	Dr (Cr)	Dr (Cr)	Dr (Cr)	Dr (Cr)
Income statement				
Sales	(500,000)	(150,000)		(650,000)
Inventories, Dec. 31, Year 1	45,000	22,500	(b) (7,500)	60,000
Purchases.	400,000			400,000
Shipments to Branch X	(80,000)		(a) 80,000	
Shipments from Home Office		120,000	(a) (120,000)	
Inventories, Dec. 31, Year 2	(70,000)	(30,000)	(c) 10,000	(90,000)
Operating expenses	120,000	27,500		147,500
Net income (to statement of retained earnings below). .	85,000	10,000	(d) 37,500	132,500
Totals.	-0-	-0-		-0-
Statement of retained earnings				
Retained earnings, Dec. 31, Year 1 (see page 145)	(117,000)			(117,000)
Net (income) (from income statement above)	(85,000)	(10,000)	(d) (37,500)	(132,500)
Dividends declared.	60,000			60,000

(continued)

SMALDINO COMPANY
Working Paper for Combined Financial Statements of Home Office and Branch X (concluded)
For Year Ended December 31, Year 2
(Periodic Inventory System: Billings above Cost)

	Adjusted trial balances		Eliminations	Combined
	Home office	Branch		
	Dr (Cr)	Dr (Cr)	Dr (Cr)	Dr (Cr)
Statement of retained earnings				
Retained earnings, Dec. 31, Year 2 (to balance sheet below)............				189,500
Totals.................				-0-
Balance sheet				
Cash.....................	30,000	9,000		39,000
Trade accounts receivable (net)....................	64,000	28,000		92,000
Inventories, Dec. 31, Year 2	70,000	30,000	(c) (10,000)	90,000
Allowance for overvaluation of inventories: Branch X ..	(47,500)		(a) 40,000 / (b) 7,500	
Investment in Branch X	57,000		(e) (57,000)	
Equipment	158,000			158,000
Accumulated depreciation of equipment	(15,000)			(15,000)
Trade accounts payable ...	(24,500)			(24,500)
Home office		(57,000)	(e) 57,000	
Common stock, $10 par ...	(150,000)			(150,000)
Retained earnings (from statement of retained earnings above).............				(189,500)
Totals.................	-0-	-0-	-0-	-0-

(a) To eliminate reciprocal ledger accounts for merchandise shipments.
(b) To reduce beginning inventories of branch to cost.
(c) To reduce ending inventories of branch to cost.
(d) To increase income of home office by portion of merchandise markup that was realized by branch sales.
(e) To eliminate reciprocal ledger account balances.

Reconciliation of Reciprocal Ledger Accounts

At the end of an accounting period, the balance of the Investment in Branch X ledger account in the accounting records of the home office may not agree with the balance of the Home Office account in the accounting records of Branch X, because certain transactions may have been recorded by one office but not by the other. The situation is comparable with that of reconciling the ledger account for Cash in Bank with the balance in the monthly bank statement. The lack of agreement between the reciprocal ledger account balances causes no difficulty during an accounting period, but at the end of each period the reciprocal account balances must be brought into agreement before combined financial statements are prepared.

As an illustration of the procedure for reconciling reciprocal ledger account balances at year-end, assume that the home office and branch accounting records of Mercer Company contain the following data on December 31, Year 10:

Reciprocal ledger accounts before adjustments

Investment in Branch A (in accounting records of Home Office)

Date	Explanation	Debit	Credit	Balance
Year 10				
Nov. 30	Balance			62,500 dr
Dec. 10	Cash received from branch		20,000	42,500 dr
27	Collection of branch trade accounts receivable		1,000	41,500 dr
29	Merchandise shipped to branch	8,000		49,500 dr

Home Office (in accounting records of Branch A)

Date	Explanation	Debit	Credit	Balance
Year 10				
Nov. 30	Balance			62,500 cr
Dec. 7	Cash sent to home office	20,000		42,500 cr
28	Acquired equipment	3,000		39,500 cr
30	Collection of home office trade accounts receivable		2,000	41,500 cr

Comparison of the two reciprocal ledger accounts discloses the four reconciling items described below and on page 154.

(1) A debit of $8,000 in the Investment in Branch A ledger account without a related credit in the Home Office account

On December 29, the home office shipped merchandise costing $8,000 to the branch. The home office debits its reciprocal ledger account with the branch on the date merchandise is shipped, but the branch credits its reciprocal account with the home office when the merchandise is received, perhaps a few days later. The required journal entry on December 31, Year 10, in the ***branch accounting records,*** assuming use of the perpetual inventory system, appears below:

Branch journal entry for merchandise in transit from home office

Inventories in Transit	8,000	
Home Office		8,000
To record shipment of merchandise in transit from home office.		

In determining its ending inventories, on December 31, Year 10, the branch must add to the inventories on hand the $8,000 of merchandise in transit. When the merchandise is received in Year 11, the branch debits Inventories and credits Inventories in Transit.

(2) A credit of $1,000 in the Investment in Branch A ledger account without a related debit in the Home Office account

On December 27, trade accounts receivable of the branch were collected by the home office. The collection was recorded by the home office by a debit to Cash and a credit to Investment in Branch A. No journal entry was made by Branch A; therefore, the following journal entry is required *in the accounting records of Branch A* on December 31, Year 10:

<table>
<tr><td>Branch journal entry for trade accounts receivable collected by home office</td><td>Home Office 1,000
    Trade Accounts Receivable   1,000
To record collection of accounts receivable by home office.</td></tr>
</table>

(3) A debit of $3,000 in the Home Office ledger account without a related credit in the Investment in Branch A account

On December 28, the branch acquired equipment for $3,000. Because the equipment used by the branch is carried in the accounting records of the home office, the journal entry made by the branch was a debit to Home Office and a credit to Cash. No journal entry was made by the home office; therefore, the following journal entry is required on December 31, Year 10, *in the accounting records of the home office:*

<table>
<tr><td>Home office journal entry for equipment acquired by branch</td><td>Equipment: Branch A 3,000
    Investment in Branch A   3,000
To record equipment acquired by branch.</td></tr>
</table>

(4) A credit of $2,000 in the Home Office ledger account without a related debit in the Investment in Branch A account

On December 30, trade accounts receivable of the home office were collected by Branch A. The collection was recorded by Branch A by a debit to Cash and a credit to Home Office. No journal entry was made by the home office; therefore, the following journal entry is required *in the accounting records of the home office* on December 31, Year 10:

<table>
<tr><td>Home office journal entry for trade accounts receivable collected by branch</td><td>Investment in Branch A 2,000
    Trade Accounts Receivable   2,000
To record collection of accounts receivable by Branch A.</td></tr>
</table>

The effect of the foregoing end-of-period journal entries is to update the reciprocal ledger accounts, as shown by the following reconciliation:

MERCER COMPANY—HOME OFFICE AND BRANCH A
Reconciliation of Reciprocal Ledger Accounts
December 31, Year 10

	Investment in Branch A account (in home office accounting records)	Home Office account (in branch accounting records)
Balances before adjustments	$49,500 dr	$41,500 cr
Add: (1) Merchandise shipped to branch by home office		8,000
(4) Home office trade accounts receivable collected by branch	2,000	
Less: (2) Branch trade accounts receivable collected by home office		(1,000)
(3) Equipment acquired by branch.	(3,000)	
Adjusted balances.	$48,500 dr	$48,500 cr

Transactions between Branches

Efficient operations may on occasion require that assets be transferred from one branch to another. Generally, a branch does not carry a reciprocal ledger account with another branch but records the transfer in the Home Office ledger account. For example, if Branch A ships merchandise to Branch B, Branch A debits Home Office and credits Inventories (assuming that the perpetual inventory system is used). On receipt of the merchandise, Branch B debits Inventories and credits Home Office. The home office records the transfer between branches by a debit to Investment in Branch B and a credit to Investment in Branch A.

The transfer of merchandise from one branch to another does not justify increasing the carrying amount of inventories by the freight costs incurred because of the indirect routing. The amount of freight costs properly included in inventories at a branch is limited to the cost of shipping the merchandise *directly* from the home office to its present location. Excess freight costs are recognized as expenses of the home office.

To illustrate the accounting for excess freight costs on interbranch transfers of merchandise, assume the following data. The home office shipped merchandise costing $6,000 to Branch D and paid freight costs of $400. Subsequently, the home office instructed Branch D to transfer this merchandise to Branch E. Freight costs of $300 were paid by Branch D to carry out this order. If the merchandise had been shipped directly from the home office to Branch E, the freight costs would have been $500. The journal entries required in the three sets of accounting records (assuming that the perpetual inventory system is used) are as follows:

In accounting records of *home office:*

Investment in Branch D	6,400	
Inventories		6,000
Cash..		400
To record shipment of merchandise and payment of freight costs.		

Investment in Branch E	6,500	
Excess Freight Expense—Interbranch Transfers	200	
Investment in Branch D....................................		6,700

To record transfer of merchandise from Branch D to Branch E under instruction of home office. Interbranch freight of $300 paid by Branch D caused total freight costs on this merchandise to exceed direct shipment costs by $200 ($400 + $300 − $500 = $200).

In accounting records of *Branch D:*

Freight In (or Inventories)	400	
Inventories..	6,000	
Home Office		6,400
To record receipt of merchandise from home office with freight costs paid in advance by home office.		

Home Office	6,700	
Inventories		6,000
Freight In (or Inventories)		400
Cash..		300

To record transfer of merchandise to Branch E under instruction of home office and payment of freight costs of $300.

In accounting records of *Branch E:*

Inventories..	6,000	
Freight In (or Inventories)	500	
Home Office		6,500

To record receipt of merchandise from Branch D transferred under instruction of home office and normal freight costs billed by home office.

Recognizing excess freight costs on merchandise transferred from one branch to another as expenses is an example of the accounting principle that expenses and losses should be given prompt recognition. The excess freight costs from such shipments generally result from inefficient planning of original shipments and should not be included in inventories.

In recognizing excess freight costs of interbranch transfers as expenses attributable to the home office, the assumption was that the home office makes the decisions directing all shipments. If branch managers are given authority to order transfers of merchandise between branches, the excess freight costs are recognized as expenses attributable to the branches whose managers authorized the transfers.

SEC ENFORCEMENT ACTION DEALING WITH WRONGFUL APPLICATION OF ACCOUNTING STANDARDS FOR DIVISIONS

AAER 35 The SEC's *AAER 35,* ''Securities and Exchange Commission v. Stauffer Chemical Company'' (August 13, 1984), describes a federal court's entry of a permanent injunction against a corporation engaged in the manufacture and sale of chemicals and chemical-related products. The SEC found that the corporation had overstated its earnings by means of three major misstatements, one of which was the failure to eliminate $1.1 million of intracompany profits in inventories shipped from one of the corporation's divisions to another division. The court also ordered the corporation to file timely with the SEC a *Form 8-K,* ''Current Report,'' describing its restatement of its previously reported revenue and earnings for the effects of the three major misstatements.

REVIEW QUESTIONS

1 Some branches maintain complete accounting records and prepare financial statements much the same as an autonomous business enterprise. Other branches perform only limited accounting functions, with most accounting activity concentrated in the home office. Assuming that a branch has a fairly complete set of accounting records, what criterion or principle would you suggest be used in deciding whether various types of expenses applicable to the branch should be recognized by the home office or by the branch?

2 Explain the use of *reciprocal ledger accounts* in home office and branch accounting systems in conjunction with the periodic inventory system.

3 The president of Sandra Company informs you that a branch is being opened and requests your advice as follows: ''I have been told that we may bill merchandise shipped to the branch at cost, at retail selling prices, or anywhere in between. Do certified public accountants really have that much latitude in the application of generally accepted accounting principles?''

4 Jesse Corporation operates 10 branches in addition to its home office and bills merchandise shipped by the home office to the branches at 10% above home office cost. All plant assets are carried in the home office accounting records. The home office also conducts an advertising program that benefits all branches. Each branch maintains its own accounting records and prepares separate financial statements. In the home office, the accounting department prepares financial statements for the home office and combined financial statements for the enterprise as a whole.

Explain the purpose of the financial statements prepared by the branches, the home office financial statements, and the combined financial statements.

5   The policies of Armenia Company provide that equipment used by its branches is to be carried in the accounting records of the home office. Acquisitions of new equipment may be made either by the home office or by the branches with the approval of the home office. Slauson Branch, with the approval of the home office, acquired equipment at a cost of $17,000. Describe the journal entries for the Slauson Branch and the home office to record the acquisition of the equipment.

6   Explain the use of and journal entries for a home office's Allowance for Overvaluation of Inventories: Branch ledger account.

7   The reciprocal ledger account balances of Meadow Company's branch and home office are not in agreement at year-end. What factors might have caused this?

8   Ralph Company operates a number of branches but centralizes its accounting records in the home office and maintains control of branch operations. The home office found that Branch D had ample inventories of a certain item of merchandise but that Branch E was almost out of the item. Therefore, the home office instructed Branch D to ship merchandise with a cost of $5,000 to Branch E. What journal entry should Branch D make, and what principle should guide the treatment of freight costs? (Assume that Branch D uses the perpetual inventory system.)

EXERCISES

Ex. 4-1   Select the best answer for each of the following multiple-choice questions:

1   If the home office of a business enterprise ships merchandise to the branch at a markup of 20% of home office cost, the markup on billed price of the merchandise is:
a 16⅔%
b 18%
c 20%
d 25%
e Some other percentage

2   On September 26, Year 9, the home office of Statewide Company shipped merchandise costing $100,000 at a billed price of $120,000 to Florida Branch via the Panama Canal; the merchandise had not reached the branch by September 30, Year 9, the end of the accounting period. Both the home office and Florida Branch use the perpetual inventory system. The appropriate accounting treatment by Florida Branch on September 30, Year 9, is:
a No journal entry
b Debit Inventories in Transit and credit Home Office, $120,000
c Debit Inventories in Transit and credit Inventories, $120,000
d Debit Home Office and credit inventories, $100,000

3   Does the home office of a business enterprise use an Allowance for Overvaluation of Inventories: Branch ledger account if it bills merchandise shipments to the branch at:

	Home office cost?	Home office cost plus a markup?	Retail selling price?
a	Yes	Yes	Yes
b	Yes	Yes	No
c	No	Yes	No
d	No	Yes	Yes

4   If a cash remittance is in transit from the branch to the home office of a business enterprise on May 31, Year 4, on that date the:

a Home office debits Cash in Transit and credits Investment in Branch

b Branch debits Home Office and credits Cash in Transit

c Home office debits Investment in Branch and credits Cash in Transit

d Branch debits Cash in Transit and credits Home Office

5   In the working paper for combined financial statements of a business enterprise whose home office bills merchandise shipments to the branch at a markup above home office cost, the elimination for the Allowance for Overvaluation of Inventories: Branch (allowance) ledger account is:

a Debit Allowance; credit Cost of Goods Sold and Inventories.

b Debit Cost of Goods Sold and Inventories; credit Allowance.

c Debit Allowance and credit Home Office.

d Debit Investment in Branch and credit Allowance.

6   Is a Shipments to Branch ledger account used by the home office of a business enterprise under the:

	Perpetual inventory system?	Periodic inventory system?
a	Yes	Yes
b	Yes	No
c	No	Yes
d	No	No

7   Which of the following forms of journal entry (explanation omitted) is appropriate when the branch of a business enterprise collects an interest-bearing note receivable of the home office?

a Cash XXX

       Home Office Notes Receivable.................................... XXX

       Home Office Interest Revenue XXX

b Cash XXX

       Home Office.. XXX

c Home Office... XXX

       Cash XXX

d Home Office Notes Receivable... XXX

       Home Office Interest Revenue XXX

       Cash XXX

8　Arcadia Branch of Pasadena Company prepared the following journal entry:

Home Office	*10,000*	
Cash		*10,000*

To record acquisition of equipment to be carried in home office ac-counting records.

The appropriate journal entry (explanation omitted) for the home office of Arcadia Company is:

a　*Equipment: Arcadia Branch* . . . .　*10,000*

　　　Investment in Arcadia Branch . . . .　　　*10,000*

b　*Investment in Arcadia Branch* . . . .　*10,000*

　　　Equipment: Arcadia Branch . . . .　　　*10,000*

c　*Equipment: Arcadia Branch* . . . .　*10,000*

　　　Equipment (Home Office) . . . .　　　*10,000*

d　*Equipment* . . . .　*10,000*

　　　Home Office . . . .　　　*10,000*

9　The August 1, Year 3, credit balance of the home office's Allowance for Over-valuation of Inventories: Marina Branch was $30,000 ($100,000 × 0.30). A single credit to the account, $90,000 ($300,000 × 0.30), was posted on August 25, Year 3. On August 31, Year 3, Marina Branch reported an ending inventory of $140,000 (at billed prices) of merchandise received from the home office. The ***adjusted balance*** of the home office's Allowance for Overvaluation of Inventories: Marina Branch, on August 31, Year 3, is:

a $42,000

b $78,000

c $120,000

d $140,000

e Some other amount

10　An Allowance for Overvaluation of Inventories: Branch ledger account is in-cluded in the accounting records of:

a The home office only

b The branch only

c Either, or both, the home office or/and the branch

d Neither the home office nor the branch

11　May transactions underlying journal entries to the home office ledger account Equipment: Branch be initiated by:

	The home office?	*The branch?*
a	*No*	*No*
b	*No*	*Yes*
c	*Yes*	*No*
d	*Yes*	*Yes*

12　The Investment in Branch ledger account of the home office of a business enterprise is:

a Displayed as an investment in the combined balance sheet of home office and branch

b A current asset account of the home office

c Debited when the branch acquires plant assets to be accounted for by the home office

d Eliminated in the preparation of combined financial statements for the home office and the branch

13   The typical balances in the reciprocal ledger accounts of the home office and a branch of a business enterprise are:

	Investment in Branch ledger account	Home Office ledger account
a	Debit	Debit
b	Debit	Credit
c	Credit	Debit
d	Credit	Credit

14   Excess freight costs incurred in a branch's shipment of home office–provided merchandise to another branch are recognized as an expense by the:

a Shipping branch

b Receiving branch

c Home office

d Shipping branch or receiving branch, as circumstances warrant

15   The purpose of the Allowance for Overvaluation of Inventories: Branch ledger account of the home office of a business enterprise is to:

a Reduce the carrying amount of the branch's inventories to home office cost

b Reduce the carrying amount of the home office's Investment in Branch ledger account to a cost basis with respect to shipments to branch

c Enable the home office to use the equity method of accounting for operating results of the branch

d Recognize the difference between the selling price and home office–billed price of home office–supplied merchandise sold by the branch

Ex. 4-2   On September 1, Year 4, Pasadena Company established a branch in San Marino. Following are the first three transactions between the home office and San Marino branch of Pasadena Company:

Sept. 1   Home office sent $10,000 to branch for an imprest bank account.

2   Home office shipped merchandise costing $60,000 to the branch, billed at a markup of 20% on billed price.

3   Branch acquired office equipment for $3,000, to be carried in home office accounting records.

Both the home office and the San Marino branch of Pasadena Company use the perpetual inventory system.

Prepare the journal entries (omit explanations) for the foregoing transactions:

a In the accounting records of the home office.

b In the accounting records of the San Marino branch.

Ex. 4-3   On September 1, Year 9, Western Company established the Eastern Branch. Separate accounting records were set up for the branch. Both the home office and the Eastern Branch use the periodic inventory system. Among the intracompany transactions were the following:

Sept. 1   Home office mailed a check for $50,000 to the branch. The check was received by the branch on September 3.

      4   Home office shipped merchandise costing $95,000 to the branch at a billed price of $125,000. The branch received the merchandise on September 8.

     11   The branch acquired a truck for $34,200. The home office maintains the plant assets of the branch in its accounting records.

   Prepare journal entries (omit explanations) for the foregoing intracompany transactions in the accounting records of (a) the home office and (b) the Eastern Branch.

Ex. 4-4   Among the journal entries of the home office of Watt Corporation for the month of January, Year 9, were the following:

Year 9

Jan. 2   Investment in Wilshire Branch   100,000
                Inventories   80,000
                Allowance for Overvaluation of Inventories: Wil-
                  shire Branch.   20,000
          To record merchandise shipped to branch.

     18   Equipment: Wilshire Branch   5,000
                Investment in Wilshire Branch   5,000
          To record acquisition of equipment by branch for cash.

     31   Investment in Wilshire Branch   8,000
                Operating Expenses.   8,000
          To record allocation of operating expenses to branch.

   Prepare related journal entries for the Wilshire Branch of Watt Corporation; the branch uses the perpetual inventory system.

Ex. 4-5   Among the journal entries for business transactions and events of the Hoover Street Branch of Usc Company during January, Year 3, were the following:

Year 3

Jan. 12   Inventories   60,000
                Home Office   60,000
          To record the receipt of merchandise shipped Jan. 10 from
          the home office and billed at a markup of 20% on billed
          price.

(continued)

25	Cash...	25,000	
	Home Office....................................		25,000
	To record collection of trade accounts receivable of home office.		

31	Operating expenses	18,000	
	Home Office....................................		18,000
	To record operating expenses allocated by home office.		

Prepare appropriate journal entries for the home office of Usc Company.

Ex. 4-6 Among the journal entries of the home office of Turbo Company for the month ended August 31, Year 5, were the following:

Aug. 6	Investment in Branch................................	10,000	
	Cash		10,000
	To record payment of trade account payable of branch.		

14	Cash	6,000	
	Investment in Branch...........................		6,000
	To record collection of trade account receivable of branch.		

22	Equipment: Branch..................................	20,000	
	Investment in Branch...........................		20,000
	To record branch acquisition of equipment for cash, to be carried in home office accounting records.		

Prepare appropriate journal entries (omit explanations) for the branch of Turbo Company.

Ex. 4-7 Prepare journal entries in the accounting records of the home office and the Exeter Branch of Wardell Company to record each of the following transactions or events (omit explanations):

a Home office transferred cash of $5,000 and merchandise (at home office cost) of $10,000 to the branch. Both the home office and the branch use the perpetual inventory system.

b Home office allocated operating expenses of $1,500 to the branch.

c Exeter Branch informed the home office that it had collected $416 on a note payable to the home office. Principal amount of the note was $400.

d Exeter Branch made sales of $12,500, terms 2/10, n/30, and incurred operating expenses of $2,500. The cost of goods sold was $8,000, and the operating expenses were paid in cash.

e Exeter Branch had a net income of $500. (Debit Income Summary in the accounting records of the branch.)

Ex. 4-8 Leland Company has a policy of accounting for all plant assets of its branches in the accounting records of the home office. Contrary to this policy, the accountant for Davis Branch prepared the following journal entries for the equipment acquired by the Davis Branch at the direction of the home office:

Year 3

Aug. 1 Equipment *20,000*
            Cash *20,000*
            To record acquisition of equipment with an economic life of
            10 years and a net residual value of $2,000.

Dec. 31 Depreciation Expense *750*
            Accumulated Depreciation of Equipment *750*
            To recognize depreciation of equipment by the straight-line
            method ($18,000 × ⁵⁄₁₂₀ = $750).

Prepare appropriate journal entries for the Davis Branch and the home office on December 31, Year 3, the end of the fiscal year, assuming that the home office had prepared no journal entries for the equipment acquired by the Davis Branch on August 1, Year 3. Neither set of accounting records has been closed.

Ex. 4-9   The home office of Figueroa Company ships merchandise to the Nine-Zero Branch at a billed price that includes a markup on home office cost of 25%. The Inventories ledger account of the branch, under the perpetual inventory system, showed a December 31, Year 1, debit balance, $120,000; a debit for a shipment received January 16, Year 2, $500,000; total credits for goods sold during January, Year 2, $520,000; and a January 31, Year 2, debit balance, $100,000 (all amounts are home office billed prices).

Prepare a working paper for the home office of Figueroa Company to analyze the flow of merchandise to Nine-Zero Branch during January, Year 2.

Ex. 4-10   The flow of merchandise from the home office of Southern Cal Company to its 32 Branch during the month of April, Year 9, may be analyzed as follows:

SOUTHERN CAL COMPANY
Flow of Merchandise for 32 Branch
For Month Ended April 30, Year 9

	Billed price	*Cost*	*Markup*
Beginning inventories....................	$180,000	$150,000	$ 30,000
Add: Shipment from home office (Apr. 16) ..	540,000	450,000	90,000
Available for sale......................	$720,000	$600,000	$120,000
Less: Ending inventories	120,000	100,000	20,000
Cost of goods sold	$600,000	$500,000	$100,000

From the foregoing information, reconstruct a three-column ledger account Allowance for Overvaluation of Inventories: 32 Branch for the home office of Southern Cal Company, beginning with the March 31, Year 9, balance, $30,000 credit.

Ex. 4-11   On May 31, Year 8, the Portland Street Branch (the only branch) of Trapp Company reported a net income of $80,000 for May, Year 8, and a $240,000 ending inventory at billed price of merchandise received from the home office at a 25% markup on billed price. Prior to adjustment, the May 31, Year 8, balance of the home office's Allowance for Overvaluation of Inventories: Portland Street Branch was $200,000 credit.

Prepare journal entries (omit explanations) on May 31, Year 8, for the home office of Trapp Company to reflect the foregoing facts.

Ex. 4-12 Tillman Textile Company has a single branch in Toledo. On March 1, Year 1, the home office accounting records included an Allowance for Overvaluation of Inventories: Toledo Branch ledger account with a credit balance of $32,000. During March, merchandise costing $36,000 was shipped to the Toledo Branch and billed at a price representing a 40% markup on the billed price. On March 31, the branch prepared an income statement indicating a net loss of $11,500 for March and ending inventories at billed prices of $25,000.

    a Prepare a working paper to compute the home office cost of the branch inventories on March 1, assuming a uniform markup on all shipments to the branch.

    b Prepare a journal entry to adjust the Allowance for Overvaluation of Inventories: Toledo Branch ledger account on March 31 in the accounting records of the home office.

Ex. 4-13 The home office of Glendale Company, which uses the perpetual inventory system, bills shipments of merchandise to the Montrose Branch at a markup of 25% on the billed price. On August 31, Year 5, the credit balance of the home office's Allowance for Overvaluation of Inventories: Montrose Branch ledger account was $60,000. On September 17, Year 5, the home office shipped merchandise to the branch at a billed price of $400,000. The branch reported an ending inventory, at billed price, of $160,000 on September 30, Year 5.

Prepare journal entries involving the Allowance for Overvaluation of Inventories: Montrose Branch ledger account of the home office of Glendale Company on September 17 and 30, Year 5. Show supporting computations in the explanations for the entries.

Ex. 4-14 On January 31, Year 6, the unadjusted credit balance of the Allowance for Overvaluation of Inventories: Vermont Avenue Branch of the home office of Searl Company was $80,000. The branch reported a net income of $60,000 for January, Year 6, and an ending inventory on January 31, Year 6, of $81,000, at billed prices that included a markup on home office cost of 50%.

Prepare journal entries (omit explanations) for the home office of Searl Company on January 31, Year 6, for the foregoing facts.

Ex. 4-15 The home office of Gomez Company bills its only branch at a markup of 25% above home office cost for all merchandise shipped to that Perez Branch. Both the home office and the branch use the periodic inventory system. During Year 5, the home office shipped merchandise to the branch at a billed price of $30,000. Perez Branch inventories for Year 5 were as follows:

	Jan. 1	Dec. 31
Purchased from home office (at billed price)	$15,000	$19,500
Purchased from outsiders.	6,800	8,670

Prepare journal entries (including adjusting entry) for the home office of Gomez Company for Year 5 to reflect the foregoing information.

Ex. 4-16 Samore, Inc., bills its only branch for merchandise shipments at a markup of 30% above home office cost. The branch sells the merchandise at a markup of 10% above billed price. Shortly after the close of business on January 28, Year 7, some of the branch merchandise was destroyed by fire. The following additional information is available:

Inventories, Jan. 1 (at billed prices from home office)......................	$15,600
Inventories, Jan. 28, of merchandise not destroyed (at selling prices)	7,150
Shipments from home office from Jan. 1 to Jan. 28 (at billed prices)	71,500
Sales from Jan. 1 to Jan. 28..	51,840
Sales returns from Jan. 1 to Jan. 28 (merchandise actually returned)	3,220
Sales allowances from Jan. 1 to Jan. 28 (price adjustments)	300

a Prepare a working paper to compute the estimated cost (to the home office) of the merchandise destroyed by fire at the branch of Samore, Inc., on January 28, Year 7.

b Prepare a journal entry for the branch to recognize the uninsured fire loss on January 28, Year 7. Both the home office and the branch use the perpetual inventory system.

Ex. 4-17 On May 31, Year 6, the unadjusted balances of the Investment in Troy Branch ledger account of the home office of Argos Company and the Home Office account of the Troy Branch of Argos Company were $380,000 debit and $140,000 credit, respectively.

Additional Information

(1) On May 31, Year 6, the home office had shipped merchandise to the branch at a billed price of $280,000; the branch did not receive the shipment until June 3. Both the home office and the branch use the perpetual inventory system.

(2) On May 31, Year 6, the branch had sent a $10,000 "dividend" to the home office, which did not receive the check until June 2.

(3) On May 31, Year 6, the home office had prepared the following journal entry, without notifying the branch:

Cash	50,000	
Investment in Troy Branch		50,000
To record collection of a trade accounts receivable of branch.		

Prepare journal entries (omit explanations) on May 31, Year 6, for (**a**) the home office and (**b**) the Troy Branch of Argos Company to reconcile the reciprocal ledger accounts.

CASES

Case 4-1 The management of Longo Company, which has a June 30 fiscal year and sells merchandise at its home office and six branches, is considering closing Santee Branch because of its declining sales volume and excessive operating expenses. Longo's contract with Lewis Hanson, manager of Santee Branch, provides that Hanson is to receive a termination bonus of 15% of the branch's net income in its final period of operations, but no bonus in the event of a net loss in the final period. The contract is silent as to the measurement of the branch's net income or loss.

For the period July 1 through October 31, Year 5, the date Santee Branch ceased operations, its income statement prepared in the customary fashion by the branch accountant reported a net loss of $10,000. Hanson pointed out to Longo management that the loss was net of $30,000 advertising expenses that had been apportioned to the branch by Longo's home office in September, Year 5, prior to Longo management's decision to close the branch on October 31. Hanson alleged that it was inappropriate for the branch to absorb advertising costs for a period in which it would no longer be making sales presumably initiated in part by the advertising. The controller of Longo responded that under the same line of reasoning, the branch's October 31, Year 5, inventories, which included a $60,000 markup over home office cost, should be reduced by that amount, with a corresponding increase in the branch's net loss, because the home office would never realize the markup through future sales by Santee Branch.

Instructions

Do you agree with the Santee Branch manager, with the controller of Longo Company, with both, or with neither? Explain.

Case 4-2   Fortunato Company, which had operated successfully in a single location for many years, opened a branch operation in another city. The products sold by Fortunato in its home office required federal and state regulatory agency approval; the home office had secured such approval long ago. However, new approval of those agencies was required before Fortunato was authorized to produce and sell the same products at the new branch.

After the branch had been established and had begun testing its manufacturing equipment and considering development of possible new products other than those manufactured by the home office, management of Fortunato met to discuss accounting for start-up costs of the new branch prior to its authorization to manufacture and sell products. Controller Robert Engle pointed out that when the home office had been established, it was a ***development stage enterprise*** prior to obtaining approval for production and sale of its products, with specialized financial statements display requirements provided by ***FASB Statement No. 7,*** "Accounting and Reporting by Development Stage Enterprises." Engle added that Fortunato, as currently an operating enterprise, was not authorized to use such specialized requirements for the new branch. The vice president for legal affairs, Nancy Kubota, stated that the current regulatory agency environment was much stricter than it had been when Fortunato's home office obtained authorization for its production and sales, and that a several-month waiting period might be anticipated before approval of the branch's operations. Pending such approval, the branch could not legally even manufacture products for stockpiling in inventories.

Chief executive officer Michael Kantor expressed dismay at the prospect described by Kubota, stating that a long period of "marking time" at the branch, with no revenue available to cover operating costs, would generate substantial losses for Fortunato as a whole unless the costs could be deferred as start-up costs. Financial vice president Mary Sage asked Engle if there were any published financial accounting standards for start-up costs. Engle replied in the negative; the Financial Accounting Standards Board, in issuing ***Statement No. 7,*** specifically declined to establish accounting standards for start-up costs of operating (as opposed to development stage) enterprises. Sage asked Engle if he was aware of any business enterprises that deferred start-up costs of new branches. Engle responded that enterprises that did so typically had many branches and short start-up periods. Engle pointed out that given the uncertain regulatory agency climate, there was no assurance that Fortunato's branch *definitely* would obtain approval of its operations and thus that the branch's start-up costs would be *contingent assets* at best.

Instructions

Do generally accepted accounting principles sanction Fortunato Company's deferral of start-up costs of the new branch, for amortization as expenses once the branch receives regulatory agency approval for manufacturing and selling its products? Explain, giving consideration to the accepted definitions of *assets, contingent assets, expenses, losses,* and *research and development costs.*

Case 4-3   Kevin Carter, CPA, a member of the IMA, the FEI, and the AICPA (see Chapter 1), is the newly hired controller of Oilers, Inc., a closely held manufacturer of replacement parts for oil well drilling equipment. Oilers distributes its products through its home office and 14 branches located near oil fields in several southwestern states. Shortly after being employed, Carter learned that the reciprocal ledger accounts at Oilers' home office and 14 branches were out of balance by substantial amounts and that no member of the home office accounting department could remember when— if ever—the reciprocal ledger accounts had been in balance. In response to Carter's astonished inquiries, the home office chief accountant stated that:

(1) Oilers, Inc., had never been audited by independent CPAs, and it had no internal audit staff.
(2) Management of Oilers, in reviewing financial statements of the 14 branches, concentrated on branch income statements and were unconcerned about the out-of-balance status of the branches' Home Office ledger accounts.
(3) To facilitate elimination of the reciprocal ledger account balances in the working paper for combined financial statements of the home office and 14 branches of Oilers, the chief accountant debited Miscellaneous Expense or credited Miscellaneous Revenue for the aggregate amount of the unlocated differences. These "plug" amounts were reported in the federal and state income tax returns filed by Oilers.

Instructions

What is your advice to Kevin Carter? Should he permit the practice described above to continue? If not, should he request management of Oilers to contract for an independent audit? Alternatively, should he authorize the accountant at each of the 14 branches to adjust the branch's Home Office ledger account balance to agree with the home office's reciprocal Investment in Branch account balance, with the unlocated difference debited to Miscellaneous Expense or credited to Miscellaneous Revenue, as appropriate? Should some other course of action be taken? Explain.

Case 4-4   Langley, Inc., operates a number of branches as well as a home office. Each branch stocks a complete line of merchandise obtained almost entirely from the home office.

The branches also handle their billing, approve customer credit, and make cash collections. Each branch has its own bank account, and each maintains accounting records. However, all plant assets at the branches are carried in the accounting records of the home office and are depreciated by the straight-line method at 10% a year, with no residual value. Depreciation expense is not recognized in the branch accounting records.

On July 1, Year 1, the manager of Lola Branch acquired office equipment. The equipment had a cash price of $2,400 but was acquired on the installment plan with no down payment and 24 monthly payments of $110 beginning August 1, Year 1. No journal entry was made for this transaction by the branch until August 1, when the first monthly payment was recorded by a debit to Miscellaneous Expense. The same journal entry was made in each of the four remaining months of Year 1.

On December 2, the branch manager became aware that equipment could be acquired by the branches only with prior approval by the home office. Regardless of whether the home office or the branches acquired plant assets, such assets were to be carried in the accounting records of the home office, but any gain or loss on the disposal of equipment was to be recognized in the accounting records of the branches. To avoid criticism, the manager of the Lola Branch immediately disposed of the office equipment acquired July 1 by sale for $1,500 cash to an independent store. The manager then paid the balance due on the installment contract using a personal check and the $1,500 check received from sale of the equipment. In consideration of the advance payment of the remaining installments on December 3, the equipment dealer agreed to a $150 reduction in the $240 interest portion of the contract. No journal entry was prepared for the sale of the equipment or the settlement of the liability.

Assume that you are a CPA engaged to audit the financial statements of Langley, Inc. During your visit to the Lola Branch you analyze the Miscellaneous Expense ledger account and investigate the five monthly debits of $110. This investigation discloses the acquisition and subsequent disposal of the office equipment. After some hesitation, the branch manager gives you a full explanation of the events.

Instructions

a Describe (do not prepare) the journal entries that should have been made by Lola Branch for the foregoing transactions and events.

b Describe (do not prepare) the journal entries that should have been made by the home office of Langley, Inc., for the foregoing transactions and events.

c Prepare a single journal entry for Lola Branch to correct its account records.

d Prepare a single journal entry for the home office of Langley, Inc., to correct its accounting records.

PROBLEMS

Pr. 4-1 Hartman, Inc., established the Reno Branch on January 2, Year 3. During the first year of operations, Hartman's home office shipped merchandise to the Reno Branch that cost $300,000. Billings were made at prices marked up 20% above home office cost. Freight costs of $15,000 were paid by the home office. Sales by the branch were $450,000, and branch operating expenses were $96,000, all for cash. On December

31, Year 3, the branch took a physical inventory that showed merchandise on hand of $72,000 at billed prices. Both the home office and the branch use the periodic inventory system.

Instructions

Prepare journal entries for the Reno Branch and the home office of Hartman, Inc., to record the foregoing transactions and events, ending inventories, and adjusting and closing entries on December 31, Year 3. (Allocate a proportional amount of freight costs to the ending inventories of the branch.)

Pr. 4-2   Included in the accounting records of the home office and Wade Branch, respectively, of Lobo Company were the following ledger accounts for the month of January, Year 5:

Investment in Wade Branch (in home office accounting records)

Date	Explanation	Debit	Credit	Balance
Year 5				
Jan. 1	Balance			39,200 dr
9	Shipment of merchandise	4,000		43,200 dr
21	Receipt of cash		1,600	41,600 dr
27	Collection of branch trade accounts receivable		1,100	40,500 dr
31	Shipment of merchandise	6,000		46,500 dr
31	Payment of branch trade accounts payable	2,000		48,500 dr

Home Office (in Wade Branch accounting records)

Date	Explanation	Debit	Credit	Balance
Year 5				
Jan. 1	Balance			39,200 cr
10	Receipt of merchandise		4,000	43,200 cr
19	Remittance of cash	1,600		41,600 cr
28	Acquisition of furniture	1,200		40,400 cr
30	Return of merchandise	2,200		38,200 cr
31	Remittance of cash	2,500		35,700 cr

Instructions

a Prepare a working paper to reconcile the reciprocal ledger accounts of Lobo Company's home office and Wade Branch to the corrected balances on January 31, Year 5.

b Prepare journal entries on January 31, Year 5, for the (1) home office and (2) Wade Branch of Lobo Company to bring the accounting records up to date. Both the home office and the branch use the perpetual inventory system.

Pr. 4-3   The home office of Styler Corporation operates a branch to which it bills merchandise at prices marked up 20% above home office cost. The branch obtains merchandise only from the home office and sells it at prices averaging markups 10% above the prices billed by the home office. Both the home office and the branch maintain perpetual inventory records and both close their accounting records on December 31.

On March 10, Year 9, a fire at the branch destroyed a part of the inventories. Immediately after the fire, a physical inventory of merchandise on hand and not damaged amounted to $16,500 at retail selling prices. On January 1, Year 9, the inventories of the branch at billed prices had been $18,000. Shipments from the home office during the period January 1 to March 10 were billed to the branch in the amount of $57,600. The accounting records of the branch show that net sales during this period were $44,880.

Instructions

Prepare journal entries on March 10, Year 9, to record the uninsured loss from fire in the accounting records of (**a**) the branch and (**b**) the home office of Styler Company. Show supporting computations for all amounts. Assume that the loss was reported at billed prices by the branch to the home office and that it was recorded in the intra-company reciprocal ledger accounts.

Pr. 4-4 On December 31, Year 10, the Investment in Branch Q ledger account in the accounting records of the home office of Yugo Company shows a debit balance of $55,500. You ascertain the following facts in analyzing this account:

(1) On December 31, Year 10, merchandise billed at $5,800 was in transit from the home office to the branch. The periodic inventory system is used by both the home office and the branch.

(2) The branch had collected home office trade accounts receivable of $560; the home office was not notified.

(3) On December 29, Year 10, the home office had mailed a check for $2,000 to the branch, but the accountant for the home office had recorded the check as a debit to the Charitable Contributions ledger account; the branch had not received the check as of December 31, Year 10.

(4) Branch net income for December, Year 10, was recorded erroneously by the home office at $840 instead of $480. The credit was recorded by the home office in the Income: Branch Q ledger account.

(5) On December 28, Year 10, the branch had returned supplies costing $220 to the home office; the home office had not recorded the receipt of the supplies. The home office records acquisitions of supplies in the Inventory of Supplies ledger account.

Instructions

a Assuming that all other transactions and events have been recorded properly, prepare a working paper to compute the unadjusted balance of the Home Office ledger account in the accounting records of Yugo Company's Branch Q on December 31, Year 10.

b Prepare journal entries for the home office of Yugo Company on December 31, Year 10, to bring its accounting records up to date. Closing entries have not been made.

c Prepare journal entries for Branch Q of Yugo Company on December 31, Year 10, to bring its accounting records up to date.

d Prepare a reconciliation on December 31, Year 10, of the Investment in Branch Q ledger account in the accounting records of the home office and the Home Office account in the accounting records of Branch Q of Yugo Company. Use a single column for each account and start with the unadjusted balances.

Pr. 4-5 Trudie Company's home office bills shipments of merchandise to its Savoy Branch at 140% of home office cost. During the first year after the branch was opened, the following were among the transactions and events completed:

(1) The home office shipped merchandise with a home office cost of $110,000 to Savoy Branch.
(2) Savoy Branch sold for $80,000 cash merchandise that was billed by the home office at $70,000, and incurred operating expenses of $16,500 (all paid in cash).
(3) The physical inventories taken by Savoy Branch at the end of the first year were $82,460 at billed prices from the home office.

Instructions

a Assuming that the perpetual inventory system is used both by the home office and by Savoy Branch, prepare for the first year:
  (1) All journal entries, including closing entries, in the accounting records of Savoy Branch of Trudie Company
  (2) All journal entries, including the adjustment of the inventories overvaluation account, in the accounting records of the home office of Trudie Company

b Assuming that the periodic inventory system is used both by the home office and by Savoy Branch, prepare for the first year:
  (1) All journal entries, including the closing entry, in the accounting records of Savoy Branch of Trudie Company
  (2) All journal entries, including the adjustment of the inventories overvaluation account, in the accounting records of the home office of Trudie Company

Pr. 4-6 You are making an audit for the year ended December 31, Year 1, of the financial statements of Kosti-Marian Company, which carries on merchandising operations at both a home office and a branch. The unadjusted trial balances of the home office and the branch are shown below and on page 173.

KOSTI-MARIAN COMPANY
Unadjusted Trial Balances
December 31, Year 1

	Home office Dr (Cr)	Branch Dr (Cr)
Cash	$ 22,000	$ 10,175
Inventories, Jan. 1, Year 1	23,000	11,550
Investment in branch	60,000	
Allowance for overvaluation of branch inventories, Jan. 1, Year 1	(1,000)	
Other assets (net).	197,000	48,450

(continued)

KOSTI-MARIAN COMPANY
Unadjusted Trial Balances (concluded)
December 31, Year 1

	Home office Dr (Cr)	Branch Dr (Cr)
Current liabilities	(35,000)	(8,500)
Common stock, $2.50 par	(200,000)	
Retained earnings, Jan. 1, Year 1	(34,000)	
Dividends declared.	15,000	
Home office		(51,000)
Sales.	(169,000)	(144,700)
Purchases	190,000	
Shipments to branch	(110,000)	
Shipments from home office		104,500
Freight-in from home office		5,225
Operating expenses.	42,000	24,300
Totals	$ -0-	$ -0-

The audit for the year ended December 31, Year 1, disclosed the following:

(1) The branch deposits all cash receipts in a local bank for the account of the home office. The audit working papers for the cash cutoff include the following:

Amount	Date deposited by branch	Date recorded by home office
$1,050	Dec. 27, Year 1	Dec. 31, Year 1
1,100	Dec. 30, Year 1	Not recorded
600	Dec. 31, Year 1	Not recorded
300	Jan. 2, Year 2	Not recorded

(2) The branch pays operating expenses incurred locally from an imprest cash account that is maintained with a balance of $2,000. Checks are drawn once a week on the imprest cash account, and the home office is notified of the amount needed to replenish the account. On December 31, Year 1, an $1,800 reimbursement check was in transit from the home office to the branch.

(3) The branch receives all its merchandise from the home office. The home office bills the merchandise shipments at a markup of 10% above home office cost. On December 31, Year 1, a shipment with a billed price of $5,500 was in transit to the branch. Freight costs of common carriers typically are 5% of billed price. Freight costs are considered to be inventoriable costs. Both the home office and the branch use the periodic inventory system.

(4) Beginning inventories in the trial balance are shown at the respective costs to the home office and to the branch. The physical inventories on December 31, Year 1, were as follows:

Home office, at cost	$30,000
Branch, at billed price (excluding shipment in transit and freight)	9,900

Instructions

a Prepare journal entries to adjust the accounting records of the home office of Kosti-Marian Company on December 31, Year 1.

b Prepare journal entries to adjust the accounting records of Kosti-Marian Company's branch on December 31, Year 1.

c Prepare a working paper for combined financial statements of Kosti-Marian Company (use the format on pages 151–152). Compute the amounts in the adjusted trial balances for the home office and the branch by incorporating the journal entries in **a** and **b** with the amounts in the unadjusted trial balances.

Pr. 4-7 On January 4, Year 5, Solis Company opened its first branch, with instructions to Steven Carr, the branch manager, to perform the functions of granting credit, billing customers, accounting for receivables, and making cash collections. The branch paid its operating expenses by checks drawn on its bank account. The branch obtained merchandise solely from the home office; billings for these shipments *were at cost to the home office.* The adjusted trial balances for the home office and the branch on December 31, Year 5, were as follows:

SOLIS COMPANY
Adjusted Trial Balances
December 31, Year 5

	Home office Dr (Cr)	Branch Dr (Cr)
Cash	$ 46,000	$ 14,600
Notes receivable	7,000	
Trade accounts receivable (net)	80,400	37,300
Inventories	95,800	24,200
Investment in branch	82,700	
Furniture and equipment (net)	48,100	
Trade accounts payable	(41,000)	
Common stock, $2 par	(200,000)	
Retained earnings, Dec. 31, Year 4	(25,000)	
Dividends declared	30,000	
Home office		(82,700)
Sales	(394,000)	(101,100)
Cost of goods sold	200,500	85,800
Operating expenses	69,500	21,900
Totals	$ -0-	$ -0-

The physical inventories on December 31, Year 5, were in agreement with the perpetual inventory records of the home office and the branch.

Instructions

a Prepare a four-column working paper for combined financial statements of the home office and branch of Solis Company for the year ended December 31, Year 5.

b Prepare closing entries on December 31, Year 5, in the accounting records of the branch of Solis Company.

c Prepare adjusting and closing entries pertaining to branch operations on December 31, Year 5, in the accounting records of the home office of Solis Company.

Pr. 4-8 The unadjusted general ledger trial balances on December 31, Year 3, for Calco Corporation's home office and its only branch are shown below:

CALCO CORPORATION
Unadjusted Trial Balances
December 31, Year 3

	Home office Dr (Cr)	Branch Dr (Cr)
Cash	$ 28,000	$ 23,000
Trade accounts receivable (net)	35,000	12,000
Inventories, Jan. 1, Year 3 (at cost to home office)	70,000	15,000
Investment in branch	30,000	
Equipment (net)	90,000	
Trade accounts payable	(46,000)	(13,500)
Accrued liabilities	(14,000)	(2,500)
Home office		(19,000)
Common stock, $10 par	(50,000)	
Retained earnings, Jan. 1, Year 3	(48,000)	
Dividends declared...................................	10,000	
Sales...	(450,000)	(100,000)
Purchases	290,000	24,000
Shipments from home office		45,000
Operating expenses...................................	55,000	16,000
Totals	$ -0-	$ -0-

Your audit disclosed the following:

(1) On December 10, Year 3, the branch manager acquired equipment for $500, but failed to notify the home office. The branch accountant, knowing that branch equipment is carried in the home office ledger, recorded the proper journal entry in the branch accounting records. It is Calco's policy not to recognize depreciation on equipment acquired in the last half of a year.

(2) On December 27, Year 3, Mojo, Inc., a customer of the branch, erroneously paid its account of $2,000 to the home office. The accountant made the correct journal entry in the home office accounting records but did not notify the branch.

(3) On December 30, Year 3, the branch remitted cash of $5,000, which had not been received by the home office as of December 31, Year 3.

(4) On December 31, Year 3, the branch erroneously recorded the December allocated expenses from the home office as $500 instead of $5,000.

(5) On December 31, Year 3, the home office shipped merchandise billed at $3,000 to the branch; the shipment had not been received by the branch as of December 31, Year 3.

(6) The inventories on December 31, Year 3, excluding the shipment in transit,

were: home office—$60,000 (at cost); branch—$20,000 (consisting of $18,000 from home office at billed prices and $2,000 from suppliers). Both the home office and the branch use the periodic inventory system.

(7) The home office erroneously billed shipments to the branch at a markup of 20% above home office cost, although the billing should have been at cost. The Sales ledger account was credited for the invoices' price by the home office.

Instructions

a Prepare journal entries for the home office of Calco Corporation on December 31, Year 3, to bring the accounting records up to date and to correct any errors. Record ending inventories by an offsetting credit to the Income Summary ledger account. Do not prepare other closing entries.

b Prepare journal entries for the branch of Calco Corporation on December 31, Year 3, to bring the accounting records up to date and to correct any errors. Record ending inventories at cost to the home office by an offsetting credit to the Income Summary ledger account. Do not prepare other closing entries.

c Prepare a working paper to summarize the operations of Calco Corporation for the year ended December 31, Year 3. Disregard income taxes and use the following column headings:

Revenue and expenses	Home office	Branch	Combined

Pr. 4-9   The reciprocal ledger accounts below and on page 177 were included in the accounting records of the home office and the Lee Branch of Kreshek Company on April 30, Year 2.

Investment in Lee Branch

Date	Explanation	Debit	Credit	Balance
Year 2				
Feb. 1	Balance			124,630 dr
6	Shipment of merchandise, 160 units @ $49	7,840		132,470 dr
17	Note receivable collected by branch	2,500		134,970 dr
Mar. 31	Cash deposited by branch		2,000	132,970 dr
Apr. 2	Merchandise returned by branch		450	132,520 dr
26	Loss on disposal of branch equipment	780		133,300 dr
28	Operating expenses charged to branch	1,200		134,500 dr
29	Corrected loss on disposal of branch equipment from $780 to $250		530	133,970 dr

Home Office

Date	Explanation	Debit	Credit	Balance
Year 2				
Feb. 1	Balance			124,630 cr
8	Merchandise from home office, 160 units @ $49		7,480	132,110 cr
14	Received shipment directly from supplier, invoice to be paid by home office		2,750	134,860 cr
15	Note receivable collected for home office		2,500	137,360 cr
Mar. 30	Deposited cash in account of home office	2,000		135,360 cr
31	Returned merchandise to home office	450		134,910 cr
Apr. 29	Paid repair bill for home office	375		134,535 cr
30	Excess merchandise returned to home office (billed at cost)	5,205		129,330 cr
30	Preliminary net income for quarter (before any required corrections)		13,710	143,040 cr

You have been retained by Kreshek to assist it with some accounting work preliminary to the preparation of financial statements for the quarter ended April 30, Year 2.

Additional Information

(1) Branch equipment is carried in the accounting records of the home office; the home office notifies the branch periodically as to the amount of depreciation applicable to equipment used by the branch. Gains or losses on disposal of branch equipment are reported to the branch and included in the income statement of the branch.

(2) Because of the error in recording the shipment from the home office on February 8, Year 2, the sale of the 160 units has been debited improperly by the branch to cost of goods sold at $46.75 a unit.

(3) On April 30, Year 2, the branch collected trade accounts receivable of $350 belonging to the home office, but the branch employee who recorded the collection mistakenly treated the trade accounts receivable as belonging to the branch.

(4) The branch recorded the preliminary net income of $13,710 by a debit to Income Summary and a credit to Home Office, although the revenue and expense ledger accounts had not been closed.

Instructions

a Reconcile the reciprocal ledger accounts of the home office and Lee Branch of Kreshek Company to the correct balances on April 30, Year 2. Use a four-column working paper (debit and credit columns for the Investment in Lee Branch account

in the home office accounting records and debit and credit columns for the Home
Office account in the branch accounting records). Start with the unadjusted balances on April 30, Year 2, and work to corrected balances, including explanations
of all adjusting or correcting items.

b Prepare journal entries for the Lee Branch of Kreshek Company on April 30, Year
2, to bring its accounting records up to date, assuming that corrections still may be
made to revenue and expense ledger accounts. The branch uses the perpetual
inventory system. Do not prepare closing entries.

c Prepare journal entries for the home office of Kreshek Company on April 30, Year
2, to bring its accounting records up to date. The home office uses the perpetual
inventory system and has not prepared closing entries. Do not prepare closing
entries.

Pr. 4-10　　Casden's, a single proprietorship owned by Alan Casden, sells merchandise at both
its home office and a branch. The home office bills merchandise shipped to the
branch at 125% of home office cost, and is the only supplier for the branch. Shipments of merchandise to the branch have been recorded improperly by the home
office by credits to Sales for the billed price. Both the home office and the branch use
the perpetual inventory system.

Casden's has engaged you to audit its financial statements for the year ended
December 31, Year 5. This is the first time the proprietorship has retained an independent accountant. You were provided with the following unadjusted trial balances:

CASDEN'S
Unadjusted Trial Balances
December 31, Year 5

	Home office Dr (Cr)	Branch Dr (Cr)
Cash	$ 31,000	$ 13,000
Trade accounts receivable (net)	20,000	22,000
Inventories...	40,000	8,000
Investment in branch..................................	45,000	
Equipment (net)	150,000	
Trade accounts payable	(23,000)	
Accrued liabilities		(2,000)
Note payable, due Year 8..............................	(51,000)	
Alan Casden, capital, Jan. 1, Year 5	(192,000)	
Alan Casden, drawing..................................	50,000	
Home office		(10,000)
Sales...	(390,000)	(160,000)
Cost of goods sold....................................	250,000	93,000
Operating expenses....................................	70,000	36,000
Totals	$ -0-	$ -0-

Additional Information

(1) On January 1, Year 5, inventories of the home office amounted to $25,000 and
inventories of the branch amounted to $6,000. During Year 5, the branch was
billed for $105,000 for shipments from the home office.

(2) On December 28, Year 5, the home office billed the branch for $12,000, representing the branch's share of operating expenses paid by the home office. This billing had not been recorded by the branch.

(3) All cash collections made by the branch were deposited in a local bank to the bank account of the home office. Deposits of this nature included the following:

Amount	Date deposited by branch	Date recorded by home office
$5,000	Dec. 28, Year 5	Dec. 31, Year 5
3,000	Dec. 30, Year 5	Not recorded
7,000	Dec. 31, Year 5	Not recorded
2,000	Jan. 2, Year 6	Not recorded

(4) Operating expenses incurred by the branch were paid from an imprest bank account that was reimbursed periodically by the home office. On December 30, Year 5, the home office had mailed a reimbursement check in the amount of $3,000, which had not been received by the branch as of December 31, Year 5.

(5) A shipment of merchandise from the home office to the branch was in transit on December 31, Year 5.

Instructions

a Prepare journal entries to adjust the accounting records of Casden's home office on December 31, Year 5. Establish an allowance for overvaluation of branch inventories.

b Prepare journal entries to adjust the accounting records of Casden's branch on December 31, Year 5.

c Prepare a working paper for combined financial statements of Casden's on December 31, Year 5 (use the format on page 145). Compute the amounts for the adjusted trial balances for the home office and the branch by incorporating the journal entries in **a** and **b** with the amounts in the unadjusted trial balances.

d After the working paper in **c** is completed, prepare all required adjusting and closing entries on December 31, Year 5, in the accounting records of Casden's home office.

Part 2

Business Combinations and Consolidated Financial Statements

Business combinations have been a hallmark of the U.S. economy for many years. Statutory mergers, statutory consolidations, acquisitions of assets, and acquisitions of common stock result in a single economic and accounting entity in place of the two or more predecessor entities. Each of the two methods of accounting for business combinations—purchase and pooling of interests—has shortcomings that are not easily resolved.

The preparation of consolidated financial statements for a parent company and its subsidiaries involves many complexities. The treatment of goodwill, the computation and financial statement classification of minority interest, and the elimination of intercompany profits (gains) or losses are among the issues that must be resolved if consolidated statements are to achieve the objective of representational faithfulness.

5

Business Combinations

Business combinations are events or transactions in which two or more business enterprises, or their net assets, are brought under common control in a single accounting entity. Other terms frequently applied to business combinations are **mergers** and **acquisitions.**

The Financial Accounting Standards Board has suggested the following definitions for terms commonly used in discussions of business combinations:[1]

1   **Combined enterprise**   The accounting entity that results from a business combination

2   **Constituent companies**   The business enterprises that enter into a business combination

3   **Combinor**   A constituent company entering into a business combination whose owners as a group end up with control of the ownership interests in the combined enterprise

4   **Combinee**   A constituent company other than the combinor in a business combination

Business combinations may be divided into two classes—friendly takeovers and unfriendly takeovers. In a **friendly takeover,** the boards of directors of the constituent companies generally work out the terms of the business combination amicably and submit the proposal to stockholders of all constituent companies for approval. A target combinee in an **unfriendly takeover** typically resists the proposed business combination by resorting to one or more defensive tactics with the following colorful designations:

1   **Pac-man defense**   A threat to undertake an unfriendly takeover of the prospective combinor

---

[1] *FASB Discussion Memorandum,* ''An Analysis of Issues Related to Accounting for Business Combinations and Purchased Intangibles,'' FASB (Stamford: 1976), p. 3.

2   *White knight* A search for a candidate to be the combinor in a friendly takeover

3   *Scorched earth* The disposal, by sale or by a spin-off to stockholders, of one or more profitable business segments

4   *Shark repellent* An acquisition of substantial amounts of outstanding common stock for the treasury or for retirement, or the incurring of substantial long-term debt in exchange for outstanding common stock

5   *Poison pill* An amendment of the articles of incorporation or bylaws to make it more difficult to obtain stockholder approval for a takeover

6   *Greenmail* An acquisition of common stock presently owned by the prospective combinor at a price substantially in excess of the prospective combinor's cost, with the stock thus acquired placed in the treasury or retired

In the first section of this chapter I discuss reasons for the popularity of business combinations and techniques for arranging them. Then, the two methods of accounting for business combinations, that is, *purchase* and *pooling of interests,* are explained and illustrated. In the final section I evaluate the propriety of purchase accounting and pooling-of-interests accounting.

BUSINESS COMBINATIONS: WHY AND HOW?

Why do business enterprises enter into a business combination? Although a number of reasons have been cited, probably the overriding one for *combinors* in recent years has been *growth.* Business enterprises have major operating objectives other than growth, but that goal increasingly has motivated combinor managements to undertake business combinations. Advocates of this *external* method of achieving growth point out that it is much more rapid than growth through *internal* means. There is no question that expansion and diversification of product lines, or enlarging the market share for current products, is achieved readily through a business combination with another enterprise. However, the disappointing experiences of many combinors engaging in business combinations suggest that much may be said in favor of more gradual and reasoned growth through internal means, using available management and financial resources.

Other reasons often advanced in support of business combinations are obtaining new management strength or better use of existing management and achieving manufacturing or other operating economies. In addition, a business combination may be undertaken for the income tax advantages available to one or more parties to the combination.

Critics have alleged that the foregoing reasons attributed to the ''urge to merge'' (business combinations) do not apply to unfriendly takeovers. These critics complain that the ''sharks'' who engage in unfriendly takeovers, and the investment bankers and attorneys who counsel them, are motivated by the prospect of substantial gains resulting from the sale of business segments of a combinee following the business combination.

Antitrust Considerations

One obstacle faced by large corporations that undertake business combinations is the possibility of antitrust litigation. The U.S. government on occasion has opposed concentration of economic power in large business enterprises. Consequently, business combinations frequently have been challenged by the Federal Trade Commission or the Antitrust Division of the Department of Justice, under the provisions of Section 7 of the Clayton Act, which reads in part as follows:

> . . . no corporation engaged in commerce shall acquire, directly or indirectly, the whole or any part of the stock or other share capital and no corporation subject to the jurisdiction of the Federal Trade Commission shall acquire the whole or any part of the assets of another corporation engaged also in commerce, where in any line of commerce in any section of the country the effect of such acquisition may be substantially to lessen competition or to tend to create a monopoly.

The breadth of the preceding legislation has led to federal antitrust action against all types of business combinations: ***horizontal*** (combinations involving enterprises in the same industry), ***vertical*** (combinations between an enterprise and its customers or suppliers), and ***conglomerate*** (combinations between enterprises in unrelated industries or markets).

Methods for Arranging Business Combinations

The four common methods for carrying out a business combination are statutory merger, statutory consolidation, acquisition of common stock, and acquisition of assets.

Statutory Merger   As its name implies, a statutory merger is executed under provisions of applicable state laws. In a statutory merger, the boards of directors of the constituent companies approve a plan for the exchange of voting common stock (and perhaps some preferred stock, cash, or long-term debt) of one of the corporations (the *survivor*) for all the outstanding voting common stock of the other corporations. Stockholders of all constituent corporations must approve the terms of the merger; some states require approval of a two-thirds majority of stockholders. The surviving corporation issues its common stock or other consideration to the stockholders of the other corporations in exchange for all their holdings, thus acquiring ownership of those corporations. The other corporations ***then are dissolved and liquidated and thus cease to exist as separate legal entities,*** and their activities often are continued as ***divisions*** of the survivor, which now owns the ***net assets*** (assets minus liabilities), rather than the outstanding common stock, of the liquidated corporations.

To summarize, the procedures in a statutory merger are as follows:

1   The boards of directors of the constituent companies work out the terms of the merger.

2   Stockholders of the constituent companies approve the terms of the merger, in accordance with applicable corporate bylaws and state laws.

3   The survivor issues its common stock or other consideration to the stockholders of the other constituent companies in exchange for all their outstanding voting common stock of those companies.

4   The survivor dissolves and liquidates the other constituent companies, receiving in exchange for its common stock investments the net assets of those companies.

Statutory Consolidation   A statutory consolidation also is consummated in accordance with applicable state laws. However, in a consolidation a *new corporation is formed to issue its common stock* for the outstanding common stock of two or more existing corporations, *which then go out of existence.* The new corporation thus acquires the net assets of the defunct corporations, whose activities may be continued as divisions of the new corporation.

To summarize, the procedures in a statutory consolidation are as follows:

1   The boards of directors of the constituent companies work out the terms of the consolidation.

2   Stockholders of the constituent companies approve the terms of the consolidation, in accordance with applicable corporate bylaws and state laws.

3   A new corporation is formed to issue its common stock to the stockholders of the constituent companies in exchange for all their outstanding voting common stock of those companies.

4   The new corporation dissolves and liquidates the constituent companies, receiving in exchange for its common stock investments the net assets of those companies.

Acquisition of Common Stock   One corporation (the *investor*) may issue preferred or common stock, cash, debt, or a combination thereof to acquire from present stockholders all or a majority of the voting common stock of another corporation (the *investee*). This stock acquisition program may function through direct acquisition in the stock market, through negotiations with the principal stockholders of a closely held corporation, or through a tender offer to stockholders of a publicly owned corporation. A *tender offer* is a publicly announced intention to acquire, for a stated amount of consideration, a maximum number of shares of the combinee's common stock ''tendered'' by holders thereof to an agent, such as an investment banker or a commercial bank. The price per share stated in the tender offer usually is well above the prevailing market price of the combinee's common stock. If more than 50% of the combinee's voting common stock is acquired, that corporation becomes *affiliated* with the combinor *parent company* as a *subsidiary,* but *is not dissolved and liquidated and remains a separate legal entity.* Business combinations arranged through common stock acquisitions require authorization by the combinor's board of directors and may require ratification by the combinee's stockholders. Most unfriendly takeovers are accomplished by this means.

Business combinations that result in a parent company–subsidiary relationship are discussed in Chapters 6 and 8.

Acquisition of Assets A business enterprise may acquire from another enterprise all or most of the gross assets or net assets of the other enterprise for cash, debt, preferred or common stock, or a combination thereof. The transaction generally must be approved by the boards of directors and stockholders of the constituent companies. The selling enterprise *may continue its existence as a separate entity or it may be dissolved and liquidated;* it does not become an *affiliate* of the combinor.

Establishing the Price for a Business Combination

An important early step in planning a business combination is deciding on an appropriate price to pay. The amount of cash or debt securities, or the number of shares of preferred or common stock, to be issued in a business combination generally is determined by variations of the following methods:

1 Capitalization of expected average annual earnings of the combinee at a desired rate of return

2 Determination of current fair value of the combinee's net assets (including goodwill)

The price for a business combination consummated for cash or debt generally is expressed in terms of the total dollar amount of the consideration issued. When common stock is issued in a business combination, the price is expressed as a ratio of the number of shares of the combinor's common stock to be exchanged for each share of the combinee's common stock.

Illustration of Exchange Ratio The negotiating officers of Palmer Corporation have agreed with the stockholders of Simpson Company to acquire all 20,000 outstanding shares of Simpson common stock for a total price of $1,800,000. Palmer's common stock presently is trading in the market at $65 a share. Stockholders of Simpson agree to accept 30,000 shares of Palmer's common stock at a value of $60 a share in exchange for their stock holdings in Simpson. The exchange ratio is expressed as 1.5 shares of Palmer's common stock for each share of Simpson's common stock, in accordance with the following computation:

Computation of exchange ratio in business combination	*Number of shares of Palmer Corporation common stock to be issued* *30,000*
	Number of shares of Simpson Company common stock to be exchanged *20,000*
	Exchange ratio: 30,000 ÷ 20,000 .... *1.5:1*

METHODS OF ACCOUNTING FOR BUSINESS COMBINATIONS

Purchase Accounting

Because the majority of business combinations involve an identified combinor and one or more combinees, many accountants consider it logical to account for *all* business combinations, regardless of how consummated, as the *acquisition of assets.* Thus, assets (including goodwill) acquired in a business combination for cash would be recognized at the amount of cash paid, and assets acquired in a business combination involving the issuance of debt, preferred stock, or common stock would be recognized at the current fair value of the assets or of the debt or stock, whichever was more clearly evident. This approach is known as *purchase accounting* for business combinations and was widely used prior to the increase in popularity of pooling-of-interests accounting. *APB Opinion No. 16,* ''Business Combinations,'' set forth the concept of purchase accounting as follows.[2]

> Accounting for a business combination by the purchase method follows principles normally applicable under historical-cost accounting to record acquisitions of assets and issuances of stock and to accounting for assets and liabilities after acquisition.

Determination of the Combinor

Because the carrying amounts of the net assets of the combinor are not affected by a business combination, the combinor must be accurately identified. The Accounting Principles Board provided the following guidance for identifying the combinor:[3]

> A corporation which distributes cash or other assets or incurs liabilities to obtain the assets or stock of another company is clearly the [combinor]. . . . The Board concludes that presumptive evidence of the [combinor] in combinations effected by an exchange of stock is obtained by identifying the former common stockholder interests of a [constituent] company which either retain or receive the larger portion of the voting rights in the combined [enterprise]. That corporation should be treated as the [combinor] unless other evidence clearly indicates that another corporation is the [combinor].

Computation of Cost of a Combinee

The cost of a combinee in a business combination accounted for by the purchase method is the total of (1) the amount of consideration paid by the combinor, (2) the combinor's *direct* ''out-of-pocket'' costs of the combination, and (3) any *contingent consideration* that is determinable on the date of the business combination.

Amount of Consideration   This is the total amount of cash paid, the current fair value of other assets distributed, the present value of debt securities issued, and the current fair (or market) value of equity securities issued by the combinor.

Direct Out-of-Pocket Costs   Included in this category are some legal fees, some accounting fees, and finder's fees. A *finder's fee* is paid to the investment banking firm or other organizations or individuals that investigated the combinee, assisted in determining the price of the business combination, and otherwise rendered services to bring about the combination.

---

[2] *APB Opinion No. 16,* ''Business Combinations,'' AICPA (New York: 1970), p. 311.
[3] Ibid., p. 313.

Costs of registering with the SEC and issuing *debt securities* in a business combination are debited to Bond Issue Costs; they are not part of the cost of the combinee. Costs of registering with the SEC and issuing *equity securities* are not direct costs of the business combination but are offset against the proceeds from the issuance of the securities. *Indirect* out-of-pocket costs of the combination, such as salaries of officers of constituent companies involved in negotiation and completion of the combination, are recognized as expenses incurred by the constituent companies.

Contingent Consideration Contingent consideration is additional cash, other assets, or securities that may be issuable in the future, contingent on future events such as a specified level of earnings or a designated market price for a security that had been issued to complete the business combination. Contingent consideration that is *determinable* on the consummation date of a combination is recorded as part of the cost of the combination; contingent consideration *not determinable* on the date of the combination is recorded when the contingency is resolved and the additional consideration is paid or issued (or becomes payable or issuable).

Illustration of Contingent Consideration The contract for Norton Company's acquisition of the net assets of Robinson Company provided that Norton would pay $800,000 cash for Robinson's net assets (including goodwill), which would be included in the Robb Division of Norton Company. The following contingent consideration also was included in the contract:

1 Norton was to pay Robinson $100 a unit for all sales by Robb Division of a slow-moving product that had been written down to scrap value by Robinson prior to the business combination. No portion of the $800,000 price for Robinson's net assets involved the slow-moving product.

2 Norton was to pay Robinson 25% of any pre-tax accounting income in excess of $500,000 (excluding income from sale of the slow-moving product) of Robb Division for each of the four years subsequent to the business combination.

On January 2, Year 1, the date of completion of the business combination, Robinson Company had firm, noncancelable sales orders for 500 units of the slow-moving product. The sales orders and all units of the slow-moving product were transferred to Norton by Robinson.

Norton's cost of the net assets acquired from Robinson includes $50,000 (500 × $100 = $50,000) for the *determinable* contingent consideration attributable to the backlog of sales orders for the slow-moving product. However, because any pre-tax accounting income of Robb Division for the next four years cannot be determined on January 2, Year 1, no provision for the 25% contingent consideration is included in Norton's cost on January 2, Year 1. The subsequent accounting for such contingent consideration is described on pages 214 to 215.

Allocation of Cost of a Combinee

APB Opinion No. 16 provided the following principles for allocating cost of a combinee in a purchase-type business combination:[4]

---

[4] Ibid., p. 318.

First, all identifiable assets acquired . . . and liabilities assumed in a business combination . . . should be assigned a portion of the cost of the acquired company, normally equal to their fair values at date of acquisition.

Second, the excess of the cost of the acquired company over the sum of the amounts assigned to identifiable assets acquired less liabilities assumed should be recorded as *goodwill.* [Emphasis added.]

Identifiable Assets and Liabilities *APB Opinion No. 16* provided guidelines for assigning values to a purchased combinee's identifiable assets and liabilities.[5] Among these were present values for receivables and liabilities; net realizable values for marketable securities, finished goods and goods in process inventories, and for plant assets held for sale or for temporary use; appraised values for intangible assets, land, natural resources, and nonmarketable securities; and replacement cost for inventories of material and plant assets held for long-term use.

In addition, the Financial Accounting Standards Board has provided the following guidelines for matters not dealt with in *APB Opinion No. 16:*

1   A part of the cost of a purchased combinee is allocable to identifiable tangible and intangible assets that resulted from research and development activities of the combinee or are to be used in research and development activities of the combined enterprise. Subsequently, such assets are to be expensed, as required by *FASB Statement No. 2,* "Accounting for Research and Development Costs," unless they may be used for other than research and development activities in the future.[6]

2   In a purchase-type business combination, leases of the combinee are classified by the combined enterprise as they were by the combinee unless the provisions of a lease are modified to the extent it must be considered a new lease.[7] Thus, unmodified capital leases of the combinee are treated as capital leases by the combined enterprise, and the leased property and related liability are recognized in accordance with the guidelines of *APB Opinion No. 16.*

3   A combinee in a purchase-type business combination may have *preacquisition contingencies,* which are contingent assets (other than potential income tax benefits of a loss carryforward), contingent liabilities, or contingent impairments of assets, that existed prior to completion of the business combination. If so, an *allocation period,* generally not longer than one year from the date the combination is completed, may be used to determine the current fair value of a preacquisition contingency. A portion of the cost of a purchased combinee is allocated to a preacquisition contingency whose fair value is determined during the allocation period. Otherwise, an estimated amount is assigned to a preacquisition contingency if it appears probable that an asset existed, a liability had been incurred, or an asset had been impaired at the completion of the combination. Any adjustment of the carrying amount of a

---

[5] Ibid., pp. 318–320.

[6] *FASB Interpretation No. 4,* "Applicability of *FASB Statement No. 2* to Business Combinations Accounted for by the Purchase Method," FASB (Stamford: 1975), pp. 1–3.

[7] *FASB Interpretation No. 21,* "Accounting for Leases in a Business Combination," FASB (Stamford: 1978), pp. 6–7.

preacquisition contingency subsequent to the end of the allocation period is included in the measurement of net income for the accounting period of the adjustment.[8]

Goodwill   Goodwill frequently is recognized in purchase-type business combinations because the total cost of the combinee exceeds the current fair value of identifiable net assets of the combinee. The amount of goodwill recognized on the date the business combination is consummated may be adjusted subsequently when contingent consideration becomes issuable, as illustrated on page 214.[9]

''Negative Goodwill''   In some purchase-type business combinations (known as *bargain purchases*), the current fair values assigned to the identifiable net assets acquired exceed the total cost of the combinee. A bargain purchase is most likely to occur for a combinee with a history of losses or when common stock prices are extremely low. The excess of the current fair values over total cost is applied pro rata to reduce (but not below zero) the amounts initially assigned to noncurrent assets other than long-term investments in marketable securities.[10] If the foregoing proration does not extinguish the *bargain-purchase excess,* a deferred credit, sometimes termed *negative goodwill,* is established. Negative goodwill means an excess of current fair value of the combinee's identifiable net assets over their cost to the combinor. It is amortized over the period benefited, not to exceed 40 years.[11]

Illustration of Purchase Accounting for Statutory Merger, with Goodwill

On December 31, Year 1, Mason Company (the combinee) was merged into Saxon Corporation (the combinor or surviving company). Both companies used the same accounting principles for assets, liabilities, revenue, and expenses and both had a December 31 fiscal year. Saxon issued 150,000 shares of its $10 par common stock (current fair value $25 a share) to Mason's stockholders for all 100,000 issued and outstanding shares of Mason's no-par, $10 stated value common stock. In addition, Saxon paid the following out-of-pocket costs associated with the business combination:

Combinor's out-of-pocket costs of purchase-type business combination

Accounting fees:	
For investigation of Mason Company as prospective combinee	$ 5,000
For SEC registration statement for Saxon common stock	$ 60,000
Legal fees:	
For the business combination	10,000
For SEC registration statement for Saxon common stock	50,000
Finder's fee	51,250
Printer's charges for printing securities and SEC registration statement	23,000
SEC registration statement fee	750
Total out-of-pocket costs of business combination	$200,000

[8] *FASB Statement No. 38,* ''Accounting for Preacquisition Contingencies of Purchased Enterprises,'' FASB (Stamford: 1980), pp. 2–4.
[9] *APB Opinion No. 16,* pp. 315–316.
[10] Ibid., p. 318.
[11] Ibid., p. 321.

There was no contingent consideration in the merger contract.

Immediately prior to the merger, Mason Company's condensed balance sheet was as follows:

Combinee's balance
sheet prior to merger
purchase-type
business combination

MASON COMPANY (Combinee)
Balance Sheet (prior to business combination)
December 31, Year 1

Assets

Current assets	$1,000,000
Plant assets (net)	3,000,000
Other assets	600,000
Total assets	$4,600,000

Liabilities & Stockholders' Equity

Current liabilities	$ 500,000
Long-term debt	1,000,000
Common stock, no-par, $10 stated value	1,000,000
Additional paid-in capital	700,000
Retained earnings	1,400,000
Total liabilities & stockholders' equity	$4,600,000

Using the guidelines in *APB Opinion No. 16,* ''Business Combinations,'' (see page 190) the board of directors of Saxon Corporation determined the current fair values of Mason Company's identifiable assets and liabilities (identifiable net assets) as follows:

Current fair values of
combinee's identifiable
net assets

Current assets	$1,150,000
Plant assets	3,400,000
Other assets	600,000
Current liabilities	(500,000)
Long-term debt (present value)	(950,000)
Identifiable net assets of combinee	$3,700,000

The condensed journal entries on page 193 are required for Saxon Corporation (the combinor) to record the merger with Mason Company on December 31, Year 1, as a purchase-type business combination.

Note that no adjustments are made in the journal entries on page 193 to reflect the current fair values of Saxon's identifiable net assets or goodwill, because Saxon is the *combinor* in the business combination.

Accounting for the income tax effects of purchase-type business combinations is considered in Chapter 10.

Mason Company (the combinee) prepares the condensed journal entry on page 194 to record the dissolution and liquidation of the company on December 31, Year 1.

SAXON CORPORATION (Combinor)
Journal Entries
December 31, Year 1

Investment in Mason Company Common Stock		
(150,000 × $25)	3,750,000	
Common Stock (150,000 × $10).		1,500,000
Paid-in Capital in Excess of Par.		2,250,000

To record merger with Mason Company as a purchase.

Investment in Mason Company Common Stock ($5,000 +		
$10,000 + $51,250)	66,250	
Paid-in Capital in Excess of Par ($60,000 + $50,000 +		
$23,000 + $750)	133,750	
Cash.		200,000

To record payment of out-of-pocket costs incurred in merger with Mason Company. Accounting, legal, and finder's fees in connection with the merger are recognized as an investment cost; other out-of-pocket costs are recorded as a reduction in the proceeds received from issuance of common stock.

Current Assets	1,150,000	
Plant Assets	3,400,000	
Other Assets.	600,000	
Discount on Long-Term Debt	50,000	
Goodwill.	116,250	
Current Liabilities.		500,000
Long-Term Debt		1,000,000
Investment in Mason Company Common Stock		3,816,250

To allocate cost of Mason Company investment to identifiable assets and liabilities, with the remainder to goodwill. (Income tax effects are disregarded.) Amount of goodwill is computed as follows:

Total cost of investment		
($3,750,000 + $66,250)	$3,816,250	
Less: Carrying amount of		
identifiable net assets		
($4,600,000 −		
$1,500,000).	$3,100,000	
Excess (deficiency) of		
current fair values of		
identifiable net assets		
over carrying		
amounts:		
Current assets	150,000	
Plant assets	400,000	
Long-term debt.	50,000	3,700,000
Amount of goodwill		$ 116,250

MASON COMPANY (Combinee)
Journal Entry
December 31, Year 1

Current Liabilities...	500,000	
Long-Term Debt...	1,000,000	
Common Stock, $10 stated value	1,000,000	
Paid-in Capital in Excess of Stated Value	700,000	
Retained Earnings...	1,400,000	
Current Assets......................................		1,000,000
Plant Assets (net)		3,000,000
Other Assets..		600,000

To record liquidation of company in conjunction with merger
with Saxon Corporation.

Illustration of Purchase Accounting for Acquisition of Net Assets, with "Negative Goodwill"

On December 31, Year 1, Davis Corporation acquired the net assets of Fairmont Corporation directly from Fairmont for $400,000 cash, in a purchase-type business combination. Davis paid legal fees of $40,000 in connection with the combination. The condensed balance sheet of Fairmont prior to the business combination, with related current fair value data, is presented below:

Balance sheet of
combinee prior to
purchase-type
business combination

FAIRMONT CORPORATION (Combinee)
Balance Sheet (prior to business combination)
December 31, Year 1

	Carrying amounts	Current fair values
Assets		
Current assets	$ 190,000	$ 200,000
Investment in marketable securities	50,000	60,000
Plant assets (net).......................................	870,000	900,000
Intangible assets (net)	90,000	100,000
Total assets......................................	$1,200,000	$1,260,000
Liabilities & Stockholders' Equity		
Current liabilities	$ 240,000	$ 240,000
Long-term debt...	500,000	520,000
Total liabilities....................................	$ 740,000	$ 760,000
Common stock, $1 par..................................	$ 600,000	
Deficit..	(140,000)	
Total stockholders' equity	$ 460,000	
Total liabilities & stockholders' equity	$1,200,000	

Thus, Davis acquired identifiable net assets with a current fair value of $500,000 ($1,260,000 − $760,000 = $500,000) for a total cost of $440,000 ($400,000 + $40,000 = $440,000). The $60,000 excess of current fair value of the net assets over their cost to Davis ($500,000 − $440,000 = $60,000) is prorated to the plant assets and intangible assets in the ratio of their respective current fair values, as follows:

Allocation of excess of current fair value over cost of identifiable net assets of combinee in purchase-type business combination

$$\text{To plant assets: } \$60,000 \times \frac{\$900,000}{\$900,000 + \$100,000} \quad \cdots\cdots\cdots\cdots\cdots\cdots\cdots \quad \$54,000$$

$$\text{To intangible assets: } \$60,000 \times \frac{\$100,000}{\$900,000 + \$100,000} \quad \cdots\cdots\cdots\cdots\cdots\cdots \quad 6,000$$

Total excess of current fair value of identifiable net assets over combinor's
cost. $60,000

No part of the $60,000 excess is allocated to current assets or to the investment in marketable securities.

The journal entries below record Davis Corporation's acquisition of the net assets of Fairmont Corporation and payment of $40,000 legal fees:

Combinor's journal entries for purchase-type business combination (acquisition of net assets)

DAVIS CORPORATION (Combinor)
Journal Entries
December 31, Year 1

Investment in Net Assets of Fairmont Corporation	400,000	
Cash		400,000
To record acquisition of net assets of Fairmont Corporation.		
Investment in Net Assets of Fairmont Corporation	40,000	
Cash		40,000
To record payment of legal fees incurred in acquisition of net assets of Fairmont Corporation.		
Current Assets	200,000	
Investments in Marketable Securities	60,000	
Plant Assets ($900,000 − $54,000)	846,000	
Intangible Assets ($100,000 − $6,000)	94,000	
Current Liabilities		240,000
Long-Term Debt		500,000
Premium on Long-Term Debt ($520,000 − $500,000)		20,000
Investment in Net Assets of Fairmont Corporation		440,000
To allocate cost of net assets acquired to identifiable net assets, with excess of current fair value of the net assets over their cost prorated to noncurrent assets other than investments in marketable securities. (Income tax effects are disregarded.)		

Pooling-of-Interests Accounting

The original premise of the pooling-of-interests method was that certain business combinations *involving the exchange of common stock* between an *issuer* and the stockholders of a combinee were more in the nature of a *combining of existing stockholder interests* than an *acquisition of assets* or *raising of capital.* Combining of existing stockholder interests was evidenced by combinations involving common stock exchanges between corporations of approximately equal size. The stockholders and managements of these corporations continued their relative interests and activities in the combined enterprise as they previously did in the constituent companies. Because neither of the like-size constituent companies could be considered the *combinor* under the criteria set forth on page 188, the pooling-of-interests method of accounting provided for carrying forward to the accounting records of the combined enterprise the combined assets, liabilities, and retained earnings of the constituent companies at their *carrying amounts* in the accounting records of the constituent companies. The current fair value of the common stock issued to effect the business combination and the current fair value of the combinee's net assets *are disregarded* in pooling-of-interests accounting. Further, because there is no identifiable combinor in a pooling-type business combination, the term *issuer* identifies the corporation that issues its common stock to accomplish the combination.

Illustration of Pooling-of-Interests Accounting for Statutory Merger

The Saxon Corporation–Mason Company merger business combination described on pages 191 to 192 would be accounted for as a pooling of interests by the journal entries below, in Saxon Corporation's (the survivor's) accounting records:

Survivor's journal entries for pooling-type business combination (statutory merger)

SAXON CORPORATION (Survivor) Journal Entries December 31, Year 1		
Current Assets	1,000,000	
Plant Assets (net)	3,000,000	
Other Assets	600,000	
Current Liabilities		500,000
Long-Term Debt		1,000,000
Common Stock, $10 par		1,500,000
Paid-in Capital in Excess of Par		200,000
Retained Earnings		1,400,000
To record merger with Mason Company as a pooling of interests.		
Expenses of Business Combination	200,000	
Cash		200,000
To record payment of out-of-pocket costs incurred in merger with Mason Company.		

Because a pooling-type business combination is a combining of existing stockholder interests rather than an acquisition of assets, an Investment in Mason Company Net Assets ledger account is not used in the foregoing journal entries. Instead, in the first journal entry, Mason's assets, liabilities, and retained earnings are assigned their carrying amounts in Mason's premerger balance sheet (see page 192). Because the common stock issued by Saxon Corporation must be recorded at *par* (150,000 shares $\times$ $10 = $1,500,000), the $200,000 credit to paid-in capital in excess of par is a *balancing amount* for the journal entry. It may be verified as shown below:

<table>
<tr><td>Computation of survivor's credit to paid-in capital in excess of par</td><td>Total paid-in capital of Mason Company prior to merger
($1,000,000 + $700,000)..</td><td>$1,700,000</td></tr>
<tr><td></td><td>Less: Par value of Saxon Corporation common stock issued in merger....</td><td>1,500,000</td></tr>
<tr><td></td><td>Amount credited to Saxon Corporation's Paid-in Capital in Excess of Par
  ledger account ....</td><td>$ 200,000</td></tr>
</table>

If the par value of common stock issued by Saxon Corporation had *exceeded* the total paid-in capital of Mason Company, Saxon's Paid-in Capital in Excess of Par ledger account would have been *debited* in the illustrated journal entry. If the balance of Saxon's Paid-in Capital in Excess of Par account were insufficient to absorb the debit, Saxon's Retained Earnings account would be reduced.

In the second journal entry on page 196, *all* the out-of-pocket costs of the business combination were *recognized as expenses* because a pooling-type business combination is neither an acquisition of assets nor a raising of capital. The expenses of business combination are not deductible for income tax purposes; thus Saxon Corporation does not adjust its income taxes expense and liability ledger accounts.

Mason Company's journal entry to record the dissolution and liquidation of the company would be identical to the journal entry illustrated on page 194.

Popularity of Pooling Accounting

The pooling method of accounting for business combinations was sanctioned initially by the AICPA in *Accounting Research Bulletin No. 40,* "Business Combinations." However, *ARB No. 40* provided few criteria for identifying the business combinations that qualified for pooling accounting and was therefore unsatisfactory as a guide for this accounting method. Subsequently, *ARB No. 48,* "Business Combinations," superseded the previous pronouncement with an expanded discussion of the pooling method. *ARB No. 48* continued to permit pooling accounting for most business combinations involving an exchange of common stock. However, *ARB No. 48* also failed to provide definitive guidelines for identifying the business combinations that qualified for pooling accounting. As a result, a substantial number of business combinations arranged during the 1950s and 1960s were accounted for as poolings, despite the fact that the "combining of existing stockholder interests" aspect was absent.

Why had pooling accounting become so popular? Some of the reasons are apparent from the following comparison of the combined Saxon Corporation journal entries illustrated on pages 193 and 196 for the merger with Mason Company:

Comparison of
combinor's/issuer's
journal entries—
purchase and pooling

	Purchase accounting	Pooling accounting
Current Assets.	1,150,000	1,000,000
Plant Assets.	3,400,000	3,000,000
Other Assets	600,000	600,000
Discount on Long-Term Debt. . .	50,000	
Goodwill	116,250	
Expenses of Business		
Combination.		200,000
Current Liabilities	500,000	500,000
Long-Term Debt	1,000,000	1,000,000
Common Stock, $10 par.	1,500,000	1,500,000
Paid-in Capital in Excess		
of Par.	2,116,250	200,000
Retained Earnings		1,400,000
Cash	200,000	200,000

To record merger with Mason Company.

Differences in Net Assets   The first difference to consider in comparing the foregoing journal entries is that the net assets recorded under the purchase method ($3,616,250) exceed the pooling-method net assets ($2,900,000) by $716,250. The composition of the $716,250 is summarized below:

Composition of
difference in net assets
—purchase versus
pooling

Excess of purchase asset values over pooling asset values:

Current assets ($1,150,000 − $1,000,000).	$150,000
Plant assets ($3,400,000 − $3,000,000).	400,000
Goodwill	116,250

Excess of pooling liability values over purchase liability values:

Long-term debt [$1,000,000 − ($1,000,000 − $50,000)].	50,000
Excess of purchase net assets values over pooling net assets values.	$716,250

Assuming that the $400,000 difference in plant assets is attributable to *depreciable* assets, total expenses of Saxon Corporation for years subsequent to December 31, Year 1, will be $716,250 larger under purchase accounting than under pooling accounting. Assume, for example, that the $150,000 difference in current assets is attributable to inventories that will be allocated to cost of goods sold on the first-in, first-out basis; the average economic life of the depreciable plant assets is 10 years; the goodwill is to be amortized over a 40-year period; and the long-term debt has a remaining five-year term to maturity.[12] Saxon Corporation's *pre-tax income* for the

---

[12] For simplicity, the discount on long-term debt is amortized by the straight-line method. Theoretically, and in actual practice, the *interest* method described in intermediate accounting textbooks is used when the difference between the two methods is material in amount.

year ending December 31, Year 2 (the year following the merger), would be nearly $203,000 less under purchase accounting than under pooling accounting, attributable to the following larger postmerger expenses under purchase accounting:

Difference in pre-tax income—purchase versus pooling	

Cost of goods sold	$150,000
Depreciation expense ($400,000 × 1/10).	40,000
Amortization expense ($116,250 × 1/40).	2,906
Interest expense ($50,000 × 1/5)	10,000
Excess of Year 2 pre-tax income under pooling accounting rather than under purchase accounting	$202,906

It is true that pre-tax income for the year ended December 31, Year 1 (the year of the merger), is reduced $200,000 in pooling accounting, because the pooling method included the immediate *expensing* of the out-of-pocket costs of the business combination. However, this situation tends to be obscured by the fact that the income statements of Saxon Corporation and Mason Company would be combined in pooling accounting for the *entire* year ended December 31, Year 1 (as described on pages 207 to 208).

In summary, the favorable effect of pooling accounting on post-combination earnings has been the main reason for the popularity of this accounting method for business combinations.

Difference in Total Paid-in Capital The increase in Saxon Corporation's total paid-in capital is $1,916,250 less ($3,616,250 − $1,700,000 = $1,916,250) under pooling accounting than under purchase accounting. Of this difference, $1,200,000 ($1,400,000 − $200,000 = $1,200,000) is attributable to a net increase in Saxon Corporation's retained earnings under the pooling accounting method. If state laws make this $1,200,000 available as a basis for dividend declarations by Saxon, another advantage of the pooling method of accounting is readily apparent.

Impact of Different Price-Earnings Ratios Even more dramatic than the preceding advantages inherent in the pooling-of-interests method of accounting is the potential impact on the market price of Saxon Corporation's common stock if the price-earnings ratios for Saxon's and Mason's common stock differed significantly prior to the merger. Suppose, for example, that Saxon Corporation and Mason Company had the financial information on page 200 prior to the business combination.

After consummation of the business combination as a pooling, Saxon Corporation's income statement for the year ended December 31, Year 1, reports the combined enterprise's net income as $875,000 ($500,000 + $375,000 = $875,000)—the total of the separate net incomes of the constituent companies. "Pooled" earnings per share for Saxon thus is increased to approximately $0.76. This increased amount of earnings per share is computed by dividing combined earnings of $875,000 by 1,150,000 (1,000,000 + 150,000 = 1,150,000), the *effective* number of shares of Saxon's common stock considered to have been outstanding during the year ended December 31, Year 1. If the price-earnings ratio for Saxon's common

Selected financial
information prior to
business combination

	Saxon Corporation	Mason Company
Year ended Dec. 31, Year 1:		
Net income	$500,000*	$375,000
Earnings per share of common stock	$0.50	$3.75
On Dec. 31, Year 1:		
Number of shares of common stock outstanding	1,000,000†	100,000†
Market price per share	$25	$30
Price-earnings ratio	50	8

* Net of $200,000 expenses of business combination.
† Outstanding during entire year.

stock continued unchanged, the stock's market price would increase after the merger to $38 a share ($0.76 × 50 = $38), a 52% increase ($13 ÷ $25 = 0.52). Saxon Corporation probably would attain the reputation of an "exciting growth company," and Saxon's directors likely would seek out other prospects for pooling-type business combinations.

Less spectacular advantages attributed to the pooling method of accounting for business combinations result from the fact that the carrying amounts of assets and liabilities of the combinee are not restated. Pooling accounting thus parallels income tax accounting if the business combination qualifies as a "tax-free corporate reorganization." Further, goodwill amortization (not deductible in the computation of taxable income) is not required in the pooling method.

Past Abuses of Pooling Accounting

The attractive features of pooling accounting described in the preceding section, together with the absence of firm guidelines for poolings in *ARB No. 48,* led to a number of serious abuses of the method in the past. Among these abuses were retroactive poolings; retrospective poolings; part-pooling, part-purchase accounting; treasury stock issuances; issuances of unusual securities; creation of "instant earnings"; contingent payouts; and "burying" the costs of pooling-type business combinations.

Retroactive Poolings   After *ARB No. 48* was issued, some accountants interpreted its provisions as permitting pooling accounting for many business combinations that already had been accounted for as purchases under *ARB No. 40.* Accordingly, a significant number of business combinations that had been recorded as purchases in the late 1950s and early 1960s were *restated retroactively* as poolings in subsequent years. *Such restatements raised questions in the minds of users of financial statements as to the integrity of both the initial and the revised accounting for the business combinations.*

Retrospective Poolings   The theory that the constituent companies in a pooling-type business combination were *effectively combined* in accounting periods preceding the actual business combination led to the practice of *retrospective poolings.*

This technique involved the consummation of pooling business combinations *after the close of an issuer's fiscal year but prior to the preparation of its annual financial statements.* The income statement that ultimately was issued included the operating results of the subsequently pooled combinee on a retrospective basis. Thus, a desired earnings per share amount might have been attained simply by a working paper adjustment.

Part-Pooling, Part-Purchase Accounting   Some business combinations involving the issuance of common stock as well as cash and debt were accounted for as *poolings* to the extent of the common stock issuance and as *purchases* for the remainder of the consideration. This hybrid method was inconsistent with an orderly structure of financial accounting theory.

Treasury Stock Issuances   Pooling accounting required the exchange of common stock between the issuer and the combinee's stockholders. One method devised to avoid the potential dilution of earnings per share resulting from common stock issuances was the cash acquisition of treasury stock and its subsequent reissuance in a pooling-type business combination. If substance is emphasized over form, such a combination is effected for *cash,* not for *previously unissued stock.*

Issuances of Unusual Securities   As another means of minimizing the dilutive effects of common stock issuances in poolings, many unusual securities were devised to consummate business combinations. These securities, generally in the form of either preferred stock or a special class of common stock, were in most cases convertible to the issuer's voting common stock. In substance, these unusual securities were not equivalent to voting common stock, yet the business combinations involving these securities frequently were treated as poolings.

Creation of "Instant Earnings"   The discussion on pages 197 to 199, comparing the purchase and pooling journal entries for Saxon Corporation, indicated how pooling accounting might *instantly increase earnings per share* for the year of a business combination. Another technique for creating instant earnings was the sale of a combinee's assets shortly after the pooling combination. Because the selling price generally exceeded the carrying amounts of the assets, a gain was recognized. The selling price generally *approximated* the current fair value of the issuer's common stock issued in the pooling combination. Thus, the instant earnings were fictitious because the gain in effect represented proceeds from the common stock issued to effect the combination.

Contingent Payouts   If the "combining of existing stockholder interests" feature of a pooling combination were genuine, there would be no unresolved contingencies with respect to the number of shares of common stock to be issued in the combination. Nevertheless, a large number of business combinations involving contingent issuances of additional shares of common stock or cash were accounted for as poolings.

"Burying" the Costs of Pooling-Type Business Combinations   The out-of-pocket costs of most pooling-type business combinations effected before 1970 were *debited to paid-in capital in excess of par rather than to expenses of the combined enterprise.* The accounting method violated the basic assumption that a pooling is in substance neither an *acquisition* of one business enterprise by another nor an *obtaining of new capital.*

Abuses of Purchase Accounting

Purchase accounting was not free of abuses during the 1950s and 1960s. The principal abuse of purchase accounting was the failure to allocate the cost of a combinee to the identifiable net assets acquired and to goodwill. Instead, an "Excess of Cost over Net Assets Acquired" ledger account was debited with the excess of the cost over the *carrying amounts* of the combinee's net assets and displayed in the post-combination balance sheet as an intangible asset—usually not subject to amortization. Consequently, reported earnings subsequent to these purchase-type combinations were the same as though pooling accounting had been used. Also, as in pooling-type business combinations, "instant earnings" often were created by the disposal of understated identifiable assets shortly after the purchase-type combination.

Action by the AICPA

The AICPA's Accounting Principles Board reacted to the abuses of pooling accounting and purchase accounting by tightening the accounting standards for poolings and by limiting drastically the range of situations in which pooling would be allowed. The Board's action is summarized in the following paragraph of *APB Opinion No. 16,* "Business Combinations":[13]

> The Board concludes that the purchase method and the pooling of interests method are both acceptable in accounting for business combinations, although *not as alternatives* in accounting for the same business combination. A business combination which meets specified conditions requires accounting by the pooling of interests method. A new basis of accounting is not permitted for a combination that meets the specified conditions, and the assets and liabilities of the combining companies are combined at their recorded amounts. All other business combinations should be accounted for as an acquisition of one or more companies by a corporation. The cost to an acquiring corporation of an entire acquired company should be determined by the principles of accounting for the acquisition of an asset. That cost should then be allocated to the identifiable individual assets acquired and liabilities assumed based on their fair values; the unallocated cost should be recorded as goodwill. [Emphasis added.]

By this action the Accounting Principles Board eliminated many of the abuses of pooling accounting and purchase accounting described on pages 200 to 202. Retrospective poolings and part-pooling, part-purchase accounting were expressly prohibited. Substantial restrictions were placed on the use of treasury stock and hybrid securities to consummate pooling-type combinations. Pooling accounting was forbidden for a combination containing any contingent payout provisions or plans to dispose of assets acquired in the combination. Out-of-pocket costs of pooling-type

---

[13] *APB Opinion No. 16,* p. 283.

combinations were required to be expensed, even though these costs were not deductible for income tax purposes. However, the concept of relative equal size of constituent companies as a prerequisite for poolings (see page 196) was dropped.

Conditions Requiring Pooling Accounting

The Accounting Principles Board provided 12 conditions for business combinations that were to be accounted for as poolings. The conditions, ***all of which were to be satisfied for pooling to be appropriate,*** were divided into three groups as follows:

1 ***Attributes of the combining companies*** The conditions in this group were designed to assure that the pooling-type business combination was truly a combining of two or more enterprises whose common stockholder interests were ***previously independent*** of each other.

2 ***Manner of combining ownership interests*** The conditions in this group supported the requirement for pooling accounting that an exchange of stock to combine existing voting common stock interests actually took place, in substance as well as in form.

3 ***Absence of planned transactions.*** The planned transactions prohibited by this group of conditions were those that would be inconsistent with the combining of entire existing interests of common stockholders.

A business combination that meets the Accounting Principles Board's 12 conditions is accounted for as a pooling, regardless of the legal form of the combination (statutory merger, statutory consolidation, acquisition of common stock, or acquisition of assets). An acquisition of assets may be construed as an ''exchange of voting common stock interests'' if all the other specified conditions for a pooling are met.

The following summary includes the 12 conditions established by the Accounting Principles Board for pooling accounting:[14]

1 ***Attributes of the constituent companies***
a Each of the constituent companies is autonomous and has not been a subsidiary or division of another corporation within two years before the plan of combination is initiated.
b Each of the constituent companies is independent of the other companies.

2 ***Manner of combining ownership interests***
a The combination is effected in a single transaction or is completed in accordance with a specific plan within one year after the plan is initiated.
b A corporation offers and issues only common stock with rights identical to those of the majority of its outstanding voting common stock in exchange for substantially all the voting common stock interest of another company on the date the plan of combination is consummated.
c None of the constituent companies changes the equity interest of the voting common stock in contemplation of effecting the combination either within two years

---

[14] Adapted from *APB Opinion No. 16,* ''Business Combinations,'' AICPA (New York: 1970), pp. 295–304.

before the plan of combination is initiated or between the dates the combination is initiated and consummated; changes in contemplation of effecting the combination may include distributions to stockholders and additional issuances, exchanges, and retirements of securities.

d Each of the constituent companies acquires shares of its outstanding voting common stock only for purposes other than business combinations, and no company acquires more than a normal number of such shares between the dates the plan of combination is initiated and consummated.

e The ratio of the interest of an individual common stockholder to those of other common stockholders in a constituent company remains the same as a result of the exchange of common stock to effect the combination.

f The voting rights to which the common stock ownership interests in the resulting combined enterprise are entitled are exercisable by the stockholders; the stockholders are neither deprived of nor restricted in exercising those rights for a period.

g The combination is resolved on the date the plan is consummated, and no provisions of the plan relating to the issue of securities or other consideration are pending.

3   *Absence of planned transactions*

a The combined enterprise does not agree directly or indirectly to retire or acquire all or part of the common stock issued to effect the combination.

b The combined enterprise does not enter into other financial arrangements for the benefit of the former stockholders of a constituent company, such as a guaranty of loans secured by common stock issued in the combination, which in effect negates the exchange of common stock.

c The combined enterprise does not intend or plan to dispose of a significant part of the assets of the constituent companies within two years after the combination other than disposals in the ordinary course of business of the former separate companies and to eliminate duplicate facilities or excess capacity.

Many of the foregoing conditions are self-explanatory; however, four of them warrant discussion.

Independence of Constituent Companies   On the dates of initiation and consummation of a business combination, no constituent company may have more than a 10% ownership of the outstanding voting common stock of another constituent company. Otherwise, the companies could not be considered independent of each other, because ownership of more than 10% of an investee's common stock often enables the investor to have some degree of influence over the investee.

Substantially All Voting Common Stock   This condition requires that at least 90% of the combinee's outstanding voting common stock be exchanged for the issuer's voting common stock. The following are ***excluded*** from the computation of the number of shares exchanged:

1   Shares acquired before the date the business combination is initiated and held by either the issuer or its subsidiaries on that date

2   Shares acquired by either the issuer or its subsidiaries after the combination is initiated, other than in exchange for the issuer's voting common stock

3   Shares of the combinee still outstanding on the date the combination is consummated

In addition, any voting common stock of the issuer owned or acquired by the combinee before the business combination must be considered. These issuer shares are converted to equivalent shares of the combinee for the 90% test.

To illustrate the application of the "independence" and "90% of voting common stock" tests, assume that on March 13, Year 2, Patton Corporation and Sherman Company initiated a plan of business combination. Under the plan, 1½ shares of Patton's voting common stock (1,000,000 shares issued and outstanding prior to March 13, Year 2) were to be exchanged for each outstanding share of Sherman's common stock (100,000 shares issued and 99,500 shares outstanding prior to March 13, Year 2).

At this time, Patton owned 7,500 shares of Sherman's common stock, and Sherman owned 6,000 shares of Patton's voting common stock; in addition, 500 shares of Sherman's common stock were in Sherman's treasury. Neither Patton's ownership of 7.54% of Sherman's outstanding common stock (7,500 ÷ 99,500 = 7.54%) or Sherman's ownership of 0.6% of Patton's outstanding common stock (6,000 ÷ 1,000,000 = 0.6%) exceeds the 10% limitation of the *independence of constituent companies requirement.* On March 26, Year 2, Patton acquired in the open market for cash 1,000 shares (1.005%) of Sherman's outstanding common stock; and on June 30, Year 2, Patton issued 136,500 shares of its voting common stock in exchange for 91,000 outstanding shares of Sherman's common stock to complete the business combination.

Computation of the 90% requirement follows:

Computation of "substantially all voting common stock" pooling requirement		

Total Sherman Company shares issued, June 30, Year 2   100,000
Less: Shares in Sherman's treasury   500
Total Sherman shares outstanding, June 30, Year 2   99,500
Less:
 Sherman shares owned by Patton Corporation, Mar. 13, Year 2 . .   7,500
 Sherman shares acquired by Patton for cash, Mar. 26, Year 2 . . .   1,000
 Equivalent number of Sherman shares represented by Patton's
  common stock owned by Sherman, Mar. 13, Year 2
  (6,000 ÷ 1½)   4,000   12,500
Effective number of Sherman shares acquired June 30, Year 2,
 in exchange for Patton's common stock   87,000
Application of 90% requirement (99,500 × 90%)   89,550

Thus, the 91,000 shares of Sherman Company common stock actually exchanged on June 30, Year 2, are in effect restated to 87,000 shares. Because the restated amount is less than 90% of Sherman's 99,500 shares outstanding, the business combination *does not qualify for pooling accounting.*

Restrictions on Treasury Stock   To preclude the treasury stock abuses described on page 201, *APB Opinion No. 16* provided that any treasury stock issued in a business combination qualifying for pooling accounting must have been acquired in accordance with a systematic plan of treasury stock acquisitions. The systematic plan of acquisitions must have been established *for at least two years prior to the initiation of a combination;* and the treasury stock acquisitions must be required for stock option and stock purchase plans or for other recurring stock distributions. Treasury stock meeting the foregoing restrictions is said to be *untainted.* Any untainted treasury stock issued to effect a pooling-type business combination *is accounted for as though it had been retired and then issued as previously unissued stock.*

No Pending Provisions   For pooling accounting to be appropriate for a business combination, no additional common stock must be contingently issuable to former stockholders of a combinee after a combination has been initiated. In addition, no common stock must have been issued to an escrow agent pending the resolution of a contingency.

Financial Statements Following a Business Combination

Under both purchase accounting and pooling accounting, the balance sheet for a combined enterprise issued as of the date of a business combination accomplished through a statutory merger, statutory consolidation, or acquisition of assets includes all the assets and liabilities of the constituent companies. (The *consolidated* balance sheet issued immediately following a combination that results in a parent-subsidiary relationship is described in Chapters 6 and 8.) In a balance sheet following a purchase-type business combination, assets and liabilities of the combinor are at carrying amount, assets acquired from the combinee are at current fair value (adjusted for any negative goodwill as illustrated on page 195), and *retained earnings is that of the combinor only.* In a balance sheet following a pooling-type business combination, assets and liabilities of all constituent companies are at carrying amount, and *retained earnings is the total for all constituent companies.*

The form of the combined enterprise's income statement for the accounting period in which a business combination is completed depends on whether purchase accounting or pooling accounting is used to record the combination.

Purchase   The income statement of the combined enterprise for the accounting period in which a purchase-type business combination occurred includes the operating results of the combinee *after the date of the combination only.* For example, under purchase accounting, Saxon Corporation's postmerger income statement for the year ended December 31, Year 1, would be identical to Saxon's premerger income statement shown on page 207, except that net income would be $700,000 and operating expenses would be $1,683,333. (The $200,000 out-of-pocket costs of the business combination are not recognized as expenses in purchase accounting; $66,250 is part of the cost to Saxon of Mason's net assets, and $133,750 is a reduction in Saxon's paid-in capital in excess of par.)

Pooling The income statement of the combined enterprise for the accounting period in which a pooling-type business combination took place includes the results of operations of the constituent companies *as though the combination had been completed at the beginning of the period.* According to *APB Opinion No. 20,* "Accounting Changes," a business combination accounted for by the pooling method results in a *change in the reporting entity.*[15] Comparative financial statements for preceding periods are restated in order to show financial information for the new reporting entity for all periods.[16] Intercompany transactions prior to the combination must be eliminated from the combined income statements in a manner comparable with that described in Chapter 4 for branches.

This presentation stems from the concept that a business combination accounted for as a pooling is a *combining of existing stockholder interests* rather than an *acquisition of assets.* Because stockholder interests are combined, previous financial statements showing changes in those interests also are combined.

To illustrate, assume that the income statements of Saxon Corporation and Mason Company for the year ended December 31, Year 1 (prior to completion of their *pooling-type* merger described on pages 196 to 197), were as follows:

Income statements of constituent companies prior to pooling-type business combination

SAXON CORPORATION AND MASON COMPANY
Separate Income Statements
For Year Ended December 31, Year 1

	Saxon Corporation	Mason Company
Sales and other revenue	$10,000,000	$5,000,000
Costs and expenses:		
Cost of goods sold	$ 7,000,000	$3,000,000
Operating expenses	1,883,333*	1,274,500
Interest expense	150,000	100,500
Income taxes expense	466,667	250,000
Total costs and expenses	$ 9,500,000	$4,625,000
Net income	$ 500,000	$ 375,000

* Includes $200,000 expenses of business combination.

Assume also that Mason's interest expense includes $25,000 paid to Saxon on a loan that was repaid prior to December 31, Year 1, and that Saxon's sales and other revenue include $25,000 interest revenue received from Mason.

The working paper for the postmerger income statement of Saxon Corporation under pooling accounting is illustrated on page 208. The amounts in the Combined column are reported in Saxon's published postmerger income statement for the year ended December 31, Year 1.

---

[15] *APB Opinion No. 20,* "Accounting Changes," AICPA (New York: 1971), p. 388.
[16] Ibid., p. 398.

SAXON CORPORATION
Working Paper for Combined Income Statement (Pooling of Interests)
For Year Ended December 31, Year 1

	Saxon Corporation	Mason Company	Eliminations	Combined
Sales and other revenue	10,000,000	5,000,000	(a) (25,000)	14,975,000
Costs and expenses:				
Cost of goods sold.	7,000,000	3,000,000		10,000,000
Operating expenses	1,883,333	1,274,500		3,157,833
Interest expense ..	150,000	100,500	(a) (25,000)	225,500
Income taxes expense	466,667	250,000		716,667
Total costs and expenses	9,500,000	4,625,000	(25,000)	14,100,000
Net income	500,000	375,000	-0-	875,000

Explanation of combination elimination:
(a) To eliminate intercompany interest received by Saxon Corporation from Mason Company.

Disclosure of Business Combinations in a Note to the Financial Statements

Because of the complex nature of business combinations and their effects on the financial position and operating results of the combined enterprise, extensive disclosure is required for the periods in which they occur.

Purchase   The Accounting Principles Board required disclosure of the following aspects of a purchase-type business combination in a note to the financial statements for the period in which the business combination took place:[17] name and brief description of the combinee; period for which combinee's operating results are included in the income statement of the combined enterprise; cost of the combinee, including number of shares and value per share of common stock issued, and nature of and accounting treatment for contingent consideration; amortization policy for goodwill recorded in the combination; and pro forma operating results for the combined enterprise for the current and preceding accounting periods as though the combination had occurred at the beginning of the preceding period. Subsequently, the Financial Accounting Standards Board waived the pro forma disclosures for nonpublic enterprises whose debt and equity securities are not publicly traded.[18]

The following note to the financial statements of Vulcan Materials Company, a

---

[17] *APB Opinion No. 16,* pp. 322–323.
[18] *FASB Statement No. 79,* '' Elimination of Certain Disclosures for Business Combinations by Nonpublic Enterprises,'' FASB (Stamford: 1984), p. 2.

publicly owned company, illustrates the required disclosures for a purchase-type business combination:[19]

> On September 6, 1990, the Company purchased all of the stock of Reed Crushed Stone Company, Inc., Reed Terminal Company, Inc., and BRT Transfer Terminal, Inc. The purchase price paid for the three companies was $113,602,000 including $13,404,000 referable to cash, cash items and short-term investments. Funds for payment of the purchase price were obtained by the Company through issuance and sale of short-term notes. The purchase price was calculated in accordance with the stock purchase agreements and was based upon management's expectations for the future and the value of the assets and liabilities of the three companies.
>
> The acquisition has been accounted for as a purchase transaction and, accordingly, the purchase price was allocated to the assets acquired and liabilities assumed based on estimated fair values at the date of acquisition.
>
> The excess of the purchase price over the fair value of the tangible assets acquired is approximately $18,032,000, including the effect of deferred income taxes, and will be amortized on a straight-line basis over 20 years.
>
> Pro forma results of the Company's operations, assuming the acquisition occurred at the beginning of 1989, are shown in the following table. These unaudited pro forma results have been prepared for comparative purposes only and do not purport to be indicative of what would have occurred had the acquisition been made at the beginning of 1989, or of the results which may occur in the future.

	(Thousands of dollars, except per share amounts)	
	1990	*1989*
Net sales	$1,147,987	$1,136,041
Earnings from continuing operations before income taxes	178,147	202,906
Net earnings from continuing operations	119,105	133,603
Primary and fully diluted earnings per share of common stock from continuing operations	3.07	3.31

> The assets of the acquired companies include a large limestone quarry which provides stone to markets on the Mississippi River system, to the western Kentucky area and to rail customers from Illinois to Mississippi; a number of deck barges which are used to ship stone to the river markets; and a stone distribution business in Memphis, Tennessee. In addition, BRT Transfer Terminal operates three terminals which blend and transload coal from rail to barge and barge to barge. During Reed's last three fiscal years before the acquisition, stone shipments have averaged about 9.5 million tons per year. The acquired businesses have continued their operations and now function as subsidiary companies in Vulcan's Construction Materials segment.

---

[19] AICPA, *Accounting Trends & Techniques,* 45th ed. (New York: 1991), p. 72.

Pooling of Interests Among the disclosures required for a pooling-type business combination in a note to the financial statements of the combined enterprise are the following:[20] name and brief description of the combinee, number of shares of common stock issued in the combination, and separate operating results of the constituent companies for the period prior to the combination that were included in the operating results of the combined enterprise for the year in which the combination occurred.

The following note to the financial statements of Rubbermaid Incorporated, a publicly owned company, illustrates the required disclosures for a pooling-type business combination:[21]

In October 1990, 6,236,758 Common Shares were issued in exchange for all the Outstanding Common Shares of Eldon Industries, Inc. (Eldon), primarily a manufacturer and marketer of office products.

The acquisition has been accounted for as a pooling of interests, and accordingly, the accompanying financial information has been restated to include the accounts of Eldon for all periods presented. Net sales and net earnings of the separate companies for the period preceding the acquisition were [dollars in thousands]:

| | January 1, 1990 Through October 29, 1990 | Years Ended December 31, | |
		1989	1988
Net Sales:			
Rubbermaid	$1,184,249	$1,343,873	$1,193,539
Eldon	88,732	108,492	98,045
Combined	$1,272,981	$1,452,365	$1,291,584
Net Earnings:			
Rubbermaid	$ 117,366	$ 116,410	$ 99,290
Eldon	6,440	8,574	7,568
Combined	$ 123,806	$ 124,984	$ 106,858

Comparison of Purchase and Pooling Accounting

The table on page 211 summarizes the principal aspects of purchase accounting and pooling-of-interests accounting for business combinations.

Other Topics in Accounting for Business Combinations

Purchase-Type Statutory Consolidation Because a new corporation issues common stock to effect a statutory consolidation, one of the constituent companies in a purchase-type statutory consolidation must be identified as the combinor, under the criteria described on page 188. Once the combinor has been identified, the new corporation recognizes net assets acquired from the combinor at their carrying amount in the combinor's accounting records; however, net assets acquired from the combinee are recognized by the new corporation at their current fair values.

To illustrate, assume the balance sheets on page 212 of the constituent companies involved in a purchase-type statutory consolidation on December 31, Year 1.

---

[20] *APB Opinion No. 16*, p. 310.
[21] AICPA, *Accounting Trends & Techniques,* 45th ed. (New York: 1991, p. 66.)

Comparison of Purchase Accounting and Pooling-of-Interests Accounting for Business Combinations

Aspect	Purchase accounting	Pooling-of-interests accounting
Underlying premise	Acquisition of assets	Combining of stockholder interests
Applicability	Combinations not meeting all 12 criteria for pooling accounting	Combinations meeting all 12 criteria for pooling accounting
Accounting recognition of investment in combinee	At cost, including amount of consideration, direct out-of-pocket costs, and determinable contingent consideration	At carrying amount of combinee's net assets (all out-of-pocket costs are recognized as expenses of the issuer)
Valuation of combinee's net assets in combined enterprise	At current fair values on date of combination	At carrying amounts on date of combination
Goodwill recognition	Yes, if combinor's cost exceeds current fair value of combinee's identifiable net assets	No
Retained earnings of constituent companies combined on date of business combination	No	Yes
Financial statements and notes for period of business combination:		
Balance sheet	Combinor's net assets at carrying amount; combinee's net assets at current fair value	Both issuer's and combinee's net assets at carrying amount
Income statement	Combinor's operations for entire period; combinee's operations from date of combination to end of period	Both issuer's and combinee's operations for entire period as though combination took place at beginning of period; prior periods restated comparably
Disclosures of operations in notes	Pro forma for combined enterprise for current and preceding period as though combination took place at beginning of preceding period	Separately for constituent companies for period prior to combination

LAMSON CORPORATION AND DONALD COMPANY
Separate Balance Sheets (prior to business combination)
December 31, Year 1

	Lamson Corporation	Donald Company
Assets		
Current assets	$ 600,000	$ 400,000
Plant assets (net)	1,800,000	1,200,000
Other assets	400,000	300,000
Total assets	$2,800,000	$1,900,000
Liabilities & Stockholders' Equity		
Current liabilities	$ 400,000	$ 300,000
Long-term debt	500,000	200,000
Common stock, $10 par	430,000	620,000
Additional paid-in capital.	300,000	400,000
Retained earnings	1,170,000	380,000
Total liabilities & stockholders' equity	$2,800,000	$1,900,000

The current fair values of both companies' liabilities were equal to carrying amounts. Current fair values of identifiable assets were as follows for Lamson and Donald, respectively: current assets, $800,000 and $500,000; plant assets, $2,000,000 and $1,400,000; other assets, $500,000 and $400,000.

On December 31, Year 1, in a statutory consolidation approved by shareholders of both constituent companies, a new corporation, LamDon Corporation, issued 74,000 shares of no-par, no-stated-value common stock with an agreed value of $60 a share, based on the following valuations assigned by the negotiating directors to the two constituent companies' identifiable net assets and goodwill:

Computation of number of shares of common stock issued in statutory consolidation

	Lamson Corporation	Donald Company
Current fair value of identifiable net assets:		
Lamson: $800,000 + $2,000,000 + $500,000 −		
$400,000 − $500,000	$2,400,000	
Donald: $500,000 + $1,400,000 + $400,000 −		
$300,000 − $200,000		$1,800,000
Goodwill	180,000	60,000
Net assets' current fair value	$2,580,000	$1,860,000
Number of shares of LamDon common stock to be issued		
to constituent companies' stockholders, at $60 a share		
agreed value	43,000	31,000

Because the former stockholders of Lamson Corporation receive the largest interest in the common stock of LamDon Corporation ($^{43}/_{74}$, or 58%), Lamson is the combinor in the purchase-type business combination. Assuming that LamDon paid out-of-pocket costs of the statutory consolidation after it was consummated on December 31, Year 1, LamDon's journal entries would be as follows:

Journal entries for new corporation for purchase-type business combination (statutory consolidation)

LAMDON CORPORATION
Journal Entries
December 31, Year 1

Investment in Lamson Corporation and Donald Company Common Stock (74,000 × $60)	4,440,000	
Common Stock, no par		4,440,000

To record consolidation of Lamson Corporation and Donald Company as a purchase.

Investment in Lamson Corporation and Donald Company Common Stock	110,000	
Common Stock, no par	90,000	
Cash		200,000

To record payment of direct costs incurred in consolidation of Lamson Corporation and Donald Company. Accounting, legal, and finder's fees in connection with the consolidation are recorded as investment cost; other out-of-pocket costs are recorded as a reduction in the proceeds received from the issuance of common stock.

Current Assets ($600,000 + $500,000)	1,100,000	
Plant Assets ($1,800,000 + $1,400,000)	3,200,000	
Other Assets ($400,000 + $400,000)	800,000	
Goodwill	850,000	
Current Liabilities ($400,000 + $300,000)		700,000
Long-Term Debt ($500,000 + $200,000)		700,000
Investment in Lamson Corporation and Donald Company Common Stock ($4,440,000 + $110,000)		4,550,000

To allocate cost of investment to identifiable assets and liabilities, at carrying amount for combinor Lamson Corporation's net assets and at current fair value for combinee Donald Company's net assets. (Income tax effects are disregarded.) Amount of goodwill is computed as follows:

Total cost of investment ($4,440,000 + $110,000)	$ 4,550,000
Less: Carrying amount of Lamson's identifiable net assets	(1,900,000)
Current fair value of Donald's identifiable net assets	(1,800,000)
Amount of goodwill	$ 850,000

Note in the foregoing journal entry that because of the combinor's net assets' being recognized at carrying amount and because of the $110,000 direct out-of-pocket costs of the business combination, the amount of goodwill is $850,000, rather than $240,000 ($180,000 + $60,000 = $240,000), the amount assigned by the negotiating directors to goodwill in the determination of the number of shares of common stock to be issued in the combination (see page 212).

Subsequent Issuance of Contingent Consideration   As indicated on page 189, contingent consideration that is *determinable* on the date of a purchase-type business combination is included in the measurement of cost of the combinee. Any other contingent consideration is recorded when the contingency is resolved and the additional consideration becomes issuable or is issued.

Returning to the Norton Company illustration on page 189, assume that by December 31, Year 1, the end of the first year following Norton's acquisition of the net assets of Robinson Company, another 300 units of the slow-moving product had been sold, and Norton's Robb Division had pre-tax accounting income of $580,000 (exclusive of income from the slow-moving product). On December 31, Year 1, Norton prepares the following journal entry to record the resolution of contingent consideration:

Journal entry for contingent consideration involving subsequent sales and earnings	Goodwill 50,000	
	Payable to Robinson Company............................	50,000
	To record payable contingent consideration applicable to January 2,	
	Year 1, business combination as follows:	
	Sales of slow-moving product (300 × $100) $30,000	
	Pre-tax income of Robb Division	
	[($580,000 − $500,000) × 0.25] 20,000	
	Total payable $50,000	

The additional goodwill recognized in the foregoing journal entry is amortized over the remaining economic life of the goodwill recognized in the business combination.[22]

Some purchase-type business combinations involve contingent consideration based on subsequent market prices of debt or equity securities issued to effect the combination. Unless the subsequent market price equals at least a minimum amount on a subsequent date or dates, additional securities, cash, or other assets must be issued by the combinor to compensate for the deficiency.

For example, assume the following journal entry for the statutory merger of Soltero Corporation and Mero Company on January 2, Year 4:

Journal entry for purchase-type business combination (statutory merger)	Investment in Mero Company Common Stock (120,000 × $12) 1,440,000	
	Common Stock, $5 stated value (120,000 × $5)	600,000
	Paid-in Capital in Excess of Stated Value.............	840,000
	To record merger with Mero Company as a purchase.	

---

[22] *APB Opinion No. 16*, p. 316.

Assume that terms of the Soltero-Mero business combination required Soltero to issue additional shares of its common stock to the former stockholders of Mero if the market price of Soltero's common stock was less than $12 a share on December 31, Year 4. Assuming that the market price of Soltero's common stock was $10 on that date, Soltero prepares the following journal entry on that date:

Journal entry for contingent consideration involving subsequent market price of common stock

Paid-in Capital in Excess of Stated Value (24,000 × $5)	120,000	
Common Stock to Be Issued for Contingent Consideration		120,000

To record additional shares of common stock to be issued under terms of Jan. 2, Year 4, merger with Mero company, as follows:

Required value of common stock issued in merger	
(120,000 × $12).	$1,440,000
Less: Market value of common stock, Dec. 31,	
Year 4 (120,000 × $10)	1,200,000
Market value of additional common stock to be	
issued.	$ 240,000
Number of additional shares of common stock to	
be issued ($240,000 ÷ $10)	24,000

The foregoing journal entry is in accord with the following provisions of *APB Opinion No. 16,* ''Business Combinations'':[23]

> . . . the issuance of additional securities or distribution of other consideration does not affect the cost of the [combinee], regardless of whether the amount specified is a security price to be maintained or a higher security price to be achieved. On a later date when the contingency is resolved and additional consideration is distributable, the [combinor] should record the current fair value of the additional consideration issued or issuable. However, the amount previously recorded for securities issued at the date of [the business combination] should simultaneously be reduced to the lower current value of those securities. Reducing the value of debt securities previously issued to their later fair value results in recording a discount on debt securities. The discount should be amortized from the date the additional securities are issued.

APPRAISAL OF ACCOUNTING STANDARDS FOR BUSINESS COMBINATIONS

The accounting standards for business combinations described and illustrated in the preceding pages of this chapter may be criticized on grounds that they are not consistent with the conceptual framework for financial accounting and reporting.

---

[23] Ibid., pp. 316–317.

Criticism of Purchase Accounting

The principal criticisms of purchase accounting center on the recognition of good-will. Many accountants take exception to the *residual* basis for valuing goodwill established in *APB Opinion No. 16.* These critics contend that part of the amounts thus assigned to goodwill probably apply to other *identifiable* intangible assets. Accordingly, goodwill in a business combination should be valued *directly* by use of methods described in intermediate accounting textbooks. Any remaining cost not directly allocated to all identifiable tangible and intangible assets and to goodwill would be apportioned to those assets based on the amounts assigned in the first valuation process.

The mandatory amortization of goodwill, prescribed in *APB Opinion No. 17,* "Intangible Assets," is considered by some accountants to be inappropriate for goodwill attributable to a business combination. These accountants recommend treating the amount assigned to goodwill in a business combination as a reduction of stockholders' equity of the combined enterprise.

The accounting described on page 191 for the excess of current fair values over total cost in a bargain-purchase business combination also has been challenged. Critics maintain there is no theoretical support for the arbitrary reduction of previously determined current fair values of assets by an apportioned amount of the bargain-purchase excess. They suggest the amortization treatment described on page 191 for the *entire* bargain-purchase excess.

Other accountants question whether current fair values of the *combinor's* net assets—especially goodwill—should be disregarded in accounting for a purchase-type business combination. They maintain it is inconsistent to reflect current fair values for net assets of the *combinee only,* in view of the significance of many combinations involving large constituent companies.

Criticism of Pooling Accounting

The principal objections to pooling accounting are summarized below:

1 Despite the elaborate framework for pooling accounting established in *APB Opinion No. 16,* this accounting method is founded upon a questionable assumption. This assumption—that some business combinations involving exchanges of voting common stock result in a combining of existing stockholder interests rather than an acquisition of assets—is difficult to support in accounting theory. Two *Accounting Research Studies* recommended abolishing the pooling accounting method for business combinations between independent constituent companies.[24]

2 There is no explicit disclosure of the current fair value of the issuer's common stock exchanged in a business combination accounted for as a pooling. The disclosure required by *APB Opinion No. 16* is limited to stating the number of shares of common stock issued in a pooling-type business combination.

3 The assets of the combinee in a pooling-type business combination are not

[24] Arthur R. Wyatt, *Accounting Research Study No. 5,* "A Critical Study of Accounting for Business Combinations," AICPA (New York: 1963), p. 105; George R. Catlett and Norman O. Olson, *Accounting Research Study No. 10,* "Accounting for Goodwill," AICPA (New York: 1968), pp. 106, 109.

accounted for at their cost to the issuer. In the illustrated pooling accounting for the merger of Saxon Corporation and Mason Company (page 196), the net assets of Mason were entered in Saxon's accounting records at $3,100,000, the carrying amounts in Mason's accounting records. This amount is $716,250 less than the *cost* of Mason's net assets of $3,816,250 as reflected in the purchase accounting illustration.

4   A consequence of the misstatement of asset values is that net income for each accounting period subsequent to a pooling-type business combination is misstated.

The foregoing are powerful criticisms and are difficult to refute. Despite its alleged flaws, purchase accounting for business combinations appears conceptually superior in every respect to pooling-of-interests accounting.

FASB Study of Accounting for Business Combinations

In recognition of the unsatisfactory state of accounting for business combinations, the Financial Accounting Standards Board initiated a study of the subject shortly after the Board's inception. A lengthy *FASB Discussion Memorandum,* "An Analysis of Issues Related to Accounting for Business Combinations and Purchased Intangibles," was issued. Subsequently, however, the FASB removed the business combinations and purchased intangibles project from its agenda "because of [its] low priority in relation to other existing and potential projects."[25] The FASB possibly was influenced by the infrequency of pooling accounting for business combinations of large publicly owned companies.[26] However, the FASB's decision may be questioned, in light of the criticisms of current accounting standards for business combinations described in the foregoing section.

SEC ENFORCEMENT ACTIONS DEALING WITH WRONGFUL APPLICATION OF ACCOUNTING STANDARDS FOR BUSINESS COMBINATIONS

AAER 38   AAER 38, "Securities and Exchange Commission v. Corda Diversified Technologies Inc., et al." (September 10, 1984), reports a federal court's entry of an injunction against a corporate manufacturer and marketer of residential, commercial, and industrial hardware and its CEO, CFO, and independent auditors. The SEC stated that the corporation, which formerly had been a publicly owned "shell" with no operations, had wrongly been identified as the combinor in a purchase-type business combination with a privately owned company. Because the former stockholders of the privately owned corporation controlled 75% of the outstanding common stock of the "shell" following the business combination, the privately owned company was the combinor. Nonetheless, it was improperly accounted for as the combinee,

---

[25] *Status Report,* FASB (Stamford: Apr. 10, 1981), p. 3.
[26] The 45th edition of *Accounting Trends & Techniques,* issued by the AICPA in 1991, showed that pooling-type business combinations comprised only 7.1% of the 882 business combinations reported by the 600 surveyed companies during the past four years.

and its assets were carried at current fair values in the consolidated financial statements. The result was that consolidated total assets, reported as $15,119,727, were overstated at least $9 million. In a related enforcement action, reported in *AAER 39*, ". . . In the Matter of Smith & Stephens Accountancy Corporation and James J. Smith" (September 10, 1984), the SEC permanently prohibited the independent auditors of the manufacturing corporation from appearing or practicing before the SEC, with the proviso that, under specified conditions, the auditors could apply for reinstatement after two years.

AAER 275   In *AAER 275*, ". . . In the Matter of Charles C. Lehman, Jr." (September 28, 1990), the SEC reported the permanent disbarment of a CPA from appearing or practicing before it, with the proviso that the CPA might, if he complied with specified conditions, apply for reinstatement in eighteen months. According to the SEC, the CPA, on behalf of the firm of which he was managing partner, improperly expressed an unqualified audit opinion on the financial statements of a combined enterprise following a merger in which the *survivor* was improperly identified as the *combinor.* The *merging company* actually was the combinor because following the business combination its former sole stockholder owned 82.8% of the outstanding common stock of the survivor. The consequence of the misidentification of the combinor was the overstatement of a principal asset of the combined enterprise by 12,045% ($1,342,600 compared with $11,055).

REVIEW QUESTIONS

1   Define *business combination.*

2   Differentiate between a *statutory merger* and a *statutory consolidation.*

3   Identify two methods that may be used, individually or jointly, to determine an appropriate price to pay for a combinee in a business combination.

4   How is the combinor in a purchase-type business combination determined?

5   State how each of the following out-of-pocket costs of a merger purchase-type business combination is accounted for by the combinor:
a Printing costs for proxy statement mailed to combinor's stockholders in advance of special meeting to ratify terms of the merger
b Legal fees for negotiating the merger
c CPA firm's fees for auditing financial statements in SEC registration statement covering shares of common stock issued in the merger
d Printing costs for common stock issued in the merger
e Legal fees for SEC registration statement covering shares of common stock issued in the merger
f CPA firm's fees for advice on income tax aspects of the merger

6   The word *goodwill* often appears in connection with purchase-type business combinations. Explain the meaning of *goodwill* and *negative goodwill.*

7   **a** Define *contingent consideration* in a business combination.

    b If a plan for a business combination includes a provision for contingent consideration, is pooling accounting appropriate for the combination? Explain.

8 How is the cost of a combinee allocated in a purchase-type business combination?

9 Define the term *preacquisition contingencies.*

10 Distinguish between a *purchase* and a *pooling of interests* in terms of the entity relationships between the constituent companies and the combined enterprise. (Do not discuss accounting differences.)

11 If a business combination meets the 12 conditions requiring treatment as a pooling, what is the accounting effect as compared with a purchase interpretation?

12 How do the journal entries to the Paid-in Capital in Excess of Par (or Stated Value) ledger account differ in purchase accounting and pooling accounting?

13 Discuss some of the reasons for the popularity of pooling accounting for business combinations.

14 Identify five abuses of pooling accounting during the 1960s.

15 Differentiate *retrospective poolings* from *retroactive poolings.*

16 Critics have charged that pooling accounting creates *instant earnings.* How is this accomplished?

17 What information is disclosed in a note to the financial statements of a combined enterprise following a pooling-type business combination?

18 How has purchase accounting for business combinations been criticized?

19 Comment on the following quotation:

> It is our judgment that the weight of logic and consistency supports the conclusion that business combinations between independent entities are exchange transactions involving a transfer of assets and that the accounting action to account for exchange transactions is necessary to reflect properly the results of business combinations.

EXERCISES

Ex. 5-1 Select the best answer for each of the following multiple-choice questions:

1 Is *cost of the combinee* a characteristic of a business combination accounted for as a:

	Purchase?	*Pooling of interests?*
a	Yes	Yes
b	Yes	No
c	No	Yes
d	No	No

2   Are direct out-of-pocket costs of a business combination recognized as expenses if the combination is accounted for as a:

	Purchase?	Pooling of interests?
a	Yes	Yes
b	Yes	No
c	No	Yes
d	No	No

3   A target company's defense against an unfriendly takeover that involves the disposal of one or more profitable business segments of the target is termed:

a Pac-man defense   **b** Scorched earth   **c** Shark repellent   **d** Poison pill

4   Are the combinees *always* liquidated in business combinations accomplished by a(n):

	Statutory merger?	Statutory consolidation?	Acquisition of common stock?	Acquisition of assets
a	Yes	Yes	Yes	No
b	Yes	Yes	No	Yes
c	Yes	Yes	No	No
d	Yes	No	No	Yes

5   *Direct* out-of-pocket costs (debited to the Investment ledger account) of a purchase-type business combination involving the combinor's issuance of bonds do not include:

a Legal fees

b Finder's fee

c Bond issue costs

d CPA firm fees related to effecting the combination

6   In a merger business combination, retained earnings of the combined enterprise in its balance sheet on the date of the combination includes the combinee's retained earnings in:

a A purchase-type combination only

b A pooling-type combination only

c Both a purchase-type and a pooling-type combination

d Neither a purchase-type nor a pooling-type combination

7   One of the 12 conditions established by the Accounting Principles Board for pooling-of-interests accounting for business combinations is that one corporation exchanges its common stock for:

a All the outstanding voting common stock of another corporation

b More than 50% of the outstanding voting common stock of another corporation

c At least 80% of the outstanding voting common stock of another corporation

d At least 90% of the outstanding voting common stock of another corporation

8   Is an Investment in Combinee Common Stock ledger account used in accounting for a statutory merger that qualifies for:

	Purchase accounting?	Pooling accounting?
a	Yes	Yes
b	Yes	No
c	No	Yes
d	No	No

9 The term *survivor* is associated with a business combination accomplished through:

a A statutory merger
b A statutory consolidation
c An acquisition of common stock
d An acquisition of assets

10 Does the date-of-combination cost of the combinee in a purchase-type business combination include:

	Determinable contingent consideration?	Nondeterminable contingent consideration?
a	Yes	Yes
b	Yes	No
c	No	Yes
d	No	No

11 In the balance sheet of a combined enterprise on the date of a purchase-type business combination, *unallocated* negative goodwill is displayed:

a In stockholders' equity
b In a note to financial statements
c As a contra to total assets
d As a deferred credit

12 Which of the following is *not* included in the 12 conditions established by the APB in *Opinion No. 16* for pooling-of-interests accounting for a business combination?

a Autonomy of the constituent companies
b Relative sizes of the constituent companies
c Manner of combining ownership interests
d Absence of planned transactions

13 May a business combination involving the issuance of treasury stock possibly be accounted for as a:

	Pooling of interests?	Purchase?
a	Yes	Yes
b	Yes	No
c	No	Yes
d	No	No

14 Which of the following is a characteristic of a business combination accounted for as a pooling of interests?

a Acquisition of assets

b Combining of existing stockholder interests

c Raising of capital

d All of the foregoing

e None of the foregoing

15 Are separate operating results of the constituent companies for the portion of the accounting period prior to the business combination disclosed in a note to the financial statements of the combined enterprise for the accounting period of a business combination accounted for as a:

	Purchase?	*Pooling of interests?*
a	Yes	Yes
b	Yes	No
c	No	Yes
d	No	No

Ex. 5-2   The balance sheet of Mel Company on January 31, Year 2, showed current assets, $100,000; other assets, $800,000; current liabilities, $80,000; long-term debt, $240,000; common stock (10,000 shares, $10 par), $100,000; and retained earnings, $480,000. On that date, Mel merged with Sal Corporation in a business combination in which Sal issued 35,000 shares of its $1 par (current fair value $20 a share) common stock to stockholders of Mel in exchange for all their outstanding common stock. The current fair values of Mel's liabilities were equal to their carrying amounts; the current fair values of Mel's current assets and other assets were $120,000 and $850,000, respectively, on January 31, Year 2. Also on that date, Sal paid direct out-of-pocket costs of the business combination, $40,000, and costs of registering and issuing its common stock, $70,000.

Prepare journal entries (omit explanations) for Sal Corporation to record its merger with Mel Company as a purchase. (Disregard income taxes.)

Ex. 5-3   The condensed balance sheet of Geo Company on March 31, Year 8, is shown below:

GEO COMPANY
Balance Sheet (prior to business combination)
March 31, Year 8

Assets

Cash.	$ 20,000
Other current assets.	140,000
Plant assets (net)	740,000
Total assets	$900,000

Liabilities & Stockholders' Equity

Current liabilities	$ 80,000
Long-term debt	200,000
Common stock, $2 par.	180,000
Additional paid-in capital	120,000
Retained earnings.	320,000
Total liabilities & stockholders' equity.	$900,000

On March 31, Year 8, Master Corporation paid $700,000 cash for all the net assets of Geo (except cash) in a purchase-type business combination. The carrying amounts of Geo's other current assets and current liabilities were the same as their current fair values. However, current fair values of Geo's plant assets and long-term debt were $920,000 and $190,000, respectively. Also on March 31, Master paid the following out-of-pocket costs for the business combination with Geo:

Legal fees...	$ 10,000
Finder's fee...	70,000
CPA firm's fee for audit of Geo Company's March 31, Year 8, financial state-	
ments..	20,000
Total out-of-pocket costs of business combination	$100,000

Prepare a working paper to compute the amount of goodwill or negative good-will in the business combination of Master Corporation and Geo Company on March 31, Year 8. (Disregard income taxes.)

Ex. 5-4 The balance sheet of Combinee Company on January 31, Year 5, was as follows:

COMBINEE COMPANY
Balance Sheet (prior to business combination)
January 31, Year 5

Assets		**Liabilities & Stockholders' Equity**	
Current assets	$ 300,000	Current liabilities	$ 200,000
Plant assets	600,000	Long-term debt............	300,000
Other assets..............	100,000	Common stock, no	
		par or stated value........	100,000
		Retained earnings.........	400,000
		Total liabilities	
		& stockholders'	
Total assets	$1,000,000	equity.................	$1,000,000

On January 31, Year 5, Combinor Company issued $700,000 face amount of 6%, 20-year bonds due January 31, Year 25, with a present value of $625,257 at a 7% yield, to Combinee Company for its net assets. On January 31, Year 5, the current fair values of Combinee's liabilities equaled their carrying amounts; however, current fair values of combinee's assets were as follows:

Current assets	$320,000
Plant assets	680,000
Other assets..	120,000

Also on January 31, Year 5, Combinor paid out-of-pocket costs of the combination as follows:

Accounting, legal, and finder's fees	$ 80,000
Costs of registering 6% bonds with SEC................................	110,000
Total out-of-pocket costs...	$190,000

Prepare journal entries (omit explanations) for Combinor Company to record its acquisition of the net assets of Combinee Company. (Disregard income taxes.)

Ex. 5-5   On March 31, Year 9, Combinor Company issued 100,000 shares of its $1 par common stock (current fair value $5 a share) for the net assets of Combinee Company. Also on that date, Combinor paid the following out-of-pocket costs in connection with the combination:

Finder's, accounting, and legal fees relating to business combination	$ 70,000
Costs associated with SEC registration statement	50,000
Total out-of-pocket costs of business combination	$120,000

The balance sheet of Combinee on March 31, Year 9, with related current fair values, was as follows:

COMBINEE COMPANY
Balance Sheet (prior to business combination)
March 31, Year 9

Assets	Carrying amounts	Current fair values
Current assets	$200,000	$260,000
Plant assets (net).	400,000	480,000
Other assets	140,000	150,000
Total assets	$740,000	

Liabilities & Stockholders' Equity		
Current liabilities	$ 80,000	$ 80,000
Long-term debt.	260,000	260,000
Common stock, no par or stated value	150,000	
Retained earnings	250,000	
Total liabilities & stockholders' equity	$740,000	

Prepare journal entries (omit explanations) for Combinor Company on March 31, Year 9, to record the business combination with Combinee Company as a purchase. (Disregard income taxes.)

Ex. 5-6   On May 31, Year 3, Byers Corporation acquired for $560,000 cash all the net assets except cash of Sellers Company, and paid $60,000 cash to a law firm for legal services in connection with the business combination. The balance sheet of Sellers on May 31, Year 3, was as follows:

SELLERS COMPANY
Balance Sheet (prior to business combination)
May 31, Year 3

Assets		Liabilities & Stockholders' Equity	
Cash.	$ 40,000	Liabilities	$ 620,000
Other current assets (net) . .	280,000	Common stock, $1 par	250,000
Plant assets (net).	760,000	Retained earnings	330,000
Intangible assets (net)	120,000	Total liabilities &	
Total assets	$1,200,000	stockholders' equity	$1,200,000

The present value of Sellers's liabilities on May 31, Year 3, was $620,000. The current fair values of its noncash assets were as follows on May 31, Year 3:

Other current assets...	*$300,000*
Plant assets	*780,000*
Intangible assets	*130,000*

Prepare journal entries (omit explanations) for Byers Corporation on May 31, Year 3, to record the acquisition of the net assets of Sellers Company except cash. (Disregard income taxes.)

Ex. 5-7   On September 26, Year 4, Acquirer Corporation paid $160,000 cash to Disposer Company for all its net assets except cash, and $10,000 direct out-of-pocket costs of the purchase-type business combination. There was no contingent consideration. Current fair values of Disposer's identifiable net assets on September 26, Year 4, were as follows:

	Current fair values
Cash..	*$ 10,000*
Other current assets	*120,000*
Plant assets...	*150,000*
Intangible assets	*50,000*
Current liabilities..	*90,000*
Long-term debt (face amount $60,000)...............................	*50,000*

Prepare journal entries (omit explanations) for Acquirer Corporation on September 26, Year 4, to record the purchase-type business combination. (Disregard income taxes.)

Ex. 5-8   On December 31, Year 7, Issuer Company issued 100,000 shares of its $1 par common stock (current fair value $5 a share) for all the outstanding common stock of Combinee Company in a statutory merger. Also on that date, Issuer paid the following out-of-pocket costs in connection with the combination:

Accounting, finder's, and legal fees relating to business combination........	*$ 70,000*
Costs associated with SEC registration statement	*50,000*
Total out-of-pocket costs of business combination	*$120,000*

The balance sheet of Combinee on December 31, Year 7, is as shown on page 226.
Prepare journal entries (omit explanations) for Issuer Company on December 31, Year 7, to record the business combination with Combinee Company as a pooling of interests. (Disregard income taxes.)

COMBINEE COMPANY
Balance Sheet (prior to business combination)
December 31, Year 7

Assets

Current assets	$200,000
Plant assets (net)	400,000
Other assets.	140,000
Total assets	$740,000

Liabilities & Stockholders' Equity

Current liabilities	$ 80,000
Long-term debt	260,000
Common stock, no par or stated value.	150,000
Retained earnings.	250,000
Total liabilities & stockholders' equity.	$740,000

Ex. 5-9   The balance sheet of Combinee Company on September 24, Year 8, was as follows:

COMBINEE COMPANY
Balance Sheet (prior to business combination)
September 24, Year 8

Current assets	$ 200,000	Current liabilities	$ 100,000
Plant assets	700,000	Long-term debt.	300,000
Other assets	100,000	Common stock, no par or	
		stated value.	200,000
		Retained earnings	400,000
		Total liabilities &	
Total assets	$1,000,000	stockholders' equity	$1,000,000

On that date, Issuer Corporation issued 100,000 shares of its $1 par ($30 current fair value) common stock for all the outstanding common stock of Combinee Company in a statutory merger qualifying for pooling-of-interests accounting, and paid $180,000 out-of-pocket costs in connection with the combination.

Prepare journal entries (omit explanations) for (a) Issuer Corporation and (b) Combinee Company to record the statutory merger. (Disregard income taxes.)

Ex. 5-10   The balance sheet of Nestor Company on February 28, Year 7, with related current fair values of assets and liabilities, is on page 227.

On February 28, Year 7, Bragg Corporation issued 600,000 shares of its $1 par common stock (current fair value $25 a share) to Lucy Rowe, sole stockholder of Nestor Company, for all 500,000 shares of Nestor common stock owned by her, in a pooling-type merger business combination. Because the merger was negotiated privately and Rowe signed a "letter agreement" not to dispose of the Bragg common stock she received, the Bragg stock was not subject to SEC registration requirements. Thus, only $8,000 in legal fees was incurred to effect the merger; these fees were paid in cash by Bragg on February 28, Year 7.

Prepare journal entries for Bragg Corporation on February 28, Year 7, to record the business combination with Nestor Company. (Disregard income taxes.)

NESTOR COMPANY
Balance Sheet (prior to business combination)
February 28, Year 7

	Carrying amounts	Current fair values
Assets		
Current assets	$ 500,000	$ 580,000
Plant assets (net)	1,000,000	1,150,000
Other assets.	300,000	350,000
Total assets	$1,800,000	
Liabilities & Stockholders' Equity		
Current liabilities	$ 300,000	$ 300,000
Long-term debt	400,000	380,000
Common stock, $1 par.	500,000	
Additional paid-in capital	200,000	
Retained earnings.	400,000	
Total liabilities & stockholders' equity.	$1,800,000	

Ex. 5-11 The condensed balance sheet of Maxim Company on December 31, Year 4, prior to the business combination with Sorrel Corporation, was as follows:

MAXIM COMPANY
Balance Sheet (prior to business combination)
December 31, Year 4

Assets

Current assets	$ 400,000
Plant assets (net).	1,200,000
Other assets	200,000
Total assets.	$1,800,000

Liabilities & Stockholders' Equity

Current liabilities	$ 300,000
Common stock, $1 par.	400,000
Additional paid-in capital	200,000
Retained earnings	900,000
Total liabilities & stockholders' equity	$1,800,000

On December 31, Year 4, Sorrel issued 800,000 shares of its $1 par common stock (current fair value $3 a share) for all the outstanding common stock of Maxim in a statutory merger that qualified for pooling-of-interests accounting. Also on December 31, Year 4, Sorrel paid the following out-of-pocket costs of the business combination with Maxim:

Finder's and legal fees relating to business combination.	$30,000
Costs associated with SEC registration statement.	40,000
Total out-of-pocket costs of business combination	$70,000

On December 31, Year 4, the current fair values of Maxim's other assets and current liabilities equaled their carrying amounts; current fair values of Maxim's current assets and plant assets were $500,000 and $1,500,000, respectively. Sorrell had additional paid-in capital of $800,000 on December 31, Year 4.

Prepare journal entries for Sorrel Corporation on December 31, Year 4, to record the pooling-type business combination with Maxim Company. (Disregard income taxes.)

Ex. 5-12   On August 31, Year 2, Issuer Corporation entered into a statutory merger (a pooling-type business combination) with Combinee Company, by issuing 100,000 shares of $1 par common stock having a current fair value of $20 a share for all 50,000 outstanding shares of Combinee's no-par, no-stated-value common stock. Also, Issuer paid the following out-of-pocket costs of the combination on August 31, Year 2:

Finder's and legal fees relating to business combination..................	$100,000
Costs associated with SEC registration statement	150,000
Total out-of-pocket costs of business combination	$250,000

On August 31, Year 2, Combinee's balance sheet included the following:

	Carrying amounts	Current fair values
Current assets........................	$ 500,000	$ 600,000
Plant assets (net)	2,600,000	2,800,000
Current liabilities......................	400,000	400,000
Long-term debt	1,000,000	1,000,000
Common stock	800,000	
Retained earnings	900,000	

Prepare journal entries (omit explanations) for Issuer Corporation to record the statutory merger (pooling-type business combination) with Combinee Company. (Disregard income taxes.)

Ex. 5-13   Gamma Corporation was organized in a statutory consolidation to combine the resources of Alpha Company and Beta, Inc., in a pooling-type business combination. On January 2, Year 1, Gamma issued 65,000 shares of its $10 par common stock in exchange for all the outstanding common stock of Alpha and Beta. The stockholders' equity components of Alpha and Beta on January 2, Year 1, were as follows:

	Alpha Company	Beta, Inc.	Totals
Common stock, $1 par.......................	$150,000	$450,000	$600,000
Additional paid-in capital	20,000	55,000	75,000
Retained earnings..........................	110,000	210,000	320,000
Total stockholders' equity	$280,000	$715,000	$995,000

Prepare a working paper to compute the balance of Gamma's Paid-in Capital in Excess of Par ledger account immediately after the business combination. Disregard out-of-pocket costs of the business combination.

Ex. 5-14   Tom Corporation offered to exchange two shares of its common stock for each share of Muir Company common stock. On the date of the offer, Tom owned 3,000 shares (3%) of Muir's common stock and Muir owned 500 shares (0.05%) of Tom's common stock. In later cash transactions, Tom acquired 2,000 shares (2%) of Muir's outstanding common stock and Muir acquired 2,500 shares (0.25%) of Tom's outstanding common stock. At all times the number of shares of common stock outstanding was 1,000,000 for Tom and 100,000 for Muir. After consummation of the business combination, Tom owned 100,000 shares of Muir common stock.

Prepare a working paper to compute the number of shares of Muir Company common stock considered exchanged in determining whether the business combination of Tom Corporation and Muir Company should be accounted for as a pooling of interests.

Ex. 5-15   On November 1, Year 4, Sullivan Corporation issued 50,000 shares of its common stock in exchange for all the common stock of Mears Company in a statutory merger. Out-of-pocket costs of the business combination may be disregarded. Sullivan tentatively recorded the shares of common stock issued at par and debited the Investment in Mears Company Common Stock ledger account for $500,000. Mears Company was liquidated and became Mears Division of Sullivan Corporation. The net income of Sullivan Corporation and Mears Company or Mears Division during Year 4 was as follows:

	Jan. 1 through Oct. 31	Nov. 1 through Dec. 31
Sullivan Corporation	$420,000	$80,000*
Mears Company	350,000	
Mears Division of Sullivan Corporation		50,000

* Excludes any portion of Mears Division net income.

Condensed balance sheet information and other data for Year 4 follow:

	Sullivan Corporation		Mears Company Oct. 31	Mears Division of Sullivan Corporation Dec. 31
	Oct. 31	Dec. 31		
Assets	$3,500,000	$4,080,000	$4,000,000	$4,150,000
Liabilities	500,000	500,000	1,000,000	1,100,000
Common stock, $10 par	2,000,000	2,500,000	2,000,000	
Retained earnings	1,000,000	1,080,000*	1,000,000	
Market price per share of common stock	100	130	20	

* Excludes any portion of Mears Division net income.

Neither Sullivan nor Mears Company declared or paid dividends during Year 4. In recent months, Sullivan's common stock had been trading at about 40 times earnings; prior to November 1, Year 4, Mears Company common stock had been trading at 10 times earnings.

Answer the following questions, *assuming that the difference between current fair values and carrying amounts of Mears Company's identifiable net assets applies to land.* Show supporting computations and disregard income taxes.

a Assuming that the merger is accounted for as a pooling, what is Sullivan's net income for Year 4?

b What is the amount of the Year 4 earnings per share for Sullivan on a pooling basis?

c If the merger had been accounted for as a purchase, what would Sullivan's net income have been for Year 4?

d What is Sullivan's earnings per share for Year 4 on a purchase basis?

e What is the amount of retained earnings on a pooling basis at the end of Year 4?

f What is the amount of retained earnings on a purchase basis at the end of Year 4?

Ex. 5-16   On December 31, Year 7, Tucker Corporation acquired all the net assets of Loring Company for 100,000 shares of Tucker's $2 par common stock having a current fair value of $16 a share. Terms of the purchase-type business combination required Tucker to issue additional shares of common stock to Loring on December 31, Year 8, if the market price of the common stock was less than $16 a share on that date. Sufficient shares would be issued to make the aggregate market value of the total shares issued to Loring equal to $1,600,000 on December 31, Year 8. The market price of Tucker's common stock on that date was $10 a share.

Prepare a journal entry for Tucker Corporation on December 31, Year 8, to record the additional shares of common stock issuable to Loring Company on that date.

CASES

Case 5-1   When a business combination is effected by an exchange of common stock, the transaction is accounted for either as a purchase or as a pooling of interests. The accounting methods are not optional and may yield significantly different results as to financial position and results of operations of the combined enterprise.

Instructions
Discuss the supportive arguments for each of the following methods of accounting for business combinations:
a Purchase method
b Pooling-of-interests method

Do not discuss the rules for distinguishing between a purchase and a pooling of interests.

Case 5-2   The boards of directors of Carter Corporation, Fulton Company, Russell, Inc., and Towne Corporation are meeting jointly to discuss plans for a statutory merger. Each of the corporations has one class of common stock outstanding; Fulton also has one class of preferred stock outstanding. Although terms of the business combination have not as yet been settled, Carter will be the survivor. Because the directors want to conform to generally accepted accounting principles, they have asked you to attend the meeting as an adviser.

Instructions

Consider each question below independently of the others, and answer each in accordance with generally accepted accounting principles. Explain your answers.

a Assume that the merger will be consummated August 31, Year 5. Explain the rationale underlying the accounting and how the balance sheet amounts of each of the four corporations will appear in Carter's balance sheet on September 1, Year 5, if the merger is accounted for as a:

(1) Pooling of interests, with Carter the issuer

(2) Purchase, with Carter the combinor

b Assume that the merger will be consummated August 31, Year 5. Explain how the income statement amounts of each of the four corporations will be accounted for in Carter's income statement for the year ended December 31, Year 5, if the merger is accounted for as a:

(1) Pooling of interests, with Carter the issuer

(2) Purchase, with Carter the combinor

c Some of the directors believe that the terms of the merger should be agreed on immediately and that the method of accounting to be used may be chosen at some later date. Others believe that the terms of the merger and the accounting method to be used are closely related. Which position is correct? Explain.

d Carter and Towne are comparable in size; Russell and Fulton are much smaller. How do these facts affect the choice of accounting method for the merger?

e Fulton was formerly a subsidiary of Garson Corporation, which has no other relationship to any of the four companies discussing the business combination. Garson voluntarily spun off Fulton 18 months ago. What effect, if any, do these facts have on the choice of accounting method for the merger?

f Carter owns 2,000 of Fulton's 10,000 outstanding shares of preferred stock and 15,000 of Russell's 100,000 outstanding shares of common stock. All of Carter's holdings were acquired during the first three months of Year 5. What effect, if any, do these facts have on the choice of accounting method?

g Because the directors feel that one of Towne's major divisions will not be compatible with the operations of the combined enterprise, they anticipate that it will be sold as soon as possible after the business combination is consummated. They expect to have no trouble in finding a buyer. What effect, if any, does this fact have on the choice of accounting method?

Case 5-3 You have been engaged to audit the financial statements of Solamente Corporation for the fiscal year ended May 31, Year 6. You discover that on June 1, Year 5, Mika Company was merged into Solamente in a purchase-type business combination. You also find that both Solamente and Mika (prior to its liquidation) incurred legal fees, accounting fees, and printing costs for the business combination; both companies debited those costs to an intangible asset ledger account entitled "Cost of Business Combination." In its journal entry to record the business combination with Mika,

Solamente increased its Cost of Business Combination account by an amount equal to the balance of Mika's comparable ledger account.

Instructions

Evaluate Solamente's accounting for the out-of-pocket costs of the business combination with Mika.

Case 5-4   Satchell Corporation and Mobley Company, both of which have only voting common stock outstanding, are considering a statutory merger whereby Satchell would be the survivor. The terms of the business combination provide that the transaction would be carried out by Satchell's exchanging one share of its unissued common stock for each two shares of Mobley's outstanding common stock. Prior to the date of the contemplated exchange, Satchell had acquired 5% of Mobley's outstanding common stock, which it holds as an investment. Mobley, on the date of the contemplated exchange, owned 2% of Satchell's outstanding common stock. All the remaining outstanding common stock of Mobley would be acquired by Satchell in the contemplated exchange. Neither of the two companies has ever had any affiliation as a subsidiary or division of any other company.

Instructions

a How is a determination made as to whether a business combination is accounted for as a pooling of interests or as a purchase? (Do not enumerate specific criteria.)

b Based only on the foregoing facts, discuss the criteria that would qualify or disqualify the Satchell-Mobley business combination for pooling accounting.

Case 5-5   On February 15, Year 6, officers of Shane Corporation agreed with George Merlo, sole stockholder of Merlo Company and Merlo Industries, Inc., to acquire all his common stock ownership in the two companies as follows:

(1) 10,000 shares of Shane's $1 par common stock (current fair value $25 a share) would be issued to George Merlo on February 28, Year 6, for his 1,000 shares of $10 par common stock of Merlo Company. In addition, 10,000 shares of Shane common stock would be issued to George Merlo on February 28, Year 11, if aggregate net income of Merlo Company for the five-year period then ended exceeded $300,000.

(2) $250,000 cash would be paid to George Merlo on February 28, Year 6, for his 10,000 shares of $1 par common stock of Merlo Industries, Inc. In addition $250,000 in cash would be paid to George Merlo on February 28, Year 11, if aggregate net income of Merlo Industries, Inc., for the five-year period then ended exceeded $300,000.

Both Merlo Company and Merlo Industries, Inc., were to be merged into Shane on February 28, Year 6, and were to continue operations after that date as divisions of Shane. George Merlo also agreed not to compete with Shane for the period March 1, Year 6, through February 28, Year 11. Because the merger was negotiated privately and George Merlo signed a "letter agreement" not to dispose of the Shane common stock he received, the business combination was not subject to the jurisdiction of the SEC. Out-of-pocket costs of the business combination may be disregarded.

Selected financial statement data of the three constituent companies as of February 28, Year 6 (prior to the merger), were as follows:

	Shane Corporation	Merlo Company	Merlo Industries, Inc.
Total assets	$25,000,000	$ 500,000	$ 600,000
Stockholders' equity	10,000,000	200,000	300,000
Net sales	50,000,000	1,500,000	2,500,000
Earnings per share	5	30	3

The controller of Shane prepared the following condensed journal entries to record the merger on February 28, Year 6:

Assets	500,000	
Liabilities		300,000
Common Stock		10,000
Common Stock to Be Issued		10,000
Paid-in Capital in Excess of Par		180,000
To record merger with Merlo Company as a pooling of interests.		

Assets	650,000	
Goodwill	150,000	
Liabilities		300,000
Payable to George Merlo		250,000
Cash		250,000
To record merger with Merlo Industries, Inc., as a purchase, with assets and liabilities of Merlo Industries, Inc., recorded at current fair values and goodwill to be amortized over a 40-year economic life.		

Instructions

Do you concur with the controller's journal entries? Explain.

Case 5-6 In a discussion of accounting standards for business combinations, student Joan asserted that, because the 12 conditions for pooling-of-interests accounting set forth in *APB Opinion No. 16,* "Business Combinations," do not include a relative-size-of-constituent-companies test, as did prior pronouncements, the alleged combining of existing stockholder interests concept supporting pooling accounting is not met. Student George disagreed, avowing that the 12 conditions clearly are consistent with a combining of stockholder interests, which may occur despite a significant difference in the relative size of the constituent companies.

Instructions

Do you agree with student Joan or student George? Explain.

Case 5-7 The directors of Issuer Corporation and Combinee Company are meeting to draft a plan for a statutory merger business combination that would meet the 12 conditions for pooling-of-interests accounting specified by *APB Opinion No. 16,* "Business Combinations." Negotiations have proceeded well; however, controller Beth James of Issuer has stunned the directors by stating that, because of Issuer's recent acquisition (from a dissident stockholder) for cash and retirement of 150,000 shares of its common stock (15% of previously outstanding shares), it is her view that pooling accounting would be inappropriate for the proposed business combination because part of the 400,000 shares slated to be issued by Issuer in the merger would be "tainted treasury stock." James pointed out that, had state law permitted, the acquired Issuer common stock would have been carried in the treasury rather than retired.

Instructions

Do you concur with Beth James's interpretation of the status of Issuer Corporation's 150,000 shares of retired common stock? Explain.

PROBLEMS

Pr. 5-1   On January 31, Year 8, La Salle Corporation acquired for $540,000 cash all the net assets except cash of De Soto Company and paid $60,000 cash to a law firm for legal services in connection with the business combination. The balance sheet of De Soto Company on January 31, Year 8, prior to the business combination, was as follows:

DE SOTO COMPANY
Balance Sheet (prior to business combination)
January 31, Year 8

Assets		Liabilities & Stockholders' Equity	
Cash	$ 40,000	Liabilities.	$ 620,000
Other current assets (net). . .	280,000	Common stock, no par or	
Plant assets (net)	760,000	stated value	250,000
Intangible assets (net)	120,000	Retained earnings	330,000
		Total liabilities & stock-	
Total assets	$1,200,000	holders' equity	$1,200,000

The present value of De Soto's liabilities on January 31, Year 8, was $620,000. The current fair values of its noncash assets were as follows on January 31, Year 8:

Other current assets	$300,000
Plant assets	874,000
Intangible assets	76,000

Instructions

Prepare journal entries for La Salle Corporation on January 31, Year 8, to record the acquisition of the net assets of De Soto Company except cash. Show computations in the explanations for the journal entries where appropriate. (Disregard income taxes.)

Pr. 5-2   The balance sheet of Cooper Company on August 31, Year 2, with related current fair value data, was as follows:

COOPER COMPANY
Balance Sheet (prior to business combination)
August 31, Year 2

Assets	Carrying amounts	Current fair values
Current assets..	$180,000	$ 220,000
Plant assets (net).....................................	640,000	700,000
Intangible assets (net)................................	80,000	90,000
Total assets.......................................	$900,000	$1,010,000

Liabilities and Stockholders' Equity		
Current liabilities....................................	$ 80,000	$ 80,000
Long-term debt.......................................	200,000	190,000
Total liabilities.....................................	$280,000	$ 270,000
Common stock, no par or stated value	$400,000	
Retained earnings	220,000	
Total stockholders' equity..........................	$620,000	
Total liabilities & stockholders' equity	$900,000	

On August 31, Year 2, Lionel Corporation issued $1 million face amount of 10-year, 10% bonds (interest payable each February 28 and August 31), to yield 14%, for all the net assets of Cooper. Bond issue costs paid on August 31, Year 2, totaled $60,000, and the accounting and legal fees to effect the business combination, paid on August 31, Year 2, were $40,000.

Instructions

Prepare journal entries on August 31, Year 2, to record Lionel Corporation's acquisition of the net assets of Cooper Company. Show the computation of goodwill in the explanation of the relevant journal entry. (Disregard income taxes.)

Pr. 5-3 The journal entries for the purchase-type business combination of Wabash Corporation and Indiana Company on December 31, Year 5, were as follows:

WABASH CORPORATION
Journal Entries
December 31, Year 5

Investment in Indiana Company Common Stock..........	10,000,000	
12% Bonds Payable.............................		10,000,000
To record merger with Indiana Company as a purchase.		

Investment in Indiana Company Common Stock..........	150,000	
Bond Issue Costs	50,000	
Cash		200,000
To record payment of costs incurred in merger with Indiana Company.		

WABASH CORPORATION

Journal Entries (concluded)

December 31, Year 5

Current Assets ($3,140,000 + $560,000)	3,700,000	
Plant Assets ($9,070,000 + $330,000)	9,400,000	
Goodwill	400,000	
Current Liabilities		3,350,000
Investment in Indiana Company Common Stock. . . .		10,150,000

To allocate cost of Indiana Company investment to identifiable assets and liabilities, with the remainder to goodwill. (Income tax effects are disregarded.) Amount of goodwill is computed as follows:

Total cost of investment

   ($10,000,000 + $150,000). $10,150,000

  Less: Carrying amount of

      identifiable net assets

      [($3,140,000 +

      $9,070,000) −

      $3,350,000] $8,860,000

      Excess of current fair

      values of identifiable

      net assets over

      carrying amounts

      ($560,000 +

      $330,000).   890,000   9,750,000

  Amount of goodwill . . . . $ 400,000

Additional Information

(1) The stockholders' equity section of Indiana Company's balance sheet on December 31, Year 5 (prior to the merger), included the following:

Common stock, $1 par	$5,000,000
Retained earnings	3,860,000
Total stockholders' equity.	$8,860,000

(2) There was no contingent consideration in connection with the business combination.

Instructions

Prepare journal entries for Wabash Corporation for the business combination on December 31, Year 5, under the assumption that, instead of issuing bonds, Wabash had issued 1 million shares of its no-par, no-stated-value common stock with a current fair value of $10 a share to effect the combination, that the bond issue costs were costs of issuing common stock, that all other facts remained the same, and that the combination qualified for pooling-of-interests accounting rather than purchase accounting.

Pr. 5-4 The balance sheet of Combinee Company on October 31, Year 5, was as follows:

COMBINEE COMPANY
Balance Sheet (prior to business combination)
October 31, Year 5

Assets

Cash	$ 60,000
Other current assets	420,000
Plant assets (net)	920,000
Total assets	$1,400,000

Liabilities & Stockholders' Equity

Current liabilities	$ 180,000
Long-term debt	250,000
Common stock, $5 par	200,000
Additional paid-in capital	320,000
Retained earnings	450,000
Total liabilities & stockholders' equity	$1,400,000

Combinor Corporation's board of directors established the following current fair values for Combinee's identifiable net assets other than cash:

Other current assets	$ 500,000
Plant assets (net)	1,000,000
Current liabilities	180,000
Long-term debt	240,000

Accordingly, on October 31, Year 5, Combinor issued 100,000 shares of its $10 par (current fair value $13) common stock for all the net assets of Combinee in a purchase-type business combination. Also on October 31, Year 5, Combinor paid the following out-of-pocket costs in connection with the combination:

Finder's fee, accounting fees, and legal fees	$180,000
Costs associated with SEC registration statement	120,000
Total out-of-pocket costs of business combination	$300,000

Instructions

Prepare journal entries for Combinor Corporation on October 31, Year 5, to record the business combination with Combinee Company. (Disregard income taxes.)

Pr. 5-5 Condensed balance sheets of Conner Company and Capsol Company on July 31, Year 9, are on page 238.

On July 31, Year 9, Conner and Capsol entered into a statutory consolidation. The new company, Consol Corporation, issued 45,000 shares of $10 par common stock for all the outstanding common stock of Conner and 30,000 shares for all the outstanding common stock of Capsol. Out-of-pocket costs of the business combination may be disregarded.

	Conner Company	Capsol Company
Total assets	$700,000	$670,000
Total liabilities	$300,000	$300,000
Common stock, $25 par	200,000	250,000
Additional paid-in capital.............................	80,000	130,000
Retained earnings (deficit)	120,000	(10,000)
Total liabilities & stockholders' equity...................	$700,000	$670,000

Instructions

a Prepare a journal entry for Consol Corporation on July 31, Year 9, to record the business combination as a pooling of interests.

b Prepare journal entries for Consol Corporation on July 31, Year 9, to record the business combination as a purchase. Assume that Capsol is the combinor; that current fair values of identifiable assets are $800,000 for Conner and $700,000 for Capsol; that each company's liabilities are fairly stated at $300,000; and that the current fair value of Consol's common stock is $14 a share. (Disregard income taxes.)

Pr. 5-6   The condensed balance sheets of Silva Corporation, the issuing company, prior to and subsequent to its March 1, Year 4, merger with Marvel Company, are as follows:

SILVA CORPORATION
Balance Sheets (prior to and subsequent to business combination)
March 1, Year 4

	Prior to business combination	Subsequent to business combination
Assets		
Current assets	$ 500,000	$ 850,000
Plant assets (net)	1,000,000	1,800,000
Total assets	$1,500,000	$2,650,000
Liabilities & Stockholders' Equity		
Current liabilities	$ 350,000	$ 600,000
Long-term debt	100,000	150,000
Common stock, $1 par..........................	400,000	700,000
Additional paid-in capital	310,000	570,000
Retained earnings................................	340,000	630,000
Total liabilities & stockholders' equity............	$1,500,000	$2,650,000

Prior to the business combination, Marvel had total assets of $1,200,000 and total liabilities of $300,000. Out-of-pocket costs of the business combination were paid by Silva on March 1, Year 4.

Instructions

Reconstruct the journal entries that Silva Corporation prepared on March 1, Year 4, to record the business combination with Marvel Company. (Disregard income taxes.)

Pr. 5-7   On October 31, Year 9, Solomon Corporation issued 20,000 shares of its $1 par (current fair value $20) common stock for all the outstanding common stock of Midland Company in a statutory merger. Out-of-pocket costs of the business combination paid by Solomon on October 31, Year 9, were as follows:

Direct costs of the business combination................................	$20,870
Costs of registering and issuing common stock..........................	31,130
Total out-of-pocket costs of business combination	$52,000

Midland's balance sheet on October 31, Year 9, follows:

MIDLAND COMPANY
Balance Sheet (prior to business combination)
October 31, Year 9

Assets

Inventories	$140,000
Other current assets...	80,000
Plant assets (net)	380,000
Total assets	$600,000

Liabilities & Stockholders' Equity

Payable to Solomon Corporation..	$ 75,000
Other liabilities	225,000
Common stock, $3 par..	30,000
Additional paid-in capital	120,000
Retained earnings..	150,000
Total liabilities & stockholders' equity................................	$600,000

Additional Information

(1) The current fair values of Midland's other current assets and all its liabilities equaled the carrying amounts on October 31, Year 9.

(2) Current fair values of Midland's inventories and plant assets were $170,000 and $420,000, respectively, on October 31, Year 9.

(3) Solomon's October 31, Year 9, balance sheet included an asset entitled Receivable from Midland Company in the amount of $75,000.

Instructions

Prepare Solomon Corporation's journal entries on October 31, Year 9, to record the business combination with Midland Company:

a As a purchase (Disregard income taxes.)

b As a pooling of interests

Pr. 5-8   The balance sheet on March 31, Year 7, and the related current fair value data for Edgar Company were as follows:

EDGAR COMPANY
Balance Sheet (prior to business combination)
March 31, Year 7

	Carrying amounts	*Current fair values*
Assets		
Current assets	$ 500,000	$ 575,000
Plant assets (net)	1,000,000	1,200,000
Patent (net).	100,000	50,000
Total assets	$1,600,000	
Liabilities & Stockholders' Equity		
Current liabilities	$ 300,000	$ 300,000
Long-term debt	400,000	450,000
Common stock, $10 par	100,000	
Retained earnings.	800,000	
Total liabilities & stockholders' equity.	$1,600,000	

On April 1, Year 7, Value Corporation issued 50,000 shares of its no-par, no-stated-value common stock (current fair value $14 a share) and $225,000 cash for the net assets of Edgar Company, in a purchase-type business combination. Of the $125,000 out-of-pocket costs paid by Value on April 1, Year 7, $50,000 were accounting, legal, and finder's fees related to the business combination, and $75,000 were costs related to the issuance of common stock.

Instructions

Prepare journal entries for Value Corporation on March 31, Year 7, to record the business combination with Edgar Company. (Disregard income taxes.)

Pr. 5-9   Molo Company merged into Stave Corporation in a business combination completed April 30, Year 5. Out-of-pocket costs paid by Stave on April 30, Year 5, in connection with the combination were as follows:

Finder's, accounting, and legal fees relating to the business combination	$15,000
Cost associated with SEC registration statement for securities issued to complete the business combination	10,000
Total out-of-pocket costs of business combination	$25,000

The individual balance sheets of the constituent companies immediately prior to the merger were as follows:

STAVE CORPORATION AND MOLO COMPANY
Balance Sheets (prior to business combination)
April 30, Year 5

	Stave Corporation	*Molo Company*
Assets		
Current assets	$ 4,350,000	$ 3,000,000
Plant assets (net)	18,500,000	11,300,000
		(continued)

STAVE CORPORATION AND MOLO COMPANY
Balance Sheets (prior to business combination) (concluded)
April 30, Year 5

	Stave Corporation	*Molo Company*
Assets		
Patents (net).....................................	450,000	200,000
Deferred charges	150,000	
Total assets	$23,450,000	$14,500,000

Liabilities & Stockholders' Equity		
Liabilities.......................................	$ 2,650,000	$ 2,100,000
Common stock, $10 par............................	12,000,000	
Common stock, $5 par.............................		3,750,000
Additional paid-in capital	4,200,000	3,200,000
Retained earnings................................	5,850,000	5,450,000
Less: Treasury stock, at cost, 100,000 shares........	(1,250,000)	
Total liabilities & stockholders' equity..............	$23,450,000	$14,500,000

Additional Information

(1) The current fair values of the identifiable assets and liabilities of Stave Corporation and of Molo Company were as follows on April 30, Year 5:

STAVE CORPORATION AND MOLO COMPANY
Current Fair Values of Identifiable Net Assets
April 30, Year 5

	Stave Corporation	*Molo Company*
Current assets......................................	$ 4,950,000	$ 3,400,000
Plant assets (net)...................................	22,000,000	14,000,000
Patents	570,000	360,000
Deferred charges	150,000	
Liabilities...	(2,650,000)	(2,100,000)
Identifiable net assets	$25,020,000	$15,660,000

(2) There were no intercompany transactions prior to the business combination.

(3) Before the business combination, Stave had 3,000,000 shares of common stock authorized, 1,200,000 shares issued, and 1,100,000 shares outstanding. Molo had 750,000 shares of common stock authorized, issued, and outstanding. The treasury stock of Stave was ''untainted.''

(4) Molo Company was dissolved and liquidated on completion of the merger.

Instructions

Prepare journal entries for Stave Corporation on April 30, Year 5, to record the business combination with Molo Company under each of the following independent assumptions:

a Stave exchanged 400,000 shares of previously unissued common stock and 100,000 shares of treasury stock for all the outstanding common stock of Molo.

All the conditions for pooling accounting enumerated in ***APB Opinion No. 16,*** "Business Combinations," were met.

b Stave paid $3,100,000 cash and issued 10% bonds at face amount of $16,900,000 for all the outstanding common stock of Molo. The current fair value of the bonds was equal to their face amount. (Disregard income taxes.)

Pr. 5-10   As of the close of business August 31, Year 2, Mullin Company merged into Samos Corporation in a business combination meeting the 12 conditions for pooling accounting listed in ***APB Opinion No. 16,*** "Business Combinations." Premerger income statements of the constituent companies for the year ended August 31, Year 2, were as follows:

SAMOS CORPORATION AND MULLIN COMPANY
Income Statements (prior to business combination)
For Year Ended August 31, Year 2

	Samos Corporation	Mullin Company
Revenue:		
Net sales	$800,000	$550,000
Interest	20,000	
Rent		50,000
Total revenue	$820,000	$600,000
Costs and expenses:		
Cost of goods sold	$480,000	$300,000
Operating expenses	75,000	50,000
Interest expense	15,000	10,000
Income taxes expense	100,000	96,000
Total costs and expenses	$670,000	$456,000
Net income	$150,000	$144,000

During the year prior to the merger, Mullin had obtained from and repaid to Samos a $100,000, 15%, 90-day loan; Samos had rented for the entire year a sales office owned by Mullin with a monthly rent of $500 plus 1% of net sales; and Samos had sold to Mullin, at Samos's regular markup, goods costing $120,000, all of which Mullin sold during the year ended August 31, Year 2, to outside customers at Mullin's regular markup.

Instructions

a Prepare working paper eliminations (in journal entry format) for Samos Corporation's postmerger income statement for the year ended August 31, Year 2. (Disregard income taxes.)

b Prepare a working paper for the postmerger income statement of Samos Corporation for the year ended August 31, Year 2.

Pr. 5-11   On June 30, Year 2, Capsule Company and Compari Company entered into a statutory consolidation. A new company, Cap-Com Corporation, issued 100,000 shares of its 500,000 authorized shares of no-par, $5 stated value common stock as follows:

(1) 60,000 shares for all 10,000 outstanding shares of Capsule's $2 par common stock

(2) 40,000 shares for all 15,000 outstanding shares of Compari's $1 par common stock

Costs of $50,000 associated with the statutory consolidation (legal and audit fees, printing charges, SEC fees) were paid in cash on June 30, Year 2 (prior to the consolidation), by Capsule on behalf of Cap-Com. There were no other intercompany transactions.

Following are condensed financial statements of Capsule and Compari for the year ended June 30, Year 2, prior to the consolidation:

CAPSULE COMPANY AND COMPARI COMPANY
Balance Sheets (prior to business combination)
June 30, Year 2

	Capsule Company	Compari Company
Assets		
Current assets	$ 200,000	$ 300,000
Receivable from Cap-Com Corporation	50,000	
Plant assets (net)	700,000	500,000
Other assets	60,000	10,000
Total assets	$1,010,000	$ 810,000
Liabilities & Stockholders' Equity		
Current liabilities	$ 160,000	$ 80,000
Long-term debt	200,000	90,000
Common stock	20,000	15,000
Additional paid-in capital	80,000	150,000
Retained earnings	550,000	475,000
Total liabilities & stockholders' equity	$1,010,000	$ 810,000

CAPSULE COMPANY AND COMPARI COMPANY
Statements of Income and Retained Earnings (prior to business combination)
For Year Ended June 30, Year 2

Net sales	$2,000,000	$3,000,000
Costs and expenses:		
Cost of goods sold	$1,200,000	$2,000,000
Operating expenses	400,000	500,000
Interest expense	15,000	10,000
Income taxes expense	154,000	196,000
Total costs and expenses	$1,769,000	$2,706,000
Net income	$ 231,000	$ 294,000
Retained earnings, beginning of year	319,000	181,000
Retained earnings, end of year	$ 550,000	$ 475,000

Capsule costs its inventories on the first-in, first-out basis; Compari uses last-in, first-out cost for inventories. As part of the consolidation contract, Compari agreed to change its inventories valuation method from last-in first-out to first-in, first-out. Relevant data for Compari are as follows:

	Last-in, first-out cost	First-in, first-out cost
Inventories, June 30, Year 2.......	$100,000	$150,000
Inventories, June 30, Year 1.......	90,000	130,000

Instructions

a Prepare an adjusting entry on June 30, Year 2, to change Compari Company's inventories from last-in, first-out cost to first-in, first-out cost. Compari's income tax rate is 40%. (*Note:* In accordance with **APB Opinion No. 20,** ''Accounting Changes,'' a change from last-in, first-out to another inventory valuation method requires the retroactive adjustment of retained earnings.)

b Prepare a June 30, Year 2, journal entry for Cap-Com Corporation to record the statutory consolidation as a pooling of interests. Do not include revenue and expenses in the journal entry.

c Prepare a working paper to compute the pooled net income of Cap-Com Corporation for the year ended June 30, Year 2.

Pr. 5-12   Coolidge Corporation agreed to pay $850,000 cash and issue 50,000 shares of its $10 par ($20 current fair value a share) common stock on September 30, Year 4, to Hoover Company for all the net assets of Hoover except cash. In addition, Coolidge agreed that if the market value of its common stock was not $20 a share or more on September 30, Year 5, a sufficient number of additional shares of common stock would be issued to Hoover to make the aggregate market value of its Coolidge common shareholdings equal to $1 million on that date.

The balance sheet of Hoover on September 30, Year 4, with related current fair values of assets and liabilities, is on page 245.

Out-of-pocket costs of the business combination paid by Coolidge on September 30, Year 4, were as follows:

Audit fees—SEC registration statement	$ 30,000
Finder's fee...	35,000
Legal fees—business combination.......................................	15,000
Legal fees—SEC registration statement.................................	20,000
Printing costs—securities and SEC registration statement.................	25,000
SEC registration fee..	350
Total out-of-pocket costs of business combination	$125,350

HOOVER COMPANY
Balance Sheet (prior to business combination)
September 30, Year 4

	Carrying amounts	Current fair values
Assets		
Cash..	$ 100,000	$ 100,000
Trade accounts receivable (net)	300,000	300,000
Inventories	600,000	680,000
Short-term prepayments	20,000	20,000
10% investment in Truman Company common stock		
(long-term, marketable)..............................	100,000	180,000
Land..	500,000	650,000
Other plant assets (net)...............................	1,000,000	1,250,000
Patent (net)..	80,000	100,000
Total assets	$2,700,000	
Liabilities & Stockholders' Equity		
Current liabilities	$ 700,000	$ 700,000
Long-term debt	500,000	480,000
Common stock, $5 par................................	600,000	
Additional paid-in capital	400,000	
Retained earnings.....................................	500,000	
Total liabilities & stockholders' equity.................	$2,700,000	

Instructions

a Prepare the September 30, Year 4, journal entries for Coolidge Corporation to reflect the foregoing transactions and events. (Disregard income taxes.)

b Assume that on September 30, Year 5, the market value of Coolidge Corporation's common stock was $16 a share. Prepare a journal entry to record the issuance of additional shares of Coolidge common stock to Hoover Company on that date and the payment of cash in lieu of fractional shares, if any.

6

Consolidated Financial Statements: On Date of Purchase-Type Business Combination

Chapter 5 includes the terms *investor* and *investee* in the discussion of business combinations involving a combinor's acquisition of common stock of a combinee corporation. If the investor acquires a controlling interest in the outstanding common stock of the investee, a *parent-subsidiary relationship* is established. The investee becomes a *subsidiary* of the acquiring *parent company* (investor) but remains a separate legal entity.

Strict adherence to the legal aspects of such a business combination would require the issuance of separate financial statements for the parent company and the subsidiary on the date of the combination, and also for all subsequent accounting periods of the affiliation. However, such strict adherence to legal form disregards the substance of most parent-subsidiary relationships. A parent company and its subsidiary are a *single economic entity.* In recognition of this fact, *consolidated financial statements* are issued to report the financial position and operating results of a parent company and its subsidiaries as though they comprised a *single accounting entity.*

Nature of Consolidated Financial Statements

Consolidated financial statements are similar to the combined financial statements described in Chapter 4 for a home office and its branches. Assets, liabilities, revenue, and expenses of the parent company and its subsidiaries are totaled; intercompany transactions and balances are eliminated; and the final consolidated amounts are reported in the consolidated balance sheet, income statement, statement of stockholders' equity, and statement of cash flows.

However, the separate legal entity status of the parent and subsidiary corporations necessitates consolidation eliminations that generally are more complex than the combination eliminations described and illustrated in Chapter 4 for a home office and its branches. Before illustrating consolidation eliminations, it is appropriate to examine some basic principles of consolidation.

Should All Subsidiaries Be Consolidated?

In the past, a wide range of consolidation practices existed among major corporations in the United States. For example, the forty-second edition of *Accounting Trends & Techniques* (published in 1988), the AICPA's annual survey of accounting practices in the published financial statements of 600 companies, reported the following:[1]

1   A total of 456 companies consolidated all significant subsidiaries, but 136 companies excluded some significant subsidiaries from the consolidated financial statements. (The remaining 8 companies surveyed did not issue consolidated financial statements.)

2   The principal types of subsidiaries excluded from consolidation were foreign subsidiaries, finance-related subsidiaries, and real estate subsidiaries. "Finance-related subsidiaries" included finance companies, insurance companies, banks, and leasing companies.

In the author's opinion, such wide variations in consolidation policy were undesirable and difficult to justify from a theoretical point of view. The purpose of consolidated financial statements is to present for a single accounting entity the combined resources, obligations, and operating results of a family of related corporations; consequently, there is no reason for excluding from consolidation any subsidiary that is *controlled.* The argument that finance-related subsidiaries should not be consolidated with parent manufacturing or retailing enterprises because of their unique features is difficult to justify when one considers the wide variety of production, marketing, and service enterprises that are consolidated in a *conglomerate* or highly diversified family of corporations.

In *FASB Statement No. 94,* "Consolidation of All Majority-Owned Subsidiaries," issued in 1987, the Financial Accounting Standards Board required the consolidation of nearly all subsidiaries, effective for financial statements for fiscal years ending after December 15, 1988. Only subsidiaries not actually controlled (as described in the following paragraph) were exempted from consolidation.

The Meaning of Controlling Interest

Traditionally, an investor's direct or indirect ownership of *more than 50%* of an investee's outstanding common stock has been required to evidence the controlling interest underlying a parent-subsidiary relationship. However, even though such a common stock ownership exists, other circumstances may negate the parent company's *actual* control of the subsidiary. For example, a subsidiary that is in liquidation or reorganization in court-supervised bankruptcy proceedings is not controlled by its parent company. Also, a foreign subsidiary in a country having severe production, monetary, or income tax restrictions may be subject to the authority of the foreign country rather than of the parent company.

It is important to recognize that a parent company's control of a subsidiary may be achieved *indirectly.* For example, if Plymouth Corporation owns 85% of the

---

[1] *Accounting Trends & Techniques,* 42nd ed., AICPA (New York: 1988), p. 45.

outstanding common stock of Selwyn Company and 45% of Talbot Company's common stock, and Selwyn also owns 45% of Talbot's common stock, both Selwyn and Talbot are controlled by Plymouth, because it effectively controls 90% of Talbot. This effective control consists of 45% owned directly and 45% indirectly. Additional examples of indirect control are in Chapter 11.

Criticism of Traditional Concept of Control

Some accountants have challenged the traditional definition of **control** described in the preceding section, which emphasizes *legal form.* These accountants maintain that an investor owning less than 50% of an investee's voting common stock *in substance* may control the affiliate, especially if the remaining common stock is scattered among a large number of stockholders who do not attend stockholder meetings or give proxies. Effective control of an investee also is possible if the individuals comprising management of the investor corporation own a substantial number of shares of common stock of the investee or successfully solicit proxies from the investee's other stockholders.

Furthering the foregoing views, in *Financial Reporting Release No. 25,* the Securities and Exchange Commission (SEC) required companies subject to its jurisdiction to emphasize *economic substance* over *legal form* in adopting a consolidation policy.[2] Subsequently, the Financial Accounting Standards Board issued a *Discussion Memorandum,* ''An Analysis of Issues Related to Consolidation Policy and Procedures,'' which dealt at length with the question of *ownership* (legal form) versus *control* (economic substance) as a basis for consolidation.[3]

Unconsolidated Subsidiaries in Consolidated Financial Statements

Generally accepted accounting principles typically require the use of the *cost method* of accounting for investments in unconsolidated subsidiaries because the subsidiaries generally are neither *controlled* nor *significantly influenced* by the parent company.[4] The cost method of accounting, which is discussed and illustrated in Chapter 7, displays the parent company's share of the dividends declared by an unconsolidated subsidiary as revenue in the consolidated income statement.

CONSOLIDATION OF WHOLLY OWNED SUBSIDIARY ON DATE OF PURCHASE-TYPE BUSINESS COMBINATION

There is no question of *control* of a wholly owned subsidiary. Thus, to illustrate consolidated financial statements for a parent company and a wholly owned purchased subsidiary, assume that on December 31, Year 1, Palm Corporation issued 10,000 shares of its $10 par common stock (current fair value $45 a share) to stock-

---

[2] *Codification of Financial Reporting Policies,* Securities and Exchange Commission (Washington: 1986), Sec. 105.

[3] *FASB Discussion Memorandum,* ''. . . Consolidation Policy and Procedures,'' FASB (Norwalk: 1991), pp. 7–9.

[4] *FASB Statement No. 94,* ''Consolidation of All Majority-Owned Subsidiaries,'' FASB (Stamford: 1987), p. 21.

holders of Starr Company for all the outstanding $5 par common stock of Starr. There was no contingent consideration. Out-of-pocket costs of the business combination paid by Palm on December 31, Year 1, consisted of the following:

<table>
<tr><td rowspan="3">Combinor's out-of-pocket costs of business combination</td><td>Finder's and legal fees relating to business combination . . . .</td><td>$50,000</td></tr>
<tr><td>Costs associated with SEC registration statement for Palm common stock . . .</td><td>35,000</td></tr>
<tr><td>Total out-of-pocket costs of business combination . . . .</td><td>$85,000</td></tr>
</table>

Assume also that the business combination qualified for purchase accounting because all 12 specified conditions for pooling accounting (pages 203 to 204) were not met. Starr Company was to continue its corporate existence as a wholly owned subsidiary of Palm Corporation. Both constituent companies had a December 31 fiscal year and used the same accounting principles and procedures; thus, no adjusting entries were required for either company prior to the combination. The income tax rate for each company was 40%.

Financial statements of Palm Corporation and Starr Company for the year ended December 31, Year 1, prior to consummation of the business combination, are shown on page 250.

The December 31, Year 1, current fair values of Starr Company's identifiable assets and liabilities were the same as their carrying amounts, except for the three assets listed below:

<table>
<tr><td rowspan="4">Current fair values of selected assets of combinee</td><td></td><td>*Current fair values, Dec. 31, Year 1*</td></tr>
<tr><td>Inventories . . . .</td><td>$135,000</td></tr>
<tr><td>Plant assets (net) . . . .</td><td>365,000</td></tr>
<tr><td>Patent (net). . . . .</td><td>25,000</td></tr>
</table>

Because Starr was to continue as a separate corporation and generally accepted accounting principles do not sanction write-ups of assets of a going concern, Starr did not prepare journal entries for the business combination. Palm Corporation recorded the combination as a purchase on December 31, Year 1, with the journal entries on page 251.

The first journal entry on page 251 is similar to the entry illustrated in Chapter 5 (page 193) for a statutory merger accounted for as a purchase. An Investment in Common Stock ledger account is debited with the current fair value of the combinor's common stock issued to effect the business combination, and the paid-in capital accounts are credited in the usual manner for any common stock issuance. In the second journal entry, the ***direct*** out-of-pocket costs of the business combination are debited to the Investment in Common Stock ledger account, and the costs that are

PALM CORPORATION AND STARR COMPANY
Separate Financial Statements (prior to purchase-type business combination)
For Year Ended December 31, Year 1

Income Statements	Palm Corporation	Starr Company
Revenue:		
Net sales	$ 990,000	$600,000
Interest revenue	10,000	
Total revenue	$1,000,000	$600,000
Costs and expenses:		
Cost of goods sold	$ 635,000	$410,000
Operating expenses	158,333	73,333
Interest expense	50,000	30,000
Income taxes expense	62,667	34,667
Total costs and expenses	$ 906,000	$548,000
Net income	$ 94,000	$ 52,000

Statements of Retained Earnings

	Palm Corporation	Starr Company
Retained earnings, beginning of year	$ 65,000	$100,000
Add: Net income	94,000	52,000
Subtotals	$ 159,000	$152,000
Less: Dividends	25,000	20,000
Retained earnings, end of year	$ 134,000	$132,000

Balance Sheets

Assets

	Palm Corporation	Starr Company
Cash	$ 100,000	$ 40,000
Inventories	150,000	110,000
Other current assets	110,000	70,000
Receivable from Starr Company	25,000	
Plant assets (net)	450,000	300,000
Patent (net)		20,000
Total assets	$ 835,000	$540,000

Liabilities & Stockholders' Equity

	Palm Corporation	Starr Company
Payable to Palm Corporation		$ 25,000
Income taxes payable	$ 26,000	10,000
Other liabilities	325,000	115,000
Common stock, $10 par	300,000	
Common stock, $5 par		200,000
Additional paid-in capital	50,000	58,000
Retained earnings	134,000	132,000
Total liabilities & stockholders' equity	$ 835,000	$540,000

Combinor's journal entries for purchase-type business combination (acquisition of 100% of subsidiary's common stock)

PALM CORPORATION (Combinor)
Journal Entries
December 31, Year 1

Investment in Starr Company Common Stock (10,000 × $45) ...	450,000	
Common Stock (10,000 × $10)		100,000
Paid-in Capital in Excess of Par		350,000

To record issuance of 10,000 shares of common stock for all the outstanding common stock of Starr Company in a purchase-type business combination.

Investment in Starr Company Common Stock.................	50,000	
Paid-in Capital in Excess of Par	35,000	
Cash		85,000

To record payment of out-of-pocket costs of business combination with Starr Company. Finder's and legal fees relating to the combination are recorded as additional costs of the investment; costs associated with the SEC registration statement are recorded as an offset to the previously recorded proceeds from the issuance of common stock.

associated with the SEC registration statement, being costs of issuing the common stock, are applied to reduce the proceeds of the common stock issuance.

Unlike the journal entries for a merger accounted for as a purchase illustrated in Chapter 5, the foregoing journal entries do not include any debits or credits to record individual assets and liabilities of Starr Company in the accounting records of Palm Corporation. The reason is that Starr was not *liquidated* as in a merger; it remains a separate legal entity.

After the foregoing journal entries have been posted, the affected ledger accounts of Palm Corporation (the combinor) are as follows:

Ledger accounts of combinor affected by purchase-type business combination

Cash				
Date	**Explanation**	**Debit**	**Credit**	**Balance**
Year 1				
Dec. 31	Balance forward			100,000 dr
31	Out-of-pocket costs of business combination		85,000	15,000 dr

(continued)

Investment in Starr Company Common Stock

Date	Explanation	Debit	Credit	Balance
Year 1				
Dec. 31	Issuance of common stock in business combination	450,000		450,000 dr
31	Direct out-of-pocket costs of business combination	50,000		500,000 dr

Common Stock, $10 Par

Date	Explanation	Debit	Credit	Balance
Year 1				
Dec. 31	Balance forward			300,000 cr
31	Issuance of common stock in business combination		100,000	400,000 cr

Paid-in Capital in Excess of Par

Date	Explanation	Debit	Credit	Balance
Year 1				
Dec. 31	Balance forward			50,000 cr
31	Issuance of common stock in business combination		350,000	400,000 cr
31	Costs of issuing common stock in business combination	35,000		365,000 cr

Preparation of Consolidated Balance Sheet without a Working Paper   Purchase accounting for the business combination of Palm Corporation and Starr Company requires a *fresh start* for the consolidated entity. This reflects the theory that a business combination that meets the requirements for purchase accounting is an *acquisition of the combinee's net assets* (assets less liabilities) by the combinor. The operating results of Palm and Starr prior to the date of their business combination are those of two separate *economic* — as well as *legal* — entities. Accordingly, a consolidated balance sheet is the only *consolidated* financial statement issued by Palm on December 31, Year 1, the date of the purchase-type business combination of Palm and Starr.

The preparation of a consolidated balance sheet for a parent company and its wholly owned subsidiary may be accomplished without the use of a supporting working paper. The parent company's investment account and the subsidiary's stockholder's equity accounts do not appear in the consolidated balance sheet because they are essentially *reciprocal* (intercompany) accounts. Under purchase accounting theory, the parent company (combinor) assets and liabilities (other than intercompany ones) are reflected at *carrying amounts,* and the subsidiary (combinee) assets and liabilities (other than intercompany ones) are reflected at ***current fair values***, in the consolidated balance sheet. Goodwill is recognized to the extent the cost of the parent's investment in 100% of the subsidiary's outstanding common stock exceeds the current fair value of the subsidiary's ***identifiable*** net assets.

Applying the foregoing principles to the Palm Corporation and Starr Company parent-subsidiary relationship, the following consolidated balance sheet is produced:

PALM CORPORATION AND SUBSIDIARY
Consolidated Balance Sheet
December 31, Year 1

Assets

Current assets:		
Cash ($15,000 + $40,000)		$ 55,000
Inventories ($150,000 + $135,000)		285,000
Other ($110,000 + $70,000)		180,000
Total current assets		$ 520,000
Plant assets (net) ($450,000 + $365,000)		815,000
Intangible assets:		
Patent (net) ($0 + $25,000)	$ 25,000	
Goodwill (net)	15,000	40,000
Total assets		$1,375,000

Liabilities & Stockholders' Equity

Liabilities:		
Income taxes payable ($26,000 + $10,000)		$ 36,000
Other ($325,000 + $115,000)		440,000
Total liabilities		$ 476,000
Stockholders' equity:		
Common stock, $10 par	$400,000	
Additional paid-in capital	365,000	
Retained earnings	134,000	899,000
Total liabilities & stockholders' equity		$1,375,000

The following are significant aspects of the foregoing consolidated balance sheet:

1 The first amounts in the computations of consolidated assets and liabilities (except goodwill) are the parent company's carrying amounts; the second amounts are the subsidiary's current fair values.

2 Intercompany accounts (parent's investment, subsidiary's stockholder's equity, and intercompany receivable/payable) are excluded from the consolidated balance sheet.

3   *Goodwill* in the consolidated balance sheet is the cost of the parent company's investment ($500,000) less the current fair value of the subsidiary's identifiable net assets ($485,000), or $15,000. The $485,000 current fair value of the subsidiary's identifiable net assets is computed as follows: $40,000 + $135,000 + $70,000 + $365,000 + $25,000 − $25,000 − $10,000 − $115,000 = $485,000.

Working Paper for Consolidated Balance Sheet   The preparation of a consolidated balance sheet on the date of a purchase-type business combination usually requires the use of a *working paper for consolidated balance sheet,* even for a parent company and a wholly owned subsidiary. The form of the working paper, with the individual balance sheet amounts included for both Palm Corporation and Starr Company, is on page 255.

Developing the Elimination   As indicated on page 252, Palm Corporation's Investment in Starr Company Common Stock ledger account in the working paper for consolidated balance sheet is similar to a home office's Investment in Branch account, as described in Chapter 4. However, Starr Company is a *separate corporation,* not a *branch;* therefore, Starr has the three conventional stockholder's equity accounts rather than the single Home Office reciprocal account used by a branch. Accordingly, the elimination for the *intercompany* accounts of Palm and Starr must *decrease to zero* the Investment in Starr Company Common Stock account of Palm and the three stockholder's equity accounts of Starr. Decreases in assets are effected by *credits,* and decreases in stockholders' equity accounts are effected by *debits;* therefore, the elimination for Palm Corporation and subsidiary on December 31, Year 1 (the date of the purchase-type business combination), is begun as follows (a journal entry format is used to facilitate review of the elimination):

<table>
<tr><td>Elimination of
intercompany accounts</td><td>Common Stock—Starr ....</td><td>200,000</td><td></td></tr>
<tr><td></td><td>Additional Paid-in Capital—Starr ....</td><td>58,000</td><td></td></tr>
<tr><td></td><td>Retained Earnings—Starr ....</td><td>132,000</td><td></td></tr>
<tr><td></td><td></td><td>390,000</td><td></td></tr>
<tr><td></td><td>Investment in Starr Company Common Stock—Palm ....</td><td></td><td>500,000</td></tr>
</table>

The footing of $390,000 of the debit items of the foregoing partial elimination represents the *carrying amount* of the net assets of Starr Company and is $110,000 less than the credit item of $500,000, which represents the cost of Palm Corporation's investment in Starr. As indicated on page 249, part of the $110,000 difference is attributable to the excess of current fair values over carrying amounts of certain *identifiable* assets of Starr. This excess is summarized on page 256 (the current fair values of all other assets and liabilities are equal to their carrying amounts).

Form of working paper
for consolidated
balance sheet

Wholly owned subsidiary on date of purchase-type business combination

PALM CORPORATION AND SUBSIDIARY
Working Paper for Consolidated Balance Sheet
December 31, Year 1

	Palm Corporation	Starr Company	Eliminations increase (decrease)	Consolidated
Assets				
Cash	15,000	40,000		
Inventories......	150,000	110,000		
Other current				
assets.........	110,000	70,000		
Intercompany				
receivable				
(payable)	25,000	(25,000)		
Investment in				
Starr Company				
common stock..	500,000			
Plant assets (net)	450,000	300,000		
Patent (net)		20,000		
Goodwill (net) ...				
Total assets...	1,250,000	515,000		
Liabilities & Stockholders' Equity				
Income taxes				
payable........	26,000	10,000		
Other liabilities ..	325,000	115,000		
Common stock,				
$10 par........	400,000			
Common stock,				
$5 par.........		200,000		
Additional paid-in				
capital.........	365,000	58,000		
Retained				
earnings.......	134,000	132,000		
Total liabilities & stock- holders' equity	1,250,000	515,000		

Differences between current fair values and carrying amounts of combinee's identifiable assets

	Current fair values	Carrying amounts	Excess of current fair values over carrying amounts
Inventories...........................	$135,000	$110,000	$25,000
Plant assets (net).....................	365,000	300,000	65,000
Patent (net)...........................	25,000	20,000	5,000
Totals..............................	$525,000	$430,000	$95,000

Generally accepted accounting principles do not presently permit the write-up of a going concern's assets to their current fair values. Thus, to conform to the requirements of purchase accounting for business combinations, the foregoing excess of current fair values over carrying amounts must be incorporated in the consolidated balance sheet of Palm Corporation and subsidiary by means of the elimination. *Increases* in assets are recorded by *debits;* thus, the elimination for Palm Corporation and subsidiary begun on page 254 is *continued* as follows (in journal entry format):

Use of elimination to reflect current fair values of combinee's identifiable assets

Common Stock—Starr......................................	200,000	
Additional Paid-in Capital—Starr	58,000	
Retained Earnings—Starr	132,000	
Inventories—Starr ($135,000 − $110,000)	25,000	
Plant Assets (net)—Starr ($365,000 − $300,000).............	65,000	
Patent (net)—Starr ($25,000 − $20,000).....................	5,000	
	485,000	
Investment in Starr Company Common Stock—Palm		500,000

The revised footing of $485,000 of the debit items of the foregoing partial elimination is equal to the *current fair value* of the *identifiable* tangible and intangible net assets of Starr Company. Thus, the $15,000 difference ($500,000 − $485,000 = $15,000) between the cost of Palm Corporation's investment in Starr and the current fair value of Starr's identifiable net assets represents *goodwill of Starr,* in accordance with purchase accounting theory for business combinations, described in Chapter 5 (pages 187 to 191). Consequently, the December 31, Year 1, elimination for Palm Corporation and subsidiary is completed with a $15,000 *debit* to Goodwill—Starr.

Completed Elimination and Working Paper for Consolidated Balance Sheet

The completed elimination for Palm Corporation and subsidiary (in journal entry format) is below, and the related working paper for consolidated balance sheet is on page 258.

Completed working paper elimination for wholly owned purchased subsidiary on date of business combination

PALM CORPORATION AND SUBSIDIARY
Working Paper Elimination
December 31, Year 1

(a) Common Stock—Starr. 200,000

　　Additional Paid-in Capital—Starr. 58,000

　　Retained Earnings—Starr. 132,000

　　Inventories—Starr ($135,000 − $110,000). 25,000

　　Plant Assets (net)—Starr ($365,000 − $300,000) 65,000

　　Patent (net)—Starr ($25,000 − $20,000) 5,000

　　Goodwill (net)—Starr ($500,000 − $485,000) 15,000

　　　　Investment in Starr Company Common Stock—Palm . 　　　　　　500,000

To eliminate intercompany investment and equity accounts of subsidiary on date of business combination; and to allocate excess of cost over carrying amount of identifiable assets acquired, with remainder to goodwill. (Income tax effects are disregarded.)

The following features of the working paper for consolidated balance sheet on the date of the purchase-type business combination should be emphasized:

1 The elimination is not entered in either the parent company's or the subsidiary's accounting records; it is only a part of the working paper for preparation of the consolidated balance sheet.

2 The elimination is used to reflect differences between current fair values and carrying amounts of the subsidiary's identifiable net assets because the subsidiary did not write up its assets to current fair values on the date of the business combination.

3 The Eliminations column in the working paper for consolidated balance sheet reflects *increases* and *decreases,* rather than *debits* and *credits.* Debits and credits are not appropriate in a working paper dealing with *financial statements* rather than *trial balances.*

4 *Intercompany receivables* and *payables* are placed on the same line of the working paper for consolidated balance sheet and are combined to produce a consolidated amount of zero.

Wholly owned subsidiary on date of purchase-type business combination

PALM CORPORATION AND SUBSIDIARY
Working Paper for Consolidated Balance Sheet
December 31, Year 1

	Palm Corporation	Starr Company	Eliminations increase (decrease)	Consolidated
Assets				
Cash	15,000	40,000		55,000
Inventories	150,000	110,000	(a) 25,000	285,000
Other current assets	110,000	70,000		180,000
Intercompany receivable (payable)	25,000	(25,000)		
Investment in Starr Company common stock . .	500,000		(a) (500,000)	
Plant assets (net)	450,000	300,000	(a) 65,000	815,000
Patent (net)		20,000	(a) 5,000	25,000
Goodwill (net) . . .			(a) 15,000	15,000
Total assets . . .	1,250,000	515,000	(390,000)	1,375,000
Liabilities & Stockholders' Equity				
Income taxes payable	26,000	10,000		36,000
Other liabilities . .	325,000	115,000		440,000
Common stock, $10 par	400,000			400,000
Common stock, $5 par		200,000	(a) (200,000)	
Additional paid-in capital	365,000	58,000	(a) (58,000)	365,000
Retained earnings	134,000	132,000	(a) (132,000)	134,000
Total liabilities & stock-holders' equity	1,250,000	515,000	(390,000)	1,375,000

5   The respective corporations are identified in the working paper elimination. The reason for precise identification is explained in Chapter 9 dealing with the eliminations of intercompany profits (or gains).

6   The consolidated paid-in capital amounts are those of the parent company only. Subsidiaries' paid-in capital amounts *always* are eliminated in the process of consolidation.

7   Consolidated retained earnings on the date of a purchase-type business combination includes only the retained earnings of the parent company. This treatment is consistent with the theory that purchase accounting reflects a fresh start in an acquisition of net assets (assets less liabilities), not a combining of existing stockholder interests.

8   The amounts in the Consolidated column of the working paper for consolidated balance sheet reflect the financial position of a *single economic entity* comprising *two legal entities,* with all *intercompany* balances of the two entities eliminated.

Consolidated Balance Sheet   The amounts in the Consolidated column of the working paper for consolidated balance sheet are presented in the customary fashion in the *consolidated balance sheet* of Palm Corporation and subsidiary on page 260. In the interest of brevity, notes to financial statements and other required disclosures are omitted. The consolidated amounts are the same as those in the consolidated balance sheet on page 253.

In addition to the *consolidated* balance sheet on December 31, Year 1, on page 260, Palm Corporation's published financial statements for the year ended December 31, Year 1, include the *unconsolidated* income statement and statement of retained earnings illustrated on page 250 and an unconsolidated statement of cash flows.

CONSOLIDATION OF PARTIALLY OWNED SUBSIDIARY ON DATE OF PURCHASE-TYPE BUSINESS COMBINATION

The consolidation of a parent company and its *partially owned* subsidiary differs from the consolidation of a wholly owned subsidiary in one major respect—the recognition of minority interest. *Minority interest,* or *noncontrolling interest,* is a term applied to the claims of stockholders other than the parent company to the net income or losses and net assets of the subsidiary. The minority interest in the subsidiary's net income or losses is displayed in the consolidated income statement, and the minority interest in the subsidiary's net assets is displayed in the consolidated balance sheet.

To illustrate the consolidation techniques for a purchase-type business combination involving a partially owned subsidiary, assume the following facts. On December 31, Year 1, Post Corporation issued 57,000 shares of its $1 par common stock (current fair value $20 a share) to stockholders of Sage Company in exchange for 38,000 of the 40,000 outstanding shares of Sage's $10 par common stock in a purchase-type business combination. Thus, Post acquired a 95% interest (38,000 ÷

PALM CORPORATION AND SUBSIDIARY
Consolidated Balance Sheet
December 31, Year 1

Assets

Current assets:

Cash..		$ 55,000
Inventories..		285,000
Other		180,000
Total current assets		$ 520,000
Plant assets (net)...		815,000
Intangible assets:		
Patent (net)	$ 25,000	
Goodwill (net)	15,000	40,000
Total assets		$1,375,000

Liabilities & Stockholders' Equity

Liabilities:

Income taxes payable..		$ 36,000
Other		440,000
Total liabilities..		$ 476,000
Stockholders' equity:		
Common stock, $10 par	$400,000	
Additional paid-in capital.............................	365,000	
Retained earnings	134,000	899,000
Total liabilities & stockholders' equity............................		$1,375,000

40,000 = 0.95) in Sage, which became Post's subsidiary. There was no contingent consideration. Out-of-pocket costs of the combination, paid in cash by Post on December 31, Year 1, were as follows:

Combinor's out-of-
pocket costs of
business combination

Finder's and legal fees relating to business combination...................	$ 52,250
Costs associated with SEC registration statement	72,750
Total out-of-pocket costs of business combination	$125,000

Financial statements of Post Corporation and Sage Company for their fiscal year ended December 31, Year 1, prior to the business combination, are on page 261. There were no intercompany transactions prior to the combination.

POST CORPORATION AND SAGE COMPANY
Separate Financial Statements (prior to purchase-type business combination)
For Year Ended December 31, Year 1

	Post Corporation	Sage Company
Income Statements		
Net sales	$5,500,000	$1,000,000
Costs and expenses:		
Cost of goods sold................................	$3,850,000	$ 650,000
Operating expenses	925,000	170,000
Interest expense.................................	75,000	40,000
Income taxes expense	260,000	56,000
Total costs and expenses	$5,110,000	$ 916,000
Net income	$ 390,000	$ 84,000
Statements of Retained Earnings		
Retained earnings, beginning of year	$ 810,000	$ 290,000
Add: Net income..................................	390,000	84,000
Subtotals	$1,200,000	$ 374,000
Less: Dividends	150,000	40,000
Retained earnings, end of year....................	$1,050,000	$ 334,000
Balance Sheets		
Assets		
Cash	$ 200,000	$ 100,000
Inventories......................................	800,000	500,000
Other current assets	550,000	215,000
Plant assets (net).................................	3,500,000	1,100,000
Goodwill (net)	100,000	
Total assets....................................	$5,150,000	$1,915,000
Liabilities & Stockholders' Equity		
Income taxes payable.............................	$ 100,000	$ 16,000
Other liabilities	2,450,000	930,000
Common stock, $1 par	1,000,000	
Common stock, $10 par...........................		400,000
Additional paid-in capital..........................	550,000	235,000
Retained earnings	1,050,000	334,000
Total liabilities & stockholders' equity	$5,150,000	$1,915,000

The December 31, Year 1, current fair values of Sage Company's identifiable assets and liabilities were the same as their carrying amounts, except for the following assets:

Current fair values of selected assets of combinee

	Current fair values, Dec. 31, Year 1
Inventories	$ 526,000
Plant assets (net)	1,290,000
Leasehold...	30,000

Sage Company did not prepare journal entries related to the business combination because Sage is continuing as a separate corporation, and generally accepted accounting principles do not permit the write-up of assets of a going concern to current fair values. Post recorded the combination with Sage as a purchase by means of the journal entries below:

Combinor's journal entries for purchase-type business combination (acquisition of 95% of subsidiary's common stock)

POST CORPORATION (Combinor)
Journal Entries
December 31, Year 1

Investment in Sage Company Common Stock		
(57,000 × $20)...	1,140,000	
Common Stock (57,000 × $1)......................		57,000
Paid-in Capital in Excess of Par.....................		1,083,000

To record issuance of 57,000 shares of common stock for 38,000 of the 40,000 outstanding shares of Sage Company common stock in a purchase-type business combination.

Investment in Sage Company Common Stock	52,250	
Paid-in Capital in Excess of Par...........................	72,750	
Cash..		125,000

To record payment of out-of-pocket costs of business combination with Sage Company. Finder's and legal fees relating to the combination are recorded as additional costs of the investment; costs associated with the SEC registration statement are recorded as an offset to the previously recorded proceeds from the issuance of common stock.

After the foregoing journal entries have been posted, the affected ledger accounts of Post Corporation are as follows:

Ledger accounts of combinor affected by purchase-type business combination

Cash

Date	Explanation	Debit	Credit	Balance
Year 1				
Dec. 31	Balance forward			200,000 dr
31	Out-of-pocket costs of business combination		125,000	75,000 dr

(continued)

Investment in Sage Company Common Stock

Date	Explanation	Debit	Credit	Balance
Year 1				
Dec. 31	Issuance of common stock in business combination	1,140,000		1,140,000 dr
31	Direct out-of-pocket costs of business combination	52,250		1,192,250 dr

Common Stock, $1 Par

Date	Explanation	Debit	Credit	Balance
Year 1				
Dec. 31	Balance forward			1,000,000 cr
31	Issuance of common stock in business combination		57,000	1,057,000 cr

Paid-in Capital in Excess of Par

Date	Explanation	Debit	Credit	Balance
Year 1				
Dec. 31	Balance forward			550,000 cr
31	Issuance of common stock in business combination		1,083,000	1,633,000 cr
31	Costs of issuing common stock in business combination	72,750		1,560,250 cr

Working Paper for Consolidated Balance Sheet   Because of the complexities caused by the minority interest in the net assets of a partially owned subsidiary and the measurement of goodwill acquired in the business combination, it is advisable to use a working paper for preparation of a consolidated balance sheet for a parent company and its partially owned subsidiary on the date of the purchase-type business combination. The format of the working paper is identical to that illustrated on page 255.

Developing the Elimination   The preparation of the elimination for a parent company and a partially owned purchased subsidiary parallels that for a wholly owned purchased subsidiary described earlier in this chapter. First, the *intercompany* accounts are reduced to zero, as shown on page 264 (in journal entry format).

The footing of $969,000 of the debit items of the partial elimination on page 264 represents the *carrying amount* of the net assets of Sage Company and is $223,250 less than the credit item of $1,192,250. Part of this $223,250 difference is the excess of the total of the cost of Post Corporation's investment in Sage Company and the *minority interest* in Sage Company's net assets over the carrying amounts of Sage's identifiable net assets. This excess may be computed as follows, from the data

Elimination of intercompany accounts of parent company and purchased subsidiary on date of business combination		

Common Stock—Sage 400,000
Additional Paid-in Capital—Sage 235,000
Retained Earnings—Sage 334,000

  969,000

  Investment in Sage Company Common Stock—Post ...   1,192,250

provided on page 262 (the current fair values of all other assets and liabilities of Sage are equal to their carrying amounts):

Difference between current fair values and carrying amounts of combinee's identifiable assets	Current fair values	Carrying amounts	Excess of current fair values over carrying amounts
Inventories...........................	$ 526,000	$ 500,000	$ 26,000
Plant assets (net)......................	1,290,000	1,100,000	190,000
Leasehold	30,000		30,000
Totals	$1,846,000	$1,600,000	$246,000

Under current generally accepted accounting principles, the foregoing differences are not entered in Sage Company's accounting records. Thus, to conform with the requirements of purchase accounting, the differences must be reflected in the consolidated balance sheet of Post Corporation and subsidiary by means of the elimination, which is continued below:

Use of elimination to reflect current fair values of identifiable assets of purchased subsidiary on date of business combination		

Common Stock—Sage 400,000
Additional Paid-in Capital—Sage 235,000
Retained Earnings—Sage 334,000
Inventories—Sage ($526,000—$500,000) 26,000
Plant Assets (net)—Sage ($1,290,000 − $1,100,000) 190,000
Leasehold—Sage 30,000

  1,215,000

  Investment in Sage Company Common Stock—Post ..   1,192,250

The revised footing of $1,215,000 of the debit items of the above partial elimination represents the ***current fair value*** of Sage Company's ***identifiable*** tangible and intangible net assets on December 31, Year 1.

Two items now must be recorded to complete the elimination for Post Corporation and subsidiary. First, the ***minority interest*** in the identifiable net assets (at current fair values) of Sage Company is recorded by a ***credit.*** The minority interest is computed as follows:

Computation of minority interest in combinee's identifiable net assets	Current fair value of Sage Company's identifiable net assets	$1,215,000
	Minority interest ownership in Sage Company's identifiable net assets (100% minus Post Corporation's 95% interest)	0.05
	Minority interest in Sage Company's **identifiable** net assets ($1,215,000 × 0.05)	$ 60,750

Second, the goodwill **acquired by Post Corporation** in the business combination with Sage Company is recorded by a **debit.** The goodwill is computed below:

Computation of goodwill acquired by combinor	Cost of Post Corporation's 95% interest in Sage Company	$1,192,250
	Less: Current fair value of Sage Company's identifiable net assets acquired by Post ($1,215,000 × 0.95)	1,154,250
	Goodwill **acquired by Post Corporation**	$ 38,000

The working paper elimination for Post Corporation and subsidiary may now be completed as follows:

Completed working paper elimination for partially owned purchased subsidiary on date of business combination

POST CORPORATION AND SUBSIDIARY
Working Paper Elimination
December 31, Year 1

(a) Common Stock—Sage	400,000	
Additional Paid-in Capital—Sage	235,000	
Retained Earnings—Sage	334,000	
Inventories—Sage ($526,000 − $500,000)	26,000	
Plant Assets (net)—Sage ($1,290,000 − $1,100,000)	190,000	
Leasehold—Sage	30,000	
Goodwill (net)—Post ($1,192,250 − $1,154,250)	38,000	
Investment in Sage Company Common Stock—Post		1,192,250
Minority Interest in Net Assets of Subsidiary		60,750
To eliminate intercompany investment and equity accounts of subsidiary on date of business combination; to allocate excess of cost over carrying amount of identifiable assets acquired, with remainder to goodwill; and to establish minority interest in identifiable net assets of subsidiary on date of business combination ($1,215,000 × 0.05 = $60,750). (Income tax effects are disregarded.)		

Working Paper for Consolidated Balance Sheet The working paper for the consolidated balance sheet on December 31, Year 1, for Post Corporation and subsidiary follows:

Partially owned subsidiary on date of purchase-type business combination

POST CORPORATION AND SUBSIDIARY
Working Paper for Consolidated Balance Sheet
December 31, Year 1

	Post Corporation	Sage Company	Eliminations increase (decrease)		Consolidated
Assets					
Cash..............................	75,000	100,000			175,000
Inventories	800,000	500,000	(a)	26,000	1,326,000
Other current assets................	550,000	215,000			765,000
Investment in Sage Company common stock	1,192,250		(a)	(1,192,250)	
Plant assets (net)	3,500,000	1,100,000	(a)	190,000	4,790,000
Leasehold.........................			(a)	30,000	30,000
Goodwill (net)......................	100,000		(a)	38,000	138,000
Total assets	6,217,250	1,915,000		(908,250)	7,224,000
Liabilities & Stockholders' Equity					
Income taxes payable	100,000	16,000			116,000
Other liabilities....................	2,450,000	930,000			3,380,000
Minority interest in net assets of sub- sidiary			(a)	60,750	60,750
Common stock, $1 par..............	1,057,000				1,057,000
Common stock, $10 par		400,000	(a)	(400,000)	
Additional paid-in capital	1,560,250	235,000	(a)	(235,000)	1,560,250
Retained earnings..................	1,050,000	334,000	(a)	(334,000)	1,050,000
Total liabilities & stockholders' equity.	6,217,250	1,915,000		(908,250)	7,224,000

Nature of Minority Interest

The appropriate classification and presentation of minority interest in consolidated financial statements has been a perplexing problem for accountants, especially because it is recognized *only in the consolidation process* and does not result from a business transaction or event of either the parent company or the subsidiary. Two concepts for consolidated financial statements have been developed to account for minority interest—the *parent company concept* and the *economic unit concept.* The FASB has described these two concepts as follows:[5]

---

[5] *FASB Discussion Memorandum,* ". . . Consolidation Policy and Procedures," FASB (Norwalk: 1991), p. 24.

The parent company concept emphasizes the interests of the parent's shareholders. As a result, the consolidated financial statements reflect those stockholders' interests in the parent itself, plus their undivided interests in the net assets of the parent's subsidiaries. The consolidated balance sheet is essentially a modification of the parent's balance sheet with the assets and liabilities of all subsidiaries substituted for the parent's investment in subsidiaries.

. . . [T]he stockholders' equity of the parent company is also the stockholders' equity of the consolidated entity. Similarly, the consolidated income statement is essentially a modification of the parent's income statement with the revenues, expenses, gains, and losses of subsidiaries substituted for the parent's income from investment in the subsidiaries.

The economic unit concept emphasizes control of the whole by a single management. As a result, under this concept (sometimes called the entity theory in the accounting literature), consolidated financial statements are intended to provide information about a group of legal entities—a parent company and its subsidiaries—operating as a single unit. The assets, liabilities, revenues, expenses, gains, and losses of the various component entities are the assets, liabilities, revenues, expenses, gains, and losses of the consolidated entity. Unless all subsidiaries are wholly owned, the business enterprise's proprietary interest (its residual owners' equity—assets less liabilities) is divided into the controlling interest (stockholders or other owners of the parent company) and one or more noncontrolling interests in subsidiaries. Both the controlling and the noncontrolling interests are part of the proprietary group of the consolidated entity, even though the noncontrolling stockholders' ownership interests relate only to the affiliates whose shares they own.

In accordance with the foregoing quotation, the ***parent company concept*** of consolidated financial statements apparently treats the minority interest in net assets of a subsidiary as a *liability.* This liability is increased each accounting period subsequent to the date of a purchase-type business combination by an ***expense*** representing the minority's share of the subsidiary's net income (or decreased by the minority's share of the subsidiary's net loss). Dividends declared by the subsidiary to minority stockholders decrease the liability to them. Consolidated net income is ***net*** of the minority's share of the subsidiary's net income, as illustrated in Chapter 7.

In the ***economic unit concept,*** the minority interest in the subsidiary's net assets is displayed in the stockholders' equity section of the consolidated balance sheet. The consolidated income statement displays the minority interest in the subsidiary's net income as a ***subdivision of total consolidated net income,*** similar to the distribution of net income of a partnership (see page 45).

In the author's opinion, the economic unit concept of reporting minority interest overemphasizes the ***legal aspects*** of the separate corporate organizations comprising a parent-subsidiary relationship. In substance, minority stockholders are a special class of creditors of the consolidated entity, because in the usual case they exercise ***no ownership control whatsoever*** over the operations of either the parent company or the subsidiary. If consolidated financial statements are to present fairly the operating results and financial position of a single economic entity, the niceties of minority stockholders' ownership of a part of the subsidiary should be disregarded. Consequently, *the parent company concept of accounting for minority interest in subsidiary is stressed throughout this book.*[6]

Consolidated Balance Sheet for Partially Owned Subsidiary

The consolidated balance sheet of Post Corporation and its partially owned subsidiary, Sage Company, follows. The consolidated amounts are taken from the working paper for consolidated balance sheet on page 266.

POST CORPORATION AND SUBSIDIARY
Consolidated Balance Sheet
December 31, Year 1

Assets

Current assets:

Cash		$ 175,000
Inventories		1,326,000
Other		765,000
Total current assets		$2,266,000
Plant assets (net)		4,790,000
Intangible assets:		
Leasehold	$ 30,000	
Goodwill (net)	138,000	168,000
Total assets		$7,224,000

Liabilities & Stockholders' Equity

Liabilities:

Income taxes payable		$ 116,000
Other		3,380,000
Minority interest in net assets of subsidiary		60,750
Total liabilities		$3,556,750
Stockholders' equity:		
Common stock, $1 par	$1,057,000	
Additional paid-in capital	1,560,250	
Retained earnings	1,050,000	3,667,250
Total liabilities & stockholders' equity		$7,224,000

The display of minority interest in net assets of subsidiary in the liabilities section of the consolidated balance sheet of Post Corporation and subsidiary is consistent with the parent company concept of consolidated financial statements. It

---

[6] Tables in the 45th edition of *Accounting Trends & Techniques,* issued by the AICPA in 1991, imply that the 135 (of 600) publicly owned companies reporting minority interest in net assets of subsidiaries displayed the amounts among liabilities (p. 225) and that the 56 companies reporting minority interest in net income of subsidiaries displayed the amounts among expenses (p. 355), consistent with the parent company concept. (The difference in the 135 and 56 numbers presumably results from materiality considerations.)

should be noted that *there is no ledger account for minority interest in net assets of subsidiary, in either the parent company's or the subsidiary's accounting records.*

Alternative Methods for Valuing Minority Interest and Goodwill

The computation of minority interest in net assets of subsidiary and goodwill on page 265 is based on two premises. First, the *identifiable net assets* of a partially owned purchased subsidiary should be valued on a single basis—*current fair value,* in accordance with purchase accounting theory for business combinations. Second, only the subsidiary goodwill *acquired by the parent company* should be recognized, in accordance with the cost method for valuing assets.

Two alternatives to the procedure described above have been suggested. The first alternative would assign current fair values to a partially owned purchased subsidiary's identifiable net assets *only to the extent of the parent company's ownership interest therein.* Under this alternative, $233,700 ($246,000 × 0.95 = $233,700) of the total difference between current fair values and carrying amounts of Sage Company's identifiable net assets summarized on page 264 would be reflected in the aggregate debits to inventories, plant assets, and leasehold in the working paper elimination for Post Corporation and subsidiary on December 31, Year 1. The minority interest in net assets of subsidiary would be based on the *carrying amounts* of Sage Company's identifiable net assets, rather than on their *current fair values,* and would be computed as follows: $969,000 × 0.05 = $48,450. Goodwill would be $38,000, as computed on page 265. Supporters of this alternative argue that current fair values of a combinee's identifiable net assets should be reflected in consolidated financial statements only to the extent (percentage) that they have been *acquired by the combinor.* The balance of the combinee's net assets, and the related minority interest in the net assets, should be reflected in consolidated financial statements at the carrying amounts in the subsidiary's accounting records. Thus, identifiable net assets of the subsidiary would be valued on a *hybrid* basis, rather than at full current fair values as required by purchase accounting theory.

The other alternative for valuing minority interest in net assets of subsidiary and goodwill is to obtain a current fair value for *100%* of a partially owned purchased subsidiary's *total* net assets, either through independent measurement of the minority interest or by *inference* from the cost of the parent company's investment in the subsidiary. Independent measurement of the minority interest might be accomplished by reference to quoted market prices of publicly traded common stock owned by minority stockholders of the subsidiary. The computation of minority interest and goodwill of Sage Company by inference from the cost of Post Corporation's investment in Sage is on page 270. Supporters of this approach contend that a *single valuation method* should be used for all net assets of a purchased subsidiary—including goodwill—regardless of the existence of a minority interest in the subsidiary. They further maintain that the goodwill should be attributed to the *subsidiary,* rather than to the *parent company,* as is done for a wholly owned purchased subsidiary, in accordance with the theory of purchase accounting for business combinations.

Total cost of Post Corporation's investment in Sage Company............	$1,192,250
Post's percentage ownership of Sage....................................	0.95
Implied current fair value of 100% of Sage's total net assets	
($1,192,250 ÷ 0.95)...	$1,255,000
Minority interest ($1,255,000 × 0.05)...................................	$ 62,750
Goodwill ($1,255,000 − $1,215,000, the current fair value of Sage's **identi-**	
fiable net assets)	$ 40,000

A summary of the three methods for valuing minority interest and goodwill of apartially owned purchased subsidiary (derived from the December 31, Year 1, business combination of Post Corporation and Sage Company) follows:

	Total identifiable net assets	Minority interest in net assets of subsidiary	Goodwill
1 Identifiable net assets recorded at current fair value; minority interest in net assets of subsidiary based on identifiable net assets...............................	$1,215,000	$60,750	$38,000
2 Identifiable net assets recorded at current fair value only to extent of parent company's interest; balance of net assets and minority interest in net assets of subsidiary reflected at carrying amounts	1,202,700*	48,450	38,000
3 Current fair value, through independent measurement or inference, assigned to total net assets of subsidiary, including goodwill	1,215,000	62,750	40,000

* $969,000 + ($246,000 × 0.95) = $1,202,700

The author has chosen to reflect, in subsequent chapters of this book, the method illustrated in the elimination on page 265 (method **1** above) because it is consistent with purchase accounting for business combinations.

"Negative Goodwill" in Consolidated Balance Sheet

A purchase-type business combination that results in a parent company-subsidiary relationship may involve an excess of current fair values of the subsidiary's identifiable net assets over the cost of the parent company's investment in the subsidiary's common stock. If so, the accounting standards described in Chapter 5 (page 191) are applied. The excess of current fair values over cost is applied pro rata to reduce the amounts initially assigned to noncurrent assets other than long-term investments in marketable securities. Any remaining excess is established as a deferred credit and is amortized over a maximum period of 40 years.

Illustration of "Negative Goodwill": Wholly Owned Subsidiary On December 31, Year 1, Plowman Corporation acquired all the outstanding common stock of Silbert Company for $850,000 cash, including direct out-of-pocket costs of the purchase-type business combination. Stockholders' equity of Silbert totaled $800,000, consisting of common stock, $100,000; additional paid-in capital, $300,000; and retained earnings, $400,000. The current fair values of Silbert's identifiable net assets were the same as their carrying amounts, except for the following:

Current fair values of selected assets of combinee

	Current fair values	Carrying amounts	Differences
Inventories............................	$ 339,000	$320,000	$19,000
Long-term investments in marketable securities	61,000	50,000	11,000
Plant assets (net).......................	1,026,000	984,000	42,000
Intangible assets (net)..................	54,000	36,000	18,000

Thus, the current fair values of Silbert's identifiable net assets exceeded the amount paid by Plowman by $40,000 [($800,000 + $19,000 + $11,000 + $42,000 + $18,000) − $850,000 = $40,000]. This $40,000 "negative goodwill" is offset against amounts originally assigned to Silbert's plant assets and intangible assets in proportion to their current fair values ($1,026,000 : $54,000 = 95 : 5). The December 31, Year 1, working paper elimination for Plowman Corporation and subsidiary is shown below:

Working paper elimination for wholly owned purchased subsidiary with "negative goodwill" on date of business combination

PLOWMAN CORPORATION AND SUBSIDIARY
Working Paper Elimination
December 31, Year 1

(a) Common Stock—Silbert	100,000	
Additional Paid-in Capital—Silbert	300,000	
Retained Earnings—Silbert	400,000	
Inventories—Silbert ($339,000 − $320,000)	19,000	
Long-Term Investments in Marketable Securities—Silbert ($61,000 − $50,000)	11,000	
Plant Assets (net)—Silbert [($1,026,000 − $984,000) − ($40,000 × 0.95)]...........	4,000	
Intangible Assets (net)—Silbert [($54,000 − $36,000) − ($40,000 × 0.05)]...............	16,000	
Investment in Silbert Company Common Stock— Plowman......................................		850,000

To eliminate intercompany investment and equity accounts of subsidiary on date of business combination; and to allocate $40,000 excess of current fair values of subsidiary's identifiable net assets over cost to subsidiary's plant assets and intangible assets in ratio of $1,026,000 : $54,000, or 95% : 5%. (Income tax effects are disregarded.)

Illustration of "Negative Goodwill": Partially Owned Subsidiary The Plowman Corporation – Silbert Company business combination described in the foregoing section is now changed by assuming that Plowman acquired **98%**, rather than **100%**, of Silbert's common stock for $833,000 ($850,000 × 0.98 = $833,000) on December 31, Year 1, with all other facts remaining unchanged. The excess of current fair values of Silbert's identifiable net assets over Plowman's cost is $39,200 [($890,000 × 0.98) − $833,000 = $39,200]. Under these circumstances, the working paper elimination for Plowman Corporation and subsidiary on December 31, Year 1, is as shown below:

PLOWMAN CORPORATION AND SUBSIDIARY
Working Paper Elimination
December 31, Year 1

(a) Common Stock—Silbert	100,000	
Additional Paid-in Capital—Silbert	300,000	
Retained Earnings—Silbert	400,000	
Inventories—Silbert ($339,000 − $320,000)	19,000	
Long-Term Investments in Marketable Securities—Silbert ($61,000 − $50,000)	11,000	
Plant Assets (net)—Silbert [($42,000 − ($39,200 × 0.95)]	4,760	
Intangible Assets (net)—Silbert [$18,000 − ($39,200 × 0.05)]	16,040	
Investment in Silbert Company Common Stock— Plowman		833,000
Minority Interest in Net Assets of Subsidiary ($890,000 × 0.02)		17,800

To eliminate intercompany investment and equity accounts of subsidiary on date of business combination; to allocate parent company's share of excess ($39,200) of current fair values of subsidiary's identifiable net assets over cost to subsidiary's plant assets and intangible assets in ratio of 95% : 5%; and to establish minority interest in net assets of subsidiary on date of business combination. (Income tax effects are disregarded.)

Disclosure of Consolidation Policy

The "Summary of Significant Accounting Policies" note to financial statements required by **APB Opinion No. 22,** "Disclosure of Accounting Policies," generally includes a description of consolidation policy reflected in consolidated financial statements. The following excerpt from an annual report of Unocal Corporation, a publicly owned corporation, is typical:[7]

Principles of Consolidation
For the purposes of this report, Unocal Corporation (Unocal) and its consolidated subsidiary, Union Oil Company of California (Union Oil), will be referred to as the company.

[7] *Accounting Trends & Techniques,* 45th ed., AICPA (New York: 1991), p. 54.

The consolidated financial statements of the company include the accounts of subsidiaries more than 50 percent owned, except for certain Brazilian subsidiaries which are accounted for by the cost method due to currency restrictions imposed by the Brazilian government. Investments in affiliates owned 50 percent or less are accounted for by the equity method. Under the equity method, the investments are stated at cost plus the company's equity in undistributed earnings after acquisition. Income taxes estimated to be payable when earnings are distributed are included in deferred income taxes.

Another example of disclosure of consolidation policy is shown in Note 1 to the financial statements of The Walt Disney Company in the appendix at the end of Chapter 20.

Advantages and Shortcomings of Consolidated Financial Statements

Consolidated financial statements are useful principally to stockholders and prospective investors of the parent company. These users of consolidated financial statements are provided with comprehensive financial information for the economic unit represented by the parent company and its subsidiaries, without regard for legal separateness of the individual companies.

Creditors of each consolidated company and minority stockholders of subsidiaries have only limited use for consolidated financial statements, because such statements do not show the financial position or operating results of the individual companies comprising the consolidated group. In addition, creditors of the constituent companies cannot ascertain the asset coverages for their respective claims. But perhaps the most telling criticism of consolidated financial statements in recent years has come from financial analysts. These critics have pointed out that consolidated financial statements of diversified companies (conglomerates) are impossible to classify into a single industry. Thus, say the financial analysts, consolidated financial statements of a conglomerate cannot be used for comparative purposes. The problem of financial reporting by diversified companies is considered in Chapter 20.

"Push-Down Accounting" for a Purchased Subsidiary

A thorny question for accountants has been the appropriate basis of accounting for assets and liabilities of a purchased subsidiary that, because of loan agreements, legal requirements, or other commitments, issues separate financial statements to outsiders following the purchase-type business combination. Some accountants have maintained that because generally accepted accounting principles do not permit the write-up of assets by a going concern, the purchased subsidiary should report assets, liabilities, revenue, and expenses in its separate financial statements at amounts based on carrying amounts prior to the business combination. Other accountants have recommended that the values assigned to the purchased subsidiary's net assets in the consolidated financial statements be "pushed down" to the subsidiary for incorporation in its separate financial statements. These accountants believe that the business combination is an event that warrants recognition of current fair values of the subsidiary's net assets in its separate statements.

In *Staff Accounting Bulletin No. 54,* the Securities and Exchange Commission staff sanctioned *push-down accounting* for separate financial statements of purchased subsidiaries that are substantially wholly owned by a parent company subject to the SEC's jurisdiction.[8] (The securities laws administered by the SEC, and the SEC's own rules, sometimes require a parent company to include separate financial statements of a subsidiary in its reports to the SEC.) This action by the SEC staff was followed several years later by the FASB's issuance of a *Discussion Memorandum,* ". . . New Basis Accounting," which solicited views on when, if ever, a business enterprise should adjust the carrying amounts of its net assets, including goodwill, to current fair values, including push-down accounting situations.[9]

In the absence of definitive guidelines from the Financial Accounting Standards Board, companies that have applied push-down accounting apparently have used accounting techniques analogous to quasi-reorganizations (which are discussed in intermediate accounting textbooks) or to reorganizations under the U.S. Bankruptcy Code (discussed in Chapter 16). That is, the restatement of identifiable assets and liabilities of the purchased subsidiary and the recognition of goodwill are accompanied by a write-off of the subsidiary's retained earnings; the balancing amount is an increase in additional paid-in capital of the subsidiary.[10]

To illustrate push-down accounting, I return to the Post Corporation–Sage Company business combination, specifically to the working paper for consolidated balance sheet on page 266. To apply the push-down accounting techniques described in the previous paragraph, the following *working paper adjustment* to the Sage Company balance sheet amounts would be required:

Working paper adjustment for push-down accounting for subsidiary's separate balance sheet		

Inventories	26,000	
Plant Assets (net)	190,000	
Leasehold	30,000	
Goodwill	38,000	
Retained Earnings	334,000	
Additional Paid-in Capital		618,000

To adjust carrying amounts of identifiable net assets, to recognize goodwill, and to write off retained earnings in connection with push-down accounting for separate financial statements.

Sage Company's separate balance sheet reflecting push-down accounting is on page 275. A note to financial statements would describe Sage Company's business combination with Post Corporation and its adjustments to reflect push-down accounting in its balance sheet.

Note that the $38,000 goodwill in Sage Company's separate balance sheet was attributed to Post Corporation in the working paper elimination on page 265. As explained in Chapter 7, the attribution to Post Corporation is required to avoid applying any amortization of the goodwill to minority stockholders' interest in net income of Sage.

---

[8] *Staff Accounting Bulletin No. 54,* Securities and Exchange Commission (Washington: 1983).
[9] *FASB Discussion Memorandum,* ". . . New Basis Accounting," FASB (Norwalk: 1991), pp. 1–2.
[10] Hortense Goodman and Leonard Lorensen, *Illustrations of "Push Down" Accounting,* AICPA (New York: 1985).

SAGE COMPANY
Balance Sheet (push-down accounting)
December 31, Year 1

Assets

Current assets:

Cash..	$ 100,000
Inventories ($500,000 + $26,000)................................	526,000
Other	215,000
Total current assets	$ 841,000
Plant assets (net) ($1,100,000 + $190,000)...........................	1,290,000
Leasehold	30,000
Goodwill..	38,000
Total assets	$2,199,000

Liabilities & Stockholders' Equity

Liabilities:

Income taxes payable..		$ 16,000
Other		930,000
Total liabilities...		$ 946,000
Stockholders' equity:		
Common stock, $10 par	$400,000	
Additional paid-in capital ($235,000 + $618,000)..........	853,000	1,253,000
Total liabilities & stockholders' equity		$2,199,000

SEC ENFORCEMENT ACTIONS DEALING WITH WRONGFUL APPLICATION OF ACCOUNTING STANDARDS FOR CONSOLIDATED FINANCIAL STATEMENTS

AAER 34 "Securities and Exchange Commission v. Digilog, Inc. and Ronald Moyer," reported in *AAER 34* (July 5, 1984), deals with the issue of whether Corporation A, though *in form* not a conventional subsidiary, *in substance* was controlled by Corporation B and thus should have been a party to consolidated financial statements with Corporation B, which developed, manufactured, and sold electronic equipment. In reporting a federal court's entry of a permanent injunction against Corporation B and its CEO, the SEC opined that, although Corporation A's initial issuance of 50 shares of common stock was to the CEO of Corporation B (for $50,000), Corporation B nonetheless substantively controlled Corporation A for the following reasons:

1 Corporation B provided initial working capital of $450,000 to Corporation A in exchange for promissory notes convertible within five years to 90% of the authorized common stock of Corporation A.

2 Corporation B sublet office space and provided accounting, financial, and administrative services to Corporation A.

3   Corporation B sold equipment, software, furniture, and other items to Corporation A for cash and a $92,000 interest-bearing promissory note.

4   Corporation B ultimately made loans and extended credit to, and guaranteed bank loans of, Corporation A that totaled $4.9 million.

5   All promissory notes issued by Corporation A to Corporation B were secured by the former's accounts receivable, inventories, and equipment.

Despite Corporation B's management's having been informed by its independent auditors that its financial statements need not be consolidated with those of Corporation A, the SEC ruled to the contrary, maintaining that *substance* prevailed over *form* (Corporation B's CEO, rather than Corporation B itself, owned all 50 shares of Corporation A's outstanding common stock). In a related enforcement action, reported in *AAER 45,* ''. . . In the Matter of Coopers & Lybrand and M. Bruce Cohen, C.P.A.'' (November 27, 1984), the SEC reported its acceptance of the undisclosed terms of a ''Consent and Settlement'' with the CPA firm and its engagement partner that had audited Corporation B's unconsolidated financial statements.

REVIEW QUESTIONS

1   Discuss the similarities and dissimilarities between consolidated financial statements for a parent company and its subsidiaries and combined financial statements for the home office and branches of a single legal entity.

2   The use of consolidated financial statements for reporting to stockholders is common. Under some conditions, certain subsidiaries may be excluded from consolidation. List the conditions under which subsidiaries sometimes are excluded from consolidated financial statements.

3   The controller of Pastor Corporation, which has just become the parent of Sexton Company in a purchase-type business combination, inquires if a consolidated income statement is required for the year ended on the date of the combination. What is your reply? Explain.

4   If a business combination resulting in a parent-subsidiary relationship is accounted for as a purchase, the identifiable net assets of the subsidiary must be reflected in the consolidated balance sheet at their current fair values on the date of the business combination. Does this require the subsidiary to enter the current fair values of the identifiable net assets in its accounting records? Explain.

5   Are eliminations for the preparation of consolidated financial statements entered in the accounting records of the parent company or of the subsidiary? Explain.

6   Differentiate between a *working paper for consolidated balance sheet* and a *consolidated balance sheet.*

7   Describe three methods that have been proposed for valuing minority interest and goodwill in the consolidated balance sheet of a parent company and its partially owned purchased subsidiary.

8 Compare the ***parent company concept*** and the ***economic unit concept*** of consolidated financial statements as they relate to the display of minority interest in net assets of subsidiary in a consolidated balance sheet.

9 The principal limitation of consolidated financial statements is their lack of separate information about the assets, liabilities, revenue, and expenses of the individual companies included in the consolidation. List the problems that users of consolidated financial statements encounter as a result of this limitation.

10 What is ***push-down accounting?***

EXERCISES

Ex. 6-1 Select the best answer for each of the following multiple-choice questions:

1 A parent company's correctly prepared journal entry to record the out-of-pocket costs of the acquisition of the subsidiary's outstanding common stock in a purchase-type business combination was as follows (explanation omitted):

Investment in Sullivan Company Common Stock 36,800
    Cash 36,800

The implication of the foregoing journal entry is that the consideration issued by the parent company for the outstanding common stock of the subsidiary was:
a Cash
b Bonds
c Common stock
d Cash, bonds, or common stock

2 The traditional definition of ***control*** for a parent company – subsidiary relationship (parent's ownership of more than 50% of the subsidiary's outstanding common stock) emphasizes:
a Legal form
b Economic substance
c Both legal form and economic substance
d Neither legal form nor economic substance

3 An investor company that owns more than 50% of the outstanding voting common stock of an investee may not ***control*** the investee if:
a The investee is in reorganization in bankruptcy proceedings.
b There is a large minority interest in the investee.
c A part of the investor company's ownership is ***indirect.***
d The investee is a finance-related enterprise.

4 ***FASB Statement No. 94,*** ''Consolidation of All Majority Owned Subsidiaries,'' exempted from consolidation:
a No subsidiaries of the parent company
b Foreign subsidiaries of the parent company
c Finance-related subsidiaries of the parent company
d Subsidiaries not controlled by the parent company

5   The method of accounting typically used for a parent company's investment in an unconsolidated subsidiary is the:

a Cost method

b Equity method

c Purchase method

d Pooling method

6   If, on the date of the business combination, C = consideration given to the former stockholders of wholly owned subsidiary Stacey Company by Passey Corporation; DOP = direct out-of-pocket costs of the combination; CA = carrying amount, and CFV = current fair value of Stacey's identifiable net assets; and GW = goodwill:

a C + DOP = CA + GW

b C − DOP = CFV − GW

c C + DOP = CFV + GW

d C = CA + GW − DOP

7   In a completed working paper elimination (in journal entry format) for a parent company and its wholly owned purchased subsidiary on the date of the business combination, the total of the debits generally equals the:

a Parent company's total cost of its investment in the subsidiary

b Carrying amount of the subsidiary's identifiable net assets

c Current fair value of the subsidiary's identifiable net assets

d Total paid-in capital of the subsidiary

8   In a working paper elimination (in journal entry format) for the consolidated balance sheet of a parent company and its wholly owned subsidiary on the date of a purchase-type business combination, the subtotal of the debits to the subsidiary's stockholder's equity accounts equals the:

a Current fair value of the subsidiary's *identifiable* net assets

b Current fair value of the subsidiary's *total* net assets, including goodwill

c Balance of the parent company's investment ledger account

d Carrying amount of the subsidiary's *identifiable* net assets

9   In the working paper for consolidated balance sheet prepared on the date of the purchase-type business combination of a parent company and its wholly owned subsidiary, whose liabilities had current fair values equal to their carrying amounts, the total of the Eliminations column is equal to:

a The current fair value of the subsidiary's *identifiable* net assets

b The total stockholder's equity of the subsidiary

c The current fair value of the subsidiary's *total* net assets, including goodwill

d An amount that is not determinable

10   On the date of the purchase-type business combination of Pobre Corporation and its wholly owned subsidiary, Sabe Company, Pobre paid (1) $100,000 to the former stockholders of Sabe for their stockholders' equity of $65,000 and (2) $15,000 for direct out-of-pocket costs of the combination. Goodwill recognized in the business combination was $10,000. The current fair value of Sabe's identifiable net assets was:

a $65,000   **b** $75,000   **c** $105,000   **d** $115,000   **e** $125,000

11 Differences between current fair values and carrying amounts of the identifiable net assets of a subsidiary on the date of a purchase-type business combination are recognized in a:

a Working paper elimination
b Subsidiary journal entry
c Parent company journal entry
d Note to the consolidated financial statements

12 In a purchase-type business combination resulting in a parent company–wholly owned subsidiary relationship, goodwill developed in the working paper elimination is attributed:

a In its entirety to the subsidiary
b In its entirety to the parent company
c To both the parent company and the subsidiary, in the ratio of current fair values of identifiable net assets
d In its entirety to the consolidated entity

13 In a consolidated balance sheet of a parent company and its partially owned purchased subsidiary, minority interest in net assets of subsidiary is displayed as a:

a Liability under the economic unit concept but a part of consolidated stockholders' equity under the parent company concept
b Part of consolidated stockholders' equity under the economic unit concept but a liability under the parent company concept
c Liability under both the economic unit concept and the parent company concept
d Part of consolidated stockholders' equity under both the economic unit concept and the parent company concept

14 On the date of the purchase-type business combination of a parent company and its partially owned subsidiary, under the computation method used in this book, the amount assigned to minority interest in net assets of subsidiary is based on the:

a Cost of the parent company's investment in the subsidiary's common stock
b Carrying amount of the subsidiary's *identifiable* net assets
c Current fair value of the subsidiary's *identifiable* net assets
d Current fair value of the subsidiary's *total* net assets, including goodwill

15 Is a minority interest in net assets of subsidiary displayed in the consolidated balance sheet of a parent company and its:

	Wholly owned subsidiary?	Partially owned subsidiary?
a	Yes	Yes
b	Yes	No
c	No	Yes
d	No	No

16 The debits in the working paper elimination (in journal entry format) for the consolidated balance sheet of Parent Corporation and 90%-owned purchased Subsidiary Company totaled $2,080,000, including a debit of $80,000 to Goodwill—Parent. The credit elements of the elimination are:

	Investment in Subsidiary Company Common Stock—Parent	Minority Interest in Net Assets of Subsidiary
a	$2,000,000	$ 80,000
b	$1,880,000	$200,000
c	$1,872,000	$208,000
d	.... Some other amounts	

17 The cost of Paul Corporation's 80% investment in Seth Company's outstanding voting common stock was $1,200,000, and the current fair value of Seth's identifiable net assets, which had a carrying amount of $1,000,000, was $1,250,000. Under the computation method used in this book, Goodwill—Paul and Minority Interest in Net Assets of Subsidiary are, respectively:

a $200,000 and $250,000
b $200,000 and $200,000
c $250,000 and $300,000
d Some other amounts

18 Has push-down accounting for a purchased subsidiary's separate financial statements been sanctioned by the:

	FASB?	SEC?
a	Yes	Yes
b	Yes	No
c	No	Yes
d	No	No

Ex. 6-2 On March 31, Year 2, Pyre Corporation acquired for $8,200,000 cash all the outstanding common stock of Stark Company when Stark's balance sheet showed net assets of $6,400,000. Out-of-pocket costs of the business combination may be disregarded. Stark's identifiable net assets had current fair values different from carrying amounts as follows:

	Carrying amounts	Current fair values
Plant assets (net)	$10,000,000	$11,500,000
Other assets	1,000,000	700,000
Long-term debt	6,000,000	5,600,000

Prepare a working paper to compute the amount of goodwill to be displayed in the consolidated balance sheet of Prye Corporation and subsidiary on March 31, Year 2.

Ex. 6-3 Single Company's balance sheet on December 31, Year 6, is on page 281.
On December 31, Year 6, Phyll Corporation acquired all the outstanding common stock of Single for $1,560,000 cash, including direct out-of-pocket costs. On that date, the current fair value of Single's inventories was $450,000 and the current fair

SINGLE COMPANY
Balance Sheet (prior to business combination)
December 31, Year 6

Assets

Cash	$ 100,000
Trade accounts receivable (net)	200,000
Inventories	510,000
Plant assets (net)	900,000
Total assets	$1,710,000

Liabilities & Stockholders' Equity

Current liabilities	$ 310,000
Long-term debt	500,000
Common stock, $1 par	100,000
Additional paid-in capital	200,000
Retained earnings	600,000
Total liabilities & stockholders' equity	$1,710,000

value of Single's plant assets was $1,000,000. The current fair values of all other assets and liabilities of Single were equal to their carrying amounts.

a Prepare a working paper to compute the amount of goodwill to be displayed in the December 31, Year 6, consolidated balance sheet of Phyll Corporation and subsidiary.

b Prepare a working paper to compute the amount of consolidated retained earnings to be displayed in the December 31, Year 6, consolidated balance sheet of Phyll Corporation and subsidiary, assuming that Phyll's unconsolidated balance sheet on that date included retained earnings of $2,500,000.

Ex. 6-4   Shown below and on page 282 are the December 31, Year 3, balance sheets of two companies prior to their business combination.

PELERIN CORPORATION AND SOUTH COMPANY
Separate Balance Sheets (prior to business combination)
December 31, Year 3
(000 omitted)

	Pelerin Corporation	South Company
Assets		
Cash	$ 3,000	$ 100
Inventories (at first-in, first-out cost, which approximates current fair value)	2,000	200
Plant assets (net)	5,000	700*
Total assets	$10,000	$1,000

(continued)

PELERIN CORPORATION AND SOUTH COMPANY
Separate Balance Sheets (prior to business combination) (concluded)
December 31, Year 3
(000 omitted)

	Pelerin Corporation	South Company
Liabilities & Stockholders' Equity		
Current liabilities....................................	$ 600	$ 100
Common stock, $1 par...............................	1,000	100
Additional paid-in capital	3,000	200
Retained earnings....................................	5,400	600
Total liabilities & stockholders' equity	$10,000	$1,000

* Current fair value, Dec. 31, Year 3, $1,500,000.

a On December 31, Year 3, Pelerin Corporation acquired all the outstanding common stock of South Company for $2,000,000 cash. Prepare a working paper to compute the amount of goodwill to be displayed in the consolidated balance sheet of Pelerin Corporation and subsidiary on December 31, Year 3.

b On December 31, Year 3, Pelerin Corporation acquired all the outstanding common stock of South Company for $1,600,000 cash. Prepare a working paper to compute the amount of plant assets to be displayed in the consolidated balance sheet of Pelerin Corporation and subsidiary on December 31, Year 3.

Ex. 6-5   The separate balance sheets of Painter Corporation and Sawyer Company following their business combination, in which Painter acquired all of Sawyer's outstanding common stock, were as follows:

PAINTER CORPORATION AND SAWYER COMPANY
Separate Balance Sheets (following business combination)
May 31, Year 6

	Painter Corporation	Sawyer Company
Assets		
Inventories...	$ 60,000	$ 30,000
Other current assets	140,000	110,000
Investment in Sawyer Company common stock..........	250,000	
Plant assets (net)....................................	220,000	160,000
Goodwill (net)	10,000	
Total assets.......................................	$680,000	$300,000
Liabilities & Stockholders' Equity		
Current liabilities....................................	$100,000	$ 70,000
Bonds payable	104,000	30,000
Common stock, $1 par...............................	200,000	80,000
Additional paid-in capital	116,000	70,000
Retained earnings....................................	160,000	50,000
Total liabilities & stockholders' equity	$680,000	$300,000

On May 31, Year 6, the current fair values of Sawyer's inventories and plant assets (net) were $40,000 and $180,000, respectively; the current fair values of its other assets and its liabilities were equal to their carrying amounts.

Prepare a consolidated balance sheet for Painter Corporation and subsidiary on May 31, Year 6, without using a working paper. (Disregard income taxes.)

Ex. 6-6   On May 31, Year 4, Pristine Corporation acquired for $950,000 cash, including direct out-of-pocket costs of the business combination, all the outstanding common stock of Superb Company. There was no contingent consideration involved in the combination. Superb was to be a subsidiary of Pristine.

Additional Information for May 31, Year 4

(1) Superb's stockholders' equity prior to the combination was as follows:

Common stock, $1 par.	$100,000
Additional paid-in capital.	200,000
Retained earnings.	450,000
Total stockholders' equity.	$750,000

(2) Superb's liabilities had current fair values equal to their carrying amounts. Current fair values of Superb's inventories, land, and building (net) exceeded carrying amounts by $60,000, $40,000, and $50,000, respectively.

Prepare a working paper elimination, in journal entry format (omit explanation) for the consolidated balance sheet of Pristine Corporation and subsidiary on May 31, Year 4. (Disregard income taxes.)

Ex. 6-7   The condensed separate and consolidated balance sheets of Perth Corporation and its subsidiary, Sykes Company, on the date of their business combination, follow:

PERTH CORPORATION AND SUBSIDIARY
Separate and Consolidated Balance Sheets (following business combination)
June 30, Year 3

	Perth Corporation	Sykes Company	Consolidated
Assets			
Cash.	$ 100,000	$ 40,000	$ 140,000
Inventories.	500,000	90,000	610,000
Other current assets.	250,000	60,000	310,000
Investment in Sykes Company common			
stock.	440,000		
Plant assets (net).	1,000,000	360,000	1,440,000
Goodwill (net).	100,000		120,000
Total assets.	$2,390,000	$550,000	$2,620,000

(continued)

PERTH CORPORATION AND SUBSIDIARY
Separate and Consolidated Balance Sheets (following business combination) (concluded)
June 30, Year 3

	Perth Corporation	Sykes Company	Consolidated
Liabilities & Stockholders' Equity			
Income taxes payable...............	$ 40,000	$ 35,000	$ 75,000
Other liabilities	580,600	195,000	775,600
Common stock.....................	1,020,000	200,000	1,020,000
Additional paid-in capital	429,400	210,000	429,400
Retained earnings (deficit)...........	320,000	(90,000)	320,000
Total liabilities & stockholders' equity	$2,390,000	$550,000	$2,620,000

Reconstruct the working paper elimination for Perth Corporation and subsidiary on June 30, Year 3 (in journal entry format), indicated by the above data. (Disregard income taxes.)

Ex. 6-8 On November 1, Year 4, Prox Corporation issued 10,000 shares of its $10 par ($30 current fair value) common stock for 85 of the 100 outstanding shares of Senna Company's $100 par common stock, in a purchase-type business combination. Out-of-pocket costs of the business combination were as follows:

Legal and finder's fees associated with the business combination	$36,800
Costs incurred for SEC registration statement for Prox common stock........	20,000
Total out-of-pocket costs of business combination	$56,800

On November 1, Year 4, the current fair values of Senna's identifiable net assets were equal to their carrying amounts. On that date, Senna's stockholders' equity consisted of the following:

Common stock, $100 par	$ 10,000
Additional paid-in capital	140,000
Retained earnings...	70,000
Total stockholders' equity	$220,000

Prepare journal entries for Prox Corporation on November 1, Year 4, to record the business combination with Senna Company. (Disregard income taxes.)

Ex. 6-9 On February 28, Year 9, Ploy Corporation acquired 88% of the outstanding common stock of Skye Company for $50,000 cash and 5,000 shares of Ploy's $10 par common stock with a current fair value of $20 a share. Out-of-pocket costs of the purchase-type business combination paid by Ploy on February 28, Year 9, were as follows:

Finder's and legal fees relating to business combination...................	$15,000
Costs associated with SEC registration statement.........................	10,000
Total out-of-pocket costs of business combination	$25,000

On February 28, Year 9, Skye's stockholders' equity consisted of common stock, $1 par, $10,000; additional paid-in capital, $30,000; and retained earnings, $60,000. Carrying amounts of the three following identifiable assets or liabilities of Skye were *less than current fair values* on February 28, Year 9, by the amounts indicated:

Inventories	$20,000
Plant assets (net)	80,000
Bonds payable, due February 28, Year 14	30,000

a Prepare journal entries for Ploy Corporation on February 28, Year 9, to record the business combination with Skye Company. (Disregard income taxes.)

b Prepare a working paper to compute the following amounts for the consolidated balance sheet of Ploy Corporation and subsidiary on February 28, Year 9:

(1) Goodwill (neither Ploy nor Skye had goodwill in its separate balance sheet)

(2) Minority interest in net assets of subsidiary

Ex. 6-10 Pullin Corporation acquired 70% of the outstanding common stock of Style Company on July 31, Year 8. The unconsolidated balance sheet of Pullin immediately after the purchase-type business combination and the consolidated balance sheet of Pullin Corporation and subsidiary were as follows:

PULLIN CORPORATION
Unconsolidated and Consolidated Balance Sheets
July 31, Year 8

	Unconsolidated	Consolidated
Assets		
Current assets	$106,000	$146,000
Investment in Style Company common stock	100,000	
Plant assets (net)	270,000	370,000
Goodwill		11,100
Total assets	$476,000	$527,100
Liabilities & Stockholders' Equity		
Current liabilities	$ 15,000	$ 28,000
Minority interest in net assets of subsidiary		38,100
Common stock, no par or stated value	350,000	350,000
Retained earnings	111,000	111,000
Total liabilities & stockholders' equity	$476,000	$527,100

Of the excess payment for the investment in Style Company common stock, $10,000 was ascribed to undervaluation of Style's plant assets and the remainder was ascribed to goodwill. Current assets of Style included a $2,000 receivable from Pullin that arose before the business combination.

a Prepare a working paper to compute the total current assets in Style Company's separate balance sheet on July 31, Year 8.

b Prepare a working paper to compute the total stockholders' equity in Style Company's separate balance sheet on July 31, Year 8.

c Prepare a working paper to show how the goodwill of $11,100 included in the July

31, Year 8, consolidated balance sheet of Pullin Corporation and subsidiary was computed.

Ex. 6-11   Polter Corporation acquired 80% of the outstanding common stock of Santo Company on October 31, Year 6, for $800,000, including direct out-of-pocket costs of the business combination. The working paper elimination (in journal entry format) on that date was as follows (explanation omitted):

POLTER CORPORATION AND SUBSIDIARY
Working Paper Elimination
October 31, Year 6

Common Stock—Santo	50,000	
Additional Paid-in Capital—Santo	60,000	
Retained Earnings—Santo	490,000	
Inventories—Santo	50,000	
Plant Assets (net)—Santo	100,000	
Goodwill—Polter [$800,000 − ($750,000 × 0.80)]	200,000	
Investment in Santo Company Common Stock—Polter		800,000
Minority Interest in Net Assets of Subsidiary		
($750,000 × 0.20)		150,000

Assuming that a value is to be imputed for 100% of Santo Company's net assets (including goodwill) from Polter Corporation's $800,000 cost, prepare a working paper to compute the debit to Goodwill and the credit to Minority Interest in Net Assets of Subsidiary in the foregoing working paper elimination.

Ex. 6-12   Combinor Corporation and Combinee Company had been operating separately for five years. Each company had a minimal amount of liabilities and a simple capital structure consisting solely of common stock. Combinor, in exchange for its unissued common stock, acquired 80% of the outstanding common stock of Combinee. Combinee's identifiable net assets had a current fair value of $800,000 and a carrying amount of $600,000. The current fair value of the Combinor common stock issued in the business combination was $700,000. Out-of-pocket costs of the combination may be disregarded.

Prepare a working paper to compute the minority interest in net assets of subsidiary and the goodwill that would be displayed in the consolidated balance sheet of Combinor Corporation and subsidiary, under three alternative methods of computation as illustrated on page 270.

Ex. 6-13   On May 31, Year 8, Pismo Corporation acquired for $760,000 cash, including direct out-of-pocket costs of the business combination, 80% of the outstanding common stock of Sobol Company. There was no contingent consideration involved in the combination. Sobol was to be a subsidiary of Pismo.

Additional Information for May 31, Year 8

(1) Sobol Company's stockholders' equity prior to the combination was as follows:

Common stock, no par or stated value	$300,000
Retained earnings	400,000
Total stockholders' equity	$700,000

(2) Differences between current fair values and carrying amounts of Sobol's identifiable assets were as follows (the current fair values of Sobol's other assets and its liabilities equaled their carrying amounts):

	Current fair values	Carrying amounts	Differences
Inventories...........	$ 120,000	$ 80,000	$ 40,000
Land	300,000	250,000	50,000
Building (net).........	800,000	740,000	60,000
Totals	$1,220,000	$1,070,000	$150,000

Prepare a working paper elimination, in journal entry format (omit explanation) for the consolidated balance sheet of Pismo Corporation and subsidiary on May 31, Year 8. (Disregard income taxes.)

Ex. 6-14 The working paper elimination (in journal entry format) on August 31, Year 5, for the consolidated balance sheet of Payton Corporation and subsidiary is shown below. On that date, Payton acquired most of the outstanding common stock of Sutton Company for cash.

PAYTON CORPORATION AND SUBSIDIARY
Working Paper Elimination
August 31, Year 5

Common Stock—Sutton.......................................	60,000	
Additional Paid-in Capital—Sutton............................	35,250	
Retained Earnings—Sutton....................................	50,100	
Inventories—Sutton..	3,900	
Plant Assets (net)—Sutton...................................	28,500	
Patent—Sutton..	4,500	
Goodwill—Payton	5,280	
Investment in Sutton Company Common Stock—Payton ..		165,660
Minority Interest in Net Assets of Subsidiary		21,870

To eliminate intercompany investment and equity accounts of subsidiary on date of business combination; to allocate excess of cost over current fair values of identifiable net assets acquired to goodwill; and to establish minority interest in net assets of subsidiary on date of purchase-type business combination. (Income tax effects are disregarded.)

Answer the following questions (show supporting computations):

a What percentage of the outstanding common stock of the subsidiary was acquired by the parent company?

b What was the aggregate current fair value of the subsidiary's identifiable net assets on August 31, Year 5?

c What amount would be assigned to goodwill under the method that infers a total current fair value for the subsidiary's total net assets, based on the parent company's investment?

d What amount would be assigned to minority interest in subsidiary under the method described in **c**?

CASES

Case 6-1   The minority interest in net assets of a subsidiary might be displayed in one of three ways in a consolidated balance sheet.

Instructions

Discuss the propriety of displaying the minority interest in net assets of subsidiary in the consolidated balance sheet:

a As a liability

b As a part of stockholders' equity

c In a separate classification between liabilities and stockholders' equity

Case 6-2   On January 2, Year 2, the board of directors of Photo Corporation assigned to a voting trust 15,000 shares of the 60,000 shares of Soto Company common stock owned by Photo. The trustee of the voting trust controls 40,000 of Soto's 105,000 shares of issued common stock, of which 5,000 shares are in Soto's treasury. The term of the voting trust is three years.

Instructions

Are consolidated financial statements appropriate for Photo Corporation and Soto Company for the three years ending December 31, Year 4? Explain.

Case 6-3   On July 31, Year 5, Paley Corporation transferred all right, title, and interest in several of its current research and development projects to Carla Saye, sole stock-holder of Saye Company, in exchange for 55 of the 100 shares of Saye Company common stock owned by Carla Saye. On the same date, Martin Morgan, who is not related to Paley Corporation, Saye Company, or Carla Saye, acquired for $45,000 cash the remaining 45 shares of Saye Company common stock owned by Carla Saye. Carla Saye notified the directors of Paley Corporation of the sale of common stock to Morgan.

Because Paley had recognized as expense the costs related to the research and development when the costs were incurred, Paley's controller prepared the following journal entry to record the business combination with Saye Company:

Investment in Saye Company Common Stock (55 × $1,000)	*55,000*	
Gain on Disposal of Intangible Assets		*55,000*

To record transfer of research and development projects to Carla
Saye in exchange for 55 shares of Saye Company common stock.
Valuation of the investment is based on an unrelated cash issuance
of Saye Company common stock on this date.

Instructions

a Do you concur with the foregoing journal entry? Explain.

b Should the $55,000 gain be displayed in a consolidated income statement of Paley Corporation and subsidiary on July 31, Year 5? Explain.

Case 6-4   On May 31, Year 6, Patrick Corporation acquired at 100, $500,000 face amount of Stear Company's 10-year, 12%, convertible bonds due May 31, Year 11. The bonds were convertible to 50,000 shares of Stear's voting common stock ($1 par), of which

40,000 shares were issued and outstanding on May 31, Year 6. The controller of Patrick, who also is one of three Patrick officers who serve on the five-member board of directors of Stear, proposes to issue consolidated financial statements for Patrick Corporation and Stear Company on May 31, Year 6.

Instructions

Do you agree with the Patrick controller's proposal? Explain.

Case 6-5 In Year 6, Pinch Corporation, a chain of discount stores, began a program of business combinations with its principal suppliers. On May 31, Year 6, the close of its fiscal year, Pinch paid $8,500,000 cash and issued 100,000 shares of its common stock (current fair value $20 a share) for all 10,000 outstanding shares of common stock of Silver Company. Silver was a furniture manufacturer whose products were sold in Pinch's stores. Total stockholders' equity of Silver on May 31, Year 6, was $9,000,000. Out-of-pocket costs attributable to the business combination itself (as opposed to the SEC registration statement for the 100,000 shares of Pinch's common stock) paid by Pinch on May 31, Year 6, totaled $100,000.

In the consolidated balance sheet of Pinch Corporation and subsidiary on May 31, Year 6, the $1,600,000 [$8,500,000 + (100,000 × $20) + $100,000 − $9,000,000] difference between the parent company's cost and the carrying amounts of the subsidiary's identifiable net assets was allocated in accordance with purchase accounting as follows:

Inventories.	$ 250,000
Plant assets	850,000
Patents.	300,000
Goodwill.	200,000
Total excess of cost over carrying amounts of subsidiary's net assets . . .	$1,600,000

Under terms of the indenture for a $1,000,000 bond liability of Silver, Pinch was obligated to maintain Silver as a separate corporation and to issue a separate balance sheet for Silver each May 31. Pinch's controller contends that Silver's balance sheet on May 31, Year 6, should value net assets at $10,600,000—their cost to Pinch. Silver's controller disputes this valuation, claiming that generally accepted accounting principles require issuance of a historical cost balance sheet for Silver on May 31, Year 6.

Instructions

a Present arguments supporting the Pinch controller's position.
b Present arguments supporting the Silver controller's position.
c Which position do you prefer? Explain.

Case 6-6 In *Statement of Financial Accounting Concepts No. 6,* "Elements of Financial Statements," the Financial Accounting Standards Board defined *liabilities* and *expenses* as follows:[11]

---

[11] *Statement of Financial Accounting Concepts No. 6,* "Elements of Financial Statements," FASB (Norwalk: 1985), pp. 13, 30.

Liabilities are probable future sacrifices of economic benefits arising from present obligations of a particular entity to transfer assets or provide services to other entities in the future as a result of past transactions or events.

Expenses are outflows or other using up of assets or incurrences of liabilities (or a combination of both) from delivering or producing goods, rendering services, or carrying out other activities that constitute the entity's ongoing major or central operations.

Instructions

Given the foregoing definitions, do you consider appropriate the parent company concept of consolidated financial statements, which considers minority interest in net assets of subsidiary to be a liability and minority interest in net income of subsidiary to be an expense? Explain.

Case 6-7   The board of directors of Purdido Corporation have just directed Purdido's officers to abandon further efforts to complete an acquisition of all the outstanding common stock of Sontee Company in a purchase-type business combination that would have resulted in a parent company–subsidiary relationship between Purdido and Sontee. After learning of the board's decision, Purdido's chief financial officer instructed the controller, a CPA who is a member of the AICPA, the FEI, and the IMA (see Chapter 1), to analyze the out-of-pocket costs of the abandoned proposed combination. After some analysis of Purdido's accounting records, the controller provided the following summary to the CFO:

PURDIDO CORPORATION
Out-of-Pocket Costs of Abandoned Business Combination
April 17, Year 5

Legal fees relating to proposed business combination	$120,000
Finder's fee relating to proposed business combination	0*
Costs associated with proposed SEC registration statement for Purdido com-	
mon stock to have been issued in the business combination	180,000
Total out-of-pocket costs of abandoned business combination	$300,000

* Finder's fee was contingent on successful completion of the business combination.

Noting that recognition of the entire $300,000 as expense on April 17, Year 5, would have a depressing effect on earnings of Purdido for the quarter ending June 30, Year 5, the CFO instructed the controller to expense only $120,000 and to debit the $180,000 amount to the Paid-in Capital in Excess of Par ledger account. In response to the controller's request for justification of such a debit, the CFO confided that Purdido's board was presently engaged in exploring other business combination opportunities, and that the costs incurred on the proposed SEC registration statement thus had future benefits to Purdido.

Instructions

May the controller of Purdido Corporation ethically comply with the CFO's instructions? Explain.

Case 6-8 Assume you are a CPA and a member of the AICPA, the FEI, and the IMA (see Chapter 1). You are CFO of a publicly owned corporation whose CEO is planning to become the sole stockholder of a newly established corporation in a situation with characteristics similar to those described in Securities and Exchange Commission *AAER 34,* "Securities and Exchange Commission v. Digilog, Inc. and Ronald Moyer" (described on pages 275 to 276). When you inform the CEO of the SEC's findings in *AAER 34,* the CEO informs you that the corporation's independent auditors have provided a copy of a reply by the AICPA's Technical Information Service to a question involving a situation similar to that in *AAER 34* and that the Technical Information Service answer was that consolidated financial statements were *not* required. The CEO gives you Section 1400.07, "Reporting on Company Where Option to Acquire Control Exists," of the *AICPA Technical Practice Aids* and orders you not to insist on consolidation of "his" corporation's financial statements.

Instructions

What are your ethical obligations in this matter? Explain.

Case 6-9 Charles Griffin, CPA, a member of the AICPA, IMA, and FEI (see Chapter 1), has just been appointed controller of Penter Corporation, a publicly owned client of Griffin's former employer, Wayland & Company, CPAs. Griffin's first task, assigned to him by CFO Ann Carter, CPA, is to prepare for the December 31, Year 6, annual audit of Penter's consolidated financial statements by Wayland & Company. Carter informs Griffin that she is considering a change to the economic unit concept from the previously used parent company concept for displaying minority interest in net assets of subsidiary. She shows Griffin the consolidated balance sheets on page 292 for Penter Corporation and subsidiary prepared by her under the two concepts.

Carter points out that the financial ratios for the November 30, Year 6, consolidated balance sheet are improved by a change to the economic unit concept as follows:

	Parent company concept	Economic unit concept
Debt ratio.	84.7%	78.6%
Equity ratio	15.3%	21.4%
Debt-to-equity ratio	553.3%	366.7%
Common stockholders' equity (book value) per		
share.	$12.50	$17.50

Carter expresses the view that the change to the economic unit concept from the parent company concept would be a *reclassification* rather than a *change in accounting principle,* and that prior years' consolidated financial statements presented for comparative purposes might likewise be restated without any disclosure in a note to the financial statements, as would be required by *APB Opinion No. 20,* "Accounting Changes."

PENTER CORPORATION AND SUBSIDIARY
Consolidated Balance Sheets
November 30, Year 6
(amounts in thousands)

	Parent company concept	Economic unit concept
Assets		
Current assets	$1,000	$1,000
Plant assets (net)..........................	8,000	8,000
Other assets	600	600
Goodwill (net)	200	200
Total assets............................	$9,800	$9,800
Liabilities & Stockholders' Equity		
Current liabilities...........................	$ 500	$ 500
Long-term debt.............................	7,200	7,200
Minority interest in net assets of subsidiary	600	
Total liabilities...........................	$8,300	$7,700
Common stock, no par or stated value, 120		
shares outstanding	$ 500	$ 500
Retained earnings	1,000	1,000
Minority interest in net assets of subsidiary		600
Total stockholders' equity	$1,500	$2,100
Total liabilities & stockholders' equity	$9,800	$9,800

In response to Griffin's inquiry as to whether Carter's request was motivated by any sound accounting theory, in addition to the enhanced financial ratios, Carter states that she does not believe that minority interest in net assets of subsidiary meets the following FASB definition of a *liability,* provided in *Statement of Financial Accounting Concepts No. 6:*[12]

> Liabilities are probable future sacrifices of economic benefits arising from present obligations of a particular entity to transfer assets or provide services to other entities in the future as a result of past transactions or events.

Knowing that if Carter's suggested change is reflected in Penter's consolidated financial statements for Year 6, he will have to defend the change to the Wayland & Company auditors, Charles Griffin researches the following sections of *AICPA Professional Standards,* volume 1, "U.S. Auditing Standards": AU420.16, AU508.77, AU508.11f, and AU9420.31.

Instructions

Research the cited standards and state whether, in your opinion, Charles Griffin will be able to defend Ann Carter's position with Wayland & Company, CPAs. Explain your views.

---

[12] *Statement of Financial Accounting Concepts No. 6,* "Elements of Financial Statements," FASB (Norwalk: 1985), p. 13.

PROBLEMS

Pr. 6-1 On September 30, Year 6, Parr Corporation paid $1,000,000 to shareholders of Sane Company for 90,000 of Sane's 100,000 outstanding shares of no-par, no-stated-value common stock; additionally, Parr paid direct out-of-pocket costs of the combination totaling $80,000 on that date. Carrying amount and current fair value of Sane's identifiable net assets on September 30, Year 6, were analyzed as follows:

Common stock, no par	$400,000
Retained earnings	500,000
Total carrying amount of identifiable net assets	$900,000
Add: Differences between current fair value and carrying amount:	
Inventories (first-in, first-out cost)	30,000
Plant assets (net)	60,000
Total current fair value of identifiable net assets	$990,000

Instructions

a Prepare journal entries for Parr Corporation on September 30, Year 6, to record the business combination with Sane Company. (Disregard income taxes.)

b Prepare a working paper elimination for Parr Corporation and subsidiary (in journal entry format) on September 30, Year 6. (Disregard income taxes.)

Pr. 6-2 On September 30, Year 1, Philly Corporation issued 100,000 shares of its no-par, no-stated-value common stock (current fair value $12 a share) for 18,800 shares of the outstanding $20 par common stock of Stype Company. The $150,000 out-of-pocket costs of the business combination paid by Philly on September 30, Year 1, were allocable as follows: 60% to finder's, legal, and accounting fees directly related to the business combination; 40% to the SEC registration statement for Philly's common stock issued in the business combination. There was no contingent consideration.

Immediately prior to the business combination, separate balance sheets of the constituent companies were as follows:

PHILLY CORPORATION AND STYPE COMPANY
Separate Balance Sheets (prior to business combination)
September 30, Year 1

Assets	Philly Corporation	Stype Company
Cash	$ 200,000	$ 100,000
Trade accounts receivable (net)	400,000	200,000
Inventories (net)	600,000	300,000
Plant assets (net)	1,300,000	1,000,000
Total assets	$2,500,000	$1,600,000

Liabilities & Stockholders' Equity		
Current liabilities	$ 800,000	$ 400,000
Long-term debt		100,000
Common stock, no par or stated value	1,200,000	
Common stock, $20 par		400,000
Retained earnings	500,000	700,000
Total liabilities & stockholders' equity	$2,500,000	$1,600,000

Current fair values of Stype's identifiable net assets differed from their carrying amounts as follows:

	Current fair values, Sept. 30, Year 1
Inventories	$ 340,000
Plant assets (net)	1,100,000
Long-term debt	90,000

Instructions

a Prepare journal entries for Philly Corporation on September 30, Year 1, to record the business combination with Stype Company as a purchase. (Disregard income taxes.)

b Prepare a working paper for consolidated balance sheet and related working paper elimination (in journal entry format) for Philly Corporation and subsidiary on September 30, Year 1. Amounts in the working papers should reflect the journal entries in **a**. (Disregard income taxes.)

Pr. 6-3   Separate balance sheets of Pellman Corporation and Shire Company on May 31, Year 4, together with current fair values of Shire's identifiable net assets, are as follows:

PELLMAN CORPORATION AND SHIRE COMPANY
Separate Balance Sheets (prior to business combination)
May 31, Year 4

	Pellman Corporation	Shire Company Carrying amounts	Shire Company Current fair values
Assets			
Cash.	$ 550,000	$ 10,000	$ 10,000
Trade accounts receivable (net)	700,000	60,000	60,000
Inventories	1,400,000	120,000	140,000
Plant assets (net)	2,850,000	610,000	690,000
Total assets	$5,500,000	$800,000	
Liabilities & Stockholders' Equity			
Current liabilities	$ 500,000	$ 80,000	$ 80,000
Long-term debt	1,000,000	400,000	440,000
Common stock, $10 par	1,500,000	100,000	
Additional paid-in capital	1,200,000	40,000	
Retained earnings.	1,300,000	180,000	
Total liabilities & stockholders' equity. . . .	$5,500,000	$800,000	

On May 31, Year 4, Pellman acquired all 10,000 shares of Shire's outstanding common stock by paying $300,000 cash to Shire's stockholders and $50,000 cash for finder's and legal fees relating to the business combination. There was no contingent consideration, and Shire became a subsidiary of Pellman.

Instructions

a Prepare journal entries for Pellman Corporation to record the business combination with Shire Company on May 31, Year 4. (Disregard income taxes.)

b Prepare a working paper for consolidated balance sheet of Pellman Corporation and subsidiary on May 31, Year 4, and the related working paper elimination (in journal entry format). Amounts in the working papers should reflect the journal entries in **a**. (Disregard income taxes.)

Pr. 6-4 On April 30, Year 6, Powell Corporation issued 30,000 shares of its no-par, no-stated-value common stock having a current fair value of $20 a share for 8,000 shares of Seaver Company's $10 par common stock. There was no contingent consideration; out-of-pocket costs of the business combination, paid by Seaver on behalf of Powell on April 30, Year 6, were as follows:

Finder's and legal fees relating to business combination	$40,000
Costs associated with SEC registration statement	30,000
Total out-of-pocket costs of business combination	$70,000

Separate balance sheets of the constituent companies on April 30, Year 6, prior to the business combination, were as follows:

POWELL CORPORATION AND SEAVER COMPANY
Separate Balance Sheets (prior to business combination)
April 30, Year 6

	Powell Corporation	Seaver Company
Assets		
Cash	$ 50,000	$ 150,000
Trade accounts receivable (net)	230,000	200,000
Inventories	400,000	350,000
Plant assets (net)	1,300,000	560,000
Total assets	$1,980,000	$1,260,000
Liabilities & Stockholders' Equity		
Current liabilities	$ 310,000	$ 250,000
Long-term debt	800,000	600,000
Common stock, no par or stated value	500,000	
Common stock, $10 par		100,000
Additional paid-in capital		360,000
Retained earnings (deficit)	370,000	(50,000)
Total liabilities & stockholders' equity	$1,980,000	$1,260,000

Current fair values of Seaver's identifiable net assets were the same as their carrying amounts, except for the following:

	Current fair values, Apr. 30, Year 6
Inventories	$440,000
Plant assets (net)	780,000
Long-term debt	620,000

Instructions

a Prepare a journal entry for Seaver Corporation on April 30, Year 6, to record its payment of out-of-pocket costs of the business combination on behalf of Powell Corporation.

b Prepare journal entries for Powell Corporation to record the purchase-type business combination with Seaver Company on April 30, Year 6. (Disregard income taxes.)

c Prepare a working paper for consolidated balance sheet of Powell Corporation and subsidiary on April 30, Year 6, and the related working paper elimination (in journal entry format). Amounts in the working papers should reflect the journal entries in **a** and **b**. (Disregard income taxes.)

Pr. 6-5   On July 31, Year 10, Pyr Corporation issued 20,000 shares of its $2 par common stock (current fair value $10 a share) for all 5,000 shares of outstanding $5 par common stock of Soper Company, which was to remain a separate corporation. Out-of-pocket costs of the business combination, paid by Pyr on July 31, Year 10, are shown below:

Finder's and legal fees related to business combination	$20,000
Costs associated with SEC registration statement for Pyr common stock	10,000
Total out-of-pocket costs of business combination	$30,000

The constituent companies' separate balance sheets on July 31, Year 10, prior to the business combination, follow:

PYR CORPORATION AND SOPER COMPANY
Separate Balance Sheets (prior to business combination)
July 31, Year 10

	Pyr Corporation	Soper Company
Assets		
Current assets	$ 800,000	$150,000
Plant assets (net).....................................	2,400,000	300,000
Goodwill (net)		20,000
Total assets...	$3,200,000	$470,000
Liabilities & Stockholders' Equity		
Current liabilities.....................................	$ 400,000	$120,000
Long-term debt.......................................	1,000,000	200,000
Common stock, $2 par	800,000	
Common stock, $5 par		25,000
Additional paid-in capital	400,000	50,000
Retained earnings....................................	600,000	75,000
Total liabilities & stockholders' equity	$3,200,000	$470,000

Soper's goodwill resulted from its July 31, Year 4, acquisition of the net assets of Solo Company.

Soper's assets and liabilities having July 31, Year 10, current fair values different from their carrying amounts were as follows:

	Carrying amounts	Current fair values
Inventories...	$ 60,000	$ 65,000
Plant assets (net)...................................	300,000	340,000
Long-term debt.....................................	200,000	190,000

There were no intercompany transactions prior to the business combination, and there was no contingent consideration in connection with the combination.

Instructions

a Prepare Pyr Corporation's journal entries on July 31, Year 10, to record the business combination with Soper Company as a purchase. (Disregard income taxes.)

b Prepare a working paper elimination (in journal entry format) and the related working paper for consolidated balance sheet of Pyr Corporation and subsidiary on July 31, Year 10. Amounts in the working papers should reflect the journal entries in **a**. (Disregard income taxes.)

Pr. 6-6 The unconsolidated and consolidated balance sheets of Pali Corporation and subsidiary on August 31, Year 6, the date of Pali's business combination with Soda Company, are as follows:

PALI CORPORATION
Unconsolidated and Consolidated Balance Sheets
August 31, Year 6

Assets	Unconsolidated	Consolidated
Cash.......................................	$ 120,000	$ 160,000
Trade accounts receivable (net)................	380,000	540,000
Inventories	470,000	730,000
Investment in Soda Company common stock.....	380,000	
Plant assets (net)	850,000	1,470,000
Goodwill.......................................		8,000
Total assets	$2,200,000	$2,908,000

Liabilities & Stockholders' Equity		
Current liabilities	$ 430,000	$ 690,000
Long-term debt................................	550,000	730,000
Premium on long-term debt.....................		20,000
Minority interest in net assets of subsidiary.......		248,000
Common stock, $1 par.........................	500,000	500,000
Additional paid-in capital	440,000	440,000
Retained earnings.............................	280,000	280,000
Total liabilities & stockholders' equity..........	$2,200,000	$2,908,000

On August 31, Year 6, Pali had paid cash of $3 a share for 60% of the outstanding shares of Soda's $1 par common stock and $20,000 cash for legal fees in connection with the business combination. There was no contingent consideration. The equity (book value) of Soda's common stock on August 31, Year 6, was $2.80 a share, and the amount of Soda's retained earnings was twice as large as the amount of its additional paid-in capital. The excess of current fair value of Soda's plant assets over their carrying amount on August 31, Year 6, was 1⅔ times as large as the comparable excess for Soda's inventories on that date. The current fair values of Soda's cash, trade accounts receivable (net), and current liabilities were equal to their carrying amounts on August 31, Year 6.

Instructions

Reconstruct the working paper elimination (in journal entry format) for the working paper for consolidated balance sheet of Pali Corporation and subsidiary on August 31, Year 6. (Disregard income taxes.)

Pr. 6-7 On October 31, Year 4, Pagel Corporation acquired 83% of the outstanding common stock of Sayre Company in exchange for 50,000 shares of Pagel's no-par, $2 stated value ($10 current fair value a share) common stock. There was no contingent consideration. Out-of-pocket costs of the business combination paid by Pagel on October 31, Year 4, were as follows:

Legal and finder's fees related to business combination	$34,750
Costs associated with SEC registration statement for Pagel's common stock .	55,250
Total out-of-pocket costs of business combination	$90,000

There were no intercompany transactions between the constituent companies prior to the business combination. Sayre was to be a subsidiary of Pagel. The separate balance sheets of the constituent companies prior to the business combination are on page 299.

Current fair values of Sayre's identifiable net assets were the same as their carrying amounts on October 31, Year 4, except for the following:

	Current fair values
Inventories.	$ 620,000
Plant assets (net).	1,550,000
Patents (net)	95,000
Long-term debt.	1,225,000

PAGEL CORPORATION AND SAYRE COMPANY
Separate Balance Sheets (prior to business combination)
October 31, Year 4

	Pagel Corporation	Sayre Company
Assets		
Cash	$ 250,000	$ 150,000
Inventories..	860,000	600,000
Other current assets	500,000	260,000
Plant assets (net)..................................	3,400,000	1,500,000
Patents (net)		80,000
Total assets....................................	$5,010,000	$2,590,000
Liabilities & Stockholders' Equity		
Income taxes payable..............................	$ 40,000	$ 60,000
Other current liabilities	390,000	854,000
Long-term debt....................................	950,000	1,240,000
Common stock, no-par, $2 stated value...............	1,500,000	
Common stock, $10 par............................		100,000
Additional paid-in capital...........................	1,500,000	
Retained earnings	630,000	336,000
Total liabilities & stockholders' equity	$5,010,000	$2,590,000

Instructions

a Prepare Pagel Corporation's journal entries on October 31, Year 4, to record the business combination with Sayre Company as a purchase. (Disregard income taxes.)

b Prepare working paper eliminations (in journal entry format) on October 31, Year 4, and the related working paper for the consolidated balance sheet of Pagel Corporation and subsidiary. Amounts in the working papers should reflect the journal entries in **a**. (Disregard income taxes.)

Pr. 6-8 On January 31, Year 3, Porcino Corporation issued $50,000 cash, 6,000 shares of $2 par common stock (current fair value $15 a share), and a 5-year, 14%, $50,000 promissory note payable for all 10,000 shares of Secor Company's outstanding common stock, which were owned by Lawrence Secor. The only out-of-pocket costs paid by Porcino to complete the business combination were legal fees of $10,000, because Porcino's common stock issued in the combination was not subject to the registration requirements of the SEC. There was no contingent consideration, and 14% was the fair rate of interest for the promissory note issued by Porcino in connection with the business combination.

Separate balance sheets of Porcino and Secor on January 31, Year 3, prior to the business combination, were as follows:

PORCINO CORPORATION AND SECOR COMPANY
Separate Balance Sheets (prior to business combination)
January 31, Year 3

	Porcino Corporation	Secor Company
Assets		
Inventories	$ 380,000	$ 60,000
Other current assets.	640,000	130,000
Plant assets (net)	1,520,000	470,000
Intangible assets (net)	160,000	40,000
Total assets	$2,700,000	$ 700,000
Liabilities & Stockholders' Equity		
Current liabilities	$ 420,000	$ 200,000
Long-term debt	650,000	300,000
Common stock, $2 par.	800,000	
Common stock, $15 par		150,000
Additional paid-in capital	220,000	160,000
Retained earnings (deficit)	610,000	(110,000)
Total liabilities & stockholders' equity.	$2,700,000	$ 700,000

Current fair values of Secor's identifiable net assets that differed from their carrying amounts on January 31, Year 3, were as follows:

	Current fair values
Inventories.	$ 70,000
Plant assets (net).	540,000
Intangible assets (net).	60,000
Long-term debt.	350,000

Instructions

a Prepare journal entries for Porcino Corporation on January 31, Year 3, to record its business combination with Secor Company. (Disregard income taxes.)

b Prepare a working paper for consolidated balance sheet of Porcino corporation and subsidiary on January 31, Year 3, and the related working paper elimination (in journal entry format). Amounts in the working papers should reflect the journal entries in **a**. (Disregard income taxes.)

Pr. 6-9   On June 30, Year 7, Pandit Corporation issued a $300,000 note payable, due $60,000 a year with interest at the fair rate of 15% beginning June 30, Year 8, for 8,500 of the 10,000 outstanding shares of $10 par common stock of Singh Company. Legal fees of $20,000 incurred by Pandit in connection with the business combination were paid on June 30, Year 7.

Separate balance sheets of the constituent companies, immediately following the business combination, are shown below:

PANDIT CORPORATION AND SINGH COMPANY
Separate Balance Sheets (following business combination)
June 30, Year 7

	Pandit Corporation	Singh Company
Assets		
Cash	$ 80,000	$ 60,000
Trade accounts receivable (net)	170,000	90,000
Inventories	370,000	120,000
Investment in Singh Company common stock	320,000	
Plant assets (net)	570,000	240,000
Goodwill (net)	50,000	
Total assets	$1,560,000	$510,000
Liabilities & Stockholders' Equity		
Trade accounts payable	$ 220,000	$120,000
Income taxes payable	100,000	40,000
15% note payable, due $60,000 annually	300,000	
Common stock, $10 par	250,000	100,000
Additional paid-in capital	400,000	130,000
Retained earnings	290,000	120,000
Total liabilities & stockholders' equity	$1,560,000	$510,000

Additional Information

(1) An independent audit of Singh Company's financial statements for the year ended June 30, Year 7, disclosed that Singh's July 1, Year 6, inventories had been overstated $60,000 due to double counting; and that Singh had omitted from its inventories on June 30, Year 7, merchandise shipped FOB shipping point by a vendor on June 30, Year 7, at an invoiced amount of $35,000. Corrections of Singh's inventories errors are not reflected in Singh's balance sheet.

(2) Both Pandit and Singh had an income tax rate of 40%.

(3) Current fair values of Singh's net assets reported in Singh's balance sheet on June 30, Year 7, differed from carrying amounts as follows:

	Current fair values
Inventories	$150,000
Plant assets (net)	280,000

Instructions

a Prepare a journal entry or entries (including income tax effects) to correct the inventories' misstatements in Singh Company's financial statements for the year ended June 30, Year 7. Singh's accounting records have not been closed for the year ended June 30, Year 7.

b Prepare a working paper elimination (in journal entry format) and a working paper for the consolidated balance sheet of Pandit Corporation and subsidiary on June 30, Year 7. Amounts in the working papers for Singh Company should reflect the adjusting journal entry or entries prepared in **a**. (Disregard income taxes.)

Pr. 6-10   Shown below are the separate balance sheets of Pliny Corporation and Sylla Company on December 31, Year 6, prior to their business combination:

PLINY CORPORATION AND SYLLA COMPANY
Separate Balance Sheets (prior to business combination)
December 31, Year 6

	Pliny Corporation	Sylla Company
Assets		
Inventories...	$ 800,000	$ 300,000
Other current assets	1,200,000	500,000
Long-term investments in marketable securities.........		200,000
Plant assets (net)....................................	2,500,000	900,000
Intangible assets (net)...............................	100,000	200,000
Total assets......................................	$4,600,000	$2,100,000
Liabilities & Stockholders' Equity		
Current liabilities....................................	$1,400,000	$ 300,000
10% note payable, due June 30, Year 16...............	2,000,000	
12% bonds payable, due Dec. 31, Year 11		500,000
Common stock, $1 par..............................	600,000	200,000
Additional paid-in capital............................	200,000	400,000
Retained earnings	400,000	700,000
Total liabilities & stockholders' equity	$4,600,000	$2,100,000

On December 31, Year 6, Pliny paid $100,000 cash and issued $1,500,000 face amount of 14%, 10-year bonds for all the outstanding common stock of Sylla, which became a subsidiary of Pliny. On the date of the business combination, 16% was the fair rate of interest for the bonds of both Pliny and Sylla, both of which paid interest on June 30 and December 31. There was no contingent consideration involved in the business combination, but Pliny paid the following out-of-pocket costs on December 31, Year 6:

Finder's and legal fees relating to business combination....................	$50,000
Costs associated with SEC registration statement for Pliny's bonds..........	40,000
Total out-of-pocket costs of business combination	$90,000

In addition to the 12% bonds payable, Sylla had identifiable net assets with current fair values that differed from carrying amounts on December 31, Year 6, as follows:

	Current fair values
Inventories.	$330,000
Long-term investments in marketable securities.	230,000
Plant assets (net).	940,000
Intangible assets (net).	220,000

Instructions

a Prepare journal entries for Pliny Corporation to record the business combination with Sylla Company on December 31, Year 6. Use present value tables to compute the present value, rounded to the nearest dollar, of the 14% bonds issued by Pliny. (Disregard income taxes.)

b Prepare a working paper for consolidated balance sheet for Pliny Corporation and subsidiary on December 31, Year 6, and the related working paper elimination (in journal entry format). Use present value tables to compute the present value, rounded to the nearest dollar, of the 12% bonds payable of Sylla. Amounts in the working papers should reflect the journal entries in **a**. (Disregard income taxes.)

Pr. 6-11   You have been engaged to audit the financial statements of Parthenia Corporation and subsidiary for the year ended June 30, Year 6. The working paper for consolidated balance sheet of Parthenia and subsidiary on June 30, Year 6, prepared by Parthenia's inexperienced accountant, is on page 304.

In the course of your audit, you reviewed the following June 30, Year 6, journal entries in the accounting records of Parthenia Corporation:

Investment in Storey Company Common Stock	220,000	
Goodwill	60,000	
Cash		280,000

To record acquisition of 4,000 shares of Storey Company's outstanding common stock in a purchase-type business combination, and to record acquired goodwill as follows:

Cash paid for Storey common stock.	$280,000
Less: Stockholders' equity of Storey, June 30,	
Year 6	220,000
Goodwill acquired	$ 60,000

Expenses of Business Combination.	10,000	
Cash		10,000

To record payment of legal fees in connection with business combination with Storey Company.

PARTHENIA CORPORATION AND SUBSIDIARY
Working Paper for Consolidated Balance Sheet
June 30, Year 6

	Parthenia Corporation	Storey Company	Eliminations increase (decrease)	Consolidated
Assets				
Cash.................................	60,000	50,000		110,000
Trade accounts receivable (net).........	120,000	90,000		210,000
Inventories	250,000	160,000		410,000
Investment in Storey Company common				
stock................................	220,000		(a) (220,000)	
Plant assets (net)......................	590,000	500,000		1,090,000
Goodwill (net).........................	60,000			60,000
Total assets	1,300,000	800,000	(220,000)	1,880,000
Liabilities & Stockholders' Equity				
Current liabilities	200,000	280,000		480,000
Long-term debt........................	500,000	300,000		800,000
Common stock, $5 par.................	100,000			100,000
Common stock, $10 par................		50,000	(a) (50,000)	
Additional paid-in capital	200,000	70,000	(a) (70,000)	200,000
Retained earnings.....................	300,000	100,000	(a) (100,000)	300,000
Total liabilities & stockholders' equity ...	1,300,000	800,000	(220,000)	1,880,000

Your inquiries of directors and officers of Parthenia and your review of supporting documents disclosed the following current fair values for Storey's identifiable net assets that differ from carrying amounts on June 30, Year 6:

	Current fair values
Inventories..	$180,000
Plant assets (net)...	530,000
Long-term debt...	260,000

Instructions

a Prepare a journal entry to correct Parthenia Corporation's accounting for its June 30, Year 6, business combination with Storey Company. Parthenia's accounting records have not been closed. (Disregard income taxes.)

b Prepare a corrected working paper for consolidated balance sheet of Parthenia Corporation and subsidiary on June 30, Year 6, and related working paper elimination (in journal entry format). Amounts in the working papers should reflect the journal entries in **a**. (Disregard income taxes.)

7

Consolidated Financial Statements: Subsequent to Date of Purchase-Type Business Combination

Subsequent to the date of a business combination, the parent company must account for the operating results of the subsidiary: the net income or net loss and dividends declared and paid by the subsidiary. In addition, a number of intercompany transactions and events that frequently occur in a parent company–subsidiary relationship must be recorded.

In this chapter the accounting for operating results of purchased subsidiaries is described and illustrated. Accounting for operating results of pooled subsidiaries and for intercompany transactions not involving a profit (gain) or a loss is illustrated in Chapter 8; Chapter 9 includes a discussion of accounting for intercompany transactions involving a profit (gain) or a loss.

ACCOUNTING FOR OPERATING RESULTS OF WHOLLY OWNED PURCHASED SUBSIDIARIES

In accounting for the operating results of consolidated purchased subsidiaries, a parent company may choose the *equity method* or the *cost method* of accounting.

Equity Method

In the equity method of accounting, the parent company recognizes its share of the subsidiary's net income or net loss, adjusted for depreciation and amortization of differences between current fair values and carrying amounts of a purchased subsidiary's net assets on the date of the business combination, as well as its share of dividends declared by the subsidiary. Thus, the equity method of accounting for a subsidiary's operating results is similar to home office accounting for a branch's operations, as described in Chapter 4.

306

Proponents of the equity method of accounting maintain that the method is consistent with the accrual basis of accounting because it recognizes increases or decreases in the carrying amount of the parent company's investment in the subsidiary when they are *realized* by the subsidiary as net income or net loss, not when they are *paid* by the subsidiary as dividends. Thus, proponents claim, the equity method stresses the *economic substance* of the parent company–subsidiary relationship because the two companies constitute a single economic entity for financial accounting. Proponents of the equity method also claim that dividends declared by a subsidiary do not constitute revenue to the parent company, as maintained by advocates of the cost method; instead, dividends are a liquidation of a portion of the parent company's investment in the subsidiary.

Cost Method

In the cost method of accounting, the parent company accounts for the operations of a subsidiary only to the extent that dividends are declared by the subsidiary. Dividends declared by the subsidiary from net income subsequent to the business combination are recognized as revenue by the parent company; dividends declared by the subsidiary in excess of post-combination net income constitute a reduction of the carrying amount of the parent company's investment in the subsidiary. Net income or net loss of the subsidiary is *not recognized* by the parent company when the cost method of accounting is used.

Supporters of the cost method contend that the method appropriately recognizes the *legal form* of the parent company–subsidiary relationship. Parent company and subsidiary are separate legal entities; accounting for a subsidiary's operations should recognize the separateness, according to proponents of the cost method. Thus, a parent company realizes revenue from an investment in a subsidiary when the subsidiary declares a dividend, not when the subsidiary reports net income. The cost method of accounting is illustrated in the appendix at the end of this chapter (pages 344 to 351).

Choosing between Equity Method and Cost Method

Consolidated financial statement amounts are the same, regardless of whether a parent company uses the equity method or the cost method to account for a subsidiary's operations. However, the working paper eliminations used in the two methods are different, as illustrated in subsequent sections of this chapter.

The equity method of accounting is appropriate for *pooled* subsidiaries as well as *purchased* subsidiaries. The cost method, on the other hand, is compatible with *purchase accounting* only. In purchase accounting, the parent company's original investment in the subsidiary is recorded at *cost.* Hence, accounting for operating results of purchased subsidiaries by the cost method may be considered a logical extension of purchase accounting. However, in pooling accounting the parent company's investment on the date of the business combination is recorded *at the parent's share of the carrying amount of the subsidiary's net assets.* As a result, the parent company's Investment in Subsidiary Common Stock ledger account reflects the parent's equity in the subsidiary's net assets on the date of the business combination; *there is no cost of a pooled subsidiary.* The equity method of accounting for a pooled subsidiary's operations thus is consistent with pooling accounting, as illustrated in Chapter 8, and is stressed in this book.

Illustration of Equity Method for Wholly Owned Purchased Subsidiary for First Year after Business Combination

Assume that Palm Corporation appropriately had used purchase accounting for the December 31, Year 1, business combination with its wholly owned subsidiary, Starr Company (see pages 248 to 249 for a description of the purchase-type business combination), and that Starr had a net income of $60,000 (income statement is on page 315) for the year ended December 31, Year 2. Assume further that on December 20, Year 2, Starr's board of directors declared a cash dividend of $0.60 a share on the 40,000 outstanding shares of common stock owned by Palm. The dividend was payable January 8, Year 3, to stockholders of record December 29, Year 2.

Starr's December 20, Year 2, journal entry to record the dividend declaration is as follows:

<table>
<tr><td style="text-align:right; font-style:italic;">Wholly owned subsidiary's journal entry for declaration of dividend</td><td colspan="3">Year 2</td></tr>
<tr><td></td><td>Dec. 20</td><td>Dividends Declared (40,000 × $0.60) ....</td><td>24,000</td><td></td></tr>
<tr><td></td><td></td><td>Intercompany Dividends Payable ....</td><td></td><td>24,000</td></tr>
<tr><td></td><td></td><td colspan="3">To record declaration of dividend payable Jan. 8, Year 3, to stockholders of record Dec. 29, Year 2.</td></tr>
</table>

Starr's credit to the Intercompany Dividends Payable ledger account indicates that the liability for dividends payable to the parent company *must be eliminated* in the preparation of consolidated financial statements for the year ended December 31, Year 2.

Under the equity method of accounting, Palm Corporation prepares the following journal entries to record the dividend and net income of Starr for the year ended December 31, Year 2:

<table>
<tr><td style="text-align:right; font-style:italic;">Parent company's equity-method journal entries to record operating results of wholly owned purchased subsidiary</td><td colspan="3">Year 2</td></tr>
<tr><td></td><td>Dec. 20</td><td>Intercompany Dividends Receivable ....</td><td>24,000</td><td></td></tr>
<tr><td></td><td></td><td>Investment in Starr Company Common Stock .....</td><td></td><td>24,000</td></tr>
<tr><td></td><td></td><td colspan="3">To record dividend declared by Starr Company, payable Jan. 8, Year 3, to stockholders of record Dec. 29, Year 2.</td></tr>
<tr><td></td><td>31</td><td>Investment in Starr Company Common Stock ....</td><td>60,000</td><td></td></tr>
<tr><td></td><td></td><td>Intercompany Investment Income ....</td><td></td><td>60,000</td></tr>
<tr><td></td><td></td><td colspan="3">To record 100% of Starr Company's net income for the year ended Dec. 31, Year 2. (Income tax effects are disregarded.)</td></tr>
</table>

The parent's first journal entry records the dividend declared by the subsidiary in the Intercompany Dividends Receivable account and is the counterpart of the subsidiary's journal entry to record the declaration of the dividend. The credit to the Investment in Starr Company Common Stock account in the first journal entry reflects an underlying premise of the equity method of accounting: dividends declared by a subsidiary represent a return of a portion of the parent company's investment in the subsidiary.

The parent's second journal entry records the parent's 100% share of the subsidiary's net income for Year 2. The subsidiary's net income *accrues* to the parent company under the equity method of accounting, similar to the accrual of interest on a note receivable or an investment in bonds.

The income tax effects of Palm Corporation's accrual of its share of Starr Company's net income are disregarded at this time. Income tax allocation problems associated with all aspects of parent company and subsidiary accounting are considered in Chapter 10.

Adjustment of Purchased Subsidiary's Net Income Because it is assumed in this chapter that Palm Corporation's business combination with Starr Company was accounted for as a *purchase,* Palm must prepare a third equity-method journal entry on December 31, Year 2, to adjust Starr's net income for depreciation and amortization attributable to the differences between the current fair values and carrying amounts of Starr's net assets on December 31, Year 1, the date of the Palm–Starr business combination. Because such differences are not recorded by the subsidiary, the subsidiary's net income *is overstated* from the point of view of the consolidated entity.

Assume that the December 31, Year 1 (date of business combination), differences between the current fair values and carrying amounts of Starr Company's net assets were as follows (see Chapter 6, pages 249 and 256):

Differences between current fair values and carrying amounts of wholly owned purchased subsidiary's assets on date of business combination	Inventories (first-in, first-out cost)		$ 25,000
	Plant assets (net):		
	Land	$15,000	
	Building (economic life 15 years)	30,000	
	Machinery (economic life 10 years)	20,000	65,000
	Patent (economic life 5 years)		5,000
	Goodwill (economic life 30 years)		15,000
	Total...		$110,000

Palm Corporation prepares the following additional equity-method journal entry to reflect the effects of depreciation and amortization of the differences between the current fair values and carrying amounts of Starr Company's net assets on Starr's net income for the year ended December 31, Year 2:

Parent company's equity-method journal entry to record operating results of wholly owned purchased subsidiary attributable to depreciation and amortization of subsidiary's net assets	**Year 2**		
	Dec. 31 Intercompany Investment Income.....................	30,500	
	Investment in Starr Company Common Stock.....		30,500
	To amortize differences between current fair values and carrying amounts of Starr Company's net assets on Dec. 31, Year 1, as follows:		

(continued)

Inventories—to cost of goods sold	$25,000
Building—depreciation ($30,000 ÷ 15).	2,000
Machinery—depreciation ($20,000 ÷ 10) . . .	2,000
Patent—amortization ($5,000 ÷ 5).	1,000
Goodwill—amortization ($15,000 ÷ 30).	500
Total amortization applicable to Year 2. . . .	$30,500

(Income tax effects are disregarded.)

After the three foregoing journal entries are posted, Palm Corporation's Investment in Starr Company Common Stock and Intercompany Investment Income ledger accounts are as shown below:

Ledger accounts of parent company using equity method of accounting for wholly owned purchased subsidiary

Investment in Starr Company Common Stock

Date	Explanation	Debit	Credit	Balance
Year 1				
Dec. 31	Issuance of common stock in business combination	450,000		450,000 dr
31	Direct out-of-pocket costs of business combination	50,000		500,000 dr
Year 2				
Dec. 20	Dividend declared by Starr		24,000	476,000 dr
31	Net income of Starr	60,000		536,000 dr
31	Amortization of differences between current fair values and carrying amounts of Starr's net assets		30,500	505,500 dr

Intercompany Investment Income

Date	Explanation	Debit	Credit	Balance
Year 2				
Dec. 31	Net income of Starr		60,000	60,000 cr
31	Amortization of differences between current fair values and carrying amounts of Starr's net assets	30,500		29,500 cr

Developing the Elimination Palm Corporation's use of the equity method of accounting for its investment in Starr Company resulted in a balance in the Investment account that is a mixture of two components: (1) the carrying amount of Starr's identifiable net assets and (2) the excess on the date of business combination of the current fair values of the subsidiary's net assets (including goodwill) over their carrying amounts, net of depreciation and amortization ("current fair value excess"). These components are analyzed as follows:

PALM CORPORATION
Analysis of Investment in Starr Company Common Stock Ledger Account
For Year Ended December 31, Year 2

	Carrying amount	Current fair value excess	Total	
Beginning balances (date of business combination)	$390,000	$110,000	$500,000	
Net income of Starr.	60,000		60,000	Intercompany investment income, $29,500
Amortization of differences between current fair values and carrying amounts of Starr's net assets		(30,500)	(30,500)	
Dividend declared by Starr	(24,000)		(24,000)	
Ending balances	$426,000	$ 79,500	$505,500	

The $426,000 ending balance of the Carrying Amount column agrees with the total stockholder's equity of Starr Company on December 31, Year 2 (see balance sheet section of working paper for consolidated financial statements on page 315), as follows:

Wholly owned subsidiary's stockholder's equity, Dec. 31, Year 2

Common stock, $5 par.	$200,000
Additional paid-in capital	58,000
Retained earnings.	168,000
Total stockholder's equity	$426,000

Unamortized differences between current fair values and carrying amounts of wholly owned purchased subsidiary's assets one year subsequent to business combination

	Balances, Dec. 31, Year 1 (p. 309)	Amortization for Year 2 (pp. 309–310)	Balances, Dec. 31, Year 2
Inventories . . .	$ 25,000	$(25,000)	
Plant assets (net):			
Land.	$ 15,000		$15,000
Building. . . .	30,000	$ (2,000)	28,000
Machinery. .	20,000	(2,000)	18,000
Total plant assets . .	$ 65,000	$ (4,000)	$61,000
Patent	$ 5,000	$ (1,000)	$ 4,000
Goodwill	15,000	(500)	14,500
Totals . . .	$110,000	$(30,500)	$79,500

The $79,500 ending balance of the Current Fair Value Excess column agrees with the December 31, Year 2, total of the unamortized balances for each of the respective assets of Starr Company, as shown on page 311.

It is evident from the analysis of Palm Corporation's Investment ledger account that the working paper elimination subsequent to the date of a purchase-type business combination must include accounts that appear in the constituent companies' income statements and statements of retained earnings, as well as in their balance sheets, because *all three basic financial statements must be consolidated for accounting periods subsequent to the date of a purchase-type business combination.* (A consolidated statement of cash flows is prepared from the three basic *consolidated* financial statements and other information, as explained in Chapter 10.) The items that must be included in the elimination are (1) the subsidiary's *beginning-of-year* stockholder's equity and its dividends, and the parent's investment; (2) the parent's intercompany investment income; (3) unamortized current fair value excesses of the subsidiary; and (4) certain operating expenses of the subsidiary. Assuming that Starr Company allocates machinery depreciation and patent amortization entirely to cost of goods sold, goodwill amortization entirely to operating expenses, and building depreciation 50% each to cost of goods sold and operating expenses, the working paper elimination (in journal entry format) for Palm Corporation and subsidiary on December 31, Year 2, is as follows, with the component items numbered in accordance with the foregoing breakdown:

Working paper elimination for wholly owned purchased subsidiary for first year subsequent to date of business combination

PALM CORPORATION AND SUBSIDIARY
Working Paper Elimination
December 31, Year 2

(a) Common Stock—Starr	200,000 (1)	
Additional Paid-in Capital—Starr	58,000 (1)	
Retained Earnings—Starr	132,000 (1)	
Intercompany Investment Income—Palm	29,500 (2)	
Plant Assets (net)—Starr ($65,000 − $4,000)	61,000 (3)	
Patent (net)—Starr ($5,000 − $1,000)	4,000 (3)	
Goodwill (net)—Starr ($15,000 − $500)	14,500 (3)	
Cost of Goods Sold—Starr	29,000 (4)	
Operating Expenses—Starr	1,500 (4)	
Investment in Starr Company Common Stock— Palm		505,500 (1)
Dividends Declared—Starr		24,000 (1)

To carry out the following:

(a) Eliminate intercompany investment and equity accounts of subsidiary **at beginning of year,** and subsidiary dividend.

(b) Provide for Year 2 depreciation and amortization on differences between current fair values and carrying amounts of Starr's net assets as follows:

(continued)

PALM CORPORATION AND SUBSIDIARY
Working Paper Elimination (concluded)
December 31, Year 2

	Cost of goods sold	Operating expenses
Inventories sold	$25,000	
Building depreciation...	1,000	$1,000
Machinery depreciation.	2,000	
Patent amortization	1,000	
Goodwill amortization ..		500
Totals	$29,000	$1,500

(c) Allocate unamortized differences between combination date current fair values and carrying amounts
of Starr's net assets to appropriate assets.
(Income tax effects are disregarded.)

Comments on components of the foregoing working paper elimination, numbered to correspond with the four categories on page 312 and in the elimination, follow:

(1) As indicated in Chapter 6 (page 254), the three components of the subsidiary's stockholder's equity are reciprocal to the parent company's Investment ledger account. However, because a consolidated statement of retained earnings is to be prepared for the first year following the purchase-type business combination, the subsidiary's **beginning-of-year** retained earnings amount is eliminated, together with the subsidiary's dividends, which are a contra to the subsidiary's retained earnings. (As illustrated in the analysis on page 311, the balance of the parent company's Investment ledger account is **net** of the dividends received from the subsidiary.) The elimination of the subsidiary's beginning-of-year retained earnings makes beginning-of-year consolidated retained earnings on page 315 identical to the end-of-previous-year consolidated retained earnings (see page 258 in Chapter 6).

(2) As illustrated in the analysis on page 311, the amount of the parent company's intercompany investment income is an element of the balance of the parent's Investment ledger account. In effect, the elimination of the intercompany investment income, coupled with items described in (4) on page 312, comprises a reclassification of the intercompany investment income to the adjusted components of the subsidiary's net income in the consolidated income statement.

(3) The debits to the subsidiary's plant assets, patent, and goodwill bring into the consolidated balance sheet the unamortized differences between current fair values and carrying amounts of the subsidiary's assets on the date of the business combination (see the analysis on page 311).

(4) The increases in the subsidiary's cost of goods sold and operating expenses, totaling $30,500 ($29,000 + $1,500 = $30,500), in effect reclassify the comparable decrease in the parent company's Investment ledger account under the

equity method of accounting (see the analysis on page 311) to the appropriate categories for the consolidated income statement.

Working Paper for Consolidated Financial Statements   The working paper for consolidated financial statements for Palm Corporation and subsidiary for the year ended December 31, Year 2, is on page 315. The intercompany receivable and payable is the $24,000 dividend payable by Starr to Palm on December 31, Year 2. (The advances by Palm to Starr that were outstanding on December 31, Year 1, were repaid by Starr January 2, Year 2.)

The following aspects of the working paper for consolidated financial statements of Palm Corporation and subsidiary should be emphasized:

1   The intercompany receivable and payable, placed in adjacent columns on the same line, are offset without a formal elimination.

2   The elimination cancels all intercompany transactions and balances not dealt with by the offset technique described in **1** above.

3   The elimination cancels the subsidiary's retained earnings balance *at the beginning of the year* (the date of the business combination), so that each of the three basic financial statements may be consolidated in turn. (*All* financial statements of a parent company and a purchased subsidiary are consolidated for accounting periods subsequent to the business combination.)

4   The first-in, first-out method is used by Starr Company to account for inventories; thus, the $25,000 difference attributable to Starr's beginning inventories is allocated to cost of goods sold for the year ended December 31, Year 2.

5   Income tax effects of the elimination's increase in Starr Company's expenses are not included in the elimination. Accounting for income tax effects in consolidated financial statements is considered in Chapter 10.

6   One of the effects of the elimination is to reduce the differences between the current fair values and the carrying amounts of the subsidiary's net assets, excepting land, on the business combination date. The effect of the reduction is as follows:

Total difference on date of business combination (Dec. 31, Year 1)	$110,000
Less: Reduction in elimination (a) ($29,000 + $1,500)	30,500
Unamortized difference, Dec. 31, Year 2 ($61,000 + $4,000 + $14,500)....	$ 79,500

The joint effect of Palm Corporation's use of the equity method of accounting and the annual elimination will be to extinguish $64,500 of the $79,500 difference above through Palm's Investment in Starr Company Common Stock ledger account. *The $15,000 balance applicable to Starr's land will not be extinguished.*

7   The parent company's use of the equity method of accounting results in the equalities described on page 316.

Equity method: Wholly owned subsidiary subsequent to date of purchase-type business combination

PALM CORPORATION AND SUBSIDIARY
Working Paper for Consolidated Financial Statements
For Year Ended December 31, Year 2

	Palm Corporation	Starr Company	Eliminations increase (decrease)	Consolidated
Income Statement				
Revenue:				
Net Sales	1,100,000	680,000		1,780,000
Intercompany investment income	29,500		(a) (29,500)	
Total revenue	1,129,500	680,000	(29,500)	1,780,000
Costs and expenses:				
Cost of goods sold	700,000	450,000	(a) 29,000	1,179,000
Operating expenses.	217,667	130,000	(a) 1,500	349,167
Interest expense.	49,000			49,000
Income taxes expense.	53,333	40,000		93,333
Total costs and expenses.	1,020,000	620,000	30,500*	1,670,500
Net income.	109,500	60,000	(60,000)	109,500
Statement of Retained Earnings				
Retained earnings, beginning of year	134,000	132,000	(a) (132,000)	134,000
Net income.	109,500	60,000	(60,000)	109,500
Subtotal.	243,500	192,000	(192,000)	243,500
Dividends declared.	30,000	24,000	(a) (24,000)†	30,000
Retained earnings, end of year	213,500	168,000	(168,000)	213,500
Balance Sheet				
Assets				
Cash	15,900	72,100		88,000
Intercompany receivable (payable).	24,000	(24,000)		
Inventories	136,000	115,000		251,000
Other current assets.	88,000	131,000		219,000
Investment in Starr Company common stock.	505,500		(a) (505,500)	
Plant assets (net).	440,000	340,000	(a) 61,000	841,000
Patent (net)		16,000	(a) 4,000	20,000
Goodwill (net)			(a) 14,500	14,500
Total assets	1,209,400	650,100	(426,000)	1,433,500
Liabilities & Stockholders' Equity				
Income taxes payable	40,000	20,000		60,000
Other liabilities.	190,900	204,100		395,000
Common stock, $10 par	400,000			400,000
Common stock, $5 par		200,000	(a) (200,000)	
Additional paid-in capital.	365,000	58,000	(a) (58,000)	365,000
Retained earnings	213,500	168,000	(168,000)	213,500
Total liabilities & stockholders' equity.	1,209,400	650,100	(426,000)	1,433,500

* An **increase** in total costs and expenses and a **decrease** in net income.
† A **decrease** in dividends and an **increase** in retained earnings.

> Parent company net income = consolidated net income
>
> Parent company retained earnings = consolidated retained earnings

The equalities exist when the equity method of accounting is used *if there are no intercompany profits accounted for in the determination of consolidated net assets.* Intercompany profits (gains) are discussed in Chapter 9.

8   Despite the equalities indicated above, ***consolidated financial statements*** are superior to ***parent company financial statements*** for the presentation of financial position and operating results of parent and subsidiary companies. The effect of the consolidation process for Palm Corporation and subsidiary is to ***reclassify Palm's $29,500 share of its subsidiary's adjusted net income to the revenue and expense components of that net income.*** Similarly, Palm's $505,500 investment in the subsidiary ***is replaced by the assets and liabilities comprising the subsidiary's net assets.***

9   Purchase accounting theory requires the exclusion from consolidated retained earnings of a subsidiary's retained earnings on the date of a purchase-type business combination. Palm Corporation's use of the equity method of accounting meets this requirement. Palm's ending retained earnings amount in the working paper, which is equal to consolidated retained earnings, includes Palm's $29,500 share of the subsidiary's adjusted net income for the year ended December 31, Year 2, the first year of the parent-subsidiary relationship.

Consolidated Financial Statements   The consolidated income statement, statement of retained earnings, and balance sheet of Palm Corporation and subsidiary for the year ended December 31, Year 2, are on pages 317 to 318. The amounts in the consolidated financial statements are taken from the Consolidated column in the working paper on page 315.

Closing Entries   After consolidated financial statements have been completed, both the parent company and its subsidiaries prepare and post closing entries, to complete the accounting cycle for the year. The subsidiary's closing entries are prepared in the usual fashion. However, the parent company's use of the equity method of accounting necessitates specialized closing entries.

The equity method of accounting disregards legal form in favor of the economic substance of the relationship between a parent company and its subsidiaries. However, state corporation laws generally require separate accounting for retained earnings available for dividends to stockholders. Accordingly, Palm Corporation prepares the following closing entries on December 31, Year 2, after the consolidated financial statements have been completed:

Parent company's Dec. 31, Year 2, closing entries under the equity method of accounting for purchased subsidiary

Net Sales...	1,100,000	
Intercompany Investment Income	29,500	
Income Summary		1,129,500
To close revenue accounts.		
Income Summary..	1,020,000	
Cost of Goods Sold..............................		700,000
Operating Expenses...............................		217,667
Interest Expense		49,000
Income Taxes Expense		53,333
To close expense accounts.		
Income Summary..	109,500	
Retained Earnings of Subsidiary ($29,500 − $24,000)		5,500
Retained Earnings ($109,500 − $5,500)............		104,000
To close Income Summary account; to transfer net income legally available for dividends to retained earnings; and to segregate 100% share of adjusted net income of subsidiary not distributed as dividends by the subsidiary.		
Retained Earnings......................................	30,000	
Dividends Declared...............................		30,000
To close Dividends Declared account.		

PALM CORPORATION AND SUBSIDIARY
Consolidated Income Statement
For Year Ended December 31, Year 2

Net sales...		$1,780,000
Costs and expenses:		
Cost of goods sold	$1,179,000	
Operating expenses.................................	349,167	
Interest expense	49,000	
Income taxes expense...............................	93,333	
Total costs and expenses		1,670,500
Net income		$ 109,500
Earnings per share of common stock (40,000 shares outstanding)......		$2.74

PALM CORPORATION AND SUBSIDIARY
Consolidated Statement of Retained Earnings
For Year Ended December 31, Year 2

Retained earnings, beginning of year	$ 134,000
Add: Net income	109,500
Subtotal	$ 243,500
Less: Dividends ($0.75 a share)	30,000
Retained earnings, end of year	$ 213,500

PALM CORPORATION AND SUBSIDIARY
Consolidated Balance Sheet
December 31, Year 2

Assets

Current assets:		
Cash		$ 88,000
Inventories		251,000
Other		219,000
Total current assets		$ 558,000
Plant assets (net)		841,000
Intangible assets:		
Patent (net)	$ 20,000	
Goodwill (net)	14,500	34,500
Total assets		$1,433,500

Liabilities & Stockholders' Equity

Liabilities:		
Income taxes payable		$ 60,000
Other		395,000
Total liabilities		$ 455,000
Stockholders' equity:		
Common stock, $10 par	$ 400,000	
Additional paid-in capital	365,000	
Retained earnings	213,500	978,500
Total liabilities & stockholders' equity		$1,433,500

After the foregoing closing entries have been posted, Palm Corporation's Retained Earnings and Retained Earnings of Subsidiary ledger accounts are as shown on page 319.

The third closing entry on page 317 excludes from Palm Corporation's retained earnings the amount of Palm's net income not available for dividends to Palm's stockholders—$5,500. This amount is computed as shown on page 319.

Parent company's ledger accounts for retained earnings

Retained Earnings

Date	Explanation	Debit	Credit	Balance
Year 1				
Dec. 31	Balance			134,000 cr
Year 2				
Dec. 31	Close net income available for dividends		104,000	238,000 cr
31	Close Dividends Declared account	30,000		208,000 cr

Retained Earnings of Subsidiary

Date	Explanation	Debit	Credit	Balance
Year 2				
Dec. 31	Close net income not available for dividends		5,500	5,500 cr

Adjusted net income of Starr Company recorded by Palm Corporation in Intercompany Investment Income ledger account	$29,500
Less: Dividends declared by Starr to Palm	24,000
Amount of Starr's adjusted net income not distributed as a dividend to Palm ..	$ 5,500

Palm's Retained Earnings of Subsidiary ledger account thus contains the amount of Starr's adjusted net income (less net losses) *since the date of the business combination* that has not been distributed by Starr to Palm as dividends. This amount is termed the *undistributed earnings of the subsidiary* and is equal to the net increase in the balance of Palm's Investment in Starr Company Common Stock ledger account (page 310) since December 31, Year 1, the date of the business combination ($505,500 − $500,000 = $5,500). In addition, the total of the ending balances of Palm's Retained Earnings and Retained Earnings of Subsidiary ledger accounts is equal to consolidated retained earnings, as shown below:

Total of parent company's two retained earnings account balances equals consolidated retained earnings

Balances, Dec. 31, Year 2:	
Retained earnings...	$208,000
Retained earnings of subsidiary......................................	5,500
Total (equal to consolidated retained earnings, Dec. 31, Year 2—see page 318)	$213,500

Illustration of Equity Method for Wholly Owned Purchased Subsidiary for Second Year after Business Combination

In this section, the Palm Corporation–Starr Company example is continued to illustrate application of the equity method of accounting for a wholly owned purchased subsidiary for the second year following a business combination. On December 17, Year 3, Starr Company declared a dividend of $40,000, payable January 6, Year 4, to Palm Corporation, the stockholder of record December 28, Year 3. For the year ended December 31, Year 3, Starr had a net income of $90,000.

After the posting of appropriate Year 3 journal entries under the equity method of accounting, selected ledger accounts for Palm Corporation are as shown below and on page 321.

Ledger accounts of parent company under the equity method of accounting for wholly owned purchased subsidiary

Investment in Starr Company Common Stock				
Date	**Explanation**	**Debit**	**Credit**	**Balance**
Year 1				
Dec. 31	*Issuance of common stock in business combination*	*450,000*		*450,000 dr*
31	*Direct out-of-pocket costs of business combination*	*50,000*		*500,000 dr*
Year 2				
Dec. 20	*Dividend declared by Starr*		*24,000*	*476,000 dr*
31	*Net income of Starr*	*60,000*		*536,000 dr*
31	*Amortization of differences between current fair values and carrying amounts of Starr's net assets*		*30,500*	*505,500 dr*
Year 3				
Dec. 17	*Dividend declared by Starr*		*40,000*	*465,500 dr*
31	*Net income of Starr*	*90,000*		*555,500 dr*
31	*Amortization of differences between current fair values and carrying amounts of Starr's net assets*		*5,500**	*550,000 dr*

(continued)

Intercompany Investment Income

Date	Explanation	Debit	Credit	Balance
Year 2				
Dec. 31	Net income of Starr		60,000	60,000 cr
31	Amortization of differences between current fair values and carrying amounts of Starr's net assets	30,500		29,500 cr
31	Closing entry	29,500		-0-
Year 3				
Dec. 31	Net income of Starr		90,000	90,000 cr
31	Amortization of differences between current fair values and carrying amounts of Starr's net assets	5,500*		84,500 cr

* Building depreciation ($30,000 ÷ 15)	$2,000
Machinery depreciation ($20,000 ÷ 10)	2,000
Patent amortization ($5,000 ÷ 5)	1,000
Goodwill amortization ($15,000 ÷ 30)	500
Total amortization applicable to Year 3	$5,500

Developing the Elimination The working paper elimination for December 31, Year 3, is developed in much the same way as the elimination for December 31, Year 2, as follows (in journal entry format):

Working paper elimination for wholly owned purchased subsidiary for second year subsequent to date of business combination

PALM CORPORATION AND SUBSIDIARY
Working Paper Elimination
December 31, Year 3

(a) Common Stock—Starr	200,000	
Additional Paid-in Capital—Starr	58,000	
Retained Earnings—Starr ($168,000 − $5,500)	162,500	
Retained Earnings of Subsidiary—Palm	5,500	
Intercompany Investment Income—Palm	84,500	
Plant Assets (net)—Starr ($61,000 − $4,000)	57,000	
Patent (net)—Starr ($4,000 − $1,000)	3,000	
Goodwill (net)—Starr ($14,500 − $500)	14,000	
Cost of Goods Sold—Starr	4,000	
Operating Expenses—Starr	1,500	
Investment in Starr Company Common Stock—Palm .		550,000
Dividends Declared—Starr		40,000

To carry out the following:

(a) Eliminate intercompany investment and equity accounts of subsidiary **at beginning of year,** and subsidiary dividend.

(continued)

PALM CORPORATION AND SUBSIDIARY
Working Paper Elimination (concluded)
December 31, Year 3

(b) Provide for Year 3 depreciation and amortization on differences between current fair values and carrying amounts of Starr's net assets as follows:

	Cost of goods sold	Operating expenses
Building depreciation.............	$1,000	$1,000
Machinery depreciation	2,000	
Patent amortization..............	1,000	
Goodwill amortization............		500
Totals........................	$4,000	$1,500

(c) Allocate unamortized differences between combination date current fair values and carrying amounts of Starr's net assets to appropriate assets.

(Income tax effects are disregarded.)

The principal new feature of the foregoing elimination is the treatment of the beginning-of-year Retained Earnings ledger account balance of the subsidiary, Starr Company. Because consolidated retained earnings of Palm Corporation and subsidiary on December 31, Year 2, included the amount of $5,500, representing the undistributed earnings of the subsidiary for the year ended December 31, Year 2, only $162,500 ($168,000 − $5,500 = $162,500) is eliminated from the subsidiary's retained earnings balance on January 1, Year 3. In addition, the $5,500 balance (before the closing entry for Year 3) of the parent company's Retained Earnings of Subsidiary ledger account is eliminated, to avoid "double counting" of the undistributed earnings of the subsidiary as of January 1, Year 3, in the consolidated financial statements of Palm Corporation and subsidiary for the year ended December 31, Year 3.

Working Paper for Consolidated Financial Statements   The features of the December 31, Year 3, elimination for Palm Corporation and subsidiary described in the foregoing paragraph are illustrated in the *partial* working paper for consolidated financial statements on page 323. The net income and dividends for Palm Corporation are assumed for illustrative purposes.

The elimination of only $162,500 of the balance of the subsidiary's beginning-of-year retained earnings results in consolidated retained earnings of $213,500 at the beginning of the year (January 1, Year 3). This amount is equal to consolidated retained earnings on December 31, Year 2 (see page 315). In addition, the total of the

Equity method: Wholly owned subsidiary subsequent to date of purchase-type business combination

PALM CORPORATION AND SUBSIDIARY
Partial Working Paper for Consolidated Financial Statements
For Year Ended December 31, Year 3

	Palm Corporation	Starr Company	Eliminations increase (decrease)	Consolidated
Statement of Retained Earnings				
Retained earnings, beginning of year ...	208,000	168,000	(a) (162,500)	213,500
Net income.........................	244,500	90,000	(90,000)*	244,500
Subtotal	452,500	258,000	(252,500)	458,000
Dividends declared..................	60,000	40,000	(a) (40,000)†	60,000
Retained earnings, end of year........	392,500	218,000	(212,500)	398,000
Balance Sheet				
Common stock, $10 par	400,000			400,000
Common stock, $5 par		200,000	(a) (200,000)	
Additional paid-in capital.............	365,000	58,000	(a) (58,000)	365,000
Retained earnings	392,500	218,000	(212,500)	398,000
Retained earnings of subsidiary	5,500		(a) (5,500)	
Total stockholders' equity...........	1,163,000	476,000	(476,000)	1,163,000
Total liabilities & stockholders' equity....	x,xxx,xxx	xxx,xxx	(476,000)	x,xxx,xxx

*Decrease in intercompany investment income ($84,500), plus total increase in costs and expenses ($4,000 + $1,500), equals $90,000.
† A **decrease** in dividends and an **increase** in retained earnings.

parent company's two retained earnings amounts in the working paper for consolidated financial statements ($392,500 + $5,500 = $398,000) is identical to the amount of consolidated retained earnings on December 31, Year 3.

Closing Entries The amount of the undistributed earnings of Starr Company for Year 3 is $44,500, computed as follows:

Adjusted net income of Starr Company recorded by Palm Corporation in Intercompany Investment Income ledger account (page 321)..................	$84,500
Less: Dividends declared by Starr to Palm	40,000
Amount of Starr's adjusted net income not distributed as a dividend to Palm..	$44,500

In the December 31, Year 3, closing entries for Palm Corporation, $44,500 of Palm's $244,500 net income for Year 3 is closed to the Retained Earnings of Subsidiary ledger account. The remaining $200,000 ($244,500 − $44,500 = $200,000) is closed to the Retained Earnings account, because it is available for dividends to the stockholders of Palm. Following the posting of the closing entries, the two ledger accounts are as follows:

Parent company's
ledger accounts for
retained earnings

	Retained Earnings			
Date	**Explanation**	**Debit**	**Credit**	**Balance**
Year 1				
Dec. 31	Balance			134,000 cr
Year 2				
Dec. 31	Close net income available for dividends		104,000	238,000 cr
31	Close Dividends Declared account	30,000		208,000 cr
Year 3				
Dec. 31	Close net income available for dividends		200,000	408,000 cr
31	Close Dividends Declared account	60,000		348,000 cr

	Retained Earnings of Subsidiary			
Date	**Explanation**	**Debit**	**Credit**	**Balance**
Year 2				
Dec. 31	Close net income not available for dividends		5,500	5,500 cr
Year 3				
Dec. 31	Close net income not available for dividends		44,500	50,000 cr

Again, the balance of Palm's Retained Earnings of Subsidiary ledger account, $50,000, is equal to the net increase in the balance of Palm's Investment in Starr Company Common Stock account (page 320) since the date of the business combination ($550,000 − $500,000 = $50,000). Further, the total of the ending balances of the foregoing retained earnings accounts, $398,000 ($348,000 + $50,000 = $398,000) is equal to consolidated retained earnings of $398,000 on December 31, Year 3 (see page 323).

ACCOUNTING FOR OPERATING RESULTS OF PARTIALLY OWNED PURCHASED SUBSIDIARIES

Accounting for the operating results of a partially owned purchased subsidiary requires the computation of the minority interest in net income or net losses of the subsidiary. Thus, under the parent company concept of consolidated financial statements, the consolidated income statement of a parent company and its partially owned purchased subsidiary includes an expense—minority interest in net income (or loss) of subsidiary. The minority interest in net assets of the subsidiary is displayed among liabilities in the consolidated balance sheet.

Illustration of Equity Method for Partially Owned Purchased Subsidiary for First Year after Business Combination

The Post Corporation–Sage Company consolidated entity described in Chapter 6 (pages 259 to 262) is used in this section to illustrate the equity method of accounting for the operating results of a partially owned purchased subsidiary. Post owns 95% of the outstanding common stock of Sage, and minority stockholders own the remaining 5%.

Assume that Sage Company on November 24, Year 2, declared a $1 a share dividend, payable December 16, Year 2, to stockholders of record December 1, Year 2, and that Sage had a net income of $90,000 for the year ended December 31, Year 2. Sage prepares the following journal entries for the declaration and payment of the dividend:

<table>
<tr><td style="width:200px">Partially owned subsidiary's journal entries for declaration and payment of dividend</td><td colspan="3">

Year 2

Nov. 24 Dividends Declared (40,000 × $1)   40,000
              Dividends Payable ($40,000 × 0.05) *2,000*
              Intercompany Dividends Payable ($40,000 × 0.95)   *38,000*
         To record declaration of dividend payable Dec. 16, Year 2,
         to stockholders of record Dec. 1, Year 2.

Dec. 16 Dividends Payable   2,000
        Intercompany Dividends Payable   38,000
             Cash *40,000*
         To record payment of dividend declared Nov. 24, Year 2, to
         stockholders of record Dec. 1, Year 2.

</td></tr>
</table>

Post's journal entries for Year 2, under the equity method of accounting, include the following:

<table>
<tr><td style="width:200px">Parent company's equity-method journal entries to record operating results of partially owned purchased subsidiary</td><td colspan="3">

Year 2

Nov. 24 Intercompany Dividends Receivable   38,000
              Investment in Sage Company Common Stock *38,000*
         To record dividend declared by Sage Company, payable
         Dec. 16, Year 2, to stockholders of record Dec. 1, Year 2.

Dec. 16 Cash   38,000
              Intercompany Dividends Receivable *38,000*
         To record receipt of dividend from Sage Company.

     31 Investment in Sage Company Common Stock
          ($90,000 × 0.95).................................   85,500
              Intercompany Investment Income...............   *85,500*
         To record 95% of net income of Sage Company for the
         year ended Dec. 31, Year 2. (Income tax effects are disre-
         garded.)

</td></tr>
</table>

As pointed out on page 264, a purchase-type business combination involves a restatement of net asset values of the subsidiary. Sage Company's net income of $90,000 does not reflect cost expirations attributable to Sage's restated net asset values, *because the restatements were not entered in Sage's accounting records.* Consequently, the depreciation and amortization of the $246,000 difference between the current fair values of Sage's *identifiable* net assets on December 31, Year 1, the date of the business combination, and the carrying amounts of those net assets must be accounted for by Post Corporation. Assume, as in Chapter 6 (page 264), that the difference was allocable to Sage's identifiable assets as shown below:

Differences between current fair values and carrying amounts of partially owned purchased subsidiary's identifiable net assets on date of business combination	*Inventories (first-in, first-out cost)*	*$ 26,000*
	Plant assets (net):	
	Land *$60,000*	
	Building (economic life 20 years) *80,000*	
	Machinery (economic life 5 years) *50,000*	*190,000*
	Leasehold (economic life 6 years).....................................	*30,000*
	Total..	*$246,000*

In addition, Post had acquired in the business combination goodwill (to be amortized over 40 years) attributable to Sage in the amount of $38,000, computed as follows:

Computation of goodwill acquired by combinor

Cost of Post Corporation's 95% interest in Sage Company..............	*$1,192,250*
Less: 95% of $1,215,000 aggregate current fair values of Sage's identifiable	
net assets	*1,154,250*
Goodwill acquired by Post (to be amortized over 40 years)..............	*$ 38,000*

Parent company's equity-method journal entry to record amortization of partially owned purchased subsidiary's identifiable net assets

Intercompany Investment Income	*42,750*	
Investment in Sage Company Common Stock..............		*42,750*
To amortize differences between current fair values and carrying		
amounts of Sage Company's identifiable net assets on December		
31, Year 1, as follows:		
Inventories—to cost of goods sold	*$26,000*	
Building—depreciation ($80,000 ÷ 20)	*4,000*	
Machinery—depreciation ($50,000 ÷ 5)	*10,000*	
Leasehold—amortization ($30,000 ÷ 6)	*5,000*	
Total difference applicable to Year 2...............	*$45,000*	
Amortization for Year 2 ($45,000 × 0.95)............	*$42,750*	
(Income tax effects are disregarded.)		

Post Corporation prepares the additional journal entry on page 326 on December 31, Year 2, under the equity method of accounting to reflect the effects of the differences between current fair values and carrying amounts of the partially owned subsidiary's identifiable net assets.

Next, Post prepares the following journal entry on December 31, Year 2, to record the amortization of goodwill acquired by Post in the business combination with Sage:

Parent company's equity-method journal entry to record amortization of goodwill

Amortization Expense ($38,000 ÷ 40)............................	950	
Investment in Sage Company Common Stock.............		950
To amortize goodwill acquired in business combination with partially owned purchased subsidiary over an economic life of 40 years.		

Note that the amortization of the goodwill is debited to *Amortization Expense,* not to Intercompany Investment Income. The reason for this treatment is explained on page 328.

After the journal entries set forth above are posted, Post Corporation's Investment in Sage Company Common Stock and Intercompany Investment Income ledger accounts are below and on page 328.

The $42,750 balance of Post Corporation's Intercompany Investment Income account represents 95% of the $45,000 adjusted net income ($90,000 − $45,000 = $45,000) of Sage Company for the year ended December 31, Year 2.

Ledger accounts of parent company under equity method of accounting for partially owned purchased subsidiary

Investment in Sage Company Common Stock

Date	Explanation	Debit	Credit	Balance
Year 1				
Dec. 31	Issuance of common stock			
	in business combination	1,140,000		1,140,000 dr
31	Direct out-of-pocket costs			
	of business combination	52,250		1,192,250 dr
Year 2				
Nov. 24	Dividend declared by Sage		38,000	1,154,250 dr
Dec. 31	Net income of Sage	85,500		1,239,750 dr
31	Amortization of differences			
	between current fair			
	values and carrying			
	amounts of Sage's			
	identifiable net assets		42,750	1,197,000 dr
31	Amortization of goodwill		950	1,196,050 dr

Intercompany Investment Income

Date	Explanation	Debit	Credit	Balance
Year 2				
Dec. 31	Net income of Sage		85,500	85,500 cr
31	Amortization of differences between current fair values and carrying amounts of Sage's identifiable net assets	42,750		42,750 cr

Amortization of Goodwill Attributable to Partially Owned Subsidiary   As explained in Chapter 6 (page 265), goodwill in a business combination involving a *partially owned subsidiary* is attributed to the *parent company* rather than the *subsidiary* under the widely used accounting practice illustrated in this text. Consequently, amortization of the goodwill is *debited to the Amortization Expense ledger account of the parent company,* with an *offsetting credit to the Investment account.* This technique avoids charging any portion of goodwill amortization to the minority interest, which did not acquire any goodwill. Thus, this treatment differs from the amortization of goodwill attributable to a *wholly owned subsidiary.* As illustrated on page 310, amortization of a wholly owned subsidiary's goodwill is debited to the parent company's Intercompany Investment Income ledger account.

POST CORPORATION
Analysis of Investment in Sage Company Common Stock Ledger Account
For Year Ended December 31, Year 2

	Carrying amount	Current fair value excess	Goodwill	Total	
Beginning balances	$920,550	$233,700	$38,000	$1,192,250	
Net income of Sage					
($90,000 × 0.95)	85,500			85,500	⎫
Amortization of differences					
between current					Intercompany
fair values and carry-					investment
ing amounts of Sage's					income,
identifiable net assets					$42,750
($45,000 × 0.95)		(42,750)		(42,750)	⎭
Amortization of goodwill			(950)	(950)	
Dividend declared by Sage					
($40,000 × 0.95)	(38,000)			(38,000)	
Ending balances	$968,050	$190,950	$37,050	$1,196,050	

Developing the Eliminations Post Corporation's use of the equity method of accounting for its investment in Sage Company resulted in a balance in the Investment ledger account that is a mixture of three components: (1) the carrying amount of Sage's identifiable net assets; (2) the "current fair value excess," which is attributable to Sage's *identifiable* net assets; and (3) the goodwill acquired by Post in the business combination with Sage. These components are analyzed on page 328.

The minority interest in Sage's net assets (which is not recorded in a ledger account) may be analyzed similarly, except that *there is no goodwill attributable to the minority interest:*

POST CORPORATION
Analysis of Minority Interest in Net Assets of Sage Company
For Year Ended December 31, Year 2

	Carrying amount	Current fair value excess	Total	
Beginning balances..................	$48,450	$12,300	$60,750	
Net income of Sage ($90,000 × 0.05)	4,500		4,500	Minority interest in net income of subsidiary, $2,250
Amortization of differences between current fair values and carrying amounts of Sage's identifiable net assets ($45,000 × 0.05).....................		(2,250)	(2,250)	
Dividend declared by Sage ($40,000 × 0.05).....................	(2,000)		(2,000)	
Ending balances......................	$50,950	$10,050	$61,000	

The $1,019,000 ($968,050 + $50,950 = $1,019,000) total of the ending balances of the Carrying Amount columns of the two foregoing analyses agrees with the total stockholders' equity of Sage Company on December 31, Year 2 (see balance sheet section of working paper for consolidated financial statements on page 334), as follows:

Partially owned subsidiary's stockholders' equity, Dec. 31, Year 2

Common stock, $10 par..	$ 400,000
Additional paid-in capital	235,000
Retained earnings..	384,000
Total stockholders' equity	$1,019,000

The $201,000 ($190,950 + $10,050 = $201,000) total of the ending balances of the Current Fair Value Excess columns of the two analyses agrees with the December 31, Year 2, total of the unamortized balances for each of the respective identifiable assets of Sage Company, as follows:

Unamortized differences between current fair values and carrying amounts of partially owned purchased subsidiary's identifiable assets one year subsequent to business combination

	Balances, Dec. 31, Year 1 (p. 326)	Amortization for Year 2 (p. 326)	Balances, Dec. 31, Year 2
Inventories...............	$ 26,000	$(26,000)	
Plant assets (net):			
Land...................	$ 60,000		$ 60,000
Building	80,000	$ (4,000)	76,000
Machinery	50,000	(10,000)	40,000
Total plant assets	$190,000	$(14,000)	$176,000
Leasehold	$ 30,000	$ (5,000)	$ 25,000
Totals................	$246,000	$(45,000)	$201,000

Assuming that Sage Company allocates machinery depreciation and leasehold amortization entirely to cost of goods sold, and building depreciation 50% each to cost of goods sold and operating expenses, the working paper eliminations (in journal entry format) for Post Corporation and subsidiary on December 31, Year 2, are as shown below and on page 331. The reference numbers in parentheses relate to the discussion that follows the elimination.

Working paper eliminations for partially owned purchased subsidiary for first year subsequent to date of business combination

POST CORPORATION AND SUBSIDIARY
Working Paper Eliminations
December 31, Year 2

(a) Common Stock—Sage	400,000 (1)	
Additional Paid-in Capital—Sage	235,000 (1)	
Retained Earnings—Sage	334,000 (1)	
Intercompany Investment Income—Post..........	42,750 (2)	
Plant Assets (net)—Sage ($190,000 − $14,000) ...	176,000 (3)	
Leasehold (net)—Sage ($30,000 − $5,000)	25,000 (3)	
Goodwill (net)—Post ($38,000 − $950)	37,050 (3)	
Cost of Goods Sold—Sage	43,000 (4)	
Operating Expenses—Sage.....................	2,000 (4)	
Investment in Sage Company Common		
Stock—Post............................		1,196,050 (1)
Dividends Declared—Sage		40,000 (1)
Minority Interest in Net Assets of Subsidiary		
($60,750 − $2,000) [See (d) on page 331]..		58,750 (1)
To carry out the following:		
(a) Eliminate intercompany investment and equity		
accounts of subsidiary **at beginning of year,** and		
subsidiary dividends.		

(continued)

POST CORPORATION AND SUBSIDIARY
Working Paper Eliminations (concluded)
December 31, Year 2

(b) Provide for Year 2 depreciation and amortization
on differences between current fair values and
carrying amounts of Sage's identifiable net
assets as follows:

	Cost of goods sold	Operating expenses
Inventories sold	$26,000	
Building depreciation.	2,000	$2,000
Machinery deprecia-		
tion	10,000	
Leasehold amortiza-		
tion	5,000	
Totals	$43,000	$2,000

(c) Allocate unamortized differences between combination date current fair values and carrying
amounts to appropriate assets.

(d) Establish minority interest in net assets of subsidiary at beginning of year ($60,750), less minority
share of dividends declared by subsidiary during
year ($40,000 × 0.05 = $2,000).

(Income tax effects are disregarded.)

(b) Minority Interest in Net Income of Subsidiary 2,250

    Minority Interest in Net Assets of Subsidiary . . 2,250

To establish minority interest in subsidiary's adjusted
net income for Year 2 as follows:

Net income of subsidiary	$ 90,000
Net reduction of elimination (a)	
($43,000 + $2,000)	(45,000)
Adjusted net income of subsidiary	$ 45,000
Minority share ($45,000 × 0.05)	$ 2,250

Comments on components of the foregoing working paper elimination follow:

(1) As indicated in Chapter 6 (page 254), the three components of the subsidiary's
stockholders' equity are reciprocal to the parent company's Investment account.
However, because a consolidated statement of retained earnings is to be prepared
for the first year following the purchase-type business combination, the subsidiary's *beginning-of-year* retained earnings amount is eliminated, together with
the subsidiary's dividends, which are a contra to the subsidiary's retained earn-

ings. Further, the beginning-of-year minority interest, $60,750 (see page 266 of Chapter 6), is reduced by the minority's share of the subsidiary's dividends, $2,000, as a counterpart of the parent company's reduction of its Investment account balance by $38,000, its share of the subsidiary's dividends (see the analysis of the Investment account on page 328).

(2) As illustrated in the analysis on page 328, the amount of the parent company's intercompany investment income is an element of the balance of the parent's Investment ledger account. In effect, the elimination of the intercompany investment income, coupled with items described in (4) below, comprises a reclassification of the intercompany investment income to the adjusted components of the subsidiary's net income in the consolidated income statement.

(3) The debits to the subsidiary's plant assets and leasehold bring into the consolidated balance sheet the unamortized differences between current fair values and carrying amounts of the subsidiary's identifiable assets on the date of the business combination (see the analysis on page 330). Further, the debit to the parent company's goodwill brings the unamortized amount of that asset into the consolidated balance sheet.

(4) The increases in the subsidiary's cost of goods sold and operating expenses, totaling $45,000 ($43,000 + $2,000 = $45,000), in effect reclassify the comparable decreases totaling $45,000 ($42,750 + $2,250 = $45,000) in the parent company's Investment account and the minority interest in net assets of the subsidiary, respectively (see the analyses on pages 328 and 329) to the appropriate categories for the consolidated income statement.

Working Paper for Consolidated Financial Statements   The working paper for consolidated financial statements for Post Corporation and subsidiary for the year ended December 31, Year 2, is shown on pages 333 to 334.

The following aspects of the working paper for consolidated financial statements of Post Corporation and subsidiary should be emphasized:

1   Income tax effects of the increase in Sage Company's costs and expenses are not included in elimination *(a)*. Income tax effects in consolidated financial statements are considered in Chapter 10.

2   Elimination *(a)* cancels Sage's retained earnings balance ***at the beginning of the year.*** This step is essential for the preparation of all three basic consolidating financial statements.

3   The parent company's use of the equity method of accounting results in the following equalities:

Parent company net income = consolidated net income

Parent company retained earnings = consolidated retained earnings

These equalities exist in the equity method of accounting if there are no intercompany profits (gains) or losses eliminated for the determination of consolidated net assets. Intercompany profits are discussed in Chapter 9.

Equity method: Partially owned subsidiary subsequent to date of purchase-type business combination

POST CORPORATION AND SUBSIDIARY
Working Paper for Consolidated Financial Statements
For Year Ended December 31, Year 2

	Post Corporation	Sage Company	Eliminations increase (decrease)		Consolidated
Income Statement					
Revenue:					
Net sales..............	5,611,000	1,089,000			6,700,000
Intercompany investment					
income................	42,750		(a)	(42,750)	
Total revenue..........	5,653,750	1,089,000		(42,750)	6,700,000
Costs and expenses:					
Cost of goods sold	3,925,000	700,000	(a)	43,000	4,668,000
Operating expenses	556,950*	129,000	(a)	2,000	687,950
Interest and income taxes					
expense...............	710,000	170,000			880,000
Minority interest in net					
income of subsidiary.......			(b)	2,250	2,250
Total costs and expenses	5,191,950	999,000		47,250†	6,238,200
Net income	461,800	90,000		(90,000)	461,800
Statement of Retained Earnings					
Retained earnings, beginning					
of year	1,050,000	334,000	(a)	(334,000)	1,050,000
Net income	461,800	90,000		(90,000)	461,800
Subtotal.................	1,511,800	424,000		(424,000)	1,511,800
Dividends declared	158,550	40,000	(a)	(40,000)‡	158,550
Retained earnings, end of					
year	1,353,250	384,000		(384,000)	1,353,250
Balance Sheet					
Assets					
Inventories	861,000	439,000			1,300,000
Other current assets........	639,000	371,000			1,010,000
Investment in Sage Company					
common stock	1,196,050		(a)	(1,196,050)	
Plant assets (net)	3,600,000	1,150,000	(a)	176,000	4,926,000
Leasehold (net)			(a)	25,000	25,000
Goodwill (net)..............	95,000		(a)	37,050	132,050
Total assets	6,391,050	1,960,000		(958,000)	7,393,050

* Includes $950 amortization of goodwill.
† An **increase** in total costs and expenses and a **decrease** in net income.
‡ A **decrease** in dividends and an **increase** in retained earnings.

(continued)

POST CORPORATION AND SUBSIDIARY
Working Paper for Consolidated Financial Statements (concluded)
For Year Ended December 31, Year 2

	Post Corporation	Sage Company	Eliminations increase (decrease)		Consolidated
Liabilities & Stockholders' Equity					
Liabilities	2,420,550	941,000			3,361,550
Minority interest in net assets of subsidiary			(a) (b)	58,750 2,250	61,000
Common stock, $1 par.	1,057,000				1,057,000
Common stock, $10 par.		400,000	(a)	(400,000)	
Additional paid-in capital	1,560,250	235,000	(a)	(235,000)	1,560,250
Retained earnings.	1,353,250	384,000		(384,000)	1,353,250
Total liabilities & stock- holders' equity	6,391,050	1,960,000		(958,000)	7,393,050

4 One of the effects of elimination *(a)* is to reduce the differences between the current fair values of the subsidiary's identifiable net assets on the business combination date and their carrying amounts on that date. The effect of the reduction is as follows:

Aggregate difference on date of business combination (Dec. 31, Year 1). . . .	$246,000
Less: Reduction in elimination (a) ($43,000 + $2,000)	45,000
Unamortized difference, Dec. 31, Year 2 ($176,000 + $25,000).	$201,000

The joint effect of Post's use of the equity method of accounting and the annual eliminations will be to extinguish $141,000 of the remaining $201,000 difference through Post's Investment in Sage Company Common Stock ledger account. *The $60,000 applicable to Sage's land will not be extinguished.*

5 The minority interest in net assets of subsidiary on December 31, Year 2, may be verified as follows:

Sage Company's total stockholders' equity, Dec. 31, Year 2	$1,019,000
Add: Unamortized difference computed in **4**, above	201,000
Sage's adjusted stockholders' equity, Dec. 31, Year 2.	$1,220,000
Minority interest in net assets of subsidiary ($1,220,000 × 0.05).	$ 61,000

6 The minority interest in net income of subsidiary is recognized in elimination *(b)* in the amount of $2,250 (5% of the adjusted net income of Sage Company) as an increase in minority interest in net assets of subsidiary and a decrease in consolidated net income.

POST CORPORATION AND SUBSIDIARY
Consolidated Income Statement
For Year Ended December 31, Year 2

Net sales		$6,700,000
Costs and expenses:		
Cost of goods sold	$4,668,000	
Operating expenses	687,950	
Interest and income taxes expense	880,000	
Minority interest in net income of subsidiary	2,250	
Total costs and expenses		6,238,200
Net income		$ 461,800
Earnings per share of common stock (1,057,000 shares outstanding)		$ 0.44

POST CORPORATION AND SUBSIDIARY
Consolidated Statement of Retained Earnings
For Year Ended December 31, Year 2

Retained earnings, beginning of year	$1,050,000
Add: Net income	461,800
Subtotal	$1,511,800
Less: Dividends ($0.15 a share)	158,550
Retained earnings, end of year	$1,353,250

POST CORPORATION AND SUBSIDIARY
Consolidated Balance Sheet
December 31, Year 2

Assets

Current assets:		
Inventories		$1,300,000
Other		1,010,000
Total current assets		$2,310,000
Plant assets (net)		4,926,000
Intangible assets:		
Leasehold (net)	$ 25,000	
Goodwill (net)	132,050	157,050
Total assets		$7,393,050

Liabilities & Stockholders' Equity

Liabilities:		
Other than minority interest		$3,361,550
Minority interest in net assets of subsidiary		61,000
Total liabilities		$3,422,550
Stockholders' equity:		
Common stock, $1 par	$1,057,000	
Additional paid-in capital	1,560,250	
Retained earnings	1,353,250	3,970,500
Total liabilities & stockholders' equity		$7,393,050

Consolidated Financial Statements The consolidated income statement, statement of retained earnings, and balance sheet of Post Corporation and subsidiary for the year ended December 31, Year 2, are on page 335. The amounts in the consolidated financial statements are taken from the Consolidated column in the working paper on pages 333 and 334.

Closing Entries As indicated on pages 316 to 317, legal considerations necessitate the following closing entries for Post Corporation on December 31, Year 2:

Parent company's Dec. 31, Year 2, closing entries under the equity method of accounting for purchased subsidiary

Net Sales.	5,611,000	
Intercompany Investment Income	42,750	
Income Summary		5,653,750
To close revenue accounts.		
Income Summary.	5,191,950	
Cost of Goods Sold.		3,925,000
Operating Expenses.		556,950
Interest and Income Taxes Expense.		710,000
To close expense accounts.		
Income Summary.	461,800	
Retained Earnings of Subsidiary ($42,750 − $38,000)		4,750
Retained Earnings ($461,800 − $4,750).		457,050
To close Income Summary account; to transfer net income legally available for dividends to retained earnings; and to segregate 95% share of adjusted net income of subsidiary not distributed as dividends.		
Retained Earnings.	158,550	
Dividends Declared.		158,550
To close Dividends Declared account.		

After the foregoing closing entries have been posted, Post's Retained Earnings and Retained Earnings of Subsidiary ledger accounts are as follows:

Parent company's ledger accounts for retained earnings

Retained Earnings				
Date	**Explanation**	**Debit**	**Credit**	**Balance**
Year 1				
Dec. 31	Balance			1,050,000 cr
Year 2				
Dec. 31	Close net income available for dividends		457,050	1,507,050 cr
31	Close Dividends Declared account	158,550		1,348,500 cr

Retained Earnings of Subsidiary				
Date	Explanation	Debit	Credit	Balance
Year 2 Dec. 31	Close net income not available for dividends		4,750	4,750 cr

The $4,750 balance of Post's Retained Earnings of Subsidiary ledger account represents Post's share of the undistributed earnings of Sage Company for the year ended December 31, Year 2. The undistributed earnings of the subsidiary may be reconciled to the increase in Post's investment ledger account balance as follows:

Reconciliation of undistributed earnings of subsidiary	Undistributed earnings of subsidiary, year ended Dec. 31, Year 2.............	$4,750
	Less: Amortization of goodwill acquired by parent company in business combination (page 327)...	950
	Increase in balance of Investment in Sage Company Common Stock ledger account during Year 2 ($1,196,050 − $1,192,250)	$3,800

In addition, the total of the ending balances of Post's Retained Earnings and Retained Earnings of Subsidiary ledger accounts is equal to consolidated retained earnings, as shown below:

Total of parent company's two retained earnings account balances equals consolidated retained earnings	Balances, Dec. 31, Year 2: Retained earnings...	$1,348,500
	Retained earnings of subsidiary.....................................	4,750
	Total (equal to consolidated retained earnings, Dec. 31, Year 2—see page 334)	$1,353,250

Illustration of Equity Method for Partially Owned Purchased Subsidiary for Second Year after Business Combination

In this section, the Post Corporation–Sage Company example is continued to demonstrate application of the equity method of accounting for a partially owned purchased subsidiary for the second year following the business combination. On November 22, Year 3, Sage Company declared a dividend of $50,000, payable December 17, Year 3, to stockholders of record December 1, Year 3. For the year ended December 31, Year 3, Sage had a net income of $105,000. Post's share of the dividend was $47,500 ($50,000 × 0.95 = $47,500), and Post's share of Sage's net income was $99,750 ($105,000 × 0.95 = $99,750).

After the posting of appropriate Year 3 journal entries under the equity method of accounting, selected ledger accounts for Post Corporation are as shown on pages 338 to 339.

Developing the Eliminations   The working paper eliminations for December 31, Year 3, are developed in much the same way as for the eliminations for December 31, Year 2, as illustrated on pages 339 to 340 (in journal entry format).

Because consolidated retained earnings of Post Corporation and subsidiary on December 31, Year 2, included the amount of $4,750, representing the parent company's share of the undistributed earnings of the subsidiary for the year ended De-

Ledger accounts of parent company under equity method of accounting for partially owned purchased subsidiary

Investment in Sage Company Common Stock

Date	Explanation	Debit	Credit	Balance
Year 1				
Dec. 31	Issuance of common stock in business combination	1,140,000		1,140,000 dr
31	Direct out-of-pocket costs of business combination	52,250		1,192,250 dr
Year 2				
Nov. 24	Dividend declared by Sage		38,000	1,154,250 dr
Dec. 31	Net income of Sage	85,500		1,239,750 dr
31	Amortization of differences between current fair values and carrying amounts of Sage's identifiable net assets		42,750	1,197,000 dr
31	Amortization of goodwill		950	1,196,050 dr
Year 3				
Nov. 22	Dividend declared by Sage		47,500	1,148,550 dr
Dec. 31	Net income of Sage	99,750		1,248,300 dr
31	Amortization of differences between current fair values and carrying amounts of Sage's identifiable net assets		18,050*	1,230,250 dr
31	Amortization of goodwill		950	1,229,300 dr

Intercompany Investment Income

Date	Explanation	Debit	Credit	Balance
Year 2				
Dec. 31	Net income of Sage		85,500	85,500 cr
31	Amortization of differences between current fair values and carrying amounts of Sage's identifiable net assets	42,750		42,750 cr
31	Closing entry	42,750		-0-

(continued)

Intercompany Investment Income (concluded)

Date	Explanation	Debit	Credit	Balance
Year 3				
Dec. 31	Net income of Sage		99,750	99,750 cr
31	Amortization of differences between current fair values and carrying amounts of Sage's identifiable net assets	18,050*		81,700 cr

* Building depreciation ($80,000 ÷ 20) .... $ 4,000
Machinery depreciation ($50,000 ÷ 5) 10,000
Leasehold amortization ($30,000 ÷ 6) 5,000
Total amortization applicable to Year 3...................... $19,000
Post Corporation's share ($19,000 × 0.95) $18,050

cember 31, Year 2, only $379,250 ($384,000 − $4,750 = $379,250) is eliminated from the subsidiary's retained earnings on January 1, Year 3. In addition, the $4,750 balance (before the closing entry for Year 3) of the parent company's Retained Earnings of Subsidiary ledger account is eliminated, to avoid "double counting" of the undistributed earnings of the subsidiary as of January 1, Year 3, in the consolidated financial statements of Post Corporation and subsidiary for the year ended December 31, Year 3.

Working paper eliminations for partially owned purchased subsidiary for second year subsequent to date of business combination

POST CORPORATION AND SUBSIDIARY
Working Paper Eliminations
December 31, Year 3

(a) Common Stock—Sage 400,000
Additional Paid-in Capital—Sage........................ 235,000
Retained Earnings—Sage ($384,000 − $4,750).......... 379,250
Retained Earnings of Subsidiary—Post................. 4,750
Intercompany Investment Income—Post................. 81,700
Plant Assets (net)—Sage ($176,000 − $14,000)......... 162,000
Leasehold (net)—Sage ($25,000 − $5,000).............. 20,000
Goodwill (net)—Post ($37,050 − $950)................. 36,100
Cost of Goods Sold—Sage............................. 17,000
Operating Expenses—Sage............................. 2,000
Investment in Sage Company Common Stock—Post ... 1,229,300
Dividends Declared—Sage..................... 50,000
Minority Interest in Net Assets of Subsidiary ($61,000 − $2,500)............................... 58,500

(continued)

POST CORPORATION AND SUBSIDIARY
Working Paper Eliminations (concluded)
December 31, Year 3

To carry out the following:

*(a) Eliminate intercompany investment and equity accounts of subsidiary **at beginning of year,** and subsidiary dividend.*

(b) Provide for Year 3 depreciation and amortization on differences between current fair values and carrying amounts of Sage's identifiable net assets as follows:

	Cost of goods sold	Operating expenses
Building depreciation	$ 2,000	$2,000
Machinery depreciation	10,000	
Leasehold amortization	5,000	
Totals	$17,000	$2,000

(c) Allocate unamortized differences between combination date current fair values and carrying amounts to appropriate assets.

(d) Establish minority interest in net assets of subsidiary at beginning of year ($61,000), less minority share of dividends declared by subsidiary during year ($50,000 × 0.05 = $2,500).

(Income tax effects are disregarded.)

(b) Minority Interest in Net Income of Subsidiary		4,300	
Minority Interest in Net Assets of Subsidiary			4,300

To establish minority interest in subsidiary's adjusted net income for Year 3 as follows:

Net income of subsidiary	$105,000
Net reduction in elimination (a)	
($17,000 + $2,000)	(19,000)
Adjusted net income of subsidiary	$ 86,000
Minority share ($86,000 × 0.05)	$ 4,300

Working Paper for Consolidated Financial Statements   The aspects of the December 31, Year 3, eliminations for Post Corporation and subsidiary described in the foregoing paragraph are illustrated in the following *partial* working paper for consolidated financial statements. The amounts presented for Post Corporation are assumed.

Equity method: Partially owned subsidiary subsequent to date of purchase-type business combination

POST CORPORATION AND SUBSIDIARY
Partial Working Paper for Consolidated Financial Statements
For Year Ended December 31, Year 3

	Post Corporation	Sage Company	Eliminations increase (decrease)		Consolidated
Statement of Retained Earnings					
Retained earnings, beginning of year........	1,348,500	384,000	(a)	(379,250)	1,353,250
Net income...........	352,600	105,000		(105,000)*	352,600
Subtotal	1,701,100	489,000		(484,250)	1,705,850
Dividends declared.....	158,550	50,000	(a)	(50,000)†	158,550
Retained earnings, end of year..............	1,542,550	439,000		(434,250)	1,547,300
Balance Sheet					
Minority interest in net assets of subsidiary...			{ (a) { (b)	58,500 ⎫ 4,300 ⎬	62,800
Total liabilities	x,xxx,xxx	xxx,xxx		62,800	xxx,xxx
Common stock, $1 par .	1,057,000				1,057,000
Common stock, $10 par		400,000	(a)	(400,000)	
Additional paid-in capital	1,560,250	235,000	(a)	(235,000)	1,560,250
Retained earnings	1,542,550	439,000		(434,250)	1,547,300
Retained earnings of subsidiary...........	4,750		(a)	(4,750)	
Total stockholders' equity..............	4,164,550	1,074,000		(1,074,000)	4,164,550
Total liabilities & stockholders' equity .	x,xxx,xxx	x,xxx,xxx		(1,011,200)	x,xxx,xxx

* Decrease in intercompany investment income ($81,700), plus total increase in costs and expenses ($17,000 + $2,000 + $4,300), equals $105,000.
*† A **decrease** in dividends and an **increase** in retained earnings.*

The December 31, Year 3, balance of the minority interest in net assets of subsidiary may be verified as follows:

Proof of minority interest in net assets of subsidiary

Sage Company's total stockholders' equity, Dec. 31, Year 3	$1,074,000
Add: Unamortized difference between combination date current fair values and carrying amounts of Sage's identifiable net assets	
($162,000 + $20,000)	182,000
Sage's adjusted stockholders' equity, Dec. 31, Year 3...................	$1,256,000
Minority interest in net assets of subsidiary ($1,256,000 × 0.05).........	$ 62,800

Closing Entries Post Corporation's share of the undistributed earnings of Sage Company for Year 3 is $34,200, computed as follows:

<table>
<tr><td>Parent company's share of undistributed earnings of subsidiary</td><td>*Adjusted net income of Sage Company recorded by Post Corporation in Inter-company Investment Income ledger account (page **339**)* . . . .</td><td>*$81,700*</td></tr>
</table>

Parent company's share of undistributed earnings of subsidiary

Adjusted net income of Sage Company recorded by Post Corporation in Inter-
*company Investment Income ledger account (page **339**)* *$81,700*
Less: Post's share of dividends declared by Sage ($50,000 × 0.95) *47,500*
Post's share of amount of Sage's adjusted net income not distributed as divi-
dends *$34,200*

In the December 31, Year 3, closing entries for Post Corporation, $34,200 of Post's net income for Year 3 is closed to the Retained Earnings of Subsidiary ledger account. The remaining $318,400 ($352,600 − $34,200 = $318,400) is closed to the Retained Earnings account, because it is available for dividends to the stockholders of Post. Following the posting of the closing entries, the two ledger accounts are as follows:

Parent company's ledger accounts for retained earnings

Retained Earnings

Date	Explanation	Debit	Credit	Balance
Year 1				
Dec. 31	*Balance*			*1,050,000 cr*
Year 2				
Dec. 31	*Close net income available for dividends*		*457,050*	*1,507,050 cr*
31	*Close Dividends Declared account*	*158,550*		*1,348,500 cr*
Year 3				
Dec. 31	*Close net income available for dividends*		*318,400*	*1,666,900 cr*
31	*Close Dividends Declared account*	*158,550*		*1,508,350 cr*

Retained Earnings of Subsidiary

Date	Explanation	Debit	Credit	Balance
Year 2				
Dec. 31	*Close net income not available for dividends*		*4,750*	*4,750 cr*
Year 3				
Dec. 31	*Close net income not available for dividends*		*34,200*	*38,950 cr*

The $38,950 balance of Post's Retained Earnings of Subsidiary ledger account represents Post's share of the undistributed earnings of Sage Company since December 31, Year 1, the date of the business combination. The undistributed earnings of the subsidiary may be reconciled to the increase in Post's Investment ledger account balance as follows:

Reconciliation of undistributed earnings of subsidiary

Undistributed earnings of subsidiary $38,950
Less: Amortization of goodwill acquired in business combination ($950 × 2) .. 1,900
Increase in balance of Investment in Sage Company Common Stock ledger
  account since Dec. 31, Year 1, date of business combination
  ($1,229,300 − $1,192,250) $37,050

In addition, the total of the December 31, Year 3, ending balances of Post's Retained Earnings and Retained Earnings of Subsidiary ledger accounts is equal to consolidated earnings, as shown below:

Total of parent company's two retained earnings account balances equals consolidated retained earnings

Balances, Dec. 31, Year 3:
  Retained earnings $1,508,350
  Retained earnings of subsidiary 38,950
  Total (equal to consolidated retained earnings, Dec. 31, Year 3—see
    page 341) $1,547,300

Concluding Comments on Equity Method of Accounting

In today's financial accounting environment, the equity method of accounting for a subsidiary's operations is preferable to the cost method (illustrated in the appendix on pages 344 to 351) for the following reasons:

1 The equity method emphasizes *economic substance* of the parent company–subsidiary relationship, while the cost method emphasizes *legal form.* Financial accounting stresses substance over form.

2 The equity method permits the use of *parent company journal entries* to reflect many items that must be included in *working paper eliminations* in the cost method (see pages 346 to 350). Formal journal entries in the accounting records provide a better record than do working paper eliminations.

3 The equity method facilitates issuance of separate financial statements for the parent company, if required by Securities and Exchange Commission regulations or other considerations.

4 Except when intercompany profits (gains) or losses (discussed in Chapter 9) exist in assets or liabilities to be consolidated, the parent company's net income and combined retained earnings account balances are identical in the equity method to the related consolidated amounts. Thus, the equity method provides a useful self-checking technique.

5 As demonstrated in Chapter 8, the cost method is not considered appropriate for accounting for a pooled subsidiary's operations.

For these reasons, the equity method of accounting for a subsidiary's operations is emphasized in the following chapters.

APPENDIX: COST METHOD FOR PARTIALLY OWNED PURCHASED SUBSIDIARY

To illustrate the cost method of accounting for the operating results of a purchased subsidiary, the Post Corporation–Sage Company business combination, which involves a partially owned subsidiary, is used. Post acquired 95% of Sage's outstanding common stock at a total cost (including out-of-pocket costs) of $1,192,250 on December 31, Year 1. Sage's operations for the first two years following the business combination included the following:

Year ended Dec. 31,	Net income	Dividends declared
Year 2	$ 90,000	$40,000
Year 3	105,000	50,000

Illustration of Cost Method for Partially Owned Purchased Subsidiary for First Year after Business Combination

If Post Corporation used the cost method, rather than the equity method, of accounting for Sage Company's operating results for the year ended December 31, Year 2, Post would not prepare journal entries to record Sage's net income for the year. Post would record Sage's dividend declaration as follows on November 24, Year 2:

Parent company's cost-method journal entry to record dividend declared by partially owned purchased subsidiary

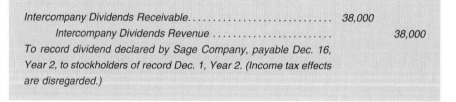

Intercompany Dividends Receivable.............................	38,000	
Intercompany Dividends Revenue		38,000
To record dividend declared by Sage Company, payable Dec. 16, Year 2, to stockholders of record Dec. 1, Year 2. (Income tax effects are disregarded.)		

Post's journal entry for receipt of the dividend from Sage would be the same under the cost method as under the equity method of accounting illustrated on page 325.

Working Paper for Consolidated Financial Statements   The working paper for consolidated financial statements and the related working paper eliminations (in journal entry format) for Post Corporation and subsidiary for the year ended December 31, Year 2, are on pages 345 to 348.

The points beginning on page 346 relative to the cost-method working papers for Post Corporation and subsidiary should be noted.

Cost method: Partially owned subsidiary subsequent to date of purchase-type business combination

POST CORPORATION AND SUBSIDIARY
Working Paper for Consolidated Financial Statements
For Year Ended December 31, Year 2

	Post Corporation	Sage Company	Eliminations increase (decrease)		Consolidated
Income Statement					
Revenue:					
Net sales	5,611,000	1,089,000			6,700,000
Intercompany dividends revenue . .	38,000		(c)	(38,000)	
Total revenue	5,649,000	1,089,000		(38,000)	6,700,000
Cost and expenses:					
Cost of goods sold	3,925,000	700,000	(b)	43,000	4,668,000
Operating expenses	556,000	129,000	(b)	2,950	687,950
Interest and income taxes expense	710,000	170,000			880,000
Minority interest in net income of					
subsidiary			(d)	2,250	2,250
Total costs and expenses	5,191,000	999,000		48,200*	6,238,200
Net income	458,000	90,000		(86,200)	461,800
Statement of Retained Earnings					
Retained earnings, beginning of year	1,050,000	334,000	(a)	(334,000)	1,050,000
Net income	458,000	90,000		(86,200)	461,800
Subtotal	1,508,000	424,000		(420,200)	1,511,800
Dividends declared	158,550	40,000	(c)	(40,000)†	158,550
Retained earnings, end of year	1,349,450	384,000		(380,200)	1,353,250
Balance Sheet					
Assets					
Inventories	861,000	439,000	(a) (b)	26,000 (26,000)	1,300,000
Other current assets	639,000	371,000			1,010,000
Investment in Sage Company common stock	1,192,250		(a)	(1,192,250)	
Plant assets (net)	3,600,000	1,150,000	(a) (b)	190,000 (14,000)	4,926,000
Leasehold (net)			(a) (b)	30,000 (5,000)	25,000
Goodwill (net)	95,000		(a) (b)	38,000 (950)	132,050
Total assets	6,387,250	1,960,000		(954,200)	7,393,050

(continued)

POST CORPORATION AND SUBSIDIARY
Working Paper for Consolidated Financial Statements (concluded)
For Year Ended December 31, Year 2

	Post Corporation	Sage Company	Eliminations increase (decrease)	Consolidated
Liabilities & Stockholders' Equity				
Liabilities..........................	2,420,550	941,000		3,361,550
Minority interest in net assets of subsidiary......................			(a) 60,750 (c) (2,000) (d) 2,250	61,000
Common stock, $1 par	1,057,000			1,057,000
Common stock, $10 par		400,000	(a) (400,000)	
Additional paid-in capital...........	1,560,250	235,000	(a) (235,000)	1,560,250
Retained earnings	1,349,450	384,000	(380,200)	1,353,250
Total liabilities & stockholders' equity	6,387,250	1,960,000	(954,200)	7,393,050

* An **increase** in total costs and expenses and a **decrease** in net income.
† A **decrease** in dividends and an **increase** in retained earnings.

1 The consolidated amounts in the cost-method working paper for consolidated financial statements are identical to the consolidated amounts in the equity-method working paper (pages 333 to 334). This outcome results from the use of different eliminations in the two methods.

2 Three cost-method eliminations, *(a), (b),* and *(c),* are required to accomplish what a single equity-method elimination, *(a)* on pages 330 to 331, does. The reason is that the parent company's accounting records are used in the equity method to reflect the parent's share of the subsidiary's adjusted net income or net loss.

Working paper eliminations (cost method) for partially owned purchased subsidiary for first year subsequent to date of business combination

POST CORPORATION AND SUBSIDIARY
Working Paper Eliminations
December 31, Year 2

(a) Common Stock—Sage	400,000	
Additional Paid-in Capital—Sage........................	235,000	
Retained Earnings—Sage..............................	334,000	
Inventories—Sage	26,000	
Plant Assets (net)—Sage	190,000	
Leasehold (net)—Sage	30,000	
Goodwill (net)—Post.................................	38,000	
Investment in Sage Company Common Stock—Post		1,192,250
Minority Interest in Net Assets of Subsidiary........		60,750

(continued)

To eliminate intercompany investment and equity accounts of subsidiary **on date of business combination** (Dec. 31, Year 1); to allocate excess of cost over carrying amounts of identifiable assets acquired, with remainder to goodwill; and to establish minority interest in net assets of subsidiary on date of business combination ($1,215,000 × 0.05 = $60,750).

(b)
Cost of Goods Sold—Sage..............................	43,000	
Operating Expenses—Sage............................	2,000	
Operating Expenses—Post.............................	950	
Inventories—Sage		26,000
Plant Assets (net)—Sage		14,000
Leasehold (net)—Sage...........................		5,000
Goodwill (net)—Post		950

(a) To provide for Year 2 depreciation and amortization on differences between business combination date current fair values and carrying amounts of Sage's identifiable assets as follows:

	Cost of goods sold	Operating expenses
Inventories sold...............	$26,000	
Building depreciation	2,000	$2,000
Machinery depreciation........	10,000	
Leasehold amortization........	5,000	
Totals	$43,000	$2,000

(b) To amortize goodwill acquired in business combination ($38,000 ÷ 40 = $950).
(Income tax effects are disregarded.)

(c)
Intercompany Dividends Revenue—Post.............	38,000	
Minority Interest in Net Assets of Subsidiary	2,000	
Dividends Declared—Sage		40,000

To eliminate intercompany dividends and minority share thereof ($40,000 × 0.05 = $2,000).

(d)
Minority Interest in Net Income of Subsidiary..........	2,250	
Minority Interest in Net Assets of Subsidiary		2,250

To establish minority interest in subsidiary's adjusted net income for Year 2 as follows:

Net income of subsidiary.................	$ 90,000
Net reduction in elimination (b)...........	(45,000)
Adjusted net income of subsidiary........	$ 45,000
Minority share ($45,000 × 0.05)	$ 2,250

3 Elimination *(a)* deals with the intercompany investment and subsidiary equity accounts **on the date of the business combination.** This elimination is identical to the one on page 265 of Chapter 6. This accounting technique is necessary because the parent's Investment in Sage Company Common Stock account is maintained at the *cost of the original investment* in the cost method.

4 The parent company's cost-method net income and retained earnings are not the same as the consolidated amounts. Thus, the consolidated amounts on December 31, Year 2, may be proved as shown below, to assure their accuracy:

<table>
<tr><td style="width:25%">Proof of consolidated
net income and
consolidated retained
earnings under cost
method</td><td>

Consolidated net income:

Net income of Post Corporation	$ 458,000
Less: Amortization of business combination goodwill	(950)
Add: Post's share of Sage Company's adjusted net income not distrib-	
uted as dividends [($45,000 − $40,000) × 0.95)]	4,750
Consolidated net income	$ 461,800

Consolidated retained earnings:

Retained earnings of Post Corporation	$1,349,450
Less: Amortization of business combination goodwill	(950)
Add: Post's share of adjusted net increase in Sage Company's retained	
earnings [($50,000 − $45,000) × 0.95]	4,750
Consolidated retained earnings.	$1,353,250

</td></tr>
</table>

Closing Entries   There are no unusual features of closing entries for a parent company that uses the cost method of accounting for a subsidiary's operating results. The Intercompany Dividends Revenue ledger account is closed with other revenue accounts to the Income Summary account. Because the parent company does not record the undistributed earnings of subsidiaries under the cost method, a Retained Earnings of Subsidiary ledger account is unnecessary in the cost method.

Illustration of Cost Method for Partially Owned Purchased Subsidiary for Second Year after Business Combination

The only journal entry prepared by Post Corporation for the Year 3 operating results of Sage Company under the cost method of accounting is to accrue $47,500 of intercompany dividends revenue ($50,000 × 0.95 = $47,500) on November 22, Year 3. The working paper eliminations (in journal entry format) follow:

Working paper
eliminations for partially
owned purchased
subsidiary for second
year subsequent to
date of business
combination

POST CORPORATION AND SUBSIDIARY
Working Paper Eliminations
December 31, Year 3

(a) Common Stock—Sage	400,000	
Additional Paid-in Capital—Sage......................	235,000	
Retained Earnings—Sage.............................	334,000	
Inventories—Sage	26,000	
Plant Assets (net)—Sage	190,000	
Leasehold (net)—Sage	30,000	
Goodwill (net)—Post.................................	38,000	
Investment in Sage Company Common Stock—Post		1,192,250
Minority Interest in Net Assets of Subsidiary		60,750

To eliminate intercompany investment and equity accounts
of subsidiary **on date of business combination** (Dec. 31,
Year 1); to allocate excess of cost over carrying amounts of
identifiable assets acquired, with remainder to goodwill; and
to establish minority interest in net assets of subsidiary on
date of business combination.

(b) Retained Earnings—Sage.............................	45,000	
Retained Earnings—Post	950	
Cost of Goods Sold—Sage............................	17,000	
Operating Expenses—Sage...........................	2,000	
Operating Expenses—Post............................	950	
Inventories—Sage		26,000
Plant Assets (net)—Sage		28,000
Leasehold—Sage...............................		10,000
Goodwill—Post		1,900

To provide for Years 2 and 3 depreciation and amortization
on differences between business combination date current
fair values and carrying amounts of Sage's identifiable
assets and of Post's goodwill. Year 2 amounts are debited to
the respective retained earnings accounts; Year 3 amounts
are debited to appropriate expense accounts.

(c) Retained Earnings—Sage ($61,000 − $60,750)	250	
Minority Interest in Net Assets of Subsidiary		250

To provide for net increase in minority interest from date of
business combination to **beginning of year.**

(continued)

POST CORPORATION AND SUBSIDIARY
Working Paper Eliminations (concluded)
December 31, Year 3

(d) Intercompany Dividends Revenue—Post 47,500
    Minority Interest in Net Assets of Subsidiary 2,500
        Dividends Declared—Sage...................... 50,000
    To eliminate intercompany dividends and minority share of
    dividends ($50,000 × 0.05 = $2,500).

(e) Minority Interest in Net Income of Subsidiary 4,300
        Minority Interest in Net Assets of Subsidiary........ 4,300
    To establish minority interest in subsidiary's adjusted net in-
    come for Year 3 as follows:
      Net income of subsidiary.................. $105,000
      Net reduction in elimination (b)............ (19,000)
      Adjusted net income of subsidiary......... $ 86,000
      Minority share ($86,000 × 0.05) .... $ 4,300

Cost method: Partially owned subsidiary subsequent to date of purchase-type business combination

POST CORPORATION AND SUBSIDIARY
Partial Working Paper for Consolidated Financial Statements
For Year Ended December 31, Year 3

	Post Corporation	Sage Company	Eliminations increase (decrease)	Consolidated
Statement of Retained Earnings				
Retained earnings, beginning of year......................	1,349,450	384,000	(a)(334,000) (b) (45,950) (c) (250)	1,353,250
Net income	319,350	105,000	(71,750)*	352,600
Subtotal	1,668,800	489,000	(451,950)	1,705,850
Dividends declared	158,550	50,000	(d) (50,000)†	158,550
Retained earnings, end of year.	1,510,250	439,000	(401,950)	1,547,300

* Decrease in intercompany dividends revenue ($47,500), plus total increase in costs and expenses ($17,000 + $2,000 + $950 + $4,300), equals $71,750.
† A **decrease** in dividends and an **increase** in retained earnings.

Because the parent company does not record depreciation and amortization applicable to the differences between the current fair values and carrying amounts of the subsidiary's identifiable net assets, elimination *(b)* on page 349 must provide for total depreciation and amortization for **both** years since the business combination. In addition, elimination *(c)* must account for the net increase in the minority interest in net assets of the subsidiary from the business combination date to the beginning of the current year.

Working Paper for Consolidated Financial Statements The *partial* working paper for consolidated financial statements on page 350 illustrates the retained earnings changes for Post Corporation and subsidiary during Year 3. The consolidated amounts are identical to those under the equity method of accounting (see page 341).

REVIEW QUESTIONS

1 "Consolidated financial statement amounts are the same, regardless of whether a parent company uses the equity method or the cost method to account for a subsidiary's operations." Why is this quotation true?

2 When there are no intercompany profits (gains) or losses in consolidated assets or liabilities, the equity method of accounting produces parent company net income that equals consolidated net income. The equity method also results in parent company retained earnings of the same amount as consolidated retained earnings. Why, then, are consolidated financial statements considered superior to separate financial statements of the parent company when the parent company uses the equity method? Explain.

3 Describe the special features of closing entries for a parent company that accounts for its subsidiary's operating results by the equity method.

4 Strake Company, a 90%-owned subsidiary of Peale Corporation, had a net income of $50,000 for the first year following the business combination. However, the working paper elimination for the minority interest in the subsidiary's net income was in the amount of $3,500 rather than $5,000. Is this difference justifiable? Explain.

5 Discuss some of the advantages that result from the use of the equity method, rather than the cost method, of accounting for a subsidiary's operating results.

6 Both Parnell Corporation and Plankton Company have wholly owned subsidiaries. Parnell has an Intercompany Dividends Revenue ledger account, and an Intercompany Investment Income account is included in the Plankton ledger. Do both companies use the same method of accounting for their subsidiaries' operating results? Explain.

7 Plumstead Corporation's 92%-owned subsidiary declared a dividend of $3 a share on its 50,000 outstanding shares of common stock. How does Plumstead record this dividend under:
a The equity method of accounting?
b The cost method of accounting?

8   Is a Retained Earnings of Subsidiary ledger account required for a parent company that uses the cost method of accounting for the subsidiary's operations? Explain.

EXERCISES

Ex. 7-1   Select the best answer for each of the following multiple-choice questions:

1   Concepts underlying the equity method and the cost method of accounting for the operating results of a purchased subsidiary may be summarized as follows:

	Equity method	*Cost method*
a	Legal form	Economic substance
b	Legal form	Legal form
c	Economic substance	Economic substance
d	Economic substance	Legal form

2   Under the equity method of accounting, dividends declared by the subsidiary to the parent company are credited to the parent's:
a Intercompany Dividends Receivable account
b Investment in Subsidiary Common Stock account
c Retained Earnings of Subsidiary account
d Retained Earnings account

3   Depending on circumstances, may a cash dividend received from a purchased subsidiary, for the investment in which the parent company uses the cost method of accounting, be recognized as:

	Revenue?	*Reduction in investment carrying amount?*
a	Yes	Yes
b	Yes	No
c	No	Yes
d	No	No

4   After completion of the parent company's equity-method journal entries for its profitable wholly owned purchased subsidiary's operating results, the balance of the parent's Intercompany Investment Income ledger is equal to the:
a Subsidiary's net income
b Subsidiary's net income, less amortization of current fair value differences of the subsidiary's identifiable net assets
c Subsidiary's net income, less amortization of current fair value differences of the subsidiary's total net assets, including goodwill
d Increase in the after-closing balance of the subsidiary's Retained Earnings ledger account

5   The end-of-period closing entries for a parent company that uses the equity method of accounting for the operating results of a wholly owned purchased subsidiary include a credit to the Retained Earnings of Subsidiary ledger account in the amount of the:
a Ending retained earnings of the subsidiary

b Net income of the subsidiary for the period

c Undistributed earnings of the subsidiary for the period

d Dividends declared by the subsidiary during the period

6   On any date, the balance of a parent company's Retained Earnings of Subsidiary account attributable to a wholly owned purchased subsidiary is equal to the:

a Balance of the subsidiary's Retained Earnings account

b Net increase in the parent's Investment in Subsidiary Common Stock account since the date of the business combination

c Total net income of the subsidiary since the date of the business combination

d Total dividends declared by the subsidiary since the date of the business combination

7   During a fiscal year, the balance of a parent company's Investment in Subsidiary Common Stock ledger account for a wholly owned purchased subsidiary, for which the parent company uses the equity method of accounting, increases by the amount of the subsidiary's:

a Adjusted net income

b Dividends

c Adjusted net income plus dividends

d Undistributed earnings

8   If the parent company uses the equity method of accounting, in the working paper eliminations for the second and succeeding years following a purchase-type business combination between the parent company and its wholly owned subsidiary, the amount eliminated for the subsidiary's retained earnings is the balance of the subsidiary's Retained Earnings Ledger account:

a At the *beginning* of the year

b On the date of the business combination

c At the *end* of the year

d At the *beginning* of the year, *less* the balance of the parent's Retained Earnings of Subsidiary account

9   The 80%-owned purchased subsidiary of a parent company reported a net income of $80,000 for the year ended May 31, Year 7. The parent company's appropriate journal entry under the equity method of accounting is (explanation omitted):

a *Investment in Subsidiary Company Common Stock* *80,000*

   Investment Income *80,000*

b *Intercompany Investment Income* *80,000*

   Investment in Subsidiary Company Common Stock *80,000*

c *Investment in Subsidiary Company Common Stock* *64,000*

   Intercompany Investment Income *64,000*

d *Intercompany Investment Income* *64,000*

   Investment in Subsidiary Company Common Stock *64,000*

10   The amortization of goodwill recognized in the purchase-type business combination of a parent company and its wholly owned subsidiary is debited to the:

a Subsidiary's Amortization Expense account

b Parent's Amortization Expense account
c Parent's Investment in Common Stock of Subsidiary account
d Parent's Intercompany Investment Income account

11 Under the equity method of accounting for a subsidiary's operating results, a parent company journal entry debiting Amortization Expense and crediting Investment in Subsidiary Common Stock is appropriate for an investment in:
a A wholly owned subsidiary only
b A partially owned subsidiary only
c Both a wholly owned and a partially owned subsidiary
d Neither a wholly owned nor a partially owned subsidiary

12 On May 31, Year 8, Plaque Corporation acquired 80% of Stanton Company's outstanding common stock in a purchase-type business combination for a total cost, including direct out-of-pocket costs, of $800,000. For the year ended May 31, Year 9, Stanton had a net income of $100,000 and declared and paid dividends of $40,000. For the year ended May 31, Year 9, *total* amortization of the current fair value excess was $30,000, and the amortization of goodwill acquired by Plaque in the business combination with Stanton was $800. The balance of Plaque's Intercompany Investment Income ledger account (prior to closing) on May 31, Year 9, is:
a $32,000
b $55,360
c $56,000
d $80,000
e Some other amount

13 A parent company uses the Retained Earnings of Subsidiary ledger account for a purchased subsidiary:
a For closing entries only
b For dividends declared by the subsidiary only
c For both dividends declared by the subsidiary and closing entries
d For neither dividends declared by the subsidiary nor closing entries

14 On May 31, Year 4, the date of the purchase-type business combination of Passey Corporation and its 80%-owned subsidiary, Sandy Company, for which Passey uses the equity method of accounting, the balance of Sandy's Retained Earnings account was $100,000, and on May 31, Year 5, the after-closing balance was $120,000. *Prior to* Passey's May 31, Year 5, closing entries, the balance of its Retained Earnings of Subsidiary ledger account is:
a Zero
b $80,000
c $100,000
d An undeterminable amount

15 At the end of an accounting period, a parent company that uses the equity method of accounting for its partially owned purchased subsidiary closes its:
a Dividends Declared ledger account
b Intercompany Dividends Receivable ledger account
c Dividends Payable ledger account
d Intercompany Dividends Payable ledger account

16 The accuracy of the minority interest in net assets of a partially owned purchased subsidiary subsequent to the date of the business combination may be verified by applying the minority interest percentage to the:

a Total stockholders' equity of the subsidiary

b Balance of the parent company's Investment in Subsidiary Common Stock account

c Total stockholders' equity of the subsidiary plus unamortized current fair value differences

d Amount in **c** plus unamortized goodwill

Ex. 7-2 The September 30, Year 5, date-of-combination current fair value differences of the net assets of Spence Company, wholly owned purchased subsidiary of Pence Corporation, were as follows:

	Current fair value	*Carrying amount*	*Difference*
Inventories (first-in,			
first-out cost)	$120,000	$100,000	$ 20,000
Plant assets (depreciable			
over 10-year life)	680,000	560,000	120,000
Identifiable intangible			
assets (amortizable			
over 5-year life)	160,000	120,000	40,000

In addition, goodwill of $45,000 having an economic life of 15 years was recognized in the Pence–Spence business combination.

During the year ended September 30, Year 6, the following occurred:

Sept. 1 Spence declared a dividend of $80,000 to Pence.
   18 Spence paid the $80,000 dividend to Pence.
   30 Spence reported a net income of $980,000 for the year to Pence.

Prepare journal entries (omit explanations) for Pence Corporation to record the operating results of Spence Company under the equity method of accounting. (Disregard income taxes.)

Ex. 7-3 Following are all details of three ledger accounts of a parent company that uses the equity method of accounting for its subsidiary's operating results:

Intercompany Dividends Receivable

Aug. 16, Year 8	36,000	Aug. 27, Year 8	36,000

Investment in Subsidiary Common Stock

Sept. 1, Year 7	630,000	Aug. 16, Year 8	36,000
Aug. 31, Year 8	72,000	Aug. 31, Year 8	5,000

Intercompany Investment Income

Aug. 31, Year 8	5,000	Aug. 31, Year 8	72,000

Draft the most logical explanation for each of the transactions or events recorded in the foregoing ledger accounts.

Ex. 7-4   The working paper elimination for a parent company and its subsidiary on the date of their purchase-type business combination was as follows:

PRISTINE CORPORATION AND SUBSIDIARY
Working Paper Elimination
May 31, Year 7

Common Stock—Superb	100,000	
Additional Paid-in Capital—Superb	200,000	
Retained Earnings—Superb	450,000	
Inventories—Superb	60,000	
Land—Superb	40,000	
Building—Superb	50,000	
Goodwill—Superb	50,000	
Investment in Superb Company Common Stock—Pristine		950,000

To eliminate intercompany investment and equity accounts of subsidiary on date of business combination; and to allocate excess of cost over carrying amount of identifiable net assets acquired, with remainder to goodwill. (Income tax effects are disregarded.)

Additional Information

(1) For the year ended May 31, Year 8, Superb had a net income of $80,000 and declared and paid a dividend of $30,000 (debited to the Dividends Declared ledger account) to Pristine.
(2) Superb uses first-in, first-out cost for inventories and straight-line depreciation and amortization for plant and intangible assets.
(3) On May 31, Year 7, Superb's building had a remaining economic life of 10 years, and the consolidated goodwill had an economic life of 20 years.
(4) Superb includes depreciation in cost of goods sold and goodwill amortization in operating expenses.

Prepare a working paper elimination, in journal entry format (omit explanation) for Pristine Corporation and subsidiary on May 31, Year 8. (Disregard income taxes.)

Ex. 7-5   The working paper elimination (in journal entry format) for Polar Corporation and its wholly owned subsidiary, Solar Company, on July 31, Year 4, the date of the purchase-type business combination, is on page 357.

Additional Information

(1) For the year ended July 31, Year 5, Solar declared dividends (debiting the Dividends Declared ledger account) of $20,000 and had a net income of $50,000, for which Polar applied the equity method of accounting.
(2) Solar uses a 10-year economic life for depreciable plant assets, with depreciation expense included in cost of goods sold, and a 20-year economic life for goodwill, with amortization expense included in operating expenses.

POLAR CORPORATION AND SUBSIDIARY
Working Paper Elimination
July 31, Year 4

(a) Common Stock, no-par—Solar	50,000	
Retained Earnings—Solar	250,000	
Inventories (first-in, first-out cost)—Solar	30,000	
Plant Assets (depreciable, net)—Solar	120,000	
Goodwill—Solar	20,000	
Investment in Solar Company Common Stock—Polar		470,000

To eliminate intercompany investment and equity accounts of
subsidiary on date of business combination; and to allocate
excess of cost over carrying amount of identifiable assets acquired, with remainder to goodwill. (Income tax effects are disregarded.)

Prepare a working paper elimination (in journal entry format) for Polar Corporation and Subsidiary on July 31, Year 5. Omit the explanation for the elimination.
(Disregard income taxes.)

Ex. 7-6   The date-of-business combination working paper elimination (in journal entry format, explanation omitted) for the consolidated balance sheet of P Corporation and its
wholly owned subsidiary, S Company, was as follows:

P CORPORATION AND SUBSIDIARY
Working Paper Elimination
February 28, Year 6

Common Stock—S	50,000	
Retained Earnings—S	80,000	
Inventories—S (first-in, first-out cost)	10,000	
Plant Assets (net)—S (10-year economic life)...................	60,000	
Goodwill (net)—S ($210,000 − $200,000) (10-year economic life)	10,000	
Investment in S Company Common Stock—P............		210,000

On February 3, Year 7, S Corporation declared a dividend of $20,000 to its stock-
holder; on February 27, Year 7, S paid the dividend; and on February 28, Year 7, S
reported a net income of $60,000 for the year then ended. S Company includes all
depreciation and amortization in cost of goods sold.
    Prepare a working paper elimination (in journal entry format; omit explanation)
for consolidated financial statements of P Corporation and subsidiary on February
28, Year 7. (Disregard income taxes.)

Ex. 7-7   The working paper elimination (in journal entry format) for Parry Corporation and
subsidiary on October 31, Year 6, the date of the business combination, was:

PARRY CORPORATION AND SUBSIDIARY
Working Paper Elimination
October 31, Year 6

(a) *Common Stock—Samuel* 100,000
     Additional Paid-in Capital—Samuel 150,000
     Retained Earnings—Samuel 200,000
     Plant Assets (net)—Samuel (depreciable) 250,000
     Goodwill—Samuel 60,000
         Investment in Samuel Company Common Stock—Parry   760,000
     To eliminate intercompany investment and equity accounts of
     subsidiary on date of business combination; and to allocate
     excess of cost over carrying amount of identifiable assets ac-
     quired, with remainder to goodwill.

For the year ended October 31, Year 7, Samuel had a net income of $50,000, and on October 31, Year 7, Samuel declared dividends of $20,000, payable November 16, Year 7. Samuel depreciates plant assets by the straight-line method at a 10% rate and amortizes intangible assets by the straight-line method over a 40-year economic life. Samuel includes plant assets depreciation in cost of goods sold and goodwill amortization in operating expenses.

a Prepare Parry Corporation's October 31, Year 7, journal entries to record the operating results and dividend of Samuel Company under the equity method of accounting. (Disregard income taxes and omit explanations.)

b Prepare the October 31, Year 7, working paper elimination (in journal entry format) for Parry Corporation and subsidiary. (Disregard income taxes and omit explanation.)

Ex. 7-8 The working paper elimination (explanation omitted) on the date of the Pulp Corporation–Stump Company purchase-type business combination was as follows:

PULP CORPORATION AND SUBSIDIARY
Working Paper Elimination
January 31, Year 2

Common Stock, no par or stated value—Stump 100,000
Retained Earnings—Stump 180,000
Inventories (first-in, first-out cost)—Stump 20,000
Plant Assets—Stump (depreciable, 5-year life) 100,000
Goodwill—Stump (10-year life) 40,000
     Investment in Stump Company Common Stock—Pulp.   440,000

For the year ended January 31, Year 3, Stump had a net income of $240,000, and on that date it declared and paid a dividend of $120,000. Stump includes both plant asset depreciation and goodwill amortization expenses in cost of goods sold.

a Prepare journal entries (omit explanations) for Pulp Corporation on January 31, Year 3, to record the operations of Stump Company under the equity method of accounting. (Disregard income taxes.)

b Prepare a working paper elimination, in journal entry format (omit explanation), for Pulp Corporation and subsidiary on January 31, Year 3. (Disregard income taxes.)

Ex. 7-9 Palmer Corporation had the following ledger account on December 31, Year 3:

Investment in Sim Company Common Stock

Date	Explanation	Debit	Credit	Balance
Year 1				
Dec. 31	Issuance of common stock in business combination	840,000		840,000 dr
31	Direct out-of-pocket costs of business combination	40,000		880,000 dr
Year 2				
Oct. 14	Dividend declared by Sim		20,000	860,000 dr
Dec. 31	Net income of Sim	60,000		920,000 dr
31	Amortization of differences between current fair values and carrying amounts of Sim's net assets		14,500	905,500 dr
Year 3				
Oct. 18	Dividend declared by Sim		50,000	855,500 dr
Dec. 31	Net income of Sim	90,000		945,500 dr
31	Amortization of differences between current fair values and carrying amounts of Sim's net assets		4,500	941,000 dr

Prepare a three-column Retained Earnings of Subsidiary ledger account for Palmer Corporation, and post appropriate closing entries for December 31, Year 2, and December 31, Year 3, to the account.

Ex. 7-10 On March 31, Year 1, Pitt Corporation acquired for cash 90% of the outstanding common stock of Scow Company. The $100,000 excess of Pitt's investment over 90% of the current fair value (and carrying amount) of Scow's identifiable net assets was allocable to goodwill having an economic life of 25 years on March 31, Year 1. For the year ended March 31, Year 2, Scow had a net loss of $130,000 and declared no dividends.

Disregarding income taxes, prepare a working paper to compute the balance of Pitt Corporation's Intercompany Investment Income ledger account under the equity method of accounting on March 31, Year 2.

Ex. 7-11 On January 2, Year 6, Ply Corporation acquired 75% of the outstanding common stock of Spade Company for $345,000 cash, including out-of-pocket costs. The investment was accounted for by the equity method. On January 2, Year 6, Spade's identifiable net assets (carrying amount and current fair value) were $300,000. Ply determined that the excess of the cost of its investment over the current fair value of Spade's identifiable net assets had an indeterminant economic life. Spade's net income for the year ended December 31, Year 6, was $160,000. During Year 6, Ply received $60,000 cash dividends from Spade. There were no other transactions between the two enterprises.

Prepare a working paper to compute the balance of Ply Corporation's Investment in Spade Company Common Stock ledger account (after adjustment) on December 31, Year 6, disregarding income taxes.

Ex. 7-12 On January 2, Year 5, Plain Corporation acquired 80% of Sano Company's outstanding common stock for an amount of cash equal to 80% of the carrying amount (and current fair value) of Sano's identifiable net assets on that date. The balances of Plain's and Sano's Retained Earnings ledger accounts on January 2, Year 5, were $500,000 and $100,000, respectively. During Year 5, Plain had a net income of $200,000 under the equity method of accounting and declared dividends of $50,000, and Sano had a net income of $40,000 and declared dividends of $20,000. There were no other intercompany transactions between Plain and Sano.

Prepare a working paper to compute the consolidated retained earnings of Plain Corporation and subsidiary on December 31, Year 5. (Disregard income taxes.)

Ex. 7-13 Pinson Corporation owned a 90% interest in a purchased subsidiary, Solomon Company, which was accounted for by the equity method. During Year 5, Pinson had income, exclusive of intercompany investment income, of $145,000, and Solomon had a net income of $120,000. Solomon declared and paid a $40,000 dividend during Year 5. There were no differences between the current fair values and carrying amounts of Solomon's identifiable net assets on the date of the business combination, and there was no goodwill in the business combination.

Prepare a working paper to compute the consolidated net income of Pinson Corporation and subsidiary for Year 5. (Disregard income taxes.)

Ex. 7-14 The working paper elimination (explanation omitted) on the date of the Pallid Corporation–Sallow Company purchase-type business combination was as follows:

PALLID CORPORATION AND SUBSIDIARY
Working Paper Elimination
January 31, Year 10

Common Stock, no par or stated value—Sallow	50,000	
Retained Earnings—Sallow...................................	90,000	
Inventories (first-in, first-out cost)—Sallow....................	10,000	
Plant Assets—Sallow (depreciable, 10-year life)	50,000	
Goodwill—Pallid (20-year life)................................	20,000	
Investment in Sallow Company Common Stock—Pallid....		190,000
Minority Interest in Net Assets of Subsidiary		
($200,000 × 0.15)		30,000

For the year ended January 31, Year 11, Sallow had a net income of $120,000, and on that date it declared dividends totaling $60,000, to be paid February 28, Year 11.

a Prepare journal entries (omit explanations) for Pallid Corporation on January 31, Year 11, to record the operations of Sallow Company under the equity method of accounting. (Disregard income taxes.)

b Prepare working paper eliminations, in journal entry format (omit explanations), for Pallid Corporation and subsidiary on January 31, Year 11. Sallow includes depreciation in cost of goods sold. (Disregard income taxes.)

Ex. 7-15 The retained earnings ledger accounts of Putter Corporation and its 80%-owned purchased subsidiary, Simmer Company, were as follows for the two years following their business combination on May 31, Year 6. There were no intercompany profits (gains) or losses in transactions between the two enterprises during the two years ended May 31, Year 8.

Putter Corporation:

Retained Earnings

Date	Explanation	Debit	Credit	Balance
Year 6				
May 31	Balance			640,000 cr
Year 7				
May 31	Close net income available for dividends ($140,000 − $28,000)		112,000	752,000 cr
31	Close Dividends Declared account	60,000		692,000 cr
Year 8				
May 31	Close net income available for dividends ($180,000 − $52,000)		128,000	820,000 cr
31	Close Dividends Declared account	90,000		730,000 cr

Retained Earnings of Subsidiary

Date	Explanation	Debit	Credit	Balance
Year 7				
May 31	Close net income not available for dividends [($80,000 − $15,000 − $30,000) × 0.80]		28,000	28,000 cr
Year 8				
May 31	Close net income not available for dividends [($120,000 − $5,000 − $50,000) × 0.80]		52,000	80,000 cr

Simmer Company:

Retained Earnings

Date	Explanation	Debit	Credit	Balance
Year 6				
May 31	Balance			100,000 cr
Year 7				
May 31	Close net income		80,000	180,000 cr
31	Close Dividends Declared account	30,000		150,000 cr
Year 8				
May 31	Close net income		120,000	270,000 cr
31	Close Dividends Declared account	50,000		220,000 cr

Prepare the statement of retained earnings section of the working paper for consolidated financial statements of Putter Corporation and subsidiary for the year ended May 31, Year 8.

Ex. 7-16 Selected ledger account balances for Parton Corporation on May 31, Year 5, were as follows:

Investment in (80% owned) Starter Company common stock ($60,000 net increase from May 31, Year 4)	$620,000 dr
Intercompany investment income	95,000 cr
Amortization expense (attributable to goodwill in business combination with Starter Company)	5,000 dr
Dividends declared	50,000 dr
Sales (no contra accounts)	840,000 cr
Cost of goods sold	378,000 dr
Operating expenses and income taxes expense	212,000 dr

Prepare closing entries (omit explanations) for Parton Corporation on May 31, Year 5.

Ex. 7-17 The balance of Putnam Corporation's Investment in Salisbury Company Common Stock ledger account on September 30, Year 6, was $265,000. The 20% minority interest in net assets of subsidiary in the consolidated balance sheet of Putnam Corporation and subsidiary on September 30, Year 6, was $60,000. For the year ended September 30, Year 7, Salisbury had a net income of $50,000 and declared and paid dividends of $18,750. Amortization for the year ended September 30, Year 7, was as follows:

Differences between current fair values and carrying amounts of Salisbury's identifiable net assets on date of business combination	$4,500
Goodwill acquired by Putnam in business combination	1,000

Prepare a working paper to compute the following:

a Balance of Putnam Corporation's Investment in Salisbury Company Common Stock ledger account on September 30, Year 7
b Balance of Putnam Corporation's Intercompany Investment Income ledger account on September 30, Year 7, before closing entry
c Amount of closing entry credit to Putnam's Retained Earnings of Subsidiary ledger account on September 30, Year 7
d Minority interest in net income of subsidiary in consolidated income statement of Putnam Corporation and subsidiary for year ended September 30, Year 7
e Minority interest in net assets of subsidiary in consolidated balance sheet of Putnam Corporation and subsidiary on September 30, Year 7

Ex. 7-18 Seal Company, wholly owned purchased subsidiary of Presto Corporation, had a net income of $90,000 and had paid dividends of $35,000 for the first year following the business combination. Goodwill computed in accordance with purchase accounting amounted to $64,000 on the date of the business combination and had an economic life of 20 years. Exclusive of Seal's operations, Presto had income of $180,000 for the first year following the business combination.

Disregarding income taxes, compute the net income of Presto Corporation under **(a)** the equity method and **(b)** the cost method of accounting for the operating results of Seal Company.

CASES

Case 7-1 You have recently become the controller of Precision Corporation, a manufacturing enterprise that has begun a program of expansion through business combinations. On February 1, Year 4, two weeks prior to your controllership appointment, Precision had completed the acquisition of 85% of the outstanding common stock of Sloan Company for $255,000 cash, including out-of-pocket costs. You are engaged in a discussion with Precision's chief accountant concerning the appropriate accounting method for Precision's interest in Sloan Company's operating results. The chief accountant strongly supports the cost method of accounting, offering the following arguments:

(1) The cost method recognizes that Precision and Sloan are separate legal entities.
(2) The existence of a 15% minority interest in Sloan requires emphasis on the legal separateness of the two companies.
(3) A parent company recognizes revenue under the cost method only when the subsidiary declares dividends. Such dividend revenue is consistent with the revenue realization principle of financial accounting. The Intercompany Investment Income account recorded in the equity method of accounting does not fit the definition of realized revenue.
(4) Use of the equity method of accounting might result in Precision's declaring dividends to its shareholders out of ''paper'' retained earnings that belong to Sloan.
(5) The cost method is consistent with other aspects of historical-cost accounting, because working paper eliminations, rather than journal entries in ledger accounts, are used to recognize amortization of differences between current fair values and carrying amounts of Sloan's identifiable net assets.

Instructions
Prepare a rebuttal to each of the chief accountant's arguments.

Case 7-2 John Raymond, chief financial officer of publicly owned Punjab Corporation, is concerned about the negative impact on Punjab's quarterly earnings resulting from its December 31, Year 6, purchase-type business combination with wholly owned Selvidge Company, its only subsidiary. With the end of the first quarter of Year 7 approaching and the required filing of *Form 10-Q,* ''Quarterly Report,'' with the Securities and Exchange Commission, Raymond has considered the required depreciation and amortization of the current fair value excesses resulting from the business combination, as follows:

Depreciable plant assets (5-year remaining composite economic life to Selvidge)	$200,000
Patent (3-year remaining economic life, 8-year remaining legal life to Selvidge)	96,000
Goodwill	160,000

Reviewing controller Nancy Wade's forecasts of pre-tax income of Punjab and Selvidge in their separate income statements for the three months ending March 31, Year 7, Raymond made the following estimates:

Forecasted pre-tax income for 3 months ended Mar. 31, Year 7:

Punjab Corporation		$ 80,000
Selvidge Company		40,000
Total		$120,000
Per share (100,000 weighted-average shares expected to be outstanding)		$1.20
Less: Depreciation and amortization of date-of-business combination current fair value excess:		
Plant assets ($200,000 × ⅕ × ¼)	$10,000	
Patent ($96,000 × ⅓ × ¼)	8,000	
Goodwill ($160,000 × ¹⁄₄₀ × ¼)	1,000	19,000
Adjusted forecasted pre-tax income		$101,000
Per share		$1.01

Pointing out to Wade that the nearly 16% decrease in forecasted earnings per share ($0.19 ÷ $1.20 = 15.8%) would be difficult to explain to Punjab's board of directors, Raymond asked her to increase the remaining composite economic life of Selvidge's depreciable plant assets to 10 years from 5 years and to use the remaining legal life, rather than the remaining economic life, of the patent as its basis of amortization. In reply, Wade informed Raymond that before acquiescing to his request, she would have to research the following literature of accounting and auditing:

APB Opinion No. 17, "Intangible Assets," paragraph 27

APB Opinion No. 20, "Accounting Changes," paragraphs 10, 31, and 33

AICPA Professional Standards, vol. 1, "U.S. Auditing Standards," Sections AU342.05 and AU420.14

Instructions

After researching the foregoing references, state your opinion as to how Nancy Wade should respond to John Raymond's request.

PROBLEMS

Pr. 7-1 The working paper elimination for Prem Corporation and its subsidiary, Supp Company, on December 31, Year 3, the date of the purchase-type business combination, is on page 365 (in journal entry format).

On December 8, Year 4, Supp declared, and on December 18, Year 4, paid, a dividend to Prem of $6,000, and it had a net income of $30,000 for Year 4. Prem used the equity method of accounting for Supp's operating results.

PREM CORPORATION AND SUBSIDIARY
Working Paper Elimination
December 31, Year 3

(a) Common Stock—Supp	*10,000*	
Additional Paid-in Capital—Supp	*40,000*	
Retained Earnings—Supp	*50,000*	
Inventories—Supp (first-in, first-out cost)	*20,000*	
Plant Assets—Supp (economic life 10 years).	*60,000*	
Goodwill—Supp (economic life 40 years)	*12,000*	
Investment in Supp Company Common Stock—Prem. .		*192,000*

To eliminate intercompany investment and equity accounts of subsidiary on date of business combination; and to allocate excess of cost over carrying amount of identifiable assets acquired, with remainder to goodwill. (Income tax effects are disregarded.)

Instructions

a Set up a three-column ledger account for Prem Corporation's Investment in Supp Company Common Stock ledger account, bring forward the December 31, Year 3, debit balance of $192,000, and post the required entries to the account for Year 4. (Disregard income taxes.)

b Prepare a working paper elimination (in journal entry format) for Prem Corporation and subsidiary on December 31, Year 4, disregarding income taxes. Supp Company includes straight-line depreciation expense in cost of goods sold and amortization expense in operating expenses.

Pr. 7-2 On September 5, Year 6, Soy Company, the 80%-owned purchased subsidiary of Pro Corporation, declared a cash dividend of $1 a share on its 100,000 outstanding shares of $1 par common stock. The dividend was paid on September 26, Year 6. For the year ended September 30, Year 6, the first year of the Pro-Soy affiliation, Soy had a net income of $300,000. In addition to goodwill of $80,000 having a 40-year economic life, the September 30, Year 5 (date of the business combination) working paper elimination (in journal entry format) for Pro Corporation and subsidiary included the following debits:

Inventories (first-in, first-out cost)—Soy.	*$60,000*
Plant assets (net) (all depreciable over a 10-year economic life, straight-line	
method)—Soy.	*80,000*
Discount on long-term debt (5-year remaining term)—Soy.	*20,000*

Instructions

Prepare journal entries for Pro Corporation on September 5, 26, and 30, Year 6, to record its equity method of accounting for the operating results of Soy Company. Use the straight-line method of amortization for discount on long-term debt, and disregard income taxes.

Pr. 7-3 The working paper elimination (in journal entry format) for Promo Corporation and subsidiary on March 31, Year 7, the date of the purchase-type business combination, was as follows:

PROMO CORPORATION AND SUBSIDIARY
Working Paper Elimination
March 31, Year 7

(a) Common Stock, $1 par—Sanz	50,000	
Additional Paid-in Capital—Sanz	100,000	
Retained Earnings—Sanz	150,000	
Inventories—Sanz (first-in, first-out cost)	20,000	
Land—Sanz...	50,000	
Other Plant Assets—Sanz (economic life 10 years).........	80,000	
Goodwill—Sanz (economic life 40 years)	40,000	
Investment in Sanz Company Common Stock—Promo		490,000

To eliminate intercompany investment and equity accounts of
subsidiary on date of business combination; and to allocate
excess of cost over carrying amounts of identifiable assets
acquired, with remainder to goodwill. (Income tax effects are
disregarded.)

For the year ended March 31, Year 8, Sanz had a net income of $60,000. Sanz declared a cash dividend of $0.40 a share on March 1, Year 8, and paid the dividend on March 15, Year 8. (Sanz had not declared or paid dividends during the year ended March 31, Year 7.) Sanz uses the straight-line method for depreciation expense and amortization expense, both of which are included in operating expenses.

Instructions

a Prepare journal entries for Promo Corporation to record the operating results of Sanz Company for the year ended March 31, Year 8, under the equity method of accounting. (Disregard income taxes.)

b Prepare three-column ledger accounts for Promo Corporation's Investment in Sanz Company Common Stock and Intercompany Investment Income ledger accounts, and post the journal entries in **a**.

c Prepare a working paper elimination for Promo Corporation and subsidiary on March 31, Year 8 (in journal entry format). (Disregard income taxes.)

Pr. 7-4   Penn Corporation's October 31, Year 4, journal entries to record the operations of its 80%-owned purchased subsidiary, Soper Company, during the first year following the business combination, were as follows:

Intercompany Dividends Receivable............................	16,000	
Investment in Soper Company Common Stock.............		16,000

To record $1 a share dividend declared by Soper Company, payable
Nov. 7, Year 4, to stockholders of record Oct. 31, Year 4.

Investment in Soper Company Common Stock	40,000	
Intercompany Investment Income........................		40,000

To record 80% of Soper Company's net income for the year ended
Oct. 31, Year 4. (Income tax effects are disregarded.)

Intercompany Investment Income	22,400	
Investment in Soper Company Common Stock		22,400

To amortize differences between current fair values and carrying
amounts of Soper Company's identifiable net assets on Oct. 31,
Year 3:

Inventories—to cost of goods sold	$20,000
Plant assets—depreciation ($80,000 ÷ 10)	8,000
Total difference	$28,000
Amortization ($28,000 × 0.80)	$22,400

(Income tax effects are disregarded.)

Amortization Expense ($40,000 ÷ 20 years)	2,000	
Investment in Soper Company Common Stock		2,000

To amortize goodwill acquired in business combination with partially
owned purchased subsidiary over an economic life of 20 years.

Additional Information

(1) Penn had acquired 16,000 shares of Soper's $1 par common stock on October 31, Year 3, at a total cost, including out-of-pocket costs, of $240,000. The minority interest in net assets of subsidiary on that date was $50,000.

(2) On October 31, Year 4, the balances of Soper's Common Stock, Paid-in Capital in Excess of Par, and Retained Earnings ledger accounts were in the ratio of 1:3:5, respectively.

(3) Soper allocates depreciation expense 75% to cost of goods sold and 25% to operating expenses.

Instructions

Prepare working paper eliminations (in journal entry format) for Penn Corporation and subsidiary on October 31, Year 4. (Suggestion: Use T accounts to determine balances of ledger accounts of the parent company and subsidiary.) (Disregard income taxes.)

Pr. 7-5 On January 2, Year 6, Pewter Corporation made the following investments:

(1) Acquired for cash 80% of the 1,000 shares of outstanding common stock of Stewart Company at $70 a share. The stockholders' equity of Stewart on January 2, Year 6, consisted of the following:

Common stock, no par or stated value.	$50,000
Retained earnings.	20,000
Total stockholders' equity	$70,000

(2) Acquired for cash 70% of the 3,000 shares of outstanding common stock of Skate Company at $40 a share. The stockholders' equity of Skate on January 2, Year 6, consisted of the following:

Common stock, $20 par	$ 60,000
Additional paid-in capital	20,000
Retained earnings	40,000
Total stockholders' equity	$120,000

Out-of-pocket costs of the two business combinations may be disregarded. An analysis of the retained earnings of each company for Year 6 follows:

	Pewter Corporation	Stewart Company	Skate Company
Balances, beginning of year	$240,000	$ 20,000	$ 40,000
Net income (loss)	104,600*	36,000	(12,000)
Cash dividends declared and paid, Dec. 31, Year 6	(40,000)	(16,000)	(9,000)
Balances, end of year	$304,600*	$ 40,000	$ 19,000

* Before giving effect to journal entries in **a**(2), below.

Instructions

a Prepare journal entries for Pewter Corporation to record the following for Year 6:
(1) Investments in subsidiaries' common stock
(2) Parent company's share of subsidiaries' net income or net loss (disregarding income taxes), under the equity method of accounting
(3) Parent company's share of subsidiaries' dividends declared, under the equity method of accounting (Do not prepare journal entries for receipt of cash.)

b Prepare a working paper to compute the amount of minority interest in each subsidiary's net assets on December 31, Year 6.

c Prepare a working paper to compute the amount to be reported as consolidated retained earnings of Pewter Corporation and subsidiaries on December 31, Year 6.

Pr. 7-6 Analyses of the Investment in State Company Common Stock ledger account of Parks Corporation (State's parent company), the minority interest in net assets of State, and the differences between current fair values and carrying amounts of State's identifiable net assets on May 31, Year 3, the date of the Parks–State business combination, were as on page 369 for the year ended May 31, Year 4.

State had 10,000 shares of $1 par common stock outstanding on May 31, Year 4, that had been issued for $5 a share when State was organized. There has been no

PARKS CORPORATION
Analysis of Investment in State Company Common Stock Ledger Account
For Year Ended May 31, Year 4

	Carrying amount	Current fair value excess	Goodwill	Total	
Beginning balances.......	$400,000	$80,000	$50,000	$530,000	
Net income of State Company	80,000			80,000	Intercompany investment income, $72,800
Amortization of differences between current fair values and carrying amounts of State's identifiable net assets....		(7,200)		(7,200)	
Amortization of goodwill ...			(2,000)	(2,000)	
Dividend declared by State	(30,000)			(30,000)	
Ending balances..........	$450,000	$72,800	$48,000	$570,800	

PARKS CORPORATION
Analysis of Minority Interest in Net Assets of State Company
For Year Ended May 31, Year 4

	Carrying amount	Current fair value excess	Total	
Beginning balances	$100,000	$20,000	$120,000	
Net income of State Company	20,000		20,000	Minority interest in net income of subsidiary, $18,200
Amortization of differences between current fair values and carrying amounts of State's identifiable net assets		(1,800)	(1,800)	
Dividend declared by State..............	(7,500)		(7,500)	
Ending balances	$112,500	$18,200	$130,700	

PARKS CORPORATION
Analysis of Differences between Current Fair Values and Carrying
Amounts of State Company's Identifiable Net Assets
For Year Ended May 31, Year 4

	Balances, May 31, Year 3	Amortization for Year 4	Balances, May 31, Year 4
Plant assets (net):			
Land	$ 39,000		$39,000
Buildings	36,000	$4,000	32,000
Machinery	25,000	5,000	20,000
Total plant assets	$100,000	$9,000	$91,000

change in State's paid-in capital since State's organization. State includes straight-line depreciation expense on plant assets in cost of goods sold. Dividends were declared by State on May 31, Year 4.

Instructions

a Reconstruct Parks Corporation's journal entries for the year ended May 31, Year 4, to record the operating results of State Company under the equity method of accounting. (Disregard income taxes.)

b Prepare working paper eliminations for Parks Corporation and subsidiary (in journal entry format) on May 31, Year 4. (Disregard income taxes.)

Pr. 7-7 Paseo Corporation acquired 82% of Steppe Company's outstanding common stock for $328,000 cash on March 31, Year 8. Out-of-pocket costs of the business combination may be disregarded. Steppe's stockholders' equity on March 31, Year 8, was as follows:

Common stock, $2 par..	$ 50,000
Additional paid-in capital	75,000
Retained earnings...	135,000
Total stockholders' equity	$260,000

Additional Information

(1) All of Steppe's identifiable net assets were fairly valued at their March 31, Year 8, carrying amounts except for the following:

	Carrying amounts	Current fair values
Land...	$100,000	$120,000
Building (net) (10-year economic life).......................	200,000	250,000
Patent (net) (8-year economic life)	60,000	80,000

(2) Any goodwill resulting from the business combination was to be amortized over the maximum period of 40 years. Steppe used the straight-line method for depreciation and amortization. Steppe included depreciation expense in cost of goods sold and amortization expense in operating expenses.

(3) During the year ended March 31, Year 9, Steppe had a net income of $1.20 a share and declared and paid no dividends. There were no intercompany transactions between Paseo and Steppe.

Instructions

a Prepare Paseo Corporation's journal entries to record Steppe Company's operating results for the year ended March 31, Year 9, under the equity method of accounting. (Disregard income taxes.)

b Prepare working paper eliminations (in journal entry format) for Paseo Corporation and subsidiary on March 31, Year 9. (Disregard income taxes.)

Pr. 7-8 Pavich Corporation acquired 75% of the outstanding common stock of Sisler Company on October 1, Year 6, for $547,500, including direct out-of-pocket costs. Sisler's stockholders' equity on October 1, Year 6, was as follows:

Common stock, $5 par..	$250,000
Additional paid-in capital	100,000
Retained earnings..	200,000
Total stockholders' equity	$550,000

Additional Information

(1) Current fair values of Sisler's identifiable net assets exceeded their carrying amounts as follows:

	Excess of current fair values over carrying amounts
Inventories (first-in, first-out cost).............................	$30,000
Plant assets (net) (economic life 10 years)	50,000
Patents (net) (economic life 5 years)	20,000

(2) Pavich amortized goodwill over a 40-year economic life, and both Pavich and Sisler included depreciation expense in cost of goods sold and amortization expense in operating expenses. Both companies used the straight-line method for depreciation and amortization.

(3) For the two years ended September 30, Year 8, Sisler had net income and declared and paid dividends as follows:

Year ended Sept. 30	Net income	Dividends
Year 7	$ 80,000	$10,000
Year 8	120,000	75,000

Instructions

a Prepare journal entries for Pavich Corporation on September 30, Year 7, and September 30, Year 8, to record under the equity method of accounting the operating results of Sisler Company for the two years ended on those dates. Do not prepare entries for the declaration of Sisler's dividends; assume the dividends were received by Pavich on September 30 of each year. (Disregard income taxes.)

b Prepare working paper eliminations (in journal entry format) for Pavich Corporation and subsidiary on September 30, Year 7, and September 30, Year 8. (Disregard income taxes.)

c Prepare a three-column ledger account for Pavich Corporation's Retained Earnings of Subsidiary ledger account, showing the closing entries posted to that account on September 30, Year 7, and September 30, Year 8.

Pr. 7-9 The working paper elimination for Plumm Corporation and its wholly owned purchased subsidiary, Stamm Company, on the date of the business combination was as follows (in journal entry format):

PLUMM CORPORATION AND SUBSIDIARY
Working Paper Elimination
November 30, Year 1

Common Stock—Stamm	80,000	
Additional Paid-in Capital—Stamm	200,000	
Retained Earnings—Stamm	220,000	
Inventories—Stamm	20,000	
Goodwill—Stamm	40,000	
Investment in Stamm Company Common Stock—Plumm.		560,000

To eliminate intercompany investment and equity accounts of subsidiary on date of business combination; and to allocate excess of cost over carrying amounts of identifiable assets acquired, with remainder to goodwill having an economic life of 40 years. (Income tax effects are disregarded.)

Separate financial statements of Plumm and Stamm for the year ended November 30, Year 2, were as follows:

PLUMM CORPORATION AND STAMM COMPANY
Separate Financial Statements (for first year following business combination)
For Year Ended November 30, Year 2

	Plumm Corporation	Stamm Company
Income Statements		
Revenue:		
Net sales	$ 800,000	$415,000
Intercompany investment income	69,000	
Total revenue	$ 869,000	$415,000
Costs and expenses:		
Cost of goods sold	$ 500,000	$110,000
Operating expenses	233,333	155,000
Income taxes expense	26,667	60,000
Total costs and expenses	$ 760,000	$325,000
Net income	$ 109,000	$ 90,000
Statements of Retained Earnings		
Retained earnings, beginning of year	$ 640,000	$220,000
Net income	109,000	90,000
Subtotals	$ 749,000	$310,000
Dividends	60,000	30,000
Retained earnings, end of year	$ 689,000	$280,000
Balance Sheets		
Assets		
Investment in Stamm Company common stock	$ 599,000	
Other	1,840,000	$960,000
Total assets	$2,439,000	$960,000

(continued)

PLUMM CORPORATION AND STAMM COMPANY
Separate Financial Statements (for first year following business combination) (concluded)
For Year Ended November 30, Year 2

	Plumm Corporation	Stamm Company
Liabilities & Stockholders' Equity		
Liabilities	$ 650,000	$400,000
Common stock, $1 par	500,000	80,000
Additional paid-in capital	600,000	200,000
Retained earnings	689,000	280,000
Total liabilities & stockholders' equity	$2,439,000	$960,000

Instructions

a Reconstruct the journal entries for Plumm Corporation on November 30, Year 2, under the equity method of accounting, to record the operating results of Stamm Company for the year ended November 30, Year 2, including Stamm's dividend declared and paid on that date. (Do not prepare a journal entry for the declaration of the dividend.) (Disregard income taxes.)

b Prepare a working paper for consolidated financial statements of Plumm Corporation and subsidiary for the year ended November 30, Year 2, and the related working paper elimination (in journal entry format). Include goodwill amortization in operating expenses. (Disregard income taxes.)

Pr. 7-10 Ping Corporation acquired 80% of the outstanding common stock of Stang Company on December 31, Year 2, for $120,000. On that date, Stang had one class of common stock outstanding with a carrying amount of $100,000 and retained earnings of $30,000. Ping had a $50,000 deficit in retained earnings.

Additional Information

(1) Ping acquired the Stang common stock from Stang's major stockholder primarily to acquire control of signboard leases owned by Stang. The leases were to expire on December 31, Year 7, and Ping's executives estimated that the leases, which were not renewable, were worth at least $20,000 more than their carrying amount when the Stang common stock was acquired. Stang includes signboard leases amortization in other expenses.

(2) The separate financial statements for both companies for the year ended December 31, Year 6, were as on page 374.

(3) Stang declared a 9% cash dividend on December 20, Year 6, payable January 16, Year 7, to stockholders of record December 31, Year 6. Ping carried its investment at cost and had not recorded Stang's dividend on December 31, Year 6. Ping neither declared nor paid dividends during Year 6.

Instructions

a Prepare adjusting entries for Ping Corporation on December 31, Year 6, to convert its accounting for Stang Company's operating results to the equity method of accounting. (Disregard income taxes.)

PING CORPORATION AND SUBSIDIARY
Separate Financial Statements (prior to business combination)
For Year Ended December 31, Year 6

	Ping Corporation	Stang Company
Income Statements		
Net sales	$ 420,000	$300,000
Costs and expenses:		
Cost of goods sold	$ 315,000	$240,000
Other expenses	65,000	35,000
Total costs and expenses	$ 380,000	$275,000
Net income	$ 40,000	$ 25,000
Statements of Retained Earnings		
Retained earnings, beginning of year	$ 15,000	$ 59,000
Net income	40,000	25,000
Subtotals	$ 55,000	$ 84,000
Dividends.		9,000
Retained earnings, end of year	$ 55,000	$ 75,000
Balance Sheets		
Assets		
Current assets	$ 172,000	$199,100
Investment in Stang Company common stock	120,000	
Land	25,000	10,500
Building and equipment	200,000	40,000
Accumulated depreciation	(102,000)	(7,000)
Signboard leases (net)		8,400
Total assets	$ 415,000	$251,000
Liabilities & Stockholders' Equity		
Dividends payable		$ 9,000
Other current liabilities	$ 60,000	67,000
Common stock, no par or stated value	300,000	100,000
Retained earnings	55,000	75,000
Total liabilities & stockholders' equity	$ 415,000	$251,000

b Prepare a working paper for consolidated financial statements of Ping Corporation and subsidiary on December 31, Year 6, and the related working paper eliminations (in journal entry format). Amounts for Ping Corporation should reflect the adjusting entries in **a**. (Disregard income taxes.)

Pr. 7-11   On June 30, Year 6, Petal Corporation acquired for cash of $19 a share, including out-of-pocket costs, all the outstanding common stock of Sepal Company. Both companies continued to operate as separate entities. Petal adopted the equity method of accounting for Sepal's operating results.

Additional Information

(1) On June 30, Year 6, Sepal's balance sheet was as follows:

SEPAL COMPANY
Balance Sheet (prior to business combination)
June 30, Year 6

Assets

Cash..	$ 700,000
Trade accounts receivable (net).......................................	600,000
Inventories	1,400,000
Plant assets (net)	3,300,000
Other assets..	500,000
Total assets	$6,500,000

Liabilities & Stockholders' Equity

Trade accounts payable and other current liabilities....................	$ 700,000
Long-term debt...	2,600,000
Other liabilities	200,000
Common stock, $1 par...	1,000,000
Additional paid-in capital	400,000
Retained earnings..	1,600,000
Total liabilities & stockholders' equity...............................	$6,500,000

(2) On June 30, Year 6, Sepal's assets and liabilities having current fair values that were different from carrying amounts were as follows:

	Current fair values
Plant assets (net)...	$16,400,000
Other assets..	200,000
Long-term debt..	2,200,000

The differences between current fair values and carrying amounts resulted in a debit or credit to depreciation or amortization for the consolidated financial statements for the six-month period ended December 31, Year 6, as follows:

Plant assets (net)...	$500,000 debit
Other assets...	10,000 credit
Long-term debt...	5,000 debit
Total..	$495,000 debit

(3) The amount paid by Petal in excess of the current fair value of the identifiable net assets of Sepal was attributable to expected superior future earnings of Sepal and was to be amortized over the maximum allowable period.

(4) The Year 6 net income or net loss for each company was as follows:

	Petal Corporation	Sepal Company
Jan. 1 to June 30	$ 250,000	$ (750,000)
July 1 to Dec. 31.................................	1,070,000	1,250,000

The $1,070,000 net income of Petal included Petal's equity in the adjusted net income of Sepal for the six months ended December 31, Year 6.

(5) On December 31, Year 6, the end of the fiscal year, the separate balance sheets for both companies were as follows:

PETAL CORPORATION AND SUBSIDIARY
Separate Balance Sheets (six months subsequent to business combination)
December 31, Year 6

	Petal Corporation	Sepal Company
Assets		
Cash...	$ 3,500,000	$ 625,000
Trade accounts receivable (net).....................	1,400,000	1,500,000
Inventories.......................................	1,000,000	2,500,000
Investment in Sepal Company common stock	19,720,000	
Plant assets (net).................................	2,000,000	3,100,000
Other assets	100,000	475,000
Total assets.....................................	$27,720,000	$8,200,000
Liabilities & Stockholders' Equity		
Trade accounts payable and other current liabilities	$ 1,500,000	$1,100,000
Long-term debt....................................	4,000,000	2,600,000
Other liabilities	750,000	250,000
Common stock, $1 par.............................	10,000,000	1,000,000
Additional paid-in capital	5,000,000	400,000
Retained earnings.................................	6,470,000	2,850,000
Total liabilities & stockholders' equity	$27,720,000	$8,200,000

Instructions

Prepare a consolidated balance sheet for Petal Corporation and its wholly owned subsidiary, Sepal Company, on December 31, Year 6. Do not use a working paper, but show supporting computations. (Disregard income taxes.)

8

Consolidated Financial Statements: Pooling-Type Business Combination

In this chapter, I discuss consolidated financial statements of parent corporations and pooled subsidiaries, both on, and subsequent to, the date of the pooling-type business combination. The chapter concludes with illustrations of intercompany transactions that do not involve a profit (gain) or a loss.

Consolidated financial statements on the date of a pooling-type business combination differ in several respects from consolidated financial statements on the date of a purchase-type business combination. Among these differences are the following:

1 All four financial statements of the parent company and pooled subsidiary are consolidated on the date of a pooling-type combination, in accordance with the theory that a pooling is a combining of past and present stockholder interests. In contrast, only a consolidated balance sheet is appropriate on the date of a purchase-type combination.

2 Current fair values of the subsidiary's net assets are not reflected in the consolidated balance sheet for a pooled subsidiary as they are for a purchased subsidiary, and no goodwill is recognized.

3 Consolidated retained earnings on the date of a pooling-type combination includes the parent company's share of the subsidiary's retained earnings on that date. In contrast, only the amount of the parent company's retained earnings is included in consolidated retained earnings on the date of a purchase-type combination.

Illustrated in the two sections that follow are the consolidation of a wholly owned pooled subsidiary and the consolidation of a partially owned pooled subsidiary, both on, and subsequent to, the date of the business combination.

CONSOLIDATION OF WHOLLY OWNED POOLED SUBSIDIARY ON DATE OF BUSINESS COMBINATION

To illustrate the consolidated financial statements for a wholly owned pooled subsidiary on the date of a business combination, the Palm Corporation–Starr Company business combination described in Chapter 6 (pages 248 to 249) is used, assuming that the combination qualified for pooling accounting rather than for purchase accounting. As indicated in Chapter 6, on December 31, Year 1, the end of a fiscal year, Palm issued 10,000 shares of its $10 par common stock for all the outstanding common stock of Starr and paid out-of-pocket costs of $85,000 in connection with the combination. Separate financial statements of Palm and Starr prior to the combination are on page 379; these statements are identical to those on page 250 of Chapter 6.

The following journal entries are prepared by Palm on December 31, Year 1, to record the combination as a pooling:

Issuing company's journal entries for pooling-type business combination

PALM CORPORATION (Issuing Company)
Journal Entries
December 31, Year 1

Investment in Starr Company Common Stock		
($200,000 + $58,000 + $132,000)	*390,000*	
Common Stock (10,000 × $10)		*100,000*
Paid-in Capital in Excess of Par ($258,000 − $100,000)		*158,000*
Retained Earnings of Subsidiary		*132,000*

To record issuance of 10,000 shares of common stock for all the outstanding common stock of Starr Company in a pooling-type business combination.

Expenses of Business Combination	*85,000*	
Cash		*85,000*

To record payment of out-of-pocket costs of business combination with Starr Company.

The first of the foregoing journal entries records Palm's investment in Starr's common stock at the ***carrying amount*** of Starr's stockholders' equity on December 31, Year 1 ($200,000 + $58,000 + $132,000 = $390,000). In addition, a Retained Earnings of Subsidiary ledger account is established to record the amount of Starr's retained earnings on December 31, Year 1. This separate account emphasizes that Starr's retained earnings are not a source of dividends to Palm's stockholders, as is often true in a statutory merger. The first journal entry thus reflects the underlying theory of pooling accounting—the ***combination of existing stockholder interests*** —while recognizing the separate corporate identity (in a legal sense) of the pooled subsidiary.

In the second journal entry, all out-of-pocket costs of the business combination are recognized as expenses. As explained in Chapter 5 (page 197), this procedure is required in a pooling-type combination.

Although Palm's expenses are increased in the second journal entry, there is no adjustment of Palm's income taxes expense or liability accounts. Costs of a pooling-type combination expensed for financial accounting are not deductible for income

PALM CORPORATION AND STARR COMPANY
Separate Financial Statements (prior to pooling-type business combination)
For Year Ended December 31, Year 1

Income Statements	Palm Corporation	Starr Company
Revenue:		
Net sales	$ 990,000	$600,000
Interest revenue	10,000	
Total revenue	$1,000,000	$600,000
Costs and expenses:		
Cost of goods sold.................................	$ 635,000	$410,000
Operating expenses	158,333	73,333
Interest expense...................................	50,000	30,000
Income taxes expense	62,667	34,667
Total costs and expenses	$ 906,000	$548,000
Net income	$ 94,000	$ 52,000

Statements of Retained Earnings

	Palm Corporation	Starr Company
Retained earnings, beginning of year	$ 65,000	$100,000
Add: Net income.....................................	94,000	52,000
Subtotals	$ 159,000	$152,000
Less: Dividends	25,000	20,000
Retained earnings, end of year........................	$ 134,000	$132,000

Balance Sheets

Assets

	Palm Corporation	Starr Company
Cash...	$ 100,000	$ 40,000
Inventories..	150,000	110,000
Other current assets	110,000	70,000
Receivable from Starr Company.......................	25,000	
Plant assets (net)....................................	450,000	300,000
Patent (net)		20,000
Total assets.......................................	$ 835,000	$540,000

Liabilities & Stockholders' Equity

	Palm Corporation	Starr Company
Payable to Palm Corporation		$ 25,000
Income taxes payable.................................	$ 26,000	10,000
Other liabilities	325,000	115,000
Common stock, $10 par..............................	300,000	
Common stock, $5 par		200,000
Additional paid-in capital	50,000	58,000
Retained earnings	134,000	132,000
Total liabilities & stockholders' equity	$ 835,000	$540,000

tax purposes. The U.S. Treasury Department considers such costs to be capital expenditures, rather than expenditures that may be either deducted when incurred or amortized over a period of years.

After the foregoing journal entries have been posted, the affected financial statement items for Palm Corporation have the following balances:

<table>
<tr><td rowspan="9">Balances of financial statement items of issuing company affected by business combination</td><td>* Operating expenses ($158,333 + $85,000) ....</td><td>$243,333</td></tr>
<tr><td>Net income ($94,000 − $85,000) ....</td><td>9,000</td></tr>
<tr><td>Cash ($100,000 − $85,000) ....</td><td>15,000</td></tr>
<tr><td>Investment in Starr Company common stock ....</td><td>390,000</td></tr>
<tr><td>Common stock, $10 par ($300,000 + $100,000) ....</td><td>400,000</td></tr>
<tr><td>Additional paid-in capital ($50,000 + $158,000) ....</td><td>208,000</td></tr>
<tr><td>Retained earnings ($134,000 − $85,000) ....</td><td>49,000</td></tr>
<tr><td>Retained earnings of subsidiary ....</td><td>132,000</td></tr>
<tr><td>* Controlling account for Expenses of Business Combination ledger account.</td><td></td></tr>
</table>

Preparation of Consolidated Financial Statements without a Working Paper   If a business combination qualifies for pooling accounting, all four financial statements are consolidated for the accounting period that includes the date of the combination. This is consistent with the assumption that a pooling is a combining of existing stockholder interests, rather than an acquisition of assets.

In a pooling-type business combination involving a wholly owned subsidiary, the Investment in Subsidiary Common Stock ledger account is similar to the Investment in Branch account illustrated in Chapter 4 for a home office. However, the subsidiary's three stockholder's equity accounts (which total $390,000), rather than a single Home Office (or Parent Company) account, offset Palm Corporation's Investment in Starr Company Common Stock account, which has a balance of $390,000.

In view of the foregoing, consolidated financial statements for a parent company and a wholly owned subsidiary may be prepared without the use of a working paper. Assuming that Palm Corporation's interest revenue of $10,000 (page 379) was attributable to a loan by Palm to Starr Company prior to the pooling-type business combination, the consolidated income statement, statement of retained earnings, and balance sheet for Palm Corporation and Starr Company may be prepared as shown on page 381. (The illustration of a consolidated statement of cash flows is included in Chapter 10, so that more fundamental issues may be addressed in this chapter.)

PALM CORPORATION AND SUBSIDIARY
Consolidated Income Statement
For Year Ended December 31, Year 1

Net sales ($990,000 + $600,000)		$1,590,000
Costs and expenses:		
Cost of goods sold ($635,000 + $410,000)	$1,045,000	
Operating expenses ($243,333 + $73,333)	316,666	
Interest expense ($50,000 + $30,000 − $10,000)	70,000	
Income taxes expense ($62,667 + $34,667)	97,334	1,529,000
Net income ($9,000 + $52,000).......................................		$ 61,000
Earnings per share of common stock (40,000 shares outstanding)		$ 1.53

PALM CORPORATION AND SUBSIDIARY
Consolidated Statement of Retained Earnings
For Year Ended December 31, Year 1

Retained earnings, beginning of year, as previously reported...........		$ 65,000
Add: Adjustment to reflect pooling of interests with Starr Company......		100,000
Retained earnings, beginning of year, as restated.....................		$ 165,000
Add: Net income		61,000
Subtotal...		$ 226,000
Less: Dividends:		
Palm Corporation ($0.83⅓ a share)...................	$ 25,000	
Starr Company, prior to business combination.........	20,000	45,000
Retained earnings, end of year		$ 181,000

PALM CORPORATION AND SUBSIDIARY
Consolidated Balance Sheet
December 31, Year 1

Assets

Current assets:		
Cash ($15,000 + $40,000)		$ 55,000
Inventories ($150,000 + $110,000).................................		260,000
Other ($110,000 + $70,000)..		180,000
Total current assets		$ 495,000
Plant assets (net) ($450,000 + $300,000)............................		750,000
Patent (net) ($0 + $20,000)		20,000
Total assets		$1,265,000

Liabilities & Stockholders' Equity

Liabilities:		
Income taxes payable ($26,000 + $10,000).........................		$ 36,000
Other ($325,000 + $115,000)		440,000
Total liabilities..		$ 476,000
Stockholders' equity:		
Common stock, $10 par	$ 400,000	
Additional paid-in capital............................	208,000	
Retained earnings.................................	181,000	789,000
Total liabilities & stockholders' equity		$1,265,000

In reviewing the consolidated financial statements of Palm Corporation and subsidiary, the following should be noted:

1   Intercompany items are excluded from the consolidated amounts as follows:

Palm Corporation's intercompany interest revenue	$ 10,000
Starr Company's intercompany interest expense	10,000
Palm Corporation's receivable from Starr Company	25,000
Starr Company's payable to Palm Corporation	25,000
Palm Corporation's investment in Starr Company common stock (from p. 380)	390,000
Starr Company's total paid-in capital ($200,000 + $58,000)	258,000
Palm Corporation's retained earnings of subsidiary	132,000

The latter amount is excluded from the consolidated balance sheet so that consolidated retained earnings in the statement of consolidated retained earnings may be brought forward to the consolidated balance sheet.

2   Other than the foregoing, amounts in the separate income statements and balance sheets of the two constituent companies (from page 379) are totaled to arrive at the consolidated amounts.

3   Because a pooling-of-interests business combination represents a *change in the reporting entity,*[1] the consolidated statement of retained earnings for Palm Corporation and subsidiary displays an ''adjustment to reflect pooling of interests with Starr Company.'' This adjustment represents the retroactive application of the pooling accounting method to include Starr's beginning-of-Year 1 retained earnings of $100,000 with Palm's comparable amount of $65,000. Further, Starr's dividends to its former stockholders are displayed separately because *they were not intercompany dividends declared to Palm.*

Working Paper for Consolidated Financial Statements   The preparation of a working paper for consolidated financial statements and related working paper elimination for a parent company and a wholly owned pooled subsidiary is uncomplicated because of the absence of current fair value excesses and goodwill in the subsidiary. The working paper elimination for Palm corporation and subsidiary on December 31, Year 1, is on page 384; the related working paper for consolidated financial statements is on page 383.

In reviewing the working paper for consolidated financial statements for a pooling-type business combination, note the following points:

1   A consolidated statement of cash flows is not illustrated at this point in order to focus attention on more fundamental issues. Once the consolidated balance sheet, consolidated income statement, and consolidated statement of retained earnings are available, a consolidated statement of cash flows may be prepared from comparative

[1] *APB Opinion No. 20,* ''Accounting Changes,'' AICPA (New York: 1971), p. 388.

Wholly owned subsidiary on date of pooling-type business combination

PALM CORPORATION AND SUBSIDIARY
Working Paper for Consolidated Financial Statements
For Year Ended December 31, Year 1

	Palm Corporation	Starr Company	Eliminations increase (decrease)	Consolidated
Income Statement				
Revenue:				
Net sales	990,000	600,000		1,590,000
Intercompany revenue (expense).......	10,000	(10,000)		
Total revenue	1,000,000	590,000		1,590,000
Costs and expenses:				
Cost of goods sold...................	635,000	410,000		1,045,000
Operating expenses...................	243,333	73,333		316,666
Interest expense.....................	50,000	20,000		70,000
Income taxes expense	62,667	34,667		97,334
Total costs and expenses...........	991,000	538,000		1,529,000
Net income............................	9,000	52,000		61,000
Statement of Retained Earnings				
Retained earnings, beginning of year	65,000	100,000		165,000
Net income............................	9,000	52,000		61,000
Subtotal	74,000	152,000		226,000
Dividends declared.....................	25,000	20,000		45,000
Retained earnings, end of year...........	49,000	132,000		181,000
Balance Sheet				
Assets				
Cash	15,000	40,000		55,000
Inventories..............................	150,000	110,000		260,000
Other current assets	110,000	70,000		180,000
Intercompany receivables (payable)	25,000	(25,000)		
Investment in Starr Company common stock	390,000		(a) (390,000)	
Plant assets (net).......................	450,000	300,000		750,000
Patent (net)		20,000		20,000
Total assets...........................	1,140,000	515,000	(390,000)	1,265,000
Liabilities & Stockholders' Equity				
Income taxes payable	26,000	10,000		36,000
Other liabilities.........................	325,000	115,000		440,000
Common stock, $10 par	400,000			400,000
Common stock, $5 par		200,000	(a) (200,000)	
Additional paid-in capital................	208,000	58,000	(a) (58,000)	208,000
Retained earnings	49,000	132,000		181,000
Retained earnings of subsidiary	132,000		(a) (132,000)	
Total liabilities & stockholders' equity ...	1,140,000	515,000	(390,000)	1,265,000

PALM CORPORATION AND SUBSIDIARY
Working Paper Elimination
December 31, Year 1

(a) Common Stock—Starr..................................	200,000	
Additional Paid-in Capital—Starr.........................	58,000	
Retained Earnings of Subsidiary—Palm..................	132,000	
Investment in Starr Company Common Stock—Palm.		390,000

To eliminate intercompany investment and related accounts for stockholder's equity of subsidiary on date of business combination.

consolidated statements and supplementary data relating to depreciation, amortization, and other items. A consolidated statement of cash flows is illustrated in Chapter 10.

2   Intercompany revenue and expenses and intercompany receivables and payables are placed on the same line in adjacent columns of the income statement section and balance sheet section, respectively, of the working paper, so that they are offset without a formal elimination. There are no other intercompany items that require use of the Eliminations column in the income statement and retained earnings statement sections of the working paper.

3   Each pair of financial statements is consolidated in turn, in the sequence of the conventional accounting cycle. Thus, the consolidated net income of $61,000 is carried forward to the consolidated statement of retained earnings, and the consolidated retained earnings amount of $181,000 is carried forward to the consolidated balance sheet.

4   Dividends declared by Starr Company *are not eliminated* in the statement of retained earnings section of the working paper *because the dividends were paid prior to the pooling-type business combination to the former stockholders of Starr, not to Palm Corporation.*

5   Consolidated retained earnings include the retained earnings of both Palm and Starr, in accordance with the pooling theory of accounting for a business combination. Thus, the separate Retained Earnings of Subsidiary amount of Palm is eliminated, so that the individual Retained Earnings amounts of the parent company and subsidiary *may be combined.*

Consolidated Financial Statements   The consolidated financial statements of Palm Corporation and subsidiary (page 385) are identical to those on page 381 and include the amounts in the Consolidated column of the working paper for consolidated financial statements on page 383. Because all intercompany transactions and balances have been eliminated in the computation of the consolidated amounts, these balances reflect only the transactions of Palm and Starr with *outside parties.*

PALM CORPORATION AND SUBSIDIARY
Consolidated Income Statement
For Year Ended December 31, Year 1

Net sales		$1,590,000
Costs and expenses:		
Cost of goods sold	$1,045,000	
Operating expenses	316,666	
Interest expense	70,000	
Income taxes expense	97,334	1,529,000
Net income		$ 61,000
Earnings per share of common stock (40,000 shares outstanding)		$ 1.53

PALM CORPORATION AND SUBSIDIARY
Consolidated Statement of Retained Earnings
For Year Ended December 31, Year 1

Retained earnings, beginning of year, as previously reported		$ 65,000
Add: Adjustment to reflect pooling of interests with Starr Company		100,000
Retained earnings, beginning of year, as restated		$ 165,000
Add: Net income		61,000
Subtotal		$ 226,000
Less: Dividends:		
Palm Corporation ($0.83⅓ a share)	$ 25,000	
Starr Company, prior to business combination	20,000	45,000
Retained earnings, end of year		$ 181,000

PALM CORPORATION AND SUBSIDIARY
Consolidated Balance Sheet
December 31, Year 1

Assets

Current assets:		
Cash		$ 55,000
Inventories		260,000
Other		180,000
Total current assets		$ 495,000
Plant assets (net)		750,000
Patent (net)		20,000
Total assets		$1,265,000

Liabilities & Stockholders' Equity

Liabilities:		
Income taxes payable		$ 36,000
Other		440,000
Total liabilities		$ 476,000
Stockholders' equity:		
Common stock, $10 par	$ 400,000	
Additional paid-in capital	208,000	
Retained earnings	181,000	789,000
Total liabilities & stockholders' equity		$1,265,000

CONSOLIDATION OF WHOLLY OWNED POOLED SUBSIDIARY SUBSEQUENT TO DATE OF BUSINESS COMBINATION

In the following section, the Palm Corporation–Starr Company example is continued to illustrate the preparation of consolidated financial statements subsequent to the date of a pooling-type business combination.

The Equity Method of Accounting for Pooled Subsidiaries

A parent company's investment account for a subsidiary acquired in a pooling-type business combination originally reflects the parent's share of the *carrying amount* of the subsidiary's net assets. Thus, there is no *cost of the investment* in a pooled subsidiary; the investment is recorded as the *parent's equity in the subsidiary's net assets.* It follows that the *equity method of accounting* is appropriate for the operating results of a pooled subsidiary subsequent to the business combination, and that the *cost method of accounting* is not appropriate for a pooled subsidiary.

To illustrate the equity method of accounting for a wholly owned pooled subsidiary, return to the December 31, Year 1, business combination of Palm Corporation and Starr Company and assume that it has been accounted for as a pooling, as described on pages 377 to 378.

For the year ended December 31, Year 2, Starr had a net income of $60,000. Starr's board of directors on December 20, Year 2, declared a cash dividend of $0.60 a share on the 40,000 outstanding shares of Starr common stock. The dividend was payable January 8, Year 3, to the stockholder of record on December 29, Year 2.

Under the equity method of accounting, Palm prepares the following journal entries to record the operating results of Starr for the year ended December 31, Year 2:

<table>
<tr><td>Parent company's equity-method journal entries to record operating results of wholly owned pooled subsidiary</td><td>

Year 2

Dec. 20 *Intercompany Dividends Receivable (40,000 × $0.60)* . . . *24,000*
           Investment in Starr Company Common Stock *24,000*
      To record dividend declared by Starr Company, payable Jan. 8, Year 3, to stockholders of record Dec. 29, Year 2.

31 *Investment in Starr Company Common Stock* *60,000*
          Intercompany Investment Income *60,000*
      To record 100% of Starr Company's net income for the year ended Dec. 31, Year 2. (Income tax effects are disregarded.)

</td></tr>
</table>

After the foregoing journal entries are posted, Palm's Investment in Starr Company Common Stock ledger account is as shown below:

Investment ledger account of parent company using equity method of accounting for wholly owned pooled subsidiary

Investment in Starr Company Common Stock

Date	Explanation	Debit	Credit	Balance
Year 1				
Dec. 31	Issuance of common stock in business combination			390,000 dr
Year 2				
Dec. 20	Dividend declared by Starr		24,000	366,000 dr
31	Net income of Starr	60,000		426,000 dr

The $426,000 balance of Palm's Investment in Starr Company Common Stock ledger account on December 31, Year 2, exactly offsets the total stockholder's equity of Starr on that date (see Starr's December 31, Year 2, balance sheet on page 389), as shown below:

Total stockholder's equity of wholly owned pooled subsidiary equals balance of parent company's Investment ledger account

Starr Company's stockholder's equity:	
Common stock, $5 par.	$200,000
Additional paid-in capital	58,000
Retained earnings.	168,000
Total stockholder's equity of Starr Company	$426,000

The Investment in Starr Company Common Stock ledger account thus reflects Palm's 100% equity in the net assets of Starr at carrying amount.

Working Paper for Consolidated Financial Statements Because of the additional intercompany amounts resulting from the equity method of accounting, a working paper is advisable for the preparation of consolidated financial statements for years subsequent to that of the business combination. The working paper for consolidated financial statements for Palm Corporation and subsidiary for the year ended December 31, Year 2, is on page 389; the working paper elimination (in journal entry format) is on page 388. The intercompany receivable and payable is the $24,000 dividend payable by Starr to Palm on December 31, Year 2. [The $25,000 of advances by Palm Corporation to Starr Company that were outstanding on December 31, Year 1 (see page 382), were repaid by Starr on January 2, Year 2.]

The following aspects of the working paper for consolidated financial statements for Palm Corporation and subsidiary should be emphasized:

1 The intercompany receivable and payable, placed in adjacent columns on the same line, are offset without a formal elimination.

Working paper
elimination for wholly
owned pooled
subsidiary for first year
subsequent to date of
business combination

PALM CORPORATION AND SUBSIDIARY
Working Paper Elimination
December 31, Year 2

(a) *Common Stock—Starr* 200,000
    Additional Paid-in Capital—Starr 58,000
    Retained Earnings of Subsidiary—Palm 132,000
    Intercompany Investment Income—Palm 60,000
        Investment in Starr Company Common Stock—Palm .   426,000
        Dividends Declared—Starr   24,000
    To eliminate intercompany investment, related accounts for
    *stockholder's equity of subsidiary at **beginning of year,** and*
    investment income from subsidiary.

2   Elimination (*a*) cancels all intercompany transactions and balances not dealt with by the offset described in **1** on page 387.

3   *Consolidated net income* is the same as the *parent company's net income.* Also, *consolidated retained earnings* is equal to the total of the parent company's two retained earnings amounts in the working paper, as shown below:

Total of parent
company's two
retained earnings
amounts in working
paper equals
consolidated retained
earnings

Palm Corporation's retained earnings amounts:
  Retained earnings $159,000
  Retained earnings of subsidiary 132,000
    Total (equal to consolidated retained earnings) $291,000

This equality results from Palm's use of the equity method of accounting for its investment in Starr.

4   The working paper elimination cancels the parent company's retained earnings of subsidiary amount because it carries a balance equal to the subsidiary's retained earnings *at the beginning of Year 2.* In this manner, each of the three financial statements (income statement, statement of retained earnings, and balance sheet) may be consolidated.

Consolidated Financial Statements   The consolidated financial statements of Palm Corporation and subsidiary on page 390 are prepared from the amounts in the Consolidated column of the working paper for consolidated financial statements (page 389). The consolidated statement of retained earnings is prepared in the customary manner, because the business combination took place in the prior accounting period.

Equity method: Wholly owned subsidiary subsequent to date of pooling-type business combination

PALM CORPORATION AND SUBSIDIARY
Working Paper for Consolidated Financial Statements
For Year Ended December 31, Year 2

	Palm Corporation	Starr Company	Eliminations increase (decrease)	Consolidated
Income Statement				
Revenue:				
Net sales............................	1,100,000	680,000		1,780,000
Intercompany investment income	60,000		(a) (60,000)	
Total revenue.....................	1,160,000	680,000	(60,000)	1,780,000
Costs and expenses:				
Costs of goods sold	700,000	450,000		1,150,000
Operating expenses..................	217,667	130,000		347,667
Interest expense	49,000			49,000
Income taxes expense................	53,333	40,000		93,333
Total costs and expenses...........	1,020,000	620,000		1,640,000
Net income..........................	140,000	60,000	(60,000)	140,000
Statement of Retained Earnings				
Retained earnings, beginning of year.....	49,000	132,000		181,000
Net income...........................	140,000	60,000	(60,000)	140,000
Subtotals............................	189,000	192,000	(60,000)	321,000
Dividends declared....................	30,000	24,000	(a) (24,000)*	30,000
Retained earnings, end of year	159,000	168,000	(36,000)	291,000
Balance Sheet				
Assets				
Intercompany receivable (payable).......	24,000	(24,000)		
Investment in Starr Company common stock	426,000		(a) (426,000)	
Other assets...........................	679,900	674,100		1,354,000
Total assets	1,129,900	650,100	(426,000)	1,354,000
Liabilities & Stockholders' Equity				
Liabilities..............................	230,900	224,100		455,000
Common stock, $10 par	400,000			400,000
Common stock, $5 par.................		200,000	(a) (200,000)	
Additional paid-in capital	208,000	58,000	(a) (58,000)	208,000
Retained earnings.....................	159,000	168,000	(36,000)	291,000
Retained earnings of subsidiary	132,000		(a) (132,000)	
Total liabilities & stockholders' equity...	1,129,900	650,100	(426,000)	1,354,000

*A **decrease** in dividends and an **increase** in retained earnings.

PALM CORPORATION AND SUBSIDIARY
Consolidated Income Statement
For Year Ended December 31, Year 2

Net sales		$1,780,000
Costs and expenses:		
Cost of goods sold	$1,150,000	
Operating expenses	347,667	
Interest expense	49,000	
Income taxes expense	93,333	1,640,000
Net income		$ 140,000
Earnings per share of common stock (40,000 shares outstanding)		$ 3.50

PALM CORPORATION AND SUBSIDIARY
Consolidated Statement of Retained Earnings
For Year Ended December 31, Year 2

Retained earnings, beginning of year	$ 181,000
Add: Net income	140,000
Subtotal	$ 321,000
Less: Dividends ($0.75 a share)	30,000
Retained earnings, end of year	$ 291,000

PALM CORPORATION AND SUBSIDIARY
Consolidated Balance Sheet
December 31, Year 2

Assets

Other assets	$1,354,000

Liabilities & Stockholders' Equity

Liabilities		$ 455,000
Stockholders' equity:		
Common stock, $10 par	$ 400,000	
Additional paid-in capital	208,000	
Retained earnings	291,000	899,000
Total liabilities & stockholders' equity		$1,354,000

Closing Entries The equity method of accounting disregards legal form in favor of the economic substance of the relationship between a parent company and its subsidiary. However, state corporation laws generally necessitate a careful accounting for retained earnings available for dividends. Accordingly, Palm Corporation prepares the following closing entries on December 31, Year 2, after the consolidated financial statements have been completed:

Parent company's closing entries under equity method of accounting for pooled subsidiary	*Net Sales*... 1,100,000	
	Intercompany Investment Income 60,000	
	Income Summary	*1,160,000*
	To close revenue accounts.	
	Income Summary....................................... 1,020,000	
	Cost of Goods Sold..............................	*700,000*
	Operating Expenses..............................	*217,667*
	Interest Expense	*49,000*
	Income Taxes Expense	*53,333*
	To close expense accounts.	
	Income Summary....................................... 140,000	
	Retained Earnings of Subsidiary ($60,000 − $24,000)	*36,000*
	Retained Earnings ($140,000 − $36,000)...........	*104,000*
	To close Income Summary account; to transfer net income legally available for dividends to retained earnings; and to segregate 100% share of net income of subsidiary not distributed as dividends by the subsidiary.	
	Retained Earnings....................................... 30,000	
	Dividends Declared..............................	*30,000*
	To close Dividends Declared account.	

The third closing entry excludes from Palm Corporation's retained earnings the amount of Palm's net income not available for dividends to Palm's stockholders—$36,000. This amount is computed as follows:

Computation of undistributed earnings of subsidiary	*Net income of Starr recorded by Palm Corporation*........................ $60,000
	Less: Dividends declared by Starr to Palm 24,000
	*Amount of Starr's **net income not distributed** as a dividend to Palm (undistributed earnings of subsidiary)* $36,000

After the foregoing closing entries have been posted, Palm's Retained Earnings and Retained Earnings of Subsidiary ledger accounts are as follows:

Parent company's ledger accounts for retained earnings

Retained Earnings

Date	Explanation	Debit	Credit	Balance
Year 1				
Dec. 31	Balance			49,000 cr
Year 2				
Dec. 31	Close net income available for dividends		104,000	153,000 cr
31	Close Dividends Declared account	30,000		123,000 cr

Retained Earnings of Subsidiary

Date	Explanation	Debit	Credit	Balance
Year 1				
Dec. 31	Pooling-type business combination		132,000	132,000 cr
Year 2				
Dec. 31	Close net income not available for dividends		36,000	168,000 cr

The $168,000 after-closing balance of Palm's Retained Earnings of Subsidiary ledger account is equal to the after-closing balance of Starr's Retained Earnings ledger account (see Starr's balance sheet on page 389). In addition, the $291,000 total ($123,000 + $168,000 = $291,000) of the balances of Palm's two ledger accounts for retained earnings is equal to consolidated retained earnings of Palm Corporation and subsidiary on December 31, Year 2.

In the December 31, Year 3, working paper elimination for Palm Corporation and subsidiary, the December 31, Year 2, balance of Palm's Retained Earnings of Subsidiary ledger account would be eliminated. For example, if Starr Company declared a dividend of $40,000 and had a net income of $90,000 for the year ended December 31, Year 3, the working paper elimination (in journal entry format) for Palm Corporation and subsidiary on that date would be as illustrated below:

Working paper elimination for wholly owned pooled subsidiary for second year subsequent to date of business combination

PALM CORPORATION AND SUBSIDIARY
Working Paper Elimination
December 31, Year 3

(a) Common Stock—Starr...............................	200,000	
Additional Paid-in Capital—Starr.........................	58,000	
Retained Earnings of Subsidiary—Palm...................	168,000	
Intercompany Investment Income—Palm..................	90,000	
Investment in Starr Company Common Stock—Palm		
($426,000 + $90,000 − $40,000).................		476,000
Dividends Declared—Starr.........................		40,000

To eliminate intercompany investment, related accounts for stockholder's equity of subsidiary at **beginning of year,** and investment income from subsidiary.

CONSOLIDATION OF PARTIALLY OWNED POOLED SUBSIDIARY ON DATE OF BUSINESS COMBINATION

Under the assumption that the Post Corporation–Sage Company business combination described on pages 259 and 260 qualified for pooling accounting rather than for purchase accounting, it is used in this section to illustrate consolidated financial statements for a partially owned pooled subsidiary on the date of the business combination. As indicated in Chapter 6, on December 31, Year 1, the end of a fiscal year, Post issued 57,000 shares of its $1 par common stock in exchange for 38,000 of the 40,000 outstanding shares of Sage's common stock, and paid $125,000 out-of-pocket costs of the business combination. Separate financial statements of the two companies prior to the combination are on page 394; these statements are identical to those on page 261.

Post's December 31, Year 1, journal entries to record the business combination with Sage as a pooling are shown below. Note that the first of the journal entries records Post's **95% share** of the net assets (carrying amount $969,000) and retained earnings of Sage.

Issuing company's journal entries for pooling-type business combination

POST CORPORATION (Issuing Company) Journal Entries December 31, Year 1		
Investment in Sage Company Common Stock		
[($400,000 + $235,000 + $334,000) × 0.95]	920,550	
Common Stock (57,000 × $1)		57,000
Paid-in Capital in Excess of Par		
($635,000 × 0.95) − $57,000]		546,250
Retained Earnings of Subsidiary ($334,000 × 0.95)		317,300
To record issuance of 57,000 shares of common stock for 38,000 of the 40,000 shares of outstanding common stock of Sage Company in a pooling-type business combination.		
Expenses of Business Combination.	125,000	
Cash		125,000
To record payment of out-of-pocket costs of business combination with Sage Company.		

As pointed out on pages 378 and 380, out-of-pocket costs of a pooling-type business combination expensed for financial accounting are not deductible or amortizable for income tax purposes. Thus, although the second of the foregoing journal entries increases Post Corporation's expenses, its income taxes expense and liability accounts are not adjusted. The costs of the business combination represent a ***permanent difference,*** rather than a ***temporary difference,*** between Post's pre-tax accounting income and taxable income. There is no income tax advantage to a pooling corporation for out-of-pocket costs of the business combination, just as an acquiring

POST CORPORATION AND SAGE COMPANY
Separate Financial Statements (prior to pooling-type business combination)
For Year Ended December 31, Year 1

	Post Corporation	Sage Company
Income Statements		
Net sales	$5,500,000	$1,000,000
Costs and expenses:		
Costs of goods sold................................	$3,850,000	$ 650,000
Operating expenses	925,000	170,000
Interest expense..................................	75,000	40,000
Income taxes expense	260,000	56,000
Total costs and expenses	$5,110,000	$ 916,000
Net income	$ 390,000	$ 84,000
Statements of Retained Earnings		
Retained earnings, beginning of year	$ 810,000	$ 290,000
Add: Net income....................................	390,000	84,000
Subtotals	$1,200,000	$ 374,000
Less: Dividends	150,000	40,000
Retained earnings, end of year......................	$1,050,000	$ 334,000
Balance Sheets		
Assets		
Cash	$ 200,000	$ 100,000
Inventories..	800,000	500,000
Other current assets	550,000	215,000
Plant assets (net)...................................	3,500,000	1,100,000
Goodwill (net)	100,000	
Total assets......................................	$5,150,000	$1,915,000
Liabilities & Stockholders' Equity		
Income taxes payable................................	$ 100,000	$ 16,000
Other liabilities	2,450,000	930,000
Common stock, $1 par	1,000,000	
Common stock, $10 par		400,000
Additional paid-in capital............................	550,000	235,000
Retained earnings	1,050,000	334,000
Total liabilities & stockholders' equity	$5,150,000	$1,915,000

corporation receives no income tax benefits from the amortization of purchased goodwill.

After the foregoing journal entries have been posted in the ledger, Post Corporation's relevant financial statement items have the following balances:

<table>
<tr><td rowspan="9">Balances of financial statement items of issuing company affected by business combination</td></tr>
<tr><td>* Operating expenses ($925,000 + $125,000) ....</td><td>$1,050,000</td></tr>
<tr><td>Net income ($390,000 − $125,000) ....</td><td>265,000</td></tr>
<tr><td>Cash ($200,000 − $125,000) ....</td><td>75,000</td></tr>
<tr><td>Investment in Sage Company common stock........................</td><td>920,550</td></tr>
<tr><td>Common stock ($1,000,000 + $57,000) ....</td><td>1,057,000</td></tr>
<tr><td>Additional paid-in capital ($550,000 + $546,250) ....</td><td>1,096,250</td></tr>
<tr><td>Retained earnings ($1,050,000 − $125,000) ....</td><td>925,000</td></tr>
<tr><td>Retained earnings of subsidiary.....................................</td><td>317,300</td></tr>
</table>

Controlling account for Expenses of Business Combination ledger account.

Working Paper for Consolidated Financial Statements   As stated on page 263 of Chapter 6, efficiency requires the use of a working paper to prepare consolidated financial statements of a parent company and a partially owned subsidiary. The working paper for consolidated financial statements for Post Corporation and subsidiary is on page 396; the working paper eliminations (in journal entry format) are below.

POST CORPORATION AND SUBSIDIARY
Working Paper Eliminations
December 31, Year 1

(a) Common Stock—Sage 400,000
    Additional Paid-in Capital—Sage 235,000
    Retained Earnings—Sage ($290,000 × 0.05) 14,500
    Retained Earnings of Subsidiary—Post................... 317,300
        Investment in Sage Company Common Stock—Post .   920,550
        Dividends Declared—Sage ($40,000 × 0.05)   2,000
        Minority Interest in Net Assets of Subsidiary
          ($46,250 − $2,000)   44,250
    To eliminate intercompany investment and establish minority interest in net assets of subsidiary at **beginning of year** [($400,000 + $235,000 + $290,000) × 0.05 = $46,250], less minority interest in dividends ($40,000 × 0.05 = $2,000).

(b) Minority Interest in Net Income of Subsidiary 4,200
        Minority Interest in Net Assets of Subsidiary.........   4,200
    To establish minority interest in net income of subsidiary for year ended Dec. 31, Year 1 ($84,000 × 0.05 = $4,200).

Partially owned subsidiary on date of pooling-type business combination

POST CORPORATION AND SUBSIDIARY
Working Paper for Consolidated Financial Statements
For Year Ended December 31, Year 1

	Post Corporation	Sage Company	Eliminations increase (decrease)	Consolidated
Income Statement				
Net sales........................	5,500,000	1,000,000		6,500,000
Costs and expenses:				
Cost of goods sold	3,850,000	650,000		4,500,000
Operating expenses	1,050,000	170,000		1,220,000
Interest expense	75,000	40,000		115,000
Income taxes expense.............	260,000	56,000		316,000
Minority interest in net income of sub-				
sidiary			(b) 4,200	4,200
Total costs and expenses	5,235,000	916,000	4,200*	6,155,200
Net income	265,000	84,000	(4,200)	344,800
Statement of Retained Earnings				
Retained earnings, beginning of year...	810,000	290,000	(a) (14,500)	1,085,500
Net income	265,000	84,000	(4,200)	344,800
Subtotal...........................	1,075,000	374,000	(18,700)	1,430,300
Dividends declared	150,000	40,000	(a) (2,000)†	188,000
Retained earnings, end of year	925,000	334,000	(16,700)	1,242,300
Balance Sheet				
Assets				
Cash...............................	75,000	100,000		175,000
Inventories	800,000	500,000		1,300,000
Other current assets................	550,000	215,000		765,000
Investment in Sage Company common				
stock............................	920,550		(a) (920,550)	
Plant assets (net)	3,500,000	1,100,000		4,600,000
Goodwill (net)......................	100,000			100,000
Total assets	5,945,550	1,915,000	(920,550)	6,940,000
Liabilities & Stockholders' Equity				
Income taxes payable	100,000	16,000		116,000
Other liabilities	2,450,000	930,000		3,380,000
Minority interest in net assets of sub-			{ (a) 44,250	48,450
sidiary..............................			{ (b) 4,200	
Common stock, $1 par...............	1,057,000			1,057,000
Common stock, $10 par..............		400,000	(a) (400,000)	
Additional paid-in capital	1,096,250	235,000	(a) (235,000)	1,096,250
Retained earnings...................	925,000	334,000	(16,700)	1,242,300
Retained earnings of subsidiary........	317,300		(a) (317,300)	
Total liabilities & stockholders' equity.	5,945,550	1,915,000	(920,550)	6,940,000

*An **increase** in costs and expenses and a **decrease** in net income.
† A **decrease** in dividends and an **increase** in retained earnings.

The following should be noted in a review of the working paper for consolidated financial statements of Post Corporation and subsidiary under the pooling theory:

1   In elimination *(a)*, the minority stockholders' 5% interest in the subsidiary's beginning-of-year retained earnings balance and dividends declared by the subsidiary prior to the business combination are eliminated, so that these amounts will be excluded from the consolidated statement of retained earnings, under the parent company concept.

2   The $4,200 debit to Minority Interest in Net Income of Subsidiary in elimination *(b)* is entered in the income statement section of the working paper for consolidated financial statements; the $14,500 debit to the Retained Earnings account of Sage Company in elimination *(a)* is entered in the ***beginning-of-year*** line in the statement of retained earnings section of the working paper. All eliminations that affect consolidated statements other than the consolidated balance sheet are entered directly in the appropriate consolidated statements sections.

3   As in the previously illustrated working papers for consolidated financial statements in this chapter, the net income totals of the income statement section are brought forward to the statement of retained earnings section, and the end-of-year retained earnings amounts in the latter section are forwarded to the consolidated balance sheet section.

4   The combined effect of the $14,500 and $4,200 debit items of eliminations *(a)* and *(b)* is to include in end-of-year consolidated retained earnings only Post Corporation's 95% interest in the end-of-year retained earnings of Sage company. Thus, total amount of consolidated retained earnings on December 31, Year 1, is composed of the following:

Composition of consolidated retained earnings at end of year	

Retained earnings of Post Corporation...............................	$ 925,000
95% of retained earnings of Sage Company ($334,000 × 0.95)	317,300
Consolidated retained earnings, end of year..........................	$1,242,300

5   The combined effect of the $44,250 and $4,200 credit items of eliminations *(a)* and *(b)* is to reflect the minority interest in the net assets of the subsidiary on December 31, Year 1 ($48,450), at its correct amount of 5% of Sage Company's total stockholders' equity ($400,000 + $235,000 + $334,000 = $969,000; $969,000 × 0.05 = $48,450) on that date.

Consolidated Financial Statements   The consolidated financial statements for Post Corporation and subsidiary incorporate the amounts in the Consolidated column of the working paper for consolidated financial statements, as shown on pages 398 and 399.

The consolidated financial statements of a parent company and its partially owned subsidiary are similar in format to those for a parent company and its wholly owned subsidiary illustrated on page 385. The principal difference is the display of

POST CORPORATION AND SUBSIDIARY
Consolidated Income Statement
For Year Ended December 31, Year 1

Net sales		$6,500,000
Costs and expenses:		
Cost of goods sold	$4,500,000	
Operating expenses	1,220,000	
Interest expense	115,000	
Income taxes expense	316,000	
Minority interest in net income of subsidiary	4,200	6,155,200
Net income		$ 344,800
Earnings per share of common stock (1,057,000 shares outstanding)		$ 0.33

POST CORPORATION AND SUBSIDIARY
Consolidated Statement of Retained Earnings
For Year Ended December 31, Year 1

Retained earnings, beginning of year, as previously reported		$ 810,000
Add: Adjustment to reflect pooling of interests with Sage Company		275,500
Retained earnings, beginning of year, as restated		$1,085,500
Add: Net income		344,800
Subtotal		$1,430,300
Less: Dividends:		
Post Corporation ($0.15 a share)	$ 150,000	
Sage Company, prior to business combination	38,000	188,000
Retained earnings, end of year		$1,242,300

POST CORPORATION AND SUBSIDIARY
Consolidated Balance Sheet
December 31, Year 1

Assets

Current assets:	
Cash	$ 175,000
Inventories	1,300,000
Other	765,000
Total current assets	$2,240,000
Plant assets (net)	4,600,000
Goodwill (net)	100,000
Total assets	$6,940,000

(continued)

POST CORPORATION AND SUBSIDIARY
Consolidated Balance Sheet (concluded)
December 31, Year 1

Liabilities & Stockholders' Equity

Liabilities:

Income taxes payable...		$ 116,000
Other		3,380,000
Minority interest in net assets of subsidiary........................		48,450
Total liabilities...		$3,544,450

Stockholders' equity:

Common stock, $1 par...............................	$1,057,000	
Additional paid-in capital.............................	1,096,250	
Retained earnings....................................	1,242,300	3,395,550
Total liabilities & stockholders' equity............................		$6,940,000

minority interest in net income of the subsidiary in the consolidated income statement and minority interest in net assets of the subsidiary in the consolidated balance sheet. In addition, the amounts attributable to the subsidiary in the consolidated statement of retained earnings are the **parent company's 95% share only,** as the following computations demonstrate:

Computation of
amounts in
consolidated statement
of retained earnings

Adjustment to beginning-of-year retained earnings to reflect pooling of interests ($290,000 × 0.95)	$275,500
Dividends of subsidiary prior to business combination ($40,000 × 0.95).....	$ 38,000

CONSOLIDATION OF PARTIALLY OWNED POOLED SUBSIDIARY SUBSEQUENT TO DATE OF BUSINESS COMBINATION

The Post Corporation–Sage Company pooling-type business combination example is continued in this section to illustrate the preparation of consolidated financial statements for a parent company and its partially owned pooled subsidiary for the year following the business combination.

Assume that on November 24, Year 2, Sage Company declared a $1 a share dividend, payable December 16, Year 2, to stockholders of record December 1,

Year 2, and that Sage had a net income of $90,000 for the year ended December 31, Year 2. The following journal entries record the dividend in the accounting records of Sage:

<table>
<tr><td rowspan="10">Partially owned subsidiary's journal entries for declaration and payment of dividend</td><td colspan="3">Year 2</td></tr>
<tr><td>Nov. 24</td><td>Dividends Declared (40,000 × $1)......................</td><td>40,000</td><td></td></tr>
<tr><td></td><td>Dividends Payable ($40,000 × 0.05)............</td><td></td><td>2,000</td></tr>
<tr><td></td><td>Intercompany Dividends Payable ($40,000 × 0.95)</td><td></td><td>38,000</td></tr>
<tr><td></td><td>To record declaration of dividend payable Dec. 16, Year 2, to stockholders of record Dec. 1, Year 2.</td><td></td><td></td></tr>
<tr><td>Dec. 16</td><td>Dividends Payable ....</td><td>2,000</td><td></td></tr>
<tr><td></td><td>Intercompany Dividends Payable ....</td><td>38,000</td><td></td></tr>
<tr><td></td><td>Cash ....</td><td></td><td>40,000</td></tr>
<tr><td></td><td>To record payment of dividend declared Nov. 24, Year 2, to stockholders of record Dec. 1, Year 2.</td><td></td><td></td></tr>
</table>

The following journal entries are required in the accounting records of Post under the equity method of accounting.

<table>
<tr><td rowspan="11">Parent company's equity-method journal entries to record operating results of partially owned pooled subsidiary</td><td colspan="3">Year 2</td></tr>
<tr><td>Nov. 24</td><td>Intercompany Dividends Receivable ....</td><td>38,000</td><td></td></tr>
<tr><td></td><td>Investment in Sage Company Common Stock ....</td><td></td><td>38,000</td></tr>
<tr><td></td><td>To record dividend declared by Sage Company, payable Dec. 16, Year 2, to stockholders of record Dec. 1, Year 2.</td><td></td><td></td></tr>
<tr><td>Dec. 16</td><td>Cash ....</td><td>38,000</td><td></td></tr>
<tr><td></td><td>Intercompany Dividends Receivable ....</td><td></td><td>38,000</td></tr>
<tr><td></td><td>To record receipt of dividend from Sage Company.</td><td></td><td></td></tr>
<tr><td>31</td><td>Investment in Sage Company Common Stock ($90,000 × 0.95).....................................</td><td>85,500</td><td></td></tr>
<tr><td></td><td>Intercompany Investment Income................</td><td></td><td>85,500</td></tr>
<tr><td></td><td>To record 95% of net income of Sage Company for year ended Dec. 31, Year 2. (Income tax effects are disregarded.)</td><td></td><td></td></tr>
</table>

After the foregoing journal entries are posted, Post Corporation's Investment in Sage Company Common Stock ledger account is as shown on page 401.

The $968,050 balance of Post Corporation's Investment in Sage Company Common Stock ledger account on December 31, Year 2, is equal to 95% of Sage's total stockholders' equity on that date, as computed on page 401.

Investment ledger account of parent company under equity method of accounting for partially owned pooled subsidiary				

Investment in Sage Company Common Stock

Date	Explanation	Debit	Credit	Balance
Year 1 Dec. 31	Issuance of common stock in business combination			920,550 dr
Year 2 Nov. 24	Dividend declared by Sage		38,000	882,550 dr
Dec. 31	Net income of Sage	85,500		968,050 dr

95% of total stockholders' equity of partially owned pooled subsidiary equals balance of parent company's investment ledger account

Sage Company's stockholders' equity:	
Common stock, $10 par...	$ 400,000
Additional paid-in capital	235,000
Retained earnings...	384,000
Total stockholders' equity of Sage Company	$1,019,000
95% of Sage's stockholders' equity ($1,019,000 × 0.95)..............	$ 968,050

Thus, the Investment in Sage Company Common Stock account reflects Post's 95% equity in the net assets of Sage at Sage's carrying amount.

Working Paper for Consolidated Financial Statements The working paper for consolidated financial statements for Post Corporation and subsidiary for the year ended December 31, Year 2, is on page 403; the working paper eliminations (in journal entry format) are below and on page 402.

Working paper eliminations for partially owned pooled subsidiary for first year subsequent to business combination

POST CORPORATION AND SUBSIDIARY
Working Paper Eliminations
December 31, Year 2

(a) Common Stock—Sage	400,000	
Additional Paid-in Capital—Sage	235,000	
Retained Earnings—Sage ($334,000 × 0.05)..............	16,700	
Retained Earnings of Subsidiary—Post....................	317,300	
Intercompany Investment Income—Post..................	85,500	
Investment in Sage Company Common Stock—Post .		968,050
Dividends Declared—Sage		40,000
Minority Interest in Net Assets of Subsidiary ($48,450 − $2,000)		46,450

To eliminate intercompany investment and related accounts for stockholders' equity of subsidiary at **beginning of year,** and investment income from subsidiary; and to establish minority interest in net assets of subsidiary at beginning of year ($48,450) less minority dividends ($40,000 × 0.05 = $2,000).

(continued)

> **POST CORPORATION AND SUBSIDIARY**
> **Working Paper Eliminations** (concluded)
> **December 31, Year 2**
>
> *(b) Minority Interest in Net Income of Subsidiary 4,500*
> *   Minority Interest in Net Assets of Subsidiary 4,500*
> *   To establish minority interest in net income of subsidiary for*
> *   year ended Dec. 31, Year 2 ($90,000 × 0.05 = $4,500).*

The following aspects of the working paper for consolidated financial statements for Post Corporation and subsidiary are worthy of emphasis:

1   *Consolidated net income is the same as the parent company's net income.* Also, the amount of consolidated retained earnings is equal to the total of the parent company's two retained earnings amounts in the working paper, as follows:

Total of parent company's two retained earnings amounts equals consolidated retained earnings

> *Post Corporation's retained earnings amounts:*
> *   Retained earnings . . . .* $1,271,950
> *   Retained earnings of subsidiary . . . .*   317,300
> *   Total (equal to consolidated retained earnings) . . . .* $1,589,250

2   The combined effect of the $46,450 and $4,500 credit amounts in eliminations *(a)* and *(b)* is to present the minority interest in net assets of subsidiary on December 31, Year 2, at the correct amount of 5% of Sage Company's total stockholders' equity on that date ($400,000 + $235,000 + $384,000 = $1,019,000; $1,019,000 × 0.05 = $50,950).

Consolidated Financial Statements   The consolidated financial statements of Post Corporation and subsidiary on page 404 are prepared from the Consolidated column of the working paper for consolidated financial statements on page 403.

Equity method: Partially owned subsidiary subsequent to date of pooling-type business combination

POST CORPORATION AND SUBSIDIARY
Working Paper for Consolidated Financial Statements
For Year Ended December 31, Year 2

	Post Corporation	Sage Company	Eliminations increase (decrease)	Consolidated
Income Statement				
Revenue:				
Net sales	5,611,000	1,089,000		6,700,000
Intercompany investment income	85,500		(a) (85,500)	
Total revenue	5,696,500	1,089,000	(85,500)	6,700,000
Costs and expenses:				
Cost of goods sold.	3,925,000	700,000		4,625,000
Operating expenses	556,000	129,000		685,000
Interest and income taxes expense.	710,000	170,000		880,000
Minority interest in net income of sub-				
sidiary			(b) 4,500	4,500
Total costs and expenses	5,191,000	999,000	4,500*	6,194,500
Net income	505,500	90,000	(90,000)	505,500
Statement of Retained Earnings				
Retained earnings, beginning of year	925,000	334,000	(a) (16,700)	1,242,300
Net income	505,500	90,000	(90,000)	505,500
Subtotal	1,430,500	424,000	(106,700)	1,747,800
Dividends declared	158,550	40,000	(a) (40,000)†	158,550
Retained earnings, end of year.	1,271,950	384,000	(66,700)	1,589,250
Balance Sheet				
Assets				
Investment in Sage Company common				
stock.	968,050		(a) (968,050)	
Other assets	5,195,000	1,960,000		7,155,000
Total assets.	6,163,050	1,960,000	(968,050)	7,155,000
Liabilities & Stockholders' Equity				
Liabilities	2,420,550	941,000		3,361,550
Minority interest in net assets of subsidiary			(a) 46,450 / (b) 4,500	50,950
Common stock, $1 par	1,057,000			1,057,000
Common stock, $10 par		400,000	(a) (400,000)	
Additional paid-in capital	1,096,250	235,000	(a) (235,000)	1,096,250
Retained earnings	1,271,950	384,000	(66,700)	1,589,250
Retained earnings of subsidiary	317,300		(a) (317,300)	
Total liabilities & stockholders' equity . . .	6,163,050	1,960,000	(968,050)	7,155,000

*An **increase** in costs and expenses and a **decrease** in net income.
† A **decrease** in dividends and an **increase** in retained earnings.

POST CORPORATION AND SUBSIDIARY
Consolidated Income Statement
For Year Ended December 31, Year 2

Net sales		$6,700,000
Costs and expenses:		
Cost of goods sold	$4,625,000	
Operating expenses	685,000	
Interest and income taxes expense	880,000	
Minority interest in net income of subsidiary	4,500	6,194,500
Net income		$ 505,500
Earnings per share of common stock (1,057,000 shares outstanding) . . .		$ 0.48

POST CORPORATION AND SUBSIDIARY
Consolidated Statement of Retained Earnings
For Year Ended December 31, Year 2

Retained earnings, beginning of year	$1,242,300
Add: Net income	505,500
Subtotal	$1,747,800
Less: Dividends ($0.15 a share)	158,550
Retained earnings, end of year	$1,589,250

POST CORPORATION AND SUBSIDIARY
Consolidated Balance Sheet
December 31, Year 2

Assets

Other assets	$7,155,000

Liabilities & Stockholders' Equity

Liabilities:		
Other liabilities		$3,361,550
Minority interest in net assets of subsidiary		50,950
Total liabilities		$3,412,500
Stockholders' equity:		
Common stock, $1 par	$1,057,000	
Additional paid-in capital	1,096,250	
Retained earnings	1,589,250	3,742,500
Total liabilities & stockholders' equity		$7,155,000

Closing Entries Post Corporation prepares the closing entries on page 405 on December 31, Year 2, after the consolidated financial statements have been completed.

After the posting of the foregoing closing entries, Post's Retained Earnings and Retained Earnings of Subsidiary ledger accounts are as illustrated on page 405.

The $364,800 after-closing balance of Post's Retained Earnings of Subsidiary ledger account equals 95% of the after-closing balance of Sage's Retained Earnings

Parent company's closing entries under equity method of accounting for pooled subsidiary

Net Sales	5,611,000	
Intercompany Investment Income	85,500	
Income Summary		5,696,500
To close revenue accounts.		
Income Summary	5,191,000	
Cost of Goods Sold		3,925,000
Operating Expenses		556,000
Interest and Income Taxes Expense		710,000
To close expense accounts.		
Income Summary	505,500	
Retained Earnings of Subsidiary		
[($90,000 − $40,000) × 0.95]		47,500
Retained Earnings ($505,500 − $47,500)		458,000
To close Income Summary account; to transfer net income legally available for dividends to retained earnings; and to segregate 95% share of net income of subsidiary not distributed as dividends by subsidiary.		
Retained Earnings	158,550	
Dividends Declared		158,550
To close Dividends Declared account.		

Parent company's ledger accounts for retained earnings

Retained Earnings

Date	Explanation	Debit	Credit	Balance
Year 1				
Dec. 31	Balance			925,000 cr
Year 2				
Dec. 31	Close net income available for dividends		458,000	1,383,000 cr
31	Close Dividends Declared account	158,550		1,224,450 cr

Retained Earnings of Subsidiary

Date	Explanation	Debit	Credit	Balance
Year 1				
Dec. 31	Pooling-type business combination		317,300	317,300 cr
Year 2				
Dec. 31	Close net income not available for dividends		47,500	364,800 cr

ledger account ($384,000 × 0.95 = $364,800). In addition, the $1,589,250 total ($1,224,450 + $364,800 = $1,589,250) of Post's two ledger accounts for retained earnings is equal to consolidated retained earnings of Post Corporation and subsidiary on December 31, Year 2.

In the December 31, Year 3, working paper eliminations for Post Corporation and Subsidiary, the December 31, Year 2, balance of Post's Retained Earnings of Subsidiary ledger account would be eliminated. For example, if Sage Company declared dividends of $50,000 ($47,500 to Post and $2,500 to minority stockholders) and had a net income of $105,000 ($99,750 to Post and $5,250 to minority stockholders) for the year ended December 31, Year 3, the working paper eliminations (in journal entry format) for Post Corporation and subsidiary on that date would be as follows:

Working paper eliminations for partially owned pooled subsidiary for second year subsequent to business combination

POST CORPORATION AND SUBSIDIARY
Working Paper Eliminations
December 31, Year 3

(a) Common Stock—Sage 400,000
    Additional Paid-in Capital—Sage 235,000
    Retained Earnings—Sage ($384,000 × 0.05) 19,200
    Retained Earnings of Subsidiary—Post................. 364,800
    Intercompany Investment Income—Post................ 99,750
        Investment in Sage Company Common Stock—
        Post ($968,050 + $99,750 − $47,500) 1,020,300
        Dividends Declared—Sage 50,000
        Minority Interest in Net Assets of Subsidiary
        ($50,950 − $2,500)............................ 48,450
    To eliminate intercompany investment and related accounts for stockholders' equity of subsidiary at **beginning of year,** and investment income from subsidiary; and to establish minority interest in net assets of subsidiary at beginning of year ($50,950) less minority dividends ($2,500).

(b) Minority Interest in Net Income of Subsidiary 5,250
        Minority Interest in Net Assets of Subsidiary........ 5,250
    To establish minority interest in net income of subsidiary for year ended Dec. 31, Year 3.

ACCOUNTING FOR INTERCOMPANY TRANSACTIONS NOT INVOLVING PROFIT (GAIN) OR LOSS

Subsequent to the date of a business combination, a parent company and its subsidiaries may enter into a number of business transactions with each other. Both the parent and the subsidiary companies should account for these intercompany transactions in a manner that facilitates the consolidation process. To this end, *separate ledger accounts should be established for all intercompany assets, liabilities, revenue, and expenses.* These separate accounts clearly identify the intercompany items that must be eliminated in the preparation of consolidated financial statements. The accounting techniques described above are designed to assure that consolidated financial statements include only those balances and transactions resulting from the *consolidated group's dealings with outsiders.*

Among the types of business transactions (other than dividends) consummated between a parent company and its subsidiaries are the following:

Sales of merchandise

Sales of land or depreciable plant assets

Sales of intangible assets

Leases of property under sales-type/capital leases

Loans on promissory notes or open account

Leases of property under operating leases

Rendering of services

The first four types of transactions listed above usually involve an element of profit (gain) or loss, which complicates the preparation of consolidated financial statements. Discussion of these intercompany transactions is in Chapter 9.

Loans on Notes or Open Account

Parent companies generally have more extensive financial resources or bank lines of credit than do their subsidiaries. Also, it may be more economical in terms of favorable interest rates for the parent company to carry out all the affiliated group's borrowings from financial institutions. Under these circumstances, the parent company may make loans to its subsidiaries for their working capital or other needs. Generally, the rate of interest on such loans exceeds the parent company's borrowing rate.

To illustrate, assume that during the year ended December 31, Year 3, Palm Corporation made the following cash loans to its wholly owned subsidiary, Starr Company, on promissory notes:

Loans by parent company to wholly owned subsidiary

Date of note	Term of note, months	Interest rate, %	Amount
Feb. 1, Year 3	6	10	$10,000
Apr. 1, Year 3	6	10	15,000
Sept. 1, Year 3	6	10	21,000
Nov. 1, Year 3	6	10	24,000

To differentiate properly between intercompany loans and loans with outsiders, Palm Corporation and Starr Company would use the following ledger accounts to record the foregoing transactions (assuming all promissory notes were paid when due):

Ledger accounts of parent company and subsidiary for intercompany loan transactions

PALM CORPORATION LEDGER				STARR COMPANY LEDGER			
Intercompany Notes Receivable				**Intercompany Notes Payable**			
Feb. 1	10,000	Aug. 1	10,000	Aug. 1	10,000	Feb. 1	10,000
Apr. 1	15,000	Oct. 1	15,000	Oct. 1	15,000	Apr. 1	15,000
Sept. 1	21,000					Sept. 1	21,000
Nov. 1	24,000					Nov. 1	24,000

Intercompany Interest Receivable				**Intercompany Interest Payable**			
Dec. 31	1,100					Dec. 31	1,100

Intercompany Interest Revenue				**Intercompany Interest Expense**			
		Aug. 1	500	Aug. 1	500		
		Oct. 1	750	Oct. 1	750		
		Dec. 31	1,100	Dec. 31	1,100		

In the working paper for consolidated financial statements for Palm Corporation and subsidiary for the year ended December 31, Year 3, the foregoing ledger accounts appear as shown below:

PALM CORPORATION AND SUBSIDIARY
Partial Working Paper for Consolidated Financial Statements
For Year Ended December 31, Year 3

	Palm Corporation	Starr Company	Eliminations increase (decrease)	Consolidated
Income Statement				
Intercompany revenue (expenses)........	2,350	(2,350)		
Balance Sheet				
Intercompany receivables (payables)	46,100*	(46,100)		

* $45,000 + $1,100 = $46,100

It is apparent from the above illustration that careful identification of intercompany ledger account balances in the accounting records of the affiliated companies is essential for correct elimination of the intercompany items in the working paper for consolidated financial statements.

Discounting of Intercompany Notes If an intercompany note receivable is discounted at a bank by the payee, the note in effect is payable to an *outsider* — the discounting bank. Consequently, discounted intercompany notes are *not eliminated* in a working paper for consolidated financial statements.

Suppose, for example, that on December 1, Year 3, Palm Corporation had discounted at a 12% discount rate the $24,000 note receivable from Starr Company. Palm would prepare the following journal entry:

<table>
<tr><td rowspan="6" style="text-align:right">Parent company's
journal entry for
discounting of note
receivable from
subsidiary</td><td>Cash ($25,200 − $1,260) . . . .</td><td>23,940</td><td></td></tr>
<tr><td>Interest Expense ($1,260 discount − $1,000*) . . . .</td><td>260</td><td></td></tr>
<tr><td>   Intercompany Notes Receivable . . . .</td><td></td><td>24,000</td></tr>
<tr><td>   Intercompany Interest Revenue ($24,000 × 0.10 × 1/12) . . .</td><td></td><td>200</td></tr>
<tr><td colspan="3">To record discounting of 10%, six-month note receivable from
Starr Company dated Nov. 1, Year 3, at a discount rate of 12%.
Cash proceeds are computed as follows:</td></tr>
<tr><td colspan="3">
Maturity value of note
  [$24,000 + ($24,000 × 0.10 × 6/12)] $25,200
  Less: Discount ($25,200 × 0.12 × 5/12).   1,260
  Proceeds $23,940

* Interest on note that accrues to discounting bank during discount period
</td></tr>
</table>

The foregoing journal entry recognizes intercompany interest revenue for the one month the note was held by Palm. This approach is required because Starr recognizes in its accounting records one month of intercompany interest expense on the note.

To assure proper accountability for the $24,000 note, Palm should notify Starr of the discounting. Starr would then prepare the following journal entry on December 1, Year 3:

<table>
<tr><td rowspan="5" style="text-align:right">Subsidiary journal entry
for parent company's
discounting of note
payable by subsidiary
to parent company</td><td>Intercompany Notes Payable . . . .</td><td>24,000</td><td></td></tr>
<tr><td>Intercompany Interest Expense . . . .</td><td>200</td><td></td></tr>
<tr><td>   Notes Payable . . . .</td><td></td><td>24,000</td></tr>
<tr><td>   Interest Payable . . . .</td><td></td><td>200</td></tr>
<tr><td colspan="3">To transfer 10%, six-month note payable to Palm Corporation dated
Nov. 1, Year 3, from intercompany notes to outsider notes. Action is
necessary because Palm Corporation discounted the note on this
date.</td></tr>
</table>

In the foregoing journal entry, Starr credited Interest Payable rather than Intercompany Interest Payable for the $200 accrued interest on the note. This approach is required because the discounting bank, not Palm, is now the payee for the total maturity value of the note.

Under the note discounting assumption, the ledger accounts related to intercompany notes would appear in the December 31, Year 3, working paper for consolidated financial statements as follows:

PALM CORPORATION AND SUBSIDIARY
Partial Working Paper for Consolidated Financial Statements
For Year Ended December 31, Year 3

	Palm Corporation	Starr Company	Eliminations increase (decrease)	Consolidated
Income Statement				
Intercompany revenue (expenses)........	2,150*	(2,150)*		
Balance Sheet				
Intercompany receivables (payables)	21,700†	(21,700)†		

* $200 less than in illustration on page 408 because $24,000 discounted note earned interest for one month rather than two months.
† $21,000 note dated Sept. 1, Year 3, plus $700 accrued interest.

Leases of Property under Operating Leases

If a parent company leases property to a subsidiary, or vice versa, it is essential that both affiliates use the same accounting principles for the lease. If the lease is an *operating lease,* the lessor affiliate recognizes the rental payments as intercompany rent revenue, and the lessee affiliate recognizes the payments as intercompany rent expense. (For a *sales-type/capital lease,*[2] the lessor affiliate recognizes a sale of the property, and the lessee affiliate accounts for the lease as an acquisition of the property. Accounting for a capital lease offen involves intercompany profits or losses,which are discussed in Chapter 9.)

To illustrate consolidation techniques for an intercompany *operating lease,* assume that Palm Corporation leased space for a sales office to Starr Company under a 10-year lease dated February 1, Year 3. The lease required monthly rentals of $2,500 payable in advance the first day of each month beginning February 1, Year 3.

In the income statement section of the working paper for consolidated financial statements for the year ended December 31, Year 3, Palm's $27,500 intercompany rent revenue would be offset against Starr's intercompany rent expense in a manner similar to the offset of intercompany interest revenue and expense illustrated above. There would be no intercompany assets or liabilities to be offset in an operating lease for which rent is paid in advance at the beginning of each month.

Rendering of Services

One affiliate may render services to another, with resultant intercompany fee revenue and expenses. A common example is the *management fee* charged to subsidiaries by a parent company that is a holding company with no significant operations.

---

[2] The accounting for operating leases and capital leases is explained in intermediate accounting textbooks.

Management fees often are billed monthly by the parent company, computed as a percentage of the subsidiary's net sales, number of employees, total assets, or some other measure. No new consolidation problems are introduced by intercompany fee revenue and expenses. However, care must be taken to make certain that both the parent company and the subsidiary record the fee billings in the same accounting period.

Income Taxes Applicable to Intercompany Transactions

The intercompany revenue and expense transactions illustrated in this chapter do not include an element of intercompany profit (gain) or loss for the consolidated entity. This is true because the revenue of one affiliate exactly offsets the expense of the other affiliate in the income statement section of the working paper for consolidated financial statements. Consequently, there are no income tax effects associated with the elimination of the intercompany revenue and expenses, whether the parent company and its subsidiaries file separate income tax returns or a consolidated income tax return.

Summary: Intercompany Transactions and Balances

The preceding sections have emphasized the necessity of clearly identifying intercompany ledger account balances in the accounting records of both the parent company and the subsidiary. This careful identification facilitates the elimination of intercompany items in the preparation of consolidated financial statements. Sometimes, the separate financial statements of a parent company and a subsidiary include differing amounts for intercompany items that should offset. Before preparation of the working paper for consolidated financial statements, journal entries should be prepared to correct intercompany balances or to bring such balances up to date.

REVIEW QUESTIONS

1   Depending on circumstances, a business combination may be accounted for as a purchase or as a pooling of interests. Discuss the differences between (1) a consolidated balance sheet prepared on the date of a purchase-type business combination and (2) a consolidated balance sheet prepared on the date of a pooling-type business combination.

2   For the year ended October 31, Year 2, Staley Company had a net income of $60,000. On that date, Pryor Corporation acquired most of the outstanding common stock of Staley Company in exchange for Pryor's unissued common stock. The working paper eliminations (in journal entry format) for Pryor Corporation and subsidiary for the year ended October 31, Year 2, included the following (explanation omitted):

Minority Interest in Net Income of Subsidiary	1,200	
Minority Interest in Net Assets of Subsidiary.................		1,200

a Was the business combination of Pryor Corporation and Staley Company accounted for as a purchase or as a pooling of interests? Explain.

b What percentage of Staley's outstanding common stock was exchanged for Pryor's common stock? Explain.

3   The retained earnings balances of Pelham Corporation and Skeene Company on September 30, Year 5, were $2,000,000 and $800,000, respectively. At the close of business that date, Skeene became a subsidiary of Pelham when Pelham acquired 95% of Skeene's outstanding common stock.

What is the amount of consolidated retained earnings in the consolidated balance sheet of Pelham Corporation and subsidiary on September 30, Year 5, if the business combination is accounted for as:

a A purchase? Explain.
b A pooling of interests? Explain.

4   Explain the purpose of the parent company's Retained Earnings of Subsidiary ledger account used for a pooled subsidiary.

5   Why is the equity method of accounting for a subsidiary's operating results consistent with the pooling-of-interests theory of accounting for a business combination?

6   Describe a special feature of the closing entries for a parent company that uses the equity method of accounting for the operating results of a pooled subsidiary.

7   How does the balance of a parent company's Retained Earnings of Subsidiary ledger account for a pooled subsidiary differ from the balance of the same account for a purchased subsidiary?

8   How should a parent company and subsidiary account for intercompany transactions and balances to assure their correct elimination in the preparation of consolidated financial statements? Explain.

9   What are five common intercompany transactions between a parent company and its subsidiary?

10 Primak Corporation rents a sales office to its wholly owned subsidiary under an operating lease requiring rent of $2,000 a month, payable the first day of the month. What are the income tax effects of the elimination of Primak's $24,000 rent revenue and the subsidiary's $24,000 rent expense in the preparation of a consolidated income statement? Explain.

11 Is an intercompany note receivable that has been discounted by a bank eliminated in the preparation of a consolidated balance sheet? Explain.

EXERCISES

Ex. 8-1   Select the best answer for each of the following multiple-choice questions:
1   In the journal entry to record a pooling-type business combination with a wholly owned subsidiary, a parent company debits its Investment in Subsidiary Common Stock account in the amount of the:
a Total stockholder's equity of the subsidiary
b Current fair value of the par value common stock issued by the parent
c Stated value of the no-par value common stock issued by the parent
d Current fair value of the subsidiary's identifiable net assets

2   Does the working paper elimination (in journal entry format) on the date of the pooling-type business combination of Paul Corporation and its wholly-owned subsidiary, Saul Company, include a debit to:

	Retained Earnings—Saul?	Retained Earnings of Subsidiary—Paul?
a	Yes	Yes
b	Yes	No
c	No	Yes
d	No	No

3 The caption "Adjustment to reflect pooling of interests with subsidiary" is displayed in a consolidated:
a Income statement
b Statement of retained earnings
c Balance sheet
d Statement of cash flows

4 The fact that a pooling-of-interests business combination occurred during an accounting period is evidenced by appropriate disclosure in that period's consolidated:
a Income statement
b Statement of retained earnings
c Balance sheet
d Income statement, statement of retained earnings, and balance sheet

5 Consolidated retained earnings at the end of an accounting period for a parent company and its pooled subsidiary may be verified by reference to the working paper for consolidated financial statement amount or amounts for the:
a Parent company's retained earnings plus its retained earnings of subsidiary
b Parent company's retained earnings only
c Parent company's retained earnings plus the subsidiary's retained earnings
d Parent company's retained earnings plus its retained earnings of subsidiary plus the subsidiary's retained earnings

6 Does a parent company having a wholly owned pooled subsidiary prepare a journal entry to its Retained Earnings of Subsidiary ledger account:

	To record the business combination?	In an end-of-period closing entry?
a	Yes	Yes
b	Yes	No
c	No	Yes
d	No	No

7 Does the working paper elimination to eliminate a parent company's investment in a profitable, wholly owned pooled subsidiary include a debit to Intercompany Investment Income if the consolidated financial statements are prepared:

	On the date of the business combination?	Subsequent to the date of the business combination?
a	Yes	Yes
b	No	No
c	Yes	No
d	No	Yes

8   In a pooling-type business combination with a 96%-owned subsidiary having total paid-in capital of $100,000 and retained earnings of $200,000, the parent company issued 120,000 shares of $1 par common stock; prior to the combination, the parent had total paid-in capital of $600,000 attributable to 200,000 shares of outstanding common stock. In its journal entry to record the business combination, the parent company:

a Debits Paid-in Capital in Excess of Par, $20,000
b Debits Paid-in Capital in Excess of Par, $24,000
c Credits Paid-in Capital in Excess of Par, $240,000
d Credits Retained Earnings, $200,000

9   In the working paper elimination (in journal entry format) on the date of a pooling-type business combination involving a partially owned subsidiary, is there a debit to the:

	Parent's Retained Earnings of Subsidiary account?	Subsidiary's Retained Earnings account?
a	Yes	No
b	No	Yes
c	No	No
d	Yes	Yes

10   In a consolidated balance sheet prepared on the date of a pooling-type business combination involving a parent company and its partially owned subsidiary, consolidated retained earnings includes:

a The parent company's retained earnings only
b Both the parent company's and the subsidiary's retained earnings
c The parent company's retained earnings plus the parent's share of the subsidiary's retained earnings
d The parent company's retained earnings plus the subsidiary's retained earnings minus the minority interest in net assets of subsidiary

11   On May 26, Year 7, Pewter Corporation loaned $100,000 to its 80%-owned subsidiary, Selas Company, on a 90-day, 16% note. On June 25, Year 7, Pewter discounted the note at a bank discount rate of 18%. In the journal entry to record the discounting, Pewter debits Cash in the amount of:

a $ 97,000
b $ 98,500
c $100,880
d $102,440
e Some other amount

12   Does a subsidiary's journal entry to record the parent company's discounting of a promissory note receivable from the subsidiary at the bank generally include a:

	Debit to Intercompany Interest Expense?	Credit to Intercompany Interest Payable?
a	Yes	Yes
b	Yes	No
c	No	Yes
d	No	No

13 Which of the following statements is correct with respect to an intercompany operating lease, with the parent company as lessor?

a The subsidiary may capitalize the present value of the minimum lease payments.

b There are no income tax effects associated with the relevant eliminations.

c An intercompany profit element must be eliminated.

d The parent company debits Intercompany Rent Expense for the rental payments.

Ex. 8-2 On November 1, Year 4, Pollitt Corporation issued 10,000 shares of its $10 par ($30 current fair value) common stock for 99 of the 100 outstanding shares of Simon Company's $100 par common stock, in a pooling-type business combination. Out-of-pocket costs of the business combination were as follows:

Legal and accounting fees and finder's fee associated with business combination	$15,000
Costs incurred for SEC registration statement for Pollitt's common stock	20,000
Total out-of-pocket costs of business combination	$35,000

On November 1, Year 4, Simon Company's stockholders' equity was as follows:

Common stock, $100 par	$ 10,000
Additional paid-in capital	140,000
Retained earnings...	70,000
Total stockholders' equity	$220,000

Prepare journal entries for Pollitt Corporation on November 1, Year 4, to record the business combination with Simon Company.

Ex. 8-3 The separate January 2, Year 3, balance sheets of two companies prior to their business combination follow:

POULT CORPORATION AND SAKI COMPANY
Separate Balance Sheets (prior to business combination)
January 2, Year 3

	Poult Corporation	Saki Company
	('000 omitted)	
Assets		
Cash..	$ 6,000	$ 200
Inventories..	4,000	400
Plant assets (net)...	10,000	1,400
Total assets...	$20,000	$2,000
Liabilities & Stockholders' Equity		
Current liabilities...	$ 1,200	$ 200
Common stock, $1 par.....................................	2,000	200
Additional paid-in capital	6,000	400
Retained earnings	10,800	1,200
Total liabilities & stockholders' equity	$20,000	$2,000

On January 2, Year 3, Poult Corporation acquired all the outstanding common stock of Saki Company by issuing 200,000 shares of common stock (current fair value $20 a share) in a pooling-type business combination.

Prepare a working paper to compute the amount of consolidated additional paid-in capital in the January 2, Year 3, consolidated balance sheet of Poult Corporation and subsidiary.

Ex. 8-4   On May 31, Year 6, Pone Corporation issued 10,000 shares of its $10 par common stock ($25 current fair value per share) for all 1,000 outstanding shares of Scone Company's $1 par common stock in a pooling-type business combination. Pone also paid out-of-pocket costs of the combination totaling $25,000 on May 31, Year 6. On that date, Scone's stockholders' equity consisted of common stock, $1,000; additional paid-in capital, $189,000; and retained earnings, $30,000.

Prepare journal entries for Pone Corporation on May 31, Year 6 (omit explanations), and a working paper elimination (in journal entry format) for Pone Corporation and subsidiary on May 31, Year 6 (omit explanation).

Ex. 8-5   On February 28, Year 4, the stockholders' equity sections of P Corporation's and S Company's separate balance sheets prior to their business combination were as follows:

P CORPORATION AND SUBSIDIARY
Stockholders' Equity Sections of Balance Sheets (prior to business combination)
February 28, Year 4

	P Corporation	S Company
Common stock, $1 par	$100,000	$ 50,000
Additional paid-in capital	50,000	30,000
Retained earnings	90,000	80,000
Total stockholders' equity	$240,000	$160,000

On February 28, Year 4, P Corporation issued 60,000 shares of its common stock for all the outstanding common stock of S Company in a pooling-type business combination in which S became a subsidiary of P. Also on that date, P paid the following out-of-pocket costs for the combination:

Legal and accounting fees and finder's fee	$15,000
Costs of registering and issuing common stock	10,000
Total out-of-pocket costs	$25,000

a Prepare journal entries (omit explanations) for P Corporation on February 28, Year 4, to record the business combination with S Company.

b Prepare a working paper elimination (in journal entry format, explanation omitted) for consolidated financial statements of P Corporation and subsidiary on February 28, Year 4.

Ex. 8-6 The working paper elimination (explanation omitted) on the date of the Pistil Corporation–Stamen Company pooling-type business combination was as follows:

PISTIL CORPORATION AND SUBSIDIARY
Working Paper Elimination
January 31, Year 9

Common stock, no par or stated value—Stamen..............	100,000	
Retained Earnings of Subsidiary—Pistil......................	300,000	
Investment in Stamen Company Common Stock—Pistil ..		400,000

For the year ended January 31, Year 10, Stamen had a net income of $40,000, and on that date it declared a dividend of $30,000, to be paid February 28, Year 10.

a Prepare journal entries (omit explanations) for Pistil Corporation on January 31, Year 10, to record the operations of Stamen Company under the equity method of accounting. (Disregard income taxes.)

b Prepare a working paper elimination, in journal entry format (omit explanation), for Pistil Corporation and subsidiary on January 31, Year 10.

Ex. 8-7 Saticoy Company, the wholly owned pooled subsidiary of Porterville Corporation, had a net income of $80,000 and declared dividends of $20,000 for the year ended December 31, Year 6. Porterville had total revenue of $2,000,000, exclusive of intercompany investment income, and total costs and expenses of $1,200,000 for the year ended December 31, Year 6. Porterville declared dividends of $180,000 during Year 6.

Prepare Porterville Corporation's closing entries on December 31, Year 6.

Ex. 8-8 On February 28, Year 8, Prone Corporation entered into a pooling-type business combination with Supine Company by issuing 100,000 shares of $1 par common stock for 9,800 shares of Supine's 10,000 outstanding shares of no-par, no-stated-value common stock and paying $50,000 out-of-pocket costs. On the date of the combination, Supine's stockholders' equity was as follows:

Common stock, no par or stated value.................................	$200,000
Retained earnings..	300,000
Total stockholders' equity	$500,000

a Prepare journal entries for Prone Corporation on February 28, Year 8, for the business combination with Supine Company. Omit explanations.

b Prepare working paper eliminations (in journal entry format) for Prone Corporation and subsidiary on February 28, Year 8, assuming Supine had a net income of $50,000, but declared no dividends, for the year ended February 28, Year 8. Omit explanations.

Ex. 8-9 The working paper eliminations (in journal entry format) for Pillar Corporation and its 99%-owned pooled subsidiary on March 31, Year 2, the date of the business combination, are on page 418. Prior to the business combination with Pillar, Scanlon had declared and paid dividends of $30,000 during the year ended March 31, Year 2.

PILLAR CORPORATION AND SUBSIDIARY
Working Paper Eliminations
March 31, Year 2

(a) Common Stock—Scanlon.................................   200,000
    Additional Paid-in Capital—Scanlon......................   300,000
    Retained Earnings of Subsidiary—Pillar..................   396,000
    Retained Earnings—Scanlon............................   3,500
      Investment in Scanlon Company Common Stock—
        Pillar...   891,000
      Dividends Declared—Scanlon......................   300
      Minority Interest in Net Assets of Subsidiary..........   8,200
    To eliminate intercompany investment and establish minority
    interest in net assets of subsidiary at beginning of year, less
    minority dividends.

(b) Minority Interest in Net Income of Subsidiary   800
      Minority Interest in Net Assets of Subsidiary..........   800
    To establish minority interest in net income of subsidiary for
    year ended March 31, Year 2.

Prepare a separate statement of retained earnings for Scanlon Company for the year ended March 31, Year 2, prior to the business combination with Pillar Corporation.

Ex. 8-10   Shown below is the statement of retained earnings section of the working paper for consolidated financial statements for Panda Corporation and subsidiary for the year ended March 31, Year 7, the date that Panda exchanged 10,000 shares of its common stock for 92% of the outstanding common stock of Silas Company in a pooling-type business combination.

	Panda Corporation	Silas Company	Eliminations increase (decrease)	Consolidated
Retained earnings, beginning of year........	100,000	50,000	(a) (4,000)	146,000
Net income ..	60,000	40,000	(3,200)	96,800
Subtotals ..	160,000	90,000	(7,200)	242,800
Dividends declared	20,000			20,000
Retained earnings, end of year..	140,000	90,000	(7,200)	222,800

Prior to the business combination, Panda had 100,000 shares of common stock outstanding for many years.

Prepare a consolidated statement of retained earnings for Panda Corporation and subsidiary for the year ended March 31, Year 7.

Ex. 8-11   The working paper elimination for Perdio Corporation and subsidiary on September 30, Year 7 (in journal entry format), is shown below. On that date, Perdio Corporation had combined with Sergio Company in a purchase-type business combination. Sergio's net income for the year ended September 30, Year 7, was $10,000, and Sergio had neither declared nor paid dividends during that year. There were no intercompany transactions between the two companies prior to the business combination.

PERDIO CORPORATION AND SUBSIDIARY
Working Paper Elimination
September 30, Year 7

(a) Common Stock—Sergio	50,000	
Additional Paid-in Capital—Sergio	60,000	
Retained Earnings—Sergio	70,000	
Inventories—Sergio	20,000	
Plant Assets (net)—Sergio	40,000	
Goodwill—Perdio	18,000	
Investment in Sergio Company Common Stock—		
Perdio		234,000
Minority Interest in Net Assets of Subsidiary.		24,000

To eliminate intercompany investment and equity accounts of subsidiary on date of business combination; to allocate excess of cost over carrying amounts of identifiable assets acquired, with remainder to goodwill; and to establish minority interest in net assets of subsidiary on date of business combination ($240,000 × 0.10 = $24,000). (Income tax effects are disregarded.)

Prepare working paper eliminations (in journal entry format) for Perdio Corporation and subsidiary under the assumption that the business combination of Perdio and Sergio Company had been accounted for as a pooling rather than as a purchase.

Ex. 8-12   Pender Corporation uses the equity method of accounting for the operating results of its 97%-owned pooled subsidiary, Sebo Company. For Year 6, Pender had net sales of $2,000,000 and total costs and expenses of $1,700,000. Sebo had a net income of $150,000 and declared dividends of $70,000.

Prepare Pender Corporation's journal entries under the equity method of accounting to record its share of Sebo Company's dividends and net income for Year 6. (Disregard income taxes.)

Ex. 8-13   During the year ended October 31, Year 5, Strickland Company, 96%-owned pooled subsidiary of Prykop Corporation, had a net income of $50,000 and declared dividends of $20,000 on October 20, Year 5, payable November 10, Year 5, to stockholders of record October 31, Year 5.

a Prepare journal entries for Prykop Corporation under the equity method of accounting to record Strickland Company's operating results and dividend declaration for the year ended October 31, Year 5. (Disregard income taxes.)

b Prepare the working paper elimination (in journal entry format) for the minority interest in Strickland Company's net income for the year ended October 31, Year 5.

Ex. 8-14 Power Corporation completed a pooling-type business combination with Stern Company on December 31, Year 6. Exchanged in the combination were 48,000 of Stern's 50,000 shares of outstanding common stock. Stern had a net income of $0.80 a share for Year 7 and declared dividends of $0.35 a share on December 13, Year 7, payable January 6, Year 8, to stockholders of record December 23, Year 7. There were no other intercompany transactions during Year 7.

Prepare journal entries to record:

a Stern Company's dividend declaration in its accounting records.

b Stern Company's operating results for Year 7 in Power Corporation's accounting records under the equity method of accounting. (Disregard income taxes.)

Ex. 8-15 Poplar Corporation erroneously used the cost method of accounting for the operating results of its 94%-owned pooled subsidiary, Squire Company, with which Poplar had combined on May 31, Year 3. Details of Squire's Retained Earnings ledger account for the three years since that date follow:

Retained Earnings

May 26, Year 4 Dividends	30,000	May 31, Year 3 Balance	470,000
May 31, Year 5 Net loss	20,000	May 31, Year 4 Net income	60,000
May 24, Year 6 Dividends	30,000	May 31, Year 6 Net income	80,000

Prepare a correcting entry for Poplar Corporation on May 31, Year 6, to convert its accounting for its subsidiary's operating results to the equity method. The entry should include the ledger account or accounts necessary for Poplar's income statement for the year ended May 31, Year 6. (Disregard income taxes.)

Ex. 8-16 On December 31, Year 3, Plodder Corporation and Slasher Company combined in a pooling-type business combination that required the working paper eliminations (in journal entry format) on page 421 for consolidated financial statements. For the year ended December 31, Year 4, Slasher declared and paid dividends totaling $60,000 and had a net income of $100,000.

Prepare working paper eliminations (in journal entry format) for Plodder Corporation and subsidiary on December 31, Year 4. Omit explanations and disregard income taxes.

PLODDER CORPORATION AND SUBSIDIARY
Working Paper Eliminations
December 31, Year 3

(a) Common Stock—Slasher..............................	100,000	
Additional Paid-in Capital—Slasher......................	150,000	
Retained Earnings—Slasher ($200,000 × 0.10)...........	20,000	
Retained Earnings of Subsidiary—Plodder ($250,000 × 0.90)	225,000	
Investment in Slasher Company Common Stock—		
Plodder (500,000 × 0.90).........................		450,000
Dividends Declared—Slasher ($30,000 × 0.10)......		3,000
Minority Interest in Net Assets of Subsidiary		
($45,000 − $3,000)..............................		42,000

To eliminate intercompany investment and establish minority
interest in net assets of subsidiary at beginning of year
[($100,000 + $150,000 + $200,000) × 0.10 = $45,000], less
minority interest in dividends (30,000 × 0.10 = $3,000).

(b) Minority Interest in Net Income of Subsidiary...............	8,000	
Minority Interest in Net Assets of Subsidiary..........		8,000

To establish minority interest in net income of subsidiary for
year ended December 31, Year 3 ($80,000 × 0.10 = $8,000).

Ex. 8-17 Plon Corporation owns 90% of the outstanding common stock of Stubb Company, acquired in a pooling-type business combination January 31, Year 1. For the year ended January 31, Year 2, Plon's unconsolidated income statement was as follows:

PLON CORPORATION
Income Statement (unconsolidated)
For Year Ended January 31, Year 2

Revenue:	
Net sales..	$500,000
Intercompany investment income	27,000
Intercompany revenue..	23,000
Total revenue...	$550,000
Costs and expenses...	510,000
Net income..	$ 40,000

During the year ended January 31, Year 2, both Plon and Stubb had declared and paid dividends of $15,000.

Prepare closing entries for Plon Corporation on January 31, Year 2.

Ex. 8-18 The unconsolidated income statement of Press Corporation, parent company of 98%-owned pooled subsidiary, Stress Company, for the first year following the business combination was as follows (in thousands):

PRESS CORPORATION
Unconsolidated Income Statement
For Year Ended May 31, Year 5
(000 omitted)

Revenue:		
Net sales.		$10,000
Intercompany investment income		980
Total revenue.		$10,980
Costs and expenses:		
Cost of goods sold	$7,600	
Operating expenses.	1,380	
Income taxes expense.	800	
Total costs and expenses.		9,780
Net income.		$1,200

During the year ended May 31, Year 5, Press declared and paid dividends totaling $300,000 and Stress declared and paid dividends totaling $400,000 (000 *not* omitted). Both Press and Stress debit dividends declared to Dividends Declared contra-retained earnings ledger accounts.

Prepare closing entries (omit explanations) for Press Corporation on May 31, Year 5.

Ex. 8-19 On March 13, Year 7, Parker Corporation loaned $100,000 to its subsidiary, Sark Company, on a 90-day, 8% promissory note. On April 12, Year 7, Parker discounted the Sark note at First National Bank at a 10% discount rate.

Prepare a working paper to compute the debit to the Cash ledger account in Parker Corporation's April 12, Year 7, journal entry to record the discounting of the Sark Company note. Round to the nearest dollar.

Ex. 8-20 On March 1, Year 2, Payton Corporation loaned $10,000 to its subsidiary, Slagle Company, on a 90-day, 7% promissory note. On March 31, Year 2, Payton discounted the Slagle note at a bank at a 9% discount rate.

Prepare Payton Corporation's journal entry on March 31, Year 2, to record the discounting of the Slagle Company note. Round all amounts to the nearest dollar.

Ex. 8-21 On March 31, Year 4, Scully Company, the wholly owned subsidiary of Planke Corporation, prepared the following journal entry at the instruction of Planke:

Intercompany Notes Payable	18,000	
Intercompany Interest Expense	135	
Notes Payable.		18,000
Interest Payable		135

To transfer 9%, 60-day-note payable to Planke Corporation dated March 1, Year 4, from intercompany notes to outsider notes. Action is necessary because Planke discounted the note at 10% on this date.

Prepare a journal entry for Planke Corporation on March 31, Year 4, to record the discounting of the Scully Company note with the bank. Use a 360-day year.

Ex. 8-22   Palos Verdes Corporation had the following events and transactions with its 90%-owned pooled subsidiary, South Gate Company, during the year ended May 31, Year 9:

Year 8
June 1   Palos Verdes loaned South Gate $120,000 on a 90-day, 12% promissory note.
July 1   Palos Verdes discounted the South Gate note at a bank at a 15% discount rate.
Year 9
May 1   South Gate declared a dividend totaling $80,000.
May 10   South Gate paid the dividend declared May 1, Year 9.
May 31   South Gate reported a net income of $200,000 for the year ended May 31, Year 9.

Prepare journal entries for Palos Verdes Corporation (omit explanations) for the foregoing transactions and events. Use the equity method of accounting where appropriate. (Disregard income taxes.)

CASES

Case 8-1   On March 1, Year 6, Perlmuth Corporation signed a preliminary agreement to consummate a business combination with Stabler Company that met the prerequisites for pooling accounting. A condition precedent of the combination was that the Perlmuth Corporation common stock issued to Ralph Stabler, sole shareholder of Stabler Company, would be registered with the Securities and Exchange Commission. However, Perlmuth withdrew its registration statement for the common stock because of adverse stock market conditions. Accordingly, the business combination was never completed.

On April 30, Year 7, Progress Corporation issued its common stock, which was registered with the SEC, for all the outstanding common stock of Stabler Company. All the requirements of pooling accounting appeared to be met in the Progress-Stabler business combination. However, on learning of Perlmuth's aborted combination with Stabler Company, the independent auditors for Progress questioned whether the following requirement for pooling accounting, set forth in *APB Opinion No. 16,* ''Business Combinations,'' applied:

Each of the combining companies is autonomous and has not been a subsidiary or division of another corporation within two years before the plan of combination is initiated.

Instructions
Does the Progress Corporation–Stabler Company business combination qualify for pooling accounting? Explain.

Case 8-2   As independent auditor of a new client, Aqua Water Corporation, you are reviewing the working paper for consolidated financial statements prepared by Arthur Brady, Aqua Water's accountant. Aqua Water distributes water to homeowners in a suburb of a large city. Aqua Water purchases the water from its subsidiary, Aqua Well Company. Aqua Water organized Aqua Well five years ago and acquired all its common stock for cash on that date.

During the course of your audit, you have learned the following:

(1) Both Aqua Water and Aqua Well are public utilities subject to the jurisdiction of the state's Public Utilities Commission.
(2) Aqua Well charges Aqua Water for the transmission of water from wells to consumers. The transmission charge, at the customary utility rate, was approved by the state's Public Utilities Commission.
(3) Aqua Well charges Aqua Water separately for the volume of water delivered to Aqua Water's customers.
(4) Your audit working papers show the following audited amounts for the two companies' separate financial statements:

	Aqua Water Corporation	Aqua Well Company
Total revenue	$3,500,000	$ 300,000
Net income	300,000	50,000
Total assets	5,700,000	1,000,000
Stockholders' equity	2,500,000	600,000

The working paper for consolidated financial statements prepared by Aqua Water Corporation's accountant appears in order, except that Aqua Well's Transmission Revenue amount of $60,000 is not offset against Aqua Water's Transmission Expense amount of $60,000. The accountant explained that, because the transmission charge by Aqua Well is at the customary utility rate approved by the state's Public Utilities Commission, the charge should not be treated as intercompany revenue and expense. Furthermore, Brady points out, the working paper for consolidated financial statements does offset Aqua Well's Water Sales amount of $200,000 against Aqua Water's Purchases amount of $200,000.

Instructions

Do you concur with the accountant's (Brady's) position? Explain.

PROBLEMS

Pr. 8-1   The stockholders' equity sections of Payne Corporation's and Sybil Company's balance sheets on December 31, Year 5, were as follows:

PAYNE CORPORATION AND SYBIL COMPANY
Stockholders' Equity Sections of Balance Sheets (prior to business combination)
December 31, Year 5

	Payne Corporation	Sybil Company
Common stock, $1 par	$200,000	$100,000
Additional paid-in capital	100,000	60,000
Retained earnings	180,000	160,000
Total stockholders' equity	$480,000	$320,000

On December 31, Year 5, Payne issued 60,000 shares of its common stock for 90% of the outstanding common stock of Sybil Company in a pooling-type business combination in which Sybil became a subsidiary of Payne. Also on that date, Payne paid the following out-of-pocket costs of the combination:

Legal fees, accounting fees, and finder's fee	$40,000
Costs of registering and issuing common stock	30,000
Total out-of-pocket costs of business combination	$70,000

During the year ended December 31, Year 5, Sybil had a net income of $20,000 but did not declare or pay dividends.

Instructions

a Prepare journal entries for Payne Corporation on December 31, Year 5, to record the business combination with Sybil Company. (Disregard income taxes.)

b Prepare working paper eliminations, in journal entry format, for Payne Corporation and subsidiary on December 31, Year 5.

Pr. 8-2 The working paper eliminations (explanations omitted) on the date of the Pope Corporation–Sande Company pooling-type business combination were as follows:

POPE CORPORATION AND SUBSIDIARY
Working Paper Eliminations
January 31, Year 10

(a) Common Stock, no par or stated value—Sande	50,000	
Retained Earnings—Sande ($170,000 × 0.08)	13,600	
Retained Earnings of Subsidiary—Pope ($220,000 × 0.92) .	202,400	
Investment in Sande Company Common Stock—Pope		
($270,000 × 0.92)		248,400
Dividends Declared—Sande ($30,000 × 0.08)		2,400
Minority Interest in Net Assets of Subsidiary		
[($220,000 × 0.08) − $2,400]		15,200
(b) Minority Interest in Net Income of Subsidiary ($80,000 × 0.08)	6,400	
Minority Interest in Net Assets of Subsidiary		6,400

(As indicated by the foregoing eliminations, the January 31, Year 9, balance of Sande's retained earnings, $170,000, was increased by net income of $80,000 and decreased by dividends declared of $30,000 during the year ended January 31, Year 10, to a balance of $220,000 on that date.)

For the year ended January 31, Year 11, Sande had a net income of $60,000, and on that date it declared a dividend of $20,000, to be paid February 28, Year 11.

Instructions

a Prepare journal entries for Pope Corporation on January 31, Year 11, to record the operations of Sande Company under the equity method of accounting. (Disregard income taxes.)

b Prepare working paper eliminations, in journal entry format, for Pope Corporation and subsidiary on January 31, Year 11.

Pr. 8-3   On January 2, Year 6, Petro Corporation issued 200,000 shares of its common stock in exchange for 100,000 shares of Swiss Company's outstanding common stock in a pooling-type business combination. The current fair value of Petro's common stock was $40 a share on the date of the combination. The balance sheets of Petro and Swiss immediately before the combination contained the following information:

Petro Corporation

Common stock, $5 par; authorized 1,000,000 shares; issued and out-	
standing 600,000 shares	$ 3,000,000
Additional paid-in capital	6,000,000
Retained earnings	11,000,000
Total stockholders' equity	$20,000,000

Swiss Company

Common stock, $10 par; authorized 250,000 shares; issued and outstand-	
ing 100,000 shares	$1,000,000
Additional paid-in capital	2,000,000
Retained earnings	4,000,000
Total stockholders' equity	$7,000,000

Additional Information

(1) Net income for the year ended December 31, Year 6, was $1,150,000 for Petro and $350,000 for Swiss. The net income for Petro does not include its share of Swiss Company's net income.

(2) During Year 6, Petro declared and paid $900,000 in dividends to its stockholders and Swiss declared and paid $220,000 in dividends to Petro.

Instructions

Prepare the stockholders' equity section of the consolidated balance sheet of Petro Corporation and subsidiary on December 31, Year 6. Prepare a supporting exhibit for consolidated retained earnings. (Disregard income taxes.)

Pr. 8-4   On October 21, Year 9, Prentiss Corporation loaned to its 92%-owned pooled subsidiary, Scopes Company, $100,000 on a 90-day, 7½% promissory note. On October

31, Year 9, Prentiss discounted the Scopes note at City Bank, at a discount rate of 9% a year.

Instructions

Prepare journal entries for the foregoing business transactions and events:
a In the accounting records of Prentiss Corporation
b In the accounting records of Scopes Company
Round all amounts to the nearest dollar.

Pr. 8-5 On July 31, Year 7, Pinto Corporation issued 15,000 shares of its $100 par common stock for 9,700 shares of Savoy Company's 10,000 outstanding shares of $50 par common stock. Out-of-pocket costs of $150,000 were paid by Pinto on July 31, Year 7. The business combination qualified for pooling accounting, and Savoy became a subsidiary of Pinto. Immediately following the combination, Pinto's accounting records included the following ledger account balances:

Investment in Savoy Company Common Stock.....................	$1,789,650 dr
Paid-in Capital in Excess of Par	2,100,000 cr
Retained Earnings of Subsidiary (Savoy Company)...................	625,650 cr

Savoy had a net income of $60,000 and declared no dividends for the year ended July 31, Year 7.

Instructions

a Reconstruct Pinto Corporation's journal entries to record the pooling-type business combination with Savoy Company on July 31, Year 7.
b Prepare working paper eliminations (in journal entry format) for Pinto Corporation and subsidiary on July 31, Year 7.

Pr. 8-6 On September 30, Year 1, the end of a fiscal year, Pirtle Corporation issued 100,000 shares of its $5 par common stock (current fair value $12 a share) for 18,800 shares of the outstanding $20 par common stock of Solis Company. The $150,000 out-of-pocket costs of the business combination paid by Pirtle on September 30, Year 1, were allocable as follows: 60% to accounting fees, legal fees, and finder's fee directly related to the business combination, and 40% to the SEC registration statement for Pirtle common stock issued in the business combination.

Immediately prior to the business combination, stockholders' equity amounts of the two companies were as follows:

	Pirtle Corporation	Solis Company
Common stock	$4,000,000	$ 400,000
Additional paid-in capital............................	1,500,000	
Retained earnings	3,000,000	700,000*
Total stockholders' equity.........................	$8,500,000	$1,100,000

* Net income $260,000, dividends declared $120,000, for year ended Sept. 30, Year 1.

Instructions

a Prepare Pirtle Corporation's journal entries on September 30, Year 1, to record the business combination with Solis Company as a pooling.

b Prepare working paper eliminations (in journal entry format) for Pirtle Corporation and subsidiary on September 30, Year 1.

Pr. 8-7 Pillsbury Corporation has begun making working capital loans to its wholly owned subsidiary, Sarpy Company, on 7½% promissory notes. The following 120-day loans were made prior to June 30, Year 3, the close of the fiscal year:

May 1, Year 3.	$15,000
May 31, Year 3.	20,000

On June 6, Year 3, Pillsbury discounted the May 1 note at a bank, at a 9% discount rate. The bank used a 360-day year and based the discount on the maturity value of the note.

Instructions

Prepare journal entries to record the note transactions and related June 30, Year 3, adjustments:
a In the accounting records of Pillsbury Corporation
b In the accounting records of Sarpy Company
Round all amounts to the nearest dollar.

Pr. 8-8 Separate statements of retained earnings for Pedro Corporation and Santo Company for the year ended May 31, Year 2 (prior to their business combination), follow:

PEDRO CORPORATION AND SANTO COMPANY
Separate Statements of Retained Earnings (prior to business combination)
For Year Ended May 31, Year 2

	Pedro Corporation	Santo Company
Retained earnings, beginning of year	$500,000	$290,000
Net income	100,000	80,000
Subtotals	$600,000	$370,000
Dividends.	40,000	25,000
Retained earnings, end of year.	$560,000	$345,000

On May 31, Year 2, Pedro issued 50,000 shares of its $1 par common stock for 54,600 of the 60,000 outstanding shares of $3 par common stock of Santo. Total paid-in capital attributable to Santo's common stock was $7 a share. The $30,000 out-of-pocket costs of the pooling-type business combination were paid by Pedro on May 31, Year 2. There were no intercompany transactions prior to the date of the combination.

Instructions

Prepare a working paper to compute the following:
a Minority interest in net income of Santo Company for the year ended May 31, Year 2.

b Consolidated net income for Pedro Corporation and subsidiary for the year ended May 31, Year 2. (Disregard income taxes.)

c Minority interest in net assets of Santo Company on May 31, Year 2.

d Consolidated retained earnings of Pedro Corporation and subsidiary on May 31, Year 2. (Disregard income taxes.)

Pr. 8-9 The accountant of Purvis Corporation prepared the following journal entries on March 1, Year 8:

Investment in Semel Company Common Stock	783,000	
Minority Interest in Net Assets of Subsidiary	16,000	
Common Stock.		49,000
Paid-in Capital in Excess of Par of Subsidiary.		300,000
Retained Earnings of Subsidiary.		450,000

To record issuance of 4,900 shares of $10 par common stock for 9,800 of 10,000 outstanding shares of Semel Company $5 par common stock in pooling-type business combination; to bring forward Semel's Paid-in Capital in Excess of Par and Retained Earnings accounts at their carrying amounts in Semel's accounting records; and to provide for minority interest in Semel's net assets ($800,000) on March 1, Year 8.

Investment in Semel Company Common Stock	80,000	
Paid-in Capital in Excess of Par	70,000	
Cash		150,000

To record payment of out-of-pocket costs of business combination with Semel Company as follows:

Finder's fee, accounting fees, and legal fees relating to business combination	$ 80,000
Costs associated with SEC registration statement .	70,000
Total out-of-pocket costs of business combination	$150,000

Instructions

a Prepare journal entries to correct Purvis Corporation's accounting for its business combination with Semel Company on March 1, Year 8.

b Assuming that Semel Company had a net income of $100,000 and declared no dividends for the fiscal year ended February 28, Year 9, prepare (1) a journal entry under the equity method of accounting to record Semel's net income in the accounting records of Purvis Corporation on February 28, Year 9; and (2) working paper eliminations (in journal entry format) required for the preparation of consolidated financial statements for Purvis Corporation and subsidiary for the year ended February 28, Year 9. (Disregard income taxes.)

Pr. 8-10 The working paper eliminations (in journal entry format) for Poole Corporation and subsidiary on October 31, Year 4, the date of the pooling-type business combination, were as follows:

POOLE CORPORATION AND SUBSIDIARY
Working Paper Eliminations
October 31, Year 4

(a) *Common Stock—Soule*..................................	*100,000*	
Additional Paid-in Capital—Soule........................	*150,000*	
Retained Earnings—Soule ($160,000 × 0.10)	*16,000*	
Retained Earnings of Subsidiary—Poole ($200,000 × 0.90) .	*180,000*	
Investment in Soule Company Common Stock—Poole		
($450,000 × 0.90)..............................		*405,000*
Minority Interest in Net Assets of Subsidiary		
($410,000 × 0.10)..............................		*41,000*
To eliminate intercompany investment and establish minority		
interest in net assets of subsidiary at beginning of year (Nov. 1,		
Year 3).		
(b) *Minority Interest in Net Income of Subsidiary ($40,000 × 0.10)*	*4,000*	
Minority Interest in Net Assets of Subsidiary..........		*4,000*
To establish minority interest in net income of subsidiary for		
year ended Oct. 31, Year 4.		

During the year ended October 31, Year 5, Soule had a net income of $50,000, and on October 31, Year 5, Soule declared dividends of $20,000.

Instructions

a Prepare Poole Corporation's October 31, Year 5, journal entries to record the operating results and dividends of Soule Company under the equity method of accounting. (Disregard income taxes.)

b Prepare the October 31, Year 5, working paper eliminations (in journal entry format) for Poole Corporation and subsidiary.

Pr. 8-11 Pittsburgh Corporation completed a business combination with Syracuse Company on April 30, Year 7. Immediately thereafter, Pittsburgh began making cash advances to Syracuse at a 10% annual interest rate. In addition, Syracuse agreed to pay a monthly management fee to Pittsburgh of 2% of monthly net sales. Payment was to be made no later than the tenth day of the month following Syracuse's accrual of the fee.

During your audit of the financial statements of Pittsburgh Corporation and Syracuse Company as of July 31, Year 7, the end of the fiscal year, you discovered that each company has set up only one ledger account—entitled Intercompany Account—to record all intercompany transactions. Details of the two accounts on July 31, Year 7, are as follows:

PITTSBURGH CORPORATION LEDGER
Intercompany Account—Syracuse Company

Date	Explanation	Debit	Credit	Balance
Year 7				
May 2	Cash advance paid	4,500		4,500 dr
May 27	Cash advance paid	9,000		13,500 dr
June 11	Management fee received		2,000	11,500 dr
June 12	Repayment of May 2 advance and interest		4,550	6,950 dr
June 21	Cash advance paid	10,000		16,950 dr
July 11	Management fee received		2,200	14,750 dr
July 27	Repayment of May 27 advance and interest		9,150	5,600 dr
July 31	Cash advance paid	5,000		10,600 dr

SYRACUSE COMPANY LEDGER
Intercompany Account—Pittsburgh Corporation

Date	Explanation	Debit	Credit	Balance
Year 7				
May 3	Cash advance received		4,500	4,500 cr
May 28	Cash advance received		9,000	13,500 cr
June 10	Management fee paid ($100,000 × 0.02)	2,000		11,500 cr
June 11	Repayment of May 2 advance and interest	4,550		6,950 cr
June 22	Cash advance received		10,000	16,950 cr
July 10	Management fee paid ($110,000 × 0.02)	2,200		14,750 cr
July 26	Repayment of May 27 advance and interest	9,150		5,600 cr

Your audit working papers show audited net sales of $330,000 for Syracuse Company for the three months ended July 31, Year 7. You agreed to the companies' use of a 360-day year for computing interest.

Instructions

a Prepare correcting entries for Pittsburgh Corporation on July 31, Year 7. Establish appropriate separate intercompany accounts in the journal entries.

b Prepare correcting entries for Syracuse Company on July 31, Year 7. Establish appropriate separate intercompany accounts in the journal entries.

c Prepare a partial working paper for consolidated financial statements to include the intercompany accounts established in a and b.

9

Consolidated Financial Statements: Intercompany Profits (Gains) and Losses

Many business transactions between a parent company and its subsidiaries involve a profit (gain) or loss. Among these transactions are intercompany sales of merchandise, intercompany sales of plant assets, intercompany leases of property under capital/sales-type leases, and intercompany sales of intangible assets. Until intercompany profits or losses in such transactions are *realized* through the sale of the asset to an *outsider* or otherwise, the profits or losses must be eliminated in the preparation of consolidated financial statements.

In addition, a parent or subsidiary company's acquisition of its affiliate's bonds *in the open market* may result in a *realized gain or loss to the consolidated entity.* Such a realized gain or loss is not recognized in the separate income statement of either the parent company or the subsidiary, but it must be recognized in the consolidated income statement.

In this chapter I discuss and illustrate the working paper eliminations for intercompany transactions of the types described above. The focus is on intercompany transactions involving *profits (gains),* although such transactions also may involve losses.

Importance of Eliminating or Including Intercompany Profits (Gains) and Losses

At the outset, I must stress the importance of eliminating *unrealized* intercompany profits (gains) and losses and recognizing *realized* gains or losses in the preparation of consolidated income statements. Failure to eliminate *unrealized* profits and losses would result in consolidated income statements that report not only results of transactions with those outside the consolidated entity but also the results of *related-party* activities within the affiliated group. Similarly, nonrecognition of *realized* gains and losses would misstate consolidated net income. The parent company's management would have free rein to manipulate consolidated net income if unrealized intercompany profits and losses were not eliminated in the preparation of consolidated income statements.

INTERCOMPANY SALES OF MERCHANDISE

Intercompany sales of merchandise are a natural outgrowth of *vertical* business combinations, which involve a combinor and one or more of its customers or suppliers as combinees. *Downstream* intercompany sales of merchandise are those from a parent company to its subsidiaries. *Upstream* intercompany sales are those from subsidiaries to the parent company. *Lateral* intercompany sales are between two subsidiaries of the same parent company.

The *intercompany sales* of merchandise between a parent company and its subsidiary are similar to the *intracompany shipments* of merchandise by a home office to a branch, described in Chapter 4.

Intercompany Sales of Merchandise at Cost

Intercompany sales of merchandise may be made at a price equal to the selling company's cost. If so, the working paper elimination is the same, whether all the goods were sold by the purchasing affiliate or whether some of the goods remained in the purchaser's inventories on the date of the consolidated financial statements. For example, assume that Palm Corporation (the parent company) during the year ended December 31, Year 3, sold merchandise costing $150,000 to Starr Company (the subsidiary) at a selling price equal to the cost of the merchandise. Assume further that Starr's December 31, Year 3, inventories included $25,000 of merchandise obtained from Palm and that Starr still owed Palm $15,000 for merchandise purchases on December 31, Year 3. (Starr also had purchased merchandise from other suppliers during Year 3.)

Partial working paper for consolidated financial statements— intercompany sales of merchandise at cost

PALM CORPORATION AND SUBSIDIARY
Partial Working Paper for Consolidated Financial Statements
For Year Ended December 31, Year 3

	Palm Corporation	Starr Company	Eliminations increase (decrease)	Consolidated
Income Statement				
Intercompany revenue (expenses) . . .	*			
Balance Sheet				
Intercompany receivable (payable).	15,000	(15,000)		

* Palm Corporation's $150,000 intercompany sales and intercompany cost of goods sold are offset in Palm's separate income statement in the working paper.

Journal entries for parent company's downstream sales of merchandise to subsidiary at cost and subsidiary's sales of merchandise to outsiders

Explanations	Palm Corporation journal entries	Starr Company journal entries

(1) Palm Corporation sold merchandise to Starr Company.	Intercompany Accounts Receivable 150,000
	    Intercompany Sales 150,000
		Inventories 150,000
		    Intercompany Accounts
		        Payable 150,000

	Intercompany Cost of Goods Sold 150,000 Inventories 150,000	

(2) Starr paid cash to Palm for merchandise purchased.	Cash 135,000
	    Intercompany Accounts Receivable 135,000
		Intercompany Accounts Payable .. 135,000
		    Cash 135,000

(3) Starr sold merchandise purchased from Palm (Starr's selling prices are assumed).		Trade Accounts Receivable 160,000
		    Sales 160,000
		
		Cost of Goods Sold 125,000
		    Inventories 125,000

The two companies would prepare the aggregate journal entries illustrated on page 434 for the foregoing transactions, assuming that both companies used the perpetual inventory system.

The working paper for consolidated financial statements for Palm Corporation and subsidiary for the year ended December 31, Year 3, would include the data on page 433 with regard to intercompany sales of merchandise only.

Note that Starr Company's cost of goods sold for Year 3 and inventories on December 31, Year 3, are not affected by working paper eliminations. From a consolidated entity viewpoint, both Starr's cost of goods sold and Starr's inventories are stated at *cost;* no element of intercompany profit or loss is involved.

Unrealized Intercompany Profit in Ending Inventories

More typical than the intercompany sales of merchandise at cost described in the preceding section are intercompany sales involving a gross profit. The gross profit margin may be equal to, more than, or less than the margin on sales to outsiders. The selling affiliate's intercompany gross profit is *realized* through the purchasing affiliate's sales of the acquired merchandise to outsiders. Consequently, any merchandise purchased from an affiliated company that remains unsold on the date of a consolidated balance sheet results in the *overstatement* (from a *consolidated* point of view) of the purchaser's ending inventories. The overstatement is equal to the amount of the selling affiliate's *unrealized* intercompany gross profit included in the ending inventories. This overstatement is canceled through an appropriate working paper elimination in the preparation of consolidated financial statements.

Suppose, for example, that Sage Company (the 95%-owned subsidiary) during the year ended December 31, Year 3, began selling merchandise to Post Corporation (the parent company) at a gross profit margin of 20%. Sales by Sage to Post for the year totaled $120,000, of which $40,000 remained unsold by Post on December 31, Year 3. On that date, Post owed $30,000 to Sage for merchandise. Both companies used the perpetual inventory system.

The transactions described in the foregoing paragraph are recorded in summary form by the two companies as illustrated on page 436.

The intercompany gross profit in Sage's sales to Post during the year ended December 31, Year 3, is analyzed below:

Analysis of gross profit margin in partially owned subsidiary's upstream sales of merchandise to parent company for first year

	Selling price	Cost	Gross profit (25% of cost; 20% of selling price)
Beginning inventories			
Add: Sales........	$120,000	$96,000	$24,000
Subtotals	$120,000	$96,000	$24,000
Less: Ending inventories	40,000	32,000	8,000
Cost of goods sold.	$ 80,000	$64,000	$16,000

Journal entries for partially owned subsidiary's upstream sales of merchandise to parent company at a gross profit and parent's sales of the merchandise to outsiders

Explanations	Post Corporation journal entries	Sage Company journal entries

(1) Sage Company sold merchandise to Post Corporation.	Inventories........................ 120,000
	    Intercompany Accounts
	    Payable........................ 120,000
		Intercompany Accounts Receivable........................ 120,000
		    Intercompany Sales........ 120,000
		Intercompany Cost of Goods Sold. 96,000
		    Inventories 96,000

(2) Post paid cash to Sage for merchandise purchased.	Intercompany Accounts Payable .. 90,000
	    Cash............................ 90,000
		Cash............................ 90,000
		    Intercompany Accounts Receivable........................ 90,000

(3) Post sold merchandise purchased from Sage (Post's selling prices are assumed).	Trade Accounts Receivable....... 100,000
	    Sales 100,000
	Cost of Goods Sold............. 80,000
	    Inventories 80,000	

The analysis on page 435 shows that the intercompany gross profit on sales by Sage to Post totaled $24,000, and that $16,000 of this intercompany profit was realized through Post's sales of the acquired merchandise to outside customers. The remaining $8,000 of intercompany profit remains **unrealized** in Post's inventories on December 31, Year 3.

The following working paper elimination (in journal entry format) is required for Sage's intercompany sales of merchandise to Post for the year ended December 31, Year 3:

Working paper elimination for first year of intercompany sales of merchandise at a gross profit margin

POST CORPORATION AND SUBSIDIARY
Partial Working Paper Eliminations
December 31, Year 3

(b) Intercompany Sales—Sage	120,000	
Intercompany Cost of Goods Sold—Sage		96,000
Cost of Goods Sold—Post		16,000
Inventories—Post		8,000

To eliminate intercompany sales, cost of goods sold, and unrealized intercompany profit in inventories. (Income tax effects are disregarded.)

The effects of the foregoing elimination are as follows: First, it eliminates Sage's intercompany sales to Post and the related intercompany cost of goods sold; this avoids the overstatement of the **consolidated** amounts for sales and cost of goods sold, which should represent merchandise transactions with customers outside the consolidated entity. Second, the elimination removes the intercompany gross profit from Post's cost of goods sold, thus restating it to the cost of the **consolidated entity.** Finally, the elimination reduces the consolidated inventories to **actual cost** for the consolidated entity.

Entering the preceding elimination in the working paper for consolidated financial statements results in the consolidated amounts shown on page 438 (amounts for total sales to outsiders and cost of goods sold are assumed).

Note that the $120,000 elimination of intercompany sales, less the $112,000 total ($16,000 + $96,000 = $112,000) of the two cost of goods sold eliminations, equals $8,000—the amount of the intercompany profit eliminated from inventories. This $8,000 unrealized intercompany profit is attributable to Sage Company—the **seller** of the merchandise—and **must be taken into account in the computation of the minority interest in Sage's net income** for the year ended December 31, Year 3. The $8,000 also enters into the computation of Sage's portion of consolidated retained earnings on December 31, Year 3. These procedures are illustrated in the following sections.

If the intercompany sales of merchandise are made by a parent company or by a wholly owned subsidiary, there is no effect on any minority interest in net income or

Partial working paper
for consolidated
financial statements—
first year of
intercompany sales of
merchandise at a gross
profit

POST CORPORATION AND SUBSIDIARY
Partial Working Paper for Consolidated Financial Statements
For Year Ended December 31, Year 3

	Post Corporation	Sage Company	Eliminations increase (decrease)	Consolidated
Income Statement				
Revenue:				
Sales	5,800,000	1,200,000		7,000,000
Intercompany sales .		120,000	(b) (120,000)	
Costs and expenses:				
Cost of goods sold .	4,100,000	760,000	(b) (16,000)	4,844,000
Intercompany cost of goods sold .		96,000	(b) (96,000)	
Balance Sheet				
Assets				
Intercompany receivable (payable).	(30,000)	30,000		
Inventories	900,000	475,000	(b) (8,000)	1,367,000

loss, ***because the selling affiliate does not have minority stockholders.*** Thus, it is important to identify, by company name, the financial statement items that are affected by working paper eliminations for intercompany sales of merchandise, so that the minority interest in net income or loss of a partially owned subsidiary that makes upstream or lateral sales of merchandise at a gross profit may be computed correctly.

Intercompany Profit in Beginning and Ending Inventories

The working paper elimination for intercompany sales of merchandise is complicated by intercompany profits in the ***beginning*** inventories of the purchaser. It is generally assumed that, on a first-in, first-out basis, the intercompany profit in the purchaser's ***beginning*** inventories is realized through sales of the merchandise to outsiders during the ensuing accounting period. Only the intercompany profit in ***ending*** inventories remains unrealized at the end of the period.

Continuing the illustration from the preceding section, assume that Sage Company's intercompany sales of merchandise to Post Corporation during the year ended December 31, Year 4, are analyzed as follows:

Analysis of gross profit margin in partially owned subsidiary's upstream sales of merchandise to parent company for second year

	Selling price	Cost	Gross profit (25% of cost; 20% of selling price)
Beginning inventories	$ 40,000	$ 32,000	$ 8,000
Add: Sales.	$150,000	120,000	30,000
Subtotals	$190,000	$152,000	$38,000
Less: Ending inventories	60,000	48,000	12,000
Cost of goods sold.	$130,000	$104,000	$26,000

Sage's intercompany sales and intercompany cost of goods sold for the year ended December 31, Year 3, had been closed with other income statement amounts to Sage's Retained Earnings ledger account. Consequently, from a *consolidated* point of view, Sage's December 31, Year 3, retained earnings was overstated by $7,600 (95% of the $8,000 unrealized intercompany profit in Post's inventories on December 31, Year 3). The remaining $400 of unrealized profit on December 31, Year 3, is attributable to the minority interest in net assets of Sage Company, the *seller* of the merchandise. The following working paper elimination (in journal entry format) on December 31, Year 4, reflects these facts:

Working paper elimination for second year of intercompany sales of merchandise at a gross profit margin

POST CORPORATION AND SUBSIDIARY
Partial Working Paper Eliminations
December 31, Year 4

(b) Retained Earnings—Sage ($8,000 × 0.95)*	7,600	
Minority Interest in Net Assets of Subsidiary ($8,000 × 0.05).	400	
Intercompany Sales—Sage	150,000	
Intercompany Cost of Goods Sold—Sage		120,000
Cost of Goods Sold—Post		26,000
Inventories—Post		12,000

To eliminate intercompany sales, cost of goods sold, and unrealized intercompany profit in inventories. (Income tax effects are disregarded.)

* As indicated in Chapter 7 (page 314), this elimination is posted to the **beginning-of-year** retained earnings in the statement of retained earnings section of the working paper for consolidated financial statements.

Intercompany Profit in Inventories and Amount of Minority Interest

Accountants have given considerable thought to intercompany profits in purchases and sales transactions of partially owned subsidiaries. There is general agreement that all the unrealized intercompany profit in a partially owned subsidiary's ending inventories should be eliminated for consolidated financial statements. *This holds true whether the sales to the subsidiary are downstream from the parent company or are made by a wholly owned subsidiary of the same parent.*

There has been no such agreement on the treatment of intercompany profit in the parent company's or a subsidiary's inventories from upstream or lateral sales by a partially owned subsidiary. Two alternative approaches have been suggested.

1   The first approach is elimination of intercompany profit *only to the extent of the parent company's ownership interest* in the selling subsidiary's common stock. This approach is based on the *parent company concept* of consolidated financial statements (see Chapter 6, pages 266 to 267), in which the minority interest is considered to be a *liability* of the consolidated entity. If the minority stockholders are considered *outside creditors,* intercompany profit in the parent company's ending inventories has been *realized* to the extent of the minority stockholders' interest in the selling subsidiary.

2   The second approach is elimination of *all the intercompany profit.* The *economic unit concept* of consolidated financial statements (see Chapter 6, page 267), in which the minority interest is considered to be a *part of consolidated stockholders' equity*, underlies this approach. If minority stockholders are *part owners* of consolidated assets, their share of intercompany profits in inventories has not been realized.

The AICPA sanctioned the second approach, in the following passage from *Accounting Research Bulletin No. 51:*[1]

> The amount of intercompany profit or loss to be eliminated . . . is not affected by the existence of a minority interest. The complete elimination of the intercompany profit or loss is consistent with the underlying assumption that the consolidated statements represent the financial position and operating results of a single business enterprise. *The elimination of the intercompany profit or loss may be allocated proportionately between the majority and minority interests.* [Emphasis added.]

Consequently, intercompany profits or losses in inventories resulting from *upstream or lateral sales of merchandise by a partially owned subsidiary* must be considered in the computation of minority interest in net income of the subsidiary, and in the computation of the portion of retained earnings of the subsidiary to be included in consolidated retained earnings. The subsidiary's net income must be *increased* by the *realized* intercompany profit in the purchasing affiliate's *beginning* inventories and *decreased* by the *unrealized* intercompany profit in the purchasing affiliate's *ending* inventories. Failure to do so would attribute the entire intercom-

---

[1] *ARB No. 51,* "Consolidated Financial Statements," AICPA (New York: 1959), p. 45.

pany profit effects to the *consolidated* net income. (See page 465 for an illustration of the computation of minority interest in net income of a partially owned subsidiary that makes intercompany sales of merchandise.)

Should Net Profit or Gross Profit Be Eliminated?

Some accountants have discussed the propriety of eliminating intercompany *net profit,* rather than *gross profit,* in inventories of the consolidated entity. There is little theoretical support for such a proposal. First, elimination of intercompany net profit would in effect capitalize operating (selling and administrative) expenses in consolidated inventories. Selling expenses are always period costs, and only in unusual circumstances are some administrative expenses capitalized in inventories as product costs. Second, the measurement of net profit for particular merchandise requires many assumptions as to allocations of common costs.

INTERCOMPANY SALES OF PLANT ASSETS

Intercompany sales of plant assets differ from intercompany sales of merchandise in two respects. First, intercompany sales of plant assets between affiliated companies are rare transactions. In contrast, intercompany sales of merchandise occur frequently, once a program of such sales has been established. Second, the relatively long economic lives of plant assets require the passage of many accounting periods before intercompany gains or losses on sales of these assets are realized in transactions with outsiders. Conversely, intercompany profits in consolidated inventories at the end of one accounting period usually are realized through sale of the merchandise to outsiders during the ensuing period. These differences are illustrated in the working paper eliminations for intercompany gains or losses on sales of plant assets described in the following sections.

Intercompany Gain on Sale of Land

Suppose that, during the year ended December 31, Year 3, Post Corporation (the parent company) sold to Sage Company (the partially owned subsidiary) for $175,000 a parcel of land that had cost Post $125,000. Sage acquired the land for a new building site. The two companies would record the transaction as follows (disregarding income tax effects to Post Corporation):

Journal entries for parent company's downstream sale of land to partially owned subsidiary

Post Corporation journal entry			Sage Company journal entry		
Cash.............	175,000		Land..............	175,000	
Land.........		125,000	Cash		175,000
Intercompany			To record acquisition		
Gain on Sale			of land from Post		
of Land		50,000	Corporation.		
To record sale of land					
to Sage Company.					

In consolidated financial statements for the year ended December 31, Year 3, the land must be valued at its historical cost to the consolidated entity. Also, the $50,000 intercompany gain must be eliminated, because it has not been *realized* in a transaction with an outsider. Accordingly, the following working paper elimination (in journal entry format) is required on December 31, Year 3:

Working paper elimination for year of intercompany sale of land at a gain

POST CORPORATION AND SUBSIDIARY
Partial Working Paper Eliminations
December 31, Year 3

(c) Intercompany Gain on Sale of Land—Post 50,000
    Land—Sage 50,000
    To eliminate unrealized intercompany gain on sale of land. (Income tax effects are disregarded.)

The working paper elimination is entered as follows in the working paper for consolidated financial statements for the year ended December 31, Year 3:

Partial working paper for consolidated financial statements— year of intercompany sale of land at a gain

POST CORPORATION AND SUBSIDIARY
Partial Working Paper for Consolidated Financial Statements
For Year Ended December 31, Year 3

	Post Corporation	Sage Company	Eliminations increase (decrease)	Consolidated
Income Statement				
Intercompany gain on sale of land	50,000		(c) (50,000)	
Balance Sheet				
Land (for building site)		175,000	(c) (50,000)	125,000

Because land is not a depreciable plant asset, in subsequent years no journal entries affecting the land would be made by Sage unless the land were resold to an outsider (or back to Post). Nevertheless, in ensuing years, as long as Sage owns the land, its $175,000 cost to Sage is overstated $50,000 for consolidated financial statement purposes. Because the gain of $50,000 on the sale of land was closed with other income statement amounts to Post's Retained Earnings ledger account on December 31, Year 3, the working paper elimination (in journal entry format) on page 443 is required for Year 4 and subsequent years.

The working paper elimination on page 443 has no effect on the minority interest in the net income or net assets of the subsidiary, because *the unrealized gain was attributable entirely to the parent company, the seller.*

Working paper elimination for years subsequent to intercompany sale of land at a gain

POST CORPORATION AND SUBSIDIARY
Partial Working Paper Eliminations
December 31, Year 4

(c) Retained Earnings—Post 50,000
    Land—Sage....................................... 50,000
    To eliminate unrealized intercompany gain in land. (Income tax effects are disregarded.)

Suppose that, instead of constructing a building on the land, Sage sold the land to an outsider for $200,000 during the year ended December 31, Year 5. Sage would prepare the following journal entry to record the sale:

Subsidiary's journal entry for sale of land to an outsider

Cash 200,000
    Land 175,000
    Gain on Sale of Land................................. 25,000
To record sale of land to an outsider.

The consolidated income statement for the year ended December 31, Year 5, must show that, for **consolidated** purposes, a **$75,000 gain was realized** on Sage's sale of the land. This $75,000 gain consists of the $25,000 gain recognized by Sage and the $50,000 intercompany gain on Post's sale of the land to Sage two years earlier. The following working paper elimination (in journal entry format) is required on December 31, Year 5:

Working paper elimination to recognize realization of intercompany gain on sale of land

POST CORPORATION AND SUBSIDIARY
Partial Working Paper Eliminations
December 31, Year 5

(c) Retained Earnings—Post 50,000
    Gain on Sale of Land—Post.......................... 50,000
    To recognize $50,000 gain on Post Corporation's sale of land to Sage Company resulting from sale of land by Sage to an outsider. (Income tax effects are disregarded.)

No further eliminations with respect to the land would be required after Year 5.

Intercompany Gain on Sale of Depreciable Plant Asset

Periodic depreciation expense causes a significant difference in the working paper eliminations for an unrealized intercompany gain on the sale of a depreciable plant asset, compared with the eliminations described in the preceding section. Because the unrealized intercompany gain must be eliminated from the valuation of the depreciable asset in a consolidated balance sheet, the appropriate gain element also must be eliminated from the related depreciation expense in a consolidated income statement. This concept is illustrated in the following pages.

Intercompany Gain on Date of Sale of Depreciable Plant Asset   The date-of-sale working paper elimination for the intercompany sale of a depreciable plant asset is identical to the comparable elimination for land. On the date of sale, no depreciation expense has been recognized by the affiliate that acquired the plant asset.

To illustrate, assume that on December 31, Year 3, Sage Company (the partially owned subsidiary) sold machinery to Post Corporation (the parent company). Details of the sale and depreciation policy of the machinery follow:

Selling price of machinery to Post Corporation	$60,000
Cost of machinery to Sage Company when acquired Jan. 2, Year 1	50,000
Estimated residual value:	
To Sage Company, Jan. 2, Year 1	$ 4,000
To Post Corporation, Dec. 31, Year 3	4,000
Economic life:	
To Sage Company, Jan. 2, Year 1	10 years
To Post Corporation, Dec. 31, Year 3	5 years
Annual depreciation expense (straight-line method):	
To Sage Company ($46,000 × 0.10)	$ 4,600
To Post Corporation ($56,000 × 0.20)	11,200

Details of machinery sold upstream to parent company by partially owned subsidiary

The two companies would account for the sale on December 31, Year 3, as follows (disregarding income tax effects to Sage):

Journal entries for partially owned subsidiary's upstream sale of machinery to parent company

Post Corporation journal entry	Sage Company journal entry
Machinery 60,000	Cash 60,000
Cash 60,000	Accumulated Depre-
To record acquisition	ciation ($4,600 × 3). 13,800
of machinery from	Machinery 50,000
Sage Company.	Intercompany
	Gain on Sale
	of Machinery. 23,800
	To record sale of ma-
	chinery to Post Cor-
	poration.

The following working paper elimination (in journal entry format) is required for consolidated financial statements on December 31, Year 3, the date of intercompany sale of the machinery:

Working paper
elimination on date of
intercompany sale of
machinery at a gain

POST CORPORATION AND SUBSIDIARY
Partial Working Paper Eliminations
December 31, Year 3

(d) *Intercompany Gain on Sale of Machinery—Sage* 23,800
         Machinery—Post. 23,800
    To eliminate unrealized intercompany gain on sale of machinery.
    (Income tax effects are disregarded.)

The elimination results in the machinery's being valued in the consolidated balance sheet at its carrying amount to Sage Company—the seller—as follows:

Effect of elimination of
unrealized
intercompany profit on
upstream sale of
machinery

Cost of machinery to Post Corporation (acquirer parent company) $60,000
Less: Amount of elimination—intercompany gain 23,800
Difference—equal to carrying amount [cost ($50,000), less accumulated depreciation ($13,800)] of machinery to Sage Company (seller subsidiary). $36,200

Elimination of the $23,800 intercompany gain on the sale of machinery *is taken into account in the computation of the minority interest in the net income of the partially owned subsidiary—the seller—*for Year 3. The $23,800 elimination also enters into the computation of *Sage's retained earnings,* for consolidation purposes, on December 31, Year 3. These matters are illustrated on page 465.

Intercompany Gain Subsequent to Date of Sale of Depreciable Plant Asset   An appropriate intercompany gain element must be eliminated from depreciation ex-

Working paper
elimination for first year
subsequent to
intercompany sale of
machinery at a gain

POST CORPORATION AND SUBSIDIARY
Partial Working Paper Eliminations
December 31, Year 4

(d) *Retained Earnings—Sage ($23,800 × 0.95)* 22,610
    Minority Interest in Net Assets of Subsidiary ($23,800 × 0.05).. 1,190
    Accumulated Depreciation—Post 4,760
         Machinery—Post. 23,800
         Depreciation Expense—Post 4,760
    To eliminate unrealized intercompany gain in machinery and in related depreciation. (Income tax effects are disregarded.) Gain element in straight-line depreciation computed as $23,800 × 0.20 = $4,760, based on five-year economic life.

pense for a plant asset acquired by one affiliate from another at a gain. The working paper elimination (in journal entry format) on page 445 for Post Corporation and subsidiary on December 31, Year 4 (one year after the intercompany sale of machinery), illustrates this point.

Because Sage Company's intercompany gain on sale of the machinery was closed to Sage's Retained Earnings ledger account on December 31, Year 3, the working paper elimination on December 31, Year 4, corrects the overstatement of Sage's *beginning-of-year* retained earnings from the viewpoint of the consolidated entity. In addition, the minority interest's share of the overstatement in the beginning retained earnings of Sage is recorded.

The intercompany gain eliminated from Post Corporation's depreciation expense may be verified as follows:

<table>
<tr><td>Verification of intercompany gain element in depreciation expense of parent company</td><td>*Post's annual straight-line depreciation expense [($60,000 − $4,000) × 0.20]*</td><td>$11,200</td></tr>
<tr><td></td><td>*Less: Straight-line depreciation expense for a five-year economic life, based on*
Sage's carrying amount on date of sale [($36,200 − $4,000) × 0.20] . . . .</td><td>6,440</td></tr>
<tr><td></td><td>*Difference—equal to intercompany gain element in Post's annual depreciation*
expense. . . . .</td><td>$ 4,760</td></tr>
</table>

Intercompany Gain in Depreciation and Minority Interest From the point of view of the consolidated entity, the intercompany gain element of the acquiring affiliate's annual depreciation expense represents a *realization* of a portion of the intercompany gain by the selling affiliate. Depreciation, in this view, is in effect an *indirect sale* of a portion of the machinery to the customers of Post Corporation—the acquirer of the machinery. The selling prices of Post's products produced by the machinery are established at amounts adequate to cover all costs of producing the products, including depreciation expense.

Thus, the $4,760 credit to Post's depreciation expense in the December 31, Year 4, working paper elimination illustrated on page 445 in effect *increases* Sage's net income for consolidated purposes. *This increase must be considered in the computation of the minority interest in the subsidiary's net income* for the year ended December 31, Year 4, *and of the amount of the subsidiary's retained earnings included in consolidated retained earnings on that date,* as illustrated on page 476.

Intercompany Gain in Later Years Working paper eliminations for later years in the economic life of the machinery sold at an intercompany gain must reflect the fact that the intercompany gain element in the *acquiring affiliate's* annual depreciation expense in effect represents a *realization* of the intercompany gain by the *selling affiliate.* For example, the working paper elimination (in journal entry format) for Post Corporation and subsidiary on December 31, Year 5 (two years following the intercompany sale of the machinery), is as follows:

Working paper
elimination for second
year subsequent to
intercompany sale of
machinery at a gain

POST CORPORATION AND SUBSIDIARY
Partial Working Paper Eliminations
December 31, Year 5

(d) Retained Earnings—Sage [($23,800 − $4,760) × 0.95]   18,088
Minority Interest in Net Assets of Subsidiary
[($23,800 − $4,760) × 0.05]   952
Accumulated Depreciation—Post ($4,760 × 2)   9,520
Machinery—Post   23,800
Depreciation Expense—Post   4,760
To eliminate unrealized intercompany gain in machinery and re-
lated depreciation. (Income tax effects are disregarded.)

The credit amounts of the foregoing elimination for Year 5 are the same as those for Year 4. The credit amounts will remain unchanged for all working paper eliminations during the remaining economic life of the machinery, because of the parent company's use of the straight-line method of depreciation. The $19,040 total ($18,088 + $952 = $19,040) of the debits to Sage's retained earnings and to the minority interest in net assets of subsidiary represents the **unrealized** portion of the intercompany gain **at the beginning of Year 5.** Each succeeding year, the unrealized portion of the intercompany gain **decreases,** as indicated by the following summary of the working paper elimination **debits** for those years:

Debit elements of
working paper
eliminations for third,
fourth, and fifth years
subsequent to
intercompany sale of
machinery at a gain

POST CORPORATION AND SUBSIDIARY
Partial Working Paper Eliminations—Debits Only
December 31, Year 6 through Year 8

	Year ended Dec. 31,		
	Year 6	Year 7	Year 8
Debits			
(d) Retained earnings—Sage	$13,566	$ 9,044	$ 4,522
Minority interest in net assets of subsidiary . . .	714	476	238
Accumulated depreciation—Post	14,280	19,040	23,800

Working paper
elimination following
end of economic life of
machinery sold at an
intercompany gain

POST CORPORATION AND SUBSIDIARY
Partial Working Paper Eliminations
December 31, Year 9

Accumulated Depreciation—Post   23,800
Machinery—Post   23,800
To eliminate intercompany gain in machinery and related accumu-
lated depreciation. (Income tax effects are disregarded.)

At the end of Year 8, the entire $23,800 of intercompany gain has been realized through Post Corporation's annual depreciation expense. Thereafter, the working paper elimination (in journal entry format) on page 447 is required for the machinery until it is sold or scrapped.

INTERCOMPANY LEASE OF PROPERTY UNDER CAPITAL/ SALES-TYPE LEASE

Land and buildings, machinery and equipment, and other property may be transferred from one affiliate to another under a lease that is a *sales-type lease* to the lessor and a *capital lease* to the lessee.[2] If so, a number of intercompany ledger accounts must be established by both the lessor and the lessee to account for the lease.

To illustrate, assume that on January 2, Year 3, Palm Corporation (the parent company) leased equipment to Starr Company (the wholly owned subsidiary) under a sales-type lease requiring Starr to pay Palm $10,000 on each January 2, Year 3 through Year 6, with a bargain purchase option of $1,000 payable on January 2, Year 7. Palm's implicit interest rate, which was known to Starr and was less than Starr's incremental borrowing rate, was 8%. The economic life of the equipment to Starr was six years, with no residual value. The cost of the leased equipment, which had been carried in Palm's Inventories ledger account, was $30,000, and there were no initial direct costs under the lease.

The present value of the minimum lease payments, which constitutes Palm's *net investment in the lease,* is computed as follows (using present value tables):

Computation of present value of minimum lease payments

Present value of $10,000 each year for four years at 8% ($10,000 × 3.577097)	$35,771
Present value of $1,000 in four years at 8% ($1,000 × 0.735030)	735
Palm Corporation's net investment in the lease	$36,506

The journal entries of Palm Corporation and Starr Company for Year 3, the first year of the lease, are illustrated on page 449, and selected ledger accounts for both companies relative to the lease are shown on pages 450 through 452.

Working paper eliminations (in journal entry format) for Palm Corporation and subsidiary for the first two years of the intercompany lease are on page 453 (intercompany interest revenue and intercompany interest expense self-eliminate on the same line of the income statement section of the working paper for consolidated financial statements).

---

[2] Accounting for leases is discussed and illustrated in intermediate accounting textbooks.

Parent company's
(lessor's) journal
entries for first year of
intercompany sales-
type lease

PALM CORPORATION
Journal Entries

Year 3

Jan. 2 Intercompany Lease Receivables

[($10,000 × 4) + $1,000] 41,000

Intercompany Cost of Goods Sold 30,000

Intercompany Sales 36,506

Unearned Intercompany Interest Revenue

($41,000 − $36,506) 4,494

Inventories 30,000

To record sales-type lease with Starr Company at incep-
tion and cost of leased equipment.

2 Cash 10,000

Intercompany Lease Receivables 10,000

To record receipt of first payment on intercompany lease.

Dec. 31 Unearned Intercompany Interest Revenue

[($31,000 − $4,494) × 0.08] 2,120

Intercompany Interest Revenue 2,120

To recognize interest earned for first year of intercompany
sales-type lease.

Subsidiary's (lessee's)
journal entries for first
year of intercompany
capital lease

STARR COMPANY
Journal Entries

Year 3

Jan. 2 Leased Equipment—Capital Lease 36,506

Intercompany Liability under Capital Lease (net) .. 36,506

To record intercompany capital lease at inception.

2 Intercompany Liability under Capital Lease (net)......... 10,000

Cash 10,000

To record lease payment for first year of intercompany
lease.

Dec. 31 Intercompany Interest Expense

[($36,506 − $10,000) × 0.08] 2,120

Intercompany Interest Payable 2,120

To record accrued interest on intercompany lease obliga-
tion on Dec. 31, Year 3.

31 Depreciation Expense ($36,506 ÷ 6) 6,084

Leased Equipment—Capital Lease 6,084

To record depreciation expense (straight-line method) for
first year of intercompany lease. (Six-year economic life of
leased equipment is used because lease contains a bar-
gain purchase option.)

Parent company's
(lessor's) ledger
accounts for
intercompany sales-
type lease

PALM CORPORATION
Ledger Accounts
Intercompany Lease Receivables

Date	Explanation	Debit	Credit	Balance
Year 3				
Jan. 2	Inception of lease	41,000		41,000 dr
2	Receipt of first payment		10,000	31,000 dr
Year 4				
Jan. 2	Receipt of second payment		10,000	21,000 dr
Year 5				
Jan. 2	Receipt of third payment		10,000	11,000 dr
Year 6				
Jan. 2	Receipt of fourth payment		10,000	1,000 dr
Year 7				
Jan. 2	Receipt of purchase option		1,000	-0-

Unearned Intercompany Interest Revenue

Date	Explanation	Debit	Credit	Balance
Year 3				
Jan. 2	Inception of lease			
	($41,000 − $36,506)		4,494	4,494 cr
Dec. 31	Interest for year			
	[($31,000 − $4,494) × 0.08]	2,120		2,374 cr
Year 4				
Dec. 31	Interest for year			
	[($21,000 − $2,374) × 0.08]	1,490		884 cr
Year 5				
Dec. 31	Interest for year			
	[($11,000 − $884) × 0.08]	809		75 cr
Year 6				
Dec. 31	Interest for year			
	[($1,000 − $75) × 0.08]	75*		-0-

* Adjusted $1 for rounding.

Intercompany Interest Revenue

Date	Explanation	Debit	Credit	Balance
Year 3				
Dec. 31	Interest for Year 3		2,120	2,120 cr
31	Closing entry	2,120		-0-
Year 4				
Dec. 31	Interest for Year 4		1,490	1,490 cr
31	Closing entry	1,490		-0-
Year 5				
Dec. 31	Interest for Year 5		809	809 cr
31	Closing entry	809		-0-
Year 6				
Dec. 31	Interest for Year 6		75*	75 cr
31	Closing entry	75		-0-

* Adjusted $1 for rounding.

Subsidiary's (lessee's) ledger accounts for intercompany capital lease

STARR COMPANY
Ledger Accounts
Leased Equipment—Capital Lease

Date	Explanation	Debit	Credit	Balance
Year 3				
Jan. 2	Capital lease at inception	36,506		36,506 dr
Dec. 31	Depreciation for Year 3		6,084	30,422 dr
Year 4				
Dec. 31	Depreciation for Year 4		6,084	24,338 dr
Year 5				
Dec. 31	Depreciation for Year 5		6,084	18,254 dr
Year 6				
Dec. 31	Depreciation for Year 6		6,084	12,170 dr
Year 7				
Dec. 31	Depreciation for Year 7		6,085*	6,085 dr
Year 8				
Dec. 31	Depreciation for Year 8		6,085*	-0-

* Adjusted $1 for rounding.

Intercompany Liability under Capital Lease

Date	Explanation	Debit	Credit	Balance
Year 3				
Jan. 2	Capital lease at inception		36,506	36,506 cr
2	First lease payment	10,000		26,506 cr
Year 4				
Jan. 2	($10,000 − $2,120 interest)	7,880		18,626 cr
Year 5				
Jan. 2	($10,000 − $1,490 interest)	8,510		10,116 cr
Year 6				
Jan. 2	($10,000 − $809 interest)	9,191		925 cr
Year 7				
Jan. 2	($1,000 − $75 interest)	925		-0-

(continued)

STARR COMPANY
Ledger Accounts (concluded)
Intercompany Interest Expense

Date	Explanation	Debit	Credit	Balance
Year 3				
Dec. 31	($26,506 × 0.08)	2,120		2,120 dr
31	Closing entry		2,120	-0-
Year 4				
Dec. 31	($18,626 × 0.08)	1,490		1,490 dr
31	Closing entry		1,490	-0-
Year 5				
Dec. 31	($10,116 × 0.08)	809		809 dr
31	Closing entry		809	-0-
Year 6				
Dec. 31	($925 × 0.08)	75*		75 dr
31	Closing entry		75	-0-

* Adjusted $1 for rounding.

Depreciation Expense

Date	Explanation	Debit	Credit	Balance
Year 3				
Dec. 31	($36,506 ÷ 6)	6,084		6,084 dr
31	Closing entry		6,084	-0-
Year 4				
Dec. 31	($36,506 ÷ 6)	6,084		6,084 dr
31	Closing entry		6,084	-0-
Year 5				
Dec. 31	($36,506 ÷ 6)	6,084		6,084 dr
31	Closing entry		6,084	-0-
Year 6				
Dec. 31	($36,506 ÷ 6)	6,084		6,084 dr
31	Closing entry		6,084	-0-
Year 7				
Dec. 31	($36,506 ÷ 6)	6,085*		6,085 dr
31	Closing entry		6,085	-0-
Year 8				
Dec. 31	($36,506 ÷ 6)	6,085*		6,085 dr
31	Closing entry		6,085	-0-

* Adjusted $1 for rounding.

Working paper
elimination for first year
of intercompany sales-
type/capital lease

PALM CORPORATION AND SUBSIDIARY
Partial Working Paper Eliminations
December 31, Year 3

(b) Intercompany Liability under Capital Lease—Starr 26,506
    Intercompany Interest Payable—Starr 2,120
    Unearned Intercompany Interest Revenue—Palm 2,374
    Intercompany Sales—Palm 36,506
             Intercompany Cost of Goods Sold—Palm 30,000
             Intercompany Lease Receivables—Palm 31,000
             Leased Equipment—Capital Lease—Starr
             ($36,506 − $30,000 − $1,084) 5,422
             Depreciation Expense—Starr
             [($36,506 − $30,000) ÷ 6] 1,084
To eliminate intercompany accounts associated with intercompany lease and to defer unrealized portion of intercompany gross profit on sales-type lease. (Income tax effects are disregarded.)

Working paper
elimination for second
year of intercompany
sales-type/capital lease

PALM CORPORATION AND SUBSIDIARY
Partial Working Paper Eliminations
December 31, Year 4

(b) Intercompany Liability under Capital Lease—Starr 18,626
    Intercompany Interest Payable—Starr 1,490
    Unearned Intercompany Interest Revenue—Palm 884
    Retained Earnings—Palm [($36,506 − $30,000) − $1,084] 5,422
             Intercompany Lease Receivables—Palm 21,000
             Leased Equipment—Capital Lease—Starr
             ($5,422 − $1,084) 4,338
             Depreciation Expense—Starr 1,084
To eliminate intercompany accounts associated with intercompany lease and to defer unrealized portion of intercompany gross profit on sales-type lease. (Income tax effects are disregarded.)

The eliminations on page 453 have features comparable with both eliminations for intercompany sales of merchandise (page 439) and eliminations for intercompany sales of plant assets (page 445). For example, the elimination of December 31, Year 3, removes the parent company's intercompany sales ($36,506) and cost of goods sold ($30,000), because the leased equipment had been carried in the parent's Inventories ledger account and the sales-type lease (from the parent's viewpoint) occurred during Year 3. The subsidiary's (lessee's) depreciation expense of $1,084 for Year 3 represents the realization of a portion of the parent's gross profit margin on the intercompany sale. In the Year 4 elimination, the original $6,506 ($36,506 − $30,000 = $6,506) unrealized gross profit element in the subsidiary's leased equipment has been reduced by the $1,084 reduction of the subsidiary's Year 3 depreciation expense.

INTERCOMPANY SALES OF INTANGIBLE ASSETS

The working paper eliminations for intercompany gains on sales of intangible assets are similar to those for intercompany gains in depreciable plant assets, except that no accumulated amortization ledger account may be involved. The unrealized intercompany gain of the selling affiliate is realized through periodic amortization expense recognized by the acquiring affiliate.

To illustrate, assume that on January 2, Year 4, Palm Corporation sold to Starr Company, its wholly owned subsidiary, for $40,000 a patent carried in Palm's accounting records at $32,000. The patent had a remaining economic life of four years on January 2, Year 4, and was amortized by the straight-line method. The appropriate working paper elimination (in journal entry format) on December 31, Year 4, follows:

Working paper elimination for year of intercompany sale of patent at a gain

PALM CORPORATION AND SUBSIDIARY
Partial Working Paper Eliminations
December 31, Year 4

(c) Intercompany Gain on Sale of Patent—Palm ($40,000 − $32,000)   8,000
    Amortization Expense—Starr ($8,000 ÷ 4).   2,000
    Patent—Starr ($8,000 − $2,000).   6,000
    To eliminate unrealized intercompany gain in patent and related amortization. (Income tax effects are disregarded.)

The working paper elimination (in journal entry format) for December 31, Year 5, is as follows:

<table>
<tr><td>Working paper
elimination for year
following year of
intercompany sale of
patent at a gain</td><td>

PALM CORPORATION AND SUBSIDIARY
Partial Working Paper Eliminations
December 31, Year 5

(c) *Retained Earnings—Palm ($8,000 − $2,000)*................... *6,000*
          Amortization Expense—Starr ($8,000 ÷ 4)..............   *2,000*
          Patent—Starr ($6,000 − $2,000).......................   *4,000*
    To eliminate unrealized intercompany gain in patent and related
    amortization. (Income tax effects are disregarded.)

</td></tr>
</table>

ACQUISITION OF AFFILIATE'S BONDS

The intercompany profits (gains) or losses on intercompany sales of merchandise, plant assets, and intangible assets and on leases of property under capital/sales-type leases are, on the date of sale, *unrealized* gains or losses resulting from business transactions between two affiliated corporations. Intercompany gains and losses may be *realized by the consolidated entity* when one affiliate acquires in the open market outstanding bonds of another affiliate. The gain or loss on such a transaction is *imputed,* because the transaction is not consummated between the two affiliates. No realized or unrealized intercompany gain or loss would result from the *direct* acquisition of one affiliate's bonds by another affiliate, because the cost of the investment to the acquirer would be *exactly offset* by the issuance proceeds of the debt.

Illustration of Acquisition of Affiliate's Bonds

Assume that on January 2, Year 3, Sage Company (the partially owned subsidiary) issued to the public $500,000 face amount of 10% bonds due January 1, Year 8. The bonds were issued at a price to yield a 12% return to investors. Interest was payable annually on January 1. Bond issue costs are disregarded in this example.

    The net proceeds of the bond issue to Sage were $463,952, computed as follows:[3]

<table>
<tr><td>Computation of
proceeds of bonds
issued by partially
owned subsidiary</td><td>

Present value of $500,000 in five years at 12%, with interest paid annually
  ($500,000 × 0.567427).. *$283,713*
Add: Present value of $50,000 each year for five years at 12%
  ($50,000 × 3.604776).. *180,239*
Proceeds of bond issue.. *$463,952*

</td></tr>
</table>

---

[3] Intermediate accounting textbooks generally contain a discussion of computations of bond issuance proceeds using present value tables. (Annual interest payments are assumed to simplify the illustration; bonds typically pay interest semiannually.)

During the year ended December 31, Year 3, Sage prepared the following journal entries for the bonds, including the amortization of bond discount by the *interest method:*

Partially owned subsidiary's journal entries for issuance of bonds payable and accrual of interest

Year 3

Jan. 2	Cash	463,952	
	Discount on Bonds Payable	36,048	
	Bonds Payable		500,000
	To record issuance of 10% bonds due Jan. 1, Year 8, at a discount to yield 12%.		

Year 3

Dec. 31	Interest Expense ($463,952 × 0.12)	55,674	
	Interest Payable ($500,000 × 0.10)		50,000
	Discount on Bonds Payable		5,674
	To record accrual of annual interest on 10% bonds.		

On December 31, Year 3, the balance of Sage's Discount on Bonds Payable ledger account was $30,374 ($36,048 − $5,674 = $30,374).

Assume that on December 31, Year 3, Post Corporation (the parent company) had cash available for investment. With a market yield rate of 15% on that date, Sage Company's 10% bonds might be acquired at a substantial discount. Consequently, Post acquired in the open market on December 31, Year 3, $300,000 face amount (or 60% of the total issue of $500,000) of the bonds for $257,175 plus $30,000 accrued interest for one year ($300,000 × 0.10 = $30,000). The $257,175 acquisition cost is computed as follows:

Computation of parent company's acquisition cost for bonds of partially owned subsidiary

Present value of $300,000 in four years at 15%, with interest paid annually ($300,000 × 0.571753)	$171,526
Add: Present value of $30,000 each year for four years at 15% ($30,000 × 2.854978)	85,649
Cost to Post Corporation of $300,000 face amount of bonds	$257,175

Post prepared the following journal entry on December 31, Year 3, to record the acquisition of Sage's bonds:

Parent company's journal entry to record open-market acquisition of bonds of partially owned subsidiary

Investment in Sage Company Bonds	257,175	
Intercompany Interest Receivable	30,000	
Cash		287,175
To record acquisition of $300,000 face amount of Sage Company's 10% bonds due Jan. 1, Year 8, and accrued interest for one year.		

Upon receiving notification of the parent company's acquisition of the bonds, Sage Company prepared the following journal entry on December 31, Year 3, to record the *intercompany* status of a portion of its bonds payable:

<table>
<tr><td style="width:30%; vertical-align:top; text-align:right;">Partially owned subsidiary's journal entry to record parent company's open-market acquisition of subsidiary's outstanding bonds</td><td>

Bonds Payable	300,000	
Discount on Intercompany Bonds Payable ($30,374 × 0.60)	18,224	
Interest Payable ($50,000 × 0.60)	30,000	
Intercompany Bonds Payable		300,000
Discount on Bonds Payable.		18,224
Intercompany Interest Payable		30,000
To transfer to intercompany accounts all amounts attributable to bonds acquired by parent company in open market.		

</td></tr>
</table>

From the standpoint of the consolidated entity, Post Corporation's acquisition of Sage Company's bonds is equivalent to the *extinguishment* of the bonds at a *realized* gain of $24,601, computed as follows:

<table>
<tr><td style="width:30%; vertical-align:top; text-align:right;">Computation of realized gain on parent company's open-market acquisition of subsidiary's outstanding bonds</td><td>

Carrying amount of Sage Company's bonds acquired by Post Corporation on	
Dec. 31, Year 3 ($300,000 − $18,224)	$281,776
Less: Cost of Post Corporation's investment	257,175
Realized gain on extinguishment of bonds	$ 24,601

</td></tr>
</table>

The $24,601 realized gain *is not recorded* in the accounting records of either the parent company or the subsidiary. Instead, it is recognized in the following working paper elimination (in journal entry format) on December 31, Year 3:

<table>
<tr><td style="width:30%; vertical-align:top; text-align:right;">Working paper elimination to recognize gain on intercompany extinguishment of bonds payable</td><td>

POST CORPORATION AND SUBSIDIARY
Partial Working Paper Eliminations
December 31, Year 3

(e) Intercompany Bonds Payable—Sage	300,000	
Discount on Intercompany Bonds Payable—Sage. . . .		18,224
Investment in Sage Company Bonds—Post		257,175
Gain on Extinguishment of Bonds—Sage.		24,601
To eliminate subsidiary's bonds acquired by parent and to recognize gain on the extinguishment of the bonds. (Income tax effects are disregarded.)		

</td></tr>
</table>

Disposition of Gain on Extinguishment of Bonds The working paper elimination illustrated above attributes the gain on Post Corporation's acquisition of its subsidiary's bonds to Sage Company—the subsidiary. This treatment of the gain follows from the assumption that the parent company's open-market acquisition of the subsidiary's bonds was, in substance, the extinguishment of the bonds by the subsidiary.

The parent company acted as *agent* for the subsidiary in the open-market transaction; thus, the gain is attributed to the subsidiary. Under this approach, the accounting for the gain on the acquisition of the subsidiary's bonds is the same as if the *subsidiary itself* had acquired and retired the bonds.

The entire realized gain of $24,601 is displayed in the consolidated income statement of Post Corporation and subsidiary for the year ended December 31, Year 3.[4] If the gain is *material,* it is displayed as an *extraordinary item,* net of applicable income taxes.[5]

Minority Interest in Gain on Extinguishment of Bonds   As discussed in the preceding section, the gain on Post Corporation's acquisition of its subsidiary's bonds is attributed to the partially owned subsidiary. It follows that *the gain should be considered in the computation of the minority interest in the subsidiary's net income* for the year ended December 31, Year 3. Also, the gain is included in the computation of the amount of the subsidiary's retained earnings to be included in consolidated retained earnings on December 31, Year 3. These procedures are illustrated on page 465.

Accounting for Gain in Subsequent Years

In the four years following Post Corporation's acquisition of Sage Company's bonds, the gain *realized but unrecorded* on the date of acquisition is in effect *recorded* by the consolidated entity through the differences in the two affiliates' amortization and accumulation of bond discount. (It is essential that the affiliate that acquired the bonds at a discount undertake an accumulation program consistent with that of the affiliate that issued the bonds; thus, Post Corporation should adopt the interest method of amortization used by Sage.) To illustrate this concept, the accounting for the bond interest by the two companies for the year ended December 31, Year 4, is on page 459, and the ledger accounts of both companies relative to the intercompany bonds are illustrated on pages 460 and 461 for the four years the bonds remain outstanding.

A comparison of the yearly journal entries to Post Corporation's Intercompany Interest Revenue ledger account and Sage Company's Intercompany Interest Expense account demonstrates that the difference between the annual entries in the two

Total of differences between parent's intercompany interest revenue and subsidiary's intercompany interest expense is equal to realized gain on parent's acquisition of subsidiary's bonds

Year ended Dec. 31,	Post Corporation's intercompany interest revenue	Sage Company's intercompany interest expense	Difference—representing recording of realized gain
Year 4	$ 38,576	$ 33,813	$ 4,763
Year 5	39,863	34,271	5,592
Year 6	41,342	34,783	6,559
Year 7	43,044	35,357	7,687
Totals	$162,825	$138,224	$24,601

[4] *APB Opinion No. 26,* ''Early Extinguishment of Debt,'' AICPA (New York: 1973), pp. 501–502.
[5] *FASB Statement No. 64,* ''Extinguishments of Debt . . . ,'' FASB (Stamford: 1982), p. 2.

accounts represents the ***recording,*** in the separate companies' accounting records, of the $24,601 gain ***realized but unrecorded*** when the parent company acquired the subsidiary's bonds in the open market. A summary of the differences between the two intercompany interest amounts is on page 458.

Affiliated companies' journal entries for bonds for year after intercompany acquisition of the bonds

	Post Corporation journal entries		Sage Company journal entries		
Year 4					
Jan. 2	Cash 30,000		Intercompany Interest Pay-		
	Intercompany Interest		able	30,000	
	Receivable.	30,000	Interest Payable	20,000	
	To record receipt of accrued		Cash		50,000
	interest on Sage Company's		To record payment of ac-		
	10% bonds.		crued interest on 10% bonds.		
Dec. 31	Intercompany Interest Re-		Intercompany Interest Ex-		
	ceivable 30,000		pense	33,813	
	Investment in Sage Company		Interest Expense.	22,542	
	Bonds	8,576	Intercompany Interest		
	Intercompany Interest		Payable		30,000
	Revenue.	38,576	Interest Payable		20,000
	To accrue annual interest on		Discount on Intercom-		
	Sage Company's 10% bonds		pany Bonds Payable .		3,813
	($257,175 × 0.15 = $38,576).		Discount on Bonds		
			Payable		2,542
			To accrue annual interest on		
			10% bonds, Interest is com-		
			puted as follows:		
			Intercompany ($300,000 −		
			$18,224) × 0.12 =		
			$33,813		
			Other ($200,000 −		
			$12,150) × 0.12 =		
			$22,542		

Parent company's
ledger accounts for
intercompany bonds

POST CORPORATION
Ledger Accounts
Investment in Sage Company Bonds

Date	Explanation	Debit	Credit	Balance
Year 3				
Dec. 31	Acquisition of $300,000 face			
	amount of bonds	257,175		257,175 dr
Year 4				
Dec. 31	Accumulation of discount			
	($38,576 − $30,000)	8,576		265,751 dr
Year 5				
Dec. 31	Accumulation of discount			
	($39,863 − $30,000)	9,863		275,614 dr
Year 6				
Dec. 31	Accumulation of discount			
	($41,342 − $30,000)	11,342		286,956 dr
Year 7				
Dec. 31	Accumulation of discount			
	($43,044 − $30,000)	13,044		300,000 dr

Intercompany Interest Revenue

Date	Explanation	Debit	Credit	Balance
Year 4				
Dec. 31	($257,175 × 0.15)		38,576	38,576 cr
31	Closing entry	38,576		-0-
Year 5				
Dec. 31	($265,751 × 0.15)		39,863	39,863 cr
31	Closing entry	39,863		-0-
Year 6				
Dec. 31	($275,614 × 0.15)		41,342	41,342 cr
31	Closing entry	41,342		-0-
Year 7				
Dec. 31	($286,956 × 0.15)		43,044*	43,044 cr
31	Closing entry	43,044		-0-

* Adjusted $1 for rounding.

SAGE COMPANY
Ledger Accounts
Intercompany Bonds Payable

Date	Explanation	Debit	Credit	Balance
Year 3				
Dec. 31	Bonds acquired by parent company		300,000	300,000 cr

Discount on Intercompany Bonds Payable

Date	Explanation	Debit	Credit	Balance
Year 3				
Dec. 31	Bonds acquired by parent company	18,224		18,224 dr
Year 4				
Dec. 31	Amortization ($33,813 − $30,000)		3,813	14,411 dr
Year 5				
Dec. 31	Amortization ($34,271 − $30,000)		4,271	10,140 dr
Year 6				
Dec. 31	Amortization ($34,783 − $30,000)		4,783	5,357 dr
Year 7				
Dec. 31	Amortization ($35,357 − $30,000)		5,357	-0-

Intercompany Interest Expense

Date	Explanation	Debit	Credit	Balance
Year 4				
Dec. 31	[($300,000 − $18,224) × 0.12]	33,813		33,813 dr
31	Closing entry		33,813	-0-
Year 5				
Dec. 31	[($300,000 − $14,411) × 0.12]	34,271		34,271 dr
31	Closing entry		34,271	-0-
Year 6				
Dec. 31	[($300,000 − $10,140) × 0.12]	34,783		34,783 dr
31	Closing entry		34,783	-0-
Year 7				
Dec. 31	[($300,000 − $5,357) × 0.12]	35,357		35,357 dr
31	Closing entry		35,357	-0-

Working Paper Elimination on December 31, Year 4 The working paper elimination (in journal entry format) for the bonds and interest on December 31, Year 4, is as follows:

Working paper
elimination for first year
subsequent to
intercompany
acquisition of bonds

POST CORPORATION AND SUBSIDIARY
Partial Working Paper Eliminations
December 31, Year 4

(e) *Intercompany Interest Revenue—Post*	*38,576*	
Intercompany Bonds Payable—Sage	*300,000*	
Discount on Intercompany Bonds Payable—Sage. . . .		*14,411*
Investment in Sage Company Bonds—Post		*265,751*
Intercompany Interest Expense—Sage.		*33,813*
Retained Earnings—Sage ($24,601 × 0.95)		*23,371*
Minority Interest in Net Assets of Subsidiary		
($24,601 × 0.05).		*1,230*

*To eliminate subsidiary's bonds owned by parent company,
and related interest revenue and expense; and to increase
subsidiary's **beginning** retained earnings by amount of unamortized realized gain on the extinguishment of the bonds.
(Income tax effects are disregarded.)*

The foregoing working paper elimination effectively reduces consolidated income before minority interest by $4,763 ($38,576 − $33,813 = $4,763). As on
page 458, the $4,763 is the difference between the eliminated intercompany interest
revenue of the parent company and the eliminated intercompany interest expense of
the subsidiary. Failure to eliminate intercompany interest in this manner would result
in a $4,763 overstatement of pre-minority interest consolidated income for Year 4,
because the *entire* $24,601 realized gain on the parent company's acquisition of the
subsidiary's bonds was recognized in the consolidated income statement for Year
3—the year the bonds were acquired—as evidenced by the $24,601 credited to
Retained Earnings—Sage and to Minority Interest in Net Assets of Subsidiary in the
elimination.

The $4,763 reduction of consolidated income before minority interest is attrib-
utable to the subsidiary, because the original realized gain to which the $4,763 relates
was allocated to the subsidiary. Consequently, *the $4,763 must be considered in the
computation of minority interest in net income of the subsidiary* for the year ended
December 31, Year 4. The $4,763 also enters into the computation of the amount of
the subsidiary's retained earnings included in consolidated retained earnings. These
amounts associated with Sage Company's bonds are reflected in the working paper
for consolidated financial statements for the year ended December 31, Year 4, as
illustrated on pages 475 and 476.

Working Paper Elimination on December 31, Year 5   The working paper elimination (in journal entry format) on December 31, Year 5, is on page 463.

Comparable working paper eliminations are appropriate for Years 6 and 7. After
Sage Company paid the bonds in full on maturity (January 2, Year 8), no further
working paper eliminations for the bonds would be required.

Working paper
elimination for second
year subsequent to
intercompany
acquisition of bonds

POST CORPORATION AND SUBSIDIARY		
Partial Working Paper Eliminations		
December 31, Year 5		
(e) Intercompany Interest Revenue—Post 39,863		
Intercompany Bonds Payable—Sage 300,000		
Discount on Intercompany Bonds Payable—Sage....		10,140
Investment in Sage Company Bonds—Post		275,614
Intercompany Interest Expense—Sage.............		34,271
Retained Earnings—Sage		
[($24,601 − $4,763) × 0.95]		18,846
Minority Interest in Net Assets of Subsidiary		
[($24,601 − $4,763) × 0.05]		992
To eliminate subsidiary's bonds owned by parent company,		
and related interest revenue and expense; and to increase		
subsidiary's **beginning** retained earnings by amount of un-		
amortized realized gain on the extinguishment of the bonds.		
(Income tax effects are disregarded.)		

Reissuance of Intercompany Bonds

The orderly amortization of a realized gain on the acquisition of an affiliate's bonds is disrupted if the acquiring affiliate sells the bonds to outsiders before they mature. A *transaction* gain or loss on such a sale is not *realized* by the consolidated entity. Logic requires that a working paper elimination be prepared to treat the transaction gain or loss as premium or discount on the reissued bonds, as appropriate. These complex issues are rarely encountered; thus, they are not illustrated here.

ILLUSTRATION OF EFFECT OF INTERCOMPANY PROFITS (GAINS) ON MINORITY INTEREST

To illustrate the effect of intercompany profits (gains) on the computation of minority interest in the net income of a partially owned subsidiary, return to the example of Post Corporation and its 95%-owned purchased subsidiary, Sage Company. The working paper eliminations for Post Corporation and subsidiary (in journal entry format) on pages 464 and 465 are taken from pages 339 and 340 of Chapter 7, and from pages 437, 442, 445, and 457 of this chapter. These eliminations are followed by a *revised* elimination (which differs from the one on page 340 of Chapter 7) for minority interest in net income of subsidiary.

POST CORPORATION AND SUBSIDIARY
Working Paper Eliminations
December 31, Year 3

(a) Common Stock—Sage	400,000	
Additional Paid-in Capital—Sage........................	235,000	
Retained Earnings—Sage ($384,000 − $4,750)..........	379,250	
Retained Earnings of Subsidiary—Post.................	4,750	
Intercompany Investment Income—Post.................	81,700	
Plant Assets (net)—Sage ($176,000 − $14,000)	162,000	
Leasehold—Sage ($25,000 − $5,000)...................	20,000	
Goodwill—Post ($37,050 − $950)......................	36,100	
Cost of Goods Sold—Sage.............................	17,000	
Operating Expenses—Sage	2,000	
Investment in Sage Company Common Stock—Post		1,229,300
Dividends Declared—Sage.......................		50,000
Minority Interest in Net Assets of Subsidiary		
($61,000 − $2,500).............................		58,500

To carry out the following:

(1) Eliminate intercompany investment and equity accounts of subsidiary **at beginning of year,** and subsidiary dividends.

(2) Provide for Year 3 depreciation and amortization on differences between current fair values and carrying amounts of Sage's identifiable net assets as follows:

	Cost of goods sold	Operating expenses
Building depreciation......	$ 2,000	$2,000
Machinery depreciation....	10,000	
Leasehold amortization....	5,000	
Totals	$17,000	$2,000

(3) Allocate unamortized differences between combination date current fair values and carrying amounts to appropriate assets.

(4) Establish minority interest in net assets of subsidiary at beginning of year ($61,000), less minority share of dividends declared by subsidiary during year ($50,000 × 0.05 = $2,500).

(Income tax effects are disregarded.)

(b) Intercompany Sales—Sage	120,000	
Intercompany Cost of Goods Sold—Sage		96,000
Cost of Goods Sold—Post		16,000
Inventories—Post...............................		8,000

To eliminate intercompany sales, cost of goods sold, and unrealized profit in inventories. (Income tax effects are disregarded.)

(continued)

POST CORPORATION AND SUBSIDIARY
Working Paper Eliminations (concluded)
December 31, Year 3

(c) Intercompany Gain on Sale of Land—Post   50,000
　　　　Land—Sage . . . .　　　　　　50,000
　　To eliminate unrealized intercompany gain on sale of land.
　　(Income tax effects are disregarded.)

(d) Intercompany Gain on Sale of Machinery—Sage   23,800
　　　　　Machinery—Post . . . .　　　　　　23,800
　　To eliminate unrealized intercompany gain on sale of ma-
　　chinery. (Income tax effects are disregarded.)

(e) Intercompany Bonds Payable—Sage   300,000
　　　　　Discount on Intercompany Bonds Payable—Sage . .　　　　18,224
　　　　　Investment in Sage Company Bonds—Post . . . .　　　257,175
　　　　　Gain on Extinguishment of Bonds—Sage . . . .　　　　24,601
　　To eliminate subsidiary's bonds acquired by parent, and to
　　recognize gain on the extinguishment of the bonds. (Income
　　tax effects are disregarded.)

(f) Minority Interest in Net Income of Subsidiary   3,940
　　　　　Minority Interest in Net Assets of Subsidiary . . . .　　　　3,940
　　To establish minority interest in subsidiary's adjusted net in-
　　come for Year 3 as follows:
　　　Net income of subsidiary . . . .　$105,000
　　　Adjustments for working paper eliminations:
　　　　(a) ($17,000 + $2,000) . . . .　(19,000)
　　　　(b) . . . .　(8,000)
　　　　(d) . . . .　(23,800)
　　　　(e) . . . .　24,601
　　　Adjusted net income of subsidiary . . . .　$ 78,801
　　　Minority share ($78,801 × 0.05) . . . .　$ 3,940

In elimination (f) above, the effects of the other eliminations on the subsidiary's net income are applied to compute the adjusted net income of the subsidiary, for consolidation purposes. The minority percentage then is applied to compute the minority interest in net income of the subsidiary. The rationale for these procedures follows:

Elimination (a) increases costs and expenses of the subsidiary, thus decreasing the subsidiary's net income, a total of $19,000.

Elimination (b) reduces the subsidiary's gross profit margin on sales by $24,000 ($120,000 − $96,000 = $24,000); however, $16,000 of the gross profit margin was

Equity method: Partially owned subsidiary subsequent to date of purchase-type business combination

POST CORPORATION AND SUBSIDIARY
Partial Working Paper for Consolidated Financial Statements
For Year Ended December 31, Year 3

	Post Corporation	Sage Company	Eliminations increase (decrease)		Consolidated
Statement of Retained Earnings					
Retained earnings, beginning of year	1,348,500	384,000	(a)	(379,250)	1,353,250
Net income	352,600	105,000		(161,839)*	295,761
Subtotals	1,701,100	489,000		(541,089)	1,649,011
Dividends declared	158,550	50,000	(a)	(50,000)†	158,550
Retained earnings, end of year.	1,542,550	439,000		(491,089)	1,490,461
Balance Sheet					
Liabilities & Stockholders' Equity					
Minority interest in net assets of subsidiary. . . .			{ (a) (f)	58,500 } 3,940 }	62,440
Total liabilities.	x,xxx,xxx	xxx,xxx		62,440	x,xxx,xxx
Common stock, $1 par . .	1,057,000				1,057,000
Common stock, $10 par .		400,000	(a)	(400,000)	
Additional paid-in capital.	1,560,250	235,000	(a)	(235,000)	1,560,250
Retained earnings	1,542,550	439,000		(491,089)	1,490,461
Retained earnings of subsidiary.	4,750		(a)	(4,750)	
Total stockholders' equity	4,164,550	1,074,000		(1,130,839)	4,107,711
Total liabilities & stockholders' equity. .	x,xxx,xxx	x,xxx,xxx		(1,068,399)	x,xxx,xxx

* Net decrease in revenue (and gains): $81,700 + $120,000 + $50,000 + $23,800 − $24,601 . . . . $250,899
Less: Net decrease in costs and expenses: $96,000 + $16,000 − $19,000 − $3,940. 89,060
Decrease in combined net incomes to compute consolidated net income $161,839
† A *decrease* in dividends and an *increase* in retained earnings.

realized by the parent company in its sales to outsiders. The net effect on the subsidiary's net income is a decrease of $8,000 ($24,000 − $16,000 = $8,000).

Elimination (c) removes a gain of the parent company; it does not affect the subsidiary's net income.

Elimination (d) removes a gain of the subsidiary and reduces the subsidiary's net income by $23,800.

Elimination (e) attributes a gain on extinguishment of bonds to the subsidiary, thus increasing the subsidiary's net income by $24,601.

Working Paper for Consolidated Financial Statements A partial working paper for consolidated financial statements for Post Corporation and subsidiary for the year ended December 31, Year 3, is shown on page 466. The amounts for Post Corporation and Sage Company are the same as in the illustration on page 341 of Chapter 7. The illustration demonstrates that, when intercompany profits exist, consolidated net income is not the same as the parent company's net income under the equity method of accounting for the subsidiary's operations; nor is consolidated retained earnings the same as the total of the parent company's two retained earnings amounts. ($1,542,550 + $4,750 = $1,547,300; consolidated retained earnings is $1,490,461.) In the comprehensive illustration that follows, I demonstrate how consolidated net income and consolidated retained earnings may be verified when intercompany profits (gains) are involved in the consolidation process.

COMPREHENSIVE ILLUSTRATION OF WORKING PAPER FOR CONSOLIDATED FINANCIAL STATEMENTS

In Chapters 6 through 9 I explain and illustrate a number of aspects of working papers for consolidated financial statements. The comprehensive illustration that follows incorporates most of these aspects. The illustration is for Post Corporation and its partially owned purchased subsidiary, Sage Company, for the year ended December 31, Year 4.

The ledger accounts for Post Corporation's Investment in Sage Company Common Stock, Retained Earnings, and Retained Earnings of Subsidiary, and for Sage Company's Retained Earnings, are below and on pages 468 and 469. Closing entries for Year 4 are not yet recorded in the retained earnings accounts. Review of these accounts should aid in understanding the illustrative working paper for consolidated financial statements on pages 472 and 473 and the related working paper eliminations (in journal entry format) on pages 474 through 476.

POST CORPORATION LEDGER ACCOUNTS
Investment in Sage Company Common Stock

Date	Explanation	Debit	Credit	Balance
Year 1				
Dec. 31	Total cost of business combination	1,192,250		1,192,250 dr
Year 2				
Nov. 24	Dividend declared by Sage		38,000	1,154,250 dr
Dec. 31	Net income of Sage	85,500		1,239,750 dr
31	Amortization of differences		42,750	1,197,000 dr
31	Amortization of goodwill		950	1,196,050 dr

(continued)

POST CORPORATION LEDGER ACCOUNTS
Investment in Sage Company Common Stock (concluded)

Date	Explanation	Debit	Credit	Balance
Year 3				
Nov. 22	Dividend declared by Sage		47,500	1,148,550 dr
Dec. 31	Net income of Sage	99,750		1,248,300 dr
31	Amortization of differences		18,050	1,230,250 dr
31	Amortization of goodwill		950	1,229,300 dr
Year 4				
Nov. 25	Dividend declared by Sage		57,000	1,172,300 dr
Dec. 31	Net income of Sage	109,250		1,281,550 dr
31	Amortization of differences		18,050	1,263,500 dr
31	Amortization of goodwill		950	1,262,550 dr

Retained Earnings

Date	Explanation	Debit	Credit	Balance
Year 1				
Dec. 31	Balance			1,050,000 cr
Year 2				
Dec. 31	Close net income available for dividends		457,050	1,507,050 cr
31	Close Dividends Declared account	158,550		1,348,500 cr
Year 3				
Dec. 31	Close net income available for dividends		318,400	1,666,900 cr
31	Close Dividends Declared account	158,550		1,508,350 cr

Retained Earnings of Subsidiary

Date	Explanation	Debit	Credit	Balance
Year 2				
Dec. 31	Close net income not available for dividends		4,750	4,750 cr
Year 3				
Dec. 31	Close net income not available for dividends		34,200	38,950 cr

	SAGE COMPANY LEDGER ACCOUNT			
	Retained Earnings			
Date	**Explanation**	**Debit**	**Credit**	**Balance**
Year 1				
Dec. 31	*Balance*		*334,000*	*334,000 cr*
Year 2				
Dec. 31	*Close net income*		*90,000*	*424,000 cr*
31	*Close Dividends Declared account*	*40,000*		*384,000 cr*
Year 3				
Dec. 31	*Close net income*		*105,000*	*489,000 cr*
31	*Close Dividends Declared account*	*50,000*		*439,000 cr*

Following are important features of the working paper for consolidated financial statements and related working paper eliminations for Post Corporation and subsidiary for the year ended December 31, Year 4:

1   Intercompany investment income of Post Corporation for Year 4 is computed as follows:

<table>
<tr><td>Computation of
intercompany
investment income</td><td>

$115,000 (Sage Company's net income for Year 4) × 0.95 . . . .   *$109,250*
Less: $19,000 [(Year 4 amortization of differences between current fair values
  and carrying amounts of Sage Company's identifiable net assets on date of
  business combination) × 0.95] *18,050*
Intercompany investment income of Post Corporation for Year 4 . . . .   *$ 91,200*

</td></tr>
</table>

2   Post Corporation's intercompany revenue of $14,000 is a management fee from Sage Company, computed as 1% of Sage's $1,400,000 net sales for Year 4 ($1,400,000 × 0.01 = $14,000).

3   The income tax effects of Post Corporation's use of the equity method of accounting for its subsidiary's operations are not reflected in Post's income taxes expense for Year 4. Income tax effects associated with the equity method of accounting are considered in Chapter 10.

4   Consolidated retained earnings of Post Corporation and subsidiary at the beginning of Year 4 ($1,490,461) is identical to consolidated retained earnings at the end of Year 3 (see page 466).

5   The net intercompany payable of Post Corporation on December 31, Year 4, is computed on page 470.

<table>
<tr><td>Computation of net
intercompany payable
of parent company</td><td></td></tr>
</table>

Computation of net intercompany payable of parent company	

Computation of net intercompany payable of parent company

Accounts payable to Sage Company for merchandise purchases..........		$47,500
Less: Interest receivable from Sage Company (page 459).......	$30,000	
Management fee receivable from Sage Company.........	14,000	44,000
Net intercompany payable...		$ 3,500

6   Elimination *(a)* continues the amortization of differences between current fair values and carrying amounts of the subsidiary's net assets on the date of the business combination of Post Corporation and Sage Company (see Chapter 7, page 330).

7   The $62,800 minority interest at the beginning of the year, *excluding intercompany profits (gains) effects,* as set forth in the explanation for elimination *(a)(4)*, is computed as follows:

Computation of minority interest at beginning of year

Stockholders' equity of Sage Company, Dec. 31, Year 3:		
Common stock, $10 par...		$ 400,000
Additional paid-in capital		235,000
Retained earnings...		439,000
Total stockholders' equity		$1,074,000
Add: Unamortized differences between current fair values and carrying amounts of Sage's identifiable net assets, Dec. 31, Year 3 (see page 464):		
Plant assets...	$162,000	
Leasehold..	20,000	182,000
Total adjusted net assets of Sage, Dec. 31, Year 3....................		$1,256,000
Minority interest therein ($1,256,000 × 0.05)		$ 62,800

8   Eliminations *(b)*, *(c)*, *(d)*, and *(e)* are identical to the eliminations illustrated in this chapter on pages 439, 443, 445, and 462, respectively. For posting to the working paper for consolidated financial statements, elimination *(d)* was condensed. The credit to Depreciation Expense in elimination *(d)* is posted to Cost of Goods Sold in the income statement section of the working paper.

9   The effects of eliminations *(a)* through *(e)* on the computation of minority interest in net income of the subsidiary, in elimination *(f)*, are analyzed below and on page 471.

Elimination (a) increases costs and expenses of the subsidiary, thus decreasing the subsidiary's net income, a total of $19,000.

Elimination (b) reduces the subsidiary's gross profit margin on sales by $30,000 ($150,000 − $120,000 = $30,000); however, $26,000 of gross profit margin was realized by the parent company in its sales to outsiders. The net effect on the subsidiary's net income is a decrease of $4,000 ($30,000 − $26,000 = $4,000).

Elimination (c) does not affect the net income of the subsidiary.

Elimination (d) includes a $4,760 credit to the parent company's depreciation expense, which in effect is a realization of a portion of the intercompany profit on the subsidiary's sale of machinery to the parent company (see page 446). Thus, the subsidiary's net income is increased by $4,760.

Elimination (e) decreases intercompany interest revenue by $38,576 and decreases intercompany interest expense by $33,813. The difference, $4,763 ($38,576 − $33,813 = $4,763), is a reduction of the subsidiary's net income, to avoid double counting of the realized but unrecorded gain on the extinguishment of the subsidiary's bonds in the prior year (see page 462).

10 Because of the elimination of intercompany profits (gains), consolidated net income for the year ended December 31, Year 4, does not equal the parent company's equity-method net income. Consolidated net income may be verified as follows:

Verification of consolidated net income	Net income of Post Corporation		$460,200
	Less: Post's share of adjustments to subsidiary's net income for intercompany profits (gains):		
	Elimination (b) ($150,000 − $120,000 − $26,000).	$(4,000)	
	Elimination (d).	4,760	
	Elimination (e) ($38,576 − $33,813)	(4,763)	
	Total	$(4,003)	
	Post's share [$(4,003) × 0.95]		(3,803)
	Consolidated net income		$456,397

11 Similarly, consolidated retained earnings on December 31, Year 4, does not equal the total of the two parent company retained earnings amounts in the working paper for consolidated financial statements. Consolidated retained earnings may be verified as follows:

Verification of consolidated retained earnings	Total of Post Corporation's two retained earnings amounts ($1,810,000 + $38,950)		$1,848,950
	Adjustments:		
	Post's share of adjustments to subsidiary's net income (see **10**, above).		(3,803)
	Intercompany gain in Post's retained earnings—elimination (c)		(50,000)
	Post's share of adjustments to subsidiary's beginning retained earnings for intercompany profits (gains):		
	Elimination (b)	$ (7,600)	
	Elimination (d)	(22,610)	
	Elimination (e)	23,371	(6,839)
	Consolidated retained earnings.		$1,788,308

12 The consolidated amounts in the working paper for consolidated financial statements represent the financial position and operating results of Post Corporation and subsidiary resulting from the consolidated entity's transactions with *outsiders*. All intercompany transactions, profits (gains), and balances have been eliminated in the computation of the consolidated amounts.

Equity method: Partially owned subsidiary subsequent to purchase-type business combination

POST CORPORATION AND SUBSIDIARY
Working Paper for Consolidated Financial Statements
For Year Ended December 31, Year 4

	Post Corporation	Sage Company	Eliminations increase (decrease)	Consolidated
Income Statement				
Revenue:				
Net sales	5,900,000	1,400,000		7,300,000
Intercompany sales		150,000	(b) (150,000)	
Intercompany interest revenue	38,576		(e) (38,576)	
Intercompany invest- ment income	91,200		(a) (91,200)	
Intercompany revenue (expenses)	14,000	(14,000)		
Total revenue	6,043,776	1,536,000	(279,776)	7,300,000
Costs and expenses:			(a) 17,000	
			(b) (26,000)	
Cost of goods sold	4,300,000	950,000	(d) (4,760)	5,236,240
Intercompany cost of goods sold		120,000	(b) (120,000)	
Operating expenses	986,058	217,978	(a) 2,000	1,206,036
Intercompany interest expense		33,813	(e) (33,813)	
Interest expense	51,518	22,542		74,060
Income taxes expense . .	246,000	76,667		322,667
Minority interest in net income of subsidiary . . .			(f) 4,600	4,600
Total costs and ex- penses	5,583,576	1,421,000	(160,973)*	6,843,603
Net income	460,200	115,000	(118,803)	456,397
Statement of Retained Earnings			(a) (400,050)	
			(b) (7,600)	
Retained earnings, begin-			(c) (50,000)	
ning of year	1,508,350	439,000	(d) (22,610)	1,490,461
			(e) 23,371	
Net income	460,200	115,000	(118,803)	456,397
Subtotal	1,968,550	554,000	(575,692)	1,946,858
Dividends declared	158,550	60,000	(a) (60,000)†	158,550
Retained earnings, end of year	1,810,000	494,000	(515,692)	1,788,308

* A **decrease** in total costs and expenses and an **increase** in net income.
† A **decrease** in dividends and an **increase** in retained earnings.

(continued)

POST CORPORATION AND SUBSIDIARY
Working Paper for Consolidated Financial Statements (concluded)
For Year Ended December 31, Year 4

	Post Corporation	Sage Company	Eliminations increase (decrease)		Consolidated
Balance Sheet					
Assets					
Intercompany receivables (payables)	(3,500)	3,500			
Inventories.	950,000	500,000	(b)	(12,000)	1,438,000
Other current assets	760,000	428,992			1,188,992
Investment in Sage Company stock.	1,262,550		(a)	(1,262,550)	
Investment in Sage Company bonds	265,751		(e)	(265,751)	
Plant assets (net).	3,700,000	1,300,000	(a) (d)	148,000 (19,040)	5,128,960
Land (for building site) . . .		175,000	(c)	(50,000)	125,000
Leasehold (net)			(a)	15,000	15,000
Goodwill (net)	85,000		(a)	35,150	120,150
Total assets	7,019,801	2,407,492		(1,411,191)	8,016,102
Liabilities & Stockholders' Equity					
Bonds payable		200,000			200,000
Intercompany bonds payable.		300,000	(e)	(300,000)	
Discount on bonds payable.		(9,608)			(9,608)
Discount on intercompany bonds payable		(14,411)	(e)	(14,411)*	
Other liabilities	2,553,601	802,511			3,356,112
Minority interest in net assets of subsidiary.			(a) (b) (d) (e) (f)	59,800 (400) (1,190) 1,230 4,600	64,040
Common stock, $1 par . . .	1,057,000				1,057,000
Common stock, $10 par . .		400,000	(a)	(400,000)	
Additional paid-in capital .	1,560,250	235,000	(a)	(235,000)	1,560,250
Retained earnings	1,810,000	494,000		(515,692)	1,788,308
Retained earnings of subsidiary.	38,950		(a)	(38,950)	
Total liabilities & stockholders' equity	7,019,801	2,407,492		(1,411,191)	8,016,102

*A **decrease** in discount on intercompany bonds payable and an **increase** in total liabilities and stockholders' equity.

POST CORPORATION AND SUBSIDIARY
Working Paper Eliminations
December 31, Year 4

(a) Common Stock—Sage 400,000

Additional Paid-in Capital—Sage....................... 235,000

Retained Earnings—Sage ($439,000 − $38,950)......... 400,050

Retained Earnings of Subsidiary—Post................. 38,950

Intercompany Investment Income—Post................. 91,200

Plant Assets (net)—Sage ($162,000 − $14,000) 148,000

Leasehold (net)—Sage ($20,000 − $5,000).............. 15,000

Goodwill (net)—Post ($36,100 − $950)................. 35,150

Cost of Goods Sold—Sage............................. 17,000

Operating Expenses—Sage 2,000

   Investment in Sage Company Common Stock—

   Post.. 1,262,550

   Dividends Declared—Sage...................... 60,000

   Minority Interest in Net Assets of Subsidiary........ 59,800

To carry out the following:

(1) Eliminate intercompany investment and equity accounts of subsidiary at **beginning** of year, and subsidiary dividend.

(2) Provide for Year 4 depreciation and amortization on differences between current fair values and carrying amount of Sage's identifiable net assets as follows:

	Cost of goods sold	Operating expenses
Building depreciation	$ 2,000	$2,000
Machinery depreciation....	10,000	
Leasehold amortization....	5,000	
Totals	$17,000	$2,000

(3) Allocate unamortized differences between combination date current fair values and carrying amounts to appropriate assets.

(4) Establish minority interest in net assets of subsidiary at beginning of year, excluding intercompany profits effects ($62,800), less minority share of dividends declared by subsidiary during year ($60,000 × 0.05 = $3,000).

(Income tax effects are disregarded.)

(continued)

POST CORPORATION AND SUBSIDIARY
Working Paper Eliminations (continued)
December 31, Year 4

(b) Retained Earnings—Sage............................	7,600	
Minority Interest in Net Assets of Subsidiary.............	400	
Intercompany Sales—Sage	150,000	
Intercompany Cost of Goods Sold—Sage		120,000
Cost of Goods Sold—Post		26,000
Inventories—Post..............................		12,000

To eliminate intercompany sales, cost of goods sold, and unrealized profits in inventories. (Income tax effects are disregarded.)

(c) Retained Earnings—Post	50,000	
Land—Sage......................................		50,000

To eliminate unrealized intercompany gain in land. (Income tax effects are disregarded.)

(d) Retained Earnings—Sage............................	22,610	
Minority Interest in Net Assets of Subsidiary.............	1,190	
Accumulated Depreciation—Post	4,760	
Machinery—Post...............................		23,800
Depreciation Expense—Post		4,760

To eliminate unrealized intercompany gain in machinery and in related depreciation. (Income tax effects are disregarded.)

(e) Intercompany Interest Revenue—Post..................	38,576	
Intercompany Bonds Payable—Sage...................	300,000	
Discount on Intercompany Bonds Payable—Sage ..		14,411
Investment in Sage Company Bonds—Post........		265,751
Intercompany Interest Expense—Sage		33,813
Retained Earnings—Sage		23,371
Minority Interest in Net Assets of Subsidiary........		1,230

To eliminate subsidiary's bonds owned by parent company, and related interest revenue and expense; and to increase subsidiary's beginning retained earnings by amount of unamortized realized gain on the extinguishment of the bonds. (Income tax effects are disregarded.)

(continued)

POST CORPORATION AND SUBSIDIARY
Working Paper Eliminations (concluded)
December 31, Year 4

(f) Minority Interest in Net Income of Subsidiary		4,600	
Minority Interest in Net Assets of Subsidiary			4,600

To establish minority interest in subsidiary's adjusted net income for Year 4, as follows:

Net income of subsidiary	$115,000	
Adjustments for working paper eliminations:		
(a) ($17,000 + $2,000)	(19,000)	
(b) ($150,000 − $120,000 − $26,000) . . .	(4,000)	
(d)	4,760	
(e) ($38,576 − $33,813)	(4,763)	
Adjusted net income of subsidiary	$ 91,997	
Minority share ($91,997 × 0.05)	$ 4,600	

REVIEW QUESTIONS

1 How are consolidated financial statements affected if unrealized intercompany profits (gains) resulting from transactions between a parent company and its subsidiaries are not eliminated? Explain.

2 What consolidated financial statement categories are affected by intercompany sales of merchandise at a profit? Explain.

3 How is the unrealized intercompany profit in a subsidiary's *beginning* inventories resulting from the parent company's sales of merchandise to the subsidiary accounted for in a working paper elimination (in journal entry format)? Explain.

4 How is minority interest in net income of a partially owned subsidiary affected by working paper eliminations for intercompany profits? Explain.

5 Some accountants advocate the elimination of intercompany profit in the parent company's ending inventories only to the extent of the parent's ownership interest in the partially owned selling subsidiary. What is an argument in opposition to this treatment of intercompany profit in the parent company's ending inventories?

6 How do intercompany sales of plant assets and intangible assets differ from intercompany sales of merchandise?

7 Is an intercompany gain on the sale of land ever *realized?* Explain.

8 Sayles Company, a 90%-owned subsidiary of Partin Corporation, sold to Partin for $10,000 a machine with a carrying amount of $8,000, no residual value, and an economic life of four years. Explain how the intercompany gain element of Partin Corporation's annual depreciation expense for the machine is accounted for in the working paper for consolidated financial statements.

9 In what ways do working paper eliminations (in journal entry format) for intercompany leases of property under capital/sales-type leases resemble eliminations for intercompany sales of plant assets and intangible assets? Explain.

10 ''No intercompany gain or loss should be recognized when a parent company acquires in the open market outstanding bonds of its subsidiary, because the transaction is not an *intercompany* transaction.'' Do you agree with this statement? Explain.

11 What accounting problems result from the reissuance by a subsidiary of parent company bonds that had been acquired in the open market by the subsidiary? Explain.

12 Intercompany profits (gains) or losses in inventories, plant assets, intangible assets, or bonds result in consolidated net income that differs from the parent company's equity-method net income. Why is this true? Explain.

EXERCISES

Ex. 9-1 Select the best answer for each of the following multiple-choice questions:

1 An unrealized intercompany profit in a parent company's beginning inventory, resulting from the parent's purchase of merchandise from its partially owned subsidiary, requires the following in a working paper elimination (in journal entry format):
a A credit to Inventories—Parent
b A debit to Minority Interest in Net Assets of Subsidiary
c A credit to Cost of Goods Sold—Subsidiary
d A debit to Retained Earnings—Parent
e A debit to Retained Earnings of Subsidiary—Parent

2 Does the working paper elimination (in journal entry format) for sales of merchandise by a wholly owned subsidiary to a partially owned subsidiary of the same parent company include a debit or credit, as appropriate, to:

	Cost of goods sold— wholly owned subsidiary?	Cost of goods sold— partially owned subsidiary?
a	Yes	No
b	No	Yes
c	No	No
d	Yes	Yes

3 In a working paper elimination (in journal entry format) for intercompany sales of merchandise by a parent company to its partially owned subsidiary, unrealized intercompany profit in the subsidiary's beginning inventories is:
a Debited to Retained Earnings—Subsidiary and to Minority Interest in Net Income of Subsidiary
b Debited to Retained Earnings—Parent
c Credited to Beginning Inventories—Subsidiary
d Debited to Retained Earnings of Subsidiary—Parent

4   Does the working paper elimination (in journal entry format) for intercompany sales of merchandise by a parent company to its partially owned subsidiary include *credits* to:

	Cost of goods sold— Parent?	Cost of goods sold— Subsidiary?
a	Yes	Yes
b	Yes	No
c	No	Yes
d	No	No

5   Is there a debit to Retained Earnings—Parent in the working paper elimination (in journal entry format) attributable to the parent's sale of land at a gain to the subsidiary:

	For the accounting period of the sale?	For accounting periods subsequent to the sale?
a	Yes	No
b	Yes	Yes
c	No	Yes
d	No	No

6   The intercompany gain on the sale of a depreciable plant asset is realized by the consolidated entity:

a At no time
b When the plant asset is sold to an outsider
c When the sale occurs
d As the acquirer depreciates the plant asset

7   The relevant working paper elimination (in journal entry format) for years following a parent company's sale of a depreciable plant asset to its partially owned subsidiary does not include a debit or credit to:

a Minority Interest in Net Assets of Subsidiary
b Depreciation Expense—Subsidiary
c Retained Earnings—Parent
d Accumulated Depreciation—Subsidiary

8   On June 1, Year 4, Soporific Company, the 90%-owned purchased subsidiary of Pungent Corporation, sold to Pungent at a $75,000 gain a machine with an economic life of five years and no residual value. Pungent uses the sum-of-the-years'-digits method of depreciation for machinery. The working paper elimination for Pungent Corporation and Subsidiary for the fiscal year ended May 31, Year 5, does *not* include:

a A debit of $7,500 to Minority Interest in Net Assets of Subsidiary
b A credit of $25,000 to Depreciation Expense—Pungent
c A credit of $75,000 to Machinery—Pungent
d A debit of $25,000 to Accumulated Depreciation—Pungent

9   The working paper elimination for an intercompany capital/sales-type lease has features similar to the elimination of intercompany sales of:

a Merchandise only

b Plant assets only

c Both merchandise and plant assets

d Neither merchandise nor plant assets

10 On May 31, Year 7, Parke Corporation sold for $80,000 to its 85%-owned subsidiary, Stark Company, a patent with a carrying amount to Parke of $60,000 and a remaining economic life to Stark of five years. Stark credits amortization of intangible assets directly to the asset account. Disregarding income taxes, the May 31, Year 8, working paper elimination (in journal entry format) for consolidated financial statements of Parke Corporation and subsidiary includes a credit to Patents — Stark in the amount of:

a $60,000

b $48,000

c $20,000

d $16,000

e Some other amount

11 The realized extinguishment gain resulting from a parent company's open-market acquisition of its subsidiary's outstanding bonds is recognized in the accounting period of the parent's acquisition in the:

a Parent company's journal entry to record the acquisition of the bonds

b Subsidiary's journal entry to record the extinguishment of the bonds

c Working paper elimination at the end of the accounting period in which the parent company acquired the bonds

d Affiliates' journal entries for intercompany interest revenue and expense subsequent to the parent company's acquisition of the bonds

12 The difference between periodic intercompany interest revenue and intercompany interest expense related to a parent company's open-market acquisition of its subsidiary's bonds at a discount represents:

a A realized gain on the acquisition of the bonds

b An unrealized gain on the acquisition of the bonds

c The accounting-records recognition of the gain on the acquisition of the bonds

d An amount to be closed to the parent's Retained Earnings of Subsidiary account

13 The May 31, Year 2, working paper eliminations (in journal entry format) for the consolidated financial statements of Polo Corporation and its 80%-owned subsidiary, Solo Company, included a credit to Gain on Extinguishment of Bonds — Solo in the amount of $120,000. The Solo bonds were to mature on May 31, Year 8. Disregarding income taxes, the May 31, Year 3, working paper elimination (in journal entry format) for consolidated financial statements of Polo Corporation and subsidiary includes a:

a $120,000 credit to Retained Earnings — Solo

b $20,000 debit to Minority Interest in Net Assets of Subsidiary

c $96,000 credit to Retained Earnings — Solo

d $120,000 credit to Retained Earnings of Subsidiary — Polo

Ex. 9-2 Peggy Corporation supplies all the merchandise sold by its wholly owned subsidiary, Sally Company. Both Peggy and Sally use the perpetual inventory system. Peggy bills merchandise to Sally at a price 25% in excess of Peggy's cost. For the year ended November 30, Year 8, Peggy's sales to Sally were $120,000 at billed prices. At billed prices, Sally's December 1, Year 7, inventories were $18,000, and its November 30, Year 8, inventories were $24,000.

Prepare for Peggy Corporation and subsidiary an analysis of intercompany sales, cost of goods sold, and gross profit in inventories for the year ended November 30, Year 8. Your analysis should show selling price, cost, and gross profit for each of the three intercompany items.

Ex. 9-3   The intercompany sales of merchandise by Patter Corporation to its wholly owned subsidiary, Smatter Company, for the year ended February 28, Year 3, may be analyzed as follows:

	Selling price	Cost	Gross profit
Beginning inventories	$100,000	$ 75,000	$ 25,000
Add: Sales	800,000	600,000	200,000
Subtotals.	$900,000	$675,000	$225,000
Less: Ending inventories.	150,000	112,500	37,500
Cost of goods sold	$750,000	$562,500	$187,500

Prepare a working paper elimination for Patter Corporation and subsidiary on February 28, Year 3. Omit explanation and disregard income taxes.

Ex. 9-4   Pele Corporation acquired 70% of the outstanding common stock of Shad Company on August 1, Year 2. During the year ended July 31, Year 3, Pele sold merchandise to Shad in the amount of $120,000; the merchandise was priced at 20% above Pele's cost. Shad had 30% of this merchandise in inventories on July 31, Year 3.

Prepare a working paper elimination (in journal entry format) for Pele Corporation and subsidiary on July 31, Year 3. (Disregard income taxes.)

Ex. 9-5   During the year ended December 31, Year 7, Spring Company, a 75%-owned subsidiary of Polydom Corporation, sold merchandise costing $600,000 to Solano Company, a 90%-owned subsidiary of Polydom, at a markup of 25% on selling price. Included in Solano's December 31, Year 7, inventories were goods acquired from Spring at a billed price of $200,000, representing a $40,000 increase over the comparable inventories on December 31, Year 6.

Prepare a working paper elimination (in journal entry format) for Polydom Corporation and subsidiaries on December 31, Year 7. (Disregard income taxes.)

Ex. 9-6   Polar Corporation entered into purchase-type business combinations with Solar Company, an 80%-owned subsidiary, and Stellar Company, a 70%-owned subsidiary, on September 30, Year 5. During the year ended September 30, Year 6, intercompany sales of merchandise by the two subsidiaries were as follows:

	Solar sales to Stellar	Stellar sales to Solar
Cost of merchandise sold	$120,000	$180,000
Markup on selling price	20%	25%
Selling price of merchandise (cost to purchaser) in Sept. 30, Year 6, inventories of purchaser	$ 40,000	$ 60,000

Prepare working paper eliminations (in journal entry format; omit explanations) for Polar Corporation and subsidiaries on September 30, Year 6. (Disregard income taxes.)

Ex. 9-7 Among the working paper eliminations (in journal entry format) of Parke Corporation and subsidiary on December 31, Year 5, was the following (explanation omitted):

Retained Earnings—Selma ($18,750 × 0.90)...................	16,875	
Minority Interest in Net Assets of Subsidiary ($18,750 × 0.10)	1,875	
Accumulated Depreciation—Parke	12,500	
Machinery—Parke......................................		25,000
Depreciation Expense (straight-line)—Parke ($25,000 ÷ 4) .		6,250

Answer the following questions:

a What is the probable explanation of the foregoing elimination?

b How many years have elapsed since the underlying intercompany transaction? Explain.

c How does the credit to Depreciation Expense—Parke enter into the measurement of consolidated net income for Parke Corporation and subsidiary for the year ended December 31, Year 5? Explain.

Ex. 9-8 On October 1, Year 4, the beginning of a fiscal year, Patria Corporation acquired equipment for $14,500 from its 90%-owned subsidiary, Selena Company. The equipment was carried at $9,000 in Selena's accounting records and had an economic life of 10 years on October 1, Year 4. Patria uses the sum-of-the-years'-digits depreciation method.

Prepare a working paper elimination (in journal entry format) for Patria Corporation and subsidiary on September 30, Year 6. (Disregard income taxes.)

Ex. 9-9 On January 2, Year 1, Steve Company, an 80%-owned subsidiary of Paulo Corporation, sold to its parent company for $20,000 a machine with a carrying amount of $16,000, a five-year economic life, and no residual value. Both Paulo and Steve use the straight-line method of depreciation for all machinery.

Compute the missing amounts in the working paper eliminations (in journal entry format) for Paulo Corporation and subsidiary that follow. Use the identifying numbers for the missing amounts in your solution.

	December 31, Year 2		December 31, Year 4	
Minority Interest in Net Assets of Subsidiary	(1)		(4)	
Retained Earnings—Steve	(2)		(5)	
Accumulated Depreciation—Paulo	(3)		(6)	
Machinery—Paulo......................		4,000		4,000
Depreciation Expense—Paulo		800		800
To eliminate unrealized intercompany gain in machinery and in related depreciation. (Income tax effects are disregarded.)				

Ex. 9-10 The working paper elimination (in journal entry format) on December 31, Year 3, the

date that Pelion Corporation entered into a sales-type lease with its subsidiary, Styron Company, was as follows:

Intercompany Liability under Capital Lease—Styron	15,849	
Unearned Intercompany Interest Revenue—Pelion	4,151	
Intercompany Sales—Pelion	20,849	
Intercompany Cost of Goods Sold—Pelion		17,000
Intercompany Lease Receivables—Pelion.		20,000
Leased Equipment—Capital Lease—Styron		
($20,849 − $17,000)		3,849

To eliminate intercompany accounts associated with intercompany lease and to defer unrealized portion of intercompany gross profit on sales-type lease. (Income tax effects are disregarded.)

Pelion's (the lessor's) implicit interest rate, known to Styron (the lessee) and less than Styron's incremental borrowing rate, was 10%, and the leased equipment had a 10-year economic life with no residual value. Five lease payments of $5,000 each, beginning on December 31, Year 3, were required under the lease. Styron uses the straight-line method of depreciation.

Prepare a working paper elimination (in journal entry format) for Pelion Corporation and subsidiary on December 31, Year 4. (Disregard income taxes.)

Ex. 9-11   On March 1, Year 6, the beginning of a fiscal year, Smart Company, the wholly owned subsidiary of Pawley Corporation, sold to Pawley for $80,000 a patent with a carrying amount of $60,000 and a four-year remaining economic life. Pawley credits amortization directly to intangible asset ledger accounts and includes amortization with operating expenses.

Prepare a working paper elimination for Pawley Corporation and subsidiary on February 28, Year 7. (Omit explanation and disregard income taxes.)

Ex. 9-12   Solaw Company, the wholly owned subsidiary of Polka Corporation, issued 10%, five-year bonds on May 1, Year 1, at their face amount of $100,000. Interest is payable annually each May 1, beginning Year 2. On April 30, Year 2, the end of a fiscal year, Polka acquired in the open market 40% of Solaw's outstanding bonds at a 12% yield, plus accrued interest for one year.

Prepare a working paper to compute the amount of cash paid by Polka Corporation for Solaw Company's bonds on April 30, Year 2, and the gain on the extinguishment of the bonds. Round all computations to the nearest dollar. (Disregard income taxes.)

Ex. 9-13   On November 1, Year 5, the beginning of a fiscal year, Sinn Company, the 90%-owned subsidiary of Parr Corporation, issued to the public $100,000 face amount of five-year, 9% bonds, interest payable each November 1, for $103,993—an 8% yield. Bond issue costs may be disregarded. On October 31, Year 6, Parr acquired in the open market $60,000 face amount of Sinn's 9% bonds for $58,098—a 10% yield. The realized gain on the transaction displayed in the October 31, Year 6, consolidated income statement of Parr Corporation and subsidiary was $3,889. Sinn and Parr use the interest method of amortization of bond premium and accumulation of bond discount.

Prepare a working paper to compute the missing amounts in the working paper elimination (in journal entry format) below. Round all amounts to the nearest dollar. (Disregard income taxes.)

PARR CORPORATION AND SUBSIDIARY
Partial Working Paper Eliminations
October 31, Year 7

Intercompany Interest Revenue—Parr	(1)	
Intercompany Bonds Payable—Sinn...............................	60,000	
Premium on Intercompany Bonds Payable—Sinn	(2)	
Investment in Sinn Company Bonds—Parr		(3)
Intercompany Interest Expense—Sinn		(4)
Retained Earnings—Sinn.		(5)
Minority Interest in Net Assets of Subsidiary		389

To eliminate subsidiary's bonds owned by parent company, and related interest revenue and expense; and to increase subsidiary's beginning retained earnings by amount of unamortized realized gain on the extinguishment of the bonds. (Income tax effects are disregarded.)

Ex. 9-14 Palimino Corporation acquired a 70% interest in Sokal Company in Year 2. For the years ended December 31, Year 3 and Year 4, Sokal had a net income of $80,000 and $90,000, respectively. During Year 3, Sokal sold merchandise to Palimino for $10,000 at a gross profit of $2,000. The merchandise was resold during Year 4 by Palimino to outsiders for $15,000.

Compute the minority interest in Sokal Company's net income for the years ended December 31, Year 3 and Year 4. (Disregard income taxes.)

CASES

Case 9-1 Powell Corporation has begun selling idle machinery from a discontinued product line to a wholly owned subsidiary, Seeley Company, which needs the machinery in its operations. Powell had transferred the machinery from the Machinery ledger account to an Idle Machinery account, had written down the machinery to net realizable value based on quotations from used machinery dealers, and had terminated depreciation of the idle machinery when the product line was discontinued.

During the year ended December 31, Year 3, Powell's sales of idle machinery to Seeley totaled $50,000 and were accounted for by Powell and Seeley in the following aggregate journal entries:

Powell Corporation Journal Entries

Cash.	50,000	
Sales of Idle Machinery...................................		50,000
To record sales of idle machinery to Seeley Company.		

Cost of Idle Machinery Sold	40,000	
Idle Machinery.		40,000
To write off net realizable value of idle machinery sold to Seeley Company.		

Seeley Company Journal Entries

Machinery	50,000	
Cash		50,000

To record acquisition of used machinery from Powell Corporation.

Depreciation Expense	5,000	
Accumulated Depreciation of Machinery		5,000

To provide, in accordance with regular policy, depreciation for one-half year in year of acquisition of machinery, based on economic life of five years and no residual value.

On December 31, Year 3, the accountant for Powell Corporation prepared the following working paper elimination (in journal entry format):

Retained Earnings—Powell	10,000	
Machinery—Seeley		10,000

To eliminate unrealized intercompany gain in machinery.

Instructions

Evaluate the foregoing journal entries and working paper elimination.

Case 9-2   Sawhill Company, one of two wholly owned subsidiaries of Peasley Corporation, is in liquidation under Chapter 7 of the U.S. Bankruptcy Code. On October 31, Year 8, the close of a fiscal year, Sawhill sold trade accounts receivable with a carrying amount of $50,000 to Shelton Company, the other wholly owned subsidiary of Peasley Corporation, for a gain of $10,000. Shelton debited the $10,000 to a deferred charge ledger account, which was to be amortized to expense in proportion to the amounts collected on the trade accounts receivable Shelton had acquired from Sawhill. The $10,000 gain was displayed in the consolidated income statement of Peasley Corporation and Shelton Company for the year ended October 31, Year 8; Sawhill Company was not included in the consolidated financial statements on that date because it was in liquidation. Peasley used the equity method of accounting for its investments in both Shelton and Sawhill.

Instructions

Evaluate the accounting described above.

PROBLEMS

Pr. 9-1   Parley Corporation owns 90% of the outstanding common stock of Silton Company. Both Parley and Silton have a February 28 (or 29) fiscal year-end. On March 1, Year 4, Silton sold to Parley for $100,000 a warehouse carried in Silton's Leasehold Improvements ledger account on that date at a net amount of $80,000. Parley was amortizing the warehouse on the straight-line basis over the remaining term of the operating lease, which was to expire February 28, Year 14.

On March 1, Year 5, Parley acquired in the open market for $48,264 cash (a 10% yield) one-half of Silton's $100,000 face amount 8% bonds due February 28, Year 7.

The bonds had been issued at their face amount on March 1, Year 2, with interest payable annually on February 28, beginning in Year 3. Both Silton and Parley use the interest method of amortization and accumulation of bond discount.

Instructions

Prepare working paper eliminations (in journal entry format) on February 28, Year 6, for Parley Corporation and subsidiary. (Disregard income taxes.)

Pr. 9-2 Peke Corporation sells merchandise to its 75%-owned subsidiary, Stoke Company, at a markup of 25% on cost. Stoke sells merchandise to Peke at a markup of 25% on selling price. Merchandise transactions between the two companies for the year ended June 30, Year 2, were as follows, at selling prices:

	Peke sales to Stoke	Stoke sales to Peke
July 1, Year 1, inventories of purchaser	$ 48,000	$ 30,000
Sales during year	600,000	800,000
Subtotals	$648,000	$830,000
Less: June 30, Year 2, inventories of purchaser	60,000	40,000
Cost of goods sold during year	$588,000	$790,000

Instructions

Prepare working paper eliminations (in journal entry format) on June 30, Year 2, for Peke Corporation and subsidiary. (Disregard income taxes.)

Pr. 9-3 For the year ended April 30, Year 7, Scala Company, the 90%-owned pooled subsidiary of Padua Corporation, had a net income of $120,000. During the year ended April 30, Year 7, the following intercompany transactions and events occurred:

(1) Padua sold merchandise to Scala for $180,000, at a markup of 20% on Padua's cost. Merchandise acquired from Padua in Scala's inventories totaled $54,000 on May 1, Year 6, and $84,000 on April 30, Year 7, at billed prices.

(2) On May 1, Year 6, Scala sold to Padua for $80,000 a machine with a carrying amount to Scala of $56,000. Padua established a remaining economic life of eight years, no residual value, and the straight-line method of depreciation for the machine.

(3) On April 30, Year 7, Padua acquired in the open market $200,000 face amount of Scala's 10%, ten-year bonds for $158,658, a yield rate of 14%. Scala had issued $400,000 face amount of the bonds on October 31, Year 6, for $354,120, a yield rate of 12%. The bonds paid interest each April 30 and October 31; Padua acquired its bond investment after the interest for April 30, Year 7, had been paid to the previous bondholders. Both Scala and Padua use the interest method of amortization or accumulation of bond discount.

Instructions

Prepare working paper eliminations (in journal entry format) for Padua Corporation and subsidiary on April 30, Year 7, including minority interest in net income of subsidiary. Disregard the elimination for the intercompany investment in the subsidiary's common stock; also disregard income taxes.

Pr. 9-4 On July 1, Year 8, the beginning of a fiscal year, Pacific Corporation and its wholly owned subsidiary, Sommer Company, entered into the following intercompany transactions and events:

(1) Pacific sold to Sommer for $16,000 a machine with a carrying amount of $12,000 ($30,000 cost less $18,000 accumulated depreciation). Sommer estimated a remaining economic life of eight years and no residual value for the machine. Sommer uses the straight-line method of depreciation for all plant assets.

(2) Pacific acquired in the open market for $361,571 (a 12% yield) four-fifths of Sommer's outstanding 8% bonds due June 30, Year 11 (after June 30, Year 8, interest had been paid on the bonds). Sommer's accounting records on July 1, Year 8, included the following ledger account balances:

8% bonds payable, due June 30, Year 11	$500,000 cr
Discount on 8% bonds payable	24,870 dr

The 8% bonds (interest payable each June 30) had been issued by Sommer July 1, Year 6, to yield 10%. Bond issue costs may be disregarded. Interest expense recognized by Sommer through Year 8 was as follows:

Year ended June 30, Year 7	$46,209
Year ended June 30, Year 8	46,830

Both Sommer and Pacific use the interest method of amortization or accumulation of bond discount.

Instructions

a Prepare journal entries for Pacific Corporation to record the two transactions or events with Sommer Company on July 1, Year 8, and intercompany interest revenue for the year ended June 30, Year 9. (Disregard income taxes.)

b Prepare working paper eliminations (in journal entry format) for Pacific Corporation and subsidiary on June 30, Year 9. (Disregard income taxes.)

Pr. 9-5 On August 31, Year 4, the end of a fiscal year, Silver Company, a wholly owned subsidiary of Pollard Corporation, issued to the public, at a yield rate of 11%, $800,000 face amount of 10%, ten-year bonds, with interest payable each February 28 and August 31. Bond issue costs may be disregarded. On August 31, Year 5, after Silver's interest payment, Pollard acquired in the open market $600,000 face amount of Silver's 10% bonds for $535,034, at a yield rate of 12%. On that date, Silver's Discount on Bonds Payable account had a debit balance of $44,985. Both companies use the interest method of amortization or accumulation of bond discount, and both companies close their accounting records only at the end of the fiscal year.

Instructions

a Set up three-column ledger accounts for Pollard Corporation's Investment in Silver Company Bonds and Intercompany Interest Revenue and for Silver Company's Intercompany Bonds Payable, Discount on Intercompany Bonds Payable, and Intercompany Interest Expense. Record in the ledger accounts all transactions involving Silver's 10% bonds from August 31, Year 5, through August 31, Year 6. Round all amounts to the nearest dollar. Disregard income taxes, and do not prepare closing entries.

b Prepare working paper eliminations (in journal entry format) for Pollard Corporation and subsidiary on August 31, Year 5, and August 31, Year 6. (Disregard income taxes.)

Pr. 9-6   On December 31, Year 7, Procus Corporation entered into a three-year sales-type lease with its 90%-owned subsidiary, Stoffer Company, for equipment having an economic life of six years, no residual value, and a cost in Procus's Inventories ledger account of $32,000. The lease required Stoffer to pay Procus $20,000 on December 31, Year 7, Year 8, and Year 9, and $5,000 (a bargain purchase option) on December 31, Year 10. Procus's implicit interest rate (known to Stoffer and less than Stoffer's incremental borrowing rate) was 7%, and Stoffer uses the straight-line method of depreciation. The present value of the minimum lease payments was $60,242.

Instructions

a Set up three-column ledger accounts for Procus Corporation's Intercompany Lease Receivables, Unearned Intercompany Interest Revenue, and Intercompany Interest Revenue ledger accounts and for Stoffer Company's Leased Equipment —Capital Lease, Intercompany Liability under Capital Lease, and Intercompany Interest Expense accounts; record in the accounts all transactions and events related to the leased property for the six years ended December 31, Year 13. (Round all amounts to the nearest dollar; disregard income taxes.)

b Prepare working paper eliminations (in journal entry format) for Procus Corporation and subsidiary on December 31, Year 7, and December 31, Year 8. (Disregard income taxes.)

Pr. 9-7   Patrick Corporation issued 100,000 shares of its $10 par common stock to acquire all the outstanding $10 par common stock of Shannon Company on December 31, Year 9, the end of a fiscal year, in a pooling-type business combination. In addition, Patrick acquired for $220,424, at a 12% yield rate, $250,000 face amount of Shannon's 9%, ten-year bonds due June 30, Year 15, with interest payable each June 30 and December 31. After completion of the business combination and journal entries to transfer merchandise transactions between Patrick and Shannon prior to the business combination to appropriate intercompany ledger accounts, the separate financial statements of the two companies were as shown on page 488.

On December 31, Year 9, one-half of the merchandise acquired by Patrick from Shannon prior to the pooling-type business combination remained unsold.

PATRICK CORPORATION AND SHANNON COMPANY
Separate Financial Statements (following business combination)
For Year Ended December 31, Year 9

	Patrick Corporation	Shannon Company
Income Statements		
Revenue:		
Net sales	$15,000,000	$10,000,000
Intercompany sales		600,000
Total revenue	$15,000,000	$10,600,000
Costs and expenses:		
Cost of goods sold	$ 6,000,000	$ 6,000,000
Intercompany cost of goods sold		480,000
Operating expenses	5,350,000	2,137,000
Interest expense	150,000	108,000
Income taxes expense	1,400,000	750,000
Total costs and expenses	$12,900,000	$ 9,475,000
Net income	$ 2,100,000	$ 1,125,000

Statements of Retained Earnings		
Retained earnings, beginning of year	$ 2,400,000	$ 275,000
Add: Net income	2,100,000	1,125,000
Subtotals	$ 4,500,000	$ 1,400,000
Less: Dividends declared	800,000	270,000
Retained earnings, end of year	$ 3,700,000	$ 1,130,000

Balance Sheets		
Assets		
Cash	$ 750,000	$ 300,000
Trade accounts receivable (net)	1,950,000	450,000
Intercompany accounts receivable		300,000
Inventories	2,100,000	950,000
Investment in Shannon Company common stock	2,205,000	
Investment in Shannon Company bonds	220,424	
Plant assets (net)	4,660,000	2,000,000
Other assets	564,576	350,000
Total assets	$12,450,000	$ 4,350,000

Liabilities & Stockholders' Equity		
Intercompany accounts payable	$ 300,000	
Other current liabilities	1,450,000	$ 945,000
Bonds payable	1,500,000	950,000
Intercompany bonds payable		250,000
Common stock, $10 par	3,000,000	900,000
Additional paid-in capital	1,370,000	175,000
Retained earnings	3,700,000	1,130,000
Retained earnings of subsidiary	1,130,000	
Total liabilities & stockholders' equity	$12,450,000	$ 4,350,000

Instructions

a Prepare a working paper for consolidated financial statements and related working paper eliminations (in journal entry format) for Patrick Corporation and subsidiary on December 31, Year 9. (Disregard income taxes.)

b Prepare a consolidated statement of retained earnings for Patrick Corporation and subsidiary for the year ended December 31, Year 9.

Pr. 9-8 Power Corporation acquired 80% of Snyder Company's 1,250 shares of outstanding $100 par common stock on July 1, Year 6, for $158,600, including out-of-pocket costs of the purchase-type business combination. The excess of the current fair value of Snyder's identifiable net assets over their carrying amounts on July 1, Year 6, was attributable as follows:

To inventories	$3,000
To equipment (five-year remaining economic life on July 1, Year 6)	4,000
To goodwill (five-year remaining economic life on July 1, Year 6)	Remainder of excess

In addition, on July 1, Year 6, Power acquired in the open market at face amount $40,000 of Snyder Company's 6% bonds payable. Interest is payable by Snyder each July 1 and January 1.

Separate financial statements for Power Corporation and Snyder Company for the period ended December 31, Year 6, were as follows:

POWER CORPORATION AND SNYDER COMPANY
Separate Financial Statements
For Periods Ended December 31, Year 6

	Power Corporation (year ended 12-31-6)	Snyder Company (six months ended 12-31-6)
Income Statements		
Revenue:		
Net sales	$ 902,000	$400,000
Intercompany sales	60,000	105,000
Intercompany interest revenue (expense)	1,200	(1,200)
Intercompany investment income	13,280	
Intercompany loss on sale of equipment	(2,000)	
Total revenue	$ 974,480	$503,800
Costs and expenses:		
Cost of goods sold	$ 720,000	$300,000
Intercompany cost of goods sold	50,000	84,000
Operating expenses and income taxes expense . .	124,480	99,800
Total costs and expenses	$ 894,480	$483,800
Net income	$ 80,000	$ 20,000

(continued)

POWER CORPORATION AND SNYDER COMPANY
Separate Financial Statements (concluded)
For Periods Ended December 31, Year 6

	Power Corporation (year ended 12-31-6)	Snyder Company (six months ended 12-31-6)
Statements of Retained Earnings		
Retained earnings, beginning of period	$ 220,000	$ 50,000
Add: Net income	80,000	$ 20,000
Subtotals	$ 300,000	$ 70,000
Less: Dividends declared	36,000	9,000
Retained earnings, end of period	$ 264,000	$ 61,000
Balance Sheets		
Assets		
Intercompany receivables (payables)	$ 100	$ (100)
Inventories, at first-in, first-out cost	300,000	75,000
Investment in Snyder Company common stock	164,340	
Investment in Snyder Company bonds	40,000	
Plant assets	794,000	280,600
Accumulated depreciation of plant assets	(260,000)	(30,000)
Other assets	610,900	73,400
Total assets	$1,649,340	$398,900
Liabilities & Stockholders' Equity		
Dividends payable		$ 1,600
Bonds payable	$ 600,000	45,000
Intercompany bonds payable		40,000
Other liabilities	376,340	114,300
Common stock, $100 par	360,000	125,000
Additional paid-in capital	49,000	12,000
Retained earnings	264,000	61,000
Total liabilities & stockholders' equity	$1,649,340	$398,900

Additional Information

(1) Intercompany sales data for the six months ended December 31, Year 6, are shown below:

	Power Corporation	Snyder Company
Intercompany accounts payable, Dec. 31, Year 6	$13,000	$ 5,500
Intercompany purchases in inventories, Dec. 31, Year 6	25,000	18,000

(2) On October 1, Year 6, Power had sold to Snyder for $12,000 equipment having a carrying amount of $14,000 on that date. Snyder established a five-year remaining economic life, no residual value, and the straight-line method of depreciation for the equipment. Snyder includes depreciation expense in operating expenses.

(3) Dividends were declared by Snyder as follows:

Sept. 30, Year 6	$1,000
Dec. 31, Year 6	8,000
Total dividends declared	$9,000

Instructions

Prepare a working paper for consolidated financial statements and related working paper eliminations (in journal entry format) for Power Corporation and subsidiary for the year ended December 31, Year 6. (Disregard income taxes.)

Pr. 9-9 On January 2, Year 1, Pritchard Corporation issued 5,000 shares of its $10 par common stock in exchange for all 3,000 shares of Spangler Company's $20 par common stock outstanding on that date. Out-of-pocket costs of the pooling-type business combination may be disregarded. Separate financial statements of the two companies for the year ended December 31, Year 1, follow:

PRITCHARD CORPORATION AND SPANGLER COMPANY
Separate Financial Statements
For Year Ended December 31, Year 1

Income Statements	Pritchard Corporation	Spangler Company
Revenue:		
Net sales	$499,850	$298,240
Intercompany sales	40,000	6,000
Intercompany interest revenue (expense)	300	(480)
Intercompany investment income	10,200	
Intercompany gain on sale of equipment		2,000
Total revenue	$550,350	$305,760
Costs and expenses:		
Cost of goods sold	$400,000	$225,000
Intercompany cost of goods sold	30,000	4,800
Operating expenses and income taxes expense	88,450	65,760
Total costs and expenses	$518,450	$295,560
Net income	$ 31,900	$ 10,200

Statements of Retained Earnings		
Retained earnings, beginning of year	$ 67,000	$ 22,100
Add: Net income	31,900	10,200
Subtotals	$ 98,900	$ 32,300
Less: Dividends declared		4,500
Retained earnings, end of year	$ 98,900	$ 27,800

Balance Sheets		
Assets		
Intercompany receivables (payables)	$ 21,300	$(22,980)
Inventories	81,050	49,840
Investment in Spangler Company common stock	112,300	
Plant assets	83,200	43,500

(continued)

PRITCHARD CORPORATION AND SPANGLER COMPANY
Separate Financial Statements (concluded)
For Year Ended December 31, Year 1

Balance Sheets	*Pritchard Corporation*	*Spangler Company*
Assets		
Accumulated depreciation of plant assets	(12,800)	(9,300)
Other assets	71,150	56,200
Total assets.	$356,200	$117,260
Liabilities & Stockholders' Equity		
Liabilities	$ 56,700	$ 9,460
Common stock, $10 par	120,000	
Common stock, $20 par		60,000
Additional paid-in capital	58,500	20,000
Retained earnings	98,900	27,800
Retained earnings of subsidiary	22,100	
Total liabilities & stockholders' equity	$356,200	$117,260

Additional Information

(1) On December 31, Year 1, Spangler owed Pritchard $16,000 on open account and $8,000 on 12% demand notes dated July 1, Year 1 (interest payable at maturity). Pritchard had discounted $3,000 of the notes received from Spangler with a bank on July 1, Year 1, without notifying Spangler of this action.

(2) During Year 1, Pritchard sold to Spangler for $40,000 merchandise that cost $30,000. Spangler's December 31, Year 1, inventories included $10,000 of this merchandise priced at Spangler's cost.

(3) On July 1, Year 1, Spangler had sold equipment with a carrying amount of $15,000 to Pritchard for $17,000. Pritchard recognized depreciation on the equipment in the amount of $850 for Year 1. The remaining economic life of the equipment on the date of sale was 10 years. Pritchard includes depreciation expense in operating expenses.

(4) Spangler had shipped merchandise to Pritchard on December 31, Year 1, and recorded an intercompany account receivable of $6,000 for the sale. Spangler's cost for the merchandise was $4,800. Because the merchandise was in transit, Pritchard did not record the transaction. The terms of the sale were FOB shipping point.

(5) Spangler declared a dividend of $1.50 a share on December 31, Year 1, payable on January 10, Year 2. Pritchard made no journal entry for the dividend declaration.

Instructions

a Prepare adjusting entries for Pritchard Corporation and Spangler Company on December 31, Year 1.

b Prepare a working paper for consolidated financial statements and related working paper eliminations (in journal entry format) for Pritchard Corporation and subsidiary on December 31, Year 1. Amounts in the working paper should reflect the adjusting entries in **a**. (Disregard income taxes.)

10

Consolidated Financial Statements: Income Taxes, Cash Flows, and Installment Acquisitions

This chapter considers two topics that have relevance for every business combination and parent company–subsidiary relationship: (1) income taxes and (2) the consolidated statement of cash flows. In addition, this chapter deals with accounting for installment acquisitions of a subsidiary in a purchase-type business combination.

INCOME TAXES IN BUSINESS COMBINATIONS AND CONSOLIDATIONS

Accounting for income taxes for a consolidated entity has received considerable attention from accountants in recent years, primarily because of the emphasis on income tax allocation and disclosure in financial statements. Accounting for income taxes in business combinations and consolidated financial statements may be subdivided into three sections: (1) income taxes attributable to current fair values of a purchased subsidiary's identifiable net assets, (2) income taxes attributable to undistributed earnings of subsidiaries, and (3) income taxes attributable to unrealized and realized intercompany profits (gains).

Income Taxes Attributable to Current Fair Values of Purchased Subsidiary's Identifiable Net Assets

Income tax accounting requirements for business combinations often differ from financial accounting requirements. A purchase-type business combination, which requires a revaluation of the combinee's identifiable net assets, may meet the requirements for a "tax-free corporate reorganization" under the Internal Revenue Code, in which a new income tax basis may not be required for the combinee's net assets. Similarly, a pooling-type business combination, in which there is no revaluation of the combinee's net assets, may not be a "tax-free corporate reorganization," and the income tax basis of the combinee's net assets may be changed. In such

493

situations, a ***temporary difference*** may result between provisions for depreciation and amortization in the combinee's financial statements and income tax returns.

In recognition of this problem, the Financial Accounting Standards Board made the following provision for income tax considerations in the valuation of a purchased combinee's net assets:[1]

> A deferred tax liability or asset shall be recognized in accordance with the requirements of this Statement for differences between the assigned values and the tax bases of the assets and liabilities (except the portion of goodwill for which amortization is not deductible for tax purposes, unallocated ''negative goodwill,'' leveraged leases, . . .) recognized in a purchase business combination. . . .

To illustrate the application of the above, assume that the purchase-type business combination of Principia Corporation and the combinee, Sandusky Company, completed on June 1, Year 7, met the requirements for a ''tax-free corporate reorganization'' for income tax purposes. Principia paid $800,000 (including direct out-of-pocket costs of the business combination) for all of Sandusky's identifiable net assets except cash. The current fair values of Sandusky's identifiable net assets were equal to their carrying amounts, except for the following assets:

Differing current fair values and carrying amounts of assets				

Assets	Current fair values	Tax bases/ carrying amounts	Current fair value excess	Economic life
Inventories (first-in, first-out cost)	$ 100,000	$ 80,000	$ 20,000	
Land....................	250,000	220,000	30,000	
Building	640,000	500,000	140,000	20 years
Machinery..............	120,000	100,000	20,000	5 years
Totals.................	$1,110,000	$900,000	$210,000	

If the carrying amounts (equal to current fair values) of Sandusky's other identifiable assets and liabilities were $390,000 and $650,000, respectively, and the income tax rate is 40%, Principia's journal entries to record the business combination with Sandusky Company on June 1, Year 7, would be as follows:

Journal entries for purchase-type business combination including deferred income tax liability

Investment in Net Assets of Sandusky Company	800,000	
Cash		800,000
To record acquisition of net assets of Sandusky Company except cash, and direct out-of-pocket costs of the business combination.		

(continued)

[1] *FASB Statement No. 109,* ''Accounting for Income Taxes,'' FASB (Norwalk, 1992), p. 12.

Inventories	100,000	
Land	250,000	
Building.	640,000	
Machinery.	120,000	
Other Identifiable Assets.	390,000	
Goodwill {$800,000 − [($1,110,000 + $390,000) − ($84,000 + $650,000)]}.	34,000	
Deferred Income Tax Liability ($210,000 × 0.40).		84,000
Other Liabilities.		650,000
Investment in Net Assets of Sandusky Company		800,000
To allocate cost of Sandusky's net assets to identifiable net assets; to establish liability for deferred income tax attributable to differences between current fair values and tax bases of assets; and to allocate remainder of cost to goodwill.		

The deferred income tax liability established in the foregoing journal entry will be extinguished when the temporary differences between current fair values and tax bases of the inventories and plant assets are realized through sale or depreciation. For example, assuming the inventories were sold during the year ended May 31, Year 8, the deferred tax liability would be reduced by $12,400, computed as follows:

Income tax effect of reversing temporary differences	Cost of goods sold (inventories current fair value excess).	$20,000
	Building depreciation attributable to current fair value excess ($140,000 ÷ 20)	7,000
	Machinery depreciation attributable to current fair value excess ($20,000 ÷ 5)	4,000
	Total reversing temporary differences	$31,000
	Income tax effect ($31,000 × 0.40).	$12,400

Assuming Principia Corporation had pre-tax accounting income of $420,000 (net of nondeductible goodwill amortization of $850) for the year ended May 31, Year 8, and there were no temporary differences between pre-tax accounting income and taxable income other than those resulting from the business combination with Sandusky Company, Principia's journal entry for income taxes on May 31, Year 8, is as follows:

Journal entry for income taxes	Income Taxes Expense [($420,000 + $850) × 0.40].	168,340
	Deferred Income Tax Liability	12,400
	Income Taxes Payable [($420,850 + $31,000) × 0.40] . . .	180,740
	To record income taxes expense for Year 8.	

In the foregoing journal entry, nondeductible goodwill amortization expense of $850 is added to both pre-tax accounting income and taxable income, because it is not a temporary difference between the two amounts.

Income Taxes Attributable to Undistributed Earnings of Subsidiaries

In 1992, the Financial Accounting Standards Board revised prior accounting standards for income taxes attributable to undistributed earnings of subsidiaries in the following provisions:[2]

1   A deferred income tax liability is to be recognized for an excess of the financial reporting carrying amount of an investment in a domestic subsidiary over its tax basis if the excess arose in fiscal years beginning after December 15, 1992.

2   A deferred income tax liability need not be recognized for an excess of the financial reporting carrying amount over the tax basis of an investment in a foreign subsidiary if the excess essentially is permanent in duration.

The substance of the foregoing is that currently a deferred income tax liability must be provided by the parent company for the undistributed earnings of its domestic subsidiaries.

Illustration of Income Tax Allocation for Undistributed Earnings of Subsidiaries

Pinkley Corporation owns 75% of the outstanding common stock of Seabright Company, which it acquired for cash on April 1, Year 2. Goodwill acquired by Pinkley in the purchase-type business combination was $30,000; Seabright's identifiable net assets were fairly valued at their carrying amounts. For the year ended March 31, Year 3, Pinkley had pre-tax accounting income, exclusive of goodwill amortization and intercompany investment income under the equity method of accounting, of $100,000. Seabright's pre-tax accounting income was $50,000, and dividends declared and paid by Seabright during Year 3 totaled $10,000. The income tax rate for both companies is 40%. Income tax laws provide for a dividend-received deduction rate of 80% on dividends from less-than-80%-owned domestic corporations. Neither Pinkley nor Seabright had any temporary differences; neither had any income subject to preference income tax rates; and there were no intercompany profits resulting from transactions between Pinkley and Seabright.

Seabright's journal entry to accrue income taxes on March 31, Year 3, is as follows:

<table>
<tr><td>Subsidiary's journal entry for accrual of income taxes</td><td>Income Taxes Expense.. 20,000
    Income Taxes Payable   20,000
To record income taxes expense for Year 3 ($50,000 × 0.40 = $20,000).</td></tr>
</table>

On March 31, Year 3, Pinkley prepares the following journal entries for income taxes payable, the subsidiary's operating results, and deferred income tax liability:

---

[2] Ibid., pp. 12–13.

PINKLEY CORPORATION
Journal Entries
March 31, Year 3

Amortization Expense	750	
Investment in Seabright Company Common Stock.		750

To record amortization of goodwill for Year 3 ($30,000 ÷ 40 = $750).

Income Taxes Expense.	40,000	
Income Taxes Payable		40,000

To record income taxes expense for Year 3 on income exclusive of goodwill amortization (not deductible) and intercompany investment income ($100,000 × 0.40 = $40,000).

Cash	7,500	
Investment in Seabright Company Common Stock.		7,500

To record dividend declared and paid by subsidiary ($10,000 × 0.75 = $7,500).

Investment in Seabright Company Common Stock.	22,500	
Intercompany Investment Income.		22,500

To accrue share of subsidiary's net income for Year 3 ($30,000* × 0.75 = $22,500).

Income Taxes Expense.	1,800	
Income Taxes Payable		600
Deferred Income Tax Liability		1,200

To provide for income taxes on intercompany investment income from subsidiary as follows:

Net income of subsidiary	$30,000
Less: Depreciation and amortization attributable to	
differences between current fair values and carrying	
amounts of subsidiary's net assets	-0-
Income of subsidiary subject to income taxes	$30,000
Parent company's share ($30,000 × 0.75)	$22,500
Less: Dividend-received deduction ($22,500 × 0.80)	18,000
Amount subject to income taxes.	$ 4,500
Income taxes expense ($4,500 × 0.40)	$ 1,800
Taxes currently payable based on dividend received	
($7,500 × 0.20 × 0.40)	$ 600
Taxes deferred until earnings remitted by subsidiary	1,200
Income taxes expense	$ 1,800

* $50,000 − $20,000 = $30,000

Income Taxes Attributable to Intercompany Profits (Gains)

Federal income tax laws permit an affiliated group of corporations to file a consolidated income tax return rather than separate returns. Intercompany profits (gains) and losses are eliminated in a consolidated income tax return just as they are in consolidated financial statements. An "affiliated group" for federal income tax purposes is defined as follows:[3]

> . . . the term "affiliated group" means one or more chains of includible corporations connected through stock ownership with a common parent corporation which is an includible corporation if—
>
> (1) Stock possessing at least 80 percent of the voting power of all classes of stock and at least 80 percent of each class of the nonvoting stock of each of the includible corporations (except the common parent corporation) is owned directly by one or more of the other includible corporations; and
>
> (2) The common parent corporation owns directly stock possessing at least 80 percent of the voting power of all classes of stock and at least 80 percent of each class of the nonvoting stock of at least one of the other includible corporations
>
> As used in this subsection, the term "stock" does not include nonvoting stock which is limited and preferred as to dividends, ...

If a parent company and its subsidiaries do not qualify for the "affiliated group" status, or if they otherwise elect to file *separate income tax returns,* the provisions of *FASB Statement No. 109,* "Accounting for Income Taxes," for the recognition of deferred tax assets and liabilities apply.[4] (Accounting for income taxes is discussed in depth in intermediate accounting textbooks.) The deferral of income taxes accrued or paid on unrealized intercompany profits is best illustrated by returning to the intercompany profits examples in Chapter 9.[5]

Income Taxes Attributable to Unrealized Intercompany Profits in Inventories

For unrealized intercompany profits in inventories at the end of the first year of an affiliated group's operations, return to the working paper elimination (in journal entry format) on page 437 for Post Corporation and Sage Company on December 31, Year 3, which is as follows:

<table>
<tr><td rowspan="5">Elimination of
unrealized
intercompany profit in
ending inventories</td><td>Intercompany Sales—Sage....................................</td><td align="right">120,000</td><td></td></tr>
<tr><td>   Intercompany Cost of Goods Sold—Sage...............</td><td></td><td align="right">96,000</td></tr>
<tr><td>   Cost of Goods Sold—Post............................</td><td></td><td align="right">16,000</td></tr>
<tr><td>   Inventories—Post ....</td><td></td><td align="right">8,000</td></tr>
<tr><td>To eliminate intercompany sales, cost of goods sold, and unrealized
intercompany profit in inventories.</td><td></td><td></td></tr>
</table>

---

[3] United States, *Internal Revenue Code of 1986,* sec. 1504(a).

[4] *FASB Statement, No. 109,* pp. 3–4, 42–43.

[5] In the examples that follow, it is assumed that the provisions of *FASB Statement No. 109,* "Accounting for Income Taxes" for recognizing deferred tax assets without a valuation allowance are met.

If Post and Sage file *separate income tax returns* for Year 3 and the income tax rate is 40%, the following additional elimination (in journal entry format) is required on December 31, Year 3:

Elimination for income taxes attributable to unrealized intercompany profit in ending inventories	*Deferred Income Tax Asset—Sage* 3,200	
	Income Taxes Expense—Sage	3,200
	To defer income taxes provided on separate income tax returns of subsidiary applicable to unrealized intercompany profits in parent company's inventories on Dec. 31, Year 3 ($8,000 × 0.40 = $3,200).	

The $3,200 reduction in the income taxes expense of Sage Company (the partially owned subsidiary) enters into the computation of the minority interest in net income of the subsidiary for the year ended December 31, Year 3.

With regard to unrealized intercompany profits in beginning and ending inventories, I refer to the working paper elimination (in journal entry format, on page 439) for the year ended December 31, Year 4, which follows:

Elimination of intercompany profits in beginning and ending inventories	*Retained Earnings—Sage ($8,000 × 0.95)* 7,600	
	Minority Interest in Net Assets of Subsidiary ($8,000 × 0.05) 400	
	Intercompany Sales—Sage 150,000	
	Intercompany Cost of Goods Sold—Sage	120,000
	Cost of Goods Sold—Post	26,000
	Inventories—Post	12,000
	To eliminate intercompany sales, cost of goods sold, and unrealized intercompany profit in inventories.	

Assuming *separate income tax returns* for Post Corporation and Sage Company for Year 4 and an income tax rate of 40%, the following additional eliminations (in journal entry format) are appropriate on December 31, Year 4:

Eliminations for income taxes attributable to intercompany profits in ending and beginning inventories	*Deferred Income Tax Asset—Sage* 4,800	
	Income Taxes Expense—Sage	4,800
	To defer income taxes provided on separate income tax returns of subsidiary applicable to unrealized intercompany profits in parent company's inventories on Dec. 31, Year 4 ($12,000 × 0.40 = $4,800).	
	Income Taxes Expense—Sage 3,200	
	Retained Earnings—Sage ($3,200 × 0.95; or $7,600 × 0.40) .	3,040
	Minority Interest in Net Assets of Subsidiary ($3,200 × 0.05; or $400 × 0.40)	160
	To provide for income taxes attributable to realized intercompany profits in parent company's inventories on Dec. 31, Year 3 ($8,000 × 0.40 = $3,200).	

The second elimination above reflects the income tax effects of the ***realization*** by the consolidated group, on a first-in, first-out basis, of the intercompany profits in the parent company's ***beginning*** inventories.

Income Taxes Attributable to Unrealized Intercompany Gain in Land   Under generally accepted accounting principles, gains and losses from sales of plant assets are not extraordinary items.[6] Thus, intraperiod income tax allocation is not appropriate for such gains and losses.

The intercompany gain on Post Corporation's sale of land to Sage Company during Year 3 is eliminated by the following December 31, Year 3, working paper elimination (in journal entry format, from page 442):

Elimination of
unrealized
intercompany gain in
land

Intercompany Gain on Sale of Land—Post	*50,000*	
Land—Sage		*50,000*
To eliminate unrealized intercompany gain on sale of land.		

If Post and Sage filed ***separate income tax returns*** for Year 3, the following elimination (in journal entry format) accompanies the one illustrated above, assuming an income tax rate of 40%:

Elimination for income
taxes attributable to
unrealized
intercompany gain in
land—for accounting
period of sale

Deferred Income Tax Asset—Post.	*20,000*	
Income Taxes Expense—Post		*20,000*
To defer income taxes provided on separate income tax returns of		
parent company applicable to unrealized intercompany gain in sub-		
sidiary's land on Dec. 31, Year 3 ($50,000 × 0.40 = $20,000).		

In years subsequent to Year 3, as long as the subsidiary owns the land, the following elimination (in journal entry format) accompanies the elimination that debits Retained Earnings—Post and credits Land—Sage for $50,000:

Elimination for income
taxes attributable to
unrealized
intercompany gain in
land—for accounting
periods subsequent to
sale

Deferred Income Tax Asset—Post.	*20,000*	
Retained Earnings—Post.		*20,000*
To defer income taxes attributable to unrealized intercompany gain		
in subsidiary's land.		

In a period in which the subsidiary resold the land to an outsider, the appropriate elimination would be a debit to Income Taxes Expense—Post and a credit to Retained Earnings—Post, in the amount of $20,000, because the $50,000 gain that previously was unrealized would be realized on behalf of Post by Sage, the seller of the land to an outsider.

---

[6] *APB Opinion No. 30,* ''Reporting the Results of Operations,'' AICPA (New York: 1973), pp. 566 and 568.

Income Taxes Attributable to Unrealized Intercompany Gain in a Depreciable Plant Asset

As pointed out in Chapter 9, the intercompany gain on the sale of a depreciable plant asset is realized through the periodic depreciation of the asset. Therefore, the related deferred income taxes reverse as depreciation expense is taken on the asset.

To illustrate, refer to the illustration in Chapter 9, page 445, of the December 31, Year 3, working paper elimination (in journal entry format) for the unrealized intercompany gain in Post Corporation's machinery, which is reproduced below:

Elimination of unrealized intercompany gain in machinery	*Intercompany Gain on Sale of Machinery—Sage*................ 23,800	
	Machinery—Post	*23,800*
	To eliminate unrealized intercompany gain on sale of machinery.	

Assuming *separate income tax returns* and an income tax rate of 40%, the tax-deferral elimination on December 31, Year 3 (the date of the intercompany sale of machinery), is as follows:

Elimination for income taxes attributable to unrealized intercompany gain in machinery—for accounting period of sale	*Deferred Income Tax Asset—Sage* 9,520	
	Income Taxes Expense—Sage...........................	*9,520*
	To defer income taxes provided on separate income tax returns of subsidiary applicable to unrealized intercompany gain in parent company's machinery on Dec. 31, Year 3 ($23,800 × 0.40 = $9,520).	

The $9,520 increase in the subsidiary's net income is included in the computation of the minority interest in the subsidiary's net income for Year 3. For the year ended December 31, Year 4, the elimination (in journal entry format) of the intercompany gain (see page 445) is as follows:

Elimination of intercompany gain in machinery and in related depreciation	*Retained Earnings—Sage ($23,800 × 0.95)*..................... 22,610	
	Minority Interest in Net Assets of Subsidiary ($23,800 × 0.05) 1,190	
	Accumulated Depreciation—Post............................ 4,760	
	Machinery—Post	*23,800*
	Depreciation Expense—Post	*4,760*
	To eliminate unrealized intercompany gain in machinery and in related depreciation. Gain element in depreciation computed as $23,800 × 0.20 = $4,760, based on five-year economic life.	

For the year ended December 31, Year 4, the elimination (in journal entry format) for income taxes attributable to the intercompany gain is on page 502.

Comparable working paper eliminations would be necessary on December 31, Years 5, 6, 7, and 8.

<table>
<tr>
<td>

Elimination for income
taxes attributable to
intercompany gain in
machinery—for first
year subsequent to sale

</td>
<td>

Income Taxes Expense—Sage 1,904
Deferred Income Tax Asset—Sage ($9,520 − $1,904) 7,616
     Retained Earnings—Sage ($9,520 × 0.95; or $22,610 × 0.40)   9,044
     Minority Interest in Net Assets of Subsidiary ($9,520 × 0.05; or
       $1,190 × 0.40) 476
To provide for income taxes expense on intercompany gain realized
through parent company's depreciation ($4,760 × 0.40 = $1,904); and
to defer income taxes attributable to remainder of unrealized gain.

</td>
</tr>
</table>

Income Taxes Attributable to Intercompany Gain on Extinguishment of Bonds

As pointed out in Chapter 9, a gain or loss is recognized in consolidated financial statements for one affiliate's open-market acquisition of another affiliate's bonds. Thus, income taxes attributable to the gain or loss should be provided for in a working paper elimination.

Referring to Post Corporation's December 31, Year 3, open-market acquisition of Sage Company's bonds (see page 457), there is the following working paper elimination (in journal entry format) on December 31, Year 3:

<table>
<tr>
<td>

Elimination for realized
gain on extinguishment
of affiliate's bonds

</td>
<td>

Intercompany Bonds Payable—Sage 300,000
    Discount on Intercompany Bonds Payable—Sage 18,224
    Investment in Sage Company Bonds—Post 257,175
    Gain on Extinguishment of Bonds—Sage 24,601
To eliminate subsidiary's bonds acquired by parent; and to recog-
nize gain on the extinguishment of the bonds.

</td>
</tr>
</table>

The appropriate elimination (in journal entry format) to accompany the one above is as follows, assuming that (1) the income tax rate is 40%, (2) *separate income tax returns are filed,* and (3) the gain on extinguishment of bonds is not material and thus is not reported as an extraordinary item in the consolidated income statement of Post Corporation and subsidiary for Year 3:

<table>
<tr>
<td>

Elimination for income
taxes attributable to
realized gain on
extinguishment of
affiliate's bonds—for
accounting period of
extinguishment

</td>
<td>

Income Taxes Expense—Sage 9,840
    Deferred Income Tax Liability—Sage 9,840
To provide for income taxes attributable to subsidiary's realized gain on
parent company's acquisition of the subsidiary's bonds ($24,601
× 0.40 = $9,840).

</td>
</tr>
</table>

The additional expense of the subsidiary recognized in the foregoing elimination enters into the computation of the minority interest in net income of the subsidiary for Year 3.

In periods subsequent to the date of the acquisition of the bonds, the *actual* income taxes expense of both the parent company and the subsidiary reflect the effects of the intercompany interest revenue and intercompany interest expense. The income tax effects of the difference between intercompany interest revenue and expense represent the reversal of the $9,840 deferred income tax liability recorded in the foregoing elimination. For example, the working paper elimination (in journal entry format) for intercompany bonds of Post Corporation and subsidiary on December 31, Year 4 (see page 462), is repeated below:

<table>
<tr><td style="width:200px;text-align:right;vertical-align:top">Elimination for
intercompany bonds
one year after
acquisition</td><td>

Intercompany Interest Revenue—Post *38,576*
Intercompany Bonds Payable—Sage *300,000*
    Discount on Intercompany Bonds Payable—Sage *14,411*
    Investment in Sage Company Bonds—Post *265,751*
    Intercompany Interest Expense—Sage *33,813*
    Retained Earnings—Sage ($24,601 × 0.95) *23,371*
    Minority Interest in Net Assets of Subsidiary
      ($24,601 × 0.05) *1,230*
To eliminate subsidiary's bonds owned by parent company, and related interest revenue and expense; and to increase subsidiary's beginning related earnings by the amount of unamortized realized gain on the extinguishment of the bonds.
</td></tr>
</table>

The foregoing elimination is accompanied by the following additional elimination (in journal entry format) on December 31, Year 4:

<table>
<tr><td style="width:200px;text-align:right;vertical-align:top">Elimination for income
taxes attributable to
gain on acquisition of
affiliate's bonds—for
first year subsequent to
acquisition</td><td>

Retained Earnings—Sage ($9,840 × 0.95; or $23,371 × 0.40) *9,348*
Minority Interest in Net Assets of Subsidiary ($9,840 × 0.05; or
  $1,230 × 0.40) *492*
    Income Taxes Expense—Sage [($38,576 − $33,813) × 0.40]   *1,905*
    Deferred Income Tax Liability—Sage ($9,840 − $1,905) *7,935*
*To reduce the subsidiary's income taxes expense for amount attributable to **recorded** intercompany gain (for consolidation purposes) on subsidiary's bonds; and to provide for remaining deferred income taxes on unrecorded portion of gain.*
</td></tr>
</table>

Summary: Income Taxes Attributable to Intercompany Profits (Gains) In this section I illustrate the interperiod allocation of income taxes attributable to intercompany profits (gains) of affiliated companies that *file separate income tax returns.* The elimination of unrealized intercompany profits (gains) causes a temporary difference in which taxable income exceeds pre-tax accounting income in the accounting period of the intercompany gain; thus, assuming provisions of *FASB Statement No. 109,* ''Accounting for Income Taxes,'' for recognizing deferred tax assets without a valuation allowance are met, deferred income tax assets must be accounted for in working paper eliminations that accompany the profit (gain) eliminations. In the case of intercompany bonds, pre-tax accounting income exceeds taxable income of the accounting period of the realized gain; thus, a deferred income tax liability must be provided in a working paper elimination.

The illustrative working paper eliminations for Post Corporation and subsidiary for the year ended December 31, Year 4, outlined in the preceding pages, are summarized below and on page 505.

All the following eliminations except *(d)* and *(e)* affect the net income of Sage Company, the partially owned subsidiary. The appropriate amounts in those eliminations are included in the computation of minority interest in net income of subsidiary for Year 4.

POST CORPORATION AND SUBSIDIARY
Partial Working Paper Eliminations
December 31, Year 4

(b) Retained Earnings—Sage ($8,000 × 0.95) 7,600
    Minority Interest in Net Assets of Subsidiary ($8,000 × 0.05). 400
    Intercompany Sales—Sage 150,000
        Intercompany Cost of Goods Sold—Sage 120,000
        Cost of Goods Sold—Post 26,000
        Inventories—Post 12,000
    To eliminate intercompany sales, cost of goods sold, and unrealized intercompany profit in inventories.

(c) Deferred Income Tax Asset—Sage 4,800
        Income Taxes Expense—Sage 4,800
    To defer income taxes provided on separate income tax returns of subsidiary applicable to unrealized intercompany profits in parent company's inventories on Dec. 31, Year 4 ($12,000 × 0.40 = $4,800).

    Income Taxes Expense—Sage 3,200
        Retained Earnings—Sage ($3,200 × 0.95; or
          $7,600 × 0.40) 3,040
        Minority Interest in Net Assets of Subsidiary
          ($3,200 × 0.05; or $400 × 0.40) 160
    To provide for income taxes attributable to realized intercompany profits in parent company's inventories on Dec. 31, Year 3 ($8,000 × 0.40 = $3,200).

(d) Retained Earnings—Post 50,000
        Land—Sage 50,000
    To eliminate unrealized intercompany gain in land.

(e) Deferred Income Tax Asset—Post 20,000
        Retained Earnings—Post 20,000
    To defer income taxes attributable to unrealized intercompany gain in subsidiary's land ($50,000 × 0.40 = $20,000).

(continued)

(f) Retained Earnings—Sage ($23,800 × 0.95) 22,610

Minority Interest in Net Assets of Subsidiary ($23,800 × 0.05) 1,190

Accumulated Depreciation—Post......................... 4,760

Machinery—Post 23,800

Depreciation Expense—Post....................... 4,760

To eliminate unrealized intercompany gain in machinery and in related depreciation. Gain element in depreciation computed as $23,800 × 0.20 = $4,760, based on five-year economic life.

(g) Income Taxes Expense—Sage.......................... 1,904

Deferred Income Tax Asset—Sage ($9,520 − $1,904)...... 7,616

Retained Earnings—Sage ($9,520 × 0.95; or

$22,610 × 0.40) 9,044

Minority Interest in Net Assets of Subsidiary

($9,520 × 0.05; or $1,190 × 0.40) 476

To provide for income taxes expense on intercompany gain realized through parent company's depreciation ($4,760 × 0.40 = $1,904); and to defer income taxes attributable to remainder of unrealized gain.

(h) Intercompany Interest Revenue—Post 38,576

Intercompany Bonds Payable—Sage 300,000

Discount on Intercompany Bonds Payable—Sage.... 14,411

Investment in Sage Company Bonds—Post 265,751

Intercompany Interest Expense—Sage.............. 33,813

Retained Earnings—Sage ($24,601 × 0.95)......... 23,371

Minority Interest in Net Assets of Subsidiary

($24,601 × 0.05)................................ 1,230

To eliminate subsidiary's bonds owned by parent company, and related interest revenue and expense; and to increase subsidiary's beginning retained earnings by amount of unamortized realized gain on the extinguishment of the bonds.

(i) Retained Earnings—Sage ($9,840 × 0.95;

or $23,371 × 0.40) 9,348

Minority Interest in Net Assets of Subsidiary ($9,840 × 0.05;

or $1,230 × 0.40) 492

Income Taxes Expense—Sage

[($38,576 − $33,813) × 0.40] 1,905

Deferred Income Tax Liability—Sage

($9,840 − $1,905)................................ 7,935

To reduce the subsidiary's income taxes expense for amount attributable to **recorded** intercompany gain (for consolidation purposes) on subsidiary's bonds; and to provide for remaining deferred income taxes on unrecorded portion of gain.

CONSOLIDATED STATEMENT OF CASH FLOWS

The consolidated financial statements issued by publicly owned companies include a statement of cash flows. This statement may be prepared as described in intermediate accounting textbooks; however, when the statement is prepared on a consolidated basis, a number of problems arise. Some of these are described below:

1   Depreciation and amortization expense, as reported in the consolidated income statement, is added to combined net income, *including the minority interest in net income of subsidiary,* in a consolidated statement of cash flows. The depreciation and amortization expense in a purchase-type business combination is based on the current fair values of the assets, including any goodwill, of subsidiaries on the date of the business combination. Net income applicable to minority interests is included in the computation of net cash provided by operating activities because 100% of the cash of all subsidiaries is included in a consolidated balance sheet.

2   Only cash dividends paid by the parent company and cash dividends paid by partially owned subsidiary companies *to minority stockholders* are reported as cash flows from financing activities. Cash dividends paid by subsidiaries to the parent company have no effect on consolidated cash because cash is transferred entirely *within the affiliated group* of companies. Dividends paid to minority stockholders that are material in amount may be listed separately or disclosed parenthetically in a consolidated statement of cash flows.

3   A cash acquisition by the parent company of additional shares of common stock directly from a subsidiary does not change the amount of consolidated cash and thus is not reported in a consolidated statement of cash flows.

4   A cash acquisition by the parent company of additional shares of common stock from minority stockholders reduces consolidated cash. Consequently, such an acquisition is reported in a consolidated statement of cash flows in the cash flows from investing activities section.

5   A cash sale of part of the investment in a subsidiary company increases consolidated cash (and the amount of minority interest) and thus is reported with cash flows from investing activities in a consolidated statement of cash flows. A gain or loss from such a sale represents an adjustment to combined net income of the parent company and its subsidiaries in the measurement of net cash flow from operating activities.

Illustration of Consolidated Statement of Cash Flows

Parent Corporation has owned 100% of the common stock of Sub Company for several years. The business combination of Parent and Sub was a pooling-type combination. Sub has outstanding only one class of common stock, and its total stockholder's equity on December 31, Year 10, was $500,000. On January 2, Year 11, Parent sold 30% of its investment in Sub's common stock to outsiders for $205,000, which was $55,000 more than the carrying amount of the stock in Parent's accounting records. Sub had a net income of $100,000 for Year 11 and paid cash dividends of $60,000 near the end of Year 11. During Year 11, Parent issued additional common stock and cash of $290,000 in exchange for plant assets with a current fair value of $490,000. The consolidated entity had additional long-term borrowings of $93,000 during Year 11, and interest payments during the year totaled $62,000, none of which was capitalized. Income tax payments totaled $234,000.

The consolidated income statement for Year 11, the consolidated statement of stockholders' equity for Year 11, and the comparative consolidated balance sheets on December 31, Year 10 and Year 11, are below and on page 508.

PARENT CORPORATION AND SUBSIDIARY
Consolidated Income Statement
For Year Ended December 31, Year 11

Sales and other revenue (including gain of $55,000 on sale of investment in Sub Company common stock)..		$2,450,000
Costs and expenses:		
Cost of goods sold..	$1,500,000	
Depreciation and amortization expense	210,000	
Other operating expenses	190,000	1,900,000
Income before income taxes		$ 550,000
Income taxes expense..		250,000
Combined net income		$ 300,000
Less: Minority interest in net income of subsidiary		30,000
Consolidated net income..		$ 270,000
Earnings per share of common stock...		$ 5.14

PARENT CORPORATION AND SUBSIDIARY
Consolidated Statement of Stockholders' Equity
For Year Ended December 31, Year 11

	Common stock, $10 par	Additional paid-in capital	Retained earnings	Total
Balances, beginning of year...............	$500,000	$300,000	$ 670,000	$1,470,000
Issuance of 5,000 shares of common stock for plant assets	50,000	150,000		200,000
Net income.............................			270,000	270,000
Cash dividends declared and paid ($2.91 a share)			(160,000)	(160,000)
Balances, end of year	$550,000	$450,000	$ 780,000	$1,780,000

(continued)

PARENT CORPORATION AND SUBSIDIARY
Consolidated Balance Sheets
December 31, Year 11 and Year 10

Assets	Year 11	Year 10
Cash	$ 300,000	$ 240,000
Other current assets	900,000	660,000
Plant assets	3,000,000	2,510,000
Less: Accumulated depreciation of plant assets	(1,300,000)	(1,100,000)
Intangible assets (net)	240,000	250,000
Total assets	$ 3,140,000	$ 2,560,000
Liabilities & Stockholders' Equity		
Current liabilities (no notes payable)	$ 505,000	$ 490,000
Long-term debt	693,000	600,000
Minority interest in net assets of subsidiary	162,000	
Common stock, $10 par	550,000	500,000
Additional paid-in capital	450,000	300,000
Retained earnings	780,000	670,000
Total liabilities & stockholders' equity	$ 3,140,000	$ 2,560,000

PARENT CORPORATION AND SUBSIDIARY
Working Paper for Consolidated Statement of Cash Flows (indirect method)
For Year Ended December 31, Year 11

	Balances Dec. 31, Year 10	Transactions for Year 11 Debit	Transactions for Year 11 Credit	Balances Dec. 31, Year 11
Cash	240,000	(x) 60,000		300,000
Other current assets less current liabilities	170,000	(5) 225,000		395,000
Plant assets	2,510,000	(6) 290,000 (9) 200,000		3,000,000
Intangible assets (net)	250,000		(2) 10,000	240,000
Totals	3,170,000			3,935,000
Accumulated depreciation	1,100,000		(2) 200,000	1,300,000
Long-term debt	600,000		(7) 93,000	693,000
Minority interest in net assets of subsidiary		(8) 18,000	(3) 30,000 (4) 150,000	162,000
Common stock, $10 par	500,000		(9) 50,000	550,000
Additional paid-in capital	300,000		(9) 150,000	450,000
Retained earnings	670,000	(8) 160,000	(1) 270,000	780,000
Totals	3,170,000	953,000	953,000	3,935,000

(continued)

PARENT CORPORATION AND SUBSIDIARY
Working Paper for Consolidated Statement of Cash Flows (indirect method) (concluded)
For Year Ended December 31, Year 11

	Balances Dec. 31, Year 10	Transactions for Year 11		Balances Dec. 31, Year 11
		Debit	Credit	
Operating activities				
Net income		(1) 270,000		
Add: Depreciation and am-				
ortization expense . . .		(2) 210,000		
Minority interest in				
net income of sub-				From operating
sidiary		(3) 30,000		activities,
Less: Gain on sale of in-				$230,000
vestment in Sub				
Company common				
stock			(4) 55,000	
Net increase in net				
current assets			(5) 225,000	
Investing activities				
Sale of investment in Sub				From investing
Company common stock . .		(4) 205,000		activities
Acquisition of plant assets . .			(6) 290,000	($85,000)
Financing activities				
Long-term borrowings		(7) 93,000		From financing
Payment of dividends, in-				activities
cluding $18,000 to minority				($85,000)
shareholders of Sub Com-				
pany			(8) 178,000	
Subtotals		808,000	748,000	
Increase in cash			(x) 60,000	
Totals		808,000	808,000	

The working paper for consolidated statement of cash flows for Year 11 is on page 508 and above. The consolidated statement of cash flows (indirect method) for Parent Corporation and subsidiary for Year 11 is on page 510.

PARENT COMPANY AND SUBSIDIARY
Consolidated Statement of Cash Flows (indirect method)
For Year Ended December 31, Year 11

Net cash provided by operating activities **(Exhibit 1)**...............		$ 230,000
Cash flows from investing activities:		
Disposal of investment in Sub Company common stock .	$ 205,000	
Acquisition of plant assets	(290,000)	
Net cash used in investing activities........................		(85,000)
Cash flows from financing activities:		
Long-term borrowings	$ 93,000	
Dividends paid, including $18,000 to minority stockholders of Sub Company...........................	(178,000)	
Net cash used in financing activities		(85,000)
Net increase in cash...		$ 60,000
Cash, beginning of year		240,000
Cash, end of year..		$ 300,000

Exhibit 1 Cash flows from operating activities:		
Net income..		$ 270,000
Adjustments to reconcile net income to net cash provided by operating activities:		
Depreciation and amortization expense		210,000
Minority interest in net income of subsidiary....................		30,000
Gain on disposal of investment in Sub Company common stock ...		(55,000)
Net increase in net current assets		(225,000)*
Net cash provided by operating activities		$ 230,000

Exhibit 2 Supplemental disclosure of cash flow information:		
Cash paid during the year for:		
Interest (none capitalized)		$ 62,000
Income taxes...		234,000

Exhibit 3 Noncash investing and financing activities:		
Common stock issued for plant assets		$ 200,000

* This amount was aggregated to condense the illustration; **FASB Statement No. 95**, "Statement of Cash Flows," FASB (Stamford: 1987), p. 9, requires disclosure, as a minimum, of changes in receivables and payables pertaining to operating activities and in inventories.

The following items in the consolidated statement of cash flows warrant emphasis:

1   Net cash provided by operating activities *includes* the minority interest in net income of Sub Company.

2   Net cash provided by operating activities *excludes* the gain of $55,000 from sale of the investment in Sub Company common stock; thus, the proceeds of $205,000 are reported as a component of cash flows from investing activities in the consolidated statement of cash flows.

3   Only the dividends paid to stockholders of Parent Corporation ($160,000) and to minority stockholders of Sub Company ($18,000) are reported as cash flows from financing activities.

4   The issuance of common stock by Parent Corporation to acquire plant assets is a *noncash transaction* [coded (9) in the working paper on page 508] that is reported in Exhibit 3 at the bottom of the consolidated statement of cash flows.

INSTALLMENT ACQUISITION OF SUBSIDIARY

A parent company may obtain control of a subsidiary in a series of installment acquisitions of the subsidiary's common stock, rather than in a single transaction constituting a business combination. Such a combination is a *purchase,* because a *pooling may not be effected in installments.*[7]

In accounting for installment acquisitions of common stock of the eventual subsidiary, accountants are faced with a difficult question: At what point in the installment acquisition sequence should current fair values be determined for the subsidiary's identifiable net assets, in accordance with purchase accounting for business combinations? A practical answer is: Current fair values for the subsidiary's net assets should be ascertained on the date when the parent company attains control of the subsidiary. On that date, the purchase-type business combination is completed.

However, this answer is not completely satisfactory, because generally accepted accounting principles require use of the equity method of accounting for investments in common stock sufficient to enable the investor to influence significantly the operating and financial policies of the investee.[8] A 20% common stock investment is presumed, in the absence of contrary evidence, to be the minimum ownership interest for exercising significant operating and financial influence over the investee. *APB Opinion No. 18,* "The Equity Method of Accounting for Investments in Common Stock," requires retroactive application of the equity method of accounting when an investor's ownership interest reaches 20%. The following example illustrates these points.

Illustration of Installment Acquisition of Parent Company's Controlling Interest

Prinz Corporation, which has a February 28 fiscal year, acquired 9,500 shares of Scarp Company's 10,000 shares of outstanding $5 par common stock as follows (out-of-pocket costs are disregarded):

---

[7] As indicated in Chapter 5, pooling accounting is appropriate only for business combinations involving the exchange of 90% or more of the combinee's common stock in a single transaction or in accordance with a specific plan.

[8] *APB Opinion No. 18,* "The Equity Method of Accounting for Investments in Common Stock," AICPA (New York: 1971), pp. 355–356.

Date	Number of shares of Scarp Company common stock acquired	Method of payment by Prinz Corporation	Carrying amount of Scarp Company's identifiable net assets
Mar. 1, Year 2 ..	1,000	$ 10,000 cash	$80,000
Mar. 1, Year 3 ..	2,000	22,000 cash	85,000
Mar. 1, Year 4 ..	6,500	28,000 cash	90,000
		50,000, 15%	
		5-year	
		promissory note	
Totals........	9,500	$110,000	

The foregoing analysis indicates that Prinz made investments at a cost of $10, $11, and $12 a share in Scarp's common stock on dates when the stockholders' equity (book value) per share of Scarp's common stock was $8, $8.50, and $9, respectively. The practicality of ascertaining current fair values for Scarp's net assets on March 1, Year 4, the date Prinz attained control of Scarp, is apparent.

In addition to the Common Stock ledger account with a balance of $50,000 (10,000 × $5 = 50,000) and a Paid-in Capital in Excess of Par account with a balance of $10,000, Scarp had a Retained Earnings account that showed the following changes:

Retained Earnings

Date	Explanation	Debit	Credit	Balance
Year 2				
Mar. 1	Balance			20,000 cr
Year 3				
Feb. 10	Dividends declared ($1 a share)	10,000		10,000 cr
28	Net income		15,000	25,000 cr
Year 4				
Feb. 17	Dividends declared ($1 a share)	10,000		15,000 cr
28	Net income		15,000	30,000 cr

Parent Company's Journal Entries for Installment Acquisition

Prinz prepares the following journal entries (in addition to the usual end-of-period adjusting and closing entries) to record its investment in Scarp's common stock. (All dividends declared by Scarp are assumed to have been paid in cash on the declaration date, and income tax effects are disregarded.)

PRINZ CORPORATION
Journal Entries

Year 2

Mar. 1 Investment in Scarp Company Common Stock 10,000

           Cash   10,000

         To record acquisition of 1,000 shares of Scarp Company's
         outstanding common stock.

Year 3

Feb. 10 Cash... 1,000

           Dividend Revenue   1,000

         To record receipt of $1 a share cash dividend on 1,000
         shares of Scarp Company common stock.

Mar. 1 Investment in Scarp Company Common Stock 22,000

           Cash..   22,000

         To record acquisition of 2,000 shares of Scarp Company's
         outstanding common stock.

1 Investment in Scarp Company Common Stock 450

           Retained Earnings of Investee...................   450

         To change retroactively accounting for investment in Scarp
         Company to equity method from cost method; and to
         record retroactively 10% share of Scarp Company's net
         income for year ended Feb. 28, Year 3, as follows:

           Share of Scarp's net income, Year 3
            ($15,000 × 0.10) $1,500
           Less: Amortization of goodwill acquired
             Mar. 1, Year 2: $10,000 cost, minus
             ($80,000 × 0.10) = $2,000 goodwill;
             $2,000 ÷ 40 years = amortization for
             Year 3...................................   50
           Subtotal $1,450
           Less: Dividend revenue recognized in Year 3 .   1,000
           Prior period adjustment to Retained Earnings
             of Investee ledger account................. $ 450

Year 4

Feb. 17 Cash... 3,000

           Investment in Scarp Company Common Stock   3,000

         To record receipt of $1 a share cash dividend on 3,000
          shares of Scarp Company's common stock.

(continued)

PRINZ CORPORATION
Journal Entries (concluded)

Year 4

Feb. 28   Investment in Scarp Company Common Stock   4,500
                    Investment Income   4,500
          To record share of Scarp Company's net income for year
          ended Feb. 28, Year 4 ($15,000 × 0.30 = $4,500).

     28   Investment Income   175
                    Investment in Scarp Company Common Stock   175
          To record amortization of goodwill for Year 4 as follows:
            Acquisition of Mar. 1, Year 2: $2,000 ÷ 40 . . . $ 50
            Acquisition of Mar. 1, Year 3: $22,000 cost,
            minus ($85,000 × 0.20) = $5,000 goodwill;
            $5,000 ÷ 40 = amortization for Year 4   125
                    Total amortization . . . . $ 175

Mar. 1   Investment in Scarp Company Common Stock   78,000
                    Cash   28,000
                    Notes Payable   50,000
          To record acquisition of 6,500 shares of Scarp Company's
          outstanding common stock for cash and a 15%, five-year
          promissory note.

Prinz's acquisition of 6,500 shares of Scarp's outstanding common stock on March 1, Year 4, is a purchase-type business combination. Accordingly, on that date Prinz should apply the principles of purchase accounting described in Chapters 5 and 6, including the valuation of Scarp's identifiable net assets at their current fair values. Any excess of the $78,000 cost of Prinz's investment over Prinz's 65% share of the current fair value of Scarp's identifiable net assets is assigned to goodwill and amortized over a period of 40 years or less.

Criticism of Foregoing Approach   The foregoing illustration of accounting for the installment acquisition of an eventual subsidiary's common stock may be criticized for its handling of goodwill. On three separate dates spanning two years, goodwill was recognized in Prinz's three acquisitions of outstanding common stock of Scarp. Furthermore, the three goodwill amounts are amortized over three different 40-year (or shorter) periods.

It might be argued that the current fair values of Scarp's identifiable net assets should be determined on each of the three dates Prinz acquired Scarp common stock. However, such a theoretically precise application of accounting principles for long-term investments in common stock appears unwarranted in terms of cost-benefit analysis. Until Prinz attained control of Scarp, the amortization elements of Prinz's investment income presumably would not be material. Thus, the goodwill approach illustrated in the preceding section of this chapter appears to be practical and consistent with the following passage from *APB Opinion No. 18:*[9]

> The carrying amount of an investment in common stock of an investee that qualifies for the equity method of accounting . . . may differ from the underlying equity in net assets of the investee . . . if the investor is unable to relate the difference to specific accounts of the investee, the difference should be considered to be goodwill and amortized over a period not to exceed forty years, ...

Working Paper for Consolidated Financial Statements

The working paper for consolidated financial statements and related working paper eliminations for Prinz Corporation and subsidiary on March 1, Year 4, and for subsequent accounting periods are prepared in accordance with the procedures for purchased subsidiaries outlined in prior chapters. Prinz's retroactive application of the equity method of accounting for its investment in Scarp's common stock results in the Investment in Scarp Company Common Stock and Retained Earnings of Subsidiary (Investee) ledger accounts on March 1, Year 4, as shown below:

Selected ledger accounts of parent company

Investment in Scarp Company Common Stock

Date	Explanation	Debit	Credit	Balance
Year 2				
Mar. 1	Acquisition of 1,000 shares	10,000		10,000 dr
Year 3				
Mar. 1	Acquisition of 2,000 shares	22,000		32,000 dr
1	Retroactive application of equity method of accounting	450		32,450 dr
Year 4				
Feb. 17	Dividends received ($1 a share)		3,000	29,450 dr
28	Share of net income	4,500		33,950 dr
28	Amortization of goodwill		175	33,775 dr
Mar. 1	Acquisition of 6,500 shares	78,000		111,775 dr

Retained Earnings of Subsidiary (Investee)

Date	Explanation	Debit	Credit	Balance
Year 3				
Mar. 1	Retroactive application of equity method of accounting		450	450 cr
Year 4				
Feb. 28	Closing entry—share of Scarp Company adjusted net income not declared as a dividend ($4,500 − $175 − $3,000)		1,325	1,775 cr

---

[9] Ibid., p. 360.

If the current fair value of Scarp's identifiable net assets on March 1, Year 4, was $90,000, the same as the carrying amount of the net assets on that date, the working paper elimination (in journal entry format) for Prinz and subsidiary on March 1, Year 4, is as illustrated below:

Working paper elimination on date of business combination for partially owned purchased subsidiary acquired in installments

PRINZ CORPORATION AND SUBSIDIARY
Working Paper Elimination
March 1, Year 4

(a) Common Stock, $5 par—Scarp........................... 50,000
     Additional Paid-in Capital—Scarp........................ 10,000
     Retained Earnings—Scarp ($30,000 − $1,775) 28,225
     Retained Earnings of Subsidiary (Investee)—Prinz 1,775
     Goodwill (net)—Prinz ($1,900 + $4,875 + $19,500) 26,275
            Investment in Scarp Company Common Stock—Prinz .   111,775
            Minority Interest in Net Assets of Subsidiary...........   4,500
     To eliminate intercompany investment and equity accounts of
     subsidiary on date of purchase-type business combination; to
     allocate excess of cost over current fair value (equal to carrying
     amounts) of identifiable net assets acquired to goodwill; and to
     establish minority interest in net assets of subsidiary on date of
     business combination ($90,000 × 0.05 = $4,500).

Goodwill of $26,275 recognized in the foregoing working paper elimination comprises the following three components:

Components of net goodwill on date of purchase-type business combination accomplished in installments

Installment acquisition of	Mar. 1, Year 2	Mar. 1, Year 3	Mar. 1, Year 4
Cost of Scarp Company common stock acquired....................	$10,000	$22,000	$78,000
Less: Share of carrying amount of Scarp's identifiable net assets acquired:			
Mar. 1, Year 2 ($80,000 × 0.10)	8,000		
Mar. 1, Year 3 ($85,000 × 0.20)		17,000	
Mar. 1, Year 4 ($90,000 × 0.65)			58,500
Goodwill (gross)	$ 2,000	$ 5,000	$19,500
Less: Amortization over 40 years:			
Year ended Feb. 28, Year 3.......	(50)		
Year ended Feb. 28, Year 4.......	(50)	(125)	
Goodwill (net), Mar. 1, Year 4	$ 1,900	$ 4,875	$19,500

On March 1, Year 4, the date the purchase-type business combination of Prinz Corporation and Scarp Company was completed, only a consolidated balance sheet is appropriate, for reasons discussed in Chapter 6. Following is the working paper for consolidated balance sheet of Prinz and Scarp on March 1, Year 4, that reflects the working paper elimination on page 516. Amounts for Prinz and Scarp, other than those illustrated in the elimination, are assumed. Also, there were no intercompany transactions between the two companies prior to March 1, Year 4.

Partially owned subsidiary on date of purchase-type business combination accomplished in installments.

PRINZ CORPORATION AND SUBSIDIARY
Working Paper for Consolidated Balance Sheet
March 1, Year 4

	Prinz Corporation	Scarp Company	Eliminations increase (decrease)	Consolidated
Assets				
Current assets.......	400,000	140,000		540,000
Investment in Scarp Company common stock	111,775		(a) (111,775)	
Plant assets (net)	1,200,000	160,000		1,360,000
Goodwill (net)			(a) 26,275	26,275
Total assets	1,711,775	300,000	(85,500)	1,926,275
Liabilities & Stockholders' Equity				
Current liabilities	200,000	60,000		260,000
Long-term debt	800,000	150,000		950,000
Minority interest in net assets of subsidiary ..			(a) 4,500	4,500
Common stock, $1 par	150,000			150,000
Common stock, $5 par		50,000	(a) (50,000)	
Additional paid-in capital.................	350,000	10,000	(a) (10,000)	350,000
Retained earnings	210,000	30,000	(a) (28,225)	211,775
Retained earnings of subsidiary..........	1,775		(a) (1,775)	
Total liabilities & stockholders' equity	1,711,775	300,000	(85,500)	1,926,275

The $1,775 portion of Scarp's retained earnings attributable to Prinz's 30% ownership of Scarp common stock prior to the business combination *is not eliminated.* Thus, consolidated retained earnings on March 1, Year 4, the date of the purchase-type business combination, includes the $1,775 amount plus Prinz's own retained earnings of $210,000, for a total of $211,775.

For fiscal years subsequent to March 1, Year 4, Prinz recognizes intercompany investment income equal to 95% of the operating results of Scarp. In addition, Prinz debits the Amortization Expense ledger account for each period's amortization of the three goodwill amounts acquired by Prinz in the installment investments in Scarp's common stock.

REVIEW QUESTIONS

1   Under what circumstances do income taxes enter into the measurement of current fair values of a combinee's identifiable net assets in a purchase-type business combination?

2   What standards were established in *FASB Statement No. 109,* "Accounting for Income Taxes," for undistributed earnings of subsidiaries?

3   Are income tax allocation procedures necessary in working paper eliminations for a parent company and subsidiaries that file consolidated income tax returns? Explain.

4   A parent company and its subsidiary file separate income tax returns. How does the consolidated deferred income tax asset associated with the intercompany gain on the parent company's sale of a depreciable plant asset to its subsidiary reverse? Explain.

5   Are cash dividends declared to minority stockholders included in a consolidated statement of cash flows? Explain.

6   How is the equity method of accounting applied when a parent company attains control of a subsidiary in a series of common stock acquisitions? Explain.

7   At what stage in the installment acquisition of an eventual subsidiary's outstanding common stock does the parent company ascertain the current fair values of the subsidiary's identifiable net assets? Explain.

8   What amounts comprise consolidated retained earnings on the date of a purchase-type business combination that involved installment acquisitions of the subsidiary's outstanding common stock?

EXERCISES

Ex. 10-1   Select the best answer for each of the following multiple-choice questions:

1   In a purchase-type business combination that is a "tax-free corporate reorganization" for income tax purposes, may the temporary differences between current fair values and tax bases of the combinee's inventories and plant assets be realized through the assets':

	Sale?	Depreciation?
a	Yes	Yes
b	Yes	No
c	No	Yes
d	No	No

2 The appropriate format for a parent company's journal entry to provide for income taxes on intercompany investment income from a 65%-owned domestic subsidiary that declared and paid dividends less than the amount of that income is:

a Deferred Income Tax Asset XXX
    Income Taxes Expense. XXX
        Income Taxes Payable XXX

b Deferred Income Tax Liability XXX
    Income Taxes Expense. XXX
        Income Taxes Payable XXX

c Deferred Income Tax Asset XXX
        Income Taxes Expense XXX
        Income Taxes Payable XXX

d Income Taxes Expense. XXX
        Income Taxes Payable XXX
        Deferred Income Tax Liability XXX

3 Is a deferred income tax liability typically recognized by a combinor/parent company for:

	Differences between current fair values and carrying amounts of the identifiable net assets of a purchased subsidiary?	Undistributed earnings of a 65%-owned domestic subsidiary?
a	Yes	Yes
b	Yes	No
c	No	Yes
d	No	No

4 If a parent company and its subsidiary file separate income tax returns, a deferred income tax liability is recognized in working paper eliminations for a:
a Parent company's open-market acquisition of its subsidiary's outstanding bonds
b Subsidiary's sale of merchandise to its parent company
c Wholly-owned subsidiary's sale of land to a partially-owned subsidiary
d Partially-owned subsidiary's sale of an intangible asset to a wholly-owned subsidiary

5 In a consolidated statement of cash flows, cash flows from financing activities include, for a partially owned subsidiary:
a Cash dividends paid to the parent company only
b Cash dividends paid to minority stockholders only
c Both cash dividends paid to the parent company and cash dividends paid to minority stockholders
d Neither cash dividends paid to the parent company nor cash dividends paid to minority stockholders

6 How is the parent company's cash acquisition of additional shares of previously unissued common stock directly from a subsidiary displayed in a consolidated statement of cash flows?

a As an operating cash flow
b As an investing cash flow
c As a financing cash flow
d It is not reported

7   In a consolidated statement of cash flows (indirect method), a gain on the parent company's disposal of a portion of its investment in the subsidiary for cash is displayed with:
a Cash flows from investing activities
b Cash flows from financing activities
c Noncash investing and financing activities (exhibit)
d Cash flows from operating activities (exhibit)

8   In a consolidated statement of cash flows under the indirect method, the parent company's investment income from an influenced investee that paid no dividends is displayed in:
a Cash flows from investing activities
b Cash flows from operating activities
c The exhibit reconciling net income to net cash flows from operating activities
d None of the foregoing sections

9   In a consolidated statement of cash flows prepared under the indirect method, minority interest in net income of subsidiary is added to consolidated net income for the computation of net cash provided by operating activities because:
a Cash dividends paid to minority stockholders by a partially owned subsidiary are excluded from cash flows from financing activities.
b An increase in minority interest in net assets of subsidiary is displayed with cash flows from investing activities.
c A decrease in minority interest in net assets of subsidiary is displayed with cash flows from financing activities.
d 100% of the cash of all subsidiaries is included in a consolidated balance sheet.

10   In an installment acquisition of a controlling interest in a subsidiary, the investor uses a Retained Earnings of Investee/Subsidiary ledger account:
a Beginning with the date of the first investment, regardless of amount
b Beginning when the investment aggregates at least 20%
c Beginning when the controlling interest is acquired
d In none of the foregoing circumstances

11 If, on the date an investor corporation acquires an influencing interest in an investee company in a second or subsequent installment acquisition of the investee's common stock, there was goodwill implicit in the cost of the investor's prior installment acquisition(s), the goodwill is:
a Disregarded
b Amortized retroactively only
c Amortized prospectively only
d Amortized both retroactively and prospectively

Ex. 10-2   Salvo Corporation merged with Mango Company in a purchase-type business combination. As a result, goodwill was recognized. For income tax purposes, the business combination was considered to be a tax-free corporate reorganization. One of Mango's assets was a building with an appraised value of $150,000 on the date of the business combination. The building had a carrying amount of $90,000, net of accumulated depreciation based on the double-declining-balance method of depreciation, for financial accounting. Current fair values of other assets were equal to carrying amounts.

Assuming a 40% income tax rate, prepare a working paper to compute the amount of the deferred income tax liability that Salvo Corporation recognizes with respect to the building as a result of the business combination.

Ex. 10-3 On May 31, Year 3, Combinor Corporation acquired for $560,000 cash all the net assets except cash of Combinee Company, and paid $60,000 cash to a law firm for legal services in connection with the business combination. The balance sheet of Combinee Company on May 31, Year 3, was as follows:

COMBINEE COMPANY
Balance Sheet (prior to business combination)
May 31, Year 3

Assets		*Liabilities & Stockholders' Equity*	
Cash......................	$ 40,000	Liabilities	$ 620,000
Other current assets (net) ..	280,000	Common stock, $1 par.....	250,000
Plant assets (net)..........	760,000	Retained earnings.........	330,000
Intangible assets (net)	120,000	Total liabilities &	
Total assets	$1,200,000	stockholders' equity	$1,200,000

The present value of Combinee's liabilities on May 31, Year 3, was $620,000. The current fair values of its noncash assets were as follows on that date:

Other current assets..	$300,000
Plant assets	780,000
Intangible assets	130,000

The income tax rate is 40%.

Prepare journal entries (omit explanations) for Combinor Corporation on May 31, Year 3, to record the acquisition of the net assets of Combinee Company except cash, but including deferred income tax liability.

Ex. 10-4 On November 1, Year 5, the date of the purchase-type business combination of Prudence Corporation and its 70%-owned subsidiary, Sagacity Company, the current fair values of Sagacity's identifiable net assets equaled their carrying amounts, and goodwill having on economic life of 10 years was recognized in the amount of $60,000 in the working paper elimination for the consolidated balance sheet of Prudence Corporation and subsidiary on that date. For the year ended October 31, Year 6, Sagacity had a net income of $140,000 and declared and paid dividends of $50,000 on that date.

Assuming that the income tax rate is 40% and Prudence qualifies for the 80% dividend-received deduction, prepare journal entries (omit explanations) for Prudence Corporation, under the equity method of accounting, for the operations of Sagacity Company for the year ended October 31, Year 6, including income tax allocation.

Ex. 10-5   During the year ended October 31, Year 6, Shipp Company, a wholly owned subsidiary of Ponte Corporation, sold merchandise to Stack Company, an 80%-owned subsidiary of Ponte, at billed prices totaling $630,000, representing Shipp's usual 40% markup on cost. Stack's beginning and ending inventories for the year included merchandise purchased from Shipp at the following total billed prices:

Nov. 1, Year 5 . . . . $35,000

Oct. 31, Year 6. 77,000

Ponte, Shipp, and Stack file separate income tax returns, and each has an income tax rate of 40%.

Prepare October 31, Year 6, working paper eliminations (in journal entry format, explanations omitted) for Ponte Corporation and subsidiaries, including income tax allocation, assuming that the provisions of *FASB Statement No. 109,* ''Accounting for Income Taxes,'' for recognizing a deferred tax asset without a valuation allowance are met.

Ex. 10-6   During the year ended November 30, Year 9, Pederson Corporation sold merchandise costing $100,000 to its 80%-owned subsidiary, Solomon Company, at a gross profit rate of 20%. On November 30, Year 9, Solomon's inventories included merchandise acquired from Pederson at a billed price of $30,000—a $10,000 increase over the comparable amount in Solomon's November 30, Year 8, inventories. Both Pederson and Solomon file separate income tax returns, and both are subject to an income tax rate of 40%.

Prepare working paper eliminations (in journal entry format) for merchandise transactions and related income tax allocation for Pederson Corporation and subsidiary on November 30, Year 9, assuming that the provisions of *FASB Statement No. 109,* ''Accounting for Income Taxes,'' for recognizing a deferred tax asset without a valuation allowance are met.

Ex. 10-7   The sales of merchandise by Sol Company, 80%-owned subsidiary of Pol Corporation, to Stu Company, 70%-owned subsidiary of Pol, during the year ended October 31, Year 7, may be analyzed as follows:

	Selling price	*Cost*	*Gross profit*
Beginning inventories.	$ 80,000	$ 60,000	$ 20,000
Sales	400,000	300,000	100,000
Subtotals.	$480,000	$360,000	$120,000
Ending inventories	90,000	67,500	22,500
Cost of goods sold	$390,000	$292,500	$ 97,500

Pol, Sol, and Stu file separate income tax returns, and each has an income tax rate of 40%.

Prepare working paper eliminations, including income taxes allocation, in journal entry format (omit explanations) for Pol Corporation and subsidiaries on October 3, Year 7, assuming that the provisions of *FASB Statement No. 109,* ''Accounting for Income Taxes,'' for recognizing a deferred tax asset without a valuation allowance are met.

Ex. 10-8 The following working paper eliminations (in journal entry format) were prepared by the accountant for Purdue Corporation on February 28, Year 5, the end of a fiscal year:

PURDUE CORPORATION AND SUBSIDIARY
Working Paper Eliminations
February 28, Year 5

Intercompany Gain on Sale of Machinery—Purdue	12,000	
Machinery—Scarsdale		12,000

To eliminate unrealized intercompany gain on February 28, Year 5, sale of machine with a six-year economic life, no residual value, and straight-line depreciation method.

Deferred Income Tax Asset—Purdue ($12,000 × 0.40)	4,800	
Income Taxes Expense—Purdue.		4,800

To defer income taxes provided in separate income tax returns of parent company applicable to unrealized intercompany gain in subsidiary's machinery on February 28, Year 5.

Prepare working paper eliminations (in journal entry format, explanations omitted) for Purdue Corporation and subsidiary on February 28, Year 6, assuming that the provisions of **FASB Statement No. 109,** ''Accounting for Income Taxes,'' for recognizing a deferred tax asset without a valuation allowance are met.

Ex. 10-9 The working paper eliminations (in journal entry format) of Pegler Corporation and its wholly owned subsidiary, Stang Company, on October 31, Year 9, included the following:

(b) Retained Earnings—Stang.	10,000	
Intercompany Sales—Stang.	240,000	
Intercompany Cost of Goods Sold—Stang.		120,000
Cost of Goods Sold—Pegler		60,000
Inventories—Pegler.		70,000

To eliminate intercompany sales, cost of goods sold, and unrealized intercompany profit in inventories.

(c) Retained Earnings—Pegler	40,000	
Accumulated Depreciation—Stang.	60,000	
Machinery—Stang		80,000
Depreciation Expense—Stang		20,000

To eliminate unrealized intercompany gain in machinery and in related depreciation. Gain element in depreciation computed as $80,000 ÷ 4 = $20,000, based on four-year economic life of machinery.

Both Pegler and Stang file separate tax returns, and both have an income tax rate of 40%.

Prepare required additional working paper eliminations (in journal entry format; omit explanations) for Pegler Corporation and subsidiary on October 31, Year 9, assuming that the provisions of *FASB Statement No. 109,* "Accounting for Income Taxes," for recognizing a deferred tax asset without a valuation allowance are met.

Ex. 10-10   On October 31, Year 5, Salvador Company, 80%-owned subsidiary of Panama Corporation, sold to its parent company for $20,000 a patent with a carrying amount of $15,000 on that date. Remaining legal life of the patent on October 31, Year 5, was five years; the patent was expected to produce revenue for Panama during the entire five-year period. Panama and Salvador file separate income tax returns; their income tax rate is 40%. Panama uses an Accumulated Amortization of Patent ledger account.

Assuming that the provisions of *FASB Statement No. 109,* "Accounting for Income Taxes," for recognizing a deferred tax asset without a valuation allowance are met, prepare working paper eliminations (in journal entry format), including income tax allocation, for Panama Corporation and subsidiary with respect to the patent: **(a)** on October 31, Year 5, and **(b)** on October 31, Year 6.

Ex. 10-11   The following working paper elimination (in journal entry format) was prepared for Plumm Corporation and subsidiary on March 31, Year 3:

Intercompany Interest Revenue—Plumm ($456,447 × 0.10)	45,645	
Intercompany 8% Bonds Payable—Sam	500,000	
Discount on Intercompany 8% Bonds Payable—Sam		
($22,429 − $2,981)		19,448
Investment in Sam Company Bonds—Plumm		
($456,447 + $5,645)		462,092
Intercompany Interest Expense—Sam ($477,571 × 0.09)		42,981
Retained Earnings—Sam ($477,571 − $456,447)		21,124

To eliminate subsidiary's bonds owned by parent company, and related interest revenue and expense; and to increase subsidiary's beginning retained earnings by amount of unamortized realized gain on the extinguishment of the bonds.

Plumm and Sam file separate income tax returns, and both are subject to a 40% income tax rate.

Prepare a working paper elimination (in journal entry format) for Plumm Corporation and subsidiary on March 31, Year 3, for the income tax effects of the foregoing elimination. Omit the explanation for the elimination.

Ex. 10-12   On October 31, Year 2, P Corporation acquired in the open market $500,000 face amount of the 10%, ten-year bonds due October 31, Year 11, of its wholly owned subsidiary, S Company. The bonds had been issued by S on October 31, Year 1, to yield 12%. P's investment was at a 15% yield rate. Both P and S file separate income tax returns, both companies are subject to an income tax rate of 40%, and neither company has any items requiring interperiod or intraperiod income tax allocation other than the S Company bonds, on which interest is payable each October 31. Working paper eliminations (in journal entry format) related to the bonds on October 31, Year 2, and October 31, Year 3, with certain amounts omitted, are as follows:

P CORPORATION AND SUBSIDIARY
Partial Working Paper Eliminations
October 31, Year 2

Intercompany Bonds Payable—S...........................	500,000	
Discount on Intercompany Bonds Payable—S..........		53,283
Investment in S Company Bonds—P		380,710
Gain on Extinguishment of Bonds—S.................		66,007*

To eliminate subsidiary's bonds acquired by parent, and to recognize gain on the extinguishment of the bonds.

Income Taxes Expense—S................................	(1)	
Deferred Income Tax Liability—S.....................		(2)

To provide for income taxes attributable to subsidiary's realized gain on parent company's acquisition of the subsidiary's bonds.

* Not material.

P CORPORATION AND SUBSIDIARY
Partial Working Paper Eliminations
October 31, Year 3

Intercompany Interest Revenue—P...........................	57,107	
Intercompany Bonds Payable—S	500,000	
Discount on Intercompany Bonds Payable—S...........		49,725
Investment in S Company Bonds—P...................		387,817
Intercompany Interest Expense—S....................		53,558
Retained Earnings—S		66,007

To eliminate subsidiary's bonds owned by parent company, and related interest revenue and expense; and to increase subsidiary's beginning retained earnings by amount of unamortized realized gain on the extinguishment of the bonds.

Retained Earnings—S	(3)	
Income Taxes Expense—S............................		(4)
Deferred Income Tax Liability—S		(5)

To reduce the subsidiary's income taxes expense for amount attributable to recorded intercompany gain (for consolidation purposes) on subsidiary's bonds; and to provide for remaining deferred income taxes on unrecorded portion of gain.

Prepare a working paper to compute the five missing amounts in the foregoing working paper eliminations.

Ex. 10-13 Prieto Corporation declared and paid cash dividends of $250,000 on its common stock and distributed a 5% common stock dividend in Year 5. The market value of the shares distributed pursuant to the 5% stock dividend was $600,000. Prieto owns 100% of the common stock of S Company and 75% of the common stock of SS Company. In Year 5, S declared and paid cash dividends of $100,000 on its common stock and $25,000 on its $5 cumulative preferred stock. None of the preferred stock is owned by Prieto. In Year 5, SS declared and paid cash dividends of $44,000 on its common stock, the only class of capital stock issued.

Prepare a working paper to compute the amount to be displayed as cash flows for the payment of dividends in the Year 5 consolidated statement of cash flows for Prieto Corporation and subsidiaries.

Ex. 10-14 The consolidated statement of cash flows (indirect method) for Paradise Corporation and its partially owned subsidiaries is to be prepared for Year 2. Using the following letters, indicate how each of the 13 items listed below should be displayed in the statement.

A–O = Add to combined net income in the computation of net cash provided by operating activities

D–O = Deduct from combined net income in the computation of net cash provided by operating activities

IA = A cash flow from investing activities

FA = A cash flow from financing activities

N = Not included or separately displayed in the consolidated statement of cash flows, but possibly disclosed in a separate exhibit

(1) The minority interest in net income of subsidiaries is $37,500.

(2) Paradise issued a note payable to a subsidiary company in exchange for plant assets with a current fair value of $180,000.

(3) Paradise distributed a 10% stock dividend; the additional shares of common stock issued had a current fair value of $675,000.

(4) Paradise declared and paid a cash dividend of $200,000.

(5) Long-term debt of Paradise in the amount of $2 million was converted to its common stock.

(6) A subsidiary sold plant assets to outsiders at the carrying amount of $80,000.

(7) Paradise's share of the net income of an influenced investee totaled $28,000. The investee did not declare or pay cash dividends in Year 2.

(8) Consolidated depreciation and amortization expense totaled $285,000.

(9) A subsidiary amortized $3,000 of premium on bonds payable owned by outsiders.

(10) Paradise sold its entire holdings in an 80%-owned subsidiary for $3 million.

(11) Paradise merged with Sun Company in a pooling-type business combination; 150,000 shares of common stock with a current fair value of $4.5 million were issued by Paradise for 98% of Sun's outstanding common stock.

(12) Paradise received cash dividends of $117,000 from its subsidiaries.

(13) The subsidiaries of Paradise declared and paid cash dividends of $21,500 to minority stockholders.

Ex. 10-15 On August 1, Year 6, Packard Corporation acquired 1,000 of the 10,000 outstanding shares of Stenn Company's $1 par common stock for $5,000. Stenn's identifiable net assets had a current fair value and carrying amount of $40,000 on that date. Stenn had a net income of $3,000 and declared and paid dividends of the same amount for the year ended July 31, Year 7. On August 1, Year 7, Packard acquired 4,500 more shares of Stenn's outstanding common stock for $22,500. The current fair values and carrying amounts of Stenn's identifiable net assets were still $40,000 on that date.

Stenn had a net income of $7,500 and declared no dividends for the year ended July 31, Year 8.

Prepare journal entries for Packard Corporation for the foregoing business transactions and events for the two years ended July 31, Year 8. (Omit explanations and disregard income tax effects.)

CASES

Case 10-1   In a discussion of accounting standards established in *FASB Statement No. 109,* ''Accounting for Income Taxes,'' student Laura is critical of the requirement to establish a deferred tax asset or liability for differences between the assigned values and the tax bases of most assets and liabilities recognized in a purchase-type business combination (see page 494). Laura points out that, in the usual situation of assigned values in excess of tax bases, the recognition of a deferred tax liability for the resultant differences has the effect of increasing goodwill (or decreasing ''negative goodwill'') otherwise recognized in the purchase-type business combination. Laura questions whether, on the date of the business combination, the so-called deferred income tax liability is really a *liability,* as defined in paragraph 35 of *FASB Concepts Statement No. 6,* ''Elements of Financial Statements.'' Student Jason responds that in paragraphs 75 through 79 of *FASB Statement No. 109,* the FASB deals with the issue raised by Laura and concludes that deferred income tax liabilities resulting from purchase-type business combinations are indeed *liabilities.*

Instructions

Do you agree with student Jason that the FASB's conclusion should put to rest criticisms of *FASB Statement No. 109* such as that expressed by student Laura? Explain.

Case 10-2   On April 1, Year 4, the beginning of a fiscal year, Paddock Corporation acquired 70% of the outstanding common stock of domestic subsidiary Serge Company in a purchase-type business combination. In your audit of the consolidated financial statements of Paddock Corporation and subsidiary for the year ended March 31, Year 5, you discover that Serge had a net income of $50,000 for the year but did not declare or pay any cash dividends. Nonetheless, Paddock did not record a deferred income tax liability applicable to Serge's undistributed earnings, net of the 80% dividend-received deduction, despite Paddock's having adopted the equity method of accounting for Serge's operating results.

In response to your inquiries, the controller of Paddock pointed out that Serge's severe cash shortage made the declaration and payment of cash dividends by Serge doubtful for the next several years. Therefore, stated the controller, a provision for deferred income taxes on Serge's undistributed earnings for the year ended March 31, Year 5, is inappropriate under generally accepted accounting principles.

Instructions

Do you agree with the controller's interpretation of generally accepted accounting principles for the undistributed earnings of Serge Company? Explain.

Case 10-3   The recognition of goodwill on a *residual* basis in purchase-type business combinations has been criticized by some accountants (see page 216). In the accounting for purchase-type business combinations accomplished in installments, described on pages 511 through 518, more than one amount of goodwill may be recognized.

Instructions

Assume that you are asked to advise the Financial Accounting Standards Board on alternatives to recognizing multiple amounts of goodwill in purchase-type business combinations accomplished in installments. What alternatives would you recommend? Explain.

PROBLEMS

Pr. 10-1   This problem consists of two unrelated parts.

   a The merchandise sales by Pro Corporation's wholly owned subsidiary, Spa Company, to Pro's 80%-owned subsidiary, Sol Company, may be analyzed as follows for the year ended October 31, Year 6:

	Selling price	Cost	Gross profit (33⅓ of cost; 25% of selling price)
Beginning inventories..........	$ 100,000	$ 75,000	$ 25,000
Sales........................	2,000,000	1,500,000	500,000
Subtotals...................	$2,100,000	$1,575,000	$525,000
Ending inventories	300,000	225,000	75,000
Cost of goods sold	$1,800,000	$1,350,000	$450,000

Pro, Spa, and Sol use the perpetual inventory system, file separate income tax returns, and have an income tax rate of 40%.

Instructions

Prepare working paper eliminations (in journal entry format), including income taxes allocation, for Pro Corporation and subsidiaries on October 31, Year 6.

   b The following working paper eliminations (in journal entry format) were prepared by the accountant for Primrose Corporation, which had a single wholly owned subsidiary:

PRIMROSE CORPORATION AND SUBSIDIARY
Partial Working Paper Eliminations
April 30, Year 5

Intercompany 8% Bonds Payable—Safflower................	1,000,000	
Discount on Intercompany 8% Bonds Payable—Safflower		124,622
Investment in Safflower Company 8% Bonds—Primrose		770,602
Gain on Extinguishment of Bonds—Safflower.........		104,776

To eliminate subsidiary's bonds (interest payable Apr. 30 and Oct. 31), which had been issued to yield 10% and were acquired by parent company at a 12% yield; and to recognize gain on the extinguishment of the bonds.

(continued)

PRIMROSE CORPORATION AND SUBSIDIARY
Partial Working Paper Eliminations (concluded)
April 30, Year 5

Income Taxes Expense—Safflower ($104,776 × 0.40)	41,910	
Deferred Income Tax Liability—Safflower		41,910

To provide for income taxes attributable to subsidiary's realized
gain on parent company's acquisition of the subsidiary's bonds.

Instructions

Prepare comparable working paper eliminations for Primrose Corporation and subsidiary on October 31, Year 5.

Pr. 10-2   The working paper eliminations (in journal entry format) for intercompany bonds of Pullet Corporation and its wholly owned subsidiary on November 30, Year 3, the end of a fiscal year, follow. The bonds, which had been issued by Sagehen Company for a five-year term on November 30, Year 2, to yield 10%, were acquired in the open market by Pullet on November 30, Year 3, to yield 12%. Interest on the bonds is payable at the rate of 8% each November 30, Year 3 through Year 7. Both companies use the interest method of amortization or accumulation of bond premium or discount.

PULLET CORPORATION AND SUBSIDIARY
Partial Working Paper Eliminations
November 30, Year 3

Intercompany Bonds Payable—Sagehen	60,000	
Discount on Intercompany Bonds Payable—Sagehen		3,804
Investment in Sagehen Company Bonds—Pullet		52,710
Gain on Extinguishment of Bonds—Sagehen		3,486*

To eliminate subsidiary's bonds acquired by parent; and to recognize gain on the extinguishment of the bonds.

Income Taxes Expense—Sagehen ($3,486 × 0.40)	1,394	
Deferred Income Tax Liability—Sagehen		1,394

To provide for income taxes attributable to subsidiary's realized gain
on parent company's acquisition of the subsidiary's bonds.
* Not material.

Instructions

a   Prepare journal entries for both Pullet Corporation and Sagehen Company to recognize intercompany interest revenue and expense, respectively, on November 30, Year 4. Disregard Sagehen's bonds owned by outsiders.

b   Prepare working paper eliminations (in journal entry format) for Pullet Corporation and subsidiary on November 30, Year 4, including allocation of income taxes.

Pr. 10-3   On January 2, Year 1, Presto Corporation issued 10,000 shares of its $1 par (current fair value $40) common stock for all 50,000 shares of Shuey Company's outstanding common stock in a statutory merger that was a purchase-type business combination.

Out-of-pocket costs in connection with the combination, paid by Presto on January 2, Year 1, were as follows:

Finder's fee, accounting fees, and legal fees relating to the business combination $60,000
Costs associated with SEC registration statement for securities issued to complete the business combination 30,000
Total out-of-pocket costs of business combination $90,000

For income tax purposes, the business combination qualified as a "Type A tax-free corporate reorganization." The balance sheet of Shuey Company on January 2, Year 1, with associated current fair values of assets and liabilities, was as follows:

SHUEY COMPANY
Balance Sheet (prior to business combination)
January 2, Year 1

	Carrying amounts	Current fair values
Assets		
Cash	$ 20,000	$ 20,000
Short-term investments	30,000	45,000
Trade accounts receivable (net)	80,000	80,000
Inventories	120,000	160,000
Short-term prepayments	10,000	10,000
Plant assets (net)	430,000	490,000
Intangible assets (net)	110,000	130,000
Total assets	$800,000	$935,000
Liabilities & Stockholders' Equity		
Liabilities:		
Notes payable	$ 60,000	$ 60,000
Trade accounts payable	90,000	90,000
Income taxes payable	30,000	30,000
Long-term debt	300,000	300,000
Total liabilities	$480,000	$480,000
Stockholders' equity:		
Common stock, $2 par	$100,000	
Additional paid-in capital	100,000	
Retained earnings	120,000	
Total stockholders' equity	$320,000	
Total liabilities & stockholders' equity	$800,000	

The income tax rate for both Presto and Shuey is 40%.

Instructions

Prepare journal entries for Presto Corporation to record the purchase-type business combination with Shuey Company on January 2, Year 1, including deferred income taxes.

Pr. 10-4 Separate balance sheets of Pellerin Corporation and its subsidiary, Sigmund Company, on the dates indicated, are as follows. Both companies have a December 31 fiscal year.

PELLERIN CORPORATION AND SIGMUND COMPANY
Separate Balance Sheets
Various Dates, Year 3

	Pellerin Corporation	Sigmund Company		
	Dec. 31, Year 3	Jan. 2, Year 3	Sept. 30, Year 3	Dec. 31, Year 3
Assets				
Cash	$ 400,000	$ 550,000	$ 650,000	$ 425,000
Fees and royalties receivable.........		250,000	450,000	500,000
Investment in Sigmund Company common stock.....	2,240,000			
Patents (net)		1,000,000	850,000	800,000
Other assets (net)...	4,360,000			200,000
Total assets	$7,000,000	$1,800,000	$1,950,000	$1,925,000
Liabilities & Stockholders' Equity				
Liabilities...........	$ 400,000	$ 200,000	$ 150,000	$ 275,000
Common stock, $10 par	5,000,000	1,000,000	1,000,000	1,000,000
Retained earnings...	1,600,000	600,000	800,000	650,000
Total liabilities & stockholders' equity..........	$7,000,000	$1,800,000	$1,950,000	$1,925,000

Additional Information

(1) Pellerin had acquired 30,000 shares of Sigmund's outstanding common stock on January 2, Year 3, at a cost of $480,000; and 60,000 shares on September 30, Year 3, at a cost of $1,760,000. Pellerin obtained control over Sigmund because of the valuable patents owned by Sigmund.

(2) Sigmund amortizes the cost of patents on a straight-line basis. Any amount allocated to patents as a result of the business combination is to be amortized over the five-year remaining economic life of the patents from January 2, Year 3.

(3) Sigmund declared and paid a cash dividend of $300,000 on December 31, Year 3. Pellerin had not recorded either the declaration or the receipt of the dividend.

Instructions

Prepare journal entries for Pellerin Corporation on December 31, Year 3, to account for its investments in Sigmund Company under the equity method of accounting.

Disregard income taxes, and do not prepare journal entries for Pellerin's *acquisition* of the investments in Sigmund.

Pr. 10-5 Consolidated financial statements of Porcelain Corporation and its 80%-owned subsidiary, Skinner Company, for the year ended December 31, Year 8, including a comparative consolidated balance sheet on December 31, Year 7, are as follows:

PORCELAIN CORPORATION AND SUBSIDIARY
Consolidated Income Statement
For Year Ended December 31, Year 8

Revenue:		
Net sales		$1,200,000
Gain on disposal of plant assets		50,000
Total revenue		$1,250,000
Costs and expenses:		
Cost of goods sold	$700,000	
Depreciation expense	40,000	
Amortization expense (goodwill)	20,000	
Other operating expenses	120,000	
Interest expense	50,000	
Income taxes expense	192,000	
Minority interest in net income of subsidiary	10,000	1,132,000
Net income		$ 118,000
Earnings per share of common stock		$ 1.97

PORCELAIN CORPORATION AND SUBSIDIARY
Consolidated Statement of Stockholders' Equity
For Year Ended December 31, Year 8

	Common stock, $1 par	Additional paid-in capital	Retained earnings	Total
Balances, beginning of year	$ 60,000	$30,000	$180,000	$270,000
Issuance of 40,000 shares of common stock at $1.75 a share	40,000	30,000		70,000
Net income			118,000	118,000
Cash dividends declared and paid ($1 a share)			(60,000)	(60,000)
Balances, end of year	$100,000	$60,000	$238,000	$398,000

PORCELAIN CORPORATION AND SUBSIDIARY
Consolidated Balance Sheets
December 31, Year 8 and Year 7

	Year 8	Year 7
Assets		
Cash	$ 70,000	$ 50,000
Other current assets	230,000	150,000
Plant assets (net)	680,000	600,000
Goodwill (net)	140,000	160,000
Total assets	$1,120,000	$960,000
Liabilities & Stockholders' Equity		
Liabilities:		
Current liabilities, including current portion of note payable	$ 187,000	$110,000
Note payable, due $50,000 annually, plus interest at 10%.	450,000	500,000
Minority interest in net assets of subsidiary	85,000	80,000
Total liabilities	$ 722,000	$690,000
Stockholders' equity:		
Common stock, $1 par	$ 100,000	$ 60,000
Additional paid-in capital	60,000	30,000
Retained earnings	238,000	180,000
Total stockholders' equity	$ 398,000	$270,000
Total liabilities & stockholders' equity	$1,120,000	$960,000

Additional Information

(1) The affiliated companies acquired plant assets for $220,000 cash during the year ended December 31, Year 8. Also during the year, Skinner Company, the 80%-owned subsidiary of Porcelain, sold plant assets with a carrying amount of $100,000 to an outsider for $150,000 cash.

(2) Skinner declared and paid dividends totaling $25,000 during the year ended December 31, Year 8.

Instructions

Prepare a consolidated statement of cash flows (indirect method) for Porcelain Corporation and subsidiary for the year ended December 31, Year 8, without using a working paper. Disregard disclosure of cash paid for interest and income taxes.

Pr. 10-6 The following transactions took place between Parkhurst Corporation and its wholly owned subsidiary, Sandland Company, which file separate income tax returns, during the year ended March 31, Year 6:

(1) Parkhurst sold to Sandland at a 30% gross profit rate merchandise with a total sale price of $200,000. Sandland's March 31, Year 6, inventories included $40,000 (billed prices) of the merchandise obtained from Parkhurst—a $20,000 increase from the related April 1, Year 5, inventories amount. Both Parkhurst and Sandland use the perpetual inventory system.

(2) On April 1, Year 5, Sandland sold to Parkhurst for $50,000 a machine with a carrying amount of $30,000 on that date. The economic life of the machine to Parkhurst was five years, with no residual value. Parkhurst uses the straight-line method of depreciation for all plant assets.

(3) On February 28, Year 6, Parkhurst sold land for a plant site to Sandland for $480,000. The land had a carrying amount to Parkhurst of $360,000.

(4) On March 31, Year 6, following Sandland's payment of interest to bondholders, Parkhurst acquired in the open market for $487,537, a 16% yield, 60% of Sandland's 12%, ten-year bonds dated March 31, Year 5. The bonds had been issued to the public by Sandland on March 31, Year 5, to yield 14%. On March 31, Year 6, following the payment of interest, Sandland's accounting records included the following ledger account balances relative to the bonds:

12% bonds payable . . . . $1,000,000 cr
Discount on 12% bonds payable. . . . . 100,590 dr

Both Parkhurst and Sandland use the interest method of amortization or accumulation of bond interest. The income tax rate for both affiliated companies, which file separate income tax returns, is 40%.

Instructions

Prepare working paper eliminations (in journal entry format), including income taxes allocation, for Parkhurst Corporation and subsidiary on March 31, Year 6. Round all amounts to the nearest dollar.

Pr. 10-7 Paine Corporation owns 99% of the outstanding common stock of Spilberg Company, acquired July 1, Year 5, in a pooling-type business combination, and 90% of the outstanding common stock of Sykes Company, acquired July 1, Year 5, in a purchase-type business combination that reflected goodwill of $52,200. All identifiable net assets of Sykes were fairly valued at their carrying amounts on July 1, Year 5. Goodwill is amortized over 40 years.

Separate financial statements of Paine, Spilberg, and Sykes for the year ended June 30, Year 6, prior to income tax provisions and equity-method accruals in the accounting records of Paine, are on page 535.

Intercompany profits in June 30, Year 6, inventories resulting from Paine's sales to its subsidiaries during the year ended June 30, Year 6, are as follows:

In Spilberg Company's inventories—$6,000
In Sykes Company's inventories—$7,500

Instructions

a Prepare Paine Corporation's June 30, Year 6, journal entries for income taxes and equity-method accruals. The income tax rate for all three companies is 40%. All three companies declared dividends on June 30, Year 6. Disregard the dividend-received deduction.

b Prepare a working paper for consolidated financial statements and related working paper eliminations (in journal entry format), including income taxes allocation, for Paine Corporation and subsidiaries for the year ended June 30, Year 6. The three affiliated companies file separate income tax returns. Amounts for Paine Corporation should reflect the journal entries in **a**.

PAINE CORPORATION AND SUBSIDIARIES
Separate Financial Statements
For Year Ended June 30, Year 6

	Paine Corporation	Spilberg Company	Sykes Company
Income Statements			
Revenue:			
Net sales	$1,000,000	$ 550,000	$ 220,000
Intercompany sales	100,000		
Total revenue	$1,100,000	$ 550,000	$ 220,000
Costs and expenses:			
Cost of goods sold...............	$ 700,000	$ 357,500	$ 143,000
Intercompany cost of goods sold ..	70,000		
Operating expenses..............	130,000	125,833	43,667
Interest expense.................	50,000		
Income taxes expense		26,667	13,333
Total costs and expenses.......	$ 950,000	$ 510,000	$ 200,000
Net income........................	$ 150,000	$ 40,000	$ 20,000
Statements of Retained Earnings			
Retained earnings, beginning of year	$ 103,000	$ 300,000	$ 150,000
Add: Net income...................	150,000	40,000	20,000
Subtotals	$ 253,000	$ 340,000	$ 170,000
Less: Dividends...................	50,000	20,000	10,000
Retained earnings, end of year......	$ 203,000	$ 320,000	$ 160,000
Balance Sheets			
Assets			
Inventories........................	$1,000,000	$ 800,000	$ 700,000
Investment in Spilberg Company common stock........................	990,000		
Investment in Sykes Company common stock........................	574,200		
Other assets	1,501,300	1,260,000	790,000
Total assets.....................	$4,065,500	$2,060,000	$1,490,000
Liabilities & Stockholders' Equity			
Intercompany dividends payable.....		$ 19,800	$ 9,000
Other liabilities....................	$1,965,500	1,020,200	891,000
Common stock, $1 par	1,000,000	500,000	300,000
Additional paid-in capital...........	600,000	200,000	130,000
Retained earnings	203,000	320,000	160,000
Retained earnings of subsidiaries....	297,000		
Total liabilities & stockholders' equity.........................	$4,065,500	$2,060,000	$1,490,000

Pr. 10-8   The separate financial statements of Pickens Corporation and subsidiary for the year ended December 31, Year 8, are as follows:

PICKENS CORPORATION AND SUBSIDIARY
Separate Financial Statements
For Year Ended December 31, Year 8

Income Statements	Pickens Corporation	Skiffen Company
Revenue:		
Net sales	$ 840,000	$360,000
Intercompany sales	80,600	65,000
Intercompany gain on sale of equipment	9,500	
Intercompany interest revenue	2,702	
Intercompany investment income	44,800	
Total revenue	$ 977,602	$425,000
Costs and expenses:		
Cost of goods sold	$ 546,000	$252,000
Intercompany cost of goods sold	56,420	48,750
Interest expense	32,000	9,106
Intercompany interest expense		2,276
Other operating expenses and income taxes expense	271,382	56,868
Total costs and expenses	$ 905,802	$369,000
Net income	$ 71,800	$ 56,000

Statements of Retained Earnings

	Pickens	Skiffen
Retained earnings, beginning of year	$ 595,000	$136,000
Add: Net income	71,800	56,000
Subtotals	$ 666,800	$192,000
Less: Dividends	20,000	11,000
Retained earnings, end of year	$ 646,800	$181,000

Balance Sheets

Assets

	Pickens	Skiffen
Intercompany receivables (payables)	$ 35,800	$ (35,800)
Inventories	180,000	96,000
Investment in Skiffen Company common stock	392,570	
Investment in Skiffen Company bonds	27,918	
Plant assets (net)	781,500	510,000
Accumulated depreciation of plant assets	(87,000)	(85,000)
Other assets	333,782	146,500
Total assets	$1,664,570	$631,700

Liabilities & Stockholders' Equity

	Pickens	Skiffen
Dividends payable	$ 20,000	$ 2,200
Bonds payable	400,000	120,000
Intercompany bonds payable		30,000

(continued)

PICKENS CORPORATION AND SUBSIDIARY
Separate Financial Statements (concluded)
For Year Ended December 31, Year 8

	Pickens Corporation	Skiffen Company
Liabilities & Stockholders' Equity		
Discount on bonds payable		(4,281)
Discount on intercompany bonds payable		(1,070)
Deferred income tax liability.	15,800	
Other liabilities	164,470	24,851
Common stock, $2.50 par	400,000	250,000
Additional paid-in capital	14,000	29,000
Retained earnings	646,800	181,000
Retained earnings of subsidiary	3,500	
Total liabilities & stockholders' equity	$1,664,570	$631,700

Pickens had acquired 10% of the 100,000 outstanding shares of $2.50 par common stock of Skiffen Company on December 31, Year 6, for $38,000. An additional 70,000 shares were acquired for $315,700 on January 2, Year 8 (at which time there was no difference between the current fair values and carrying amounts of Skiffen's identifiable net assets). Out-of-pocket costs of the business combination may be disregarded.

Additional Information

(1) Pickens Corporation's ledger accounts for Investment in Skiffen Company Common Stock, Deferred Income Tax Liability, Retained Earnings, and Retained Earnings of Subsidiary were as follows (before December 31, Year 8, closing entries):

Investment in Skiffen Company Common Stock

Date	Explanation	Debit	Credit	Balance
Year 6				
Dec. 31	Acquisition of 10,000 shares	38,000		38,000 dr
Year 8				
Jan. 2	Acquisition of 70,000 shares	315,700		353,700 dr
2	Retroactive application of equity method of accounting [($40,000 − $5,000) × 0.10]	3,500		357,200 dr
Dec. 15	Dividend declared by Skiffen ($11,000 × 0.80)		8,800	348,400 dr
31	Net income of Skiffen ($56,000 × 0.80)	44,800		393,200 dr
31	Amortization of goodwill ($25,200 ÷ 40)		630	392,570 dr

(continued)

Deferred Income Tax Liability

Date	Explanation	Debit	Credit	Balance
Year 8				
Jan. 2	Income taxes applicable to un-distributed earnings of subsidi-ary ($3,500 × 0.40)*		1,400	1,400 cr
Dec. 31	Income taxes applicable to un-distributed earnings of subsidi-ary [($44,800 − $8,800) × 0.40]*		14,400	15,800 cr

* Dividend received deduction is disregarded.

Retained Earnings

Date	Explanation	Debit	Credit	Balance
Year 6				
Dec. 31	Balance			540,000 cr
Year 7				
Dec. 31	Close net income		55,000	595,000 cr

Retained Earnings of Subsidiary

Date	Explanation	Debit	Credit	Balance
Year 8				
Jan. 2	Retroactive application of equity method of accounting		3,500	3,500 cr

(2) Skiffen Company's Retained Earnings ledger account was as follows:

Retained Earnings

Date	Explanation	Debit	Credit	Balance
Year 6				
Dec. 31	Balance			101,000 cr
Year 7				
Dec. 31	Close net income		40,000	141,000 cr
31	Close Dividends Declared ac-count	5,000		136,000 cr

(3) Information relating to intercompany sales for Year 8:

	Pickens Corporation	Skiffen Company
Dec. 31, Year 8, inventory of intercompany merchandise purchases, on first-in, first-out basis	$26,000	$22,000
Intercompany payables, Dec. 31, Year 8	12,000	7,000

(4) Pickens acquired $30,000 face amount of Skiffen's 6% bonds in the open market on January 2, Year 8, for $27,016—a 10% yield. Skiffen had issued the bonds on January 2, Year 6, to yield 8% and had been paying the interest each December 31. Any gain or loss on extinguishment of the bonds is immaterial.

(5) On September 1, Year 8, Pickens sold equipment with a cost of $40,000 and

accumulated depreciation of $9,300 to Skiffen for $40,200. On September 1, Year 8, the equipment had an economic life of 10 years and no residual value. Skiffen includes depreciation expense (straight-line method) in other operating expenses.

(6) Skiffen owed Pickens $32,000 on December 31, Year 8, for noninterest-bearing cash advances.

(7) Pickens and Skiffen file separate income tax returns. The income tax rate is 40%. The dividend-received deduction is disregarded.

Instructions

Prepare a working paper for consolidated financial statements and related working paper eliminations (in journal entry format) for Pickens Corporation and subsidiary on December 31, Year 8, including income taxes allocation. Round all amounts to the nearest dollar.

Pr. 10-9 On January 2, Year 6, Plummer Corporation acquired a controlling interest of 75% in the outstanding common stock of Sinclair Company for $96,000, including direct out-of-pocket costs of the business combination. Separate financial statements for the two companies for the year ended December 31, Year 6, are on page 540.

Additional Information

(1) Sinclair sold machinery with a carrying amount of $4,000, no residual value, and a remaining economic life of five years to Plummer for $4,800 on December 31, Year 6.

(2) Sinclair's depreciable plant assets had a composite estimated remaining economic life of five years on January 2, Year 6; Sinclair uses the straight-line method of depreciation for all plant assets.

(3) Data on intercompany sales of merchandise follow:

	In purchaser's inventory, Dec. 31, Year 6	Amount payable by purchaser, Dec. 31, Year 6
Plummer Corporation to Sinclair Company	$24,300	$24,000
Sinclair Company to Plummer Corporation	18,000	8,000

(4) Both companies are subject to an income tax rate of 40%. Plummer is entitled to a dividend-received deduction of 80%. Each company will file separate income tax returns for Year 6. Except for Plummer's Intercompany Investment Income ledger account, there are no temporary differences for either company.

(5) Plummer's ledger accounts for Investment in Sinclair Company Common Stock

PLUMMER CORPORATION AND SINCLAIR COMPANY
Separate Financial Statements
For Year Ended December 31, Year 6

	Plummer Corporation	Sinclair Company
Income Statements		
Revenue:		
Net sales	$ 772,000	$ 426,000
Intercompany sales	78,000	104,000
Dividend revenue		750
Intercompany gain on sale of machinery		800
Intercompany investment income	31,163	
Other revenue	9,000	2,900
Total revenue	$ 890,163	$ 534,450
Costs and expenses:		
Cost of goods sold	$ 445,000	$ 301,200
Intercompany cost of goods sold	65,000	72,800
Depreciation expense	65,600	11,200
Other operating expenses	195,338	84,667
Income taxes expense	35,225	25,833
Total costs and expenses	$ 806,163	$ 495,700
Net income	$ 84,000	$ 38,750
Statements of Retained Earnings		
Retained earnings, beginning of year	$ 378,000	$ 112,000
Add: Net income	84,000	38,750
Subtotals	$ 462,000	$ 150,750
Less: Dividends	7,500	4,000
Retained earnings, end of year	$ 454,500	$ 146,750
Balance Sheets		
Assets		
Short-term investments		$ 18,000
Intercompany receivables (payables)	$ 16,000	(16,000)
Inventories	275,000	135,000
Other current assets	309,100	106,750
Investment in Sinclair Company common stock	124,163	
Plant assets	518,000	279,000
Accumulated depreciation	(298,200)	(196,700)
Total assets	$ 944,063	$ 326,050
Liabilities & Stockholders' Equity		
Dividends payable	$ 7,500	
Income taxes payable	35,225	$ 25,833
Other current liabilities	260,838	123,467
Common stock, $10 par	150,000	
Common stock, $5 par		20,000
Additional paid-in capital	36,000	10,000
Retained earnings	454,500	146,750
Total liabilities & stockholders' equity	$ 944,063	$ 326,050

and Intercompany Investment Income were as shown below (before December 31, Year 6, closing entries):

Investment in Sinclair Company Common Stock

Date	Explanation	Debit	Credit	Balance
Year 6				
Jan. 2	Acquisition of 3,000 shares	96,000		96,000 dr
Dec. 31	Net income of Sinclair			
	($38,750 × 0.75)	29,063		125,063 dr
31	Amortization of "negative			
	goodwill" {[($142,000 ×			
	0.75) − $96,000] ÷ 5}	2,100		127,163 dr
31	Dividend declared by Sinclair			
	($4,000 × 0.75)		3,000	124,163 dr

Intercompany Investment Income

Date	Explanation	Debit	Credit	Balance
Year 6				
Dec 31	Net income of Sinclair		29,063	29,063 cr
31	Amortization of "negative good-			
	will"		2,100	31,163 cr

Instructions

a Prepare December 31, Year 6, adjusting entries for Plummer Corporation to provide for income tax allocation resulting from Plummer's use of the equity method of accounting for the subsidiary's operating results. Round all amounts to the nearest dollar.

b Prepare a working paper for consolidated financial statements and related working paper elimination (in journal entry format), including income tax allocation, for Plummer Corporation and subsidiary on December 31, Year 6. Amounts for Plummer should reflect the journal entries in **a**.

11

Consolidated Financial Statements: Special Problems

In this chapter, the following special problems that might arise in the preparation of consolidated financial statements are discussed:

Changes in parent company's ownership interest in a subsidiary

Subsidiary with preferred stock outstanding

Stock dividends distributed by a subsidiary

Treasury stock transactions of a subsidiary

Indirect shareholdings and parent company's common stock owned by a subsidiary

CHANGES IN PARENT COMPANY'S OWNERSHIP INTEREST IN A SUBSIDIARY

Subsequent to the date of a business combination, a parent company might acquire stockholdings of the subsidiary's minority stockholders; or the parent company might sell some of its shares of subsidiary common stock to outsiders. Also, the subsidiary itself might issue additional shares of common stock to the public, or to the parent company. The accounting treatment for each of these situations is discussed in the following sections.

Parent Company Acquisition of Minority Interest

Purchase accounting is applied to the parent company's or the subsidiary's acquisition of all or part of the minority interest in net assets of the subsidiary, even though the business combination had been accounted for as a pooling.[1] Any other approach would be inconsistent with the basic premises of pooling accounting.

---

[1] *APB Opinion No. 16,* "Business Combinations," AICPA (New York: 1970), p. 294.

To illustrate the acquisition of a subsidiary's minority interest, return to the Prinz Corporation–Scarp Company illustration in Chapter 10 (pages 511 to 518) and assume that Scarp had a net income of $25,000 for the year ended February 28, Year 5, and declared dividends totaling $15,000 on February 14, Year 5. Under the equity method of accounting, Prinz Corporation's Investment in Scarp Company Common Stock and Retained Earnings of Subsidiary ledger accounts, and Scarp Company's Retained Earnings account, are as follows (before February 28, Year 5, closing entries):

Selected ledger accounts of parent company one year after business combination

PRINZ CORPORATION LEDGER
Investment in Scarp Company Common Stock

Date	Explanation	Debit	Credit	Balance
Year 2				
Mar. 1	Acquisition of 1,000 shares	10,000		10,000 dr
Year 3				
Mar. 1	Acquisition of 2,000 shares	22,000		32,000 dr
1	Retroactive application of equity method of accounting	450		32,450 dr
Year 4				
Feb. 17	Dividends received: $1 a share (3,000 × $1)		3,000	29,450 dr
28	Share of net income ($15,000 × 0.30)	4,500		33,950 dr
28	Amortization of goodwill		175	33,775 dr
Mar. 1	Acquisition of 6,500 shares	78,000		111,775 dr
Year 5				
Feb. 14	Dividends received: $1.50 a share (9,500 × $1.50)		14,250	97,525 dr
28	Share of net income ($25,000 × 0.95)	23,750		121,275 dr
28	Amortization of goodwill [$175 + ($19,500 ÷ 40)]		663	120,612 dr

Retained Earnings of Subsidiary

Date	Explanation	Debit	Credit	Balance
Year 3				
Mar. 1	Retroactive application of equity method of accounting		450	450 cr
Year 4				
Feb. 28	Closing entry—share of Scarp Company's adjusted net income not declared as a dividend ($4,500 − $175 − $3,000)		1,325	1,775 cr

Retained Earnings ledger account of subsidiary one year after business combination

SCARP COMPANY LEDGER
Retained Earnings

Date	Explanation	Debit	Credit	Balance
Year 2				
Mar. 1	Balance			20,000 cr
Year 3				
Feb. 10	Dividends declared: $1 a share	10,000		10,000 cr
28	Net income		15,000	25,000 cr
Year 4				
Feb. 17	Dividends declared: $1 a share	10,000		15,000 cr
28	Net income		15,000	30,000 cr

The working paper eliminations (in journal entry format) for the year ended February 28, Year 5, are as follows (disregarding income taxes):

Working paper eliminations for first year following business combination

PRINZ CORPORATION AND SUBSIDIARY
Working Paper Eliminations
February 28, Year 5

(a) Common Stock, $5 par—Scarp............................. 50,000
    Additional Paid-in Capital—Scarp........................ 10,000
    Retained Earnings—Scarp ($30,000 − $1,775) 28,225
    Retained Earnings of Subsidiary—Prinz 1,775
    Intercompany Investment Income—Prinz 23,750
    Goodwill (net)—Prinz ($1,850 + $4,750 + $19,012) 25,612
        Investment in Scarp Company Common Stock—Prinz .   120,612
        Dividends Declared—Scarp........................   15,000
        Minority Interest in Net Assets of Subsidiary
        ($4,500 − $750)   3,750
    To eliminate intercompany investment and equity accounts of subsidiary at **beginning of year;** to allocate excess of cost over current fair values (equal to carrying amounts) of identifiable net assets acquired to goodwill; and to establish minority interest in net assets of subsidiary at beginning of year ($4,500—see page 517), less minority share of dividends ($15,000 × 0.05 = $750).

(b) Minority Interest in Net Income of Subsidiary ($25,000 × 0.05)   1,250
        Minority Interest in Net Assets of Subsidiary..........   1,250
    To establish minority interest in net income of subsidiary for year ended February 28, Year 5.

Goodwill of $25,612 recognized in the first of the foregoing eliminations comprises the following three components:

<table>
<tr><td rowspan="2">Components of net goodwill one year after business combination</td><td>***Installment acquisition of***</td><td>***Mar. 1, Year 2***</td><td>***Mar. 1, Year 3***</td><td>***Mar. 1, Year 4***</td></tr>
</table>

Components of net goodwill one year after business combination	*Installment acquisition of*	*Mar. 1, Year 2*	*Mar. 1, Year 3*	*Mar. 1, Year 4*
	Goodwill (net), Mar. 1, Year 4			
	(page 516)	*$1,900*	*$4,875*	*$19,500*
	Less: Amortization over 40 years,			
	year ended Feb. 28, Year 5	*50*	*125*	*488*
	Goodwill (net), Feb. 28, Year 5 . .	*$1,850*	*$4,750*	*$19,012*

Assume further that on March 1, Year 5, Prinz acquired for $6,000 the 500 shares of Scarp's common stock owned by minority stockholders; the following journal entry is appropriate:

Parent company's journal entry for acquisition of minority interest	*Investment in Scarp Company Common Stock*	*6,000*	
	Cash		*6,000*
	To record acquisition of 500 shares of subsidiary's common stock from minority stockholders.		

Because the minority interest in net assets of subsidiary in the consolidated balance sheet of Prinz and subsidiary on February 28, Year 5, totaled $5,000 ($3,750 + $1,250 = $5,000), an additional $1,000 ($6,000 − $5,000 = $1,000) of goodwill must be amortized by Prinz over a maximum period of 40 years, beginning March 1, Year 5. Under the equity method of accounting, Prinz accrues 100% of Scarp's net income subsequent to March 1, Year 5, and there is no minority interest to be accounted for in consolidation.

If Prinz paid *less* than the carrying amount of the minority interest acquired, the appropriate accounting treatment of the difference is not clear. Presumably, the excess of minority interest carrying amount over Prinz's cost should be allocated pro rata to the carrying amounts of Scarp's noncurrent assets other than long-term investments in marketable securities. This approach would be consistent with the theory of purchase accounting set forth in Chapter 5 (page 191). However, assuming that the difference between carrying amount and cost is immaterial, it may be treated as an offset to goodwill arising from earlier acquisitions of Scarp's common stock and amortized over the remaining economic life of that goodwill.

Parent Company Sale of a Portion of Its Subsidiary Common Stockholdings

A parent company with a substantial ownership interest in a subsidiary may sell a portion of that interest for several reasons. Perhaps the parent company is short of cash, or the earnings of the subsidiary are unsatisfactory. The parent company may recognize that a subsidiary may be controlled effectively with just over 50% ownership of its outstanding common stock and that an 80% or 90% ownership of a subsidiary may tie up excessive amounts of capital. Some corporations in recent years have sold a portion of a newly acquired subsidiary's common stock in order to generate cash for additional business combinations.

Sale of all of an ownership interest in a subsidiary often involves accounting for and presentation of the disposal of a business segment. This topic is considered in Chapter 20.

Accounting for a parent company's sale of a part of its investment in a subsidiary is similar to the accounting for disposal of any noncurrent asset. The carrying amount of the subsidiary common stock sold is removed from the parent company's Investment in Subsidiary Common Stock ledger account, and the difference between that carrying amount and the cash or current fair value of other consideration received is recognized as a gain or loss on disposal of the stock. Under generally accepted accounting principles, the gain or loss *is not an extraordinary item* for consolidated income statement display.[2]

Unless the business combination had resulted from an installment acquisition of the subsidiary's common stock, there is no significant change in the working paper eliminations after the parent's sale of part of its ownership interest in the subsidiary. However, the minority interest in the subsidiary's net income and net assets increases. The parent company's equity-method journal entries for the subsidiary's operations are changed only for the decrease in the percentage of the parent's ownership interest in the subsidiary.

When control was acquired by installment purchases of the subsidiary's common stock, *specific identification* should be used to account for the carrying amount of the subsidiary stock sold. There must be an accompanying adjustment in the parent company's application of the equity method of accounting for the subsidiary's operating results. For example, purchased goodwill may no longer be accounted for in the working paper for consolidated financial statements if the block of subsidiary common stock to which it applies was sold by the parent company.

Illustration of Parent Company Sale of Subsidiary Stockholding Returning to the Prinz Corporation–Scarp Company affiliation, assume that Scarp declared a $15,000 dividend to Prinz on February 12, Year 6, and had a net income of $35,000 for the year ended February 28, Year 6. Under these circumstances, Prinz's Investment ledger account and Retained Earnings of Subsidiary account, and Scarp Company's Retained Earnings account (before February 28, Year 6, closing entries), are as follows:

Selected ledger accounts of parent company two years after business combination

	PRINZ CORPORATION LEDGER Investment in Scarp Company Common Stock			
Date	**Explanation**	**Debit**	**Credit**	**Balance**
Year 2				
Mar. 1	Acquisition of 1,000 shares	10,000		10,000 dr
Year 3				
Mar. 1	Acquisition of 2,000 shares	22,000		32,000 dr
1	Retroactive application of equity method of accounting	450		32,450 dr

(continued)

_____

[2] *APB Opinion No. 30,* "Reporting the Results of Operations," AICPA (New York: 1973), p. 566.

PRINZ CORPORATION LEDGER
Investment in Scarp Company Common Stock (concluded)

Date	Explanation	Debit	Credit	Balance
Year 4				
Feb. 17	Dividends received: $1 a share			
	(3,000 × $1)		3,000	29,450 dr
28	Share of net income ($15,000 ×			
	0.30)	4,500		33,950 dr
28	Amortization of goodwill		175	33,775 dr
Mar. 1	Acquisition of 6,500 shares	78,000		111,775 dr
Year 5				
Feb. 4	Dividends received: $1.50 a			
	share (9,500 × $1.50)		14,250	97,525 dr
28	Share of net income ($25,000 ×			
	0.95)	23,750		121,275 dr
28	Amortization of goodwill		663	120,612 dr
Mar. 1	Acquisition of 500 shares	6,000		126,612 dr
Year 6				
Feb. 12	Dividends received: $1.50 a			
	share (10,000 × $1.50)		15,000	111,612 dr
28	Share of net income ($35,000 ×			
	1.00)	35,000		146,612 dr
28	Amortization of goodwill			
	[$663 + ($1,000 ÷ 40)]		688	145,924 dr

Retained Earnings of Subsidiary

Date	Explanation	Debit	Credit	Balance
Year 3				
Mar. 1	Retroactive application of equity			
	method of accounting		450	450 cr
Year 4				
Feb. 28	Closing entry—share of Scarp			
	Company adjusted net income			
	not paid as a dividend			
	($4,500 − $175 − $3,000)		1,325	1,775 cr
Year 5				
Feb. 28	Closing entry—share of subsidi-			
	ary's net income not declared			
	as a dividend ($23,750 −			
	$14,250)		9,500	11,275 cr

Retained Earnings
ledger account of
subsidiary two years
after business
combination

SCARP COMPANY LEDGER
Retained Earnings

Date	Explanation	Debit	Credit	Balance
Year 2				
Mar. 1	Balance			20,000 cr
Year 3				
Feb. 10	Dividends declared: $1 a share	10,000		10,000 cr
28	Net income		15,000	25,000 cr
Year 4				
Feb. 17	Dividends declared: $1 a share	10,000		15,000 cr
28	Net income		15,000	30,000 cr
Year 5				
Feb. 14	Dividends declared: $1.50 a share	15,000		15,000 cr
28	Net income		25,000	40,000 cr

Under these circumstances, the working paper elimination (in journal entry format) for Prinz Corporation and subsidiary on February 28, Year 6, is as follows (disregarding income taxes):

Working paper
elimination for second
year following business
combination

PRINZ CORPORATION AND SUBSIDIARY
Working Paper Elimination
February 28, Year 6

(a) Common Stock, $5 par—Scarp............................ 50,000
    Additional Paid-in Capital—Scarp......................... 10,000
    Retained Earnings—Scarp ($40,000 − $11,275) 28,725
    Retained Earnings of Subsidiary—Prinz 11,275
    Intercompany Investment Income—Prinz 35,000
    Goodwill (net)—Prinz ($1,800 + $4,625 + $18,524 + $975).. 25,924
        Investment in Scarp Company Common Stock—Prinz .   145,924
        Dividends Declared—Scarp.........................   15,000
    To eliminate intercompany investment and equity accounts of subsidiary at **beginning of year;** and to allocate excess of cost over current fair values (equal to carrying amounts) of identifiable net assets acquired to goodwill.

Goodwill of $25,924 recognized in the foregoing elimination comprises the four components on page 549.

Continuing the illustration, assume that, in order to raise cash for additional business combinations, Prinz on March 1, Year 6, sold in the open market the 1,000 and 2,000 shares of Scarp common stock acquired March 1, Year 2, and March 1, Year 3, respectively, for $55,000. The sale resulted in a gain of $12,575, computed as shown on page 549.

Installment acquisition of	Mar. 1, Year 2	Mar. 1, Year 3	Mar. 1, Year 4	Mar. 1, Year 5
Goodwill (net) Feb. 28, Year 5 (page 545).	$1,850	$4,750	$19,012	
Add: Goodwill acquired Mar. 1, Year 5 [$6,000 − $5,000 (page 545)].				$1,000
Less: Amortization over 40 years, year ended Feb. 28, Year 6	50	125	488	25
Goodwill (net), Feb. 28, Year 6.	$1,800	$4,625	$18,524	$ 975

Components of net goodwill two years after business combination

Computation of gain on parent company's sale of portion of subsidiary stockholdings

Proceeds of sale.		$ 55,000
Less: Carrying amount of 1,000 shares of Scarp common stock acquired Mar. 1, Year 2:		
Cost	$10,000	
Add: Share of Scarp's net income, Years 3−6 ($90,000 × 0.10)	9,000	
Less: Share of Scarp's dividends, Years 3−6 ($50,000 × 0.10)	(5,000)	
Amortization of goodwill ($50 × 4)	(200)	(13,800)
Carrying amount of 2,000 shares of Scarp common stock acquired Mar. 1, Year 3:		
Cost	$22,000	
Add: Share of Scarp's net income, Years 4−6 ($75,000 × 0.20)	15,000	
Less: Share of Scarp's dividends, Years 4−6 ($40,000 × 0.20)	(8,000)	
Amortization of goodwill ($125 × 3)	(375)	(28,625)
Gain on sale of portion of subsidiary stockholdings		$ 12,575

The following journal entry is prepared by Prinz Corporation on March 1, Year 6, to record the sale of part of its investment in Scarp Company common stock:

Parent company's journal entry to record sale of portion of investment in subsidiary

Cash.	55,000	
Investment in Scarp Company Common Stock ($13,800 + $28,625)		42,425
Realized Gain on Disposal of Investment in Subsidiary.		12,575
To record sale of 3,000 shares of Scarp Company common stock at a gain.		

The $12,575 realized gain in the foregoing journal entry is displayed in the consolidated income statement of Prinz Corporation and subsidiary for the year ending February 28, Year 7, because it was *realized* in a transaction with *outsiders*.

For a consolidated balance sheet of Prinz Corporation and subsidiary on March 1, Year 6, following Prinz's sale of Scarp common stock, the following working paper elimination (in journal entry format) is required:

PRINZ CORPORATION AND SUBSIDIARY
Working Paper Elimination
March 1, Year 6

(a) Common Stock, $5 par—Scarp. 50,000	
Additional Paid-in Capital—Scarp. 10,000	
Retained Earnings—Scarp ($40,000 + $20,000 − $31,275). . 28,725	
Retained Earnings of Subsidiary—Prinz	
($11,275 + $35,000 − $15,000) 31,275	
Goodwill (net)—Prinz ($25,924 − $1,800 − $4,625). 19,499	
Investment in Scarp Company Common Stock	
($145,924 − $42,425)	103,499
Minority Interest in Net Assets of Subsidiary	
[($50,000 + $10,000 + $60,000) × 0.30].	36,000

To eliminate intercompany investment and equity accounts of subsidiary; to allocate excess of cost over current fair values (equal to carrying amounts) of identifiable net assets acquired to goodwill; and to establish minority interest in net assets of subsidiary.

The foregoing elimination recognizes only the goodwill applicable to Prinz Corporation's March 1, Year 4, and March 1, Year 5, acquisitions of Scarp Company common stock. The total goodwill of $19,499 comprises the following:

Mar. 1, Year 4, acquisition [$19,500 − ($488 × 2)].	$18,524
Mar. 1, Year 5, acquisition ($1,000 − $25)	975
Total goodwill, Mar. 1, Year 6.	$19,499

Also reflected in the foregoing elimination is the minority interest in net assets of subsidiary that resulted from Prinz's disposal of 30% of its investment in Scarp's common stock. The amount of the minority interest is developed from the carrying amount of Scarp's identifiable net assets of $120,000 ($50,000 + $10,000 + $60,000 = $120,000) on March 1, Year 6.

Subsidiary's Issuance of Additional Shares of Common Stock to the Public

Instead of obtaining funds by selling a portion of its ownership interest in a subsidiary, the parent company may instruct the subsidiary to issue additional shares of common stock to the public, with the parent company and minority stockholders waiving their preemptive right to acquire part of the common stock. The cash obtained would be available to the consolidated group through intercompany transactions. Because the parent company does not acquire shares of common stock on a pro rata basis along with present minority stockholders in the subsidiary's stock issuance, as in a stock rights offering, the parent's percentage ownership interest in the subsidiary changes. In addition, unless the subsidiary issues additional common stock to the public at a price per share equal to the per-share carrying amount of the subsidiary's outstanding common stock, there is a realized gain or loss to the parent company. These two points are illustrated in the following section.

Illustration of Subsidiary's Issuance of Additional Common Stock to the Public On January 2, Year 1, Paulson Corporation acquired 80% of the outstanding common stock of Spaulding Company for $240,000. Out-of-pocket costs of the business combination are disregarded in this illustration. Spaulding's stockholders' equity on January 2, Year 1, was as follows:

Stockholders' equity of subsidiary on date of purchase-type business combination

Common stock, $5 par.	$ 50,000
Additional paid-in capital	75,000
Retained earnings.	100,000
Total stockholders' equity	$225,000

The current fair values of Spaulding's identifiable net assets on January 2, Year 1, were equal to their carrying amounts. Thus, the $60,000 excess of the cost of Paulson's investment ($240,000) over 80% of the $225,000 current fair value of Spaulding's identifiable net assets ($225,000 × 0.80 = $180,000) was attributable to goodwill, which is to be amortized over 40 years.

For the year ended December 31, Year 1, Spaulding had a net income of $20,000 and declared and paid cash dividends of $10,000 ($1 a share). On December 31, Year 1, Spaulding issued 2,000 shares of common stock in a public offering at $33 a share, net of costs of issuing the stock, for a total of $66,000. (Both Paulson and the existing minority stockholders waived their preemptive right to acquire additional shares of Spaulding's common stock.) Thus, after the closing process, Spaulding's stockholders' equity on December 31, Year 1, amounted to $301,000 ($225,000 + $20,000 − $10,000 + $66,000 = $301,000) and consisted of the following amounts:

Stockholders' equity of purchased subsidiary after its issuance of common stock to public

Common stock, $5 par ($50,000 + $10,000)	$ 60,000
Additional paid-in capital ($75,000 + $56,000)	131,000
Retained earnings ($100,000 + $20,000 − $10,000).	110,000
Total stockholders' equity	$301,000

Paulson's investment ledger account under the equity method of accounting is as follows after the subsidiary's issuance of common stock:

Parent company's
investment account
after subsidiary's
issuance of common
stock to public

Investment in Spaulding Company Common Stock				
Date	**Explanation**	**Debit**	**Credit**	**Balance**
Year 1				
Jan. 2	Acquisition of 8,000 shares in business combination	240,000		240,000 dr
Dec. 31	Dividends received ($10,000 × 0.80)		8,000	232,000 dr
31	Share of net income ($20,000 × 0.80)	16,000		248,000 dr
31	Amortization of goodwill ($60,000 ÷ 40)		1,500	246,500 dr
31	Nonoperating gain on subsidiary's issuance of common stock to public	12,667		259,167 dr

The December 31, Year 1, increase of $12,667 in Paulson's investment ledger account is offset by a credit to a nonoperating gain account. The $12,667 is Paulson's share (for which Paulson paid nothing) of the increase in Spaulding's net assets resulting from Spaulding's issuance of common stock to the public at $33 a share. The $33 a share issuance price exceeds the $30.81 carrying amount ($246,500 ÷ 8,000 shares = $30.81) a share of Paulson's Investment account prior to Spaulding's common stock issuance. The $12,667 debit to Paulson's investment ledger account is computed as follows:

Computation of gain to
parent company
resulting from
subsidiary's issuance
of common stock to
public

	Total	**Paulson's share**		**Minority's share**	
Carrying amount of Spaulding Company's identifiable net assets after common stock issuance to public..	$301,000	(66⅔%)†	$200,667	(33⅓%)	$100,333
Carrying amount of Spaulding Company's identifiable net assets before common stock issuance to public..	235,000*	(80%)	188,000‡	(20%)	47,000
Difference	$ 66,000		$ 12,667§		$ 53,333

* $225,000 + $20,000 − $10,000 = $235,000
† 8,000 ÷ (10,000 + 2,000) = 66⅔%
‡ Paulson's share of Spaulding's identifiable net assets [($225,000 + $20,000 − $10,000) × 0.80] $188,000
Add: Unamortized goodwill ($60,000 − $1,500) 58,500
Balance of Paulson's Investment in Spaulding Company Common Stock ledger account $246,500
§ Nonoperating gain to parent company; Paulson's journal entry (explanation omitted) is as follows:

Investment in Spaulding Company Common Stock 12,667
    Gain from Subsidiary's Issuance of Common Stock 12,667

The foregoing analysis reflects the effect of the decrease of Paulson's percentage interest in Spaulding's outstanding common stock from 80% before the public stock issuance to 66⅔% after the issuance. Nevertheless, the issuance price of $33 a share exceeded the $30.81 carrying amount per share of Paulson's original investment in Spaulding, thus resulting in the $12,667 nonoperating gain to Paulson. At one time, the ***nonoperating gain*** treatment accorded to the $12,667 increase in Paulson's interest in Spaulding was not acceptable to the Securities and Exchange Commission. However, in ***Staff Accounting Bulletin 51,*** the SEC sanctioned such treatment in certain circumstances, specifying the following disclosure requirements.[3]

> Gains (or losses) arising from issuances by a subsidiary of its own stock, if recorded in income by the parent, shall be presented as a separate line item in the consolidated income statement without regard to materiality and clearly be designated as nonoperating income. An appropriate description of the transaction should be included in the notes to the financial statements.

The working paper eliminations (in journal entry format) below are appropriate for Paulson Corporation and subsidiary following Spaulding's common stock issuance on December 31, Year 1, assuming that there were no other intercompany transactions or profits for Year 1:

Working paper eliminations on date of subsidiary's issuance of common stock to public

PAULSON CORPORATION AND SUBSIDIARY
Working Paper Eliminations
December 31, Year 1

(a) *Common Stock—Spaulding*	*60,000*	
Additional Paid-in Capital—Spaulding	*131,000*	
Retained Earnings—Spaulding	*100,000*	
Goodwill (net)–Paulson ($60,000 − $1,500)	*58,500*	
Intercompany Investment Income—Paulson		
($20,000 × 0.80)	*16,000*	
Investment in Spaulding Company Common Stock—		
Paulson		*259,167*
Dividends Declared—Spaulding		*10,000*
Minority Interest in Net Assets of Subsidiary		
($45,000 − $2,000 + $53,333)		*96,333*

*To eliminate intercompany investment and related equity accounts of subsidiary (retained earnings of subsidiary at the **beginning of year**); to eliminate subsidiary's dividends declared; to record unamortized balance of goodwill on Dec. 31, Year 1; and to provide for minority interest in net assets of subsidiary at beginning of year ($225,000 × 0.20 = $45,000), less dividends to minority stockholders ($10,000 × 0.20 = $2,000), plus minority interest's share of proceeds of public stock issuance ($66,000 − $12,667 = $53,333).*

(continued)

---

[3] *Staff Accounting Bulletin 51,* Securities and Exchange Commission (Washington: 1983).

PAULSON CORPORATION AND SUBSIDIARY
Working Paper Eliminations (concluded)
December 31, Year 1

(b) Minority Interest in Net Income of Subsidiary   4,000
         Minority Interest in Net Assets of Subsidiary.   4,000
     To provide for minority interest in subsidiary's Year 1 net in-
     come as follows: $20,000 × 0.20 interest throughout Year
     1 = $4,000.

Note that Paulson's $12,667 nonoperating gain is not eliminated in the forego-
ing eliminations; it was *realized* through the subsidiary's transaction with *outsiders.*

Subsidiary's Issuance of Additional Shares of Common Stock to Parent Company

Instead of issuing additional common stock to the public, a subsidiary might issue
the additional stock to the parent company. This eventuality might occur if the parent
company desired to increase its total investment in the subsidiary, or if the parent
wished to reduce the influence of minority stockholders of the subsidiary.

To illustrate, return to the Paulson Corporation–Spaulding Company illustration and assume that on December 31, Year 1, Spaulding had issued 2,000 shares of

Computation of loss to parent company resulting from subsidiary's issuance of common stock to parent company

	Total	Paulson's share		Minority's share	
Carrying amount of Spauld-ing Company's identifiable net assets after common stock issuance to parent . .	$301,000	(83⅓%)*	$250,833	(16⅔%)	$50,167
Carrying amount of Spauld-ing Company's identifiable net assets before common stock issuance to parent . .	235,000	(80%)	188,000†	(20%)	47,000
Difference	$ 66,000		$ 62,833		$ 3,167‡

* (8,000 + 2,000) ÷ (10,000 + 2,000) = 83⅓%

† Paulson's share of Spaulding's identifiable net assets	$188,000
Add: Unamortized goodwill ($60,000 − $1,500)	58,500
Balance of Paulson's Investment in Spaulding Company Common Stock ledger account	$246,500

‡ Nonoperating loss to parent company; Paulson's journal entry (explanation omitted) is
as follows:

Loss from Subsidiary's Issuance of Common Stock	3,167	
Investment in Spaulding Company Common Stock		3,167

common stock to Paulson, rather than to the public, at $33 a share, for a total of $66,000, and that the minority stockholders waived their preemptive rights to acquire additional common stock. Under these circumstances, Paulson's investment account increases to a balance of $309,333 ($246,500 + $66,000 cost of common stock acquired − $3,167 nonoperating loss = $309,333). The nonoperating loss of $3,167 is computed as shown on page 554.

Paulson's $3,167 loss is *realized* because, although it arose in a transaction with Spaulding, Paulson paid $66,000 for an investment valued at $62,833; the minority stockholders (*creditors* under the parent company concept) were the beneficiaries of the $3,167 difference. Thus, Paulson's $3,167 loss is displayed in the consolidated income statement of Paulson Corporation and subsidiary for the year ended December 31, Year 1.

The working paper eliminations (in journal entry format) for Paulson Corporation and subsidiary following Spaulding's common stock issuance on December 31, Year 1, are as follows:

Working paper eliminations on date of subsidiary's issuance of common stock to parent company

PAULSON CORPORATION AND SUBSIDIARY
Working Paper Eliminations
December 31, Year 1

(a) Common Stock—Spaulding...........................	60,000	
Additional Paid-in Capital—Spaulding..................	131,000	
Retained Earnings—Spaulding.........................	100,000	
Goodwill (net)—Paulson ($60,000 − $1,500)	58,500	
Intercompany Investment Income—Paulson		
($20,000 × 0.80).....................................	16,000	
Investment in Spaulding Company Common Stock—		
Paulson ($250,833 + $58,500)		309,333
Dividends Declared—Spaulding...................		10,000
Minority Interest in Net Assets of Subsidiary		
($45,000 − $2,000 + $3,167)		46,167

To eliminate intercompany investment and related equity accounts of subsidiary (retained earnings of subsidiary at the **beginning of year**); to eliminate subsidiary's dividends declared; to record unamortized balance of the goodwill on Dec. 31, Year 1; and to provide for minority interest in net assets of subsidiary at beginning of year ($225,000 × 0.20 = $45,000), less dividends to minority stockholders ($10,000 × 0.20 = $2,000), plus minority interest's share of proceeds of common stock issuance to parent company ($3,167).

(b) Minority Interest in Net Income of Subsidiary	4,000	
Minority Interest in Net Assets of Subsidiary.........		4,000

To provide for minority interest in subsidiary's Year 1 net income as follows: $20,000 × 0.20 interest throughout Year 1 = $4,000.

SUBSIDIARY WITH PREFERRED STOCK OUTSTANDING

Some combinees in a business combination have outstanding preferred stock. If a parent company acquires all of a subsidiary's preferred stock, together with all or a majority of its common stock, the working paper for consolidated financial statements and working paper eliminations are similar to those illustrated in Chapters 6 through 10. If less than 100% of the subsidiary's preferred stock is acquired by the parent company, the preferences associated with the preferred stock must be considered in the computation of the minority interest in the net assets and net income of the subsidiary.

Illustration of Minority Interest in Subsidiary with Preferred Stock

Suppose, for example, that on July 1, Year 4, Praeger Corporation paid $200,000 (including direct out-of-pocket costs of the business combination) for 60% of Simmon Company's 10,000 shares of outstanding $1 par, 6% cumulative preferred stock and 80% of Simmon's 50,000 shares of outstanding $2 par common stock, which were owned pro rata by the same stockholders. The preferred stock had a liquidation preference of $1.10 a share and was callable at $1.20 a share plus cumulative preferred dividends in arrears. The stockholders' equity of Simmon on July 1, Year 4, was as shown below:

<table>
<tr><td>Stockholders' equity of
subsidiary on date of
purchase-type
business combination</td><td>6% cumulative preferred stock, $1 par, 10,000 shares outstanding ....</td><td>$ 10,000</td></tr>
<tr><td></td><td>Common stock, $2 par, 50,000 shares outstanding ....</td><td>100,000</td></tr>
<tr><td></td><td>Additional paid-in capital ....</td><td>30,000</td></tr>
<tr><td></td><td>Retained earnings...</td><td>50,000</td></tr>
<tr><td></td><td>Total stockholders' equity ....</td><td>$190,000</td></tr>
</table>

There were no cumulative preferred dividends in arrears on July 1, Year 4. The current fair values of Simmon's identifiable net assets on July 1, Year 4, were equal to their carrying amounts on that date.

The presence of the preferred stock raises two questions:

1   What part, if any, does the preferred stock play in the measurement of the goodwill recognized in the business combination?

2   Which per-share amount—$1 par, $1.10 liquidation preference, or $1.20 call price—should be used to measure the minority interest in Simmon's net assets on July 1, Year 4?

In the opinion of the author, the following are logical answers to the two questions:

1   The preferred stock does not enter into the measurement of the goodwill recognized in the business combination. Typically, preferred stockholders have no voting rights; thus, in a business combination, preferred stock may in substance be considered **debt** rather than **owners' equity.** Accordingly, the amount paid by the combinor for the subsidiary's common stock should be the basis for computation of the goodwill.

2   The call price plus any cumulative preferred dividends in arrears should be used to measure the minority interest of the preferred stockholders in Simmon's net assets on July 1, Year 4. The call price generally is the maximum claim on net assets imposed by the preferred stock contract. Furthermore, the call price is the amount that Simmon would pay, on a going-concern basis, to extinguish the preferred stock. Use of the preferred stock's liquidation value in the computation of the minority stockholders' interest in the subsidiary's net assets would stress a **quitting-concern** approach, rather than the going-concern principle. Finally, the par of the preferred stock has no significance as a measure of value for the preferred stock.

In accordance with the foregoing discussion, Praeger prepares the following journal entry to record the business combination with Simmon on July 1, Year 4. (Out-of-pocket costs of the combination are not accounted for separately in this illustration.)

Parent company's journal entry for purchase-type business combination involving subsidiary's preferred stock

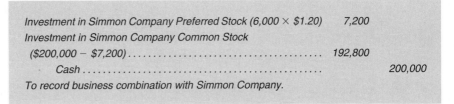

Investment in Simmon Company Preferred Stock (6,000 × $1.20)	7,200	
Investment in Simmon Company Common Stock		
($200,000 − $7,200)......................................	192,800	
Cash..		200,000
To record business combination with Simmon Company.		

The working paper elimination (in journal entry format) for Praeger and subsidiary on July 1, Year 4, is illustrated on page 558.

The following aspects of the elimination on page 558 should be emphasized:

1   Simmon's goodwill is measured as the difference between the cost assigned to Praeger's investment in Simmon's common stock and Praeger's share of the current fair value of Simmon's net assets applicable to common stock; Simmon's preferred stock does not enter the measurement of the goodwill.

2   The minority interest in the subsidiary's preferred stock is measured as the 4,000 shares of preferred stock owned by minority stockholders multiplied by the $1.20 call price per share.

3   The minority interest in the subsidiary's common stock is measured as 20% of the $178,000 ($190,000 − $12,000 = $178,000) net asset value of Simmon's common stock.

Preferred Stock Considerations Subsequent to Date of Business Combination

Regardless of whether Simmon's preferred dividend is paid or omitted in years subsequent to July 1, Year 4, the preferred dividend affects the measurement of the

Working paper
elimination on date of
business combination
involving partially
owned subsidiary
having preferred stock
outstanding

PRAEGER CORPORATION AND SUBSIDIARY
Working Paper Elimination
July 1, Year 4

Cumulative Preferred Stock—Simmon.........................	10,000	
Common Stock—Simmon..................................	100,000	
Additional Paid-in Capital—Simmon.........................	30,000	
Retained Earnings—Simmon...............................	50,000	
Goodwill—Praeger {$192,800 − [($190,000 − $12,000 call price		
of preferred stock) × 0.80]}...............................	50,400	
Investment in Simmon Company Preferred Stock—		
Praeger...		7,200
Investment in Simmon Company Common Stock—		
Praeger...		192,800
Minority Interest in Net Assets of Subsidiary—Preferred		
(4,000 × $1.20)....................................		4,800
Minority Interest in Net Assets of Subsidiary—Common		
($178,000 × 0.20)..................................		35,600

To eliminate intercompany investment and related equity accounts
of subsidiary on date of business combination; to record excess of
cost attributable to common stock over 80% share of current fair
value of subsidiary's identifiable net assets as goodwill; and to
provide for minority interest in subsidiary's preferred stock and in
net assets applicable to common stock on date of business combination.

minority interest of common stockholders in the net income of Simmon. For example, assume that Simmon had a net income of $50,000 for the fiscal year ended June
30, Year 5, and declared and paid the preferred dividend of $0.06 a share and a
common dividend of $0.50 a share on June 30, Year 5. Praeger records these ele-
ments of Simmon's operating results on June 30, Year 5, under the equity method of
accounting, as illustrated on page 559.

After the journal entries on page 559 are posted, Praeger's Investment in Simmon Company Common Stock ledger account is as follows:

Investment account of
parent company one
year subsequent to
business combination

Investment in Simmon Company Common Stock

Date	Explanation	Debit	Credit	Balance
Year 4				
July 1	Acquisition of 40,000 shares	192,800		192,800 dr
Year 5				
June 30	Dividends received: $0.50 a			
	share		20,000	172,800 dr
30	Share of net income	39,520		212,320 dr
30	Amortization of goodwill		1,260	211,060 dr

<table>
<tr><td>Parent company's
journal entries,
June 30, Year 5</td><td></td></tr>
</table>

PRAEGER CORPORATION
Journal Entries

Cash 20,360
       Investment in Simmon Company Common Stock.........   20,000
       Intercompany Dividend Revenue   360
To record receipt of dividends declared and paid by Simmon Company as follows:
   Preferred stock (6,000 × $0.06)................... $ 360
   Common stock (40,000 × $0.50).................   20,000
     Total cash received........................... $20,360

Investment in Simmon Company Common Stock.............. 39,520
       Intercompany Investment Income......................   39,520
To record share of Simmon Company's net income applicable to common stock as follows:
   Simmon Company's net income.................. $50,000
   Less: Preferred dividend (10,000 × $0.06)   600
   Net income attributable to common stock.......... $49,400
     Parent company's share ($49,400 × 0.80) $39,520
(Income tax effects are disregarded.)

Amortization Expense 1,260
       Investment in Simmon Company Common Stock.........   1,260
To provide for Year 5 amortization of Simmon Company's goodwill acquired on date of business combination as follows:
   Simmon's goodwill acquired on date of business
     combination.................................... $50,400
   Amortization (50,400 ÷ 40)...................... $ 1,260

If there are no other intercompany transactions or profits, the June 30, Year 5, working paper eliminations (in journal entry format) for Praeger Corporation and subsidiary are as shown on page 560.

Working paper
eliminations one year
subsequent to
business combination
involving partially
owned subsidiary
having preferred stock
outstanding

PRAEGER CORPORATION AND SUBSIDIARY
Working Paper Eliminations
June 30, Year 5

(a) Cumulative Preferred Stock—Simmon	10,000	
Common Stock—Simmon	100,000	
Additional Paid-in Capital—Simmon.......................	30,000	
Retained Earnings—Simmon............................	50,000	
Intercompany Dividend Revenue—Praeger................	360	
Intercompany Investment Income—Praeger	39,520	
Goodwill (net)—Praeger ($50,400 − $1,260)...............	49,140	
Investment in Simmon Company Preferred Stock—		
Praeger...		7,200
Investment in Simmon Company Common Stock—		
Praeger...		211,060
Dividends Declared—Simmon		
[(10,000 × $0.06) + (50,000 × $0.50)].............		25,600
Minority Interest in Net Assets of Subsidiary—		
Preferred ($4,800 − $240)........................		4,560
Minority Interest in Net Assets of Subsidiary—		
Common [$35,600 − ($25,000 × 0.20)]		30,600

To eliminate intercompany investment and related equity accounts of subsidiary at **beginning of year**; to eliminate subsidiary's dividends declared; to record unamortized balance of
goodwill on June 30, Year 5; and to provide for minority interest in subsidiary's preferred stock and common stock at beginning of year, less dividends to minority stockholders.

(b) Minority Interest in Net Income of Subsidiary	10,120	
Minority Interest in Net Assets of Subsidiary—		
Preferred..		240
Minority Interest in Net Assets of Subsidiary—		
Common [($50,000 − $600) × 0.20]		9,880

To provide for minority interest in net income of subsidiary for
Year 5.

In the review of the June 30, Year 5, journal entries of Praeger and the working
paper eliminations on that date, the following points should be noted:

1   Praeger Corporation's accounting for its investment in the subsidiary's preferred
stock *essentially is the cost method.* This method is appropriate as long as the
subsidiary declares and pays the cumulative preferred dividend annually. If the subsidiary had *passed* the preferred dividend of $600 for the year ended June 30, Year 5,
Praeger would have recorded the passed preferred dividend *under the equity method
of accounting* as follows:

Parent company's journal entry for *passed* cumulative preferred dividend of subsidiary

Investment in Simmon Company Preferred Stock 360
    Intercompany Investment Income............................... 360
To accrue cumulative preferred dividend passed by subsidiary's board of
directors ($600 × 0.60 = $360).

The working paper eliminations in the year of a passed cumulative preferred dividend would be the same as those illustrated on page 560, except that the minority interest in the subsidiary's preferred stock would be $240 ($600 × 0.40 = $240) larger because of the effect of the passed dividend. (Of course, no common dividend could be declared if the cumulative preferred dividend were passed.)

2 The net result of the foregoing journal entries and working paper eliminations is that the subsidiary's net income of $50,000 is allocated as follows:

Allocation of subsidiary's net income to preferred and common stockholders

	Total	Consolidated net income	Minority interest
To preferred stockholders: 10,000 shares × $0.06, in 60:40 ratio..................	$ 600	$ 360	$ 240
To common stockholders in 80:20 ratio...................	49,400	39,520	9,880
Net income of subsidiary........	$50,000	$39,880	$10,120

Other Types of Preferred Stock Treatment similar to that illustrated in the foregoing section is appropriate for the minority interest in a subsidiary having other types of outstanding preferred stock. If the preferred stock were *noncumulative,* there would be no parent company accrual of passed dividends. If the preferred stock were *participating* (which seldom is the case), the subsidiary's retained earnings would be allocated to the minority interests in preferred stock and common stock according to the terms of the *participation clause.*

STOCK DIVIDENDS DISTRIBUTED BY A SUBSIDIARY

If a parent company uses the equity method of accounting for the operating results of a subsidiary, the subsidiary's declaration and issuance of a common stock dividend has no effect on the parent's Investment in Subsidiary Common Stock ledger account. As emphasized in intermediate accounting textbooks, receipt of a stock dividend does not represent dividend revenue to the investor.

After the declaration of a common stock dividend not exceeding 20 to 25%, the subsidiary's retained earnings is reduced by an amount equal to the current fair value of the stock issued as a dividend. This reduction and the offsetting increase in the subsidiary's paid-in capital ledger accounts are incorporated in the working paper eliminations subsequent to the issuance of the stock dividend, and there is no specific elimination for the *stock dividend itself.* Thus, the amount of consolidated retained earnings is not affected by a subsidiary's stock dividend. As stated by the AICPA,[4]

> . . . the retained earnings in the consolidated financial statements should re-flect the accumulated earnings of the consolidated group not distributed to the shareholders of, or capitalized by, the parent company.

Illustration of Subsidiary Stock Dividend

On June 30, Year 5, the date of the pooling-type business combination of Pasco Corporation and its wholly owned subsidiary, Salvo Company, the working paper elimination (in journal entry format) was as follows:

Working paper elimination on date of pooling-type business combination with wholly owned subsidiary

PASCO CORPORATION AND SUBSIDIARY		
Working Paper Elimination		
June 30, Year 5		
(a) Common Stock, $1 par—Salvo	150,000	
Additional Paid-in Capital—Salvo	200,000	
Retained Earnings of Subsidiary—Pasco	250,000	
Investment in Salvo Company Common Stock—Pasco		600,000
To eliminate intercompany investment and related accounts for stockholders' equity of subsidiary on date of pooling-type business combination.		

On June 18, Year 6, Salvo distributed 15,000 shares of its $1 par common stock to Pasco as a 10% stock dividend. Salvo debited the Dividends Declared ledger account for $75,000, the current fair value of the common stock distributed as a dividend (15,000 × $5 = $75,000). Pasco prepared no journal entry for the stock dividend, but it did record the subsidiary's net income of $180,000 for the year ended June 30, Year 6, under the equity method of accounting as follows:

Parent company's equity-method journal entry to record net income of wholly owned pooled subsidiary

Investment in Salvo Company Common Stock	180,000	
Intercompany Investment Income		180,000
To record 100% of Salvo Company's net income for the year ended June 30, Year 6. (Income tax effects are disregarded.)		

On June 30, Year 6, the working paper elimination (in journal entry format) for Pasco Corporation and subsidiary is as shown on page 563.

In its closing entries on June 30, Year 6, as described in Chapter 7 (pages 316 to 317), Pasco credits its Retained Earnings of Subsidiary ledger account for $105,000, the amount of the undistributed earnings of the subsidiary ($180,000 − $75,000 = $105,000). This closing entry brings the balance of the account to $355,000

---

[4] *ARB No. 51,* "Consolidated Financial Statements," AICPA (New York: 1959), p. 46.

Working paper
elimination following
wholly owned
subsidiary's distribution
of a stock dividend

PASCO CORPORATION AND SUBSIDIARY
Working Paper Elimination
June 30, Year 6

(a) Common Stock, $1 par—Salvo ($150,000 + $15,000) 165,000

    Additional Paid-in Capital—Salvo ($200,000 + $60,000) 260,000

    Retained Earnings of Subsidiary—Pasco 250,000

    Intercompany Investment Income—Pasco 180,000

        Investment in Salvo Company Common Stock—

        Pasco ($600,000 + $180,000) 780,000

        Dividends Declared—Salvo 75,000

    To eliminate intercompany investment, related accounts for
stockholders' equity of subsidiary, and investment income
from subsidiary.

($250,000 + $105,000 = $355,000), which is the same as the after-closing balance of Salvo's Retained Earnings ledger account ($250,000 + $180,000 − $75,000 = $355,000). However, because $75,000 of Pasco's intercompany investment income is closed with the remainder of Pasco's net income to its Retained Earnings ledger account, consolidated retained earnings of Pasco Corporation and subsidiary includes $430,000 of earnings attributable to the subsidiary ($355,000 + $75,000 = $430,000).

TREASURY STOCK TRANSACTIONS OF A SUBSIDIARY

Treasury stock owned by a subsidiary on the date of a business combination is treated as *retired stock* in the preparation of consolidated financial statements because the treasury stock is not outstanding and thus was not acquired by the parent company. A working paper elimination is prepared to account for the ''retirement'' of the treasury stock by the *par* or *stated value method*, which is described in intermediate accounting textbooks.

Illustration of Treasury Stock Owned by Subsidiary on Date of Business Combination

Palance Corporation acquired all 49,000 shares of the outstanding common stock of Sizemore Company on March 1, Year 6, for $147,000, including direct out-of-pocket costs. Sizemore's stockholders' equity on that date was as follows:

Stockholders' equity of
subsidiary with treasury
stock on date of
purchase-type
business combination

Common stock, $1 par.	$ 50,000
Additional paid-in capital	25,000
Retained earnings.	50,000
Total paid-in capital and retained earnings	$125,000
Less: 1,000 shares of treasury stock, at cost	2,000
Total stockholders' equity	$123,000

On the date of the combination, the current fair values of Sizemore's identifiable net assets equaled their carrying amounts.

The working paper eliminations (in journal entry format) for Palance Corporation and subsidiary on March 1, Year 6, are as follows:

Working paper
eliminations on date of
purchase-type
business combination
with wholly owned
subsidiary having
treasury stock

PALANCE CORPORATION AND SUBSIDIARY
Working Paper Eliminations
March 1, Year 6

(a) Common Stock—Sizemore (1,000 × $1) 1,000
    Additional Paid-in Capital—Sizemore (1,000 × $0.50) 500
    Retained Earnings—Sizemore (1,000 × $0.50) 500
        Treasury Stock—Sizemore (1,000 × $2) 2,000
    To account for subsidiary's treasury stock as though it had been retired.

(b) Common Stock—Sizemore ($50,000 − $1,000) 49,000
    Additional Paid-in Capital—Sizemore ($25,000 − $500)...... 24,500
    Retained Earnings—Sizemore ($50,000 − $500)........... 49,500
    Goodwill—Sizemore ($147,000 − $123,000)............... 24,000
        Investment in Sizemore Company Common Stock—
        Palance 147,000
    To eliminate intercompany investment and equity accounts of subsidiary on date of business combination; and to allocate excess of cost over current fair values (and carrying amounts) of identifiable net assets acquired to goodwill.

In the first elimination, additional paid-in capital of the subsidiary is reduced by the pro rata portion ($25,000 ÷ 50,000 shares = $0.50 a share) applicable to the treasury stock. The remainder of the cost of the treasury stock is allocated to the subsidiary's retained earnings.

As indicated on page 542, if, subsequent to the date of a business combination, a subsidiary acquires for its treasury some or all of the shares of its common stock owned by minority stockholders, purchase accounting is applied, even if the business combination had been accounted for as a pooling of interests. Thus, in the working paper elimination that accounts for the treasury stock as though it had been retired, current fair value differences and goodwill may be recognized. [It should be emphasized that, in a *greenmail* (defined on page 184) acquisition of treasury stock, the excess of the cost of the treasury stock over its current fair value typically is recognized as an expense or a loss.[5]]

Illustration of Treasury Stock Acquired by Subsidiary Subsequent to Business Combination

On December 31, Year 1, Portola Corporation acquired 80% of the outstanding common stock of Stanley Company for $44,000, including direct out-of-pocket costs

---

[5] *FASB Technical Bulletin No. 85-6,* ''Accounting for a Purchase of Treasury Shares at a Price Significantly in Excess of the Current Market Price of the Shares . . . ,'' FASB (Stamford: 1985), p. 2.

of the business combination. Stanley's stockholders' equity on December 31, Year 1, was as follows, with current fair values of identifiable net assets equal to carrying amounts:

Stockholders' equity of subsidiary on date of purchase-type business combination

Common stock, $10 par..	$10,000
Additional paid-in capital	15,000
Retained earnings...	25,000
Total stockholders' equity	$50,000

For the year ended December 31, Year 2, Stanley declared dividends of $4,000 and had a net income of $10,000. Portola's investment ledger account appeared as follows on December 31, Year 2:

Investment ledger account of parent company one year subsequent to purchase-type business combination

Investment in Stanley Company Common Stock

Date	Explanation	Debit	Credit	Balance
Year 1				
Dec. 31	Acquisition of 800 shares	44,000		44,000 dr
Year 2				
Dec. 28	Dividends received: $4 a share ($4,000 × 0.80)		3,200	40,800 dr
31	Share of net income ($10,000 × 0.80)	8,000		48,800 dr
31	Amortization of goodwill ($4,000* ÷ 40)		100	48,700 dr

* $44,000 − ($50,000 × 0.80) = $4,000 goodwill

The working paper eliminations (in journal entry format) for Portola Corporation and subsidiary on December 31, Year 2, are as follows:

Working paper eliminations one year subsequent to purchase-type business combination involving partially owned subsidiary

PORTOLA CORPORATION AND SUBSIDIARY
Working Paper Eliminations
December 31, Year 2

(a) Common Stock, $10 par—Stanley	10,000	
Additional Paid-in Capital—Stanley	15,000	
Retained Earnings—Stanley.................................	25,000	
Intercompany Investment Income—Portola	8,000	
Goodwill (net)—Portola ($4,000 − $100)	3,900	
Investment in Stanley Company Common Stock— Portola...		48,700
Dividends Declared—Stanley		4,000
Minority Interest in Net Assets of Subsidiary ($10,000 − $800)		9,200

(continued)

PORTOLA CORPORATION AND SUBSIDIARY
Working Paper Eliminations (concluded)
December 31, Year 2

*To eliminate intercompany investment and equity accounts of subsidiary at **beginning of year**; to allocate excess of cost over current fair values (and carrying amounts) of identifiable net assets acquired to goodwill; and to establish minority interest in net assets of subsidiary at beginning of year ($50,000 × 0.20 = $10,000), less minority share of dividends declared by subsidiary during year ($4,000 × 0.20 = $800).*

(b) Minority Interest in Net Income of Subsidiary ($10,000 × 0.20) .	2,000	
Minority Interest in Net Assets of Subsidiary		2,000

To establish minority interest in subsidiary's net income for Year 2.

On January 2, Year 3, Stanley paid $7,400 (current fair value) to acquire 100 shares of its common stock from a minority stockholder. Stanley's journal entry to record the acquisition of treasury stock was as follows:

Subsidiary's journal entry for acquisition of treasury stock subsequent to business combination

Treasury Stock (100 × $74)	7,400	
Cash.		7,400

To record acquisition of common stock from a minority stockholder.

The $74 a share acquisition cost of the treasury stock exceeds the $56 a share ($11,200 ÷ 200 = $56) carrying amount of the minority interest in net assets of subsidiary by $18 ($74 − $56 = $18). Thus, assuming that the current fair values of Stanley's identifiable net assets were equal to their carrying amounts on January 2, Year 3, Stanley's acquisition of goodwill of $1,800 (100 × $18 = $1,800) is recognized in the first of the following working paper eliminations (in journal entry format) on that date:

Working paper eliminations following partially owned subsidiary's acquisition of treasury stock

---

PORTOLA CORPORATION AND SUBSIDIARY
Working Paper Eliminations
January 2, Year 3

(a) Common Stock, $10 par—Stanley (100 × $10).	1,000	
Additional Paid-in Capital—Stanley (100 × $15).	1,500	
Retained Earnings—Stanley (100 × $31).	3,100	
Goodwill—Stanley (100 × $18).	1,800	
Treasury Stock—Stanley		7,400

To account for subsidiary's treasury stock as though it had been retired.

(continued)

PORTOLA CORPORATION AND SUBSIDIARY
Working Paper Eliminations (concluded)
January 2, Year 3

(b) Common Stock, $10 par—Stanley ($10,000 − $1,000)....... 9,000
Additional Paid-in Capital—Stanley ($15,000 − $1,500)...... 13,500
Retained Earnings—Stanley ($25,000 + $10,000 − $4,000 −
$3,100 − $4,800)... 23,100
Retained Earnings of Subsidiary—Portola ($8,000 − $3,200).. 4,800
Goodwill (net)—Portola ($4,000 − $100) 3,900
Investment in Stanley Company Common Stock—
Portola 48,700
Minority Interest in Net Assets of Subsidiary
($11,200 − $5,600)............................... 5,600
To eliminate intercompany investment and equity accounts of
subsidiary; to allocate excess of cost over current fair values of
identifiable net assets acquired to goodwill; and to establish mi-
nority interest in net assets of subsidiary (100 × $56 = $5,600).

Assuming a 40-year economic life for the Stanley goodwill, for Year 3 and subsequent years Stanley prepares an end-of-period adjusting entry debiting Amortization Expense and crediting Treasury Stock $45 ($1,800 ÷ 40 = $45). The debits to Goodwill—Stanley and the credits to Treasury Stock—Stanley in working paper eliminations on December 31, Year 3, and subsequently thus will decrease $45 each year for 40 years.

INDIRECT SHAREHOLDINGS AND PARENT COMPANY'S COMMON STOCK OWNED BY A SUBSIDIARY

In the early history of business combinations resulting in parent company–subsidiary relationships, complex indirect or reciprocal shareholdings frequently were involved. *Indirect shareholdings* are those involving such relationships as one subsidiary and the parent company jointly owning a controlling interest in another subsidiary, or a subsidiary company itself being the parent company of its own subsidiary. *Reciprocal shareholdings* involve subsidiary ownership of shares of the parent company's common stock.

Indirect Shareholdings

Business combinations in recent years generally have been far less complex than those described above. There usually has been a single parent company and one or more subsidiaries, and indirect shareholdings have been the exception rather than the rule. Accountants faced with the problems of preparing a working paper for consolidated financial statements for parent company–subsidiary relationships involving indirect shareholdings must follow carefully the common stock ownership percentages and apply the equity method of accounting for the operating results of the various subsidiaries.

Illustration of Indirect Shareholdings   On December 31, Year 2, Placer Corporation acquired 160,000 shares (80%) of the outstanding common stock of Shabot Company for $476,240, and 36,000 shares (45%) of Sur Company's outstanding common stock for $182,000. Both amounts included direct out-of-pocket costs of the common stock acquisitions. On December 31, Year 2, Shabot owned 20,000 shares (25%) of Sur's outstanding common stock; accordingly, Placer acquired indirect control of Sur as well as direct control of Shabot in the business combination, as illustrated in the following diagram:

Illustration of indirect shareholdings

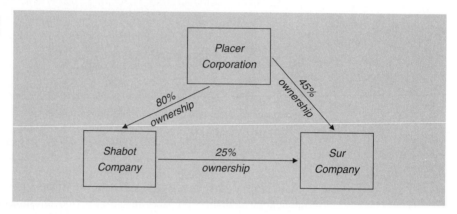

Separate balance sheets of Shabot and Sur on December 31, Year 2, prior to the business combination, follow:

SHABOT COMPANY AND SUR COMPANY
Separate Balance Sheets (prior to purchase-type business combination)
December 31, Year 2

Assets	Shabot Company	Sur Company
Current assets	$ 360,400	$190,600
Investment in Sur Company common stock	91,950	
Plant assets (net)	640,650	639,400
Total assets	$1,093,000	$830,000
Liabilities & Stockholders' Equity		
Current liabilities	$ 210,200	$ 80,500
Long-term debt	300,000	389,500
Common stock, $1 par	200,000	80,000
Additional paid-in capital	150,000	120,000
Retained earnings	222,850	160,000
Retained earnings of investee	9,950	
Total liabilities & stockholders' equity	$1,093,000	$830,000

Shabot's Investment in Sur Company Common Stock and Retained Earnings of Investee ledger accounts were as follows on December 31, Year 2:

Selected ledger accounts of subsidiary investor on date of purchase-type business combination

Investment in Sur Company Common Stock

Date	Explanation	Debit	Credit	Balance
Year 1				
Dec. 31	Acquisition of 20,000 shares	82,000		82,000 dr
Year 2				
Dec. 6	Dividends received: $0.25 a share		5,000	77,000 dr
31	Share of net income ($60,000 × 0.25)	15,000		92,000 dr
31	Amortization of goodwill ($2,000 ÷ 40)		50	91,950 dr

Retained Earnings of Investee

Date	Explanation	Debit	Credit	Balance
Year 2				
Dec. 31	Closing entry—share of Sur Company adjusted net income not paid as a dividend ($15,000 − $50 − $5,000)		9,950	9,950 cr

The foregoing ledger accounts of Shabot indicate that Shabot had applied the equity method of accounting for its investment in the influenced investee, Sur, and that the $2,000 excess of the cost of Shabot's investment over the underlying equity of Sur's identifiable net assets was allocated to goodwill having an economic life of 40 years.

The current fair values of the identifiable net assets of both Shabot and Sur equaled their carrying amounts on December 31, Year 2. Accordingly, goodwill acquired by Placer in the business combination with Shabot and Sur was measured as follows:

Computation of goodwill acquired by parent company

	Shabot Company	Sur Company
Cost of investment	$476,240	$182,000
Less: Current fair value of identifiable net assets acquired:		
Shabot ($582,800 × 0.80)	466,240	
Sur ($360,000 × 0.45).		162,000
Goodwill (economic life 40 years)	$ 10,000	$ 20,000

Working Paper for Consolidated Balance Sheet on Date of Business Combination The working paper for consolidated balance sheet of Placer Corporation and subsidiaries on December 31, Year 2, the date of the purchase-type business combination, and the related working paper eliminations (in journal entry format) are below and on page 571.

Partially owned subsidiaries on date of purchase-type business combination

PLACER CORPORATION AND SUBSIDIARIES
Working Paper for Consolidated Balance Sheet
December 31, Year 2

	Placer Corporation	Shabot Company	Sur Company	Eliminations increase (decrease)	Consolidated
Assets					
Current assets.........	1,400,000	360,400	190,600		1,951,000
Investment in Shabot Company common stock	476,240			(a) (476,240)	
Investment in Sur Company common stock........	182,000	91,950		{ (b) (91,950) ⎫ (b) (182,000) ⎬	
Plant assets (net)......	3,800,000	640,650	639,400		5,080,050
Goodwill				{ (a) 10,000 ⎫ (b) 21,950 ⎬	31,950
Total assets.........	5,858,240	1,093,000	830,000	(718,240)	7,063,000
Liabilities & Stockholders' Equity					
Current liabilities.......	600,000	210,200	80,500		890,700
Long-term debt........	3,000,000	300,000	389,500		3,689,500
Minority interest in net assets of subsidiaries........				{ (a) 116,560 ⎫ (b) 108,000 ⎬	224,560
Common stock $1 par	1,200,000	200,000	80,000	{ (a) (200,000) ⎫ (b) (80,000) ⎬	1,200,000
Additional paid-in capital..............	500,000	150,000	120,000	{ (a) (150,000) ⎫ (b) (120,000) ⎬	500,000
Retained earnings	558,240	222,850	160,000	{ (a) (222,850) ⎫ (b) (160,000) ⎬	558,240
Retained earnings of investee		9,950		(a) (9,950)	
Total liabilities & stockholders' equity........	5,858,240	1,093,000	830,000	(718,240)	7,063,000

The following two aspects of the working paper eliminations on page 571 warrant emphasis:

1   In elimination *(a)*, Shabot Company's retained earnings of investee amount on the date of the business combination is reduced to zero. Because Placer Corporation

Working paper
eliminations on date of
purchase-type
business combination
involving indirect
shareholdings

PLACER CORPORATION AND SUBSIDIARIES
Working Paper Eliminations
December 31, Year 2

(a) Common Stock, $1 par—Shabot 200,000
Additional Paid-in Capital—Shabot....................... 150,000
Retained Earnings—Shabot............................. 222,850
Retained Earnings of Investee—Shabot 9,950
Goodwill—Placer 10,000
    Investment in Shabot Company Common Stock—
      Placer.. 476,240
    Minority Interest in Net Assets of Subsidiaries
      ($582,800 × 0.20).............................. 116,560

To eliminate intercompany investment and equity accounts of Shabot Company on date of business combination; to allocate excess of cost over current fair values (and carrying amounts) of identifiable net assets acquired to goodwill; and to establish minority interest in net assets of Shabot on date of business combination.

(b) Common Stock, $1 par—Sur........................... 80,000
Additional Paid-in Capital—Sur.......................... 120,000
Retained Earnings—Sur................................ 160,000
Goodwill (net)—Placer ($1,950 + $20,000) 21,950
    Investment in Sur Company Common Stock—Placer . 182,000
    Investment in Sur Company Common Stock—Shabot 91,950
    Minority Interest in Net Assets of Subsidiaries
      ($360,000 × 0.30).............................. 108,000

To eliminate intercompany investments and equity accounts of Sur Company on date of business combination; to allocate excess of cost over current fair values (and carrying amounts) of identifiable net assets acquired to goodwill; and to establish minority interest in net assets of Sur on date of business combination.

is the parent company in the Placer–Shabot–Sur business combination, Shabot's ownership of 20,000 shares of Sur's outstanding common stock on the date of the combination is not construed as an installment acquisition by Placer; thus, consolidated retained earnings on the date of the combination does not include Shabot's share of Sur's retained earnings.

2 In elimination (b), both the $20,000 goodwill acquired by Placer (see page 569) and the goodwill implicit in Shabot's investment in Sur ($2,000 − $50 = $1,950) are included in consolidated goodwill, because the current fair values of Sur's identifiable net assets equaled their carrying amounts on the date of combination. The entire goodwill is attributable to Placer because of the existence of minority interests in both Shabot and Sur.

Working Paper Eliminations Subsequent to Business Combination   For the year ended December 31, Year 3, Shabot Company had an income of $150,000 (exclusive of investment income from Sur) and declared dividends of $60,000; Sur Company had a net income of $80,000 and declared dividends of $20,000. These operating results are recorded in the investment accounts of Placer and Shabot below and on page 573, under the equity method of accounting:

on page 573

Investment accounts of parent company and subsidiary one year subsequent to business combination

PLACER CORPORATION LEDGER
Investment in Shabot Company Common Stock

Date	Explanation	Debit	Credit	Balance
Year 2				
Dec. 31	Acquisition of 160,000 shares	476,240		476,240 dr
Year 3				
Dec. 6	Dividends received: $0.30 a share		48,000	428,240 dr
31	Share of net income [($150,000 + $20,000) × 0.80]	136,000		564,240 dr
31	Amortization of goodwill ($10,000 ÷ 40)		250	563,990 dr

Investment in Sur Company Common Stock

Date	Explanation	Debit	Credit	Balance
Year 2				
Dec. 31	Acquisition of 36,000 shares	182,000		182,000 dr
Year 3				
Dec. 6	Dividends received: $0.25 a share		9,000	173,000 dr
31	Share of net income ($80,000 × 0.45)	36,000		209,000 dr
31	Amortization of goodwill ($20,000 ÷ 40)		500	208,500 dr

SHABOT COMPANY LEDGER
Investment in Sur Company Common Stock

Date	Explanation	Debit	Credit	Balance
Year 1				
Dec. 31	Acquisition of 20,000 shares	82,000		82,000 dr
Year 2				
Dec. 6	Dividends received: $0.25 a share		5,000	77,000 dr

(continued)

SHABOT COMPANY LEDGER
Investment in Sur Company Common Stock (concluded)

Date	Explanation	Debit	Credit	Balance
Year 2				
Dec. 31	Share of net income ($60,000 × 0.25)	15,000		92,000 dr
31	Amortization of goodwill ($2,000 ÷ 40)		50	91,950 dr
Year 3				
Dec. 6	Dividends received: $0.25 a share		5,000	86,950 dr
31	Share of net income ($80,000 × 0.25)	20,000		106,950 dr
31	Amortization of goodwill ($2,000 ÷ 40)		50	106,900 dr

The working paper eliminations (in journal entry format) for Placer Corporation and subsidiaries on December 31, Year 3, are as follows:

Working paper eliminations for first year following purchase-type business combination involving indirect shareholdings

PLACER CORPORATION AND SUBSIDIARIES
Working Paper Eliminations
December 31, Year 3

(a) Common Stock, $1 par—Shabot	200,000	
Additional Paid-in Capital—Shabot	150,000	
Retained Earnings—Shabot	222,850	
Retained Earnings of Investee—Shabot	9,950	
Intercompany Investment Income—Placer	136,000	
Goodwill (net)—Placer ($10,000 − $250)	9,750	
Investment in Shabot Company Common Stock—		
Placer		563,990
Dividends Declared—Shabot		60,000
Minority Interest in Net Assets of Subsidiaries		
($116,560 − $12,000)		104,560

To eliminate intercompany investment and equity accounts of Shabot Company at **beginning of year**, and subsidiary dividends; to allocate unamortized excess of cost over current fair values of identifiable net assets to goodwill; and to establish minority interest in net assets of Shabot at beginning of year ($116,560), less dividends to minority stockholders ($60,000 × 0.20 = $12,000).

(continued)

PLACER CORPORATION AND SUBSIDIARIES
Working Paper Eliminations (concluded)
December 31, Year 3

(b) Common Stock, $1 par—Sur............................	80,000	
Additional Paid-in Capital—Sur.........................	120,000	
Retained Earnings—Sur................................	160,000	
Intercompany Investment Income—Placer.................	36,000	
Intercompany Investment Income—Shabot	20,000	
Goodwill (net)—Placer ($1,950 − $50 + $20,000 − $500) ..	21,400	
Investment in Sur Company Common Stock—Placer .		208,500
Investment in Sur Company Common Stock—Shabot		106,900
Dividends Declared—Sur.........................		20,000
Minority Interest in Net Assets of Subsidiaries		
($108,000 − $6,000)		102,000

To eliminate intercompany investment and equity accounts of Sur Company at **beginning of year,** and subsidiary dividends; to allocate unamortized excess of cost over current fair values of identifiable net assets to goodwill; and to establish minority interest in net assets of Sur at beginning of year ($108,000), less dividends to minority stockholders ($20,000 × 0.30 = $6,000).

(c) Minority Interest in Net Income of Subsidiaries		
[($170,000 × 0.20) + ($80,000 × 0.30)].................	58,000	
Minority Interest in Net Assets of Subsidiaries		58,000

To establish minority interest in subsidiaries' net income for Year 3.

Parent Company's Common Stock Owned by a Subsidiary

The traditional approach by accountants to problems of *reciprocal shareholdings* involved complex mathematical allocations of the individual affiliated companies' net income or loss to consolidated net income or loss and to minority interest. These allocations typically involved matrices or simultaneous equations.

Accountants have come to question the traditional approach to reciprocal shareholdings. The principal criticism is that strict application of mathematical allocations for reciprocal shareholdings violates the *going-concern* aspect of consolidated financial statements in favor of a *liquidation* approach. A related criticism is the emphasis of the traditional approach on *legal form* of the reciprocal shareholdings, rather than on *economic substance.* When a subsidiary acquires outstanding common stock of the parent company, it has been argued, the shares of parent company common stock owned by the subsidiary are in essence *treasury stock* to the consolidated entity. The treasury stock treatment for reciprocal shareholdings was sanctioned by the American Accounting Association and by the AICPA as follows:

Shares of the controlling company's capital stock owned by a subsidiary before the date of acquisition of control should be treated in consolidation as treasury stock. Any subsequent acquisition or sale by a subsidiary should likewise be treated in the consolidated statements as though it had been the act of the controlling company.[6]

Shares of the parent held by a subsidiary should not be treated as outstanding stock in the consolidated balance sheet.[7]

The author concurs with the view that a subsidiary's shareholdings of parent company common stock in essence are treasury stock to the consolidated entity. This position is analogous to that set forth in Chapter 9 for intercompany bondholdings. There, the point is made that a subsidiary acquiring the parent company's bonds payable in the open market is acting on behalf of the parent in the acquisition of the bonds for the consolidated entity's treasury.

To illustrate the accounting and working paper eliminations for parent company's common stock owned by a subsidiary, assume that on May 1, Year 7, the beginning of a fiscal year, Springer Company, the wholly owned subsidiary of Prospect Corporation, acquired for $50,000 in the open market 5,000 shares, or 5%, of the outstanding $1 par common stock of Prospect. On April 30, Year 8, Prospect declared and paid a cash dividend of $1.20 a share.

Springer prepares the following journal entries for its investment in Prospect's common stock, under the appropriate cost method of accounting:

Subsidiary's journal entries for investment in parent company's common stock			
Year 7			
May 1	Investment in Prospect Corporation Common Stock	50,000	
	Cash		50,000
	To record acquisition of 5,000 shares of parent company's outstanding common stock at $10 a share.		
Year 8			
Apr. 30	Cash	6,000	
	Intercompany Dividend Revenue		6,000
	To record dividend of $1.20 a share on 5,000 shares of parent company's common stock.		

The working paper eliminations (in journal entry format) for Prospect Corporation and subsidiary on April 30, Year 8, include those on page 576.

The effect of the second elimination is to remove the parent company dividends applicable to the consolidated treasury stock. The result is that, in the consolidated statement of retained earnings, dividends are in the amount of $114,000 ($120,000 − $6,000 = $114,000), representing the $1.20 a share dividend on

[6] *Accounting and Reporting Standards for Corporate Financial Statements,* "Consolidated Financial Statements," AAA (Madison: 1957), p. 44.
[7] *ARB No. 51,* p. 45.

Working paper
eliminations for parent
company common
stock owned by
subsidiary

PROSPECT CORPORATION AND SUBSIDIARY
Partial Working Paper Eliminations
April 30, Year 8

(b) Treasury Stock—Prospect   50,000
      Investment in Prospect Corporation Common Stock—
         Springer   50,000
      To transfer subsidiary's investment in parent company's com-
      mon stock to treasury stock category.

(c) Intercompany Dividend Revenue—Springer   6,000
      Dividends Declared—Prospect   6,000
      To eliminate parent company dividends received by subsidiary.

95,000 shares of parent company common stock that are outstanding from the view-point of the consolidated entity.

Concluding Comments on Special Problems

In this chapter are discussed a number of special problems that might arise in the preparation of consolidated financial statements. Not discussed are earnings per share computations for a consolidated entity, because in most circumstances the standards for earnings per share computations described in intermediate accounting textbooks apply to the computation of consolidated earnings per share. The problems that arise in earnings per share computations when a subsidiary has securities that are common stock equivalents or are otherwise *dilutive* are highly technical and too specialized to warrant inclusion in a discussion of basic concepts relating to consolidated financial statements.

REVIEW QUESTIONS

1 *APB Opinion No. 16,* "Business Combinations," requires use of the purchase method of accounting for a parent company's or a subsidiary's acquisition of all or part of the minority interest in net assets of the subsidiary, even though the business combination was a pooling-type combination. Discuss the reasoning in support of this requirement.

2 If a parent company acquires the minority interest in net assets of a subsidiary at less than carrying amount, what accounting treatment is appropriate for the difference? Explain.

3 Why does a parent company recognize a gain or a loss when a subsidiary issues common stock to the public at a price per share that differs from the carrying amount per share of the parent company's investment in the subsidiary's common stock? Explain.

4 Is a gain or a loss that is recognized by a parent company on the disposal of part of its investment in common stock of a subsidiary eliminated in the preparation of consolidated financial statements? Explain.

5 Explain how the minority interest in net assets of a subsidiary is affected by the parent company's ownership of 70% of the subsidiary's outstanding common stock and 60% of the subsidiary's outstanding 7%, cumulative, fully participating preferred stock.

6 Does the declaration of a stock dividend by a subsidiary necessitate any special treatment in working paper eliminations? Explain.

7 Describe how a subsidiary's ledger accounts are affected when it acquires for its treasury all or part of its outstanding common stock owned by minority stockholders.

8 ''The treasury stock treatment for shares of parent company common stock owned by a subsidiary overstates consolidated net income and understates the minority interest in net income of the subsidiary.'' Do you agree? Explain.

9 Shares of its common stock held by a corporation in its treasury are not entitled to dividends. However, a subsidiary receives dividends on shares of its parent company's common stock owned by the subsidiary. For consolidated financial statements, these parent company shares are considered equivalent to treasury stock of the consolidated entity. Is there an inconsistency in this treatment? Explain.

EXERCISES

Ex. 11-1 Select the best answer for each of the following multiple-choice questions:

1 If a parent company acquires for cash all the common stock owned by minority stockholders of a partially owned subsidiary, the excess of the cash paid over the minority interest in net assets of the subsidiary is recognized as:
a An expense in a parent company journal entry
b Goodwill in a working paper elimination
c An increase in the current fair values of the subsidiary's identifiable net assets in a working paper elimination
d A reduction of an additional paid-in capital ledger account balance in a parent company journal entry

2 Parsell Corporation disposed of a 20% interest in the outstanding common stock of its previously wholly owned subsidiary, Sorbell Company, on May 31, Year 4, to an outside entity at a substantial gain. A result of this event is:
a A decrease in consolidated goodwill of Parsell Corporation and subsidiary on May 31, Year 4
b The elimination of the gain in the working paper for consolidated financial statements of Parsell Corporation and subsidiary for the year ended May 31, Year 4
c An increase in minority interest in net income of subsidiary in the consolidated income statement of Parsell Corporation and subsidiary for the year ended May 31, Year 4
d All of the foregoing
e None of the foregoing

3 Is a parent company's gain on disposal of a portion of its investment in the subsidiary displayed as realized in the:

	Parent company's unconsolidated income statement?	Consolidated income statement of parent company and subsidiary?
a	Yes	Yes
b	Yes	No
c	No	Yes
d	No	No

4 The appropriate recording (explanation omitted) for a parent company to reflect the loss on its subsidiary's issuance of additional shares of common stock to the public is:

a A working paper elimination debiting Nonoperating Loss from Subsidiary's Issuance of Common Stock and crediting Investment in Subsidiary Company Common Stock

b A parent company journal entry debiting Nonoperating Loss from Subsidiary's Issuance of Common Stock and crediting Investment in Subsidiary Company Common Stock

c A subsidiary journal entry debiting an additional paid-in capital ledger account and crediting Payable to Parent Company

d A note to the consolidated financial statements only

5 If a parent company acquires additional shares of previously unissued common stock from its subsidiary, with minority stockholders of the subsidiary waiving their preemptive rights, a resultant gain or loss is:

a Recognized by the parent company and eliminated in the preparation of consolidated financial statements

b Recognized by the parent company and not eliminated in the preparation of consolidated financial statements

c Recognized by the subsidiary and eliminated in the preparation of consolidated financial statements

d Recognized in a working paper elimination for the preparation of consolidated financial statements.

6 A parent company realizes a gain or loss on its acquisition of additional common stock from a subsidiary, with the minority stockholders waiving their preemptive rights, because:

a The minority stockholders are *owners* under the economic unit concept.

b The minority stockholders are *creditors* under the parent company concept.

c The subsidiary will pay more dividends to the parent company subsequent to its acquisition of additional common stock of the subsidiary.

d The parent company will recognize more intercompany investment income or loss subsequent to its acquisition of additional common stock of the subsidiary.

7 Is a gain or loss *realized* by the parent company when a subsidiary issues additional shares of common stock to:

	The public?	The parent company?
a	No	No
b	No	Yes
c	Yes	No
d	Yes	Yes

8 The minority interest of preferred stockholders in the net assets of a partially owned purchased subsidiary preferably is measured by the preferred stock's

a Cash dividend per share

b Call price per share

c Liquidation preference per share

d Par or stated value per share

9 When a parent company acquires both preferred stock and common stock of the subsidiary in a business combination, goodwill recognized in the combination is computed based on:

a Cost allocated to preferred stock only

b Cost allocated to common stock only

c Cost allocated to both preferred stock and common stock

d Some other measure

10 Is goodwill attributable to the purchased subsidiary recognized in a working paper elimination for treasury stock of the subsidiary:

	Owned on the date of the business combination?	Acquired subsequent to the date of the business combination?
a	Yes	Yes
b	Yes	No
c	No	Yes
d	No	No

11 Treasury stock acquired by a subsidiary from minority stockholders of the subsidiary is accounted for in consolidated financial statements as:

a Treasury stock of the subsidiary

b Treasury stock of the parent company

c Treasury stock of the consolidated entity

d Retired stock of the subsidiary

12 Shares of the parent company's issued common stock that are owned by the subsidiary are treated in the consolidated balance sheet as being:

a Outstanding

b In the treasury

c Retired

d Part of the minority interest

Ex. 11-2 On March 31, Year 4, the consolidated balance sheet of Polberg Corporation and its 85%-owned subsidiary, Serrano Company, showed goodwill of $65,400 and minority interest in net assets of subsidiary of $22,800. On April 1, Year 4, Polberg paid $10,000 to minority stockholders who owned 500 of Serrano's 10,000 shares of issued common stock.

Prepare a working paper to compute goodwill and minority interest in net assets of subsidiary for display in the consolidated balance sheet of Polberg Corporation and subsidiary on April 1, Year 4.

Ex. 11-3 On January 2, Year 3, Prester Corporation organized Shire Company, paying $40,000 for 10,000 shares of Shire's $1 par common stock. On January 3, Year 3, before beginning operations, Shire issued 2,000 shares of its $1 par common stock to the public for net proceeds of $11,000; Prester did not exercise its preemptive right.

Prepare a working paper to compute the nonoperating gain or loss to Prester that resulted from Shire's issuance of common stock to the public.

Ex. 11-4   On October 31, Year 6, when the balance of Pinto Corporation's Investment in Sorrell Company Common Stock ledger account was $540,000 and the minority interest in net assets of subsidiary was $135,000, Sorrel Company, of whose 10,000 shares of outstanding common stock Pinto owned 8,000 shares, issued 2,000 shares of unissued common stock to Pinto at $72 a share. (Minority stockholders did not exercise their preemptive rights.) Prior to issuance of the 2,000 shares of common stock, the stockholders' equity of Sorrel, which had been organized by Pinto, totaled $675,000; after issuance of the 2,000 shares, Sorrel's stockholders' equity totaled $819,000.

a Prepare a three-column working paper to compute the nonoperating gain or loss to Pinto Corporation resulting from Sorrel Company's issuance of 2,000 shares of common stock to Pinto on October 31, Year 6. Use the following column headings: "Total," "Pinto's share," and "Minority's share."

b Prepare a journal entry for Pinto Corporation on October 31, Year 6, to record the nonoperating gain or loss resulting from Sorrel Company's issuance of 2,000 shares of common stock to Pinto.

Ex. 11-5   The stockholders' equity section of Stegg Company's August 31, Year 2, balance sheet was as follows:

8% cumulative preferred stock, $1 par, dividends in arrears two years, authorized, issued, and outstanding 100,000 shares, callable at $1.10 a share plus dividends in arrears	$ 100,000
Common stock, $2 par, authorized, issued, and outstanding 100,000 shares	200,000
Additional paid-in capital—common stock...........................	150,000
Retained earnings	750,000
Total stockholders' equity	$1,200,000

On August 31, Year 2, Panay Corporation acquired 50,000 shares of Stegg's outstanding preferred stock and 75,000 shares of Stegg's outstanding common stock for a total cost—including out-of-pocket costs—of $1,030,500. The current fair values of Stegg's identifiable net assets were equal to their carrying amounts on August 31, Year 2.

Answer the following questions (show supporting computations):

a What amount of the $1,030,500 total cost is assignable to Stegg's preferred stock?

b What is the minority interest of preferred stockholders in Stegg's net assets on August 31, Year 2?

c What is the amount of goodwill acquired by Panay August 31, Year 2?

d What is the minority interest of common stockholders in Stegg's net assets on August 31, Year 2?

Ex. 11-6   Simplex Company, the partially owned subsidiary of Polyglot Corporation, had a net income of $342,800 for the year ended May 31, Year 6. Simplex declared a dividend of $12 a share on its 10,000 shares of outstanding 12%, $100 par, cumulative preferred stock, and a dividend of $8 a share on its 80,000 shares of outstanding $1 par common stock. Polyglot owned 7,000 shares of preferred stock and 60,000 shares of common stock of Simplex. There were no dividends in arrears on the preferred stock.

Prepare a working paper (as on page 561) to show the allocation of Simplex Company's $342,800 net income for the year ended May 31, Year 6, to consolidated net income and to the minority interest in net income of subsidiary.

Ex. 11-7 On September 30, Year 6, prior to the declaration of a 15% stock dividend by its subsidiary, Sabro Company, on that date, Placard Corporation's accountant prepared the following tentative working paper elimination (in journal entry format):

(a) Common Stock, $2 par—Sabro............................	80,000	
Additional Paid-in Capital—Sabro.........................	40,000	
Retained Earnings—Sabro ($130,000 − $10,000)..........	120,000	
Retained Earnings of Subsidiary—Placard................	10,000	
Intercompany Investment Income—Placard................	70,000	
Goodwill—Sabro..	20,000	
Investment in Sabro Company Common Stock— Placard		340,000

To eliminate intercompany investment and equity accounts of subsidiary at **beginning of year,** and investment income from subsidiary; and to allocate excess of cost over current fair values (and carrying amounts) of identifiable net assets acquired to goodwill.

The current fair value of the dividend shares issued by Sabro was $5 a share. Placard had net sales of $840,200 and total costs and expenses of $668,500 for the year ended September 30, Year 6.

a Prepare a revised working paper elimination (in journal entry format) for Placard Corporation and subsidiary on September 30, Year 6, to reflect the effects of Sabro's stock dividend. Omit explanation, but show supporting computations.

b Prepare a single closing entry (foregoing use of the Income Summary ledger account) for Placard Corporation on September 30, Year 6. Omit explanation, but show supporting computations.

Ex. 11-8 On December 31, Year 4, the date of the purchase-type business combination between Portland Corporation and Salem Company, Salem had 50,000 shares of $5 par common stock authorized, 20,000 shares issued (total net issue proceeds were $160,000), and 500 shares in the treasury, with a total cost of $5,500. The balance of Salem's Retained Earnings ledger account was $240,000 on December 31, Year 4.

Prepare a working paper elimination (in journal entry format) for Portland Corporation and subsidiary on December 31, Year 4, to account for the subsidiary's treasury stock as though it had been retired.

Ex. 11-9 On February 28, Year 7, the stockholders' equity of Stocker Company was as follows:

Common stock, no par or stated value, 50,000 shares issued, 48,000	
shares outstanding	*$250,000*
Retained earnings	*600,000*
Total paid-in capital and retained earnings	*$850,000*
Less: 2,000 shares of treasury stock, at cost	*16,000*
Total stockholders' equity	*$834,000*

On February 28, Year 7, Priam Corporation paid $900,000 for all 48,000 shares of outstanding common stock of Stocker; on that date, current fair values of Stocker's identifiable net assets were equal to their carrying amounts. Out-of-pocket costs of the business combination may be disregarded.

Prepare working paper eliminations (in journal entry format; omit explanations) for Priam Corporation and subsidiary on February 28, Year 7.

Ex. 11-10   The stockholders' equity section of the balance sheet of Sergeant Company, the wholly owned, pooled subsidiary of Private Corporation, on May 31, Year 2, the date of the pooling-type business combination, was as follows:

Common stock, $10 par	*$100,000*
Additional paid-in capital	*50,000*
Retained earnings	*150,000*
Total paid-in capital and retained earnings	*$300,000*
Less: 500 shares of treasury stock, at cost	*7,500*
Total stockholders' equity	*$292,500*

Prepare working paper eliminations, in journal entry format (omit explanations), for Private Corporation and subsidiary on May 31, Year 2.

Ex. 11-11   The stockholders' equity of Sibley Company on February 28, Year 7, was as follows:

Common stock, no par or stated value, 100,000 shares authorized, 80,000	
shares issued	*$160,000*
Retained earnings	*640,000*
Total stockholders' equity	*$800,000*

On February 28, Year 7, Parson Corporation acquired 75,000 shares of Sibley's outstanding common stock for $790,000, including direct out-of-pocket costs of the business combination. Simultaneously, Sibley acquired for the treasury the remaining 5,000 shares of its outstanding common stock for $60,000, a fair price. The current fair values of Sibley's identifiable net assets were equal to their carrying amounts on February 28, Year 7.

Prepare working paper eliminations, in journal entry format (omit explanations), for Parson Corporation and subsidiary on February 28, Year 7.

Ex. 11-12 On January 2, Year 7, Prince Corporation organized Sabine Company with authorized common stock of 10,000 shares, $5 par. Prince acquired 4,000 shares of Sabine's common stock at $8 a share, and Samnite Company, a wholly owned subsidiary of Prince, acquired the 6,000 remaining authorized shares of Sabine's common stock at $8 a share. For the year ended December 31, Year 7, Sabine had a net income of $80,000 and declared dividends of $2 a share on December 28, Year 7, payable on January 25, Year 8.

Prepare journal entries under the equity method of accounting to record the operating results of Sabine Company for Year 7 in the accounting records of **(a)** Prince Corporation, and **(b)** Samnite Company. (Omit explanations; disregard income taxes.)

Ex. 11-13 During the year ended May 31, Year 4, Sugar Company, the wholly owned subsidiary of Peaches Corporation, prepared the following journal entries:

Year 3

June 1	Investment in Peaches Corporation Common Stock. . . .	100,000	
	Cash		100,000
	To record acquisition of 100 shares (1%) of parent company's outstanding common stock at $1,000 a share.		

Year 4

May 31	Cash	5,000	
	Intercompany Dividends Revenue		5,000
	To record dividend of $50 a share on 100 shares of parent company's common stock.		

Prepare working paper eliminations (in journal entry format, omitting explanations) for Peaches Corporation and subsidiary on May 31, Year 4.

Ex. 11-14 On August 1, Year 4, the beginning of a fiscal year, Pressman Corporation acquired 95% of the outstanding common stock of Sycamore Company in a pooling-type business combination. Among the intercompany transactions and events between Pressman and Sycamore subsequent to August 1, Year 4, were the following:

(1) On May 31, Year 5, Sycamore declared a 10% stock dividend on its 10,000 outstanding shares of $10 par common stock having a current fair value of $18 a share. The 1,000 shares of the stock dividend were issued June 18, Year 5.
(2) On July 28, Year 5, Sycamore acquired in the open market for $15,000, 1,000 of the 100,000 outstanding shares of Pressman's $1 par common stock. Pressman declared no dividends during the year ended July 31, Year 5.

Prepare working paper eliminations (in journal entry format) on July 31, Year 5, for Pressman Corporation and subsidiary, required for the foregoing intercompany transactions.

CASES

Case 11-1 Scarbo Company, a wholly owned subsidiary of Poller Corporation, was in need of additional long-term financing. Under instructions from Poller, which waived its preemptive right, Scarbo offered 5,000 shares of its previously unissued $2 par common stock to stockholders of Poller at a price of $10 a share. The offer was fully subscribed by Poller's stockholders, and the common stock was issued for $50,000 cash on June 30, Year 6.

After the common stock issuance, Poller owned 45,000 shares, or 90%, of the 50,000 outstanding shares of Scarbo common stock, and stockholders of Poller owned 5,000 shares, or 10%, of Scarbo's outstanding common stock. By comparing Poller's 90% interest in Scarbo's net assets after the common stock issuance with the parent company's 100% interest in the subsidiary's net assets before the stock issuance, Poller's accountant computed a $4,000 nonoperating gain for recognition in Poller's accounting records. The controller of Poller objected to the accountant's entry. The controller pointed out that the 5,000 shares of Scarbo common stock were issued to Poller's stockholders, not to outsiders, and that it is a basic accounting premise that a corporation does not profit from common stock issuances to its stockholders.

Instructions

Evaluate the objections of Poller Corporation's controller.

Case 11-2   Paragraph 43 of *APB Opinion No. 16*, "Business Combinations," reads in part as follows:

> The acquisition . . . of some or all of the stock held by minority stockholders of a subsidiary—whether acquired by the parent, *the subsidiary itself*, or another affiliate—should be accounted for by the purchase method. . . . [Emphasis added.]

Instructions

Given that the parent company may realize a nonoperating gain or loss when a subsidiary issues additional common stock to the public, with the parent and any present minority stockholders waiving their preemptive rights, is the accounting for a subsidiary's acquisition of all or part of minority stockholders' interest specified by the foregoing paragraph appropriate? Should the parent company recognize a gain or loss on such *shrinkages* of the subsidiary's outstanding common stock, as it does for *increases* therein? Explain.

PROBLEMS

Pr. 11-1   Scrip Company, the 80%-owned subsidiary of Pinch Corporation, had 10,000 shares of $5 par common stock outstanding on March 31, Year 5, the date of the Pinch–Scrip business combination, with total stockholders' equity of $300,000 and total paid-in capital equal in amount to retained earnings on that date. Goodwill in the amount of $40,000 (remaining economic life of 40 years) and minority interest in net assets of subsidiary of $60,000 were displayed in the consolidated balance sheet of Pinch Corporation and subsidiary on March 31, Year 5. The current fair values of Scrip's identifiable net assets equaled their carrying amounts on March 31, Year 5.

On April 1, Year 5, Pinch paid $44,000 (the current fair value) to a minority stockholder for 1,000 shares of Scrip common stock. For the year ended March 31, Year 6, Scrip had a net income of $90,000 and declared and paid dividends of $3 a share in March, Year 6.

Instructions

Prepare working paper eliminations (in journal entry format) for Pinch Corporation and subsidiary on March 31, Year 6. Pinch amortizes goodwill over a 40-year economic life. (Disregard income taxes.)

Pr. 11-2   On January 2, Year 6, Prime Corporation issued 50,000 shares of $10 par (current fair value $25 a share) common stock and paid $140,000 out-of-pocket costs for all the outstanding common stock of Showboat Company in a pooling-type business combination. On the date of the combination, Showboat's stockholders' equity consisted of the following:

Common stock, $1 par.	$400,000
Additional paid-in capital	300,000
Retained earnings.	250,000
Total paid-in capital and retained earnings	$950,000
Less: 20,000 shares of treasury stock, at cost	50,000
Total stockholders' equity	$900,000

On December 29, Year 6, Showboat declared a dividend of $0.10 a share, payable in Year 7. For the year ended December 31, Year 6, Showboat had a net income of $90,000.

Instructions

a Prepare journal entries for Prime Corporation to record the operating results of Showboat Company for Year 6, under the equity method of accounting. (Disregard income taxes.)

b Prepare working paper eliminations (in journal entry format) for Prime Corporation and subsidiary on December 31, Year 6. (Disregard income taxes.)

Pr. 11-3   The working paper eliminations (in journal entry format) for Pumble Corporation and its pooled subsidiary on October 31, Year 9, were as shown on page 586.

On November 1, Year 9, Salton issued 1,000 additional shares of $1 par common stock to Pumble for $20 a share (Salton's minority stockholders did not exercise their preemptive rights). (Out-of-pocket costs of the stock issuance may be disregarded.) On October 31, Year 10, Salton declared a dividend of $2 a share, and for the year ended October 31, Year 10, Salton had a net income of $35,000.

Instructions

a Prepare journal entries for Pumble Corporation to record the operating results of Salton Company for the year ended October 31, Year 10, under the equity method of accounting. Round Pumble's new percentage interest in Salton to two decimal places, and all dollar amounts to the nearest dollar. (Disregard income taxes.)

b Prepare working paper eliminations (in journal entry format) for Pumble Corpo-

PUMBLE CORPORATION AND SUBSIDIARY
Working Paper Eliminations
October 31, Year 9

(a) Common Stock—Salton 10,000

Additional Paid-in Capital—Salton 60,000

Retained Earnings—Salton ($80,000 × 0.02) 1,600

Retained Earnings of Subsidiary—Pumble ($80,000 × 0.98).. 78,400

Intercompany Investment Income—Pumble ($40,000 × 0.98). 39,200

Investment in Salton Company Common Stock—

Pumble ($180,000 × 0.98)   176,400

Dividends Declared—Salton   10,000

Minority Interest in Net Assets of Subsidiary

($3,000 − $200)   2,800

To eliminate intercompany investment and related accounts
for stockholders' equity of subsidiary at **beginning of year,**
and investment income from subsidiary; and to establish
minority interest in net assets of subsidiary at beginning of
year ($150,000 × 0.02 = $3,000), less minority dividends
($10,000 × 0.02 = $200).

(b) Minority Interest in Net Income of Subsidiary ($40,000 × 0.02)   800

Minority Interest in Net Assets of Subsidiary...........   800

To establish minority interest in net income of subsidiary for year
ended October 31, Year 9.

ration and subsidiary on October 31, Year 10. Round all amounts to the nearest
dollar. (Disregard income taxes.)

Pr. 11-4   On February 28, Year 5, the end of a fiscal year, the balance of Pronto Corporation's
Retained Earnings of Subsidiary ledger account (after closing) was $9,000, and the
balance of Pronto's Investment in Speedy Company Common Stock ledger account
was $75,000, which was analyzed as follows:

Share of identifiable net assets of Speedy (current fair values equaled carrying

amounts on date of business combination) ($100,000 × 0.60) $60,000

Goodwill (net) (20-year remaining economic life)..........................   15,000

Balance of Pronto's investment account, Feb. 28, Year 5 .... $75,000

The minority interest in net assets of subsidiary in the consolidated balance sheet
of Pronto Corporation and subsidiary on February 28, Year 5, was $40,000
($100,000 × 0.40 = $40,000). The stockholders' equity of Speedy Company on
February 28, Year 5, consisted of the following:

Common stock, $1 par.. $ 10,000

Additional paid-in capital   30,000

Retained earnings...   60,000

Total stockholders' equity $100,000

On March 1, Year 5, in order to reduce the minority interest in the net assets of Speedy Company, Pronto Corporation paid $32,000 to Speedy for 2,000 shares of Speedy's unissued common stock, thus increasing Pronto's ownership interest in Speedy to 66⅔% [(6,000 + 2,000) ÷ (10,000 + 2,000) = 66⅔%]. (The minority stockholders of Speedy did not exercise their preemptive rights.)

Instructions

a Prepare a journal entry for Speedy Company to record the issuance of 2,000 shares of common stock to Pronto Corporation on March 1, Year 5.

b Prepare a working paper to compute the balance of Pronto Corporation's Investment in Speedy Company Common Stock ledger account on March 1, Year 5, following the acquisition of 2,000 shares of Speedy's unissued common stock. (Include the nonoperating gain or loss resulting from Speedy's issuance of common stock to Pronto.)

c Prepare a working paper elimination (in journal entry format) for the consolidated balance sheet of Pronto Corporation and subsidiary on March 1, Year 5, following Speedy's issuance of 2,000 shares of common stock to Pronto. Disregard Speedy's operations for March 1, Year 5, and disregard income taxes.

Pr. 11-5 On October 31, Year 5, Pun Corporation acquired 80% of the outstanding common stock of Sim Company for $960,000, including goodwill of $80,000 having an economic life of 40 years. On that date, the carrying amount (equal to current fair value) of Sim's identifiable net assets was $1,100,000, represented by the following stockholders' equity:

Common stock, no par or stated value, 10,000 shares authorized, issued,	
and outstanding	*$ 500,000*
Retained earnings	*600,000*
Total stockholders' equity	*$1,100,000*

Additional Information

(1) For the year ended October 31, Year 6, Sim had a net income of $100,000 and declared and paid dividends of $40,000. Thus, the balance of Pun's Investment in Sim Company Common Stock ledger account under the equity method of accounting on October 31, Year 6, was $1,006,000, computed as follows:

Cost of 8,000 shares acquired Oct. 31, Year 5.		*$ 960,000*
Add: Share of net income ($100,000 × 0.80)		*80,000*
Subtotal		*$1,040,000*
Less: Share of dividends ($40,000 × 0.80)	*$32,000*	
Amortization of goodwill ($80,000 ÷ 40)	*2,000*	*34,000*
Balance, Oct. 31, Year 6		*$1,006,000*

(2) The after-closing balance of Pun's Retained Earnings of Subsidiary ledger account on October 31, Year 6, was $48,000 ($80,000 − $32,000 = $48,000).

(3) On November 1, Year 6, at Pun's direction, Sim paid $170,000 (the current fair

value) to a dissident minority stockholder for 1,000 shares of Sim's outstanding common stock, preparing the following journal entry:

Treasury Stock (1,000 × $170)............................ *170,000*

   Cash... *·.....*   *170,000*

To record acquisition of 1,000 shares of outstanding common

stock from a minority stockholder for the treasury.

The current fair values of Sim's identifiable net assets were the same as their carrying amounts on November 1, Year 6.

Instructions

Prepare working paper eliminations (in journal entry format) for Pun Corporation and subsidiary on November 1, Year 6, to account for Sim Company's treasury stock as though it had been retired and to eliminate the intercompany investment and equity accounts of the subsidiary. Disregard Sim's operations for November 1, Year 6, and disregard income taxes.

Pr. 11-6   Separate and consolidated financial statements of Peterson Corporation and its wholly owned subsidiary, Swanson Company, for the year ended May 31, Year 4, are on page 589. The two companies used intercompany ledger accounts only for receivables and payables.

Additional Information

(1) All of Swanson's identifiable net assets were fairly valued at their carrying amounts on May 31, Year 2—the date of the Peterson–Swanson business combination. Thus, the $50,000 excess of Peterson's investment in Swanson over the carrying amounts of Swanson's identifiable net assets was attributable to goodwill with an economic life of 40 years.

(2) During the year ended May 31, Year 4, Peterson sold merchandise to Swanson at Peterson's regular markup.

(3) Swanson had acquired 1,000 shares of Peterson's common stock on June 10, Year 3, and Peterson had acquired its treasury stock on May 26, Year 4.

Instructions

Reconstruct the working paper eliminations (in journal entry format) for Peterson Corporation and subsidiary on May 31, Year 4. (Disregard income taxes; omit explanations for eliminations.)

PETERSON CORPORATION AND SUBSIDIARY
Separate and Consolidated Financial Statements
For Year Ended May 31, Year 4

	Peterson Corporation	Swanson Company	Consolidated
Income Statements			
Revenue:			
Net sales	$10,000,000	$4,600,000	$12,900,000
Other revenue.	270,000	20,000	38,250
Total revenue	$10,270,000	$4,620,000	$12,938,250
Costs and expenses:			
Cost of goods sold.	$ 6,700,000	$3,082,000	$ 8,085,300
Operating expenses and income taxes expense	2,920,000	1,288,000	4,209,250
Total costs and expenses	$ 9,620,000	$4,370,000	$12,294,550
Net income.	$ 650,000	$ 250,000	$ 643,700
Statements of Retained Earnings			
Retained earnings, beginning of year	$ 2,420,000	$ 825,000	$ 2,529,300
Add: Net income.	650,000	250,000	643,700
Subtotals	$ 3,070,000	$1,075,000	$ 3,173,000
Less: Dividends	300,000	175,000	297,000
Retained earnings, end of year.	$ 2,770,000	$ 900,000	$ 2,876,000
Balance Sheets			
Assets			
Intercompany receivables (payables)	$ 520,000	$ (520,000)	
Short-term investments.	400,000	150,000	$ 530,000
Inventories.	1,100,000	610,000	1,693,500
Investment in Swanson Company common stock	1,097,500		
Other assets	2,800,000	1,370,000	4,170,000
Goodwill (net)			47,500
Total assets.	$ 5,917,500	$1,610,000	$ 6,441,000
Liabilities & Stockholders' Equity			
Liabilities	$ 2,075,000	$ 560,000	$ 2,635,000
Common stock, $10 par	1,000,000	150,000	1,000,000
Retained earnings	2,770,000	900,000	2,876,000
Retained earnings of subsidiary	122,500		
Treasury stock	(50,000)		(70,000)
Total liabilities & stockholders' equity	$ 5,917,500	$1,610,000	$ 6,441,000

Pr. 11-7   Separate financial statements of Pomerania Corporation and its two subsidiaries for the year ended December 31, Year 8, are on page 590.

POMERANIA CORPORATION AND SUBSIDIARIES
Separate Financial Statements
For Year Ended December 31, Year 8

	Pomerania Corporation	Slovakia Company	Sylvania Company
Income Statements			
Revenue:			
Net sales	$1,120,000	$900,000	$700,000
Intercompany sales.	140,000		
Intercompany investment income	44,000		
Total revenue	$1,304,000	$900,000	$700,000
Costs and expenses:			
Cost of goods sold.	$ 800,000	$650,000	$550,000
Intercompany cost of goods sold	100,000		
Operating expenses and income taxes expense	300,000	150,000	130,000
Total costs and expenses	$1,200,000	$800,000	$680,000
Net income	$ 104,000	$100,000	$ 20,000
Statements of Retained Earnings			
Retained earnings, beginning of year	$ 126,200	$107,000	$100,000
Add: Net income	104,000	100,000	20,000
Subtotals	$ 230,200	$207,000	$120,000
Less: Dividends	22,000	75,000	
Retained earnings, end of year.	$ 208,200	$132,000	$120,000
Balance Sheets			
Assets			
Intercompany receivables (payables)	$ 63,400	$ (41,000)	$ (22,400)
Inventories.	290,000	90,000	115,000
Investment in Slovakia Company common stock	305,600		
Investment in Slovakia Company bonds.	20,800		
Investment in Sylvania Company preferred stock	7,000		
Investment in Sylvania Company common stock	196,000		
Other assets	836,400	555,000	510,000
Total assets.	$1,719,200	$604,000	$602,600
Liabilities and Stockholders' Equity			
Dividends payable	$ 22,000	$ 6,000	
Bonds payable	285,000	125,000	$125,000
Intercompany bonds payable		25,000	
Discount on bonds payable.	(8,000)	(10,000)	
Discount on intercompany bonds payable		(2,000)	
Other liabilities	212,000	78,000	107,600
Preferred stock, $20 par.	400,000		50,000
Common stock, $10 par.	600,000	250,000	200,000
Retained earnings	208,200	132,000	120,000
Total liabilities & stockholders' equity	$1,719,200	$604,000	$602,600

Additional Information

(1) Pomerania Corporation's Investment in Slovakia Company Common Stock ledger account was as follows:

Investment in Slovakia Company Common Stock

Date	Explanation	Debit	Credit	Balance
Year 8				
Jan 2	Cost of 5,000 shares	71,400		71,400 dr
June 30	20% of dividend declared		9,000	62,400 dr
30	20% of net income for Jan. 2–			
	June 30	12,000		74,400 dr
July 1	Cost of 15,000 shares	223,200		297,600 dr
Dec. 31	80% of dividend declared		24,000	273,600 dr
31	80% of net income for July 1–			
	Dec. 31	32,000		305,600 dr

(2) The accountant for Pomerania made no equity-method journal entries for Pomerania's investments in Sylvania's preferred stock and common stock. Pomerania had acquired 250 shares of Sylvania's fully participating noncumulative preferred stock for $7,000 and 14,000 shares of Sylvania's common stock for $196,000 on January 2, Year 8. Out-of-pocket costs of the business combination may be disregarded.

(3) Sylvania's December 31, Year 8, inventories included $22,400 of merchandise purchased from Pomerania for which no payment had been made.

(4) Pomerania had acquired in the open market twenty-five $1,000 face amount 6% bonds of Slovakia for $20,800 on December 31, Year 8. The bonds had a December 31 interest payment date, and a maturity date of December 31, Year 10.

(5) Slovakia owed Pomerania $17,000 on December 31, Year 8, for a noninterest-bearing cash advance.

Instructions

a Prepare adjusting entries for Pomerania Corporation on December 31, Year 8, to account for the investments in Sylvania Company preferred stock and common stock under the equity method. (Disregard income taxes.)

b Prepare a working paper for consolidated financial statements and related working paper eliminations (in journal entry format) for Pomerania Corporation and subsidiaries on December 31, Year 8. (Disregard income taxes.)

Pr. 11-8 Plover Corporation acquired for $151,000, including direct out-of-pocket costs of the business combination, 100% of the common stock and 20% of the preferred stock of Starling Company on June 30, Year 1. On that date, Starling's retained earnings balance was $41,000. The current fair values of Starling's identifiable assets and liabilities and preferred stock were the same as their carrying amounts on June 30, Year 1.

The separate financial statements of Plover and Starling for the year ended December 31, Year 2, are on pages 592 and 593.

Transactions between Plover and Starling during the year ended December 31, Year 2, are on page 593.

PLOVER CORPORATION AND SUBSIDIARY
Separate Financial Statements
For Year Ended December 31, Year 2

	Plover Corporation	Starling Company
Income Statements		
Revenue:		
Net sales..	$1,562,000	
Intercompany sales	238,000	
Contract revenue		$1,210,000
Intercompany contract revenue.		79,000
Interest revenue	19,149	
Intercompany investment income	42,500	
Intercompany dividend revenue	500	
Intercompany gain on sale of land	4,000	
Intercompany interest revenue (expense).	851	(851)
Total revenue.	$1,867,000	$1,288,149
Costs and expenses:		
Cost of goods sold	$ 942,500	
Intercompany cost of goods sold.	212,500	
Cost of contract revenue.		$ 789,500
Intercompany cost of contract revenue		62,500
Operating expenses and income taxes expense.	497,000	360,000
Interest expense	49,000	31,149
Total costs and expenses.	$1,701,000	$1,243,149
Net income.	$ 166,000	$ 45,000
Statements of Retained Earnings		
Retained earnings, beginning of year.	$ 139,311	$ 49,500
Add: Net income	166,000	45,000
Subtotals.	$ 305,311	$ 94,500
Less: Dividends.		2,500
Retained earnings, end of year	$ 305,311	$ 92,000
Balance Sheets		
Assets		
Intercompany receivables (payables).	$ 35,811	$ 21,189
Costs and estimated earnings in excess of billings on uncompleted contracts.		30,100
Inventories	217,000	117,500
Investment in Starling Company preferred and common stock	202,000	
Land.	34,000	42,000
Other plant assets (net).	717,000	408,000
Other assets.	153,000	84,211
Total assets	$1,358,811	$ 703,000

(continued)

PLOVER CORPORATION AND SUBSIDIARY
Separate Financial Statements (concluded)
For Year Ended December 31, Year 2

Balance Sheets	Plover Corporation	Starling Company
Liabilities & Stockholders' Equity		
Dividends payable		$ 2,000
Mortgage notes payable	$ 592,000	389,000
Other liabilities.	203,000	70,000
5% noncumulative, nonparticipating preferred stock, $1 par		50,000
Common stock, no par or stated value	250,000	100,000
Retained earnings.	305,311	92,000
Retained earnings of subsidiary	8,500	
Total liabilities & stockholders' equity.	$1,358,811	$ 703,000

(1) On January 2, Year 2, Plover sold land with an $11,000 carrying amount to Starling for $15,000. Starling made a $3,000 down payment and signed an 8% mortgage note payable in 12 equal quarterly payments of $1,135, including interest, beginning March 31, Year 2. 8% was a fair interest rate.

(2) Starling produced equipment for Plover under two separate construction-type contracts. The first contract, which was for office equipment, was begun and completed during Year 2 at a cost to Starling of $17,500. Plover paid $22,000 cash for the equipment on April 17, Year 2. The second contract was begun on February 15, Year 2, but will not be completed until May of Year 3. Starling had incurred $45,000 costs under the second contract as of December 31, Year 2, and anticipated additional costs of $30,000 to complete the $95,000 contract. Starling accounts for all construction-type contracts under the percentage-of-completion method of accounting. Plover had made no journal entry in its accounting records for the uncompleted contract as of December 31, Year 2. Plover depreciates all its equipment by the straight-line method over a 10-year estimated economic life with no residual value, takes a half year's depreciation in the year of acquisition of plant assets, and includes depreciation in operating expenses.

(3) On December 1, Year 2, Starling declared a 5% cash dividend on its preferred stock, payable January 15, Year 3, to stockholders of record December 14, Year 2.

(4) Plover sold merchandise to Starling at an average markup of 12% of cost. During the year, Plover billed Starling $238,000 for merchandise shipped, for which Starling had paid $211,000 by December 31, Year 2. Starling had $11,200 of this merchandise on hand on December 31, Year 2.

Instructions

a Prepare an analysis of the Intercompany Receivables (Payables) ledger accounts of the affiliates on December 31, Year 2.

b Prepare adjusting entries for December 31, Year 2, based on your analysis in **a** above.

c Prepare a working paper for consolidated financial statements and related working paper eliminations (in journal entry format) for Plover Corporation and subsidiary for Year 2. Round all computations to the nearest dollar. The working paper should reflect the adjusting entries in **b**. (Disregard income taxes.)

Pr. 11-9 On February 1, Year 5, Pullard Corporation acquired all the outstanding common stock of Staley Company for $5,850,000, including direct out-of-pocket costs of the business combination, and 20% of Staley's preferred stock for $150,000. On the date of the combination, the carrying amounts and current fair values of Staley's identifiable assets and liabilities were as follows:

	Carrying amounts	Current fair values
Cash	$ 200,000	$ 200,000
Notes receivable	85,000	85,000
Trade accounts receivable (net)	980,000	980,000
Inventories	828,000	700,000
Land	1,560,000	2,100,000
Other plant assets	7,850,000	10,600,000
Accumulated depreciation	(3,250,000)	(4,000,000)
Other assets	140,000	50,000
Total assets	$ 8,393,000	$10,715,000
Notes payable	$ 115,000	$ 115,000
Trade accounts payable	400,000	400,000
7% bonds payable	5,000,000	5,000,000
Total liabilities	$ 5,515,000	$ 5,515,000
Preferred stock, noncumulative, nonparticipating, $5 par and call price per share, authorized, issued, and outstanding 150,000 shares	$ 750,000	
Common stock, $10 par, authorized, issued, and outstanding 100,000 shares	1,000,000	
Additional paid-in capital—common stock	122,000	
Retained earnings	1,006,000	
Total stockholders' equity	$ 2,878,000	
Total liabilities & stockholders' equity	$ 8,393,000	

Separate financial statements of Pullard and Staley for the period ended October 31, Year 5, are on page pages 595 and 596.

By the fiscal year-end, October 31, Year 5, the following transactions and events had taken place:

(1) The balance of Staley's net trade accounts receivable on February 1, Year 5, had been collected.
(2) Staley's inventories on February 1, Year 5, had been debited to cost of goods sold under the perpetual inventory system.
(3) Prior to February 1, Year 5, Pullard had acquired, at face amount, $1,500,000 of Staley's 7% bonds payable. The bonds mature on August 31, Year 11, with interest payable annually each August 31.
(4) As of February 1, Year 5, Staley's other plant assets had a composite remaining economic life of six years. Staley used the straight-line method of depreciation,

PULLARD CORPORATION AND STALEY COMPANY
Separate Financial Statements
For Period Ended October 31, Year 5

	Pullard Corporation (year ended 10/31/5)	Staley Company (9 months ended 10/31/5)
Income Statements		
Revenue:		
Net sales	$18,042,000	$ 5,530,000
Intercompany sales...........................	158,000	230,000
Intercompany investment income	505,150	
Interest revenue..............................	26,250	1,700
Intercompany interest revenue.................	78,750	
Total revenue.............................	$18,810,150	$ 5,761,700
Costs and expenses:		
Cost of goods sold	$10,442,000	$ 3,010,500
Intercompany cost of goods sold...............	158,000	149,500
Depreciation expense.........................	1,103,000	588,750
Operating expenses and income taxes expense ..	3,448,500	1,063,900
Interest expense	806,000	190,650
Intercompany interest expense		78,750
Total costs and expenses	$15,957,500	$ 5,082,050
Net income	$ 2,852,650	$ 679,650
Statements of Retained Earnings		
Retained earnings, beginning of period	$12,683,500	$ 1,006,000
Add: Net income	2,852,650	679,650
Retained earnings, end of period.................	$15,536,150	$ 1,685,650
Balance Sheets		
Assets		
Cash...	$ 822,000	$ 530,000
Notes receivable		85,000
Trade accounts receivable (net).................	2,723,700	1,346,400
Intercompany receivables	12,300	
Inventories...................................	3,204,000	1,182,000
Investment in Staley Company common stock......	6,355,150	
Investment in Staley Company preferred stock	150,000	
Investment in Staley Company bonds.............	1,500,000	
Land...	4,000,000	1,560,000
Other plant assets.............................	17,161,000	7,850,000
Accumulated depreciation	(6,673,000)	(3,838,750)
Other assets..................................	263,000	140,000
Total assets	$29,518,150	$ 8,854,650

(continued)

PULLARD CORPORATION AND STALEY COMPANY
Separate Financial Statements (concluded)
For Period Ended October 31, Year 5

	Pullard Corporation (year ended 10/31/5)	Staley Company (9 months ended 10/31/5)
Liabilities & Stockholders' Equity		
Notes payable		$ 115,000
Trade accounts payable.........................	$ 1,342,000	169,700
Intercompany payables		12,300
7% bonds payable...............................		3,500,000
Intercompany 7% bonds payable.................		1,500,000
Long-term debt.................................	10,000,000	
Preferred stock, $5 par..........................		750,000
Common stock, $10 par..........................	2,400,000	1,000,000
Additional paid-in capital	240,000	122,000
Retained earnings...............................	15,536,150	1,685,650
Total liabilities & stockholders' equity	$29,518,150	$ 8,854,650

with no residual value. Staley's depreciation expense for the nine months ended October 31, Year 5, was based on the former depreciation rates in effect prior to the business combination.

(5) The other assets consist entirely of long-term investments made by Staley and do not include any investment in Pullard.

(6) During the nine months ended October 31, Year 5, the following intercompany sales of merchandise had occurred:

	Pullard to Staley	Staley to Pullard
Net sales...	$158,000	$230,000
Included in purchaser's inventories, Oct. 31, Year 5.........	36,000	12,000
Balance unpaid, Oct. 31, Year 5	16,800	22,000

Pullard sold merchandise to Staley at cost. Staley sold merchandise to Pullard at selling prices that included a gross profit margin of 35%. There had been no intercompany sales prior to February 1, Year 5.

(7) Neither company had declared dividends during the period covered by the separate financial statements.

(8) Staley's goodwill recognized in the business combination was $1,400,000. The companies' policy is to amortize intangible assets over a 20-year economic life, and to include the amortization among operating expenses.

(9) The $505,150 balance of Pullard's Intercompany Investment Income ledger account is computed as follows:

Net income of Staley for nine months ended Oct. 31, Year 5		$679,650
Less: Amortization of differences between current fair values and carrying		
amounts of Staley's identifiable net assets on Feb. 1, Year 5:		
Inventories—to cost of goods sold	$(128,000)	
Other plant assets—depreciation {[($6,600,000 −		
$4,600,000) ÷ 6] × ¾}.	250,000	
Goodwill—amortization [($1,400,000 ÷ 20) × ¾].	52,500	174,500
Balance, Oct. 31, Year 5		$505,150

Instructions

Prepare a working paper for consolidated financial statements and related working paper eliminations (in journal entry format) for Pullard Corporation and subsidiary on October 31, Year 5. Round all computations to the nearest dollar. (Disregard income taxes.)

Part 3

Accounting for Nonbusiness Organizations

State and local governmental entities and nonprofit organizations, once an obscure area for issues of accounting theory and practice, have become prominent in recent years because of financial problems of some major cities and scandals associated with some charitable or religious organizations. The concern of taxpayers and others about the expenditures of state and local governments and accompanying taxes has made accountants aware of the necessity for more specific and logical accounting standards for governmental entities. Similarly, public concern about the many social problems that are the purview of nonprofit organizations—educational, health care, and other—has created a need for more rational accounting and more informative reporting for such organizations. The many features of nonprofit organizations that differentiate them from business enterprises necessitate the use of accounting and reporting standards that vary significantly from those applicable to business enterprises. The use of several accounting units—termed *funds*—for a single nonprofit organization and the issuance of a statement of activities rather than an income statement are only two of the unique features of accounting and reporting for nonprofit organizations.

12

Governmental Entities: General Fund

Collectively, governmental entities and nonprofit (or not-for-profit) organizations are known as *nonbusiness organizations.* The two types of nonbusiness organizations have several characteristics in common, as well as some differentiating features. Thus, it is convenient to discuss accounting principles for the two types of nonbusiness organizations in a single section of this book. Discussed in this chapter are the objectives of financial reporting for nonbusiness organizations, the nature of governmental entities, accounting standards for governmental entities, and the accounting for a governmental entity's general fund. Chapters 13 and 14 deal with accounting for other funds and account groups of a governmental entity. Accounting for nonprofit organizations is covered in Chapter 15.

OBJECTIVES OF FINANCIAL REPORTING FOR NONBUSINESS ORGANIZATIONS

For many years, neither the American Institute of Certified Public Accountants nor the Financial Accounting Standards Board gave attention to the accounting problems of nonbusiness organizations. Thus, the development of accounting principles for those organizations was left to other authorities and individual accountants. During the 1970s, a number of factors caused both the AICPA and the FASB to consider the need for a comprehensive body of accounting principles for nonbusiness organizations. Among these factors were the desperate financial condition of many U.S. cities and other local governmental entities and scandals associated with the fund-raising activities of a few nonprofit organizations.

   As a result of the factors described in the foregoing paragraph, the Financial Accounting Standards Board added financial reporting by nonbusiness organizations to the scope of its conceptual framework for financial accounting and reporting project, which is described in intermediate accounting textbooks. In *Statement of Financial Accounting Concepts No. 4,* "Objectives of Financial Reporting by Nonbusiness Organizations," the FASB developed the following objectives:[1]

---

[1] *Statement of Financial Accounting Concepts No. 4,* "Objectives of Financial Reporting by Nonbusiness Organizations," FASB (Stamford: 1980), pp. xiii–xiv.

1   Financial reporting by nonbusiness organizations should provide information that is useful to present and potential resource providers and other users in making rational decisions about the allocation of resources to those organizations.

2   Financial reporting should provide information to help present and potential resource providers and other users in assessing the services that a nonbusiness organization provides and its ability to continue to provide those services.

3   Financial reporting should provide information that is useful to present and potential resource providers and other users in assessing how managers of a nonbusiness organization have discharged their stewardship responsibilities and about other aspects of their performance.

4   Financial reporting should provide information about the economic resources, obligations, and net resources of an organization, and the effects of transactions, events, and circumstances that change resources and interests in those resources.

5   Financial reporting should provide information about the performance of an organization during a period. Periodic measurements of the changes in the amount and nature of the net resources of a nonbusiness organization and information about the service efforts and accomplishments of an organization together represent the information most useful in assessing its performance.

6   Financial reporting should provide information about how an organization obtains and spends cash or other liquid resources, about its borrowing and repayment of borrowing, and about other factors that may affect an organization's liquidity.

7   Financial reporting should include explanations and interpretations to help users understand financial information provided.

The Financial Accounting Standards Board stated that it was aware of no persuasive evidence that the seven objectives outlined in the foregoing section were inappropriate for general-purpose external financial reports of state and local governmental entities. However, the FASB deferred a final decision on the matter, pending resolution of the question of how accounting standards for state and local governmental entities should be established. The FASB explicitly recognized that accounting and reporting standards for the federal government were not addressed in *Statement of Financial Accounting Concepts No. 4.*[2] Furthermore, that *Statement* did not establish standards prescribing accounting procedures or disclosure practices for particular items or events, because such prescriptions are made by *Statements of Financial Accounting Standards.*

Shortly after its establishment (as described on page 604) the Governmental Accounting Standards Board issued *Concepts Statement No. 1,* ''Objectives of Financial Reporting,'' in which it established the following reporting objectives for *state and local* governmental entities:[3]

---

[2] Ibid., p. 2

[3] *Codification of Governmental Accounting and Financial Reporting Standards,* GASB (Norwalk: 1992), pp. 25–26.

a. Financial reporting should assist in fulfilling government's duty to be publicly accountable and should enable users to assess that accountability by:

(1) Providing information to determine whether current-year revenues were sufficient to pay for current-year services

(2) Demonstrating whether resources were obtained and used in accordance with the entity's legally adopted budget, and demonstrating compliance with other finance-related legal or contractual requirements

(3) Providing information to assist users in assessing the service efforts, costs, and accomplishments of the governmental entity

b. Financial reporting should assist users in evaluating the operating results of the governmental entity for the year by:

(1) Providing information about sources and uses of financial resources

(2) Providing information about how it financed its activities and met its cash requirements

(3) Providing information necessary to determine whether its financial position improved or deteriorated as a result of the year's operations

c. Financial reporting should assist users in assessing the level of services that can be provided by the governmental entity and its ability to meet its obligations as they become due by:

(1) Providing information about its financial position and condition

(2) Providing information about its physical and other nonfinancial resources having useful lives that extend beyond the current year, including information that can be used to assess the service potential of those resources

(3) Disclosing legal or contractual restrictions on resources and the risk of potential loss of resources.

NATURE OF GOVERNMENTAL ENTITIES

Students beginning the study of accounting for governmental entities temporarily must set aside many of the familiar accounting principles for business enterprises. Such fundamental concepts of accounting theory for business enterprises as the nature of the accounting entity and the primacy of the income statement have limited relevance in accounting for governmental entities. Consequently, the following discussion identifies the features of governmental entities that give rise to unique accounting concepts.

When thinking of governmental entities of the United States, one tends to focus on the federal government or on the governments of the 50 states. However, in addition to those major governmental entities and the governments of the several U.S. territories, there are the following governmental entities in the United States:[4]

---

[4] *Local Governmental Accounting Trends & Techniques—1990 Third Edition,* AICPA (New York: 1990), p. 1-1.

More than 3,000 counties

Nearly 17,000 townships

Over 19,000 municipalities

Nearly 15,000 school districts

Over 28,000 special districts (port authorities, airports, public buildings, libraries, and others)

Despite the wide range in size and scope of governance, the governmental entities listed above have a number of characteristics in common. Among these characteristics are the following:

1   *Organization to serve the citizenry.* A basic tenet of governmental philosophy in the United States is that governmental entities exist to serve the citizens subject to their jurisdiction. Thus, the citizens as a whole establish governmental entities through the constitutional and charter process. In contrast, business enterprises are created by only a limited number of individuals.

2   *General absence of the profit motive.* With few exceptions, governmental entities render services to the citizenry without the objective of profiting from those services. Business enterprises are motivated to earn profits.

3   *Taxation as the principal source of revenue.* The citizens subject to a governmental entity's jurisdiction provide resources to the governmental entity principally through taxation. Many of these taxes are paid on a self-assessment basis. There is no comparable revenue source for business enterprises.

4   *Impact of the legislative process.* Operations of governmental entities are for the most part initiated by various legislative enactments, such as operating budgets, borrowing authorizations, and tax levies. Business enterprises also are affected by federal, state, and local laws and regulations, but not to such a direct extent.

5   *Stewardship for resources.* A primary responsibility of governmental entities in financial reporting is to demonstrate adequate stewardship for resources provided by their citizenry. Business enterprises have a comparable responsibility to their owners, but not to the same extent as governmental entities.

The five foregoing characteristics of governmental entities are major determinants of accounting standards for such entities.

ACCOUNTING STANDARDS FOR GOVERNMENTAL ENTITIES

For many years, accounting standards for governmental entities were established by the National Council on Governmental Accounting, a 21-member organization composed primarily of local, state, and national finance officers, including two Canadian finance officers. In 1984, the Governmental Accounting Standards Board (GASB) was established as an arm of the Financial Accounting Foundation, which also oversees the Financial Accounting Standards Board. The GASB issues *Statements of Governmental Accounting Standards* for financial accounting and reporting of state and local governmental entities.

One of the first acts of the GASB was to codify governmental accounting and financial reporting standards in effect in 1984. Subsequently, the GASB issued a number of *Statements* that superseded, modified, or supplemented the standards set forth in the *Codification;* and the *Codification* was frequently revised.[5] In this chapter and in Chapters 13 and 14, I discuss and illustrate many of the governmental accounting and financial reporting standards currently in effect.

The Governmental Financial Reporting Entity

A significant question to be resolved in accounting for governmental entities is what agencies, institutions, commissions, public authorities, or other governmental organizations are to constitute the *financial reporting entity* for a governmental entity. The *Codification* provided that the governmental financial reporting entity was to consist of the following:[6]

(1) The *primary government*—a state government, a municipality or county, or a special-purpose government such as a school district or a park district meeting specified criteria

(2) Organizations for which the primary government is *financially accountable* by reason of appointing a voting majority of the governing bodies and thus either imposing its will on the organizations or being responsible to provide financial benefits to, or financial burdens on, the organizations

(3) Other organizations whose relationship with the primary government necessitates their inclusion in the financial reporting entity

The organizations described in (2) and (3) above are termed *component units.* The *Codification* provided several nonauthoritative illustrative examples of governmental financial reporting entities.[7]

Funds: The Accounting Unit for Governmental Entities

Accounting for business enterprises emphasizes the economic entity as an accounting unit. Thus, a partnership is considered to be an accounting entity separate from the partners; and consolidated financial statements are issued for a group of affiliated—but legally separate—corporations that comprise a single economic entity under common control.

There is generally no single accounting entity for a specific governmental entity, such as a city or a county. Instead, *the accounting unit for governmental entities is the fund.* The *Codification* defined *fund* as follows:[8]

---

[5] *Codification of Governmental Accounting and Financial Reporting Standards.*
[6] Ibid., pp. A-106 and A-107, A-109, and A-110.
[7] Ibid., pp. A-143 through A-155.
[8] Ibid., pp. 33.

Governmental accounting systems should be organized and operated on a fund basis. A *fund* is defined as a fiscal and accounting entity with a self-balancing set of accounts recording cash and other financial resources, together with all related liabilities and residual equities or balances, and changes therein, which are segregated for the purpose of carrying on specific activities or attaining certain objectives in accordance with special regulations, restrictions, or limitations. [Emphasis added.]

The ***Codification*** identified seven types of funds and two account groups, as follows:[9]

Governmental Funds:

1   *The General Fund*—to account for all financial resources except those required to be accounted for in another fund.

2   *Special Revenue Funds*—to account for the proceeds of specific revenue sources (other than expendable trusts or for major capital projects) that are legally restricted to expenditure for specified purposes.

3   *Capital Projects Funds*—to account for financial resources to be used for the acquisition or construction of major capital facilities (other than those financed by proprietary funds and trust funds).

4   *Debt Service Funds*—to account for the accumulation of resources for, and the payment of, general long-term debt principal and interest.

Proprietary Funds:

1   *Enterprise Funds*—to account for operations *(a)* that are financed and operated in a manner similar to private business enterprises—where the intent of the governing body is that the costs (expenses, including depreciation) of providing goods or services to the general public on a continuing basis be financed or recovered primarily through user charges; or *(b)* where the governing body has decided that periodic determination of revenues earned, expenses incurred, and/or net income is appropriate for capital maintenance, public policy, management control, accountability, or other purposes.

2   *Internal Service Funds*—to account for the financing of goods or services provided by one department or agency to other departments or agencies of the governmental entity, or to other governmental entities, on a cost-reimbursement basis.

Fiduciary Funds:

1   *Trust and Agency Funds*—to account for assets held by a governmental entity in a trustee capacity or as an agent for individuals, private organizations, other governmental entities, and/or other funds. These include *(a)* expendable trust funds, *(b)* nonexpendable trust funds, *(c)* pension trust funds, and *(d)* agency funds.

---

[9] Ibid., pp. 33–35.

Account Groups:

1 *The General Fixed Assets Account Group*—Fixed assets related to specific proprietary funds or trust funds should be accounted for through those funds. All other fixed assets of a governmental entity should be accounted for through the general fixed assets account group.

2 *The General Long-Term Debt Account Group*—Long-term liabilities of proprietary funds and trust funds should be accounted for through those funds. All other unmatured general long-term liabilities of the governmental entity, including special assessment debt for which the government is obligated in some manner, should be accounted for through the general long-term debt account group.

The *governmental funds* account for financial resources of a governmental entity that are used in day-to-day operations. The *proprietary funds* carry out governmental entity activities that closely resemble the operations of a business enterprise. *Fiduciary funds* account for resources that are not *owned* by a governmental entity, but are administered by the entity as a *custodian* or *fiduciary.* The two *account groups* are not funds; they are *memorandum records* of the governmental entity's plant assets and long-term liabilities, respectively, that are not recorded in a fund.

Every governmental entity has a general fund and the two account groups. According to the *Codification,* any additional funds should be established as required by law and sound financial administration.[10] Accounting for the general fund is discussed in subsequent sections of this chapter; accounting for other funds and the account groups is explained in Chapters 13 and 14. At this point, it is appropriate to emphasize that a governmental entity *does not have a single accounting unit* to account for its financial resources, obligations, revenues, and expenditures.

The Accrual Basis of Accounting

In the past, the governmental funds and expendable trust funds of a governmental entity used a *modified accrual basis of accounting,* in which revenues were recognized only when they became both *measurable* and *available* to finance expenditures of a fiscal period. Expenditures were recognized when the related liabilities were incurred, and short-term prepayments were not recognized as assets. The conventional accrual basis of accounting was used for other funds.

In *GASB Statement No. 11,* "Measurement Focus and Basis of Accounting—Governmental Fund Operating Statements," the Governmental Accounting Standards Board adopted the accrual basis of accounting for revenues and expenditures of governmental funds and expendable trust funds, effective for fiscal years ended after June 15, 1994.[11] Later, that effective date was postponed indefinitely. Nonetheless, because the provisions of *GASB Statement No. 11* reportedly have been adopted by some governmental entities, they are described and illustrated in the following sections of this chapter.

The accrual basis of accounting was to be applied as outlined in the following sections.

---

[10] Ibid., p. 34.
[11] Ibid., p. A-62.

Revenues Recognition   Revenues of governmental funds arise from taxation; other nonexchange transactions such as fines, licenses and permits fees, and donations; and exchange transactions such as charges for services, investments, and operating leases.[12]

Revenues from taxation—sales taxes, income taxes, property taxes, and the like—are recognized with a related receivable when the underlying transaction or event has taken place and the government has demanded the taxes by a due date on or before the fiscal year-end, or, for taxpayer-assessed taxes such as income taxes, within two months after the end of the period. Revenues from fines are recognized when the fines become enforceable. Accruals for taxes include *delinquent* taxes not received when due and *current final settlements* resulting from taxpayer audits.[13]

Revenues from licenses and permits fees generally are recognized when received in cash, assuming the fees are not refundable. Revenues from donations are recognized when the governmental entity has an enforceable claim and it is probable that the donations will be received.[14]

Revenues from exchange transactions, such as charges for services, investments in securities, and operating leases of governmental property, are recognized when earned, as for business enterprises.[15]

Expenditures Recognition   Because governmental funds of governmental entities are nonbusiness units, they account for *expenditures* of financial resources rather than *expenses matched against revenues.* In addition to *operating expenditures* for transactions and events of a day-to-day nature, such as salaries and wages, utilities, *consumption* of short-term prepayment assets and supplies inventories, and fees of independent contractors, *capital expenditures* for plant assets and *debt service expenditures* for interest on *operating debt* such as short-term loans are recognized on the accrual basis by governmental funds.[16]

Recording the Budget

The *Codification* provided the following statement regarding budgets of governmental entities:[17]

(1)   An annual budget(s) should be adopted by every governmental entity.

(2)   The accounting system should provide the basis for appropriate budgetary control.

(3)   A common terminology and classification should be used consistently throughout the budget, the accounts, and the financial reports of each fund.

Budgets are key elements of legislative control over governmental entities. The executive branch of a governmental entity proposes the budgets; the legislative

---

[12] Ibid., p. A-63.
[13] Ibid., pp. A-64, A-65, and A-70.
[14] Ibid., pp. A-70 and A-71.
[15] Ibid., pp. A-72 and A-73.
[16] Ibid., pp. A-75, A-76, A-78, and A-83.
[17] Ibid., p. 75.

branch reviews, modifies, and enacts the budgets; and finally the executive branch approves the budgets and carries out their provisions.

The two basic classifications of budgets for governmental entities are the same as those for business enterprises—annual budgets and long-term or capital budgets. *Annual budgets* include the *estimated revenues* and *appropriations* for expenditures for a specific fiscal year of the governmental entity. Annual budgets are appropriate for the general fund and special revenue funds; they sometimes are used for other governmental funds. An expendable trust fund also may have an annual budget, depending on the terms of the *trust indenture. Capital budgets,* which are used to control the expenditures for construction projects or other plant asset acquisitions, may be appropriate for capital projects funds. The annual or capital budgets often are recorded in the accounts of all these funds, to aid in accounting for compliance with legislative authorizations.

The operations of the two proprietary funds (enterprise funds and internal service funds) are similar to those of business enterprises. Consequently, annual budgets are used by these funds as a managerial planning and control device *rather than as a legislative control tool.* Thus, annual budgets of enterprise funds and internal service funds generally *are not recorded in ledger accounts by those funds.*

Types of Annual Budgets   One or more of three types of annual budgets may be used by a governmental entity.[18] An *object budget* emphasizes, by department, the *object* of each authorized expenditure. For example, under the legislative activity of the general government function, the object budget may include authorized expenditures for salaries, services, supplies, and equipment.

A *program budget* stresses measurement of total cost of a specific governmental entity *program,* regardless of how many departments of the governmental entity are involved in the program. Object of expenditure information is of secondary importance in a program budget.

In a *performance budget,* there is an attempt to relate the input of governmental resources to the output of governmental services. For example, the total estimated expenditures of the enforcement section of the taxation department might be compared with the aggregate collections of additional tax assessments budgeted for the fiscal year.

Regardless of which types of annual budgets are used by a governmental entity, the final annual budget adopted by the governmental entity's legislative body will include *estimated revenues* for the fiscal year and the *appropriations* for expenditures authorized for that year. If the estimated revenues of the budget exceed appropriations (as required by law for many governmental entities), there will be a *budgetary surplus;* if appropriations exceed estimated revenues, there will be a *budgetary deficit* in the *deficit budget.*

Journal Entry for a General Fund Budget   To illustrate the recording of an annual budget in the accounts of a general fund, assume that the Town of Verdant Glen in June, Year 5, adopted the following condensed annual budget for its General Fund for the fiscal year ending June 30, Year 6:

---

[18] *Audit and Accounting Guide,* ''Audits of State and Local Governmental Units,'' AICPA (New York: 1986), p. 51.

Budget of general fund of a governmental entity	Estimated revenues:		
	General property taxes		$700,000
	Other		140,000
	Total estimated revenues		$840,000
	Add: Estimated other financing sources (transfer from Enterprise Fund)...		10,000
	Subtotal		$850,000
	Less: Appropriations:		
	General government.	$470,000	
	Other	340,000	
	Total appropriations	$810,000	
	Estimated other financing uses (transfer to Debt Service Fund)	10,000	820,000
	Excess of estimated revenues and other financing sources over appropriations and other financing uses (budgetary surplus)		$ 30,000

The journal entry to record the annual budget on July 1, Year 5, follows:

Journal entry for budget of general fund of a governmental entity	Estimated Revenues	840,000	
	Estimated Other Financing Sources.	10,000	
	Appropriations.		810,000
	Estimated Other Financing Uses		10,000
	Budgetary Fund Balance		30,000
	To record annual budget adopted for fiscal year ending June 30, Year 6.		

An analysis of each of the ledger accounts in the foregoing journal entry follows:

1 The Estimated Revenues and Estimated Other Financing Sources ledger accounts may be considered *pseudo asset* controlling accounts because they reflect resources expected to be received by the General Fund during the fiscal year. These accounts are not actual assets, because they do not fit the accounting definition of an asset as a probable economic benefit obtained or controlled by a particular entity as a result of past transactions or events.[19] Thus, the two accounts in substance are *memorandum accounts,* useful for control purposes only, that *will be closed after the issuance of financial statements* for the General Fund for the fiscal year ending June 30, Year 6.

2 The Estimated Other Financing Sources ledger account includes the budgeted amounts of such items as proceeds from the disposal of plant assets (which also may be recognized as revenue) and *operating transfers in* from other funds.

3 The Appropriations and Estimated Other Financing Uses ledger accounts may

---

[19] *Statement of Financial Accounting Concepts No. 6,* "Elements of Financial Statements," FASB (Stamford: 1985), p. 10.

be considered *pseudo liability* controlling accounts because they reflect the legislative body's *commitments* to expend General Fund resources as authorized in the annual budget. These accounts are not genuine liabilities because they do not fit the definition of a liability as a probable future sacrifice of economic benefits arising from present obligations of a particular entity to transfer assets or provide services to other entities in the future as a result of past transactions or events.[20] The Appropriations and Estimated Other Financing Uses accounts are *memorandum accounts,* useful for control purposes only, that *will be closed after issuance of year-end financial statements* for the General Fund.

4   The Estimated Other Financing Uses account includes budgeted amounts of *operating transfers out* to other funds, which are not expenditures.

5   The Budgetary Fund Balance ledger account, as its title implies, is an account that balances the debit and credit entries to accounts of a *budget journal entry.* Although similar to the owners' equity accounts of a business enterprise in this balancing feature, the Budgetary Fund Balance account does not purport to show an ownership interest in a general fund's assets. At the end of the fiscal year, the Budgetary Fund Balance account is closed by a *journal entry that reverses the original entry for the budget.*

The journal entry to record the Town of Verdant Glen General Fund's annual budget for the year ending June 30, Year 6, is accompanied by detailed entries to subsidiary ledgers for estimated revenues, estimated other financing sources, appropriations, and estimated other financing uses. The budget of the Town of Verdant Glen General Fund purposely was condensed; in practice, the general fund's estimated revenues and appropriations would be detailed by source and function, respectively, into one or more of the following widely used subsidiary ledger categories:

Estimated revenues:	Appropriations:
Taxes	General government
Licenses and permits	Public safety
Intergovernmental revenues	Public works
Charges for services	Health and welfare
Fines and forfeits	Culture — recreation
Miscellaneous	Conservation of natural resources
	Debt service
	Intergovernmental expenditures
	Miscellaneous

In summary, budgets of a governmental entity often are recorded in the accounts of the four governmental funds. An expendable trust fund also may record a budget if required to do so by the trust indenture. *The recording of the budget initiates the accounting cycle for each of the funds listed above.* Recording the budget also facilitates the preparation of financial statements that compare actual amounts of revenues and expenditures with amounts budgeted therefore.

---

[20] Ibid., p. 13.

Encumbrances and Budgetary Control   Because of the need for the expenditures of governmental entities to be in accord with appropriations of governing legislative bodies, an *encumbrance* accounting technique is used for the general fund and special revenue funds and often for capital projects funds. When a purchase order for goods or services is issued to a supplier by one of those funds, a journal entry similar to the following is prepared for the fund:

Journal entry for encumbrances

Encumbrances.   18,413
*   Fund Balance Reserved for Encumbrances. 18,413*
To record encumbrance for purchase order No. 1685 issued to Wilson Company.

When the supplier's invoice for the ordered merchandise or services is received by the governmental entity, it is recorded and the related encumbrance is reversed as illustrated below:

Journal entries for receipt of invoice and reversal of encumbrance

Expenditures   18,507
*   Vouchers Payable 18,507*
To record invoice No. 348J received from Wilson Company under purchase order No. 1685.

Fund Balance Reserved for Encumbrances   18,413
*   Encumbrances 18,413*
To reverse encumbrance for purchase order No. 1685 issued to Wilson Company.

As indicated by the example above, the invoice amount may differ from the amount of the governmental entity's purchase order because of such items as shipping charges, sales taxes, and price changes.

The controls inherent in the encumbrance technique may be illustrated by assuming, with respect to the foregoing journal entries, that they applied to a purchase order for supplies (not available from the governmental entity's internal service fund) for the general government, the fiscal year appropriation for which totaled $85,000. The subsidiary ledger record for general government supplies would include the information on page 613 (dates are assumed). The posting of the $18,413 encumbrance on July 2 reduces the balance of the appropriation by that amount and protects against the issuance of one or more purchase orders in excess of the unexpended, unencumbered balance of $66,587. Receipt of the invoice for $18,507 and reversal of the related encumbrance of $18,413 reduces the unexpended, unencumbered balance by $94 ($18,507 − $18,413 = $94).

Thus, the encumbrance technique is a memorandum method for assuring that total expenditures for a fiscal year do not exceed appropriations. Encumbrance journal entries *are not necessary for normal recurring expenditures such as salaries and wages, utilities, and rent.* The encumbrance technique used in accounting for governmental entities has no counterpart in accounting for business enterprises.

Subsidiary ledger
account for supplies

			General Government—Supplies		
Date		**Appropriation credit**	**Encumbrance debit**	**Expenditure debit**	**Unexpended, unencumbered balance, credit**
Year 9					
July 1	Budgeted appropriation	85,000			85,000
2	P.O. 1685 to Wilson Company		18,413		66,587
6	Inv. 348J from Wilson Company		(18,413)	18,507	66,493

ACCOUNTING FOR A GOVERNMENTAL ENTITY'S GENERAL FUND

As indicated on page 606, a general fund is used to account for all transactions and events of a governmental entity not accounted for in one of the other six types of funds. Thus, the general fund as an accounting unit serves the same *residual* purpose that the general journal provides as an accounting record. Although the general fund is residual, it generally accounts for the largest aggregate dollar amounts of the governmental entity's revenues and expenditures.

In illustrating the accounting for a general fund, the example of the Town of Verdant Glen used in the preceding section is continued.

Illustration of Accounting for a General Fund

Assume that the balance sheet of the Town of Verdant Glen General Fund on June 30, Year 5 (*prior to the journal entry for the Fiscal Year 6 budget* illustrated on page 610), was as follows:

Balance sheet of a
governmental entity's
general fund at end of
preceding fiscal year

TOWN OF VERDANT GLEN GENERAL FUND
Balance Sheet
June 30, Year 5

Assets

Cash..		$160,000
Inventory of supplies		40,000
Total assets		$200,000

Liabilities & Fund Balance

Vouchers payable..		$ 80,000
Fund balance:		
Reserved for inventory of supplies.........................	$40,000	
Unreserved and undesignated	80,000	120,000
Total liabilities & fund balance		$200,000

The fund balance reserved for inventory of supplies is analogous to a ***mandatory*** restriction of retained earnings in a business enterprise. It represents a reservation of the General Fund's fund balance, so that the $40,000 nonexpendable portion of the General Fund's total assets will not be appropriated for expenditures in the legislative body's adoption of the annual budget for the General Fund for the year ending June 30, Year 6.

Assume that, in addition to the budget illustrated and recorded on page 610, the Town of Verdant Glen General Fund had the summarized transactions and events for the fiscal year ended June 30, Year 6, shown below. For the sake of simplicity, income taxes, sales taxes, short-term prepayments, and short-term loans are disregarded in this illustration.

1   Property taxes were billed in the amount of $720,000, of which $14,000 was of doubtful collectibility.

2   Property taxes collected in cash totaled $650,000; revenues from licenses and permits fees collected totaled $102,000.

3   Property taxes in the amount of $13,000 were determined to be uncollectible.

4   Purchase orders for nonrecurring expenditures were issued to outside suppliers in the total amount of $360,000.

5   Expenditures for the year totaled $760,000, of which $90,000 applied to additions to inventory of supplies, and $350,000 applied to $355,000 of the purchase orders in the total amount of $360,000 issued during the year.

6   Billings for services and supplies received from the Enterprise Fund and the Internal Service Fund totaled $30,000 and $20,000, respectively.

7   Cash payments on vouchers payable totaled $770,000. Cash payments to the Enterprise Fund and the Internal Service Fund were $25,000 and $14,000, respectively.

8   Transfers of cash to the Debt Service Fund for maturing principal and interest on general obligation serial bonds totaled $11,000.

9   A payment of $40,000 in lieu of property taxes and a subsidy of $10,000 were received from the Enterprise Fund.

10 Supplies with a cost of $80,000 were used during the year.

11 All uncollected property taxes on June 30, Year 6, were delinquent.

12 The Town Council ***designated*** $25,000 of the unreserved and undesignated fund balance for the replacement of equipment during the year ending June 30, Year 7.

After the journal entry for the budget is recorded, as illustrated on page 610, the following journal entries, numbered to correspond to the transactions or events listed above, are prepared for the Town of Verdant Glen General Fund during the year ended June 30, Year 6:

Journal entries for
general fund of a
governmental entity

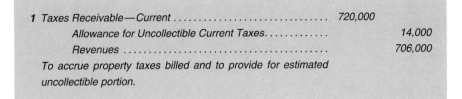

```
1  Taxes Receivable—Current ..............................   720,000
        Allowance for Uncollectible Current Taxes............           14,000
        Revenues .........................................          706,000
   To accrue property taxes billed and to provide for estimated
   uncollectible portion.
```

As indicated on page 608, ***the accrual basis of accounting for a general fund requires the accrual of property taxes because they are billed*** to the property owners by the Town of Verdant Glen. The estimated uncollectible property taxes are ***offset*** against the total taxes billed in order to measure ***actual revenues*** from property taxes for the year.

```
2  Cash ....................................................   752,000
        Taxes Receivable—Current .......................          650,000
        Revenues .........................................          102,000
   To record collections of property taxes and licenses and permits
   fees revenues for the year.
```

Under the accrual basis of accounting, revenues from licenses and permits fees are recognized on the cash basis. However, any taxes or other revenues collected in advance of the fiscal year to which they apply are credited to a liability ledger account.

If a governmental entity's general fund has a cash shortage prior to collection of property taxes, it may issue short-term ***tax anticipation notes*** to borrow cash. Typically, tax anticipation notes payable are repaid from proceeds of the subsequent tax collections.

```
3  Allowance for Uncollectible Current Taxes ....................   13,000
        Taxes Receivable—Current ..........................           13,000
   To write off receivables for property taxes that are uncollectible.
```

The foregoing journal entry represents a shortcut approach. In an actual situation, uncollectible property taxes first would be transferred, together with estimated uncollectible amounts, to the Taxes Receivable—Delinquent ledger account from the Taxes Receivable—Current account. Any amounts collected on these delinquent taxes would include revenues for interest and penalties required by law. Uncollected delinquent taxes would be transferred, together with estimated uncollectible amounts, to the Tax Liens Receivable ledger account. After the passage of an appropriate statutory period, the governmental entity might satisfy its tax lien by selling the property on which the delinquent taxes were levied.

4 Encumbrances 360,000
          Fund Balance Reserved for Encumbrances 360,000
          To record purchase orders for nonrecurring expenditures issued
          during the year.

As explained on page 612, encumbrance journal entries are used to prevent the overexpending of an appropriated amount in the budget. The journal entry to the Encumbrances ledger account is posted in detail to reduce the unexpended balances of each applicable appropriation in the subsidiary ledger for appropriations. The unexpended balance of each appropriation thus is reduced for the amount committed by the issuance of purchase orders.

5a Expenditures... 670,000
          Inventory of Supplies...................................... 90,000
               Vouchers Payable 760,000
          To record expenditures for the year.

The Expenditures ledger account is debited with all expenditures, regardless of purpose, *except for additions to the inventory of supplies and short-term prepayments* (see page 608). Principal and interest payments on long-term debt, additions to the governmental entity's plant assets not accounted for in other funds, payments for goods or services to be received in the future—all are debited to Expenditures or to Other Financing Uses rather than to asset or liability ledger accounts. (Expenditures for long-term debt principal and plant asset additions also are recorded *on a memorandum basis* in the general long-term debt and general fixed assets account groups, respectively, as explained in Chapter 13.)

The accounting for general fund expenditures described above emphasizes once again the importance of the annual budget in the accounting for a general fund. Expenditures are chargeable to amounts appropriated by the legislative body of the governmental entity. Detailed items making up the $670,000 total debit to the Expenditures ledger account in the foregoing journal entry are posted to the appropriations subsidiary ledger as reductions of unexpended balances of each appropriation.

5b Fund Balance Reserved for Encumbrances 355,000
               Encumbrances.................................... 355,000
          To reverse encumbrances applicable to vouchered expenditures totaling $350,000.

Recording actual expenditures of $350,000 (included in the $670,000 total in entry **5a** above) applicable to purchase orders totaling $355,000 makes this amount of the previously recorded encumbrances no longer necessary. Accordingly, $355,000 of encumbrances is reversed; the reversal is posted to the detailed appropriations subsidiary ledger as well as to the general ledger. Encumbrances of $5,000

($360,000 − $355,000 = $5,000) remain outstanding on June 30, Year 6, the fiscal year end.

6 Expenditures	50,000	
Payable to Enterprise Fund		30,000
Payable to Internal Service Fund		20,000
To record billings for services and supplies received from other funds.		

Billings from other funds of the governmental entity are not subject to encumbrance or vouchered for payment, as are billings from outside suppliers. Instead, billings from other funds are recorded in separate liability ledger accounts. The related debit is to the Expenditures account if the billings are for *quasi-external transactions,* such as providing services and supplies.

7 Vouchers Payable	770,000	
Payable to Enterprise Fund	25,000	
Payable to Internal Service Fund	14,000	
Cash		809,000
To record payment of liabilities during the year.		
8 Other Financing Uses	11,000	
Cash		11,000
To record transfer to Debt Service Fund for maturing principal and interest on long-term general-obligation serial bonds.		

The Other Financing Uses ledger account is debited because the payment to the Debt Service Fund is an *operating transfer out* rather than a *quasi-external transaction.*

9 Cash	50,000	
Revenues		40,000
Other Financing Sources		10,000
To record payment in lieu of property taxes ($40,000) and subsidy ($10,000) received from Enterprise Fund.		

Amounts transferred in to the General Fund from other funds are recognized as revenues if they are *quasi-external transactions,* such as payments in lieu of property taxes; otherwise, they are recognized as other financing sources if they are *operating transfers in,* such as subsidies.

10 Expenditures	80,000	
Inventory of Supplies		80,000
To record cost of supplies used during the year.		

> Unreserved and Undesignated Fund Balance................ 10,000
>   Fund Balance Reserved for Inventory of Supplies.......   10,000
> To increase inventory of supplies reserve to $50,000 to agree
> with balance of Inventory of Supplies ledger account at end of
> year ($50,000 − $40,000 = $10,000).

The immediately preceding journal entry represents a restriction of a portion of the Fund Balance account to prevent its being appropriated improperly to finance a deficit annual budget for the General Fund for the year ending June 30, Year 7. Only cash and other monetary assets of a general fund are available for appropriation to finance authorized expenditures of the succeeding fiscal year.

> 11 Taxes Receivable—Delinquent 57,000
>   Allowance for Uncollectible Current Taxes.................. 1,000
>   Taxes Receivable—Current   57,000
>   Allowance for Uncollectible Delinquent Taxes...........   1,000
> To transfer delinquent taxes and related estimated uncollectible
> amounts from the current classification.

The foregoing journal entry clears the Taxes Receivable—Current ledger account and the related contra account for uncollectible amounts so that they will be available for accrual of property taxes for the fiscal year ending June 30, Year 7.

> 12 Unreserved and Undesignated Fund Balance................ 25,000
>   Fund Balance Designated for Replacement of Equip-
>   ment   25,000
> To designate a portion of the fund balance for the replacement of
> equipment during the year ending June 30, Year 7.

The Fund Balance Designated for Replacement of Equipment ledger account is similar to a *voluntary* retained earnings appropriation of a business enterprise. It indicates that the annual budget for the Town of Verdant Glen General Fund for the year ending June 30, Year 7, must include an appropriation of $25,000 for new equipment and estimated revenues for the proceeds from disposal of the replaced equipment. The designated fund balance of $25,000 will be closed to the Unreserved and Undesignated Fund Balance ledger account on July 1, Year 6, when the annual budget for the year ending June 30, Year 7, is recorded.

Trial Balance at End of Fiscal Year for a General Fund

After all the foregoing journal entries (including the budget entry on page 610) have been posted to the general ledger of the Town of Verdant Glen General Fund, the trial balance on June 30, Year 6, is as follows:

<table>
<tr><td>Trial balance of a governmental entity's general fund at end of current fiscal year</td><td colspan="2">TOWN OF VERDANT GLEN GENERAL FUND
Trial Balance
June 30, Year 6</td></tr>
</table>

	Debit	Credit
Cash	$ 142,000	
Taxes receivable—delinquent	57,000	
Allowance for uncollectible delinquent taxes		$ 1,000
Inventory of supplies	50,000	
Vouchers payable		70,000
Payable to Enterprise Fund		5,000
Payable to Internal Service Fund		6,000
Fund balance reserved for encumbrances		5,000
Fund balance reserved for inventory of supplies		50,000
Fund balance designated for replacement of equipment		25,000
Unreserved and undesignated fund balance		45,000
Budgetary fund balance		30,000
Estimated revenues	840,000	
Estimated other financing sources	10,000	
Appropriations		810,000
Estimated other financing uses		10,000
Revenues		848,000
Other financing sources		10,000
Expenditures	800,000	
Other financing uses	11,000	
Encumbrances	5,000	
Totals	$1,915,000	$1,915,000

Financial Statements for a General Fund

The results of operations (that is, net income or net loss) is not relevant for a general fund. Instead, two financial statements—a statement of revenues, expenditures, and changes in fund balance, and a balance sheet—are appropriate. These two financial statements are shown on page 620 for the Town of Verdant Glen's General Fund for the year ended June 30, Year 6.[21]

The following aspects of the Town of Verdant Glen General Fund financial statements are significant:

1   The statement of revenues, expenditures, and changes in fund balance compares budgeted with actual amounts. This comparison aids in the appraisal of the stewardship for the General Fund's resources and the compliance with legislative appropriations. (Expenditures in excess of appropriated amounts generally are not permitted

[21] In a *Preliminary Views* document issued in 1992, the GASB discussed alternative display methods in the financial statements of a governmental entity's governmental funds. The GASB's actions may presage significant changes from the form and content of governmental fund financial statements illustrated on page 620 and in Chapter 13.

Financial statements of a governmental entity's general fund at end of current fiscal year

TOWN OF VERDANT GLEN GENERAL FUND
Statement of Revenues, Expenditures, and Changes in Fund Balance
For Year Ended June 30, Year 6

	Budget	Actual	Variance favorable (unfavorable)
Revenues:			
Taxes............................	$700,000	$706,000	$ 6,000
Other.............................	140,000	142,000	2,000
Total revenues....................	$840,000	$848,000	$ 8,000
Expenditures:*			
General government................	$470,000	$459,000	$11,000
Other.............................	340,000	341,000	(1,000)
Total expenditures	$810,000	$800,000	$10,000
Excess of revenues over expenditures ...	$ 30,000	$ 48,000	$18,000
Other financing sources (uses):			
Operating transfers in	10,000	10,000	
Operating transfers out	(10,000)	(11,000)	(1,000)
Excess of revenues and other sources over expenditures and other uses.......	$ 30,000	$ 47,000	$17,000
Fund balance, beginning of year.........	120,000	120,000	
Fund balance, end of year	$150,000	$167,000	$17,000

* Breakdown of actual amounts between general government and other categories is assumed.

TOWN OF VERDANT GLEN GENERAL FUND
Balance Sheet
June 30, Year 6

Assets

Cash..	$142,000
Taxes receivable, net of allowance for estimated uncollectible amounts, $1,000	56,000
Inventory of supplies	50,000
Total assets	$248,000

Liabilities & Fund Balance

Liabilities:		
Vouchers payable..		$ 70,000
Payable to other funds......................................		11,000
Total liabilities		$ 81,000
Fund balance:		
Reserved for encumbrances	$ 5,000	
Reserved for inventory of supplies........................	50,000	
Designated for replacement of equipment	25,000	
Unreserved and undesignated	87,000	167,000
Total liabilities & fund balance		$248,000

unless a supplementary appropriation is made by the legislative body and approved by the executive of the governmental entity.)

2 The amounts received from and paid to other funds of the Town of Verdant Glen are termed *operating transfers in* and *operating transfers out,* respectively, to distinguish them from other types of financing sources and uses that might have been received or paid by the General Fund.

3 The assets of the General Fund include only *financial resources assets* —cash, receivables, and inventories.[22] Expenditures for plant assets are not recognized as assets in the General Fund.

4 The unreserved and undesignated fund balance in the balance sheet, $87,000, is a balancing amount to make the total of the reserved, designated, and unreserved and undesignated fund balance amounts equal to $167,000, the final amount in the statement of revenues, expenditures, and changes in fund balance. After the posting of the closing entries illustrated in the next section, the ending balance of the Unreserved and Undesignated Fund Balance ledger account is $87,000 (see page 622).

Closing Entries for a General Fund

After financial statements have been prepared for the Town of Verdant Glen General Fund, the budgetary and actual revenues, expenditures, and encumbrances ledger accounts must be closed, to clear them for the next fiscal year's activities. The closing entries below are appropriate for the Town of Verdant Glen General Fund on June 30, Year 6:

Closing entries for a governmental entity's general fund at end of current fiscal year

Unreserved and Undesignated Fund Balance	5,000	
Encumbrances		5,000
To close Encumbrances ledger account.		
Appropriations	810,000	
Estimated Other Financing Uses	10,000	
Budgetary Fund Balance	30,000	
Estimated Revenues		840,000
Estimated Other Financing Sources		10,000
To close budgetary ledger accounts. (See page 610).		
Revenues	848,000	
Other Financing Sources	10,000	
Expenditures		800,000
Other Financing Uses		11,000
Unreserved and Undesignated Fund Balance		47,000
To close revenues, expenditures, and other financing sources and uses ledger accounts.		

---

[22] *Codification of Governmental Accounting and Financial Reporting Standards,* p. A-62.

The foregoing journal entries do not close the Fund Balance Reserved for Encumbrances ledger account. Thus, the reserve represents a *mandatory* restriction of the fund balance on June 30, Year 6, because the Town of Verdant Glen General Fund is committed in Fiscal Year 7 to make estimated expenditures of $5,000 attributable to budgetary appropriations carried over from Fiscal Year 6. If the Fund Balance Reserved for Encumbrances account had been closed, the Unreserved and Undesignated Fund Balance account would have been overstated by $5,000. The Unreserved and Undesignated Fund Balance ledger account balance must represent the amount of the General Fund's net assets that is available for appropriation for a *deficit budget* in Fiscal Year 7. When expenditures applicable to the $5,000 outstanding encumbrances on June 30, Year 6, are vouchered for payment in the succeeding fiscal year, the Fund Balance Reserved for Encumbrances ledger account is debited for $5,000, the Vouchers Payable account is credited for the amount to be paid, and the balancing debit or credit is entered in the Unreserved and Undesignated Fund Balance account.

The budgetary accounts are closed at the end of the fiscal year because they are no longer required for control over revenues, expenditures, and other financing sources and uses. The amounts in the journal entry that closed the budgetary accounts were taken from the journal entry to record the budget (page 610).

After the June 30, Year 6, closing entries for the Town of Verdant Glen General Fund are posted, the Unreserved and Undesignated Fund Balance ledger account is as shown below:

Unreserved and Undesignated Fund Balance ledger account of a governmental entity's general fund at end of current fiscal year

Unreserved and Undesignated Fund Balance

Date	Explanation	Debit	Credit	Balance
Year 5				
June 30	Balance			80,000 cr
Year 6				
June 30	Increase in amount reserved for inventory of supplies (page 618)	10,000		70,000 cr
30	Designation for replacement of equipment (page 618)	25,000		45,000 cr
30	Close Encumbrances account (page 621)	5,000		40,000 cr
30	Close excess of revenues and other financing sources over expenditures and other financing uses (page 621)		47,000	87,000 cr

REVIEW QUESTIONS

1   What are *nonbusiness organizations?*

2   Does the Financial Accounting Standards Board establish accounting standards for governmental entities? Explain.

3 Did the Financial Accounting Standards Board recommend objectives of financial reporting by the federal government?

4 What characteristics of governmental entities have a significant influence on the accounting for governmental entities? Explain.

5 What is a *fund* in accounting for governmental entities?

6 What is the support for each of the following accounting standards for governmental entities?
a The accrual basis of accounting
b The encumbrance accounting technique
c Recording the budget in the accounting records

7 **a** Differentiate between a *program budget* and a *performance budget.*
b Differentiate between a *budgetary deficit* and a *deficit budget.*

8 The Estimated Revenues ledger account of a governmental entity's general fund may be considered a *pseudo asset,* and the Appropriations account may be considered a *pseudo liability.* Why is this true?

9 What is the function of the Budgetary Fund Balance ledger account for a governmental entity's general fund?

10 What does the reference to a governmental entity's general fund as *residual* mean? Explain.

11 What revenues of a governmental entity's general fund generally are accrued? Explain.

12 Distinguish between the Expenditures ledger account of a governmental entity's general fund and the expense accounts of a business enterprise.

13 Explain the use of the Other Financing Sources and Other Financing Uses ledger accounts of a governmental entity's general fund.

14 The accounting records for the City of Worthington General Fund include a ledger account titled Fund Balance Reserved for Inventory of Supplies. Explain the purpose of this account.

15 Differentiate between a *reservation* and a *designation* of the fund balance of a governmental entity's general fund.

16 **a** What are the financial statements issued for a governmental entity's general fund?
b What are the principal differences between the financial statements of a governmental entity's general fund and the financial statements of a business enterprise?

EXERCISES

Ex. 12-1 Select the best answer for each of the following multiple-choice questions:

1 Which of the following is not a characteristic of a *fund* in governmental accounting?

a Fiscal and accounting entity
b Owners' equity
c Self-balancing set of accounts
d Attaining certain objectives

2   In the journal entry to record the annual budget of a governmental entity's general fund, appropriate entries to the following general fund ledger accounts are:

	Estimated Revenues	Appropriations	Estimated Other Financing Uses
a	Debit	Debit	Credit
b	Debit	Credit	Credit
c	Credit	Debit	Debit
d	Credit	Debit	Credit

3   Which of the following is a budgetary ledger account of a governmental entity's general fund?
a Encumbrances
b Other Financing Sources
c Unreserved and Undesignated Fund Balance
d Appropriations

4   Which of the following ledger accounts of a governmental entity's general fund is credited when a purchase order is approved?
a Fund Balance Reserved for Encumbrances
b Encumbrances
c Vouchers Payable
d Appropriations
e None of the foregoing

5   Which of the following ledger accounts of a governmental entity's general fund is credited when previously ordered supplies are received?
a Fund Balance Reserved for Encumbrances
b Encumbrances
c Expenditures
d Appropriations
e None of the foregoing

6   In a governmental entity's general fund journal entry on the date an invoice is received for a nonrecurring procurement under a purchase order, the appropriate entries to the following ledger accounts are:

	Encumbrances	Expenditures
a	Debit	Debit
b	Debit	Credit
c	Credit	Debit
d	Credit	Credit

7   The ledger account debited in the journal entry of a governmental entity's general fund crediting the Allowance for Uncollectible Current Taxes ledger account is:
a Doubtful Current Taxes Expense
b Unreserved and Undesignated Fund Balance

c Revenues

d Taxes Receivable—Current

e Some other ledger account

8 Repairs that have been made for a governmental entity's general fund, and for which an invoice has been received, are recorded in the general fund with a debit to:

a Expenditures

b Encumbrances

c Repairs Expense

d Appropriations

e Some other ledger account

9 The appropriate ledger accounts to be credited by a governmental entity's general fund for cash received from the entity's enterprise fund are:

	Payments in lieu of property taxes	Subsidies
a	Revenues	Other Financing Sources
b	Revenues	Revenues
c	Other Financing Sources	Revenues
d	Other Financing Sources	Other Financing Sources

10 The appropriate format of the end-of-fiscal-year journal entry (explanation omitted) to close the Encumbrances ledger account of a governmental entity's general fund is:

a Unreserved and Undesignated Fund Balance
    Encumbrances

b Fund Balance Reserved for Encumbrances
    Encumbrances

c Expenditures
    Encumbrances

d Encumbrances
    Appropriations

Ex. 12-2 The activity with respect to the General Government—Supplies subsidiary ledger account of the Ridge City General Fund included the following for the first part of the July 1, Year 3–June 30, Year 4, fiscal year:

July 1 The appropriation in the fiscal year budget was $100,000.

2 Purchase order 4-1 for $20,000 was issued to Crosby Company.

3 Supplies were received from Crosby Company under purchase order 4-1, invoice 6392 for $20,120.

5 Defective supplies with an invoice 6392 cost of $640 were returned to Crosby Company, accompanied by debit memorandum 4-6.

8 Purchase order 4-14 for $18,000 was issued to Lassen Company.

Prepare a subsidiary ledger account for General Government—Supplies for Ridge City General Fund and post entries for the foregoing events or transactions. Your ledger account should have the following columns: Date; Explanation; Appropriation credit; Encumbrance debit; Expenditure debit; Unexpended, unencumbered balance, credit.

Ex. 12-3 The post-closing trial balance of the Winston County General Fund included the following ledger account balances on June 30, Year 2:

Taxes receivable—delinquent. . . . . $30,200 dr
Allowance for uncollectible delinquent taxes . . . .   1,300 cr

The property taxes assessments for the year ending June 30, Year 3, totaled $640,000; 4% of Winston County's property taxes assessments has been uncollectible in past fiscal years.

Prepare a journal entry for the property taxes of Winston County's General Fund on July 1, Year 2, the date on which the property taxes for the year ending June 30, Year 3, were billed to taxpayers.

Ex. 12-4 On July 25, Year 3, office supplies estimated to cost $2,390 were ordered from a vendor for delivery to the office of the city manager of Gaskill. The City of Gaskill maintains a perpetual inventory system for such supplies. The supplies ordered July 25 were received on August 9, Year 3, accompanied by an invoice for $2,500.

Prepare journal entries to record the foregoing transactions in the City of Gaskill General Fund.

Ex. 12-5 The Glengarry School District General Fund had an inventory of supplies (and related reserve) of $60,200 on July 1, Year 8. For the year ended June 30, Year 9, supplies costing $170,900 were acquired; related purchase orders totaled $168,400. The physical inventory of unused supplies on June 30, Year 9, totaled $78,300. The perpetual inventory system is used to account for the inventory of supplies.

Prepare journal entries for the foregoing facts for the year ended June 30, Year 9. Omit explanations for the journal entries.

Ex. 12-6 Among the journal entries prepared by the inexperienced accountant of Rainbow County General Fund for the year ended June 30, Year 7, were the following:

Year 6
July 1 Accounts Receivable 800,000
             Cash.   800,000
         To record nonreturnable operating transfer of cash to
         Internal Service Fund to provide working capital for that
         fund.

Sept. 1 Equipment. 120,000
             Vouchers Payable.   120,000
         To record acquisition of equipment having a 10-year
         economic life and no residual value.

Prepare correcting entries on June 30, Year 7, for Rainbow County General Fund.

Ex. 12-7 From the following ledger account balances for the Town of Irving General Fund on June 30, Year 5, the end of the town's fiscal year, prepare closing entries:

Appropriations	$1,520,000
Encumbrances	10,000
Estimated revenues	1,600,000
Expenditures	1,500,000
Fund balance reserved for encumbrances	10,000
Revenues	1,616,000

Ex. 12-8 *Selected* ledger account balances of Bixby Village General Fund on June 30, Year 7, were as follows:

	Debit	Credit
Appropriations		$400,000
Budgetary fund balance		30,000
Encumbrances	$ 1,000	
Estimated other financing sources	10,000	
Estimated other financing uses		6,000
Estimated revenues	426,000	
Expenditures	395,000	
Fund balance reserved for encumbrances		1,000
Other financing sources		14,000
Other financing uses	5,000	
Revenues		440,000
Unreserved and undesignated fund balance		80,000

Prepare closing entries (omit explanations) for Bixby Village General Fund on June 30, Year 7.

Ex. 12-9 Following is the statement of revenues, expenditures, and changes in fund balance for the Village of Mortimer General Fund for the year ended June 30, Year 8. The village did not have any other financing sources or uses for the year. Unfilled purchase orders on June 30, Year 8, totaled $11,400.

VILLAGE OF MORTIMER GENERAL FUND
Statement of Revenues, Expenditures, and Changes in Fund Balance
For Year Ended June 30, Year 8

	Budget	Actual	Variance favorable (unfavorable)
Revenues:			
Taxes	$820,000	$814,200	$(5,800)
Other	160,000	162,500	2,500
Total revenues	$980,000	$976,700	$(3,300)
Expenditures:			
General government	$615,000	$618,800	$(3,800)
Other	275,000	277,400	(2,400)
Total expenditures	$890,000	$896,200	$(6,200)
Excess of revenues over expenditures	$ 90,000	$ 80,500	$(9,500)
Fund balance, beginning of year	280,400	280,400	
Fund balance, end of year	$370,400	$360,900	$(9,500)

Prepare closing entries for the Village of Mortimer General Fund on June 30, Year 8.

Ex. 12-10   On July 1, Year 9, the general ledger of the City of Winkle General Fund had the following fund balance ledger accounts:

	Balance July 1, Year 9
Reserved for inventory of supplies..................................	$ 80,600
Reserved for encumbrances......................................	18,100
Unreserved and undesignated	214,700

The budget for the year ending June 30, Year 10, showed a budgetary surplus of $20,400. Revenues for the year ended June 30, Year 10, exceeded expenditures by $37,600. There were no other financing sources or uses for the year. The physical inventory of supplies on June 30, Year 10, was $88,200, and outstanding encumbrances on June 30, Year 10, totaled $14,800.

Prepare a working paper to compute the balance of the Unreserved and Undesignated Fund Balance ledger account (after posting of closing entries) for the City of Winkle General Fund on June 30, Year 10.

Ex. 12-11   The Unreserved and Undesignated Fund Balance ledger account of the Town of Oldberry General Fund was as follows on June 30, Year 4:

Unreserved and Undesignated Fund Balance

Date	Explanation	Debit	Credit	Balance
Year 3				
June 30	Balance			62,400 cr
Year 4				
June 30	Decrease in amount reserved			
	for inventory of supplies		3,700	66,100 cr
30	Close Encumbrances ledger			
	account	6,200		59,900 cr
30	Close excess of revenues			
	($840,200) over expenditures			
	($764,800)		75,400	135,300 cr
30	Designation for replacement of			
	equipment	60,000		75,300 cr

The Town of Oldberry did not have any other financing sources or uses during the year ended June 30, Year 4.

Reconstruct the journal entries of the Town of Oldberry General Fund indicated by the foregoing information.

CASES

Case 12-1   The inexperienced accountant of Corbin City prepared the following financial statements for the city's general fund:

CORBIN CITY GENERAL FUND
Income Statement
For Year Ended June 30, Year 9

Revenues:

Taxes		$640,000
Other		180,000
Total revenues		$820,000

Expenses:

General government	$600,000	
Depreciation	60,000	
Other	120,000	780,000
Net income		$ 40,000

CORBIN CITY GENERAL FUND
Statement of Changes in Fund Balance
For Year Ended June 30, Year 9

Fund balance, beginning of year	$4,850,000
Add: Net income	40,000
Fund balance, end of year	$4,890,000

CORBIN CITY GENERAL FUND
Balance Sheet
June 30, Year 9

Assets

Cash	$ 260,000
Property taxes receivable—delinquent	80,000
Inventory of supplies	110,000
Plant assets (net)	4,620,000
Total assets	$5,070,000

Liabilities, Reserves & Fund Balance

Vouchers payable	$ 160,000
Reserve for delinquent property taxes	20,000
Fund balance	4,890,000
Total liabilities, reserves & fund balance	$5,070,000

Instructions

Identify the deficiencies of the foregoing financial statements of Corbin City General Fund. There are no arithmetic errors in the statements. Disregard notes to the financial statements.

Case 12-2 In a discussion of accounting standards for general funds of governmental entities, student Ella questioned the propriety of accruing self-assessed taxes such as income taxes and sales taxes. She pointed out that until the taxes are paid, the governmental entity has no liability-paying ability and no knowledge of the amount of taxes ultimately expected to be collected. Student Janice disagrees with Ella, stating that the budget-preparation process entails estimation of total fiscal year revenues, including revenues from sales taxes and income taxes. Janice concludes by asserting that the modified accrual basis of accounting formerly used by governmental entities' general funds to recognize revenues was overly conservative and failed to provide meaningful budget-to-actual comparisons in general funds' statements of revenues, expenditures, and changes in fund balance.

Instructions

Do you support the views of student Ella or student Janice? Explain.

Case 12-3   You have been assigned by your CPA firm, in which you are an audit manager, to conduct a staff training program in accounting for governmental entities. In preparing for the program, you have decided to anticipate questions about the reasons governmental entities must use separate funds and account groups, rather than a single accounting unit, to account for the governmental entity's transactions and events.

Instructions

Prepare a brief essay on the reasons for fund accounting by governmental entities.

PROBLEMS

Pr. 12-1   The trial balance of Weedpatch County General Fund on June 30, Year 5, was as follows (amounts in thousands):

	Debit	Credit
Cash	$ 100	
Taxes receivable—delinquent	60	
Allowance for uncollectible delinquent taxes		$ 10
Inventory of supplies	50	
Vouchers payable		40
Payable to other funds		12
Fund balance reserved for encumbrances		4
Fund balance reserved for inventory of supplies		50
Unreserved and undesignated fund balance		18
Budgetary fund balance		20
Estimated revenues	800	
Appropriations		780
Revenues		830
Expenditures	750	
Encumbrances	4	
Totals	$1,764	$1,764

The balance of the Unreserved and Undesignated Fund Balance ledger account on July 1, Year 4, was $22,000; there were balances of $6,000 and $40,000, respectively, in the Fund Balance Reserved for Encumbrances and the Fund Balance Reserved for Inventory of Supplies accounts on that date.

Instructions

Prepare a statement of revenues, expenditures, and changes in fund balance and a balance sheet (amounts in thousands) for Weedpatch County General Fund for the year ended June 30, Year 5.

Pr. 12-2 The following information was taken from the accounting records of the General Fund of the City of Lory after the accounts had been closed for the fiscal year ended June 30, Year 3:

CITY OF LORY GENERAL FUND

	Post-closing trial balance, June 30, Year 2	Transactions, events, and closing entries, July 1, Year 2, through June 30, Year 3		Post-closing trial balance, June 30, Year 3
		Debit	Credit	
Debits				
Cash...............	$700,000	$1,820,000	$1,852,000	$668,000
Taxes receivable.....	40,000	1,870,000	1,828,000	82,000
Total debits......	$740,000			$750,000
Credits				
Allowance for uncol-				
lectible taxes........	$ 8,000	8,000	10,000	$ 10,000
Vouchers payable	132,000	1,852,000	1,840,000	120,000
Fund balance:				
Reserved for				
encumbrances		1,000,000	1,070,000	70,000
Unreserved and				
undesignated	600,000	70,000	20,000	550,000
Total credits	$740,000	$6,620,000	$6,620,000	$750,000

The budget for the fiscal year ended June 30, Year 3, included estimated revenues of $2,000,000 and appropriations of $1,940,000. There were no estimated or actual other financing sources or other financing uses.

Instructions

Prepare journal entries to record the budgeted and actual transactions and events of the City of Lory General Fund for the fiscal year ended June 30, Year 3. Also prepare closing entries. Do not differentiate between current and delinquent taxes receivable.

Pr. 12-3 At the start of your audit of the financial statements of the City of Riverdale, you discovered that the city's accountant failed to maintain separate funds. The trial balance of the City of Riverdale General Fund for the year ended December 31, Year 11, on page 632 was available.

Additional Information

(1) The budget for Year 11, not recorded in the accounting records, was as follows: estimated revenues, $815,000; appropriations, $775,000. There were no estimated or actual other financing sources or other financing uses.

(2) Outstanding purchase orders on December 31, Year 11, for expenditures not recognized in the accounting records, totaled $2,500.

(3) Included in the Revenues ledger account balance was a credit of $190,000 representing the current fair value of land donated by the state as a site for construction of the River Bridge.

(4) The taxes receivable became delinquent on December 31, Year 11.

CITY OF RIVERDALE GENERAL FUND
Trial Balance
December 31, Year 11

	Debit	Credit
Cash...	$ 207,500	
Taxes receivable—current.............................	148,500	
Allowance for uncollectible current taxes.................		$ 6,000
Revenues..		992,500
Expenditures	760,000	
Donated land..	190,000	
Construction in progress—River Bridge	130,000	
River Bridge bonds payable		100,000
Contracts payable—River Bridge.......................		30,000
Vouchers payable...		7,500
Unreserved and undesignated fund balance		300,000
Totals...	$1,436,000	$1,436,000

Instructions

Prepare correcting entries on December 31, Year 11 for the City of Riverdale General Fund. Correcting entries for other funds and closing entries are not required.

Pr. 12-4   The following transactions and events affecting Canning County General Fund took place during the fiscal year ended June 30, Year 5:

(1) The following annual budget was adopted:

Estimated revenues:	
Property taxes	$4,500,000
Licenses and permits	300,000
Fines...	200,000
Total estimated revenues................................	$5,000,000

Appropriations:	
General government.......................................	$1,500,000
Police services...	1,200,000
Fire department services	900,000
Public works services	800,000
Acquisition of fire engines	400,000
Total appropriations	$4,800,000

There were no other financing sources or other financing uses budgeted.

(2) Property tax bills totaling $4,650,000 were mailed; it was estimated that $150,000 of this amount would be uncollectible. Fines of $200,000 were assessed.

(3) Property taxes totaling $3,900,000 were collected. The $150,000 previously estimated to be uncollectible remained unchanged, but $630,000 of uncollected property taxes was reclassified as delinquent. It was known that delinquent taxes would be collected soon enough after June 30, Year 5, to make these taxes available to finance obligations incurred during the year ended June 30, Year 5. (There was no balance of uncollected taxes on July 1, Year 4.)

(4) Other cash collections were as follows:

Licenses and permits	$ 270,000
Fines.	200,000
Disposal of public works equipment (carrying amount in the General Fixed Assets Account Group was $5,000).	15,000
Total other cash collections.	$ 485,000

(5) No encumbrances were outstanding on June 30, Year 4. The following purchase orders were executed:

	Total amount	Outstanding June 30, Year 5
General government.	$1,050,000	$ 60,000
Police services.	300,000	30,000
Fire department services.	150,000	15,000
Public works services.	250,000	10,000
Fire engines	400,000	
Totals.	$2,150,000	$ 115,000

(6) The following vouchers were approved for payment:

General government	$1,440,000
Police services	1,155,000
Fire department services	870,000
Public works services	700,000
Fire engines	400,000
Total vouchers approved	$4,565,000

(7) Vouchers totaling $4,600,000 were paid.

Instructions

Prepare journal entries to record the foregoing transactions and events of Canning County General Fund for the year ended June 30, Year 5. Do not prepare closing entries.

Pr. 12-5 The trial balance of Arden School District General Fund is as follows:

ARDEN SCHOOL DISTRICT GENERAL FUND
Trial Balance
December 31, Year 5

	Debit	Credit
Cash.	$ 47,250	
Short-term investments	11,300	
Taxes receivable—delinquent.	30,000	
Inventory of supplies	11,450	
Vouchers payable.		$ 20,200
Payable to Internal Service Fund		950
Fund balance reserved for encumbrances		2,800
Fund balance reserved for inventory of supplies		11,450
Unreserved and undesignated fund balance		59,400
Budgetary fund balance.		7,000
Estimated revenues	1,007,000	
Appropriations		985,000
Estimated other financing uses		15,000
Revenues		1,008,200
Expenditures	990,200	
Other financing uses	10,000	
Encumbrances.	2,800	
Totals.	$2,110,000	$2,110,000

The balance of the Fund Balance Reserved for Inventory of Supplies ledger account on December 31, Year 4, was $9,500.

Instructions

a Prepare the following financial statements for Arden School District General Fund for the year ended December 31, Year 5:

(1) Statement of revenues, expenditures, and changes in fund balance

(2) Balance sheet

b Prepare closing entries for Arden School District General Fund on December 31, Year 5.

Pr. 12-6 The summary of transactions and events on page 635 was taken from the accounting records of Melton School District General Fund before the accounting records had been closed for the year ended June 30, Year 5.

Additional Information

(1) The estimated taxes receivable for the year ended June 30, Year 5, were $2,870,000, and taxes collected during the year totaled $2,810,000.

(2) An analysis of the transactions in the Vouchers Payable ledger account for the year ended June 30, Year 5, follows:

	Debit (credit)
Current year expenditures (all subject to encumbrances).............	$(2,700,000)
Expenditures applicable to June 30, Year 4, outstanding encumbrances	(58,000)
Vouchers for payments to other funds.............................	(210,000)
Cash payments...	2,640,000
Net change...	$ (328,000)

(3) During Year 5, the General Fund was billed $142,000 for services furnished by other funds of Melton School District.

(4) On May 2, Year 5, purchase orders were issued for new textbooks at an estimated cost of $91,000. The books were to be delivered in August, Year 5.

MELTON SCHOOL DISTRICT GENERAL FUND
Summary of Transactions and Events
For Year Ended June 30, Year 5

	Post-closing balances, June 30, Year 4	Pre-closing balances, June 30, Year 5
Ledger accounts with debit balances:		
Cash.....................................	$400,000	$ 700,000
Taxes receivable	150,000	170,000
Estimated revenues........................		3,000,000
Expenditures..............................		2,700,000
Other financing uses		142,000
Encumbrances		91,000
Totals	$550,000	$6,803,000
Ledger accounts with credit balances:		
Allowance for uncollectible taxes	$ 40,000	$ 70,000
Vouchers payable	80,000	408,000
Payable to other funds	210,000	142,000
Fund balance reserved for encumbrances....	60,000	91,000
Unreserved and undesignated fund balance..	160,000	162,000
Revenues from taxes		2,800,000
Other revenues............................		130,000
Budgetary fund balance		20,000
Appropriations............................		2,810,000
Estimated other financing uses.............		170,000
Totals	$550,000	$6,803,000

Instructions

a Based on the foregoing data, reconstruct the journal entries to record all transactions and events of Melton School District General Fund for the year ended June 30, Year 5, including the recording of the budget for the year. Disregard current and delinquent taxes receivable. (Hint: The $2,000 difference between the

$60,000 fund balance reserved for encumbrances on June 30, Year 4, and the $58,000 amount vouchered for the related expenditures is credited to the Unreserved and Undesignated Fund Balance ledger account.)

b Prepare closing entries for Melton School District General Fund on June 30, Year 5.

c Prepare a post-closing trial balance for Melton School District General Fund on June 30, Year 5.

Pr. 12-7 Because the controller of the City of Romaine had resigned, the assistant controller attempted to compute the cash required to be derived from property taxes for the General Fund for the year ending June 30, Year 7. The computation was made as of January 1, Year 6, to serve as a basis for establishing the property tax rate for the fiscal year ending June 30, Year 7. The mayor of Romaine has requested you to review the assistant controller's computations and obtain other necessary information to prepare for the City of Romaine General Fund a formal estimate of the cash required to be derived from property taxes for the fiscal year ending June 30, Year 7. Following are the computations prepared by the assistant controller:

City resources other than proposed property tax levy:
Estimated General Fund cash balance, Jan. 1, Year 6.................	$ 352,000
Estimated cash receipts from property taxes, Jan. 1 to June 30, Year 6 .	2,222,000
Estimated cash revenues from investments, Jan. 1, Year 6, to June 30, Year 7...	442,000
Estimated proceeds from issuance of general obligation bonds in August, Year 6..	3,000,000
Total City resources	$6,016,000

General Fund requirements:
Estimated expenditures, Jan. 1 to June 30, Year 6....................	$1,900,000
Proposed appropriations, July 1, Year 6, to June 30, Year 7	4,300,000
Total General Fund requirements	$6,200,000

Additional Information

(1) The General Fund cash balance required for July 1, Year 7, is $175,000.

(2) Property tax collections are due in March and September of each year. You note that during February, Year 6, estimated expenditures will exceed available cash by $200,000. Pending collection of property taxes in March, Year 6, this deficiency will have to be met by the issuance of 30-day tax-anticipation notes of $200,000 at an estimated interest rate of 12% a year.

(3) The proposed general-obligation bonds will be issued by the City of Romaine Enterprise Fund to finance the construction of a new water pumping station.

Instructions

Prepare a working paper as of January 1, Year 6, to compute the property tax levy required for the City of Romaine General Fund for the fiscal year ending June 30, Year 7.

Pr. 12-8 The following data were taken from the accounting records of the Town of Tosca General Fund after the accounts had been closed for the fiscal year ended June 30, Year 3:

TOWN OF TOSCA GENERAL FUND
Data from Accounting Records
For Year Ended June 30, Year 3

	Balances July 1, Year 2	Fiscal Year 3 changes		Balances June 30, Year 3
		Debit	Credit	
Assets				
Cash	$180,000	$ 955,000	$ 880,000	$255,000
Taxes receivable.	20,000	809,000	781,000	48,000
Allowance for uncollectible				
taxes	(4,000)	6,000	9,000	(7,000)
Total assets	$196,000			$296,000
Liabilities & Fund Balance				
Vouchers payable.	$ 44,000	880,000	889,000	$ 53,000
Payable to Internal Service				
Fund	2,000	7,000	10,000	5,000
Payable to Enterprise Fund	10,000	60,000	100,000	50,000
Fund balance reserved for				
encumbrances.	40,000	40,000	47,000	47,000
Unreserved and undesig-				
nated fund balance.	100,000	47,000	88,000	141,000
Total liabilities & fund				
balance.	$196,000	$2,804,000	$2,804,000	$296,000

Additional Information

(1) The budget for Fiscal Year 3 provided for estimated revenues of $1,000,000 and appropriations of $965,000. There were no other financing sources or other financing uses budgeted.

(2) Expenditures totaling $895,000, in addition to those chargeable against the Fund Balance Reserved for Encumbrances ledger account, were made.

(3) The actual expenditure chargeable against the July 1, Year 2, Fund Balance Reserved for Encumbrances ledger account was $37,000.

Instructions

Reconstruct the journal entries, including closing entries, for the Town of Tosca General Fund indicated by the foregoing data for the year ended June 30, Year 3. Do not attempt to differentiate between current and delinquent taxes receivable.

Pr. 12-9 The post-closing trial balance of the City of Douglas General Fund on June 30, Year 4, was as follows:

CITY OF DOUGLAS GENERAL FUND
Post-Closing Trial Balance
June 30, Year 4

	Debit	Credit
Cash	$ 62,000	
Taxes receivable—delinquent	46,000*	
Allowance for uncollectible delinquent taxes		$ 8,000
Inventory of supplies	18,000	
Vouchers payable..		28,000
Fund balance reserved for inventory of supplies.............		18,000
Fund balance reserved for encumbrances..................		12,000
Unreserved and undesignated fund balance		60,000
Totals	$126,000	$126,000

* Collectible delinquent taxes were expected to be collected by Aug. 31, Year 4.

Additional Information

(1) The annual budget for the year ending June 30, Year 5, was as follows:

Estimated revenues		$400,000
Estimated other financing sources		200,000
Subtotal..		$600,000
Less: Appropriations.....................................	$560,000	
Estimated other financing uses	20,000	580,000
Budgetary surplus..		$ 20,000

(2) Property taxes were levied for the year ended June 30, Year 5, in an amount to provide revenues of $220,800, after estimated uncollectible taxes of 4% of total taxes receivable.

(3) Purchase orders issued for the year ended June 30, Year 5, totaled $518,000.

(4) Cash receipts for the year ended June 30, Year 5, were as follows:

Delinquent property taxes..	$ 38,000
Current property taxes...	226,000
Refund from vendor for overpayment of Fiscal Year 5 invoice for acquisition	
of equipment	4,000
Other revenues (licenses and permits fees)...........................	196,000
Other financing sources	200,000
Total cash receipts...	$664,000

(5) Vouchers were prepared as follows for the year ended June 30, Year 5:

Encumbrance outstanding, June 30, Year 4............................	$ 10,000
Expenditures for year ended June 30, Year 5 (including supplies, $80,000;	
related encumbrances totaled $292,000)	298,000
Other expenditures (no encumbrances)	244,000
Other financing uses (payable to Capital Projects Fund).................	20,000
Total vouchers...	$572,000

(6) Cash payments for vouchers payable during the year ended June 30, Year 5, totaled $580,000.

(7) The physical inventory of supplies on June 30, Year 5, amounted to $12,000. Supplies are accounted for under the perpetual inventory system.

(8) On June 30, Year 5, $20,000 of the unreserved and undesignated fund balance was designated for the acquisition of equipment during the year ended June 30, Year 6.

Instructions

Prepare journal entries for the foregoing transactions and events of the City of Douglas General Fund for the year ended June 30, Year 5, and closing entries on June 30, Year 5.

13

Governmental Entities: Other Governmental Funds and Account Groups

In this chapter I discuss and illustrate accounting for governmental funds other than the general fund, and for the general fixed assets and general long-term debt account groups.

OTHER GOVERNMENTAL FUNDS

Accounting for the three governmental funds (special revenue funds, capital projects funds, and debt service funds) other than the general fund incorporates many of the accounting standards discussed in Chapter 12. For example, the accrual basis of accounting is to be appropriate for all governmental funds, and recording the budget (together with encumbrance accounting) is appropriate for special revenue funds and may be useful for debt service funds and capital projects funds.

Accounting for Special Revenue Funds

As indicated on page 607, *separate* special revenue funds are established by governmental entities as mandated by legislative or executive enactments or as necessary, to account for the receipts and expenditures associated with specialized revenue sources that are earmarked by law or regulation to finance specified governmental operations. Fees for rubbish collection, state gasoline taxes, "sin taxes" on tobacco products and alcoholic beverages, and traffic violation fines are examples of governmental entity revenues that may be accounted for in separate special revenue funds. Ledger account titles, budgetary processes, and financial statements for special revenue funds are similar to those for general funds.

To illustrate the accounting for a special revenue fund, assume that on July 1, *Year 6,* the Town Council of the Town of Verdant Glen authorized the establishment of a special revenue fund—its first such fund—to account for *special assessments* levied on certain residents of the neighboring Village of Arbor. Those residents had requested the Town Council to provide street cleaning and streetlight maintenance services, which could not be furnished by the Village of Arbor. Because the property tax revenues of the Town of Verdant Glen, which among other services financed street cleaning and streetlight maintenance for *residents of the town only,* could not be used for such services elsewhere, the Town Council authorized the special assessment to finance comparable services for the requesting residents of the Village of Arbor. The Town Council adopted a budget for the Special Revenue Fund for the year ending June 30, Year 7, providing for estimated revenues (from the special assessments) of $80,000 and appropriations (for reimbursements to the General Fund for expenditures made by that fund for the services provided to the Village of Arbor residents) of $75,000. Following are additional transactions or events of the Town of Verdant Glen Special Revenue Fund for the year ending June 30, Year 7:

1 Special assessments totaling $82,000 were levied on the appropriate residents of the Village of Arbor, to be paid in full in 60 days. All the special assessments were expected to be collected.

2 Cash receipts from the special assessments were collected in full, $82,000.

3 Of the cash receipts, $63,000 was invested in U.S. Treasury bills with a face amount of $65,000. The U.S. Treasury bills matured on June 30, Year 7, and were redeemed in full on that date.

4 Billings from the Town of Verdant Glen General Fund, requesting reimbursement of expenditures of that fund, totaled $76,000; $62,000 of that amount was paid to the General Fund by June 30, Year 7.

5 On June 30, Year 7, the Town Council of the Town of Verdant Glen designated the fund balance ($8,000) of the Special Revenue Fund for reimbursement of the General Fund during the year ending June 30, Year 8.

Journal Entries for Special Revenue Fund   Journal entries of the Town of Verdant Glen Special Revenue Fund to record the foregoing events and transactions and to close the accounts for the year ended June 30, Year 7, are on pages 642 to 643.

Note that the encumbrances technique is not used by this special revenue fund *because it does not issue purchase orders for goods or services from outsiders.*

Because the $76,000 billings of the Town of Verdant Glen General Fund to the Special Revenue Fund were for reimbursement of General Fund expenditures, the General Fund credits its Expenditures ledger account in the journal entry in which it debits Receivable from Special Revenue Fund.

Financial Statements for Special Revenue Fund   The financial statements for a special revenue fund are the same as those for the general fund: a statement of revenues, expenditures, and changes in fund balance, and a balance sheet. Financial statements for the Town of Verdant Glen Special Revenue Fund for the year ended June 30, *Year 7,* are on page 643.

Journal entries for
special revenue fund of
a governmental entity

TOWN OF VERDANT GLEN SPECIAL REVENUE FUND
Journal Entries

Estimated Revenues	80,000	
Appropriations		75,000
Budgetary Fund Balance...............................		5,000

To record annual budget adopted for fiscal year ending June 30, Year 7.

Special Assessments Receivable—Current.....................	82,000	
Revenues..		82,000

To record special assessments billed, all of which are estimated to be collectible.

Cash...	82,000	
Special Assessments Receivable—Current...............		82,000

To record collection of special assessments in full during the year.

Investments	63,000	
Cash		63,000

To record acquisition of $65,000 face amount of U.S. Treasury bills, maturity June 30, Year 7.

Cash...	65,000	
Investments		63,000
Revenues..		2,000

To record receipt of cash for matured U.S. Treasury bills.

Expenditures	76,000	
Payable to General Fund		76,000

To record billings from General Fund for reimbursement of expenditures for street cleaning and streetlight maintenance for residents of the Village of Arbor.

Payable to General Fund	62,000	
Cash		62,000

To record payments to General Fund during the year.

Appropriations	75,000	
Budgetary Fund Balance..	5,000	
Estimated Revenues		80,000

To close budgetary ledger accounts.

(continued)

TOWN OF VERDANT GLEN SPECIAL REVENUE FUND
Journal Entries (concluded)

Revenues ($82,000 + $2,000)......................................	84,000	
Expenditures		76,000
Unreserved and Undesignated Fund Balance		8,000
To close Revenues and Expenditures ledger accounts.		
Unreserved and Undesignated Fund Balance	8,000	
Fund Balance Designated for Reimbursement of General		
Fund		8,000
To designate entire fund balance for reimbursement of the General		
Fund during the year ending June 30, Year 8.		

Financial statements of a governmental entity's special revenue fund

TOWN OF VERDANT GLEN SPECIAL REVENUE FUND
Statement of Revenues, Expenditures, and Changes in Fund Balance
For Year Ended June 30, Year 7

	Budget	Actual	Variance favorable (unfavorable)
Revenues:			
Special assessments.....................	$80,000	$82,000	$ 2,000
Other...................................		2,000	2,000
Total revenues	$80,000	$84,000	$ 4,000
Expenditures:			
Reimbursements of General Fund expendi-			
tures	$75,000	$76,000	$ (1,000)
Excess of revenues over expenditures (fund			
balance, end of year).....................	$ 5,000	$ 8,000	$ 3,000

TOWN OF VERDANT GLEN SPECIAL REVENUE FUND
Balance Sheet
June 30, Year 7

Assets

Cash	$22,000

Liabilities & Fund Balance

Payable to General Fund	$14,000
Fund balance designated for reimbursement of General Fund	8,000
Total liabilities & fund balance.................................	$22,000

Accounting for Capital Projects Funds

Capital projects funds of a governmental entity record the receipt and payment of cash for the construction or acquisition of the governmental entity's plant assets other than those financed by proprietary funds (enterprise funds and internal service funds) or trust funds. The resources for a capital projects fund generally are derived from proceeds of general obligation bonds, but the resources also may come from current tax revenues or from *grants* or *shared revenues* of other governmental entities.

A capital budget, rather than an annual budget, is the *control device* appropriate for a capital projects fund. The capital budget deals with both the authorized expenditures for the project and the bond proceeds or other financing sources for the project.

Journal Entries for Capital Projects Fund   On July 1, Year 5, the Town of Verdant Glen authorized a $500,000, 20-year, 7% general obligation bond issue to finance an addition to the town's high school. A capital budget was approved for the amount of the bonds, but was not to be integrated in the accounting records of the capital projects fund authorized for the project. The following journal entries illustrate receipt of proceeds of the bonds and other activities of the Town of Verdant Glen Capital Projects Fund for the year ended June 30, Year 6:

Journal entries for capital projects fund of a governmental entity

TOWN OF VERDANT GLEN CAPITAL PROJECTS FUND
Journal Entries

Cash	450,518	
Other Financing Uses: Discount on Bonds Issued	49,482	
Other Financing Sources: Bonds Issued		500,000
To record proceeds of 20-year, 7% general obligation term bonds due July 1, Year 25, interest payable Jan. 1 and July 1, to yield 8%, face amount $500,000. (Bond issue costs are disregarded.)		
Investments	335,000	
Cash		335,000
To record acquisition of $350,000 face amount of U.S. Treasury bills, maturity 26 weeks.		
Encumbrances	482,000	
Fund Balance Reserved for Encumbrances		482,000
To record contracts with architect and construction contractor and issuance of purchase orders.		
Cash	350,000	
Investments		335,000
Revenues		15,000
To record receipt of cash for matured U.S. Treasury bills.		
Expenditures	378,000	
Vouchers Payable		378,000
To record expenditures for the year.		

(continued)

TOWN OF VERDANT GLEN CAPITAL PROJECTS FUND
Journal Entries (concluded)

Fund Balance Reserved for Encumbrances....................	368,200	
Encumbrances		368,200
To reverse encumbrances applicable to vouchered expenditures.		
Vouchers Payable	327,500	
Cash...		327,500
To record payment of vouchers during the year.		
Unreserved and Undesignated Fund Balance		
($482,000 − $368,200).....................................	113,800	
Encumbrances		113,800
To close Encumbrances ledger account.		
Revenues...	15,000	
Other Financing Sources: Bonds Issued......................	500,000	
Expenditures..		378,000
Other Financing Uses: Discount on Bonds Issued........		49,482
Unreserved and Undesignated Fund Balance............		87,518
To close Revenues, Expenditures, and Other Financing Sources and Uses ledger accounts.		

The following features of the foregoing journal entries should be noted:

1   The capital budget for the high school addition was not entered in the accounting records of the Capital Projects Fund. The indenture for the 20-year, 7% general obligation bonds *(general long-term capital debt)* provided adequate control.

2   The liability applicable to the 20-year general obligation bonds was not recorded in the Capital Projects Fund. The liability for the bonds is recorded at face amount in the general long-term debt account group (see page 653).

3   The face amount of the general obligation bonds is an other financing source of the Capital Projects Fund; the discount on the bonds is an other financing use.[1] The interest earned on the short-term investment in U.S. Treasury bills represents revenues to the Capital Projects Fund.

4   The encumbrances and expenditures accounting for the Capital Projects Fund is similar to that for the General Fund illustrated in Chapter 12. Also, the closing entries for the two types of governmental funds are similar.

Expenditures for construction recorded in the Town of Verdant Glen Capital

---

[1]*Codification of Governmental Accounting and Financial Reporting Standards*, GASB (Norwalk: 1992), p. A-81.

Projects Fund are accompanied in the general fixed assets account group by a journal entry at the end of the fiscal year with a debit to Construction in Progress and a credit to Investment in Fixed Assets from Capital Projects Funds (see page 651). The accounting for the general fixed assets account group is illustrated in a subsequent section of this chapter.

At the end of each fiscal year prior to completion of a capital project, the Revenues, Other Financing Sources, Expenditures, and Encumbrances ledger accounts of the Capital Projects Fund are closed to the Unreserved and Undesignated Fund Balance account. On completion of the project, the Capital Projects Fund is terminated by a transfer of any unused cash to the Debt Service Fund or the General Fund, as appropriate; the Unreserved and Undesignated Fund Balance ledger account of the receiving fund would be credited for this *residual equity transfer.* Any cash deficiency in the Capital Projects Fund (a possibility suggested by the deficit fund balance in the balance sheet below) probably would be made up by the

Financial statements of a governmental entity's capital projects fund

TOWN OF VERDANT GLEN CAPITAL PROJECTS FUND
Statement of Revenues, Expenditures, and Changes in Fund Balance
For Year Ended June 30, Year 6

Revenues:	
Miscellaneous	$ 15,000
Expenditures:*	
Construction contracts	$ 287,600
Engineering and other	90,400
Total expenditures	$ 378,000
Excess (deficiency) of revenues over expenditures	$(363,000)
Other financing sources (uses):	
Face amount of general obligation bonds	$ 500,000
Discount on general obligation bonds	(49,482)
Excess of revenues and other sources over expenditures and other uses	
(fund balance, end of year)	$ 87,518

* Breakdown of expenditures is assumed.

TOWN OF VERDANT GLEN CAPITAL PROJECTS FUND
Balance Sheet
June 30, Year 6

Assets

Cash		$ 138,018

Liabilities & Fund Balance

Liabilities:		
Vouchers payable		$ 50,500
Fund balance:		
Reserved for encumbrances	$113,800	
Unreserved and undesignated	(26,282)	87,518
Total liabilities & fund balance		$ 138,018

General Fund; this *operating transfer* would be credited to the Other Financing Sources ledger account of the Capital Projects Fund and debited to the Other Financing Uses account of the General Fund.

Financial Statements for Capital Projects Fund A capital projects fund issues the same financial statements as a general fund: a statement of revenues, expenditures, and changes in fund balance, and a balance sheet. For the Town of Verdant Glen Capital Projects Fund, these financial statements are on page 646 for the year ended June 30, *Year 6.*

   To reiterate, the plant assets constructed with resources of the Capital Projects Fund are not displayed in that fund's balance sheet. The constructed plant assets are recorded in the governmental entity's general fixed assets account group. Furthermore, the general obligation bonds issued to finance the Capital Projects Fund are not a liability of that fund. Prior to the maturity date or dates of the bonds, the liability is carried in the general long-term debt account group (see page 653). On the date the bonds mature, the related liability is transferred to a debt service fund or to the general fund, as appropriate, from the general long-term debt account group.

Accounting for Debt Service Funds

Payments of principal and interest on long-term bonds and other long-term debt of a governmental entity, other than special assessment bonds, revenue bonds, and general obligation bonds serviced by an enterprise fund, are accounted for either in the general fund or in debt service funds. *Special assessment bonds* are repaid from the proceeds of special assessment levies against specific properties receiving benefits from the special assessment improvements; if these bonds finance construction projects for an enterprise fund, they are accounted for in that enterprise fund. *Revenue bonds* are payable from the earnings of a governmental entity's enterprise and are accounted for in the appropriate enterprise fund. In some cases, *general obligation bonds,* which are backed by the full faith and credit of the issuing governmental entity, will be repaid from the resources of a governmental entity enterprise. These general obligation bonds are displayed as liabilities of the appropriate enterprise fund.

   The liability for bonds payable from resources of the general fund or a debt service fund is not recorded in that fund until the debt matures. Prior to maturity date, the bond liability is carried in the general long-term debt account group.

   The two customary types of general obligation bonds whose servicing is recorded in debt service funds are the following:

Serial bonds, with principal payable in annual installments over the term of the bond issue

Term bonds, with principal payable in total on a fixed maturity date, generally from proceeds of an accumulated sinking fund

   Generally, legal requirements govern the establishment of debt service funds. In the absence of legal requirements or of a formal plan for accumulation of a sinking fund for repayment of a general obligation term bond, there may be no need to establish a debt service fund.

Journal Entries for Debt Service Fund   To illustrate the journal entries that are typical for a debt service fund, assume that the Town of Verdant Glen had only two general obligation bond issues outstanding during the year ended June 30, *Year 6:* A $100,000, 10% serial bond issue whose final annual installment of $10,000 was payable on January 1, Year 6, and a $500,000, 7% term bond issue due July 1, Year 25 (see page 644). The Town Council had authorized establishment of a debt service fund for the serial bonds. However, sinking fund accumulations on the term bonds were not required to begin until July 1, Year 8; therefore, a debt service fund for those bonds was unnecessary during the year ended June 30, Year 6.

Interest on both general obligation bond issues was payable each January 1 and July 1. Interest payments on the term bonds were recorded in the General Fund during the year ended June 30, Year 6, and were included in expenditures of that fund, as illustrated on page 616. Interest payments on the serial bonds were made from the Debt Service Fund to a fiscal agent, for transfer to the bondholders.

The June 30, *Year 5,* balance sheet of the Town of Verdant Glen Debt Service Fund for the serial bonds was as follows:

TOWN OF VERDANT GLEN DEBT SERVICE FUND
Balance Sheet
June 30, Year 5

Assets

Cash. $342

Liabilities & Fund Balance

Fund balance reserved for debt service. $342

Aggregate journal entries for the Town of Verdant Glen Debt Service Fund for the year ended June 30, *Year 6,* are as follows:

Aggregate journal entries for debt service fund of a governmental entity

TOWN OF VERDANT GLEN DEBT SERVICE FUND
Journal Entries

Cash.	11,000	
Other Financing Sources		11,000

To record receipt of cash from General Fund for payment of serial bond principal ($10,000) and interest ($1,000) maturing on July 1, Year 5, and Jan. 1, Year 6.

Cash with Fiscal Agent	11,000	
Cash		11,000

To record payment of cash to bank trust department acting as fiscal agent for payment of serial bond principal and interest.

(continued)

TOWN OF VERDANT GLEN DEBT SERVICE FUND
Journal Entries (concluded)

Expenditures	11,000	
Matured Bonds Payable		10,000
Matured Interest Payable		1,000
To record expenditures for interest due July 1, Year 5, and principal and interest due Jan. 1, Year 6.		
Matured Bonds Payable	10,000	
Matured Interest Payable	1,000	
Cash with Fiscal Agent		11,000
To record fiscal agent's payments of bond principal and interest.		
Expenditures	342	
Cash		342
To record payment of fiscal agent for services during year ended June 30, Year 6.		
Other Financing Sources	11,000	
Fund Balance Reserved for Debt Service	342	
Expenditures		11,342
To close fund on extinguishment of related serial bonds.		

Following are significant aspects of the foregoing journal entries:

1 There was no journal entry to record an annual budget. Generally, indentures for general obligation bonds provide sufficient safeguards (such as restricting the fund balance of the debt service fund solely for the payment of debt and related servicing costs), so that recording the budget in the Debt Service Fund is unnecessary. (Note, however, on page 610 of Chapter 12 that the General Fund's estimated other financing use for payment of $10,000 to the Debt Service Fund had been included in the General Fund's annual budget.)

2 The first journal entry is the counterpart of the General Fund journal entry no. *8* on page 617.

3 Expenditures for principal and interest payments of the Debt Service Fund are recorded only on the maturity dates of the obligations. Prior to the maturity dates, the liability for the bonds' *principal* is carried in the general long-term debt account group (see page 653). Because a debt service fund generally does not issue purchase orders, encumbrance accounting is not required.

4 The closing entry extinguishes all remaining ledger account balances of the Debt Service Fund, because the final serial principal payment had been made.

The accrual basis of accounting is appropriate for revenues of a debt service fund. Thus, any property taxes specifically earmarked for servicing of a governmental entity's general obligation bonds may be accrued as revenues in the debt service fund. The accounting for such a tax accrual is the same as that for the general fund.

For a term bond issue that requires the accumulation of a sinking fund, the journal entries for a debt service fund include the investment of cash in interest-bearing securities and the collection of interest. Under the accrual basis of accounting, interest revenue accrued on sinking fund investments at the end of the governmental entity's fiscal year is recognized in the accounting records of the debt service fund.

Financial Statements for Debt Service Fund   A balance sheet for a debt service fund is illustrated on page 648. There is no balance sheet for the Town of Verdant Glen Debt Service Fund on June 30, *Year 6,* because the fund had been extinguished. The statement of revenues, expenditures, and changes in fund balance for the Town of Verdant Glen Debt Service Fund for the year ended June 30, *Year 6,* is shown below:

Statement of revenues, expenditures, and changes in fund balance of a governmental entity's debt service fund

TOWN OF VERDANT GLEN DEBT SERVICE Statement of Revenues, Expenditures, and Changes in Fund Balance For Year Ended June 30, Year 6	
Expenditures:	
Principal retirement	$ 10,000
Interest and charges by fiscal agent	1,342
Total expenditures	$ 11,342
Excess (deficiency) of revenues over expenditures	$(11,342)
Other financing sources:	
Operating transfers in	11,000
Excess (deficiency) of revenues and other financing sources over	
expenditures	$ (342)
Fund balance, beginning of year	342
Fund balance, end of year	–0–

GENERAL FIXED ASSETS AND GENERAL LONG-TERM DEBT ACCOUNT GROUPS

The accounting standards for state and local governmental entities described in Chapter 12 (page 607) require governmental entities to use *account groups* to record plant assets other than *infrastructure* (streets, sidewalks, bridges, and the like) and long-term debt of a governmental entity not recorded in a fund. A governmental entity's general fixed assets and general long-term debt account groups are not *funds;* they are *memorandum accounts.* Their purpose is to provide in one record the governmental entity's plant assets and long-term liabilities that are not recorded in one of the governmental entity's funds. Plant assets are recorded in enterprise, trust, and internal service funds; bonds payable and other long-term liabilities are recorded in debt service and enterprise funds.

Accounting for General Fixed Assets Account Group

Plant assets in the general fixed assets account group are recorded at their cost to the governmental entity or at their current fair value if donated to the governmental entity. The offsetting credit is to a memorandum ledger account such as Investment in General Fixed Assets from (the source of the asset).

According to the Governmental Accounting Standards Board, depreciation may be recorded in the general fixed assets account group, with a debit to the appropriate Investment in General Fixed Assets ledger account and a credit to an Accumulated Depreciation account.[2] When a plant asset carried in the general fixed assets account group is disposed of by the governmental entity, the carrying amount of the asset is removed from the appropriate memorandum ledger accounts in the general fixed assets account group; any proceeds are recognized as miscellaneous revenue or as other financing sources in the general fund, and no gain or loss is recognized.

Journal Entries for General Fixed Assets Account Group   The journal enries for the Town of Verdant Glen below are typical of those for a governmental entity's general fixed assets account group:

Journal entries for general fixed assets account group of a governmental entity

TOWN OF VERDANT GLEN GENERAL FIXED ASSETS ACCOUNT GROUP Journal Entries		
Machinery and Equipment	126,400	
Investment in General Fixed Assets from General Fund		
Revenues		126,400
To record acquisition of equipment by General Fund.		
Construction in Progress	378,000	
Investment in General Fixed Assets from Capital Projects		
Funds		378,000
To record construction work in progress on high school addition.		
Land	500,000	
Buildings	800,000	
Investment in General Fixed Assets from Gifts		1,300,000
To record, at current fair value, private citizen's gift of land and a		
building to be used as a public library.		
Investment in General Fixed Assets from General Fund		
Revenues	20,000	
Accumulated Depreciation of Machinery and Equipment	70,000	
Machinery and Equipment		90,000
To record disposal of machinery and equipment.		

(continued)

---

[2] Ibid., p. 57.

TOWN OF VERDANT GLEN GENERAL FIXED ASSETS ACCOUNT GROUP
Journal Entries (concluded)

Investment in General Fixed Assets from General Fund Revenues...	40,000	
Investment in General Fixed Assets from Capital Projects Funds	280,000	
Investment in General Fixed Assets from Gifts..............	60,000	
Accumulated Depreciation of Buildings...............		240,000
Accumulated Depreciation of Machinery and Equipment		140,000
To recognize depreciation of buildings and machinery and equipment for the year ended June 30, Year 6.		

The first of the foregoing journal entries incorporates the assumption that equipment acquisitions were included in the expenditures of the Town of Verdant Glen General Fund for the year ended June 30, Year 6 (see page 616); the second journal

Statement of changes in general fixed assets of a governmental entity

TOWN OF VERDANT GLEN GENERAL FIXED ASSETS ACCOUNT GROUP
Statement of Changes in General Fixed Assets
For Year Ended June 30, Year 6

	Balances, July 1, Year 5	Additions	Retirements*	Balances, June 30, Year 6
General fixed assets				
Land....................................	$ 6,200,000	$ 500,000		$ 6,700,000
Buildings.................................	18,700,000	800,000		19,500,000
Machinery and equipment....................	720,000	126,400	$ 90,000	756,400
Construction in progress....................		378,000		378,000
Totals..................................	$25,620,000	$1,804,400	$ 90,000	$27,334,400
Accumulated depreciation				
Buildings.................................	$ 1,460,000	$ 240,000		$ 1,700,000
Machinery and equipment....................	216,000	140,000	$ 70,000	286,000
Totals..................................	$ 1,676,000	$ 380,000	$ 70,000	$ 1,986,000
Investment in general fixed assets				
From General Fund revenues................	$10,424,000	$ 126,400	$ 60,000	$10,490,400
From Capital Projects Funds................	9,618,000	378,000	280,000	9,716,000
From gifts................................	3,902,000	1,300,000	60,000	5,142,000
Totals..................................	$23,944,000	$1,804,400	$400,000	$25,348,400

* For investment in general fixed assets section, includes depreciation.

entry was made on June 30, Year 6, to record accumulated cost of the construction project of the Town of Verdant Glen Capital Projects Fund (page 644); and the fourth journal entry incorporates the assumption that proceeds of disposal of machinery and equipment were included in revenues of the Town of Verdant Glen General Fund for the year ended June 30, Year 6.

Statement of Changes in General Fixed Assets   The Governmental Accounting Standards Board requires presentation of a statement of changes in general fixed assets in a governmental entity's comprehensive annual financial report (CAFR; see Chapter 14) unless a note to the financial statements discloses such changes.[3] The statement of changes in general fixed assets for the Town of Verdant Glen for the year ended June 30, Year 6, is on page 652 (beginning-of-period and end-of-period balances are assumed).

Accounting for General Long-Term Debt Account Group

General obligation bonds of a governmental entity, both serial and term, and other long-term liabilities that are not recorded in an enterprise fund are recorded as memorandum credits in the general long-term debt account group. The offsetting memorandum debit entry is to the Amount to Be Provided ledger account. When cash and other assets for the ultimate payment of a bond issue or other long-term liabilities have been accumulated in a debt service fund, the Amount Available in Debt Service Fund ledger account is debited and the Amount to Be Provided account is credited. When the bonds or other liabilities are paid by the debt service fund, the memorandum accounts are reversed in the general long-term debt account group in a closing entry at the end of the fiscal year.

Journal entries for general long-term debt account group of a governmental entity

TOWN OF VERDANT GLEN GENERAL LONG-TERM DEBT ACCOUNT GROUP
Journal Entries

Amount Available in Debt Service Fund	10,000	
Amount to Be Provided.		10,000
To record amount received by Debt Service Fund from General Fund for retirement of principal of general obligation serial bonds.		
Serial Bonds Payable	10,000	
Amount Available in Debt Service Fund		10,000
To record Debt Service Fund payment of 10% serial bonds on January 1, Year 6.		
Amount to Be Provided.	500,000	
Term Bonds Payable.		500,000
To record issuance of 7% general obligation term bonds for construction of addition to high school.		

---

[3] Ibid., p. 58.

Journal Entries for Long-Term Debt Account Group   The journal entries on page 653 for the Town of Verdant Glen General Long-Term Debt Account Group parallel the corresponding journal entries in the Debt Service Fund (pages 648 to 649) and the Capital Projects Fund (page 644), respectively.

Statement of Changes in General Long-Term Debt   The Governmental Accounting Standards Board requires presentation of a statement of changes in general long-term debt in the comprehensive annual financial report of a governmental entity unless such changes are disclosed in a note to the financial statements.[4] Following is the statement of changes in general long-term debt of the Town of Verdant Glen for the year ended June 30, Year 6:

Statement of changes in general long-term debt of a governmental entity

TOWN OF VERDANT GLEN GENERAL LONG-TERM DEBT ACCOUNT GROUP
Statement of Changes in General Long-Term Debt
For Year Ended June 30, Year 6

	Balances, July 1, Year 5	Additions	Payments	Balances, June 30, Year 6
Term bonds				
7%, 20-year general obligation bonds due July 1, Year 25..........		$500,000		$500,000
Serial bonds				
10%, 10-year general obligation bonds, final installment due January 1, Year 6	$10,000		$10,000	
Totals.................	$10,000	$500,000	$10,000	$500,000

Capital Leases of Governmental Entities

If a capital lease is executed by a governmental entity for property not recorded in a proprietary fund (internal service fund or enterprise fund), the property is recorded in the general fixed assets account group and the lease liability is recorded in the general long-term debt account group, valued in accordance with the provisions of *FASB Statement No. 13,* ''Accounting for Leases'' (as amended and interpreted).[5] The periodic lease payments typically are included in expenditures of the general fund.

To illustrate accounting for a capital lease by a governmental entity, assume that on July 1, *Year 6,* the Town of Verdant Glen entered into a three-year capital lease for furniture and equipment for the library building donated to the town (see page

---

[4] Ibid., p. 140.
[5] Ibid., p. 361.

651). The minimum lease payments were $10,000, payable each July 1, Year 6 through Year 8. Title to the furniture and equipment was vested in the town on July 1, Year 9. The town adopted the straight-line method of depreciation, a 10-year economic life, and no residual value for the furniture and equipment. The interest rate implicit in the lease, known to the town and less than the town's incremental borrowing rate, was 8%.

The following journal entries would be required for the capital lease for the three-year lease term:

Journal entries for governmental entity's capital lease

TOWN OF VERDANT GLEN
Journal Entries for Capital Lease

In General Fund

Year 6

July	1	Expenditures	10,000	
		Cash		10,000
		To record first lease payment on three-year capital lease for library furniture and equipment.		

Year 7

July	1	Expenditures ($1,427 interest + $8,573 principal)	10,000	
		Cash		10,000
		To record second lease payment on three-year capital lease for library furniture and equipment.		

Year 8

July	1	Expenditures ($740 interest + $9,260 principal)	10,000	
		Cash		10,000
		To record third lease payment on three-year capital lease for library furniture and equipment.		

In General Long-Term Debt Account Group

Year 6

July	1	Amount to Be Provided ($10,000 × 2.783265*)	27,833	
		Liability under Capital Lease (net)		27,833
		To record liability under three-year capital lease for library furniture and equipment.		

	1	Liability under Capital Lease (net)	10,000	
		Amount to Be Provided		10,000
		To record General Fund payment of first lease payment on three-year capital lease for library furniture and equipment.		

(continued)

TOWN OF VERDANT GLEN
Journal Entries for Capital Lease (concluded)

In General Long-Term Debt Account Group

Year 7

July   1   Liability under Capital Lease (net)   8,573
Amount to Be Provided.   8,573
To record General Fund payment of second lease payment
on three-year capital lease for library furniture and equip-
ment.

Year 8

July   1   Liability under Capital Lease (net)   9,260
Amount to Be Provided.   9,260
To record General Fund payment of third lease payment on
three-year capital lease for library furniture and equip-
ment.

In General Fixed Assets Account Group

Year 6

July   1   Leased Furniture and Equipment—Capital Lease   27,833
Investment in General Fixed Assets from General
Fund Revenues   27,833
To record acquisition of library furniture and equipment
under three-year capital lease.

Year 7

June 30   Investment in General Fixed Assets from General Fund
Revenues ($27,833 ÷ 10)   2,783
Leased Furniture and Equipment—Capital Lease .   2,783
To recognize depreciation of leased library furniture and
equipment for the year ended June 30, Year 7.

(The same depreciation journal entries would be prepared on June 30, Year 8, and June 30, Year 9.)

** Present value of **annuity due** of 1 for three periods at 8%*

Accounting for Special Assessment Bonds

In *GASB Statement No. 6,* "Accounting and Financial Reporting for Special Assessments," the Governmental Accounting Standards Board terminated the use of *special assessment funds* to account for the construction of public improvements financed by special assessments against selected property owners and by related special assessment bonds.[6] Instead, special revenue funds, capital projects funds, and

---

[6] Ibid., p. 410.

debt service funds are to be used, as appropriate, for the transactions and events related to such construction projects.

With respect to special assessment bonds, which sometimes are issued by a governmental entity to finance construction projects pending the receipt of special assessments payable in annual installments, the GASB provided the following standards:[7]

> Special assessment debt for which the government is obligated in some manner . . . should be reported in the [general long-term debt account group], except for the portion, if any, that is a direct obligation of an enterprise fund, or that is expected to be repaid from operating revenues of an enterprise fund.
>
> **1** The portion of the special assessment debt that will be repaid from property owner assessments should be reported as ''special assessment debt with governmental commitment.''
>
> **2** The portion of special assessment debt that will be repaid from general resources of the government (the public benefit portion, or the amount assessed against government-owned property), should be reported in the [general long-term debt account group] like other general obligation debt. . . .
>
> Special assessment debt for which the government is not obligated in any manner should not be displayed in the government's financial statements.

To illustrate application of the foregoing standards, assume that on July 1, *Year 6,* the Town Council of the Town of Verdant Glen enacted a special assessment for paving streets and installing sidewalks in a section of the town. The total assessment was $250,000, payable by the assessed property owners in five annual installments, beginning July 1, Year 6. Interest on unpaid balances at 10% a year was payable annually by the assessed property owners, beginning July 1, Year 7. To help finance the cost of the construction project, the Town Council authorized the issuance on July 1, Year 6, of $200,000 face amount, four-year, 8% special assessment bonds, payable $50,000 a year plus interest payable annually, beginning July 1, Year 7. The Town Council authorized the establishment of a special revenue fund and a capital projects fund to account for the construction project. Under the terms of the bond indenture for the special assessment bonds, the Town of Verdant Glen was obligated to pay the special assessment bonds at maturity if the property owners defaulted on their special assessments and proceeds of lien foreclosures on the property were insufficient.

The journal entries on page 658 are required on July 1, *Year 6,* the date of the special assessment.

Some significant features of the journal entries on page 658 are as follows:

1 The capital budget for the paving and sidewalks project is not entered in the

---

[7] Ibid., p. 413.

Journal entries for governmental entity construction project financed by special assessment

TOWN OF VERDANT GLEN
Journal Entries for Construction Project Financed by Special Assessment

In Special Revenue Fund (different from that illustrated on pages 640–643):

Special Assessments Receivable—Current	50,000	
Special Assessments Receivable—Deferred	200,000	
Revenues		50,000
Deferred Revenues		200,000

To record special assessment levied on property owners benefited by paving and sidewalk project; special assessments receivable and related revenues applicable to year ended June 30, Year 7, are current, and the balance is deferred.

Cash	50,000	
Special Assessments Receivable—Current		50,000

To record receipt of current special assessment payments.

Other Financing Uses	50,000	
Cash		50,000

To record transfer of cash for financing of paving and sidewalk project to Capital Projects Fund established for that purpose.

In Capital Projects Fund (different from that illustrated on pages 643–647):

Cash	50,000	
Other Financing Sources		50,000

To record receipt of cash from Special Revenue Fund for proceeds of current installment of special assessments.

Cash	195,776	
Other Financing Uses: Discount on Bonds Issued	4,224	
Other Financing Sources: Bonds Issued		200,000

To record proceeds of $200,000 face amount of four-year, 8% special assessment bonds to yield 9%.

In General Long-Term Debt Account Group (same as that illustrated on pages 653–654):

Amount to Be Provided	200,000	
Special Assessment Bonds Payable		200,000

To record issuance of 8% special assessment bonds for paving and sidewalk project; the town is obligated to honor deficiencies on payment of the bonds.

accounting records of either the Special Revenue Fund or the Capital Projects Fund. The Town Council's approval of the special assessment and the related bonds provides adequate control.

2 Because the Special Revenue Fund will collect the special assessments as they become current, that fund also will service the special assessment bonds as they become payable. Further, the Special Revenue Fund will accrue interest receivable (at 10%) on the unpaid special assessments receivable, and interest payable (at 8%) on the special assessment bonds.

3 On June 30, Year 7, Year 8, Year 9, and Year 10, the Special Revenue Fund will prepare the following journal entry:

Special Assessments Receivable—Current......................	50,000	
Deferred Revenues	50,000	
Special Assessments Receivable—Deferred		50,000
Revenues..		50,000
To transfer special assessment installment receivable in next fiscal year and related revenues to the current category from the deferred category.		

4 The special assessment bonds and related interest are payable serially over a four-year period by the Special Revenue Fund, from proceeds of the annual collections of special assessments and related interest. Accordingly, the present value of the 8% special assessment bonds ($195,776) at the 9% yield rate is computed as follows:

Principal and interest due July 1, Year 7 [($50,000 + $16,000) × 0.917431*]	$ 60,550
Principal and interest due July 1, Year 8 [($50,000 + $12,000) × 0.841680*]	52,184
Principal and interest due July 1, Year 9 [($50,000 + $8,000) × 0.772183*]	44,787
Principal and interest due July 1, Year 10 [($50,000 + $4,000) × 0.708425*]	38,255
Present value (proceeds) of 8% special assessment bonds at 9% yield rate	$195,776

* From present value tables.

REVIEW QUESTIONS

1 Describe the taxes, fees, or other revenues of a governmental entity that often are accounted for in special revenue funds.

2 The following journal entry was prepared for the Town of Groman Special Revenue Fund, established to account for special assessments on selected property owners of the nearby Village of Angelus:

Expenditures	42,000	
Payable to General Fund		42,000
To record billings from General Fund for reimbursement of expenditures for street cleaning and streetlight maintenance for residents of the Village of Angelus.		

What ledger account does the Town of Groman General Fund credit to offset the $42,000 debit to Receivable from Special Revenue Fund? Explain.

3   How are proceeds of general obligation bonds issued at face amount by a governmental entity to finance a construction project accounted for in a capital projects fund? Explain.

4   Is a separate debt service fund established for every issue of general obligation bonds issued by a governmental entity? Explain.

5   The following journal entry (explanation omitted) appeared in the Charter County Debt Service Fund:

Cash with Fiscal Agent	83,000	
Cash		83,000

What is the probable explanation for this journal entry? Explain.

6   Is the recognition of depreciation of plant assets mandatory for a governmental entity's general fixed assets account group? Explain.

7   Explain the use of the Investment in General Fixed Assets from Gifts ledger account of a governmental entity's general fixed assets account group.

8   Is a balance sheet issued for a governmental entity's general fixed assets account group? Explain.

9   The following journal entry appeared in the accounting records of the Village of Marvell General Long-Term Debt Account Group:

Amount to Be Provided	25,000	
Amount Available in Debt Service Fund		25,000
To record amount received by Debt Service Fund from General Fund		
for retirement of principal of general obligation serial bonds.		

Is the foregoing journal entry prepared correctly? Explain.

10   Explain how each of the following accounting units of a governmental entity is affected by a capital lease for fire engines of the fire department: general fund, general long-term debt account group, general fixed assets account group.

11   Under what circumstances, if any, is a liability for special assessment bonds recorded in a governmental entity's general long-term debt account group? Explain.

EXERCISES

Ex. 13-1   Select the best answer for each of the following multiple-choice questions:

1   May funds other than the general fund be established by a governmental entity in response to:

	Legislative action?	Executive action?
a	Yes	Yes
b	Yes	No
c	No	Yes
d	No	No

2   The governmental funds of a governmental entity include all the following except:

a Special revenue funds
b Agency funds
c Debt service funds
d Capital projects funds

3   An example of a governmental fund of a governmental entity is:

a An enterprise fund
b A special revenue fund
c An agency fund
d None of the foregoing

4   The type of governmental fund of a governmental entity whose accounting most resembles that of the entity's general fund is a:

a Capital projects fund
b Debt service fund
c Special revenue fund
d Special expenditures fund

5   The governmental funds of a governmental entity for which the statement of revenues, expenditures, and changes in fund balance typically displays both budgeted and actual amounts are:

a Special revenue funds
b Capital projects funds
c Debt service funds
d None of the foregoing

6   A capital projects fund of a governmental entity is:

a A governmental fund
b A proprietary fund
c A fiduciary fund
d An account group

7   A Fund Balance Reserved for Encumbrances ledger account most likely is appropriate for a governmental entity's:

a Special revenue fund
b Capital projects fund
c Debt service fund
d Three foregoing governmental funds

8   To record the issuance of general obligation bonds at face amount to finance a governmental entity's capital project fund, the accountant for that fund credits:

a Revenues
b Other Financing Sources
c Unreserved and Undesignated Fund Balance
d General Obligation Bonds Payable

9   Is an annual budget always recorded by a governmental entity's:

	Special revenue funds?	Capital projects funds?	Debt service funds?
a	Yes	Yes	Yes
b	Yes	No	Yes
c	Yes	Yes	No
d	Yes	No	No

10   A governmental entity's general fixed assets account group is used for all plant assets of the governmental entity not recorded in:
a Capital projects funds
b Trust funds
c The general fund
d Plant asset funds

11   Are plant assets of a governmental entity accounted for in the entity's:

	General fund?	Capital projects funds?
a	Yes	Yes
b	Yes	No
c	No	Yes
d	No	No

12   Excluded from the general fixed assets account group of a governmental entity are:
a Donated plant assets
b Plant assets constructed with resources of capital projects funds
c Infrastructure
d None of the foregoing

13   A governmental entity's Amount to Be Provided ledger account is included in the accounting records of the entity's:
a Debt service funds
b Capital projects funds
c General long-term debt account group
d General fixed assets account group

14   The typical balances of the following ledger accounts of a governmental entity's general long-term debt account group are:

	Amount Available in Debt Service Fund	Amount to Be Provided
a	Debit	Credit
b	Credit	Debit
c	Debit	Debit
d	Credit	Credit

15   Are journal entries for a capital lease (for property not recorded in a proprietary fund) entered into by a governmental entity typically required in the entity's:

	General fund?	General long-term debt account group?	General fixed assets account group?
a	No	Yes	Yes
b	Yes	No	Yes
c	Yes	Yes	No
d	Yes	Yes	Yes

16 For the transactions and events related to construction of public improvements financed by special assessments, does a governmental entity use a:

	Special revenue fund?	Capital projects fund?	Debt service fund?
a	Yes	Yes	Yes
b	Yes	Yes	No
c	No	Yes	No
d	No	Yes	Yes

Ex. 13-2 On July 1, Year 4, property taxes totaling $480,000, of which 1½% was estimated to be uncollectible, were levied by the County of Larchmont Special Revenue Fund. Property taxes collected by the Special Revenue Fund during July, Year 4, totaled $142,700.

Prepare journal entries for the County of Larchmont Special Revenue Fund for the foregoing transactions and events.

Ex. 13-3 On July 1, Year 5, the City of Garbo Capital Projects Fund received the proceeds of a $1 million face amount, 6%, five-year serial bond issue, $200,000 principal plus interest payable annually, to finance the construction of a new elementary school. The bonds were issued to yield 8%.

Prepare a working paper to compute the proceeds (present value) of the City of Garbo 6% serial bonds on July 1, Year 5.

Ex. 13-4 On July 1, Year 7, the County of Pinecrest issued at face amount $1,200,000 of 30-year, 5% general obligation term bonds, interest payable each January 1 and July 1, to finance the construction of a public health center.

Prepare journal entries on July 1, Year 7, to record the foregoing transaction for all County of Pinecrest funds or account groups affected. Identify the funds or account groups.

Ex. 13-5 On April 30, Year 5, the fiscal agent for the Town of Wallen Debt Service Fund paid the final serial payment of $50,000 on the town's 8% general obligation bonds, together with semiannual interest. The Debt Service Fund had provided sufficient cash to the fiscal agent a few days earlier.

Prepare a journal entry for the Town of Wallen Debt Service Fund to record the fiscal agent's payment of bond principal and interest on April 30, Year 5.

Ex. 13-6 Among the activities of Nemo County for the fiscal year beginning July 1, Year 4, and ending June 30, Year 5, was the following:

Sept. 1, Year 4   Acquired for cash, from proceeds of general tax revenues, equipment costing $80,000 (the related purchase order was for $79,600). The equipment was to be used by the general government of Nemo County.

Prepare journal entries (omit explanations) for the foregoing activity of Nemo County. Identify by initials the funds or account groups (for example, GF, SRF, CPF, GFAAG) in which the journal entries are recorded.

Ex. 13-7   On June 30, Year 9, the end of the fiscal year, the following journal entry was prepared by the accountant for the Town of Backwoods Town Hall Capital Projects Fund:

Expenditures *950,000*
    Vouchers Payable *950,000*
To record first progress billings of architect and contractor for town
hall under construction.

Prepare a journal entry on June 30, Year 9, for the Town of Backwoods General Fixed Assets Account Group.

Ex. 13-8   A citizen of Hays City donated 10 acres of undeveloped land to the city for a future school site. The donor's cost of the land was $555,000. The current fair value of the land was $850,000 on the date of the gift.

Prepare a journal entry for the appropriate fund or account group of Hays City to record the gift. Identify the fund or account group.

Ex. 13-9   On April 30, Year 7, the Town of Noblisse General Fund received the $30,000 proceeds from disposal of a computer that had a carrying amount of $40,000. The General Fund had acquired the computer three years earlier at a cost of $100,000.

Prepare journal entries on April 30, Year 7, to record the foregoing transaction for all Town of Noblisse funds or account groups affected. Identify the funds or account groups.

Ex. 13-10   On July 1, Year 4, the City of Rogell entered into a five-year capital lease for fire-fighting equipment, with lease payments of $20,000 due each July 1, Year 4 through Year 8. Title to the equipment was to pass to the City of Rogell on June 30, Year 9. The interest rate implicit in the lease, known to Rogell and less than Rogell's incremental borrowing rate, was 8%.

Prepare journal entries on July 1, Year 4, to record the foregoing transaction for all City of Rogell funds or account groups affected. Identify the funds or account groups.

Ex. 13-11   On July 1, Year 5, the Town of Warren issued $600,000 face amount of three-year, 9% special assessment bonds, payable $200,000 a year plus interest, at a 10% yield rate, to finance a street improvement project. The town was ''obligated in some manner'' for the bonds.

Prepare journal entries on July 1, Year 5, to record the foregoing transaction for all Town of Warren funds or account groups affected. Identify the funds or account groups.

Ex. 13-12   The ledger accounts listed on page 665 are included frequently in the accounting records of governmental entities.

	Ledger account		Fund or account group
1	Bonds Payable	a	General fund
2	Fund Balance Reserved for Encum-	b	Special revenue fund
	brances	c	Capital projects fund
3	Amount to Be Provided	d	Debt service fund
4	Equipment	e	General fixed assets account group
5	Appropriations	f	General long-term debt account
6	Estimated Revenues		group
7	Taxes Receivable—Current		

Select the appropriate identifying letter to indicate the governmental entity fund or account group in which these ledger accounts might properly appear. An account might appear in more than one fund or account group.

CASES

Case 13-1 The controller of the City of Darby has asked your advice on the accounting for an installment contract payable by the city. The contract covers the cost of installing automatic gates, currency receptacles, and ticket dispensers for the 20 city-owned parking lots in the downtown district. Installation of the self-parking equipment resulted in a decrease in the required number of parking attendants for the city-owned parking lots and a reduction in the salaries and related expenditures of the City of Darby General Fund.

The contract is payable monthly in amounts equal to 40% of the month's total parking revenue for the 20 lots. Because no legal or contractual provisions require the City of Darby to establish an enterprise fund for the parking lots, both parking revenue and parking-lot maintenance and repairs expenditures are to be recorded in the City of Darby General Fund. The parking-lot sites are to be carried at cost in the City of Darby General Fixed Assets Account Group.

The city controller describes the plans for accounting for payments on the contract as follows: Monthly payments under the contract are to be debited to the Expenditures ledger account of the General Fund and to the debt service section of the expenditures subsidiary ledger. The payments also will be recorded in the General Fixed Assets Account Group as additions to the Improvements Other than Buildings ledger account. A note to the General Fund balance sheet will disclose the unpaid balance of the installment contract at the end of each fiscal year. The unpaid balance of the contract will not be included in the General Long-Term Debt Account Group because the contract does not represent a liability for borrowing of cash, as do the bond and other long-term debt liabilities of the City of Darby.

Instructions

What is your advice to the controller of the City of Darby? Explain.

Case 13-2 The chief accountant of the City of DelVille requests your advice on how to account for two special assessments, which the city has never before enacted. One special assessment was to finance street lighting and maintenance services to selected residents of the nearby Town of Minimus; the other was to finance construction of a new city hall for the City of DelVille. Special assessment bonds were not to be issued.

Instructions

What is your advice to the chief accountant of the City of DelVille? Explain.

PROBLEMS

Pr. 13-1   During the year ended June 30, Year 6, Ridge City had the following plant asset transactions and events, among others:

Year 5

Oct. 31   General Fund for cash equipment costing $20,000.

Dec. 10   A citizen donated land and a building with current fair values of $100,000 and $500,000, respectively.

Year 6

June 30   Construction in progress expenditures in the Capital Projects Fund totaled $970,000 at fiscal year end.

30   Depreciation of buildings—$250,000—and of equipment—$40,000— was attributable to plant assets acquired as follows: From General Fund revenues—$60,000; from Capital Projects Funds—$140,000; from gifts—$90,000.

Instructions

Prepare journal entries for the Ridge City General Fixed Assets Account Group for the foregoing transactions and events.

Pr. 13-2   Shown below is the trial balance of the Town of Dilbey Capital Projects Fund at the end of its first year of operations:

TOWN OF DILBEY CAPITAL PROJECTS FUND
Trial Balance
June 30, Year 8

	Debit	Credit
Cash	$ 276,036	
Vouchers payable		$ 101,000
Fund balance reserved for encumbrances		227,600
Revenues (interest on investments)		30,000
Other financing sources: Bonds issued		1,000,000
Expenditures: Construction contracts	575,200	
Expenditures: Engineering and other	180,800	
Other financing uses: Discount on bonds issued	98,964	
Encumbrances	227,600	
Totals	$1,358,600	$1,358,600

Instructions

Prepare financial statements for the Town of Dilbey Capital Projects Fund for the year ended June 30, Year 8.

Pr. 13-3 On July 1, Year 6, the Town of Logan began two construction projects: (1) an addition to the town hall and (2) a curbing construction project financed with a special assessment. The special assessment totaled $400,000, payable by the assessed citizens in five annual installments beginning July 1, Year 6, together with interest at 8% a year on the unpaid assessments. Other details for the year ended June 30, Year 7, were as follows:

	Addition to town hall	Curbing construction project
Bonds issued July 1, Year 6, at face amount........	$600,000 face amount, 7%, 20-year general obligation term bonds, interest payable Jan. 1 and July 1	$320,000 face amount 7½%, 4-year special assessment bonds, $80,000 principal and interest payable each July 1
Total encumbrances......	$530,200	$384,600
Total expenditures........	$380,600	$360,300
Encumbrances applicable to expenditures.........	$382,100	$354,700
Total cash paid on vouchers	$322,700	$347,600

Instructions

Prepare journal entries for the year ended June 30, Year 7, including year-end accruals but excluding closing entries, for **(a)** the Town of Logan Town Hall Capital Projects Fund and **(b)** the Town of Logan Special Revenue Fund (established to account for the proceeds of the special assessments). Do not prepare journal entries for the Town of Logan Curbing Construction Capital Projects Fund.

Pr. 13-4 Among the journal entries of the General Fund of Webster Village for the year ended June 30, Year 24, were the following:

Year 23

July 3 Other Financing Uses 15,000

                   Payable to Capital Projects Fund............. 15,000

         To record liability to Capital Projects Fund for operating transfer to make up that fund's cash deficiency.

Aug. 31 Other Financing Uses 210,000

                   Cash...................................... 210,000

         To record transfer to Debt Service Fund for maturing principal and final six-months interest payment on $200,000 face amount, 20-year, 10% general obligation term bonds issued Aug. 31, Year 3.

(continued)

Year 23

Nov. 30 Expenditures 60,000

                Vouchers Payable 60,000

              To record expenditure for new computer for village. Straight-line depreciation is to be used; economic life is five years, with no residual value.

    30 Fund Balance Reserved for Encumbrances 58,800

                Encumbrances 58,800

              To reverse encumbrance applicable to computer.

Year 24

Jan. 2 Other Financing Uses 20,000

                Cash 20,000

              To record operating transfer to Special Revenue Fund for village's share of street-paving project cost in Westside section; remaining $180,000 estimated cost is to be financed by a special assessment.

Instructions

Prepare journal entries for the year ended June 30, Year 24, in the other funds or account groups affected by the foregoing transactions or events of the General Fund of Webster Village. Identify the affected funds or account groups. Include a journal entry for depreciation of the computer.

Pr. 13-5 Among the activities of Calabash County for the fiscal year beginning July 1, Year 7, and ending June 30, Year 8, were the following:

July 1 Approved the annual budget for the Gasoline Tax Special Revenue Fund as follows: Appropriations, $600,000; estimated revenues, $640,000.

    5 Executed a contract for the construction of a new public library at a total cost of $5 million.

Aug. 1 Authorized a special assessment of $400,000 on residents of the North Subdivision for construction of sidewalks. The special assessment, which was payable in five annual installments beginning September 1, Year 7, with interest at 9% a year on the unpaid installments, was to be accounted for in the Special Assessment Special Revenue Fund.

Sept. 1 Acquired from proceeds of general tax revenues equipment costing $20,000 (the related purchase order was for $19,600). The equipment was to be used by the general government of Calabash County, which does not depreciate plant assets in the General Fixed Assets Account Group.

Instructions

Prepare journal entries for the year ended June 30, Year 8, for the foregoing transactions or events of Calabash County. Identify the funds or account groups in which the journal entries are recorded.

Pr. 13-6 On July 1, Year 6, the City of Arlette, which records depreciation on plant assets in the General Fixed Assets Account Group, leased under a three-year term capital lease a computer with a four-year economic life and no residual value. Lease payments of $3,000 by the General Fund were payable on July 1, Year 6, Year 7, and Year 8; a bargain purchase option of $500 was payable on June 30, Year 9. The interest rate implicit in the lease, 9%, was less than the city's incremental borrowing rate and was known to the City Council.

Instructions

Prepare journal entries with respect to the capital lease for the City of Arlette for the three years ended June 30, Year 9, in all affected funds and account groups. Identify the affected funds or account groups. The City of Arlette depreciates plant assets by the straight-line method.

Pr. 13-7 The City of Ordway's fiscal year ends on June 30. During the year ended June 30, Year 2, the city authorized the construction of a new library and the issuance of general obligation term bonds to finance the construction of the library. The authorization imposed the following restrictions:

(1) Construction cost was not to exceed $5 million.
(2) Annual interest rate was not to exceed 10%.

The city does not record capital budgets, but other appropriate ledger accounts are maintained. The following transactions or events relating to the financing and constructing of the library occurred during the year ended June 30, Year 3:

(1) On July 1, Year 2, the city issued $5 million of 30 year, 9% general obligation term bonds for $5,100,000. The semiannual interest dates were June 30 and December 31.

(2) On July 3, Year 2, the Library Capital Projects Fund invested $4,900,000 in short-term notes. This investment was at face amount, with no accrued interest. Interest on cash invested by the Library Capital Projects Fund must be transferred to the Library Debt Service Fund. During the year ending June 30, Year 3, estimated interest to be earned was $140,000.

(3) On July 5, Year 2, the City signed a construction-type contract with Premier Construction Company to build the library for $4,980,000.

(4) On January 15, Year 3, the Library Capital Projects Fund received $3,040,000, from the maturity of short-term notes acquired on July 3, Year 2. The cost of these notes was $3 million. The interest of $40,000 was transferred to the Library Debt Service Fund.

(5) On January 20, Year 3, Premier Construction Company billed the City $3 million for work performed on the new library. The contract calls for 10% retention until final inspection and acceptance of the building. The Library Capital Projects Fund paid $2,700,000 to Premier.

(6) On June 30, Year 3, the Library Capital Projects Fund prepared adjusting and closing entries.

Instructions

a Prepare journal entries for the year ended June 30, Year 2, for the foregoing transactions or events of the City of Ordway Library Capital Projects Fund. Use the following ledger account titles:

Cash
Encumbrances
Expenditures
Fund Balance Reserved for Encumbrances
Interest Receivable
Investments
Other Financing Sources
Payable to Library Debt Service Fund
Unreserved and Undesignated Fund Balance
Vouchers Payable

Do not record journal entries in any other fund or account group.

b Prepare a balance sheet for the City of Ordway Library Capital Projects Fund on June 30, Year 3.

Pr. 13-8 In a special election held on May 1, Year 3, the citizens of the City of Wilmont approved a $10 million issue of 20-year, 8% general obligation term bonds maturing in Year 23. The proceeds of the bonds will be used to help finance the construction of a new civic center. The total cost of the project was estimated at $15 million. The remaining $5 million was to be financed by an irrevocable state grant, which has been awarded. A capital projects fund was established to account for this project and was designated the Civic Center Capital Projects Fund.

The following transactions and events occurred during the fiscal year beginning July 1, Year 3, and ending June 30, Year 4:

(1) On July 1, the General Fund loaned $500,000 (noninterest-bearing) to the Civic Center Capital Projects Fund for defraying engineering and other costs.
(2) Preliminary engineering and planning costs of $320,000 were paid to Akron Company. There had been no encumbrance for this cost.
(3) On December 1, the bonds were issued to yield 9%. Interest was payable each June 1 and December 1, through Year 23.
(4) On March 15, a contract for $12 million was entered into with Carlson Construction Company for the major part of the project.
(5) Purchase orders were placed for material estimated to cost $55,000.
(6) On April 1, a partial payment of $2,500,000 was received from the state government.
(7) The material that was ordered previously was received at a cost of $51,000 and paid for.
(8) On June 15, a progress billing of $2 million was received from Carlson Construction Company for work done on the project. In accordance with the contract, the city withheld 6% of any billing until the project was completed.
(9) The General Fund was repaid the $500,000 previously loaned.

Instructions

Prepare general journal entries to record the foregoing transactions and events of the Civic Center Capital Projects Fund for the period July 1, Year 3, through June 30, Year 4, and the closing entries on June 30, Year 4. Omit explanations for the journal entries. Use the following ledger account titles in the journal entries:

Cash   Other Financing Uses
Encumbrances   Payable to General Fund
Expenditures   Receivable from State Government
Fund Balance Reserved for   Revenues
  Encumbrances   Unreserved and Undesignated Fund Balance
Other Financing Sources   Vouchers Payable

Pr. 13-9 The following deficit budget was proposed for Year 3 for the Angelus School District General Fund:

ANGELUS SCHOOL DISTRICT GENERAL FUND
Annual Budget
For Year Ending December 31, Year 3

Fund balance, Jan. 1, Year 3..	$128,000
Revenues:	
Property taxes	112,000
Investment interest...	4,000
Total..	$244,000
Expenditures:	
Operating	$120,000
County treasurer's fees	1,120
Bond interest	50,000
Projected fund balance, Dec. 31, Year 3..	72,880
Total..	$244,000

A general obligation bond issue of the School District was proposed in Year 2. The proceeds were to be used for a new school. There are no other outstanding bond issues. Information about the bond issue follows:

Principal amount	$1,000,000
Interest rate	7½%
Bonds dated	Jan. 1, Year 3
Interest payable	Jan. 1 and July 1, beginning July 1, Year 3
Maturity	Serially at the rate of $100,000 a year, starting Jan. 1, Year 5.

The School District uses a separate bank account for each fund. The General Fund trial balance on December 31, Year 2, is on page 672.

The county treasurer collects the property taxes and withholds a fee of 1% on all collections. The transactions and events for Year 3 were as follows:

Jan. 1 The proposed budget was adopted, the general obligation bond issue was authorized, and the property taxes were levied.

Feb. 28 Net property tax receipts from county treasurer, $49,500, were deposited.
Apr. 1 General obligation bonds were issued at 101 plus accrued interest. It was directed that the premium be used for payment of interest by the General Fund.
      2 The School District paid $147,000 for the new school site.
      3 A contract for $850,000 for the new school was approved.
May   1 Interest was received on short-term investments.
July 1 Interest was paid on bonds.
Aug. 31 Net property tax receipts from county treasurer, $59,400, were deposited.
Nov. 1 Payment on new school construction contract, $200,000, was made.
      1 Interest was received on short-term investments.
Dec. 31 Operating expenditures during the year were $115,000. (Disregard vouchering and encumbrances.)

ANGELUS SCHOOL DISTRICT GENERAL FUND
Trial Balance
December 31, Year 2

	Debit	Credit
Cash	$ 28,000	
Short-term investments—U.S. Treasury 6% bonds, interest payable on May 1 and Nov. 1	100,000	
Unreserved and undesignated fund balance		$128,000
Totals	$128,000	$128,000

Instructions

Prepare journal entries for Angelus School District to record the foregoing Year 3 transactions and events in the following funds or account groups. (Closing entries are not required.)

a General Fund
b Capital Projects Fund
c General Fixed Assets Account Group
d General Long-Term Debt Account Group
Angelus School District does not use a Debt Service Fund.

14

Governmental Entities: Proprietary Funds, Fiduciary Funds, and Comprehensive Annual Financial Report

■n this chapter, the coverage of accounting and reporting for governmental entities is completed with the discussion and illustration of (1) accounting for proprietary funds and fiduciary funds and (2) the comprehensive annual financial report (CAFR) published by governmental entities other than the federal government.

PROPRIETARY FUNDS

Enterprise funds and internal service funds comprise the proprietary funds of governmental entities. These funds are more similar to business enterprises than are governmental funds or fiduciary funds (trust funds and agency funds). Enterprise funds sell services to the citizens of the governmental entity and sometimes to other funds of the governmental entity, for amounts designed to produce a net income. Internal service funds, as their title indicates, sell goods or services to other funds of the governmental entity, but not to the public. Accordingly, earning significant amounts of net income is not an objective of an internal service fund.

Both enterprise funds and internal service funds use the accrual basis of accounting and issue financial statements similar to those for a business enterprise—a statement of revenues, expenses, and changes in retained earnings (which includes an amount labeled *net income*), a balance sheet, and a statement of cash flows.

The balance sheets of both types of proprietary funds are classified into current and noncurrent sections. The plant assets of the two types of proprietary funds are recorded in their accounting records, and depreciation and amortization expenses are recognized by each proprietary fund.

Because of the many similarities in the accounting cycle and the financial statements of business enterprises and proprietary funds, journal entries for proprietary funds are not illustrated in this section. Instead, the unique features of proprietary

673

funds, including differences from features of business enterprises, are emphasized, and financial statements for proprietary funds are illustrated.

Accounting for Enterprise Funds

Enterprise funds account for the operations of commercial-type activities of a governmental entity, such as utilities, airports, seaports, and recreational facilities. These commercial-type enterprises sell services to the public (and in some cases to other activities of the governmental entity) at a profit. Consequently, the accounting for enterprise funds is more akin to business enterprise accounting than the accounting for any other governmental entity fund. For example, the accrual basis of accounting is used for an enterprise fund, with short-term prepayments, depreciation expense, and doubtful accounts expense recognized in the fund's accounting records. The enterprise fund's accounting records also include the plant assets owned by the fund, as well as the liabilities for revenue bonds and any general obligation bonds payable by the fund. (General obligation bonds are a liability of an enterprise fund if their proceeds were used by the enterprise fund for construction of plant assets or other purposes.) Encumbrance accounting is not used for enterprise funds, and their annual budgets generally are not entered in the accounting records. Retained earnings of an enterprise fund may be debited with cash remittances for operating transfers to the general fund, similar to dividends declared and paid by a corporate enterprise.

However, there are a number of differences between accounting for an enterprise fund and accounting for a business enterprise. Among these differences are the following:

1   Enterprise funds are not subject to federal and state income taxes. However, an enterprise fund may make payments in lieu of property or franchise taxes to the general fund and display the payments as expenses in the statement of revenues, expenses, and changes in retained earnings. (See page 617 of Chapter 12.)

2   There is no capital stock in an enterprise fund's balance sheet. Instead, Contributions ledger accounts set forth, in the *fund equity* section of the balance sheet, the assets contributed to the enterprise fund by the governmental entity, by customers of the enterprise fund, or by other public agencies.

3   An enterprise fund has restricted assets, which are segregated from current assets in the balance sheet. Cash deposits made by customers of a utility enterprise fund, which are to help assure the customers' payment for utility services, are restricted for cash or interest-bearing investments to offset the enterprise fund's liability for the customers' deposits. Cash received from proceeds of revenue bonds issued by the enterprise fund is restricted to payments for construction of plant assets financed by issuance of the bonds. Part of the cash generated by the enterprise fund's operations must be segregated and invested for payment of interest and principal of the revenue bonds issued by the enterprise fund.

4   Current liabilities payable from restricted assets are segregated from other current liabilities of an enterprise fund in a section of the balance sheet that precedes long-term liabilities.

5   An appropriation of retained earnings generally is displayed in the balance sheet of an enterprise fund. The appropriation is equal to the cash and investments restricted to payment of revenue bond interest and principal.

6   Subsidy-type operating transfers from an enterprise fund to the general fund are displayed in the operating transfers section of the enterprise fund's statement of revenues, expenses, and changes in retained earnings.

7   The form of the statement of cash flows for proprietary funds of governmental entities was set forth in *GASB Statement No. 9,* "Reporting Cash Flows of Proprietary and Nonexpendable Trust Funds and Governmental Entities That Use Proprietary Fund Accounting," issued in 1989 by the Governmental Accounting Standards Board.[1] Among the features of an enterprise fund's statement of cash flows are the following:

(1) There are *four categories* of cash flows: from operating activities, from noncapital financing activities, from capital and related financing activities, and from investing activities. (The statement of cash flows for a business enterprise has *three categories* of cash flows.)

(2) In the indirect method, *operating income,* rather than *net income,* is reconciled to net cash provided by operating activities.

(3) Noncapital financing activities cash flows include operating grants from other governmental entities and operating transfers to or from other funds of the governmental entity.

(4) Temporary investments of cash received from borrowings for plant assets construction are reported with cash flows from capital and related financing activities, rather than with cash flows from investing activities.

Financial Statements for Enterprise Fund   Some of the foregoing discussion is illustrated in the financial statements of the Town of Verdant Glen Enterprise Fund (for the town's water utility) on pages 676 through 678.

The following aspects of the financial statements for the Town of Verdant Glen Enterprise Fund should be noted:

1   The payment in lieu of property taxes, $40,000, and the operating transfer out, $10,000, in the statement of revenues, expenses, and changes in retained earnings are counterparts of the amounts recorded by the Town of Verdant Glen General Fund in journal entry no. *9* on page 617 of Chapter 12.

2   The receivable from General Fund, $5,000, in the balance sheet is the counterpart of the related payable to Enterprise Fund in the General Fund trial balance on page 619 of Chapter 12.

---

[1] *Codification of Governmental Accounting and Financial Reporting Standards,* GASB (Norwalk: 1992), pp. 197–207.

3   The $53,000 appropriation of retained earnings for revenue bond retirement in the balance sheet may be verified as follows:

Total restricted assets	$167,000
Less: Amount attributable to customers' deposits	44,000
Difference	$123,000
Less: Amount attributable to current portion of revenue bonds and accrued	
interest ($50,000 + $20,000)	70,000
Appropriation of retained earnings	$ 53,000

4   Short-term investments, both current and restricted, in the balance sheet are *cash equivalents.* Thus, the end-of-year cash and cash equivalents in the statement of cash flows is computed as follows: $62,000 + $120,000 + $22,000 + $145,000 = $349,000.

Financial statements of a governmental entity's enterprise fund

TOWN OF VERDANT GLEN ENTERPRISE FUND
Statement of Revenues, Expenses, and Changes in Retained Earnings
For Year Ended June 30, Year 6

Operating revenues:		
Charges for services		$520,000
Operating expenses:		
Personal services	$ 82,000	
Contractual services	94,000	
Supplies	21,000	
Material	75,000	
Heat, light, and power	14,000	
Depreciation	45,000	
Payment in lieu of property taxes	40,000	
Total operating expenses		371,000
Operating income		$149,000
Nonoperating revenues (expenses):		
Operating grants	$ 43,000	
Interest revenue	12,000	
Interest expense	(46,000)	
Fiscal agent fees	(14,000)	
Total nonoperating revenues (expenses)		(5,000)
Income before operating transfers		$144,000
Operating transfer (out) to General Fund		(10,000)
Net income		$134,000
Retained earnings, beginning of year		322,000
Retained earnings, end of year		$456,000

TOWN OF VERDANT GLEN ENTERPRISE FUND
Balance Sheet
June 30, Year 6

Assets

Current assets:

Cash		$ 62,000
Short-term investments, at cost		120,000
Accounts receivable (net)		56,000
Receivable from General Fund		5,000
Inventory of supplies, at first-in, first-out cost		18,000
Short-term prepayments		2,000
Total current assets		$ 263,000
Restricted assets:		
Cash	$ 22,000	
Short-term investments, at cost	145,000	
Total restricted assets		167,000
Plant assets:		
Land	$ 192,000	
Buildings	1,285,000	
Machinery and equipment	347,000	
Subtotal	$1,824,000	
Less: Accumulated depreciation	748,000	
Total plant assets		1,076,000
Total assets		$1,506,000

Liabilities & Fund Equity

Current liabilities:		
Vouchers payable		$ 144,000
Accrued liabilities		82,000
Total current liabilities		$ 226,000
Liabilities payable from restricted assets:		
Interest payable	$ 20,000	
Current portion of revenue bonds	50,000	
Customers' deposits	44,000	
Total liabilities payable from restricted assets		114,000
Long-term debt:		
Revenue bonds, less current portion		500,000
Total liabilities		$ 840,000
Fund equity:		
Contributed capital from General Fund	$ 210,000	
Retained earnings:		
Appropriated for revenue bonds retirement	53,000	
Unappropriated	403,000	
Total fund equity		666,000
Total liabilities & fund equity		$1,506,000

TOWN OF VERDANT GLEN ENTERPRISE FUND
Statement of Cash Flows (indirect method)
For Year Ended June 30, Year 6

Net cash provided by operating activities **(Exhibit 1)**.		$ 204,000
Cash flows from noncapital financing activities:		
Payment of principal ($50,000) and interest ($2,000) of		
note payable to bank	$(52,000)	
Operating grants from state government	43,000	
Operating transfer (out) to General Fund.	(10,000)	
Net cash used in noncapital financing activities		(19,000)
Cash flows from capital and related financing activities:		
Acquisition of machinery and equipment	$(41,000)	
Payment of serial maturity of revenue bonds ($50,000) and		
annual interest on the bonds ($44,000)	(94,000)	
Payment of fiscal agent fees.	(14,000)	
Deposits received from customers.	10,000	
Net cash used in capital and related financing activities.		(139,000)
Cash flows from investing activities:		
Interest received on short-term investments		12,000
Increase in cash and cash equivalents		$ 58,000
Cash and cash equivalents, beginning of year		291,000
Cash and cash equivalents, end of year.		$ 349,000
Exhibit 1 Cash flows from operating activities:		
Operating income	$149,000	
Adjustments to reconcile operating income to net cash pro-		
vided by operating activities:		
Depreciation expense.	45,000	
Decrease in accounts receivable (net)	3,000	
Increase in receivable from General Fund.	(5,000)	
Increase in inventory of supplies	(4,000)	
Decrease in short-term prepayments	1,000	
Increase in vouchers payable.	21,000	
Decrease in accrued liabilities	(6,000)	
Net cash provided by operating activities.	$204,000	

Accounting for Internal Service Funds

An internal service fund is established to sell supplies and services to other funds of the governmental entity, but not to the public. This type of fund is created to assure uniformity and economies in the procurement of supplies and services for the governmental entity as a whole, such as stationery supplies and the maintenance and repairs of motor vehicles.

The operations of internal service funds resemble those of a business enterprise, except that internal service funds are not profit-motivated. The revenues of internal service funds should be sufficient to cover all their operating costs and expenses, with perhaps a modest profit margin. In this way, the resources of internal service funds are "revolving"; the original contribution from the general fund of the governmental entity to establish an internal service fund is expended for supplies, operating equipment, employees' salaries or wages, and other operating expenses, and the amounts expended then are recouped through billings to other funds of the governmental entity.

Although an internal service fund should use an annual budget for managerial planning and control purposes, the budget need not be entered in the accounting records of the fund. The accrual basis of accounting, including the perpetual inventory system and depreciation of plant assets, is appropriate for an internal service fund. Encumbrance accounting is not required but may be useful in controlling nonrecurring purchase orders of an internal service fund.

Because internal service funds do not issue revenue bonds and do not receive contributions or deposits from customers, the financial statements of internal service funds are nearly identical in form and content to those of business enterprises. However, similar to enterprise funds, internal service funds do not have owners' equity in their balance sheets. A Contributions ledger account balance accompanies the Retained Earnings account balance in the fund equity section of the balance sheet for an internal service fund.

Financial Statements for Internal Service Fund The financial statements for the Town of Verdant Glen Internal Service Fund that follow are illustrative of the statements for such a fund. The receivable from General Fund, $6,000, in the balance sheet is the counterpart of the related payable to Internal Service Fund in the General Fund trial balance on page 619 of Chapter 12.

Financial statements of a governmental entity's internal service fund

TOWN OF VERDANT GLEN INTERNAL SERVICE FUND
Statement of Revenues, Expenses, and Changes in Retained Earnings
For Year Ended June 30, Year 6

Operating revenues:		
Charges for services...		$162,400
Operating expenses:		
Personal services	$ 21,200	
Supplies	84,300	
Heat, light, and power	20,500	
Depreciation..	34,000	
Total operating expenses		160,000
Net income		$ 2,400
Retained earnings, beginning of year................................		26,800
Retained earnings, end of year.....................................		$ 29,200

TOWN OF VERDANT GLEN INTERNAL SERVICE FUND
Balance Sheet
June 30, Year 6

Assets

Current assets:

Cash...		$ 8,600
Receivable from General Fund....................................		6,000
Inventory of supplies, at first-in, first-out cost		64,300
Total current assets		$ 78,900

Plant assets:

Land...	$142,100	
Building..	627,500	
Machinery and equipment..............................	132,800	
Subtotal...	$902,400	
Less: Accumulated depreciation	327,800	
Total plant assets		574,600
Total assets		$653,500

Liabilities & Fund Equity

Current liabilities:

Vouchers payable		$ 14,300

Fund equity:

Contributed capital from General Fund	$610,000	
Unappropriated retained earnings.......................	29,200	
Total fund equity		639,200
Total liabilities & fund equity		$653,500

TOWN OF VERDANT GLEN INTERNAL SERVICE FUND
Statement of Cash Flows (indirect method)
For Year Ended June 30, Year 6

Net cash provided by operating activities:

Net income	$ 2,400	
Adjustments to reconcile net income to net cash provided by operating activities:		
Depreciation expense	34,000	
Decrease in receivable from General Fund	1,000	
Increase in inventory of supplies......................	(11,300)	
Increase in vouchers payable.........................	$ 2,600	
Net cash provided by operating activities........................		$ 28,700

Cash flows from capital and related financing activities:

Acquisition of machinery and equipment		(23,400)
Increase in cash...		$ 5,300
Cash, beginning of year...		3,300
Cash, end of year		$ 8,600

FIDUCIARY FUNDS

Expendable trust funds, nonexpendable trust funds, pension trust funds, and agency funds constitute the fiduciary funds of a governmental entity. The position of the governmental entity with respect to such funds is one of a ***custodian*** or a ***trustee,*** rather than an ***owner.***

In explaining the accounting principles for state and local governmental entities, the Governmental Accounting Standards Board described accounting for trust funds as follows:[2]

> Each trust fund is classified for accounting measurement purposes as either a governmental fund or a proprietary fund. Expendable trust funds are accounted for in essentially the same manner as governmental funds. Nonexpendable trust funds and pension trust funds are accounted for in essentially the same manner as proprietary funds. Agency funds are purely custodial (assets equal liabilities) and thus do not involve measurement of results of operations.

Accounting for Agency Funds

Agency funds are of short duration. Typically, agency funds are used to account for sales taxes collected by a state government on behalf of the municipalities and townships of the state, and for payroll taxes and other deductions withheld from salaries and wages payable to employees of a governmental entity. The amounts withheld subsequently are paid to a federal or state collection unit. Also, in ***GASB Statement No. 2,*** "Financial Reporting of Deferred Compensation Plans . . . ," the Governmental Accounting Standards Board required that amounts set aside by state and local governmental entities for deferred compensation to employees in accordance with Internal Revenue Code Section 457 be accounted for in an agency fund.[3] (Such deferred compensation is not taxable to the governmental entity's employee until it is withdrawn by the employee or by a designated beneficiary.)

Agency funds do not have operations during a fiscal year; thus, the only financial statements for an agency fund are a balance sheet, showing the cash or receivables of the fund and the amounts payable to other funds or governmental entities or to outsiders, and a statement of changes in assets and liabilities, illustrated as follows for the Town of Verdant Glen:

Financial statements of a governmental entity's agency fund

TOWN OF VERDANT GLEN AGENCY FUND
Balance Sheet
June 30, Year 6

Assets

Cash.. $12,600

Liabilities

Vouchers payable.. $12,600

---

[2] Ibid., pp. 46–47.
[3] Ibid., p. 293.

TOWN OF VERDANT GLEN AGENCY FUND
Statement of Changes in Assets and Liabilities
For Year Ended June 30, Year 6

	Balances, July 1, Year 5	Additions	Deductions	Balances, June 30, Year 6
Assets				
Cash	$14,200	$49,000	$50,600	$12,600
Liabilities				
Vouchers payable	$14,200	$49,000	$50,600	$12,600

Accounting for Expendable and Nonexpendable Trust Funds

Trust funds of a governmental entity are longer-lived than agency funds. An *expendable trust fund* is one whose principal and income both may be expended to achieve the objectives of the trust. A *nonexpendable trust fund* is one whose revenues are expended to carry out the objectives of the trust; the principal remains intact. For example, an *endowment* established by the grantor of a trust may specify that the revenues from the endowment are to be expended by the governmental entity for student scholarships, but the endowment principal is not to be expended. A nonexpendable trust fund requires two separate trust fund accounting entities—one for principal and one for revenues. Accounting for the two separate trust funds requires a careful distinction between transactions affecting the principal—such as changes in the investment portfolio—and transactions affecting revenues—such as cash dividends and interest on the investment portfolio. The *trust indenture,* which is the legal document establishing the trust, should specify distinctions between principal and revenues. If the trust indenture is silent with respect to such distinctions, the trust law of the governmental entity governs separation of principal trust fund and revenues trust fund transactions.

Because the governmental entity serves as a custodian for a trust fund, accounting for a trust fund should comply with the trust indenture under which the fund was established. Among the provisions that might affect the accounting for a trust fund are requirements that the annual budget for the trust fund be entered in its accounting records and that depreciation be recognized for an endowment principal trust fund that includes depreciable plant assets.

To illustrate accounting for expendable and nonexpendable trust funds, assume that Karl and Mabel Root, residents of the Town of Verdant Glen, contributed marketable securities with a market value of $100,000 on July 1, Year 5, to a trust to be administered by the Town of Verdant Glen as trustee. Principal of the gift was to be maintained in an Endowment Principal Nonexpendable Trust Fund. Revenues from the marketable securities were to be used for scholarships for qualified students to attend Verdant Glen College; the revenues and expenditures for scholarships were to be accounted for in an Endowment Revenues Expendable Trust Fund. The Bank of Verdant Glen trust department was to receive an annual trustee's fee of $500 for administering the two trust funds on behalf of the Town of Verdant Glen.

Journal entries for nonexpendable trust fund and expendable trust fund of a governmental entity

Explanation of transactions and events	Account titles	Endowment Principal Nonexpendable Trust Fund	Endowment Revenues Expendable Trust Fund
Receipt of marketable securities in trust	Investments	100,000	
	Revenues	100,000	
Accrual of revenues on marketable securities	Interest Receivable	5,000	
	Dividends Receivable	8,000	
	Revenues	13,000	
Receipt of interest and dividends	Cash	13,000	
	Interest Receivable	5,000	
	Dividends Receivable	8,000	
Recording of liability to Revenues Trust Fund for interest and dividends	Other Financing Uses	13,000	
	Payable to Revenues Trust Fund	13,000	
	Receivable from Principal Trust Fund		13,000
	Other Financing Sources		13,000
Transfer of cash from Principal Trust Fund to Revenues Trust Fund	Payable to Revenues Trust Fund	13,000	
	Cash	13,000	
	Cash		13,000
	Receivable from Principal Trust Fund		13,000
Payment of scholarships to students James Rich and Janet Wells	Expenditures		12,000
	Cash		12,000
Payment of trustee's fee	Expenditures		500
	Cash		500
Closing entries	Revenues	113,000	
	Other Financing Uses	13,000	
	Fund Balance Reserved for Endowment	100,000	
	Other Financing Sources		13,000
	Expenditures		12,500
	Fund Balance Reserved for Scholarships		500

Journal entries for the two trust funds for the year ended June 30, Year 6, are summarized on page 683.

Financial Statements of Nonexpendable Trust Fund   Because accounting for nonexpendable trust funds parallels accounting for proprietary funds, the financial statements for a nonexpendable trust fund are a statement of revenues, expenses, and changes in fund balance, a balance sheet, and a statement of cash flows. Financial statements (excluding a statement of cash flows) of the Town of Verdant Glen Endowment Principal Nonexpendable Trust Fund are shown below for the year ended June 30, Year 6:

Financial statements of a governmental entity's nonexpendable trust fund

TOWN OF VERDANT GLEN ENDOWMENT PRINCIPAL NONEXPENDABLE TRUST FUND
Statement of Revenues, Expenses, and Changes in Fund Balance
For Year Ended June 30, Year 6

Operating revenues:	
Interest	$ 5,000
Dividends	8,000
Gifts	100,000
Total operating revenues	$113,000
Operating transfers out	13,000
Net income	$100,000
Fund balance, beginning of year	-0-
Fund balance, end of year	$100,000

TOWN OF VERDANT GLEN ENDOWMENT PRINCIPAL NONEXPENDABLE TRUST FUND
Balance Sheet
June 30, Year 6

Assets

Investments	$100,000

Liabilities & Fund Balance

Fund balance reserved for endowment	$100,000

Financial Statements of Expendable Trust Fund   Accounting for expendable trust funds is comparable with accounting for governmental funds; therefore, financial statements for expendable trust funds are a statement of revenues, expenditures, and changes in fund balance, and a balance sheet only. For the Town of Verdant Glen Endowment Revenues Expendable Trust Fund, financial statements for the year ended June 30, Year 6, are on page 685.

There is no unreserved and undesignated fund balance for either of the Town of Verdant Glen trust funds, because the trust indenture required the reservation of the entire fund balance of each fund to achieve the purpose of the trust.

Financial statements of
a governmental entity's
expendable trust fund

TOWN OF VERDANT GLEN ENDOWMENT REVENUES
EXPENDABLE TRUST FUND
Statement of Revenues, Expenditures, and Changes in Fund Balance
For Year Ended June 30, Year 6

Revenues	$ -0-
Expenditures:	
Education	$ 12,000
Administration	500
Total expenditures	$ 12,500
Excess (deficiency) of revenues over expenditures	$(12,500)
Operating transfers in	13,000
Excess of revenues and other financing sources over expenditures	$ 500
Fund balance, beginning of year	-0-
Fund balance, end of year	$ 500

TOWN OF VERDANT GLEN ENDOWMENT REVENUES
EXPENDABLE TRUST FUND
Balance Sheet
June 30, Year 6

Assets

Cash	$500

Liabilities & Fund Balance

Fund balance reserved for scholarships	$500

Accounting for Pension Trust Funds

Pension trust funds are perhaps the most complex of all the funds of a governmental entity, because they involve accounting for liabilities and fund balance reserves that are computed on the basis of actuarial assumptions. These actuarial assumptions include life expectancies of employees covered by the governmental entity's defined benefit pension plans and rates of earnings on pension trust fund assets.

Pension trust funds are accounted for in essentially the same manner as proprietary funds, although pension trust funds may not have plant assets or depreciation expense. Thus, the accounting records of pension trust funds are maintained under the accrual basis of accounting and include all assets, liabilities, revenues, and expenses of the fund. The costs of administering some pension trust funds may be borne by the general fund of the governmental entity.

Because of the complexities of pension trust funds, illustrative journal entries for a pension trust fund are beyond the scope of this discussion. The following financial statements for the Town of Verdant Glen Employees' Retirement System Pension Trust Fund for the year ended June 30, Year 6, which exclude a statement of cash flows, illustrate some of the accounting concepts involved:[4]

---

[4] Ibid., pp. 431–439.

Financial statements of
a governmental entity's
pension trust fund

TOWN OF VERDANT GLEN EMPLOYEE RETIREMENT SYSTEM
PENSION TRUST FUND
Statement of Revenues, Expenses, and Changes in Fund Balance
For Year Ended June 30, Year 6

Operating revenues:

Member contributions		$131,600
Employer contributions		247,300
Investment revenues		146,200
Total operating revenues		$525,100

Operating expenses:

Annuity benefits	$134,800	
Disability benefits	87,200	
Refunds to terminated employees	38,300	
Administrative expenses	187,200	
Total operating expenses		447,500
Net operating income		$ 77,600
Fund balance, beginning of year		842,300
Fund balance, end of year		$919,900

TOWN OF VERDANT GLEN EMPLOYEE RETIREMENT SYSTEM
PENSION TRUST FUND
Balance Sheet
June 30, Year 6

Assets

Cash	$ 21,200
Interest and dividends receivable	34,800
Investments	884,600
Plant assets, less accumulated depreciation, $64,200	82,100
Total assets	$1,022,700

Liabilities

Accounts payable and accrued liabilities	102,800
Net assets available for benefits	$ 919,900

Fund balance

Actuarial present value of projected benefits payable to current retirees and beneficiaries	$ 231,500
Actuarial present value of projected benefits payable to terminated vested participants	18,600
Actuarial present value of credited projected benefits for active employees:	
Member contributions	289,200
Employer-financed portion	502,600
Total actuarial present value of credited projected benefits	$1,041,900
Unfunded actuarial present value of credited projected benefits	(122,000)
Total fund balance	$ 919,900

Following is a discussion of important features of the financial statements for the Town of Verdant Glen Employees' Retirement System Pension Trust Fund:

1   The defined benefit pension plan of the Town of Verdant Glen is a *contributory pension plan,* to which both covered employees and the town make contributions. (In a *noncontributory pension plan,* only the town would make contributions.)

2   Investment revenues of the Pension Trust Fund include gains and losses on investments as well as interest and dividends.

3   Annuity benefits are pension payments to retired former employees of the Town of Verdant Glen. Disability benefits are payments to former employees whose disabilities precluded their working until scheduled retirement dates.

4   All pension payments to retired employees had been made through June 30, Year 6; otherwise, the liabilities in the Pension Trust Fund balance sheet would include an amount for annuities payable.

5   *Projected benefits* under a defined benefit pension plan are the amount of all pension benefits attributable to employee services to the date of computation of the actuarial present value. The actuarial present value amounts are computed on the basis of estimates of mortality, employee turnover, anticipated employee earnings, rates of inflation, and the like.

6   Not illustrated for the Town of Verdant Glen Pension Trust Fund are the extensive disclosures required in notes to the financial statements of the Pension Trust Fund. These required disclosures are set forth in *GASB Statement No. 5,* "Disclosure of Pension Information by Public Employee Retirement Systems and State and Local Governmental Employers," which is incorporated in the 1992 edition of *Governmental Accounting and Financial Reporting Standards.*[5]

COMPREHENSIVE ANNUAL FINANCIAL REPORT OF GOVERNMENTAL ENTITIES

The comprehensive annual financial report (CAFR) is required by the Governmental Accounting Standards Board to be prepared by every governmental entity as a matter of public record.[6] The complex components of the CAFR are as follows:[7]

    a. Introductory Section
        (Table of contents, letter(s) of transmittal, and other material deemed appropriate by management)
    b. Financial Section
        (1) Auditor's Report
        (2) General Purpose Financial Statements (GPFS)
              (Combined Statements—Overview)

---

[5] Ibid., pp. 441–455.
[6] Ibid., p. 135.
[7] Ibid., pp. 137–138.

      (a)   Combined Balance Sheet—All Fund Types and Account Groups

      (b)   Combined Statement of Revenues, Expenditures, and Changes in Fund Balances—All Governmental Fund Types

      (c)   Combined Statement of Revenues, Expenditures, and Changes in Fund Balances—Budget and Actual—General and Special Revenue Fund Types (and similar governmental fund types for which annual budgets have been legally adopted)

      (d)   Combined Statement of Revenues, Expenses, and Changes in Retained Earnings (or Equity)—All Proprietary Fund Types

      (e)   Combined Statement of Cash Flows—All Proprietary Fund Types and Nonexpendable Trust Funds

      (f)   Notes to the financial statements

      (g)   Required Supplementary Information

      (Trust fund operations may be reported in (b), (d), and (e) above, as appropriate, or separately.)

    (3)   Combining and Individual Fund and Account Group Statements and Schedules

      (a)   Combining Statements—By Fund Type—where a governmental entity has more than one fund of a given fund type

      (b)   Individual fund and account group statements—where a governmental entity has only one fund of a given type and for account groups and/or where necessary to present prior-year and budgetary comparisons

      (c)   Schedules

         (i)   Schedules necessary to demonstrate compliance with finance-related legal and contractual provisions

        (ii)   Schedules to present information spread throughout the statements that can be brought together and shown in greater detail (for example, taxes receivable, including delinquent taxes; long-term debt; investments; and cash receipts, disbursements, and balances)

       (iii)   Schedules to present greater detail for information reported in the statements (for example, additional revenues sources detail and object of expenditure data by departments)

      (Narrative explanations useful in understanding combining and individual fund and account group statements and schedules that are not included in the notes to the financial statements should be presented on divider pages, directly on the statements and schedules, or in a separate section.)

  c.   Statistical Tables

  d.   Component Unit Financial Reports or Statements (Optional)

    The Governmental Accounting Standards Board provided that the general-purpose financial statements component of the comprehensive annual financial report of a governmental entity might be issued separately in official statements for bond offerings and for distribution to users requiring less detailed information than is contained in the comprehensive annual financial report.[8] Thus, the general-purpose financial statements component issued separately may be compared with the annual report of a publicly owned company, whereas the comprehensive annual financial report may be compared with *Form 10-K,* annual report, filed with the Securities and Exchange Commission by a publicly owned company, as described in Chapter 20.

It is evident that comprehensive annual financial reports of governmental entities may be voluminous, and perhaps even overwhelming, in content. For example, the *combined financial statements* included in the financial section of the financial report do not show single combined amounts; the statements include columns for each of the seven fund types and two account groups, possibly with optional *memorandum only* total columns for both the current year and the prior year. Comparable multicolumn presentations constitute the *combining* statements and schedules. Thus, the principal financial statements included in the annual financial reports of governmental entities are far more complex than the *consolidated* financial statements of business enterprises making up a parent company–subsidiaries group.

Appraisal of Accounting Standards for Governmental Entities

The accounting standards for governmental entities described and illustrated in this chapter and in Chapters 12 and 13 have been improved significantly since the inception of the Governmental Accounting Standards Board in 1984. However, considerable dissatisfaction still exists. Much of this dissatisfaction centers on fund accounting, accounting and financial reporting for public employee retirement systems, and plant assets and related depreciation. The increased attention to stewardship for taxpayer-provided resources of governmental entities necessitates continued improvements in the accounting and reporting for state and local governmental entities.

REVIEW QUESTIONS

1   Under what circumstances are general obligation bonds payable of a governmental entity recorded in the governmental entity's enterprise fund? Explain.

2   The accounting for a governmental entity's enterprise fund in many respects is similar to the accounting for a business enterprise; yet there are a number of differences between the two types of accounting. Identify at least three of the differences.

3   Why does a governmental entity's enterprise fund have restricted assets in its balance sheet? Explain.

4   What are the four categories of cash flows in the statement of cash flows for a governmental entity's enterprise fund?

5   How is the Contribution from General Fund ledger account displayed in the financial statements of a governmental entity's internal service fund? Explain.

6   How does the balance sheet of a governmental entity's internal service fund differ from the balance sheet of the governmental entity's enterprise fund? Explain.

---

[8] Ibid, p. 146.

7   Is a statement of revenues, expenses, and changes in fund balance issued for an agency fund of a governmental entity? Explain.

8   Accounting for a nonexpendable trust for which a governmental entity acts as custodian requires the establishment of two separate trust funds. Why is this true?

9   Explain the nature of the *contribution revenues* in the statement of revenues, expenses, and changes in fund balance of a governmental entity's pension trust fund.

10   Differentiate between a governmental entity's *comprehensive annual financial report* and its *general-purpose financial statements.*

11   Is a consolidated balance sheet appropriate for all funds and account groups of a governmental entity? Explain.

EXERCISES

Ex. 14-1   Select the best answer for each of the following multiple-choice questions:

1   Nonoperating revenues and expenses typically are displayed in the statement of revenues, expenses, and changes in retained earnings of a governmental entity's:
a Enterprise fund
b Internal service fund
c Agency fund
d Nonexpendable trust fund

2   The equity-type ledger accounts of a governmental entity's proprietary funds (enterprise funds and internal service funds) are Retained Earnings and:
a Fund Balance
b Contributed Capital from General Fund
c Governmental Equity
d Proprietary Equity

3   In the statement of cash flows (indirect method) for an enterprise fund of a governmental entity, the amount that is reconciled to net cash provided by operating activities is:
a Operating income
b Net income
c Income before operating transfers
d Nonoperating revenues (expenses)

4   May the following be displayed, as appropriate, among the liabilities of a governmental entity's enterprise fund:

	General obligation bonds payable?	*Revenue bonds payable?*
a	Yes	Yes
b	Yes	No
c	No	Yes
d	No	No

5   An agency fund of a governmental entity is a type of:

a Governmental fund

b Proprietary fund

c Fiduciary fund

d Account group

6   Is a statement of changes in assets and liabilities prepared for a governmental entity's:

	Agency fund?	Nonexpendable trust fund?	Expendable trust fund?
a	Yes	Yes	Yes
b	Yes	Yes	No
c	Yes	No	Yes
d	Yes	No	No

7   Accounting for a governmental entity's proprietary funds parallels accounting for the entity's:

a Nonexpendable trust funds only

b Expendable trust funds only

c Nonexpendable trust funds and expendable trust funds

d Agency funds

8   Is a fund balance displayed in the appropriate financial statement for a governmental entity's:

	Agency fund?	Nonexpendable trust fund?
a	Yes	Yes
b	Yes	No
c	No	Yes
d	No	No

9   Is a fund balance reserved for scholarships typically displayed in the balance sheet of a governmental entity's:

	Nonexpendable trust fund?	Expendable trust fund?
a	Yes	Yes
b	Yes	No
c	No	Yes
d	No	No

10   Is a fund balance reserved for endowment typically displayed in the balance sheet of a governmental entity's:

	Nonexpendable trust fund?	Expendable trust fund?
a	Yes	Yes
b	Yes	No
c	No	Yes
d	No	No

11 Is an unreserved and undesignated fund balance displayed in the balance sheet of a governmental entity's:

	Nonexpendable trust fund?	*Expendable trust fund?*
a	Yes	Yes
b	No	No
c	No	Yes
d	Yes	No

Ex. 14-2 The Enterprise Fund of Orchard City billed the General Fund $16,400 for utility services on May 31, Year 5.

Prepare journal entries for the May 31, Year 5, billing for both the Orchard City General Fund and the Orchard City Enterprise Fund.

Ex. 14-3 Selected ledger accounts of the Town of Goland Enterprise Fund had the following balances on June 30, Year 3:

Liabilities payable from restricted assets:	
Interest payable	$ 24,400
Current portion of revenue bonds	80,000
Customers' deposits	62,600
Restricted assets:	
Cash	42,300
Short-term investments, at cost	168,100

Prepare a working paper to compute the required balance of the Retained Earnings Appropriated for Revenue Bonds Retirement ledger account of the Town of Goland Enterprise Fund on June 30, Year 3.

Ex. 14-4 On June 18, Year 9, the Wilbert Township Enterprise Fund made a $120,000 payment in lieu of property taxes to the town's general fund.

Prepare journal entries on June 18, Year 9, for Wilbert Township General Fund and Enterprise Fund.

Ex. 14-5 Selected items taken from comparative financial statements of the Town of Liddell Enterprise Fund were as follows for the year ended June 30, Year 6:

Decrease in inventory of supplies	$ 42,600
Decrease in receivable from General Fund	21,700
Decrease in vouchers payable	12,200
Depreciation expense	81,700
Increase in accounts receivable	36,800
Increase in accrued liabilities	8,100
Increase in short-term prepayments	11,600
Net income	94,200
Operating income	125,400
Operating transfer out to General Fund	18,600
Payment in lieu of property taxes to General Fund	46,800

Prepare the cash flows from operating activities exhibit for the statement of cash flows (indirect method) for the Town of Liddell Enterprise Fund for the year ended June 30, Year 6.

Ex. 14-6   From the following trial balance, prepare appropriate financial statements (excluding a statement of cash flows):

TOWN OF DILBEY INTERNAL SERVICE FUND
Trial Balance
June 30, Year 8

	Debit	Credit
Cash.	$ 17,200	
Receivable from General Fund	12,000	
Inventory of supplies	128,600	
Plant assets	1,804,800	
Accumulated depreciation of plant assets		$ 655,600
Vouchers payable.		28,600
Contributed capital from General Fund		1,220,000
Unappropriated retained earnings.		53,600
Charges for services		324,800
Operating expenses.	320,000	
Totals.	$2,282,600	$2,282,600

Ex. 14-7   Agatha Morris, a citizen of Roark City, donated common stock valued at $620,000 to the city under a trust indenture dated July 1, Year 6. Under the terms of the indenture, the principal amount is to be kept intact; use of dividends revenues from the common stock is restricted to financing academic scholarships for college students. On December 14, Year 6, dividends of $42,000 were received on the common stock donated by Morris.

Prepare journal entries for Roark City to record the foregoing transactions and events in the appropriate funds. Identify the funds. Disregard entries for accrual of dividends. Omit explanations for the journal entries.

Ex. 14-8   Ledger account balances on June 30, Year 8, applicable to the City of Carvell Employee Retirement System Pension Trust Fund statement of revenues, expenses, and changes in fund balance for the year ended on that date, were as follows:

Administrative expenses	$294,600
Annuity benefits.	284,300
Disability benefits	52,800
Employer contributions	318,500
Fund balance, July 1, Year 7	841,000
Investment revenues	163,900
Member contributions.	211,600
Refunds to terminated employees.	61,600

Prepare a statement of revenues, expenses, and changes in fund balance for the City of Carvell Employee Retirement System Pension Trust Fund for the year ended June 30, Year 8.

Ex. 14-9   Among the transactions or events of Local Town for the month of November, Year 7, were the following:

Nov.   3   Issued at face amount $1 million of general obligation bonds, the proceeds of which were to finance construction of a new water treatment plant for water sold to residents of the town.

5   Received an invoice of $25,000 in the General Fund for equipment for which a purchase order in the amount of $24,700 had been issued earlier.

7   Acquired for $50,000 cash supplies for the central warehouse, to be issued to various departments of the town. The perpetual inventory system is used for supplies.

30   Issued bills totaling $80,000 to consumers of the water utility, for water consumption for the 30 days ended November 30.

Prepare journal entries (omit explanations) for the foregoing transactions or events of Local Town for the month of November, Year 7. Identify the fund or account group in which each journal entry is recorded.

CASES

Case 14-1   You have been requested to audit the financial statements of the funds and account groups of Ashburn City for the year ended June 30, Year 7. During the course of your audit, you learned that on July 1, Year 6, the city had issued at face amount $1 million, 20-year, 8% general obligation serial bonds to finance additional power-generating facilities for the Ashburn City electric utility. Principal and interest on the bonds were payable by the Ashburn City Electric Utility Enterprise Fund. However, for the first five years of the serial maturities of the bonds—July 1, Year 7, through July 1, Year 11—a special tax levy accounted for in the Ashburn City Special Revenue Fund was to contribute to the payment of 80% of the interest and principal of the general obligation bonds. At the end of the five-year period, it is anticipated that revenue from the electric utility's new power-generating facilities would create cash flow for the Ashburn City Electric Utility Enterprise Fund sufficient to pay all the serial maturities and interest of the general obligation bonds during the period July 1, Year 12, through July 1, Year 26.

You found that the accounting records of the Ashburn City Electric Utility Enterprise Fund included the following ledger account balances relative to the general obligation bonds on June 30, Year 7:

8% general obligation serial bonds payable ($50,000 due July 1, Year 7)	$1,000,000 cr
Interest payable (interest on the bonds is payable annually each July 1)	80,000 cr
Interest expense	80,000 dr

The statement of revenues, expenses, and changes in retained earnings for the year ended June 30, Year 7, prepared by the accountant for the Ashburn City Electric Utility Enterprise Fund showed a net loss of $40,000. You also learned that on July 1, Year 7, the Ashburn City Special Revenue Fund paid $104,000 ($130,000 × 0.80 = $104,000) and the Ashburn City Electric Utility Enterprise Fund paid the remaining $26,000 ($130,000 × 0.20 = $26,000) to the fiscal agent for the 8% general obligation serial bonds. The $130,000 was the total of the $50,000 principal and $80,000 interest due on the bonds July 1, Year 7. In the Enterprise Fund's journal entry to record payment of the bond principal and interest, the amount of $104,000 was credited to the Contribution from Special Revenue Fund ledger account.

Instructions

Do you concur with the Ashburn City Electric Utility Enterprise Fund's accounting and reporting treatment for the 8% general obligation serial bonds? Discuss.

Case 14-2 Wallace and Brenda Stuart, residents of Colby City, have donated their historic mansion, "Greystone," in trust to Colby City to serve as a tourist attraction. For a nominal charge, tourists will be guided through Greystone to observe the paintings, sculptures, antiques, and other art objects collected by the Stuarts, as well as the mansion's unique architecture.

The trust indenture executed by the Stuarts provided that the admissions charges to Greystone (which was appraised at $5 million on the date of the trust indenture) are to cover the operating expenditures associated with the tours, as well as maintenance and repairs costs for Greystone. Any excess of admissions revenues over the foregoing expenditures and costs was to be donated to Colby University for scholarships to art and architecture students. The trust indenture requires depreciation of Greystone.

Instructions

Discuss the fund accounting issues, and related accounting matters such as depreciation, that should be considered by officials of Colby City with respect to the Stuart Trust.

PROBLEMS

Pr. 14-1 Among the transactions and events of Kaspar City for the first four months of the year ended June 30, Year 9, were the following:

July 1, Year 8   Billed general property taxes, $1,600,000, of which 5% was estimated to be uncollectible.

Aug. 1   Issued $1 million, 20-year, 7% general obligation bonds to yield 6%, interest payable February 1 and August 1, to finance construction of a power-generating facility for the electricity utility.

Sept. 1   Received invoice in General Fund for a new computer for governmental accounting. Cost of the computer and related software was $10,000; the related purchase order had been issued for $10,200.

Oct. 1   Received invoice in General Fund for supplies received from Internal Service Fund, $1,200. The amount had not been subject to encumbrance.

Instructions

Prepare journal entries for the foregoing transactions or events of Kaspar City for the first four months of the fiscal year ended June 30, Year 9, in all affected funds or account groups. Identify the funds or account groups. The Internal Service Fund uses the periodic inventory system.

Pr. 14-2 The adjusted trial balance of the Town of Tolliver Enterprise Fund on June 30, Year 9, was as follows:

TOWN OF TOLLIVER ENTERPRISE FUND
Adjusted Trial Balance
June 30, Year 9

	Debit	Credit
Cash—unrestricted	$ 22,000	
Cash—restricted	38,000	
Short-term investments, at cost—unrestricted	64,000	
Short-term investments, at cost—restricted	97,000	
Accounts receivable	64,000	
Allowance for doubtful accounts		$ 12,000
Receivable from General Fund	26,000	
Receivable from Internal Service Fund	18,000	
Inventory of supplies, at average cost	47,000	
Short-term prepayments	8,000	
Land	160,000	
Buildings	830,000	
Accumulated depreciation of buildings		186,000
Machinery and equipment	247,000	
Accumulated depreciation of machinery and equipment		62,000
Vouchers payable		38,000
Contracts payable		27,000
Accrued liabilities		18,000
Interest payable		24,000
Customers' deposits		38,000
6% revenue bonds, payable $40,000 a year		400,000
Contribution from General Fund		250,000
Retained earnings appropriated for revenue bonds retirement		33,000
Unappropriated retained earnings		476,000
Charges for services		643,000
Operating grants		50,000
Interest revenue		12,000
Personal services	281,000	
Contractual services	143,000	
Material and supplies	46,000	
Heat, light, and power	38,000	
Depreciation expense	57,000	
Interest expense and fiscal agent's fees	83,000	
Totals	$2,269,000	$2,269,000

Instructions

Prepare a statement of revenues, expenses, and changes in retained earnings and a balance sheet for the Town of Tolliver Enterprise Fund for the year ended June 30, Year 9.

Pr. 14-3 In compliance with a newly enacted state law, Diggs County assumed the responsibility of collecting all property taxes levied within its boundaries as of July 1, Year 5. A composite property tax rate per $100 of net assessed valuation was developed for the fiscal year ending June 30, Year 6, and is presented below:

Diggs County General Fund	$ 6.00
Evans City General Fund.	3.00
Hickman Township General Fund	1.00
Total	$10.00

All property taxes were due in quarterly installments. After collection, taxes were to be distributed to the governmental entities represented in the composite rate. In order to administer collection and distribution of such taxes, Diggs County established a Tax Agency Fund.

Additional Information

(1) In order to reimburse Diggs County for estimated costs of administering the Tax Agency Fund, the Tax Agency Fund was to deduct 2% from the tax collections each quarter for Evans City and Hickman Township. The total amount deducted was to be remitted to the Diggs County General Fund.

(2) Current year tax levies to be collected by the Tax Agency Fund were as follows:

	Gross levy	Estimated amount to be collected
Diggs County	$3,600,000	$3,500,000
Evans City.	1,800,000	1,740,000
Hickman Township	600,000	560,000
Totals	$6,000,000	$5,800,000

(3) As of September 30, Year 5, the Diggs County Tax Agency Fund had received $1,440,000 in first-quarter payments. On October 1, Year 5, the Diggs County Tax Agency Fund made a distribution to the three governmental entities.

Instructions

For the period July 1, Year 5, through October 1, Year 5, prepare journal entries (explanations omitted) to record the foregoing transactions and events for the following funds:

Diggs County Tax Agency Fund   Evans City General Fund

Diggs County General Fund   Hickman Township General Fund

Your working paper should be organized as follows:

Account titles	Diggs County Tax Agency Fund	Diggs County General Fund	Evans City General Fund	Hickman Township General Fund
	dr(cr)	dr(cr)	dr(cr)	dr(cr)

Pr. 14-4   The Town of Northville was incorporated and began operations on July 1, Year 1. The following transactions and events occurred during the first fiscal year, July 1, Year 1, to June 30, Year 2:

(1) The Town Council adopted a budget for general operations during the year ending June 30, Year 2. Revenues were estimated at $400,000. Legal authorizations for budgeted expenditures were $394,000. There were no other financing sources or uses.

(2) Property taxes were levied in the amount of $390,000; it was estimated that 2% of this amount would be uncollectible. These taxes were available on the date of levy to finance current expenditures.

(3) During the year a resident of the town donated marketable securities valued at $50,000 to the town under a trust. The terms of the trust indenture specified that the principal amount was to be kept intact; use of revenues generated by the securities was restricted to financing college scholarships for students. Revenues earned and received on these marketable securities amounted to $5,500 through June 30, Year 2.

(4) A General Fund transfer of $55,000 was made to establish an Internal Service Fund to provide for a permanent investment in inventory of supplies.

(5) The Town Council decided to install lighting in the Town Park, and a special assessment project was authorized to install the lighting at a cost of $75,000. The assessments were levied for $72,000, with the town contributing $3,000 from the General Fund. All assessments were collected during the year, as was the General Fund contribution.

(6) A contract for $75,000 was approved for the installation of the lighting. On June 30, Year 2, the lighting was completed but not approved. The contractor was paid all but 5%, which was retained to ensure compliance with the terms of the contract. Encumbrances accounts are maintained.

(7) During the year, the Internal Service Fund purchased supplies at a cost of $41,900.

(8) Cash collections recorded by the General Fund during the year were as follows:

Property taxes.	*$386,000*
Licenses and permits fees	*7,000*

(9) The Town Council decided to build a town hall at an estimated cost of $500,000 to replace space occupied in rented facilities. The town does not record project authorizations. General obligation term bonds bearing interest at 6% were to be issued. On June 30, Year 2, the bonds were issued at their face amount of $500,000, payable June 30, Year 22. No contracts had been signed for this project and no expenditures had been made.

(10) A fire truck was acquired for $16,000, and the voucher was approved and paid by the General Fund. This expenditure previously had been encumbered for $15,000.

Instructions

Prepare journal entries for the Town of Northville to record each of the foregoing transactions and events in the appropriate fund or account group. Omit explanations for the journal entries. Do not prepare closing entries for any fund. Organize your working paper as follows:

Transaction or event no.	Fund or account group	Account titles	Debit	Credit

Number each journal entry to correspond with the transactions or events described on page 698. Use the funds (show fund symbol in working paper) and account titles below:

Endowment Principal Trust Fund (EPF)
    Cash
    Investments
    Other Financing Uses
    Payable to Endowment Revenues Trust Fund
    Revenues

Endowment Revenues Trust Fund (ERF)
    Cash
    Other Financing Sources
    Receivable from Endowment Principal Trust Fund

General Fixed Assets Account Group (GFA)
    Improvements (Other than Buildings)
    Investment in General Fixed Assets from Capital Projects Funds
    Investment in General Fixed Assets from General Fund Revenues
    Machinery and Equipment

General Fund (GF)
    Allowance for Uncollectible Current Taxes
    Appropriations
    Budgetary Fund Balance
    Cash
    Encumbrances
    Estimated Revenues
    Expenditures
    Fund Balance Reserved for Encumbrances
    Other Financing Uses
    Payable to Special Revenue Fund
    Revenues
    Taxes Receivable—Current
    Vouchers Payable

General Long-Term Debt Account Group (GLTD)
    Amount to Be Provided
    Term Bonds Payable

Internal Service Fund (ISF)
    Cash
    Contribution from General Fund
    Inventory of Supplies

Special Revenue Fund (SRF)
  Cash
  Other Financing Sources
  Receivable from General Fund
  Revenues
  Special Assessments Receivable — Current

Town Hall Capital Projects Fund (TH)
  Cash
  Other Financing Sources

Town Park Lighting Capital Projects Fund (TPL)
  Cash
  Encumbrances
  Expenditures
  Fund Balance Reserved for Encumbrances
  Vouchers Payable

Pr. 14-5 The City of Cavendish operates a central garage in an Internal Service Fund to provide garage space and repairs for all city-owned and -operated vehicles. The Internal Service Fund was established by a contribution of $200,000 from the General Fund on July 1, Year 1, at which time the building was acquired. The post-closing trial balance of the Internal Service Fund on June 30, Year 3, was as follows:

CITY OF CAVENDISH INTERNAL SERVICE FUND
Post-Closing Trial Balance
June 30, Year 3

	Debit	Credit
Cash	$150,000	
Receivable from General Fund	20,000	
Inventory of material and supplies	80,000	
Land	60,000	
Building	200,000	
Accumulated depreciation of building		$ 10,000
Machinery and equipment	56,000	
Accumulated depreciation of machinery and equipment		12,000
Vouchers payable		38,000
Contribution from General Fund		200,000
Unappropriated retained earnings		306,000
Totals	$566,000	$566,000

Additional Information for the Year Ended June 30, Year 4

(1) Material and supplies were purchased on account for $74,000.
(2) The perpetual inventory balance of material and supplies on June 30, Year 4, was $58,000, which agreed with the physical count on that date.
(3) Salaries and wages paid to employees totaled $230,000, including related fringe benefits.
(4) A billing was received from the Enterprise Fund for utility charges totaling $30,000, and was paid.

(5) Depreciation of the building was recognized in the amount of $5,000. Depreciation of the machinery and equipment amounted to $8,000.

(6) Billings to other funds for services rendered to them were as follows:

General Fund.	$262,000
Enterprise Fund.	84,000
Special Revenue Fund	32,000

(7) Unpaid interfund receivable balances on June 30, Year 4, were as follows:

General Fund.	$ 6,000
Special Revenue Fund.	16,000

(8) Vouchers payable on June 30, Year 4, were $14,000.

Instructions

For the period July 1, Year 3, through June 30, Year 4, prepare journal entries to record all the transactions and events for the City of Cavendish Internal Service Fund. Omit explanations for the entries. Use the following account titles, in addition to those included in the June 30, Year 3, post-closing trial balance:

Charges for Services	Receivable from Enterprise Fund
Operating Expenses (controlling account)	Receivable from Special Revenue Fund
Payable to Enterprise Fund	

Pr. 14-6 Your audit of the financial statements of the Town of Novis for the year ended June 30, Year 6, disclosed that the town's inexperienced accountant was uninformed regarding governmental accounting standards and recorded all transactions and events in the General Fund. The following Town of Novis General Fund trial balance was prepared by the accountant:

TOWN OF NOVIS GENERAL FUND
Trial Balance
June 30, Year 6

	Debit	Credit
Cash	$ 12,900	
Accounts receivable	1,200	
Taxes receivable—current	8,000	
Town property	16,100	
Vouchers payable		$ 15,000
Bonds payable	48,000	
Unreserved and undesignated fund balance		23,200
Appropriations		350,000
Expenditures	332,000	
Estimated revenues	290,000	
Revenues		320,000
Totals	$708,200	$708,200

Your audit disclosed the following:

(1) The accounts receivable balance was due from the town's water utility for the sale of obsolete equipment on behalf of the General Fund. Accounts for the water utility operated by the town are maintained in the Water Utility Enterprise Fund.

(2) The total property tax levy for the year was $270,000. The town's tax collection experience in recent years indicates an average loss of 3% of the total property tax levy for uncollectible taxes.

(3) On June 30, Year 6, the town retired at face amount 12% general obligation serial bonds totaling $30,000. The bonds had been issued on July 1, Year 5, in the total amount of $150,000. Interest paid during the year also was recorded in the Bonds Payable ledger account. There was no debt service fund for the serial bonds.

(4) On July 1, Year 5, to service various departments the Town Council authorized a supply room with an inventory not to exceed $10,000. During the year supplies totaling $12,300 were purchased and debited to Expenditures. The physical inventory taken on June 30, Year 6, disclosed that supplies totaling $8,400 had been used. No internal service fund was authorized by the Town Council.

(5) Expenditures for Year 6 included $2,600 applicable to purchase orders issued in the prior year. Outstanding purchase orders on June 30, Year 6, not entered in the accounting records, amounted to $4,100.

(6) The amount of $8,200, receivable from the state during Fiscal Year 6 for the town's share of state gasoline taxes, had not been entered in the accounting records, because the state was late in remitting the $8,200.

(7) Equipment costing $7,500, which had been acquired by the General Fund, was removed from service and sold for $900 during the year, and new equipment costing $17,000 was acquired. These transactions were recorded in the Town Property ledger account. The town does not recognize depreciation in the General Fixed Assets Account Group.

Instructions

a Prepare adjusting and closing entries for the Town of Novis General Fund on June 30, Year 6.

b Prepare a post-closing trial balance for the Town of Novis General Fund for the year ended June 30, Year 6.

c Prepare adjusting entries for any other funds or account groups of the Town of Novis. (The town's accountant had recorded all the foregoing transactions or events in the General Fund, and had prepared no journal entries for other funds or account groups.)

Pr. 14-7   Selected financial statements of the Village of Rosner Enterprise Fund are as follows:

VILLAGE OF ROSNER ENTERPRISE FUND
Statement of Revenues, Expenses, and Changes in Retained Earnings
For Year Ended June 30, Year 8

Operating revenues:		
Charges for services...		$282,000
Operating expenses:		
Personal services..	$ 41,000	
Contractual services	26,000	
Material and supplies	37,000	
Heat, light, and power...................................	11,000	
Depreciation	36,000	
Payment in lieu of property taxes........................	15,000	
Total operating expenses		166,000
Operating income		$116,000
Nonoperating revenues (expenses):		
Operating grant	$ 20,000	
Interest revenue..	8,000	
Interest expense..	(40,000)	
Total nonoperating revenues (expenses).........................		(12,000)
Income before operating transfers....................................		$104,000
Operating transfer (out) to General Fund.............................		(5,000)
Net income		$ 99,000
Retained earnings, beginning of year		82,000
Retained earnings, end of year......................................		$181,000

VILLAGE OF ROSNER ENTERPRISE FUND
Balance Sheets
June 30, Year 8 and Year 7

	June 30	
	Year 8	Year 7
Assets		
Current assets:		
Cash and short-term investments	$ 41,000	$ 32,000
Accounts receivable (net)................................	82,000	76,000
Receivable from General Fund............................	12,000	8,000
Inventory of supplies....................................	21,000	23,000
Short-term prepayments.................................	4,000	5,000
Total current assets..................................	$160,000	$144,000
Restricted assets:		
Cash and short-term investments	118,000	106,000
Plant assets (net).......................................	641,000	614,000
Total assets..	$919,000	$864,000

(continued)

VILLAGE OF ROSNER ENTERPRISE FUND
Balance Sheets (concluded)
June 30, Year 8 and Year 7

	June 30 Year 8	Year 7
Liabilities & Fund Equity		
Current liabilities:		
Vouchers payable	$ 67,000	$ 73,000
Accrued liabilities	46,000	39,000
Total current liabilities	$113,000	$112,000
Liabilities payable from restricted assets:		
Interest payable	$ 20,000	$ 20,000
Customers deposits	55,000	50,000
Total liabilities payable from restricted assets	$ 75,000	$ 70,000
Long-term debt:		
10% revenue bonds payable	$400,000	$400,000
Total liabilities	$588,000	$582,000
Fund equity:		
Contributed capital from General Fund	$150,000	$200,000
Retained earnings:		
Appropriated for revenue bond retirement	43,000	36,000
Unappropriated	138,000	46,000
Total fund equity	$331,000	$282,000
Total liabilities & fund equity	$919,000	$864,000

Additional Information for the Year Ended June 30, Year 8

(1) The 10% revenue bonds, which pay interest January 1 and July 1, are due serially $50,000 a year beginning July 1, Year 9.

(2) New customers' deposits totaled $7,000; refunds of customers' deposits amounted to $2,000.

(3) Plant assets with a carrying amount of $22,000 were disposed of for that amount; new plant assets were acquired for cash.

(4) A partial refund of contributed capital was made to the General Fund.

(5) The short-term investments are cash equivalents.

Instructions

Prepare a statement of cash flows (indirect method) for the Village of Rosner Enterprise Fund for the year ended June 30, Year 8.

15

Nonprofit Organizations

A *nonprofit* (or *not-for-profit*) *organization* is a legal and accounting entity that is operated for the benefit of society as a whole, rather than for the benefit of an individual proprietor or a group of partners or stockholders. Thus, the concept of net income is not meaningful for a nonprofit organization. Instead, as does the internal service fund of a governmental entity described in Chapter 14, a nonprofit organization strives only to obtain revenues sufficient to cover its expenses.

Nonprofit organizations comprise a significant segment of the U.S. economy. As pointed out by the Financial Accounting Standards Board:[1]

> Not-for-profit organizations include cemetery organizations, civic organizations, colleges and universities, cultural institutions, fraternal organizations, hospitals, labor unions, libraries, museums, performing arts organizations, political parties, private and community foundations, private elementary and secondary schools, professional associations, public broadcasting stations, religious organizations, research and scientific organizations, social and country clubs, trade associations, voluntary health and welfare organizations, and zoological and botanical societies. They do not include governmental units.

For many years, the accounting standards and practices that constitute generally accepted accounting principles were not considered to be entirely applicable to nonprofit organizations. The following quotation, which formerly appeared in various auditing publications of the AICPA, outlines this situation:[2]

> . . . the statements . . . of a not-for-profit organization . . . may reflect accounting practices differing in some respects from those followed by enterprises organized for profit. In some cases generally accepted accounting principles applicable to not-for-profit organizations have not been clearly defined. In those

---

[1] *Invitation to Comment,* "Financial Reporting by Not-for-Profit Organizations: Form and Content of Financial Statements," FASB (Norwalk: 1989), p. 17.
[2] *Statement on Auditing Standards No. 1,* "Codification of Auditing Standards and Procedures," AICPA (New York: 1973), p. 136.

705

areas where the independent auditor believes generally accepted accounting principles have been clearly defined, he may state his opinion as to the conformity of the financial statements either with *generally accepted accounting principles* or (less desirably) with *accounting practices* for not-for-profit organizations in the particular field, and in such circumstances he may refer to financial position and results of operations. In those areas where he believes generally accepted accounting principles have not been clearly defined, the provisions covering special reports as discussed under cash basis and modified accrual basis statements are applicable.

In the period 1972 to 1974, the unsettled state of accounting for nonprofit organizations was improved by the AICPA's issuance of three *Audit and Accounting Guides* or *Industry Audit Guides:* "Hospital Audit Guide," "Audits of Colleges and Universities," and "Audits of Voluntary Health and Welfare Organizations." All three were subsequently amended, and in 1992 the "Hospital Audit Guide" was superseded by "Audits of Providers of Health Care Services." The status of an *Audit and Accounting Guide* or an *Industry Audit Guide* is set forth in each guide; the following language in "Audits of Providers of Health Care Services" is typical: [3]

> This audit and accounting guide presents recommendations of the AICPA Health Care Committee on the application of generally accepted auditing standards to audits of financial statements of providers of health care services. This guide also presents the committee's recommendations on and descriptions of financial accounting and reporting principles and practices for providers of health care services. The AICPA Accounting Standards Executive Committee and members of the AICPA Auditing Standards Board have found this guide to be consistent with existing standards and principles covered by Rules 202 and 203 of the AICPA Code of Professional Conduct. AICPA members should be prepared to justify departures from this guide.

The three *Guides* listed above deal with only three types of nonprofit organizations. Thus, in 1978, the AICPA issued *Statement of Position 78-10,* later incorporated in "Audits of Certain Nonprofit Organizations," which applies to at least 18 types of nonprofit organizations, ranging from cemetery societies to zoological and botanical societies.

The existence of four separate sources of authoritative support for generally accepted accounting principles for nonprofit organizations has led to many inconsistencies among the accounting standards for such organizations. In time, the Financial Accounting Standards Board may resolve these inconsistencies as a result of its work on accounting concepts for nonbusiness organizations, in *Statement of Financial Accounting Concepts No. 4,* "Objectives of Financial Reporting by Nonbusiness Organizations" (see Chapter 12, pages 601 to 602), *Statement of Financial Accounting Concepts No. 6,* "Elements of Financial Statements," and *Invitation to*

---

[3] *Audit and Accounting Guide,* "Audits of Providers of Health Care Services," AICPA (New York: 1992), p. iii.

Comment: Financial Reporting by Nonprofit Organizations . . . (the basis for *FASB Statement No. 117* discussed in this chapter).

Characteristics of Nonprofit Organizations

Nonprofit organizations are in certain respects hybrid because they have some characteristics similar to those of governmental entities and other characteristics similar to those of business enterprises.

Among the features of nonprofit organizations that resemble characteristics of governmental entities are the following:

1 *Service to society.* Nonprofit organizations render services to society as a whole. The members of this society may range from a limited number of citizens of a community to almost the entire population of a city, state, or nation. Similar to the services rendered by governmental entities, the services of nonprofit organizations are of benefit to the many rather than the few.

2 *No profit motivation.* Nonprofit organizations do not operate with the objective of earning a profit. Consequently, nonprofit organizations generally are exempt from federal and state income taxes. Governmental entities, except for enterprise funds, have the same characteristics. (As pointed out in Chapter 14, enterprise funds sometimes are assessed an amount in lieu of property taxes by the legislative branch of the government.)

3 *Financing by the citizenry.* As with governmental entities, most nonprofit organizations depend on the general population for a substantial portion of their support, because revenues from charges for their services are not intended to cover all their operating costs. Exceptions are professional societies and the philanthropic foundations established by wealthy individuals or families. Whereas the citizenry's contributions to government revenues are mostly ***involuntary taxes,*** their contributions to nonprofit organizations are ***voluntary donations.***

4 *Stewardship for resources.* Because a substantial portion of the resources of a nonprofit organization is donated, the organization must account for the resources on a stewardship basis similar to that of governmental entities. The stewardship requirement makes ***fund accounting*** appropriate for many nonprofit organizations, as it is for governmental entities.

5 *Importance of budget.* The four preceding characteristics of nonprofit organizations cause their ***annual budget*** to be as important as for governmental entities. Nonprofit organizations may employ an ***object budget,*** a ***program budget,*** or a ***performance budget.*** These types of annual budgets are described in Chapter 12.

Among the characteristics of nonprofit organizations that resemble those of business enterprises are the following:

1 *Governance by board of directors.* As with a business corporation, a nonprofit corporation is governed by elected or appointed directors, trustees, or governors. In contrast, the legislative and executive branches of a governmental entity share the responsibilities for its governance.

2   *Measurement of cost expirations.* Governance by a board of directors means that a nonprofit organization does not answer to a lawmaking body as does a governmental entity. One consequence is that *cost expirations,* or *expenses,* rather than *expenditures,* are reported in the *statement of activities* (see page 720) of most nonprofit organizations. Allocation of expenses (including depreciation) and revenues to the appropriate accounting period thus is a common characteristic of nonprofit organizations and business enterprises.

3   *Use of accrual basis of accounting.* Nonprofit organizations employ the same accrual basis of accounting used by business enterprises.

FUND ACCOUNTING BY NONPROFIT ORGANIZATIONS

The accounting unit for many nonprofit organizations is the *fund,* which is defined in Chapter 12 (page 606). Separate funds may be necessary to distinguish between assets that may be used as authorized by the board of directors and assets whose use is restricted by donors. Funds commonly used by some of the nonprofit organizations covered in this chapter include the following:

Unrestricted fund (sometimes called *unrestricted current fund, general fund,* or *current unrestricted fund*)

Restricted fund (sometimes called *restricted current fund* or *current restricted fund*)

Endowment fund

Agency fund (sometimes called *custodian fund*)

Annuity fund and life income fund (sometimes called *living trust fund*)

Loan fund

Plant fund (sometimes called *land, building, and equipment fund*)

Unrestricted Fund

In many respects, an *unrestricted fund* is similar to the *general fund* of a governmental entity. The unrestricted fund includes all the assets of a nonprofit organization that are available for use as authorized by the board of directors and are not restricted for specific purposes. Thus, similar to the general fund of a governmental entity, an unrestricted fund is *residual* in nature.

Revenues and Gains of Unrestricted Fund   The revenues and gains of an unrestricted fund are derived from a number of sources. For example, a hospital derives general (unrestricted) fund revenues from patient services, educational programs, research and other grants, unrestricted gifts, unrestricted income from endowment funds, and miscellaneous sources such as donated material and services. A university's sources of unrestricted fund revenues and gains include student tuition and fees; governmental grants and contracts; gifts and private grants; unrestricted income from endowment funds; and revenue from auxiliary activities such as student residences, food services, and intercollegiate athletics. The principal revenue sources of voluntary health and welfare organizations' unrestricted funds (and all other funds) are cash donations and pledges. Revenues may also include membership dues, interest, dividends, and gains on disposal of investments. A nonprofit professional society receives revenues from membership dues, fees for educational programs, advertising, and sales of publications.

Revenues for Services A nonprofit organization's revenues for services are accrued at full rates, *even though part or all of the revenue is to be waived or reduced.*[4] Suppose, for example, that nonprofit Community Hospital's patient service revenues records for June, Year 3, include the following amounts:

<table>
<tr><td style="text-align:right">Patient service
revenues components
of a nonprofit hospital</td><td>Gross patient service revenues (before charity care or contractual adjustments) ....</td><td style="text-align:right">$100,000</td></tr>
<tr><td></td><td>Charity care for indigent patients..</td><td style="text-align:right">8,000</td></tr>
<tr><td></td><td>Amount to be received from Civic Welfare, Inc., as a partial reimbursement for
   charity care...</td><td style="text-align:right">3,000</td></tr>
<tr><td></td><td>Contractual adjustment allowed to Blue Cross...........................</td><td style="text-align:right">16,000</td></tr>
<tr><td></td><td>Provision for doubtful accounts ....</td><td style="text-align:right">12,000</td></tr>
</table>

The following journal entries are appropriate for the Community Hospital General Fund on June 30, Year 3:

<table>
<tr><td style="text-align:right">Journal entries for
patient service
revenues of general
fund of a nonprofit
hospital</td><td>Accounts Receivable ....</td><td style="text-align:right">92,000</td><td></td></tr>
<tr><td></td><td>   Patient Service Revenues ($100,000 − $8,000)............</td><td></td><td style="text-align:right">92,000</td></tr>
<tr><td></td><td>To record gross patient service revenues for month of June at full
rates, exclusive of charity care.</td><td></td><td></td></tr>
<tr><td></td><td>Accounts Receivable ....</td><td style="text-align:right">3,000</td><td></td></tr>
<tr><td></td><td>   Patient Service Revenues................................</td><td></td><td style="text-align:right">3,000</td></tr>
<tr><td></td><td>To record amount receivable from Civic Welfare, Inc. ($3,000), as a
partial reimbursement for charity care.</td><td></td><td></td></tr>
<tr><td></td><td>Contractual Adjustments ....</td><td style="text-align:right">16,000</td><td></td></tr>
<tr><td></td><td>   Accounts Receivable ....</td><td></td><td style="text-align:right">16,000</td></tr>
<tr><td></td><td>To record contractual adjustments allowed to Blue Cross for June.</td><td></td><td></td></tr>
<tr><td></td><td>Doubtful Accounts Expense ....</td><td style="text-align:right">12,000</td><td></td></tr>
<tr><td></td><td>   Allowance for Doubtful Accounts.........................</td><td></td><td style="text-align:right">12,000</td></tr>
<tr><td></td><td>To provide for doubtful accounts receivable for June.</td><td></td><td></td></tr>
</table>

---

[4] *FASB Statement No. 117,* "Financial Statements of Not-for-Profit Organizations," FASB (Norwalk: 1993), p. 8.

In the first journal entry for Community Hospital, the value of the ***charity care*** provided to indigent patients is not accrued as accounts receivable or revenues because the underlying health care services provided by the hospital were never expected to result in cash flows to the hospital.[5] The account receivable in the second journal entry resulted from a commitment by another nonprofit organization to contribute toward the value of charity care provided by Community Hospital. The contractual adjustments recorded in the third journal entry above illustrate a unique feature of a hospital's operations. Many accounts receivable of a hospital are collectible from a ***third-party payor,*** rather than from the patient receiving services. Among third-party payors are the U.S. government (Medicare and Medicaid programs), state programs such as Medical in California, Blue Cross, and private medical insurance carriers. The hospital's contractual agreements with third-party payors generally provide for payments by the third parties at less than full billing rates.

In the statement of activities of Community Hospital for June, Year 3, the balances of the Contractual Adjustments ledger account on June 30, Year 3, is deducted from the balance of the Patient Service Revenues account to compute net patient service revenue for the month. The balance of the Allowance for Doubtful Accounts ledger account is offset against the balance of the Accounts Receivable account in the balance sheet, and write-offs of accounts receivable are recorded in the customary fashion. For example, the uncollectible accounts receivable of nonpaying patients who had been billed for services would be written off by Community Hospital by the following journal entry in the Unrestricted Fund on June 30, Year 3:

<table>
<tr><td rowspan="8">Journal entry to write off uncollectible accounts receivable of a nonprofit hospital</td><td colspan="3">*Allowance for Doubtful Accounts* ....   *5,100*</td></tr>
<tr><td colspan="3">   *Accounts Receivable* ....   *5,100*</td></tr>
<tr><td colspan="3">*To write off uncollectible accounts receivable of nonpaying patients,*</td></tr>
<tr><td colspan="3">*as follows:*</td></tr>
<tr><td colspan="3">   *J. R. English.* ....   *$1,500*</td></tr>
<tr><td colspan="3">   *R. L. Knight* ....   *1,100*</td></tr>
<tr><td colspan="3">   *S. O. Newman.* ....   *2,500*</td></tr>
<tr><td colspan="3">   *Total.* ....   *$5,100*</td></tr>
</table>

In contrast to the ***contra-revenue*** presentation of contractual adjustments in the statement of activities of a nonprofit hospital, the comparable tuition remissions or exemptions of a nonprofit university or college are included with ***expenses for student aid*** in that entity's statement of activities.[6] This is one of many examples of divergent accounting standards established for various nonprofit organizations by the American Institute of Certified Public Accountants.

Donated Material, Services, and Facilities   In addition to cash contributions, nonprofit organizations often receive donations of material, services, and facilities. For example, a hospital may receive free drugs, or a university may receive free operat-

---

[5] "Audits of Providers of Health Care Services," p. 41.
[6] *Industry Audit Guide,* "Audits of Colleges and Universities," Second Edition, AICPA (New York: 1975), pp. 20, 28–29.

ing supplies. The donated material is recorded in the Inventories ledger account at its current fair value, with a credit to a revenues account in an unrestricted fund, as illustrated in the following journal entry for the General Fund of Community Hospital:

<table>
<tr><td>Journal entry for material donated to a nonprofit hospital</td><td>Inventories. 5,000
    Contributions Revenue. 5,000
To record donated drugs at current fair value.</td></tr>
</table>

Donated services are recorded in an unrestricted fund as salaries expense, with an offset to a revenues account, if the services are rendered to the nonprofit organization by skilled individuals. The value assigned to the services is the going rate for comparable employees or contractors of the entity, less any meals or other living costs absorbed for the donor of the services by the nonprofit organization. The Financial Accounting Standards Board established the following requirements for recognizing donated services in the accounting records of a nonprofit organization:[7]

Contributions of services shall be recognized if the services received (a) create or enhance nonfinancial assets or (b) require specialized skills, are provided by individuals possessing those skills, and would typically need to be purchased if not provided by donation. Services requiring specialized skills are provided by architects, carpenters, doctors, electricians, lawyers, nurses, plumbers, teachers, and other professionals and craftsmen. Contributed services . . . that do not meet the above criteria shall not be recognized.

To illustrate the accounting for donated services that meet the foregoing criteria, assume that the services of volunteer nurses' aides were valued at $26,400 for the month of June, Year 3, by Community Hospital, and that the value of meals provided at no cost to the volunteers during the month was $2,100. The following journal entry is appropriate for the General Fund of Community Hospital on June 30, Year 3:

<table>
<tr><td>Journal entry for services donated to a nonprofit hospital</td><td>Salaries Expense 24,300
    Contributions Revenue 24,300
To record donated services at current fair value of $26,400 less
$2,100 value of meals provided to donors.</td></tr>
</table>

Significant donated facilities are recognized as revenue at their current fair value, offset by a debit to an asset or an expense account, as appropriate. For example, if the fair rental value of the building used by Archer School, a nonprofit private elementary school, is $8,000 a month, but the building's owner waived rental pay-

---

[7] *FASB Statement No. 116,* ''Accounting for Contributions Received and Contributions Made,'' FASB (Norwalk: 1993), p. 3.

ments, Archer School prepares the following journal entry each month in its Unrestricted Fund:

Journal entry for
donated facilities

Rent Expense.   8,000
    Contributions Revenue.   8,000
*To record current fair value of rental of school building whose use was
donated.*

Pledges   A *pledge* is a commitment by a prospective donor to contribute a specific amount of cash or property to a nonprofit organization on a future date or in installments. Because a pledge is in writing and signed by the *pledgor,* it resembles in form the *promissory note* used in business. However, pledges often are not enforceable contracts.

Under the accrual basis of accounting, ***unconditional*** pledges are recognized as receivables and revenues in the unrestricted fund, with appropriate provision for doubtful pledges.[8] Pledges due in future accounting periods or having restrictions as to their use generally are accounted for in a restricted fund (see page 717).[9]

To illustrate the accounting for pledges, assume that Civic Welfare, Inc., a voluntary health and welfare organization, received unconditional pledges totaling $200,000 in a fund-raising drive. Based on past experience, 15% of the pledges were considered to be doubtful of collection. The journal entries below are appropriate:

Journal entries to
recognize receivable
for pledges and
doubtful pledges of a
nonprofit voluntary
health and welfare
organization

Pledges Receivable.   200,000
    Contributions Revenue   200,000
To record receivable for pledges.

Doubtful Pledges Expense.   30,000
    Allowance for Doubtful Pledges   30,000
*To record provision for doubtful pledges ($200,000 × 0.15 =
$30,000).*

Contributions revenue is displayed in the statement of activities, as is doubtful pledges expense. Pledges receivable are displayed in the balance sheet net of the allowance for doubtful pledges. The write-off of uncollectible pledges is recorded by a debit to the Allowance for Doubtful Pledges ledger account and a credit to the Pledges Receivable account.

Revenues from Pooled Investments   Many of the funds of nonprofit organizations have cash available for investments in securities and other money-market instruments. To provide greater efficiency and flexibility in investment programs, the investment resources of all funds of a nonprofit organization may be pooled for

[8] Ibid., p. 3.
[9] Ibid., p. 4.

investment by a single portfolio manager. The pooling technique requires a careful allocation of investment revenues, including gains and losses, to each participating fund.

To illustrate the pooling of investments, assume that on January 2, Year 5, four funds of Civic Welfare, Inc., a nonprofit voluntary health and welfare organization, pooled their investments (to be managed by the Unrestricted Fund), as follows:

Pooling of investments by nonprofit voluntary health and welfare organization on Jan. 2, Year 5

	Cost	Current fair values	Original equity, %
Unrestricted Fund...........................	$ 20,000	$ 18,000	15
Restricted Fund.............................	15,000	21,600	18
Plant Fund.................................	10,000	20,400	17
Wilson Endowment Fund...................	55,000	60,000	50
Totals	$100,000	$120,000	100

The original equity percentages in the above tabulation are based on *current fair value,* not on *cost.* The current fair values of the pooled investments on January 2, Year 5, represent a common ''measuring rod'' not available in the cost amounts, which represent current fair values on various dates the investments were acquired by the respective funds.

Realized gains (or losses) and interest and dividend revenue of the pooled investments during Year 5 are allocated to the four funds in the ratio of the original equity percentages. For example, if $18,000 net realized gains of the investment pool during Year 5 were *reinvested,* and if interest and dividend revenue of $9,000 was realized and *distributed* by the pool during Year 5, these amounts are allocated as shown below:

Allocation of Year 5 revenue from pooled investments to respective funds

	Original equity, %	Net realized gains	Interest and dividends revenue
Unrestricted Fund.............................	15	$ 2,700	$1,350
Restricted Fund	18	3,240	1,620
Plant Fund....................................	17	3,060	1,530
Wilson Endowment Fund.......................	50	9,000	4,500
Totals	100	$18,000	$9,000

Each of the funds participating in the investment pool debits Investments and credits Gains on Sale of Investments or Investment Income for its share of the $18,000 net realized gains of the pooled investments. However, assuming that *all* the interest and dividends revenue, regardless of the fund to which it is attributable, is available for unrestricted use by Civic Welfare, Inc., the entire $9,000 interest and dividends revenue is recognized as revenue by the Unrestricted Fund.[10]

---

[10] *Industry Audit Guide,* ''Audits of Voluntary Health and Welfare Organizations,'' AICPA (New York, 1974), pp. 6–7.

If another fund of Civic Welfare, Inc., entered the investment pool on December 31, Year 5, the original equity percentages would be revised, based on the December 31, Year 5, current fair values of the investment portfolio. For example, if the Harris Endowment Fund entered the Civic Welfare, Inc., investment pool (which had total investments with a current fair value of $144,000) on December 31, Year 5, with investments having a cost of $32,000 and a current fair value of $36,000 on that date, the equity percentages would be revised as illustrated below:

	Cost*	Current fair values†	Revised equity, %
Revision of fund equities in pooled investments on Dec. 31, Year 5			
Unrestricted Fund..........................	$ 22,700	$ 21,600	12.0
Restricted Fund	18,240	25,920	14.4
Plant Fund..............................	13,060	24,480	13.6
Wilson Endowment Fund...................	64,000	72,000	40.0
Subtotals	$118,000	$144,000	
Harris Endowment Fund...................	32,000	36,000	20.0
Totals	$150,000	$180,000	100.0

*Cost for four original pool member funds includes $18,000 realized gains of Year 5.
† Current fair value of original pooled investments totaling $144,000 on December 31, Year 5, allocated to original pool member funds based on original equity percentages computed on page 713.

Realized gains (or losses) and interest and dividends revenue for accounting periods subsequent to December 31, Year 5, are *allocated in the revised equity percentages.* The revised equity percentages are maintained until the membership of the investment pool changes again.

Expenses and Losses of Unrestricted Fund   A nonprofit organization typically recognizes all expenses in its unrestricted fund. As indicated on page 718, losses may be recognized in other funds as well as in the unrestricted fund.

Expenses of a nonprofit organization may be classified in two groups: program services and supporting services. *Program services* are the organization's activities that result in the distribution of goods and services to beneficiaries, customers, or members that fulfill the purposes or mission of the organization. *Supporting services* are all activities of the organization other than program services, such as management and general, fund-raising, and membership development activities.[11]

Depreciation Expense of Nonprofit Organizations   In *FASB Statement No. 93,* "Recognition of Depreciation by Not-for-Profit Organizations," the Financial Accounting Standards Board required recognition of depreciation on *all* long-lived tangible assets of nonprofit organizations, except for individual works of art or historical treasures having extraordinarily long economic lives, with disclosure of the following in a note to the financial statements:[12]

---

[11] *FASB Statement No. 117,* pp. 9–10.
[12] *FASB Statement No. 93,* "Recognition of Depreciation by Not-for-Profit Organizations," FASB (Stamford: 1987), p. 2.

1 Depreciation expense for the period

2 Balances of major classes of depreciable assets, by nature or function, at the balance sheet date

3 Accumulated depreciation, either by major classes of depreciable assets or in total, at the balance sheet date

4 A general description of the method or methods used in computing depreciation for major classes of depreciable assets

Expenses that are unique to nonprofit organizations include fund-raising expense, grants, and income taxes on certain unrelated business income.

Fund-Raising Expense Although fund-raising costs may benefit future accounting periods of a nonprofit organization, just as advertising costs of a business enterprise may benefit future periods, fund-raising costs generally are recognized as an expense when incurred.

Grants Expense Some nonprofit organizations make grants to individuals or to other organizations. For example, a nonprofit performing arts organization may make grants to theaters to help defray operating costs. Generally, grants are recognized as expense when the governing board of the nonprofit organization approves them. However, unpaid amounts of grants that may be revoked by the nonprofit organization are not recognized as expense until they are paid, and unpaid commitments under such grants are reported in a note to the nonprofit organization's financial statements.[13]

Income Taxes Some otherwise tax-exempt nonprofit organizations may be subject to federal and state income taxes on their *unrelated business income,* which is derived from activities not substantially related to the educational, charitable, or other basis of the organization's tax-exempt status. For example, the income that a country club derives from staging professional tennis tournaments on its tennis courts otherwise used by members might be subject to income taxes. Income taxes expense for such nonprofit organizations is subject to the interperiod tax allocation requirements for business enterprises.[14]

Assets and Liabilities of Unrestricted Fund Most assets and liabilities of a nonprofit organization's unrestricted fund are similar to the current assets and liabilities of a business enterprise. Cash, investments, accounts receivable, receivables from other funds, inventories, and short-term prepayments are typical assets of an unrestricted fund. Nonprofit organizations that use fund accounting generally account for plant assets in a plant fund, although health care entities account for such assets in the general fund.[15]

---

[13] *Audit and Accounting Guide,* "Audits of Certain Nonprofit Organizations," AICPA (New York: 1987), p. 88.
[14] Ibid.
[15] "Audits of Providers of Health Care Services," p. 55.

With respect to nonexhaustible *collections* of museums, art galleries, botanical gardens, libraries, and similar nonprofit organizations, the FASB waived recognition of such assets in the organizations' accounting records under specified conditions. However, the organization's statement of activities and a note to the financial statements must include specified disclosures regarding the collections.[16]

The liabilities of an unrestricted fund include payables, accruals, and deferred revenue similar to those of a business enterprise, as well as amounts payable to other funds.

Fund Balance of Unrestricted Fund   Because most nonprofit organizations do not have owners, the net assets of the organizations' unrestricted funds are represented by a fund balance similar to that of most funds of a governmental entity.

The board of directors of a nonprofit organization may *designate* a portion of an unrestricted fund's net assets for a specific purpose. The earmarked position is accounted for as a segregation of the unrestricted fund balance, rather than as a separate restricted fund. For example, if the board of directors of Civic Welfare, Inc., a voluntary health and welfare organization, earmarks $25,000 of the unrestricted fund's assets for the acquisition of office equipment, the following journal entry is prepared for Civic Welfare, Inc., Unrestricted Fund:

Journal entry for designation of portion of fund balance of unrestricted fund	*Undesignated Fund Balance* *25,000*	
	Designated Fund Balance—Office Equipment	*25,000*
	To record designation of portion of fund balance for acquisition of office equipment.	

The Designated Fund Balance—Office Equipment ledger account is similar to a retained earnings appropriation account of a corporation and a designated fund balance account of a governmental entity and is reported in the accounting records of Civic Welfare, Inc., as a portion of the fund balance of the Unrestricted Fund.

Restricted Fund

Nonprofit organizations establish *restricted funds* to account for assets available for current use but expendable only as authorized by the donor of the assets. Thus, a restricted fund of a nonprofit organization resembles the special revenue fund of a governmental entity, because the assets of both types of funds may be expended only for specified purposes.

The assets of restricted funds are not derived from the operations of the nonprofit organization. Instead, the assets are obtained from (1) restricted gifts or grants from individuals or governmental entities, (2) revenues from restricted fund investments, (3) gains on sales of investments of the restricted funds, and (4) restricted income from endowment funds. These assets are transferred to the unrestricted fund

---

[16] *FASB Statement No. 117,* pp. 3–4, 8.

at the time the designated expenditure is made, with a credit to an account with a title such as Net Assets Released from Restrictions.

To illustrate, assume that on July 1, Year 4, Robert King donated $50,000 to Community Hospital, a nonprofit organization, for the acquisition of beds for a new wing of the hospital. On August 1, Year 4, Community Hospital paid $51,250 for the beds. These transactions and events are recorded by Community Hospital as shown below:

Journal entries for restricted donation to nonprofit hospital

In Robert King Restricted Fund:

Year 4

July 1	Cash...	50,000	
	Contributions Revenue		50,000
	To record receipt of gift from Robert King for acquisition of beds for new wing.		
Aug. 1	Net Assets Released from Restrictions	50,000	
	Payable to Unrestricted Fund....................		50,000
	To record obligation to Unrestricted Fund for cost of beds for new wing in accordance with Robert King's gift.		

In Unrestricted Fund:

Year 4

Aug. 1	Plant Assets..	51,250	
	Cash		51,250
	To record acquisition of beds for new wing.		
1	Receivable from Robert King Restricted Fund............	50,000	
	Net Assets Released from Restrictions		50,000
	To record receivable from Robert King Restricted Fund for reimbursement of expenditures for beds.		

Endowment Fund

An *endowment fund* of a nonprofit organization is similar to a *nonexpendable trust fund* of a governmental entity, described in Chapter 14. A *permanent endowment fund* is one for which the principal must be maintained indefinitely in revenue-producing investments. Only the revenues from a permanent endowment fund's investments may be expended by the nonprofit organization. In contrast, the principal of a *term endowment fund* may be expended after the passage of a period of time or the occurrence of an event specified by the donor of the endowment principal. A *quasi-endowment fund* is established by the board of directors of a nonprofit organization, rather than by an outside donor. At the option of the board, the principal of a quasi-endowment fund later may be expended by the entity that established the fund.

The revenues of endowment funds are accounted for in accordance with the instructions of the donor or the board of directors. If there are no restrictions on the use of endowment fund income, it is transferred to the nonprofit organization's unrestricted fund. Otherwise, the endowment fund revenues are transferred to an appropriate restricted fund.

Agency Fund

An *agency fund* of a nonprofit organization is identical to its counterpart in a governmental entity. An agency fund is used to account for assets held by a nonprofit organization as a custodian. The assets are disbursed only as instructed by their owner.

For example, a nonprofit university may act as custodian of cash of a student organization. The university disburses the cash as directed by the appropriate officers of the student organization. The undistributed cash of the student organization is reported as a *liability* of the university's agency fund, rather than as a *fund balance,* because the university has no equity in the fund.

Annuity and Life Income Funds

Annuity Fund   Assets may be contributed to a nonprofit organization with the stipulation that the organization pay specified fixed amounts periodically to designated recipients, for a specified time period. An *annuity fund* is established by the nonprofit organization to account for this arrangement. At the end of the specified time period for the periodic payments, the unexpended assets of the annuity fund are transferred to the unrestricted fund or to a restricted fund or endowment fund specified by the donor.

The journal entries on page 719 illustrate the accounting for the Ruth Collins Annuity Fund of Ridgedale College, a nonprofit college, for the fund's first fiscal year, ending June 30, Year 2. Note that, in the first journal entry on June 30, Year 2, the revenues and gains on the annuity fund's share of the investment pool are credited to the Annuity Payable ledger account. This is necessary because the actuarial computation of the annuity on the date of establishment of the annuity fund valued the annuity liability at its *then present value.*

Life Income Fund   A *life income fund* is used to account for stipulated payments to a named beneficiary (or beneficiaries) during the beneficiary's lifetime. In a life income fund, only the *income* is paid to the beneficiary. Thus, payments to a life income fund's beneficiary vary from one accounting period to the next, but payments from an annuity fund are fixed in amount.

Loan Fund

A *loan fund* may be established by any nonprofit organization, but loan funds most frequently are included in the accounting records of colleges and universities. Student loan funds generally are *revolving;* that is, as old loans are repaid, new loans are made from the receipts. Loans receivable are carried in the loan fund at estimated realizable value; provisions for doubtful loans are debited directly to the Fund Balance ledger account, not to an expense account. Interest on loans is credited to the Fund Balance account, ordinarily on the cash basis of accounting.

Journal entries for
annuity fund of a
nonprofit college

Year 1				
July	*1*	*Cash*	*50,000*	
		Annuity Payable		*35,000*
		Contributions Revenue		*15,000*
		To record receipt of cash from Andrea Collins for an annuity of $6,000 a year each June 30 to Ruth Collins for her lifetime. Liability is recorded at the actuarially computed present value of the annuity, based on life expectancy of Ruth Collins.		
	1	*Investments*	*45,000*	
		Cash		*45,000*
		To record acquisition of interest in Ridgedale College's investment pool.		
Year 2				
June 30		*Cash*	*1,500*	
		Investments	*2,000*	
		Annuity Payable		*3,500*
		To record share of revenues and gains of Ridgedale College investment pool.		
	30	*Annuity Payable*	*6,000*	
		Cash		*6,000*
		To record payment of current year's annuity to Ruth Collins.		
	30	*Contributions Revenue*	*15,000*	
		Annuity Payable		*1,000*
		Fund Balance		*14,000*
		To close revenue account and adjust annuity liability based on revised actuarial valuation of Ruth Collins annuity.		

Plant Fund

The components of plant funds vary among nonprofit organizations. In addition to plant assets, plant funds may include cash and investments earmarked for additions to plant assets and mortgage notes payable and other liabilities collateralized by the plant assets. Sinking-fund assets set aside for retirement of debt incurred to acquire plant assets also may be in plant funds.

FINANCIAL STATEMENTS OF NONPROFIT ORGANIZATIONS

The wide variety of nonprofit organizations described on page 705, together with the various inconsistent pronouncements of the AICPA on accounting for nonprofit organizations, contributed in the past to an assortment of form, content, display, and terminology techniques for financial statements of such organizations. To lend more uniformity to financial reporting by nonprofit organizations without imposing inflexible standards, the FASB issued *FASB Statement No. 117,* "Financial Statements of Not-for-Profit Organizations." Among its provisions were the following: [17]

1   Financial statements of nonprofit organizations shall be a statement of financial position, a statement of activities, a statement of cash flows, and notes to the financial statements.

2   The statement of financial position shall report the amounts of the organization's total assets, total liabilities, and total net assets.

3   The statement of financial position shall report the amounts for each of the three classes of the organization's net assets: permanently restricted, temporarily restricted, and unrestricted.

4   The statement of activities shall report the amount of the change in the organization's net assets for the period with a caption such as *changes in net assets* or *change in equity.*

5   The statement of activities shall report the amount of the changes in each of the three classes of the organization's net assets: permanently restricted, temporarily restricted, and unrestricted.

6   The statement of activities shall report gross amounts of revenues and expenses of the organization, except that investment revenues may be reported net of expenses and gains or losses on disposal of plant assets may be reported net.

7   The statement of activities or a note thereto shall report expenses by functional classifications such as program services and supporting services.

8   The statement of cash flows shall be similar in format—direct method or indirect method—to one that is issued for a business enterprise.

The financial statements on pages 721 to 723 illustrate one format of financial statements that complies with the foregoing standards.

---

[17] *FASB Statement No. 117,* pp. 4–10.

NONPROFIT ORGANIZATION
Statement of Activities
For Year Ended June 30, Year 4
(amounts in thousands)

Changes in unrestricted net assets:
Revenues and gains:

Contributions	$ 9,000
Fees	6,000
Investment income	7,000
Net realized and unrealized gains on investments	8,000
Other	1,000
Total unrestricted revenues and gains	$ 31,000
Net assets released from restrictions	16,000
Total unrestricted revenues, gains, and other support	$ 47,000

Expenses:

Programs	$ 28,000
Management and general	3,000
Fund raising	2,000
Total expenses	$ 33,000
Increase in unrestricted net assets	$ 14,000

Changes in temporarily restricted net assets:

Contributions	$ 9,000
Investment income	3,000
Net realized and unrealized gains on investments	3,000
Net assets released from restrictions	(16,000)
Decrease in temporarily restricted net assets	$ (1,000)

Changes in permanently restricted net assets:

Contributions	$ 2,000
Investment income	10,000
Net realized and unrealized gains on investments	6,000
Increase in permanently restricted net assets	$ 18,000
Increase in net assets	$ 31,000
Net assets, beginning of year	252,200
Net assets, end of year	$283,200

The following features of the financial statements on pages 721 to 723 may be noted:

1 In the statement of activities, contributions, investment income, and gains or losses are common to changes in all three categories of net assets—unrestricted, temporarily restricted, and permanently restricted. Fees and other operating revenues and expenses are associated with changes in unrestricted net assets only.

Assets

Cash and cash equivalents.	$ 100
Short-term investments	1,500
Accounts and interest receivable (net).	2,300
Pledges receivable (net)	3,000
Inventories and short-term prepayments	700
Long-term investments	220,000
Cash and investments restricted to acquisition of plant assets.	5,300
Plant assets (net)	62,000
Total assets	$294,900

Liabilities & Net Assets

Liabilities:	
Accounts payable	$ 3,000
Grants payable	1,000
Annuities payable	1,700
Long-term debt	6,000
Total liabilities	$ 11,700
Net assets:	
Unrestricted	$ 92,000
Temporarily restricted	50,000
Permanently restricted.	141,200
Total net assets.	$283,200
Total liabilities & net assets	$294,900

2 In the statement of financial position, restricted cash and investments are displayed separately, as they are in the balance sheet of an enterprise fund of a governmental entity (see page 677).

3 In the statement of cash flows (indirect method), the $17,000 of net realized and unrealized gains on investments is the total of the following in the statement of activities:

Net realized and unrealized gains on investments from:	
Unrestricted net assets	$ 8,000
Temporarily restricted net assets.	3,000
Permanently restricted net assets	6,000
Total.	$17,000

4 For a nonprofit organization that uses fund accounting, unrestricted net assets typically are those in the unrestricted (or general) fund. Temporarily restricted net assets generally are those in restricted funds, loan funds, term and quasi-endowment funds, annuity and life income funds, and plant funds. The most significant source of permanently restricted net assets is permanent endowment funds.

NONPROFIT ORGANIZATION
Statement of Cash Flows (indirect method)
For Year Ended June 30, Year 4
(amounts in thousands)

Net cash provided by operating activities **(Exhibit 1)**.....................		$19,000
Cash flows from investing activities:		
Acquisition of investments	$(29,000)	
Acquisition of plant assets	(2,000)	
Disposal of plant assets..................................	12,600	
Net cash used in investing activities...............................		(18,400)
Cash flows from financing activities:		
Contributions received..................................	$ 3,000	
Interest and dividends received and reinvested............	1,000	
Payment of annuities payable	(2,000)	
Payment of long-term debt..............................	(3,000)	
Net cash used in financing activities		(1,000)
Net decrease in cash and cash equivalents.............................		$ (400)
Cash and cash equivalents, beginning of year..........................		500
Cash and cash equivalents, end of year		$ 100

Exhibit 1 Cash flows from operating activities:	
Increase in net assets	$31,000
Adjustments to reconcile increase in net assets to net cash	
provided by operating activities:	
Depreciation expense	7,000
Increase in accounts and interest receivable.......................	(1,000)
Increase in pledges receivable	(1,000)
Decrease in inventories and short-term prepayments	2,000
Increase in accounts payable	2,000
Decrease in grants payable.......................................	(4,000)
Net realized and unrealized gains on investments	(17,000)
Net cash provided by operating activities	$ 19,000

Exhibit 2 Cash paid during the year for interest (none capi-	
talized)...	$ 400

Exhibit 3 Noncash investing and financing activities:	
Plant assets acquired by donations	$ 2,200

Concluding Observations on Accounting for Nonprofit Organizations

The FASB's issuance of *Statements No. 93, 116,* and *117* has supplanted many of the previously accepted—but inconsistent—accounting standards for the numerous types of nonprofit organizations listed on page 705. More reforms may be necessary, however, in the form and content of financial statements issued by those organizations. For example, should there be a caption, "Excess of revenues over expenses," somewhere in a nonprofit organization's statement of activities? Should budgeted amounts be compared with actual operating results in the statement of activities? May some measure of performance—for example, effectiveness of use of contributions—be reported? Perhaps more research into the needs of users of financial statements of nonprofit organizations may yield answers to these and other questions.

REVIEW QUESTIONS

1   What is a *nonprofit organization?*

2   List four types of nonprofit organizations in the United States.

3   What role did the AICPA's *Accounting and Auditing Guides* or *Industry Audit Guides* play in the establishment of accounting standards for nonprofit organizations? Explain.

4   What are three characteristics of nonprofit organizations that resemble those of governmental entities?

5   What characteristics of nonprofit organizations resemble those of business enterprises?

6   Nonprofit hospitals and universities often reduce their basic revenue charges to patients and students, respectively. How are these reductions reflected in the revenue accounting for the two types of nonprofit organizations? Explain.

7   **a** Does a nonprofit organization recognize donated material in its accounting records? Explain.
   b Does a nonprofit organization recognize donated services in its accounting records? Explain.

8   How are expenses classified in the statement of activities of a nonprofit organization that receives significant support from the public? Explain.

9   Explain the accounting for grants that may be revoked by the board of trustees of a nonprofit performing arts organization.

10   How are collections reported in the financial statements of a nonprofit museum? Explain.

11   Differentiate between an *annuity fund* and a *life income fund* of a nonprofit organization.

12   Define the following terms applicable to nonprofit organizations:
a *Designated Fund Balance*

b *Third-party payor*

c *Pledge*

d *Charity care*

e *Term endowment fund*

13 Identify the financial statements that are issued by a nonprofit organization.

EXERCISES

Ex. 15-1 Select the best answer for each of the following multiple-choice questions:

1 A fund of a nonprofit organization that has no counterpart in the funds of a governmental entity is a(n):

a Unrestricted fund

b Restricted fund

c Endowment fund

d Loan fund

2 The records of Rehab Hospital, a nonprofit organization, had the following amounts on June 30, Year 7:

Charity care	$ 40,000
Contractual adjustments	80,000
Patient service revenues (gross)	620,000
Provision for doubtful accounts	70,000

Net patient service revenues for Rehab Hospital for the year ended June 30, Year 7, amount to:

a $620,000   b $550,000   c $500,000   d $430,000   e Some other amount

3 Operating room supplies donated to a nonprofit hospital are:

a Recorded on a memorandum basis in the general journal

b Credited to the Fund Balance ledger account

c Accounted for in the unrestricted fund (general fund)

d Not accounted for in the hospital's basic accounting records

4 The original equity percentages assigned to pooled investments of the various funds of a nonprofit organization are based on the investments':

a Cost

b Carrying amounts

c Current fair values

d Revenue-generating capacity

5 Fund-raising costs of a nonprofit organization generally are:

a Recognized as an asset and amortized over the accounting periods benefited

b Offset against the contributions revenue received

c Recognized as an expense when incurred

d Accounted for in some other manner

6 Some otherwise tax-exempt nonprofit organizations may be subject to federal and state income taxes on their:

a Revenues

b Support

c Endowment income

d Unrelated business income

7   Assets of a nonprofit organization that may not be recognized in the organization's statement of financial position are:

a Pledges receivable

b Donated plant assets

c Collections

d Donated goods

8   The type of endowment fund of a nonprofit organization, the principal of which must be maintained indefinitely in revenue-producing investments, is a:

a Permanent endowment fund

b Quasi-endowment fund

c Term endowment fund

d Nonexpendable endowment fund

9   The type of endowment fund that is established by a nonprofit organization's board of directors rather than an outside donor is a:

a Permanent endowment fund

b Term endowment fund

c Quasi-endowment fund

d Directors' endowment fund

10   Endowment funds of nonprofit organizations whose principal ultimately may be expended by the organization are:

a Quasi-endowment funds only

b Term endowment funds only

c Both quasi- and term endowment funds

d Neither permanent, term, nor quasi-endowment funds

11   An annuity fund of a nonprofit organization resembles the organization's:

a Endowment funds

b Restricted funds

c Life income funds

d Loan funds

12   The fund of a nonprofit university that is *revolving* is a(n):

a Annuity fund

b Life income fund

c Loan fund

d Endowment fund

13   The statement of financial position of a nonprofit organization displays the organization's assets, liabilities, and:

a Fund balance

b Equity

c Excess of assets over liabilities

d Net assets

Ex. 15-2 Gross patient service revenues of Neighborhood Hospital, a nonprofit organization, for the month of May, Year 7, totaled $860,000. Charity care to indigent patients totaled $80,000, of which $50,000 was to be received by Neighborhood Hospital from City Charities. Contractual adjustments allowed to Blue Cross amounted to $140,000. Doubtful accounts expense was estimated at $20,000.

Prepare journal entries (omit explanations) for Neighborhood Hospital on May 31, Year 7.

Ex. 15-3 For the month of September, Year 6, its first month of operations, Redwood Hospital's patient service revenue records included the following:

Amount to be received from United Way for indigent patients	$ 16,500
Charity care for indigent patients..	32,000
Contractual adjustments allowed for Medicare patients...................	18,500
Gross patient service revenues (excluding charity care and contractual adjustments)...	225,000
Doubtful accounts expense (no accounts were written off)................	14,600

Prepare a working paper to show how the foregoing information is displayed in the financial statements of nonprofit Redwood Hospital for the month of September, Year 6.

Ex. 15-4 Selected ledger account balances for Recuperative Hospital, a nonprofit organization, on October 31, Year 1, the end of its first month of operations, were as follows:

Accounts receivable..	$174,000 dr
Allowance for doubtful accounts	24,000 cr
Contractual adjustments...	32,000 dr
Doubtful accounts expense	24,000 dr
Patient service revenues	206,000 cr

In addition, Recuperative had charity care totaling $10,000, of which $6,000 was to be reimbursed by Local Services, a nonprofit organization. Because Recuperative billed patients on October 31, Year 1, it had not collected any accounts receivable as of that date.

Reconstruct the journal entries (omit explanations) prepared by Recuperative Hospital on October 31, Year 1.

Ex. 15-5 The library of the nonprofit University of South Park (USP) received books with a current fair value of $16,000 from various publishers at no cost on June 15, Year 4. The library's operations are accounted for in USP's Unrestricted Fund.

Prepare a journal entry for the Unrestricted Fund of University of South Park on June 15, Year 4.

Ex. 15-6 In your audit of the financial statements of Cordova Hospital, a nonprofit organization, for the year ended March 31, Year 6, you note the following journal entry in the General Fund:

Inventories	200	
Cash		200
To record purchase of medicine and drugs from manufacturer at nominal cost. Current fair value of the items totals $6,400.		

Prepare a journal entry to correct the accounting records of the General Fund of Cordova Hospital on March 31, Year 6.

Ex. 15-7   During the month of October, Year 4, volunteer instructors' aides rendered services at no cost to Warner College, a nonprofit organization. Salary rates for comparable employees to Warner College applied to the services gave a total value of $3,400. Complimentary meals given to the volunteers at the Warner College cafeteria during October, Year 4, cost $180. The volunteer's services met the specifications for donated services in *FASB Statement No. 116,* ''Accounting for Contributions Received and Contributions Made.''

Prepare a journal entry for the Warner College Unrestricted Fund on October 31, Year 4, for the services donated to Warner College during the month of October, Year 4. (Disregard income taxes and other withholdings.)

Ex. 15-8   The value of services donated by docents of Modern Museum, a nonprofit organization, totaled $68,000 for the year ended June 30, Year 6. Also during that year, Modern Museum used rent-free facilities for storage that would have been leased to a business enterprise by the owner for the rent of $96,000 a year.

Prepare journal entries dated June 30, Year 6, for the foregoing support of Modern Museum.

Ex. 15-9   Community Welfare, Inc, accounts for pledges in accordance with *FASB Statement No. 116,* ''Accounting for Contributions Received and Contributions Made.'' During the month of November, Year 6, Community Welfare received unrestricted pledges totaling $500,000, of which 20% was estimated to be uncollectible, and wrote off uncollectible pledges totaling $30,000. During that month, $240,000 was collected on pledges.

Prepare journal entries (dated November 30, Year 6) for Community Welfare, Inc., with respect to pledges. (Omit explanations for the journal entries.)

Ex. 15-10   The ''Summary of Significant Accounting Policies'' note to the financial statements prepared by the controller of Wabash Hospital (a nonprofit organization) for the year ended June 30, Year 3, included the following sentence: ''Pledges for contributions are recorded when the cash is received.'' Another note read as follows:

Pledges   Unrestricted pledges receivable, received, and collected during the year ended June 30, Year 3, were as follows:

Pledges receivable, July 1, Year 2 (10% doubtful)	$ 50,000
New pledges received during year ended June 30, Year 3	300,000
Pledges receivable, July 1, Year 2, determined to be uncollectible during year	(15,000)
Pledges collected in cash during year ended June 30, Year 3	$(275,000)
Pledges receivable, June 30, Year 3 (12% doubful)	$ 60,000

All pledges are due six months from the date of the pledge. Pledge support is recorded in the General Fund.

Assume that you are engaged in the first annual audit of the financial statements of Wabash Hospital for the year ended June 30, Year 3, and are satisfied with the propriety of the amounts recorded in the hospital's ''Pledges'' note. Prepare an adjusting entry for the General Fund of Wabash Hospital on June 30, Year 3.

Ex. 15-11 On July 1, Year 5, three funds of Wilmington College pooled their individual investments, as follows:

	Cost	Current fair values
Restricted Fund.	$ 80,000	$ 90,000
Quasi-Endowment Fund	120,000	126,000
Annuity Fund	150,000	144,000
Totals.	$350,000	$360,000

During the year ended June 30, Year 6, the Wilmington College investment pool, managed by the Unrestricted Fund, reinvested realized gains of $10,000 and received dividends and interest totaling $18,000.

Prepare journal entries on June 30, Year 6, for each of the three Wilmington College funds to record the results of the investment pool's operations during Fiscal Year 6. Do not use Receivable from Unrestricted Fund ledger accounts.

Ex. 15-12 Artistry Unlimited, a nonprofit performing arts organization, received a gift of $50,000 on July 1, Year 7, to be awarded as grants to students of ballet for the school year beginning in September, Year 7. On September 1, Year 7, grants totaling $45,000 were awarded to nine students of ballet. Artistry Unlimited does not use fund accounting.

Prepare journal entries for Artistry Unlimited on July 1 and September 1, Year 7.

Ex. 15-13 On July 1, Year 2, Technology Specialists, a nonprofit research and scientific organization, awarded a $30,000, three-year research grant to Martin Grey. The grant was payable in three annual installments of $10,000, beginning July 1, Year 2; however, the governing board of Technology Specialists reserved the right to revoke the remaining unpaid amount of the grant on appropriate notice to Grey on June 30, Year 3, or June 30, Year 4.

Prepare a journal entry for Technology Specialists on July 1, Year 2, and an appropriate note to its financial statements for the year ended June 30, Year 3.

Ex. 15-14 From the following ledger account balances (amounts in thousands) of the General Fund of No-Prof Hospital, a nonprofit organization, prepare a statement of financial position as of June 30, Year 5. No-Prof has only a general fund.

Accounts with debit balances		Accounts with credit balances	
Accounts receivable (net)	$ 900	Accounts payable and accrued	
Cash and cash equivalents	100	liabilities	$ 550
Cash restricted to acquisition		Advances from third-party	
of plant assets	200	payors	200
Investments restricted to acqui-		Deferred revenues.	100
sition of plant assets	400	Fund balance designated for	
Inventory of supplies.	200	plant assets.	600
Plant assets (net).	3,100	Housing bonds payable	400
Short-term prepayments	50	Mortgage bonds payable	500
		Notes payable (current)	300
		Undesignated fund balance.	2,300
Total	$4,950	Total	$4,950

CASES

Case 15-1   During the June 20, Year 10, meeting of the board of directors of Roakdale Associations, a nonprofit voluntary health and welfare organization, the following discussion transpired:

> *Chair:* "We shall now hear the report from the controller."
>
> *Controller:* "Our unrestricted contributions are at an all-time high. I projected an Unrestricted Fund excess of revenues over expenses of $100,000 for the year ending June 30."
>
> *Chair:* "That's too large an amount for us to have a successful fund-raising drive next year. I'll entertain a motion that $80,000 of unrestricted contributions be transferred to a Restricted Fund."
>
> *Director Walker:* "So moved."
>
> *Director Hastings:* "Second."
>
> *Chair:* "All those in favor say *aye*."
>
> *All Directors:* "Aye."
>
> *Chair:* "The chair directs the controller to prepare the necessary journal entries for the Unrestricted Fund and a Restricted Fund."

Instructions

Do you concur with the action taken by the board of directors of Roakdale Association? Explain.

Case 15-2   The board of trustees of Toledo Day Care Center, a nonprofit organization, has asked you, as independent auditor for the center, to attend a meeting of the board of trustees and participate in the discussion of a proposal to create one or more endowment funds. At the meeting, the board members ask you numerous questions regarding the operations and the accounting treatment of endowment funds. Among the questions posed by trustees were the following:

(1) Are only the revenues of an endowment fund expendable for current operations?

(2) Under what circumstances, if any, may endowment fund principal be expended at the discretion of the board?

(3) Must a separate set of accounting records be established for each endowment fund, or may all endowment fund operations be accounted for in a single restricted fund?

Instructions

Prepare a reply for each of the trustees' questions. Number your replies to correspond with the question numbers.

Case 15-3   In your audit of the financial statements of Science Unlimited, a nonprofit research and scientific organization, for the year ended June 30, Year 7, you find that products created by Science Unlimited are sold at prices less than production costs. Unsold products are carried at an arbitrary amount in two sections of Science Unlimited's statement of financial position—$10,000 "base stock" as a plant asset and the remainder as a current asset. No provision is made for distribution, handling, or storage costs.

Instructions

Do you concur with the way Science Unlimited presents unsold products in its statement of financial position? Explain. (Adapted from *AICPA Technical Practice Aids.*)

Case 15-4 Station KKLL, a nonprofit public broadcasting station, is authorized to acquire surplus broadcasting equipment from the U.S. government at nominal prices. In your audit of the financial statements of Station KKLL for the year ended June 30, Year 9, you discover that a radio station tower antenna with a current fair value of $8,000 had been acquired from the U.S. government for $500, which was the amount debited to the Broadcasting Equipment ledger account. Under terms of the acquisition, Station KKLL is not permitted to resell the antenna for a period of four years.

Instructions

Do you concur with Station KKLL's accounting for the acquisition of the antenna? Explain. (Adapted from *AICPA Technical Practice Aids.*)

Case 15-5 The accountant for Nonprofit Religious Organization proposes to estimate the fair value of services donated by deacons, elders, ushers, and other volunteer laypersons and recognize the amount as both expense and support in the organization's statement of activities.

Instructions

Do you concur with the accountant's proposal? Explain.

PROBLEMS

Pr. 15-1 Ledger account balances (in alphabetical sequence) to be included in the statement of activities for Seaside Hospital (a nonprofit organization that has only a general fund) for the year ended June 30, Year 7, are as follows:

	Debit	Credit
	(in thousands)	
Administrative services expenses	$280	
Contractual adjustments	140	
Depreciation expense	340	
Doubtful accounts expense	80	
Fiscal service expense	180	
General services expense	360	
Nursing services expense	560	
Other operating revenue		$ 180
Other professional services expense	260	
Patient service revenues		1,560
Unrestricted contributions		380
Unrestricted income from investments		280

Instructions

Prepare a statement of activities for Seaside Hospital (amounts in thousands) for the year ended June 30, Year 7, ending with increase (decrease) in unrestricted net assets.

Pr. 15-2   Among the transactions and events of Holley School, a nonprofit, private secondary school, for the year ended June 30, Year 4, were the following:

(1) Paid $50,000 from the Unrestricted Fund for classroom computers, to be carried in the Plant Fund.
(2) Received an unrestricted cash gift of $200,000.
(3) Disposed of for $110,000 common stocks that had been carried in the Quasi-Endowment Fund at $100,000. There were no restrictions on use of the proceeds attributable to the gain.
(4) Constructed a new school building at a total cost of $2 million. Payment was by $250,000 cash from the Plant Fund and $1,750,000 obtained on a 5% mortgage note payable.

Instructions

Prepare journal entries for the foregoing transactions and events of Holley School for the year ended June 30, Year 4. Use the following ledger account titles in the journal entries:

Plant Fund
  Buildings
  Cash
  Equipment
  Fund Balance
  Mortgage Note Payable

Quasi-Endowment Fund
  Cash
  Investments
  Payable to Unrestricted Fund

Unrestricted Fund
  Cash
  Contributions
  Investment Income
  Receivable from Quasi-Endowment Fund
  Undesignated Fund Balance

Pr. 15-3   The adjusted trial balance of Nonprofit Trade Association, which does not use fund accounting, for June 30, Year 4, was as follows:

NONPROFIT TRADE ASSOCIATION
Adjusted Trial Balance
June 30, Year 4

	Debit	Credit
Cash...	$ 7,000	
Short-term investments	217,000	
Accounts receivable..................................	28,000	
Allowance for doubtful accounts		$ 3,000

(continued)

NONPROFIT TRADE ASSOCIATION
Adjusted Trial Balance (concluded)
June 30, Year 4

	Debit	Credit
Publications inventory	61,000	
Long-term investments	120,000	
Plant assets	55,000	
Accumulated depreciation of plant assets................		22,000
Other assets...	28,000	
Accounts payable		36,000
Accrued liabilities		12,000
Deferred membership dues		131,000
Fund balance, July 1, Year 3		285,000
Membership dues		184,000
Conferences and meetings revenue.....................		321,000
Publication and advertising sales		143,000
Special assessments revenue		50,000
Investment income, including net gains.................		11,000
Member services expense	56,000	
Conferences and meetings expense	166,000	
Technical services expense	218,000	
Communications expense.............................	61,000	
General administration expenses	154,000	
Membership development expense	27,000	
Totals...	$1,198,000	$1,198,000

Instructions

Prepare a statement of activities and a statement of financial position for Nonprofit Trade Association for the year ended June 30, Year 4.

Pr. 15-4 On July 1, Year 6, the four funds of Suburban Welfare Services, a nonprofit organization, formed an investment pool managed by the Unrestricted Fund. On that date, cost and current fair values of the investment pool were as follows:

	Cost	Current fair values
Unrestricted Fund	$ 50,000	$ 59,400
Restricted Fund	20,000	16,200
Plant Fund..	80,000	89,100
Arnold Life Income Fund	100,000	105,300
Totals	$250,000	$270,000

Additional Information

(1) During the six months ended December 31, Year 6, the investment pool, managed by the Unrestricted Fund, reinvested realized gains totaling $15,000 and received dividends and interest totaling $25,000, which was distributed to the participating funds.

(2) On December 31, Year 6, the Restricted Fund withdrew from the pool and was awarded securities in the amount of its share of the pool's aggregate December 31, Year 6, current fair value of $300,000.

(3) On January 2, Year 7, the Edwards Endowment Fund entered the Suburban Welfare Services investment pool with investments having a cost of $70,000 and a current fair value of $78,000.

(4) During the six months ended June 30, Year 7, the investment pool reinvested realized gains totaling $40,000 and received dividends and interest totaling $60,000, which was distributed to the participating funds.

Instructions

a Prepare a working paper for the Suburban Welfare Services investment pool, computing the following (round all percentages to two decimal places):
(1) Original equity percentages, July 1, Year 6
(2) Revised equity percentages, January 2, Year 7

b Prepare journal entries to record the operations of the Suburban Welfare Services investment pool in the accounting records of the Unrestricted Fund. Use Payable to Restricted Fund, Payable to Plant Fund, and Payable to Arnold Life Income Fund ledger accounts for amounts payable to other funds.

Pr. 15-5   Among the transactions and events of the General Fund of Harbor Hospital, a non-profit organization, for the month of October, Year 8, were the following:

(1) Gross patient service revenues of $80,000 were billed to patients. Indigent patient charity care amounted to $4,000, of which amount $2,500 was receivable from Bovard Welfare Organization. Provision was made for contractual adjustments allowed to Medicaid of $6,000, and doubtful accounts of $8,000.

(2) Donated services approximating $10,000 at going salary rates were received from volunteer nurses. Meals costing $200 were served to the volunteer nurses at no charge by the Harbor Hospital cafeteria.

(3) New pledges, due in three months, totaling $5,000 were received from various donors. Collections on pledges amounted to $3,500, and the provision for doubtful pledges for October, Year 8, was $800.

(4) The $500 monthly annuity established for Arline E. Walters by Walters's contribution to Harbor Hospital three years ago was paid on behalf of the Arline E. Walters Annuity Fund.

(5) The amount of $3,000, received from the Charles Watson Restricted Fund, was expended for new surgical equipment, as authorized by the donor.

Instructions

a Prepare journal entries for the October, Year 8, transactions and events of the Harbor Hospital General Fund. Number each group of entries to correspond to the number of each transactions group.

b Prepare journal entries required for the Harbor Hospital Arline E. Walters Annuity Fund and Charles Watson Restricted Fund as indicated by the transactions and events of the General Fund.

Pr. 15-6   The statements of financial position of Wigstaff Foundation, a nonprofit research and scientific organization that does not use fund accounting, on June 30, Year 8 and Year 7, were as follows:

WIGSTAFF FOUNDATION
Statements of Financial Position
June 30, Year 8 and Year 7

	Year 8	Year 7
Assets		
Current assets:		
Cash	$ 650,000	$ 630,000
Accounts receivable (net)	744,000	712,000
Unbilled contract revenue and reimbursable grant costs.	976,000	780,000
Short-term prepayments	80,000	76,000
Total current assets	$2,450,000	$2,198,000
Long-term investments	$ 840,000	$ 780,000
Plant assets:		
Land...	$ 440,000	$ 440,000
Building..	958,000	958,000
Furniture and equipment............................	334,000	312,000
Subtotals.......................................	$1,732,000	$1,710,000
Less: Accumulated depreciation	518,000	370,000
Total plant assets	$1,214,000	$1,340,000
Total assets	$4,504,000	$4,318,000

Liabilities & Net Assets

	Year 8	Year 7
Current liabilities:		
Accounts payable and accrued liabilities..............	$ 836,000	$ 776,000
Restricted grant advances	522,000	420,000
Current portion of long-term debt	176,000	164,000
Total current liabilities	$1,534,000	$1,360,000
Long-term debt (collateralized by plant assets)	618,000	794,000
Total liabilities	$2,152,000	$2,154,000
Net assets:		
Net equity in plant assets	$ 596,000	$ 546,000
Undesignated.....................................	1,756,000	1,618,000
Total unrestricted net assets	$2,352,000	$2,164,000
Total liabilities & net assets	$4,504,000	$4,318,000

Additional Information for year ended June 30, Year 8

(1) The increase in unrestricted net assets was $188,000.

(2) There were no disposals of plant assets or long-term investments. Furniture and equipment was acquired for cash, as were long-term investments.

(3) The ''net equity in plant assets'' designation of the fund balance represents the difference between total plant assets and long-term debt collateralized by plant assets.

Instructions

Prepare a statement of cash flows (indirect method) for Wigstaff foundation for the year ended June 30, Year 8. A working paper is not required.

Pr. 15-7 The post-closing trial balance of Mid-City Sports Club, a nonprofit social club, on June 30, Year 8, was as follows:

MID-CITY SPORTS CLUB
Post-Closing Trial Balance
June 30, Year 8

	Debit	Credit
Cash	$ 9,000	
Investments	58,000	
Inventories	5,000	
Land	10,000	
Building	164,000	
Accumulated depreciation of building		$130,000
Furniture and equipment	54,000	
Accumulated depreciation of furniture and equipment		46,000
Accounts payable		12,000
Membership certificates (100 × $1,000)		100,000
Cumulative increase in net assets		12,000
Totals	$300,000	$300,000

Additional Information for year ended June 30, Year 9

(1) Dues revenue was $20,000.
(2) Snack bar and soda fountain sales totaled $28,000.
(3) Interest received on investments amounted to $6,000.
(4) Amounts vouchered for payment were as follows:

Clubhouse expenses	$17,000
Snack bar and soda fountain supplies (perpetual inventory system)	26,000
General and administrative expenses	11,000

(5) Vouchers paid totaled $55,000.
(6) The members were assessed $10,000 on June 30, Year 9, payable within one year, for capital improvements to the clubhouse. All the assessments were considered collectible, although none was collected on June 30, Year 9. (Credit Contributions Revenue.)
(7) An unrestricted gift of $5,000 was received.
(8) Depreciation expense of $4,000 for the building and $8,000 for the furniture and equipment was allocable as follows: $9,000 to clubhouse expense, $2,000 to snack bar and soda fountain expense, and $1,000 to general and administrative expense.
(9) The June 30, Year 9, physical inventory of snack bar and soda fountain supplies totaled $1,000.

Instructions

a Prepare journal entries (omit explanations) for the events and transactions of Mid-City Sports Club for the year ended June 30, Year 9.

b Prepare a statement of activities and a statement of financial position for Mid-City Sports Club for the year ended June 30, Year 9.

Pr. 15-8 Following is the post-closing trial balance of the unrestricted fund and the restricted fund of State University, a nonprofit organization, on June 30, Year 8:

STATE UNIVERSITY
Post-Closing Trial Balance
June 30, Year 8
(amounts in thousands)

	Unrestricted Fund	Restricted Fund
Cash and cash equivalents	$210	$ 7
Accounts receivable (student tuition and fees)	350	
Allowance for doubtful accounts.	(9)	
State appropriation receivable	75	
Investments.		60
Totals	$626	$67
Accounts payable.	$ 45	
Deferred revenues.	66	
Fund balance	515	$67
Totals	$626	$67

The following transactions and events occurred during the year ended June 30, Year 9, at actual amounts:

(1) On July 7, Year 8, a gift of $100,000 was received from an alumnus. The alumnus requested that one-half of the gift be used for the acquisition of books for the university library and that the remainder be used for the establishment of a scholarship. The alumnus further requested that the revenue generated by the scholarship fund be used annually to award a scholarship to a qualified student, with the principal remaining intact. On July 20, Year 8, the board of trustees resolved that the cash of the newly established scholarship (endowment) fund would be invested in bank certificates of deposit. On July 21, Year 8, the certificates of deposit were acquired.

(2) Revenues from student tuition and fees applicable to the year ended June 30, Year 9, amounted to $1,900,000. Of this amount, $66,000 had been collected in the prior year and $1,686,000 had been collected during the year ended June 30, Year 9. In addition, on June 30, Year 9, the university had received cash of $158,000, representing tuition and fees for the session beginning July 1, Year 9.

(3) During the year ended June 30, Year 9, State University had collected $349,000 of the outstanding accounts receivable at the beginning of the year. The balance was determined to be uncollectible and was written off against the allowance ledger account. On June 30, Year 9, the allowance account was increased by $3,000.

(4) During the year, interest of $6,000 was earned and collected on late student fee payments.

(5) During the year, the state appropriation was received. An additional unrestricted appropriation of $50,000 was made by the state, but had not been paid to State University as of June 30, Year 9.

(6) Unrestricted cash gifts totaling $25,000 were received from alumni of the university.

(7) During the year, restricted fund investments of $21,000 were sold for $26,000. Investment earnings amounting to $1,900 were received. (Credit Fund Balance.)

(8) During the year, unrestricted operating expenses of $1,777,000 were recognized. On June 30, Year 9, $59,000 of these expenses remained unpaid.

(9) Restricted cash of $13,000 was spent for authorized purposes during the year. An equal amount was transferred from fund balance to revenues of the restricted fund.

(10) The accounts payable on June 30, Year 8, were paid during the year.

(11) During the year, $7,000 interest was earned and received on the certificates of deposit acquired in accordance with the board of trustees resolution discussed in item (1). (Credit Fund Balance.)

Instructions

Prepare journal entries for State University to record the transactions or events for the year ended June 30, Year 9. Each journal entry should be numbered to correspond with the transaction or event described above. (Omit explanations for the journal entries.)

The working paper should be organized as follows:

Transaction number	Ledger accounts	Unrestricted Fund dr(cr)	Restricted Fund dr(cr)	Endowment Fund dr(cr)
(1)				

Use the following ledger account titles in the journal entries:

Unrestricted Fund
  Accounts Payable
  Accounts Receivable
  Allowance for Doubtful Accounts
  Cash
  Deferred Revenues
  Expenses
  Revenues
  State Appropriation Receivable

Restricted Fund
  Cash
  Expenditures
  Fund Balance

Investments
Revenues

Endowment Fund
Cash
Fund Balance
Investments

Pr. 15-9 Following is the post-closing trial balance of the three funds of Resthaven Hospital, a nonprofit organization, on December 31, Year 6:

RESTHAVEN HOSPITAL
Post-Closing Trial Balance
December 31, Year 6
(amounts in thousands)

	General Fund	Plant Replacement and Expansion Fund	Endowment Fund
Cash	$ 20	$ 54	$ 6
Accounts receivable	37		
Allowance for doubtful accounts	(7)		
Inventory of supplies	14		
Investments		71	260
Land	370		
Buildings	1,750		
Accumulated depreciation of buildings	(430)		
Equipment	680		
Accumulated depreciation of equipment	(134)		
Totals	$2,300	$125	$266
Accounts payable	$ 16		
Accrued liabilities	6		
Mortgage bonds payable	150		
Fund balance designated for plant assets	2,116		
Undesignated fund balance	12	$125	$266
Totals	$2,300	$125	$266

Additional Information for Year 7, Actual Amounts

(1) Gross debits to Accounts Receivable for hospital services were as follows:

Room and board	$ 780,000
Other professional services	321,000
Gross debits to Accounts Receivable	$1,101,000

(2) Deductions from gross revenues were contractual adjustments of $15,000. Doubtful accounts expense was $30,000.

(3) The General Fund paid $18,000 to retire mortgage bonds payable with that face amount.

(4) The General Fund received unrestricted gifts of $50,000 and revenues from Endowment Fund investments of $6,500. The General Fund had been designated to receive the revenues on Endowment Fund investments.

(5) Equipment costing $26,000 was acquired. An x-ray machine that had cost $24,000 and had a carrying amount of $2,400 was disposed of for $500.

(6) Vouchers totaling $1,191,000 were issued for the following:

Administrative services expense	$ 120,000
Interest expense	95,000
General services expense	225,000
Nursing services expense	520,000
Other professional services expense	165,000
Inventory of supplies	60,000
Accrued liabilities, Dec. 31, Year 6	6,000
Total vouchers issued	$1,191,000

(7) Collections on accounts receivable totaled $985,000. Accounts receivable written off as uncollectible amounted to $11,000.

(8) Cash payments on accounts payable were $825,000.

(9) Supplies of $37,000 were issued for nursing services.

(10) On December 31, Year 7, accrued interest on Plant Replacement and Expansion Fund investments was $800.

(11) Depreciation of buildings and equipment was as follows:

Buildings	$ 44,000
Equipment	73,000
Total depreciation	$117,000

(12) On December 31, Year 7, an accrual $6,100 was made for interest on the mortgage bonds payable.

Instructions

For the period January 1, Year 7, through December 31, Year 7, prepare journal entries (omit explanations) to record the transactions and events described above for the following funds of Resthaven Hospital:

General Fund
Plant Replacement and Expansion Fund
Endowment Fund

Each journal entry should be numbered to correspond with the transactions or events described above.

The working paper should be organized as follows:

Transaction number	Ledger accounts	General Fund dr(cr)	Plant Replacement and Expansion Fund dr(cr)	Endowment Fund dr(cr)
(1)				

In addition to the ledger accounts included in the December 31, Year 6, post-closing trial balance of Resthaven Hospital, the following accounts are pertinent:

Unrestricted Fund
Administrative Services Expense
Contractual Adjustments
Depreciation Expense
Doubtful Accounts Expense
General Services Expense
Interest Expense
Loss on Disposal of Plant Assets
Nursing Services Expense
Other Professional Services Expense
Patient Service Revenues
Unrestricted Gift Revenues
Unrestricted Revenues from Endowment Fund

Plant Replacement and Expansion Fund
Interest Receivable

Pr. 15-10 A partial statement of financial position for Libra College on June 30, Year 5, follows:

LIBRA COLLEGE
Partial Statement of Financial Position
June 30, Year 5

	Current Funds Unrestricted	Restricted
Assets		
Cash...	$200,000	$ 10,000
Investments..		210,000
Accounts receivable, tuition and fees (net of $15,000 allowance for doubtful accounts)......................	360,000	
Short-term prepayments............................	40,000	
Total assets......................................	$600,000	$220,000
Liabilities & Net Assets		
Accounts payable..................................	$100,000	$ 5,000
Payable to other funds	40,000	
Deferred revenues.................................	25,000	
Net assets (fund balances)	435,000	215,000
Total liabilities & net assets........................	$600,000	$220,000

Additional Information for Year Ended June 30, Year 6

(1) Cash collected from tuition and fees totaled $3 million, of which $362,000 was for accounts receivable on June 30, Year 5, $2,500,000 was for Fiscal Year 6 tuition, and $138,000 was for Fiscal Year 7 tuition.

(2) Deferred revenues (for tuition and fees) on June 30, Year 5, were earned.

(3) The balance of accounts receivable on June 30, Year 5, was written off, and the required June 30, Year 6, balance of the Allowance for Doubtful Accounts ledger account was estimated at $10,000.

(4) On June 30, Year 6, an unrestricted appropriation of $60,000 was received from the state government.

(5) Unrestricted cash gifts of $80,000 were received, of which $30,000 was transferred to the Student Loan Fund by the board of trustees of Libra College.

(6) Investment income of $18,000 was realized and collected; investments costing $25,000 were disposed of for $31,000; and the Restricted Fund acquired investments for $40,000.

(7) Unrestricted general expenses of $2,500,000 were incurred; on June 30, Year 6, unrestricted accounts payable totaled $75,000.

(8) The restricted accounts payable balance on June 30, Year 5, was paid.

(9) The $40,000 payable to other funds was paid to the Plant Fund.

(10) One-fourth of the June 30, Year 5, short-term prepayments expired and pertained to general expenses; there were no additional short-term prepayments made.

Instructions

For the year ended June 30, Year 6, prepare journal entries (omit explanations) for the transactions and events described above for the Unrestricted Fund and the Restricted Fund of Libra College. Each journal entry should be numbered to correspond with the transactions of events described above.

The working paper should be organized as follows:

Transaction number	Ledger accounts	Unrestricted Fund dr(cr)	Restricted Fund dr(cr)
(1)			

In addition to the ledger accounts included in the June 30, Year 5, partial balance sheet of Libra College, the following accounts are pertinent:

Unrestricted Fund
  Educational and General Expenses
  Government Grants Revenues
  Private Gifts Revenues
  Provision for Doubtful Tuition and Fees
  State Appropriation Receivable
  Tuition and Fees Revenues

Pr. 15-11 The adjusted trial balances of the two funds of Handicapped Children Association, a nonprofit voluntary health and welfare organization, on June 30, Year 4, were as follows:

HANDICAPPED CHILDREN ASSOCIATION CURRENT FUNDS
Adjusted Trial Balances
June 30, Year 4

	Unrestricted Fund		Restricted Fund	
	Debit	Credit	Debit	Credit
Cash..........................	$ 40,000		$ 9,000	
Pledges receivable	12,000			
Bequest receivable			5,000	
Allowance for doubtful pledges......		$ 3,000		
Interest receivable................	1,000			
Investments, at cost	100,000			
Accounts payable and accrued liabili-				
ties............................		50,000		$ 1,000
Deferred revenues................		2,000		
Restricted fund balance				3,000
Designated fund balance		12,000		
Undesignated fund balance.........		26,000		
Contributions revenue.............		320,000		15,000
Membership dues revenue		25,000		
Program service fees revenue		30,000		
Investment income................		10,000		
Hearing-impaired children's program				
expenses......................	120,000			
Vision-impaired children's program				
expenses......................	150,000			
Management and general expenses .	45,000		4,000	
Fund-raising expenses.............	8,000		1,000	
Provision for doubtful pledges.......	2,000			
Totals	$478,000	$478,000	$19,000	$19,000

Instructions

Prepare financial statements, excluding a statement of cash flows, for Handicapped Children Association for the year ended June 30, Year 4.

Part 4

Accounting for Fiduciaries

A business enterprise that enters federal bankruptcy proceedings involving liquidation changes from a going concern to a quitting concern. This necessitates a departure from the accounting equation Assets = Liabilities + Equity to the equation Assets = Accountability. The accountability applies to the trustee in the bankruptcy liquidation, who is responsible for realizing the debtor's nonexempt assets and for paying liabilities to the extent possible in accordance with provisions of the Bankruptcy Code. In addition, the reorganization of a business enterprise under the Bankruptcy Code necessitates specialized accounting and reporting practices.

Accounting for an estate or a trust also involves the equation Assets = Accountability. Both the personal representative for an estate and the trustee for a trust are fiduciaries that must report to the supervising court in a specialized manner. Thus, accounting for estates and trusts also involves unique accounting and reporting practices.

16

Bankruptcy: Liquidation and Reorganization

Business failures are a common occurrence in the U.S. economy. Poor management, excessive debt, and inadequate accounting are the most commonly cited causes of business failures. The situation that precedes the typical business failure is inability of a business enterprise to pay liabilities as they become due. Unsecured creditors often resort to lawsuits to satisfy their unpaid claims against a business enterprise. Secured creditors may force foreclosure proceedings for real property or may repossess personal property that collateralizes a *security agreement.* The Internal Revenue Service may seize the assets of a business enterprise that has failed to pay FICA and income taxes withheld from its employees.

A business enterprise may be unable to pay its liabilities as they become due even though the current fair values of its assets exceed its liabilities. For example, an enterprise may experience a severe cash shortage in times of price inflation because of the lag between the purchase or production of goods at inflated costs and the recovery of the inflated costs through increased selling prices.

More typical of the failing business enterprise than the conditions described in the foregoing paragraph is the state of insolvency. *Insolvent* is defined in the Bankruptcy Code as follows:[1]

"insolvent" means—

(A) with reference to an entity other than a partnership, financial condition such that the sum of such entity's debts is greater than all of such entity's property, at a fair valuation, exclusive of—

 (i) property transferred, concealed, or removed with intent to hinder, delay, or defraud such entity's creditors; and

(ii) property that may be exempted from property of the estate under . . . this title; and

(B) with reference to a partnership, financial condition such that the sum of such partnership's debts is greater than the aggregate of, at a fair valuation—

---

[1] *Bankruptcy Code,* sec. 101 (26).

(i) all of such partnership's property, exclusive of the kind specified in subparagraph (A) (i) of this paragraph; and

(ii) the sum of the excess of the value of each general partner's separate property, exclusive of property of the kind specified in subparagraph (A) (ii) of this paragraph, over such partner's separate debts;

The terms *insolvent* and *bankrupt* often are used as interchangeable adjectives. Such usage is technically incorrect; *insolvent* refers to the financial condition of a person or business enterprise, and *bankrupt* refers to a legal state. In this chapter, various legal and accounting issues associated with bankruptcy are discussed.

THE BANKRUPTCY CODE

The U.S. Constitution authorizes Congress to establish uniform laws on the subject of bankruptcies throughout the United States. For the first 89 years under the Constitution, the United States had a national bankruptcy law for a total of only 16 years. During the periods in which national bankruptcy laws were not in effect, state laws on insolvency prevailed. In 1898 a Bankruptcy Act was enacted that, as amended, remained in effect for 80 years. Enactment of the Bankruptcy Act caused state laws on insolvency to be relatively dormant. In 1978 the Bankruptcy Reform Act established the present Bankruptcy Code, and in 1980 the Bankruptcy Tax Act established a uniform group of income tax rules for bankruptcy and insolvency.

The U.S. Supreme Court may prescribe by general rules the various legal practices and procedures under the Bankruptcy Code. Thus, the Bankruptcy Rules established by the Supreme Court constitute important interpretations of provisions of the Bankruptcy Code.

BANKRUPTCY LIQUIDATION

The process of *bankruptcy liquidation* under Chapter 7 of the Bankruptcy Code involves the realization (sale) of the assets of an individual or a business enterprise and the distribution of the cash proceeds to the creditors of the individual or enterprise. Creditors having *security interests* collateralized by specific assets of the debtor generally are entitled to obtain satisfaction of all or part of their claims from the assets pledged as collateral. The Bankruptcy Code provides for priority treatment for certain unsecured creditors; their claims are satisfied in full, if possible, from proceeds of realization of the debtor's noncollateralized assets. Unsecured creditors without priority receive cash, in proportion to the amounts of their claims, from proceeds available from the realization of the debtor's assets. Thus, there are four classes of creditors in a bankruptcy liquidation: *fully secured creditors, partially secured creditors, unsecured creditors with priority,* and *unsecured creditors without priority.*

Debtor's (Voluntary) Petition

The Bankruptcy Code provides that any "person," except a railroad, an insurance company, a bank, a credit union, or a savings and loan association, may file a petition in a federal bankruptcy court for *voluntary liquidation.* The official form for a *debtor's bankruptcy petition,* also known as a *voluntary petition,* must be accompanied by supporting exhibits of the petitioner's debts and property. The debts are classified as follows: (1) creditors having priority; (2) creditors holding security; and (3) creditors having unsecured claims without priority. The debtor's property is reported as follows: real property, personal property, property not otherwise scheduled, and property claimed as exempt. Valuations of property are at *market* or *current fair values.* Also accompanying the debtor's bankruptcy petition is a *statement of affairs* (not to be confused with the *accounting* statement of affairs illustrated on page 755 of this chapter), which contains a series of questions concerning all aspects of the debtor's financial condition and operations.

Creditors' (Involuntary) Petition

If a debtor other than a farmer, a nonprofit organization, or one of the types precluded from filing voluntary petitions owes unpaid amounts to 12 or more unsecured creditors who are not employees, relatives, stockholders, or other "insiders," three or more of the creditors having unsecured claims totaling $5,000 or more may file in a federal bankruptcy court a *creditors' petition for bankruptcy,* also known as an *involuntary petition.* If fewer than 12 creditors are involved, one or more creditors having unsecured claims of $5,000 or more may file the petition. The creditors' petition for bankruptcy must claim either (1) the debtor is not paying debts as they come due or (2) within 120 days prior to the date of the petition, a custodian was appointed for or had taken possession of the debtor's property.

Unsecured Creditors with Priority

The Bankruptcy Code provides that the following unsecured debts are to be paid in full, in the order specified if adequate cash is not available for all, out of a debtor's estate before any cash is paid to other unsecured creditors:

1 Administrative costs.

2 Claims arising in the course of the debtor's business or financial affairs after the commencement of a creditors' bankruptcy proceeding but before appointment of a trustee or order for relief.

3 Claims for wages, salaries, and commissions, including vacation, severance, and sick leave pay not in excess of $2,000 per claimant, earned within 90 days before the date of filing the petition for bankruptcy or cessation of the debtor's business.

4 Claims for contributions to employee benefit plans arising within 180 days before the date of filing the petition for bankruptcy or cessation of the debtor's business. The limit of such claims is $2,000 times the number of employees covered by the plans, less the aggregate amount paid to the covered employees under priority **3** above.

5   Claims for cash deposited for goods or services for the personal, family, or household use of the depositor, not in excess of $900.

6   Claims of governmental entities for various taxes or duties, subject to varying time limitations.

Property Claimed as Exempt

Certain property of a bankruptcy petitioner is not includable in the debtor's estate. The Bankruptcy Code excludes from coverage of the Code the various allowances provided in the laws of either the United States or the state of the debtor's residence, whichever is more beneficial to the debtor. Typical of these allowances are residential property exemptions provided by homestead laws and exemptions for life insurance policies payable on death to the spouse or a relative of the debtor.

Role of Court in Liquidation

The *federal bankruptcy court* in which a debtor's or creditors' petition for bankruptcy liquidation is filed oversees all aspects of the bankruptcy proceedings.

One of the first acts of the court is either to dismiss the debtor's or creditors' bankruptcy petition or to grant an *order for relief* under the Bankruptcy Code. The filing of a debtor's petition in bankruptcy is in effect an order for relief; in a creditors' petition, order for relief is made by the court after a hearing at which the debtor may attempt to refute the creditors' allegations that the debtor was not paying debts as they came due. Any suits that are pending against a debtor for whom a debtor's or creditors' bankruptcy petition is filed generally are *stayed* until order for relief or dismissal of the petition; after order for relief such suits are further stayed until the question of the debtor's *discharge* is determined by the court. Further, the court appoints an interim trustee after the order for relief, to serve permanently or until a trustee is elected by the creditors.

Role of Creditors

Within a period of 10 to 30 days after an order for relief, the bankruptcy court must call a meeting of the creditors. At the meeting, the "outsider" creditors appoint a trustee to manage the debtor's estate. A majority vote in number and amount of claims of all unsecured and nonpriority creditors present is required for actions by creditors.

Role of Trustee

The trustee elected by the creditors or appointed by the court assumes custody of the debtor's nonexempt property. The principal duties of the trustee are to continue operating the debtor's business if directed by the court, realize the free assets of the debtor's estate, and pay cash to unsecured creditors. The trustee is responsible for keeping accounting records to enable the filing of a final report with the bankruptcy court.

The Bankruptcy Code empowers the trustee to invalidate a *preference,* defined as the transfer of cash or property to an "outsider" creditor for an existing debt, made while the debtor was insolvent and within 90 days of filing of the bankruptcy petition, provided the transfer caused the creditor to receive more cash or property than would be received in the bankruptcy liquidation. The trustee may recover from the creditor the cash or property constituting the preference and include it in the debtor's estate.

Discharge of Debtor

Once the debtor's property has been liquidated, all secured and priority creditor claims have been paid, and all remaining cash has been paid to unsecured, nonpriority creditors, the debtor may receive a *discharge,* defined as the release of the debtor from all unliquidated debts except the following:

1   Taxes payable by the debtor to the United States or to any state or subdivision, including taxes attributable to improper preparation of tax returns by the debtor.

2   Debts resulting from the debtor's obtaining money or property under false pretenses or representations, or willful conversion of the property of others.

3   Debts not scheduled by the debtor in support of the bankruptcy petition, such creditors not being informed of the bankruptcy proceedings.

4   Debts arising from embezzlement or other fraudulent acts by the debtor acting in a fiduciary capacity.

5   Amounts payable for alimony or child support.

6   Debts for willful and malicious injuries to the persons or property of others.

7   Debts for fines, penalties, or forfeitures payable to governmental entities, other than for tax penalties.

8   With certain exceptions, debts for educational loans made, insured, or guaranteed by governmental entities or by nonprofit universities or colleges.

A debtor will not be discharged if any crimes, misstatements, or other malicious acts were committed by the debtor in connection with the court proceedings. In addition, a debtor will not be discharged if the current bankruptcy petition was filed *within six years* of a previous bankruptcy discharge to the same debtor.

Role of Accountant in Bankruptcy Liquidation

The accountant's role in liquidation proceedings is concerned with proper reporting of the financial condition of the debtor and adequate accounting and reporting for the trustee for the debtor's estate, as described in the following sections.

Financial Condition of Debtor Enterprise: The Statement of Affairs

A business enterprise that enters liquidation proceedings is a *quitting concern,* not a *going concern.* Consequently, a balance sheet, which reports the financial position of a going concern, is inappropriate for an enterprise in liquidation.

The financial statement designed for a business enterprise entering liquidation is the *statement of affairs* (not to be confused with the legal bankruptcy form with the same title described on page 749). The purpose of the statement of affairs is to display the assets and liabilities of the debtor enterprise from a *liquidation* viewpoint, because liquidation is the outcome of the bankruptcy proceedings. Thus, assets displayed in the statement of affairs are valued at *current fair values;* carrying amounts of the assets are presented on a memorandum basis. In addition, assets and liabilities in the statement of affairs are classified according to the rankings and priorities set forth in the Bankruptcy Code; the current/noncurrent classification used in a balance sheet for a going concern is not appropriate for the statement of affairs.

Illustration of Statement of Affairs   The balance sheet of Sanders Company on June 30, Year 4, the date that Sanders filed a debtor's (voluntary) bankruptcy petition, is on page 753.

Other information available from notes to financial statements and from estimates of current fair values of assets follows:

1   Notes receivable with a face amount plus accrued interest totaling $15,300, and a current fair value of $13,300, collateralize the notes payable to Pacific National Bank.

2   Finished goods are expected to be sold at a markup of 33⅓% over cost, with disposal costs estimated at 20% of selling prices. Estimated cost to complete goods in process is $15,400, of which $3,700 would be cost of material and factory supplies used. The estimated selling price of goods in process when completed is $40,000, with disposal costs estimated at 20% of selling prices. Estimated current fair values for material and factory supplies not required to complete goods in process are $8,000 and $1,000, respectively. All short-term prepayments are expected to be consumed in the course of liquidation.

3   Land and buildings, which collateralize the first mortgage bonds payable, have a current fair value of $95,000. Machinery with a carrying amount of $18,200 and current fair value of $10,000 collateralizes notes payable to suppliers in the amount of $12,000, including accrued interest. The current fair value of the remaining machinery is $9,000, net of disposal costs of $1,000, and the current fair value of tools after the amounts used to complete the goods in process inventory is $3,255.

4   Salaries and wages payable are debts having priority under the Bankruptcy Code.

5   Costs of administering the bankruptcy liquidation are estimated at $1,905.

The statement of affairs for Sanders Company on June 30, Year 4, is on page 755.

The following points should be stressed in the review of the June 30, Year 4, statement of affairs for Sanders Company:

1   The "Carrying amount" columns in the statement of affairs serve as a tie-in to the balance sheet of Sanders on June 30, Year 4, as well as a basis for computing expected losses or gains on realization of assets.

2   Assets are assigned to one of three groups: pledged for fully secured liabilities, pledged for partially secured liabilities, and free. This grouping of assets facilitates

SANDERS COMPANY
Balance Sheet
(prior to filing of debtor's bankruptcy petition)
June 30, Year 4

Assets

Current assets:

Cash	$ 2,700
Notes receivable and accrued interest, less allowance for doubtful notes, $6,000	13,300
Trade accounts receivable, less allowance for doubtful accounts, $23,240	16,110

Inventories, at first-in, first-out cost:

Finished goods	12,000
Goods in process	35,100
Material	19,600
Factory supplies	6,450
Short-term prepayments	950
Total current assets	$106,210

Plant assets, at cost:

Land	$ 20,000	
Buildings (net)	41,250	
Machinery (net)	48,800	
Tools (net)	14,700	
Total plant assets (net)		124,750
Total assets		$230,960

Liabilities & Stockholders' Equity

Current liabilities:

Notes payable:

Pacific National Bank, including accrued interest		$ 15,300
Suppliers, including accrued interest		51,250
Trade accounts payable		52,000
Salaries and wages payable		8,850
Property taxes payable		2,900
Interest payable on first mortgage bonds		1,800
FICA and income taxes withheld and accrued		1,750
Total current liabilities		$133,850
First mortgage bonds payable		90,000
Total liabilities		$223,850

Stockholders' equity:

Common stock, $100 par, 750 shares authorized, issued, and outstanding	$ 75,000	
Deficit	(67,890)	7,110
Total liabilities & stockholders' equity		$230,960

the computation of estimated amounts available for unsecured creditors—those with priority and those without priority.

3 Liabilities are grouped in the categories reported by a debtor in the exhibits supporting a debtor's bankruptcy petition (see page 749): unsecured with priority, fully secured, partially secured, and unsecured without priority.

4 A *contra (offset)* technique used where the *legal right of setoff* exists. For example, amounts due to fully secured creditors are deducted from the estimated current fair value of the assets serving as collateral; and unsecured liabilities with priority are deducted from estimated amounts available to unsecured creditors from the proceeds of free asset realization.

5 An estimated settlement per dollar of unsecured liabilities without priority is computed by dividing the estimated amount available for unsecured, nonpriority creditors by the total unsecured liabilities, thus:

$$\frac{\$60,960}{\$95,250} = 64 \text{ cents on the dollar}$$

This computation enables the bankruptcy trustee to estimate the amount of cash that will be available to unsecured, nonpriority creditors in a liquidation proceeding.

Estimated Amounts to Be Recovered by Each Class of Creditors

By reference to the statement of affairs on page 755, the accountant for the trustee in bankruptcy for Sanders Company may prepare the following summary of estimated amounts to be recovered by each class of Sanders's creditors:

SANDERS COMPANY
Estimated Amounts to Be Recovered by Creditors
June 30, Year 4

Class of creditors	Total claims	Computation	Estimated recovery
Unsecured with priority	$ 15,405	100%	$ 15,405
Fully secured	91,800	100%	91,800
Partially secured	27,300	$23,300 + ($4,000 × 0.64)	25,860
Unsecured without priority..	91,250	64%	58,400
Totals.................	$225,755*		$191,465†

* $15,405 + $91,800 + $15,300 + $12,000 + $39,250 + $52,000 = $225,755.
† $95,000 + $13,300 + $10,000 + ($76,365 − $3,200) = $191,465.

Accounting and Reporting for Trustee

Traditionally, the accounting records and reports for trustees have been extremely detailed and elaborate. However, the provisions of the applicable Bankruptcy Rule are general; therefore, simple accounting records and reports should be adequate.

SANDERS COMPANY
Statement of Affairs
June 30, Year 4

Assets

Carrying amounts	Assets	Current fair values	Estimated amount available	Loss or (gain) on realization
	Assets pledged for fully secured liabilities:			
$ 20,000	Land	$95,000		
41,250	Building			
	Less: Fully secured liabilities			
	(contra)	91,800	$ 3,200	$(33,750)
	Assets pledged for partially secured liabilities:			
13,300	Notes and interest receivable (deducted contra)	$13,300		
18,200	Machinery (deducted contra)	$10,000		8,200
	Free assets:			
2,700	Cash	$ 2,700	2,700	
16,110	Trade accounts receivable	16,110	16,110	
	Inventories:			
12,000	Finished goods	12,800	12,800	(800)
35,100	Goods in process	20,300*	20,300*	14,800
19,600	Material	8,000	8,000	11,600
6,450	Factory supplies	1,000	1,000	5,450
950	Short-term prepayments	–0–	–0–	950
30,600	Machinery	9,000	9,000	21,600
14,700	Tools	3,255	3,255	11,445
	Total estimated amount available		$76,365	$ 39,495
	Less: Unsecured liabilities with priority (contra)		15,405	
	Estimated amount available for unsecured, nonpriority creditors (64¢ on the dollar)		$60,960	
	Estimated deficiency to unsecured, nonpriority creditors (36¢ on the dollar)		34,290	
$230,960			$95,250	

Liabilities & stockholders' equity

Carrying amounts	Liabilities & stockholders' equity	Amount unsecured
	Unsecured liabilities with priority:	
	Estimated administrative costs	$ 1,905
$ 8,850	Salaries and wages payable	8,850
2,900	Property taxes payable	2,900
1,750	FICA and income taxes withheld and accrued	1,750
	Total (deducted contra)	$15,405
	Fully secured liabilities:	
90,000	First mortgage bonds payable	$90,000
1,800	Accrued interest on first mortgage bonds payable	1,800
	Total (deducted contra)	$91,800
	Partially secured liabilities:	
15,300	Notes and accrued interest payable to Pacific National Bank	$15,300
	Less: Net realizable value of notes receivable pledged as collateral (contra)	13,300
		$ 2,000
12,000	Notes and accrued interest payable to suppliers	$12,000
	Less: Estimated realizable value of machinery pledged as collateral (contra)	10,000
		2,000
	Unsecured liabilities without priority:	
39,250	Notes payable to suppliers	39,250
52,000	Trade accounts payable	52,000
7,110	Stockholders' equity	
$230,960		$95,250

* Estimated selling price .... $ 40,000
Less: Estimated "out-of-pocket" completion costs (15,400 – $3,700) ..... (11,700)
Estimated disposal costs ($40,000 × 0.20) ...... (8,000)
Net realizable value .... $ 20,300

The author recommends the following with respect to the trustee's accounting records for a liquidating debtor:

1   The accounting records of the debtor should be used during the period that a trustee carries on the operations of the debtor's business.

2   An *accountability* technique should be used once the trustee begins realization of the debtor's assets. In the accountability method of accounting, the assets and liabilities for which the trustee is responsible are entered in the accounting records of the trustee at their statement of affairs valuations, with a balancing debit to a memorandum-type ledger account with a title such as Estate Deficit. The amount of the debit to Estate Deficit is equal to the estimated deficiency to unsecured creditors reported in the statement of affairs. Appropriate cash receipts and cash payments journal entries are made for the trustee's realization of assets and payment of liabilities. No "gain" or "loss" ledger account is necessary because a business enterprise in liquidation does not require an income statement. Differences between cash amounts realized or paid and carrying amounts of the related assets or liabilities are debited or credited to the Estate Deficit ledger account.

Journal entry for
bankruptcy trustee

SANDERS COMPANY, IN BANKRUPTCY
Arline Wells, Trustee
Journal Entry
June 30, Year 4

Cash	2,700	
Notes and Interest Receivable	13,300	
Trade Accounts Receivable	16,110	
Finished Goods Inventory	12,800	
Goods in Process Inventory	20,300	
Material Inventory	8,000	
Factory Supplies	1,000	
Land and Buildings	95,000	
Machinery ($10,000 + $9,000)	19,000	
Tools	3,255	
Estate Deficit	34,290 (1)	
Estimated Administrative Costs		1,905
Notes and Interest Payable		66,550
Trade Accounts Payable		52,000
Salaries and Wages Payable		8,850
Property Taxes Payable		2,900
FICA and Income Taxes Withheld and Accrued		1,750
Interest Payable on First Mortgage Bonds		1,800
First Mortgage Bonds Payable		90,000

To record current fair values of assets and liabilities of Sanders Company, in bankruptcy liquidation proceedings.

(1) Equal to estimated deficiency to unsecured, nonpriority creditors in the statement of affairs on page 755.

3 The *interim* and *final reports* of the trustee to the bankruptcy court are a statement of cash receipts and cash payments, a statement of realization and liquidation, and, for interim reports, supporting exhibits of assets not yet realized and liabilities not yet liquidated.

Illustration of Accountability Technique Assume that Arline Wells, the trustee in the voluntary bankruptcy liquidation proceedings for Sanders Company (see page 752), took custody of the assets of Sanders on June 30, Year 4. The accountant for the trustee prepared the journal entry shown on page 756 on June 30, Year 4.

When the trustee realizes assets of Sanders, the appropriate journal entry is a debit to Cash, credits to the asset ledger accounts, and a debit or credit to the Estate Deficit account for a loss or gain on realization, respectively. Costs of administering the estate that exceed the $1,905 liability also are debited to the Estate Deficit ledger account.

Statement of Realization and Liquidation The traditional statement of realization and liquidation was a complex and not too readable accounting presentation. A form of realization and liquidation statement that should be more useful to the bankruptcy court than the traditional statement is shown below. This financial statement is based on the assumed activities of the trustee for the estate of Sanders Company during the month of July, Year 4, including operating the business long enough to complete and sell the goods in process inventory.

Interim statement of realization and liquidation for trustee in bankruptcy liquidation

SANDERS COMPANY, IN BANKRUPTCY
Arline Wells, Trustee
Statement of Realization and Liquidation
For Month Ended July 31, Year 4

	Current fair values, June 30, Year 4	Realization proceeds	Loss or (gain)	
Estate deficit, June 30, Year 4				$34,290
Assets realized:				
Trade accounts receivable	$14,620	$12,807	$ 1,813	
Finished goods inventory .	12,800	11,772	1,028	
Goods in process				
inventory	14,820	15,075	(255)	
Totals	$42,240	$39,654		2,586
Liabilities with priority liquidated at carrying amounts:				
Salaries and wages payable		$ 8,850		
Property taxes payable		2,900		
FICA and income taxes withheld and accrued		1,750		
Total liabilities with priority liquidated		$13,500		
Administrative costs paid, $1,867 ($1,905 had been estimated)				(38)
Estate deficit, July 31, Year 4				$36,838

An accompanying statement of cash receipts and cash payments for the month ended July 31, Year 4, would show the sources of the $39,654 total realization proceeds, and the dates, check numbers, payees, and amounts of the $13,500 paid for liabilities with priority and the $1,867 paid for administrative costs. Supporting exhibits would summarize assets not yet realized and liabilities not yet paid.

Liquidation involves realization of the assets of the debtor's estate. In many cases, an insolvent debtor may be restored to a sound financial footing if it can defer payment of its debts. Chapter 11 of the Bankruptcy Code, dealing with reorganization, enables a debtor to continue operations under court protection from creditor lawsuits while it formulates a plan to pay its debts. Reorganization is discussed in the next section.

BANKRUPTCY REORGANIZATION

Chapter 11 of the Bankruptcy Code provides for the court-supervised reorganization of a debtor business enterprise. Typically, a reorganization involves the reduction of amounts payable to some creditors, other creditors' acceptance of equity securities of the debtor for their claims, and a restructuring of the par or stated value of the common stock of the debtor.

A debtor's (voluntary) petition for reorganization may be filed by a railroad or by any "person" eligible to petition for liquidation (see page 749) except a stockbroker or a commodity broker. Requirements for a creditors' (involuntary) petition for reorganization are the same as the requirements for a liquidation petition (see page 749).

Appointment of Trustee or Examiner

During the process of reorganization, management or owners of the business enterprise may continue to operate the enterprise as *debtor in possession.* Alternatively, the bankruptcy court may appoint a trustee to manage the enterprise. A trustee is appointed because of fraud, dishonesty, incompetence, or gross mismanagement by current owners or managers, or to protect the interests of creditors or stockholders of the enterprise. In some reorganization cases not involving a trustee, the court may appoint an examiner to investigate possible fraud or mismanagement by the current managers or owners of the enterprise; the appointment of an examiner is limited to enterprises having unsecured liabilities, other than payables for goods, services, or taxes, exceeding $5 million.

Among the powers and duties of the trustee are the following:

1   Prepare and file in court a list of creditors of each class and their claims and a list of stockholders of each class.

2   Investigate the acts, conduct, property, liabilities, and business operations of the enterprise, consider the desirability of continuing operations, and formulate a plan for such continuance for submission to the bankruptcy judge if management of the debtor has not done so.

3 Report to the bankruptcy judge any facts ascertained as to fraud against or mismanagement of the debtor enterprise.

Plan of Reorganization

The plan of reorganization submitted by the management or the trustee to the bankruptcy court is given to the debtor enterprise's creditors and stockholders, to the U.S. Secretary of the Treasury, and possibly to the Securities and Exchange Commission. The plan must include provisions altering or modifying the interests and rights of the creditors and stockholders of the debtor enterprise, as well as a number of additional provisions. The SEC may review the plan and may be heard in the bankruptcy court's consideration of the plan. Before a plan of reorganization is confirmed by the bankruptcy court, the plan must be accepted by a majority of the creditors, whose claims must account for two-thirds of the total liabilities, and by stockholders owning at least two-thirds of the outstanding capital stock of each class. If one or more classes of stockholders or creditors has not accepted a plan, the bankruptcy court may confirm the plan if the plan is *fair and equitable* to the nonacceptors. Confirmation of the plan of reorganization by the bankruptcy court makes the plan binding on the debtor enterprise, on all creditors and owners of the enterprise, and on any other enterprise issuing securities or acquiring property under the plan.

Accounting for a Reorganization

The accounting for a reorganization typically requires journal entries for adjustments of carrying amounts of assets; reductions of par or stated value of capital stock (with recognition of resultant paid-in capital in excess of par or stated value); extensions of due dates of notes payable; exchanges of debt securities for equity securities; and the elimination of a retained earnings deficit. The latter entry is associated with *fresh start reporting* for a reorganized enterprise whose liabilities exceed the *reorganization value* (essentially current fair value) of its assets.[2] Because of changes in the ownership of common stock of such an enterprise as a result of the reorganization, it is no longer controlled by its former stockholder group, and it essentially is a new reporting enterprise whose assets and liabilities should be valued at current fair values and whose stockholders' equity consists only of paid-in capital.[3]

It is important for accountants to be thoroughly familiar with the plan of reorganization, in order to account properly for its implementation. Accountants must be careful to avoid charging post-reorganization operations with losses that arose before the reorganization.

To illustrate the accounting for a reorganization, assume that Sanders Company (see pages 752 to 755) filed a petition for reorganization, rather than for liquidation, on June 30, Year 4, with Sanders management as debtor in possession. The plan of reorganization, which was approved by stockholders and all unsecured creditors and confirmed by the bankruptcy court, included the following:

---

[2] *Statement of Position 90-7,* "Financial Reporting by Entities in Reorganization under the Bankruptcy Code," AICPA (New York: 1990), p. 16.
[3] Ibid., p. 24.

1   Deposit $25,000 with escrow agent, as soon as cash becomes available, to cover liabilities with priority and costs of reorganization proceedings.

2   Amend articles of incorporation to provide for 10,000 shares of authorized common stock of $1 par. The new common stock is to be exchanged on a share-for-share basis for the 750 shares of outstanding $100 par common stock.

3   Extend due date of unsecured notes payable to suppliers totaling $15,250 for four years, until May 31, Year 9. Increase the interest rate on the notes from the stated rate of 14% to 18%, the current fair rate of interest.

4   Exchange 1,600 shares of new $1 par common stock (at current fair value of $15 a share) for unsecured notes payable to suppliers totaling $24,000.

5   Pay suppliers 70 cents per dollar of trade accounts payable owed.

The following journal entries, numbered to correspond with the provisions of the reorganization plan outlined above, were recorded by Sanders Company as cash became available from operations:

Journal entries for
bankruptcy
reorganization

SANDERS COMPANY
Journal Entries

(1) Cash with Escrow Agent	25,000	
Cash..		25,000
To record deposit of cash with escrow agent under terms of bankruptcy reorganization.		
Salaries and Wages Payable	8,850	
Property Taxes Payable....................................	2,900	
FICA and Income Taxes Withheld and Accrued...............	1,750	
Cash with Escrow Agent		13,500
To record escrow agent's payment of liabilities with priority.		
Costs of Bankruptcy Proceedings	11,000	
Cash with Escrow Agent		11,000
To record escrow agent's payment of costs of bankruptcy proceedings.		
(2) Common Stock, $100 par	75,000	
Common Stock, $1 par...............................		750
Paid-in Capital in Excess of Par.......................		74,250
To record issuance of 750 shares of $1 par common stock in exchange for 750 shares of $100 par common stock.		

(continued)

SANDERS COMPANY
Journal Entries (concluded)

(3) 14% Notes Payable to Suppliers, due May 31, Year 5 .... *15,250*
         18% Notes Payable to Suppliers, due May 31, Year 9 ...   *15,250*
To record extension of due dates of notes payable to suppliers
and increase of interest rate to 18% from 14%.

(4) Notes Payable to Suppliers *24,000*
         Common Stock, $1 par. *1,600*
         Paid-in Capital in Excess of Par. *22,400*
To record exchange of 1,600 shares of $1 par common stock for
$24,000 face amount of notes payable, at current fair value of
$15 a share.

(5) Trade Accounts Payable *52,000*
         Cash. *36,400*
         Gain from Discharge of Indebtedness in Bankruptcy. *15,600*
To record payment of $0.70 per dollar of accounts payable to
suppliers.

Assuming that fresh start reporting is appropriate for Sanders Company after the plan of reorganization has been carried out, the following journal entry is appropriate for eliminating the $67,890 retained earnings deficit of Sanders on June 30, Year 4:

Journal entry to eliminate deficit

Paid-in Capital in Excess of Par *63,290*
Gain from Discharge of Indebtedness in Bankruptcy *15,600*
         Costs of Bankruptcy Proceedings. *11,000*
         Retained Earnings *67,890*
To eliminate deficit on June 30, Year 4, and close bankruptcy gain
and costs to Paid-in Capital in Excess of Par ledger account.

The effect of the foregoing journal entries is to show a "clean slate" for Sanders Company as a result of the approved bankruptcy reorganization and the write-off of the retained earnings deficit existing on the date of the petition for reorganization. The extension of due dates of some liabilities, conversion of other liabilities to common stock, and liquidation of trade accounts payable at less than their face amount should enable Sanders to resume operations as a going concern. For a reasonable number of years following the reorganization, Sanders might "date" the retained earnings in its balance sheets to disclose that the earnings were accumulated after the reorganization.

Disclosure of Reorganization

The elaborate and often complex issues involved in a bankruptcy reorganization are disclosed in a note to the financial statements for the period in which the plan of reorganization was carried out.

Evaluation of Bankruptcy Code

Since its enactment in 1978, the Bankruptcy Code has been criticized by credit grantors as being too liberal and thus popularizing bankruptcy as a means of avoiding payment of debts. Supporters of the Bankruptcy Code have alleged that lax credit-granting policies have caused the upsurge in bankruptcy petitions since the Code was enacted. Committees of Congress have reacted to these allegations by restudying provisions of the Bankruptcy Code for possible amendments.

REVIEW QUESTIONS

1   Define *insolvency* as that term is used in the Bankruptcy Code for an entity other than a partnership.

2   What are *Bankruptcy Rules?*

3   Identify the various classes of creditors whose claims are dealt with in bankruptcy liquidations.

4   Describe the process of *liquidation* under the Bankruptcy Code.

5   Differentiate between a *debtor's petition* and a *creditors' petition.*

6   May any business enterprise file a debtor's bankruptcy petition for liquidation? Explain.

7   Who may file a *creditors' petition* for bankruptcy liquidation?

8   What is a *statement of affairs* under the Bankruptcy Code?

9   List the unsecured debts having priority over other unsecured debts under the provisions of the Bankruptcy Code.

10   Describe the priority of claims for wages and salaries under the Bankruptcy Code.

11   Describe the authority of a bankruptcy trustee with respect to a *preference.*

12   What are the effects of a *discharge* in bankruptcy liquidation proceedings? Explain.

13   What use is made of the accounting financial statement known as a *statement of affairs?* Explain.

14   Describe the *accountability* method of accounting used by a trustee in a bankruptcy liquidation.

15   For what types of bankruptcy reorganizations might an *examiner* be appointed by the court?

16 What is the role of the Securities and Exchange Commission in a bankruptcy reorganization?

17 Must all classes of creditors accept a reorganization plan before the plan may be confirmed by the bankruptcy court? Explain.

18 What is *fresh start reporting* for a business enterprise reorganized under Chapter 11 of the Bankruptcy Code, and under what circumstances is it appropriate?

EXERCISES

Ex. 16-1 Select the best answer for each of the following multiple-choice questions:

1 The numbers of categories of assets and liabilities displayed in the statement of affairs for a debtor enterprise undergoing liquidation in bankruptcy are:

	Assets	*Liabilities*
a	*Four*	*Four*
b	*Four*	*Three*
c	*Three*	*Four*
d	*Three*	*Three*

2 A *creditors' (involuntary) petition for bankruptcy* must claim:
a The debtor is not paying debts as they come due.
b A custodian was appointed for or had taken possession of the debtor's property within 120 days prior to the date of the petition.
c Either **a** or **b**.
d Both **a** and **b**.

3 The appointment of a trustee is required for:
a A bankruptcy liquidation only
b A bankruptcy reorganization only
c Both a bankruptcy liquidation and a bankruptcy reorganization
d Neither a bankruptcy liquidation nor a bankruptcy reorganization

4 The debit to the Estate Deficit ledger account in the journal entry to open accounting records for a trustee in a bankruptcy liquidation is equal to the statement of affairs (financial statement) amount entitled:
a Loss on realization
b Total estimated amount available
c Estimated amount available for unsecured, nonpriority creditors
d Estimated deficiency to unsecured, nonpriority creditors

5 The outcome of a bankruptcy reorganization often includes:
a A change in the par or stated value of the debtor's common stock
b The write-off of a retained earnings deficit
c A gain from discharge of indebtedness in bankruptcy
d All the foregoing

6 A *voluntary* petition in bankruptcy is filed by:
a The debtor only

b Creditors of the debtor only
c Either the debtor or creditors of the debtor
d The debtor and creditors of the debtor jointly

7   The plan of reorganization for a business enterprise under Chapter 11 of the Bankruptcy Code provided for (1) the extension to December 17, Year 12, of the due date of a 10%, five-year promissory note dated December 17, Year 4, with a principal of $100,000 on which interest was payable at maturity and (2) an increase of the interest rate on the note to 12%. If the bankruptcy court approves the plan of reorganization on December 17, Year 7, the appropriate journal entry (explanation omitted) to be prepared by the enterprise is:

a *10% Note Payable* *100,000*
   Interest Payable ($100,000 × 0.10 × 3) *30,000*
      12% Note Payable *130,000*

b *10% Note Payable* *100,000*
      12% Note Payable *100,000*

c *10% Note Payable* *100,000*
   Interest Expense ($100,000 × 0.02 × 3). *6,000*
      12% Note Payable *100,000*
      Interest Payable *6,000*

d *10% Note Payable* *100,000*
   Costs of Bankruptcy Proceedings *6,000*
      12% Note Payable *106,000*

8   In a bankruptcy liquidation under Chapter 7 of the Bankruptcy Code, *creditors having priority* include:
a Fully secured creditors only
b Partially secured creditors only
c Both fully secured and partially secured creditors
d Neither fully secured nor partially secured creditors

9   Is a *statement of realization and liquidation* prepared for a debtor corporation undergoing bankruptcy:

	Liquidation?	*Reorganization?*
a	*Yes*	*Yes*
b	*Yes*	*No*
c	*No*	*Yes*
d	*No*	*No*

10 *Bankrupt* as an adjective appropriately refers to:
a Insolvency
b A legal state
c An economic state
d An unwillingness to pay debts

11 In a statement of affairs (financial statement) for a debtor enterprise undergoing bankruptcy liquidation, the total of assets pledged for partially secured liabilities is displayed with:

a The debtor's assets only

b The debtor's liabilities only

c Both the debtor's assets and its liabilities

d Unsecured liabilities with priority

12 Is a Costs of Bankruptcy Proceedings ledger account typically used by a debtor enterprise involved in a bankruptcy:

	Liquidation?	*Reorganization?*
a	Yes	Yes
b	Yes	No
c	No	Yes
d	No	No

13 In a bankruptcy liquidation statement of affairs (financial statement), "estimated deficiency" relates to:

a All creditors

b Partially secured creditors

c Both **a** and **b**

d Neither **a** nor **b**

14 The U.S. Bankruptcy Code provides, in a Chapter 7 liquidation, for priority treatment for:

a Certain unsecured creditors

b All unsecured creditors

c Fully secured creditors

d Partially secured creditors

15 In the statement of affairs for liquidating Oswald Company on June 30, Year 4, estimated amount available for unsecured, nonpriority creditors was $61,000; estimated deficiency to unsecured, nonpriority creditors was $34,000; and unsecured liabilities with priority totaled $15,000. The total estimated amount available was:

a $49,000

b $76,000

c $95,000

d $110,000

e Some other amount

Ex. 16-2 The December 18, Year 7, statement of affairs of Downside Company, which is in bankruptcy liquidation, included the following:

Assets pledged for fully secured liabilities	$100,000
Assets pledged for partially secured liabilities	40,000
Free assets	120,000
Fully secured liabilities	80,000
Partially secured liabilities	50,000
Unsecured liabilities with priority	60,000
Unsecured liabilities without priority	90,000

Prepare a working paper to show the estimated amount of assets expected to be received by each of the four classes of creditors of Downside Company in its bankruptcy liquidation.

Ex. 16-3   Amounts related to the statement of affairs of Foldup Company, in bankruptcy liquidation on April 30, Year 5, were as follows:

Assets pledged for fully secured liabilities	$ 80,000
Assets pledged for partially secured liabilities	50,000
Free assets	280,000
Fully secured liabilities	60,000
Partially secured liabilities	80,000
Unsecured liabilities with priority	40,000
Unsecured liabilities without priority	330,000

Prepare a working paper to compute the ***total estimated deficiency*** to unsecured, nonpriority creditors, and the ***cents per dollar*** that such creditors may expect to receive from Foldup Company.

Ex. 16-4   Data from the April 30, Year 1, statement of affairs of Windup Company, which was undergoing bankruptcy liquidation, included the following:

Assets pledged for fully secured liabilities	$70,000
Assets pledged for partially secured liabilities	30,000
Free assets	50,000
Fully secured liabilities	60,000
Partially secured liabilities	40,000
Unsecured liabilities with priority	30,000
Unsecured liabilities without priority	50,000

Prepare a working paper to show how Windup Company's assets on April 30, Year 1, are expected to be apportioned to Windup's creditors' claims on that date.

Ex. 16-5   Components of the December 17, Year 3, statement of affairs of Liquo Company, which was undergoing liquidation under Chapter 7 of the Bankruptcy Code, included the following:

Assets pledged for fully secured liabilities, at current fair value	$150,000
Assets pledged for partially secured liabilities, at current fair value	104,000
Free assets, at current fair value	80,000
Fully secured liabilities	60,000
Partially secured liabilities	120,000
Unsecured liabilities with priority	14,000
Unsecured liabilities without priority	224,000

Prepare a working paper dated December 17, Year 3, to compute the amount expected to be paid to each class of creditors of Liquo Company. The following column headings, are suggested: Class of creditor, Total claims, Computation, Estimated amount. The total of the Estimated amount column should equal total assets, $334,000.

Ex. 16-6   Scott Company filed a debtor's bankruptcy petition on June 25, Year 2, and its statement of affairs included the following amounts:

	Carrying amounts	Current fair values
Assets		
Assets pledged for fully secured liabilities................	$160,000	$190,000
Assets pledged for partially secured liabilities	90,000	60,000
Free assets	200,000	140,000
Totals..	$450,000	$390,000

Liabilities	
Unsecured liabilities with priority.........................	$ 20,000
Fully secured liabilities..................................	130,000
Partially secured liabilities..............................	100,000
Unsecured liabilities without priority	260,000
Total...	$510,000

Assuming that Scott Company's assets realized cash at the current fair values and the business was liquidated by the bankruptcy trustee, prepare a working paper to compute the amount of cash that the partially secured creditors should receive.

Ex. 16-7   The statement of affairs for Wick Corporation shows that approximately 78 cents on the dollar probably will be paid to unsecured creditors without priority. Wick owes Stark Company $23,000 on a promissory note, plus accrued interest of $940. Inventories with a current fair value of $19,200 collateralize the note payable.

Prepare a working paper to compute the amount that Stark Company should receive from the trustee of Wick Corporation, assuming that actual payments to unsecured creditors without priority amount to 78 cents on the dollar. Round all amounts to the nearest dollar.

Ex. 16-8   Decker Company filed a debtor's bankruptcy petition on August 15, Year 7, and its statement of affairs included the following amounts:

	Carrying amounts	Current fair values
Assets		
Assets pledged for fully secured liabilities................	$150,000	$185,000
Assets pledged for partially secured liabilities	90,000	60,000
Free assets	210,000	160,000
Totals..	$450,000	$405,000

Liabilities	
Unsecured liabilities with priority.........................	$ 35,000
Fully secured liabilities..................................	130,000
Partially secured liabilities..............................	100,000
Unsecured liabilities without priority	270,000
Total...	$535,000

Assuming that Decker Company's assets realized cash at the current fair values and the business was liquidated by the bankruptcy trustee, prepare a working paper to compute the amount of cash available to pay unsecured liabilities without priority.

Ex. 16-9 Prepare a working paper to compute the estimated amount expected to be paid to each class of creditors, using the following data taken from the statement of affairs for Kent Corporation:

Assets pledged for fully secured liabilities (current fair value, $75,000)	$ 90,000
Assets pledged for partially secured liabilities (current fair value, $52,000)	74,000
Free assets (current fair value, $40,000)	70,000
Unsecured liabilities with priority	7,000
Fully secured liabilities	30,000
Partially secured liabilities	60,000
Unsecured liabilities without priority	112,000

Ex. 16-10 The following information for Progress Book Company on May 31, Year 5, was obtained by an accountant retained by Progress Book's creditors:

(1) Furniture and fixtures: Carrying amount, $70,000; current fair value, $60,500; pledged on a note payable of $42,000 on which unpaid interest of $800 has accrued.

(2) Book manuscripts owned: Carrying amount, $15,000; current fair value, $7,200; pledged on a note payable of $9,000; interest on the note is paid to date.

(3) Books in process of production: Accumulated cost (direct material, direct labor, and factory overhead), $37,500; estimated sales value on completion, $60,000; additional out-of-pocket costs of $14,200 will be required to complete the books in process.

Prepare the headings for the asset side of a statement of affairs for Progress Book Company on May 31, Year 5, and illustrate how each of the three items described is displayed in the statement.

Ex. 16-11 Edward Ross, the trustee in bankruptcy for Winslow Company, set up accounting records based on the April 30, Year 5, statement of affairs for Winslow. The trustee completed the following transactions and events early in May, Year 5:

May 2 Sold for $10,000 cash the finished goods inventory with a statement of affairs valuation of $10,500.

3 Paid wages with a statement of affairs valuation of $8,000.

4 Collected $6,000 on trade accounts receivable with a statement of affairs valuation of $6,200. The remainder was considered to be uncollectible.

7 Paid trustee fee for one week, $500. (Debit Estimated Administrative Costs.)

Prepare journal entries (omit explanations) for Edward Ross, trustee in bankruptcy for Winslow Company, for the transactions and events described above.

Ex. 16-12 From the following traditional form of statement of realization and liquidation, prepare a more concise statement of realization and liquidation similar to the one illustrated on page 757:

REED COMPANY, IN BANKRUPTCY
Selma Ross, Trustee
Statement of Realization and Liquidation
For Month of January, Year 2

Assets to be realized:			*Liabilities to be liquidated:*	
Trade accounts receivable ..	$ 7,500		Notes payable	$ 5,000
Inventories	12,500		Trade accounts payable.....	30,000
Equipment................	10,000		Interest payable...........	150
Subtotal................	$30,000		Subtotal................	$35,150
Supplementary charges:			*Liabilities assumed:*	
Administrative costs	2,950		Interest payable...........	50
Interest expense	50		*Assets realized:*	
Liabilities liquidated:			Trade accounts receivable ..	6,500
Trade accounts payable.....	6,000		Inventories	14,500
Liabilities not liquidated:			*Assets not realized:*	
Notes payable	5,000		Equipment................	10,000
Trade accounts payable.....	24,000		Net loss	2,000
Interest payable...........	200			
Total...................	$68,200		Total...................	$68,200

Ex. 16-13 Following are selected provisions of the plan of reorganization for Kolb Company, which is emerging from Bankruptcy Code Chapter 11 reorganization on July 27, Year 4:

(1) Amended articles of incorporation to provide for 100,000 shares of authorized common stock, $5 par, to be exchanged on a share-for-share basis for 50,000 shares of outstanding no-par, no-stated-value common stock with a carrying amount of $600,000

(2) Exchanged 10,000 shares of the new $5 par common stock for trade accounts payable totaling $70,000

(3) Paid 80 cents per dollar for full settlement of other trade accounts payable totaling $60,000

Prepare journal entries (omit explanations) for Kolb Company on July 27, Year 4, to reflect the foregoing elements of its plan of reorganization.

Ex. 16-14 Among the provisions of the reorganization of Hayward Company under Chapter 11 of the Bankruptcy Code were the following:

(1) Issued 1,000 shares of $5 par common stock in exchange for 1,000 shares of $100 par common stock outstanding

(2) Issued 200 shares of $5 par common stock (current fair value $10 a share) for notes payable to suppliers with unpaid principal of $2,500 and accrued interest of $500

(3) Paid $8,000 to suppliers in full settlement of trade accounts payable of $10,000

Prepare journal entries (omit explanations) for Hayward Company for the foregoing provisions, all of which were completed on January 20, Year 7.

CASES

Case 16-1   In auditing the financial statements of Delbert Company for the six months ended December 31, Year 10, you find items **a** through **e** below had been debited or credited to the Retained Earnings ledger account during the six months immediately following a bankruptcy reorganization, which was effective July 1, Year 10:

a Debit of $25,000 arising from an additional income tax assessment applicable to Year 9.

b Credit of $48,000 resulting from gain on disposal of equipment that was no longer used in the business. This equipment had been written down by a $50,000 increase in the Accumulated Depreciation ledger account on July 1, Year 10.

c Debit of $15,000 resulting from the loss on plant assets destroyed in a fire on November 2, Year 10.

d Debit of $32,000 representing cash dividends declared on preferred stock.

e Credit of $60,400, the net income for the six-month period ended December 31, Year 10.

Instructions

For each of the foregoing items, state whether it is correctly debited or credited to the Retained Earnings ledger account. Give a brief reason for your conclusion.

Case 16-2   You have been asked to conduct a training program explaining the preparation of a statement of affairs (financial statement) for the staff of Bixby & Canfield, CPAs.

Instructions

Explain how each of the following is presented in a statement of affairs (financial statement) for a corporation in bankruptcy liquidation proceedings:

a Assets pledged for partially secured liabilities
b Unsecured liabilities with priority
c Stockholders' equity

PROBLEMS

Pr. 16-1   On July 24, Year 8, the date the plan of reorganization of Re-Org Company was approved by the bankruptcy court, Re-Org's stockholders' equity was as follows:

Common stock, no par or stated value, authorized 100,000 shares, issued
and outstanding 60,000 shares....................................... $ 580,000
Deficit ....   (260,000)
   Total stockholders' equity.. $ 320,000

Included in Re-Org's plan of reorganization were the following:

(1) Authorize payment of $50,000 unrecorded bankruptcy administrative costs by escrow agent holding special Re-Org cash account.

(2) Amend articles of incorporation to change common stock to $1 par from no-par, no-stated-value stock.

(3) Exchange 10% unsecured $120,000 promissory note payable to supplier (inter-

est unpaid for three months) for a 12%, two-year promissory note in the total amount of unpaid principal and accrued interest on the 10% note.

(4) Pay suppliers 80 cents on the dollar (from Re-Org cash account) for their claims totaling $100,000.

(5) Eliminate deficit against paid-in capital resulting from (2) and gain resulting from (4).

Instructions

Assuming the foregoing were completed on July 24, Year 8, prepare journal entries (omit explanations) for Re-Org Company on that date. Use the following ledger account titles:

Cash	Interest Payable
Cash with Escrow Agent	10% Note Payable
Common Stock, no par	12% Note Payable
Common Stock, $1 par	Paid-in Capital in Excess of Par
Costs of Bankruptcy Proceedings	Retained Earnings (Deficit)
Gain from Discharge of Indebtedness in Bankruptcy	Trade Accounts Payable

Pr. 16-2 The following information was available on October 31, Year 5, for Dodge Company, which cannot pay its liabilities when they are due:

	Carrying amounts
Cash...	$ 4,000
Trade accounts receivable (net): Current fair value equal to carrying amount	46,000
Inventories: Net realizable value, $18,000; pledged on $21,000 of notes payable	39,000
Plant assets: Current fair value, $67,400; pledged on mortgage note payable	134,000
Accumulated depreciation of plant assets...............................	27,000
Supplies: Current fair value, $1,500	2,000
Wages payable, all earned during October, Year 5......................	5,800
Property taxes payable	1,200
Trade accounts payable	60,000
Notes payable, $21,000 secured by inventories.........................	40,000
Mortgage note payable, including accrued interest of $400	50,400
Common stock, $5 par..	100,000
Deficit..	59,400

Instructions

a Prepare a statement of affairs for Dodge Company on October 31, Year 5, in the form illustrated on page 755.

b Prepare a working paper to compute the estimated percentage of claims each group of creditors should expect to receive if Dodge Company petitions for liquidation in bankruptcy.

Pr. 16-3 Robaire Corporation was in financial difficulty because of declining sales and poor cost controls. Its stockholders and principal creditors had asked for an estimate of the financial results of the realization of the assets, the payment of liabilities, and the liquidation of Robaire. Thus, the accountant for Robaire prepared the statement of affairs shown on page 773.

On January 2, Year 4, Robaire filed a debtor's petition for liquidation under the Bankruptcy Code. Charles Stern was appointed as trustee by the bankruptcy court to take custody of the assets, make payments to creditors, and implement an orderly liquidation. The trustee completed the transactions and events shown below during January, Year 4.

Jan. 2 Recorded the assets and liabilities of Robaire Corporation in a separate set of accounting records. The assets were recorded at current fair value, and all liabilities were recorded at the estimated amounts payable to the various groups of creditors.

  7 Disposed of the land and buildings at an auction for $52,000 cash and paid $42,550 to the mortgagee. The payment included interest of $50 that accrued in January.

  10 Made cash payments as follows:

Wages payable	$1,500
FICA and income taxes withheld and accrued	800
Completion of inventories	400
Administrative costs of liquidation	600

  31 Received cash from Jan. 8 to Jan. 31 as follows:

Collection of trade accounts receivable at carrying amount, including $10,000 of assigned accounts	$17,500
Sale of inventories	18,000
Disposal of Public Service Company bonds	920

  31 Made additional cash payments as follows:

Administrative costs of liquidation	$ 1,250
Note payable to bank (from proceeds of collection of assigned accounts receivable)	10,000
Fifty cents on the dollar to unsecured creditors	30,500

Instructions

a Prepare journal entries for the foregoing events and transactions of the trustee for Robaire Corporation.

b Prepare a statement of realization and liquidation for the trustee of Robaire Corporation for the month of January, Year 4. Use the form illustrated on page 757.

c Prepare a trial balance for the trustee of Robaire Corporation on January 31, Year 4.

Pr. 16-4 Javits Corporation advised you that it is facing bankruptcy proceedings. As the independent auditor for Javits, you knew of its financial condition.

The unaudited balance sheet of Javits on July 10, Year 10, was as shown on page 774.

ROBAIRE COMPANY
Statement of Affairs
December 31, Year 3

Assets

Carrying amounts	Assets	Current fair values	Estimated amount available	Loss or (gain) on realization
	Assets pledged for fully secured liabilities:			
$ 4,000	Land	$20,000		$(16,000)
25,000	Buildings	30,000		(5,000)
	Total	$50,000		
	Less: Fully secured liabilities (contra)	42,500	$ 7,500	
	Assets pledged for partially secured liabilities:			
10,000	Trade accounts receivable (deducted contra)	$10,000		
	Free assets:			
700	Cash	$ 700	700	
10,450	Trade accounts receivable	10,450	10,450	
40,000	Inventories	$19,350		
	Less: Cost to complete	400	18,950	18,950	21,050
9,100	Factory supplies	–0–	–0–	9,100
5,750	Public Service Company bonds	900	900	4,850
38,000	Machinery and equipment	18,000	18,000	20,000
	Total estimated amount available		$56,500	$ 34,000
	Less: Unsecured liabilities with priority (contra)		5,500	
	Estimated amount available for unsecured, nonpriority creditors		$51,000	
	Estimated deficiency to unsecured, nonpriority creditors		10,000	
$143,000			$61,000	

Liabilities & stockholders' equity

Carrying amounts	Liabilities & stockholders' equity	Amount unsecured
	Unsecured liabilities with priority:	
	Estimated administrative costs	$ 3,200
$ 1,500	Wages payable	1,500
800	FICA and income taxes withheld and accrued	800
	Total (deducted contra)	$ 5,500
	Fully secured liabilities:	
42,000	Mortgage note payable	$42,000
500	Interest payable	500
	Total (deducted contra)	$42,500
	Partially secured liabilities:	
25,000	Notes payable to bank	$25,000
	Less: Assigned trade accounts receivable	10,000	$15,000
	Unsecured liabilities without priority:	
20,000	Notes payable to suppliers	20,000
26,000	Trade accounts payable	26,000
27,200	Stockholders' equity	
$143,000		$61,000

JAVITS CORPORATION
Balance Sheet
July 10, Year 10

Assets

Cash..	$ 12,000
Short-term investments, at cost	20,000
Trade accounts receivable, less allowance for doubtful accounts	90,000
Finished goods inventory...	60,000
Material inventory	40,000
Short-term prepayments...	5,000
Land	13,000
Buildings (net)...	90,000
Machinery (net)	120,000
Goodwill (net)	20,000
Total assets...	$470,000

Liabilities & Stockholders' Equity

Notes payable to banks	$135,000
Trade accounts payable..	94,200
Wages payable...	15,000
Mortgage notes payable..	130,000
Common stock...	100,000
Retained earnings (deficit)...	(4,200)
Total liabilities & stockholders' equity	$470,000

Additional Information

(1) Cash included a $500 travel advance that had been spent.

(2) Trade accounts receivable of $40,000 had been pledged as collateral for notes payable to banks in the amount of $30,000. Credit balances of $5,000 were netted in the accounts receivable total. All accounts were expected to be collected except those for which an allowance had been established.

(3) Short-term investments consisted of U.S. government bonds costing $10,000 and 500 shares of Owens Company common stock. The current fair value of the bonds was $10,000; the current fair value of the stock was $18 a share. The bonds had accrued interest receivable of $200. The short-term investments had been pledged as collateral for a $20,000 note payable to bank.

(4) Estimated realizable value of finished goods was $50,000 and of material was $30,000. For additional out-of-pocket costs of $10,000 the material would realize $59,900 as finished goods.

(5) Short-term prepayments were expected to be consumed during the liquidation period.

(6) The current fair values of plant assets were as follows: land, $25,000; buildings, $110,000; machinery, $65,000.

(7) Trade accounts payable included $15,000 withheld FICA and income taxes and $6,000 payable to creditors who had been reassured by the president of Javits that they would be paid. There were unrecorded employer's FICA taxes in the amount of $500.

(8) Wages payable were not subject to any limitations under the Bankruptcy Code.

(9) Mortgage notes payable consisted of $100,000 secured by land and buildings, and a $30,000 installment contract secured by machinery. Total unrecorded accrued interest for these liabilities amounted to $2,400.

(10) Probable judgment on a pending damage suit was estimated at $50,000.

(11) Costs other than accounting fees to be incurred in connection with the liquidation were estimated at $10,000.

(12) You had not submitted an invoice for $5,000 for the April 30, Year 10, annual audit of Javits, and you estimate a $1,000 fee for liquidation work.

Instructions

a Prepare correcting entries for Javits Corporation on July 10, Year 10.

b Prepare a statement of affairs for Javits Corporation on July 10, Year 10. Amounts in the statement should reflect the journal entries in **a**.

Pr. 16-5 The adjusted trial balance of Laurel Company on June 30, Year 6, is on page 776.

Additional Information

(1) Notes receivable of $25,000 were pledged to collateralize the $18,000 note payable to City Bank. Interest of $500 was accrued on the pledged notes receivable, and interest of $600 was accrued on the $18,000 note payable to the bank. All the pledged notes receivable were considered collectible. Of the remaining notes receivable, a $1,000 noninterest-bearing note was uncollectible. The note had been received for an unconditional cash loan.

(2) Trade accounts receivable included $7,000 from Boren Company, which currently was being liquidated. Creditors were expected to realize 40 cents on the dollar. The allowance for doubtful accounts was adequate to cover any other uncollectible accounts. A total of $3,200 of the remaining collectible trade accounts receivable was pledged as collateral for the notes payable to Municipal Trust Company of $6,000 with accrued interest of $180 on June 30, Year 6.

(3) Inventories, valued at first-in, first-out cost, were expected to realize 25% of cost on a forced liquidation sale after the write-off of $10,000 of obsolete stock.

(4) Land and buildings, which had been appraised at 110% of their carrying amount, were mortgaged as collateral for the bonds. Interest of $1,820 was accrued on the bonds on June 30, Year 6. Laurel expected to realize 20% of the cost of its machinery and equipment, and 50% of the cost of its furniture and fixtures after incurring refinishing costs of $800.

(5) Estimated costs of liquidation were $4,500. Depreciation and accruals had been adjusted to June 30, Year 6.

(6) Laurel had net operating loss carryovers for income tax purposes of $22,000 for the year ended June 30, Year 5, and $28,000 for the year ended June 30, Year 6. The income tax rate expected to be in effect when the operating loss carryovers were used was 40%.

LAUREL COMPANY
Adjusted Trial Balance
June 30, Year 6

	Debit	Credit
Cash	$ 14,135	
Notes receivable	29,000	
Interest receivable	615	
Trade accounts receivable	24,500	
Allowance for doubtful accounts		$ 800
Inventories	48,000	
Land	10,000	
Building	50,000	
Accumulated depreciation of building		15,000
Machinery and equipment	33,000	
Accumulated depreciation of machinery and equipment		19,000
Furniture and fixtures	21,000	
Accumulated depreciation of furniture and fixtures		9,500
Goodwill	9,600	
Note payable to City Bank		18,000
Notes payable to Municipal Trust Company		6,000
Notes payable to suppliers		24,000
Interest payable on notes		1,280
Trade accounts payable		80,520
Wages payable		1,400
FICA and income taxes withheld and accrued		430
Mortgage bonds payable		32,000
Interest payable on mortgage bonds		1,820
Common stock		70,000
Retained earnings—deficit	39,900	
Totals	$279,750	$279,750

Instructions
Prepare a statement of affairs for Laurel Company on June 30, Year 6.

Pr. 16-6 Bilbo Corporation, which is in bankruptcy reorganization, had $105,000 of dividends in arrears on its 7% cumulative preferred stock on March 31, Year 20. While retained earnings was adequate to permit the payment of accumulated dividends, Bilbo's management did not want to weaken its working capital position. They also realized that a portion of the plant assets was no longer used by Bilbo. Therefore, management proposed the following plan of reorganization, which was accepted by stockholders and confirmed by the bankruptcy court, to be effective on April 1, Year 20:

(1) The preferred stock was to be exchanged for $300,000 face amount and current fair value of 15%, ten-year bonds. Dividends in arrears were to be settled by the issuance of 12,000 shares of $10 par, 15%, noncumulative preferred stock having a current fair value equal to par.

(2) Common stock was to be assigned a par of $50 a share.

(3) Goodwill was to be written off; plant assets were to be written down, based on appraisal and estimates of current fair value, by a total of $103,200, consisting of a $85,400 increase in the Accumulated Depreciation ledger account balance and a $17,800 decrease in plant assets; other current assets were to be written down by $10,460 to reduce trade accounts receivable and inventories to net realizable values.

The balance sheet of Bilbo Corporation on March 31, Year 20, follows:

BILBO CORPORATION
Balance Sheet
March 31, Year 20

Assets

Cash...		$ 30,000
Other current assets...		252,890
Plant assets	$1,458,250	
Less: Accumulated depreciation....................	512,000	946,250
Goodwill (net)...		50,000
Total assets		$1,279,140

Liabilities & Stockholders' Equity

Current liabilities	$ 132,170
7% cumulative preferred stock, $100 par ($105,000 dividends in arrears), 3,000 shares authorized, issued, and outstanding	300,000
Common stock, no par or stated value, 9,000 shares authorized, issued, and outstanding...	648,430
Additional paid-in capital: preferred stock	22,470
Retained earnings..	176,070
Total liabilities & stockholders' equity............................	$1,279,140

Instructions

a Prepare journal entries for Bilbo Corporation to give effect to the plan of reorganization on April 1, Year 20.

b Prepare a balance sheet for Bilbo Corporation on April 30, Year 20, assuming that net income for April was $15,000. The operations resulted in $11,970 increase in cash, $18,700 increase in other current assets, $7,050 increase in current liabilities, and $8,620 increase in the Accumulated Depreciation ledger account.

17

Estates and Trusts

Estates and trusts are accounting entities as well as taxable entities. The individuals or business enterprises that manage the property in estates and trusts are *fiduciaries;* they exercise stewardship for the property in accordance with the provisions of a will, a trust document, or state laws.

This chapter deals first with the legal aspects of estates, including wills, and then discusses and illustrates the accounting for estates; the last section covers the legal and accounting aspects of trusts.

LEGAL AND ACCOUNTING ASPECTS OF ESTATES

State laws (generally termed *probate codes*) regulate the administration and distribution of property in estates of decedents, missing persons, and other individuals subject to protection of courts. The many variations among the probate codes of the 50 states led to the drafting of a *Uniform Probate Code,* developed by the National Conference of Commissioners on Uniform State Laws and approved by the American Bar Association. Although the Code has not yet been adopted by all states, it is used in this chapter to illustrate the important legal issues underlying the accounting for estates.

Provisions of Uniform Probate Code Governing Estates

The Uniform Probate Code identifies an *estate* as all the property of a decedent, trust, or other person whose affairs are subject to the Code.[1] *Person* is defined as an individual, a corporation, an organization, or other legal entity. The Code also provides that the real and personal property of a decedent is to be awarded to the persons specified in the decedent's *will.* In the absence of a will—a condition known as *intestacy*—the decedent's property goes to *heirs,* as described in the Code. Thus, the intentions of a *testator* (a person creating a will) control the disposition of a decedent's property.[2]

---

[1] Uniform Probate Code, Sec. 1-201(11).
[2] Ibid., Sec. 2-603.

Wills   The Code provides that a will shall be in writing, signed by the testator, or in the testator's name by some other person in the testator's presence and by the testator's direction, and also signed by at least two witnesses. The chief exception to these requirements is a *holographic will*—a will having its essential provisions and signature in the handwriting of the testator.

Probate of Wills   The *probate* of a will is action by the probate court (also known as *surrogate* or *orphan's* court) to validate the will. The Code provides for two types of probate—*informal* and *formal.* Informal probate is initiated by the application of an interested party filed with a court official known as a *registrar.* After thorough review of the completeness and propriety of an application for informal probate, the registrar issues a written statement of informal probate, thus making the will effective.

Formal probate is litigation to determine whether a decedent left a valid will; it is initiated by a petition filed by an interested party requesting the probate court to order probate of the will. The petition also may request a finding that the decedent died *intestate* (without a valid will). During the court hearings, any party to the formal probate proceedings may oppose the will; however, the burden of proof that the will is invalid is on the contestant of the will. After completion of the hearings, the court enters an order for formal probate of a will found to be valid, or an order that the decedent died intestate. Generally, no formal or informal probate proceedings may be undertaken more than three years after the decedent's death.

Appointment of Personal Representative   In both informal and formal probate proceedings, the probate court appoints a *personal representative* of the decedent to administer the decedent's estate. A personal representative named in the decedent's will is called an *executor.* If the decedent died intestate, the court-appointed personal representative is known as an *administrator.* The Code requires the probate court to issue *letters testamentary* to the personal representative before administration of the estate may begin. Because personal representatives are fiduciaries, they must observe standards of care in administering estates that prudent persons would observe in dealing with the property of others. The personal representative is entitled to reasonable compensation for services.

Powers and Duties of Personal Representative   The personal representative of a decedent is empowered to take possession and control of the decedent's property, and to have title to the property in trust for the benefit of creditors and beneficiaries of the estate. The personal representative also has many additional powers, such as the right to continue any single proprietorship of the decedent for not more than four months following the date of the personal representative's appointment and the authority to allocate items of revenue and expenses of the estate to either *estate principal* (corpus) or *estate income,* as provided by the will or by law. Such allocations comprise the chief accounting problem for an estate and are discussed in a subsequent section of this chapter (pages 781 to 782).

Not later than 30 days after appointment, the personal representative must inform the decedent's *devisees* or heirs of the appointment. A *devisee* is any person or trust named in a will to receive real or personal property of the decedent in a transfer known as a *devise.* Within three months after appointment, the personal representative must prepare an inventory of property owned by the decedent on the date of death, together with a list of any liens against the property. The property in the inventory must be stated at current fair value on the date of death. The personal representative may retain the services of an appraiser to obtain the current fair values of property. The inventory of decedent's property is filed with the probate court. If other property of the decedent is discovered after the filing of the original inventory, the personal representative must file a supplementary inventory with the probate court.

Exempt Property and Allowances   In a manner similar to the bankruptcy law discussed in Chapter 16, the Uniform Probate Code provides for certain exemptions from claims against the estate property, even by devisees. These exemptions are as follows:

1   *Homestead allowance.*   The decedent's surviving spouse, or surviving minor and dependent children, are entitled to a *homestead allowance* of a specified amount. This allowance is in addition to any share of the estate property passing to the spouse or children pursuant to the provisions of the will.

2   *Exempt property.*   The decedent's surviving spouse or children are entitled to an aggregate specified value of automobiles, household furniture and furnishings, appliances, and personal effects.

3   *Family allowance.*   The surviving spouse and children who were being supported by the decedent are entitled to a reasonable cash allowance, payable in a lump sum not exceeding a specified amount, or in installments not exceeding one-twelfth of the specified lump sum each month for one year, during the administration of the estate. The family allowance has priority over all claims against the estate other than the homestead allowance.

Claims of Creditors against the Estate   The personal representative for an estate is required to publish a notice once a week for three successive weeks, in a newspaper of general circulation, requesting creditors of the estate to present their claims within four months after the date of the first publication, or be forever barred. If the estate property not exempt under the Code is insufficient to pay all creditors' claims in full, the personal representative pays the claims in the following order:

1   Costs of administering the estate

2   Decedent's funeral costs and medical and hospital costs of the decedent's last illness

3   Debts and taxes with preference under federal or state laws

4   All other claims

Four months after publication of the first notice to estate creditors, the personal representative initiates payment of claims in the order outlined above, after first providing for homestead, family, and exempt property allowances.

Distributions to Devisees   The personal representative also has the duty of distributing estate property to the devisees named in the will. The property is to be distributed in kind to the extent possible, rather than first being realized in cash and then distributed.

If estate property that is not exempt is insufficient to cover creditors' claims as well as all devises, the devises *abate* (are reduced) in the sequence provided for in the decedent's will. If the will is silent as to order of abatement, the Uniform Probate Code provides the following *abatement sequence:*

1   Property not specifically mentioned in the will

2   *Residuary devises,* which are devises of all estate property remaining after general and specific devises are satisfied

3   *General devises,* which are gifts of an amount of money or a number of countable monetary items, such as 500 shares of Mercury Company common stock

4   *Specific devises,* which are gifts of identified objects, such as named paintings, automobiles, stock certificates, or real property

Devises may be granted to the devisees *in trust,* which requires the establishment of a *testamentary trust,* that is, one provided for by a will. Trusts are discussed in a subsequent section of this chapter.

Estate and Inheritance Taxes   The federal estate tax assessed against the net assets of an estate, and inheritance taxes assessed by various states against devisees and heirs of a decedent, often called *death taxes,* must be charged to the devisees as outlined in the will. If the will is silent on this point, the Code provides that death taxes are to be apportioned to the devisees in the ratio of their interests (equity) in the estate.

Closing the Estate   No earlier than six months after the date of appointment, a personal representative may close an estate by filing a statement with the probate court. The written content of this statement is described in the Uniform Probate Code; this legal statement usually is accompanied by a financial statement known as a *charge and discharge statement.*

Provisions of Revised Uniform Principal and Income Act Governing Estates

I have noted on page 779 that the primary accounting problem for an estate is the allocation of revenue and expenses to principal and income. This allocation is important because many wills provide that income of a testamentary trust is paid to an *income beneficiary,* and that trust principal is paid to a different *principal beneficiary* (or *remainderman*). A proper accounting for principal and income is essential before the estate is closed.

The Revised Uniform Principal and Income Act provides guidelines for allocation in the absence of instructions in the will or trust instrument. Many states have adopted all or part of the Act, often with modifications. The provisions of the Act include the following:

1 *Income* is defined as the return in money or property derived from the use of principal, including rent, interest, cash dividends, or any other revenue received during administration of an estate.

2 *Principal* is defined as property set aside by its owner to be held in trust for eventual delivery to a remainderman. Principal includes proceeds of insurance on principal property, stock dividends, and liquidating dividends. Any accrued revenue on the date of death of the testator is included in the principal of the estate.

3 Premium or discount on investments in bonds included in principal is not amortized. All proceeds from sale or redemption of bonds are principal.

4 Income is charged with a reasonable provision for depreciation, computed in accordance with generally accepted accounting principles, on all depreciable property except property used by a beneficiary, such as a residence or a personal automobile. Income also is charged with costs of administering and preserving income-producing property. Such costs include property taxes, ordinary repairs, and property insurance.

5 Principal is charged with expenditures incurred in preparing principal property for sale or rent, cost of investing and reinvesting principal property, major repairs to principal property, and income taxes on receipts or gains allocable to principal.

6 Court costs, attorneys' fees, trustees' fees, and accountants' fees for periodic reporting to the probate court are allocated as appropriate to principal and to income.

Illustration of Accounting for an Estate

Now that certain legal issues involved in estates have been discussed, it is appropriate to illustrate the accounting for estates, including the charge and discharge statement rendered by the personal representative at the closing of the estate. Estate accounting is carried out in accordance with the *accountability* technique illustrated in Chapter 16. The accounting records of the personal representative include only those items for which the representative is accountable, under the equation Assets = Accountability.

The illustration on pages 784 to 788 of journal entries in accounting for an estate is based on the following information for the estate of Jessica Davis:

1 Jessica Davis, a single woman, died March 18, Year 3, after a brief illness that required her to be hospitalized. Her will, approved for informal probate on March 25, Year 3, contained the following devises:

a General devises of $10,000 cash to each of three household employees: Alice Martin, Angelo Bari, and Nolan Ames. Devisees must waive claims for unpaid wages on date of death.

b Specific devise of *all* 200 shares of Preston Company common stock to Nancy Grimes, a niece.

c Specific devise of paintings, other art objects, clothing, jewelry, and personal effects to Frances Davis Grimes, sister of Jessica Davis.

d Specific devise of residence, furniture, and furnishings to Wallace Davis, brother of Jessica Davis.

e General devise of $5,000 cash to Universal Charities, a nonprofit organization.

f Residue of estate in trust (First National Bank, Trustee) to Nancy Grimes; income to be paid to her at the end of each calendar quarter until her twenty-first birthday on October 1, Year 8, at which time the principal also is to be paid to Nancy Grimes.

2   Paul Hasting, attorney for Jessica Davis and executor of her estate, published the required newspaper notice to creditors on March 26, April 2, and April 9, Year 3. The following claims were received from creditors within the four-month statutory period:

List of claims against estate of Jessica Davis

Funeral costs (Wade Mortuary)	$ 810
Hospital costs (Suburban Hospital)	1,928
Doctor's fees (Charles Carson, M.D.)	426
Morningside Department Store charge account	214
Various residence bills	87
Total claims against estate of Jessica Davis	$3,465

List of property included in estate of Jessica Davis

Description of estate property	Current fair values, Mar. 18, Year 3
Bank checking account	$ 2,157
Bank savings account (including accrued interest)	30,477
Savings and loan association 2-year certificate of deposit maturing June 30, Year 3 (including accrued interest)	26,475
Salary earned for period Mar. 1 to Mar. 8, Year 3	214
Claim against medical insurance carrier	1,526
Social security benefits receivable	14,820
Proceeds of life insurance policy (payable to estate)	25,000
Marketable securities:	
Common stock of Preston Company, 200 shares	8,000
Common stock of Arthur Corporation, 100 shares	6,500
Residence	40,800*
Furniture and furnishings	2,517
Paintings and other art objects	16,522
Clothing, jewelry, personal effects	625
Automobile	2,187
Total current fair value of estate property	$177,820

*Subject to unpaid mortgage note of $15,500, due $500 monthly on the last day of the month, plus interest at 10% a year on the unpaid balance.

3   Hasting prepared final individual federal and state income tax returns for Jessica Davis for the period January 1 to March 18, Year 3. The federal return showed income tax due in the amount of $457; the state return showed no tax due.

4   Hasting prepared the inventory of property owned by Jessica Davis shown on page 783 on March 18, Year 3.

5   Subsequent to preparing the foregoing inventory, Hasting discovered a certificate for 600 shares of Campbell Company common stock with a market value of $18,000.

6   Hasting prepared the federal estate tax return for the Estate of Jessica Davis, Deceased. The return showed a tax due of $18,556. Hasting also prepared state inheritance tax returns for the devisees showing taxes due of $5,020.

7   Hasting administered the estate, charging a fee of $2,500, and closed the estate by filing the required legal documents and a charge and discharge statement prepared by a CPA who was a member of Hasting's law firm.

PAUL HASTING, EXECUTOR
Of the Will of Jessica Davis, Deceased
Journal Entries

Year 3

Mar. 18	*Principal Cash (bank checking account)*	2,157	
	Savings Account	30,477	
	Certificate of Deposit (including accrued interest)	26,475	
	Salary Receivable	214	
	Medical Insurance Claim Receivable	1,526	
	Social Security Benefits Receivable	14,820	
	Life Insurance Claim Receivable	25,000	
	Marketable Securities	14,500	
	Residence	40,800	
	Furniture and Furnishings	2,517	
	Paintings and Other Art Objects	16,522	
	Clothing, Jewelry, Personal Effects	625	
	Automobile	2,187	
	Mortgage Note Payable		15,500
	Interest Payable ($15,500 × 0.10 × $^{18}/_{360}$)		78
	Estate Principal Balance ($177,820 − $15,578) . .		162,242
	To record inventory of property owned by decedent Jessica Davis on date of death, net of lien against residence.		
25	*Marketable Securities*	18,000	
	Property Discovered		18,000
	To record property discovered subsequent to filing of original inventory of property.		

(continued)

PAUL HASTING, EXECUTOR
Of the Will of Jessica Davis, Deceased
Journal Entries (continued)

Year 3

Mar. 31	Principal Cash......................................	70,511	
	Income Cash	55	
	Savings Account.............................		30,477
	Salary Receivable		214
	Social Security Benefits Receivable.............		14,820
	Life Insurance Claim Receivable................		25,000
	Interest Revenue		55

To record realization of various property, including $55
interest received on savings account for period Mar. 18
through 31, Year 3.

31	Distributions to Income Beneficiaries..................	55	
	Income Cash...............................		55

To distribute income cash to residuary devisee Nancy
Grimes, as required by the will.

Apr. 2	Principal Cash......................................	2,050	
	Loss on Disposal of Principal Property	137	
	Automobile.................................		2,187

To record disposal of automobile.

4	Devises Distributed	5,000	
	Principal Cash..............................		5,000

To record distribution of general devise to Universal Charities.

16	Liabilities Paid.....................................	3,922	
	Principal Cash..............................		3,922

To record following liabilities paid:

Funeral costs (Wade Mortuary)	$	810
Hospital costs (Suburban Hospital)........		1,928
Doctor's fees (Charles Carson, M.D.)......		426
Final federal income tax..................		457
Morningside Department Store charge account..................................		214
Various residence bills		87
Total................................	$	3,922

(continued)

PAUL HASTING, EXECUTOR
Of the Will of Jessica Davis, Deceased
Journal Entries (continued)

Year 3

Apr. 19 Principal Cash 1,526

         Medical Insurance Claim Receivable 1,526

     To record collection of medical insurance claim.

24 Principal Cash 1,000

     Income Cash 1,500

          Payable to Devisees 1,000

          Dividend Revenue 1,500

     To record receipt of quarterly cash dividends on common
     stock, as follows:

     Preston Company (payable to Nancy

          Grimes) .... $ 1,000

     Arthur Corporation 300

     Campbell Company 1,200

          Total .... $ 2,500

25 Receivable from Devisees 23,576

          Principal Cash 23,576

     To record payment of federal estate tax and state inheri-
     tance taxes on behalf of devisees, as follows:

     Federal estate tax $18,556

     State inheritance taxes 5,020

          Total $23,576

26 Principal Cash 6,295

          Receivable from Devisees 6,295

     To record receipt of cash from specific devisees for their
     shares of federal estate tax and state inheritance taxes
     as follows:

     Frances Davis Grimes ($23,576 × 0.102)* . $ 2,405

     Wallace Davis ($23,576 × 0.165)* 3,890

          Total .... $ 6,295

* See explanation on page 789.

(continued)

PAUL HASTING, EXECUTOR
Of the Will of Jessica Davis, Deceased
Journal Entries (continued)

Year 3

Apr. 27   *Devises Distributed* *30,000*

             Receivable from Devisees *4,173*

             Principal Cash *25,827*

*To record payment of cash to general devisees, less
amounts receivable for their shares of federal estate tax
and state inheritance taxes, as follows:*

    $10,000 devises payable to Alice
    Martin, Angelo Bari, Nolan Ames
    ($10,000 × 3) *$30,000*
    Less: Share of death taxes ($23,576 ×
    0.059* × 3) *4,173*
      Net cash paid *$25,827*

30   *Mortgage Note Payable* *15,500*

    Interest Payable *78*

    Devises Distributed *52,886*

    Payable to Devisees *1,000*

        Marketable Securities *8,000*

        Residence *40,800*

        Furniture and Furnishings *2,517*

        Paintings and Other Art Objects *16,522*

        Clothing, Jewelry, Personal Effects *625*

        Principal Cash *1,000*

*To transfer to devisee Nancy Grimes cash for dividend
received on Preston Company common stock; and to
record distribution of specific devises as follows:*

    Specific devise to Nancy Grimes:
    200 shares of Preston Company common
    stock .... *$ 8,000*
    Specific devise to Frances Davis Grimes:
    Paintings, other art objects, clothing,
    jewelry, personal effects *17,147*
    Specific devise to Wallace Davis:
    Residence, net of mortgage note payable,
    with furniture and furnishings *27,739*
      Total *$52,886*

(continued)

PAUL HASTING, EXECUTOR
Of the Will of Jessica Davis, Deceased
Journal Entries (concluded)

Year 3

May	1	Administrative Costs	2,500	
		Principal Cash..............................		2,500
		To record payment of executor's fee.		
	3	Devises Distributed	85,797	
		Distributions to Income Beneficiaries..................	1,500	
		Principal Cash (balance of account).............		21,714
		Income Cash.................................		1,500
		Certificate of Deposit..........................		26,475
		Marketable Securities		24,500
		Receivable from Devisees (balance of account)..		13,108
		To record distribution of residuary devise (principal and		
		income) to First National Bank, trustee for Nancy Grimes,		
		devisee.		

The foregoing journal entries are entered in the accounting records for the Estate of Jessica Davis, Deceased. (Dates for journal entries are assumed.) Comments relating to specific journal entries that require particular emphasis follow:

March 18 Journal Entry   This entry records the executor's inventory of estate property, including accrued interest and unpaid salary on the date of death. Because the decedent was a single woman, there was no homestead allowance, family allowance, or exempt property. The mortgage note payable (and any accrued interest) applicable to the residence is recognized as a liability for accountability purposes. Claims of unsecured creditors *are not* recorded as liabilities because the accounting records for an estate are not designed to record all aspects of the estate's financial position; accounting records for an estate reflect only the executor's accountability for property and any direct claims against the property.

March 31 Journal Entries   A separate ledger account, Income Cash, is used to record cash receipts attributable to income. In accordance with provisions of the will of Jessica Davis, the income of $55 attributable to the residuary devise to Nancy Grimes is distributed to her at the end of the calendar quarter.

April 2 Journal Entry   No depreciation was recognized on the automobile prior to its disposal, because it was not a revenue-producing asset for the estate.

April 16 Journal Entry   The Liabilities Paid ledger account represents a reduction of the executor's accountability for estate property; it is neither an asset account nor an expense account, but rather an account in which distributions to estate creditors are recorded.

April 24 Journal Entry Dividends received on marketable securities required segregation in the accounting records, because the securities are allocable to separate devises, as follows:

1 Preston Company common stock, $1,000: Allocable to specific devise to Nancy Grimes

2 Arthur Corporation and Campbell Company common stocks, $1,500: Allocable to residuary devise to Nancy Grimes

Although Nancy Grimes is the recipient of both devises, the residuary devise ultimately will be placed in a testamentary trust for the devisee.

April 25 Journal Entry The will of Jessica Davis was silent regarding allocation of estate and inheritance taxes. Consequently, in accordance with the provisions of the Uniform Probate Code, the federal estate tax and state inheritance taxes are allocated in the ratio of interests of devisees, other than the nontaxable nonprofit organization, in the estate. The following summary shows this ratio.

Ratio of devisee interests in estate of Jessica Davis

PAUL HASTING, EXECUTOR
Of the Will of Jessica Davis, Deceased
Ratio of Devisee Interests
April 25, Year 3

Devisee	Current fair value of estate interest	Ratio to total of all estate interests
Alice Martin	$ 10,000	5.9%
Angelo Bari	10,000	5.9
Nolan Ames.	10,000	5.9
Nancy Grimes (specific devise).	8,000	4.7
Frances Davis Grimes.	17,147 (1)	10.2
Wallace Davis	27,739 (2)	16.5
Nancy Grimes (residuary devise)	85,797	50.9
Totals	$168,683 (3)	100.0%

(1) $16,522 + $625 = $17,147
(2) ($40,800 + $2,517) − ($15,500 + $78) = $27,739
(3) $162,242 + $18,000 − $137 − $5,000 − $3,922 − $2,500 = $168,683

April 26 and April 27 Journal Entries The executor requested the specific devisees to pay in cash their shares of the federal estate tax and state inheritance taxes. The executor withheld the general devisees' death taxes from the cash payable to them.

May 1 Journal Entry The entire fee of the executor was charged to estate principal because the time spent by Paul Hasting on income property was insignificant. The allocation of fees is more appropriate for a trust than for an estate of relatively short duration.

May 3 Journal Entry   No adjusting entries are required for interest on the certificate of deposit or any declared but unpaid dividends on the marketable securities. An accrual-basis cutoff for an estate is appropriate only at the time the executor prepares the inventory of estate property in order to facilitate the distinction between estate principal and estate income. If the will provides that the accrual basis of accounting must be used, the executor must comply.

In the preceding illustration, federal and state income taxes on the estate were disregarded. In addition, it was assumed that devisee Wallace Davis immediately occupied the decedent's residence, so that depreciation on the residence was not required as it would be if rent revenue were realized from a lease. A further assumption was that devisee Wallace Davis paid the March 31 and April 30, Year 3, installments on the mortgage note secured by the residence.

Trial Balance   A trial balance of the ledger accounts of the Estate of Jessica Davis on May 3, Year 3, is as follows:

PAUL HASTING, EXECUTOR
Of the Will of Jessica Davis, Deceased
Trial Balance
May 3, Year 3

	Dr (Cr)
Principal	
Estate principal balance	$(162,242)
Property discovered	(18,000)
Loss on disposal of principal property	137
Liabilities paid	3,922
Devises distributed	173,683
Administrative costs	2,500
Total	$ -0-
Income	
Interest revenue	$ (55)
Dividend revenue	(1,500)
Distributions to income beneficiaries	1,555
Total	$ -0-

Charge and Discharge Statement   The executor's charge and discharge statement and supporting exhibits for the Estate of Jessica Davis are shown on pages 791 to 793. The items in the statement were taken from the trial balance above. Although the executor's activities essentially ended May 3, the Uniform Probate Code precludes closing an estate earlier than six months after the issuance of letters testamentary.

The charge and discharge statement shows the executor's *accountability,* not the financial position or cash transactions of the estate. The statement discloses the

PAUL HASTING, EXECUTOR
Of the Will of Jessica Davis, Deceased
Charge and Discharge Statement
For Period March 18 through September 18, Year 3

First, as to Principal

I charge myself as follows:

Inventory of estate property, Mar. 18, Year 3 *(Exhibit 1)*..	$162,242	
Property discovered *(Exhibit 2)*.......................	18,000	$180,242
I credit myself as follows:		
Loss on disposal of principal property *(Exhibit 3)*	$ 137	
Liabilities paid *(Exhibit 4)*	3,922	
Devises distributed *(Exhibit 5)*........................	173,683	
Administrative costs *(Exhibit 6)*.......................	2,500	180,242
Balance, Sept. 18, Year 3		$ -0-

Second, as to Income

I charge myself as follows:

Interest revenue (bank savings account)	$ 55	
Dividend revenue *(Exhibit 7)*	1,500	$ 1,555
I credit myself as follows:		
Distributions of income *(Exhibit 8)*		1,555
Balance, Sept. 18, Year 3		$ -0-

charges to the executor for estate principal and estate income property for which the executor is accountable, and the credits to the executor for the dispositions made of estate property.

Closing Entry for Estate   Once the executor's closing statement and charge and discharge statement have been accepted by the probate court, the accountant for the estate may prepare an appropriate closing entry. The closing entry for the estate of Jessica Davis on September 18, Year 3, follows:

Journal entry to close
estate of Jessica Davis

Estate Principal Balance.....................................	162,242	
Property Discovered	18,000	
Interest Revenue	55	
Dividend Revenue	1,500	
Loss on Disposal of Principal Property		137
Liabilities Paid..		3,922
Devises Distributed		173,683
Administrative Costs		2,500
Distributions to Income Beneficiaries...................		1,555
To close estate of Jessica Davis in accordance with probate court authorization.		

PAUL HASTING, EXECUTOR
Of the Will of Jessica Davis, Deceased
Exhibits Supporting Charge and Discharge Statement
For Period March 18 through September 18, Year 3

Exhibit 1—Inventory of estate property, Mar. 18, Year 3:

Bank checking account		$ 2,157
Bank savings account (including accrued interest)		30,477
Savings and loan association 2-year certificate of deposit maturing June		
30, Year 3 (including accrued interest)		26,475
Salary earned for period Mar. 1 to 8, Year 3.		214
Claim against medical insurance carrier		1,526
Social security benefits receivable		14,820
Proceeds of life insurance policy (payable to estate)		25,000
Marketable securities:		
Common stock of Preston Company, 200 shares.		8,000
Common stock of Arthur Corporation, 100 shares		6,500
Residence	$40,800	
Less: Balance of mortgage note payable, including accrued		
interest of $78.	15,578	25,222
Furniture and furnishings.		2,517
Paintings and other art objects		16,522
Clothing, jewelry, personal effects.		625
Automobile		2,187
Total inventory of estate property		$162,242

Exhibit 2—Property discovered:

On Mar. 25, Year 3, a certificate for 600 shares of Campbell Company common stock was discovered among the decedent's personal effects. All other securities were located in the decedent's safe deposit box at First National Bank (valued at market value on date of Jessica Davis's death)	$ 18,000

Exhibit 3—Loss on disposal of principal property:

Disposal of automobile, Apr. 3, Year 3:	
Carrying amount	$ 2,187
Less: Cash proceeds	2,050
Loss on disposal of principal property	$ 137

Exhibit 4—Liabilities paid:

Wade Mortuary	$ 810
Suburban Hospital	1,928
Charles Carson, M.D..	426
Final federal income tax	457
Morningside Department Store	214
Various residence bills.	87
Total liabilities paid.	$ 3,922

(continued)

PAUL HASTING, EXECUTOR
Of the Will of Jessica Davis, Deceased
Exhibits Supporting Charge and Discharge Statement (concluded)
For Period March 18 through September 18, Year 3

Exhibit 5—Devises distributed:

General devise to Universal Charities: Cash	$ 5,000
General devise to Alice Martin: Cash	10,000
General devise to Angelo Bari: Cash	10,000
General devise to Nolan Ames: Cash	10,000
Specific devise to Nancy Grimes: 200 shares of Preston Company common stock	8,000
Specific devise to Frances Davis Grimes: Paintings, other art objects, clothing, jewelry, personal effects	17,147
Specific devise to Wallace Davis: Residence, net of mortgage note payable, with furniture and furnishings	27,739
Residuary devise to Nancy Grimes: Cash, certificate of deposit, 100 shares of Arthur Corporation common stock, and 600 shares of Campbell Company common stock (in trust)	85,797
Total devises distributed	$173,683

Exhibit 6—Administrative costs:

Fee of executor (charged entirely to principal because income administration activities were nominal)	$ 2,500

Exhibit 7—Dividend revenue:

Arthur Corporation common stock	$ 300
Campbell Company common stock	1,200
Total dividend revenue	$ 1,500

Exhibit 8—Distributions of income:

Mar. 31, Year 3: To residuary devisee Nancy Grimes	$ 55
May 3, Year 3: To First National Bank, trustee for Nancy Grimes	1,500
Total distributions of income	$ 1,555

The example of estate accounting in this chapter was simplified in terms of details and time required for the liquidation of the estate. In practice, many estates —especially those involved in formal probate proceedings—take several months and sometimes years to settle. For many estates, preparation of the federal estate tax return is a complex task. Furthermore, the estate of an intestate decedent involves complicated legal issues. An accountant involved in accounting for an estate must be familiar with provisions of the decedent's will and with appropriate state probate laws and principal and income laws, and should work closely with the attorney and executor (or administrator) for the estate.

LEGAL AND ACCOUNTING ASPECTS OF TRUSTS

A trust created by a will, as illustrated in the preceding sections of this chapter, is a *testamentary trust.* A trust created by the act of a living person is an *inter vivos,* or *living, trust.* The parties to a trust are (1) the *settlor* (also known as the *donor* or *trustor*)—the individual creating the trust, (2) the *trustee*—the fiduciary individual or corporation holding legal title to the trust property and carrying out the provisions of the *trust document* for a fee, and (3) the *beneficiary*—the party for whose benefit the trust was established. As noted on page 781, the income from trust property may be distributed to an *income beneficiary,* but the principal of a trust ultimately goes to a *principal beneficiary* (also known as the *remainderman*).

Provisions of Uniform Probate Code Governing Trusts

The Uniform Probate Code contains detailed sections dealing with trust registration, jurisdiction of courts concerning trusts, duties and liabilities of trustees, and powers of trustees. The Code requires that a trustee of a trust must register the trust with the appropriate state probate court. Registration subjects the trust to the jurisdiction of the court. The court's jurisdiction may include appointing or removing a trustee, reviewing the trustee's fees, and reviewing or settling interim or final accountings of the trustee. The trustee is required by the Code to administer the trust expeditiously for the benefit of the beneficiaries, and to use standards of care appropriate for a prudent person in dealing with the property of others. The trustee must keep the trust beneficiaries reasonably informed as to the administration of the trust, and furnish the beneficiaries a statement of the trust accounts annually (or more frequently if necessary) and at the termination of the trust.

Provisions of Revised Uniform Principal and Income Act Governing Trusts

The provisions for allocations between principal and income that are set forth in the Revised Uniform Principal and Income Act (see pages 781 and 782) are applicable to trusts as well as to estates.

Illustration of Accounting for a Trust

The journal entries in the accounting records of a trust usually differ from those of an estate because of the longer life of a trust. Whereas the personal representative for an estate attempts to complete the administration of the estate as expeditiously as possible, the trustee for a trust must comply with the provisions of the trust document during the stated term of the trust. Accordingly, the trustee's activities include investment of trust property and maintenance of accounting records for both trust principal and trust income.

To illustrate the accounting issues for a trust, return to the testamentary trust provided by the will of Jessica Davis (see page 783). The trust was created by the residuary devise to Nancy Grimes, which required the trustee to pay income from the trust to Grimes at the end of each calendar quarter until her twenty-first birthday (October 1, Year 8), at which time the trust principal would be paid to Grimes. Thus, Grimes is both the income beneficiary and the principal beneficiary.

The journal entries below and on page 796 illustrate the activities of First National Bank, trustee for Nancy Grimes, during the quarter ended June 30, Year 3. The journal entries for the Nancy Grimes Trust are essentially *cash-basis* entries; there is no need to accrue interest or dividends on trust investments at the end of a quarter because conventional financial statements generally are not prepared for a trust.

NANCY GRIMES TRUST
First National Bank, Trustee
Journal Entries

Year 3

May 3	Principal Cash...................................... 21,714	
	Income Cash.. 1,500	
	Certificate of Deposit (including accrued interest)........ 26,475	
	Marketable Securities 24,500	
	Trust Principal Balance.........................	72,689
	Trust Income Balance..........................	1,500
	To record receipt of principal and income property in trust	
	from Paul Hasting, executor of estate of Jessica Davis.	

6	Marketable Securities 19,900	
	Interest Receivable 180	
	Principal Cash.................................	20,080
	To record acquisition of following securities:	

$15,000 face amount of 12% bonds of
   Warren Company, due Mar. 31, Year 23 ... $15,000
   Accrued interest......................... 180
$5,000 face amount of commercial paper of
   Modern Finance Company, due July 5, Year
   3, acquired at 12% discount 4,900
      Total cash paid $20,080

June 30	Principal Cash...................................... 26,475	
	Income Cash.. 612	
	Certificate of Deposit..........................	26,475
	Interest Revenue	612
	To record proceeds of matured certificate of deposit and	
	interest since Mar. 18, Year 3.	

30	Administrative Costs 250	
	Expenses Chargeable to Income 250	
	Principal Cash.................................	250
	Income Cash..................................	250
	To record payment of trustee fee for period May 3–June	
	30, Year 3, chargeable equally to principal and to income.	

(continued)

NANCY GRIMES TRUST
First National Bank, Trustee (concluded)
Journal Entries

Year 3

June 30 Marketable Securities 25,000
              Principal Cash.   25,000
         To record acquisition of 14% U.S. Treasury notes due June
         30, Year 8, at face amount.

     30 Distributions to Income Beneficiary   1,862
              Income Cash.   1,862
         To record regular quarterly distribution to income benefi-
         ciary Nancy Grimes.

The May 3, Year 3, opening journal entry for the trust is the counterpart of the journal entry for the Estate of Jessica Davis on the same date (see page 788), except that the amount receivable from the trust beneficiary for federal estate tax and state inheritance tax was offset against the gross amount of the devise, and the $72,689 difference ($85,797 − $13,108 = $72,689) was recorded as the trust principal balance.

Trial Balance   The trial balance of the Nancy Grimes Trust on June 30, Year 3, is shown on page 797.

Charge and Discharge Statement for Trust   A charge and discharge statement for the trustee of the Nancy Grimes Trust would resemble the charge and discharge statement for an estate illustrated on pages 791 to 793. The major difference would be an exhibit for the details of the $72,439 ($72,689 − $250 = $72,439) trust principal balance on June 30, Year 3.

Periodic Closing Entry for Trust   A closing entry should be made for a trust at the end of each period for which a charge and discharge statement is prepared to clear the nominal accounts for the next reporting period. The closing entry for the Nancy Grimes Trust on June 30, Year 3, is as illustrated below:

Periodic closing entry
for a trust

Trust Principal Balance	250	
Trust Income Balance.	1,500	
Interest Revenue	612	
Administrative Costs.		250
Expenses Chargeable to Income.		250
Distributions to Income Beneficiary.		1,862
To close nominal accounts of trust.		

NANCY GRIMES TRUST
First National Bank, Trustee
Trial Balance
June 30, Year 3

	Dr (Cr)
Principal	
Principal cash	$ 2,859
Marketable securities	69,400
Interest receivable	180
Trust principal balance	(72,689)
Administrative costs	250
Totals	$ -0-
Income	
Trust income balance	$ (1,500)
Interest revenue	(612)
Expenses chargeable to income	250
Distributions to income beneficiary	1,862
Totals	$ -0-

At the time specified in the trust document for transfer of the trust principal to the principal beneficiary, a journal entry is made to debit the Distributions to Principal Beneficiary ledger account and credit the various trust principal asset accounts. A closing entry for the termination of the trust would then be required, in the form of the comparable estate journal entry illustrated on page 791.

REVIEW QUESTIONS

1 Is the Uniform Probate Code in effect throughout the United States?

2 Define the following terms:
a *Estate*
b *Intestacy*
c *Testator*
d *Executor*
e *Administrator*
f *Letters testamentary*
g *Devise*
h *Remainderman*
i *Inter vivos trust*
j *Settlor*

3 Compare *informal probate* with *formal probate* of a will.

4 Compare the standards of care required of a ***personal representative*** with the standards of care required of a ***trustee.***

5   Why must there be a distinction between *principal* and *income* in the administration of an estate?

6   Describe the *exempt property and allowances* provisions of the Uniform Probate Code.

7   What type of *devise* is each of the following?
a The beach house at 1411 Ocean Avenue, Long Beach, California
b $25,000 cash
c $60,000 face amount of U.S. Treasury bonds
d 1,000 shares of Rogers Corporation common stock represented by certificate No. G-1472
e All my remaining property

8   Is the accrual basis of accounting ever used for an estate or a trust? Explain.

9   Explain the requirements for depreciation accounting contained in the Revised Uniform Principal and Income Act.

10   Describe the use of the Property Discovered ledger account in accounting for an estate.

11   Compare a personal representative's *charge and discharge statement* for an estate with the financial statements issued by a business enterprise.

12   Discuss the similarities and differences in the journal entries for estates and for trusts.

EXERCISES

Ex. 17-1   Select the best answer for each of the following multiple-choice questions:

1   In a charge and discharge statement prepared for the executor of a decedent's estate, devises distributed are displayed in the section:
a First, as to Principal, I charge myself as follows
b First, as to Principal, I credit myself as follows
c Second, as to Income, I charge myself as follows
d Second, as to Income, I credit myself as follows

2   Under the Uniform Probate Code, the personal representative of a decedent's estate gives first priority to creditors' claims classified as:
a Costs of administering the estate
b Decedent's funeral costs and medical and hospital costs of the decedent's last illness
c Debts and taxes with preference under federal or state laws
d Any of the foregoing, at the election of the personal representative

3   A personal representative named in a decedent's will is termed:
a An executor
b An administrator

c A trustee

d A probate officer

4 Is the Property Discovered ledger account used by the personal representative of a decedent's estate to record the current fair value of:

	Property in date-of-death inventory?	*Property located subsequent to date-of-death inventory?*
a	Yes	Yes
b	Yes	No
c	No	Yes
d	No	No

5 Principal Cash and Income Cash ledger accounts typically are used by:

a The personal representative of an estate only

b The trustee of a testamentary trust only

c Both the personal representative of an estate and the trustee of a testamentary trust

d Neither the personal representative of an estate nor the trustee of a testamentary trust

6 In the *abatement sequence* provided by the Uniform Probate Code, *specific devises* are abated:

a First   **b** Second   **c** Third   **d** Last

7 The Estate Principal Balance ledger account in the accounting records of the executor of a decedent's will is:

a An asset account

b A liability account

c An accountability account

d A fund balance account

8 Which of the following terms is inconsistent with a decedent's estate created by a will?

a Letters testamentary

b Administrator

c Devises

d Homestead allowance

9 May court costs, attorneys' fees, trustees' fees, and accountants' fees related to a decedent's estate be allocated to:

	Principal?	*Income?*
a	Yes	Yes
b	Yes	No
c	No	Yes
d	No	No

10 A Property Discovered ledger account balance in the accounting records of the executor of an estate is displayed in the executor's charge and discharge statement under:

a First, as to Principal, I charge myself as follows

b First, as to Principal, I credit myself as follows
c Second, as to Income, I charge myself as follows
d Second, as to Income, I credit myself as follows

11 If nonexempt property of a decedent's estate is insufficient to cover creditors' claims as well as all devises, the devises *abate* in the following sequence:
a General devises, specific devises, residuary devises
b Specific devises, residuary devises, general devises
c Residuary devises, specific devises, general devises
d Residuary devises, general devises, specific devises

12 The executor of a decedent's estate gives preference to paying costs of administering the estate prior to:
a Decedent's funeral costs
b Medical and hospital costs of decedent's last illness
c Debts with preference under federal or state laws
d Taxes with preference under federal or state laws
e Any of the foregoing claims against the estate

13 A *charge and discharge statement* is prepared by:
a The executor of an estate only
b The trustee of a trust only
c Both the executor of an estate and the trustee of a trust
d Neither the executor of an estate nor the trustee of a trust

Ex. 17-2 Indicate whether each of the following items would be charged to trust principal or to trust income of a testamentary trust, assuming that the Revised Uniform Principal and Income Act is to be followed:
a Depreciation of building
b Legal fees for managing trust property
c Special assessment tax levied on real property for street improvements
d Interest on mortgage note payable
e Loss on disposal of trust investments
f Major repairs to real property prior to disposal of the property

Ex. 17-3 After the payment of all estate liabilities, excepting the executor's fee of $40,000, the following property remained in the Estate of Allen Baker, deceased, on April 30, Year 3:

	Amount	% of Total
Cash in checking account.	$13,860	21%
Bank certificate of deposit maturing April 30, Year 3, including accrued interest.	21,120	32
100 shares of BBM Company common stock, at current fair value on date of death.	9,900	15
$20,000 face amount Southeastern Airlines 7% bonds due Year 8, at current fair value on date of death.	21,120	32
Total estate property	$66,000	100%

The following devises remained to be distributed by the executor:

(1) Barbara Baker (wife)—certificate no. X4738 for $20,000 face amount of Southeastern Airlines 7% bonds due Year 8
(2) Carl Baker (son)—50 shares of BBM Company common stock
(3) Danielle Baker (daughter)—50 shares of BBM Company common stock
(4) Edie Baker (niece)—residue of estate

Prepare a working paper to show how total estate property should be distributed by the executor on April 30, Year 3.

Ex. 17-4 After payment of all liabilities of the Estate of Rhoda Ross, deceased, and the completion of distributions to income beneficiaries, the trial balance of the estate was as follows on December 17, Year 6:

	Dr (Cr)
Principal	
Principal cash	$ 100,000
200 shares of Excel Corporation common stock, at current fair value	60,000
$50,000 face amount of 10% Engle Corporation bonds, plus accrued in-	
terest at date of death, at current fair value	55,000
Estate principal balance	(200,000)
Gain on disposal of principal property	(15,000)
Total	$ -0-

Remaining devises to be distributed were as follows:

(1) All 200 shares of Excel Corporation common stock to Leah Ross, daughter
(2) $25,000 face amount of 10% Engle Corporation bonds to Ward Ross, son
(3) $60,000 checking account balance (included in principal cash) in acct. no. 6158 at Bank of America to University of Carlin, a nonprofit organization
(4) $50,000 cash to Music Center Fund, a nonprofit organization
(5) Residue of estate to Roberta Jones, sister

Prepare a working paper to show how the foregoing devises are to be distributed on December 17, Year 6. The following column headings are suggested: Devisee, Type of devise, Gross devise amount, Abated amount, Net devise amount. The Net devise amount column should total $215,000, the carrying amount (and current fair value) of the estate principal property.

Ex. 17-5 Prepare journal entries (omit explanations) for the following selected transactions of the executor of the will of Lincoln Johnson, deceased:

Year 2
Dec. 6   Executor Grant Hayes discovered a certificate for 1,000 shares of Coburn Company common stock with a current fair value of $6 a share. Hayes had filed the inventory of estate property with the probate court on November 14, Year 2.

14   Hayes distributed a general devise of $2,500 cash to Garfield Arthur, Johnson's nephew.

26   Hayes was authorized by the probate court to receive a fee of $1,000 (all allocable to principal) for services to date. Hayes prepared the check.

31   Hayes paid liabilities of the Estate of Lincoln Johnson in the amount of $9,200.

Ex. 17-6   Selected transactions and events completed by the executor of the will of D. C. Kane, who died on October 15, Year 10, are listed below:

Oct. 20   Inventory of estate property (at current fair value) was filed with the court as follows:

Cash...	*$ 88,800*
Real property	*148,000*
Arriba Company common stock.............................	*60,000*
Carter Corporation bonds ($40,000 face amount)	*40,000*
Accrued interest on Carter Corporation bonds	*600*
Personal and household effects.............................	*23,500*

29   A certificate for 150 shares of Basin Corporation common stock valued at $9,000 was found in the coat pocket of an old suit belonging to the decedent.

Nov. 10   A cash dividend of $520 was received on the Arriba Company common stock. The stock had been willed as a specific devise to Edward Kane, son of D. C. Kane.

15   Liabilities of D. C. Kane in the amount of $30,000 were paid.

22   Administrative costs of $3,240 were paid. All costs are chargeable to principal.

29   Bonds of Carter Corporation were sold at 94, plus accrued interest of $1,050.

30   Arriba Company common stock and the cash dividend of $520 received on November 10 were transferred to Edward Kane.

Prepare journal entries to record the foregoing transactions and events in the accounting records of the executor of the will of D. C. Kane, deceased. Omit explanations for the journal entries.

Ex. 17-7   The inexperienced accountant for Lillian Crane, executor of the will of Marion Wilson, deceased, prepared the following journal entries, among others:

Year 5

Apr. 25   Marketable Securities................................ *10,400*
                    Estate Principal Balance *10,400*
          To record supplemental inventory for property discovered
          subsequent to filing of original inventory.

30   Distribution Expense.................................. *800*
                    Income Cash *800*
          To record distribution of income cash to residuary devisee,
          as required by the will.

(continued)

Year 5

May 27	*Accounts Payable*	*7,400*	
	Principal Cash		*7,400*

To record following liabilities paid:

Funeral costs	*$2,500*	
Hospital bills	*3,800*	
Doctor's fees	*1,100*	
Total	*$7,400*	

Prepare journal entries for Lillian Crane, executor of the will of Marion Wilson, deceased, on May 31, Year 5, to correct the foregoing journal entries. Do not reverse the foregoing entries.

Ex. 17-8 The accountant for the executor of the will of Howard Jones, deceased, prepared the following trial balance on December 18, Year 4, the date the estate was closed:

MARIAN SMITH, EXECUTOR
Of the Will of Howard Jones, Deceased
Trial Balance
December 18, Year 4

	Dr (Cr)
Principal	
Estate Principal balance (June 18, Year 4)	*$(150,000)*
Property discovered	*(20,000)*
Gain on disposal of principal property	*(1,000)*
Liabilities paid	*40,000*
Devises distributed	*125,000*
Administrative costs	*6,000*
Total	*$ -0-*
Income	
Interest revenue	*$ (10,000)*
Dividend revenue	*(15,000)*
Distributions to income beneficiaries	*25,000*
Total	*-0-*

Prepare a charge and discharge statement for Marian Smith, executor of the will of Howard Jones, deceased, on December 18, Year 4. (Disregard supporting exhibits.)

Ex. 17-9 Barbara Coleman, executor of the will of Robert Kaplan, who died on August 10, Year 2, prepared the following trial balance on February 10, Year 3:

BARBARA COLEMAN, EXECUTOR
Of the Will of Robert Kaplan, Deceased
Trial Balance
February 10, Year 3

	Dr (Cr)
Principal cash	$ 26,000
Income cash	490
Estate principal balance	(117,000)
Property discovered	(1,800)
Gain on disposal of principal property	(1,200)
Administrative costs	3,000
Liabilities paid	24,500
Devises distributed	66,500
Interest revenue	(3,590)
Distributions to income beneficiaries	2,000
Expenses chargeable to income	1,100
Total	$ -0-

Prepare an *interim* charge and discharge statement for the period August 10, Year 2, through February 10, Year 3. (Do not prepare supporting exhibits.)

Ex. 17-10   The trial balance of Wanda Wardlow, Executor of the will of William Wardlow, deceased, on June 30, Year 9, the filing date for the final charge and discharge statement, included the following:

Administrative costs	$ 5,000
Property discovered	36,000
Devises distributed	347,366
Distributions to income beneficiaries	3,110
Dividend revenue	3,000
Estate principal balance	324,484
Interest revenue	110
Liabilities paid	7,844
Loss on disposal of principal property	274

Prepare a closing entry for Wanda Wardlow, Executor of the will of William Wardlow, deceased, on June 30, Year 9.

Ex. 17-11   Pursuant to the will of Gina Adams, the residue of her estate after probate of the will is to be transferred to a testamentary trust. The following trial balance was prepared from the ledger of the estate on June 30, Year 5:

	Dr (Cr)
Principal cash	$ 115,000
Income cash	6,750
Marketable securities	105,000
Estate principal balance	(265,000)
Property discovered	(13,000)
Gain on disposal of principal property	(12,000)

(continued)

	Dr (Cr)
Administrative costs...	5,400
Liabilities paid	16,000
Devises distributed...	48,600
Interest revenue	(4,000)
Dividend revenue	(4,500)
Expenses chargeable to income.....................................	1,750
Total	$ -0-

a Prepare journal entries to transfer the residuary devise to the trustee and to close the accounting records of the estate.

b Prepare a journal entry to open the accounting records of the trust.

Ex. 17-12 The trial balance of the Wilson Woodrow Trust on April 30, Year 7, a date on which the trustee rendered a charge and discharge statement to the probate court, included the following:

	Debit	Credit
Administrative costs (chargeable to principal)................	$ 1,700	
Distributions to income beneficiary	2,000	
Expenses chargeable to income	800	
Interest revenue...		$ 1,600
Marketable securities	80,000	
Principal cash...	30,000	
Trust income balance		1,200
Trust principal balance		111,700
Totals	$114,500	$114,500

Prepare a closing entry for the Wilson Woodrow Trust on April 30, Year 7.

CASES

Case 17-1 At a meeting in his office, Carl Roberts, managing partner of Roberts & Webb, CPAs, is asked by Albert Hopp, a wealthy tax client, to approve Hopp's naming Roberts as executor of his and his terminally ill wife's wills and as trustee of their testamentary trusts. Hopp tells Roberts that a bank trust department would not be as effective in the roles as Roberts because of the complexities of Hopp's investments, liabilities, and tax matters. Roberts informs Hopp that, as a partner in his firm, Roberts would have to use firm personnel in administering the estate and trust, and that such an arrangement might create a conflict of interest between Roberts as trustee and Roberts as partner. Roberts explained to Hopp that, under the quality control procedures established by Roberts & Webb for the acceptance of new clients, he would have to consult with his three partners before accepting the engagement as executor of the Hopp wills and testamentary trusts.

Instructions

If you were a partner in the Roberts & Webb firm, would you approve Carl Roberts's acceptance of the proffered executor and trustee appointments by the Hopps? Explain.

Case 17-2   The estate of Mary Carr included the following securities on the date of death, April 16, Year 2 (all of which are a part of the residuary devise):

(1) Sand Company 12% bonds due June 16, Year 12: face amount $100,000; current fair value on April 16, Year 2 (excluding accrued interest), $103,500; interest payable June 16 and December 16 of each year.

(2) Palko Corporation common stock, 5,000 shares; current fair value on April 16, Year 2, $68,000; dividend of $1 a share declared April 1, payable May 1 to stockholders of record April 14.

(3) Palko Corporation 8%, $100 par, cumulative preferred stock, 1,000 shares; current fair value on April 16, Year 2, $97,500. Dividends are paid semiannually January 1 and July 1, and there are no dividends in arrears.

Instructions

a Inform the executor of the will of Mary Carr, deceased, which of the foregoing items constitute income and which constitute principal of the estate.

b If the dividends were in arrears on the Palko Corporation 8%, $100 par, cumulative preferred stock, would your answer to **a** be any different? Explain.

Case 17-3   James Saliba transferred a manufacturing enterprise and 10,000 shares of MP Company common stock to Fidelity Trust Company to be held in trust for the benefit of his son, Robert, for life, with the remainder to go to Robert's son, Edward. Fidelity Trust Company insured the enterprise with Boston Insurance Company under two policies. One policy was a standard fire insurance policy covering the buildings and equipment. The other policy covered any loss of income during periods when the enterprise was inoperable as a result of fire or other catastrophe. The buildings and equipment subsequently were destroyed by fire, and Boston Insurance Company paid claims under both policies to Fidelity Trust Company.

Shortly after the 10,000 shares of MP Company common stock had been transferred to Fidelity Trust Company, MP Company declared a dividend of 10 shares of Monte Oil Corporation common stock for each 100 shares of MP Company common stock held. The Monte Oil common stock had been acquired as an investment by MP Company.

During the same year, MP Company directors split the common stock 2 for 1. After the distribution of the new shares, Fidelity Trust Company disposed of 10,000 shares of MP Company common stock.

Instructions

How should Fidelity Trust Company handle the events that have been described above as to distribution between the income beneficiary and the remainderman? State reasons for making the distribution in the manner that you recommend.

Case 17-4   In reviewing the accounting records of Stanley Koyanagi, executor of the will of Edward Dunn, who died January 16, Year 7, you study the will and other documents, which reveal that (1) Dunn's son received a specific devise of the decedent's only rental property and 12% bonds of Padre Corporation, $50,000 face amount, due March 1, Year 21; (2) Dunn's daughter was the beneficiary of a life insurance policy (face amount $100,000) on which the decedent had paid the premiums; and (3) Dunn's widow had been left the remainder of the estate in trust.

Your review also reveals the following transactions and events occurring from the time of Dunn's death to March 1, Year 7:

(1) Jan. 17 $3,195 was received from the redemption of $3,000 face amount of Camm Corporation 13% bonds that matured on January 15, Year 7.

(2) Jan. 20 $500 was received from Pittson Corporation as a cash dividend of $1 a share on common stock, declared December 1, Year 6, payable January 15, Year 7, to stockholders of record January 2, Year 7.

(3) Jan. 20 $5,040 was paid to Witter & Company, stockbrokers, for the acquisition of five Seaboard, Inc., 14% bonds due June 30, Year 18.

(4) Jan. 21   30 shares of common stock were received from Ragusa Company, constituting a 2% stock dividend declared December 14, Year 6, distributable January 20, Year 7, to stockholders of record January 15, Year 7.

(5) Feb. 1 $200 quarterly interest was paid by the executor on a promissory note payable due January 31, Year 8.

(6) Feb. 1   Dunn's physician was paid $2,500 for services rendered during Dunn's last illness.

(7) Feb. 2 $600 was received from East Corporation as a cash dividend of $0.25 a share on common stock, declared January 18, Year 7, payable January 30, Year 7, to stockholders of record January 27, Year 7.

(8) Feb. 3 $575 rent revenue for February was received and deposited in the bank.

(9) Feb. 10 $890 was paid for property taxes covering the period from February 1 to July 31, Year 7.

(10) Mar. 1 $1,802 was paid to the Internal Revenue Service as the remaining income taxes owed by the decedent for Year 6 taxable income.

Instructions

Indicate whether each transaction should be:

Allocated between principal and income

Allocated between principal and beneficiaries (devisees)

Attributed solely to income

Attributed solely to principal

Attributed solely to beneficiaries (devisees)

State reasons supporting your conclusions as to how each transaction should be handled.

PROBLEMS

Pr. 17-1   Mildred Young died on June 5, Year 10. Michael Synn was named executor in the will that had been prepared by Young's attorney. On December 31, Year 10, the accountant for the executor prepared the following trial balance:

MICHAEL SYNN, EXECUTOR
Of the Will of Mildred Young, Deceased
Trial Balance
December 31, Year 10

	Dr (Cr)
Principal cash	$ 25,700
Income cash	13,000
Investments in bonds.	268,300
Investments in common stocks	224,300
Household effects.	39,500
Gains on disposal of principal property	(2,200)
Property discovered.	(16,800)
Liabilities paid	36,200
Administrative costs.	10,000
Devises distributed.	15,000
Estate principal balance	(600,000)
Dividend revenue	(14,200)
Interest revenue	(18,500)
Expenses chargeable to income.	720
Distributions to income beneficiaries	18,980
Total	$ -0-

Instructions
The amount in the Estate Principal Balance ledger account represents the inventory of estate property on June 5, Year 10. Prepare an interim charge and discharge statement for the executor of the will of Mildred Young for the period June 5 through December 31, Year 10. Supporting exhibits are not required for any items except the listing of property comprising the estate principal balance on December 31, Year 10.

Pr. 17-2   Pablo Garcia died on March 1, Year 8, leaving a valid will in which he named Mark Castro as executor and trustee pending final distribution of estate property to Manuel Montejano, a nephew. The will instructed the executor to transfer Garcia's personal effects and automobile to the nephew, to pay estate taxes, outstanding liabilities, and administrative costs of the estate, and to transfer the remaining estate property to a trust for the benefit of the nephew. Income from the estate and the trust was to be paid to the nephew, who was to receive the principal (corpus) upon graduation from State University.

The inventory of estate property on March 1, Year 8, consisted of the following:

Cash	*$ 44,440*
Certificate of deposit at Standard Savings Bank (includes accrued interest of	
$1,100)	*101,100*
Personal effects	*13,200*
Automobile	*2,800*
Investments in common stocks	*77,000*

The following transactions or events were completed by the executor through December 10, Year 8:

(1) Discovered a savings account of $6,290 in the name of Pablo Garcia. (Debit Principal Cash.)
(2) Paid administrative costs for the estate, $5,200. All costs are chargeable to principal.
(3) Disposed of common stock with a carrying amount of $20,000 for $26,020, net of commissions.
(4) Transferred personal effects and automobile to Manuel Montejano.
(5) Received income as follows (there were no expenses chargeable to income): Interest, $5,200 (includes accrued interest on certificate of deposit on March 1, Year 8); dividends, $1,400.
(6) Distributed the income of the estate to Manuel Montejano.
(7) Paid liabilities of decedent, $8,050.
(8) Paid estate taxes, $32,000. (Debit Estate Taxes Paid.)
(9) Closed the accounting records of the estate and transferred property to the Manuel Montejano Trust.

Instructions

a Prepare journal entries to record the foregoing transactions or events and to close the accounting records of the estate. Disregard homestead allowance, exempt property, and family allowance.
b Prepare a charge and discharge statement immediately after the transfer of estate property to the Manuel Montejano Trust. Do not prepare any supporting exhibits.
c Prepare a journal entry to open the accounting records for the testamentary trust, the Manuel Montejano Trust.

Pr. 17-3 Janet Mann died on May 31, Year 1. Her will provided that all liabilities and costs were to be paid and that the property was to be distributed as follows:

(1) Personal residence to George Mann, widower of Janet Mann.
(2) U.S. Treasury 12% bonds and Permian Company common stock—to be placed in trust. All income to go to George Mann during his lifetime.
(3) Sonar Corporation 9% bonds—devised to Eleanor Mann, daughter of Janet Mann.
(4) Cash—a devise of $15,000 to Dudley Mann, son of Janet Mann.
(5) Residue of estate—to be divided equally between the two children of Janet Mann—Eleanor and Dudley.

Additional Information

(1) The will further provided that during the administration period George Mann was to be paid $1,500 a month from estate income. Estate and inheritance taxes

were to be borne by the residue of the estate. Dudley Mann was named as executor and trustee.

(2) The following inventory of the decedent's property was prepared:

Personal residence..	$245,000
Jewelry—diamond ring..	14,600
City National Bank—checking account; balance May 31, Year 1..........	43,000
$200,000 U.S. Treasury 12% bonds, due Year 20, interest payable Mar. 1 and Sept. 1 (includes accrued interest of $6,000)......................	206,000
$10,000 Sonar Corporation 9% bonds, due Year 10, interest payable May 31 and Nov. 30..	9,900
Permian Company common stock, 800 shares..........................	64,000
Dividends receivable on Permian Company common stock..............	800
XY Company common stock, 700 shares...............................	70,000

(3) The executor opened an estate checking account and transferred the decedent's checking account balance to it. Other deposits in the estate checking account through July 1, Year 2, were as follows:

Interest received on $200,000 U.S. Treasury 12% bonds:	
Sept. 1, Year 1..	$12,000
Mar. 1, Year 2	12,000
Dividends received on Permian Company common stock:	
June 15, Year 1, declared May 7, Year 1, payable to holders to record May 27, Year 1...	800
Sept. 15, Year 1	800
Dec. 15, Year 1	1,200
Mar. 15, Year 2..	1,500
June 15, Year 2..	1,500
Net proceeds of June 19, Year 1, disposal of 700 shares of XY Company common stock..	68,810

(4) Payments were made from the estate's checking account through July 1, Year 2, for the following:

Liabilities of decedent paid (including funeral costs)......................	$12,000
Additional prior years' federal and state income taxes, plus interest to May 31, Year 1	1,810
Year 1 income taxes of Janet Mann for the period Jan. 1, Year 1, through May 31, Year 1, in excess of amounts paid by the decedent on declarations of estimated tax	9,100
Federal and state fiduciary income taxes, fiscal years ending June 30, Year 1, and June 30, Year 2...	2,400
Estate and inheritance taxes	43,000
Monthly payments to George Mann, 13 payments of $1,500	19,500
Attorney's and accountant's fees (allocated entirely to principal)...........	25,000

(5) The executor, Dudley Mann, waived a fee. However, he desired to receive his mother's diamond ring in lieu of the $15,000 cash devise. All parties agreed to this in writing, and the probate court's approval was secured. All devises other

than the assets to be held in trust and the residue of the estate were delivered on July 1, Year 1.

Instructions

Prepare a charge and discharge statement as to principal and income, with supporting exhibits, to accompany the formal court accounting on behalf of the executor of the will of Janet Mann, deceased, for the period from May 31, Year 1, through July 1, Year 2. In accordance with the will, the executor accrued the interest and dividends on the estate investments to July 1, Year 2. Disregard homestead allowance, exempt property, and family allowance.

Pr. 17-4 The will of Frederick Doheny directed that the executor, Richard Cordes, liquidate the entire estate within two years of the date of death and pay the net proceeds and income to United Charities. Frederick Doheny, a bachelor, died on February 1, Year 10, after a brief illness.

An inventory of the decedent's property was prepared, and the current fair value of all items was determined. The preliminary inventory, before the computation of any appropriate income accruals on the property in inventory, follows:

	Current fair values
Union Bank checking account...	$ 33,500
$60,000 face amount Sun City bonds, interest rate 12%, payable Jan. 1 and	
July 1, maturity date July 1, Year 14.................................	59,000
2,000 shares Ron Corp. common stock	220,000
Term life insurance: beneficiary, Estate of Frederick Doheny	20,000
Residence ($86,500) and furniture ($23,500)	110,000

During Year 10, the following transactions or events occurred:

(1) The interest on the Sun City bonds was received. The bonds were disposed of on July 1, for $59,000, and the proceeds and interest accrued on February 1, Year 10 ($600), were paid to United Charities.

(2) Ron Corp. paid cash dividends of $1 a share on March 1 and December 1, and distributed a 10% stock dividend on July 1. All dividends had been declared 45 days before each payment date and were payable to holders of record as of 40 days before each payment date. In September, 1,000 shares of Ron Corp. common stock were disposed of for $105 a share, and the proceeds were paid to United Charities.

(3) The personal residence was rented furnished at $900 a month commencing April 1, Year 10. The rent was paid monthly, in advance. Property taxes of $1,200 for the calendar Year 10 were paid. The house and furnishings had estimated economic lives of 40 years and 8 years, respectively. The part-time gardener was paid four months' wages totaling $500 on April 30 for services performed, and then was released.

(4) The Union Bank checking account was closed, and the balance of $8,500 was transferred to a bank checking account for the estate.

(5) The proceeds of the term life insurance were received on March 1 and deposited in the bank checking account for the estate.

(6) The following cash payments were made:
   (a) Funeral costs and costs of last illness, $3,500.
   (b) Amount due on Year 9 income taxes of decedent, $700.
   (c) Attorney's and accountant's fees, $20,000, of which $3,025 was allocated to income.

(7) On December 31, the balance of the undistributed income, except for $500, was paid to United Charities. The balance of the cash on hand derived from the principal of the estate also was paid to United Charities on December 31. On December 31, the executor resigned and waived all fees.

Instructions

Prepare a charge and discharge statement, together with supporting exhibits, for the executor of the will of Frederick Doheny, deceased, for the period February 1 through December 31, Year 10. Disregard depreciation.

Part 5

International Accounting

Once an obscure matter, *International Accounting Standards* have come into prominence as a result of several forces: increased international trade and securities investments; the breakup of the former Union of Soviet Socialist Republics; the political, monetary, and economic union activities of the twelve member countries of the European Community; and other political and economic changes in central Europe and the Far East. Both *International Accounting Standards* and pronouncements of the U.S. Financial Accounting Standards Board have addressed issues involved in accounting for transactions denominated in a foreign currency and the translation of foreign currency financial statements.

18

International Accounting Standards; Accounting for Foreign Currency Transactions

Recent political events—such as the dissolution of the Union of Soviet Socialist Republics and the autonomy of its former satellite nations in Eastern Europe—and economic events—such as increased international trading in securities and the projected economic and currency unification of the European Community[1]—have focused attention on the pressing need for more uniformity in international accounting standards. Two organizations in the forefront of attempts to achieve such uniformity are the International Accounting Standards Committee (IASC) and the International Organization of Securities Commissions (IOSCO). In this chapter, I first discuss the work of the IASC, as abetted by the IOSCO; later, accounting for a multinational enterprise's business transactions denominated in a foreign currency is described and illustrated.

INTERNATIONAL ACCOUNTING STANDARDS

International Accounting Standards Committee

The International Accounting Standards Committee was formed in 1973 by professional accounting organizations of 10 countries. Currently its membership includes accounting groups from about 80 countries. Headquartered in London, the IASC is governed by a board of up to 17 members, of whom 13 are representatives of member country organizations and up to 4 are representatives of other international organizations having an interest in accounting, such as the Organization for Economic Cooperation and Development and the United Nations Commission on Transnational Corporations. To be issued, International Accounting Standards

---

[1] Member nations of the European Community (EC) are Belgium, Denmark, France, Germany, Greece, Ireland, Italy, Luxembourg, the Netherlands, Portugal, Spain, and the United Kingdom.

require the approval of three-fourths of the board members; these standards have no authoritative support unless they are adopted by standard-setting bodies in the member countries, such as the Financial Accounting Standards Board. The American Institute of Certified Public Accountants, as a member of the ISAC, is committed to using its best efforts to persuade the FASB to adopt International Accounting Standards; however, to date there is no clear evidence of this commitment's being accomplished.

Through 1990, the IASC had issued 31 *International Accounting Standards,* dealing with such accounting issues as consolidated financial statements, depreciation, segment reporting, leases, revenue recognition, business combinations, and related-party disclosures. To promote adoption of the *Standards,* the IASC has in the past accommodated alternative accounting treatments in several of its pronouncements. For example, in *International Accounting Standard 2,* the IASC sanctioned the first-in, first-out; weighted-average; last-in, first-out; or base stock method of assigning cost to inventories. And in *International Accounting Standard 11,* the IASC permitted either the percentage-of-completion method or the completed-contract method of accounting for construction-type contracts.

In an effort to narrow the diversity in financial accounting among its members, the IASC issued in 1989 *Exposure Draft 32,* ''Comparability of Financial Statements,'' which would amend 13 International Accounting Standards to eliminate some previously approved alternative accounting methods. For example, *International Accounting Standard 2* would be amended to make first-in, first-out and weighted-average the required or preferred methods of assigning cost to inventories. The base stock method would be disallowed, but the last-in, first-out method would be permitted as an alternative treatment, *provided that a reconciliation of reported net income with net income under the required or preferred methods is presented.* Likewise, *International Accounting Standard 11* would be amended to prohibit use of the completed-contract method for construction-type contracts. All told, *Exposure Draft 32* would eliminate 23 alternative accounting methods that had been sanctioned in prior *International Accounting Standards.*

Among the *International Accounting Standards* issued by the IASC are four that deal with topics covered in this book: joint ventures, business combinations, consolidated financial statements, and influenced investees. A fifth standard dealing with changes in foreign exchange rates is dealt with elsewhere in this chapter and in Chapter 19. In the following section, I draw on *AICPA Professional Standards,* vol. 2, . . . ''International Accounting . . . as of June 1, 1992,'' to describe briefly the four standards listed above.

IAS 31, **''Financial Reporting of Interests in Joint Ventures''**   In this pronouncement, the IASC permitted either the *proportionate consolidation method (proportionate share method* in Chapter 3, pp. 109–111) or the *equity method* for a venturer's investment in a *jointly controlled entity,* which might be a corporation or a partnership. As pointed out in Chapter 3, U.S. accounting standards require the equity method of accounting for investments in corporate joint ventures but permit either the equity method or the proportionate share method of accounting for investments in unincorporated joint ventures.

IAS 22, **"Accounting for Business Combinations"** The IASC required purchase-type accounting for all business combinations except those deemed a *uniting of interests,* defined as a combination in which the stockholders of the constituent companies combine into one entity the whole of the net assets and operations of those companies to achieve a continuing mutual sharing of the risks and benefits of the combined enterprise. For a uniting of interests-type combination, pooling-of-interests accounting *may* be used. Further, goodwill in a purchase-type business combination may be charged immediately to stockholders' equity of the combined enterprise instead of being amortized to future accounting periods. Minority interest in net assets of a purchased subsidiary may be valued by either method **1** or method **2** on page 270 of Chapter 6.

IAS 27, **"Consolidated Financial Statements and Accounting for Investments in Subsidiaries"** Among the provisions of *IAS 27* are the following:

1 Consolidation policy is based on *control* rather than solely on *ownership* (see Chapter 6, page 248).

2 Intercompany transactions, profits or gains, and losses are eliminated in full, regardless of an existing minority interest.

3 Minority interest in net income of subsidiary is displayed separately in the consolidated income statement. Minority interest in net assets of subsidiary is displayed separately from liabilities and stockholders' equity in the consolidated balance sheet. Thus, the IASC rejected both the parent company concept and the economic unit concept (see Chapter 6, pages 266–268).

4 In the unconsolidated financial statements of a parent company, investments in subsidiaries that are included in the consolidated statements may be accounted for by either the equity method, as required by the SEC (see Chapter 7, page 343), or the cost method.

IAS 28, **"Accounting for Investments in Associates"** Apart from using the term *associate* for an *influenced investee,* as that U.S. terminology is applied (see Chapter 10, page 511), the provisions of *IAS 28* resemble those of *APB Opinion No. 18,* "The Equity Method of Accounting for Investments in Common Stock."

International Organization of Securities Commissions

Securities regulators from about 50 countries constitute the membership of the IOSCO, whose goal is to ease the impact of differences in securities trading regulations among its members. Recently, the IOSCO, whose U.S. member is the Securities and Exchange Commission, undertook to determine whether IASC standards were appropriate for financial reports filed in IOSCO member countries to meet securities trading requirements. Additionally, a working group consisting of U.S., French, and Ontario (Canada) IOSCO members undertook to identify accounting areas where the IASC has not issued pronouncements. These activities by the IOSCO should enhance the IASC's influence in finding wider acceptance of *International Accounting Standards.*

ACCOUNTING FOR FOREIGN CURRENCY TRANSACTIONS

In most countries, a foreign country's currency is treated as though it were a ***commodity,*** or a ***money-market instrument.*** In the United States, for example, foreign currencies are bought and sold by the international banking departments of commercial banks. These foreign currency transactions are entered into on behalf of the banks' multinational enterprise customers, and for the banks' own account.

The buying and selling of foreign currencies as though they were commodities result in variations in the ***exchange rate*** between the currencies of two countries. For example, a daily newspaper might quote exchange rates for the British pound (£) as follows, based on the prior day's transactions in the pound:

	Foreign currency in dollars	Dollars in foreign currency
Britain (pound)	1.6065	0.6225

The first column indicates that £1 could be exchanged for approximately $1.61; the second column indicates that $1 could be exchanged for approximately £0.62. Note that the two exchange rates are ***reciprocals*** (1 ÷ 1.6065 = 0.6225).

The exchange rate illustrated above is the ***selling spot rate*** charged by the bank for current sales of the foreign currency. The bank's ***buying spot rate*** for the currency typically is less than the selling spot rate; the ***agio*** (or ***spread***) between the selling and buying spot rates represents gross profit to a trader in foreign currency. In addition to spot rates, there are ***forward rates,*** which apply to foreign currency transactions to be consummated on a future date. Forward rates apply to ***forward exchange contracts,*** which are discussed in a subsequent section of this chapter.

To illustrate the application of exchange rates, assume that a U.S. business enterprise required £10,000 (10,000 British pounds) to pay for merchandise acquired from a British supplier. At the $1.6065 selling spot rate, the U.S. multinational enterprise would pay $16,065 (£10,000 × $1.6065 = $16,065) for the 10,000 British pounds.

Factors influencing fluctuations in exchange rates include a nation's balance of payments surplus or deficit, differing global rates of inflation, money-market variations (such as interest rates) in individual countries, capital investments levels, and monetary actions of central banks of various nations.

FASB Statement No. 52

In December 1981, the Financial Accounting Standards Board issued ***FASB Statement No. 52,*** "Foreign Currency Translation," in which it established accounting standards for matters involving foreign currencies. The accounting standards established by the FASB for foreign currency transactions such as purchases and sales of merchandise, loans, and forward exchange contracts are discussed in the following sections.

Transactions Involving Foreign Currencies

A *multinational* (or *transnational*) *enterprise* is a business enterprise that carries on operations in more than one nation, through a network of branches, divisions, influenced investees, joint ventures, and subsidiaries. Multinational enterprises obtain material and capital in countries where such resources are plentiful. Multinational enterprises manufacture their products in nations where wages and other operating costs are lowest, and they sell their products in countries that provide the most profitable markets. Many of the largest multinational enterprises are headquartered in the United States.

A multinational enterprise headquartered in the United States engages in sales, purchases, and loans with independent foreign enterprises as well as with its branches, divisions, influenced investees, or subsidiaries in other countries. If the transactions with independent foreign enterprises are *denominated* (or expressed) in terms of the U.S. dollar, no accounting problems arise for the U.S. multinational enterprise. The sale, purchase, or loan transaction is recorded in dollars in the accounting records of the U.S. enterprise; the independent foreign enterprise must obtain the dollars necessary to complete the transaction through the foreign exchange department of its bank.

Often, however, the transactions described above are negotiated and settled in terms of the foreign enterprise's *local currency unit* (LCU). In such circumstances, the U.S. enterprise must account for the transaction denominated in foreign currency in terms of U.S. dollars. This accounting, described as *foreign currency translation,* is accomplished by applying the appropriate exchange rate between the foreign currency and the U.S. dollar.

Purchase of Merchandise from a Foreign Supplier

To illustrate a purchase of merchandise from a foreign supplier, assume that on April 18, Year 6, Worldwide Corporation purchased merchandise from a German supplier at a cost of 100,000 deutsche marks (DM). The April 18, Year 6, selling spot rate was DM1 = $0.45.[2] Because Worldwide was a customer of good credit standing, the German supplier made the sale on 30-day open account.

Assuming that Worldwide uses the perpetual inventory system, it records the April 18, Year 6, purchase as follows:

Journal entry for purchase of merchandise from German supplier, payment to be made in deutsche marks

Inventories	*45,000*	
Trade Accounts Payable		*45,000*

To record purchase on 30-day open account from German supplier for DM100,000, translated at selling spot rate of DM1 = $0.45 (DM100,000 × $0.45 = $45,000).

The *selling* spot was used in the journal entry, because it was the rate at which the liability to the German supplier could have been settled on April 18, Year 6.

---

[2] Exchange rates fluctuate significantly over time; thus, the exchange rates illustrated in this chapter may differ significantly from current exchange rates.

Transaction Gains and Losses

During the period that the trade account payable to the German supplier remains unpaid, the *selling* spot rate for deutsche marks may change. If the selling spot rate *decreases,* Worldwide will realize a *transaction gain;* if the *selling* spot rate *increases,* Worldwide will incur a *transaction loss.* Transaction gains and losses are included in the measurement of net income for the accounting period in which the spot rate changes.[3]

To illustrate, assume that on April 30, Year 6, the selling spot rate for deutsche marks was DM1 = $0.446 and Worldwide prepares financial statements monthly. The accountant for Worldwide records the following journal entry with respect to the trade account payable to the German supplier:

Journal entry to record transaction gain on date financial statements are prepared	*Trade Accounts Payable...*	*400*	
	Transaction Gains and Losses		*400*
	To recognize transaction gain applicable to April 18, Year 6, purchase from German supplier, as follows:		
	Liability recorded on Apr. 18, Year 6.....................	*$45,000*	
	Less: Liability translated at Apr. 30, Year 6, selling spot rate:		
	DM1 = $0.446 (DM100,000 × $0.446 = $44,600).......	*44,600*	
	Transaction gain	*$ 400*	

Assume further that the selling spot rate on May 18, Year 6, was DM1 = $0.44. The May 18, Year 6, journal entry for Worldwide's payment of the liability to the German supplier is shown below:

Journal entry for payment of liability to German supplier denominated in deutsche marks	*Trade Accounts Payable......................................*	*44,600*	
	Transaction Gains and Losses		*600*
	Cash		*44,000*
	To record payment for DM100,000 draft to settle liability to German supplier, and recognition of transaction gain (DM100,000 × $0.44 = $44,000).		

Two-Transaction Perspective and One-Transaction Perspective   The journal entries above and on page 821 reflect the *two-transaction perspective* for interpreting a foreign trade transaction. Under this concept, which was sanctioned by the Financial Accounting Standards Board in *FASB Statement No. 52,* Worldwide's dealings with the German supplier essentially were *two separate transactions.* One transaction was the purchase of the merchandise; the second transaction was the acquisition of the foreign currency required to pay the liability for the merchandise purchased. Supporters of the two-transaction perspective argue that an importer's or exporter's assumption of a risk of fluctuations in the exchange rate for a foreign currency is a *financing* decision, not a *merchandising* decision.

---

[3] *FASB Statement No. 52,* "Foreign Currency Translation," FASB (Stamford: 1981), p. 6.

Advocates of an opposing viewpoint, the *one-transaction perspective,* maintain that Worldwide's total transaction gain of $1,000 ($400 + $600 = $1,000) on its purchase from the German supplier should be applied to reduce the cost of the merchandise purchased. Under this approach, Worldwide would not prepare a journal entry on April 30, Year 6, but would prepare the following journal entry on May 18, Year 6 (assuming that all the merchandise purchased on April 18 had been sold by May 18):

<table>
<tr><td rowspan="6" style="text-align:left; vertical-align:top;">Journal entry under
one-transaction
perspective</td><td>Trade Accounts Payable . . . .</td><td>45,000</td><td></td></tr>
<tr><td>   Cost of Goods Sold . . . .</td><td></td><td>1,000</td></tr>
<tr><td>   Cash . . . .</td><td></td><td>44,000</td></tr>
<tr><td colspan="3">To record payment for DM100,000 (DM100,000 × $0.44 = $44,000)
to settle liability to German supplier, and offset of resultant transac-
tion gain against cost of goods sold.</td></tr>
</table>

In effect, supporters of the one-transaction perspective for foreign trade activities consider the original amount recorded for a foreign merchandise purchase as an *estimate,* subject to adjustment when the exact cash outlay required for the purchase is known. Thus, the one-transaction proponents emphasize the *cash-payment* aspect, rather than the *bargained-price* aspect, of the transaction.

The author concurs with the FASB's support for the two-transaction perspective for foreign trade transactions and for loans receivable and payable denominated in a foreign currency. The separability of the merchandising and financing aspects of a foreign trade transaction is an undeniable fact. In delaying payment of a foreign trade purchase transaction, an importer has made a decision to assume the risk of exchange rate fluctuations. This risk assumption is measured by the transaction gain or loss recorded at the time of payment for the purchase of merchandise (or on the dates of intervening financial statements).

Sale of Merchandise to a Foreign Customer

Assume that on May 17, Year 6, Worldwide Corporation, which uses the perpetual inventory system, sold merchandise acquired from a U.S. supplier for $12,000 to a French customer for 100,000 French francs (FF), with payment due June 16, Year 6. On May 17, Year 6, the buying spot rate for the franc was FF1 = $0.18. Worldwide prepares the following journal entries on May 17, Year 6:

<table>
<tr><td rowspan="7" style="text-align:left; vertical-align:top;">Journal entries for sale
of merchandise to
French customer,
payment to be received
in francs</td><td>Trade Accounts Receivable . . . .</td><td>18,000</td><td></td></tr>
<tr><td>   Sales . . . .</td><td></td><td>18,000</td></tr>
<tr><td colspan="3">To record sale on 30-day open account to French customer for
FF100,000, translated at buying spot rate of FF1 = $0.18
(FF100,000 × $0.18 = $18,000).</td></tr>
<tr><td>Cost of Goods Sold . . . .</td><td>12,000</td><td></td></tr>
<tr><td>   Inventories . . . .</td><td></td><td>12,000</td></tr>
<tr><td colspan="3">To record cost of merchandise sold to French customer.</td></tr>
</table>

Assuming that the buying spot rate for the franc was FF1 = $0.17 on May 31, Year 6, when Worldwide prepared its customary monthly financial statements, the following journal entry is appropriate:

<table>
<tr><td rowspan="9" style="vertical-align:top">Journal entry to record transaction loss on date financial statements are prepared</td><td colspan="3">*Transaction Gains and Losses.................................. 1,000*</td></tr>
</table>

Journal entry to record transaction loss on date financial statements are prepared

Transaction Gains and Losses.................................... 1,000
*   Trade Accounts Receivable 1,000*
To recognize transaction loss applicable to May 17, Year 6, sale to
French customer, as follows:
*   Asset recorded on May 17, Year 6.................... $18,000*
*   Less: Asset translated at May 31, Year 6, buying spot*
*   rate: FF1 = $0.17 (FF100,000 × $0.17 = $17,000) 17,000*
*   Transaction loss .... $ 1,000*

If on June 16, Year 6, the date when Worldwide received a draft for FF100,000 from the French customer, the franc had **strengthened** against the dollar to a buying spot rate of FF1 = $0.176, Worldwide's journal entry would be as follows:

Journal entry for receipt from French customer denominated in francs

Cash... 17,600
*   Trade Accounts Receivable 17,000*
*   Transaction Gains and Losses 600*
To record receipt and conversion to dollars of FF100,000 draft in
payment of receivable from French customer, and recognition of
transaction gain (FF100,000 × $0.176 = $17,600).

Loan Payable in a Foreign Currency

If a U.S. multinational enterprise elects to borrow a foreign currency to pay for merchandise acquired from a foreign supplier, the following journal entries would be illustrative (Sfr is the symbol for the Swiss franc):

Journal entries for loan payable in a foreign currency

Year 4
Apr. 30 Inventories... 69,000
*   Trade Accounts Payable 69,000*
*   To record purchase from Swiss supplier for Sfr100,000,*
*   translated at selling spot rate of Sfr1 = $0.69 (Sfr100,000*
*   × $0.69 = $69,000).*

*   30 Trade Accounts Payable 69,000*
*   Notes Payable 69,000*
*   To record borrowing of Sfr100,000 from bank on 30-day,*
*   6% loan to be repaid in Swiss francs, and payment of liabil-*
*   ity to Swiss supplier.*

(continued)

Year 4
May 30 Notes Payable 69,000
       Interest Expense ($69,000 × 0.06 × 30/360)........... 345
       Transaction Gains and Losses....................... 201
          Cash... 69,546
       To record payment for Sfr100,500 draft to settle
       Sfr100,000, 30-day, 6% note, together with Sfr500 interest
       (Sfr100,000 × 0.06 × 30/360 = Sfr500) at selling spot rate
       of Sfr1 = $0.692 (Sfr100,500 × 0.692 = $69,546).

Loan Receivable in a Foreign Currency

A U.S. multinational enterprise's receipt of a promissory note denominated in a foreign currency might be illustrated by the journal entries on page 826 (BF is the symbol for the Belgian franc).

Conclusions Regarding Transactions Involving Foreign Currencies

From the foregoing examples, it is evident that *increases* in the selling spot rate for a foreign currency required by a U.S. multinational enterprise to settle a liability denominated in that currency generate *transaction losses* to the enterprise because more U.S. dollars are required to obtain the foreign currency. Conversely, *decreases* in the selling spot rate produce *transaction gains* to the enterprise because fewer U.S. dollars are required to obtain the foreign currency. In contrast, *increases* in the buying spot rate for a foreign currency to be received by a U.S. multinational enterprise in settlement of a receivable denominated in that currency generate *transaction gains* to the enterprise; *decreases* in the buying spot rate produce *transaction losses*. Mastery of these relationships assures a clearer understanding of the effects of changes in exchange rates for foreign currencies.

Forward Exchange Contracts

Forward exchange contracts are another type of transaction involving foreign currencies. A *forward exchange contract* is an agreement to exchange currencies of different countries on a specified future date at the forward rate in effect when the contract was made. Forward rates may be larger or smaller than spot rates for a foreign currency, depending on the foreign currency dealer's expectations regarding fluctuations in exchange rates for the currency.

    FASB Statement No. 52 established accounting standards for the following types of forward exchange contracts:

1   Contracts not intended to hedge a net investment in a foreign enterprise or an identifiable foreign currency commitment or for speculation

2   Contracts intended to hedge an identifiable foreign currency commitment

3   Contracts for speculation in a foreign currency

The three types of forward exchange contracts, including illustrative journal entries, are discussed in the following sections.

Journal entries for loan
receivable in a foreign
currency

Year 8

May 31 Notes Receivable   30,000
                 Sales   30,000
           To record sale to Belgian customer for 60-day, 9% promis-
           sory note for BF1,000,000, translated at buying spot rate
           of BF1 = $0.03 (BF1,000,000 × $0.03 = $30,000).

     31 Cost of Goods Sold   25,000
                 Inventories   25,000
           To record cost of merchandise sold to Belgian customer.

June 30 Notes Receivable   3,200
           Interest Receivable ($33,200 × 0.09 × 30/360)   249
                 Interest Revenue   249
                 Transaction Gains and Losses   3,200
           To recognize transaction gain applicable to May 31, Year
           8, sale to Belgian customer and to accrue interest on note
           receivable from the customer, valued at the buying spot
           rate of BF 1 = $0.0332. Transaction gain is computed as
           follows:

               Receivable translated at June 30, Year 8,
                 buying spot rate (BF1,000,000 × $0.0332) . . . $33,200
                 Receivable recorded on May 31, Year 8   30,000
                 Transaction gain . . . . $ 3,200

July 30 Cash (BF1,015,000 × $0.0316)   32,074
           Transaction Gains and Losses   1,612
                 Notes Receivable   33,200
                 Interest Receivable   249
                 Interest Revenue [(BF1,000,000 × $0.0316) ×
                 0.09 × 30/360]   237
           To record receipt and conversion to dollars of BF1,015,000
           draft to settle 60-day, 9% note, together with BF15,000
           interest (BF1,000,000 × 0.09 × 60/360 = BF15,000), and
           recognition of transaction loss of $1,612 [(BF1,000,000 +
           BF7,500) × ($0.0332 − $0.0316) = $1,612].

Forward Exchange Contract Not Intended to Hedge or for Speculation   To
hedge is to take measures to reduce or eliminate a potential unfavorable outcome of a
future event. Returning to the illustration of Worldwide Corporation (pages 821–
823), assume that on April 5, Year 6, in anticipation of initiating import transactions
with various German suppliers, Worldwide acquired a 60-day forward exchange
contract for DM500,000. Because Worldwide had no specific contractual or other
commitment to pay deutsche marks on April 5, Year 6, and had no plans to buy and
sell deutsche marks as a speculative investment activity, the forward exchange contract was not a hedge or for speculation. Exchange rates for the deutsche mark on
April 5, Year 6, were as follows:

Exchange rates for
deutsche mark

Spot rates:

Buying *$0.443*

Selling *0.452*

Forward rates:

30-day contracts *0.464*

60-day contracts *0.478*

90-day contracts *0.489*

Thus, the liability for the DM500,000, 60-day forward exchange contract acquired by Worldwide on April 5, Year 6, was $239,000 (DM500,000 × $0.478 = $239,000). The present value of the liability is equal to the $226,000 *selling spot rate* value of the contract (DM500,000 × $0.452 = $226,000). The *discount* on the forward exchange contract, measured by the foreign currency amount of the contract multiplied by the difference between the forward rate and the spot rate on the date of the contract, is *interest cost* that is recognized as interest expense over the term of the contract.

Worldwide's April 5, Year 6, journal entry to record the acquisition of the forward exchange contract is as follows:

Journal entry for
acquisition of forward
exchange contract for
deutsche marks

Investment in Forward Exchange Contract

(DM500,000 × $0.452 selling spot rate) *226,000*

Discount on Forward Exchange Contract Payable

[DM500,000 × ($0.478 − $0.452)] *13,000*

Forward Exchange Contract Payable

(DM500,000 × $0.478 forward rate) *239,000*

To record acquisition of DM500,000 forward exchange contract for
60 days at forward rate of DM1 = $0.478.

During the 60-day term of the DM500,000 forward exchange contract, Worldwide realizes a transaction gain or loss whenever the spot rate for the deutsche mark changes, because the present value of the investment in the contract likewise changes. For example, if the selling spot rate for the deutsche mark on April 30, Year 6, was DM1 = $0.446 and Worldwide prepares monthly financial statements, the following journal entry is required on April 30, Year 6:

Journal entry to
recognize transaction
loss on forward
exchange contract for
deutsche marks

Transaction Gains and Losses [DM500,000 × ($0.452 − $0.446)] *3,000*

Interest Expense ($13,000 × 25⁄60) *5,417*

Investment in Forward Exchange Contract *3,000*

Discount on Forward Exchange Contract Payable *5,417*

To recognize transaction loss on forward exchange contract resulting
from decrease of spot exchange rate for the deutsche mark to $0.446
from $0.452; and to amortize discount on contract to Apr. 30, Year 6.

If the selling spot rate for the deutsche mark was DM1 = $0.449 on May 31, Year 6, the following journal entry is appropriate on that date:

<table>
<tr><td rowspan="1" style="vertical-align:top">Journal entry to
recognize transaction
gain on forward
exchange contract for
deutsche marks</td><td>

Investment in Forward Exchange Contract
  [DM500,000 × ($0.449 − $0.446)] 1,500
Interest Expense ($13,000 × 31/60) 6,717
       Transaction Gains and Losses 1,500
       Discount on Forward Exchange Contract Payable 6,717
To recognize transaction gain on forward exchange contract resulting
from increase of spot exchange rate for the deutsche mark to $0.449
from $0.446; and to amortize discount on contract to May 31, Year 6.
</td></tr>
</table>

Assuming a selling spot rate of DM1 = $0.451 on June 4, Year 6, the maturity date of Worldwide's 60-day forward exchange contract, the following journal entries are required:

<table>
<tr><td style="vertical-align:top">Journal entry to
recognize transaction
gain on forward
exchange contract for
deutsche marks</td><td>

Investment in Forward Exchange Contract
  [DM500,000 × ($0.451 − $0.449)] 1,000
Interest Expense ($13,000 × 4/60) 866
       Transaction Gains and Losses 1,000
       Discount on Forward Exchange Contract Payable 866
To recognize transaction gain on forward exchange contract re-
sulting from increase of spot exchange rate for the deutsche mark
to $0.451 from $0.449; and to amortize discount on contract to
June 4, Year 6.
</td></tr>
<tr><td style="vertical-align:top">Journal entry to record
payment of forward
exchange contract
liability for deutsche
marks</td><td>

Investment in Deutsche Marks (DM500,000 × $0.451) 225,500
Forward Exchange Contract Payable (DM500,000 × $0.478) 239,000
      Investment in Forward Exchange Contract 225,500
      Cash 239,000
To record payment of DM500,000 forward exchange contract, and
receipt of deutsche marks.
</td></tr>
</table>

After these journal entries are posted, Worldwide's Investment in Forward Exchange Contract and Discount on Forward Exchange Contract Payable ledger accounts are as shown on page 829.

Worldwide recognized interest expense of $13,000 and a net transaction loss of $500 ($3,000 − $1,500 − $1,000 = $500) during the 60-day term of its DM500,000 forward exchange contract. In return, Worldwide benefited from knowing what its total outlay for deutsche marks would be on June 4, Year 6, the maturity date of the forward exchange contract. On receipt of the deutsche marks, Worldwide could pay for imports from German suppliers at a known U.S. dollar amount as the suppliers' invoices came due.

The transaction gains and losses amounts are displayed in Worldwide's monthly income statements. The balance of the Investment in Forward Exchange Contract ledger account is a current asset, and the balance of the Forward Exchange Contract

Selected ledger
accounts related to
forward exchange
contract for deutsche
marks

Investment in Forward Exchange Contract

Date	Explanation	Debit	Credit	Balance
Year 6				
Apr. 5	Acquisition of 60-day,			
	DM500,000 contract	226,000		226,000 dr
30	Transaction loss		3,000	223,000 dr
May 31	Transaction gain	1,500		224,500 dr
June 4	Transaction gain	1,000		225,500 dr
4	Receipt of deutsche marks		225,500	–0–

Discount on Forward Exchange Contract Payable

Date	Explanation	Debit	Credit	Balance
Year 6				
Apr. 5	Acquisition of forward exchange			
	contract	13,000		13,000 dr
30	Amortization		5,417	7,583 dr
May 31	Amortization		6,717	866 dr
June 4	Amortization		866	–0–

Payable account, less the balance of the related discount account, is a current liability in the monthly balance sheets for Worldwide. Subsequent to June 4, Year 6, any balance of the Investment in Deutsche Marks ledger account is a current asset in Worldwide's balance sheets.

Forward Exchange Contract to Hedge an Identifiable Commitment   *FASB Statement No. 52* established the following conditions for a forward exchange contract intended to hedge an identifiable foreign currency commitment:[4]

1   The foreign currency transaction is designated as, and is effective as, a hedge of a foreign currency commitment.

2   The foreign currency commitment is firm.

For a forward exchange contract meeting the stated conditions, and in an amount not exceeding the related foreign currency commitment, the following are *deferred and included in the dollar amount of the related foreign currency transaction:*

1   The discount or premium on the forward exchange contract applicable to the period of the commitment (Alternatively, the discount or premium may be amortized, as illustrated above.)[5]

2   Transaction gains during the term of the contract

---

[4] Ibid., p. 9.
[5] Ibid., p. 8.

3   Transaction losses during the term of the contract, unless deferral would cause the recognition of a loss, such as a write-down of inventories to net realizable value, in a subsequent accounting period

The amount of a forward exchange contract meeting the conditions for a hedge of an identifiable foreign currency commitment may exceed the amount of the related commitment. If so, any transaction gain or loss applicable to the amount of the forward exchange contract in excess of the commitment is deferred only to the extent that the forward contract is intended to provide a hedge on an *after-income taxes basis.* Such a deferred gain or loss is offset against the related income taxes on the transaction gains or losses in the accounting period that the income taxes are reflected in the accounting records.[6] Transaction gains and losses that are not deferred are displayed in the income statement when the exchange rate changes.

To illustrate the accounting for a forward exchange contract that is a hedge of an identifiable foreign currency commitment, assume that Worldwide Corporation on May 1, Year 6, issued a purchase order for merchandise to a German supplier at a total price of DM175,000. Delivery and payment were scheduled for June 30, Year 6.

To hedge against fluctuations in the exchange rate for the deutsche mark, Worldwide acquired on May 1, Year 6, a firm forward exchange contract for the receipt of DM175,000 on June 30, Year 6. Selected exchange rates for the deutsche mark from May 1 to June 30, Year 6, were as follows:

Exchange rates for deutsche mark

	May 1	May 31	June 30
Spot rates:			
Buying...	$0.454	$0.449	$0.455
Selling...	0.462	0.458	0.466
Forward rates:			
30-day contracts...................................	0.477	0.472	0.487
60-day contracts...................................	0.493	0.488	0.495
90-day contracts...................................	0.519	0.502	0.520

Journal entries for forward exchange contract to hedge an identifiable commitment denominated in deutsche marks

Year 6
May   1   Investment in Forward Exchange Contract
                (DM175,000 × $0.462 selling spot rate)..............   80,850
            Discount on Forward Exchange Contract Payable.......   5,425
                Forward Exchange Contract Payable
                (DM175,000 × $0.493 forward rate)...........   86,275
            To record acquisition of DM175,000 forward exchange
            contract for 60 days, at forward rate of DM1 = $0.493.

(continued)

---

[6] The complicated accounting for after-income taxes hedges is illustrated on pp. 9–13 of *FASB Statement No. 20,* ''Accounting for Forward Exchange Contracts,'' FASB (Stamford: 1977), which was superseded by *FASB Statement No. 52.*

Year 6

May 31 Deferred Transaction Gains and Losses
  [DM175,000 × ($0.462 − $0.458)] 700
    Investment in Forward Exchange Contract   700
  To defer transaction loss resulting from decrease of spot
  exchange rate for the deutsche mark to DM1 = $0.458
  from DM1 = $0.462.

June 30 Investment in Forward Exchange Contract
  [DM175,000 × ($0.466 − $0.458)] 1,400
    Deferred Transaction Gains and Losses   1,400
  To defer transaction gain resulting from increase of spot
  exchange rate for the deutsche mark to DM1 = $0.466
  from DM1 = $0.458.

  30 Inventories ($81,550 − $700 + $5,425) 86,275
  Deferred Transaction Gains and Losses ($1,400 − $700) 700
    Discount on Forward Exchange Contract Payable.   5,425
    Trade Accounts Payable (DM175,000 × $0.466)..   81,550
  To record purchase of merchandise from German supplier
  for DM175,000, translated at selling exchange rate of
  DM1 = $0.466; and to increase cost of merchandise for
  discount on forward exchange contract, less deferred net
  transaction gain on contract.

  30 Forward Exchange Contract Payable 86,275
  Investment in Deutsche Marks 81,550
    Investment in Forward Exchange Contract
      ($80,850 − $700 + $1,400)   81,550
    Cash...   86,275
  To record payment of forward exchange contract, and re-
  ceipt of deutsche marks.

  30 Trade Accounts Payable............................. 81,550
    Investment in Deutsche Marks   81,550
  To record settlement of liability to German supplier.

Worldwide's journal entries for acquisition of the forward exchange contract, receipt of the merchandise from the German supplier, payment of the forward exchange contract, and payment of the supplier's invoice, are on page 830 and above.

The result of the foregoing journal entries is that the merchandise purchased by Worldwide from the German supplier is measured at the total cost, including financing costs, of the transaction with the supplier. These costs are summarized on page 832.

Total cost of
merchandise
purchased from
German supplier

Invoice cost of merchandise (DM175,000 × $0.466 selling spot rate on date received)	$81,550
Add: Discount on forward exchange contract for deutsche marks	5,425
Less: Net deferred transaction gain on forward exchange contract	(700)
Total cost of merchandise	$86,275

The illustrated accounting is appropriate because the forward exchange contract was acquired to hedge an identifiable foreign currency commitment. Acquisition of such a contract enabled Worldwide to predetermine its total cost of the merchandise purchased from the German supplier at $86,275, the cash outlay for the forward exchange contract.

Forward Exchange Contract for Speculation   There is no separate accounting treatment for the discount or premium on a forward exchange contract acquired for speculation in the foreign currency involved. The speculation forward exchange contract is similar to a short-term investment in a marketable bond that will not be held to maturity; thus, the accounting for discount or premium is similar for these two types of investments.

The transaction gain or loss on a speculation forward exchange contract is measured by multiplying the foreign currency amount of the contract by the difference between (1) the forward rate available for the remaining term of the contract and (2) the contracted forward rate or the forward rate last used to compute a transaction gain or loss. Transaction gains and losses on speculation forward exchange contracts are included in the measurement of net income for the period in which the forward rate changes.

To illustrate, assume the following exchange rates for the deutsche mark from May 1 to June 30, Year 6:

Exchange rates for
deutsche mark

	May 1	May 31	June 30
Spot rates:			
Buying..	$0.454	$0.449	$0.455
Selling...	0.462	0.458	0.466
Forward rates:			
30-day contracts.................................	0.477	0.472	0.487
60-day contracts.................................	0.493	0.488	0.495
90-day contracts.................................	0.519	0.502	0.520

On May 1, Year 6, Speco, Inc., acquired a 60-day forward exchange contract for DM200,000, in anticipation of an increase in the spot rates for the deutsche mark during the 60-day period. The journal entries of Speco, Inc., for the forward exchange contract, assuming that Speco prepares monthly financial statements, are as follows:

<table>
<tr><td>

Journal entries for forward exchange contract acquired for speculation

</td></tr>
</table>

Year 6			
May 1	Investment in Forward Exchange Contract		
	(DM200,000 × $0.493)............................	98,600	
	Forward Exchange Contract Payable		98,600
	To record acquisition of DM200,000 forward exchange contract for 60 days, at forward rate of DM1 = $0.493.		
31	Transaction Gains and Losses		
	[DM200,000 × ($0.493 − $0.472)]	4,200	
	Investment in Forward Exchange Contract		4,200
	To recognize transaction loss on forward exchange contract resulting from difference between contracted forward rate (DM1 = $0.493) and forward rate for remaining 30-day term of contract (DM1 = $0.472).		
June 30	Investment in Deutsche Marks	94,400	
	Forward Exchange Contract Payable	98,600	
	Investment in Forward Exchange Contract		
	($98,600 − $4,200)..........................		94,400
	Cash...		98,600
	To record payment of DM200,000 forward exchange contract, and receipt of deutsche marks.		
30	Cash (DM200,000 × $0.455)	91,000	
	Transaction Gains and Losses		
	[DM200,000 × ($0.472 − $0.455)]	3,400	
	Investment in Deutsche Marks		94,400
	To record sale of DM200,000 investment at buying spot rate of DM1 = $0.455; and to recognize transaction loss.		

The increase in the spot rates for the deutsche mark that Speco, Inc., had anticipated did not occur; thus, Speco incurred a total transaction loss of $7,600 ($4,200 + $3,400 = $7,600) on the forward exchange contract for speculation.

Summary of Accounting for Forward Exchange Contracts The foregoing discussion of accounting for forward exchange contracts is summarized in the table on page 834.

International Accounting Standard 21

The provisions of *IAS 21,* ''Accounting for the Effects of Changes in Foreign Exchange Rates,'' dealing with foreign currency transactions are essentially the same as those of *FASB Statement No. 52,* ''Foreign Currency Translation.'' However, *IAS 21* is more limited in its coverage of forward exchange contracts; for example, it does not address forward contracts for speculation in a foreign currency.

Accounting for Forward Exchange Contracts

Purpose of contract	Discount or premium on contract		Transaction gains or losses on contract	
	Measurement	Accounting	Measurement	Accounting
Not intended to hedge a foreign currency commitment or for speculation	Difference between forward rate and spot rate on date of contract	Recognized as expense or revenue over term of contract	Difference between spot rates on date of measurement and date of contract (or date of most recent prior measurement)	Reported in income statement for accounting period in which exchange rate changes
Hedge of identifiable foreign currency commitment	Difference between forward rate and spot rate on date of contract	Amount related to period of commitment deferred and included in dollar basis of related foreign currency transaction	Difference between spot rates on date of measurement and date of contract (or date of most recent prior measurement)	Gains deferred and included in dollar basis of related foreign currency transaction to extent amount of contract does not exceed amount of commitment. Gain on amount in excess of commitment deferred to extent amount provides a hedge on an after-income taxes basis. Gain attributable to remainder of any excess reported in income statement for accounting period in which exchange rate changes Losses comparably deferred unless deferral would lead to recognition of loss in subsequent accounting period
Speculation	Difference between forward rate and spot rate on date of contract	Not accounted for separately	Difference between forward rate for remaining term of contract and contract rate or rate last used to compute transaction gain or loss	Reported in income statement for accounting period in which exchange rate changes

Disclosures Regarding Foreign Currency Transactions

Investments in both foreign currencies and forward exchange contracts are *financial instruments,* which are defined as follows:[7]

> A financial instrument is defined as cash, evidence of an ownership interest in an entity, or a contract that both:

---

[7] *FASB Statement No. 105,* ''Disclosure of Information about Financial Instruments with Off-Balance-Sheet Risk . . . ,'' FASB (Stamford: 1990), pp. 18, 23; *FASB Statement No. 107,* ''Disclosures about Fair Value of Financial Instruments,'' FASB (Stamford: 1991), pp. 1–2.

a Imposes on one entity a contractual obligation (1) to deliver cash or another financial instrument to a second entity or (2) to exchange other financial instruments on potentially unfavorable terms with the second entity

b Conveys to that second entity a contractual right (1) to receive cash or another financial instrument from the first entity or (2) to exchange other financial instruments on potentially favorable terms with the first entity.

In *FASB Statement No. 105,* "Disclosure of Information about Financial Instruments with Off-Balance-Sheet Risk and Financial Instruments with Concentrations of Credit Risks," the Financial Accounting Standards Board required enterprises having off-balance-sheet *credit risk*[8] or *market risk,*[9] with certain exceptions, to disclose the following in the body of the financial statements or in an accompanying note:[10]

a The face or contract amount . . .

b The nature and terms, including, at a minimum, a discussion of (1) the credit and market risk of those instruments, (2) the cash requirements of those instruments, and (3) the related accounting policy pursuant to the requirements of *APB Opinion No. 22,* "Disclosure of Accounting Policies."

The FASB stated that investments in foreign currencies did not have off-balance-sheet risk, but investments in forward exchange contracts did have such risk. The following example of such disclosure is taken from the annual report of Harnischfeger Industries, Inc., a publicly owned enterprise.[11]

Note 8—Financial Instruments with Off-Balance-Sheet Risk

The Company is a party to financial instruments with off-balance-sheet risk in the normal course of business. These financial instruments include forward contracts and financial and other guarantees and involve, to varying degrees, elements of credit and exchange fluctuation risk not recognized in the balance sheet.

The Company's off-balance-sheet exposure to credit loss in the event of nonperformance by the other party to the financial instrument is limited to its involvement in financial guarantees and consists of the unpaid balance of the underlying transactions.

The Company enters into foreign exchange contracts to hedge identifiable foreign currency receivables, payables and commitments. At October 31, 1990, the Company had contracts maturing from November 2, 1990 to April 29, 1994 to purchase or sell foreign currency as follows:

---

[8] *Credit risk* is the risk of nonperformance by a party to a financial instrument contract.
[9] *Market risk* is the risk of a decline in value or an increase in onerousness of a financial instrument resulting from future changes in market prices.
[10] *FASB Statement No. 105,* p. 7.
[11] *Accounting Trends & Techniques,* 45th ed., AICPA (New York: 1991), p. 102.

	Buy at spot rate	Sell at spot rate	Net receivable (payable)
Deutsche mark	$ 7,600	$ 30,407	$(22,807)
Pound sterling	49,942	4,786	45,156
Japanese yen	426	15,248	(14,822)
French franc.	—	34,503	(34,504)
Dutch guilder	—	35,196	(35,196)
Swedish krona.	—	20,772	(20,772)
Other	11,668	4,823	6,845
	$69,636	$145,735	$(76,099)

At October 31, 1990, the Company had guaranteed $3,599 of the secured loans of customers primarily to support certain large sales of mining machinery and equipment. In addition, in connection with the divestiture of the Construction Equipment Division in 1988, the Company guaranteed the bank loan provided to Century II by certain banks. As of October 31, 1990, the outstanding balance on the Century II bank loan amounted to $20,000.

As of October 31, 1990, 62% and 12% of the Company's accounts receivable were from companies in the pulp and paper and mining industries, respectively.

REVIEW QUESTIONS

1   What are the 12 member countries of the European Community?

2   Differentiate between the International Accounting Standards Committee (IASC) and the International Organization of Securities Commissions (IOSCO).

3   What is the U.S. term for the IASC's *jointly controlled entity?*

4   How does *IAS 22,* "Accounting for Business Combinations," differ from U.S. accounting standards for pooling-type business combinations? Explain.

5   In *IAS 27,* "Consolidated Financial Statements . . . ," did the IASC adopt the parent company concept or the economic unit concept for display of minority interest in net income and net assets of subsidiaries in consolidated financial statements? Explain.

6   Define the following terms associated with foreign currencies:
a *Exchange rate*
b *Forward rate*
c *Selling spot rate*
d *Spot rate*

7   A newspaper listed quoted spot rates for the Japanese yen (¥) as follows:

Buying rate: ¥1 = $0.0039

Selling rate: ¥1 = $0.0043

How many U.S. dollars does a U.S. enterprise have to exchange for ¥50,000 at the above rates to settle a trade account payable denominated in that amount to a Japanese supplier? Explain.

8 What is a *multinational* enterprise?

9 On March 27, Year 3, a U.S. multinational enterprise purchased merchandise on 30-day credit terms from a Philippines exporter at an invoice cost of ₱80,000. (₱ is the symbol for the Philippine peso). What U.S. dollar amount does the U.S. enterprise credit to Trade Accounts Payable if the March 27, Year 3, spot rates for the Philippine peso are as follows?

Buying rate: ₱1 = $0.11

Selling rate: ₱1 = $0.12

10 Are transaction gains or losses entered in the accounting records prior to collection of a trade account receivable or payment of a trade account payable denominated in a foreign currency? Explain.

11 Explain the *one-transaction perspective* regarding the nature of a transaction gain or loss.

12 What arguments are advanced in support of the *two-transaction perspective* for transaction gains and losses? Explain.

13 What is a *forward exchange contract?*

14 How may a U.S. multinational enterprise *hedge* against the risk of fluctuations in exchange rates for foreign currencies? Explain.

15 Differentiate between *credit risk* and *market risk* with respect to financial instruments.

EXERCISES

Ex. 18-1 Select the best answer for each of the following multiple-choice questions:

1 Financial accounting pronouncements similar in form to those issued by the Financial Accounting Standards Board are developed by the:
a International Accounting Standards Committee
b International Federation of Accountants
c European Community
d International Organization of Securities Commissions

2 The International Accounting Standards Committee has proposed to make preferable the inventory cost flow valuation method(s):
a First-in, first-out
b Average
c Last-in, first-out
d **a** and **b** only
e **a**, **b**, and **c**

3 The U.S. member of the International Accounting Standards Committee is the:
a Securities and Exchange Commission
b Financial Accounting Standards Board
c American Institute of Certified Public Accountants
d General Accounting Office

4   If the exchange rate for one British pound is $1.55, $1.00 may be exchanged for:
a 0.45 pound
b 0.65 pound
c 0.78 pound
d An indeterminate fraction of a pound

5   If $1.9672 is required to acquire one British pound, the amount of pound(s) required to acquire $1 is:
a £0.5083
b £5.0834
c £3.8702
d £0.2584

6   To acquire a draft denominated in British pounds, a business enterprise pays for the pounds at the:
a Selling spot rate
b Buying spot rate
c Forward rate
d Nominal rate

7   Vermont Corporation, a U.S. enterprise, purchased merchandise from a supplier in Germany on November 5, Year 4, for DM50,000, when the selling spot rate was $0.4295. On Vermont's December 31, Year 4, year end the spot rate was $0.4245. On January 15, Year 5, Vermont acquired DM50,000 at the selling spot of $0.4345 and paid the invoice. What amounts does Vermont report in its income statements for Year 4 and Year 5 as transaction gains or (losses)?

	Year 4	*Year 5*
a	$250	$(500)
b	(250)	-0-
c	-0-	(250)
d	-0-	-0-
e	Some other amounts	

8   On April 30, Year 3, the buying spot rate for the local currency unit (LCU) was $0.15, the selling spot rate was $0.17, and the 30-day forward rate was $0.19. If a U.S. multinational enterprise received a LCU100,000 draft from a foreign customer in settlement of a purchase made by the customer on March 31, Year 3, the U.S. enterprise may convert the LCU100,000 draft to:
a $15,000
b $17,000
c $19,000
d Some other amount

9   A U.S. multinational enterprise has an account receivable from a German customer and an account payable to an unrelated German supplier, both of which are denominated in deutsche marks. If the exchange rate for the deutsche mark *decreases,* the result to the enterprise will be realization of transaction gains or losses as follows:

	On account receivable	On account payable
a	Transaction gain	Transaction gain
b	Transaction loss	Transaction loss
c	Transaction loss	Transaction gain
d	Transaction gain	Transaction loss

10 Under *FASB Statement No. 52*, ''Foreign Currency Translation,'' is the discount or premium on a forward exchange contract that is not intended to hedge a foreign currency commitment or for speculation:

	Recognized as expense or revenue over the term of the contract?	Deferred and included in the dollar basis of the related foreign currency transaction?
a	Yes	Yes
b	Yes	No
c	No	Yes
d	No	No

11 Is interest expense recognized on a U.S. multinational enterprise's investment in a forward exchange contract:

	Not intended to hedge a foreign currency commitment or for speculation?	Intended to hedge a foreign currency commitment?
a	Yes	Yes
b	Yes	No
c	No	Yes
d	No	No

12 A Deferred Transaction Gains and Losses ledger account is appropriate for accounting for a forward exchange contract:
a Not intended to hedge an identifiable commitment or for speculation
b Intended to hedge an identifiable commitment
c For speculation
d In any of the foregoing circumstances

13 On July 24, Year 2, Importers, Inc., received from a German supplier merchandise with a translated invoice cost on that date of $80,000. The discount on the forward exchange contract acquired by Importers on June 24, Year 2, to hedge its deutsche mark commitment for the merchandise ordered on that date was $5,000. The net deferred transaction gain on the contract during the period June 24–July 24, Year 2, was $1,000. The cost of the merchandise to Importers is:
a $80,000
b $84,000
c $85,000
d $86,000
e Some other amount

Ex. 18-2 On June 26, Year 9, L.A. Company purchased merchandise from Brit Company for £10,000, terms net 30 days. On June 30, Year 9, L.A. Company prepared financial statements. On July 26, Year 9, L.A. Company wired £10,000 to Brit Company. Relevant spot exchange rates for the pound sterling (£) were as follows:

	£1 =	
	Buying rate	**Selling rate**
June 26, Year 9...	$1.63	$1.67
June 30, Year 9...	1.64	1.68
July 26, Year 9	1.62	1.66

Prepare journal entries (omit explanations) for L.A. Company on June 26 and 30 and July 26, Year 9. L.A. Company uses the perpetual inventory system.

Ex. 18-3 Walker, Inc., a U.S. corporation that prepares annual financial statements, ordered a machine (plant asset) from Pfau Company of Germany on July 15, Year 3, for DM100,000 when the selling spot rate for the deutsche mark was $0.4955. Pfau shipped the machine on September 1, Year 3, and billed Walker for DM100,000. The selling spot rate was $0.4875 on that date. Walker acquired a draft for DM100,000 and paid the invoice on October 25, Year 3, when the selling spot was $0.4855.

Prepare journal entries for Walker, Inc., to record the foregoing business transactions and events.

Ex. 18-4 On November 18, Year 6, U.S. Company, which uses the perpetual inventory system and prepares financial statements monthly, shipped merchandise costing $1,000 to France Company for 20,000 French francs (FF20,000), terms n/30. On December 18, Year 6, U.S. Company received from France Company a draft for FF20,000, which U.S. converted to U.S. dollars immediately. Spot rates for the French franc were as follows:

	FF1 =	
	Buying rate	**Selling rate**
Nov. 18, Year 6	$0.14	$0.15
Nov. 30, Year 6	0.15	0.16
Dec. 18, Year 6	0.13	0.14

Prepare journal entries for U.S. Company on November 18 and 30 and December 18, Year 6. Omit explanations for the journal entries.

Ex. 18-5 On March 25, Year 4, Lincoln Company, a U.S. multinational enterprise, sold merchandise costing $260,000 to Svenska Company, a Swedish enterprise, for 2,000,000 krona (Kr) on 30-day open account. On April 24, Year 4, Lincoln received a Kr2,000,000 draft from Svenska and converted it to U.S. dollars. Lincoln prepares monthly financial statements and uses the perpetual inventory system. Exchange rates for the krona were as follows:

	Kr1 =		
	Buying	**Selling**	**Forward**
Mar. 25, Year 4....................................	$0.19	$0.20	$0.22
Mar. 31, Year 4....................................	0.20	0.22	0.24
Apr. 24, Year 4	0.18	0.19	0.20

Prepare journal entries (omit explanations) for Lincoln Company on March 25, March 31, and April 24, Year 4.

Ex. 18-6 On March 1, Year 3, Yankee Company sold merchandise with a cost of $100,000 to a foreign customer in its local currency unit (LCU) for a LCU600,000, 60-day promissory note bearing interest of 18% a year. On April 30, Year 3, Yankee received a draft for LCU618,000, in settlement of the note receivable from the foreign customer, and converted it to U.S. dollars immediately. Relevant exchange rates for the LCU were as follows:

	LCU1 =	
	Mar. 1, Year 3	Apr. 30, Year 3
Spot rates:		
Buying......................................	$0.30	$0.33
Selling......................................	0.32	0.34
30-day forward rate	0.40	0.44

Prepare journal entries for Yankee Company on March 1, Year 3, and April 30, Year 3, for the foregoing information. Yankee uses the periodic inventory system and prepares end-of-period adjustments only on June 30, the end of its fiscal year.

Ex. 18-7 The accountant for Transglobal Company is a proponent of the one-transaction perspective of accounting for foreign trade transactions. On November 19, Year 1, Transglobal's accountant prepared the following journal entry:

Trade Accounts Payable......................................	60,000	
Cost of Goods Sold ($3,000 × 33⅓%)	1,000	
Inventories ($3,000 × 66 ⅔%).................................	2,000	
Cash		63,000

To record payment for FF315,000 draft (FF315,000 × $0.20 = $63,000) to settle liability to French supplier, and allocation of resultant transaction loss to cost of goods sold and to inventories.

Prepare a journal entry for Transglobal Company on November 19, Year 1, to correct the foregoing journal entry.

Ex. 18-8 On March 31, Year 5, Kingston Company acquired a 30-day forward exchange contract for 100,000 local currency units (LCU) of a foreign country. The contract was not acquired to hedge LCU foreign currency commitments or for speculation. On April 30, Year 5, Kingston paid cash to settle the contract and obtain the LCU100,000 draft. Kingston prepares adjusting entries and financial statements only at the end of its fiscal year, April 30. Relevant exchange rates for one unit of the local currency were as follows:

	LCU1 =	
	Mar. 31, Year 5	Apr. 30, Year 5
Spot rates:		
Buying......................................	$0.18	$0.19
Selling......................................	0.20	0.22
Forward rates:		
30-day contracts............................	0.25	0.28

Prepare journal entries for Kingston Company on March 31, Year 5, and April 30, Year 5.

Ex. 18-9   On August 6, Year 7, Concordia Company, a U.S. multinational enterprise that uses the perpetual inventory system, purchased from a Belgium supplier on 30-day open account goods costing 80,000 Belgian francs. On that date, various exchange rates for the Belgian franc (BF) were as follows:

Spot rates:
  Buying: BF1 = $0.025
  Selling: BF1 = $0.029
30-day forward rate: BF1 = $0.031

Also on August 6, Year 7, Concordia acquired a 30-day forward exchange contract for BF80,000, to hedge the BF commitment.

Prepare journal entries to record the August 6, Year 7, transactions of Concordia Company, as well as the related transactions on September 5, Year 7, on which date the selling spot rate was BF1 = $0.029. Concordia does not close its accounting records monthly or prepare monthly financial statements.

CASES

Case 18-1   Both the International Accounting Standards Committee (IASC) and the U.S. Financial Accounting Standards Board were established in 1973. Since that time, the IASC has issued more than 30 *International Accounting Standards,* but the FASB has issued more than 100 *Statements of Financial Accounting Standards.*

Instructions

Do you favor the FASB's continued outpouring of *Statements,* most of which differ at least in some respects from IASC *Standards?* Alternatively, should the FASB act as a recommender to the IASC for provisions of *Standards* that it issues? Base your answer on your perception of which course of action would best enhance the adoption of uniform accounting standards throughout the world.

Case 18-2   Many accountants believe that generally accepted accounting principles in the United States, especially those developed by the Financial Accounting Standards Board, are superior to *International Accounting Standards* or to the accounting standards of other countries. In their view, foreign enterprises wanting to have their securities traded on U.S. stock exchanges should prepare financial reports that comply with U.S. accounting standards. However, the U.S. Securities and Exchange Commission is a member of the International Organization of Securities Commissions, which is studying the possibility of allowing foreign enterprises to prepare financial reports that incorporate *International Accounting Standards* in requesting permission to have their securities traded in any country.

Instructions

Do you support or oppose the SEC's participation in the work of the IOSCO? Should or should not foreign enterprises meet financial reporting standards applicable to

U.S. enterprises if the foreign enterprises want their securities to be traded on U.S. stock exchanges? Explain.

Case 18-3 The disclosure standards established by the FASB in *FASB Statement No. 105,* "Disclosure of Information about Financial Instruments with Off-Balance-Sheet Risk . . . ," are set forth on page 835 and illustrated on pages 835 to 836.

Instructions

What is your opinion of the foregoing disclosure standards, based on your review of the illustration? Are financial statement users benefited by such disclosures? Or do such disclosures contribute to "information overload" in financial statements and financial reports? Explain.

PROBLEMS

Pr. 18-1 On August 1, Year 3, Caribbean Company, a U.S. multinational enterprise that prepares financial statements monthly, acquired a 60-day forward exchange contract for £50,000. Exchange rates for the British pound (£) on various dates in Year 3 were as follows:

	£1 =		
	Aug. 1	*Aug. 31*	*Sept. 30*
Spot rates:			
Buying	*$1.80*	*$1.82*	*$1.83*
Selling	*1.90*	*1.91*	*1.92*
Forward rates:			
30-day contracts	*1.92*	*1.94*	*1.94*
60-day contracts	*1.94*	*1.96*	*1.97*
90-day contracts	*1.97*	*1.99*	*1.98*

Instructions

Prepare journal entries for Caribbean Company's forward exchange contract during its 60-day term under the following assumptions:
a The contract was acquired for speculation.
b The contract was not acquired as a hedge of an identifiable commitment or for speculation.
c The contract was firm and was designated as a hedge of a £50,000 purchase order issued by Caribbean on August 1, Year 3, to a British supplier for merchandise to be delivered and paid for on September 30, Year 3.

Pr. 18-2 The following problem consists of two unrelated parts.
a On June 27, Year 2, U.S. Company, which uses the perpetual inventory system, purchased from French Company, for 100,000 French francs (FF), merchandise to be shipped by air that date directly to Canadian Company at a selling price of 30,000 Canadian dollars ($C). On July 27, Year 2, U.S. Company obtained for U.S. dollars and sent to French Company a draft for FF100,000 and received from Canadian Company a draft for $C30,000, which U.S. immediately converted to

U.S. dollars. U.S. Company does not prepare monthly financial statements. Relevant spot exchange rates were as follows:

	FF1 =		$C1 =	
	Buying	**Selling**	**Buying**	**Selling**
June 27, Year 2.......................	$0.19	$0.20	$0.84	$0.86
July 27, Year 2........................	0.20	0.22	0.85	0.87

Instructions

Prepare journal entries (omit explanations) for U.S. Company on June 27, Year 2, to record the purchase and sale of merchandise and on July 27, Year 2, to record the payment to French Company and the receipt from Canadian Company.

b On March 1, Year 5, Spheric Company prepared the following journal entry:

Investment in Forward Exchange Contract (DM100,000 × $0.33) . .	33,000	
Discount on Forward Exchange Contract Payable	2,000	
Forward Exchange Contract Payable (DM100,000 × $0.35) .		35,000
To record acquisition of forward exchange contract, not intended to		
hedge or for speculation, for 60 days at forward rate of DM1 = $0.35.		

The selling spot rates for the German deutsche mark (DM) on March 31 and April 30, Year 5, were as follows:

Date	DM1 =
Mar. 31, Year 5	$0.32
Apr. 30, Year 5	0.31

Instructions

Prepare journal entries (omit explanations) for Spheric Company on March 31 and April 30, Year 5. Spheric prepares monthly financial statements.

Pr. 18-3 The following problem consists of two unrelated parts.

a Zonal Corporation is a multinational company that sells merchandise to Stacey, Ltd., a customer in the United Kingdom. On November 19, Year 8, Zonal sold to Stacey merchandise costing $40,000 for £38,000. On December 19, Year 8, Zonal received from Stacey a draft for £38,000, which Zonal immediately converted to U.S. dollars. Zonal uses the perpetual inventory system and prepares monthly financial statements. Selected exchange rates for the British pound were as follows:

	£1 =		
	Nov. 19, Year 8	**Nov. 30, Year 8**	**Dec. 19, Year 8**
Spot rates:			
Buying.	$1.45	$1.44	$1.43
Selling.	1.48	1.47	1.46
Forward rate:			
30-day contract.	1.50	1.49	1.48

Instructions

Prepare journal entries (omit explanations) for Zonal Corporation on November 19, November 30, and December 19, Year 8.

b On June 30, Year 6, Iberia Company, a U.S. multinational enterprise that does not prepare monthly financial statements, sold merchandise costing $75,000 to a Portuguese customer, received in exchange a 60-day, 12% note for 7,500,000 escudos (Esc). The buying spot rate for escudos on June 30, Year 6, was Esc 1 = $0.014. On August 29, Year 6, Iberia received from the Portuguese customer a draft for Esc7,650,000, which Iberia converted on that date to U.S. dollars at the buying spot rate for escudos of Esc1 = $0.016.

Instructions
Prepare journal entries (omit explanations) for Iberia Company to record the June 30, Year 6, sale, under the perpetual inventory system, and the August 29, Year 6, conversion of the Portuguese customer's Esc7,650,000 draft to U.S. dollars.

Pr. 18-4 Imex Company, a U.S. multinational enterprise with an April 30 fiscal year, had the following transactions and events, among others, during March and April, Year 8:

| | | Exchange rates | | |
| | | Spot | | |
Date	Explanation of transactions and events	Buying	Selling	Forward
Year 8				
Mar. 6	Received merchandise purchased from Brazilian supplier on 30-day open account, cost 100,000 cruzeiros (Cr$). Acquired firm 30-day forward exchange contract for Cr$100,000 as effective hedge.	$0.006	$0.007	$0.008
18	Received merchandise purchased from Danish supplier on 30-day open account, cost 75,000 kroner (DKr).	0.12	0.13	0.14
25	Sold merchandise to Swiss customer on 30-day open account for 50,000 francs (Sfr). Cost of goods sold $15,000.	0.52	0.53	0.54
Apr. 4	Received merchandise purchased from Spanish supplier on 30-day open account for 150,000 pesetas (Ptas).	0.008	0.009	0.010
5	Liquidated Cr$100,000 forward exchange contract, and paid Brazilian supplier for Mar. 6 purchase.	0.006	0.007	0.009
17	Acquired draft for DKr75,000 for payment to Danish supplier for Mar. 18 purchase.	0.13	0.14	0.15
24	Received draft for Sfr50,000 from Swiss customer for sale of Mar. 25. Exchanged draft for U.S. dollar credit to bank checking account.	0.53	0.54	0.55
30	Obtained exchange rates quotation for Spanish peseta.	0.009	0.01	0.011

Instructions

a Prepare journal entries for Imex Company to record the foregoing transactions and events in U.S. dollars, under the perpetual inventory system.

b Prepare an adjusting entry for Imex Company on April 30, Year 8. Imex does not prepare monthly financial statements.

Pr. 18-5 On June 30, Year 7, Impo Company, which prepares monthly financial statements, acquired from Japanese Company for 500,000 yen (¥) a machine with an economic life of five years and no residual value. To pay Japanese Company, Impo borrowed ¥500,000 from Japanese Bank on a 12%, 60-day note. Impo acquired a ¥510,000 draft from U.S. Bank on August 29, Year 7, to pay the maturity value of the note to Japanese Bank. Relevant exchange rates for the yen were as follows:

	¥1 =	
	Buying rate	**Selling rate**
June 30, Year 7	$0.0081	$0.0084
July 31, Year 7	0.0080	0.0082
Aug. 29, Year 7	0.0082	0.0085

Instructions

Prepare journal entries (omit explanations) for Impo Company on June 30, July 31, and August 29, Year 7, including interest accrual and depreciation of the machine. Use 30-day months for July and August interest.

Pr. 18-6 During your first-time audit of the financial statements of Allison Company, a closely held corporation, you review the following ledger account:

Forward Exchange Contracts

Date	Explanation	Debit	Credit	Balance
Year 4				
Apr. 30	Payment for 60-day contract for ¥100,000 at ¥1 = $0.00801	801		801 dr
Sept. 30	Payment of 60-day contract for FF50,000 at FF1 = $0.185	9,250		10,051 dr
30	Payment of 60-day contract for DM10,000 at DM1 = $0.632	6,320		16,371 dr

Your study of underlying records discloses the following:

(1) Allison, as a nonpublic company, prepares financial statements at the end of its September 30 fiscal year only.

(2) The offsetting credits for the debits to Forward Exchange Contracts were to Cash.

(3) No other journal entries had been prepared by Allison for the forward exchange contracts.

(4) The contract for Japanese yen (¥) was not intended to hedge an identifiable foreign currency commitment or for speculation. The yen were used for travel expenses in Japan prior to September 30, Year 4.

(5) The contract for French francs (FF) hedged a FF50,000 purchase commitment to a French supplier for merchandise received and paid for September 30, Year 4, all of which was on hand on that date.

(6) The contract for deutsche marks was for speculation; the marks were on hand on September 30, Year 4.

(7) Selling spot rates for the three currencies were as follows:

¥1: Mar. 1, Year 4, $0.00792; Apr. 30, Year 4, $0.00797

FF1: Aug. 1, Year 4, $0.173; Sept. 30, Year 4, $0.170

DM1: Aug. 1, Year 4, $0.601; Sept. 30, Year 4, $0.612

Instructions

Prepare three journal entries, one for each forward exchange contract, for Allison Company on September 30, Year 4, to correct the accounting for the three contracts. Show supporting computations in the explanations for the entries.

19

Translation of Foreign Currency Financial Statements

When a U.S. multinational enterprise prepares consolidated or combined financial statements that include the operating results, financial position, and cash flows of foreign subsidiaries or branches, the U.S. enterprise must *translate* the amounts in the financial statements of the foreign entities from the entities' *functional currency* to U.S. dollars. Similar treatment must be given to investments in other foreign investees for which the U.S. enterprise uses the equity method of accounting.

Functional Currency

The Financial Accounting Standards Board has defined the *functional currency* of a foreign entity as follows:[1]

> An entity's functional currency is the currency of the primary economic environment in which the entity operates; normally, that is the currency of the environment in which an entity primarily generates and expends cash. . . .
>
> For an entity with operations that are relatively self-contained and integrated within a particular country, the functional currency generally would be the currency of that country. However, a foreign entity's functional currency might not be the currency of the country in which the entity is located. For example, the parent's currency generally would be the functional currency for operations that are a direct and integral component or extension of the parent company's operations.

> To assist in the determination of the functional currency of a foreign entity, the FASB provided the following guidelines:[2]

> The salient economic factors set forth below, and possibly others, should be considered both individually and collectively when determining the functional currency.

---

[1] *FASB Statement No. 52,* "Foreign Currency Translation," FASB (Stamford: 1981), pp. 3–4.
[2] Ibid., pp. 25–27.

a Cash flow indicators
   (1) Foreign Currency—Cash flows related to the foreign entity's individual assets and liabilities are primarily in the foreign currency and do not directly impact the parent company's cash flows.
   (2) Parent's Currency—Cash flows related to the foreign entity's individual assets and liabilities directly impact the parent's cash flows on a current basis and are readily available for remittance to the parent company.

b Sales price indicators
   (1) Foreign Currency—Sales prices for the foreign entity's products are not primarily responsive on a short-term basis to changes in exchange rates but are determined more by local competition or local government regulation.
   (2) Parent's Currency—Sales prices for the foreign entity's products are primarily responsive on a short-term basis to changes in exchange rates; for example, sales prices are determined more by worldwide competition or by international prices.

c Sales market indicators
   (1) Foreign Currency—There is an active local sales market for the foreign entity's products, although there also might be significant amounts of exports.
   (2) Parent's Currency—The sales market is mostly in the parent's country or sales contracts are denominated in the parent's currency.

d Expense indicators
   (1) Foreign Currency—Labor, materials, and other costs for the foreign entity's products or services are primarily local costs, even though there also might be imports from other countries.
   (2) Parent's Currency—Labor, materials, and other costs for the foreign entity's products or services, on a continuing basis, are primarily costs for components obtained from the country in which the parent company is located.

e Financing indicators
   (1) Foreign Currency—Financing is primarily denominated in foreign currency, and funds generated by the foreign entity's operations are sufficient to service existing and normally expected debt obligations.
   (2) Parent's Currency—Financing is primarily from the parent or other dollar-denominated obligations, or funds generated by the foreign entity's operations are not sufficient to service existing and normally expected debt obligations without the infusion of additional funds from the parent company. Infusion of additional funds from the parent company for expansion is not a factor, provided funds generated by the foreign entity's expanded operations are expected to be sufficient to service that additional financing.

f Intercompany transactions and arrangements indicators
   (1) Foreign Currency—There is a low volume of intercompany transactions and there is not an extensive interrelationship between the operations of the foreign entity and the parent company. However, the foreign entity's

operations may rely on the parent's or affiliates' competitive advantages, such as patents and trademarks.

(2) Parent's Currency—There is a high volume of intercompany transactions and there is an extensive interrelationship between the operations of the foreign entity and the parent company. Additionally, the parent's currency generally would be the functional currency if the foreign entity is a device or shell corporation for holding investments, obligations, intangible assets, etc., that could readily be carried on the parent's or an affiliate's books.

The foregoing guidelines indicate the importance of determining the appropriate functional currency for a foreign entity. The functional currency of the foreign entity underlies the application of the ***monetary principle*** (discussed in intermediate accounting textbooks) for the entity.

Alternative Methods for Translating Foreign Entities' Financial Statements

If the exchange rate for the functional currency of a foreign subsidiary or branch remained constant instead of fluctuating, translation of the foreign entity's financial statements to U.S. dollars would be simple. All financial statement amounts would be translated to U.S. dollars at the constant exchange rate. However, exchange rates fluctuate frequently. Thus, accountants charged with translating amounts in a foreign entity's financial statements to U.S. dollars face a problem similar to that involving inventory valuation during a period of purchase price fluctuations. Which exchange rate or rates should be used to translate the foreign entity's financial statements? A number of answers were proposed for this question prior to the issuance of ***FASB Statement No. 52,*** ''Foreign Currency Translation.'' The several methods for foreign currency translation may be grouped into three basic classes: ***current/noncurrent, monetary/nonmonetary,*** and ***current rate.*** (A fourth method, the ***temporal method,*** essentially is the same as the monetary/nonmonetary method.) The three classes differ principally in translation techniques for balance sheet amounts.

Current/Noncurrent Method   In the ***current/noncurrent method*** of translation, current assets and current liabilities are translated at the exchange rate in effect on the balance sheet date of the foreign entity (the ***current rate***). All other assets and liabilities, and the elements of owners' equity, are translated at the ***historical rates*** in effect at the time the assets, liabilities, and equities first were recognized in the foreign entity's accounting records. In the income statement, depreciation expense and amortization expense are translated at historical rates applicable to the related assets, while all other revenue and expenses are translated at an ***average*** exchange rate for the accounting period.

The current/noncurrent method of translating foreign investees' financial statements was sanctioned by the AICPA for many years. This method supposedly best reflected the ***liquidity*** aspects of the foreign entity's financial position by showing the current U.S. dollar equivalents of its working capital components. Today, the current/noncurrent method has few supporters. The principal theoretical objection to the current/noncurrent method is that, with respect to inventories, it represents a departure from historical cost. Inventories are translated at the *current rate,* rather than at *historical rates* in effect when the inventories were acquired, if the current/ noncurrent method of translating foreign currency accounts is applied.

Monetary/Nonmonetary Method The *monetary/nonmonetary method* of translating foreign currencies focuses on the characteristics of assets and liabilities of the foreign entity, rather than on their balance sheet classifications. This method is founded on the same monetary/nonmonetary aspects of assets and liabilities that are employed in historical-cost/constant-purchasing-power accounting, described in intermediate accounting textbooks. *Monetary assets and liabilities* — those representing claims or obligations expressed in a fixed monetary amount — are translated at the current exchange rate. All other assets, liabilities, and owners' equity amounts are translated at appropriate historical rates. In the income statement, average exchange rates are applied to all revenue and expenses except depreciation expense, amortization expense, and cost of goods sold, which are translated at appropriate historical rates.

Supporters of the monetary/nonmonetary method emphasized its retention of the historical-cost principle in the foreign entity's financial statements. Because the foreign entity's financial statements are consolidated or combined with those of the U.S. multinational enterprise, consistent accounting principles are applied in the consolidated or combined financial statements. The monetary/nonmonetary method essentially was sanctioned by the Financial Accounting Standards Board prior to the issuance of *FASB Statement No. 52.*

Current Rate Method Critics of the monetary/nonmonetary method point out that this method emphasizes the *parent company* aspects of a foreign entity's financial position and operating results. By reflecting the foreign entity's changes in assets and liabilities, and operating results, as though they were made in the parent company's *reporting currency,* the monetary/nonmonetary method misstates the actual financial position and operating results of the foreign entity.

Critics of the monetary/nonmonetary method of foreign currency translation generally have supported the *current rate method.* Under the current rate method, all balance sheet amounts other than owners' equity are translated at the current exchange rate. Owners' equity amounts are translated at historical rates.

To emphasize the *functional currency* aspects of the foreign entity's operations, all revenue and expenses may be translated at the current rate on the respective transaction dates, if practical. Otherwise, an average exchange rate is used for all revenue and expenses.

Standards for Translation Established by the Financial Accounting Standards Board

FASB Statement No. 52 adopted the current rate method, as described in the preceding section of this chapter, for *translating* a foreign entity's financial statements from the entity's *functional currency* to the *reporting currency* of the parent company, which for a U.S. enterprise is the U.S. dollar.[3] If a foreign entity's accounting

---

[3] Ibid., p. 5.

records are maintained in a currency other than its functional currency, account balances must be **remeasured** to the functional currency before the foreign entity's financial statements may be translated.[4] **Remeasurement** essentially is accomplished by the monetary/nonmonetary method of translation described on page 851. If a foreign entity's functional currency is the U.S. dollar, **remeasurement** eliminates the need for **translation** of the entity's financial statements. Because remeasurement, if required, **must precede translation,** remeasurement techniques are illustrated in the next section.

Remeasurement of a Foreign Entity's Accounts

The Financial Accounting Standards Board provided the following guidelines for remeasurement:[5]

> The remeasurement process should produce the same result as if the entity's books of record had been initially recorded in the functional currency. To accomplish that result, it is necessary to use historical exchange rates between the functional currency and another currency in the remeasurement process for certain accounts (the current rate will be used for all others), . . . it is also necessary to recognize currently in income all . . . gains and losses from remeasurement of monetary assets and liabilities that are not denominated in the functional currency (for example, assets and liabilities that are not denominated in dollars if the dollar is the functional currency).

The following list includes the nonmonetary balance sheet items and related revenue and expense amounts that should be **remeasured using historical rates** to produce the same result in terms of the functional currency that would have occurred if those items had been recorded initially in the functional currency. (All other items are remeasured using the current rate.)

Marketable securities carried at cost:
   Equity securities
   Debt securities not intended to be held until maturity
Inventories carried at cost
Short-term prepayments such as insurance, advertising, and rent
Plant assets and accumulated depreciation of plant assets
Patents, trademarks, licenses, formulas, goodwill, other intangible assets, and accumulated amortization of intangible assets
Deferred charges and credits, except deferred income tax assets and liabilities
Deferred revenue
Common stock
Preferred stock carried at issuance price
Examples of revenue and expenses related to nonmonetary items:
   Cost of goods sold
   Depreciation of plant assets

---

[4] Ibid.
[5] Ibid., pp. 31–32.

Amortization of intangible assets such as goodwill, patents, licenses, etc.

Amortization of deferred charges or credits except deferred income tax assets and liabilities

The appropriate historical or current exchange rate generally is the rate applicable to conversion of the foreign currency for dividend remittances.[6] Accordingly, a U.S. multinational enterprise having foreign branches, investees, or subsidiaries typically uses the buying spot rate on the balance sheet date or applicable historical date to remeasure the foreign currency financial statements.

Illustration of Remeasurement of a Foreign Entity's Account Balances

To illustrate the remeasurement of a foreign entity's account balances to the entity's functional currency from another currency, return to the Smaldino Company illustration in Chapter 4, with merchandise shipments by the home office billed to the branch in excess of home office cost. Assume that both the home office and the branch use the perpetual inventory system, that the branch is located in France, and that the functional currency of the branch is the U.S. dollar, although the branch maintains its accounting records in the French franc (FF), the *local currency*.

Year 1 transactions and events of Smaldino's home office and branch illustrated in Chapter 4 are repeated below. Following each transaction is the exchange rate for the French franc on the date of the transaction or event.

Transactions or Events for Year 1

(1) Cash of $1,000 was sent by the home office to the French branch (FF1 = $0.20).

(2) Merchandise with a cost of $60,000 was shipped by the home office to the French branch at a billed price of $90,000 (FF1 = $0.20).

(3) Equipment was acquired by the French branch for FF2,500, to be carried in the home office accounting records (FF1 = $0.20).

(4) Sales by the French branch on credit amounted to FF500,000 (FF1 = $0.16). Cost of goods sold was FF337,500.

(5) Collections of trade accounts receivable by the French branch amounted to FF248,000 (FF1 = $0.25).

(6) Payments for operating expenses by the French branch totaled FF80,000 (FF1 = $0.25).

(7) Cash of FF156,250 was remitted by the French branch to home office (FF1 = $0.24).

(8) Operating expenses incurred by the home office charged to the French branch totaled $3,000 (FF1 = $0.24).

The exchange rate on December 31, Year 1, was FF1 = $0.23.

The foregoing transactions or events are recorded by the home office and by the French branch with the following journal entries (explanations omitted):

---

[6] Ibid., p. 11.

SMALDINO COMPANY
Home Office and Branch Journal Entries
For Year 1

Home office accounting records (U.S. dollars)			French branch (Branch X) accounting records (French francs)		
(1) Investment in Branch X........	1,000		Cash	5,000	
Cash		1,000	Home Office...........		5,000
(2) Investment in Branch X........	90,000		Inventories	450,000	
Inventories		60,000	Home Office...........		450,000
Allowance for Overvalua-					
tion of Inventories:					
Branch X.............		30,000			
(3) Equipment: Branch X.........	500		Home Office..................	2,500	
Investment in Branch X..		500	Cash		2,500
(4) None			Trade Accounts Receivable....	500,000	
			Cost of Goods Sold	337,500	
			Sales..................		500,000
			Inventories		337,500
(5) None			Cash	248,000	
			Trade Accounts Receiv-		
			able		248,000
(6) None			Operating Expenses...........	80,000	
			Cash		80,000
(7) Cash	37,500		Home Office..................	156,250	
Investment in Branch X..		37,500	Cash		156,250
(8) Investment in Branch X........	3,000		Operating Expenses...........	12,500	
Operating Expenses		3,000	Home Office...........		12,500

Home office reciprocal
ledger account with
branch (in dollars)

Investment in Branch X (French Branch)

Date	Explanation	Debit	Credit	Balance
	Cash sent to branch	$ 1,000		$ 1,000 dr
	Merchandise shipped to branch	90,000		91,000 dr
	Equipment acquired by branch, carried in home office accounting records		$ 500	90,500 dr
	Cash received from branch		37,500	53,000 dr
	Operating expenses billed to branch	3,000		56,000 dr

In the home office accounting records, the Investment in Branch X (French branch) ledger account (in dollars before the accounts are closed) is on page 854.

In the branch accounting records, the Home Office ledger account (in francs before the accounts are closed) is on page 854.

Branch reciprocal ledger account with home office (in francs)

	Home Office			
Date	**Explanation**	**Debit**	**Credit**	**Balance**
	Cash received from home office		FF 5,000	FF 5,000 cr
	Merchandise received from home office		450,000	455,000 cr
	Equipment acquired by branch	FF 2,500		452,500 cr
	Cash sent to home office	156,250		296,250 cr
	Operating expenses billed by home office		12,500	308,750 cr

The branch trial balance (in francs) on December 31, Year 1, is shown below:

SMALDINO COMPANY
Branch X (French Branch) Trial Balance
December 31, Year 1

	Debit	Credit
Cash	FF 14,250	
Trade accounts receivable	252,000	
Inventories	112,500	
Home office		FF308,750
Sales		500,000
Cost of goods sold	337,500	
Operating expenses	92,500	
Totals	FF808,750	FF808,750

Remeasurement of Branch Trial Balance   Remeasurement of the branch trial balance is illustrated on page 856.

In the review of the remeasurement of the French branch trial balance, the following should be noted:

1   Monetary assets are remeasured at the current rate; the single nonmonetary asset —inventories—is remeasured at the appropriate historical rate.

2   To achieve the same result as remeasurement of the Home Office ledger account transactions at appropriate historical rates, the balance of the home office's Investment in Branch X account (in dollars) is substituted for the branch's Home Office

Working paper for
remeasurement of
branch trial balance to
functional currency
from local currency

SMALDINO COMPANY
Remeasurement of Branch X (French Branch) Trial Balance to U.S. Dollars
December 31, Year 1

	Balance (French francs) dr (cr)	Exchange rates	Balance (U.S. dollars) dr (cr)
Cash..........................	FF 14,250	$0.23 (1)	$ 3,278
Trade accounts receivable	252,000	0.23 (1)	57,960
Inventories	112,500	0.20 (2)	22,500
Home office	(308,750)	(3)	(56,000)
Sales	(500,000)	0.215 (4)	(107,500)
Cost of goods sold	337,500	0.20 (2)	67,500
Operating expenses.............	92,500	0.215 (4)	19,887
Subtotals....................	FF –0–		$ 7,625
Transaction gain	–0–		(7,625)
Totals.......................	FF –0–		$ –0–

(1) Current rate (on Dec. 31, Year 1)
(2) Historical rate (when goods were shipped to branch by home office)
(3) Balance of Investment in Branch X ledger account in home office accounting records
(4) Average of beginning (FF1 = $0.20) and ending (FF1 = $0.23) exchange rates for Year 1

account (in francs). All equity ledger accounts—regardless of legal form of the investee—are remeasured at historical rates.

3   A simple average of beginning-of-year and end-of-year exchange rates is used to remeasure revenue and expense accounts other than cost of goods sold, which is remeasured at the appropriate historical rates. In practice, a quarterly, monthly, or even daily weighted average might be computed.

4   A balancing amount labeled ***transaction gain,*** which is *not* a ***ledger account,*** is used to reconcile the total debits and total credits of the branch's remeasured trial balance. This transaction gain is included in the measurement of the branch's net income for Year 1, because it results from the branch's transactions' having been recorded in French ***francs,*** the branch's local currency, rather than in ***dollars,*** the branch's functional currency.[7]

After the trial balance of the French branch has been remeasured from French francs to U.S. dollars, combined financial statements for home office and branch may be prepared as illustrated in Chapter 4, because the branch's functional currency is the U.S. dollar.

Translation of a Foreign Entity's Financial Statements

As indicated on page 851, if a foreign entity's financial statement amounts are expressed in a functional currency other than the U.S. dollar, those amounts must be translated to dollars by the current rate method. The following sections illustrate

[7] Ibid., p. 31.

translation of the financial statements of a foreign influenced investee and a foreign subsidiary.

Translation of Financial Statements of Foreign Influenced Investee To illustrate the translation of the financial statements of a foreign investee whose functional currency is its local currency, assume that on May 31, Year 6, Colossus Company, a U.S. multinational company, acquired 30% of the outstanding common stock of a corporation in Venezuela, which is termed Venezuela Investee. Although the investment of Colossus enabled it to exercise influence over the operations and financial policies of Venezuela Investee, that entity's functional currency was the bolivar (B). Colossus acquired its investment in Venezuela Investee for B600,000, which Colossus acquired at the selling spot rate of B1 = $0.25, for a total cost of $150,000. Out-of-pocket costs of the investment may be disregarded. Stockholders' equity of Venezuela Investee on May 31, Year 6, was as follows:

Stockholders' equity of foreign investee on date of investment	

Common stock..	B 500,000
Additional paid-in capital	600,000
Retained earnings...	900,000
Total stockholders' equity	B2,000,000

There was no difference between the cost of Colossus Company's investment and its equity in the net assets of Venezuela Investee (B2,000,000 × 0.30 = B600,000, the cost of the investment).

Translation of Venezuela Investee's financial statements from the functional currency to the U.S. dollar *reporting currency* for the year ended May 31, Year 7, is illustrated below and on page 858. The exchange rates for the bolivar were as follows:

Exchange rates for Venezuelan bolivar	

May 31, Year 6..	$0.25
May 31, Year 7..	0.27
Average for year ended May 31, Year 7.................................	0.26

Working paper for *translation* of investee financial statements to reporting currency from functional currency

VENEZUELA INVESTEE
Translation of Financial Statements to U.S. Dollars
For Year Ended May 31, Year 7

	Venezuelan bolivars	Exchange rates	U.S. dollars
Income Statement			
Net sales..........................	B6,000,000	$0.26 (1)	$1,560,000
Costs and expenses.................	4,000,000	0.26 (1)	1,040,000
Net income	B2,000,000		$ 520,000

(continued)

VENEZUELA INVESTEE
Translation of Financial Statements to U.S. Dollars (concluded)
For Year Ended May 31, Year 7

	Venezuelan bolivars	Exchange rates	U.S. dollars
Statement of Retained Earnings			
Retained earnings, beginning of year....	B 900,000	0.25 (2)	$ 225,000
Add: Net income	2,000,000		520,000
Subtotals..........................	B2,900,000		$ 745,000
Less: Dividends*	600,000	0.27 (3)	162,000
Retained earnings, end of year	B2,300,000		$ 583,000
Balance Sheet			
Assets			
Current assets	B 200,000	0.27 (3)	$ 54,000
Plant assets (net)	4,500,000	0.27 (3)	1,215,000
Other assets..........................	300,000	0.27 (3)	81,000
Total assets	B5,000,000		$1,350,000
Liabilities & Stockholders' Equity			
Current liabilities	B 100,000	0.27 (3)	$ 27,000
Long-term debt.......................	1,500,000	0.27 (3)	405,000
Common Stock	500,000	0.25 (2)	125,000
Additional paid-in capital	600,000	0.25 (2)	150,000
Retained earnings....................	2,300,000		583,000
Cumulative translation adjustments......			60,000
Total liabilities & stockholders' equity ..	B5,000,000		$1,350,000

* Dividends were declared on May 31, Year 7.

(1) Average rate for year ended May 31, Year 7
(2) Historical rate (on May 31, Year 6, date of Colossus Company's investment)
(3) Current rate (on May 31, Year 7)

In the review of the translation of the foreign investee's financial statements illustrated on page 857 and above, the following features may be emphasized:

1   All assets and liabilities are translated at the current rate.

2   The paid-in capital amounts and the beginning retained earnings are translated at the historical rate on the date of Colossus Company's acquisition of its investment in Venezuela Investee.

3   The average rate for the year ended May 31, Year 7, is used to translate all revenue and expenses in the income statement.

4   A balancing amount labeled *cumulative translation adjustments,* which is *not* a *ledger account,* is used to reconcile total liabilities and stockholders' equity with total assets in the translated balance sheet of Venezuela Investee. Cumulative translation adjustments are displayed in the stockholders' equity section of the translated balance sheet.[8]

Following the translation of Venezuela Investee's financial statements from bolivars (the *functional currency* of Venezuela Investee) to U.S. dollars (the *reporting currency* of Colossus Company), Colossus prepares the following journal entries in U.S. dollars under the equity method of accounting for an investment in common stock:

Investor company's journal entries under equity method of accounting

Investment in Venezuela Investee Common Stock
  ($520,000 × 0.30)   156,000
    Investment income.   156,000
To record 30% of net income of Venezuela Investee. (Income tax
effects are disregarded.)

Dividends Receivable ($162,000 × 0.30).   48,600
    Investment in Venezuela Investee Common Stock   48,600
To record dividends receivable from Venezuela Investee.

After the foregoing journal entries are posted, the Investment ledger account of Colossus Company (in U.S. dollars) is as follows:

Investment ledger account of investor

Investment in Venezuela Investee Common Stock

Date	Explanation	Debit	Credit	Balance
Year 6				
May 31	Acquisition of 30% of common			
	stock	150,000		150,000 dr
Year 7				
May 31	Share of net income	156,000		306,000 dr
31	Share of dividends		48,600	257,400 dr

The $257,400 balance of the Investment account is equal to Colossus Company's share of the total stockholders' equity, *excluding cumulative translation adjustments,* in the translated balance sheet of Venezuela Investee [($125,000 + $150,000 + $583,000) × 0.30 = $257,400]. Cumulative translation adjustments, which are not operating revenues, gains, expenses, or losses, do not enter into the computation of the translated net income or dividends of Venezuela Investee; therefore, no portion of cumulative translation adjustments is reflected in the investor's Investment ledger account. Cumulative translation adjustments are displayed in the stockholders' equity section of Venezuela Investee's translated balance sheet until

---

[8] Ibid., p. 6.

sale or liquidation of Colossus Company's investment in Venezuela Investee. At that time, the amount of the cumulative translation adjustments is included in the measurement of the gain or loss on sale or liquidation of the investment in Venezuela Investee.[9]

Translation and Consolidation of Financial Statements of Foreign Subsidiary

To illustrate the translation and consolidation of financial statements of a foreign subsidiary whose functional currency is its local currency, assume that on August 31, Year 3, SoPac Corporation, a U.S. enterprise with no subsidiaries, acquired at the selling spot rate of $NZ1 = $0.52 a draft for 500,000 New Zealand dollars (symbol $NZ), which it used to acquire all 10,000 authorized shares of $NZ50 par common stock of newly organized Anzac, Ltd., a New Zealand enterprise. The out-of-pocket costs of the acquisition were immaterial and thus recognized as expense by SoPac, which prepared the following journal entry for the investment:

Journal entry for investment in foreign subsidiary

Year 3

Aug. 31	*Investment in Anzac, Ltd., Common Stock ($NZ500,000 × $0.52)*	*260,000*	
	Cash		*260,000*
	To record acquisition of 10,000 shares of $NZ50 par common stock of Anzac, Ltd.		

ANZAC, LTD.
Balance Sheet
August 31, Year 4

Assets

Cash	$NZ 10,000
Trade accounts receivable (net)	40,000
Inventories	180,000
Short-term prepayments	4,000
Plant assets (net)	320,000
Intangible assets (net)	20,000
Total assets	$NZ574,000

Liabilities & Stockholder's Equity

Notes payable	$NZ 20,000
Trade accounts payable	30,000
Total liabilities	$NZ 50,000
Common stock, $NZ50 par	$NZ500,000
Retained earnings	24,000
Total stockholder's equity	$NZ524,000
Total liabilities & stockholder's equity	$NZ574,000

---

[9] Ibid.

Anzac, Ltd., was self-contained in New Zealand, where it conducted all its operations. Thus, the functional currency of Anzac was the New Zealand dollar. Further, to enhance Anzac's growth, the board of directors of SoPac decided that Anzac should pay no dividends to SoPac in the foreseeable future.

For the year ended August 31, Year 4, Anzac prepared the balance sheet on page 860 and the income statement below (a statement of cash flows is disregarded).

ANZAC, LTD.
Income Statement
For Year Ended August 31, Year 4

Revenue:		
Net sales		*$NZ240,000*
Other		*60,000*
Total revenue		*$NZ300,000*
Costs and expenses:		
Cost of goods sold	*$NZ180,000*	
Operating expenses and income taxes expense	*96,000*	
Total costs and expenses		*276,000*
Net income (retained earnings, end of year)		*$NZ 24,000*

Translation of the financial statements of Anzac, Ltd., from the functional currency to the U.S. dollar *reporting currency* for the year ended August 31, Year 4, is illustrated on page 862. The exchange rates for the New Zealand dollar were as follows:

Aug. 31, Year 3	*$0.52*
Aug. 31, Year 4	*0.50*
Average for year ended Aug. 31, Year 4	*0.51*

Following the translation of the financial statements of Anzac, Ltd., from New Zealand dollars (the functional currency of Anzac) to U.S. dollars (the reporting currency of SoPac Corporation), SoPac prepares the following journal entry in U.S. dollars under the equity method of accounting for an investment in common stock:

Parent company's journal entry under equity method of accounting	*Year 4*		
	Aug. 31	*Investment in Anzac, Ltd., Common Stock* *12,240*	
		Intercompany Investment Income	*12,240*
		To record 100% of net income of Anzac, Ltd. (Income tax effects are disregarded.)	

After the foregoing journal entry is posted, the balance of SoPac's Investment in Anzac, Ltd., Common Stock ledger account is $272,240 ($260,000 + $12,240 = $272,240), which is equal to the total stockholder's equity of Anzac, Ltd., *excluding cumulative translation adjustments,* in the translated balance sheet of Anzac

Working paper for **translation** of subsidiary financial statements to reporting currency from functional currency

ANZAC, LTD.
Translation of Financial Statements to U.S. Dollars
For Year Ended August 31, Year 4

	New Zealand dollars	Exchange rate	U.S. dollars
Income Statement			
Net sales............................	$NZ240,000	$0.51 (1)	$122,400
Other revenue	60,000	0.51 (1)	30,600
Total revenue.......................	$NZ300,000		$153,000
Cost of goods sold	$NZ180,000	0.51 (1)	$ 91,800
Operating expenses and income taxes expense	96,000	0.51 (1)	48,960
Total costs and expenses.............	$NZ276,000		$140,760
Net income (retained earnings, end of year)................................	$NZ 24,000		$ 12,240
Balance Sheet			
Cash	$NZ 10,000	0.50 (2)	$ 5,000
Trade accounts receivable (net)	40,000	0.50 (2)	20,000
Inventories	180,000	0.50 (2)	90,000
Short-term prepayments	4,000	0.50 (2)	2,000
Plant assets (net)	320,000	0.50 (2)	160,000
Intangible assets (net)	20,000	0.50 (2)	10,000
Total assets	$NZ574,000		$287,000
Notes payable	$NZ 20,000	$0.50 (2)	$ 10,000
Trade accounts payable	30,000	0.50 (2)	15,000
Common stock........................	500,000	0.52 (3)	260,000
Retained earnings.....................	24,000		12,240
Cumulative translation adjustments			(10,240)
Total liabilities & stockholder's equity...	$NZ574,000		$287,000

(1) Average for year ended Aug. 31, Year 4
(2) Current rate (on Aug. 31, Year 4)
(3) Historical rate (on Aug. 31, Year 3, date of SoPac Corporation's investment)

($260,000 + $12,240 = $272,240). SoPac is now enabled to prepare the working paper elimination (in journal entry format), the working paper for consolidated financial statements, and the consolidated financial statements that follow (other amounts for SoPac are assumed).

SOPAC CORPORATION AND SUBSIDIARY
Working Paper Elimination
August 31, Year 4

(a) *Common Stock—Anzac* 260,000

Intercompany Investment Income—SoPac................. 12,240

Investment in Anzac, Ltd., Common Stock—SoPac..... 272,240

To eliminate intercompany investment and equity account of subsidiary **at beginning of year.** *(Income tax effects are disregarded.)*

Equity method: wholly owned subsidiary subsequent to date of purchase-type business combination

SOPAC CORPORATION AND SUBSIDIARY
Working Paper for Consolidated Financial Statements
For Year Ended August 31, Year 4

	SoPac Corporation	*Anzac, Ltd.*	*Eliminations increase (decrease)*	*Consolidated*
Income Statement				
Revenue:				
Net sales	840,000	122,400		962,400
Intercompany investment income.......	12,240		*(a) (12,240)*	
Other................................	120,000	30,600		150,600
Total revenue	972,240	153,000	(12,240)	1,113,000
Costs and expenses:				
Cost of goods sold..................	720,000	91,800		811,800
Operating expenses and income taxes				
expense...........................	160,000	48,960		208,960
Total costs and expenses	880,000	140,760		1,020,760
Net income	92,240	12,240	(12,240)	92,240
Statement of Retained Earnings				
Retained earnings, beginning of year	480,000			480,000
Net income	92,240	12,240	(12,240)	92,240
Subtotal	572,240	12,240	(12,240)	572,240
Dividends declared	30,000			30,000
Retained earnings, end of year...........	542,240	12,240	(12,240)	542,240

(continued)

SOPAC CORPORATION AND SUBSIDIARY
Working Paper for Consolidated Financial Statements (concluded)
For Year Ended August 31, Year 4

	SoPac Corporation	Anzac, Ltd.	Eliminations increase (decrease)	Consolidated
Balance Sheet				
Assets				
Cash...................................	80,000	5,000		85,000
Trade accounts receivable (net)..........	270,000	20,000		290,000
Inventories.............................	340,000	90,000		430,000
Short-term prepayments................	12,000	2,000		14,000
Investment in Anzac, Ltd., common stock .	272,240		(a) (272,240)	
Plant assets (net)......................	618,000	160,000		778,000
Intangible assets (net)..................	80,000	10,000		90,000
Total assets.........................	1,672,240	287,000	(272,240)	1,687,000
Liabilities & Stockholders' Equity				
Notes payable.........................	50,000	10,000		60,000
Trade accounts payable................	80,000	15,000		95,000
Long-term debt........................	400,000			400,000
Common stock.........................	600,000	260,000	(a) (260,000)	600,000
Retained earnings	542,240	12,240	(12,240)	542,240
Cumulative translation adjustments.......		(10,240)		(10,240)
Total liabilities & stockholders' equity ...	1,672,240	287,000	(272,240)	1,687,000

SOPAC CORPORATION AND SUBSIDIARY
Consolidated Income Statement
For Year Ended August 31, Year 4

Revenue:		
Net sales		$ 962,400
Other		150,600
Total revenue		$1,113,000
Costs and expenses:		
Cost of goods sold.....................................	$811,800	
Operating expenses and income taxes expense............	208,960	
Total costs and expenses		1,020,760
Net income		$ 92,240
Earnings per share of common stock (60,000 shares outstanding)........	$	1.54

SOPAC CORPORATION AND SUBSIDIARY
Consolidated Statement of Retained Earnings
For Year Ended August 31, Year 4

Retained earnings, beginning of year	$480,000
Add: Net income	92,240
Subtotal	$572,240
Less: Dividends ($0.50 a share)	30,000
Retained earnings, end of year	$542,240

SOPAC CORPORATION AND SUBSIDIARY
Consolidated Balance Sheet
August 31, Year 4

Assets

Current assets:		
Cash	$	85,000
Trade accounts receivable (net)		290,000
Inventories		430,000
Short-term prepayments		14,000
Total current assets	$	819,000
Plant assets (net)		778,000
Intangible assets (net)		90,000
Total assets		$1,687,000

Liabilities & Stockholders' Equity

Current liabilities:			
Notes payable		$	60,000
Trade accounts payable			95,000
Total current liabilities		$	155,000
Long-term debt			400,000
Total liabilities		$	555,000
Stockholders' equity:			
Common stock, $10 par	$600,000		
Retained earnings	542,240		
Cumulative translation adjustments	(10,240)		
Total stockholders' equity			1,132,000
Total liabilities & stockholders' equity			$1,687,000

Summary: Remeasurement and Translation   Principal features of the foregoing discussion of remeasurement of a foreign entity's accounts and translation of a foreign entity's financial statements are summarized in the table on page 866.

Other Aspects of Foreign Currency Translation

In addition to the topics discussed thus far, the four topics described in the following sections are included in *FASB Statement No. 52*.

Comparison of *Remeasurement* and *Translation*

Feature	Remeasurement	Translation
Underlying concept	Foreign entity's accounts should reflect transactions and events as though recorded in the **functional currency** rather than the **local currency.**	Foreign entity's financial statements should reflect financial results and relationships created in the economic environment of the foreign operations.
When required	(1) Foreign entity's accounts are maintained in **local currency** instead of **functional currency.** (2) Foreign entity is operating in a **highly inflationary economy** (see page 867).	Foreign entity's **functional currency** is not the **reporting currency.**
Method used	Monetary/nonmonetary method	Current rate method
Display of balancing amount	In income statement as transaction gain or loss	In balance sheet, stockholders' equity section, as cumulative translation adjustments

Transaction Gains and Losses Excluded from Net Income   The Financial Accounting Standards Board required that gains and losses from the following foreign currency transactions be accounted for in the same manner as ***translation adjustments:***[10]

1   Foreign currency transactions that are designated as, and are effective as, economic hedges of a net investment in a foreign entity, commencing as of the designation date

2   Intercompany foreign currency transactions that are of a long-term investment nature (that is, settlement is not planned or anticipated in the foreseeable future), when the entities to the transaction are consolidated, combined, or accounted for by the equity method . . .

To illustrate an economic hedge of a net investment in a foreign entity, return to the Venezuela Investee illustration on pages 857 to 860 and assume that, to hedge its investment, Colossus Company borrowed B1,020,000 from a Venezuela bank on May 31, Year 7. B1,020,000 is equal to the carrying amount, in bolivars, of Colossus Company's investment on May 31, Year 7 [(B500,000 + B600,000 + B2,300,000) $\times$ 0.30 = B1,020,000]. If the exchange rate for the bolivar was B1 = $0.28 on May 31, Year 8, Colossus had a transaction loss of $10,200 [B1,020,000 $\times$ ($0.28 − $0.27) = $10,200] during the year ended May 31, Year 8, on the loan payable to the Venezuela bank. Disregarding income taxes, no part of the $10,200 transaction loss is recognized by Colossus if cumulative translation adjustments in the May 31, Year 8, translated balance sheet of Venezuela Investee are at

---

[10] Ibid., p. 8.

least $70,200, which is a $10,200 increase ($70,200 − $60,000 = $10,200) over the May 31, Year 7, balance. If, however, cumulative translation adjustments are less than $70,200 on May 31, Year 8, Colossus Company recognizes an appropriate part of the transaction loss. For example, if cumulative translation adjustments in the May 31, Year 8, translated balance sheet are $64,500, Colossus prepares the following journal entry on May 31, Year 8:

Investor company's journal entry for transaction loss on hedging loan	*Transaction Gains and Losses.....................................*	*5,700*	
	Loan Payable to Venezuela Bank..........................		*5,700*

To recognize transaction loss on loan obtained to hedge investment in Venezuela Investee as follows:

Liability recorded on May 31, Year 7 (B1,020,000 × $0.27)..............................	$275,400
Less: Liability translated at spot rate B1 = $0.28 (B1,020,000 × $0.28).............................	285,600
Difference..	$ (10,200)
Less: Increase in cumulative translation adjustments of investee ($64,500 − $60,000)......................	4,500
Transaction loss recognized.......................	$ (5,700)

Functional Currency in Highly Inflationary Economies The Financial Accounting Standards Board required that the functional currency of a foreign entity in a highly inflationary economy be identified as the reporting currency (the U.S. dollar for a U.S. multinational enterprise). The FASB defined a ***highly inflationary economy*** as one having cumulative inflation of 100% or more over a three-year period.[11] Thus, financial statements of a foreign entity in a country experiencing severe inflation are remeasured in U.S. dollars, regardless of the criteria for determination of the functional currency described on pages 848 to 850.

Income Taxes Related to Foreign Currency Translation Conventional interperiod and intraperiod income tax allocation procedures were prescribed by the Financial Accounting Standards Board for the income tax effects of foreign currency translation, as follows:[12]

1 Interperiod tax allocation for temporary differences associated with transaction gains and losses that are reported in different accounting periods for financial accounting and income taxes [Interperiod tax allocation is discussed in intermediate accounting textbooks.]

2 Interperiod tax allocation for temporary differences associated with translation adjustments that do not meet the criteria for nonrecognition of deferred tax liabilities for undistributed earnings of foreign subsidiaries (See Chapter 10, page 496.)

---

[11] Ibid., p. 5.
[12] Ibid., pp. 9–10.

3   Intraperiod tax allocation for translation adjustments included in the stockholders' equity section of the balance sheet [Intraperiod tax allocation is discussed in intermediate accounting textbooks.]

Disclosure of Foreign Currency Translation   The Financial Accounting Standards Board required disclosure, in the income statement or in a note to the financial statements, of the aggregate transaction gains or losses of an accounting period. Further, the FASB required disclosure of changes in cumulative translation adjustments during an accounting period, in a separate financial statement, in a note to financial statements, or in a statement of stockholders' equity. The minimum required disclosure is:[13]

1   Beginning and ending amounts of cumulative translation adjustments

2   Aggregate adjustments during the accounting period for translation adjustments, hedges of net investments, and long-term intercompany transactions

3   Income taxes allocated to translation adjustments during the period

4   Decreases resulting from sale or liquidation of an investment in a foreign entity

Following is an example of disclosure of foreign currency matters in a note to the financial statements of Johnson & Johnson, a publicly owned enterprise:[14]

8. Foreign Currency Translation

For translation of its international currencies, the Company has determined that the local currencies of its international subsidiaries are the functional currencies except those in highly inflationary economies, which are defined as those which have had compound cumulative rates of inflation of 100% or more during the past three years.

In consolidating international subsidiaries, balance sheet currency effects are recorded as a separate component of stockholders' equity. This equity account includes the results of translating all balance sheet assets and liabilities at current exchange rates, except for those located in highly inflationary economies, principally Brazil, which are reflected in operating results. These translation adjustments do not exist in terms of functional cash flows; such adjustments are not reported as part of operating results since realization is remote unless the international businesses were sold or liquidated.

An analysis of the changes during 1990 and 1989 in the separate component of stockholders' equity for cumulative currency translation adjustments follows:

(Dollars in millions)	*1990*	*1989*
Beginning of year	*$ (9)*	*(22)*
Translation adjustments	*250*	*13*
End of year	*241*	*(9)*

---

[13] Ibid., pp. 12–13.
[14] *Accounting Trends & Techniques,* 45th ed., AICPA (New York: 1991), pp. 249–250.

Net currency transaction and translation gains and losses included in other expense were after-tax losses of $124, $141 and $61 million in 1990, 1989 and 1988, respectively, incurred principally in Latin America.

International Accounting Standard 21

The provisions of *IAS 21,* "Accounting for the Effects of Changes in Foreign Exchange Rates," dealing with translation of foreign currency financial statements are comparable with those of *FASB No. 52,* "Foreign Currency Translation." A difference is that *IAS 21* states a preference for applying price-level adjustments (a topic discussed in intermediate accounting textbooks and covered in *IAS 15,* "Information Reflecting the Effects of Changing Prices") prior to the translation of financial statements of foreign entities operating in highly inflationary economies.

Appraisal of Accounting Standards for Foreign Currency Translation

FASB Statement No. 52 was approved by the Financial Accounting Standards Board by a bare four-to-three majority, which indicates the degree of dissatisfaction with the standards it established for foreign currency translation. Among the criticisms of *FASB Statement No. 52* are the following:

1 It established an indefensible distinction between *transaction gains and losses* arising from *remeasurement* and *translation adjustments* resulting from *translation.* Both *remeasurement* and *translation* involve comparable activities—the restatement of amounts in a foreign currency to another currency—thus, they should be accounted for in the same manner.

2 It provided for the inclusion of an item in stockholders' equity—cumulative translation adjustments—that does not meet the traditional definition of *owners' equity.*

3 It abandoned the historical-cost principle by sanctioning use of the current rate method for translation of foreign currency financial statements.

It appears that *FASB Statement No. 52* has been accepted by the business community. *FASB Statement No. 8,* "Accounting for the Translation of Foreign Currency Transactions and Foreign Currency Financial Statements," which was superseded by *FASB Statement No. 52,* was in effect for little more than six years, during which time it was the subject of continuous controversy. *FASB Statement No. 8* was criticized for its requirements that translation adjustments be included in the measurement of net income and that the monetary/nonmonetary method be used to translate a foreign entity's financial statements. Critics of *FASB Statement No. 8* alleged that those requirements resulted in uncontrollable and misleading fluctuations in earnings of U.S. multinational enterprises.

REVIEW QUESTIONS

1 What is the *functional currency* of a foreign entity?

2 Differentiate between the *current/noncurrent method* and the *current rate method* of translating foreign currency financial statements.

3   What exchange rate is used to remeasure to U.S. dollars (the functional currency) the balance of the Intercompany Accounts Payable ledger account of a foreign subsidiary of a U.S. parent company? Explain.

4   Differentiate *remeasurement to functional currency* from *foreign currency translation.*

5   Differentiate between *transaction gains and losses* and *translation adjustments.*

6   What *transaction gains and losses* are excluded from the measurement of net income?

7   What is the functional currency of a foreign investee in a highly inflationary economy?

8   What disclosures relating to foreign currency matters are required in the financial statements or in a note to the financial statements of U.S. multinational enterprises?

9   List three criticisms of *FASB Statement No. 52,* ''Foreign Currency Translation.''

EXERCISES

Ex. 19-1   Select the best answer for each of the following multiple-choice questions:

1   The functional currency of a foreign subsidiary might be any of the following except the:
a Local currency
b Reporting currency
c Supplemental Drawing Rights of the International Monetary Fund
d Currency in which the subsidiary maintains its accounting records

2   If a foreign subsidiary of a U.S. multinational enterprise has a functional currency other than its local currency and the U.S. dollar, the subsidiary's financial statements must be:
a Remeasured to the U.S. dollar only
b Translated to the U.S. dollar only
c Remeasured to the functional currency and translated to the U.S. dollar
d Translated to the functional currency and remeasured to the U.S. dollar

3   Gains and losses resulting from remeasurement of foreign currency financial statements to functional currency should be included as:
a A part of equity in the balance sheet
b An extraordinary item in the income statement for the accounting period in which remeasurement takes place
c An ordinary item in the income statement for losses but deferred for gains
d An ordinary item in the income statement for the accounting period in which remeasurement takes place

4 According to *FASB Statement No. 52*, "Foreign Currency Translation," re-measurement of a foreign subsidiary's accounting records to the subsidiary's functional currency should be accomplished by the:

a Monetary/nonmonetary method

b Current rate method

c Current/noncurrent method

d Functional currency method

5 The monetary/nonmonetary method of foreign currency translation currently is used for:

a Remeasurement but not for translation

b Translation but not for remeasurement

c Both remeasurement and translation

d Neither remeasurement nor translation

6 According to *FASB Statement No. 52*, "Foreign Currency Translation," the appropriate method of restatement from a foreign currency to the U.S. dollar for each of the following is:

	Remeasurement	*Translation*
a	*Current rate*	*Monetary/nonmonetary*
b	*Monetary/nonmonetary*	*Current rate*
c	*Monetary/nonmonetary*	*Monetary/nonmonetary*
d	*Current rate*	*Current rate*

7 Displayed in the income statement of a U.S. multinational enterprise are:

a Transaction gains and losses only

b Cumulative translation adjustments only

c Both transaction gains and losses and cumulative translation adjustments

d Neither transaction gains and losses nor cumulative translation adjustments

8 With respect to a foreign subsidiary's financial statements, are transaction gains and losses recognized in:

	Remeasurement from local currency to functional currency?	*Translation from functional currency to reporting currency?*
a	*Yes*	*Yes*
b	*Yes*	*No*
c	*No*	*Yes*
d	*No*	*No*

9 Do *cumulative translation adjustments* result from:

	Remeasurement of a branch's trial balance?	*Translation of a foreign investee's financial statements?*
a	*Yes*	*No*
b	*No*	*Yes*
c	*No*	*No*
d	*Yes*	*Yes*

10 Cumulative translation adjustments arising from translation of the financial statements of a foreign entity are reported in:

a Stockholders' equity of the foreign entity

b Revenue or expenses of the foreign entity

c Consolidated net income of the parent company and the foreign entity

d Paid-in capital of the parent company

Ex. 19-2 Among the journal entries of the Belgian branch of Logan Company for the month of April, Year 4, were the following, denominated in Belgian francs (BF):

```
Apr.  4   Cash.........................................  BF10,000
                Home Office............................                BF10,000
          To record receipt and conversion to francs of $2,400
          draft sent by the home office on Apr. 1, Year 4.


     16   Home Office..................................  BF50,000
                Cash .................................                  BF50,000
          To record payment for equipment to be carried in the
          home office accounting records.


     28   Home Office..................................  BF 4,000
                Cash .................................                  BF 4,000
          To record dispatch of BF4,000 draft to home office.
```

Spot exchange rates for Belgian francs during April, Year 4, were as follows:

	BF1 =	
	Buying	**Selling**
Apr. 1	$0.22	$0.24
4	0.23	0.25
16	0.21	0.22
28	0.23	0.24
30	0.22	0.23

The home office of Logan Company received and converted the BF4,000 draft to U.S. dollars on April 30, Year 4.

Prepare journal entries, denominated in U.S. dollars, for the home office of Logan Company to reflect appropriately the foregoing transactions and events of the Belgian branch.

Ex. 19-3 A wholly owned foreign subsidiary of Multiverse Company had selected expense accounts stated in local currency units (LCU) for the year ended November 30, Year 10, as follows:

Doubtful accounts expense...	LCU 60,000
Patent amortization expense (patent acquired Dec. 1, Year 7)..........	40,000
Rent expense...	100,000

The functional currency of the foreign subsidiary is the U.S. dollar. The exchange rates for the LCU for various dates or periods were as follows:

Dec. 1, Year 7..	$0.25
Nov. 30, Year 10	0.20
Average for year ended Nov. 30, Year 10	0.22

Prepare a working paper to compute the total dollar amount to be included in the remeasured income statement of Multiverse Company's foreign subsidiary for the year ended November 30, Year 10, for the foregoing expense accounts.

Ex. 19-4 The foreign subsidiary of Paloma Company, a U.S. multinational enterprise, had plant assets on December 31, Year 5, with a cost of 3,600,000 local currency units (LCU). Of this amount, plant assets with a cost of LCU2,400,000 were acquired in Year 3, when the exchange rate was LCU1 = $0.625; and plant assets with a cost of LCU1,200,000 were acquired in Year 4, when the exchange rate was LCU1 = $0.556. The exchange rate on December 31, Year 5, was LCU1 = $0.500, and the weighted-average exchange rate for Year 5 was LCU1 = $0.521. The foreign subsidiary depreciated plant assets by the straight-line method over a 10-year economic life with no residual value. The U.S. dollar was the functional currency of the foreign subsidiary.

Prepare a working paper to compute for Year 5 the depreciation expense for Paloma Company's foreign subsidiary, in U.S. dollars, for the remeasured income statement.

Ex. 19-5 Following is the franc-denominated trial balance of the French Branch of USA Corporation on June 30, Year 5, the end of the first month of the branch's operations:

USA CORPORATION
French Branch Trial Balance
June 30, Year 5

Cash	FF 15,000	
Trade accounts receivable	250,000	
Inventories	115,000	
Home office		FF360,000
Sales		450,000
Cost of goods sold	340,000	
Operating expenses	90,000	
Totals	FF810,000	FF810,000

Additional Information

(1) All the merchandise in the branch's inventories on June 30, Year 5, had been shipped by the home office on June 1, Year 5, when the exchange rate was FF1 = $0.20.

(2) The balance of the home office's Investment in French Branch ledger account on June 30, Year 5, was $70,000.

(3) The exchange rate on June 30, Year 5, was FF1 = $0.18.

Prepare a working paper to remeasure the June 30, Year 5 trial balance of French Branch of USA Corporation to U.S. dollars, the branch's functional currency.

Ex. 19-6 The trial balance of the German Branch of Global Company, a U.S. multinational enterprise, on April 30, Year 7, the end of the first month of the branch's operations, was as follows [denominated in deutsche marks (DM)]:

GLOBAL COMPANY
German Branch Trial Balance
April 30, Year 7

	Debit	Credit
Cash...	DM 15,000	
Trade accounts receivable............................	260,000	
Inventories...	120,000	
Home office...		DM280,000
Sales..		550,000
Cost of goods sold..................................	340,000	
Operating expenses	95,000	
Totals...	DM830,000	DM830,000

The balance of Global Company's home office's Investment in German Branch ledger account on April 30, Year 7, was $46,000. Relevant exchange rate for the deutsche mark were as follows:

	DM1 =
Apr. 1, Year 7 (date of Global's home office's only shipment of merchandise to	
the branch)..	$0.15
Apr. 30, Year 7	0.13
Average for April, Year 7..	0.14

Prepare a working paper to remeasure the April 30, Year 7, trial balance of the German Branch of Global Company to U.S. dollars, its functional currency, from German deutsche marks. Round all amounts to the nearest dollar. Use the following columns in your working paper:

Balance (DM) dr (cr)	Exchange rates	Balance ($) dr (cr)

Ex. 19-7   The translated balance sheet items of Spanish Company, wholly owned foreign subsidiary of U.S. corporation, which owned all of Spanish's authorized common stock, were as follows on November 30, Year 9:

Additional paid-in capital	$100,000
Common stock...	50,000
Cumulative translation adjustments (credit balance)......................	30,000
Current assets	180,000
Current liabilities	80,000
Long-term debt	120,000
Other assets..	60,000
Plant assets (net)	260,000
Retained earnings..	120,000

Prepare a balance sheet for Spanish Company on November 30, Year 9.

Ex. 19-8   For the year ended December 31, Year 7, its first year of operations after its establishment by its parent company, Stateside Corporation, wholly owned Overseas Company had the following financial statement amounts, denominated in its functional currency, the local currency unit (LCU):

Total revenue	LCU800,000
Total expenses	600,000
Total assets	900,000
Total liabilities.	500,000
Stockholders' equity:	
Common stock, LCU1 par.	200,000
Retained earnings (no dividends declared)	200,000

Exchange rates for the LCU were as follows:

Jan. 2, Year 7 (date Overseas was established)	LCU1 = $0.44
Dec. 31, Year 7	LCU1 = $0.48
Average for Year 7	LCU1 = $0.46

Prepare a working paper to compute the cumulative translation adjustments to be displayed in the translated balance sheet, stockholder's equity section, of Overseas Company on December 31, Year 7.

Ex. 19-9   On December 31, Year 7, Investor Corporation, a U.S. multinational enterprise, had a 20% influencing investment in the common stock of Foreign Investee Company, whose stockholders' equity totaled 1,500,000 local currency units (LCU), its functional currency, on that date. The translated balance sheet of Foreign Investee on December 31, Year 7, included in stockholders' equity cumulative translation adjustments of $47,600 (credit balance). On January 2, Year 8, to hedge its net investment in Foreign Investee, Investor borrowed LCU300,000 when the exchange rate was LCU1 = $0.20, which was the same exchange rate in effect on December 31, Year 7. On December 31, Year 8, the exchange rate for the local currency unit was LCU1 = $0.24, and cumulative translation adjustments in Foreign Investee's translated balance sheet amounted to $50,300 (credit balance).

Prepare a journal entry for Investor Corporation on December 31, Year 8, to recognize the change in the exchange rate for the LCU from LCU1 = $0.20 on December 31, Year 7, to LCU1 = $0.24 on December 31, Year 8.

CASES

Case 19-1   Ostmark Company, a U.S. multinational enterprise, has a subsidiary in Austria. On April 1, Year 3, Ostmark acquired for $50,000 a draft for 500,000 Austrian schillings (S) and remitted it to the Austrian subsidiary as a long-term, noninterest-bearing advance. The advance was to be repaid ultimately in U.S. dollars. The Austrian schilling is the functional currency of the subsidiary.

You were engaged as independent auditor for the audit of the March 31, Year 4, consolidated financial statements of Ostmark Company and subsidiaries (including the Austrian subsidiary). On March 31, Year 4, the selling spot rate for the schilling was S1 = $0.05. Ostmark's controller translated the Payable to Ostmark Company liability in the Austrian subsidiary's balance sheet from S500,000 to $25,000

(S500,000 × $0.05 = $25,000). Because the $25,000 translated balance of the subsidiary's Payable to Ostmark Company liability did not offset the $50,000 balance of Ostmark's Receivable from Austrian Subsidiary ledger account on March 31, Year 4, Ostmark's controller prepared the following working paper elimination (in journal entry format) on March 31, Year 4:

Cumulative Translation Adjustments—Austrian Subsidiary	25,000	
Receivable from Austrian Subsidiary—Ostmark.		25,000

To record translation adjustment resulting from decline in exchange rate for the schilling to S1 = $0.05 on March 31, Year 4, from S1 = $0.10 on April 1, Year 3.

Instructions

Evaluate the accounting treatment described above.

Case 19-2   Suppose that the following resolution were to be debated in your accounting class:

RESOLVED, that *FASB No. 52,* "Foreign Currency Translation," established an indefensible distinction between transaction gains and losses arising from remeasurement and translation adjustments arising from translation.

Instructions

Which side—affirmative or negative—would you support in the debate? Explain.

Case 19-3   *FASB No. 52,* "Foreign Currency Translation," essentially gives to management of a U.S. multinational enterprise the responsibility for determining the functional currency of the enterprise's foreign branches, divisions, influenced investees, joint ventures, and subsidiaries, except for foreign entities that operate in highly inflationary economies, which must use the reporting currency as the functional currency.

Instructions

Given that remeasurement from a local currency to the functional currency produces transaction gains and losses displayed in the enterprise's income statement, while translation from the functional currency to the reporting currency generates cumulative translation adjustments displayed in the stockholders' equity section of the balance sheet, is there any incentive for management to determine that the local currency of a foreign entity is *not* its functional currency? Explain.

PROBLEMS

Pr. 19-1   On March 1, Year 2, Transcontinent Company, a U.S. multinational enterprise, established a branch in Mideastia, a foreign country. Transcontinent's home office sent cash and merchandise (billed at cost) to the Mideastia Branch only on March 1, Year 2, and the branch made sales and incurred rent and other operating expenses in Mideastia during the month of March, Year 2. Transcontinent's home office maintained accounts in its ledger for the branch's plant assets. Because the Mideastia Branch's operations were an integral component of Transcontinent's home office's operations, the U.S. dollar was the functional currency of the Mideastia Branch;

however, the branch maintained its accounting records in the local currency unit (LCU).

The trial balance of the Mideastia Branch on March 31, Year 2, was as follows:

TRANSCONTINENT COMPANY
Mideastia Branch Trial Balance
March 31, Year 2

	Debit	Credit
Cash	LCU 2,000	
Trade accounts receivable	58,000	
Allowance for doubtful accounts		LCU 1,000
Inventories	126,000	
Home office		220,000
Sales		184,000
Cost of goods sold	160,000	
Operating expenses	59,000	
Totals	LCU405,000	LCU405,000

Appropriate exchange rates for the Mideastia Branch's local currency unit were as follows:

Mar. 1, Year 2	$0.60
Mar. 31, Year 2	0.64
Average for March, Year 2	0.62

Instructions

Prepare a working paper to remeasure the March 31, Year 2, trial balance of Mideastia Branch of Transcontinent Company to U.S. dollars, the branch's functional currency, from local currency units. The March 31, Year 2, balance (before closing entries) of the Investment in Mideastia Branch ledger account in Transcontinent's home office's ledger was $132,000. Use the following headings for your working paper:

Account title	Balance (LCUs) dr (cr)	Exchange rates	Balance (U.S. dollars) dr (cr)

Pr. 19-2 The trial balance in local currency units (LCU) of Foreign Branch of Sarasota Company on April 30, Year 7, the end of the branch's first month of operations, is on page 878. The functional currency of Foreign Branch is the U.S. dollar.

Additional Information

(1) Foreign Branch sells a single product, which it acquires from the home office of Sarasota Company.
(2) The Investment in Foreign Branch ledger account in the accounting records of the home office of Sarasota Company (prior to end-of-period adjusting and closing entries) is on page 878.

SARASOTA COMPANY
Foreign Branch Trial Balance
April 30, Year 7

	Balance dr (cr)
Cash	LCU 10,000
Trade accounts receivable	50,000
Inventories (1,600 units at first-in, first-out cost)	124,375
Home office	(104,565)
Sales (2,100 units at LCU133)	(279,300)
Cost of goods sold	152,289
Operating expenses.	47,201
Total	LCU -0-

Investment in Foreign Branch ($)

Date	Explanation	Debit	Credit	Balance
Year 7				
Apr. 1	Cash sent to branch	10,000		10,000 dr
1	1,000 units of merchandise shipped to branch × $80 a unit	80,000		90,000 dr
3	Equipment acquired by branch (recorded in Home Office accounting records)		5,500	84,500 dr
10	1,200 units of merchandise shipped to branch × $81 a unit	97,200		181,700 dr
20	1,500 units of merchandise shipped to branch × $82 a unit	123,000		304,700 dr
29	Cash received from branch		210,000	94,700 dr
30	Operating expenses billed to branch	25,000		119,700 dr

(3) The Home Office ledger account in the accounting records of the Foreign Branch of Sarasota Company (prior to end-of-period closing entries) follows:

Home Office (LCU)

Date	Explanation	Debit	Credit	Balance
Year 7				
Apr. 2	Cash received from home office		9,091	9,091 cr
2	1,000 units of merchandise received from home office × LCU72.73		72,730	81,821 cr
2	Equipment acquired by branch	5,000		76,821 cr
11	1,200 units of merchandise received from home office × LCU72.32		86,784	163,605 cr
21	1,500 units of merchandise received from home office × LCU78.10		117,150	280,755 cr
28	Cash sent to home office	200,000		80,755 cr
30	Operating expenses billed by home office		23,810	104,565 cr

(4) Exchange rates for the local currency unit (LCU) of the country in which Foreign Branch operates were as follows during April, Year 7:

Apr. 1–Apr. 6..	*$1.10*
Apr. 7–Apr. 18..	*1.12*
Apr. 19–Apr. 30..	*1.05*

Instructions

Prepare a working paper to remeasure the April 30, Year 7, trial balance of Foreign Branch of Sarasota Company to U.S. dollars, its functional currency, from local currency units. Compute all exchange rates to the nearest cent.

Pr. 19-3 On December 1, Year 5, Pan-Europe Corporation, a U.S. multinational enterprise, formed a foreign subsidiary, which issued all of its currently outstanding common stock to Pan-Europe on that date. Selected items from the subsidiary's trial balances, all of which are shown in local currency units (LCU), are as follows:

	Nov. 30, Year 7	Nov. 30, Year 6
Trade accounts receivable (net of allowance for doubtful accounts of LCU2,200 on Nov. 30, Year 7, and LCU2,000 on Nov. 30, Year 6)	*LCU40,000*	*LCU35,000*
Inventories, at first-in, first-out cost.....................	*80,000*	*75,000*
Plant assets (net of accumulated depreciation of LCU31,000 on Nov. 30, Year 7, and LCU14,000 on Nov. 30, Year 6)...	*163,000*	*150,000*
Long-term debt	*100,000*	*120,000*
Common stock, authorized 10,000 shares, LCU10 par, issued and outstanding 5,000 shares on Nov. 30, Year 7, and Nov. 30, Year 6.................................	*50,000*	*50,000*

Additional Information

(1) Relevant exchange rates were as follows:

Dec. 1, Year 5–June 30, Year 6	*2LCU to $1*
July 1, Year 6–Sept. 30, Year 6....................................	*1.8LCU to $1*
Oct. 1, Year 6–May 31, Year 7	*1.7LCU to $1*
June 1, Year 7–Nov. 30, Year 7	*1.5LCU to $1*
Average monthly rate for year ended Nov. 30, Year 6	*1.9LCU to $1*
Average monthly rate for year ended Nov. 30, Year 7	*1.6LCU to $1*

(2) An analysis of the trade accounts receivable (net) balances follows:

	Year ended November 30,	
	Year 7	**Year 6**
Trade accounts receivable:		
Balances, beginning of year	LCU 37,000	
Sales (LCU36,000 a month in Year 7 and LCU		
31,000 a month in Year 6)	432,000	LCU 372,000
Collections.................................	(423,600)	(334,000)
Write-offs (April, Year 7, and November, Year 6) .	(3,200)	(1,000)
Balances, end of year........................	LCU 42,200	LCU 37,000
Allowance for doubtful accounts:		
Balances, beginning of year	LCU 2,000	
Doubtful accounts expense	3,400	LCU 3,000
Write-offs (April, Year 7, and November, Year 6) .	(3,200)	(1,000)
Balances, end of year........................	LCU 2,200	LCU 2,000

(3) An analysis of inventories, for which the first-in, first-out inventory method is used, follows:

	Year ended November 30,	
	Year 7	**Year 6**
Inventories, beginning of year......................	LCU 75,000	
Purchases (May, Year 7, and May, Year 6)...........	335,000	LCU375,000
Goods available for sale...........................	LCU410,000	LCU375,000
Inventories, end of year	80,000	75,000
Cost of goods sold................................	LCU330,000	LCU300,000

(4) On December 1, Year 5, Pan-Europe's foreign subsidiary acquired land for LCU24,000 and depreciable plant assets for LCU140,000. On June 4, Year 7, additional depreciable plant assets were acquired for LCU30,000. Plant assets are being depreciated by the straight-line method over a 10-year economic life with no residual value. A full year's depreciation is taken in the year of acquisition of plant assets.

(5) On December 15, Year 5, 14% serial bonds with a face amount of LCU120,000 were issued. The bonds were to mature serially each year through December 15, Year 11, and interest was payable semiannually on June 15 and December 15. The first principal payment was made on December 15, Year 6.

Instructions

Prepare a working paper to remeasure the foregoing items to U.S. dollars, the functional currency of Pan-Europe Corporation's foreign subsidiary, on November 30, Year 7, and November 30, Year 6, respectively. Show supporting computations. Round all exchange rates to the nearest cent.

Pr. 19-4 On August 1, Year 8, Westpac Corporation, a U.S. multinational enterprise, established a sales branch in Singapore. The transactions and events of Westpac's home office with the Singapore branch, and the branch's own transactions and events, during August, Year 8, are described below. Following each transaction or event is the appropriate spot exchange rate for the Singapore dollar (S$).

(1) Cash of $50,000 sent to branch (S$1 = $0.45)
(2) Merchandise with a cost of $75,000 shipped to branch at a billed price of $100,000 (S$1 = $0.45)
(3) Rent of leased premises for August paid by branch, S$1,000 (S$1 = $0.45)
(4) Store and office equipment acquired by branch for S$5,000, to be carried in home office accounting records (S$1 = $0.45)
(5) Sales by branch on credit, S$25,000 (S$1 = $0.46). Cost of goods sold, S$15,000
(6) Collections of trade accounts receivable by branch, S$20,000 (S$1 = $0.455)
(7) Payment of operating expenses by branch, S$5,000 (S$1 = $0.47)
(8) Cash remitted to home office by branch, S$10,000 (S$1 = $0.44)
(9) Operating expenses incurred by home office charged to branch, $2,000 (S$1 = $0.445)
(10) Uncollectible account receivable written off by branch, S$1,000 (S$1 = $0.44)

Instructions

Prepare journal entries for the home office of Westpac Corporation in U.S. dollars, and for the Singapore branch in Singapore dollars, to record the foregoing transactions or events. Both home office and branch use the perpetual inventory system and the direct write-off method of accounting for uncollectible accounts. Round all amounts to the nearest dollar. Omit journal entry explanations.

Pr. 19-5   Portero Corporation, a U.S. multinational enterprise, combined with Sudamerica Company on January 2, Year 3, by the acquisition at carrying amount of all of Sudamerica's outstanding common stock. Sudamerica is located in Nicaduras, whose monetary unit, the local currency of Sudamerica, is the peso ($N). Sudamerica's functional currency is the U.S. dollar. Sudamerica's accounting records were continued without change. A trial balance, in Nicaduran pesos, on January 2, Year 3, follows:

SUDAMERICA COMPANY
Trial Balance (Nicaduran pesos)
January 2, Year 3

	Debit	Credit
Cash	$N 3,000	
Trade accounts receivable.	5,000	
Inventories (first-in, first-out cost).	32,000	
Plant assets.	204,000	
Accumulated depreciation of plant assets		$N 42,000
Trade accounts payable.		81,400
Common stock		50,000
Retained earnings		70,600
Totals	$N244,000	$N244,000

Sudamerica's trial balance, in Nicaduran pesos, on December 31, Year 4, follows:

SUDAMERICA COMPANY
Trial Balance (Nicaduran pesos)
December 31, Year 4

	Debit	Credit
Cash	$N 25,000	
Trade accounts receivable	20,000	
Allowance for doubtful accounts		$N 500
Receivable from Portero Corporation	33,000	
Inventories (first-in, first-out cost)	110,000	
Plant assets	210,000	
Accumulated depreciation of plant assets		79,900
Notes payable		60,000
Trade accounts payable		22,000
Income taxes payable		40,000
Common stock		50,000
Retained earnings		100,600
Sales—local		170,000
Sales—foreign		200,000
Cost of goods sold	207,600	
Depreciation expense	22,400	
Other operating expenses	60,000	
Income taxes expense	40,000	
Gain on disposal of plant assets		5,000
Totals	$N728,000	$N728,000

Additional Information

(1) All of Sudamerica's foreign sales are made to Portero and are accumulated in the Sales—Foreign ledger account. The balance of the Receivable from Portero Corporation account (a current asset) is the total of unpaid invoices. All foreign sales are billed in U.S. dollars. The reciprocal accounts in Portero's accounting records show total Year 4 purchases as $471,000 and the total of unpaid invoices as $70,500 (before end-of-period adjusting entries). Portero remits pesos to pay for the purchases.

(2) Depreciation is computed by the straight-line method over a 10-year economic life with no residual value for all depreciable assets. Machinery costing $N20,000 was acquired by Sudamerica on December 31, Year 3, and no depreciation was recorded for this machinery in Year 3. There have been no other depreciable plant assets acquired since January 2, Year 3, and no assets are fully depreciated.

(3) No journal entries have been made in the Retained Earnings ledger account of Sudamerica since its acquisition other than the net income for Year 3.

(4) The exchange rates for the Nicaduran peso follow:

Jan 2, Year 3	$2.00
Year 3 average...	2.10
Dec. 31, Year 3	2.20
Year 4 average...	2.30
Dec. 31, Year 4	2.40

Instructions

Prepare a working paper to remeasure the trial balance of Sudamerica Company for the year ended December 31, Year 4, from Nicaduran pesos to U.S. dollars, Sudamerica's functional currency. The working paper should show the trial balance amounts in pesos, the exchange rates, and the amounts in dollars.

Pr. 19-6 Hightower Company, a U.S. multinational enterprise, established a branch in Brazentina in Year 2. The branch carried its accounting records in the Brazentina peso (BP), although its functional currency was the U.S. dollar.

You were engaged to audit Hightower's combined financial statements for the year ended December 31, Year 9. You retained a licensed professional accounting firm in Brazentina to audit the branch accounts. The firm reported that the branch accounts were fairly stated in pesos, except that a Brazentina franchise fee and any possible adjustments required by home office accounting procedures were not recorded. Trial balances for the home office and the branch of Hightower Company on December 31, Year 9, are on page 884.

Additional Information

(1) The Brazentina peso was devalued July 1, Year 9, from BP1 = $0.25 to BP1 = $0.20. The former exchange rate had been in effect since Year 1.

(2) Included in the balance of the home office's Investment in Brazentina Branch ledger account was a $4,000 billing for merchandise shipped during Year 9. The branch did not receive the shipment during Year 9. Home office sales to the branch are marked up 33⅓% on home office cost and shipped FOB home office. Branch sales to home office are made at branch cost. There were no seasonal fluctuations in branch sales to outsiders during the year.

(3) The branch had beginning and ending inventories valued at first-in, first-out cost of BP80,000 [exclusive of the amount in (2), above], of which one-half on each date had been acquired from the home office. The home office had December 31, Year 9, inventories valued at first-in, first-out cost of $520,000.

(4) The Branch Market Research ledger account balance is the unamortized portion of a $15,000 fee paid by the home office in January, Year 8, to a U.S. firm for market research for the branch. Currency restrictions prevented the branch from paying the fee. The home office agreed to accept merchandise from the branch over a five-year period, during which the market research fee was to be amortized.

(5) There were no changes in the branch's plant assets during Year 9.

(6) The government of Brazentina imposes a franchise fee of 10 pesos per 100 pesos of income before franchise fee of the branch, in exchange for certain exclusive trading rights granted to the branch. The fee is payable each May 1 for the

HIGHTOWER COMPANY
Home Office and Branch
Trial Balances
December 31, Year 9

	Home office (U.S. dollars) dr (cr)	Branch (Brazentina pesos) dr (cr)
Cash	$ 90,000	BP 110,000
Trade accounts receivable (net)	160,000	150,000
Inventories, beginning of year	510,000	80,000
Short-term prepayments.	18,000	
Investment in Brazentina Branch	10,000	
Branch market research	12,000	
Plant assets.	750,000	1,000,000
Accumulated depreciation of plant assets	(350,000)	(650,000)
Current liabilities.	(240,000)	(220,000)
Long-term debt	(200,000)	(230,000)
Home office		(30,000)
Common stock	(300,000)	
Retained earnings	(145,000)	
Sales.	(4,035,000)	(1,680,000)
Intracompany sales	(160,000)	
Purchases	3,010,000	1,180,000
Intracompany purchases	140,000	
Depreciation expense	50,000	100,000
Other operating expenses and income taxes expense	680,000	190,000
Totals	$ -0-	BP -0-

preceding calendar year's trading rights; it had not been recorded by the branch on December 31, Year 9.

Instructions

a Prepare journal entries on December 31, Year 9, to correct the accounting records of:

(1) The home office of Hightower Company

(2) The Brazentina branch of Hightower Company

b Prepare a working paper to combine the financial statement of Hightower Company's home office and Brazentina branch, with all amounts stated in U.S. dollars. Formal combined financial statements are not required. Do not prepare formal combination eliminations; instead, explain the eliminations, including supporting computations, at the bottom of the working paper. Disregard income taxes. Assume that the branch purchases occurred evenly throughout Year 9.

The following column headings are suggested for the working paper:

Home office adjusted trial balance—dr (cr)

Branch adjusted trial balance:

In Brazentina pesos—dr (cr)

Exchange rates (remeasurement)
In dollars—dr (cr)
Eliminations—dr (cr)
Home office and branch combined—dr (cr)

Pr. 19-7 The financial statements of Eagle Corporation, a U.S. multinational enterprise, and its wholly owned Canadian subsidiary, Mapleleaf Company, at the end of the first year following Eagle's establishment of Mapleleaf, were as follows ($C is the symbol for the Canadian dollar, the functional currency of Mapleleaf):

EAGLE CORPORATION AND MAPLELEAF COMPANY
Separate Financial Statements
For Year Ended December 31, Year 5

	Eagle Corporation	Mapleleaf Company
Income Statements		
Total revenue...	$1,200,000	$C800,000
Total costs and expense.............................	900,000	700,000
Net income..	$ 300,000	$C100,000
Statements of Retained Earnings		
Retained earnings, beginning of year	$ 500,000	
Net income..	300,000	$C100,000
Subtotal..	$ 800,000	$C100,000
Dividends declared...................................	200,000	
Retained earnings, end of year.......................	$ 600,000	$C100,000
Balance Sheets		
Assets		
Current assets.......................................	$ 700,000	$C400,000
Investment in Mapleleaf Company common stock	160,000	
Plant assets (net)	1,600,000	500,000
Intangible assets (net)...............................	240,000	
Total assets.......................................	$2,700,000	$C900,000
Liabilities & Stockholders' Equity		
Current liabilities....................................	$ 400,000	$C200,000
Long-term debt	500,000	400,000
Common stock	1,200,000	200,000
Retained earnings	600,000	100,000
Total liabilities & stockholders' equity................	$2,700,000	$C900,000

Exchange rates for the Canadian dollar were as follows during Year 5:

	$C1 =
Jan. 2, Year 5 (date Mapleleaf Company was established)	$0.80
Dec. 31, Year 5...	0.78
Average for Year 5...	0.79

Instructions

a Prepare a working paper to translate the financial statements of Mapleleaf Company from Canadian dollars, its functional currency, to U.S. dollars, the reporting currency.

b Prepare a journal entry for Eagle Corporation on December 31, Year 5, to account for its investment in Mapleleaf Company under the equity method of accounting. (Disregard income taxes).

c Prepare a working paper for consolidated financial statements of Eagle Corporation and subsidiary on December 31, Year 5, and a related working paper elimination (in journal entry format). (Disregard income taxes.)

Pr. 19-8 Separate financial statements of Panamer Corporation, a U.S. multinational enterprise, and its two subsidiaries for the year ended December 31, Year 6, are shown below and on page 887 (IN is the symbol for the Itican peso):

PANAMER CORPORATION AND SUBSIDIARIES
Separate Financial Statements
For Year Ended December 31, Year 6

	Panamer Corporation (dollars)	U.S. Subsidiary (dollars)	Itican Subsidiary (pesos)
Income Statements			
Revenue:			
Sales..........................	$400,000	$21,000	IN381,000
Intercompany sales to U.S. Subsidiary...........................	10,000		
Total revenue	$410,000	$21,000	IN381,000
Costs and expenses:			
Cost of goods sold..............	$300,000	$15,000	IN300,000
Intercompany cost of goods sold ..	7,500		
Depreciation expense	3,000	550	17,500
Selling expenses	34,500	2,400	16,500
Other operating expenses	40,000	1,383	23,667
Income taxes expense	10,000	667	9,333
Total costs and expenses.......	$395,000	$20,000	IN367,000
Net income.......................	$ 15,000	$ 1,000	IN 14,000
Statements of Retained Earnings			
Retained earnings, beginning of year	$ 25,000	$ 2,000	IN 7,000
Net income......................	15,000	1,000	14,000
Subtotals	$ 40,000	$ 3,000	IN 21,000
Dividends declared................		1,000	
Retained earnings, end of year......	$ 40,000	$ 2,000	IN 21,000

(continued)

PANAMER CORPORATION AND SUBSIDIARIES
Separate Financial Statements (concluded)
For Year Ended December 31, Year 6

	Panamer Corporation (dollars)	U.S. Subsidiary (dollars)	Itican Subsidiary (pesos)
Balance Sheets			
Assets			
Cash	$ 10,000	$ 1,500	IN 10,000
Trade accounts receivable (net)	30,000	8,000	35,000
Intercompany receivables (payables)	4,000	(900)	
Inventories	20,000		83,000
Investment in U.S. Subsidiary common stock.......................	9,000		
Investment in Itican Subsidiary common stock.......................	12,000		
Plant assets......................	45,000	5,500	175,000
Accumulated depreciation of plant assets..........................	(15,000)	(2,000)	(75,000)
Total assets....................	$115,000	$12,100	IN228,000
Liabilities & Stockholders' Equity			
Trade accounts payable	$ 25,000		IN 7,000
Dividends payable		$ 100	
Long-term debt			100,000
Common stock, 1,000 shares	50,000	10,000	100,000
Retained earnings	40,000	2,000	21,000
Total liabilities & stockholders' equity...........................	$115,000	$12,100	IN228,000

Additional Information

(1) On December 31, Year 5, Panamer had acquired 900 of the 1,000 outstanding shares of common stock of U.S. Subsidiary for $9,000, and all 1,000 shares of the outstanding common stock of Itican Subsidiary for $12,000. The identifiable net assets of both combinees were fairly valued at their carrying amounts on December 31, Year 5. Panamer adopted the equity method of accounting for its investments in both subsidiaries.

(2) Both of Panamer's subsidiaries depreciate plant assets by the straight-line method over 10-year economic lives, with no residual values. None of the subsidiaries' plant assets was fully depreciated on December 31, Year 5, or on December 31, Year 6. There were no additions to or retirements of Itican Subsidiary's plant assets during Year 6.

(3) On December 31, Year 6, Panamer shipped merchandise billed at $4,000 to U.S. Subsidiary. There were no intercompany sales to Itican Subsidiary.

(4) On December 18, Year 6, U.S. Subsidiary declared a dividend of $1 a share, payable January 16, Year 7, to stockholders of record January 10, Year 7.

(5) Relevant exchange rates for the Itican peso, which is the functional currency of Itican Subsidiary, were as follows:

Dec. 31, Year 5, through Mar. 31, Year 6 .... $0.12

Apr. 1, Year 6, through Dec. 31, Year 6 .... $0.08

Instructions

a Prepare a working paper to translate Itican Subsidiary's financial statements from Itican pesos, its functional currency, to U.S. dollars. Use weighted-average exchange rates where appropriate.

b Prepare correcting entries for Panamer Corporation and for U.S. Subsidiary on December 31, Year 6.

c Prepare a working paper for consolidated financial statements and working paper eliminations (in journal entry format) for Panamer Corporation and subsidiaries on December 31, Year 6. The working papers should reflect the translated balances in **a** and the adjustments in **b**. (Disregard income taxes.)

20

Segments;
Interim Reports;
Reporting for the SEC

This chapter deals with three topics that have received considerable attention from accountants. Reporting for segments of a business enterprise and interim reports have been the subjects of pronouncements of the Financial Accounting Standards Board, the American Institute of Certified Public Accountants, and the Securities and Exchange Commission (SEC). In addition, the specialized requirements of accounting and reporting for the SEC by enterprises subject to its jurisdiction have undergone substantial modifications in recent years. All three topics are of considerable significance for accountants who deal with publicly owned corporations.

SEGMENT REPORTING

An *industry segment* is "a component of an enterprise engaged in providing a product or service or a group of related products and services primarily to unaffiliated customers (i.e., customers outside the enterprise) for a profit." [1] Other terms usually considered synonymous with "industry segment" are *business segment* and *line of business.*

The wave of *conglomerate* business combinations in recent years, involving companies in different industries or markets, led to consideration of appropriate methods for reporting financial data for industry segments. Financial analysts and others interested in comparing one diversified business enterprise with another found that consolidated financial statements did not supply enough information for meaningful comparative statistics regarding operations of the diversified enterprises in specific industries.

Background of Segment Reporting

The Financial Accounting Standards Board has traced the history of segment reporting from the start of hearings in 1964 before the U.S. Senate Judiciary Committee's

---

[1] *FASB Statement No. 14,* "Financial Reporting for Segments of a Business Enterprise," FASB (Stamford: 1976), p. 5.

Subcommittee on Antitrust and Monopoly. The Subcommittee was considering economic concentration in American industry, especially in the so-called conglomerate (diversified) business enterprises.

Out of these hearings came discussions and debate among academicians, members of Congress, SEC officials, financial analysts, business executives, and AICPA representatives regarding the propriety of financial reporting for segments of a business enterprise. The concept of segment reporting was controversial because it was opposed to the philosophy that consolidated financial statements, rather than separate financial statements, fairly present the financial position and operating results of an economic entity, regardless of the legal or industry-segment structure of the entity.

In 1976, the Financial Accounting Standards Board issued *FASB Statement No. 14,* ''Financial Reporting for Segments of a Business Enterprise.'' The principal provisions of this *Statement* are as follows:[2]

> When an enterprise issues a complete set of financial statements that present financial position at the end of the enterprise's fiscal year and results of operations and [cash flows] for that fiscal year in conformity with generally accepted accounting principles, those financial statements shall include certain information relating to:
>
> 1   The enterprise's operations in different industries . . .
>
> 2   Its foreign operations and export sales . . .
>
> 3   Its major customers . . .
>
> If such statements are presented for more than one fiscal year, the information required by this Statement shall be presented for each such year, ...

Initially, the disclosure of segment information was required in interim financial reports as well as in annual reports. However, the FASB rescinded that requirement a year after *FASB Statement No. 14* was issued. (Interim reports are discussed in another section of this chapter.) In 1978, *FASB Statement No. 21* suspended the applicability of *FASB Statement No. 14* to nonpublic enterprises.

Operations in Different Industries

To comply with the requirements of *FASB Statement No. 14* regarding a business enterprise, management and accountants must accomplish the following:

1   Specify the *industry segments* of the enterprise.

2   Compute the following for the specified segments: *revenue, operating profit or loss,* and *identifiable assets.*

3   Determine which of the specified segments are *significant,* and thus possibly *reportable.*

---

[2] Ibid., pp. 1–2.

4   Comply with the ***maximum*** and ***minimum limitations*** for disclosure of segment information.

5   Develop the required data for disclosure other than those listed in **2** on page 890.

Specification of Industry Segments   In developing ***FASB Statement No. 14,*** the Financial Accounting Standards Board considered whether organizational lines or areas of economic activity, or a combination of both, should be used for segmentation of a business enterprise. The FASB settled on areas of economic activity — ***industries*** and ***geographical areas*** — as the bases for segmentation. In addition, the FASB required disclosure of information regarding the ***major customers*** of a business enterprise.

The FASB established the following guidelines for reporting operations in different industries:[3]

> The reportable segments of an enterprise shall be determined by (a) identifying the individual products and services from which the enterprise derives its revenue, (b) grouping those products and services by industry lines into industry segments . . . , and (c) selecting those industry segments that are significant with respect to the enterprise as a whole. . . .

The FASB decided that none of the systems that had been developed for classifying business activities was satisfactory for determining the industry segments of all business enterprises. Accordingly, the FASB ***left to enterprise management*** the determination of an enterprise's industry segments. The FASB recommended use of the enterprise's ***profit centers,*** the smallest units of activity for which revenue and expense information is accumulated for internal management purposes, as a starting point in the identification of the enterprise's industry segments.

Computation of Revenue for Specified Segments   A controversial issue in the computation of revenue for industry segments was the inclusion or exclusion of ***intersegment sales or transfers.*** Proponents of inclusion stated that intersegment sales or transfers are a significant element of the revenue of some industry segments, and that exclusion of those items would seriously understate segment revenue. Opponents countered that intersegment sales or transfers do not result from arm's-length transactions between parties of opposing interests. The Financial Accounting Standards Board essentially compromised between the two positions on intersegment sales or transfers, as indicated in the following:[4]

> *Revenue.* Sales to unaffiliated customers and sales or transfers to other industry segments of the enterprise shall be separately disclosed in presenting revenue of a reportable segment. . . . for purposes of this Statement sales or transfers to other industry segments shall be accounted for on the basis used by the enterprise to price the intersegment sales or transfers.

---

[3] Ibid., p. 8.
[4] Ibid., p. 13.

Computation of Operating Profit or Loss for Specified Segments   Even more controversial than the status of intersegment sales or transfers was the question of what measurement of operating results was appropriate for industry segments that are not separate accounting entities. The two extreme positions on reporting operating results for segments were (1) *a net income* should be reported for each segment and (2) *no income amount* should be reported for a segment. Proponents of a net income presentation for segments, while recognizing that a number of assumptions may underlie the measurement of net income, maintained that difficulties of measurement should not preclude the reporting of a segment net income amount that would be useful to investors and creditors.

The opposing position was that the arbitrary nature of many allocations of common costs, interest, and income taxes to segments makes the resultant net income amounts misleading rather than informative. Opponents of reporting segment net income cited as one allocation problem the difficulty of apportioning income taxes expense to segments. Income taxes expense is difficult to apportion because of the existence of various tax avoidance alternatives to a diversified enterprise, the differences between income tax liabilities when a consolidated income tax return is filed as compared with separate tax returns, and the existence of net operating loss carrybacks and carryforwards.

Some accountants advocated a compromise position between the two extremes. These accountants supported a segment contribution approach for reporting a segment's operating results. *Segment contribution* was defined as segment sales less *traceable expenses*—expenses directly identified with a particular segment, such as intersegment transfers in.[5]

The Financial Accounting Standards Board took the following position on disclosure of segment income:[6]

> *Profitability.* Operating profit or loss . . . , defined . . . [as a segment's revenue minus all operating expenses, including expenses not directly traceable to the segment,] . . . shall be presented for each reportable segment. As part of its segment information, an enterprise shall explain the nature and amount of any unusual or infrequently occurring items . . . reported in its consolidated income statement that have been added or deducted in computing the operating profit or loss of a reportable segment.

The FASB required that expenses not directly traceable to a segment (nontraceable expenses) should be allocated to each benefited segment on a *reasonable basis.* However, the following *should never be included* in the computation of the operating profit or loss of a reportable segment:[7]

Revenue earned at the corporate level and not derived from the operations of any industry segment

General corporate expenses (incurred at an enterprise's central administrative office)

---

[5] *FASB Discussion Memorandum,* ''An Analysis of Issues Related to Financial Reporting for Segments of a Business Enterprise,'' FASB (Stamford: 1974), pp. 29–30.
[6] *FASB Statement No. 14,* pp. 6, 13.
[7] Ibid., pp. 6–7.

Interest expense

Domestic and foreign income taxes

Equity in income or loss from influenced investees

Gain or loss on disposal of a segment

Extraordinary items

Minority interest in net income of subsidiaries

Cumulative effect of change in accounting principle

A "reasonable basis" for the allocation of nontraceable expenses might be found in a pronouncement of the Cost Accounting Standards Board (CASB). In *Cost Accounting Standard (CAS) 403,* "Allocation of Home Office Expenses to Segments," the CASB provided a three-factor formula for the allocation of residual home office expenses to segments. The percentage of residual home office expenses to be allocated to a segment was the *arithmetic average* of the following three percentages for an accounting period:[8]

1   Segment payroll dollars divided by total payroll dollars of all segments

2   Segment operating revenue (including intersegment transfers out, and reduced by intersegment transfers in) divided by total operating revenue of all segments

3   Segment average plant assets and inventories, at carrying amounts, divided by total carrying amount of average plant assets and inventories of all segments.

Illustration of Allocation of Nontraceable Expenses   To illustrate the allocation of nontraceable expenses to industry segments under the provisions of *CAS 403,*

Data for home office and two industry segments	Home office	Chemical products	Food products	Total
Net sales (operating revenue)..............		$550,000	$ 450,000	$1,000,000
Traceable expenses.......		$300,000	$ 350,000	$ 650,000
Nontraceable expenses....	$200,000			200,000
Total expenses.........	$200,000	$300,000	$ 350,000	$ 850,000
Income before income taxes..................				$ 150,000
Income taxes expense.....				60,000
Net income..............				$ 90,000
Payroll totals	$ 60,000	$160,000	$ 240,000	$ 460,000
Average plant assets and inventories	$ 80,000	$620,000	$1,380,000	$2,080,000

---

[8] *Cost Accounting Standard 403,* CASB (Washington: 1973), sec. 403.50(c)(1).

assume the data on page 893 for the home office and two industry segments of Multiproduct Corporation for the year ended April 30, Year 7 (there were no inter-segment transfers for the year). The three-factor formula under *CAS 403* is computed for Multiproduct Corporation as follows:

Computations of three-factor formula

	Chemical products		Food products	
Ratio of segment payroll totals	$\frac{\$160,000}{\$400,000}=$	40%	$\frac{\$240,000}{\$400,000}=$	60%
Ratio of segment operating revenue	$\frac{\$550,000}{\$1,000,000}=$	55%	$\frac{\$450,000}{\$1,000,000}=$	45%
Ratio of average plant assets and inventories	$\frac{\$620,000}{\$2,000,000}=$	31%	$\frac{\$1,380,000}{\$2,000,000}=$	69%
Totals		126%		174%
Arithmetic averages (divide by 3)		42%		58%

The $200,000 amount of nontraceable expenses of the home office of Multiproduct Corporation is allocated to the two segments as follows:

Allocation of nontraceable expenses

To Chemical Products segment ($200,000 × 0.42)	$ 84,000
To Food Products segment ($200,000 × 0.58)	116,000
Total nontraceable expenses	$200,000

Operating profit (loss) for the two industry segments of Multiproduct Corporation is computed as follows:

Operating profit (loss) of two industry segments

	Chemical products	Food products	Total
Net sales	$550,000	$450,000	$1,000,000
Traceable expenses	$300,000	$350,000	$ 650,000
Nontraceable expenses	84,000	116,000	200,000
Total expenses	$384,000	$466,000	$ 850,000
Operating profit (loss)	$166,000	$(16,000)	$ 150,000

The author questions the propriety of applying such an arbitrary formula to the allocation of nontraceable expenses to segments for financial reporting. The CASB allocation formula appears to be one of expediency rather than theoretical soundness. This is borne out in the preceding illustration by the operating loss attributed to the Food Products segment of Multiproduct Corporation. The Food Products segment had higher ratios of payroll dollars and average plant assets and inventories, and thus was charged with a larger amount of nontraceable expenses. It does not necessarily follow that a direct correlation exists between nontraceable expenses and the aggregate amount of payroll dollars, plant assets, and inventories.

Computation of Identifiable Assets for Specified Segments   No significant controversy was generated by the Financial Accounting Standards Board's guidelines for the computation of identifiable assets for an industry segment, which are set forth below:[9]

> *Identifiable assets.* The identifiable assets of an industry segment are those tangible and intangible enterprise assets that are used by the industry segment, including (i) assets that are used exclusively by that industry segment and (ii) an allocated portion of assets used jointly by two or more industry segments. Assets used jointly by two or more industry segments shall be allocated among the industry segments on a reasonable basis. . . . Asset valuation allowances such as the following shall be taken into account in computing the amount of an industry segment's identifiable assets: allowance for doubtful accounts, accumulated depreciation, and marketable equity securities valuation allowance.

Determination of Significant Segments   After an enterprise has identified its industry segments, its *significant segments* must be determined. The Financial Accounting Standards Board decided that an industry segment is *significant,* and thus potentially a *reportable segment,* if it meets *one or more* of the following tests:[10]

1   Its revenue (including both sales to unaffiliated customers and intersegment sales or transfers) is 10% or more of the combined revenue (sales to unaffiliated customers and intersegment sales or transfers) of all of the enterprise's industry segments.

2   The absolute amount of its operating profit or operating loss is 10% or more of the greater, in absolute amount, of:
  (a) The combined operating profit of all industry segments that did not incur an operating loss, or
  (b) The combined operating loss of all industry segments that did incur an operating loss. . . .

3   Its identifiable assets are 10% or more of the combined identifiable assets of all industry segments.

To illustrate the determination of significant industry segments of a business enterprise, assume that the four industry segments of Diverso, Inc., had the revenue, operating profit or loss, and identifiable assets for the year ended December 31, Year 5, shown on page 896.

Segments A, B, and D of Diverso, Inc., meet the revenue test for significance because their revenue exceeds $21,000, which is 10% of total revenue of all four segments ($210,000 × 0.10 = $21,000). Segment C does not meet the revenue test for significance; its revenue of $20,000 is less than the $21,000 minimum. However, Segment C does meet the operating profit or loss test for significance, because the

---

[9] *FASB Statement No. 14,* pp. 7–8.
[10] Ibid., p. 10.

Data for test for
significant segments

	Segment				
	A	**B**	**C**	**D**	**Total**
Revenue...........	$ 60,000	$ 80,000	$ 20,000	$ 50,000	$ 210,000
Operating profit (loss)	(20,000)	30,000	(10,000)	30,000	30,000
Identifiable assets ..	500,000	400,000	100,000	300,000	1,300,000

absolute amount of its operating loss—$10,000—exceeds $6,000, which is 10% of total operating profit of Segment B and Segment D [($30,000 + $30,000) × 0.10 = $6,000]. The $60,000 total operating profit was used for the test because it exceeded the $30,000 absolute amount of the total operating losses of Segment A and Segment C ($20,000 + $10,000 = $30,000). Because all four industry segments meet either the revenue test or the operating profit or loss test for significance, the identifiable assets test is not used.

Limitations on Disclosure of Segment Information   Because of the three possible methods for a segment to be considered *significant,* as described in the preceding section, the Financial Accounting Standards Board placed both minimum and maximum limits on the number of significant segments to be considered *reportable,* and thus included in the disclosures for industry segments in the annual report of the business enterprise. If such limits had not been provided, an inordinate number of segments might have been reported. The limitations established by the FASB were as follows:[11]

1   The combined revenue from sales to unaffiliated customers of *all reportable segments* must constitute at least 75% of the combined revenue from sales to unaffiliated customers of *all industry segments* (minimum).

2   The number of reportable segments generally *should not exceed 10.* Closely related industry segments might be combined into a single reportable segment to achieve the *limit of 10* (maximum).

3   Disclosures required for reportable segments do not apply to a *dominant segment,* defined as a segment whose revenue, operating profit or loss, and identifiable assets constitute more than 90% of related combined totals for all industry segments, with no other industry segment meeting the 10% test. However, the financial statements of an enterprise having a dominant industry segment, or operating in a single industry, must identify the industry.

Required Data to Be Disclosed for Reportable Segments   In addition to revenue, operating profit or loss, and identifiable assets, the following disclosures were required by the Financial Accounting Standards Board for reportable industry segments:[12]

[11] Ibid., pp. 11, 12.
[12] Ibid., p. 14.

1   Depreciation, depletion, and amortization

2   Additions to plant assets

3   Equity in net income and net assets of influenced investees whose operations are integrated vertically with those of the segment

4   Effect of change in accounting principle on segment operating profit or loss.

Operations in Foreign Areas and Export Sales

In *FASB Statement No. 14,* the Financial Accounting Standards Board required business enterprises that operate in foreign geographic areas (individual foreign countries or groups of countries) to report information for each *significant foreign geographic area,* and in the aggregate for all other foreign geographic areas that are not significant. A foreign geographic area is considered significant if either its *revenue from sales to unaffiliated customers* or its *identifiable assets* are at least 10% of related total amounts in the enterprise's financial statements. (The concept of *operating profit or loss* is not always relevant for a foreign geographic area.) Comparable information is required for the enterprise's domestic operations, unless the domestic operations do not meet the same 10% test for significance.[13] Further, the FASB required information regarding *export sales* in the financial statements of enterprises whose export sales exceed 10% of total sales to unaffiliated customers.[14]

Major Customers

Disclosure also is required of the revenue from sales to any single *major customer,* or from sales to individual domestic or foreign governments, which represent 10% or more of total sales of the enterprise. Also, the industry segment making the sales must be identified.[15] This information is of significance to users of financial statements because of the adverse effects that might arise when a business enterprise loses a major customer.

Presentation of Segment Information, Operations in Foreign Areas, and Related Disclosures

The Financial Accounting Standards Board approved the following alternative methods for disclosure of information about the reportable segments and foreign operations of a business enterprise:[16]

1   Within financial statements, with appropriate explanatory disclosures in a note to the financial statements.

2   Entirely in a note to the financial statements.

3   In a separate exhibit that is included as an integral part of the financial state-

---

[13] Ibid., p. 17.

[14] Ibid., p. 18.

[15] Ibid., p. 19; also, *FASB Statement No. 30,* "Disclosure of Information about Major Customers," FASB (Stamford: 1979), pp. 2–3.

[16] *FASB Statement No. 14,* p. 15.

ments. If, in a report to stockholders, that exhibit is located on a page that is not clearly a part of the financial statements, the exhibit shall be referenced in the financial statements as an integral part thereof.

The financial statements of The Walt Disney Company in the Appendix illustrate the first of the foregoing methods. The basic segment information is included in the income statement on page 918; Note 12 on page 926 and the summary of significant accounting policies on page 921 provide additional data on segments of The Walt Disney Company.

SEC Requirements for Segment Information

The requirements of the Securities and Exchange Commission for reporting of segment information are in *Regulation S-K,* which outlines non-financial statement information that must be included in reports to the SEC. The SEC disclosure requirements for industry segments, in addition to the requirements of *FASB Statement No. 14,* are as follows:[17]

1   Amount or percentage of total revenue contributed by any *class of product or services* that accounted for 10% or more of total revenue during the past three years

2   The *name* of a major customer (see page 897), together with its relationship to the reporting enterprise, *if loss of the customer would have a material adverse effect on the enterprise*

3   Information about foreign operations or export sales that are *expected to be material in the future*

Regulation S-K is discussed in a subsequent section of this chapter.

Reporting the Disposal of a Business Segment

To this point, accounting standards developed by the Financial Accounting Standards Board for financial reporting for *existing* business segments have been discussed. The consideration of segment reporting is concluded with the reporting for effects of the *disposal* of a business segment.

In 1973, the Accounting Principles Board issued *APB Opinion No. 30,* "Reporting the Results of Operations. . . ." The APB's conclusions included the following with respect to disposal of a business segment:[18]

For purposes of this Opinion, the term *discontinued operations* refers to the operations of a segment of a business . . . that has been sold, abandoned, spun off, or otherwise disposed of or, although still operating, is the subject of a formal plan for disposal. . . . The Board concludes that the results of continu-

---

[17] *Codification of Financial Reporting Policies,* Securities and Exchange Commission (Washington: 1982), Sec. 503.
[18] *APB Opinion No. 30,* "Reporting the Results of Operations—. . . ," AICPA (New York: 1973), pp. 558–559.

ing operations should be reported separately from discontinued operations and that any gain or loss from disposal of a segment of a business . . . should be reported in conjunction with the related results of discontinued operations and not as an extraordinary item. Accordingly, operations of a segment that has been or will be discontinued should be reported separately as a component of income before extraordinary items and the cumulative effect of accounting changes (if applicable) in the following manner:

Income from continuing operations before income taxes	$XXXX	
Provision for income taxes	XXX	
Income from continuing operations		$XXXX
Discontinued operations (Note ___).		
Income (loss) from operations of discontinued Division X (less applicable income taxes of $ ___)	$XXXX	
Loss on disposal of Division X, including provision of $ ___ for operating losses during phase-out period (less applicable income taxes of $ ___)	XXXX	XXXX
Net income		$XXXX

Amounts of income taxes applicable to the results of discontinued operations and the gain or loss from disposal of the segment should be disclosed on the face of the income statement or in related notes. Revenues applicable to the discontinued operations should be separately disclosed in the related notes.

The provisions of *APB Opinion No. 30* are discussed in the following sections.

Income from Continuing Operations The purpose of the income from continuing operations amount is to provide a basis of comparison in the comparative income statements of a business enterprise that has discontinued a business segment. In order for the income from continuing operations amounts to be comparable, the operating results of the discontinued segment of the enterprise *must be excluded from income from continuing operations for all accounting periods presented in comparative income statements.* For example, in comparative income statements for the three years ended December 31, Year 7, for Wexler Company, a diversified enterprise with five business segments, which disposed of one of the segments during Year 7, the income from continuing operations amounts for Years 5 and 6, as well as for Year 7, exclude the operating results of the discontinued business segment.

Income (Loss) from Discontinued Operations The income or loss, net of applicable income taxes, of Wexler Company's discontinued operations (business segment) is included in its entirety in this section of Wexler's income statement for Years 5 and 6. For Year 7, the net-of-tax income or loss of the discontinued operations is for the period from January 1, Year 7, until the *measurement date,* defined as the date on which management of Wexler committed itself to a formal plan for disposal of the segment. Assuming a measurement date of September 30, Year 7, Wexler's Year 7 income statement would include the income or loss of the discontinued operations, net of income taxes, for the nine months ended September 30, Year 7, under the caption "Income (loss) from operations of discontinued business segment (described)."

Gain (Loss) on Disposal of Discontinued Operations   Included in the gain or loss recognized on discontinued operations are the following:

1   Income or loss from discontinued operations during phase-out period. The *phase-out period* is the period between the *measurement date* and the *disposal date* —the date of closing the sale of the discontinued operations or ceasing the operations of an abandoned segment.

2   The gain or loss on the sale or abandonment of the industry segment.

3   The income taxes allocated to **1** and **2** above.

If the measurement date and the disposal date are in the same accounting period, the income statement for that period displays *actual* amounts for income from continuing operations, income (loss) from discontinued operations, and gain (loss) on disposal of discontinued operations. However, if the disposal date is in an accounting period subsequent to the period of the measurement date, management of the enterprise must *estimate* on the measurement date whether disposal of the discontinued operations, including operating results of the phase-out period, will result in a gain or a loss, net of income taxes. If a *gain* is anticipated, it is not recognized until the *disposal date;* if a *loss* is expected, it must be recognized on the *measurement date.*

Computation of the gain or loss on disposal of an industry segment may be a difficult process, especially if the disposal date is a considerable period of time after the measurement date. To assist in such a computation, the Accounting Principles Board provided substantial guidance:[19]

> The determination of whether a gain or a loss results from the disposal of a segment of a business should be made at the measurement date based on estimates at that date of the net realizable value of the segment after giving consideration to any estimated costs and expenses directly associated with the disposal and, if a plan of disposal is to be carried out over a period of time and contemplates continuing operations during that period, to any estimated income or losses from operations. If it is expected that net losses from operations will be incurred between the measurement date and the expected disposal date, the computation of the gain or loss on disposal should also include an estimate of such amounts. If it is expected that income will be generated from operations during that period, the computation of the gain or loss should include the estimated income, limited however to the amount of any loss otherwise recognizable from the disposal; any remainder should be accounted for as income when realized. The Board believes that the estimated amounts of income or loss from

---

[19] Ibid., pp. 562–563.

operations of a segment between measurement date and disposal date included in the determination of loss on disposal should be limited to those amounts that can be projected with reasonable accuracy. In the usual circumstance, it would be expected that the plan of disposal would be carried out within a period of one year from the measurement date and that such projections of operating income or loss would not cover a period exceeding approximately one year.

Gain or loss from the disposal of a segment of a business should not include adjustments, costs, and expenses associated with normal business activities that should have been recognized on a going-concern basis up to the measurement date, such as adjustments of accruals on long-term contracts or write-down or write-off of receivables, inventories, property, plant, and equipment used in the business, equipment leased to others, or intangible assets. However, such adjustments, costs, and expenses which (a) are clearly a *direct* result of the decision to dispose of the segment and (b) are clearly not the adjustments of carrying amounts of costs, or expenses that should have been recognized on a going-concern basis prior to the measurement date should be included in determining the gain or loss on disposal. Results of operations before the measurement date should not be included in the gain or loss on disposal.

Costs and expenses *directly* associated with the decision to dispose include items such as severance pay, additional pension costs, employee relocation expenses, and future rentals on long-term leases to the extent they are not offset by sub-lease rentals.

Disclosure of Disposal of a Business Segment Because of the significance of discontinued operations in the financial history of a business enterprise, the Accounting Principles Board required the following disclosures:[20]

In addition to the amounts that should be disclosed in the financial statements . . . , the notes to financial statements for the period encompassing the measurement date should disclose:

1   The identity of the segment of business that has been or will be discontinued

2   The expected disposal date, if known

3   The expected manner of disposal

4   A description of the remaining assets and liabilities of the segment at the balance sheet date

5   The income or loss from operations and any proceeds from disposal of the segment during the period from the measurement date to the date of the balance sheet

An example of disclosure of discontinued operations, from the annual report of American Cyanamid Company, a publicly owned company, follows:[21]

---

[20] Ibid., pp. 563–564.
[21] AICPA, *Accounting Trends & Techniques,* 45th ed. (New York: 1991), p. 350.

	1990	1989	1988
	(Millions of dollars)		
Earnings from continuing operations	$107.8	$277.4	$254.2
Discontinued operations (Note 2):			
(Loss) earnings (after taxes of $3.7, $14.5 and $22.1)	(3.0)	14.6	41.4
Gain on sale (after taxes of $257.0)	248.0		
Net earnings	$352.8	$292.0	$295.6

NOTES TO CONSOLIDATED FINANCIAL STATEMENTS
(Millions of dollars except per share amounts)

Note 2: Discontinued Operations

During the third quarter of 1990, the businesses of the Shulton Group were sold to various parties for approximately $850.0. The 1990 consolidated statement of earnings excludes sales and expenses of discontinued operations from captions applicable to continuing operations. Prior year results have been restated to conform with this presentation. Net sales of the Shulton Group were $251.3, $608.7 and $594.1 for the period prior to the measurement date in 1990 and the years ended December 31, 1989 and 1988, respectively. The discontinued operations gain on sale of $248.0 is net of taxes of $257.0. The tax recorded on the gain differs from that computed by utilizing the U.S. federal tax rate due to accruals for which no tax benefit is available, state taxes and excess tax over book gain attributable to differences between the U.S. tax basis of foreign operations and their cosolidated book basis. The discontinued Shulton Group assets, liabilities and cash flows are not material to the company's financial statements and, accordingly, the consolidated balance sheet and statements of cash flows have not been restated.

International Accounting Standard 14

The provisions of *IAS 14,* "Reporting Financial Information by Segment," are nearly identical to those of *FASB Statement No. 14,* "Financial Reporting for Segments of a Business Enterprise." There is no separate International Accounting Standard dealing with disposal of a business segment.

Conclusions on Segment Reporting

As frequently occurs for long-outstanding financial accounting standards, the disclosure requirements established by the FASB in *FASB Statement No. 14,* "Financial Reporting for Segments of a Business Enterprise," have been criticized by some users of financial statements and financial reports of publicly owned enterprises. In reaction thereto, the FASB in 1993 issued a *Research Report,* "Reporting Disaggregated Information," and an *Invitation to Comment,* "Reporting Disaggregated Information by Business Enterprises." These actions by the FASB may represent the first step in a process leading to revision—moderate or substantial—of the disclosure standards now in effect for industry segments, foreign geographical areas, export sales, and major customers.

INTERIM FINANCIAL REPORTS

Generally, financial statements are issued for the fiscal year of a business enterprise. However, many enterprises issue complete financial statements for interim accounting periods during the course of a fiscal year. For example, a closely held company with outstanding bank loans may be required to provide monthly or quarterly financial statements to the lending bank. However, interim financial statements usually are associated with the *quarterly reports* issued by publicly owned companies to their stockholders, the Securities and Exchange Commission, and the stock exchanges that list their capital stock. The New York Stock Exchange's listing agreement requires listed companies to publish quarterly financial reports. Companies subject to the periodic reporting requirements of the SEC must file *Form 10-Q* with the SEC no later than 45 days after the end of each of the first three quarters of their fiscal years. In addition, the SEC requires disclosure of operating results for each quarter of the two most recent fiscal years in a "supplementary financial information" section of the annual report.[22]

Problems in Interim Financial Reports

Except for 10-Q quarterly reports filed with the SEC, the form, content, and accounting practices for interim financial reports were left to the discretion of business enterprises until 1973. In that year, the Accounting Principles Board issued *Opinion No. 28,* "Interim Financial Reporting." Prior to the issuance of *Opinion No. 28,* there were unresolved problems regarding interim financial reports, including the following:

1 Enterprises employed a wider variety of accounting practices and estimating techniques for interim financial reports than they used in the annual financial statements audited by independent CPAs. The enterprises' implicit view was that any misstatements in interim financial reports would be corrected by auditors' proposed adjustments for the annual financial statements.

2 Seasonal fluctuations in revenue and irregular incurrence of costs and expenses during the course of a business enterprise's fiscal year limited the comparability of operating results for interim periods of the fiscal year. Furthermore, time constraints in the issuance of interim statements limited the available time to accumulate end-of-period data for inventories, payables, and related expenses.

3 Accountants held two divergent views on the theoretical issues underlying interim financial statements. These differing views are described below:[23]

    a Under the *discrete theory,* each interim period is considered a *basic accounting period;* thus, the results of operations for each interim period are measured in essentially the same manner as for an annual accounting period. Under this theory, deferrals, accruals, and estimations at the end of each interim period are determined by following essentially the same principles and estimates or judgments that apply to annual periods.

---

[22] *Regulation S-K,* Item 302(a), Securities and Exchange Commission (Washington).
[23] *APB Opinion No. 28,* "Interim Financial Reporting," AICPA (New York: 1973), p. 521.

b Under the *integral theory,* each interim period is considered an *integral part of the annual period.* Under this theory, deferrals, accruals, and estimates at the end of each interim period are affected by judgments made at the interim date as to results of operations for the remainder of the annual period. Thus, an expense item that might be considered as falling entirely within an annual period (no fiscal year-end accrual or deferral) might be allocated among interim periods based on estimated time, sales volume, production volume, or some other basis.

The problems discussed in the preceding section led to a number of published interim income statements with substantial quarterly earnings, and income statements for the year with a substantial net loss.

APB Opinion No. 28

The stated objectives for *APB Opinion No. 28* were to provide guidance on accounting issues peculiar to interim reporting and to set forth minimum disclosure requirements for interim financial reports of publicly owned enterprises.[24] One part of the *Opinion* dealt with standards for measuring interim financial information and another covered disclosure of summarized interim financial data by publicly owned enterprises. In *APB Opinion No. 28,* the Accounting Principles Board adopted the *integral theory* that interim periods should be considered as integral parts of the annual accounting period.

The APB established guidelines for the following components of interim financial reports: revenue, costs associated with revenue, all other costs and expenses, and income taxes expense. These guidelines are discussed in the following sections.

Revenue   Revenue from products sold or services rendered *should be recognized for an interim period on the same basis as followed for the full year.* Further, business enterprises having significant seasonal variations in revenue should disclose the seasonal nature of their activities.[25]

Costs Associated with Revenue   Costs and expenses associated directly with or allocated to products sold or services rendered include costs of material, direct labor, and factory overhead. *APB Opinion No. 28* required the same accounting for these costs and expenses in interim financial reports as in fiscal-year financial statements. However, the *Opinion* provided the following exceptions with respect to the measurement of cost of goods sold for interim financial reports:[26]

1   Enterprises that use the *gross margin* method at interim dates to estimate cost of goods sold should disclose this fact in interim financial reports. In addition, any material adjustments reconciling estimated interim inventories with annual physical inventories should be disclosed.

2   Enterprises that use the *last-in, first-out inventory method* and *temporarily*

---

[24] Ibid., p. 522.
[25] Ibid., pp. 523, 527.
[26] Ibid., pp. 524–525.

deplete a base layer of inventories during an interim reporting period should include in cost of goods sold for the interim period the estimated *cost of replacing the depleted lifo base layer.*

To illustrate, assume that Megan Company, which uses the last-in, first-out inventory valuation method, temporarily depleted a base layer of inventories with a cost of $80,000 during the second quarter of the year ending December 31, Year 6. Replacement cost of the depleted base layer was $100,000 on June 30, Year 6. In addition to the usual debit to Cost of Goods Sold and credit to Inventories for the quarter ended June 30, Year 6, which would include the $80,000 amount from the base layer, Megan prepares the following journal entry on June 30, Year 6:

Cost of Goods Sold ($100,000 − $80,000).....................	*20,000*	
Liability Arising from Depletion of Base Layer of Lifo Inventories...		*20,000*
To record obligation to replenish temporarily depleted base layer of last-in, first-out inventories.		

Journal entry for temporary depletion of base layer of lifo inventories

Assuming merchandise with a total cost of $172,000 was purchased by Megan on July 6, Year 6, the following journal entry is required:

Inventories ($172,000 − $20,000)...........................	*152,000*	
Liability Arising from Depletion of Base Layer of Lifo Inventories .	*20,000*	
Trade Accounts Payable..............................		*172,000*
To record purchase of merchandise and restoration of depleted base layer of last-in, first-out inventories.		

Journal entry for restoration of base layer

3   Lower-of-cost-or-market write-downs of inventories should be provided for interim periods as for complete fiscal years, unless the interim date market declines in inventory are considered *temporary,* and not applicable at the end of the fiscal year. If an inventory market write-down in one interim period is offset by an inventory market price *increase* in a subsequent interim period, *a gain is recognized in the subsequent period to the extent of the loss recognized in preceding interim periods of the fiscal year.*

For example, assume that Reynolds Company, which uses lower-of-cost-or-market, first-in, first-out cost, for valuing its single merchandise item, had 10,000 units of merchandise with first-in, first-out cost of $50,000, or $5 a unit, in inventory

Quarterly sales and end-of-quarter replacement costs for inventory

Quarter ended	Quarterly sales (units)	End-of-quarter inventory replacement costs (per unit)
Mar. 31	*2,000*	*$6*
June 30	*1,500*	*4*
Sept. 30	*2,000*	*7*
Dec. 31	*1,200*	*3*

on January 1, Year 3. Assume further for simplicity that Reynolds made no purchases during Year 3. Quarterly sales and end-of-quarter replacement costs for inventory were as shown on page 905 during Year 3.

If the replacement cost (market) decline in the second quarter was not considered to be **temporary,** Reynolds Company's cost of goods sold for the four quarters of Year 3 would be computed as follows:

Computation of
quarterly cost of goods
sold

		Cost of goods sold	
Quarter ended	*Computation for quarter*	*For quarter*	*Cumulative*
Mar. 31	2,000 × $5	$10,000	$10,000
June 30	(1,500 × $5) + (6,500 × $1)*	14,000	24,000
Sept. 30	(2,000 × $4) − (4,500 × $1)†	3,500	27,500
Dec. 31	(1,200 × $5) + (3,300 × $2)‡	12,600	40,100

* 6,500 units remaining in inventory multiplied by $1 write-down to lower replacement cost.
† 4,500 units remaining in inventory multiplied by $1 write-up to original first-in, first-out cost.
‡ 3,300 units remaining in inventory multiplied by $2 write-down to lower replacement cost.

The $40,100 cumulative cost of goods sold for Reynolds Company for Year 3 may be verified as follows:

Verification of
cumulative cost of
goods sold

6,700 units sold during Year 3, at $5 first-in, first-out cost per unit	$33,500
Write-down of Year 3 ending inventory to replacement cost (3,300 units × $2)	6,600
Cost of goods sold for Year 3	$40,100
Alternative verification:	
Cost of goods available for sale (10,000 × $5)	$50,000
Less: Ending inventory, at lower of first-in, first-out cost or market (3,300 × $3)	9,900
Cost of goods sold for Year 3	$40,100

4   Enterprises using standard costs for inventories and cost of goods sold generally should report standard cost variances for interim periods as they do for fiscal years. Planned materials price variances and volume or capacity variances should be deferred at the end of interim periods if the variances are expected to be absorbed by the end of the fiscal year.

All Other Costs and Expenses   The following guidelines for all costs and expenses other than those associated with revenue are set forth in *APB Opinion No. 28:*[27]

> Costs and expenses other than product costs should be charged to income in interim periods as incurred, or be allocated among interim periods based on an estimate of time expired, benefit received or activity associated with the periods. Procedures adopted for assigning specific cost and expense items to an interim

[27] Ibid., pp. 525–527.

period should be consistent with the bases followed by the company in reporting results of operations at annual reporting dates. However, when a specific cost or expense item charged to expense for annual reporting purposes benefits more than one interim period, the cost or expense item may be allocated to those interim periods. . . .

The amounts of certain costs and expenses are frequently subjected to year-end adjustments even though they can be reasonably approximated at interim dates. To the extent possible such adjustments should be estimated and the estimated costs and expenses assigned to interim periods so that the interim periods bear a reasonable portion of the anticipated annual amount. Examples of such items include inventory shrinkage, allowance for uncollectible accounts, allowance for quantity discounts, and discretionary year-end bonuses.

APB Opinion No. 28 includes a number of specific applications of the foregoing guidelines.

Income Taxes Expense The techniques for recognizing income taxes expense in interim financial reports were described as follows:[28]

At the end of each interim period the company should make its best estimate of the effective tax rate expected to be applicable for the full fiscal year. The rate so determined should be used in providing for income taxes on a current year-to-date basis. The effective tax rate should reflect anticipated . . . foreign tax rates, percentage depletion, . . . and other available tax planning alternatives. However, in arriving at this effective tax rate no effect should be included for the tax related to significant unusual or extraordinary items that will be separately reported or reported net of their related tax effect in reports for the interim period or for the fiscal year.

To illustrate, assume that on March 31, Year 7, the end of the first quarter of Year 7, Carter Company's actual first quarter and forecasted fiscal year operating results were as follows:

	First quarter (actual)	Fiscal year (estimated)
Revenue...	$400,000	$1,800,000
Less: Costs and expenses other than income taxes	300,000	1,500,000
Income before income taxes........................	$100,000	$ 300,000

Actual first quarter and forecasted fiscal year pre-tax accounting income

Assume further that there were no *temporary differences* between Carter's pre-tax accounting income and taxable income, but that Carter had the following estimated *permanent differences* between pre-tax accounting income and federal and state taxable income for the fiscal year:

---

[28] Ibid., pp. 527–528.

Estimated permanent differences

Dividend received deduction	$17,000
Goodwill amortization	5,000

If Carter's *nominal* federal and state income tax rates total 40%, Carter estimates its *effective* combined income tax rate for Year 7 as follows:

Computation of estimated effective income tax rate

Estimated income before income taxes	$300,000
Add: Nondeductible goodwill amortization	5,000
Less: Dividend received deduction	(17,000)
Estimated taxable income	$288,000
Estimated combined federal and state income taxes ($288,000 × 0.40)	$115,200
Estimated effective combined federal and state income tax rate for Year 7 ($115,200 ÷ $300,000)	38.4%

Carter's journal entry for income taxes on March 31, Year 7, is as follows:

Journal entry for income taxes for first quarter of fiscal year

Income Taxes Expense	38,400	
Income Taxes Payable		38,400

To provide for estimated federal and state income taxes for the first quarter of Year 7 ($100,000 × 0.384 = $38,400).

For the second quarter of Year 7, Carter again estimates an effective combined federal and state income tax rate based on more current projections for permanent differences between pre-tax accounting income and taxable income for the entire year. However, the new effective rate *is not applied retroactively* to restate the first quarter's income taxes expense. For example, assume that Carter's second-quarter estimate of the effective combined federal and state income tax rate was 39.2% and that Carter's pre-tax income for the second quarter was $120,000 (or $220,000 for first two quarters). Carter prepares the following journal entry on June 30, Year 7, for income taxes expense for the second quarter of Year 7:

Journal entry for income taxes for second quarter of fiscal year

Income Taxes Expense	47,840	
Income Taxes Payable		47,840

To provide for estimated federal and state income taxes for the second quarter of Year 7 as follows:

Cumulative income taxes expense ($220,000 × 0.392)	$86,240
Less: Income taxes expense for first quarter	38,400
Income taxes expense for second quarter	$47,840

The foregoing computation of income taxes expense for interim periods is a highly simplified example. Many complex aspects of income taxes, such as net operating loss carrybacks and carryforwards, complicate the computations of income taxes for interim periods. *FASB Interpretation No. 18*, ''Accounting for Income Taxes in Interim Periods,'' provides guidance for complex interim period income tax computations.

Reporting Accounting Changes in Interim Periods

In 1974, the Financial Accounting Standards Board issued *FASB Statement No. 3*, ''Reporting Accounting Changes in Interim Financial Statements,'' as an amendment to *APB Opinion No. 28*. Following are the two principal provisions of *FASB Statement No. 3*:[29]

> If a cumulative effect type accounting change is made during the *first* interim period of an enterprise's fiscal year, the cumulative effect of the change on retained earnings at the *beginning of that fiscal year* shall be included in net income of the first interim period (and in last-twelve-months-to-date financial reports that include that first interim period).
>
> If a cumulative effect type accounting change is made in *other than the first* interim period of an enterprise's fiscal year, *no* cumulative effect of the change shall be included in net income of the period of the change. Instead, financial information for the pre-change interim periods of the fiscal year in which the change is made shall be restated by applying the newly adopted accounting principle to those pre-change interim periods. The cumulative effect of the change on retained earnings at the *beginning of that fiscal year* shall be included in restated net income of the first interim period of the fiscal year in which the change is made (and in any year-to-date or last-twelve-months-to-date financial reports that include the first interim period). Whenever financial information that includes those pre-change interim periods is presented, it shall be presented on the restated basis.

Disclosure of Interim Financial Data   As minimum disclosure, *APB Opinion No. 28* provided that the following data should be included in publicly owned enterprises' interim financial reports to stockholders. The data are to be reported for the most recent quarter and the year to date, or 12 months to date of the quarter's end.[30]

1   Sales or gross revenue, income taxes expense, extraordinary items (including related income tax effects), cumulative effect of a change in accounting principle or practice, and net income

2   Primary and fully diluted earnings per share data for each period presented

3   Seasonal revenue, costs, or expenses

4   Significant changes in estimates or provisions for income taxes

---

[29] *FASB Statement No. 3*, ''Reporting Accounting Changes in Interim Financial Statements,'' FASB (Stamford: 1974), p. 4.
[30] *APB Opinion No. 28*, p. 532.

5   Disposal of a business segment and extraordinary, unusual, or infrequently occurring items

6   Contingent items

7   Changes in accounting principle or estimate

8   Significant changes in financial position

An example of the disclosure of interim financial data is illustrated in the excerpt from the annual report of The Walt Disney Company, page 927 of the Appendix.

Conclusions on Interim Financial Reports

APB Opinion No. 28, FASB Statement No. 3, and *FASB Interpretation No. 18*
represented a substantial effort to upgrade the quality of interim financial reports.
However, controversy continues on the subject of interim financial reporting—
especially concerning the Accounting Principles Board's premise that an interim
period should be accounted for as an integral part of the applicable annual period. In
recognition of this controversy and other problems of interim financial reporting, the
Financial Accounting Standards Board undertook a comprehensive study of the
topic, and issued a *Discussion Memorandum* entitled "Interim Financial Accounting and Reporting." However, because of more pressing matters on its agenda, the
FASB abandoned the project a few years later.

SEC Enforcement Actions Dealing with Wrongful Application of Accounting Standards for Interim Financial Reports

AAER 170   AAER 170, "Securities and Exchange Commission v. Kaypro Corporation and Andrew F. Kay" (November 6, 1987), deals with a federal court's entry of
a permanent injunction against a corporation that developed, manufactured, and
marketed microcomputers, and against its CEO/CFO. According to the SEC, the
latter was responsible for the corporation's issuance of misleading interim reports to
the SEC in *Form 10-Q* because he sanctioned misuse of the gross margin method for
estimating quarterly ending inventories. The SEC found that quarterly cost of goods
sold amounts had been estimated at 57% of sales instead of the actual 74% of sales
determined by the corporation's independent auditor at the end of the fiscal year that
included the subject quarters.

AAER 207 and 208   AAER 207, ". . . In the Matter of Matrix Science Corp., et
al.," and *AAER 208,* "Securities and Exchange Commission v. Ronald A. Ham-
mond, John H. MacQueen and Thomas Fleming, Jr." (November 1, 1988), report
SEC enforcement actions against a corporation engaged in the design, manufacture,
and sale of electrical connectors, and against 10 of its senior and middle-manage-
ment executives, including its CFO. The SEC found that, among other misstatements, the corporation's quarterly sales, reported to the SEC in *Form 10-Q,* were
overstated because sales journals had been held open for up to two days after the end
of each quarter, to enable the corporation to report net sales amounts that approximated preestablished sales quotas for the quarter.

AAER 389 AAER 389, "Securities and Exchange Commission v. Albert Barette and Michael Strauss," (June 17, 1992) reported a permanent injunction and fines of $50,000 and $10,000, respectively, against the former CEO and former CFO of a wholly owned subsidiary of a publicly owned company. The SEC alleged that the two officials misstated the subsidiary's quarterly operating results reported to the parent company, in order to conceal the subsidiary's failure to meet internal budgetary targets. The SEC charged that because of the overstatements of some quarterly results and the understatements of others, the following pattern emerged with respect to the parent company's earnings reported to the SEC on *Form 10-Q:*

	Quarter ended (000 omitted)				
	9/30/89	*12/31/89*	*3/31/90*	*9/30/90*	*12/31/90*
Pre-tax income:					
As reported	*$2,611*	*$2,723*	*$4,100*	*$3,677*	*$3,231*
Actual	*2,262*	*2,974*	*4,529*	*3,165*	*2,569*
Overstatement (under-					
statement)	*$ 349*	*($ 251)*	*($ 429)*	*$ 512*	*$ 662*

REPORTING FOR THE SEC

The Securities and Exchange Commission (SEC) is an agency of the U.S. government created in 1934 to oversee the interstate issuances and trading of securities. Since its creation, the SEC's functions have expanded to include administration of the following statutes, among others:

Securities Act of 1933, governing interstate issuances of securities to the public

Securities Exchange Act of 1934, governing trading of securities on national securities exchanges and over the counter

Public Utility Holding Company Act of 1935, governing interstate public utility holding company systems for electricity and gas

Trust Indenture Act of 1939, governing the issuance of bonds, debentures, and similar debt securities under an indenture meeting the requirements of the Act

Investment Company Act of 1940 and *Investment Advisers Act of 1940,* governing operations of investment companies and investment advisers

This section focuses on SEC administration of the Securities Act of 1933 (the 1933 Act) and the Securities Exchange Act of 1934 (the 1934 Act).

Nature of Reporting to the SEC

Most publicly owned companies are subject to either or both the 1933 Act and the 1934 Act. Companies planning to issue securities interstate to the public generally must file a *registration statement* with the SEC. Companies whose securities are traded on national stock exchanges also must file a registration statement; in addition, periodic reports must be made to the SEC by such companies. Most large companies whose securities are traded over the counter also must report periodically to the SEC.

Registration of Securities   The SEC has developed a series of *forms* for the registration of securities. *Forms S-1, S-2, S-3, S-4,* and *F-4* are used by large companies to register securities to be issued to the public; *Form S-18* is used by small companies that issue securities for $7,500,000 or less. The principal form for registering securities for trading on a national exchange or over the counter is *Form 10.* The various forms are not a series of blanks to be filled in; they are guides for the *format of information to be included in the registration statements.*

Periodic Reporting   The principal forms established by the SEC for reporting by companies whose stock is traded on national exchanges or over the counter are *Form 10-K, Form 10-Q,* and *Form 8-K. Form 10-K* is an annual report to the SEC, which must be filed within 90 days following the close of the company's fiscal year. Much of the information required by *Form 10-K* may be *incorporated by reference* to the annual report to stockholders, which also must be filed with the SEC.

    Form 10-Q is a quarterly report to the SEC that is due within 45 days after the end of each of the first three quarters of the company's fiscal year; a quarterly report for the fourth quarter of the fiscal year is not required. The condensed financial statements that must be included in *Form 10-Q* are more extensive than the minimum disclosure requirements of *APB Opinion No. 28,* "Interim Financial Reporting" (see pages 909 to 910), but the *10-Q* financial statements need not be audited.

    Form 8-K is a current report that must be filed with the SEC within a specified number of days after the occurrence of events such as the following:

1   Change in control of the reporting company

2   Acquisition or disposal of assets by the reporting company, including business combinations

3   Bankruptcy or receivership of the reporting company

4   Change of independent auditors for the reporting company

5   Resignation of directors of the reporting company

In addition, a company may choose to report to the SEC in *Form 8-K* any other event that it considers important to stockholders.

    Another important periodic report to the SEC is a *proxy statement,* which must be filed by companies that solicit proxies for annual meetings of their stockholders. If matters other than election of directors, selection of independent auditors, and consideration of stockholder proposals are to take place at an annual meeting, a *preliminary proxy statement* must be filed with the SEC for review and comment prior to distribution of the *definitive proxy statement* to stockholders. Essentially, the proxy statement includes disclosure of all matters to be voted on at the forthcoming meeting of stockholders whose proxies are solicited. If the stockholders are to vote on authorization or issuances of securities, modification or exchanges of securities, or business combinations, the proxy statement must include financial statements of the company and of any proposed combinee.

Organization and Functions of the SEC

The SEC is administered by five commissioners appointed for five-year terms by the President and confirmed by the Senate of the United States. No more than three commissioners may be members of the same political party. Headquartered in Washington, D.C., the SEC has nine regional offices and six branch offices. In the following sections, three segments of the SEC are discussed: chief accountant, Division of Corporation Finance, and Division of Enforcement.

Chief Accountant   The chief accountant of the SEC, as an expert in accounting, is responsible for issuing pronouncements that establish the SEC's position on matters affecting accounting and auditing. The chief accountant also supervises disciplinary proceedings against accountants charged with violating the SEC's Rules of Practice. The chief accountant cooperates with the Financial Accounting Standards Board and other private organizations interested in research and standards setting in accounting and auditing.

Division of Corporation Finance   The staff of the SEC's Division of Corporation Finance reviews the *Forms* and proxy statements filed with the SEC under the 1933 Act and the 1934 Act. The extent of the reviews varies, depending on whether the filing company has a history of acceptable reporting to the SEC or is "unseasoned." Division of Corporation Finance personnel consult with the chief accountant on the propriety of accounting presentations in filings with the SEC. Changes in the various *Forms* and in *Regulation S-X* and *Regulation S-K* are the responsibility of the Division of Corporation Finance.

Division of Enforcement   The duties of the SEC's Division of Enforcement involve monitoring the compliance of companies subject to the SEC's jurisdiction with the 1933 Act and the 1934 Act. When noncompliance is ascertained, the Division of Enforcement often will request and obtain federal court injunctions prohibiting the company and its management from further violations of the two Acts. Many of the criminal indictments involving notorious management fraud in recent years have been obtained through the efforts of the SEC's Division of Enforcement.

Interaction between SEC and FASB

Both the 1933 Act and the 1934 Act empower the SEC to establish rules for the accounting principles underlying financial statements and schedules included in reports filed with the SEC. The SEC rarely has used this authority directly. Instead, it generally has endorsed actions on accounting principles by organizations in the private sector (currently the Financial Accounting Standards Board), while reserving the right to issue its own pronouncements when necessary. This posture of the SEC has been described as follows:[31]

> In ASR [Accounting Series Release] 4, the Commission stated its policy that financial statements prepared in accordance with accounting practices for which there was no substantial authoritative support were presumed to be misleading and that footnote or other disclosure would not avoid this presumption. It also stated that, where there was a difference of opinion between the Commission and a registrant as to the proper accounting to be followed in a particular case, disclosure would be accepted in lieu of correction of the financial statements themselves only if substantial authoritative support existed for the accounting practices followed by the registrant and the position of the Commission had not been expressed in rules, regulations or other official releases. For purposes of this policy, principles, standards and practices promulgated by the FASB in its Statements and Interpretations will be considered by the Commission as having substantial authoritative support, and those contrary to such FASB promulgations will be considered to have no such support.
>
> . . . Information in addition to that included in financial statements conforming to generally accepted accounting principles is also necessary. Such additional disclosures are required to be made in various fashions, such as in financial statements and schedules reported on by independent public accountants or as textual statements required by items in the applicable forms and reports filed with the Commission. The Commission will continue to identify areas where investor information needs exist and will determine the appropriate methods of disclosure to meet these needs.

Thus, the SEC differentiated between *generally accepted accounting principles* and *disclosures* in financial statements and schedules, and expressed an intention to concentrate on pronouncements on disclosures. The principal devices used by the SEC to communicate its requirements for accounting principles and disclosures have been *Regulation S-X, Regulation S-K, Accounting Series Releases, Financial Reporting Releases,* and *Staff Accounting Bulletins.*

Regulation S-X   The SEC issued *Regulation S-X* to provide guidance for the form and content of financial statements and schedules required to be filed with the SEC under the laws that it administers. Since the adoption of *Regulation S-X* in 1940, the SEC has amended the document extensively, including a thorough overhaul in 1980 *(Accounting Series Release No. 280).*

Regulation S-X consists of numerous rules subdivided into several articles. Among the significant provisions of *Regulation S-X* are Rule 3-02, which requires audited income statements and statements of cash flows for three fiscal years, and Article 12, which illustrates the form and content of schedules to be filed in support of various financial statement items. Excerpts from the annual report of The Walt

---

[31] *Codification of Financial Reporting Policies,* Securities and Exchange Commission (Washington: 1982), Sec. 101.

Disney Company in the Appendix (pages 918, 919, and 920) illustrate the required comparative financial statements.

An example of a schedule required by *Regulation S-X* is Schedule V— Property, Plant, and Equipment, which must be submitted if the total carrying amount of plant assets at both the beginning and the end of the enterprise's fiscal year exceeds 25% of total assets. Schedule V consists of the following columns:

Classification of plant assets (land, buildings, machinery and equipment, leaseholds, and the like)

Balance at beginning of period

Additions at cost

Retirements

Other changes—add (deduct)

Balance at end of period

If neither total additions nor total deductions exceed 10% of the total balance at end of period and a statement to that effect is made, only total additions, total retirements, and the balance at end of period amounts need be disclosed in Schedule V. Any additions at cost exceeding 2% of total assets at either the beginning or the end of the period must be described, and amounts in the other changes column must be described.

Regulation S-K   The SEC issued *Regulation S-K* in 1977 to provide guidance for the completion of non-financial statement disclosure requirements in the various *Forms* filed under the 1933 Act and the 1934 Act. As amended since its adoption, *Regulation S-K* contains several items of disclosure.

Accounting Series Releases (ASRs)   In 1937 the SEC initiated a program of pronouncements by the chief accountant designed to contribute to the development of uniform standards and practice in major accounting questions. Through early 1982, 307 *ASR*s were issued, with more than half of them published after January, 1974. However, fewer than half of the *ASR*s dealt solely with accounting principles and disclosures; the remainder covered auditing standards, independence of auditors, and enforcement actions of the SEC involving accountants.

Two examples of *ASR*s dealing with accounting principles and disclosures are *ASR No. 142* and *ASR No. 149.* In *ASR No. 142,* "Reporting Cash Flow and Other Related Data," the SEC concluded that financial reports *should not* present *cash flow* (net income adjusted for noncash expenses and revenue) *per share* and other comparable per-share computations, other than those based on net income, dividends, or net assets. In *ASR No. 149,* ". . . Improved Disclosure of Income Tax Expense" (as amended by *ASR No. 280*), the SEC mandated several disclosures concerning income taxes. Note 7 of the annual report of The Walt Disney Company in the Appendix (page 924) illustrates the requirements of *ASR No. 149.*

Financial Reporting Releases   In 1982, the SEC terminated the issuance of *Accounting Series Releases* and instituted *Financial Reporting Releases* for stating its views on financial reporting matters. (Enforcement actions of the SEC were to be publicized in *Accounting and Auditing Enforcement Releases.*)

Staff Accounting Bulletins (SABs)   The following excerpt from *ASR No. 180* describes the *SAB*s issued by the SEC:

> The Securities and Exchange Commission today announced the institution of a series of Staff Accounting Bulletins intended to achieve a wider dissemination of the administrative interpretations and practices utilized by the Commission's staff in reviewing financial statements. The Division of Corporation Finance and the Office of the Chief Accountant began the series today with the publication of Bulletin No. 1. . . . The statements in the Bulletin are not rules or interpretations of the Commission nor are they published as bearing the Commission's official approval; they represent interpretations and practices followed by the Division and the Chief Accountant in administering the disclosure requirements of the federal securities laws.

The following example from *SAB No. 1* (subsequently superseded by *SAB No. 40*) illustrates the contents of a typical Bulletin:

> *Facts:* Company E proposes to include in its registration statement a balance sheet showing its subordinated debt as a portion of stockholders' equity.
>
> *Question:* Is this presentation appropriate?
>
> *Interpretive Response:* Subordinated debt may not be included in the stockholders' equity section of the balance sheet. Any presentation describing such debt as a component of stockholders' equity must be eliminated. Furthermore, any caption representing the combination of stockholders' equity and any subordinated debt must be deleted.

Integration Project and Other Recent Activities of SEC

The foregoing discussion indicates the complexity of the reporting requirements of the SEC. Compliance with these requirements often is a major undertaking for companies that report to the SEC.

In the early 1980s, the SEC substantially completed an integration project designed to provide, wherever possible, uniform reporting requirements in the various *Forms* filed with the SEC. The integration was focused on providing comparable requirements for the *transaction-oriented* Securities Act of 1933 and the *status-oriented* Securities Exchange Act of 1934.[32] In a number of *ASR*s, the SEC accomplished the following:

---

[32] *Accounting Series Release No. 306,* Securities and Exchange Commission (Washington: 1982).

1   Through the *incorporation by reference* technique, enabled many companies to satisfy the reporting requirements of the 1933 Act by already-filed *Forms* provided to the SEC under the 1934 Act

2   Permitted many of the requirements of *Form 10-K* to be met by reference to the annual report to stockholders

3   Conformed many of the accounting requirements of *Regulation S-X* to generally accepted accounting principles, thus generally permitting the form and content of financial statements included in annual reports to stockholders to suffice for reports to the SEC

In addition to the integration project, the SEC has encouraged the voluntary filing of *projections of future economic performance* (also termed *financial forecasts*) in reports to it. In *Regulation S-K* the SEC provided guidelines for the preparation and disclosure of such projections. The SEC has long believed that users of financial reports would benefit from management's projections as a supplement to the historical data in the financial statements. However, the SEC has been reluctant to require projections in the various *Forms,* because there is widespread opposition to submission of financial forecasts to stockholders by accountants and business executives who fear the litigation consequences if forecasted results are not achieved.

In 1983, the SEC initiated *EDGAR,* its Electronic Data Gathering, Analysis, and Retrieval project designed to permit ''paperless'' filings with the SEC by means of direct communication over telephone lines, on diskettes, or on magnetic tapes. After substantial testing of EDGAR through a pilot project, the SEC anticipated eventual electronic filings of all *Forms* and reports by 1996.

APPENDIX: EXCERPTS FROM 1992 ANNUAL REPORT FOR THE WALT DISNEY COMPANY*

Consolidated Statement of Income

(In millions, except per share data)

Year ended September 30	1992	1991	1990
Revenues			
Theme parks and resorts	$3,306.9	$2,794.3	$2,933.2
Filmed entertainment	3,115.2	2,593.7	2,250.3
Consumer products	1,081.9	724.0	573.8
	7,504.0	6,112.0	5,757.3
Costs and Expenses			
Theme parks and resorts	2,662.9	2,247.7	2,130.3
Filmed entertainment	2,606.9	2,275.6	1,937.3
Consumer products	798.9	494.2	350.6
	6,068.7	5,017.5	4,418.2
Operating Income			
Theme parks and resorts	644.0	546.6	802.9
Filmed entertainment	508.3	318.1	313.0
Consumer products	283.0	229.8	223.2
	1,435.3	1,094.5	1,339.1
Corporate Activities			
General and administrative expenses	148.2	160.8	138.5
Interest expense	126.8	105.0	43.1
Investment and interest income	(130.3)	(119.4)	(80.8)
	144.7	146.4	100.8
Income from investment in Euro Disney	11.2	63.8	86.4
Income Before Income Taxes	1,301.8	1,011.9	1,324.7
Income taxes	485.1	375.3	500.7
Net Income	$ 816.7	$ 636.6	$ 824.0
Earnings Per Share	$ 1.52	$ 1.20	$ 1.50
Average Number of Common and Common Equivalent Shares Outstanding	536.8	532.7	549.0

See Notes to Consolidated Financial Statements

* Excerpts from The Walt Disney Company's 1992 Annual Report © 1992 The Walt Disney Company.

Consolidated Balance Sheet

(In millions)

September 30	1992	1991
Assets		
Cash and cash equivalents	$ 764.8	$ 886.1
Investments	1,407.0	782.4
Receivables	1,298.9	1,128.2
Merchandise inventories	462.8	311.6
Film and television costs	760.5	596.9
Theme parks, resorts and other property, at cost		
Attractions, buildings and equipment	6,285.3	5,628.1
Accumulated depreciation	(1,999.6)	(1,667.8)
	4,285.7	3,960.3
Projects in progress	440.1	540.9
Land	72.9	70.4
	4,798.7	4,571.6
Other assets	1,369.0	1,151.7
	$10,861.7	$9,428.5
Liabilities and Stockholders' Equity		
Accounts payable and other accrued liabilities	$ 1,791.9	$1,433.8
Income taxes payable	381.0	296.2
Borrowings	2,222.4	2,213.8
Unearned royalty and other advances	872.8	859.5
Deferred income taxes	889.0	753.9
Stockholders' equity		
Preferred stock, $.10 par value		
Authorized–100.0 and 5.0 million shares		
Issued–none		
Common stock, $.025 par value		
Authorized–1,200 million shares		
Issued–552.2 million shares and 548.6 million shares	619.9	549.7
Retained earnings	4,661.9	3,950.5
Cumulative translation adjustments	86.9	35.2
	5,368.7	4,535.4
Less treasury stock, at cost–27.8 million shares	664.1	664.1
	4,704.6	3,871.3
	$10,861.7	$9,428.5

See Notes to Consolidated Financial Statements

Consolidated Statement of Cash Flows

(In millions)

Year ended September 30	1992	1991	1990
Cash Provided by Operations Before Income Taxes	$2,132.0	$1,757.9	$1,780.3
Income taxes paid	(293.9)	(261.2)	(421.4)
	1,838.1	1,496.7	1,358.9
Investing Activities			
Theme parks, resorts and other property, net	544.4	924.6	716.3
Film and television costs	606.0	486.8	533.0
Euro Disney investment and advances	68.3	50.6	(135.1)
Investments, net	624.5	194.3	(74.2)
Other	80.5	70.0	141.9
	1,923.7	1,726.3	1,181.9
Financing Activities			
Borrowings	182.8	641.9	965.0
Reduction of borrowings	(184.6)	(124.6)	(255.9)
Repurchases of common stock	–	(181.1)	(427.5)
Cash dividends	(105.3)	(87.2)	(74.1)
Other	71.4	46.9	54.5
	(35.7)	295.9	262.0
Increase (Decrease) in Cash and Cash Equivalents	(121.3)	66.3	439.0
Cash and Cash Equivalents, Beginning of Year	886.1	819.8	380.8
Cash and Cash Equivalents, End of Year	$ 764.8	$ 886.1	$ 819.8

The difference between Income Before Income Taxes as shown on the Consolidated Statement of Income and Cash Provided By Operations Before Income Taxes is explained as follows.

Income Before Income Taxes	$1,301.8	$1,011.9	$1,324.7
Charges to Income Not Requiring Cash Outlays			
Depreciation	317.3	263.5	203.1
Amortization of film and television costs	442.3	531.0	335.2
Other	155.4	29.7	(36.7)
Changes in			
Receivables	(161.5)	(266.8)	(166.2)
Merchandise inventories	(151.2)	(42.4)	(44.9)
Prepaid expenses	(121.3)	(46.9)	(64.1)
Accounts payable and other accrued liabilities	335.9	280.1	300.0
Unearned royalty and other advances	13.3	(2.2)	(70.8)
	830.2	746.0	455.6
Cash Provided by Operations Before Income Taxes	$2,132.0	$1,757.9	$1,780.3
Supplemental Cash Flow Information:			
Interest paid	$ 89.8	$ 69.8	$ 67.3

See Notes to Consolidated Financial Statements

Management's Responsibility for Financial Statements

Management is responsible for the preparation of the Company's consolidated financial statements and related information appearing in this annual report. Management believes that the consolidated financial statements fairly reflect the form and substance of transactions and that the financial statements reasonably present the Company's financial position and results of operations in conformity with generally accepted accounting principles. Management also has included in the Company's financial statements amounts that are based on estimates and judgments which it believes are reasonable under the circumstances.

The independent accountants audit the Company's consolidated financial statements in accordance with generally accepted auditing standards and provide an objective, independent review of the fairness of reported operating results and financial position.

The Board of Directors of the Company has an Audit Review Committee composed of five non-management Directors. The Committee meets periodically with financial management, the internal auditors and the independent accountants to review accounting, control, auditing and financial reporting matters.

Report of Independent Accountants

To the Board of Directors and Stockholders of
The Walt Disney Company

In our opinion, the consolidated balance sheet (page 52) and the related consolidated statements of income (page 51) and of cash flows (page 53) present fairly, in all material respects, the financial position of The Walt Disney Company and its subsidiaries (the "Company") at September 30, 1992 and 1991, and the results of their operations and their cash flows for each of the three years in the period ended September 30, 1992, in conformity with generally accepted accounting principles. These financial statements are the responsibility of the Company's management; our responsibility is to express an opinion on these financial statements based on our audits. We conducted our audits of these statements in accordance with generally accepted auditing standards which require that we plan and perform the audits to obtain reasonable assurance about whether the financial statements are free of material misstatement. An audit includes examining, on a test basis, evidence supporting the amounts and disclosures in the financial statements, assessing the accounting principles used and significant estimates made by management, and evaluating the overall financial statement presentation. We believe that our audits provide a reasonable basis for the opinion expressed above.

Price Waterhouse

Los Angeles, California
November 25, 1992

Notes to Consolidated Financial Statements

(Tabular dollars in millions, except per share amounts)

1 Description of the Business and Summary of Significant Accounting Policies

THE WALT DISNEY COMPANY and its subsidiaries (the "Company") is a diversified international entertainment company with operations in the following businesses.

THEME PARKS AND RESORTS
The Company owns and operates the Disneyland theme park and Disneyland Hotel in California and the Walt Disney World destination resort in Florida. Walt Disney World includes the Magic Kingdom, EPCOT Center, The Disney-MGM Studios Theme Park, ten hotels and villas, a nighttime entertainment complex, a shopping village, conference centers, a campground, golf courses and other recreational facilities. Until September 30, 1992, the Company leased and operated the Queen Mary hotel and attraction in Long Beach, California. The Company earns royalties on revenues generated by the Tokyo Disneyland theme park near Tokyo, Japan, which is owned and operated by an unrelated Japanese corporation. The Company owns and operates Walt Disney Imagineering and Disney Development Company, which design and develop new theme park attractions and resort properties. Construction is continuing on the 500-unit Disney Vacation Club at Lake Buena Vista in Florida. This facility will primarily sell vacation ownership points and be operated partially as a rental property until the units are completely sold.

FILMED ENTERTAINMENT
The Company produces and acquires live action and animated motion pictures for distribution to the theatrical, television and home video markets. Original television product is also produced for network and produced for, and distributed in, syndication markets. The Company distributes its filmed product through its own distribution and marketing companies in the United States and through both its own subsidiaries and foreign distribution companies throughout the rest of the world. The Company invests in programming for and operates The Disney Channel, a pay television programming service, and a Los Angeles television station.

CONSUMER PRODUCTS
The Company licenses the name Walt Disney, its characters, literary properties, songs and music to various manufacturers, retailers, printers and publishers. Audio products are produced primarily for the children's market, while film, audio and computer software products are produced for the educational market. The Company also operates several catalog businesses primarily for the children's market. All of these products are licensed and distributed throughout the world.

The Company also has direct publishing operations in the United States in both the children's and adult markets, and in Europe primarily in the children's market. In addition, the Company owns and operates The Disney Stores, which are retail outlets for the Company's merchandise, in selected markets throughout the United States, Great Britain and Japan.

INVESTMENT IN EURO DISNEY
The Company is an equity investor in and earns royalties and other fees from the Euro Disney Resort, which opened in April 1992 near Paris, France.

Notes to Consolidated Financial Statements

The following is a summary of the Company's significant accounting policies.

Principles of Consolidation

The consolidated financial statements of the Company include the accounts of The Walt Disney Company and its subsidiaries after elimination of intercompany accounts and transactions. Investments in affiliated companies are accounted for using the equity method.

Revenue Recognition

Revenues from the theatrical distribution of motion pictures are recognized in domestic markets when motion pictures are exhibited and in foreign markets when revenues are reported by distributors. Television licensing revenues are generally recorded when the program material is available for telecasting by the licensee and when certain other conditions are met.

Revenues from participants/sponsors at the theme parks are generally recorded over the period of the applicable agreements commencing with the opening of the attraction.

Cash, Cash Equivalents and Investments

Cash and cash equivalents consist of cash on hand and marketable securities with original maturities of three months or less.

Debt securities are carried at cost, adjusted for unamortized premium or discount. Marketable equity securities are carried at the lower of aggregate cost or market. Realized gains and losses are determined on an average cost basis.

Merchandise Inventories

Cost of merchandise, materials and supplies inventories are generally determined on a moving average cost basis and are stated at the lower of cost or market.

Film and Television Costs

Film production and participation costs for each production are expensed based on the ratio of the current period's gross revenues to estimated total gross revenues from all sources on an individual production basis. Estimates of total gross revenues are reviewed periodically and amortization is adjusted accordingly.

Television broadcast rights are amortized principally on an accelerated basis over the estimated useful lives of the programs.

Theme Parks, Resorts and Other Property

Theme parks, resorts and other property are carried at cost. Depreciation is computed on the straight-line method based upon estimated useful lives ranging from three to fifty years.

Other Assets

Rights to the name, likeness and portrait of Walt Disney, goodwill and other intangible assets are being amortized over periods ranging from two to forty years.

Hedging Contracts

In the normal course of business, the Company employs a variety of off-balance-sheet financial instruments to reduce its exposure to fluctuations in interest and foreign currency exchange rates, including interest rate swap agreements and foreign currency forward exchange contracts, options and option combinations. The Company designates interest rate swaps as hedges of investments and debt, and accrues the differential to be paid or received under the agreements as interest rates change over the lives of the contracts. Gains and losses arising from foreign currency forward exchange contracts and options are deferred and recognized in income as offsets of gains and losses resulting from the underlying hedged transactions.

The Company continually monitors its positions with, and the credit quality of, the major international financial institutions which are counterparties to its off-balance-sheet financial instruments, and does not anticipate non-performance by the counterparties.

At September 30, 1992 and 1991, the Company had $2.2 billion and $1.9 billion (notional amount), respectively, of foreign currency hedge contracts outstanding, consisting principally of option strategies providing for the sale of foreign currencies. The contracts serve primarily to hedge probable, but not firmly committed, French franc, German mark, Japanese yen and other foreign currency revenues over a multi-year horizon, extending up to six years.

Earnings Per Share

Earnings per share amounts are based upon the weighted average number of common and common equivalent shares outstanding during the year.

Reclassifications

Certain reclassifications have been made in the 1991 and 1990 financial statements to conform to the 1992 presentation.

2 Cash, Cash Equivalents and Investments

At September 30, 1992, the cost and market value of marketable equity securities were $186.6 million and $205.3 million, respectively. At September 30, 1991, the cost and market value of marketable equity securities were $103.6 million and $107.7 million, respectively. For both 1992 and 1991, cost approximated market value for marketable securities other than marketable equity securities.

At September 30, 1992 and 1991, interest rate swap agreements related to certain foreign currency denominated investments converted $245 million and $120 million, respectively, of fixed rate securities to variable rate investments. At September 30, 1992, the Company received interest at the three-month lira LIBOR rate and paid interest at a weighted average fixed rate of 11.7%. The agreements expire in approximately six years.

At September 30, 1992 and 1991, the Company had outstanding interest rate swap agreements with notional amounts totaling $600 million which effectively converted variable rate investment securities to fixed rate instruments. Under these swap agreements, which expire in two to four years, the Company received interest at a weighted average fixed rate of 8.0% and paid interest at the one-month commercial paper rate at September 30, 1992.

3 Film and Television Costs

	1992	1991
Theatrical Film Costs		
Released, less amortization	$ 64.8	$111.7
In process	209.1	85.4
	273.9	197.1
Television Costs		
Released, less amortization	190.4	131.3
In process	131.0	112.0
	321.4	243.3
Television Broadcast Rights	165.2	156.5
	$760.5	$596.9

Notes to Consolidated Financial Statements

Based on management's total gross revenue estimates as of September 30, 1992, approximately 89% of unamortized film production costs applicable to released theatrical and television productions are expected to be amortized during the next three years.

4 Investment in Euro Disney

Euro Disney S.C.A. ("Euro Disney"), a publicly traded French company, operates a theme park and resort complex on a 4,800-acre site near Paris, France. Euro Disney commenced operations on April 12, 1992.

The Company has a 49% ownership interest in Euro Disney and is using the equity method of accounting for its investment. At September 30, 1992 and 1991, the investment in and advances to Euro Disney were $659.1 million and $580.9 million, respectively. The market value of the Company's investment in Euro Disney exceeded its accreted carrying value at September 30, 1992 by $797 million.

In October 1989, Euro Disney completed a public equity offering of approximately $1 billion. As a result of the offering, the Company's share of the net assets of Euro Disney exceeded its investment by approximately $375 million. The Company is recognizing this gain ratably over an eight-year period, which represents the Company's contractual obligation to manage the development and operation of the complex and maintain an ownership interest of at least 17%.

In addition to recording its equity in Euro Disney's operating results and amortization of the gain, the Company earned $33 million of royalties in 1992 under certain agreements with Euro Disney. The Company has agreed to defer its base management fees for 1992 and 1993. Payment of the deferred amount will commence no sooner than 1994 and will be contingent upon Euro Disney achieving profitability.

In June 1991, Euro Disney completed a public offering of convertible bonds of approximately $670 million. The bonds are convertible into common stock of Euro Disney at any time before they become due in 2001. If all of the holders of the bonds exercised this conversion option, the Company's ownership interest in Euro Disney would decrease to 42%.

The Company has agreed, under certain circumstances, to provide indemnification of up to $95 million in connection with the development of Euro Disney. The Company does not expect to incur any obligation with respect to this agreement.

Euro Disney's consolidated financial statements are prepared in accordance with accounting principles generally accepted in France (French GAAP). Under French GAAP, Euro Disney earned net income of FF 381 million in 1990 and FF 249 million in 1991, and incurred a net loss of FF 188 million in 1992. U.S. generally accepted accounting principles (U.S. GAAP) differ in certain significant respects from French GAAP applied by Euro Disney, principally as they relate to accounting for leases. The summarized consolidated financial statements for Euro Disney, set forth below, are stated in U.S. dollars in accordance with U.S. GAAP.

Balance Sheet	1992	1991
Cash and investments	$ 479	$1,060
Receivables	459	477
Fixed assets, net	4,346	2,399
Other assets	873	401
Total Assets	$6,157	$4,337
Accounts payable and other liabilities	$ 797	$ 796
Borrowings	3,960	2,240
Common stock	1,042	1,042
Retained earnings	358	259
Total Liabilities and Stockholders' Equity	$6,157	$4,337

Statement of Operations	1992	1991	1990
Revenues	$ 738	$ –	$ –
Costs and expenses	808	–	–
Operating income	(70)	–	–
Net interest income (expense)	(95)	76	70
Income (loss) before income taxes	(165)	76	70
Income taxes	30	(28)	–
Net Income (Loss)	$(135)	$ 48	$ 70

5 Borrowings

	Effective Interest Rate	Fiscal Year Maturity	1992	1991
Subordinated notes (a)	6.2%	2005	$1,041.4	$1,091.9
Medium term notes (b)	3.1	1993–1995	390.0	500.0
Securities sold under agreements to repurchase (c)	15.6	1993	231.2	127.3
Commercial paper (d)	3.2	1993	181.4	128.9
Other (e)	7.7	1994–2013	378.4	365.7
	6.6%		$2,222.4	$2,213.8

(a) During 1990, the Company issued $2.3 billion zero coupon subordinated notes which resulted in gross proceeds of $965 million. Holders may redeem the notes at their option for the issuance price plus accrued interest at the end of five and ten years, and upon a change in control of the Company, as defined, or at any time exchange the notes for the U.S. dollar equivalent of 19.651 shares of Euro Disney S.C.A. which is listed on the Paris Bourse. The Company has the right to call the notes at their issuance price plus accrued interest. The Company has designated a portion of its Euro Disney S.C.A. shares as a hedge offsetting the contingent liability that may arise due to the exchangeability of the notes. (See Note 13.)

(b) The Company has executed interest rate swap agreements to convert medium term notes to commercial paper-based floating rate instruments. The effect of these swaps has been reflected in the effective interest rate.

(c) Securities sold under agreements to repurchase are collateralized by certain marketable securities.

(d) The Company has available through 1994 an unsecured revolving line of bank credit of up to $310 million for general corporate purposes, including the support of commercial paper borrowings. The Company has the option to borrow at various interest rates.

(e) Foreign currency swaps effectively converted $137 million and $158 million at September 30, 1992 and 1991, respectively, of foreign debt issuances to Japanese yen or dollar obligations. The effect of these swaps has been reflected in the effective interest rate. The Company hedges the obligations converted to yen borrowings with a portion of its yen royalty receipts.

Notes to Consolidated Financial Statements

Borrowings, excluding commercial paper and securities sold under agreements to repurchase which mature in 1993, have the following scheduled maturities.

1993	$202.0
1994	161.4
1995	131.9
1996	86.2
1997	106.6

The Company capitalizes interest on assets constructed for its theme parks, resorts and other developments, and on theatrical and television productions in process. In 1992, 1991 and 1990, respectively, total interest costs incurred were $152.1, $142.4 and $90.7 million, of which $25.3, $37.4 and $47.6 million were capitalized.

6 Unearned Royalty and Other Advances

	1992	1991
Tokyo Disneyland royalty advances	$522.3	$545.8
Other	350.5	313.7
	$872.8	$859.5

In 1988, the Company monetized a substantial portion of its royalties through 2008 from certain Tokyo Disneyland operations. The Company has certain ongoing obligations under its contract with the owner and operator of Tokyo Disneyland, and accordingly royalty advances are being amortized through 2008. The maximum amount the Company may be required to fund under certain recourse provisions of the monetization agreement is $145 million. The Company does not anticipate funding any significant amount under this agreement.

7 Income Taxes

	1992	1991	1990
Income Before Income Taxes			
Domestic			
(including U.S. exports)	$1,178.9	$ 945.8	$1,270.2
Foreign subsidiaries	122.9	66.1	54.5
	$1,301.8	$1,011.9	$1,324.7
Income Tax Provision			
Current			
Federal	$ 225.8	$241.7	$ 260.4
State	40.3	34.0	50.2
Foreign subsidiaries	46.1	30.5	25.0
Other foreign	48.3	44.5	34.9
	360.5	350.7	370.5
Deferred			
Federal	109.9	10.5	110.4
State	14.7	14.1	19.8
	124.6	24.6	130.2
	$ 485.1	$ 375.3	$ 500.7

	1992	1991	1990
Components of Provision for			
Deferred Income Taxes			
Depreciation and amortization	$ 45.4	$ 56.6	$ 49.9
Licensing revenues	11.6	11.3	29.5
Capitalized interest and			
property taxes	7.5	8.9	13.1
Royalty expenses	33.7	(51.8)	(2.2)
Leveraged leasing	47.2	–	–
Other	(20.8)	(0.4)	39.9
	$ 124.6	$ 24.6	$ 130.2
Reconciliation of Effective Income Tax Rate			
Federal income tax rate	34.0%	34.0%	34.0%
State income taxes, net of			
Federal income tax benefit	2.8	3.3	3.6
Other	.5	(.2)	.2
	37.3%	37.1%	37.8%

In February 1992, the Financial Accounting Standards Board issued Statement of Financial Accounting Standards No. 109, Accounting for Income Taxes. The standard requires, among other provisions, that existing deferred tax assets and liabilities be adjusted to reflect the effect of changes in tax laws and/or rates. The Company plans to adopt this standard in 1994 and currently anticipates that it will not have a material impact on its financial condition.

8 Pension and Other Benefit Programs

The Company contributes to various pension plans under union and industry-wide agreements. Contributions are based upon the hours worked or gross wages paid to covered employees. In 1992, 1991 and 1990, the cost recognized under these plans was $26.1, $12.9 and $6.1 million, respectively. The Company's share of the unfunded liability, if any, related to these multi-employer plans is not material.

The Company also maintains pension plans covering most of its domestic salaried and hourly employees not covered by union or industry-wide pension plans and a non-qualified, unfunded retirement plan for key employees.

With respect to its defined benefit pension plans, the Company's policy is to fund, at a minimum, the amount necessary on an actuarial basis to provide for benefits in accordance with the requirements of ERISA. Benefits are generally based on years of service and/or compensation.

Pension cost is summarized as follows.

	1992	1991	1990
Service cost of current period	$48.9	$37.1	$25.4
Interest cost on projected			
benefit obligations	25.9	21.5	17.9
Gain on plan assets	(43.3)	(18.2)	(30.8)
Net amortization and deferral of			
unrecognized gain on plan assets	19.1	(1.4)	16.2
Net pension cost	$50.6	$39.0	$28.7

Notes to Consolidated Financial Statements

For 1992, 1991 and 1990, the weighted average discount rate was 9.5% and the expected long-term rate of return on plan assets was 9.5%. The assumed rate of increase in compensation was 7% for 1992, 6.6% for 1991 and 6.5% for 1990.

The funded status of the plans and the amounts included in the Company's consolidated balance sheets are as follows.

	1992	1991
Plan assets at fair value, primarily publicly traded stocks and bonds	$346.4	$270.9
Actuarial present value of projected benefit obligations		
Accumulated benefit obligations		
Vested	(277.9)	(228.5)
Non-vested	(20.1)	(10.4)
Provision for future salary increases	(57.8)	(37.7)
Deficiency in plan assets versus projected benefit obligations	(9.4)	(5.7)
Unrecognized net loss	51.5	27.9
Unrecognized prior service cost	3.4	3.8
Unrecognized net obligation	4.2	4.4
Prepaid pension cost	$ 49.7	$ 30.4

The Company sponsors a plan to provide postretirement medical benefits to most of its domestic salaried and hourly employees, and contributes to multi-employer welfare plans to provide similar benefits to certain employees under collective bargaining agreements.

In December 1990, the Financial Accounting Standards Board issued Statement of Financial Accounting Standards No. 106, Employer's Accounting for Postretirement Benefits Other Than Pensions (SFAS 106), which will require accrual of postretirement benefit costs to actuarially allocate such costs to the years during which employees render qualifying service. SFAS 106 also requires recognition no later than October 1, 1993 of the unfunded and previously unrecognized accumulated postretirement benefit obligation for all participants in the Company-sponsored plan. This "transition obligation" may be charged immediately to operations or amortized over the longer of the average remaining service period of active plan participants, or twenty years. The Company currently plans to adopt SFAS 106 in fiscal 1994, and does not anticipate that its transition obligation or ongoing expense will be material to its financial condition.

9 Stockholders' Equity

(Shares in millions)	Shares	Common Stock	Paid-in Capital	Retained Earnings
Balance at September 30, 1989	545.2	$13.5	$434.8	$2,651.2
Exercise of stock options, net	1.7	.1	54.4	
Dividends ($.13875 per share)				(74.1)
Net income				824.0
Balance at September 30, 1990	546.9	13.6	489.2	3,401.1
Exercise of stock options, net	1.7	.1	46.8	
Dividends ($.1675 per share)				(87.2)
Net income				636.6
Balance at September 30, 1991	548.6	13.7	536.0	3,950.5
Exercise of stock options, net	3.6	.1	70.1	
Dividends ($.20125 per share)				(105.3)
Net income				816.7
Balance at September 30, 1992	552.2	$13.8	$606.1	$4,661.9

On February 18, 1992, the Board of Directors approved a four-for-one stock split of the Company's common stock, which was approved by the Company's stockholders and became effective on April 20, 1992. The new shares were distributed on May 15, 1992 to holders of record on April 20, 1992. All share and per share data have been restated for all periods presented to reflect the stock split. An increase in the authorized number of shares of preferred stock of the Company from 5 million to 100 million was also approved.

In June 1989, the Company adopted a stockholders' rights plan. The plan becomes operative in certain events involving the acquisition of 25% or more of the Company's common stock by any person or group in a transaction not approved by the Company's Board of Directors. Upon the occurrence of such an event, each right, unless redeemed by the Board, entitles its holder to purchase for $350 an amount of common stock of the Company, or in certain circumstances the acquiror, having a market value of twice the purchase price. In connection with the rights plan, 7.2 million shares of preferred stock were reserved.

In 1992 and 1991 the Company recorded cumulative foreign currency translation adjustments of $86.9 million and $35.2 million, net of deferred taxes of $50.4 million and $19.5 million, respectively.

Treasury stock activity for the three years ended September 30, 1992 was as follows.

(Shares in millions)	Shares	Treasury Stock
Balance at September 30, 1989	4.0	$ 55.5
Common stock repurchases	15.9	427.5
Balance at September 30, 1990	19.9	483.0
Common stock repurchases	7.9	181.1
Balance at September 30, 1991 and 1992	27.8	$664.1

Notes to Consolidated Financial Statements

In November 1984, the Company adopted a program to repurchase up to 56 million shares. In December 1990, the Company increased the authorized share repurchase amount to 90 million shares. There were no repurchases under this program during the year ended September 30, 1992. Since adoption of the program, a total of 51.9 million shares have been repurchased at prevailing market prices.

10 Stock Incentive Plans

Under various plans, the Company may grant stock option and other awards to key executive, management and creative personnel. Transactions under the various stock option and incentive plans during 1992 were as follows.

(Shares in millions)	1992	1991	1990
Outstanding at beginning of year	44.8	43.2	38.6
Awards cancelled	(1.2)	(0.7)	(0.3)
Awards granted	4.3	4.0	6.6
Awards exercised	(3.6)	(1.7)	(1.7)
Outstanding at September 30	44.3	44.8	43.2
Exercisable at September 30	18.8	17.8	14.0

Stock option awards are granted at prices equal to at least market price on the date of grant. Options outstanding at September 30, 1992 and 1991, respectively, ranged in price from $3.23 to $37.39 and $3.23 to $32.66 per share. Options exercised during the period ranged in price from $3.23 to $32.66 per share in 1992, from $3.14 to $30.75 per share in 1991, and from $3.23 to $23.19 per share in 1990. Shares available for future option grants at September 30, 1992 were 28.4 million.

11 Detail of Certain Balance Sheet Accounts

	1992	1991
Receivables		
Trade, net of allowance	$1,033.3	$ 969.7
Euro Disney advances	119.6	109.8
Other	146.0	48.7
	$1,298.9	$1,128.2
Other Assets		
Intangibles	$ 384.5	$ 373.7
Investment in Euro Disney	539.5	471.1
Other	445.0	306.9
	$1,369.0	$1,151.7
Accounts Payable and Other Accrued Liabilities		
Accounts payable	$1,374.4	$1,111.5
Payroll and employee benefits	328.9	303.4
Other	88.6	18.9
	$1,791.9	$1,433.8

12 Business Segments

	1992	1991	1990
Capital Expenditures			
Theme parks and resorts	$ 380.9	$ 790.1	$ 519.8
Filmed entertainment	76.7	50.1	39.5
Consumer products	38.6	35.5	34.3
Corporate	48.2	48.9	122.7
	$ 544.4	$ 924.6	$ 716.3
Depreciation Expense			
Theme parks and resorts	$ 249.8	$ 213.2	$ 177.4
Filmed entertainment	29.5	23.9	12.9
Consumer products	16.8	12.4	5.8
Corporate	21.2	14.0	7.0
	$ 317.3	$ 263.5	$ 203.1
Identifiable Assets			
Theme parks and resorts	$ 5,076.8	$4,694.7	$4,056.4
Filmed entertainment	2,370.9	1,910.5	1,696.8
Consumer products	642.8	448.4	308.5
Corporate	2,231.7	1,903.8	1,596.7
Investment in Euro Disney	539.5	471.1	363.9
	$10,861.7	$9,428.5	$8,022.3
Supplemental Revenue Data			
Theme Parks and Resorts			
Admissions	$ 1,246.6	$1,093.0	$1,179.9
Merchandise, food and beverage	1,223.1	1,048.0	1,113.5
Filmed Entertainment			
Theatrical product	2,251.7	1,776.9	1,545.7
Export revenues	1,457.4	1,267.1	938.8

13 Commitments and Contingencies

The Company, together with, in some instances, certain of its directors and officers, is a defendant or co-defendant in various legal actions involving antitrust, copyright, breach of contract and various other claims incident to the conduct of its businesses. Management does not expect the Company to suffer any material liability by reason of such actions.

As of September 30, 1992, the potential liability to the Company arising from the exchangeability feature of the Company's zero coupon subordinated notes did not exceed the carrying or accreted value of the notes. (See Note 5.)

Quarterly Financial Summary

(In millions, except per share data)
(Unaudited)

	December 31	March 31	June 30	September 30
1992				
Revenues	$1,916.4	$1,629.2	$1,883.3	$2,075.1
Operating income	348.4	271.8	419.3	395.8
Net income	208.1	164.1	220.8	223.7
Earnings per share	.39	.31	.41	.42
Dividends per share	.04375	.05250	.05250	.05250
Market price per share				
High	$30\frac{3}{8}$	$39\frac{3}{8}$	$41\frac{1}{8}$	$37\frac{1}{2}$
Low	$25\frac{7}{8}$	$28\frac{1}{2}$	$34\frac{5}{8}$	$32\frac{3}{4}$
1991				
Revenues	$1,477.6	$1,423.0	$1,494.5	$1,716.9
Operating income	292.9	215.9	284.9	300.8
Net income	170.4	126.6	165.5	174.1
Earnings per share	.32	.24	.31	.33
Dividends per share	.03625	.04375	.04375	.04375
Market price per share				
High	$27\frac{1}{4}$	$32\frac{1}{2}$	31	$30\frac{3}{4}$
Low	$21\frac{1}{2}$	$23\frac{3}{8}$	$27\frac{1}{2}$	$27\frac{1}{2}$

Selected Financial Data

(In millions, except per share and other data)

	1992	1991	1990	1989	1988
Statement of Income					
Revenues	$ 7,504.0	$6,112.0	$5,757.3	$4,593.8	$3,438.2
Operating income	1,435.3	1,094.5	1,339.1	1,228.5	884.8
Interest expense	126.8	105.0	43.1	23.9	5.8
Net income	816.7	636.6	824.0	703.3	522.0
Per Share					
Net income	1.52	$1.20	$1.50	$1.27	$.95
Cash dividends	.2013	.1675	.1388	.1150	.0950
Balance Sheet					
Total assets	$10,861.7	$9,428.5	$8,022.3	$6,657.2	$5,108.9
Borrowings	2,222.4	2,213.8	1,584.6	860.6	435.5
Stockholders' equity	4,704.6	3,871.3	3,488.6	3,044.0	2,359.3
Statement of Cash Flows					
Cash flow from operations	$ 1,838.1	$1,496.7	$1,358.9	$1,275.6	$1,075.4*
Investing activities	(1,923.7)	(1,726.3)	(1,181.9)	(1,729.2)	(1,909.5)
Financing activities	(35.7)	295.9	262.0	406.4	(245.8)
Other Data					
Stockholders at year-end	310,000	189,000	175,000	143,000	124,000
Employees at year-end	58,000	58,000	52,000	47,000	39,000

Excludes $722.6 million unearned royalty advances.

REVIEW QUESTIONS

1 What is an *industry segment* of a business enterprise?

2 Is the concept of segment reporting consistent with the theory of consolidated financial statements? Explain.

3 Outline the segment reporting requirements of *FASB Statement No. 14,* ''Financial Reporting for Segments of a Business Enterprise.''

4 How is *operating profit or loss* computed for industry segments of a business enterprise?

5 Describe the formula for the allocation of residual home office expenses set forth in *Cost Accounting Standard 403,* ''Allocation of Home Office Expenses to Segments.''

6 Describe the *maximum* and *minimum* limitations on the extent of industry segment reporting by a business enterprise.

7 Differentiate between the *measurement date* and the *disposal date* for the discontinuance of a business segment. Define *phase-out period.*

8 Discuss the provisions of *APB Opinion No. 28,* ''Interim Financial Reporting,'' dealing with the accounting for costs associated with revenue in interim financial reports.

9 How is lower-of-cost-or-market accounting for inventories applied in interim financial reports?

10 Explain the technique included in *APB Opinion No. 28,* ''Interim Financial Reporting,'' for the measurement of income taxes expense in interim financial reports.

11 Identify four U.S. statutes administered by the Securities and Exchange Commission.

12 Differentiate between *Form 10-K* and *Form 8-K* filed with the Securities and Exchange Commission under the Securities Exchange Act of 1934.

13 Under what circumstances must financial statements of a business enterprise be included in a *proxy statement* issued to the enterprise's stockholders under the provisions of the Securities Exchange Act of 1934?

14 What position did the Securities and Exchange Commission take regarding its role in the establishment of accounting principles?

15 How do accountants use *Regulation S-X* in filings with the Securities and Exchange Commission?

16 What is *Regulation S-K* of the Securities and Exchange Commission?

17 What are *Financial Reporting Releases?*

18 Does the Securities and Exchange Commission require the inclusion of *financial forecasts* in filings with the SEC?

EXERCISES

Ex. 20-1 Select the best answer for each of the following multiple-choice questions:

1 For reportable industry segments of a diversified publicly owned business enterprise, all the following must be disclosed except:
a Segment contribution
b Revenue
c Operating profit or loss
d Identifiable assets

2 Which of the following is not or are not included in the measurement of the operating profit or loss of an industry segment of a business enterprise?
a General corporate expenses
b Interest expense
c Domestic and foreign income taxes
d All the foregoing
e None of the foregoing

3 Does the gain or loss on disposal of a business enterprise's discontinued business segment include the net-of-taxes:

	Income (loss) from segment's operations up to the measurement date?	Income (loss) from segment's operations during phase-out period?
a	Yes	Yes
b	Yes	No
c	No	Yes
d	No	No

4 Segment sales reduced by segment traceable and allocated nontraceable expenses yields segment:
a Net income or loss
b Contribution
c Pre-tax income or loss
d Operating profit or loss

5 *Operating profit or loss* is measured and reported for a diversified business enterprise's significant:
a Industry segments only
b Foreign geographic areas only
c Export sales only
d Industry segments and foreign geographic areas

6 Are *segment disclosures* required for:

	Nonpublic enterprises?	Interim reports?
a	Yes	Yes
b	Yes	No
c	No	Yes
d	No	No

7 Are intersegment or interarea sales or transfers included in the *revenue-based* determination of a business enterprise's:

	Significant industry segments?	Significant foreign geographic areas?
a	Yes	Yes
b	Yes	No
c	No	Yes
d	No	No

8 In *APB Opinion No. 28,* "Interim Financial Reporting," the Accounting Principles Board provided guidelines for all the following components of interim financial reports except:
a Revenue
b Costs associated with revenue
c All other costs and expenses
d Income taxes expense
e Earnings per share

9 In *interim reports,* are lower-of-cost-market write-downs of inventories required for market declines that are considered to be:

	Temporary?	Permanent?
a	Yes	Yes
b	Yes	No
c	No	Yes
d	No	No

10 In *APB Opinion No. 28,* "Interim Financial Reporting," the Accounting Principles Board adopted:
a The *integral theory* only
b The *discrete theory* only
c Both the *integral theory* and the *discrete theory*
d Neither the *integral theory* nor the *discrete theory*

11 For each of the first two quarters of its fiscal year ending May 31, Year 2, Croy Company had the following:

	Quarter ended Aug. 31, Year 1	Nov. 30, Year 1
Pre-tax accounting income	$100,000	$120,000
Estimated effective income tax rate for fiscal year	39%	38%

In accordance with *APB Opinion No. 28,* "Interim Financial Reporting," Croy Company's income taxes expense for each of the first two quarters of its Year 2 fiscal year is, respectively:
a $39,000 and $45,600
b $38,000 and $45,600
c $39,000 and $44,600

d $41,800 and $41,800

e Some other amounts

12 The *current report* filed with the SEC by a publicly owned enterprise within a specified number of days after the occurrence of specified events is:

a *Form 10-K*

b *Form 10-Q*

c *Form 8-K*

d Proxy statement

13 Disciplinary proceedings against accountants charged with violating the Rules of Practice of the Securities and Exchange Commission (SEC) are supervised by the SEC's:

a Chief accountant

b Division of Corporation Finance

c Division of Enforcement

d Commissioners

14 Currently, the Securities and Exchange Commission states its views on current financial reporting matters in:

a *Staff Accounting Bulletins*

b *Accounting Series Releases*

c *Regulation S-K*

d None of the foregoing

15 Does a publicly owned enterprise report (or incorporate by reference) quarterly operating results to the Securities and Exchange Commission in:

	Form 8-K?	Form 10-K?	Form 10-Q?
a	Yes	Yes	Yes
b	Yes	No	Yes
c	No	No	Yes
d	No	Yes	Yes

16 *Forms* and proxy statements filed with the Securities and Exchange Commission (SEC) are reviewed by the SEC's:

a Chief accountant

b Division of Corporate Finance

c Division of Enforcement

d Division of Forms and Proxy Statements

17 Changes in the SEC's *Forms, Regulation S-X,* and *Regulation S-K* are the responsibility of the SEC's:

a Division of Corporate Finance

b Chief accountant

c Division of Forms and Regulations

d Division of Enforcement

Ex. 20-2   Data for the three industry segments of Polyglot Company for the year ended June 30, Year 8, were as follows (amounts in thousands):

	Segment			
	Alpha	Beta	Gamma	Total
Sales to unaffiliated customers..............	$400	$500	$600	$1,500
Intersegment sales	50	40	30	120
Traceable expenses:				
Intersegment purchases..................	60	20	40	120
Other	200	300	500	1,000
Nontraceable expenses....................				150

Prepare a working paper to compute the revenue and operating profit of each of the industry segments of Polyglot Company for the year ended June 30, Year 8, assuming that Polyglot allocates nontraceable expenses to industry segments in the ratio of segment sales to unaffiliated customers.

Ex. 20-3   Rinker Company operates in three different industries, each of which is appropriately regarded as a reportable segment. Segment No. 1 contributed 60% of Rinker's total sales in Year 3. Sales for Segment No. 1 were $900,000 and traceable expenses were $400,000 in Year 3. Rinker's total nontraceable expenses for Year 3 were $600,000. Rinker allocates nontraceable expenses based on the ratio of a segment's sales to total sales, an appropriate method of allocation.

Prepare a working paper to compute the operating profit or loss for Rinker Company's Segment No. 1 for Year 3.

Ex. 20-4   The nontraceable expenses of Coopers Company for the year ended June 30, Year 2, totaled $310,000. The net sales, payroll totals, and average plant assets and inventories for the two industry segments of Coopers were as follows:

	Chemicals segment	Sporting goods segment
Net sales..	$1,400,000	$600,000
Payroll totals....................................	150,000	100,000
Average plant assets and inventories..............	710,000	290,000

Prepare a working paper to compute the amount of Coopers Company's nontraceable expenses to be allocated to the Chemicals segment and the Sporting Goods segment of Coopers Company for the year ended June 30, Year 2, assuming that such expenses are allocated to the two segments on the basis of the arithmetic average of the percentage of net sales, payroll totals, and average plant assets and inventories applicable to each segment.

Ex. 20-5   Canton Company allocates nontraceable expenses to its three industry segments in the ratio of net sales to unaffiliated customers. For the year ended April 30, Year 4, relevant segment data were as follows:

	Segment A	Segment B	Segment C
Revenue:			
Net sales to unaffiliated customers ...	$500,000	$300,000	$200,000
Intersegment transfers out	80,000	40,000	20,000
Costs and expenses:			
Traceable expenses................	400,000	100,000	200,000
Intersegment transfers in...........	30,000	60,000	50,000

Nontraceable expenses of Canton Company for the year ended April 30, Year 4, totaled $100,000.

Prepare a working paper to compute for each industry segment of Canton Company the following amounts for the year ended April 30, Year 4: revenue, operating expenses, operating profit or loss. Use a column for each industry segment, as shown above.

Ex. 20-6 Data with respect to the foreign geographic area operations of Emmet Company for the year ended December 31, Year 3, follow (amounts in thousands):

Foreign Geographic Areas

	Latin America	Africa	Southeast Asia	Western Europe	Total
Net sales to outsiders	$40,000	$20,000	$25,000	$ 5,000	$90,000
Interarea transfers out .	2,000	4,000	1,000	3,000	10,000
Interarea transfers in ..	4,000	3,000	2,000	1,000	10,000
Other traceable expenses	9,000	6,000	5,000	10,000	30,000
Nontraceable expenses....					20,000

Emmet allocates nontraceable expenses to industry segments only.

Prepare a working paper to determine if each foreign geographic area of Emmet Company is significant for the year ended December 31, Year 3. Disregard identifiable assets of the foreign geographic areas.

Ex. 20-7 Crossley Company had a net income of $600,000 for the year ended December 31, Year 8, after inclusion of the following events or transactions that occurred during the year:

(1) The decision was made on January 2 to dispose of the cinder block manufacturing segment.
(2) The cinder block manufacturing segment was disposed of on July 1.

(3) Operating income from January 2 to June 30 for the cinder block manufacturing segment amounted to $90,000 before income taxes.

(4) Cinder block net assets with a carrying amount of $250,000 were disposed of for $100,000.

Crossley was subject to income taxes at the rate of 40%.

a Prepare a working paper to compute Crossley Company's income from continuing operations for the year ended December 31, Year 8.

b Prepare a working paper to compute Crossley Company's total income taxes (expense and allocated) for the year ended December 31, Year 8.

Ex. 20-8   Tovar Company's accounting records for the year ended August 31, Year 4, include the following data with respect to its Wallis division, an industry segment. Sale of the net assets of that division to Expansive Enterprises, Inc., for $300,000 was authorized by Tovar's board of directors on August 31, Year 4. Closing date of the disposal was expected to be February 28, Year 5.

> *Wallis Division:*
>
> | | |
> |---|---:|
> | Net sales, year ended Aug. 31, Year 4 | $200,000 |
> | Costs and expenses, year ended Aug. 31, Year 4 | 150,000 |
> | Estimated operating losses, six months ending Feb. 28, Year 5 | 40,000 |
> | Estimated carrying amount of net assets, Feb. 28, Year 5 | 330,000 |

Tovar's income tax rate is 40%. For the year ended August 31, Year 4, Tovar had a $640,000 income from continuing operations before income taxes.

Prepare a partial income statement for Tovar Company for the year ended August 31, Year 4, to present the foregoing information. Disregard earnings per share data.

Ex. 20-9   For the year ended June 30, Year 2, Dispo Company, which has an income tax rate of 40% had the following ***pre-tax*** amounts:

> | | |
> |---|---:|
> | Income from continuing operations | $1,000,000 |
> | Loss from disposal of net assets of discontinued Division 105 (a business segment) | 60,000 |
> | Loss from operations of Division 105 from July 1, Year 1, through the measurement date, Mar. 31, Year 2 | 150,000 |
> | Loss from operations of Division 105 from Apr. 1, Year 2, through the disposal date, May 31, Year 2 | 20,000 |

Prepare a partial income statement for Dispo Company for the year ended June 30, Year 2, beginning with income from continuing operations. Disregard earnings per share.

Ex. 20-10   The income tax rate for Downsize Company was 40%, and it had no differences between pre-tax accounting income and taxable income. For the year ended November 30, Year 4, ***pre-tax*** amounts in the bottom portion of Downsize's income statement for the year then ended were as follows:

Income from continuing operations (before income taxes)................	*$500,000*
Income from operations of discontinued Webb Division (prior to measure-ment date)..	*60,000*
(Loss) on disposal of Webb Division (an industry segment)...............	*(40,000)*
(Operating losses) of Webb Division during phase-out period.............	*(50,000)*

Prepare a partial income statement, including intraperiod tax allocation, for Downsize Company for the year ended November 30, Year 4. Disregard earnings per share.

Ex. 20-11 Reducto Company had the following data for the year ended April 30, Year 9, a year in which its directors had resolved on February 28, Year 9, to dispose of Woeful Division, an industry segment, and completed the disposal on April 15, Year 9:

Income tax rate	*40%*
Pre-tax:	
Income from continuing operations....................................	*$600,000*
Loss from disposal of net assets of Woeful Division, Apr. 15, Year 9......	*70,000*
Operating losses of Woeful Division:	
May 1, Year 8–Feb. 28, Year 9.....................................	*160,000*
Mar. 1–Apr. 15, Year 9...	*40,000*

Prepare the bottom portion of Reducto Company's income statement for the year ended April 30, Year 9, beginning with income from continuing operations before income taxes. Disregard earnings per share disclosures.

Ex. 20-12 On January 2, Year 6, Luigi Company paid property taxes of $40,000 on its plant assets for Year 6. In March, Year 6, Luigi made customary annual major repairs to plant assets in the amount of $120,000. The repairs will benefit the entire Year 6. In April, Year 6, Luigi incurred a $420,000 loss from a replacement cost decline of inventories that was considered to be permanent.

Prepare a working paper to show how the foregoing items are reported in Luigi Company's quarterly income statements for the year ended December 31, Year 6.

Ex. 20-13 Lundy Company sells a single product, which it purchases from three different vendors. On May 1, Year 8, Lundy's inventory of the product consisted of 1,000 units at first-in, first-out cost of $7,500. Lundy's merchandise transactions for the year ended April 30, Year 9, were as follows:

Quarter ended	Units purchased	Cost per unit purchased	Units sold	End-of-quarter replacement cost per unit
July 31, Year 8	5,000	$8.00	4,500	$8.50
Oct. 31, Year 8	6,000	8.50	7,000	9.00
Jan. 31, Year 9	8,000	9.00	6,500	8.50*
Apr. 30, Year 9	6,000	8.50	5,500	9.50

* Decline not considered to be temporary.

Prepare a working paper to compute Lundy Company's cost of goods sold for each of the four quarters of the year ended April 30, Year 9. Show computations.

Ex. 20-14 Marmon Corporation's statutory income tax rate is 40%. Marmon forecasts pre-tax accounting income of $100,000 for the year ending April 30, Year 7, and no temporary differences between pre-tax accounting income and taxable income. Marmon forecasts the following permanent differences between pre-tax accounting income and taxable income for the year ending April 30, Year 7: dividend received deduction, $20,000; goodwill amortization, $10,000.

Prepare a working paper to compute Marmon Corporation's estimated effective income tax rate for the year ending April 30, Year 7.

Ex. 20-15 Basey Company has a fiscal year ending April 30. On July 31, Year 6, the end of the first quarter of Year 7, Basey estimated an effective income tax rate of 55% for Year 7. On October 31, Year 6, the end of the second quarter of Year 7, Basey estimated an effective income tax rate of 52% for Year 7. Pre-tax accounting income for Basey was as follows:

For three months ended July 31, Year 6 . . . . $200,000
For three months ended October 31, Year 6 250,000

Prepare journal entries for income taxes expense of Basey Company on July 31 and October 31, Year 6.

Ex. 20-16 Public Company, which uses the perpetual inventory system and the last-in, first-out method of valuing inventory, temporarily depleted a base layer of its inventories with a cost of $170,000 during the third quarter of its fiscal year ending February 28, Year 5. Replacement cost of the depleted inventory was $210,000 on November 30, Year 4. On December 18, Year 4, Public made its first purchase of merchandise during the fourth quarter, at a total cost of $360,000, on open account.

Prepare journal entries for Public Company on November 30 and December 18, Year 4.

Ex. 20-17 For its first two quarters of calendar year 6, its fiscal year, Intero Company had the following data:

Three months ended	Pre-tax accounting income for quarter	Estimated effective income tax rate for Year 6
Mar. 31, Year 6	$500,000	38.6%
June 30, Year 6	$600,000	41.2%

Prepare journal entries (omit explanations) for Intero Company to accrue income taxes expense for the first two quarters of Year 6.

Ex. 20-18 On January 31, Year 2, the end of the first quarter of its fiscal year ending October 31, Year 2, Cassidy Company had the following ledger account balances:

Income taxes expense . . . . $160,000 dr
Liability arising from depletion of base layer of lifo inventories . . . . 30,000 cr

On February 1, Year 2, Cassidy purchased merchandise costing $110,000 on account, and on April 30, Year 2, Cassidy estimated total income taxes expense of $340,000 for the six months ended on that date. Cassidy uses the perpetual inventory system.

Prepare journal entries for Cassidy Company on February 1 and April 30, Year 2, for the foregoing facts.

Ex. 20-19 Farber Company's journal entry for income taxes on September 30, Year 5, the end of its fiscal year, was as follows:

Income Taxes Expense ($31,960 + $14,100)   46,060

    Income Taxes Payable   46,060

To provide for income taxes for the year as follows:

	Federal	State
Pre-tax accounting income	$100,000	$100,000
Less: Nontaxable municipal bond inter-		
est.	(10,000)	(10,000)
Add: Nondeductible goodwill amortiza-		
tion	4,000	4,000
Taxable income, state.		$ 94,000
State income tax at 15%		$ 14,100
Less: State income tax.	(14,100)	
Taxable income, federal.	$ 79,900	
Federal income tax at 40%	$ 31,960	

Prepare a reconciliation, in percentages rounded to the nearest tenth, between the statutory federal income tax rate, 40%, and Farber Company's effective income tax rate, 46.06% ($46,060 ÷ $100,000 = 0.4606), required by **Regulation S-X,** Rule 4-08(h)(2), for a note to Farber's September 30, Year 5, financial statements filed with the Securities and Exchange Commission in **Form 10-K.** Combine any reconciling items that individually are less than 5% of the statutory federal income tax rate. Use the format on page 924.

Ex. 20-20 The ledger accounts for plant assets of Bruno Company had the following balances at the beginning and end of Year 5:

	Jan. 1, Year 5	Dec. 31, Year 5
Land.	$150,000	$200,000
Building.	800,000	800,000
Machinery and equipment	325,000	400,000

During Year 5, Bruno had acquired for $50,000 cash a parcel of land adjoining its present land to provide space for constructing an addition to its building during Year 6. The net increase of $75,000 in the Machinery and Equipment ledger account balance during Year 5 was composed of the following:

Additions at cost (none in excess of 2% of total assets). $125,000

Retirements at cost . . . .   (20,000)

Write-down of idle machinery to net realizable value. . . . .   (30,000)

  Net increase in Machinery and Equipment ledger account balance during

  Year 5. . . . . $ 75,000

Prepare a Schedule V, entitled Plant Assets, for Bruno Company to include in its **Form 10-K** filed with the SEC for Year 5. Use the format on page 915.

CASES

Case 20-1   In a classroom discussion of the provisions of *FASB Statement No. 14,* ''Financial Reporting for Segments of a Business Enterprise,'' student Jeff asserts that the standards for segment reporting and foreign geographic area reporting are flawed because of the latitude allowed to management of a diversified business enterprise in determining industry segments, allocating nontraceable expenses to segments, and determining foreign geographic areas. The results of such latitude, in Jeff's opinion, are noncompliance with the qualitative characteristic *reliability,* established as a requirement for useful financial information in *FASB Concepts Statement No. 2,* ''Qualitative Characteristics of Accounting Information.'' Jeff points out that such management-determined items are not *verifiable* or *neutral,* two ingredients of reliable financial information.

Instructions

Do you agree with student Jeff? Explain.

Case 20-2   In *APB Opinion No. 28,* ''Interim Financial Reporting,'' the Accounting Principles Board adopted the *integral theory,* rather than the *discrete theory,* for interim financial statements.

Instructions

a Present arguments in favor of the integral theory of interim financial reporting.
b Present arguments in favor of the discrete theory of interim financial reporting.
c Which theory do you prefer? Explain, disregarding the APB's adoption of the integral theory.

Case 20-3   Critics have charged that the Securities and Exchange Commission, contrary to its position as stated on page 914, essentially establishes generally accepted accounting principles in its *Financial Reporting Releases* and *Staff Accounting Bulletins.*

Instructions

Do you agree with the critics? Explain.

Case 20-4   Nanson Company, a publicly owned corporation listed on a major stock exchange, forecasted operations for the year ending December 31, Year 5, as follows:

NANSON COMPANY
Forecasted Income Statement
For Year Ending December 31, Year 5

Net sales (1,000,000 units)	$6,000,000
Cost of goods sold	3,600,000
Gross margin on sales	$2,400,000
Operating expenses	1,400,000
Operating income	$1,000,000
Nonoperating revenue and expenses	-0-
Income before income taxes	$1,000,000
Income taxes expense (current and deferred)	550,000
Net income	$ 450,000
Earnings per share of common stock	$4.50

Nanson has operated profitably for many years and has experienced a seasonal pattern of sales volume and production similar to the following ones forecasted for Year 5: Sales volume is expected to follow a quarterly pattern of 10%, 20%, 35%, 35%, respectively, because of the seasonality of the industry. Also, because of production and storage capacity limitations, it is expected that production will follow a pattern of 20%, 25%, 30%, 25%, per quarter, respectively.

At the conclusion of the first quarter of Year 5, the controller of Nanson prepared and issued the following interim income statement:

NANSON COMPANY
Income Statement
For Quarter Ended March 31, Year 5

Net sales (100,000 units)	$ 600,000
Cost of goods sold	360,000
Gross margin on sales	$ 240,000
Operating expenses	275,000
Operating loss	$ (35,000)
Loss from warehouse explosion	(175,000)
Loss before income taxes	$(210,000)
Income taxes expense	-0-
Net loss	$(210,000)
Loss per share of common stock	$ (2.10)

The following additional information was available for the first quarter just completed, but was not included in the information released by Nanson:

(1) Nanson uses a standard cost system in which standards are set at currently attainable levels on an annual basis. At the end of the first quarter, underapplied fixed factory overhead (volume variance) of $50,000 was recognized as an asset. Production during the first quarter was 200,000 units, of which 100,000 units were sold.

(2) The operating expenses were forecasted on a basis of $900,000 fixed expenses for the year plus $0.50 variable expenses per unit sold.

(3) The warehouse explosion loss met the conditions of an extraordinary loss. The warehouse had a carrying amount of $320,000; $145,000 was recovered from insurance on the warehouse. No other gains or losses were anticipated during the year from similar events or transactions, nor has Nanson had any similar losses in preceding years; thus, the full loss will be deductible as an ordinary loss for income tax purposes.

(4) The effective rate for federal and state income taxes combined was expected to average 55% of income before income taxes for Year 5. There were no permanent differences between pre-tax accounting income and taxable income.

(5) Earnings per share of common stock was computed on the basis of 100,000 shares of common stock outstanding. Nanson has only one class of common stock issued, no long-term debt outstanding, no stock option plans, and no warrants to acquire common stock outstanding.

Instructions

a Identify the weaknesses in form and content of Nanson Company's interim income statement, without reference to the additional information.

b For each of the five items of additional information, indicate the preferable treatment for interim reports and explain why that treatment is preferable.

PROBLEMS

Pr. 20-1 Data with respect to the four industry segments of Wabash Company for the year ended November 30, Year 10, follow:

	Segment				
	Alpha	**Beta**	**Gamma**	**Delta**	**Total**
Net sales to outsiders......	$40,000	$20,000	$25,000	$ 5,000	$90,000
Intersegment transfers out..	2,000	4,000	1,000	3,000	10,000
Intersegment transfers in...	4,000	3,000	2,000	1,000	10,000
Other traceable expenses ..	9,000	6,000	5,000	10,000	30,000
Nontraceable expenses					20,000

Wabash allocated nontraceable expenses to industry segments by the following reasonable method: Alpha—40%; Beta—30%; Gamma—20%; Delta—10%.

Instructions

a Prepare a working paper to compute the operating profit or loss for Wabash Company's four industry segments for the year ended November 30, Year 10.

b Prepare a working paper to determine if each industry segment of Wabash Company is *significant* for the year ended November 30, Year 10. Disregard segment identifiable assets.

Pr. 20-2 Cregar Company is "going public" early in Year 4, and is preparing to file a *Form S-1* registration statement with the SEC to register the common stock it plans to issue to the public. The accountant for Cregar prepared the following comparative income statements for inclusion in the *Form S-1:*

CREGAR COMPANY
Income Statements
For Years Ended December 31, Year 3, Year 2, and Year 1

	Year 3	Year 2	Year 1
Net sales	$10,000,000	$9,600,000	$8,800,000
Cost of goods sold....................	6,200,000	6,000,000	5,400,000
Gross margin on sales	$ 3,800,000	$3,600,000	$3,400,000
Operating expenses	2,200,000	2,400,000	2,100,000
Income from operations	$ 1,600,000	$1,200,000	$1,300,000
Gain on disposal of business segment ...	900,000		
Income before income taxes	$ 2,500,000	$1,200,000	$1,300,000
Income taxes expense	1,000,000	480,000	520,000
Net income	$ 1,500,000	$ 720,000	$ 780,000

During your audit of the foregoing income statements, you discover that Cregar contracted on January 2, Year 3, to sell for $3,200,000 the assets and product line of one of its industry segments. The sale was completed on December 31, Year 3, for a gain of $900,000 before income taxes. The discontinued operations' contribution to Cregar's income before income taxes for each year was as follows: Year 3, $640,000 loss; Year 2, $500,000 loss; Year 1, $200,000 income. Cregar's income tax rate is 40%.

Instructions

Prepare corrected partial comparative income statements for Cregar Company for the three years ended December 31, Year 3. Disregard notes to financial statements and earnings per share of common stock. Begin the income statements with income from continuing operations before income taxes. Show supporting computations.

Pr. 20-3 For the year ending July 31, Year 6, Lang Corporation forecasted pre-tax accounting income of $800,000. Lang did not anticipate any temporary differences between pre-tax accounting income and taxable income. However, the following permanent differences between accounting and taxable income for Year 6 were forecasted:

Dividend received deduction...	$150,000
Goodwill amortization..	20,000
Officers' life insurance premium expense	15,000

Additional Information

(1) Lang's combined federal and state income tax rate is 40%, and federal and state laws coincided with respect to the computation of taxable income.

(2) Lang's quarterly pre-tax accounting income for the year ended July 31, Year 6, is summarized below:

Quarter ended

Oct. 31, Year 5	$180,000
Jan. 31, Year 6	230,000
Apr. 30, Year 6	195,000
July 31, Year 6	225,000

(3) During Year 6, Lang did not alter its forecast of pre-tax accounting income for the year. However, effective January 31, Year 6, Lang revised its permanent difference estimate for the Year 6 dividend received deduction to $180,000 from $150,000. The actual amounts for the permanent differences computed by Lang on July 31, Year 6, were as follows:

Dividend received deduction	$175,000
Goodwill amortization..	20,000
Officers' life insurance premium expense	16,000

Instructions

a Prepare a working paper to compute the effective combined federal and state income tax rate that Lang Corporation should use for its quarterly interim financial reports for the year ended July 31, Year 6. Round all percentage computations to the nearest tenth.

  b Prepare Lang Corporation's journal entries for income taxes on October 31, Year 5, and January 31, April 30, and July 31, Year 6.

Pr. 20-4   Bixler Company, a diversified manufacturing enterprise that does not report to the Securities and Exchange Commission, had four separate operating divisions engaged in the manufacture of products in each of the following industries: food products, health aids, textiles, and office equipment.

Additional Information

(1) Financial data for the two years ended December 31, Year 8 and Year 7, are shown below:

	Net sales		Cost of goods sold		Operating expenses	
	Year 8	Year 7	Year 8	Year 7	Year 8	Year 7
Food products..........	$3,500,000	$3,000,000	$2,400,000	$1,800,000	$ 550,000	$ 275,000
Health aids............	2,000,000	1,270,000	1,100,000	700,000	300,000	125,000
Textiles...............	1,580,000	1,400,000	500,000	900,000	200,000	150,000
Office equipment........	920,000	1,330,000	800,000	1,000,000	650,000	750,000
Totals	$8,000,000	$7,000,000	$4,800,000	$4,400,000	$1,700,000	$1,300,000

(2) On January 1, Year 8, Bixler adopted a plan to dispose of the assets and product line of the office equipment division at an anticipated gain. On September 1, Year 8, the division's assets and product line were disposed of for $2,100,000 cash, at a gain of $640,000 (exclusive of operations during the phase-out period).

(3) Bixler's textiles division had six manufacturing plants that produced a variety of textile products. In April, Year 8, Bixler sold one of these plants and realized a gain of $130,000. After the sale, the operations at the plant that was sold were transferred to the remaining five textile plants that Bixler continued to operate.

(4) In August, Year 8, the main warehouse of the food products division, located on the banks of the Colton River, was flooded when the river overflowed. The resulting uninsured damage of $420,000 is not included in the financial data in (1) above. Historical records indicate that the Colton River normally overflows every four to five years, causing flood damage to adjacent property.

(5) For the two years ended December 31, Year 8 and Year 7, Bixler realized interest revenue on investments of $70,000 and $40,000, respectively. For the two years ended December 31, Year 8 and Year 7, Bixler's net income was $960,000 and $670,000, respectively. Income taxes expense for each of the two years should be computed at a rate of 40%.

Instructions

Prepare comparative income statements for Bixler Company for the years ended December 31, Year 8 and Year 7. Notes to the financial statements and earnings per share of common stock disclosures are not required.

Pr. 20-5 The accounting records of Draco Company included the following amounts for the year ended December 31, Year 6:

Cost of goods sold—*continuing operations*	$ 8,000,000
Estimated loss on disposal of Southern Division (an industry segment), to be completed in first quarter of Year 7	50,000
Income taxes payable ($540,000 × 0.40)	216,000
Interest expense	100,000
*Judgment paid in lawsuit of **Justin Company v. Draco Company**, initiated in Year 4*	80,000
Loss from bankruptcy liquidation of major customer	150,000
Loss from operations of Southern Division, discontinued effective Dec. 31, Year 6 (measurement date)	120,000
Net sales—continuing operations	10,000,000
Operating expenses—continuing operations	800,000
Uninsured loss from earthquake at Northern Division	160,000

Draco's income tax rate is 40%. Draco had no temporary differences or permanent differences between pre-tax accounting income and taxable income for Year 6. Prior to Year 6, there had not been an earthquake in the Northern Division's locality for more than 50 years.

Instructions

a Prepare an income statement for Draco Company for the year ended December 31, Year 6, in accordance with the provisions of *APB Opinion No. 30,* "Reporting the Results of Operations." Disregard earnings per share data and notes to financial statements.

b Prepare a journal entry for Draco Company's income taxes on December 31, Year 6, with appropriate intraperiod tax allocation.

Pr. 20-6 Principia Corporation was incorporated January 2, Year 4, with a public issuance of 3 million shares of $1 par common stock on that date for net proceeds of $5,750,000, net of out-of-pocket costs of the stock issuance. Immediately thereafter, Principia organized three wholly owned subsidiaries—Seattle Company and Boston Company in the United States, and London Company in the United Kingdom. Principia paid $1,500,000 cash for each subsidiary's 1,500,000 authorized shares of $1 par common stock.

The working paper for consolidated financial statements for Principia Corporation and subsidiaries is on page 944.

Additional Information

(1) Each of the affiliated companies constitutes an industry segment.
(2) Principia, Seattle, and Boston operate in the North America geographic area, and London operates in the Western Europe geographic area.
(3) None of the companies declared or paid dividends in Year 4.
(4) Each of the companies files separate income tax returns at an effective income tax rate of 40%.
(5) Intercompany receivables and payables represent loans or advances. (Receiv-

PRINCIPIA CORPORATION AND SUBSIDIARIES
Working Paper for Consolidated Financial Statements
For Year Ended December 31, Year 4
(000 omitted)

	Principia Corporation	Seattle Company	Boston Company	London Company*	Eliminations increase (decrease)		Consolidated
Income Statement							
Revenue:							
Net sales	500	400	300	200			1,400
Intercompany sales ..	40	30	20	10	(b)	(100)	
Intercompany invest-							
ment income	32				(a)	(32)	
Interest revenue	20						20
Total revenue	592	430	320	210		(132)	1,420
Costs and expenses:							
Cost of goods sold ...	375	320	210	130	(b)	(10)	1,025
Intercompany cost of							
goods sold	32	24	16	8	(b)	(80)	
Operating expenses..	133	60	40	50			283
Interest expense.....		6	9	7			22
Income taxes ex-							
pense	15	12	27	9	(b)	(6)	57
Total costs and							
expenses	555	422	302	204		(96)	1,387
Net income (and re-							
tained earnings)	37	8	18	6		(36)	33
Balance Sheet							
Assets							
Short-term investments.	80						80
Inventories	500	600	700	800	(b)	(10)	2,590
Other current assets ...	700	800	600	500			2,600
Deferred income tax							
asset					(b)	6	6
Intercompany receiv-							
ables (payables)	80	(60)	50	(70)			
Investments in subsidi-							
aries' common stock ..	4,532				(a)	(4,532)	
Plant assets (net)	800	900	700	600			3,000
Intangible assets (net)..	40	60	50	70			220
Total assets	6,732	2,300	2,100	1,900		(4,536)	8,496
Liabilities & Stockholders' Equity							
Current liabilities	945	692	432	227			2,296
6% bonds payable		100	150	167			417
Common stock, $1 par .	3,000	1,500	1,500	1,500	(a)	(4,500)	3,000
Additional paid-in							
capital	2,750						2,750
Retained earnings	37	8	18	6		(36)	33
Total liabilities &							
stockholders'							
equity..............	6,732	2,300	2,100	1,900		(4,536)	8,496

Explanation of eliminations:

(a) To eliminate intercompany investments and related equity accounts of subsidiaries.

(b) To eliminate intercompany sales, cost of goods sold, and unrealized profits in inventories, and to defer income taxes applicable to unrealized profits.

* Amounts remeasured to U.S. dollars, London's functional currency, from British pounds.

ables and payables arising from intercompany sales of merchandise had been paid in full on December 31, Year 4.)

(6) Of Principia's operating expenses, $50,000 represents nontraceable expenses allocable to each industry segment in the ratio of the **average** of each segment's Year 4 sales to outsiders and December 31, Year 4, plant asset amounts. The remainder of Principia's operating expenses represents general corporate expenses.

(7) Cash not required for each segment's current operations is forwarded to Principia for the acquisition of short-term investments.

Instructions

Prepare the following for Principia Corporation and subsidiaries for Year 4 in accordance with the provisions of *FASB Statement No. 14,* ''Financial Reporting for Segments of a Business Enterprise'':

a Working paper to determine whether each industry segment constitutes a significant segment.

b Disclosures of information about the operations of Principia Corporation and subsidiaries in different industries. Use the following format:

PRINCIPIA CORPORATION AND SUBSIDIARIES
Information about the Companies' Operations in Different Industries
For Year Ended December 31, Year 4
(000 omitted)

	Principia industry	Seattle industry	Boston industry	London industry	Elimi-nations	Con-solidated
Sales to unaffiliated customers..........						
Intersegment sales.........						
Total revenue						
Operating profit (loss)........						
Interest revenue.........						
General corporate expenses.						
Interest expense........						
Income before income taxes .						
Identifiable assets, Dec. 31, Year 4....						
Corporate assets...						
Total assets, Dec. 31, Year 4...						

c Disclosures of information about the operations of Principia Corporation and subsidiaries in different geographic areas. Use the following format:

PRINCIPIA CORPORATION AND SUBSIDIARIES
Information about the Companies' Operations in Different Geographic Areas
For Year Ended December 31, Year 4
(000 omitted)

	North America	Western Europe	Elimi- nations	Con- solidated
Sales to unaffiliated customers . .				
Transfers between geographic areas				
Total revenue.				
Operating profit (loss)				
Interest revenue				
General corporate expenses				
Interest expense				
Income before income taxes				
Identifiable assets, Dec. 31, Year 4				
Corporate assets.				
Total assets, Dec. 31, Year 4.				

Show supporting computations. Disregard requirements for disclosure of export sales, major customers, depreciation and amortization, and additions to plant assets.

Pr. 20-7 This problem consists of three unrelated parts.

a For the year ended April 30, Year 4, Lobeck Company had a net income of $600,000. Lobeck's income tax rate is 40%, and there were no permanent differences or temporary differences between pre-tax accounting income and taxable income.

On February 28, Year 4, in accordance with a decision of Lobeck's board of directors on December 31, Year 3, Lobeck disposed of its Texas Division, a business segment, for a pre-tax loss of $50,000. The $120,000 pre-tax operating loss of Texas Division for the 10 months ended February 28, Year 4, was incurred as follows:

Eight months ended Dec. 31, Year 3.	$ 80,000
Two months ended Feb. 28, Year 4	40,000
Total pre-tax operating loss.	$120,000

Instructions

Prepare the bottom portion of Lobeck Company's income statement for the year ended April 30, Year 4, beginning with "Income from continuing operations before income taxes." Disregard earnings per share of common stock.

b For the year ended December 31, Year 7, Spratt Company had the following:

Quarter ended	Pre-tax accounting income (and taxable income)	Estimated effective income tax rate for Year 7
Mar. 31, Year 7	$100,000	45%
June 30, Year 7	120,000	46%
Sept. 30, Year 7	140,000	44%
Dec. 31, Year 7	150,000	43%

Instructions

Prepare journal entries for Spratt Company's income taxes expense on March 31, June 30, September 30, and December 31, Year 7. Omit explanations for the journal entries.

c During the three months ended March 31, Year 3, the third quarter of its fiscal year ended June 30, Year 3, Jackson Company temporarily depleted its base layer of last-in, first-out inventories having a lifo cost of $120,000 and a replacement cost on March 31, Year 3, of $210,000. On April 30, Year 3, Jackson purchased replacement merchandise with a cost of $370,000, on open account.

Instructions

Prepare journal entries for Jackson Company on March 31, Year 3, and April 30, Year 3, for the foregoing business transactions and events. Omit explanations for the journal entries.

GLOSSARY

abatement sequence The order of reduction of devises in the will of a decedent whose estate property is insufficient to pay all the decedent's liabilities and cover all devises; the order is as follows: property not specifically mentioned in the will, residuary devises, general devises, specific devises

account group A set of memorandum ledger accounts established by a governmental entity to account for plant assets (general fixed assets account group) or long-term debt (general long-term debt account group) not recorded in a fund of the governmental entity

accountability method The method of accounting used by a trustee in bankruptcy or by the personal representative of a decedent's estate, evidenced by the equation Assets = Accountability

Accounting and Auditing Enforcement Releases (AAERs) A series of pronouncements initiated by the Securities and Exchange Commission (SEC) in 1982 to report its enforcement actions involving accountants and accounting issues

Accounting Series Releases (ASRs) Pronouncements of the chief accountants of the SEC from 1937 to 1982 designed to contribute to the development of uniform standards and practice in major accounting questions

acquisition of assets A business combination in which one business enterprise acquires the gross or net assets of another enterprise by paying cash or issuing equity or debt securities

acquisition of common stock A business combination in which an investor enterprise issues cash or equity or debt securities to acquire a controlling interest in the outstanding common stock of an investee enterprise, which is not liquidated but becomes a subsidiary of the investor parent company

administrator The personal representative of an intestate decedent, who is appointed by the probate court

affiliate A business enterprise that is controlled or significantly influenced by another enterprise

agency funds Fiduciary funds of a governmental entity, of short duration, that account for sales taxes, payroll taxes, and other such amounts collected by the governmental entity for later payment to other governmental entities entitled to the taxes and other amounts; also, funds of nonprofit organizations used for assets held by the organizations as custodian

agio (spread) The difference between the selling spot rate and the buying spot rate of a foreign currency

American Institute of Certified Public Accountants (AICPA) The national professional organization of certified public accountants licensed by the states and territories of the United States

annual budget A budget prepared for the general fund and special revenue funds of a governmental entity; includes estimated revenues, estimated other financing sources, appropriations, and estimated other financing uses for a fiscal year

annuity fund A fund established by a nonprofit organization to account for assets contributed to the organization, the income from which is the source of fixed periodic payments to designated recipients for a specified time period

appropriations Authorized expenditures of a governmental entity's general fund and special revenue funds, as approved by the legislative and executive authorities of the entity and set forth in the annual budget

associate The International Accounting Standards Committee term for *influenced investee*

bankrupt   A legal state in which an insolvent debtor is given protection from creditors' claims by the Bankruptcy Court

Bankruptcy Code   The federal law governing bankruptcies in the United States

bankruptcy liquidation   The procedure under Chapter 7 of the Bankruptcy Code in which a trustee realizes the debtor's nonexempt assets and pays creditors as specified in the Bankruptcy Code

bankruptcy reorganization   The procedure under Chapter 11 of the Bankruptcy Code in which a business enterprise is protected from creditors' claims while it develops a plan for restructuring its liabilities and stockholders' equity

bargain purchase excess   The excess of the current fair value of the combinee's identifiable net assets in a purchase-type business combination over the cost to the combinor

beneficiary   The party for whose benefit a trust is established

branch   A business unit of an enterprise, located at some distance from the home office, that carries merchandise obtained from the home office, makes sales, approves customers' credit, and makes collections from its customers

budgetary deficit   An excess of appropriations and estimated other financing uses over estimated revenues and estimated other financing sources in the annual budget of a governmental entity's general fund

budgetary surplus   An excess of estimated revenues and estimated other financing sources over appropriations and estimated other financing uses in the annual budget of a governmental entity's general fund and special revenue funds

business combination   An event or a transaction in which two or more business enterprises, or their net assets, are brought under common control in a single accounting entity

buying spot rate   The exchange rate paid by a foreign currency dealer ''on the spot''

capital budget   A budget prepared for a capital projects fund of a governmental entity; includes the estimated resources available for a capital project and the estimated costs of completion of the project

capital expenditures   Expenditures for plant assets of a governmental entity

capital lease   A lease that, from the viewpoint of the lessee, is equivalent to the *acquisition,* rather than the *rental,* of property from the lessor

capital projects funds   Governmental funds that record the receipt and payment of cash for the construction or acquisition of the governmental entity's plant assets other than those financed by proprietary funds or trust funds

cash distribution program   A plan prepared for a liquidating partnership to show the appropriate sequence for paying cash as it becomes available to partnership creditors and to partners

cash equivalents   Short-term investments that are readily marketable and have maturity dates no longer than three months

certificate   A document evidencing formation of a limited partnership, filed with the county recorder of the principal place of business of the limited partnership

change in the reporting entity   A type of accounting change, dealt with in *APB Opinion No. 20,* ''Accounting Changes,'' that requires an adjustment to beginning-of-period retained earnings—for example, a pooling-type business combination

charge and discharge statement   The financial statement prepared on behalf of the personal representative of a decedent's estate, submitted to the probate court; a comparable financial statement prepared on behalf of the trustee of a trust

charity care   Health services provided by nonprofit hospitals to indigent patients, there being no expectation of resultant cash flows to the hospital

collections   Nonexhaustible resources of nonprofit museums, art galleries, botanical gardens, libraries, and similar nonprofit organizations, for which a valuation is impracticable of determination and depreciation is inappropriate

combined enterprise   The accounting entity that results from a business combination

combinee   A constituent company other than the combinor in a business combination

combinor   A constituent company entering into a business combination whose owners as a group end up with control of the ownership interests in the combined enterprise

component unit   An organization included in a governmental financial reporting entity because the primary government is financially accountable for the organization or because of the relationship of the organization to the primary government

comprehensive annual financial report (CAFR)   The annual report required by the Governmental Accounting Standards Board to be prepared by every governmental entity as a matter of public record

conflict of interest   A situation in which an individual reaps an inappropriate personal benefit from his or her acts in an official capacity

conglomerate A group of affiliated business enterprises in unrelated industries or markets

conglomerate combination A business combination between enterprises in unrelated industries or markets

consolidated financial statements Financial statements of a single economic entity composed of several legal entities (parent company and subsidiaries)

constituent companies The business enterprises that enter into a business combination

contingent consideration Additional cash, other assets, or securities that may be issuable in the future, contingent on future events such as a specified level of earnings or a designated market price for a security that had been issued to complete a business combination

contractual adjustments Discounts from full billing rates of nonprofit hospitals provided in contracts with third-party payors such as Medicare and Medicaid

contributory pension plan A pension plan that requires contributions from employees as well as employers

"cooking the books" Fraudulent financial reporting

Cost Accounting Standard 403 A pronouncement of the federal Cost Accounting Standards Board entitled "Allocation of Home Office Expenses to Segments"

cost method The method of accounting for an investment in a purchased subsidiary that recognizes revenue only to the extent the subsidiary declares dividends from retained earnings accumulated after the date of the business combination

credit risk The risk of nonperformance by a party to a financial instrument contract

creditors' (involuntary) petition A bankruptcy petition initiated by creditors of an insolvent debtor in accordance with provisions of the Bankruptcy Code

cumulative preferred stock Preferred stock that requires dividends "passed" in one year to be declared and paid in a subsequent year, together with that year's regular dividends, to preferred stockholders before dividends may be declared and paid to common stockholders

cumulative translation adjustments A balancing amount resulting from the translation of a foreign entity's financial statements from the entity's functional currency to the reporting currency of the parent company or investor enterprise

current/noncurrent method A method of translating foreign currency financial statements in which current assets and liabilities are translated at the current exchange rate on the balance sheet date, while other assets, other liabilities, and owners' equity elements are translated at historical rates. Depreciation and amortization expenses are translated at historical rates; all other revenue and expenses are translated at an average rate for the accounting period

current rate method A method of translating foreign currency financial statements in which all balance sheet amounts other than owners' equity are translated at the current exchange rate, while owners' equity elements are translated at historical rates. All revenue and expense items are translated at the appropriate current rate or at an average of current rates

"cute accounting" Stretching the form of accounting standards to the limit, regardless of the substance of the underlying business transaction or events

death taxes Federal estate taxes on the principal of a decedent's estate and state inheritance taxes on devisees receiving devises

debt service expenditures Expenditures for interest on operating debt of a governmental entity, such as short-term loans

debt service funds Governmental funds that account for payments of principal and interest on long-term bonds and other long-term debt of a governmental entity other than special assessment bonds, revenue bonds, and general obligation bonds serviced by an enterprise fund

debtor in possession Management of a business enterprise undergoing reorganization under Chapter 11 of the Bankruptcy Code that continues to operate the enterprise during the reorganization

debtor's (voluntary) petition A bankruptcy petition initiated by an insolvent debtor

defined benefit pension plan A pension plan under which the basis of computation of pension benefits for retired employees usually involves employee compensation, years of service, and age on date of retirement

designated fund balance A segregated amount of the fund balance of a nonprofit organization's unrestricted fund that evidences the earmarking of the fund's net assets for a purpose specified by the organization's governing board

devise A transfer of real or personal property in a will

devisee The recipient of a devise

direct out-of-pocket costs Some legal fees, some accounting fees, and finder's fee incurred specifically to accomplish a business combination

discharge Forgiveness of all except specified unpaid liabilities of a debtor that underwent liquidation under Chapter 7 of the Bankruptcy Code

discontinued operations Operations of a business (industry) segment that has been sold, abandoned, spun off, or otherwise disposed of, or, although still operating, is the subject of a formal plan for disposal

discrete theory A theory of interim financial reporting that considers each interim period a basic accounting period whose operating results are measured in essentially the same manner as for an annual accounting period

disposal date   The date of closing the sale of discontinued operations or ceasing the operations of an abandoned business segment

dissolution   A change in the relationship among partners of a partnership, caused by any partner's ceasing to be associated in the carrying on of the partnership business

division   A segment of a business enterprise that generally has more autonomy than a branch; a segment that often was formerly an independent enterprise, but subsequently was a constituent company—typically the combinee—in a business combination

downstream intercompany sales   Sales of merchandise by a parent company to a subsidiary of the parent

drawing   A partner's withdrawal of cash or other assets from a partnership in accordance with terms of the partnership contract

economic unit concept   A concept of consolidated financial statements of a parent company and one or more partially owned subsidiaries that views the consolidated enterprise as a single entity with ownership by parent company stockholders and subsidiary minority stockholders

EDGAR   The Electronic Data Gathering, Analysis, and Retrieval project of the SEC, designed to permit "paperless" filings with the SEC over telephone lines, on diskettes, or on magnetic tapes

encumbrance accounting   An accounting method for governmental funds of a governmental entity that entails a debit to Encumbrances and a credit to Fund Balance Reserved for Encumbrances when purchase orders or contracts for nonrecurring expenditures are issued by the funds

endowment   A gift placed in trust that generally requires the principal of the gift to be maintained intact, with revenues from the investment of the gift used for the purposes specified by the donor of the gift

endowment fund   A nonprofit organization's fund whose principal must be maintained intact permanently or temporarily and whose income is expendable by the organization for a specified or elective purpose

enterprise funds   Proprietary funds of a governmental entity that account for commercial-type activities of the entity, such as utilities, airports, seaports, and recreational facilities

equity method   The method of accounting for an investment in a corporate or an unincorporated joint venture that increases the venturer's Investment account balance for the venturer's share of venture net income and decreases the account balance for the venturer's share of venture net losses, dividends, or other cash remittances; also, the method of accounting for an investment in a purchased or a pooled subsidiary that increases the parent company's Investment account balance for the parent's share of subsidiary net income and decreases the account balance for the parent's share of subsidiary net losses and dividends

estate   All the property of a decedent, trust, or other person whose affairs are subject to the Uniform Probate Code

exchange rate   The ratio between one unit of each of two foreign currencies

executor   The personal representative of a decedent, named in the decedent's will

exempt property   Property of a decedent excluded from claims of the decedent's creditors and devisees, including aggregate specified value of automobiles, household furniture and furnishings, and personal effects

expendable trust funds   Fiduciary funds of a governmental entity, of long duration, that account for the receipt and expenditure of revenues produced by the principal of the trust, which is nonexpendable

family allowance   A reasonable cash allowance, payable in a lump sum not exceeding a specified amount, to the decedent's spouse or children during the administration of the estate

fiduciaries   The individuals or business enterprises that manage the property in estates and trusts

fiduciary funds   Trust funds and agency funds of a governmental entity that account for resources that are not owned by the entity but are administered by the entity as a custodian or fiduciary

financial accountability   A situation in which a primary government appoints a majority of the governing body of another organization and thus imposes its will on the organization or is responsible for providing financial benefits to, or financial burdens on, the other organization

Financial Executives Institute (FEI)   The national professional organization of financial vice presidents, controllers, and treasurers of business enterprises

financial forecast   Prospective financial statements that present an entity's expected financial position, results of operations, and cash flows

financial instrument   Cash, evidence of an ownership interest in an entity, or a contract that imposes both a right on one entity and an obligation on another entity to exchange cash or other financial instruments

financial reporting entity   The primary government and

other component units that comprise the governmental entity that issues financial reports

Financial Reporting Releases (FRRs) A series of pronouncements initiated by the SEC in 1982 to state its views on financial reporting matters

financial resources Cash, claims to cash such as receivables and investments, inventories, and short-term prepayments of governmental funds of a governmental entity

finder's fee A fee paid to an investment banker or other organization or individuals that investigated the combinee, assisted in determining the price, and otherwise rendered services to bring about a business combination

foreign currency transaction A transaction of a business enterprise that is denominated in a currency other than the local currency of the enterprise

foreign currency translation Restating a transaction denominated in a foreign currency to the local currency of the transacting enterprise

foreign geographic area Individual foreign countries or groups of countries for which a diversified business enterprise reports revenues and identifiable assets

Form 8-K A current report filed by a publicly owned company with the SEC within a specified number of days following the occurrence of specified events or events elected to be reported by the company

Form 10 A registration statement filed by a publicly owned company with the SEC in connection with trading of the company's securities on a national exchange or over the counter

Form 10-K The annual report filed by a publicly owned company with the SEC within 90 days following the close of the company's fiscal year

Form 10-Q A quarterly report filed by a publicly owned company with the SEC within 45 days following the close of each of the company's first three fiscal-year quarters

formal probate Litigation to determine whether a decedent left a valid will

Forms S-1, S-2, S-3, S-4, S-18, F-4 Registration statements filed with the SEC by companies that issue securities to the public interstate

forward exchange contract An agreement to exchange currencies of different countries on a specified future date at the forward rate in effect when the contract was made

forward rate The rate of exchange between foreign currencies to be exchanged on a future date

fresh start reporting A method of financial reporting applied to certain business enterprises emerging from reorganization under Chapter 11 of the Bankruptcy Code in which assets and liabilities are stated at current fair values and retained earnings deficits are written off against additional paid-in capital

friendly takeover A business combination in which the boards of directors of the constituent companies generally work out the terms of the combination amicably and submit the proposal to stockholders of all constituent companies for approval

fully secured creditors Creditors of a debtor in bankruptcy whose claims are collateralized by debtor's assets having current fair values in excess of the amount of the claims

functional currency The currency of the primary economic environment in which the entity operates; normally, that is the currency of the environment in which the entity primarily generates and expends cash

fund In governmental accounting, a fiscal and accounting entity with a self-balancing set of accounts recording cash and other financial resources, together with all related liabilities and residual equities or balances, and changes therein, which are segregated for the purpose of carrying on specific activities or attaining certain objectives in accordance with special regulations, restrictions, or limitations; with respect to a nonprofit organization, a fiscal and accounting entity with a self-balancing set of accounts recording cash and other financial resources, together with all related liabilities and residual equities or balances, and changes therein, which are segregated for the purpose of carrying on specific activities or attaining certain objectives in accordance with special regulations, restrictions, or limitations

general devise A decedent's gift of an amount of money or a number of countable monetary items

general fixed assets account group The memorandum set of accounts of a governmental entity in which are recorded plant assets other than infrastructure that are not recorded in a fund

general long-term capital debt Liabilities expected to be paid from the financial resources of governmental funds and that provide long-term financing to acquire a governmental entity's plant assets, including infrastructure, or for nonrecurring projects or activities that have long-term economic benefit

general long-term debt account group The memorandum set of accounts of a governmental entity in which are recorded long-term liabilities not recorded in a fund

general obligation bonds Bonds issued by a governmental entity that are backed by the full faith and credit of the entity and supported by its taxation power

general partnership A partnership in which all the

partners are responsible for liabilities of the firm and all have authority to act for the firm

goodwill In general, an unidentifiable intangible asset whose cost measures the value of excess earnings of an acquired business enterprise; in a business combination, the excess of the combinor's cost in a purchase-type business combination over the current fair values of the combinee's identifiable net assets

governmental funds The general fund, special revenue funds, capital projects funds, and debt service funds of a governmental entity that account for financial resources of the entity used in day-to-day operations

grant A contribution of cash or other assets received by a governmental entity from another government to be used or expended for a specific purpose, activity, or facility

greenmail A tactic used to resist an unfriendly takeover business combination in which the target combinee acquires its common stock presently owned by the prospective combinor at a price substantially in excess of the prospective combinor's cost, with the stock thus acquired placed in the treasury or retired

hedge Measures taken to reduce or eliminate a potential unfavorable outcome of a future event

heirs Recipients of property of an intestate decedent, as specified by state probate codes

highly inflationary economy An economy having cumulative inflation of 100% or more over a three-year period

holographic will A will having its essential provisions and signature in the handwriting of the testator

home office The principal business unit of an enterprise that has branches or divisions

homestead allowance A specified amount of a decedent's property allocated to a decedent's spouse or surviving minor or dependent children, in addition to property passing to those persons by devises

horizontal combination A business combination between enterprises in the same industry

income beneficiary The recipient of income of a testamentary trust

industry segment (business segment, line of business) A component of an enterprise engaged in providing a product or service or a group of related products and services primarily to unaffiliated customers for a profit

informal probate A proceeding by the registrar of a probate court that results in the registrar's making a decedent's will effective by means of a written statement

infrastructure Streets, sidewalks, bridges, and the like of a governmental entity

insider trading Purchasing or selling a security while in posession of material, nonpublic information or communicating such information in connection with a securities transaction

insolvent Unable to pay liabilities when due because of insufficient assets and poor borrowing potential

instant earnings Enhanced earnings of the combined enterprise following a pooling-type business combination that result from combining the constituent companies' earnings for all reporting periods prior to, as well as subsequent to, the combination; also, earnings generated in the past by selling segments of a combinee in a pooling-type combination at amounts substantially in excess of their carrying amounts used by the combined enterprise

Institute of Management Accountants (IMA) The national professional organization of accountants in industry (formerly the National Association of Accountants)

integral theory A theory of interim financial reporting that considers each interim period an integral part of the annual period

inter vivos (living) trust A trust created by a living person

interest method A technique for computing interest revenue or expense that applies the yield rate of bonds to their present value at the beginning of the period for which interest is to be measured

internal service funds Proprietary funds of a governmental entity that sell supplies and services to other funds of the entity, but not to the public

International Accounting Standards Committee (IASC) An organization of accounting groups from about 80 countries, headquartered in London, whose mission is to develop accounting standards for potential adoption in the countries of the member accounting groups

International Organization of Securities Commissions (IOSCO) An organization of securities regulators from about 50 countries whose goal is to ease the impact of differences in securities trading regulations among its members

intestacy The absence of a will for a decedent

intestate Without a valid will

issuer The constituent company in a pooling-type business combination that issues its common stock in exchange for the common stock of the combinee

joint venture A partnership of limited duration and with limited projects or other activities

jointly controlled entity The International Accounting Standards Committee term for *joint venture*

lateral intercompany sales Sales of merchandise by one subsidiary of a parent company to another subsidiary of that parent

letters testamentary Authorization document for the personal representative of an estate to begin administration of the estate

life income fund A fund established by a nonprofit organization to account for assets contributed to the organization, the income from which, in whatever amount, is distributed in periodic payments to designated recipients for a specified time period

limited partnership A partnership having, in addition to one or more general partners, one or more partners with no responsibility for liabilities of the partnership and with restrictions on activities related to the partnership

liquidation (of partnership) The winding up of partnership activities, usually by selling assets, paying liabilities, and distributing any remaining cash to partners

loan fund A fund typically established by a nonprofit school, college, or university for loans to students

local currency unit One unit of currency of the country in which a business enterprise is located

market risk The risk of a decline in value or an increase in onerousness of a financial instrument resulting from future changes in market prices

marshaling of assets A provision of the Uniform Partnership Act that specifies the respective rights of partnership creditors and partners' personal creditors to partnership assets and to partners' personal assets

master limited partnership A large limited partnership engaged in ventures such as oil and gas exploration and real estate development that issues units registered with the Securities and Exchange Commission

measurement date The date on which management of a business enterprise commits itself to a formal plan for disposal of a business segment of the enterprise

minority interest (noncontrolling interest) The claim of stockholders other than the parent company to the net assets and net income or losses of a partially owned subsidiary

modified accrual basis of accounting An accounting method applied to the governmental funds of a governmental entity in which revenues are recognized only when they are measurable and available

monetary assets Cash and other assets representing claims expressed in a fixed monetary amount

monetary liabilities Liabilities representing obligations expressed in a fixed monetary amount

monetary/nonmonetary method A method of translating foreign currency financial statements in which monetary assets and monetary liabilities are translated at the current exchange rate on the balance sheet date; nonmonetary assets and liabilities and owners' equity elements are translated at historical rates. Depreciation and amortization expenses and cost of goods sold are translated at historical rates; all other revenue and expenses are translated at an average rate for the accounting period

monetary principle The principle that money is assumed to be a useful standard measuring unit for reporting the effects of business transactions and events

multinational (transnational) enterprise A business enterprise that carries on operations in more than one nation, through a network of branches, divisions, influenced investees, joint ventures, and subsidiaries

negative goodwill The remainder of a bargain purchase excess that cannot be apportioned to reduce the amounts assigned to the combinee's noncurrent assets other than investments in marketable securities

net assets Total assets less total liabilities; equal to stockholders' equity of a corporation

nonbusiness organizations Governmental entities and nonprofit organizations

noncontributory pension plan A pension plan that requires contributions from the employer but not from employees

noncumulative preferred stock Preferred stock whose owners have no future claim for dividends ''passed'' in any year

nonexpendable trust funds Fiduciary funds of a governmental entity, of long duration, that account for the principal of the trust, which must be maintained intact

nonprofit organization A legal and accounting entity that is operated for the benefit or society as a whole, rather than for the benefit of an individual proprietor or a group of partners or stockholders

object budget An annual budget of a governmental entity's general fund that emphasizes, by department, the object of each authorized expenditure

operating debt Short-term loans obtained by the general fund of a governmental entity

operating expenditures Expenditures for day-to-day operations of the governmental funds of a governmental entity, such as for salaries and wages, utilities, and consumption of short-term prepayments and inventories of supplies

operating transfers Transfers of financial resources among governmental funds of a governmental entity for other than quasi-external transactions

order for relief Action by the Bankruptcy Court to protect the debtor from creditors' claims during the bankruptcy procedure

other financing sources Sources of financial resources of a governmental fund other than revenues, such as operating transfers in and gains on disposals of plant assets

other financing uses Uses of financial resources of a governmental fund other than expenditures, such as operating transfers out and losses on disposals of plant assets

pac-man defense A tactic used to resist an unfriendly takeover business combination in which the target company itself threatens a takeover of the prospective combinor

par value method A method of accounting for the retirement of treasury stock in which the cost of the treasury stock is allocated pro rata to reduce (1) the Common Stock ledger account balance by the par or stated value, if any, of the treasury shares; (2) an appropriate additional paid-in capital account for the excess over par or stated value attributable to the original issuance of the treasury shares; and (3) Retained Earnings for any unallocated cost remaining

parent company An investor enterprise that obtains a controlling interest in the outstanding common stock of an investee (subsidiary)

parent company concept A concept of consolidated financial statements of a parent company and one or more partially owned subsidiaries that views the consolidated entity as an extension of the parent company with the minority interest in the net assets of subsidiary considered to be a liability, and the minority interest in net income of subsidiary an expense, of the consolidate entity

partially secured creditors Creditors of a debtor in bankruptcy whose claims are collateralized by debtor's assets having current fair values less than the amount of the claims

participating preferred stock Preferred stock whose owners, after receiving the specified dividend on the preferred stock, may receive an additional dividend if the common stockholders are paid dividends in excess of the specified preferred dividend

partnership An association of two or more persons to carry on, as co-owners, a business for profit

pension trust funds Fiduciary funds of a governmental entity, of long duration, that account for the receipt and expenditure of amounts contributed by employer and employees to provide resources for post-retirement pensions and other benefits to former employees

performance budget An annual budget of a governmental entity's general fund that attempts to relate the input of governmental resources to the output of governmental services

periodic inventory system The method of accounting for inventory in which the Inventories ledger account is used only at the end of an accounting period to reflect the value of the ending inventory of merchandise or manufactured products

permanent difference A difference between pre-tax accounting income and taxable income that does not "turn around" in one or more subsequent accounting periods

permanent endowment fund An endowment fund whose principal never may be disbursed by the nonprofit organization

perpetual inventory system The method of accounting for inventory in which the Inventories ledger account is debited for purchases of merchandise or the cost of goods manufactured and credited for the cost of goods sold

personal representative The executor or administrator of a decedent's estate

phase-out period The period between the measurement date and the disposal date for a business segment

plant fund A fund of a nonprofit organization that accounts for plant assets, and often for cash and investments earmarked for additions to plant assets as well as mortgage notes and other liabilities collateralized by the organization's plant assets

pledge A commitment by a prospective donor to contribute a specific amount of cash or property to a nonprofit organization on a future date or in installments

pledgor The maker of a pledge

poison pill A tactic used to resist an unfriendly takeover business combination in which the target company amends its articles of incorporation or bylaws to make it more difficult to obtain stockholder approval for a takeover

pooling of interests A business combination interpreted as a combining of existing stockholder interests rather than an acquisition of assets or raising of capital

preference The transfer of cash or property to a creditor by an insolvent debtor within 90 days of the filing of a bankruptcy petition by or on behalf of the debtor, provided that the transfer caused the creditor to receive more cash or property than would be received in the bankruptcy liquidation

primary government A state government, a municipality or county, or a special-purpose government such as a school district or a park district meeting specified criteria

principal beneficiary (remainderman) The recipient of the principal of a trust

prior period adjustment In a statement of partners' capital, an adjustment to partners' beginning capital balances to correct an error in the financial statements of a prior period

probate Action by the probate court to validate a decedent's will

probate (orphan's, surrogate) court The state court established to probate decedents' wills

professional corporation A form of corporation authorized by some states, having various requirements as to professional licensing of stockholders, transfers of stock ownership, and malpractice insurance coverage

profit center The smallest unit of activity of a business enterprise for which revenue and expense information is accumulated for internal management purposes

program budget An annual budget of a governmental entity's general fund that stresses measurement of total cost of a specific governmental entity program, regardless of how many departments of the governmental entity are involved in the program

program services Activities of a nonprofit organization that result in the distribution of goods and services to beneficiaries, customers, or members that fulfill the purposes or mission of the organization

projected benefits The amount of all benefits under a defined benefit pension plan attributable to employee services to the date of computation of the actuarial present value

promissory note An unconditional promise in writing, signed by the maker, to pay a certain sum of money on demand or at a fixed or determinable future time to order of a payee or bearer

proportionate consolidation method The International Accounting Standards Committee term for the *proportionate share method* of accounting for an investment in a joint venture

proportionate share method The method of accounting for an investment in an unincorporated joint venture that allocates to the venturer's assets, liabilities, revenue, gains, expenses, and losses the venturer's pro rata share of the venture's comparable items

proprietary funds Enterprise funds and internal services funds of a governmental entity that carry out governmental activities closely resembling the operations of a business enterprise

proxy statement A statement filed by a publicly owned company with the SEC prior to the company's solicitation of proxies from stockholders prior to a meeting of stockholders

purchase A business combination interpreted as an acquisition of assets or raising of capital rather than a combining of existing stockholder interests

push-down accounting Accounting for net assets of a purchased subsidiary at their current fair values as established in the business combination, rather than at carrying amounts, in separate financial statements of the subsidiary

quasi-endowment fund An endowment fund established by the governing board of a nonprofit organization, the principal of which may be expended at the direction of the board

quasi-external transactions Transactions of the general fund of a governmental entity with proprietary funds of the entity, such as for goods and services provided by the proprietary funds

realization Conversion of noncash assets of a liquidating partnership to cash

reciprocal accounts The Investment in Branch ledger account in the home office accounting records and the Home Office account in the branch accounting records; also, the Investment in Subsidiary Common Stock ledger account in the parent company's accounting records and the stockholders' equity accounts in the subsidiary's accounting records

registrar The officer of a probate court authorized to carry out informal probate of decedents' wills

registration statement A document filed with the SEC by a company that issues securities to the public interstate

Regulation S-K A pronouncement of the SEC that provides guidance for the completion of non-financial statement disclosure requirements in the various *Forms* filed with the SEC

Regulation S-X A pronouncement of the SEC that provides guidance on the form and content of financial statements included in the various *Forms* filed with the SEC

remeasurement Restatement of account balances of a foreign entity to its functional currency from its local currency

reorganization value The current fair value of the total assets of a business enterprise undergoing reorganization under Chapter 11 of the Bankruptcy Code

reportable segment A business segment whose revenue, operating profit or loss, identifiable assets, and other information is reported by a diversified business enterprise

reporting currency The currency of the parent company, home office, or investor enterprise of a foreign entity

residual equity transfer An amount received by the general fund of a governmental entity from a capital projects fund of the entity to clear a final fund balance of the latter fund

residuary devise A devise of all property of a decedent remaining after specific and general devises are distributed

restricted fund A fund established by a nonprofit organization to account for contributed assets available for current use but expendable only as authorized by the donor of the assets

revenue bonds Bonds issued by an enterprise fund of a governmental entity to finance a construction project of the entity; the bonds' principal and interest are paid from revenues generated by the construction project

Revised Uniform Principal and Income Act A law in effect in part or in full in many states, which provides for allocation of transactions of the personal representative of an estate between principal and income, in the absence of appropriate instructions in the will

right of offset A legal doctrine that permits offsetting of a loan receivable from or payable to a partner of a liquidating partnership against that partner's capital account balance

sales-type lease A lease that, from the viewpoint of the lessor, is equivalent to the *sale,* rather than the *rental,* of property to the lessee

scorched earth A tactic used to resist an unfriendly takeover business combination in which the target company sells or spins off to stockholders one or more profitable business segments

Securities and Exchange Commission (SEC) The federal agency charged with overseeing issuance and trading of securities interstate by publicly owned companies

security interest A legal claim of a secured creditor of a debtor to designated personal property of the debtor

segment contribution Segment sales less traceable expenses

segment identifiable assets Tangible and intangible assets used by an industry segment, including both exclusively used assets and an allocated portion of jointly used assets

segment operating profit or loss Segment revenue less segment traceable expenses and allocated nontraceable expenses

segment revenue Segment sales to unaffiliated customers and sales or transfers to other industry segments of the enterprise

selling spot rate The exchange rate charged by a foreign currency dealer ''on the spot''

settlor (donor, trustor) The creator of a trust

shared revenues Revenues received by a governmental entity from another government that had levied the taxes or fees to be shared

shark repellent A tactic used to resist an unfriendly takeover business combination in which the target company acquires substantial amounts of its outstanding common stock for the treasury or for retirement or incurs substantial long-term debt in exchange for its outstanding common stock

significant segment A business segment whose revenue, operating profit or loss, or identifiable assets constitute 10% or more of specified total amounts for all industry segments of the enterprise

special assessment bonds Bonds issued by a governmental entity, principal and interest of which are paid from special assessments on specific taxpayers benefited by the construction project financed in part by the bonds

special assessments Taxes levied by a governmental entity on specific taxpayers to be benefited by the construction project financed in part by the assessments

special revenue funds Governmental funds that account for receipts and expenditures associated with specialized revenue sources that are earmarked by law or regulation to finance specified government operations

specific devise A decedent's gift of identified objects, such as named paintings, automobiles, stock certificates, or real property

spot rate The rate of exchange between two foreign currencies to be exchanged ''on the spot''

Staff Accounting Bulletins (SABs) Pronouncements of the SEC staff regarding administrative interpretations and practices used by the staff in reviewing financial statements filed with the SEC

statement of activities A financial statement that displays the changes in net assets—unrestricted, temporarily restricted, and permanently restricted—of a nonprofit organization

statement of affairs (financial statement) A ''quitting concern'' financial statement prepared on behalf of a debtor undergoing bankruptcy liquidation that classifies nonexempt assets and liabilities of the debtor according to provisions of the Bankruptcy Code

statement of affairs (legal document) A document accompanying a debtor's petition that contains a series of questions concerning all aspects of the debtor's financial position and operations

statement of cash flows A financial statement that displays the cash flows from operating activities, investing activities, and financing activities of a nonprofit organization

statement of financial position A financial statement that displays the assets, liabilities, and net assets— permanently restricted, temporarily restricted, and unrestricted—of a nonprofit organization

statement of partners' capital The financial statement issued by a partnership to display changes in partners' capital from investments, net income or loss, and drawings during an accounting period

statement of realization and liquidation A financial statement prepared for a liquidating partnership that displays realization of noncash assets, allocation of resultant gains or losses to partners, payment of partnership liabilities, and distribution of any remaining cash to partners; also, a financial statement prepared on behalf of a trustee in a bankruptcy liquidation that sets forth assets realized and liabilities paid, with ''gains'' and ''losses'' thereon applied to the estate deficit

statutory consolidation A business combination in which a new corporation issues common stock for all the outstanding common stock of two or more other corporations that are then dissolved and liquidated, with their net assets owned by the new corporation

statutory merger A business combination in which one corporation (the survivor) acquires all the outstanding common stock of one or more other corporations that are then dissolved and liquidated, with their net assets owned by the survivor

subsidiary An investee enterprise controlled by an investor enterprise (parent company)

support Resources obtained by nonprofit organizations through contributions from individuals, governmental entities, and other organizations

supporting services All activities of a nonprofit organization other than program services, such as management and general, fund-raising, and membership development activities

survivor The constituent company in a statutory merger that is not dissolved and liquidated

temporary difference A difference between the tax basis of an asset or a liability and its reported amount in the financial statements that will result in taxable or deductible amounts in future years when the reported amount of the asset or liability is recovered or settled, respectively (taken from *FASB Statement No. 109,* p. 132); a difference between pretax accounting income and taxable income that ''turns around'' in one or more subsequent accounting periods

term endowment fund An endowment fund whose principal may be expended after a specified time period or the occurrence of a specified event

testamentary trust A trust created by a will

testator The maker of a will

third-party payor An organization such as Medicare or Medicaid that pays for services rendered by a nonprofit hospital to patients

traceable expenses Expenses directly identified with a particular business segment, such as intersegment transfers in

transaction gains and losses Gains and losses recognized on transactions denominated in a foreign currency

translation Restatement of financial statement amounts of a foreign entity from its functional currency to the reporting currency of the parent company or investor enterprise

trust document The document establishing a trust

trust indenture The legal document that creates a trust

trustee The fiduciary individual or corporation holding title to trust property and carrying out provisions of the trust document

undistributed earnings of subsidiary The parent company's share, under the equity method of accounting, of the adjusted net income less dividends of the subsidiary

unfriendly takeover A prospective business combination in which the target company resists the proposed takeover

Uniform Probate Code A law in effect in part or in full in many states, which provides for procedures used in probating wills

uniting of interests The International Accounting Standards Committee term for a *pooling-of-interests* business combination

units Securities evidencing ownership interests in a limited partnership

unrelated business income Income derived by a nonprofit organization from activities not substantially related to the educational, charitable, or other basis of the organization's tax-exempt status

unrestricted fund A nonprofit organization's fund that includes all assets of the organization available for use as authorized by the governing board and not restricted for specific purposes

unsecured creditors with priority Creditors of a debtor in a bankruptcy proceeding whose unsecured claims are paid in accordance with provisions of the Bankruptcy Code prior to the payment of claims of other unsecured creditors

unsecured creditors without priority Creditors of a debtor in a bankruptcy proceeding whose unsecured claims do not have priority under the Bankruptcy Code

untainted treasury stock Treasury stock issued in a pooling-type business combination that had been acquired by the issuer in accordance with a systematic plan for reasons other than business combinations, such as for stock option and purchase plans

upstream intercompany sales Sales of merchandise by a subsidiary to its parent company

vertical combination A business combination between an enterprise and its customers or suppliers

white knight A tactic used to resist an unfriendly takeover business combination in which the target company seeks out a candidate to be the combinor in a friendly takeover

will A document that awards a testator's property to devisees following the testator's death

Index

961